An Introduction to

Financial Markets and Institutions

Maureen Burton
California State Polytechnic University – Pomona

Reynold Nesiba
Augustana College

Ray Lombra
Pennsylvania State University – University Park

THOMSON
SOUTH-WESTERN

Australia · Canada · Mexico · Singapore · Spain · United Kingdom · United States

THOMSON

SOUTH-WESTERN

An Introduction to Financial Markets and Institutions

Maureen Burton, Reynold Nesiba, and Ray Lombra

Editor-in-Chief:
Jack Calhoun

VP/Team Director:
Michael P. Roche

Executive Editor:
Michael R. Reynolds

Senior Developmental Editor:
Susanna C. Smart

Senior Marketing Manager:
Charlie Stutesman

Senior Production Editor:
Kara ZumBahlen

Manufacturing Coordinator:
Sandee Milewski

Production House/Compositor:
Shepherd, Inc.

Printer:
Quebecor World, Versailles, KY

**Design Project Coordinator
and Internal Design:**
Rik Moore

Cover Design:
Rik Moore

Cover Illustration:
Jane Sterrett, Stock Illustration Source

Photo Researcher:
Deanna Ettinger

Library of Congress Cataloging-
in-Publication Data
Burton, Maureen.
  An introduction to financial
markets and institutions / Mau-
reen Burton, Reynold Nesiba,
Ray Lombra.
    p. cm.
  Includes index.
  ISBN 0-324-06696-1
    1. Finance. 2. Financial insti-
tutions. 3. Capital market. I.
Title: Financial markets and
institutions. II. Lombra, Ray-
mond E. III. Nesiba, Reynold F.
(Reynold Frank), 1966- IV. Title.

HG173.B873 2002
332—dc21   2001057785

Maureen Burton

Maureen Burton received a BA from the University of Missouri at Columbia in 1971, an MA from California State University, Fullerton in 1979, and a Ph.D. from the University of California at Riverside in 1986. All were in economics. She taught at Chaffey College from 1984 to 1987 and at Cal Poly Pomona since 1987, where she is a full professor. At Cal Poly Pomona, she has served as Coordinator of the Graduate Program in Economics and as Chair of the Economics Department. In addition to other publications, she co-authored an introductory text, *Economics* (Harper Collins, 1987), with S. Craig Justice and *The Financial System and the Economy, 3rd edition* (South-Western Publishing, 2002) with Ray Lombra. Her main areas of research include monetary theory and financial markets.

Reynold Nesiba

Received a BA in economics from the University of Denver in 1989 and an MA (1991) and Ph.D. (1995) in economics from the University of Notre Dame. Since 1995, Dr. Nesiba has been teaching economics at Augustana College in Sioux Falls, South Dakota, where he currently serves as Associate Professor of Economics, Dr. Nesiba has authored and/or co-authored work that appeared in the *Journal of Economic Issues*, the *Journal of Urban Affairs, Cityscape*, and the *Encyclopedia of Political Economy*. In addition, he authored the study guide and test bank for the second edition of Burton and Lombra's *The Financial System & the Economy* (also published by South-Western/Thompson Learning). Nesiba's current research interests include community reinvestment, discrimination in mortgage lending, subprime mortgage lending, and other finance-oriented topics.

Ray Lombra

Born in Hamden, Connecticut, Ray Lombra received a BA in economics from Providence College in 1967 and an MA and Ph.D. from Penn State University in 1971. He served as a senior staff economist at the Board of Governors of the Federal Reserve System from 1971–1977 and specialized in financial markets analysis and the formulation and implementation of monetary policy. He joined the faculty of Penn State University in 1977, and has taught money and banking at the undergraduate level and monetary theory and policy at the graduate level for 26 years. He is a winner of the College distinguished teaching award for innovations and instruction and is the author and editor of 5 books and over 80 scholarly publications. Articles on monetary policy, the determination of interest rates, stock prices, and exchange rates, financial innovation, globalization, and expectations formation have appeared in leading journals including the *Quarterly Journal of Economics*, the *Journal of Money, Credit and Banking*, the *Journal of Monetary Economics*, and the *Review of Economics and Statistics*.

Dedication

To a most wonderful son, David Zehntner
    —Maureen Burton

To my pitch-playing buddies, Anita, Nathaniel and Brandon
    —Reynold Nesiba

To my loving wife, Bobbi
    —Ray Lombra

Brief Contents

Contents

preface

Technological innovation, deregulation, global competition, and financial crises have significantly changed financial markets and institutions. The growth of international trade and flexible exchange rates has escalated the development of international currency markets. Financial institutions have entered nontraditional venues on both the asset and liability sides of their balance sheets. Laws now allow interstate banking and the merger of security firms, insurance companies, and banks. As a result, mega-mergers have occurred in the financial services industry that change the scope, size, and activities of financial institutions and the markets in which they exist. At the same time, advances in information and computer technologies have fostered the development of new financial instruments and products, and new and creative ways to hedge and manage risks in a global environment. Managers of financial institutions must now make decisions in this new and dynamic milieu where technological innovations are the driving force.

In the late 1990s, financial market participants struggled to deal with international financial instability that caused increased volatility in global and domestic financial markets. In the early 2000s, financial market participants face new challenges as they continue to adapt to the changing financial environment. Even before the September 11, 2001 terrorist attacks on the World Trade Center and the Pentagon, falling stock prices raised global uncertainty and slowed rates of economic growth among key industrialized countries. The attacks further threatened the economic health of financial markets and institutions that shut down during the following week. Controversy continues over monetary policy and the Fed's responses to events of 2001 that included massive injections of funds into financial markets, 11 decreases in interest rates during 2001, and the first coordination of monetary policy between the Fed and the newly created Eurosystem.

Given this climate, the motivation in developing this text is twofold: First, to capture the ongoing changes in financial markets and institutions, particularly with regard to technology and globalization. Second, to present an analytical framework that enables students to understand and anticipate changes in the financial system and the accompanying changes in financial markets and institutions.

Intended Audience

An Introduction to Financial Markets and Institutions is intended for an introductory undergraduate course in financial markets and institutions. The emphasis is on helping students intuitively understand the workings of contemporary financial markets and institutions without burying them in algebra.

A strength of the text is its clear and engaging writing style and strong intuitive approach. It avoids encyclopedic coverage while balancing a mix of financial theory and institutional detail. Students find it easy to understand and enjoyable to read. The text makes use of many examples and analogies to illustrate how financial innovation, technology, and globalization affect financial markets and institutions.

Contents of the Text

An Introduction to Financial Markets and Institutions covers the traditional material found in a financial markets and institutions text and incorporates many of the recent changes and controversies within financial markets and the financial services industry.

The chapters contain many features that include examples, historical and international perspectives, and projections about the future, bringing the material to life for students. Because financial markets are evolving at such a rapid pace, we emphasize the dynamics of how the current status of financial markets and institutions evolved and where they are likely to be heading, rather than placing emphasis on "facts" regarding their current state. To help us do this, we view the examples/illustrations as the nails in the wall on which we hang the analysis; our experience suggests it is the real-world dimension to the text and the examples that stays with students well beyond the lecture and, indeed, the course.

Topics covered in these features include recent mega-mergers among financial institutions, changes in the payments mechanism due to technology, the implicit guarantee of government sponsored enterprise securities, the causes of the Asian crisis, Europe's new single currency, and the Fed's response to the attack on the World Trade Center and the Pentagon. In addition, we examine a wide array of institutional detail ranging from disruptions in the repurchase agreement market, the anatomy of a eurodollar transaction, savings institutions in other countries, and the intersection of CRA, credit unions, and corporate taxes. We also examine international life insurance markets, alleged racial bias in the property and casualty insurance industry, and securitization of small business lending, among other topics.

The text contains annotated suggested readings that give the students some idea about how the readings are related to the material in the chapters. In addition, the Suggested Readings sections contain Internet addresses that pertain to financial markets and institutions.

Internet addresses appear throughout the text as margin notes to direct students to sites relevant to the topics being discussed. Many chapters have review and analytical questions and problems, some of which direct the student to go to an Internet address to locate and analyze financial market data.

Organization of the Text

The text is divided into six parts:

Part 1 consists of a four-chapter introduction and overview of financial markets, instruments, and institutions, including a chapter on the role and impact of the Federal Reserve on financial markets and institutions.

Part 2 contains four chapters on financial prices, including interest rates and exchange rates. This part also contains a chapter on market efficiency and how all financial prices and the flow of funds among sectors adjust throughout the economy.

Part 3 consists of five chapters on financial markets, including chapters on the money market, the corporate and government bond markets, the stock market, the mortgage market, and the international financial system.

Part 4 consists of seven chapters on financial institutions, including banks and other depository institutions, insurance companies, pension plans, finance companies, security firms, mutual funds, and financial conglomerates. Regulation in the financial services industry is also covered.

Part 5 consists of three chapters on managing financial risk and includes chapters on financial management and innovation, on the development and use of financial forward, futures, and options agreements and markets, and on the growth and role of asset-backed securities and other financial derivatives.

Part 6 consists of two chapters that provide an up-to-date look at monetary policy from a domestic and global perspective. Recent changes in the modus operandi of the Federal Reserve and the need for global monetary policy coordination are discussed.

This text is designed to be flexible. After completing Part 1, an instructor can emphasize financial prices (Part 2), financial markets (Part 3), financial institutions (Part 4), management of financial risk (Part 5), or monetary policy (Part 6) depending on the focus of the class. In parts that are not being emphasized, chapters may be skipped.

Other Special Coverage

Several other features of *An Introduction to Financial Markets and Institutions* deserve mention.

- Chapter 7 presents unique coverage that integrates the efficient markets hypothesis with equilibrium from the perspective of the flow-of-funds among sectors. Financial prices adjust so that risk-adjusted after-tax rates of return are equalized, and when there is a change in perceived risk or returns, financial prices change. This, in turn, alters the composition of lenders and borrowers within any sector, subsequently altering the flows.

- In Chapter 9, we discuss the change from a multiple-price auction to a uniform-price method adopted by the Treasury in November of 1998. We also cover the newly created 4-week Treasury bill, first auctioned in August of 2001, as well as discussion of how institutions use these instruments to manage their finances.

- Chapter 10 discusses the government securities' buy back program and its implications for the corporate bond market. Chapter 12 looks at the growth of Fannie Mae and Freddie Mac and their impact on the mortgage market. Chapter 20 gives an overview of the securities industry including investment banks, securities brokers and dealers, mutual funds, government sponsored enterprises, hedge funds, real estate investment trusts, and financial conglomerates.

- Chapter 21's discussion of risk assessment and management emphasizes the "Five Cs of Credit" to assess credit risk and income gap analysis. The more technically challenging approach of duration gap analysis is included in the chapter appendix. The subsequent two chapters (22 and 23) on forwards, futures, and options and asset-backed securities and other derivatives do not require coverage of duration analysis.

- Finally, Chapters 24 and 25 look at how the Fed's policy formulation and implementation has changed in recent years and the impact of these changes on financial markets.

Pedagogical Features of the Text

In addition to presenting the material in a clear and concise manner, we have incorporated the following pedagogical tools to enhance the student's understanding.

- **Learning objectives** at the beginning of each chapter tell the student where the chapter is heading and what questions will be answered by studying the chapter.
- **RECAP** sections are integrated throughout each chapter to summarize analytical material the student should know before moving forward and also to check if the student has mastered the preceding material.
- Highlighted features include:
  - **A Closer Look:** These features delve more deeply into the topic being discussed and enhance chapter material.
  - **Looking Out:** These boxed features add relevant international material that shows the interrelationships of global financial systems.
  - **Looking Back:** These features provide historical background of the foundations of current economic circumstances.
  - **Looking Forward:** These features do just that—look forward and make projections about possible future situations within the financial system and economies.
- **Cracking the Code** features show students how to interpret the financial pages of daily newspapers, including futures and options prices, stock, bond, mutual fund prices, foreign exchange, and Treasury bill and Treasury bond quotes.
- **Key Terms** are bold-faced in the text where they are defined, listed at the end of each chapter, and also appear in the margins with definitions.
- **Summary of Major Points** reinforce the chapter content and aid in study for exams and quizzes, as well as provide another check for students to make sure they have not missed an important concept of the chapter.
- End-of-Chapter materials include:
  - Annotated **Suggested Readings** that direct the student to related material and include relevant information available on the Internet.
  - **Review Questions, Analytical Questions,** and **Internet Exercises** appear at the end of most chapters.
- End-of-text materials include a **Glossary.**

Supplements to the Text

- *Study Guide:* The study guide, written by Francis E. Laatsch of Bowling Green State University, focuses on helping students test their knowledge of the text material. The study guide includes chapter summaries for each chapter and simulates test questions for key concepts with numerous true/false, multiple choice, fill-in, and essay questions for every chapter. Each chapter also includes Internet exercises to help students become proficient at doing online research in financial topics. Answers are provided at the end of the study guide.
- *Instructor's Manual and Test Bank:* The instructor's manual includes solutions to all chapter questions and is created by the text authors. The test bank, writ-

ten by Vivian Nazar of Ferris State University, contains over 1,200 test questions, including true/false, multiple choice, and essay questions.

- *ExamView™ Computerized Testing*: The *ExamView™* computerized testing program contains all of the questions in the printed test bank. *ExamView™* is an easy-to-use test creation software compatible with Microsoft Windows. Instructors can add or edit questions, instructions, and answers, and select questions by previewing them on the screen—selecting them randomly or by number. Instructors can also create and administer quizzes online, whether over the Internet, a local area network (LAN), or a wide area network (WAN).

- **PowerPoint™ Slides:** PowerPoint presentation slides have been specially created for this new text. These user-friendly slides can serve as lecture enhancement for instructors, as well as study aids for students. They are available on the text web site.

- *Text Web Site:* The text Web Site at *http://burton.swcollege.com* provides a wealth of resources for students and instructors alike. The site contains Learning and Teaching Resources with access to some supplements, Internet updates and direct links to sites from the text, and Talk-to-the-Author, and is enhanced by the South-Western Finance Resource Center with *Finance in the News, Finance Links Online, Thomson Investors Network, Finance Interactive, CaseNet,* Wall Street *Analyst Reports* from the Gale Group, and more.

Acknowledgements

Many people have made important contributions to this text. Special thanks go to Mike Reynolds and to Susan Smart, editors at South-Western Publishing who were always supportive, creative, and helpful. The text's production editor, Kara ZumBahlen, did a first rate job. All of our editors provided immediate answers, support, and assistance. We are glad to have the opportunity to work with such professionals.

Other people also deserve special recognition. Dr. Bryan Taylor, President of Global Financial Data, in Los Angeles, California, read much of the manuscript, answered numerous questions, provided much of the data, and gave invaluable criticisms and suggestions. Professor Emeritus George Galbreath and Professor James Sutton gave invaluable suggestions and support to the completion of this project. Jan Brue Enright and Lisa Brunick of the Mikkelsen Library at Augustana College went well beyond the call of duty to provide exemplary, expert, and expeditious research assistance. We also benefited from the real world knowledge and experience of Jeff Jorgensen at the Sioux Empire Federal Credit Union, Tom Wadsworth at Dain Rauscher, and Rich Nesiba at New York Life who provided critical and constructive comments on the chapters related to their respective areas of expertise; gratitude also goes to Jonathan Lindley at NASCUS, who provided timely information regarding alternative share insurance for credit unions. We are also grateful to our families for their comfort, support, and understanding of our obsessive compulsive desires to create this text.

We are indebted to many current and former students who have assisted in myriad ways. Roberto Ayala, Adam DeAvilan, Benton Wolverton, and Patrick Flynn provided valuable research assistance. Maggie Goodwin assisted on several chapters by proofreading, assembling annotated suggested readings, and writing drafts of various boxed features. Megan Malde and Nathan Golz tested many of the end-of-the chapter questions and Internet exercises while assisting with the accompanying instructor's manual. We also thank the following reviewers, whose comments improved the quality of this text and which were greatly appreciated.

Frank J. Bonello
University of Notre Dame

Joseph Cheng
Ithaca College

James F. Cotter
New Mexico State University

Gary Dymski
University of California—Riverside

Elyas Elyiasiani
Temple University

Milton Esbitt
Dominican University

Owen Gregory
University of Illinois—Chicago

Jon A. Hooks
Albion College

Clark L. Maxam
Montana State University

Vivian Nazar
Ferris State University

Ronnie J. Phillips
Colorado State University

Robert Schweitzer
University of Delaware—Newark

Vijaya Subrahmanyam
Clark Atlanta University

J. Van Fenstermaker
Towson University

John C. Wassom
Western Kentucky University

Martin Wolfson
University of Notre Dame

L. Randall Wray
University of Missouri—Kansas City

David A. Zalewski
Providence College

part

INTRODUCTION

chapter

1   Introduction and Overview

Learning Objectives *After reading this chapter, you should know:*

- The subject matter of economics and finance
- The general role of financial markets and institutions in a modern economy
- The major functions of the financial system and financial intermediaries
- What saving is and its uses
- How the financial system channels funds from lenders to borrowers
- The role of the Federal Reserve and its regulatory and monetary policy responsibilities

" "

Well begun is half done.
—Aristotle

What This Book Is About

Why do investors now have so many different ways to invest funds? Should a firm that wants to finance new investment spending issue stocks or bonds? Why do homebuyers now have a choice among many types of fixed and variable interest rate mortgage loans? Why have financial institutions and financial regulations changed so dramatically in the last 20 years? Why does the international value of the dollar fluctuate so much and how does that affect exports, imports, and flows of funds among countries? What is meant by the "globalization of finance"? How does the state of the federal government budget affect financial markets, institutions, and prices? How have technological changes affected financial markets? What are the complex financial instruments known as derivatives? Why do banks and other financial institutions pay so much attention to what the Federal Reserve is doing? Why have there been so many mergers between financial institutions in recent years?

We could go on, but you get the idea. This list of questions represents only a sample of the issues that motivate the discussions found throughout this text. As the questions indicate, these matters affect many aspects of our daily lives.

This chapter begins your study of financial markets, institutions, and instruments in a global economy. It is designed to introduce the subject matter and provide an overview of the key concepts and relationships. Most of the details are ignored, and most terms are not rigorously defined and examined; this is an introduction! However, don't underestimate the importance of a good beginning.

Economic and Financial Analysis of an Ever-changing System

Economics is the study of how a society decides what gets produced, how it gets produced, and who gets what. More specifically, given unlimited wants on the part of society, economics is concerned with the following processes:

1. How scarce resources (labor, capital, and natural resources) are allocated in the production process among competing uses.[1]
2. How income generated in the production and sale of goods and services is distributed among members of society.
3. How people allocate their income through spending, saving, borrowing, and lending decisions.

For methodological convenience, economics is traditionally divided into the study of the causes and consequences of individual decision-making units such as households and business firms in a particular market and the study of the causes and the effects resulting from the sum of decisions made by all firms or households in many markets. The former type of analysis is called **microeconomics;** the latter, more aggregative analysis is called **macroeconomics.**

Finance is, broadly speaking, the study of the financial or monetary aspects of the production, spending, borrowing, and lending decisions already mentioned. More to the point, finance deals with the raising and using of money by individuals, firms, governments, and foreign investors. We are familiar with our decisions to spend, borrow, lend, or save. Our everyday language includes such terms as interest

Economics
The study of how society decides what gets produced and how, and who gets what.

Microeconomics
The branch of economics that studies the behavior of individual decision-making units such as households and business firms.

Macroeconomics
The branch of economics that studies the aggregate, or total, behavior of all households and firms.

Finance
The study of how the financial system coordinates and channels the flow of funds from lenders to borrowers—and vice versa—and how new funds are created by financial intermediaries during the borrowing process.

---

[1]When economists use the term capital, they mean machinery and equipment that are utilized to produce other goods and services. For example, a sewing machine that produces shirts is capital.

rates, checking accounts, debit cards, banks, and credit cards. Finance in this context deals with how individuals, to quote *Webster's Dictionary,* "manage money."

At a more aggregative, macro level, finance is concerned with how financial markets and institutions coordinate and channel the flow of funds from lenders to borrowers and vice versa, and how new funds may be created by financial intermediaries during the borrowing process. The channeling and coordination process and its effects on the cost and availability of funds in the economy link developments in the financial system to developments in the rest of the economy. This text emphasizes this aspect of financial analysis.

The production and sale of goods and services within the economic system are intimately related to the deposits, stocks and bonds, and other financial instruments that are bought and sold in the financial system. Thus, what happens on Wall Street can have a profound effect on what happens on Main Street and vice versa.

Because the financial system is vital to a healthy economy, the government regulates and supervises its operation. Such regulatory policy is aimed at promoting a smooth-running, efficient financial system. By establishing and enforcing operating regulations for financial markets and institutions, regulators seek to promote competition and efficiency while preserving the safety and soundness of the system.

Complicating our analysis of the interaction between the financial system and the economy is the fact that the financial system is not stagnant. It continually evolves and changes, sometimes at a faster pace than at other times. For various reasons to be discussed in later chapters, the past two decades have seen rapid change, including increased globalization of financial markets, institutions, and instruments. The system is different from what it was 20 years ago, and it will be different 20 years hence. The major forces behind these changes are changes in government regulations, advances in technology, and innovations in the ways people spend, save, and borrow funds.

In recent decades, firms and individuals have developed new ways to raise and use money. Today, many manifestations of these financial innovations are all around us. For example, most checking accounts now earn interest, and 24-hour automatic teller machines (ATMs) are common. Debit cards and credit cards are widely accepted at grocery stores, gas stations, and department stores. Home equity lines of credit allow homeowners to borrow against the equity in their homes by writing checks as the need arises. Investors have an increasing array of mutual funds and other domestic and global financial instruments to choose from. Stocks and bonds can be purchased for low fees over the Internet at a fraction of the brokerage fees charged by full-service brokerage firms. None of these innovations was widely available 20 years ago. New ways for financial and nonfinancial firms to manage risks have been developed. Brokerage firms, such as Merrill Lynch, have merged with real estate companies, insurance companies, credit card companies, and retail firms. All of this merger activity in the financial services industry has created new types of financial institutions that transcend national borders. Although still in an infantile stage in the United States, the use of smart cards and stored-value cards (as well as other ways to make electronic payments) is expected to explode in the very near future. These developments, most of which have been made possible because of changes in technology, have had or will have an impact on spending, saving, borrowing, and lending decisions. Not surprisingly then, we shall examine the causes and consequences of these changes in the financial system.

Because of these financial innovations and other factors, Congress and the regulatory authorities such as the Federal Reserve have had to reconsider the costs and benefits associated with certain regulations. From the early 1970s until the late 1980s, regulatory changes were mostly in the direction of **deregulation,** which is the removing or phasing out of some existing regulations. Some regulations were eliminated

Deregulation
The removing or phasing out of existing regulations.

because many people felt that they had become increasingly ineffective as firms and households found ways to get around them. Other regulations were removed because they were believed to inhibit competition and weaken rather than strengthen the financial system. During the late 1980s and early 1990s, however, crises in various financial markets, sometimes requiring taxpayer bailouts, slowed the drive to deregulate and led to attempts at "re-regulation." By the late 1990s, the recovery of the financial services industry and a booming economy led to the passage of major legislation. The new legislation further removed regulations that impinged on the behavior and structure of financial institutions. This, coupled with continuing advances in computer technologies, promised dramatic changes in the financial system in the near future. As the financial system continues to evolve, we can expect that new and different ways of regulating will be introduced, analyzed, and tested. Nevertheless, the goals of regulation to ensure the safety and soundness of the financial system while fostering efficiency and competition will remain the same.

Finance in Our Daily Lives

Simply put, an individual's financial objective is to make payments when due and to manage funds efficiently until they are needed. To make payments we need **money**—that is, something that is acceptable in payment, whether it's for a cup of coffee or rent on a beach house.[2] As you read this book, keep in mind that only money can generally be used for payments.

Money
Something acceptable and generally used as payment for goods and services.

In our daily lives, we receive income periodically (weekly, monthly, etc.), but our expenditures are more or less continuous, depending, of course, on our lifestyles. Given this lack of synchronization between the receipt of income and expenditures, we need to manage our money over, say, a month, so that funds will be available when we make purchases of goods and services—called *consumption spending.* Income that is not spent on consumption is called **saving.** Part of household saving may be spent directly on investment goods, such as new houses.[3] With the remainder of saving, individuals will acquire financial instruments, which also have to be managed.

Saving
Income not spent on consumption.

How might the funds not used for consumption or investment in new houses be managed? We could take currency (paper money), put it in an empty coffee can, and bury it in the backyard. We also could put the funds into a savings or money market account to earn some interest. Another alternative is to buy corporate bonds, shares of common stock, Treasury bills, or other financial assets. What we buy depends on how we wish to balance the key financial characteristics of concern to savers: the expected return (gain) and the risk of loss associated with acquiring and holding a particular asset. Some assets, like Treasury bills, are relatively riskless; if you own such bills, you can be pretty sure the government will pay the interest and principal you are due. Other assets, such as bonds issued by new corporations not yet earning significant profits, may offer a much higher return, but they also carry the risk that the firm will declare bankruptcy and you will get nothing! Moreover, if an unexpected need arises and you need to get back the funds you originally loaned, you want your funds to be invested in liquid assets that can be converted quickly to cash without substantial loss. Balancing such considerations is

---

[2]Credit cards are not money. When a credit card is used, the user is taking out a loan by authorizing the institution that issued the credit card to make a payment with money on his or her behalf. Ultimately, the individual must pay credit card balances with money.

[3]As used here, investment in houses refers to expenditures for new residential construction, whereby a service is rendered over a period of time.

EXHIBIT 1-1
SSUs and DSUs

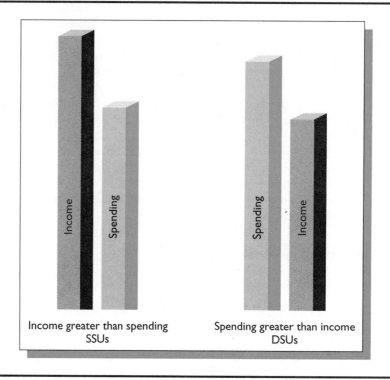

the essence of managing a portfolio—that is, a collection of financial assets—be it by an individual or by a financial institution.

Income is the flow of revenue (receipts) we receive over time for our services. With this income, we can buy and consume goods. If we have funds left over after consumption, we are saving. We have to decide how to allocate those funds among the various types of financial assets available or to invest them in real assets such as new houses. If, however, we spend more than we earn, we have a deficit and have to decide how to finance it. When we spend less on consumption and investment goods than our current income, we are called **surplus spending units (SSUs).** If the opposite is true, we have a deficit and are called **deficit spending units (DSUs).** Exhibit 1-1 portrays SSUs and DSUs.

So far we have restricted our analysis to individuals and households, but business firms may also spend more or less than their income. Business firms do not spend on consumption, so all business income is saving except income distributed as dividends to the owners of the firms. With their saving, business firms make investment expenditures in capital and inventories or acquire financial assets. A firm's investment expenditures often exceed its available funds.[4] In this case, the firm incurs financial liabilities by issuing financial claims against itself. Note that every financial instrument is an asset to the owner (purchaser) of the instrument and a liability to the issuer. SSUs acquire (purchase) financial assets while DSUs incur (issue) financial liabilities. Exhibit 1-2 shows the uses of saving for households and business firms.

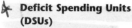 **Surplus Spending Units (SSUs)**
Spending units such as households and firms whose income exceeds their spending.

Deficit Spending Units (DSUs)
Spending units such as households and firms whose spending exceeds their income.

---

[4]Firms may also make investment expenditures to replace worn-out capital.

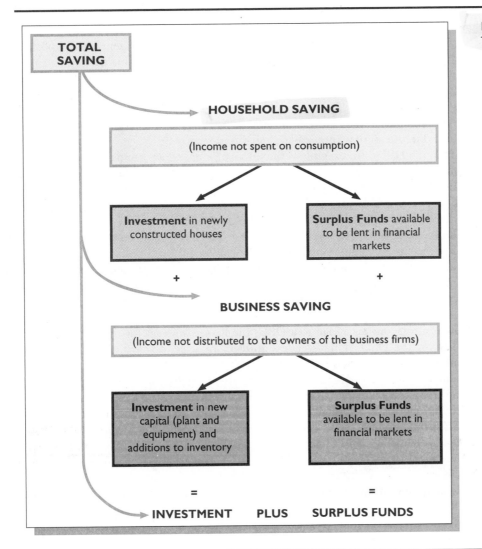

EXHIBIT 1-2
The Uses of Saving

The fact that some people or business firms are in deficit positions while others are in surplus positions creates an opportunity or a need for a way to match them up. The financial system links up these SSUs and DSUs. The government and foreign sectors may also spend more or less than their current available funds and, hence, are SSUs or DSUs.

RECAP Economics studies how scarce resources are allocated among conflicting wants. Finance studies how the financial system coordinates and channels the flows of funds from SSUs to DSUs. SSUs spend less than their current income. DSUs spend more than their current income. Household saving may be used for investment in new housing or to acquire financial assets. Business saving may be used for investment in capital and inventories or to acquire financial assets. Financial instruments are financial assets to the holder of the instrument and financial liabilities to the issuer.

Introducing the Financial System

A well-organized, efficient, smoothly functioning financial system is an important component of a modern, highly specialized economy. The financial system provides a mechanism whereby an individual unit (firm or household) that is an SSU may conveniently make funds available to DSUs who intend to spend more than their current income. The key word here is "conveniently."

The financial system is composed of financial markets and financial institutions. **Financial markets** are the markets where SSUs can lend their funds directly to DSUs. An example is the market for corporate bonds. General Motors can sell bonds to finance, say, the construction of a new plant in Mexico, and Emma from Kansas can purchase some of the bonds with the income she does not spend on goods and services. This is called **direct finance.** Purchasing stocks is another example of direct finance. **Financial institutions** are firms that provide financial services to SSUs and DSUs. The most important financial institutions are **financial intermediaries**—various institutions such as banks, savings and loan associations, and credit unions—that serve as go-betweens to link up SSUs and DSUs. Here the linkage between saver and borrower is indirect. For example, a household might deposit some surplus funds in a savings account at a bank. The deposit is an asset for the household and a liability for the bank. If the bank, in turn, makes a loan to a DSU, the loan is an asset for the bank and a liability for the DSU. This is called **indirect finance.** Even though the ultimate lender is the SSU, the DSU owes repayment of the loan to the financial intermediary, and the financial intermediary owes repayment of the deposit to the SSU regardless of whether or not the loan is repaid by the DSU. Other financial institutions that are not financial intermediaries merely link up (for a fee) the SSUs who purchase direct claims on the DSUs. Stock brokerage firms are examples of financial institutions that are not financial intermediaries. They do not give off their own liability but merely arrange for the SSUs to purchase the stocks or bonds issued by DSUs.

Exhibit 1-3 pulls together the discussion on this point. SSUs can lend funds either directly in the financial markets or indirectly through financial intermediaries. If they lend funds in the financial markets, they acquire direct or primary financial claims against the income of the borrower, even if they purchased the stock or bond through a financial institution such as a stockbroker. DSUs borrow funds by issuing these financial claims in the market. To the holder/purchaser, the claims are financial assets owned, but to the issuer, the claims are financial liabilities owed. For example, the General Motors bonds mentioned previously are assets to Emma and liabilities to General Motors.

If SSUs lend funds through financial intermediaries, they acquire indirect or secondary financial claims on those intermediaries, which, in turn, acquire direct claims on DSUs. Putting funds into a savings account is a classic example of acquiring a secondary claim on a financial institution. The institution will, in turn, make loans directly to a DSU. Through lending activities, some financial intermediaries may also create new funds (money), which meet the needs of a growing economy. In either case, whether funds flow directly from SSUs or indirectly from intermediaries, credit is extended.

More on Financial Intermediaries

One might ask, "Why do we need financial institutions that are also financial intermediaries? Why don't savers lend directly to borrowers and acquire direct

Financial Markets
Markets in which spending units trade financial claims.

Direct Finance
When SSUs lend their funds directly to DSUs.

Financial institutions
Firms that provide financial services to SSUs and DSUs; the most important financial institutions are financial intermediaries.

Financial Intermediaries
Financial institutions that borrow from SSUs for the purpose of lending to DSUs.

Indirect Finance
When DSUs borrow from financial intermediaries that have acquired the funds to lend from SSUs.

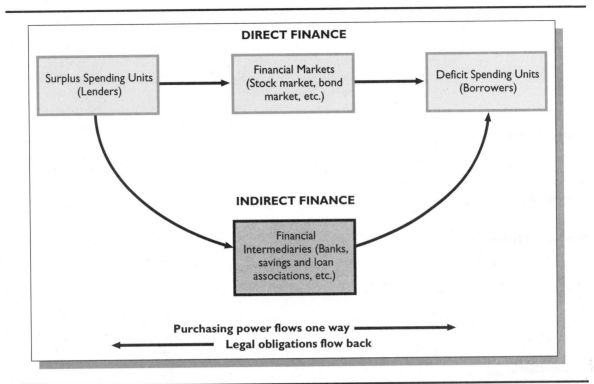

DIRECT FINANCE

Surplus Spending Units (Lenders) → Financial Markets (Stock market, bond market, etc.) → Deficit Spending Units (Borrowers)

INDIRECT FINANCE

Financial Intermediaries (Banks, savings and loan associations, etc.)

Purchasing power flows one way ⟶
⟵ Legal obligations flow back

EXHIBIT 1-3
The Financial System

claims on the ultimate DSUs?" To answer this, let us begin with the initial choices and decisions that we would face as a household. If we are working, we have a steady flow of income. If we spend only part of our income on consumption and investment goods, then we are a surplus household, or SSU. If we spend more than our income, then we must borrow, making us a deficit household, or DSU. Since deciding what to do with a surplus is more pleasant than worrying about how to finance a deficit, let us assume that we spend only part of our income on consumption and investment. Now what should we do with our surplus?

An SSU basically has two decisions to make. The first choice is between holding the surplus in the form of cash (paper currency and coin) or lending it out.[5] Because cash does not earn interest, we would probably decide to lend out at least a portion of our surplus funds to earn some interest income. This leads us to the second decision the surplus household must make: How and where is the surplus to be loaned? We could go directly to the financial markets and purchase a new bond being issued by a corporation, either through a broker or directly from the corporation. Presumably, we would not pick a bond at random. For example, we might look for a bond issued by a reputable, creditworthy borrower that will be likely to pay the promised interest on schedule and also to repay the principal, or the original amount of the loan, when the bond matures in, say, 10 years. In short, we would appraise the risk or probability of **default,** which is the failure of the borrower to pay interest, repay principal, or both.

Default
When a borrower fails to repay a financial claim.

---

[5]There is another option. If we owe back debts, we could employ surplus funds to pay off those debts.

To minimize the risk of our surplus being wiped out by the default of a particular borrower, we might want to spread our risks out and diversify. We can accomplish this by spreading our surplus over a number of DSUs.[6] In nontechnical terms, we would avoid putting all of our eggs into one basket. Moreover, most SSUs are not experts in appraising and diversifying risk and would thus hire a broker for advice about the primary claims issued by DSUs.

All of this would, of course, take time and effort. As a result, many prefer to place their surplus funds in financial intermediaries. Financial intermediaries acquire the funds of SSUs by offering claims on themselves. In other words, the SSU has really made a loan to the financial intermediary and therefore has a financial claim on the intermediary in the amount of the surplus. To determine its profit, the financial intermediary subtracts what it pays to SSUs for the use of the funds from what it earns on the loans and other investments it makes with those funds.

The financial intermediaries pool the funds they acquire from many individual SSUs and then use the funds to make loans to businesses and households, purchase bonds, and so forth. The intermediaries are actually lending out the surpluses they accept from individual SSUs while also appraising and diversifying the risk associated with lending directly to DSUs. Because the intermediaries specialize in this kind of work, it is reasonable to presume that they know what they are doing and, on average, do a better job than individual SSUs could do without hiring a broker or other financial adviser. Put a bit more formally, financial intermediaries minimize the costs—called **transactions costs**—associated with borrowing and lending.

Another reason why SSUs often entrust their funds to financial intermediaries is that the secondary (indirect) claims offered by intermediaries are often more attractive to many SSUs than the primary (direct) claims available in financial markets. In many cases, for example, the secondary claims of intermediaries are insured by an agency of the federal government such as the Federal Deposit Insurance Corporation (FDIC).[7] Therefore, the risk of default associated with holding a secondary claim is often less than with a primary claim.

In addition, secondary claims are attractive because they are often more liquid than primary claims. **Liquidity** refers to the ease of exchanging a financial claim for cash without loss of value. Different types of claims possess varying degrees of liquidity. A claim easily exchanged for cash, such as a savings deposit, is highly liquid; exchanging a less-liquid claim involves more significant time, cost, and/or inconvenience. A rare oil painting is an example of a less-liquid asset.

Suppose you loaned funds directly to a small, obscure corporation and the loan's term of maturity (the time from when you gave the firm the funds until it must pay back the principal) was 2 years. You have a financial claim in the form of a loan contract, and the corporation has your surplus funds. What would happen if after 1 year you suddenly wanted the funds back for some emergency expenditure? You

Transactions Costs
The costs associated with borrowing and lending or making other exchanges.

Liquidity
The ease with which a financial claim can be converted to cash without loss of value.

---

[6]If we have only a small amount of surplus funds available, it may be extremely difficult to diversify to a significant extent. As we shall see in later chapters, small investors can use mutual funds to accomplish this objective.

[7]The FDIC enables the public to feel confident that funds deposited in a bank or savings and loan, up to a limit (currently $100,000), are safe. If the institution fails, the FDIC will step in and pay off the depositors. When financial institutions were failing daily during the early years of the Great Depression in the 1930s, the government became convinced of the pressing need for such an agency. See *http://www.fdic.gov/*.

might ask the corporation to pay you back at once, before the due date of the loan. If this option is closed because the borrower is unwilling or unable to pay off the loan immediately, you might try to sell the claim on the borrower to someone else who is willing to hold it until maturity. Although there are organized markets for the buying and selling of certain types of existing financial claims, such markets do not exist for all types of claims. The hassle associated with unloading the loan contract in a time of crisis should be obvious. To avoid such inconvenience, many SSUs prefer to hold claims on financial intermediaries and let the "experts" worry about any problems.

Depository Institutions and Other Types of Intermediaries

Depository institutions, consisting of commercial banks, savings and loan associations, credit unions, and mutual savings banks, are the most familiar and the largest group of financial intermediaries. Not surprisingly, their principal source of funds is the deposits of individuals, business firms, and governments, both domestic and foreign. Depository institutions are particularly popular with SSUs because the secondary claims purchased by SSUs from depository institutions—that is, the deposits—are often insured and therefore relatively safe. **Checkable deposits,** as the name implies, are subject to withdrawal by writing a check to a third party, and are now offered by all depository institutions. Such deposits are money per se because they can be used in their present form as a means of payment. Because depository institutions issue checkable deposits, they are a central part of the process that determines the nation's money supply. Other claims on depository institutions such as savings deposits, although not money, are also quite liquid.

Other types of intermediaries offer specialized secondary claims. For example, insurance companies offer financial protection against early death (life companies) or property losses (casualty companies), while pension plans provide financial resources for one's old age. All of these specialized intermediaries collect savings in the form of premium payments or contributions from those who participate in the plans. Each intermediary then uses the funds acquired to purchase a variety of primary claims from DSUs. Investment-type intermediaries, such as mutual funds and money market funds, pool the surplus funds of many small savers and invest them in financial markets, thereby offering the small savers greater opportunities to diversify than they would otherwise realize. Finance companies borrow by issuing short- and long-term debt instruments and lend the proceeds to households to finance consumer purchases and to firms to finance inventories. Exhibit 1-4 highlights the various types of intermediaries.

Depository Institutions
Financial intermediaries that issue checkable deposits.

Checkable Deposits
Deposits that are subject to withdrawal by writing a check.

RECAP When SSUs lend directly to DSUs, direct finance occurs. When SSUs put their funds in financial intermediaries, which then lend to DSUs, indirect finance occurs. Financial intermediaries are a type of financial institution that acquires the funds of SSUs by issuing claims on themselves. They use the funds to purchase the financial claims of DSUs. The most important financial intermediaries are depository institutions that issue checkable deposits. Other financial intermediaries include life and casualty insurance companies, pension funds, mutual funds and money market mutual funds, and finance companies.

EXHIBIT 1-4
Types of Financial
Intermediaries

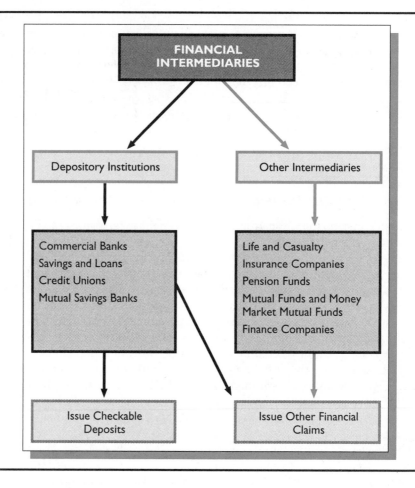

The Federal Reserve System

Federal Reserve (Fed)
The central bank of the
United States that
regulates the banking
system and determines
monetary policy.

Financial markets and institutions are greatly influenced by the **Federal Reserve.**
The Federal Reserve is a quasi-independent government agency that serves as our
nation's central bank. Its influence begins with the depository institutions and their
role in the money supply process and then spreads to other intermediaries and
financial markets in general.

The Fed, as it is often called, has a profound influence on the behavior of depository institutions through its regulatory policy and its ability to affect interest rates
and the total volume of funds available for borrowing and lending. In recent years,
depository institutions have experienced a declining share of the funds available for
lending from SSUs to DSUs, while other financial intermediaries and financial
markets have received an increasing share.[8] In addition, international financial
flows (borrowing and lending that transcends national borders) have increased
greatly. Because the Fed has more influence on domestic depository institutions
than on other financial intermediaries and financial markets, there is concern that

---

[8]Even some firms that are not primarily financial in nature are engaging in credit extension. Examples of very large, nonfinancial institutions that have entered the lending business include General Electric (GE), Sears, and General Motors (GM), all of which now issue credit cards.

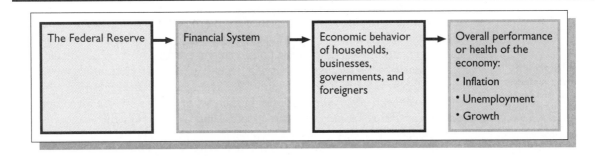

EXHIBIT 1-5
The Influence of the Fed's Monetary Policy

the Fed's ability to influence the economy through traditional avenues has actually declined. Nevertheless, the Fed continues to maintain a leading role in determining the overall health of the U.S. economy and of financial markets and institutions. The Fed's influence on depository institutions spreads through a number of channels to other financial intermediaries and more generally to the transfer of funds from SSUs to DSUs in financial markets. By affecting interest rates and the volume of funds transferred from SSUs to DSUs, the Fed can influence the aggregate, or total, demand for goods and services in the economy and, hence, the overall health of the economy. A general representation of this relationship is shown in Exhibit 1-5. The middle of this figure—the financial system and economic behavior of spending units—represents the essential anatomy or structure of the economy. The task before us is to learn how each part of the economy operates and how the collective activity of the parts is affected by the Fed's **monetary policy**—that is, the Fed's efforts to promote the overall health and stability of the economy.

Monetary Policy
The Fed's efforts to promote the overall health and stability of the economy.

In terms of Exhibit 1-3, the Fed monitors the performance of the financial system and the economy with an eye toward augmenting or reducing the supply of funds flowing from SSUs through financial markets and financial intermediaries to DSUs. Any action the Fed undertakes sets off a chain of reactions as depicted in Exhibit 1-5.

As we begin to think about the Fed's conduct of monetary policy and its effects on the economy, an analogy might be helpful. Think of the U.S. economy as a human patient to be observed and hopefully understood. Just as a human body is made of many parts (arms, legs, torso), the U.S. economy is composed of many sectors (household, business, government, and foreign). Money and the acts of spending and saving and lending and borrowing are analogous to the blood and the circulatory system of the body. We want to study how the behavior of money and credit extension (borrowing and lending) affects the well-being of households, business firms, and, more generally, the overall economy. By focusing on the borrowing and lending of money and on spending and saving, we shall see how the major sectors of the economy interact to produce goods and services and to generate income.

The health of the U.S. economy varies over time. At times the economy appears to be well and functioning normally; at other times, it appears listless and depressed; and at still other times, it seems hyperactive—characterized by erratic, unstable behavior. By studying how all of the key parts of the economy fit together, we should be able to learn something about the illnesses that can strike this patient. What causes a particular type of illness (say, inflation or unemployment)? How is the illness diagnosed? What medicines or cures can be prescribed? If more than one treatment is possible, which will work best? Are any undesirable side effects associated with particular medications? Are the doctors who diagnose the problems and administer the treatment (the policymakers) ever guilty of malpractice?

Answers to all of these questions will depend in part on "what makes the patient tick" and how we define "good health." A human patient's health is determined by the deviations, if any, from a well-established set of precise criteria involving temperature, reflexes, blood chemistry, appetite, and so forth. For the economy, however, we have no well-established, precise criteria that allow us to judge its health. Rather, loosely defined goals or objectives such as "full" employment or "low" inflation are used. If everyone agrees on these goals, including how to define and measure them, and the economy seems to be operating in the neighborhood of the goals, then we might say that the economy is in good health. If we are heading toward the goals, we would say that the economy's health is improving. If the economy seems to be deviating from the goals, however, we would say that its health is not good and that prescriptive measures may be necessary to improve matters.

The Role of Policy: Changing Views

Good health for the economy, as with humans, has both short- and long-run dimensions. Over the long run, we and policymakers would like to have the economy grow such that the quality of life and standard of living for an increasing population can improve. In the short run, we would like to minimize the fluctuations or deviations from the long-run growth path. In economics, these short-run fluctuations of the economy are part of what is appropriately called the business cycle. Exhibit 1-6 illustrates the various stages of the **business cycle** and shows how they are related to the longer-run growth of the economy. The economy, like most of us, has its ups and downs. During a recovery, or **expansion,** economic activity, as measured by the total quantity of goods and services being bought and sold, increases and unemployment falls. During a **recession,** or contraction, economic

**http://www.
minneapolisfed.org/
sylloge/history.html**
*Provides a brief history of
the Federal Reserve.*

**http://www.
minneapolisfed.org/
info/policy/index.html**
*Explains more on monetary
policy.*

Business Cycle
Short-run fluctuations in
economic activity as
measured by the output of
goods and services.

Expansion
The phase of the business
cycle in which economic
activity increases and
unemployment falls.

Recession
The phase of the business
cycle in which economic
activity falls and
unemployment rises.

EXHIBIT 1-6
Long-Run Economic
Growth and the
Business Cycle

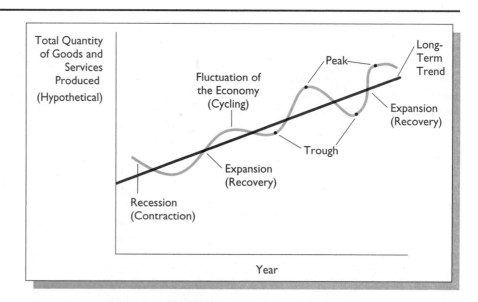

activity falls and unemployment rises. Just before the peak, all is bright and the economy/patient seems truly healthy. At the trough, all is bleak and the economy/patient appears quite ill. Over the longer run, we can calculate the average growth rate (trend), which smoothes out the expansions and contractions.

The key question is whether policymakers can, in fact, "manage" the economy successfully. Can they use monetary policy to minimize the short-run fluctuations of the economy over its long-run growth path? Can they use government spending and taxing decisions (**fiscal policy**) to speed up or slow economic activity as needed? Can they, over time, change the growth rate of output? Since a look at the historical record does not provide an encouraging answer to this question, many have wondered about the appropriate role of policy in a complex modern economy.

The medical profession requires considerable study and knowledge of causes and possible treatments before practitioners can diagnose and deal with an ailment. Despite the best efforts of eminent researchers, we still do not know how to cure some diseases. So too in economics; cures for all the economic ills we may encounter are not known.

Why are the goals that policymakers are trying to achieve on behalf of society so elusive? The answers are complex and fall into three possible areas.[9] First, the diagnosticians may not understand all the causes of the problems. What this really means is that we do not fully understand how the economy functions. Second, policymakers may be reluctant to use the currently known medicines to treat the patient because they have undesirable side effects, which may, in fact, be worse than the disease. Third, the cure for the problem may not yet be known, so more research will be needed to find a useful therapeutic approach. Thus far we have assumed that the economy's illness can only be cured by the doctors and their medicines. But could the patient get better by itself?

Prior to the Great Depression of the 1930s, many economists tended to see the economy as inherently stable, having strong, self-correcting tendencies. The prevailing belief was that the economy would never drift away from full-employment equilibrium for long; any disturbance or shock that pushed the economy away from full employment would automatically set in motion forces that tend to move the economy back to full-employment equilibrium.[10] Thus, before the Depression, many economists felt that there was no need for corrective government action when the economy was disturbed because any movement away from equilibrium would be temporary and self-correcting. This view of the economy provided an economic rationale for the government to pursue a **laissez-faire,** hands-off policy.

The Great Depression altered this view of the economy's internal dynamics. Between 1929 and 1933, the unemployment rate increased from about 3 percent to about 25 percent. The downturn was experienced worldwide and persisted until the start of World War II. Few could argue, in the face of such evidence, that the problem was correcting itself. The economist John Maynard Keynes and others suggested that once the economy's full-employment equilibrium was disturbed, its self-correcting powers were likely to be overwhelmed by other forces. The net result would be that the economy could operate below full employment for some time.

Fiscal Policy
Government spending and taxing decisions to speed up or slow down the level of economic activity.

Laissez-Faire
The view that government should pursue a hands-off policy with regard to the economy.

http://www.yardeni. com/public/cycles.html
Provides business cycle expansion and contraction tables.

---

[9]The complex answers are tackled in Part Six of this text.

[10]Equilibrium is a concept used by economists to help analyze the economy. It refers to a state of the economy from which there is no tendency to deviate—a state of rest. Of course, in reality, the economy is constantly being bombarded with disturbances and is hardly ever "at rest." The concept of equilibrium, then, is an analytical device that helps us sort out the influences of many different factors, which, in the real world, are often all changing at the same time.

	GROWTH		
	Inflation	*Unemployment*	*(Output)*
1960s	2.4%	4.75%	4.4%
1970s	7.0	6.25	3.2
1980s	5.5*	8.25	2.8
1990s	3.3	5.7**	3.7
2000–2001***	3.6	4.1	2.2

*Actually, if 1980 and 1981 are not considered, inflation averaged just under 4 percent for the remainder of the 1980s.

**From mid 1997 through the rest of the decade, unemployment was below 5 percent.

***Annualized through second quarter 2001 only.

SOURCE: *http://www.stls.frb.org/fred/*

This new perspective gave the government an economic rationale for attempting to stabilize overall economic activity. A consensus formed that a highly developed market economy, if left to itself, would be unstable. As a result, "activist" stabilization policy has been practiced by both Democratic and Republican administrations since the mid-1930s.

Despite the activist policies, the economy's performance in the 1970s and the early 1980s gave rise to doubts about the government's ability to stabilize the economy. As Exhibit 1-7 shows, the growth trend of the economy was below that achieved in the 1960s and the fluctuations around the trend were quite large. The unemployment and inflation rates were both higher in the 1970s and early 1980s than they had been in the 1960s. These developments raised many questions. Does the government know how to proceed to restore the patient's health? If it acts without adequate knowledge, can policy make things worse rather than better? Many people reverted to the pre-Depression view that "less government intervention in the economy is better." But reducing the role of government may be difficult. Attempts to do so in the 1980s resulted in larger government deficits and not less government.

Although the economy experienced healthy growth from about 1983 until the late 1980s, many believed that this growth was produced by large government deficits and increases in military spending. Chronic trade deficits, problem loans to less-developed countries, troubles within the savings and loan industry, and the collapse of the junk bond market were of concern to many.

The recession of the early 1990s caused anxiety, not because of its depth or length, but because the recovery was so sluggish. Growth remained lethargic well into the first half of 1993, and in some regions beyond that. The clear perception was that the economy was broken and needed to be fixed. The election of Bill Clinton to the presidency in 1992 focused on one issue: getting the economy back on track.

By early 1994, economic growth had accelerated, and even though inflation rates remained subdued, the Fed became concerned that the high economic growth rate could precipitate inflation. Beginning in February 1994, the Fed attempted to slow the growth rate of the economy. Over the course of the next year, the Fed took actions to increase interest rates seven times. In July 1995, the Fed reversed course and took action that led to a small decrease in interest rates. Through 1995, the economy continued to perform well, and the inflation and unemployment rates fell. Bill Clinton was reelected in 1996 as the economy continued to expand.

In March 1997, the Fed again nudged interest rates slightly higher in fear that an overheating economy would fuel inflation. By the end of the decade, the long expansion resulted in an unemployment rate of 4 percent—the lowest rate in over 30 years. Surprisingly, there was little or no acceleration of inflation despite such low unemployment.

Stock and bond prices experienced extraordinary increases into the late 1990s, even though Alan Greenspan, the Fed chair, voiced concern in December 1996 that an "irrational exuberance" was taking over in these markets. Despite a moderate correction of stock prices in October 1997, the stock market again closed at a record high in July 1998. To some, the crisis in Asia meant good news for the U.S. economy, which was believed to be less likely to overheat. By late summer 1998, stock prices finally succumbed to international financial problems. Stock prices plummeted about 20 percent, and questions surfaced about whether the U.S. economy could withstand a global downturn. The Fed responded by lowering interest rates three times in the fall of 1998. The fiscal year ended on September 30, 1998, with a widely publicized federal government budget surplus of $70 billion—the first surplus since 1969. By the end of calendar year 1998, the lower interest rates had the desired effect, and the stock market rebounded strongly with new record highs.

The economy continued to expand into the new millennium with the stock market reaching record highs in March 2000. However, there were clouds on the horizon that suggested the record long expansion could not last forever. From March 2000 on, the technology-dominated NASDAQ index of stock prices plummeted, losing over 50 percent of its value by December 31, 2000 and the DOW, the best-known index of stock prices, ended the year 2000 down for the first time since 1988. A contested presidential election gave the appearance of a divided nation. George W. Bush, the eventual winner, expressed concerns about the economy and further emphasized the need for a large income tax cut. The Fed agreed that clouds were on the horizon. Worries that the economy was heading steeply down caused the Fed to orchestrate a relatively large decrease in interest rates in early January 2001 before the new president took office. Many factors continued to threaten the record expansion including falling profits, a languishing stock market, escalating energy prices, announcements of significant layoffs, and drops in consumer confidence. In September 2001, the attacks on the World Trade Center and the Pentagon and the resulting economic turmoil convinced most people that the economy was very close to recession if not already into one. All in all, the Fed lowered interest rates nine times between January and October of 2001.

Whether the Fed's dramatic moves in 2001 or other actions by policymakers will turn the economy around remains to be seen. One thing is clear: Monetary policymakers and those affected by changes in the financial environment—each one of us—will make better decisions if we understand as best we can financial markets and institutions and their roles in the economy.

Summary of Major Points

- Economics is concerned with how, given people's unlimited wants, scarce resources are allocated among competing uses, how income is distributed, and how people allocate their incomes through spending, saving, borrowing, and lending decisions.

- Finance focuses on the financial side of these decisions—that is, the raising and using of funds by households, firms, and governments.

- The financial system consists of financial markets and institutions that coordinate and channel the flow of funds from lenders to borrowers and creates new liquidity for an expanding economy. The characteristics of this process have changed over time as innovations, the globalization of finance, and changes in regulations have occurred.

- Spending units that spend less than their current income on consumption and investment are called surplus spending units (SSUs); they are the ultimate lenders in society. Spending units that spend more than their current income are called deficit spending units (DSUs); they are the ultimate borrowers in society. Financial instruments are financial claims that are assets to the holder (purchaser) and liabilities to the issuer.

- In allocating funds among the various types of financial assets available, SSUs are concerned about the expected return, the risk of loss, and the liquidity associated with acquiring and holding a particular asset.

- Direct finance involves lending directly to DSUs either through a broker or not through a broker. A broker arranges a trade and gives financial advice but does not issue its own liability. Indirect finance involves lending to a financial intermediary, a type of financial institution that borrows from SSUs to relend to DSUs. Financial intermediaries issue claims on themselves. The lenders receive financial claims on the financial intermediary and the borrowers receive funds from the financial intermediaries.

- Financial intermediaries exist because they help to minimize the transactions costs associated with borrowing and lending. The financial services provided include appraising and diversifying risk, offering a menu of financial claims that are relatively safe and liquid, and pooling funds from individual SSUs.

- The most important types of financial intermediaries are the depository institutions: commer-

cial banks, savings and loan associations, mutual savings banks, and credit unions. These institutions issue checkable deposits and are central to the process of determining the nation's money supply. Other types of financial intermediaries are life and casualty insurance companies, pension funds, mutual funds and money market mutual funds, and finance companies.

- The Federal Reserve is a quasi-independent government agency that serves as our nation's central bank. Its regulatory policy is aimed at promoting a smooth-running, efficient, competitive financial system. The Fed's monetary policy, which influences interest rates and the volume of funds available for borrowing and lending (credit extension), is directed at enhancing the overall health and stability of the economy. Although the Fed works primarily through depository institutions, its influence spreads from depository institutions to the financial system.

- Views on the appropriate role of policy in the economy—that is, how "activist" policymakers should be in trying to manage the economy—have varied over time. Following the relatively poor performance of the economy in the 1970s, views have shifted somewhat back toward the pre-Depression perspective that "less government intervention is better." Throughout the 1980s, the economy experienced healthy growth that was accompanied by large trade and government deficits. After a recession in the early 1990s, economic growth resumed, and the economy achieved both low inflation and low unemployment with a record long expansion into the new millennium. By late 2001, it became clear that growth had decelerated and the economy was close to, if not in, a recession.

Key Terms

Business Cycle	Federal Reserve (Fed)	Macroeconomics
Checkable Deposits	Finance	Microeconomics
Default	Financial Institutions	Monetary Policy
Deficit Spending Units (DSUs)	Financial Intermediaries	Money
Depository Institutions	Financial Markets	Recession
Deregulation	Fiscal Policy	Saving
Direct Finance	Indirect Finance	Surplus Spending Units (SSUs)
Economics	Laissez-Faire	Transactions Costs
Expansion	Liquidity	

Review Questions

1. Provide a short definition of and discuss the following terms: economics, finance, the financial system, SSUs, DSUs, direct and indirect finance, financial markets, financial intermediaries, liquidity, the business cycle, depository institutions, and monetary policy.

2. Some people have money; some people need money. Explain how the financial system links these people together.

3. Discuss the statement: "Since I have high credit card limits, I have lots of money." Are credit cards money? Why or why not? (Hint: See footnote 2.)

4. When are the surplus funds I have available to lend in financial markets equal to my saving?

5. Why do financial intermediaries exist? What services do they provide to the public? Are all financial institutions financial intermediaries?

6. What are transactions costs? Does financial intermediation increase or decrease transactions costs?

7. What is a depository institution? What is a checkable deposit? How does a depository institution differ from other intermediaries? Give three examples of depository institutions.

8. Why does the Fed monitor the economy? What actions can the Fed take to affect the overall health of the economy?

9. Does the Fed directly or indirectly affect all financial markets and institutions?

10. Why have views changed concerning the appropriate role of stabilization policies in managing the economy? Briefly discuss the historical evolution of these views.

11. What are the pros and cons of lending to my next-door neighbor rather than putting my surplus funds in a bank?

12. Define laissez-faire and fiscal policy. Who determines fiscal policy? Who determines monetary policy?

Analytical Questions

13. Rank the following assets in terms of their liquidity, from least to most liquid: cash, savings deposits, gold, a house, a rare oil painting, a checkable deposit. Explain your rank order.

14. Explain whether each of the following is an example of direct or indirect financing:

    a. John purchases stock from the biotech firm that employs him.
    b. John purchases the stock of a biotech firm through a stock broker.
    c. Mary purchases a newly issued government security.
    d. John places $3,000 in a savings account at the local savings and loan.
    e. John receives a loan from Mary.
    f. John receives a loan from Friendly Savings Bank.

15. Bill's income is $4,000. He spends $3,000 on consumption and $300 on an investment in a newly constructed house. He acquires $700 in financial assets. What is his saving? What is the amount of surplus funds he has available to lend?

16. A firm spends $100,000 on investment in plant and equipment. It has available funds of $30,000 and borrows the additional funds from a bank. Is the firm a DSU or an SSU? What is the amount of the surplus or deficit?

17. What are the phases of a business cycle? Draw a graph of a typical business cycle and label the various phases.

18. The misery index is defined as the sum of the unemployment and the inflation rates. Use Exhibit 1-7 to calculate the misery index for each decade since 1960.

Internet Exercise

Access the following Web site: **http://stats.bls. gov/**. List some key economic variables that are tracked on this Web page. What U.S. government agency is responsible for the data listed here?

Suggested Readings

If the material covered in the text is to come alive and make sense to you, we suggest you try to read *The Wall Street Journal* and *Business Week* regularly. In fact, hardly a day goes by without a report on an issue that is in some way relevant to our subject. You might also consult *The New York Times*, *The Washington Post*, or *The Los Angeles Times;* all have good financial sections. Or you can browse the financial sections of *USA Today* (**http://www.usatoday. com**) or CNN (**http://www.cnnfn.com**) on the World Wide Web.

Go to the library and thumb through the *Federal Reserve Bulletin*. A half-hour investment here will reveal the types of data collected and distributed by the Fed (contained in the second half of the *Bulletin*) and the range of issues the Fed concerns itself with (contained in the first half). A plethora of financial statistics can also be found in the Federal Reserve Bank Economic Database Web site (**http://www.stls. frb.org/fred/**).

A wealth of information about the current state of the economy and attempts at stabilization by the government can be found in *The Economic Report of the President*. It is published annually during the month of February by the U.S. Government Printing Office and is available at the reference desk of most libraries. It is also available on the Internet at **http://w3.access.gpo.gov/eop/**.

The *Statistical Abstract of the United States* contains summary data on income, expenditures, wealth, prices, and the financial system (among other things). It is published annually during December by the Bureau of the Census, Department of Commerce. The *Survey of Current Business*, published monthly by the Bureau of Economic Analysis, Department of Commerce, contains current business and income statistics. The *Statistical Abstract* is also available at the following Bureau of the Census Web site: **http://www.census.gov/ftp/pub/ statab/www**.

chapter

Money: A Unique Financial Instrument

②

Learning Objectives *After reading this chapter, you should know:*

- The functions of money and why money is different from other financial instruments
- Why the Federal Reserve publishes numerous measures of monetary aggregates including M1, M2, and M3
- The meaning of domestic nonfinancial debt (DNFD)
- How and why money and the payments system have evolved over time
- What the interest rate is
- How the supply of and demand for money—and/or credit flows—influence the interest rate

" "
*If it waddles like a duck,
and quacks like a duck,
then it is a duck.*

Conceptualization: A Key Building Block

As the week ends at the start-up Internet company, Mary, the owner, calls Randy, the head programmer, over and gives him his pay envelope. It should contain $1,000. Finding the envelope somewhat different than normal, Randy opens it and discovers a piece of paper similar to a 5-year bond that promises to pay $100 at the end of each year for the next 4 years and $1,100 at the end of 5 years. Tired and somewhat irritated, especially since his rent is due next week, Randy tells Mary he wants money and not this piece of paper. Mary tries to persuade Randy to accept the paper, which promises to pay a larger amount of money in the future, but fails and eventually produces a check made out to Randy for $1,000. The check can be cashed so that Randy can receive the full $1,000 today.

A simple story. Yet it touches on most of the key issues addressed in this chapter: Why did Randy want money instead of the paper? Why does he accept the check? Why isn't the piece of paper money? Why is it not as good as money? The answers to such questions are not as obvious as one might think. As we shall see, money is a unique financial instrument. We need to be precise about how it is defined and measured.

Defining Money

In finance, money is defined in terms of its specific functions within the financial system—that is, by what it does. By specifying precisely what it does, we can distinguish money from the other financial instruments we observe in the financial system, even those things that at first glance appear quite similar. Of particular interest is what makes money unique: What does it do that other things do not?

The primary function of money is that it serves as a generally acceptable **means of payment,** or **medium of exchange.** This function distinguishes it from all other financial instruments. As stated in Chapter 1, money is what we generally use to make payments and what others generally accept as payment. The importance of money's function as a means of payment is so obvious that it is often overlooked.

Means of Payment (Medium of Exchange)
Something generally acceptable for making payments.

Imagine a world without money where all goods were exchanged by trading for other goods, a system called **barter.** Historically, barter was how people exchanged goods and services before some form of money evolved. Bartering was typically done in agricultural societies, but is still practiced in many areas of the world today. Bartering still exists today, not only in agrarian countries, but also in our own, and bartering is alive and well on the Internet. Barter club members exchange goods and services with each other, and individuals often exchange goods for services, or services for goods. The days of paying for a good or service with two chickens and a handmade wooden stool are not over yet. However, this method of exchange is complicated and time consuming.

Barter
Trade of goods for goods.

http://www.google.com, http://www.altavista.com, or **http://www.yahoo.com**
Do a search for "barter system" in one or more of the Internet search engines, and see how many variations you can find.

For example, if you were Randy and you worked in a computer factory, you might be paid in keyboards, which would not only be difficult to exchange for other goods and services but would also be rather cumbersome to carry around. To buy groceries, for example, you would have to persuade the grocer to accept your keyboards as payment. Unless the grocer needed keyboards or knew someone who did, she would not find this as an accepted form of payment. Finding a **double coincidence of wants,** whereby the person you wished to buy from wanted what you were offering in exchange, would often be extremely difficult. Exchange under a barter system is costly in terms of search time—the time spent looking for someone who has groceries and wants computer keyboards—and is a cumbersome and inefficient way to conduct transactions. Search time and effort raise transactions costs—the costs involved with making exchanges—higher transactions costs hold down the volume of exchange in the economy. For efficiency and speed to occur in commercial transactions, societies turned to some form of money.

Because we do have something that serves as a generally accepted means of payment—money—people can exchange goods and services for money and vice versa. To illustrate, Randy, the programmer mentioned earlier, planned to exchange a week's labor for $1,000 and the $1,000 for rent. If Randy had accepted the piece of paper—a type of financial instrument—he could not have paid his rent until the financial instrument was cashed in at the end of 5 years, or until he found someone who wanted the piece of paper and would pay him cash for it, or unless he could convince his landlord to accept the piece of paper. If none of these options worked, he would have an obvious dilemma and would either have to move or be homeless. If he had been paid in money, he would have none of these problems. We see from this example that a monetary exchange eliminates the need for a double coincidence of wants and facilitates trade by reducing the transactions costs involved.

Something that becomes generally accepted as a means of payment in exchange for goods and services will necessarily also function as a **store of value.** To be accepted as a medium of exchange, the medium must store value. More specifically, because people receive money and spend it at different points in time, the medium of exchange must have a specific value that lasts for some period of time. If you are paid for your labor today and have no need to purchase anything until tomorrow, you would presumably be unwilling to accept anything in payment that is likely to decline in value before you spend it. (Could Randy have sold the piece of paper for $1,000 if the company went out of business or if there was a question that the company could make the promised payments?) People will accept something as a means of payment for goods and services when they believe that they can easily exchange it for something else of like value in the near future.

We now know that money functions as a means of payment and store of value and what these functions mean. For monetary exchange to proceed in an orderly fashion, however, there must be some method of specifying the measure of value of a unit of money. Because all domestic prices and financial records, including debts, are expressed in dollars, the dollar serves as our monetary **unit of account**—the standard measure of value. To appreciate why it is convenient to have a standardized unit of account, imagine the poor grocer and the grocer's customers who, in the absence of money and a unit of account, would have to remember that one computer keyboard equals 4 quarts of milk, one crate of oranges equals 3 pounds of cheese, and so forth. A unit of account facilitates actual transactions throughout the economy by making it possible to compare the relative values of different goods and services and to keep records about prices and debts.

In sum, money is a unique financial instrument that circulates in a modern economy and is a generally accepted means of payment. Money also functions as a store of value, and its unit of measurement becomes the unit of account and measure of value. The functions of money are portrayed in Exhibit 2-1.

Double Coincidence of Wants
In barter, the situation when each person involved in a potential exchange has what the other person wants.

Store of Value
Something that retains its value over time.

Unit of Account
A standardized accounting unit such as the dollar that provides a consistent measure of value.

EXHIBIT 2-1
The Functions
of Money

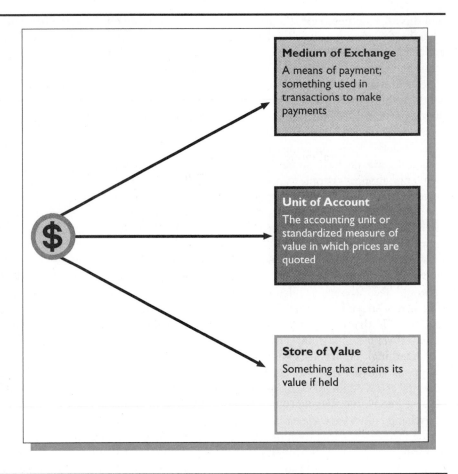

Medium of Exchange
A means of payment;
something used in
transactions to make
payments

Unit of Account
The accounting unit or
standardized measure of
value in which prices are
quoted

Store of Value
Something that retains its
value if held

The Monetary Aggregates and Domestic Nonfinancial Debt

Given our definition, measuring the quantity or stock of money in an economy should be straightforward: Add together all the things that function as a means of payment. In reality, measurement is not quite so simple. There are at least two difficulties. First, what functions as a means of payment in an economy will change over time; what is considered money will need to be revised as the economy's financial system evolves. For example, at one time, gold and silver coins were money. Now they are no longer used as a means of payment, having been replaced by paper currency, coins made out of nonprecious metals, and checkable deposits. We must keep in mind as we talk about money that we refer to more than coins and cash.

Second, some things may be difficult to classify; that is, some financial instruments are on the borderline between being and not being a means of payment. For example, **money market deposit accounts (MMDAs)** are seldom used as a means of payment because they have limited check-writing privileges—up to three checks per month. Because of the limited check-writing privileges, MMDAs are financial instruments that have some characteristics of checking accounts and, hence, are a borderline case.

Money Market Deposit Accounts (MMDAs) Financial instruments with limited check-writing privileges, offered by banks since 1982; they earn higher interest than fully checkable deposits and require a higher minimum balance.

These difficulties aside, the measurement and classification of money are vital tasks in our economy. The Fed's policy actions have often been guided in part by the money supply. Therefore, at any point in time, the Fed must have as accurate a measurement of the quantity of money as possible. Given the existence of several financial instruments that are close to being full-fledged means of payment and some controversy within the economics profession over the adequacy and narrowness of the means of payment definition, it should come as no surprise to learn that:

1. Rather than relying on only one measure, the Fed collects, publishes, and monitors data on several monetary measures.

2. The items included in the various measures have changed over time as the financial system and new means of payment have evolved and as the Fed has strived to improve its monetary measures.

3. Because changes in credit market activity can also be used to guide Fed policy actions, the Fed further covers its bases by monitoring and publishing a broad measure of outstanding credit that includes unpaid loans and debts.

The Monetary Aggregates

Among the many jobs carried out by the Fed are the collection and regular publication of financial data. Currently, the Fed publishes data on several different monetary measures. These measures are referred to as **monetary aggregates,** or collections of monetary assets. Exhibit 2-2 shows the composition of **M1, M2,** and **M3,** the main monetary aggregates. The aggregates are comprised of several different types of financial instruments, some of which clearly serve as a means of payment (currency and checkable deposits), others that clearly are not means of payment ("large" time deposits), and some that are in between (money market deposit accounts). Note that M2 consists of everything in M1 plus some other highly liquid instruments, and M3 consists of everything in M2 plus some less-liquid instruments. Thus, in general, as the aggregate gets bigger, it includes more less-liquid instruments.

The measure that *currently* corresponds most closely to the definition of money is M1. It consists of currency held by the public and checkable deposits.[1] Checkable deposits are deposits that can be withdrawn by writing a check to a third party. They consist of:

- **Demand deposits,** which are non-interest-earning checking accounts issued by banks.

- Other checkable deposits, which are interest-earning checking accounts issued by any of the depository institutions.

M1 contains the "monetary" instruments that we *currently* use in transactions, and it is generally what we have in mind throughout the text when we refer to the money supply. All of the components of M1 are means of payment. This is not true of M2 and M3; for example, large time deposits, a component of M3, cannot be used to buy groceries.

Notice that the word "currently" has been italicized in the preceding two paragraphs. The reason, hinted at in the earlier part of this section, is that as financial regulations have changed and financial practices have evolved, the Fed has refined

Monetary Aggregates
The measures of money—including M1, M2, and M3—monitored and tracked by the Fed.

M1
Currency in the hands of the public plus checkable deposits.

M2
Everything in M1 plus other highly liquid assets.

M3
Everything in M2 plus some less-liquid assets.

Demand Deposits
Non-interest-earning checking accounts issued by banks.

---

[1]M1 also includes travelers' checks, which make up a relatively insignificant portion of M1. For simplicity, we ignore travelers' checks when we discuss M1.

EXHIBIT 2-2
The Monetary
Aggregates and
Domestic
Nonfinancial Debt as
of August 2001 (in
Billions of Dollars)

M1	
Currency in the hands of the public	$ 562.4
Demand deposits at commercial banks	314.4
Other checkable deposits (Deposits that can be withdrawn by unlimited check writing)	257.5
Travelers' checks	8.8
Total M1	$ 1,143.0*
M2	
M1 plus	
Small savings and time deposits (<$100,000), including money market deposit accounts	$ 3,144.3
Individual money market mutual funds	997.6
Total M2	$ 5,284.9*
M3	
M2 plus	
Large time deposits	$ 802.1
Term repurchase agreements and term Eurodollars	586.8
Institutional money market mutual funds	997.6
Total M3	$ 7,671.4
DNFD	
Federal: Credit market debt of the U.S. government and state and local governments	$ 3,349.0
Corporate bonds	
Mortgages	
Consumer credit (including bank loans)	15,540.7
Nonfederal: Other bank loans	
Commercial paper	
Other debt instruments	
Total DNFD	$18,889.7*

*Numbers may not sum to totals because of rounding.

SOURCE: *Federal Reserve Statistical Release H.6 (508),* Board of Governors of the Federal Reserve, September 27, 2001.

Negotiable Order of Withdrawal (NOW) Accounts
Interest-earning checking accounts.

and reconstructed the various monetary measures on a number of occasions. For example, **negotiable order of withdrawal (NOW) accounts,** which are essentially interest-bearing checking accounts, were not in existence in 1970. Created in 1972 in Massachusetts and New Hampshire as the brainchild of some clever financial institution executives, these accounts were initially counted as part of M2. When their volume grew and they became legal nationwide, they were "promoted" to M1, having become a generally acceptable means of payment. Money market deposit accounts, on the other hand, are included in M2. Because of the limitations on usage (only three checks per month), the Fed has concluded that depositors generally do not use these accounts as means of payment. Hence, MMDAs are included in M2—an aggregate containing M1 and other items that are so close to money that they are often referred to as **near monies.**

Near Monies
Highly liquid financial assets that can be converted easily to transactions money (M1) without loss of value.

The other near monies included in M2 are small time deposits, passbook savings deposits, and individual money market mutual funds. Even though they are not used to make transactions, they are all fairly liquid near monies because they can easily be converted to transactions money (checkable deposits or currency) without loss of value for the principal.

The essential point to keep in mind as we end this section on measuring money is that measurement is not nearly as straightforward as one might imagine. The difficulties and ambiguities, in turn, contribute to revisions in the various measures from time to time and lead the Fed to monitor several measures rather than relying on only one. Such flexibility is required by a dynamic financial system that evolves through time as rules, regulations, and payment practices change. Now is a good time to read A Closer Look on the evolution of the payments system.

RECAP **Money is anything that functions as a means of payment (medium of exchange), a unit of account, and a store of value. Money is acceptable in payment for goods and services. The Fed monitors several measures of money. M1 (transactions money) is currency in the hands of the public plus checkable deposits: M2 includes everything in M1 plus other highly liquid instruments. M3 includes everything in M2 plus some less-liquid instruments.**

The Ongoing Evolution of the Payments System—The Role of Technology: The tendency of the financial system to change is significantly influenced by the technology used to execute transactions. The payments mechanism is the means by which transactions are completed—that is, the ways in which money is transferred among transactors.

One method of transaction is checkable deposits that are payable on demand to third parties. For example, if you write a check to your grocer, the first two parties are you and the depository institution; the grocer is the third party. The check in payment for goods purchased is an order for your bank to debit (subtract) a certain number of dollars from your checkable deposit account. The dollars are then credited (added) to the deposit account of the grocer, the third party. Thus, a checkable deposit is a means of payment, and the check is the method used to transfer ownership of the deposit from one party to another. However, the check itself is not money; it is only a method of transferring money. The balances in checkable deposits are money.

Over the years, computer and telecommunications technologies have greatly altered the way in which payments are made. Technological innovations continue to make checks much less important as a means of transferring purchasing power, and they may even become obsolete. Today we make an increasingly larger percentage of payments through an *electronic funds transfer system.* In this system, payments are made to third parties in response to electronic instructions rather than to written instructions on a paper check. Note that an electronic funds transfer system does not eliminate the need for deposit accounts; it is just a more efficient way of transferring funds from one deposit account to another. For example, if you use an ATM card to pay your grocery bill, your account is debited by the amount of your bill, and the grocer's account is credited by the same amount at the time of the exchange at the point-of-sale computer terminal. The whole system is computerized so that no written checks are necessary. At the end of the month, you receive a bank statement giving your current balance and a record of all the charges and deposits to your account. This is handled just like a checking account statement, but without all of those written checks.

Other forms of electronic funds transfer systems are stored-value cards and smart cards. *Stored-valued cards* are plastic cards that are coded for a certain amount of funds embedded on a magnetic strip. They generally have a single use only. These cards are used like credit cards and are swiped through a card reader when their owner wants to access the funds. As the funds are spent, the balance on the card is transferred electronically from the card to the card reader. Stored-value cards are popular on college campuses to pay for such things as photocopying in the library, meals in the dining hall, and parking fees. They are also used to prepay for the use of toll roads and for store gift certificates. Phone cards are also stored-value cards.

Smart cards are much more sophisticated than stored-valued cards in that they are embedded with a microprocessor chip that stores information and usually includes a "digital signature." Unlike stored-value cards, the technology of smart cards makes them applicable for multiple usages by numerous vendors. The stored information leads to greater security than stored-value cards offer because the digital signature is verified each time the card is used. The amount of the payment is deducted electronically from the card and credited to the recipient of the payment by a point-of-sale terminal. At some point, the recipient transfers smart card payments from the point-of-sale terminal to its bank. If it is transferred immediately, the payment is completed in a matter of seconds. The microprocessor checks the authenticity of the transaction by examinimg the digital signature that is embedded in the chip. Although the validity is authenticated, the transaction is kept anonymous as if cash were used. Some smart cards are issued and accepted by a single institution only. Other smart cards are accepted by multiple institutions and multiple retailers. As such, smart cards offer the possiblity of replacing cash and checks to make most payments because they may be more convenient and cheaper to use.

Currently, many employers, in cooperation with banks, pay salaries by automatically crediting their employees' bank accounts rather than by issuing the customary weekly or monthly check. Such automatic credits are also a type of electronic funds transfer system.

One of the best known and most popular forms of electronic transfer of funds is the *automatic teller machine (ATM)*. Your depository institution most likely has ATMs, which permit you to make deposits and withdrawals, even when the institution itself is closed. In all probability, your college has a few ATMs on campus. ATMs are also visible in grocery stores and at shopping malls. Recently, portable ATMs in vans have been established that can be moved to sporting event locations, concerts, etc. The vans housing the ATMs have multiple security features that prevent theft.

Domestic Nonfinancial Debt

Domestic Nonfinancial Debt (DNFD)
An aggregate that is a measure of total credit market debt owed by the domestic nonfinancial government and private sectors.

Before we leave this section on money and the monetary aggregates, we need to introduce another aggregate that the Fed keeps track of along with M1, M2, and M3. This aggregate is **domestic nonfinancial debt (DNFD),** which is a measure of outstanding loans and debts accumulated in the present and past years. Take a look at Exhibit 2-2 again for the components of DNFD.

Specifically, DNFD refers to the total credit market debt owed by the domestic nonfinancial sector including the U.S. government, state and local governments, private nonfinancial firms, and households. In this definition, "domestic" merely means U.S. entities excluding foreign entities. Nonfinancial debt excludes the debt of financial institutions—those institutions that borrow solely to relend. This debt is excluded to avoid double counting.

For example, suppose Friendly Savings and Loan borrows surplus funds from small passbook savers and relends those funds to Jorge and Maria to buy their first home. If the debt of the financial institution was counted, both Jorge and Maria's mortgage debt and Friendly's debt to the passbook savers would be included in the aggregate. This would be double counting, because the ultimate transaction went from the passbook savers to Jorge and Maria with the savings and loan in between. Furthermore, Friendly's financial debt to the passbook savers is offset by the financial claim (mortgage) Friendly holds against Jorge and Maria.

To simplify, think of DNFD as a measure of the unpaid claims lenders have against borrowers excluding the debt of financial intermediaries. DNFD is probably the best measure of outstanding nonfinancial credit that we have. When credit flows increase, DNFD (the aggregate amount of debt outstanding) goes up. Likewise, when credit flows decrease, DNFD declines. Exhibit 2-3 shows the relative size of the monetary aggregates and DNFD.

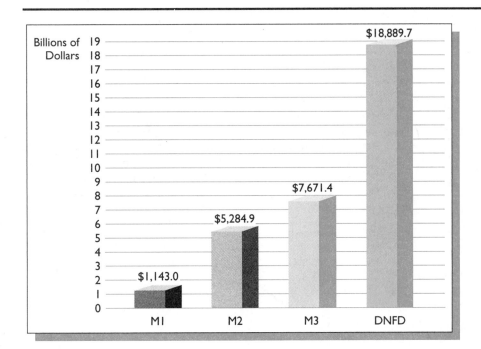

EXHIBIT 2-3

The Relative Size of the Monetary Aggregates and DNFD as of August 2001 (in Billions of Dollars)

The Economy and the Aggregates

In the early and mid-1980s, M1 was the primary measure of money that the Fed watched. Targets were set for the growth rate of M1, and the Fed monitored these targets to provide a barometer of economic activity. If M1 growth was above the target rate, the Fed would take actions that resulted in a slowdown in the growth of M1. If M1 growth was below the target, the Fed would take actions that resulted in a speedup in the growth of M1. In either case, the goal was to nudge the economy in the desired direction.

During the late 1980s, M2 gained importance and prominence in the execution of monetary policy by the Fed. During this period, the relationship between changes in M2 and economic activity seemed more stable than that between changes in M1 and economic activity. Consequently, the Fed watched the growth rate of M2 for signals about how well the economy was doing and de-emphasized the role of M1. In the early 1990s, the stable relationship between changes in M2 and changes in economic activity also seemed to break down. The growth rate of M2 moved in erratic and unpredictable ways. As a result, the Fed has also de-emphasized the use of M2 as a policy indicator.

In the early 1990s, the Fed increasingly used changes in the growth rate of DNFD as an indicator of the direction of the economy. DNFD seemed, at least at that time, to have a quite stable relationship with changes in economic activity. If credit growth was increasing, spending was likely to go up. If credit extension was slowing, the growth rate of economic activity was also likely to be slowing. Hence, the Fed was interested in monitoring changes in this broad aggregate. By the late 1990s and continuing into the early 2000s, the Fed was using many other economic variables other than the monetary aggregates and DNFD that were thought to be more relevant as barometers of economic conditions.

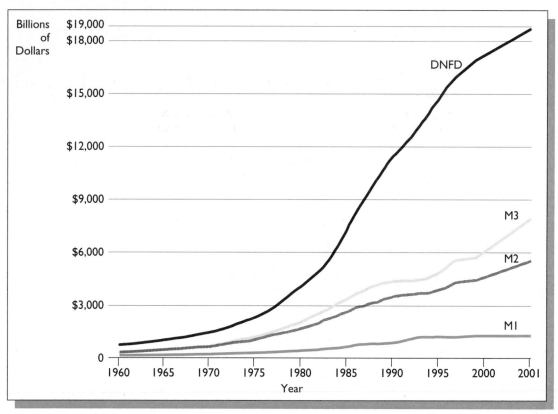

Through August 2001

EXHIBIT 2-4
The Monetary Aggregates and DNFD, 1960–2001
SOURCE: *Economic Report of the President,* February 1996, Table B-65, and the *Federal Reserve Bulletin Statistical Release H6,* September 27, 2001.

For our purposes, then, it is probably best to think of M1 as a measure of transactions money and M2 as one of several broader measures of money or other indicators (including M3 and DNFD), which may, at times, be closely related to economic activity and, therefore be closely monitored by the Fed. If you are baffled by the reasons for the changes in the relationships between the aggregates and economic activity, don't be discouraged. By the time you have completed this text, we hope to provide you with fairly good explanations of why these changes occur. Don't forget that the financial system of the economy in which we live is dynamic, innovative, and evolving. Exhibit 2-4 shows how the various aggregates have grown over time.

http://www.
federalreserve.gov/
releases/H6/current
*Provides current statistical
data on the monetary
aggregates.*

RECAP In addition to the monetary aggregates, the Fed monitors DNFD, a broad measure of credit. DNFD includes public and private debt but excludes the debt of financial institutions to avoid double counting. Sometimes a given aggregate has been more highly correlated with the level of economic activity than at other times.

LOOKING BACK: *United States Gets New Currency*

In 1996, a new $100 bill was introduced—the first U.S. currency to be redesigned since 1928. Like the old bill, the new bill had Ben Franklin's picture on it, but it was enlarged and moved to the left. To its right is a watermark that also portrays Ben Franklin. In 1997, a new $50 bill was issued, and in 1998, a new $20 bill appeared. Both new bills were comparable to the new $100 bill in that the portraits of the respective presidents on the bills were larger and moved off center to create space for a watermark. In 2000, redesigned $10 and $5 bills were issued that had features similar to the other newly issued bills.

In addition, the new $50, $20, $10, and $5 bills had a feature not found on the new $100 bill—a large, dark numeral on a light background on the back of the note. This characteristic helps millions of Americans with less than perfect vision to tell the denomination of the bill, even in dimly lighted areas.

Other new features include ink in the numeral in the lower right corner that seems to change from green to black at certain angles. Security threads that glow when exposed to ultraviolet light are woven vertically through each bill. The security thread for the $100 bill glows red, the $50 bill thread glows yellow, the $20 bill thread glows green, the $10 bill thread glows orange, and the $5 bill thread glows blue.

All of these changes make the bills more difficult to counterfeit. Recent technological advances in photocopiers, printers, and the like made it easier for counterfeiters to duplicate the old currency. According to the U.S. Secret Service, the agency that investigates counterfeiting, the changes are working in making the new bills more difficult to counterfeit.[a]

To facilitate the transition to the new bills, the Treasury Department and the Fed engaged in a public relations campaign to inform the public of the reasons for the change. Since more than two-thirds of U.S. currency circulates outside this country, the campaign went beyond the domestic economy to foreign holders of dollars, including foreign central bankers, who may have been concerned that the old bills would be recalled or worth less than their face value.[b] In all cases, old bills were not recalled, and were simply replaced as banks returned worn-out bills in the regular course of business.

Currently, there are no plans to redesign the $1 bill—something that should make vending machine owners happy. However, in late January 2000, a new dollar coin was issued by the U.S. Mint. The new coin was interestingly distributed to the public through Wal-Mart as well as the Federal Reserve.[c] Thus far, it does not seem to be in much use, as many consumers simply hoard them.

[a]Press Release for the U.S. Treasury, October 27, 1997.
[b]Press Release for the U.S. Treasury, May 9, 2000.
[c]http://www.federalreserve.gov/boarddocs/testimony/2000/20000328.htm.

The Demand for and Supply of Money

To understand money's role in the financial system, it is helpful to view money as an asset, much as someone might view an apartment house. The rent for apartments and the quantity of apartment units constructed and rented are determined by the factors affecting the supply of apartments and those affecting their demand. The analysis of money proceeds in a similar fashion. The **interest rate** is the cost to borrowers of obtaining money and the return (or yield) on money to lenders. Thus, just as rent is the cost to apartment dwellers and the return to the owner, the interest rate is the rental rate when money is borrowed or loaned, and it is known as the *cost of credit*.[2] By identifying and analyzing the factors affecting the supply of and demand for money, we gain considerable knowledge of both the "rental rate," or interest rate, associated with borrowing or lending money and the quantity of money that is

Interest Rate
The cost to borrowers of obtaining money and the return (yield) on money to lenders.

---

[2]The market in which money is borrowed and loaned is called the *credit market*. In Chapter 5, we look in depth at interest rate determination from the perspective of the credit market.

supplied and demanded. For our purposes here, we are using M1 (currency in the hands of the public plus checkable deposits) as our measure of money. As noted earlier, M1 is our narrowest definition of money used in transactions.

The Demand for Money

We begin by reviewing some of the specifics of demand and supply analysis as they pertain to money. First, the **quantity demanded of money** is the specific amount of money that spending units wish to hold at a specific interest rate (price). If we hold other factors constant and allow only the interest rate to vary, we find there is an inverse relationship between the quantity of money demanded and the interest rate. Holding other factors constant is known as invoking the *ceteris paribus* assumption.[3] Thus, in this case, we conclude, *ceteris paribus*, that when the interest rate goes up, the quantity demanded of money goes down, and when the interest rate falls, the quantity demanded of money increases.

But why is this relationship between the quantity demanded of money and the interest rate inverse? The answer is quite simple if we consider that money (even in interest-earning checking accounts) generally earns less interest than do nonmonetary assets (or near monies). Consequently, as the interest rate goes up, the opportunity cost of holding money goes up, and *ceteris paribus*, the quantity demanded of money goes down.[4] People conserve on their holdings of money balances and substitute holdings of other financial assets that pay a higher return. Thus, when the interest rate rises, "portfolio adjustments" decrease the holdings of money whose return has not increased or has increased less than that of nonmonetary assets. Exhibit 2-5 graphs various interest rate-quantity demanded combinations to get a downward-sloping demand curve for money.

By the **demand for money,** we mean the entire set of interest rate-quantity demanded combinations, or the entire downward-sloping demand curve. The demand for money by spending units is determined primarily by spending plans and by the need to pay for purchases. Spending plans and purchases, in turn, are influenced by income and generally go up when incomes go up. Thus, the demand for money to hold is positively or directly related to income. When our incomes go up, we hold more money for day-to-day transactions. (Melissa goes to the grocery store and takes her kids out for fast food more often after she gets a raise.) In addition to income and spending plans, other factors such as changes in wealth, expected inflation, and the riskiness of other financial instruments also affect the demand for money.

Exhibit 2-5 shows that when the demand for money changes, the entire demand curve shifts. For example, when the demand for money decreases, say, due to a decrease in incomes, the entire demand curve shifts to the left. Thus, we can see that changes in factors other than the interest rate affect the demand for money and cause the downward-sloping demand curve to shift. When the interest rate changes, we move along a single money demand curve, and there is a change in quantity demanded. Be certain you are clear about the difference between a change in quantity demanded and a change in demand.

Quantity Demanded of Money
The specific amount of money that spending units wish to hold at a specific interest rate (price).

Demand for Money
The entire set of interest rate—quantity demanded combinations as represented by a downward-sloping demand curve for money.

---

[3]Economists make the *ceteris paribus* assumption to investigate the relationship between two variables without having changes in other variables affect the relationship. In this book we will always assume *ceteris paribus*.

[4]The opportunity cost is the value of the next best alternative that is forgone, or given up.

The quantity of money is measured on the horizontal axis while the interest rate is measured on the vertical axis. *Ceteris paribus,* the quantity demanded of money is inversely related to the interest rate. As the interest rate falls, quantity demanded increases. As the interest rate rises, quantity demanded falls. A shift of the money demand curve means that the demand for money has changed. A shift to the right means that the demand for money has increased while a shift to the left means that the demand for money has decreased.

EXHIBIT 2-5
The Demand for Money

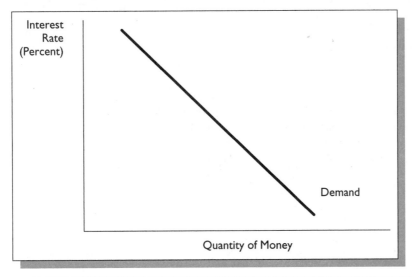

RECAP The demand for money is the amount that will be demanded at various interest rates. The quantity demanded of money is the amount that will be demanded at a specific interest rate. The demand for money is directly related to income. *Ceteris paribus,* the quantity demanded is inversely related to the interest rate. A change in demand is represented by a shift of the demand curve while a change in quantity demanded is a movement along a demand curve due to a change in the interest rate.

The Supply of Money

The **supply of money** is a little more complicated than the demand for money and warrants a brief discussion. Our most narrow definition of transactions money (M1) includes currency in the hands of the public plus checkable deposits. Financial intermediaries that issue checkable deposits (now often referred to as *depository institutions*) hold reserve assets equal to a certain fraction of checkable deposits. The **reserves** against the outstanding deposits may be held either as vault cash or, for safety reasons, as reserve deposit accounts with the Fed. The Fed enters the picture in two places:

1. A depository institution must have reserve assets equal to a certain percentage of its deposit liabilities. The Fed sets the percentage of deposit liabilities that depository institutions must hold as reserve assets. This percentage is called the **required reserve ratio.** For example, if a credit union has checkable deposits in the amount of $1,000, and the Fed has set a 10 percent required reserve ratio, then the credit union must hold $100 in reserves either as cash in its vaults or as reserve deposits with the Fed.

Supply of Money
The stock of money (M1), which includes currency in the hands of the public plus checkable deposits.

Reserves
Assets that are held as either vault cash or reserve deposit accounts with the Fed.

Required Reserve Ratio
The fraction of deposit liabilities that depository institutions must hold as reserve assets.

2. The Fed influences the amount of cash assets outstanding and, hence, the amount available for reserves.[5] We shall discuss this in greater detail in later chapters.

Commercial banks (and other depository institutions) enter the picture by influencing the amount of checkable deposits. Banks issue checkable deposits when they receive a deposit into a checking account or when they make a loan. The borrower signs the loan papers, and the intermediary (lender) credits the borrower's checking account with the amount of the loan, creating a checkable deposit. The checkable deposit is money.

Since the Fed, within some limits, controls the amount of funds available for reserves and sets the required reserve ratio, it exerts significant influence on the maximum amount of checkable deposits that depository institutions can create by making loans and, hence, has significant influence on the money supply. Exhibit 2-6 depicts the relationship between the **quantity supplied of money** and the interest rate as a vertical line (supply curve).[6] As in the case of demand, the quantity supplied of money is the specific amount that will be supplied at a specific interest rate. By the supply of money, we mean the entire set of interest rate-quantity supplied combinations—the entire vertical supply curve. By changing the quantity of reserves available to the banking system or by changing the required reserve ratio, the Fed can change the supply of money. Changes in the supply of money, initiated by the Fed, are reflected by shifts of the vertical supply curve. If the Fed speeds up the provision of reserves or reduces the required reserve ratio, the money supply curve shifts to the right, and the supply of money increases. Likewise, if the Fed slows down the provision of reserves or increases the required reserve ratio, the money supply curve shifts to the left, and the supply of money decreases.

http://www.
moneyfactory.com
*Provides interesting
information about money.*

**Quantity Supplied
of Money**
The specific amount of
money that will be
supplied at a specific
interest rate.

EXHIBIT 2-6
The Supply of Money

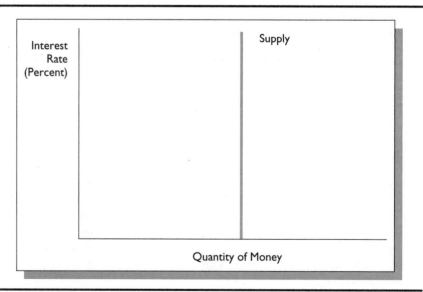

---

[5]Cash outside the Fed is either held by the public or deposited in a financial intermediary. If it is deposited, it serves as reserves for the financial intermediaries that issue checkable deposits, and it is considered a cash asset.

[6]Some economists consider the money supply curve to be upward sloping instead of a vertical line. The reasoning is that when interest rates rise, depository institutions find innovative ways around reserve requirements in order to make more loans. The loans are more profitable because interest rates are higher. In the process of making more loans, more money is created.

RECAP Depository institutions must hold reserve assets equal to a certain fraction of deposit liabilities—called the required reserve ratio—as set by the Fed. The Fed also influences the amount of cash assets outstanding and, thus, the amount available for reserves. These two factors give the Fed significant influence over the money supply. The supply curve of money is vertical. Changes in the amount of reserves or the required reserve ratio will cause the curve to shift and the supply of money to change.

Money and Interest Rates

Having previewed the factors that affect demand and supply, we are now able to see how the interaction between the supply of and demand for money determines its availability, or quantity, and its cost, or the interest rate. This is shown in Exhibit 2-7.[7] In this example, the market gravitates to i_e, or the equilibrium interest rate, where the quantity supplied of money equals the quantity demanded. If the interest rate is above i_e, there is an excess quantity supplied of money and, hence, downward pressure on the interest rate. If the rate is below equilibrium, there is an excess quantity demanded of money, and market forces will cause the interest rate to rise. Once the interest rate gravitates to i_e, the market will stay at the equilibrium rate until one of the curves shifts due to a change in either demand or supply.

Changes in the supply of or demand for money will affect the interest rate, just as changes in the supply of or demand for apartments will affect the rent on apartments. *Ceteris paribus*, if demand increases, the interest rate rises and vice versa. *Ceteris paribus*, if supply increases, the interest rate falls and vice versa. To illustrate, suppose that the Fed, through a stepped-up provision of reserves to depository institutions, succeeds in increasing the supply of money relative to the demand. As Exhibit 2-8 shows, this corresponds to a shift of the supply curve to the right. At

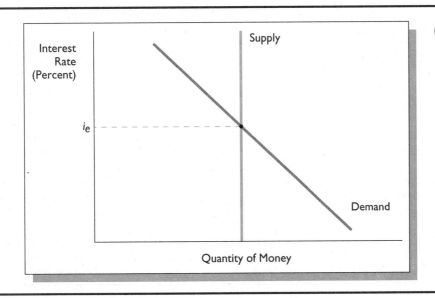

EXHIBIT 2-7
Market Equilibrium

---

[7]As is commonly known, there are many interest rates in the economy, so speaking of "the interest rate" as if there were only one is an obvious simplification. Once the fundamentals are developed, it will be much easier to extend our analysis to take into account the many different interest rates.

EXHIBIT 2-8
An Increase in the
Supply of Money

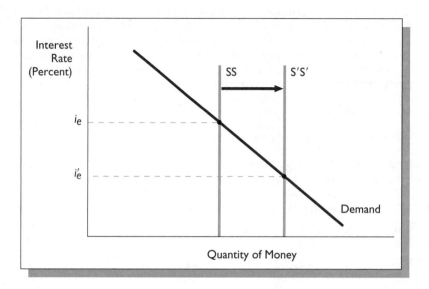

the original equilibrium interest rate (i_e), there is excess quantity supplied and, thus, downward pressure on the interest rate. The market gravitates to a new equilibrium at a lower interest rate (i'_e) where quantity demanded is equal to quantity supplied.[8] Note that the analogy continues to hold: We would expect that an increase in the supply of apartments, with no change in demand, would result in a fall in rents and, thereby, an increase in quantity demanded.

But what is the significance of the changes in interest rates caused by changes in the demand for or supply of money? In the preceding example, the fall in interest rates—reduction in the cost of borrowing—would probably encourage some spending units in the economy to borrow more money and use it to purchase more goods and services. Credit would increase and, more specifically, the increase in the supply of money would lead to an increase in the demand for goods and services. The increased demand for goods and services might lead to both an increase in the quantity of goods and services produced (supplied) in the future and an increase in the general level of prices.

Exhibit 2-9 shows how the general relationships discussed in this section are important for the economy as a whole. Remember, this is just a first approximation that does not include many details; we do not expect you to understand all the specifics yet!

http://frbatlanta.org/
publica/brochure/
fundfac/html/home/
html.
"Dollars and Cents: Fundamental Facts about U.S. Money" (2000) is a useful Internet site.

RECAP The interest rate is determined by the supply of and demand for money. Equilibrium occurs at the interest rate where the quantity demanded of money is equal to the quantity supplied. Changes in the supply of or demand for money (shifts of the supply or demand curves) affect the interest rate. *Ceteris paribus,* if demand increases, the interest rate rises and vice versa. *Ceteris paribus,* if supply increases, the interest rate falls and vice versa. Changes in interest rates affect spending that may lead to changes in output and prices.

---

[8]The *ceteris paribus* condition is very important here. For example, if the Fed takes actions that lead to increases in the money supply, then inflationary expectations may also increase. If inflationary expectations change, then the *ceteris paribus* condition is violated. In this case, increases in the money supply may lead to increases in interest rates because of the effect on inflationary expectations.

If the Fed wants to encourage an increase in economic activity, it will engage in actions that increase the money supply and credit flows and decrease interest rates. These changes will, in turn, tend to raise the demand for goods and services by households and firms. The response by producers (suppliers) of goods and services to the higher demand will probably include an expansion of output and an increase in prices.

EXHIBIT 2-9
How Money Matters:
An Illustration

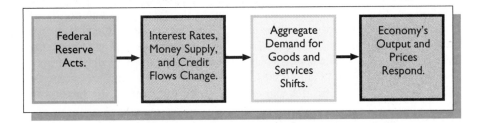

How Credit Matters: A First Approximation

So far we have been focusing on how the Fed influences spending via its influence on money or the monetary aggregates. This is all well and good in an economy where a large percentage of lending flows from commercial banks and other depository institutions such as savings and loans or credit unions. In such an economy, changes in the supply of money will be closely related to changes in the supply of **credit**—the flow of money from surplus spending units (SSUs) or financial intermediaries to deficit spending units (DSUs), and vice versa, in a given time period.

It is fairly safe to say that this situation was typical of the U.S. economy until the late 1970s and early 1980s. Previously, when commercial banks' reserves increased—perhaps orchestrated by the Fed—the banks engaged in new lending, which caused both money and credit to go up. Increases in reserves, *ceteris paribus*, will almost invariably lead to decreases in the interest rate and increases in the supply of money and credit.

We will use DNFD as a measure of credit market debt or just "credit" outstanding and changes in DNFD to represent changes in outstanding credit.[9] Credit is borrowing power. Increases in credit cause spending (and incomes) to go up.

A word of caution is needed. Since the early 1990s, changes in money and credit flows have not been as closely related as they were in previous decades. Credit flows come from the following three sources, with the last two gaining in relative importance:

Credit
The flow of money from SSUs or financial intermediaries to DSUs in a given time period, and vice versa.

1. Credit flows result from changes in credit extension by depository institutions—commercial banks, savings and loans, credit unions, and mutual savings banks. When these depository institutions make loans, they create money and extend credit.

2. Credit flows can also come from changes in lending at nondepository financial institutions and other nonfinancial institutions. For example, credit cards (Mastercards and Visas) were originally offered primarily by banks and other depository institutions. In a relatively recent development, many nonfinancial companies now offer credit cards (Sears, AT&T, AAA, etc.). In addition to these inroads by nonfinancial institutions into credit extension for consumers, corporations (both medium-size and large) have developed ways to bypass banks for their working capital and finance needs. Many avenues now exist for firms to borrow directly from lenders; this borrowing and lending then spurs economic activity.

---

[9]Recall that DNFD is a measure of private and government debt outstanding, net of the debt of financial intermediaries. It is a good measure of the outstanding credit that has been extended over a period of time in the economy.

3. In addition to domestic sources, credit flows can come from abroad. In recent years, technological advances have reduced the costs of borrowing and lending across traditional national borders. A global financial system has emerged that has resulted in a massive increase in the flows of funds among countries.

But what does all of this mean for the economy in general and the Fed in particular? Because the Fed's control over credit extension comes mainly from its influence on bank reserves and bank lending, to the extent that lending bypasses domestic depository institutions, the linkage between money and economic activity may be weakened. The commercial banking system, the primary avenue through which the Fed works, is playing a reduced role in credit extension—a development that undoubtedly is making the job of the Fed more difficult. Now would be a good time to read A Closer Look on money, credit, and the economy.

RECAP **Changes in credit extension influence changes in spending and income. Historically, the commercial banking system has been the vehicle through which credit was extended and through which the Fed exerted its influence on the economy. There was a close relationship between the monetary aggregates and economic activity. By the early 1990s, the commercial banks' share of total credit (lending) extended in the economy was declining. This weakened the Fed's traditional avenues of control over the economy, and the link between money and credit was broken.**

Money, Credit, and the Economy: The growth rate of economic activity is measured by the growth rate of *real gross domestic product (real GDP),* which is the real, or inflation-adjusted quantity of final goods and services produced in an economy in a given time period, usually a year.[10] It is fair to say that sometimes when the money supply and credit growth rates rise significantly, the general tendency is for the quantity of goods and services produced and sold (real GDP) to also grow. Conversely, when the money supply and credit growth rates drop significantly, real GDP growth also tends to fall. There is a tendency for the money supply or the flow of credit to decline around the beginning of most recessions and to increase around the beginning of most expansions. Therefore, the obvious conclusion is that money and credit flows have much to do with fluctuations in economic activity.

There is also a relationship between the growth rate of money and credit and the rate of inflation. The *consumer price index (CPI)* is a price index that measures the cost of a total of goods and services that a typical urban consumer purchases. The rate of change of the CPI measures the *inflation rate,* which is essentially the growth rate in the average level of prices paid by consumers. Whenever aggregate (total) demand for goods and services increases, there is a general tendency for output to rise quickly and for prices to rise more gradually. Likewise, whenever aggregate demand decreases, there is a tendency for output to fall fairly quickly and for prices to respond with a lag.[11] Put another way, the current inflation is heavily influenced by changes in money supply and credit growth that occurred some time in the past.

A final relationship of which we must be aware of is between changes in the growth rates of the money supply and credit and the growth rate of nominal GDP. *Nominal growth domestic product (GDP)* is the quantity of final goods and services produced in an economy during a given time period and valued at today's prices.

---

[10]Real GDP is discussed at length in most Principles of Economics texts.

[11]Although lagged changes in money and credit extension were most strongly correlated with price changes, this does not negate the fact that a weaker positive relationship exists between changes in money and credit and current price changes.

Not surprisingly, changes in money and credit are more closely correlated with changes in nominal GDP than with changes in real GDP. This is because the growth rate of nominal GDP encompasses changes in both real GDP and prices.

We can summarize by the following general proposition: A sustained and significant rise in the money supply and credit growth rates will tend to raise aggregate demand for goods and services, increase output growth, and, with a lag, may at times tend to elevate the inflation rate.[12] Conversely, a sustained fall in money supply and credit growth rates will tend to lower aggregate demand, lower output growth, and, after a time, reduce the inflation rate.

All of this suggests an important causal relationship that runs from changes in money and credit growth to key economic variables such as the inflation rate and real and nominal GDP growth. We need to emphasize that the correlations are far from perfect. In addition, the correlations do not imply causation.[13] Simply put, this lack of perfect correlation means that changes in the growth rate of the money supply and credit are not the only factors that influence inflation and economic activity. Other factors, such as current fiscal policy and expectations about future monetary and fiscal policy and future inflation, can exert a powerful influence on prices and output, especially in the short run. In fact, some economists believe that the effects of movements in these other factors are as powerful as, or more powerful than, current and past movements in the money supply and credit flows in terms of their influence on the economy. For example, if expansionary monetary policy leads to expectations of higher inflation, then interest rates may actually rise as the growth rate of money increases, as noted in footnote 8 earlier in this chapter. Finally, as we have seen, the relationship between the monetary aggregates and credit flows may also change over time, as commercial banks' share of lending changes.

In the next chapter, we take a more detailed look at other financial markets and instruments.

---

[12]This proposition assumes the economy is not starting from a position of full employment. If the economy is at full employment and there is a sustained and significant rise in the money supply and credit growth rates, the increase in aggregate demand will most likely lead to inflation with no increase in output.

[13]Events A and B are correlated if they occur together. Correlation does not mean that A caused B or vice versa.

Summary of Major Points

- The primary function of money, and the function that makes it unique, is that it serves as a generally acceptable means of payment.

- Something that becomes a generally acceptable means of payment will, of necessity, function as a store of value.

- The unit of account in the United States is the dollar. It serves as a common denominator or standardized unit of measure in which all prices and debts are quoted.

- Measuring money is not easy. What functions as money will change over time as an economy's financial system evolves, and some financial claims may be difficult to classify. Given the importance and difficulties of measurement, the Fed monitors and publishes data on several monetary aggregates.

- M1 (currency plus checkable deposits) is the best measure of the money supply currently available for transactions purposes. In the late 1980s, the Fed used M2 (everything in M1 plus other highly liquid assets) to guide its execution of monetary policy. In recent years, the behavior of M2 has become a less reliable barometer of economic activity because of the less stable relationship between M2 and economic activity. The Fed has looked to other indicators, including DNFD, to aid in the execution of policy.

- The interest rate is the cost to borrowers of obtaining money and the return (or yield) on money to lenders. It is the cost of credit. *Ceteris paribus*, the quantity demanded of money and the interest rate are inversely related.

- The demand for money is determined by the spending plans of spending units, which are usually positively or directly related to income. The supply of money is strongly influenced by the Fed through its control over reserves and the required reserve ratio.

- The interaction between the supply of and the demand for money determines the equilibrium quantity of money and the equilibrium interest rate. In general, the initial effect of either an increase in the money supply or a decrease in money demand will be a fall in the interest rate,

ceteris paribus. Conversely, the initial effect of either a decrease in the money supply or an increase in money demand will be a rise in the interest rate, *ceteris paribus.*

- Credit flows (loan extensions) are also a key determinant of changes in spending and income. As depository institutions handle a declining share of credit, the relationship between the monetary aggregates and economic activity may be diminished.

- Changes in the money supply, credit, and the interest rate will generally alter the aggregate (total) demand for goods and services in the economy. Changes in aggregate demand will, in turn, affect the overall level of output and prices. More specifically, a rise in the money supply and/or credit flows and the accompanying fall in the interest rate will generally raise aggregate demand and lead to an expansion of output and some rise in prices.

Key Terms

Barter	Medium of Exchange	Quantity Demanded of Money
Credit	Monetary Aggregates	Quantity Supplied of Money
Demand Deposits	Money Market Deposit	Required Reserve Ratio
Demand for Money	Accounts (MMDAs)	Reserves
Depository Institutions	M1	Store of Value
Domestic Nonfinancial Debt	M2	Supply of Money
(DNFD)	M3	Unit of Account
Double Coincidence of Wants	Near Monies	
Interest Rate	Negotiable Order of	
Means of Payment	Withdrawal (NOW) Accounts	

Review Questions

1. Discuss or define briefly the following terms and concepts: means of payment, store of value, unit of account, barter, monetary aggregates, domestic nonfinancial debt, and electronic funds transfer system.

2. What are the functions of money? Which function do you think is most important?

3. Suppose we define money as that which serves as a store of value. Explain why this is a poor definition.

4. Suppose something is functioning as money within an economy. What could cause the population to lose confidence in the value of the means of payment? What do you think would happen as a result?

5. How does the Fed calculate M1, M2, M3, and DNFD? Are these aggregates all money? Why or why not? Which contains the most liquid assets? Which is smallest? Which is largest?

6. Why does the Fed have so many monetary measures? Which monetary aggregate is most closely associated with transactions balances? Which monetary aggregate is most commonly used in the execution of monetary policy? Why?

7. Why is the debt of financial institutions excluded from DNFD?

8. What is the payments mechanism? What changes are occurring in this mechanism? Why are they occurring?

9. Is it necessary for the collection of assets called money to perform all of the functions described in the chapter? Why or why not?

10. Your friend took a class in money and banking 2 years ago and recalls that currency in the hands of the public is in M1. Explain to your friend why currency in the hands of the public is also included in M2 and M3.

11. Briefly define the interest rate, reserves, and the required reserve ratio.

12. Discuss the similarities between how the price of compact discs is determined in the compact disc market and how the interest rate is determined in the market for money.

13. What is the difference between the demand for money and the quantity demanded of money?

14. What is the opportunity cost of holding money?

15. Chris and Harold Yoshida are a young couple with a growing income. What will happen to their demand for money over time?

16. In what form can a depository institution hold reserves? Who determines the amount of funds available for reserves? How does the Fed influence the amount of reserves a depository institution must hold?

17. What are the sources of credit? Explain the following statement: "The money supply is measured at a point in time while the flow of credit is measured over time."

Analytical Questions

18. Would each of the following assets be good "money"? Why or why not?
    a. Gold
    b. Dirt
    c. Corn
    d. Oil (often called liquid gold)

19. In which monetary aggregate(s) is each of the following assets included?
    a. Small savings and time deposits ($100,000)
    b. Money market deposit accounts
    c. Currency in the hands of the public
    d. Checkable deposits
    e. Individual money market mutual funds
    f. Institutional money market mutual funds
    g. Large time deposits
    h. Travelers' checks

20. Show on a graph how the interest rate and the quantity demanded of money are related. Do the same for the quantity supplied of money. When is the market in equilibrium?

21. Assume the market for money is originally in equilibrium. Explain what happens to demand, supply, quantity demanded, and/or quantity supplied, *ceteris paribus*, given each of the following events:
    a. The Fed lowers reserve requirements.
    b. Households increase their spending plans.
    c. Income falls due to a severe recession.
    d. The Fed steps up its provision of reserves to depository institutions.

22. Graph each case presented in question 21.

23. What are the effects of an increase in the supply of money on interest rates, prices, and output? What are the effects of a decrease in the supply of money on interest rates, prices, and output? Do these effects occur simultaneously?

24. Substituting the words "credit flows" for "supply of money," answer question 23.

25. *Ceteris paribus*, what happens to the demand for money if incomes go down? *Ceteris paribus*, what happens to the supply of money if reserves go up? In each case, does the interest rate change? Graph each case.

26. Use a graph to show what happens to the interest rate if the demand for money is increasing while the supply of money is decreasing.

Internet Exercises

1. Use the Economic Bulletin Board to access Statistical Release H.6, the Fed's report of the most current measures of the money supply. You can employ the following root directory: **http://www.federalreserve.gov/releases/H6/current**. How does the Fed differentiate between alternative measures of the money supply such as M1, M2, and M3? Which measure of the money supply is most liquid?

2. The following root directory from the Economic Bulletin Board provides historical estimates of the money supply: **http://www.federalreserve.gov/releases/H6/hist/**.

From the data, calculate and/or observe the approximate annual (seasonally adjusted) growth rates for M1 and M2 from 1970 until today. Verify that the growth rate of M1 increased from 1971 to 1985, while the growth rate of M2 registered a downward trend over the same time period. (Hint: To calculate the approximate annual growth rates for M1 or M2 for each year, subtract the January value from the December value and then divide the result by the January value.) What were the relative growth rates of M1 and M2 in the last few years?

Suggested Readings

A beautiful book well worth the effort to locate is *Money: A History*, ed. Jonathan Williams (New York: St. Martin's Press, 1997), 256 pages.

An interesting discussion that deals with many topics about our nation's coins and currency is found in the *Testimony of Louise L. Roseman*, Director, Division of Reserve Bank Operations and Payment Systems, before a subcommittee of the U.S. House of Representatives, March 28, 2000. The testimony includes a discussion of the introduction of the new currency, the new dollar coin, anti-counterfeiting measures, and the advantages and disadvantages of high denomination banknotes. (The largest denomination U.S. note that is currently available is $100.) The testimony is available on the Internet at **http://www.federalreserve.gov/boarddocs/testimony/2000/20000328.htm**.

John Walter provides a noteworthy history of the evolution of the monetary aggregates, along with additional sources of data and further readings, in an article titled "Monetary Aggregates." It can be found in *Macroeconomic Data: A User's Guide*, published by the Federal Reserve Bank of Richmond, 1990, pp. 36–44.

E-cash, a new kind of electronic money on the Internet, is in its infant stages and may someday compete with the present system of banks, checks, and dollars. Several recent books that discuss the history and possibilities are: Elinor Harris Solomon, *Virtual Money: Understanding the Power and Risks of Money's High-Speed Journey into Electronic Space* (New York: Oxford University Press, 1997), pp. xii, 286; Donal O'Mahony, Michael Peirce, and Hitesh Tewari, *Electronic Payment Systems* (Boston: Artech House, 1997), p. 254; Daniel C. Lynch and Leslie Lundquist, *Digital Money: The New Era of Internet Commerce* (New York: John Wiley, 1996), p. 285.

For a comprehensive discussion of all forms and aspects of "electronic money," see the Payments Systems Resource Center on the Federal Reserve Bank of Chicago's Web site at **http://www.chicagofed.org/paymentsystems/index.cfm.speech/publications/BOOKLETS/electronic_money/electronic_money.html**.

For an interesting discussion of many of the topics in this chapter, see the most recent Fed Chairperson's "Monetary Policy Report to Congress" that is given in February and July of each year. The report and testimony of the Chair is available on the Internet at **http://www.federalreserve.gov/**. The reports also appear in the March and August editions of the *Federal Reserve Bulletin*.

For a more academic discussion "On the Evolution of Money and Its Implications for Price Stability" see Paul Dalziel's article by the same name, *Journal of Economic Surveys*, vol. 14, No. 4, September, 2000, pp. 373–393.

chapter

Financial Markets, Instruments, and Market Makers

3

Learning Objectives *After reading this chapter, you should know:*

- The various ways of classifying financial markets, including primary and secondary markets, money and capital markets, and spot and futures markets
- The definitions and characteristics of the major financial market instruments
- The functions of the key participants—the market makers
- How the various sectors of financial markets are connected

" "
*The worst form of inequality is to try to make unequal
things equal.*
—Aristotle

Game Talk

To understand the role of financial markets and instruments in the financial system, we need to understand the jargon employed by insiders, or market participants, when they describe and discuss the "action" in financial markets. Trade jargon is not unique to these insiders, but is pervasive in many aspects of life, including football. As the following example shows, even in this favorite American pastime the "players" need to understand the lingo.

> The time is Saturday afternoon during fall, and the place is the gridiron. When the quarterback reads a blitz (or red-dog) and man-to-man coverage, it is critical for him to call an automatic at the line of scrimmage and hit the flanker on a fly pattern. Of course, if the blitz does not materialize, the quarterback may find that he has thrown the pass into the teeth of zone coverage where the free safety can easily pick off the ball.

Such is the jargon of football. Much of this lingo is fully understood only by insiders—players, coaches, and football aficionados. Outsiders have difficulty understanding the game because they don't know the jargon, just as outsiders often have difficulty understanding financial market discussions. In this chapter, we will learn about financial markets and instruments (chiefly in the United States) and the language their participants use so that we too can understand what they are talking about.

Introducing Financial Markets

In general, a market for financial claims (instruments) can be viewed as the process or mechanism that connects the buyers and sellers of claims regardless of where they happen to be physically located. As you will see in this chapter, financial markets can be classified in many different ways. One of the most popular divides the financial markets into individual submarkets according to the type of financial claim that is traded: stock market, corporate bond market, Treasury bill market, commercial paper market, and so forth. There is, however, at least one difficulty with this classification scheme; it suggests the individual submarkets are separate, more or less unconnected compartments. A central message of this chapter is that the markets for the individual financial claims are connected and, in many respects, are more alike than different.

Another classification system, which recognizes that there are some similarities among the instruments, assigns the various financial markets to either the **money market** or the **capital market** based on the length of the term of the instruments traded there. The money market includes those markets in which securities with original maturities of 1 year or less are traded. Examples of such securities include Treasury bills, commercial paper, and negotiable certificates of deposit (CDs). As you might guess, the capital market includes those markets in which securities with original maturities of more than 1 year are traded. Examples include corporate bonds, stocks, mortgages, and Treasury bonds issued by the U.S. Treasury. Not surprisingly, some refer to the money market as the short-term market and the capital market as the long-term market.

Notice that together the money market and the capital market include all of the individual submarkets we identified in the first classification scheme. In this case, however, we are grouping instruments by their **term to maturity,** which is the length of time from when the instrument is initially issued until it matures. Put another way, the various markets may be separate institutionally, but we connect

Money Market
The market for financial assets with an original maturity of less than 1 year.

Capital Market
The market for financial assets with an original maturity of greater than 1 year.

Term to Maturity
The length of time from when a financial security is initially issued until it matures.

them analytically through the type of securities bought and sold by the participants in the markets.[1]

A third way to classify financial markets is to categorize them as the primary market and the secondary market. The **primary market** is the market in which a security is sold for the first time. The security may be called a financial instrument, claim, or IOU; all of these terms are interchangeable. For example, if a firm needs to issue new bonds or stocks to finance investment in new equipment, the initial sale of these new securities occurs in the primary market. Thus, the primary market is where the public (individuals or financial institutions) buys newly issued bonds or stocks from the firms issuing them. Once a firm has issued bonds or stocks, further trading, say, a sale of bonds a month later by an initial purchaser, occurs in the **secondary market.** Most of the transactions in financial markets occur in the secondary market as portfolios are continually adjusted. It will be helpful to think of these financial transactions in the secondary market as occurring in the "used-car lots" of our financial system.[2]

The distinction between the primary and secondary markets is somewhat conceptual. In practice, the selling of new securities in primary markets by the firms issuing them and the trading of older securities in secondary markets occur simultaneously. An analogy may help. The market for autos is made up of the market for new autos and the market for used autos. However, if you go to a GM dealer looking for these subdivisions of the auto market, the only real distinction you will observe is that the used and new cars are located on different sides of the lot.

If this is so, why bother to distinguish analytically between primary and secondary markets? To understand why, we must first learn something about the quality of secondary markets. We assess the quality of a secondary market by the cost and inconvenience associated with trading existing securities. For example, in high-quality secondary markets, securities are traded at relatively low cost and little inconvenience. Such characteristics facilitate the sale and purchase of existing securities and thereby contribute to an efficient allocation of financial resources and a smoothly functioning savings-investment process.

To illustrate the point, imagine a financial system like those in many less-developed countries where formal secondary markets do not exist. Assume now that you want to sell a security you purchased several years ago when it was first issued, say, by LHT, Inc., an emerging high-tech firm. The absence of a secondary market means that you would first have to search for someone willing and able to purchase your LHT security and then negotiate a mutually acceptable price with that person. This process would obviously be quite time-consuming and inconvenient, and the experience might discourage you from saving part of your income in this way in the future; that is, you would be less likely to buy LHT bonds in the future. If other people who own securities have similar experiences, LHT, Inc., and all

Primary Market
The market in which a security is sold for the first time.

Secondary Market
The market in which previously issued financial securities are sold.

---

[1]The nature of the connection leads some to distinguish among financial markets by whether the market facilitates the exchange of funds directly between surplus units (SSUs) and deficit spending units (DSUs), or whether funds are channeled through financial intermediaries. In a *direct market*, funds are exchanged directly; that is, direct finance occurs. In an *indirect market*, funds flow through financial intermediaries, and indirect finance occurs. As discussed in Chapter 1, indirect finance occurs when financial intermediaries exchange their own liabilities or secondary claims with SSUs for funds and then provide such funds to DSUs. In this latter transaction, financial intermediaries exchange the funds for direct claims on the DSUs.

[2]Note, however, that unlike used cars, securities usually do not fall in value through time.

firms like it, will encounter some difficulty in financing future deficits, and the amount of borrowing and lending will be less than it otherwise would have been. Assuming the deficits were to be used for planned additions to the firm's plant and equipment, the amount of investment will fall. Without this investment there will be less future growth of output and employment in the industry and the economy.

The message in this example is that the lack of a smoothly functioning secondary market will inhibit the financing of planned deficits in the primary market and thus have an adverse effect on investment and economic growth over time. In general, the strength and viability of primary markets are a direct function of the quality of secondary markets. Although the secondary market does not generate additional funds for the economy as a whole, its importance stems from the positive effect a well-developed secondary market has on the primary market. Just as selling a used car does not add to the total number of vehicles on the road, the fact that there is a market for used cars improves the market for new cars.

Another way to classify financial markets is by whether the transactions they arrange occur instantly or in the future according to terms decided today; that is, by whether the markets are spot or futures and forward markets. In **spot markets,** financial instruments trade instantaneously, and the spot price is the price of a security or financial instrument for immediate delivery. We are all familiar with spot markets. For example, if I decide to buy a share of IBM stock, I check with my broker and find out today's price for the stock. Or I may watch the financial news cable channel to check out the price of a bond for immediate delivery, say, one issued by LHT, Inc. I can also use my computer to check stock and bond prices online through my Internet account.

At other times, I may be interested in buying or selling financial instruments for delivery on some date in the future at a price determined today. In this case, I enter the **financial futures market** or the **financial forward market** where transactions are consummated today for the purchase or sale of financial instruments on a date in the future. Financial futures agreements trade U.S. government securities of several maturities, several stock market indexes, and foreign currencies on future specific dates. All quantities and futures dates are standardized. Financial forward agreements are transactions that are consummated today for the purchase or sale of financial instruments on a date in the future where the quantities and delivery dates are not standardized. Banks and other dealers and brokers customize financial forward agreements for their customers.

Financial futures and forward markets fulfill two basic functions. First, futures and forward markets may be used to reduce the risk associated with future price changes by "locking in" a future or forward price today. In recent years, financial futures and forward markets have experienced enormous growth. As financial prices have become more volatile, surplus spending units (SSUs) and deficit spending units (DSUs) have turned to financial futures and forward markets to deal with the greater risk of unanticipated price changes. Second, financial futures and forward markets can also be used to speculate. **Speculation** in financial securities is the buying or selling of securities in the hopes of profiting from future price changes. The many intricacies and nuances of financial futures and forward markets are covered in detail in Chapter 22.

Having acquired an awareness of the various ways that financial markets can be classified, we move on to the noteworthy aspects of the major financial securities

Spot Market
A market in which the trading of financial securities takes place instantaneously.

Financial Futures Markets
Organized markets that trade financial futures agreements.

Financial Forward Markets
Markets that trade financial forward agreements usually arranged by banks or other brokers and dealers.

Speculation
The buying or selling of financial securities in the hopes of profiting from future price changes.

that are traded in U.S. financial markets. Before moving on, you may want to read A Closer Look, which discusses the relationships among money, near monies, and other financial claims.

Money and Other Financial Claims: Chapter 1 explained that surplus spending units (SSUs) usually lend their surplus funds to the deficit spending units (DSUs) through the financial system (financial markets and financial intermediaries). Put another way, purchasing power is transferred from those who have it to those who need it. What is transferred, in fact, is current purchasing power, which is exchanged for another financial instrument, or a future claim on money. In effect, the SSUs "rent out" their surplus funds to DSUs for a given period of time, much as a landlord rents out an apartment. In financial markets, the SSU (lender) acquires a financial instrument, which is a claim on and liability of the DSU (borrower). The claim, an asset to the holder and a liability to the issuer, is really an IOU—a promise by the borrower to repay the original amount borrowed (the principal) plus "rent" (the interest) to the lender.

Financial (instruments) claims, other than money, are issued by DSUs or financial intermediaries. The intermediaries issue claims on themselves and then, in turn, lend to DSUs. The financial system includes many different types of financial claims, reflecting the wide variety of borrowers and lenders and the tendency to tailor particular types of claims to the preferences and needs of the SSUs and DSUs. In the 1990s, the trend among SSUs was to bypass depository institutions and to put a large share of their surplus funds into mutual funds, the most rapidly growing type of intermediary.[3]

A Closer Look

Since all financial claims, whether they be bank deposits, stocks, or Treasury bills, are claims on money, they can in some sense be compared with one another as well as with money. Traditional standards of comparison include the risk and the liquidity of various claims.

Risk refers to the variability of potential outcomes. The greater the variability, the more risky the financial instrument. Risk also refers to the possibility or probability that the value of a claim will decline. One example of risk is the possibility that a borrower will default and fail to pay back all or part of the principal or the interest. This risk is similar to the risk that a renter will burn down the apartment building or fail to pay his rent and be difficult to evict. The higher the probability of receiving less money back than expected, the riskier the financial claim is relative to money.

The liquidity of a financial claim (or asset) is determined by how easy or difficult it is to convert the asset into money. The ease (or difficulty) is defined in terms of the cost and time associated with the conversion. If significant cost or considerable time is required to convert a particular type of asset to money, it is usually referred to as *illiquid.* As the costs and time required to exchange a particular asset approach zero, the liquidity increases, with money representing perfect liquidity.[4]

---

[3]Mutual funds are investment pools in which a large number of shareholders purchase securities such as stocks and bonds.

[4]During the middle of the nineteenth century, coal miners' wages in Staffordshire, England, were paid partly in beer! Commenting on this practice, Charles Fay, a historian, remarked: "This currency was very popular and highly liquid, but it was issued to excess and difficult to store" (*Life and Labour in the Nineteenth Century* [Cambridge: Cambridge University Press, 1920], p. 197).

RECAP Financial markets can be classified as money or capital markets, as primary or secondary markets, or as spot or futures markets. Money markets trade financial instruments with an original maturity of 1 year or less. Capital markets trade financial instruments with an original maturity of more than 1 year. Primary markets trade newly issued financial instruments while secondary markets trade previously issued financial instruments. In spot markets, the trading of financial instruments takes place instantaneously. In financial futures and forward markets, the terms of the trade, including price, are arranged today but the transaction occurs at some date in the future. Financial futures agreements are standardized with regard to quantities and delivery dates. Financial forward agreements are customized with regard to delivery dates and quantities.

Major Financial Market Instruments

Financial markets perform the important role of channeling funds from SSUs to DSUs. Since the action in financial markets involves the trading of financial instruments, in effect, IOUs issued by DSUs, understanding the action requires us to be familiar with what is being traded. We first examine the instruments traded in the money market and then look at those traded in the capital market.

Money Market Instruments

The money market has undergone significant changes in the past 30 years, with new financial instruments being introduced and the amount outstanding of other instruments increasing at a far more rapid pace than the level of economic activity. In this text, we discuss the reasons for this growth and evolution when we look at the driving forces behind financial innovation. For now, we introduce and briefly describe each of the principal money market instruments. Exhibit 3-1 shows the dollar amount outstanding of the principal instruments in 1960, 1970, 1980, 1990, 1998, and 2001. Exhibit 3-2 summarizes the typical maturities, major borrowers, and degree of secondary market activity for these instruments.

U.S. Treasury Bills (T-bills)
Short-term debt instruments of the U.S. government with typical maturities of 3–12 months.

U.S. Treasury Bills

U.S. **Treasury bills (T-bills)** are short-term debt instruments of the U.S. government with typical maturities of 3–12 months. They pay a set amount at maturity

EXHIBIT 3-1
The Principal Money Market Instruments: Amount Outstanding, End of Year (in Billions of Dollars)

Type of Instrument	1960	1970	1980	1990	1998	2001[c]
Treasury bills	$37	$76	$200	$482	$691	$620
Negotiable CDs	0	45	260	NA[a]	NA[a]	NA[a]
Commercial paper[b]	5	35	99	558	1,173	1,471
Bankers' acceptances	1	4	32	52	14	7
Repurchase agreements and Fed funds	1	22	102	324	878	1,241
Eurodollars	1	20	68	NA[a]	151	214

[a]Not available.
[b]Includes commercial paper issued by financial and nonfinancial firms.
[c]As of June 30, 2001.
SOURCE: *Federal Reserve Flow of Funds Accounts, Z1,* 2nd Quarter 2001, September 18, 2001; and http://www.publicdebt.treas.gov/.

and have no explicit interest payments. In reality, they pay interest by initially selling at a discount—that is, at a price lower than the amount paid at maturity. For instance, in April 2002 you might pay $9,470 to buy a 1-year Treasury bill that can be redeemed for $10,000 in April 2003; thus, the bill effectively pays $530 in interest ($10,000 − $9,470 = $530). The yield on such a bill is 5.6 percent or $530/$9,470 [(interest amount)/(purchase price)].

U.S. Treasury bills are the most liquid of all the money market instruments because they have an active secondary market and relatively short terms to maturity. They also are the safest of all money market instruments because there is no possibility that the government will fail to pay back the amount owed when the security matures. The federal government is always able to meet its financial commitments because of its ability to increase taxes or to issue currency in fulfillment of its scheduled payments. The Cracking the Code feature explains how to interpret the information about T-bills reported on the financial pages of major newspapers.

**http://www.publicdebt.
treas.gov/**
*Provides information on
T-bills.*

Negotiable Certificates of Deposit (CDs)

A certificate of deposit (CD) is a debt instrument sold by a depository institution that pays annual interest payments equal to a fixed percentage of the original purchase price. In addition, the original purchase price is also paid back at maturity. Most CDs have a maturity of 1–12 months. Prior to 1961, most CDs were not negotiable; that is, they could not be sold to someone else and could not be redeemed from the bank before maturity without paying a significant penalty. In 1961, with the goal of making CDs more liquid and more attractive to investors, Citibank introduced the first **negotiable certificates of deposit (CDs)**. Such negotiable CDs could be resold in a secondary market, which Citibank created. Negotiable CDs have a minimum denomination of $100,000, but in practice the minimum denomination to trade in the secondary market is $2 million. Most large commercial banks and many large savings and loans now issue negotiable CDs. In addition, smaller banks are able to borrow in the market by using brokers.

**Negotiable Certificates
of Deposit (CDs)**
Certificates of deposit with
a minimum denomination
of $100,000 that can be
traded in a secondary
market, most with an
original maturity of
1–12 months.

Commercial Paper

Commercial paper is a short-term debt instrument issued by corporations such as General Motors, AT&T, and other less well-known domestic and foreign enterprises. Most commercial paper is supported by a backup line of bank credit. Prior to the 1960s, corporations usually borrowed short-term funds from banks. Since

Commercial Paper
Short-term debt
instruments issued by
corporations.

Instrument	Typical Maturities	Principal Borrowers	Secondary Market
Treasury bills	3 to 12 months	U.S. government	Very active
Negotiable CDs	1 to 6 months	Depository institutions	Modest activity
Commercial paper	1 to 270 days	Financial and business firms	Moderately active
Bankers' acceptances	90 days	Financial and business firms	Limited
Repurchase agreements	1 day, and 2 days to 3 months typical; 6 months less typical	Banks, securities dealers, other owners of securities, nonfinancial firms, governments	None, but very active primary market for short maturities
Fed funds	Chiefly 1 business day	Depository institutions	Active brokers' market
Eurodollars	Overnight, 1 week, 1 to 6 months, and longer	Banks	None

EXHIBIT 3-2
The Money Market

CRACKING THE CODE: *Treasury Bills*

Quotations for Treasury bills are shown in the accompanying table from *The Wall Street Journal,* April 13, 2001. When issued, all T-bills carry maturities of 1 year or less. As explained earlier in this chapter, Treasury bills are issued at a discount from par—that is, at a price less than $100 per $100 of face, or par, value. The investor pays, say, $99 and at maturity receives $100. The interest received is, in effect, the difference between the face value and the price paid when the bill is purchased—that is, the discount.

Maturity	Days to Mat.	Bid	Asked	Ask Chg.	Yld.
Apr 19 '01	6	4.96	4.88	−0.15	4.95
Apr 26 '01	13	3.84	3.76	−0.14	3.82
May 03 '01	20	3.87	3.79	−0.13	3.85
May 10 '01	27	3.84	3.76	−0.13	3.82
May 17 '01	34	3.81	3.77	−0.13	3.84
May 24 '01	41	3.82	3.78	−0.12	3.85
May 31 '01	48	3.87	3.83	−0.11	3.90
Jun 07 '01	55	3.78	3.74	−0.11	3.81
Jun 14 '01	62	3.78	3.76	−0.10	3.84
Jun 21 '01	69	3.80	3.78	−0.10	3.86
Jun 28 '01	76	3.83	3.81	−0.09	3.89
Jul 05 '01	83	3.91	3.89	−0.08	3.98
Jul 12 '01	90	3.90	3.89	−0.08	3.98
Jul 19 '01	97	3.90	3.88	−0.08	3.98
Jul 19 '01	97	3.89	3.88	. . . .	3.98
Jul 26 '01	104	3.90	3.88	−0.07	3.98
Aug 02 '01	111	3.91	3.89	−0.06	3.99

Source: *The Wall Street Journal,* April 13, 2001.

Look at the highlighted bill quotation. The maturity date of the bill is Jul 12 '01, which means July 12, 2001. Thus, as noted in the second column, there are 90 days to maturity, and consequently this is a 90-day Treasury bill that will mature in approximately 3 months. Dealers are bidding 3.90 percent for the issue and asking 3.89 percent. These bid and asked quotations are on what is called a discount basis. The discount is higher on the bid side than on the asked side, which means that the price at which dealers are offering to buy the T-bills is lower than the price at which they are selling the bills. The inverse relationship between yields and security prices (bills, notes, and bonds) will be discussed in Chapter 5.

Given this information, we can solve for the bid and asked prices of the bill in question, remembering that it is a 90-day bill. Leaving aside the complexities, the dollar discount from face value (that is, the face value minus the price paid) is, in effect, the interest that will be earned on an annualized basis. In our example, since we are talking about 90-day bills and there are approximately four 90-day periods in a year, we must divide the annualized bid and asked discounts by 4 to solve for the actual bid and asked prices for the bills. Thus, the price (P) will be P = face value − [(discount yield × face values)/4].

Solving for the bid price first where the face value is $100 and the bid yield is 3.90 percent, we find P = $99.025 [$99.025 = $100 − ($100 × .0390)/4]; this is what dealers are willing to pay. Likewise, since the asked yield on a discount basis is 3.89 percent, this means dealers are asking $99.0275 [$99.0275 = $100 − ($100 × .0389)/4] to sell the bill. Note that the difference between the bid and asked prices is $.0025. Lest you think that difference is trivial, it amounts to $25 per million. Since dealers trade several billion dollars of Treasury bills each day, the $25 per million adds up to a tidy sum for making a market in Treasury bills.

The last column of the highlighted quotation indicates that the annualized yield to maturity (based on the asked price) on this bill is equal to 3.98 percent; this is what we mean when we refer to the interest rate on the security. The (−.08) in the next to last column means that the annualized yield to maturity decreased yesterday.

then, corporations have come to depend on selling commercial paper to other financial intermediaries and other lenders for their immediate, short-term borrowing needs. The growth of the commercial paper market since 1960 has been impressive and is partially due to the increase in commercial paper issued by non-financial firms. Initially, only large corporations had access to the commercial paper market, but in the late 1980s and early 1990s, medium- and small-sized firms found ways to enter this market. In addition, some financial intermediaries also get funds to invest and lend by issuing commercial paper.

http://risk.ifci.ch/index.htm
Provides highlights on commercial paper.

Bankers' Acceptances

Bankers' acceptances are money market instruments created in the course of financing international trade. Banks were first authorized to issue bankers' acceptances to finance the international and domestic trade of their customers by the Federal Reserve Act in 1913. Exhibit 3-3 depicts how bankers' acceptances work. A bankers' acceptance is a bank draft (a guarantee of payment similar to a check) issued by a firm and payable on some future date. For a fee, the bank on which the draft is drawn stamps it as "accepted," thereby guaranteeing that the draft will be paid even in the event of default by the firm. If the firm fails to deposit the funds into its account to cover the draft by the future due date, the bank's guarantee

Bankers' Acceptances
Money market instruments created in the course of international trade to guarantee bank drafts due on a future date.

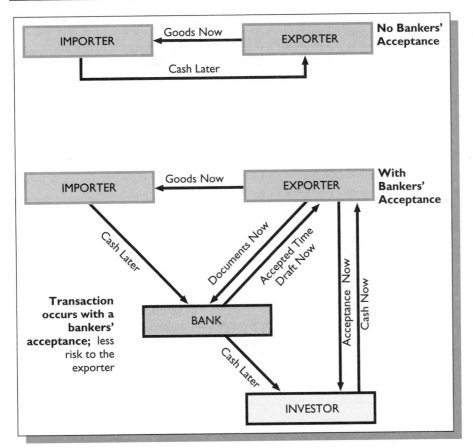

EXHIBIT 3-3
Bankers' Acceptances

SOURCE: Adapted from Ann-Marie Meulendyke, *U.S. Monetary Policy and Financial Markets* (New York: Federal Reserve Bank of New York, 1989), p. 80.

means that the bank is obligated to pay the draft. The bank's creditworthiness is substituted for that of the firm issuing the acceptance, making the draft more likely to be accepted when it is used to purchase goods abroad. The foreign exporter knows that even if the company purchasing the goods goes bankrupt, the bank draft will still be paid off. The party that accepts the draft (often another bank) can then resell the draft in a secondary market at a discount before the due date, or it can hold the draft in its portfolio as an investment. Bankers' acceptances that trade in secondary markets are similar to Treasury bills in that they are short term and sell at a discount. The amount of bankers' acceptances outstanding increased by nearly 4,000 percent ($2 billion to $75 billion) between 1960 and 1984. Since 1984, however, the acceptance market has declined due to the growth of other financing alternatives and the increased trade in currencies other than the dollar. By the middle of 2001, the amount of outstanding bankers' acceptances had fallen to $7 billion.

Repurchase Agreements

Repurchase Agreements
Short-term agreements in which the seller sells a government security to a buyer and simultaneously agrees to buy it back on a later date at a higher price.

Repurchase agreements are short-term agreements in which the seller sells a government security to a buyer and simultaneously agrees to buy the government security back on a later date at a higher price. In effect, the seller has borrowed funds for a short term, and the buyer ostensibly has made a secured loan for which the government security serves as collateral. If the seller (borrower) fails to pay back the loan, the buyer (lender) keeps the government security. For example, assume a large corporation, such as IBM, finds that it has excess funds in its checking account. It doesn't want these funds sit idle when interest can be earned. IBM uses these excess funds to buy a repurchase agreement from a bank. In the agreement, the bank sells government securities while at the same time agreeing to repurchase the government securities the next morning (or in a few days) at a price higher than the original selling price. The difference between the original selling price and the higher price the securities are bought back for is, in reality, interest. The effect of this agreement is that IBM has made a secured loan to a bank and holds the government securities as collateral until the bank repurchases them when it pays off the loan. Repurchase agreements were created in 1969. Outstanding repurchase agreements are now an important source of funds to banks.

Federal (Fed) Funds

Federal (Fed) Funds
Loans of reserves (deposits at the Fed) between depository institutions, typically overnight.

Federal (Fed) funds are typically overnight loans between depository institutions of their deposits at the Fed. This is effectively the market for excess reserves. A depository institution might borrow in the federal funds market if it finds that its reserve assets do not meet the amount required by law. It can borrow reserve deposits from another depository institution that has excess reserve deposits and choose to lend them to earn interest. The reserve deposit balances are transferred between the borrowing and lending institutions using the Fed's wire transfer system. In recent years, many large depository institutions have used this market as a permanent source of funds to lend, not just when there is a temporary shortage of required reserve assets. Financial market participants watch the federal funds rate closely to judge the tightness of credit in the financial system. When the fed funds rate is high relative to other short-term rates, it indicates that reserves are in short supply. When it is relatively low, the credit needs of depository institutions are also low.

Eurodollars

Eurodollars
Dollar-denominated deposits held abroad.

Eurodollars are dollar-denominated deposits held in banks outside the United States. For example, if an American makes a deposit denominated in U.S. dollars in a bank in England or some other foreign country, that is a Eurodollar deposit.[3] Eurodollar deposits are not subject to domestic regulations and are not covered by deposit insurance. The Eurodollar market started in the 1950s when Soviet bloc governments put dollar-denominated deposits into London banks. The funds were deposited in London because the governments were afraid that if the deposits were in the United States, they would be frozen in the event of a flare-up of Cold War tensions. Despite the easing of tensions, the Eurodollar market continues to thrive. Today, many corporations and investors hold Eurodollar deposits in a foreign country if they have trade-related dollar transactions in that country. U.S. banks can also borrow Eurodollar deposits from foreign banks or their own foreign branches when they need funds to lend and invest. In recent years, borrowings of Eurodollars, which amounted to $214 billion at the middle of 2001, have become an important source of funds for domestically chartered banks.[4]

Capital Market Instruments

The capital market is extremely important because it raises the funds needed by DSUs to carry out their spending and investment plans. A smoothly functioning capital market influences how fast the economy grows. The principal capital market instruments introduced in this section are listed in Exhibit 3-4, with the amounts outstanding in 1960, 1970, 1980, 1990, 1998, and 2001. Exhibit 3-5 describes the typical maturities, principal borrowers, and degree of secondary market activity for these instruments.

Stocks

Stocks are equity claims representing ownership of the net income and assets of a corporation. The income that stockholders receive for their ownership is called *dividends*. Preferred stock pays a fixed dividend, and in the event of bankruptcy of the corporation, the owners of preferred stock are entitled to be paid first after the corporation's other creditors are paid. Common stock pays a variable dividend, depending on the profits that are left over after preferred stockholders have been paid and retained earnings set aside.[5] The largest secondary market for outstanding shares of stock is the New York Stock Exchange. Several stock indexes measure the overall movement of common stock prices. The Dow Jones Industrial Average,

Stocks
Equity claims that represent ownership of the net assets and income of a corporation.

EXHIBIT 3-4
The Principal Capital Market Instruments: Amount Outstanding, End of Year (in Billions of Dollars)

Type of Instrument	1960	1970	1980	1990	1998	2001[b]
Corporate stock	$451	$906	$1,920	$3,530	$15,438	15,863.6
Mortgages	142	297	965	3,804	5,782	7,250.4
Corporate and foreign bonds	75	167	319	1,704	3,894	5,435.1
U.S. government securities	178	156	394	2,776	3,724	3,234.4
U.S. government agency securities[a]	10	51	170	426	1,328	4,620.4
Municipal securities	71	144	NA	NA	1,464	1,629.3

[a]Excludes federally sponsored mortgage pools.
[b]As of June 30, 2001.

SOURCE: *Federal Reserve Flow of Funds Accounts, Z1,* 2nd Quarter 2001, September 18, 2001; *Federal Reserve Bulletin,* various issues; *Banking and Monetary Statistics 1941–1970.*

---

[3]Eurodollars must be distinguished from foreign deposits that are denominated in the currency of the host country. For example, a foreign deposit results when an American converts dollars to British pounds and deposits them in a bank in England with the deposit denominated in pounds.
[4]*Federal Reserve Flow of Funds Accounts, Z1,* 2nd Quarter 2001, September 18, 2001.

Instrument	Typical Maturities	Principal Borrowers	Secondary Market
Corporate stock	—	Corporations	Very active for large corporations
Mortgages	15 to 30 years	Homeowners and other investors	Moderately active
Corporate bonds	2 to 30 years	Corporations	Active
U.S. government securities			
Notes	2 to 10 years	U.S. government	Very active
Bonds	30 years (currently)	U.S. government	Very active
U.S. government agency securities	Up to 30 years	U.S. government agency	Some activity
Municipals	2 to 30 years	State and local governments	Active

EXHIBIT 3-5
The Capital Market

http://www.ny.frb.org/
pihome/fedpoint/
fed15.html
*Discusses Fed fund
transactions.*

perhaps the best known, is based on the prices of only 30 stocks, while the Standard & Poor's 500 Stock Index is based on the prices of 500 stocks. The value of all outstanding stock was just over $20.1 trillion in early 2001, exceeding the value of any other type of security in the capital market. Stock values increased dramatically between 1990 and early 2000—due to the very bullish stock market, only to be followed by a bear market in 2001. The amount of new stock issues in any given year is typically quite small relative to the total value of shares outstanding. Chapter 11 has more on stocks.

Mortgages

Mortgages
Loans made to purchase single- or multiple-family residential housing, land, or other real structures, with the structure or land serving as collateral for the loan.

Mortgages are loans to purchase single- or multiple-family residential housing, land, or other real structures, with the structure or land serving as collateral for the loan. In the event the borrower fails to make the scheduled payments, the lender can repossess the property. Mortgages are usually made for up to 30 years, and the repayment of the principal is generally spread out over the life of the loan. Some mortgages charge a fixed interest rate that remains the same over the life of the loan; others charge a variable interest rate that is adjusted periodically to reflect changing market conditions. Savings and loan associations and mutual savings banks are the primary lenders in the residential mortgage market, although commercial banks are now also active lenders in this market.

The federal government has played an important role in the mortgage market by creating two government-sponsored enterprises that sell bonds and use the proceeds to purchase mortgages: the Federal National Mortgage Association (Fannie Mae) and the Federal Home Loan Mortgage Corporation (Freddie Mac). When the mortgages are purchased by these government-sponsored enterprises, new funds are provided to the mortgage market. A third government agency, the Government National Mortgage Association (Ginnie Mae), insures the timely payment of principal and interest on mortgages, thus also facilitating greater lending in the mortgage market.

---

[5]Note that the board of directors of a corporation may choose not to pay common stockholders dividends even if the corporation has profits left over after preferred shareholders have been paid. In this case, the income that stockholders receive will be in the form of capital gains if the stock appreciates because of the retained earnings.

Corporate Bonds

Corporate bonds are long-term bonds issued by corporations that usually (although not always) have excellent credit ratings. Maturities range from 2–30 years. The owner receives an interest payment twice a year and the principal at maturity. Because the outstanding amount of bonds for any given corporation is small, corporate bonds are not nearly as liquid as other securities such as U.S. government bonds. However, an active secondary market has been created by dealers who are willing to buy and sell corporate bonds. The principal buyers of corporate bonds are life insurance companies, pension funds, households, commercial banks, and foreign investors.

Corporate Bonds
Long-term debt instruments issued by corporations.

U.S. Government Securities

U.S. government securities are long-term debt instruments with maturities of 2–30 years issued by the U.S. Treasury to finance the deficits of the federal government. They pay semiannual dividends and return the principal at maturity. An active secondary market exists, although it is not as active as the secondary market for T-bills. Despite this, because of the ease with which they are traded, government securities are still the most liquid security traded in the capital market. The principal holders of government securities are the Federal Reserve, financial intermediaries, securities dealers, households, and foreign investors.

U.S. Government Securities
Long-term debt instruments of the U.S. government with original maturities of 2–30 years.

U.S. Government Agency Securities

U.S. government agency securities are long-term bonds issued by various government agencies including those that support commercial, residential, and agricultural real estate lending and student loans.[6] Some of these securities are guaranteed by the federal government, and some are not, even though all of the agencies are federally sponsored. Active secondary markets exist for most agency securities. Those that are guaranteed by the federal government function much like U.S. government bonds and tend to be held by the same parties that hold government securities.

U.S. Government Agency Securities
Long-term bonds issued by various government agencies including those that support real estate lending and student loans.

State and Local Government Bonds (Municipals)

State and local government bonds (municipals) are long-term instruments issued by state and local governments to finance expenditures on schools, roads, college dorms, and the like. An important attribute of municipals is that their interest payments are exempt from federal income taxes and from state taxes for investors living in the issuing state. Because of their tax status, state and local governments can issue debt at yields that are usually below those of taxable bonds of similar maturity. They carry some risk that the issuer will not be able to make scheduled interest or principal payments.[7] Payments are generally secured in one of two ways. **Revenue bonds** are used to finance specific projects, and the proceeds

State and Local Government Bonds (Municipals)
Long-term instruments issued by state and local governments to finance expenditures on schools, roads, and the like.

Revenue Bonds
Bonds used to finance specific projects with the proceeds of those projects being used to pay off the bondholders.

---

[6]The securities that are issued by Fannie Mae and Freddie Mac or insured by Ginnie Mae are called *government agency securities.* They are the agency securities that deal with residential lending and were discussed in the section on mortgages.

[7]In mid-1995, investors in Orange County, California, found out firsthand about the risks of municipal bonds after the county declared bankruptcy in December 1994. The bankruptcy resulted from a $1.7 billion loss in the county's investment portfolio due to reckless risk taking in financial markets.

General Obligation Bonds
Bonds that are paid out of the general revenues and backed by the full faith and credit of the issuer.

of those projects are used to pay off the bondholders. **General obligation bonds** are backed by the full faith and credit of the issuer; taxes can be raised to pay the interest and principal on general obligation bonds. Households in high tax brackets are the largest holders of state and local government bonds.

Now would be a good time to read the accompanying A Closer Look box, which describes some of the better-known interest rates for both money and capital market instruments.

In the next section, we discuss market makers. They are among the most important participants in financial markets because they facilitate the flow of funds from SSUs to DSUs, and vice versa.

Following the Financial News: *The Wall Street Journal* publishes the interest rates on many different financial instruments in its daily "Money Rates" column. The interest rates that are discussed most frequently in the media are:

- *Prime rate:* The interest rate that serves as a basis for quoting rates to customers; an indicator of the cost to business of borrowing from banks.
- *Federal funds rate:* The interest rate charged on overnight loans in the federal funds market; a sensitive indicator of the cost to banks of borrowing funds.
- *Treasury bill rate:* The interest rate on Treasury bills; an indicator of general levels of short-term interest rates.
- *Discount rate:* The rate charged by the Federal Reserve Banks for lending reserve asset deposits to depository institutions.
- *Federal National Mortgage Association Rate (Fannie Mae):* The interest rate on Fannie Mae mortgages; an indicator of the cost of financing conventional residential housing purchases.
- *Euro Interbank Offered Rates (EURIBOR):* The interbank rate for euro-dominated deposits among 57 euro zone banks.
- *London Interbank Offered Rate (LIBOR):* The interbank rate for dollar-denominated deposits in the London market among international banks; the interest rate that serves as a basis for quoting other international rates.

Although not included in "Money Rates," the long-term bond rate (the rate on a 30-year bond) is an important indicator of the level of long-term interest rates. Because of the length of time to maturity, small changes in interest rates cause much larger swings in bond prices—more on this later.

 RECAP The major money market instruments are U.S. T-bills, negotiable CDs, commercial paper, bankers' acceptances, repurchase agreements, fed funds, and Eurodollars. The major capital market instruments are stocks, mortgages, corporate bonds, U.S. government securities, U.S. government agency securities, and municipals.

The Role of Market Makers

Market Maker
A dealer who links up buyers and sellers of financial securities and sometimes takes positions in the securities.

The major participants in financial markets are the buyers, sellers, and **market makers.** The market makers function as coordinators who link up buyers and sellers of financial instruments. The link involves arranging and executing trades between buyers and sellers. Market makers may make markets in only one type of security, say, Treasury bills, or in several different types of securities, including stocks and corporate and government bonds. Who are these market makers? Where are they located? Why do they exist? What does "making a market" entail? These are some of the questions to which we now turn.

You probably have heard of large Wall Street firms such as Merrill Lynch, Salomon Smith Barney (part of Citigroup), Morgan Stanley, Dean Witter, and Goldman Sachs—five leaders of finance. The main offices of these financial firms are located in New York City, the financial capital of the United States. These offices are linked by telephone and telex to other major cities in the United States and the rest of the world where branch offices and regular customers are located. Like most enterprises, these firms are in business to earn profits. In this industry, profits are earned by providing financial services to the public. These services include giving advice to potential traders, conducting trades for the buyers and sellers of securities in the secondary market, and providing advice and marketing services to issuers of new securities in the primary market.[8]

To better understand the role of market makers, it will be helpful to distinguish between brokers and dealers. A **broker** simply arranges trades between buyers and sellers. A **dealer**, in addition to arranging trades between buyers and sellers, stands ready to be a principal in a transaction. More specifically, a dealer stands ready to purchase and hold securities sold by investors. The dealer carries an inventory of securities and then sells them to other investors. When we refer to market makers in this text, we are referring to dealers, the market makers.

Broker
A person who arranges trades between buyers and sellers.

Dealer
A person who arranges trades between buyers and sellers and who stands ready to be a principal in a transaction; a market maker.

As a key player in financial markets, the market maker has an important role in our financial system. In particular, a market maker helps to maintain a smoothly functioning, orderly financial market. Market makers stand ready to buy and sell and adjust prices—literally making a market. Let us assume that there are 100,000 shares of a stock for sale at a particular price. If buyers take only 80,000 shares at that price, what happens to the remaining 20,000 shares? When such a short-term imbalance occurs, rather than making inconsistent changes in prices, the market maker takes a position (buys) and holds shares over a period of time to keep the price from falling erratically. Or the market maker may alter prices until all, or most, of the shares are sold. Thus, in the short run, market makers facilitate the ongoing shuffling and rearranging of portfolios by standing ready to increase or decrease their inventory position if there is not a buyer for every seller or a seller for every buyer. These actions enhance market efficiency and contribute to an orderly, smoothly functioning financial system.

Market makers also receive, process, interpret, and disseminate information to potential buyers and sellers. Such information includes the outlook for monetary and fiscal policy; newly published data on inflation, unemployment, and output; fresh assessments of international economic conditions; information on the profits of individual firms; and analyses of trends and market shares in various industries. As holders of outstanding securities and potential issuers of new securities digest all of this information, they may take actions that bring about a change in current interest rates and the prices of stocks and bonds.

To illustrate, assume the political situation in the Middle East deteriorates, and experts believe a prolonged war, which would disrupt the exporting of oil to the rest of the world, is likely. Analysts employed by the market makers would assess the probable impact on the price of oil, the effect on U.S. oil companies' profits, and so forth.

---

[8]The packaging and marketing of new stocks and bonds issued by a corporation are part of what is often called *investment banking*—a function provided by most of the large market makers listed in the text. The term is potentially confusing, for it suggests that these market-making firms are banks; in fact, they are not full-fledged banks, even though they provide some of the same services provided by banks. This is a good example of how market jargon can be misleading. In recent years, some large banks have merged with security firms that perform investment banking services. Despite the mergers, the banks and security firms still operate as separate entities.

Such information would be disseminated to and digested by financial investors and lead some of them to buy (demand) or sell (supply) particular securities.

In general, when something affects the supply of or demand for a good, the price of that good will be affected. In the financial markets, when something affects the supply of or demand for a security, its price will move to a new equilibrium and the market maker will facilitate the adjustment. As a quick perusal of the newspaper reveals, security prices change almost every day. Because of the activity of market makers, these changes usually occur in an orderly and efficient manner. In Chapters 10 and 11, we will learn how to read the information (crack the code) on prices of stocks and bonds as reported in major newspapers.

Why Market Makers Make Markets

The willingness of a market maker to make a market for any particular security will be a function of the expected profits and risks associated with buying, selling, and holding that type of security. The profits earned by a market maker flow mainly from the revenue generated by the price it charges for conducting a transaction, the number of transactions engaged in, and any capital gains or losses associated with the market maker's inventory of securities.[9] Generally, a market maker charges a brokerage fee or commission for each transaction. The fee may be per item, such as 10 cents per share of stock, or a specified percentage of the total value of the trade, such as 1 percent of the total proceeds from a sale of bonds. Market makers also collect a fee in some markets by buying a particular security at one price—the **bid price**—and selling the security at a slightly higher price—the "offer" or **asked price.** In this case, the revenue received by a market maker is a function of the spread between the bid and asked prices and the number of transactions in which the market maker and the public engage. Competition among market makers tends to minimize transactions costs to market participants.

To sum up, market makers play a key role in facilitating the buying and selling of securities by the public, as outlined in Exhibit 3-6. First, market makers assist in raising funds to finance deficits by marketing a borrower's new securities in the primary market. Second, they advise potential buyers and sellers of securities on the course of action likely to minimize costs and maximize returns. Third, they stand ready to buy or sell outstanding securities in the secondary market. To illustrate these various roles, Exhibit 3-7 on page 59 summarizes the trading of a bond issued by All Purpose Enterprise Inc., a typical firm that wants to expand its scale of operations by building a new plan and acquiring additional inventories. Note the coordinating and connecting roles played by Merrill Lynch and Salomon Smith Barney.

Bid Price
The price at which a market maker is willing to buy securities.

Asked Price
The price at which a market maker is willing to sell securities.

Market Making and Liquidity

The quality and cost of services provided by market makers affect the transactions costs associated with buying or selling various securities. The costs and convenience associated with trading particular securities, in turn, affect the liquidity of these securities. Because transactions costs and liquidity affect portfolio decisions, the market-making function influences the allocation of financial resources in our economy. Some markets, such as the T-bill market, are characterized by high-quality

---

[9]Market makers assume a large amount of risk when they take positions in long-term bonds. They bear the risk that bond prices will fall and the value of the bonds in their portfolios will decrease. As we will see in Chapter 5, small increases in long-term interest rates can lead to large decreases in long-term bond prices.

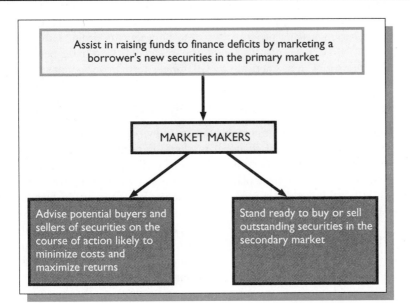

EXHIBIT 3-6
Market Makers

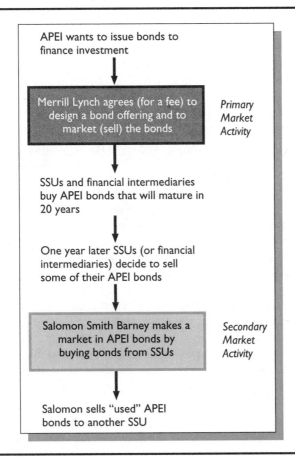

EXHIBIT 3-7
The Marketing and
Subsequent Trading
of a Corporate Bond

secondary markets. The large volume of outstanding securities encourages many firms to make markets in Treasury securities, and the volume of trading and competition among market makers produces a spread between the dealer bid and asked prices of only 0.1 to 0.2 percent—well below the spread of 0.3125 to 0.5 percent associated with transactions in less actively traded, longer-term government securities.[10]

Substitutability, Market Making, and Market Integration

Market makers play another important, but less obvious, role in helping to integrate the various subsectors of financial markets. Exhibit 3-8 shows the trading room at Salomon Smith Barney—one of the most important market makers in the world. As you can see, it is a busy place. On the floor of the trading room, the specialist in T-bills sits near the specialist in corporate bonds, who, in turn, is only 20 feet from the specialist in mortgage-backed securities. Assuming that these people talk to one another, the activity in one market is known to those operating in other markets. With each specialist disseminating information to customers via telephone and continually monitoring computer display terminals, a noticeable change in the T-bill market (say, a half percentage point decline in interest rates on T-bills), will quickly become known to buyers and sellers in other markets. Such information will, in turn, influence trading decisions in these other markets and thus affect interest rates on other securities.

This spillover from one submarket to another is important in understanding the ties that bind the various compartments of financial markets. The key concept underlying these linkages is the notion of substitutability. Whether they be individuals allocating their own savings or bank managers, portfolio managers monitor the expected returns on the array of financial assets available in financial markets. They compare the returns on assets in their portfolios to others available in the market. For example, if a higher, more attractive return becomes available on a Treasury bond as compared to a municipal bond already in the manager's portfolio, the manager may decide to sell the municipal security and buy the Treasury bond. This exchange of a lower-yielding security for a higher-yielding one is the essence of substitution. Assuming many portfolio managers undertake similar actions, the net effect is to increase the supply in the municipal securities market and the demand in the Treasury bond market. Our market makers then act in effect as auctioneers, responding to such changes in supply and demand by changing the prices at which they are willing to buy or sell securities.

So far we have restricted our discussion to domestic financial markets. Yet for almost every domestic financial market, a corresponding foreign market exists. For example, there are markets for Japanese government securities, Hong Kong stocks, Canadian mortgage-backed securities, and Greek bonds. The same factors that affect the viability of domestic markets affect the substitutability between and among domestic and foreign instruments. Most financial markets are becoming international in scope, as improvements in communication technologies have made the world a smaller place. Foreign instruments are good substitutes for domestic instruments in such a world and vice versa. The activities of the market makers are critical to "greasing the wheels" that allow for this market integration (more on this in Chapter 20).

Leaving the details aside, we have come full circle from the beginning of the chapter. We have seen that the numerous instruments traded in financial markets

---

[10]Spreads between dealer bid and asked prices for corporate bonds range up to 2 to 3 percent for securities with relatively low marketability.

EXHIBIT 3-8
A Typical Trading Room

can be classified in many different ways. We have also seen that the separate markets for the individual instruments are linked by the activities of market makers and the willingness of traders to substitute among the alternative instruments available.

Before ending this discussion, note one other aspect of the picture in Exhibit 3-8—the many computer monitors in this room from which the traders obtain numerous details on current interest rates and securities prices. Among the many bits of data watched closely by everyone on the trading floor is information relating to the operations of the Federal Reserve. In fact, if you asked these analysts and traders which type of information is most important, they would probably answer "information on Federal Reserve policy." After studying the next chapter, we are sure you will be able to see why.

Summary of Major Points

- The markets for particular types of financial claims are connected, not separate entities. The connectedness of the markets results from the buying and selling (trading) of securities by the participants in the markets—that is, the substitution among available alternative instruments.

- The money market is where securities with original maturities of 1 year or less are traded. The capital market is where securities with original maturities of more than 1 year are traded.

- Primary markets are where new securities, issued to finance current deficits, are bought and sold. Secondary markets are where outstanding securities (issued earlier) are bought and sold.

- Secondary markets are important to the operation of an efficient financial system. Well-organized, smoothly functioning, high-quality secondary markets facilitate the trading of outstanding securities at relatively low cost and little inconvenience. This, in turn, facilitates the financing of planned deficits in primary markets.

- The spot market is the market for the purchase or sale of securities for immediate delivery. In the futures and forward markets, contracts are entered into today to purchase or sell securities in the future at a price agreed upon today. Futures agreements are standardized with regard to quantities and delivery dates. Forward agreements are cutomized by banks and other brokers and dealers with regard to quantities and delivery dates to meet the needs of their customers. Futures and forward markets are used to either reduce risk or speculate.

- The principal money market instruments are U.S. Treasury bills (T-bills), negotiable certificates of deposit (CDs), commercial paper, bankers' acceptances, repurchase agreements, federal (fed) funds, and Eurodollars. The major capital market instruments are stocks, mortgages, corporate bonds, U.S. government securi-

ties, U.S. government agency securities, and state and local government bonds.

- Market makers are the specialists who function as coordinators in financial markets and link up buyers and sellers of securities. They serve three important functions: (1) they disseminate information about market conditions to buyers and sellers; (2) they connect the various markets by buying and selling in the market themselves; and (3) they provide financial services that determine the quality of primary and secondary markets. In turn, the quality of the primary and secondary markets affects the ease or difficulty associated with financing deficits, lending surpluses, and, more generally, shifting into and out of various financial instruments.

- Most domestic financial markets have a comparable foreign market, such as a foreign stock market. Market makers have assisted in integrating domestic and foreign financial markets.

Key Terms

Asked Price
Bankers' Acceptances
Bid Price
Broker
Capital Market
Commercial Paper
Corporate Bonds
Dealer
Eurodollars
Federal (Fed) Funds
Financial Forward Markets

Financial Futures Markets
General Obligation Bonds
Market Maker
Money Market
Mortgages
Negotiable Certificates of
    Deposit (CDs)
Primary Market
Repurchase Agreements
Revenue Bonds
Secondary Market

Speculation
Spot Market
State and Local Government
    Bonds (Municipals)
Stocks
Term to Maturity
U.S. Government Agency
    Securities
U.S. Government Securities
U.S. Treasury Bills (T-bills)

Review Questions

1. Distinguish between primary and secondary markets and between money and capital markets.

2. The secondary market for T-bills is active while the secondary market for federal agency securities is limited. How does this affect the primary market for each security? Why are well-developed secondary markets important for the operation of an efficient financial system?

3. What is the difference between financial futures and financial forward markets?

4. Discuss the major function of market makers in securities markets. What is the difference between a broker and a dealer?

5. If you call a local brokerage firm, you will find that the commission or brokerage fee charged for purchasing $10,000 of T-bills is less than the fee associated with purchasing $10,000 of, say, municipal bonds issued by the city of Cincinnati. Explain why.

6. Explain why it would be incorrect to view the various sectors of the financial markets as totally separate entities.

7. In Chapter 2, we saw that the Fed can change the amount of reserves available to depository institutions and the required reserve ratio. Why do market makers pay so much attention to what the Federal Reserve is doing?

8. Define commercial paper, negotiable certificates of deposit, repurchase agreements, bankers' acceptances, federal funds, and Eurodollars. In what ways are they similar, and in what ways are they different?

9. What are mortgages?

10. Define and contrast stocks and bonds. What are the advantages of owning preferred stock? What are the advantages of owning common stock?

11. What is the difference between a government security and a government agency security? Which asset would you prefer to own if safety and liquidity were important to you?

12. Would you rather own the stocks or bonds of a particular corporation if you believed that the corporation was going to earn exceptional profits next year?

13. Why are municipals attractive to individuals and corporations with high income or profits?

14. What are the fed funds rate, the Treasury bill rate, the discount rate, and the LIBOR?

15. Can the bid price ever be greater than the asked price?

Analytical Questions

16. Rank the following financial instruments in terms of their safety and liquidity:
    a. U.S. T-bills
    b. Large negotiable CDs
    c. Mortgages
    d. Government bonds
    e. Government agency securities
    f. Commercial paper
    g. Eurodollars

17. In June 2001, John pays $9,700 for a 1-year T-bill that can be redeemed for $10,000. What is the effective interest? What is the yield?

Internet Exercises

1. The Federal Reserve's *Statistical Release H-15* reports yields on several financial instruments. Access the Web site **http://www.federalreserve.gov/releases/H15/update/**. Can you distinguish between the money market instruments and capital market instruments reported at this site?

2. From the bank rate monitor Web site **http://www.bankrate.com/brml**, access the Consumer Mortgage Guide and find the local mortgage rates for 15-year fixed, 30-year fixed, and 1-year adjustable (ARM) loans in your hometown.

3. The Wong and Holt Market Report at **http://metro.turnpike.net/holt/index.html** describes daily activity in various financial markets. Access the Current Market Report and list some key indices of financial market performances available at this site. What is today's value of the Dow Jones Industrial Average and the Standard and Poor's 500? What were the most actively traded stocks on the New York Stock Exchange?

Suggested Readings

For one of the most comprehensive and readable surveys of money market instruments, see Timothy Q. Cook and Timothy D. Rowe, eds., *Instruments of the Money Market*, 7th ed. (Federal Reserve Bank of Richmond, 1993). Single copies are available for the asking. Write to the Public Service Department, Federal Reserve Bank of Richmond, P.O. Box 27622, Richmond, VA 23262-7622.

Two other books that may be of interest are *The Money Market*, rev. ed. (Homewood, IL: Dow Jones-Irwin, 1990); and *Handbook of Securities of the United States Government and Federal Agencies, and Related Money Market Instruments* (First Boston Corporation, July 1990).

Additional free publications from the Fed that may interest you include *A Pocket Guide to Selected Short-Term Instruments of the Money Market* (1987); *Commercial Paper* (Fedpoint 29); *Basic Information on Treasury Securities* (1988); *Federal Funds* (Fedpoint 15); *Understanding U.S. Government Securities Quotes* (Fedpoint 7); and *Bankers' Acceptances* (Fedpoint 12). Each of these is available by writing the Public Information Department, Federal Reserve Bank of New York, 33 Liberty Street, New York, NY 10045. Fedpoints are available on the Internet at **http://www. newyorkfed.org/pihome/fedpoint**.

For a discussion of recent developments in the commercial paper market, see Mitchell Post, "The Evolution of the U.S. Commercial Paper Market since 1980," *Federal Reserve Bulletin*, December 1992.

Some recent articles dealing with stocks are: Nathan S. Balke and Mark E. Wohar, "Why are Stock Prices So High? Dividend Growth or Discount Factor?" *Federal Reserve Bank of Dallas Working Paper No. 00-01*, January 2000; Simon Kwan, "Three Questions About New Economy Stocks," *FRBSF Economic Letter*, Federal Reserve Bank of San Francisco, No. 2000-15, May 12, 2000; Paul Jordan, "Pooled Trust Preferred Stock—A New Twist on an Older Product," *Emerging Issues*, Federal Reserve Bank of Chicago, No. S&R-00-2, March 2000; William R. Nelson, "Why Does the Change in Shares Predict Stock Returns?" *Finance and Economics Discussion Series*, Board of Governors of the Federal Reserve System, No. 1999-06, 1999.

chapter

The Federal Reserve System

Learning Objectives *After reading this chapter, you should know:*

- How the Fed is organized
- What the Federal Open Market Committee (FOMC) is
- The most important functions of the Fed
- The Fed's major policy tools
- What a "lender of last resort" is
- The controversy regarding Fed independence

" "
Speak softly and carry a big stick.
—Theodore Roosevelt

Unraveling the Fed's Mystique

"Stock Market Surges Following Fed Testimony," "Interest Rates Fall in Anticipation of Easier Fed Policy," "Fed Approves Mega Bank Merger," "Fed Actions Prevent Crisis after Bank Failure": Such headlines appear nearly every day in the nation's business and financial press. Yet, despite its prominent role in the financial system and the economy, and efforts by the Fed to be more open in recent years, the Fed and its operations are not well understood by readers of these headlines (and perhaps even the headline writers). In part, the Fed's mystique reflects the fact that its organizational structure is somewhat complex and rather different from that of other governmental entities. A considerable amount of secrecy often surrounds its deliberations and actions.

To unravel this mystique, we begin our study of the Fed with an examination of the Fed's origin, role, organization, and policy tools. This first look includes an analysis of the administrative (power) structure where policy decisions are formulated and the various functions with which the Fed is charged. Many of the details regarding the formulation of policy and the precise linkages between policy actions and the economy will be examined in later chapters. For now, we want to focus on these questions: What is the Fed? Why does the Fed appear to have such great power and influence over the economy? Who does what within the Fed? Why do they do it?

Organizational Structure of the System

Several years ago, a weekly news magazine reported that respondents in a public opinion poll considered the chair of the Board of Governors of the Federal Reserve System to be the second most influential person in the United States, topped only by the president. This poll reflected the current importance of the Federal Reserve System and monetary policy in our lives. It was not always so.

The **Federal Reserve System** was created by Congress in 1913. Experience in the United States and abroad had finally convinced lawmakers that such an institution was needed to avoid the banking crises that had periodically plagued the economy, most recently in 1907. The main purpose of the **Federal Reserve Act** was simple. It created a central bank—a kind of bank for banks—that could lend funds to commercial banks during emergencies and thus provide these banks with the funds necessary to avoid insolvency and bankruptcy. An example of such an emergency is a major crop failure that makes it impossible for farmers to pay off their bank loans. The 1913 legislation referred to this role of the Fed as providing an "elastic currency," and it is today often referred to as the **"lender of last resort"** function.

Over time, the responsibilities of the Federal Reserve have been expanded. In the midst of the Great Depression, it was clear that the limited scope and powers of the Federal Reserve System were not up to handling the nearly 8,000 bank failures that occurred during the 1930–1933 period. In the **Banking Reform Acts of 1933 and 1935,** Congress provided many of the additional policy tools and regulations that the Fed needed.

The most significant change during this period involved the underlying role of the Federal Reserve—that is, the Fed's purpose and objectives. The Fed moved into a new era because of the economic crisis of the Great Depression, the changing view of the role of government policy after this collapse (discussed in Chapter 1), and the new legislation that broadened its powers. The Federal Reserve

Federal Reserve System
The central bank of the United States that regulates the banking system and determines monetary policy.

Federal Reserve Act
The 1913 congressional statute that created the Federal Reserve System.

Lender of Last Resort
The responsibility of the Fed to provide an elastic currency by lending to commercial banks during emergencies.

Banking Reform Acts of 1933 and 1935
Statutes passed by Congress in response to the collapse of the banking system between 1930 and 1933.

LOOKING BACK: *Early Attempts at Establishing a Central Bank*

The creation of the Fed in 1913 was not the first attempt to establish a central bank in the United States. Indeed, the first effort occurred back in 1791 when the Bank of the United States was given a 20-year charter, with the government providing one-fifth of the start-up capital. The fledgling bank had elements of both a private and a central bank. Like other private banks, it made loans to businesses and individuals. Like a central bank, the new bank issued bank notes backed by gold, attempted to control the issuance of state bank notes, acted as fiscal agent for the government, and was responsible for the aggregate quantity of money and credit supplied in the economy. However, the bank was not without its detractors, who alleged that the bank represented big city "moneyed" interests. Fear and distrust, the unpopularity of centralized power, and questions about the bank's constitutionality all contributed to pressures to dissolve the bank. Its charter was allowed to run out in 1811.

The War of 1812 brought renewed pressures for a central bank that could oversee the financing of the war. Congress chartered the Second Bank of the United States in 1816. This bank also acted as fiscal agent for the U.S. government and issued bank notes redeemable in gold. Friction persisted between those who wanted a strong central bank (Federalists) and those who supported a more decentralized system (anti-Federalists). After substantially reducing the bank's powers in the early 1830s, President Andrew Jackson vetoed the rechartering of the bank, and it went out of existence in 1836.

The National Banking Acts of 1863 and 1864 succeeded in establishing a uniform national currency, but the lack of a central bank meant that there was no easy way to regulate the amount of currency in circulation. Consequently, the country experienced periodic shortages that often led to financial crises. Such crises occurred in 1873, 1884, 1893, and 1907. Nevertheless, attempts at creating a central bank that could regulate the amount of currency in circulation were not successful until 1913 when the Fed was established.

System became a full-fledged central bank. Now more than a bank for banks, it was charged with contributing to the attainment of the nation's economic and financial goals. More specifically, it was to regulate and supervise the operation of the financial system in order to (1) foster a smooth-running, efficient, competitive financial system and (2) promote the overall health and stability of the economy through its ability to influence the availability and cost of money and credit. Let us first identify the major parts of the Federal Reserve System and then discuss its functions.

The core of the Federal Reserve System is the **Board of Governors,** located in Washington, DC. The Board consists of seven members appointed by the president with the advice and consent of the U.S. Senate. A Closer Look presents brief biographical sketches of the present Board members. The full term of a Board member is 14 years, and the terms are arranged so that one term expires every 2 years. The long tenure and staggered terms were designed to insulate the Board from day-to-day political pressures and encourage the members to exercise the same independent judgment employed by Supreme Court justices. In theory, a president would be able to appoint only two of the seven members on the Board during a 4-year term. In actuality, deaths and early resignations of Board members have permitted recent presidents to name more than two new Board members during a 4-year term. Although Board members cannot be reappointed if they serve a full term, they may be reappointed if the initial appointment was to fill an unexpired term due to an early resignation or death. Board members can be removed from office only under extraordinary circumstances. It has never happened.

http://www. federalreserve.gov and **http://woodrow.mpls. frb.fed.us/info/index. html**
Provides general information on the Fed.

Board of Governors
The seven governors of the Fed appointed by the president with Senate approval for 14-year terms.

The Board of Governors*

- *Chair Alan Greenspan (b. 1926). Took office in June 2000 for a third 4-year term as chair; originally appointed to the Board to fill an unexpired term in August 1987; appointed to a full 14-year term in February 1992; term as chair expires in June 2004 and as a governor in January 2006.* **Background:** *Business economist; chair and president of Townsend-Greenspan, an economic consulting firm, 1954–1974 and 1977–1987; chair of the Council of Economic Advisers, 1974–1977; chair of the National Commission on Social Security, 1981–1983; Ph.D. in economics from New York University, 1977.*

- *Roger W. Ferguson (b. 1951). Took office in November 1997 to fill an unexpired term ending in January 2000; appointed to full 14-year term in July 2001; became vice chair in October 1999; term as vice chair expires in October 2003 and as a governor in 2014.* **Background:** *Business; partner at McKinsey & Company, Inc., an international management consulting firm, 1984–1997; attorney for Davis Polk & Wardwell of New York City, 1981–1984; Ph.D. in economics from Harvard University, 1981.*

- *Laurence H. Meyer (b. 1944). Took office in June 1996 to fill an unexpired term; term expires in January 2002.* **Background:** *Academic and business; professor of economics at Washington University, 1969–1996; president and co-founder of Laurence H. Meyer and Associates, a macroeconomic forecasting firm, 1982–1996; economist at Federal Reserve Bank of New York, 1975–1976; Ph.D. in economics from Massachusetts Institute of Technology, 1970.*

- *Edward M. Gramlich (b. 1939). Took office in November 1997 to fill an unexpired term ending in January 2008.* **Background:** *Academic; professor of economics at the University of Michigan, 1976–1997; senior fellow at the Brookings Institution, 1973–1976; director of Policy Research Division at the Office of Economic Opportunity, 1971–1973; staff member at the Federal Reserve Board, 1965–1970; Ph.D. in economics from Yale University, 1965.*

- *Susan Schmidt Bies (b. 1947). Took office in December 2001 to fill a full term ending in January 2012.* **Background:** *Academic and business; assistant professor in economics, Wayne State University, 1977–1979; associate professor of economics, Rhodes College, 1977–1979; various positions, First Tennessee National Corporation, 1979–2001; most recently, Executive Vice President for Risk Management and Auditor, 1995–2001; Ph.D. in economics from Northwestern University, 1972.*

- *Mark W. Olson (b. 1943). Took office in December 2001 to fill an unexpired term ending in January 2010.* **Background:** *Business; President and CEO of Security State Bank, Fergus Falls, Minnesota, 1976–1988; partner with Ernst & Young and its predecessor, Arthur Young & Company, 1988–1999; Staff Director of the Securities Subcommittee of the Banking, Housing, and Urban Affairs Committee, U.S. Senate, 2000–2001; B.A. in economics from Saint Olaf College, 1965.*

*When this book went to press, there was one vacancy on the Board of Governors. The vacancies were due to resignations.

**http://www.law.
cornell.edu/uscode/
12/ch3.html**
Discusses laws regulating the Fed.

The president, with the advice and consent of the Senate, appoints one of the seven Board members to be the Chair for 4 years and one to be vice chair. The choice of the Board chair is crucial, for experience shows that he becomes the chief spokesman for the Fed and, thus, a strong force in U.S. economic policy making.[1]

Federal Reserve Banks

Reserve Bank
One of the 12 Federal Reserve Banks; each is located in a large city in its district.

The original Federal Reserve Act divided the nation into 12 districts. Each Federal Reserve Bank district is served by a **Reserve Bank** located in a large city in the district. Thus, as shown in Exhibit 4-1, we have the Federal Reserve Bank of Boston, the Federal Reserve Bank of New York, and of Philadelphia, Richmond, Cleveland,

---

[1]The Board has not yet had a female chair.

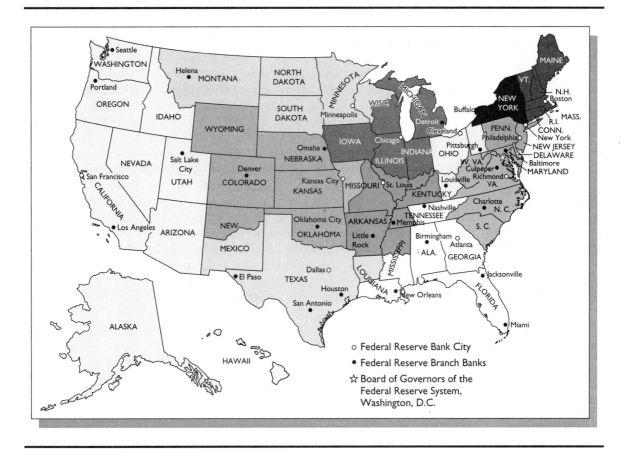

EXHIBIT 4-1
The Federal Reserve System
SOURCE: *The Federal Reserve System: Purposes and Functions* (Washington, D.C.: Board of Governors of the Federal Reserve System, 1984).

Atlanta, Chicago, Dallas, Kansas City, St. Louis, Minneapolis, and San Francisco, respectively. The three largest are the Reserve Banks of New York, Chicago, and San Francisco, which account for more than 50 percent of Fed assets. The 12 Reserve Banks have a total of 26 branches, located in major cities in the respective districts. For example, the St. Louis Fed has branches in Memphis, Tennessee and Little Rock, Arkansas. The Dallas Fed has branches in Houston, San Antonio, and El Paso, Texas. As we shall see in Chapter 15, all commercial banks that are federally chartered national banks must join the Federal Reserve System. State-chartered banks may join or not as they choose. The member banks within a Reserve Bank district (say, the Boston district) elect six of the nine directors of that Reserve Bank, and the Board of Governors appoints the other three. These directors, in turn, appoint the president and other officials of that Reserve Bank.

The original Federal Reserve Act created 12 Reserve Banks and provided for the election of directors by member commercial banks to decentralize policy-making authority.[2] Considerable antifederalist sentiment existed in Congress at the time. We will see later that, over time, the desire to decentralize authority has been stymied by the increased concentration of policy-making authority in Washington.

---

[2]In addition, no two members of the Board of Governors may come from the same Reserve Bank district. This ensures that the Board is not unduly influenced by any particular region of the country.

Federal Open Market Committee (FOMC)

Federal Open Market Committee (FOMC)
The principal policy-making body within the Federal Reserve System.

http://woodrow.mpls. frb.fed.us/info/sys/ banks.html
Lists the Federal Reserve Banks.

http://woodrow.mpls. frb.fed.us/info/policy/ fomcmin and **http://federalreserve. gov/fomc/#calendars**
Provides minutes of the FOMC meetings.

Policy Directive
A statement of the FOMC that indicates its policy consensus and sets forth operating instructions regarding monetary policy.

http://www. newyorkfed.org/ pihome/fedpoint/ fed32.html
Presents information on open market operations.

The **Federal Open Market Committee (FOMC)** is the principal policy-making body within the Federal Reserve System. The FOMC formulates monetary policy and oversees its implementation. The committee has 12 members, including all 7 members of the Board and 5 of the 12 Federal Reserve Bank presidents. The president of the New York Federal Reserve Bank always sits on the FOMC and is a permanent voting member. This is so because the New York Fed, as we shall see, implements monetary policy in accord with the FOMC's instructions. The remaining four seats are filled by the other Reserve Bank presidents who serve 1-year terms on a rotating basis. Although only five Reserve Bank presidents have voting rights on the FOMC at any one time, all 12 presidents and their senior advisers attend FOMC meetings and participate in the discussions. By law, the FOMC determines its own internal organization. By tradition, it elects the chair of the Federal Reserve Board as chair of the FOMC and the president of the New York Federal Reserve Bank as vice chair of the FOMC. With the Board having 7 of the 12 votes, you can see why most of the policy-making authority resides in Washington.

The FOMC meets in closed meetings in Washington eight times a year (about every 6 weeks or so). The **policy directive,** which is usually a two- to four-paragraph statement, is included in the minutes of an FOMC meeting.[3] This statement represents a digest of the meeting, indicates the policy consensus of the FOMC, and sets forth the operating instructions (or directive) to the Federal Reserve Bank of New York regarding the conduct of monetary policy.

Why New York? New York is the center of the U.S. financial system. Since monetary policy affects the economy by working its way through the financial system, it is logical that the New York Fed should execute policy on behalf of the entire Fed. Because FOMC decisions affect current and future economic conditions, it is also logical that economists, financial investors, and professional portfolio managers read the minutes and policy directive carefully and monitor closely the daily operations of the Federal Reserve Bank of New York.

Minutes of an FOMC meeting are published shortly after the next meeting, but interested parties do not have to wait for their release to find out what the Fed intends to do. In early 1994, the Fed began announcing policy changes made at the FOMC meetings immediately following the meetings. This removed some of the secrecy that previously surrounded the specific contents of the meetings. Despite the announcement, some confusion remained because of the wording of the announcement. In February 2000, the FOMC adopted new wording for the announcement that would convey the current stance of policy and state the FOMC's judgment about the economic outlook for the foreseeable future. Namely, the announcement would state if the FOMC believed the risks to the outlook were more weighted toward conditions that may generate heightened inflation pressures or economic weakness, or if the risks were balanced with respect to both goals.

Now that we know something about the Fed's organizational structure, let's examine what this institution and its people are charged to do.[4] As you will see, the

---

[3]Excerpts from a policy directive are reprinted in Chapter 24.

[4]In addition to the organizational structures mentioned in the body of the text, the Fed includes three advisory councils: the Consumer Advisory Council, the Federal Advisory Council, and the Thrift Institutions Advisory Council. Composed of representatives from each Federal Reserve district, they meet several times a year with the Board of Governors to provide advice on issues relating to the Fed's responsibilities in the banking, consumer finance, and depository institutions areas. Federal Reserve insiders say that, as the name suggests, the advisory councils have no real power and serve mainly as a medium for public relations and the exchange of information.

EXHIBIT 4-2
The Organizational
Structure of the
Federal Reserve
System

Board of Governors

Seven members appointed by the president of the United States and confirmed by the Senate for 14-year terms.

One of the seven governors is appointed chair by the president of the United States and confirmed by the Senate for a 4-year term.

The Board of Governors appoints three of the nine directors to each Reserve Bank.

Twelve Federal Reserve Banks

Each with nine directors who appoint the Reserve Bank president and other officers of the Reserve Banks.

Federal Open Market Committee (FOMC)

Seven members of the Board of Governors plus the president of the New York Fed and presidents of four other Reserve Banks.

Nearly 5,000 Member Commercial Banks

Elect six of the nine directors to each Reserve Bank.

Fed's responsibilities are not simple in nature or scope and, thus, are not always easily accomplished. Before moving on, however, take a look at the outline of the Fed's organizational structure in Exhibit 4-2.

RECAP The Federal Reserve System was created in 1913. It consists of 12 Reserve Banks. The Fed is governed by the Board of Governors, whose seven members are appointed by the president to 14-year terms. The Board chair is appointed for a 4-year term. The FOMC is the major policy-making body. It includes the seven Fed governors plus five Reserve Bank presidents. The president of the New York Reserve Bank is a permanent member of the FOMC, and the other four slots rotate yearly among the remaining 11 Reserve Bank presidents.

The Fed's Functions

Over the 87 plus years since its inception, the Fed's powers and responsibilities have gradually expanded. In some cases, the Fed argued that it needed more powers to accomplish its existing responsibilities or that taking on additional responsibilities was a natural adjunct to what it was already doing. Congress often responded favorably to the Fed's arguments or simply let the Fed decide on its own if it would be the best agency to handle a particular set of issues. The current list of Fed responsibilities is considerably longer and more encompassing than even the most farsighted legislator could have imagined in 1913. Fortunately, the list can be boiled down into four functional areas, as depicted in Exhibit 4-3 and outlined in the following text.

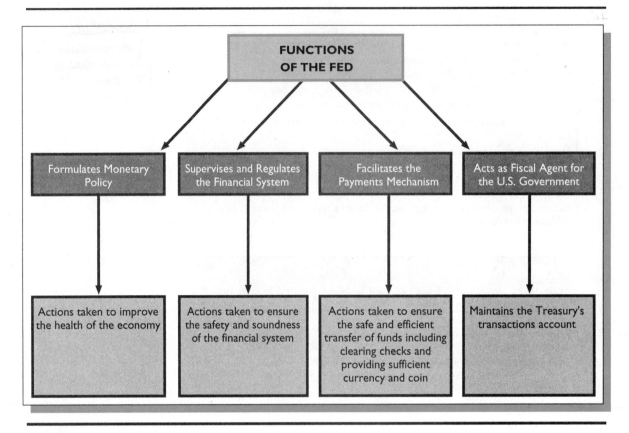

EXHIBIT 4-3
The Functions of the Fed

Formulation and Implementation of Monetary Policy

A primary responsibility of the Federal Reserve is the formulation and implementation of the nation's *monetary policy*. Broadly speaking, the conduct of monetary policy has two objectives: (1) to ensure that sufficient money and credit are available to allow the economy to expand along its long-term potential growth trend under conditions of relatively little or no inflation; and (2), in the shorter run, to minimize the fluctuations—recessions or inflationary booms—around the long-term trend.

In general, the Fed takes actions to affect the cost and availability of funds in the financial system.[5] More specifically, the Fed's actions have a direct effect on the ability of depository institutions to extend credit, on the nation's money supply, and on interest rates. Leaving many of the details for a later chapter, the key point here is that what the Fed does, or fails to do, has a pervasive effect on the environment in the financial system and the overall health and performance of the economy. For example, by taking actions that increase the availability of funds, the Fed may bring about an expansion of the money supply and a decline in interest rates, or it can do the reverse. Its decisions may, in turn, affect the spending, producing, borrowing, lending, pricing, and hiring decisions made in the rest of the economy.

---

[5]The tools the Fed has available to affect the cost and availability of funds are discussed in the next section.

Supervision and Regulation of the Financial System

The Fed, along with several other government agencies, is responsible for supervising and regulating the financial system.[6] In general, supervisory activities are directed at promoting the safety and soundness of depository institutions. From the Fed's perspective, this involves continuous oversight to ensure that banks are operated prudently and in accordance with statutes and regulations. Operationally, this means the Fed sends out teams of bank examiners (auditors) to assess the condition of individual institutions and to check compliance with existing regulations. On a more regular basis, banks must submit reports of their financial conditions and activities.

The promulgation of regulations is, of course, an activity that complements and defines the Fed's supervisory activities. Broadly speaking, regulation involves the formulation and issuance of specific rules that govern the structure and conduct of banking. The purpose of the rules is to establish a framework for bank behavior that fosters the maintenance of a safe and sound banking system and the fair and efficient delivery of services to bank customers. Operationally, the regulations (1) define which activities are permissible and which are not, (2) require banks to submit branch and merger applications to the Fed for approval, and (3) try to ensure that consumers are treated fairly when they engage in financial transactions. In later chapters, we shall see how the rules and regulations have changed over time and the implications of these changes.

Some specifics will illustrate the scope of the Fed's responsibilities and activities. The Fed is charged with ensuring that financial institutions comply with the Truth in Lending Act, the Fair Credit Billing Act, and the Equal Credit Opportunity Act. These statutes are designed to protect the customers of financial institutions from discrimination on the basis of race, sex, or age and from unfair or misleading lending practices. In addition, the Fed is responsible for ensuring compliance with the Community Reinvestment Act, which seeks to increase the availability of credit to economically disadvantaged areas and to ensure nondiscriminatory lending practices.[7] To carry out these responsibilities, the Fed monitors the advertising by institutions, investigates complaints from customers, reviews standard loan contracts used by institutions, and requires them to submit numerous reports summarizing their lending activities.

Another example of the Fed's supervisory and regulatory activities occurs when a bank encounters serious difficulties and is in danger of failing. The cause of the problems may be—and often is—related to fraudulent or misguided lending practices. Whatever the case, the Fed, along with the other relevant government agencies, tries to find an orderly solution that will preserve the public's confidence in the financial system. Often this involves finding a merger partner for the weak or failing institution, lending funds to the institution to give it time to work out its problems, and, in extreme cases, removing the bank's management. Perhaps you understand the quotation at the beginning of the chapter a bit better now.

Facilitation of the Payments Mechanism

The **payments mechanism** is at the heart of the nation's financial system. Many billions of dollars are transferred each day to pay for goods and services, settle

Payments Mechanism
The ways in which funds are transferred to make payments.

---

[6]Many of the agencies that regulate the financial system are discussed in Chapter 13. Here, it is sufficient for you to know that the Fed has the broadest set of responsibilities, some of which overlap with the activities of other regulatory agencies.

[7]The Community Reinvestment Act is discussed in greater detail in Chapter 17.

EXHIBIT 4-4
The Check-Clearing
System

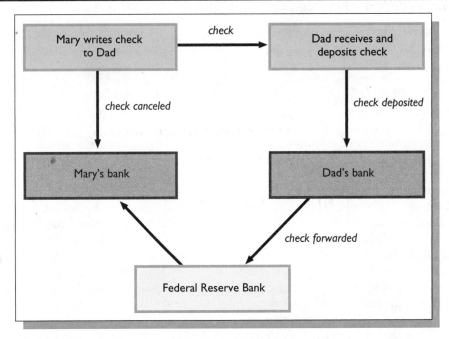

The arrows show the movement of a check through the system. The Fed plays two roles: (1) it forwards the check from the bank receiving the check (Dad's bank) to the bank on which it is written (Mary's); (2) it transfers funds from the bank on which the check is written (drawn) to the bank receiving the deposit (Dad's). When the process is complete, Mary has less funds in her account and Dad has more funds in his.

debts, and acquire securities. Since any disruption of this mechanism could prove deleterious to the economy, the Fed is committed to the development and maintenance of safe and efficient means for transferring funds—that is, making payments.

Most obviously, the Fed facilitates the transfer of funds by providing currency and coin and clearing checks. As Exhibit 4-4 illustrates, the Fed plays a central role in the transfer of funds initiated by the writing of a check.[8] The task is enormous. The Fed clears millions of checks (or similar items) each business day. Now you can see why the Fed has encouraged the adoption of technological advances, such as the electronic funds transfer system discussed in Chapter 2, which can lower the cost and speed the transfer of funds.

Operation as Fiscal Agent for the Government

As chief banker for the U.S. government, the Fed furnishes banking services to the government in a manner similar to the way private banks furnish banking services to their customers. For example, the Fed maintains the Treasury's transactions account.[9] Government disbursements, such as funds for the purchase of a missile, are made out of this account, and payments to the government, such as taxes, are made into this

---

[8]Other private institutions, known as clearinghouses, also help "clear" a substantial proportion of the checks written in the United States.

[9]The transactions account of the government held at the Fed is similar to a checking account. However, the balance in the government's transactions account is not included in any monetary aggregate and therefore is not "money."

account. The Fed also clears Treasury checks, issues and redeems government securities, and provides other financial services. It acts as the fiscal agent of the government in financial transactions with foreign governments and foreign central banks.

Now that we have explained the scope of Fed activities, we can focus on the major tools the Fed has at its disposal as it attempts to encourage and maintain a sound financial system and healthy economy.

RECAP The major responsibilities of the Fed include setting monetary policy, regulating and supervising the financial system, facilitating the payments mechanism, and acting as fiscal agent for the U.S. government.

The Fed's Major Policy Tools

When someone is suffering from a back ailment, physicians usually have several therapeutic approaches available including rest, traction, braces, muscle relaxers, and surgery. These "tools," which can be used in combination, are all designed to relieve pain and restore the patient's health. Since policymakers are similarly equipped and motivated, let's examine the Fed's major policy tools.

Open Market Operations

Open market operations are the most important monetary policy tool at the Fed's disposal. These operations, which are executed by the Federal Reserve Bank of New York under the guidance and direction of the FOMC, involve the buying or selling of U.S. government securities by the Fed. When the Fed buys securities, reserves rise, and when the Fed sells securities, reserves fall. (Details of this concept are discussed in the appendix of Chapter 14.) These operations are important because they have a direct effect on the reserves that are available to depository institutions. (Recall from Chapter 2 that depository institutions are required to hold reserve assets equal to a certain proportion of outstanding deposit liabilities.) Changes in reserves, in turn, affect the ability of depository institutions to make loans and to extend credit. When banks or other depository institutions make loans, they create checkable deposits. Thus, changes in reserves also affect the money supply. Consequently, when reserves change, the money supply and credit extension also change.

Open Market Operations
The buying and selling of government securities by the Fed to change the reserves of depository institutions.

The Discount Rate and Discount Rate Policy

Because the Fed controls the amount of required reserve assets that depository institutions must hold, it also operates a lending facility called the *discount window* through which depository institutions caught short of reserves can borrow from the Fed. The **discount rate** is the interest rate the Fed charges depository institutions that borrow reserves directly from the Fed. The discount rate is a highly visible, but less important, Fed policy tool. We say that it is "visible" because changes in the discount rate are often well publicized, for example, on the evening news broadcast.[10]

Discount Rate
The rate depository institutions are charged to borrow reserves from the Fed.

The setting of the discount rate is the general responsibility of all 12 Reserve Banks, although it can only be changed by the Board of Governors. The process works as follows: The directors of the Reserve Banks meet regularly and review

---

[10]In being widely publicized, changes in the discount rate differ from day-to-day open market operations, which are followed closely by only a small group of experts in the financial system.

matters relevant to administering the Reserve Banks, including the discount rate. If the directors see a need to change the rate, they forward their recommendation to the Board of Governors, which evaluates it and either approves or disapproves the change. Thus, the ultimate authority to change the discount rate resides with the Board. In recent years, Board members have frequently disapproved requests for rate changes, and it is rumored that they have solicited requests for rate changes from the Reserve Banks when they wanted to change the rate and no request was in hand. Is there any doubt about who calls the shots? At any rate, the Board usually approves requests for changes in the discount rate only after the broader monetary policy stance has been determined by the FOMC and is in the process of being implemented. Hence, changes in the discount rate often "lag" changes in other interest rates, particularly short-term rates.

Changes in the discount rate can have several possible effects on depository institution behavior and the economy. Most obviously, the cost of borrowing funds (reserves) from the Fed changes. If funds are withdrawn from a depository institution, not only do its deposits go down, but it also loses reserves equal to the full amount of the withdrawal. Because depository institutions are required to hold reserve assets equal to a certain proportion of their deposit liabilities, the depository institution may be caught short of reserves and, as a last resort, may borrow the needed reserves from the Fed.

Increases in the discount rate raise the cost of borrowing, while decreases lower it. Holding other factors constant, we would expect an increase in the rate to lead to a drop in the volume of borrowing from the Fed, and a decrease in the discount rate to lead to a rise in borrowing. Of course, in the real world other factors are hardly ever constant, and decisions of whether to borrow from the Fed are based on several other considerations besides the discount rate.

The Fed views borrowing as a privilege accorded to depository institutions and not as a right. Since it is a privilege, the Fed urges these institutions to borrow only when other alternatives are not available. This sentiment is spelled out in the Fed's Regulation A, which sets out the Fed's discount policy, specifying the permissible size of loans, their frequency, and the reasons for which institutions may borrow. The rules make it clear that *under normal circumstances*, borrowing from the Fed is to be for short periods, preferably no more than a few days or weeks. Institutions that borrow frequently, say, for 8 consecutive weeks or for 30 out of 35 weeks, can be examined by the Fed's team of auditors. The Fed views the borrowing privilege as a means for banks and other depository institutions to deal with temporary liquidity needs caused, for example, by unexpected deposit outflows or an unexpected surge in loan demands. The key word is temporary. If an institution borrows persistently, the Fed begins to think that the institution's management is either consciously violating the provisions of Regulation A, cannot handle the liquidity pressures, or may have a chronic problem affecting its profitability and very existence. Perhaps its solvency, which is its ability to pay off or redeem its liabilities, is questionable. At this point, the Fed will step in. If the Fed feels that the borrowing privilege is being abused, it can deny the request to borrow.

We hope you noticed that the phrase "*under normal circumstances*" in the previous paragraph was highlighted to emphasize how the Fed's discount policy usually works. Occasionally, "exceptional circumstances," such as a natural disaster, the shutdown of a large manufacturer in a small community, other developments over which an institution's management has no control, or poor management decisions, may affect an individual institution and cause it to experience severe difficulties. Borrowers may not be repaying existing loans, depositors may be withdrawing large amounts of funds, and fears over the safety and solvency of the institution may be growing.

In such circumstances, the Fed stands ready to be a lender of last resort. More specifically, the Fed will consider lending funds to the institution for an extended period to help it adjust to its new circumstances, to provide time for management reform, or to work out a merger or orderly closing of the institution. Whatever the case may be, the Fed's main concern is to minimize the risk to the public interest and the financial system. Thus, the Fed's willingness to be a lender of last resort is closely related to its regulatory and supervisory responsibilities and its overall desire to preserve the public's confidence in the safety and soundness of the financial system, in general, and depository institutions, in particular.

Reserve Requirements

The major item on the liability side of depository institutions' balance sheets is, naturally enough, deposits. The Fed requires depository institutions to hold **required reserves** equal to a proportion of checkable deposit liabilities. The Fed specifies the *required reserve ratio*, which is the fraction that must be held. For example, the required reserve ratio on checkable deposits is currently 10 percent.[11] Thus, for each $1 in checkable deposit liabilities outstanding, a depository must hold 10 cents in reserve assets.

> **Required Reserves**
> The amount of reserve assets that the Fed requires depository institutions to hold against outstanding checkable deposit liabilities.

In conjunction with its conduct of monetary policy, the Fed—the Board of Governors to be precise—may vary the required reserve ratio. To illustrate, if the Fed wants to encourage bank lending, it could lower the required reserve ratio on checkable deposits from 10 percent to 8 percent. Then depository institutions would have to hold fewer reserve assets and would have additional funds to lend or to invest in other financial assets. This seemingly small change can have a powerful effect on the supply of money and the cost and availability of credit. Despite the power of this tool, the Fed does not change the required reserve ratio very often. When it does, the Fed is more likely to lower the ratio than to increase it. In December 1990 and again in December 1992, the required reserve ratio was lowered in an effort to stimulate the economy. During 2001, the ratio was 3 percent on the first $42.8 million of checkable deposits and 10 percent thereafter. At the present time, there are no reserve requirements on time and savings deposits, although such requirements have often been imposed in the past. Rather than frequently changing the required reserve ratio, the Fed uses open market operations as its major instrument for implementing monetary policy.

In recent years, the amount of required reserves held by banks and other depository institutions has fallen dramatically because of the introduction and growth of sweep accounts. **Sweep accounts** are a financial innovation that allows depository institutions to shift customers' funds out of checkable accounts that are subject to reserve requirements and into highly liquid money market deposit accounts (MMDAs) that are not. For example, funds that were "swept" out of checkable deposits and into MMDAs totaled $5.3 billion in January 1994 when they were first tracked by the Fed. By July 2001, the cumulative funds in sweep accounts equaled $430.3 billion. Some analysts have expressed concern that the reduction in required reserves because of the growth of sweep accounts will make it more difficult for the Fed to implement monetary policy. To date, the evidence does not seem to support this concern. Sweep accounts are discussed in more depth in later chapters.

> **Sweep Accounts**
> A financial innovation that allows depository institutions to shift customers' funds out of checkable accounts that are subject to reserve requirements and into highly liquid money market deposit accounts (MMDAs) that are not.

---

[11]Actually, since 2001, the required reserve ratio has been 10 percent on checkable deposits over $42.8 million. For checkable deposits less than $42.8 million and greater than $5.5 million, the required reserve ratio is 3 percent. The first $5.5 million in checkable deposits are exempt from reserve requirements. The amount of checkable deposits against which the 3 percent and 0 percent apply is modified each year depending on the percentage change in checkable deposits. Because $42.8 million in deposits is a relatively small amount, we ignore the 3 percent and 0 percent requirements.

LOOKING OUT: *The Eurosystem: Europe's Central Bank*

The European Union consists of 15 European countries that seek greater economic and monetary integration. Twelve of the 15 member countries have adopted a single currency called the euro. The euro replaced national currencies such as the French franc, German mark, and Italian lira of the respective countries. The conversion began on January 1, 1999 and was set to be completed on March 1, 2002.[a]

The Eurosystem is made up of the European Central Bank (ECB) and the national central banks of the 12 countries in the currency union. The ECB, which was created on June 1, 1998, has capital of 5 billion euro that has been contributed on a prorata basis by the national central banks. The Eurosystem formulates and implements monetary policy for the euro zone and is independent of control by any member country. By law, the primary objective of the Eurosystem is to maintain price stability in the euro zone. In addition to directing monetary policy, the Eurosystem conducts foreign exchange operations, and holds and manages the official foreign reserves of member countries. The ECB also operates a payment system called TARGET that interlinks the national payment settlement systems of the 15 countries in the European Union in order to promote smooth operation of the payments system.

The decision-making bodies of the Eurosystem consist of the Governing Council and the Executive Board. The Executive Board consists of the President, the Vice President, and four other members, all appointed by the member countries. Minimum nonrenewable terms are 8 years. The Governing Council consists of the Executive Board plus the governors of the national central banks of the member countries. Minimum renewable terms for governors are 5 years. The national central banks of the 12 countries in the currency union continue to perform many day-to-day monetary functions.

In many ways, the national central banks take on a role similar to the 12 Federal Reserve Banks. The ECB takes on the role of the Board of Governors and the Fed Open Market Committee of the Federal Reserve System.

[a]The 15 countries are Austria, Belguim, Denmark, Finland, France, Germany, Great Britain, Greece, Ireland, Italy, Luxembourg, the Netherlands, Portugal, Spain, and Sweden. Denmark, Great Britain, and Sweden decided not to participate in the euro.

RECAP The Fed's main tools for implementing monetary policy are open market operations and setting the required reserve ratio and the discount rate. Open market operations are the most widely used tool.

Who Does What within the Fed?

Having described the Fed's organizational structure, its functions, and the major tools available to Fed policymakers, we move on to identify the group within the Fed that has primary responsibility for each tool and function. Exhibit 4-5 shows the division of responsibility within the Fed. As you can see, the Board of Governors determines reserve requirements and the discount rate while the FOMC directs open market operations.

Clearly, the Board swings the most weight within the Federal Reserve System. The Board even exercises general supervisory and budgetary control over the 12 Reserve Banks. Remember the golden rule: "He who has the gold rules!" The Reserve Banks deal directly with depository institutions. In dealing with these institutions, the Reserve Banks administer discount policy. In addition, they are an important part of the nation's check-clearing system and play an important educational role by providing financial institutions and the public with information on Fed policy and the workings of the financial system and the economy.

We can be even more specific about where the power to make policy within the Fed lies, thanks to an economist who has had a "lifelong interest in the relationship between political processes and macroeconomic outcomes, especially in the area of

Board of Governors (7 Appointed Members)
- Sets reserve requirements and approves discount rates as a part of monetary policy
- Supervises and regulates member banks, bank holding companies, and financial holding companies
- Establishes and administers protective regulations in consumer finance
- Oversees Federal Reserve Banks

Federal Reserve Banks (Reserve Banks) (12 Districts)
- Propose discount rates
- Lend funds to depository institutions (discount policy)
- Furnish currency
- Collect and clear checks and transfer funds for depository institutions
- Handle U.S. government debt and cash balances

Federal Open Market Committee (Board of Governors plus 5 Federal Reserve Bank Presidents)
- Directs open market operations (buying and selling of U.S. government securities), which are the primary instrument of monetary policy

EXHIBIT 4-5
Division of Responsibility within the Federal Reserve System

SOURCE: *The Federal Reserve System: Purposes and Functions*, (Washington, DC: Board of Governors of the Federal Reserve System, 1984), p. 5.

monetary policy."[12] According to Thomas Havrilesky, the chair of the Board of Governors has "power within the Fed's policy hierarchy because he molds the outcome of the meetings of the Board of Governors and the FOMC. The chairman plays a key role in shaping the FOMC policy directive. He expresses his own preferences and summarizes the sense of these meetings once deliberation and debate have been concluded."[13] Perhaps now you can see why this individual is such a powerful figure in U.S. policy circles.

The Federal Reserve System: An Independent Watchdog, Convenient Scapegoat, or Cunning Political Animal?

The Federal Reserve System is a quasi-government agency whose primary responsibility is to stabilize the economy. However, the Fed is just one of many government agencies that try to design policies to stabilize the economy. Others include the Council of Economic Advisers, the Treasury Department, and the Office of Management and Budget. Unlike the Fed, though, these agencies are under the direct control of the executive branch of government. Thus, the president can fire the chair of the council, the secretary of the treasury, and the budget director at any time.

As explained earlier, Congress established the Federal Reserve as an independent agency to shield it from the political process. The 14-year terms of the members of the Board ensure that the members do not have to defend their actions to Congress, the president, or the public. In addition, the Fed does not depend on an appropriation from Congress for its funding. The Fed pays its own way from the interest income it earns on loans to depository institutions and its holdings of government

---

[12]Thomas Havrilesky, *The Pressures on American Monetary Policy* (Boston: Kluwer Academic Publishers, 1993), preface.

[13]Ibid., p. 4.

Freedom of Information Act
A 1966 law that requires more openness in government and more public access to government documents.

securities. Finally, the Fed is exempt from many provisions of the **Freedom of Information Act (1966)** and "government in the sunshine" legislation, which call for government policy to be made in meetings open to the public. As a result, Fed policymakers usually meet in secret to formulate policy.

Nevertheless, the Fed is not completely outside the government. It is firmly embedded in our political system. In the short run, however, the Federal Reserve does not take orders from anyone in the executive or legislative branch of government. Its decisions regarding monetary policy are, in theory, not constrained by the whims of the president or Congress or by any partisan politics. We say "in the short run" because in the long run, Congress can pass laws that the Fed must obey. It could even abolish the Fed altogether. We think it fair to say that the Fed is aware of these possibilities and behaves accordingly.

Ever since the Fed was created, politicians and academics have argued about the desirability of its independence. The debate has largely focused on the degree to which the Fed should alter its policy in response to "suggestions" or directives from Congress or the president. Evidence suggests that since 1960, "outside forces" including Congress and the executive branch have become more aggressive in attempting to influence Fed actions. Obviously, the more responsive the Fed is to outside forces, the less independent it will be. Calls for reducing the Fed's independence in part reflect the frustration expressed by the president and some members of Congress in their often unsuccessful efforts to attain our economic goals. In recent years, this frustration has led to several attempts not only to influence the Fed but also to make it more responsive to Congress. The Fed saw such moves as a serious threat to its independence and vigorously fought off overt efforts to clip its wings.

Those who support independence do so mainly on the grounds that anything less than independence will inject politics into monetary policy operations. This argument was put forth eloquently by Alan Greenspan, Chair of the Board of Governors:

> We have to be sensitive to the appropriate degree of accountability accorded a central bank in a democratic society. If accountability is achieved by putting the conduct of monetary policy under the close influence of politicians subject to short-term election-cycle pressures, the resulting policy would likely prove disappointing over time. That is the conclusion of financial analysts, of economists, and of others who have studied the experiences of central banks around the globe, and of the legislators who built the Federal Reserve. The lure of short-run gains from gunning the economy can loom large in the context of an election cycle, but the process of reaching for such gains can have costly consequences for the nation's economic performance and standards of living over the longer term. The temptation is to step on the monetary accelerator, or at least to avoid the monetary brake, until after the next election. Giving in to such temptations is likely to impart an inflationary bias to the economy and could lead to instability, recession, and economic stagnation. Interest rates would be higher, and productivity and living standards lower, than if monetary policy were freer to approach the nation's economic goals with a longer term perspective.

The recognition that monetary policies that are in the best long-run interest of the nation may not always be popular in the short run has led not only the United States, but also most other developed nations, to limit the degree of immediate control that legislatures and administrations have over their central banks. More and more countries have been taking actions to increase the amount of separation between monetary policy and the political sphere.[14]

---

[14]Statement by Alan Greenspan, before the Committee on Banking, Finance, and Urban Affairs, U.S. House of Representatives, October 13, 1993.

Thus, proponents of continuing the Fed's independence argue that because politicians are interested in getting elected and reelected, they are short-run maximizers who do not take the long view. This could be disastrous if the long-run impacts of policy are different from its short-run impacts. For instance, to please the electorate, politicians might pursue an expansionary monetary policy that accelerates growth of economic activity, even though in the longer run this policy might increase inflation. Some have even suggested that the term of the Fed chair should be increased to further shield that individual from political influences.

On the other side of the debate, many people contend that the independence of the Fed is inconsistent with democracy. They argue that the president and Congress are held accountable for economic conditions. If unemployment is rising and inflation is rampant, the president and members of Congress will be driven from office at election time. Because the president and Congress are responsible for economic policy, they should have all the tools at their disposal. More generally, opponents of Fed independence argue that monetary policy, like other government policies, should be controlled by people directly responsible to the electorate.

Opponents of the Fed's independence would like to see reforms such as the following:

1. *A change in the status of Reserve Bank presidents on the FOMC.* Proposals include removing the Reserve Bank presidents from the FOMC, making them nonvoting members, or changing the way Reserve Bank presidents are selected so that they will be more representative of the public at large. The concern is that the Reserve Bank presidents represent the interests of the banking community because they are chosen by the Reserve Bank directors, two-thirds of whom, in turn, are elected by the member banks.

2. *A broadening of the authority of the General Accounting Office (GAO) to audit the Fed.* At present, the GAO audits all aspects of the Federal Reserve with three exceptions: (1) deliberations and decisions regarding monetary policy, (2) transactions directed by the FOMC, and (3) transactions involving foreign exchange operations. Proposals would eliminate these exceptions.

3. *Mandated disclosure of monetary policies and discussions.* Here the proposal is for fuller and more immediate disclosure of FOMC discussions and decisions. Changes in the 1990s and early 2000s with regard to policy disclosures have somewhat met this reform.

In each case, the recommended change would reduce the autonomy of the Fed and make it more accountable. In that the Fed often projects the image that monetary policy is too complicated for the public and Congress to understand, or that secrecy is essential to successful policy, it should not be surprising that members of Congress are suspicious. They want to open up the process of formulating monetary policy to examination and debate. They want more timely information about policy decisions.

Today, even though there is not a legislative requirement to do so, the FOMC releases edited minutes of its deliberations immediately after the next FOMC meeting, approximately 6 weeks later. As previously discussed, in early 1994, Chair Greenspan decided to announce several policy changes immediately after the FOMC meetings rather than waiting for the publication of minutes and the policy directive, or for the policies to be implemented. This practice was formally adopted in February 1995. In February 2000, the FOMC amended the language in the announcement to more clearly communicate the FOMC's judgment of the economic outlook in the foreseeable future. Furthermore, in 1993, the Fed agreed to publish "edited" transcripts, not just minutes, of the FOMC meetings with a 5-year delay.[15] All of these actions suggest that the Fed is becoming more open, while at the same time maintaining that the present system gives it the proper degree of accountability necessary to carry out monetary policy.

Long-time observers of the political-economic wars believe that the debate over whether the Fed should be independent is more form than substance. For one thing, they point out, Congress finds the current system quite convenient. If the economy performs badly, Congress can engage in Fedbashing—blaming the Fed for what went wrong and telling the public that the Fed, insulated by its independence, would not respond to Congress's call to "do the right thing." In 1980, Edward Kane summarized this relationship as follows:

> Whenever monetary policies are popular, incumbents can claim their influence was crucial in their adoption. On the other hand, when monetary policies prove unpopular, they can blame everything on a stubborn Federal Reserve and claim further that things would have been worse if they had not pressed Fed officials at every opportunity.[16]

Kane's synopsis is as true today as it was in 1980. Scapegoats are convenient. If the Fed were directly and completely responsible to Congress, then who would Congress have to blame when things go wrong?

To sum up, the Fed's independence is in part an illusion. It can only be maintained if the Fed operates within politically acceptable bounds. If it pursues policies at considerable variance from what the president and Congress desire, Congress can change the law! Since changes have not occurred, we can infer that current arrangements are convenient and attractive. More specifically, political decision makers gain from having the public perceive the Fed as being independent. This way the Fed can take the heat for unpopular policies, and the politicians can share the credit when things go right. At the same time, Congress and the president are probably confident that if push comes to shove, they can persuade the Fed to pursue policies conforming, at least broadly, to their wishes. This is part of what is popularly referred to as "the political economy of policy making."

In Chapters 5 and 6, we look at how interest rates are determined. It is time to move into the world of financial prices in which the Fed operates.

---

[15]The editing of the transcripts usually involves deleting a small amount of confidential material that pertains to foreign central banks or entities.

[16]Edward Kane, "Politics and Fed Policymaking: The More Things Change the More They Remain the Same," *Journal of Monetary Economics*, April 1980, pp. 199–211.

Summary of Major Points

- The Federal Reserve System was established by an act of Congress in 1913. The original Federal Reserve Act was modified and strengthened in 1933 and 1935 following the economic and financial collapse of the Great Depression.

- The Fed is charged with regulating and supervising the operation of the financial system so as to promote a smooth-running, efficient, competitive financial system and with promoting the overall health and stability of the economy through its ability to influence the availability and cost of money and credit.

- The Board of Governors, located in Washington, D.C., is the core of the Federal Reserve System. It is composed of seven members appointed by the president, with the approval of the Senate, for 14-year terms. The terms are staggered so that one expires every 2 years. The president appoints one of the governors as chair for a 4-year term.

- The country is divided into 12 districts. Each district is served by a Reserve Bank located in a large city within the district. The framers of the original Federal Reserve Act hoped to decentralize policy-making authority within the Fed through the creation of Reserve Banks.

- The Federal Open Market Committee (FOMC) is the chief policy-making body within the Fed. It is composed of 12 members: the 7 members of the Board of Governors and 5 of the 12 presidents of the Reserve Banks. The president of the New York Federal Reserve Bank is a permanent voting member, and the other four slots rotate yearly among the remaining 11 Reserve Bank presidents.

- The Fed's functions can be classified into four main areas: formulating and implementing monetary policy; supervising and regulating the financial system; facilitating the payments mechanism; and acting as fiscal agent for the government.

- The FOMC directs open market operations, the major tool for implementing monetary policy. These operations involve the buying or selling of government securities—actions that affect the volume of reserves in the banking system as well as interest rates. When the Fed buys securities, bank reserves increase. This, in turn, encourages bankers to expand loans and, hence, the money supply.

- The FOMC meets eight times each year in closed meetings in Washington. Policy changes are announced immediately after the meetings. The minutes of the FOMC meetings are released to the public immediately after the next FOMC meeting. They contain the policy directive, which is the set of instructions regarding the conduct of open market operations that is issued to the New York Fed. The New York Fed, located at the center of the nation's financial markets, executes open market operations on behalf of the FOMC and the entire Federal Reserve System. The Fed announces FOMC decisions immediately following the meeting, including a statement about its judgment about the economic outlook in the foreseeable future.

- The discount rate is the rate the Fed charges depository institutions for borrowing reserves from their district Reserve Bank. Since the Fed views borrowing as a privilege rather than a right, institutions are encouraged to borrow only when absolutely necessary and only for short periods of time.

- In exceptional circumstances, the Fed is prepared to serve as a lender of last resort. To preserve the public's confidence in the safety and soundness of the financial system, the Fed will lend for an extended period to an institution experiencing severe difficulties.

- The Fed requires depository institutions to hold reserve assets equal to a proportion of each dollar of deposit liabilities. The Fed's required reserve ratio specifies the proportion.

- There is an ongoing debate as to whether the Fed should continue to operate as an independent government agency. The Fed and others argue that independence is essential to the pursuit of economic stability. Opponents argue that such independence is inconsistent with our democratic form of government. Others observe that Congress and the president find the Fed a convenient scapegoat when the economy deteriorates. They further believe that the Fed is really not all that independent and that, at times, it does respond to political pressure. In recent years, the Fed has become more open.

Key Terms

Banking Reform Acts of 1933 and 1935	Federal Reserve Act	Payments Mechanism
Board of Governors	Federal Reserve System	Policy Directive
Discount Rate	Freedom of Information Act	Required Reserves
Federal Open Market Committee (FOMC)	Lender of Last Resort	Reserve Bank
	Open Market Operations	Sweep Accounts

Review Questions

1. Discuss each of the four major functions of the Fed. Which do you believe requires Fed autonomy? Why?

2. Give the major responsibilities of each of the following:
   a. The Board of Governors
   b. The 12 Reserve Banks
   c. The Federal Open Market Committee

3. Why was the Fed created? What effect should the existence of the Fed have on financial crises?

4. Why did Congress create 12 Federal Reserve Banks rather than one central bank?

5. What features of the Fed's structure serve to make it fairly autonomous? Is Congress able to wield any control over the Fed?

6. Why have the responsibilities of the Fed increased since its inception?

7. Discuss the major policy tools that the Fed can use to promote the overall health of the economy. What is the most widely used tool?

8. When and why are changes in the discount rate implemented? Who requests such changes? How often does the Fed change the required reserve ratio? How often does the Fed engage in open market operations?

9. What are the arguments for increasing the autonomy of the Fed? The arguments for increasing the accountability of the Fed?

10. Suppose that the Fed was less independent. How could this affect monetary policy? Suppose that the Fed was more independent. How could this affect monetary policy?

11. Why is the president of the New York Fed a permanent member of the FOMC?

12. Is the Fed more accountable to Congress or to the president? Why? Who created the Fed? Who appoints the Fed chair?

13. How does each of the following affect the money supply?
    a. The Fed lowers the required reserve ratio.
    b. The Fed lowers the discount rate.
    c. The Fed buys government securities.

14. What are sweep accounts? How do sweep accounts affect required reserves? Are balances in sweep accounts subject to reserve requirements?

Internet Exercises

1. This chapter has described the Federal Reserve System. Access the following Web site maintained by the Federal Reserve Bank of Minneapolis and answer the following questions: **http://woodrow.mpls.frb.fed. US/info/sys/index.html**.
   a. When and by whom was the Fed created?
   b. What is the Board of Governors of the Fed?
   c. Who are the current members of the Board of Governors?

2. The Federal Open Market Committee (FOMC) directs open market operations that involve the purchase or sale of government securities. Information on the FOMC can be found at the following Web site maintained by the Federal Reserve Bank of Minneapolis: **http://woodrow.mpls. frb.fed.us/info/policy/#fomc**. Access this site and answer the following questions:
   a. What is the current schedule of FOMC meeting dates?
   b. Who are the current members of the FOMC?

Suggested Readings

For an excellent monetary history and a summary of the events leading up to the legislation establishing the Federal Reserve, see Milton Friedman and Anna Jacobson Schwartz, *A Monetary History of the United States, 1867–1960* (Princeton, NJ: Princeton University Press, 1963), chapter 4.

The concern about political pressure on the central bank was well founded given the early history of banks in the United States. For a relevant discussion, see Bray Hammond, *Banks and Politics in America from the Revolution to the Civil War* (Princeton, NJ: Princeton University Press, 1957).

U.S. Monetary Policy and Financial Markets by Ann-Marie Meulendyke (1998) is a readable discussion of Fed procedures and the conduct of monetary policy. It can be obtained free of charge from the Public Information Dept., Federal Reserve Bank of New York, 33 Liberty Street, New York, NY 10045. It is also available on the Internet at **http://www.newyorkfed.org/pihome/addpub**. This site also contains several other topics about the Federal Reserve including "A Day at the Fed," "A Guide to Federal Reserve Regulations," "The Federal System Purposes and Functions," "Understanding Open market Operations," and "The Structure of the Federal Reserve System."

For two interesting articles on the Fed, see Thomas Cunningham, "Fed's Regional Structure Provides Unique insight into the Economy," *EconSouth*, Federal Reserve Bank of Atlanta, No. 2, Quarter 2, 2000, p. 1 and Joel Hellier, "Independence of the Central Bank, Growth, and Coalitions in a Monetary Union," *Journal of Post Keynesian Economics*, Vol. 22, No. 2, Winter 1999–2000, pp. 285–312.

In the body of the chapter, we saw that banks use sweep accounts to minimize the holdings of reserves. Payment of interest on reserves by the Fed would reduce the incentive to do so. See the "Testimony of Governor Laurence H. Meyer on the Payment of Interest on Reserves and Fed Surplus," before the Committee on Banking and Financial Services, U.S. House of Representatives, May 3, 2000. The testimony is available on the Fed's Web site at **http://www.federalreserve.gov/boarddocs/testimony/2000/20000503.htm**.

On May 6, 1997, the Bank of England gained substantially more independence in the conduct of monetary policy. An article that looks at the result of this greater independence is Mark M. Spiegal, "Central Bank Independence and Inflation Expectations: Evidence from the British Index-Linked Gilts," *Economic Review of the Federal Reserve Bank of San Francisco* 1 (1998): 3–14.

"The Independence of Central Banks," by Sun Bae Kim, summarizes a study showing that countries with the most independent central banks have the lowest inflation rates. Furthermore, if the central bank has a reputation for controlling inflation, this can substitute for legal independence. The article can be found in the *Weekly Letter of the San Francisco Federal Reserve Bank*, December 13, 1991.

"An Independent Central Bank in a Democratic Country: The Federal Reserve Experience" by William McDonough, offers a discussion of historical development of central banking in the United States and of the need for the Fed to be somewhat independent of the day-to-day control of the government so that it will be less likely to succumb to short-term political pressures. The article can be found in the *Federal Reserve Bank of New York Quarterly Review* 19 (Spring 1994): 1–6.

Three additional articles devoted to the question of central bank autonomy can be found in "The Papers and Proceedings of the 107th Annual Meeting of the American Economic Association in Washington, D.C., January 6–8, 1995" as published in the *American Economic Review*, May 1995. These articles are "How Independent Should the Central Bank Be?" by Alberto Alesina and Roberta Gaiti; "Central-Bank Independence Revisited" by Stanley Fischer; and "Two Fallacies Concerning Central-Bank Independence" by Bennett T. McCallum.

Other articles dealing with central bank independence are Jakob de Haan, "Commitment rather than Independence: An Institutional Design for Reducing the Inflationary Bias of Monetary Policy: A Comment on Henriette M. Prast," *Kiklos* 51:1 (1998): 119–125; Richard W. Stevenson, "Divorcing Central Banks and Politics: Independence Helps Fight Inflation," *New York Times*, May 7, 1997, p. D6; and Susanne Lohmann, "Federalism and Central Bank Independence: The Politics and German Monetary Policy," *World Politics* 50:3 (1998): 401–406.

part

FINANCIAL PRICES

chapter

5

Interest Rates and Bond Prices

Learning Objectives *After reading this chapter, you should know:*

- Why the interest rate represents the time value of money
- What compounding and discounting are
- Why interest rates and bond prices are inversely related
- The major determinants of interest rates
- The relationship between nominal and real interest rates
- How interest rates fluctuate over the business cycle

" "
Change must be measured from a known baseline.
—Evan Shute

ACCOUNT	MINIMUM BALANCE TO OBTAIN ANNUAL PERCENTAGE YIELD	10	500	10

Certificates of Deposit

| **6 Month (Simple Interest Rate) | | 4.25% | 4.35% |
| 1 Year | | 4.20% | 4.25% |

The Present versus the Future

State University currently charges students $5,000 a year for tuition. Following the appointment of an innovative financial officer, it offers enrolling freshmen a new way to pay 4 years' tuition—pay $18,000 today rather than $5,000 per year for 4 years. Would you participate in the plan?

Following her third box office smash, a Hollywood sensation has just signed a multipicture contract. As compensation, the star has been offered either $6 million today or $7.5 million in 5 years. You are her financial adviser; what should she do and why?

You win a million dollar lottery and learn that the million dollars will be paid out in equal installments of $50,000 per year over the next 20 years. Would you be willing to trade this stream of future income for one payment today? How large would that payment have to be?

The purpose of the first half of this chapter is to provide the analytical framework needed to understand and answer questions that involve comparing the present with the future, such as those just posed. As you will see, the framework developed and questions addressed, while important by themselves, are the key to the second half of the chapter, where we will examine the determinants of interest rates and the relationships among interest rates, bond prices, economic activity, and inflation. Even a casual reader of the financial pages of U.S. newspapers has seen headlines such as "Bond Prices Slump as Interest Rates Rise" or "Bond Market Rallies after Weak GDP Report" or "Inflation Fears Result in Lower Bond Prices." Understanding such headlines is the objective of the second part of the chapter.

The Time Value of Money

Interest rates have already popped up in numerous places in the text. In our earlier substantive discussion in Chapter 2, we emphasized that the interest rate is the cost to borrowers of obtaining credit and the reward to lenders for lending surplus funds. Thus, just as rent is the cost to apartment dwellers and the return to the landlord, the interest rate is the rental rate paid by borrowers and received by lenders when money is "rented out."

Money represents purchasing power; a person who has money can purchase goods or services now. If someone does not have money now and wants to make purchases, she can rent purchasing power by borrowing. Likewise, if someone else has money now and is willing to postpone purchases to the future, he can rent out purchasing power. Note carefully the role played by the interest rate here. Presumably, the willingness to postpone purchases into the future is a function of the reward—that is, the interest rate. In particular, the higher the interest rate, the greater the reward and, hence, the greater the willingness to postpone purchases into the future and lend in the present. Similar reasoning applies on the borrowing side. We can think of someone who wants to purchase goods and services but is short of the necessary funds as having two options: (1) borrow now and purchase now, or (2) save now and purchase later. Since the willingness to borrow depends on the cost, among other things, we can conclude that the higher the interest rate, the less attractive is option (1) and the more attractive is option (2).

The central point to remember from this discussion is the role the interest rate plays in linking the present with the future. Lending in the present enables spending in the future the sum of what is lent plus the interest earned. Borrowing in the present enables spending in the present, but requires paying back in the future what is borrowed plus interest. Since the interest rate is the return on lending and the cost of borrowing, it plays a pivotal role in spending, saving, borrowing, and lending decisions made in the present and bearing on the future. The concept we

Time Value of Money
The terms on which one can trade off present purchasing power for future purchasing power; the interest rate.

have been discussing is called the **time value of money.** Simply put, the interest rate represents the time value of money because it specifies the terms upon which one can trade off present purchasing power for future purchasing power. In the pages that follow, it should become crystal clear that this is one of the most important and fundamental concepts in economics and finance.

Compounding and Discounting

Compounding: Future Values

Compounding
A method used to determine the future value of a sum lent today.

Compounding is a method used to answer a simple question: What is the future value of money lent (or borrowed) today? As illustrated in Exhibit 5-1, the question is forward looking; we stand in the present (today) and ask a question about the future. To see how it works, a few examples will be helpful.

Principal
The original amount of funds lent.

Suppose Joseph M. Student agrees to lend a friend $1,000 for 1 year. The friend gives Joe an IOU for $1,000 and agrees to repay the $1,000 plus interest in a year. The amount that is originally lent is called the **principal**—in this case, $1,000. If the agreed interest rate is 6 percent, then the friend will pay a total of $1,060 ($1,000 + $60). In this example, the amount of interest is $60 ($1,000 × .06 = $60). This general relationship can be expressed as

(A)   Amount repaid = principal + interest

The amount of interest can be expressed as

(B)   Interest = principal × interest rate

Substituting Equation (B) into Equation (A) yields

(C)   Amount repaid = principal + (principal × interest rate)

Since each term on the right-hand side of Equation (C) has a common factor, it can be rearranged and rewritten as

(D)   Amount repaid = principal × (1 + i)

where i is the interest rate. Utilizing Equation (D) and our example, Joe's friend would repay

$$\$1,060 = \$1,000 \times 1.06$$

For later use, we will rewrite Equation (D) as

(5-1) $V_1 = V_0(1 + i)$

where V_1 = the funds to be received by the lender (paid by the borrower) at the end of year 1; note that this is a future value.
        V_0 = the funds lent (and borrowed) now; note that this is a present value.

Imagine now that Joe's friend borrows for 2 years instead of 1 year and makes no payments to Joe until 2 years pass. Here is where compounding comes into play.

EXHIBIT 5-1

Compounding: The Future Value of Money Lent Today

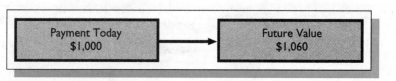

| Payment Today $1,000 | → | Future Value $1,060 |

Literally, compounding means to combine, add to, or increase. In the financial world, it refers to the increase in the value of funds that results from earning interest on interest. More specifically, interest earned after the first year is added to the original principal; the second year's interest calculation is based on this total. The funds to be received at the end of 2 years, V_2, consist of the original amount of funds lent out, V_0, plus the interest on the original amount, iV_0, plus the interest on the amount of funds owed at the end of the first year $[i(V_0 + iV_0)]$.[1] In our example:

principal + interest earned in first year + interest earned in second year =   *2 YR. LOAN*

$1,000 + .06($1,000)   + .06[$1,000 + .06($1,000)]   =

$1,000 + $60   + $63.60   = $1,123.60

Note that the implication of the last term is that interest is earned on interest; this is compounding. In the second year, Joe earns interest not only on the principal $(.06 \times \$1,000)$ but also on the interest earned in the first year $[.06 \times .06(\$1,000)]$. In effect, the interest earned in the first year is reinvested. Expressed symbolically:

(5-2) $$V_2 = V_0 + iV_0 + i(V_0 + iV_0)$$

Using some simple algebra, this equation can be reduced to[2]

(5-3) $$V_2 = V_0 (1 + i)^2$$

Equation (5-3) can be generalized for any sum of money lent (invested) for any maturity of n years:

(5-4) $$V_n = V_0(1 + i)^n$$

The future value of a sum of money invested for n years, V_n, is equal to the original sum, V_0, compounded by the interest rate $(1 + i)^n$. In our last example, $V_0 = \$1,000$, $i = .06$, $n = 2$, and $V_2 = \$1,123.60$.

The formula in Equation (5-4) is actually quite easy to use. For example, most calculators have a y^x function and $(1 + i)^n$ is a y^x calculation. Using $(1 + .11)$ for y and 10 for x, you should be able to verify that if Joe lends $1,000 for 10 years at an interest rate of 11 percent, he will receive $2,839.42 at maturity: $2,839.42 = $1,000(1.11)^{10}$.

http://www.ny.frb.org/ pihome/fedpoint/ fed28.html
Provides information on estimating yields on Treasury securities.

Discounting: Present Values

Compounding is forward looking. It addresses the question: What is the future value of money lent (or borrowed) today? As we shall see, understanding compounding is the key to really understanding what often seems to be a more difficult concept for students to grasp—**discounting.**

In effect, as shown in Exhibit 5-2, discounting is backward looking. It addresses this question: What is the **present value** of money to be received (or paid) in the future?

Perhaps the best way to learn how to answer this question and to see why such questions and answers are important is to address one of the examples mentioned at

Discounting
A method used to determine the present value of a sum to be received in the future.

Present Value
The value today of funds to be received or paid on a future date.

---

[1] The simple interest rate in this example is 6 percent. If Joe took the interest earned on the loan after 1 year but left the principal, the total return over 2 years would be $120, or $60 each year. The average annual rate of return would be 6 percent $[.06 = (\$120/\$1,000) \div 2]$. If, as in the example, no interest payment is made after 1 year—the funds being, in effect, relent or reinvested—the total return is $123.60, and the compound annual return is 6.18 percent $[.0618 = (\$123.60/\$1,000) \div 2]$. The compound rate will always be greater than the simple rate due to the interest earned on interest.

[2] For those who would like to work through all the steps, start with $V_2 = V_0 + iV_0 + i(V_0 + iV_0) = V_0 + iV_0 + iV_0 + i^2 V_0 = V_0 + 2iV_0 + i^2 V_0 = V_0 (1 + 2i + i^2) = V_0 (1 + i) (1 + i) = V_0 (1 + i)^2$.

Einstein discovers that time is actually money.

EXHIBIT 5-2

Discounting: The Present Value of Money to Be Received in the Future

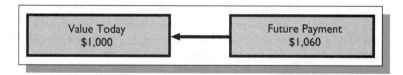

the beginning of the chapter. Remember the movie star? She has been signed to a multipicture deal, and the studio has offered her either $6 million today or $7.5 million in 5 years. Which option should she select?

To calculate the answer, we can simply rearrange Equation (5-4). In the previous example, we knew the present value, V_0, the interest rate, i, and the number of years, n, and we wanted to solve for the future value, V_n. Now we want to solve for the present value, V_0, of a sum to be received in the future ($7.5 million), so we can compare it to another present value (the $6 million). Accordingly,

(5-5)
$$V_0 = V_n / (1 + i)^n$$

Assuming we know the interest rate—say, it's 6 percent—the present value of $7.5 million to be available in 5 years is

$$\$7{,}500{,}000/(1 + .06)^5 = \$5{,}604{,}436.30$$

The present value of $6 million received today for signing the multipicture contract is, obviously, $6 million. Given an interest rate of 6 percent, the present value of $7.5 million to be received in 5 years is obviously less.[3] Accordingly, the movie star should take the $6 million today. To see more clearly why, all you need to do is turn the discounting/present value problem into a compounding/future value problem; if the actress took the $6 million today and invested it at 6 percent, she would have more than $7.5 million in 5 years. To be exact, she would have $8,029,353.47 [$6,000,000(1 + .06)^5 = $8,029,353.47]!

To be sure you are completely with us, close the book and ask yourself what the present value of $7.5 million in 5 years, given an interest rate of 6 percent, really represents. It is the sum you would need to invest today, given a 6 percent interest rate, to have $7.5 million in 5 years; that is, to have $7.5 million in 5 years given an interest rate of 6 percent, you would have to invest $5,604,436.30 today. To nail everything down, assume the interest rate is 4 percent instead of 6 percent. Would you still advise the movie star to take the $6 million today, or does the change in the interest rate point to a different option? Why or why not? The explanation and calculation are in the footnote at the bottom of the page; give the problem a try and then check your answer.[4]

RECAP Compounding is finding the future value of a present sum. Discounting is finding the present value of a future sum. The future value, V_n, of a sum, V_0, invested today for n years is $V_0(1 + i)^n$. The present value, V_0, of a sum, V_n, to be received in n years is $V_n/(1 + i)^n$.

STOP

Interest Rates, Bond Prices, and Present Values

In the previous example, we learned how to compute the present value of a single future payment. How does this help us to understand the relationship between bond prices and interest rates?

Although bonds issued by corporations and governments differ in a variety of ways, they generally share the following characteristics: They have an original maturity greater than 10 years, they have a face or **par value** (F) of $1,000 per bond, and the issuer (borrower) agrees to make equal periodic interest payments over the term to maturity of the instrument and to repay the face value at maturity. The periodic payments are called **coupon payments** (C) and are equal to the coupon rate on a bond multiplied by the face value of the bond. As we shall see in a moment, the coupon rate, which usually appears on the bond itself, is not the same as the interest rate. The distinction between the coupon rate and the coupon payment and between the coupon rate and the interest rate is often a source of considerable confusion; bear with us and you can avoid the problem.

Par Value
The face value printed on a bond; the amount the bond originally sold for.

Coupon Payments
The periodic payments made to bondholders, which are equal to the principal times the coupon rate.

---

[3]We are also assuming that she expects the interest rate to be 6 percent for the next 5 years.

[4]The present value of $7.5 million to be received in 5 years, assuming an interest rate of 4 percent, is $6,164,453.30. This is obviously more than $6 million. Put another way, if the actress took the $6 million today and lent it at 4 percent for 5 years, she would have only $7,299,917.41 at the end of the period rather than $7.5 million. The $6,164,453.30 is what she would need to lend today at 4 percent for 5 years to have $7.5 million at the end of the period. In sum, the actress should take the $7.5 million in 5 years rather than the $6 million today.

Given these characteristics, a bond represents a stream of future payments. To find its present value and, thus, the price it will trade at in financial markets, we need to compute the present value of each coupon payment and the present value of the final repayment of the face value on the maturity date. The appropriate formula is

(5-6) $$P = C_1/(1 + i)^1 + C_2/(1 + i)^2 + \ldots + C_n/(1 + i)^n + F/(1 + i)^n$$

where P = the price (present value) of the bond
C = the coupon payment on the bond (C_1 in year 1, C_2 in year 2, etc.)
F = the face or par value of the bond
i = the interest rate
n = the number of years to maturity (on a 5-year bond, n = 5)

Notice that this formula is a descendant of Equation (5-5) with $P = V_0$ and $V_n = C$ or F. The only difference is that we use Equation (5-6) to compute the present value of a number of future payments, such as occurs with a bond, while Equation (5-5) is used to compute the present value of a single future payment. To put some flesh on an otherwise bare-boned formula, let's work through a few examples. Suppose Jane is about to buy a bond that will mature in 1 year, has a face value of $1,000, carries a coupon payment of $60, and the prevailing interest rate in the market is 6 percent. What is Jane willing to pay for this bond? Utilizing Equation (5-6),

$$P = \$60/(1 + .06)^1 + \$1,000/(1 + .06)^1 =$$
$$\$56.60 + \$943.40 = \$1,000$$

This tells Jane that the price of the bond or its present value is $1,000.[5] In other words, if the interest rate is 6 percent, the present value of receiving $1,060 in 1 year is $1,000, and this is what Jane (or anybody else) will pay for the bond. Since the coupon payment is $60, the coupon rate is 6 percent (6 percent = $60/$1,000). You might also note that when the price of a bond is equal to its par value ($1,000), the coupon rate is equal to the interest rate.

Continuing with this example, Jane buys the bond for $1,000, and the next day the prevailing interest rate in the market rises to 8 percent. What effect does this have on the value (price) of Jane's bond? Remember that Jane's bond will pay her $1,060 in 1 year.[6] Imagine yourself with $1,000 to invest. How much would you pay for Jane's bond? Would you pay $1,000? We hope your answer is "no"! You could go out in the market and buy another bond yielding 8 percent for $1,000! Alternatively, you could buy Jane's bond. But you would do this if and only if it, too, was somehow made to yield 8 percent. How could this happen? The maturity of the bond (1 year), the coupon payment ($60 per $1,000 of par value), and the par value ($1,000) are all fixed. They represent the contractual arrangements entered into by the bond issuer (borrower) at the time the bond was initially issued. What's left, you ask? The price of the bond! You and other investors would be willing to pay a price for the bond that, given the receipt of $1,060 at maturity, would represent a yield over the year of 8 percent. Using Equation (5-5),

---

[5]Are you puzzled by the fact that the price of the bond in the marketplace equals the present value of the bond? If so, think of what happens in any market when a product is selling for less or more than buyers and sellers think it's really worth. If it is selling for less, quantity demanded will be greater than quantity supplied, and the price will rise in response. If it is selling for more, quantity demanded will be less than quantity supplied, and the price will fall in response. Equilibrium is reached when the prevailing price in the market is such that quantity demanded equals quantity supplied. So too in financial markets.

[6]Technically, the time to maturity is now 1 year less a day, but to simplify, we ignore the 1 day.

$$P = \$60/(1 + .08)^1 + \$1,000/(1 + .08)^1 =$$
$$\$55.55 + \$925.93 = \$981.48$$

The figure \$981.48 is the present value of \$1,060 to be received in 1 year, given that the interest rate we use to discount the future sum is 8 percent.

Put somewhat more intuitively, if you bought Jane's bond for \$981.48, you would receive \$60 of interest at maturity plus a capital gain of \$18.52; the gain is equal to the par value you get back at maturity (\$1,000) minus the price you pay at the time of purchase (\$981.48). Together the interest and the capital gain (\$60 + \$18.52 = \$78.52) give us an 8 percent yield over the year (\$78.52/\$981.48 = .08). Thus, in this example, you buy the bond at a price below its par value. This is called a **discount from par** and raises the yield on the bond, called the **yield to maturity,** from 6 percent to 8 percent. In sum, as the market interest rate rises, the price of existing bonds falls. The lower yield to maturity on existing bonds is unattractive to potential purchasers who can purchase newly issued bonds with higher yields to maturity. Therefore, the yield to maturity on previously issued bonds must somehow rise to remain competitive with the new higher level of prevailing interest rates. The yield on existing bonds rises when their prices fall. Hence, bond prices fall until the yield to maturity of the bond becomes equal to the current interest rate.

Discount from Par
When a bond sells below its face value because interest rates have increased since the bond was originally issued.

Yield to Maturity
The return on a bond held to maturity, which includes both the interest return and any capital gain or loss.

Suppose that instead of rising from 6 percent to 8 percent the day after Jane buys the bond, the interest rate in the market falls to 4 percent. You should now be able to do the arithmetic with the aid of Equation (5-6); the price (or present value) of Jane's bond will rise to \$1,019.23. What does this represent? If any of us bought Jane's bond for \$1,019.23, we would be paying a price above the par value. This is called a **premium above par**. At maturity we would get \$60 minus a capital loss of \$19.23; the loss is equal to what we pay at the time of purchase minus the par value we receive at maturity (\$1,019.23 − \$1,000 = \$19.23). The \$40.77 (\$60 − \$19.23 = \$40.77) represents a 4 percent yield over the year (\$40.77/\$1,019.23 = .04). Thus, as the market interest rate falls, the prices of existing bonds rise. The reason is that the higher yield to maturity on existing bonds is attractive to potential investors. As they buy existing bonds, the bond prices rise, reducing their yield to maturity.

Premium above Par
When a bond sells above its face value because interest rates have decreased since the bond was originally issued.

In general, then, there is an inverse relationship between the price of outstanding bonds trading in the secondary market and the prevailing level of market interest rates. As a result, one can say that if bond prices are rising, then interest rates are falling, and vice versa. These are different ways of saying the same thing, and we need not resort to the formalities of discounting and present value analysis to see the bare essentials of this relationship. For practice, go to the "Credit Markets" section in *The Wall Street Journal*, usually found about 10 pages from the back, and read the article. You should now be able to follow the description of the happenings in the market.[7]

Fluctuations in Interest Rates and Managing a Bond Portfolio

In financial circles, one often hears conversation about the interest rate; people will ask, for example, "Do you think interest rates will rise or fall?" In such discussions, the reference to interest rates is, in fact, a reference to yields to maturity or yields for short.

---

[7]You should also be able to verify that the longer the term to maturity, the greater will be the fluctuation in the price of the bond and, hence, the larger the premium above par or discount below par.

Why would the manager of a bond portfolio for a large pension fund be concerned about the likely direction of interest rates? Simply put, if rates rise sharply, for example, the value of the manager's portfolio, which contains previously purchased bonds, would fall significantly. This year's bonus for skillful management could go right out the window. Conversely, if rates fall, the prices of previously purchased bonds increase, and capital gains are in the offing. Such possibilities are what motivate managers and their advisers to pay so much attention to the factors that determine interest rates. More specifically, a portfolio manager who believes the Fed is about to engage in actions that will raise interest rates is likely to sell a considerable amount of bonds now to avoid the capital losses on bonds held that will accompany any rise in market yields. Conversely, the expectation of a fall in interest rates would encourage purchases of bonds now in anticipation of the capital gains that will accompany a fall in market rates.[8]

Positioning the pension fund to take advantage of any change in interest rates requires our portfolio manager to understand the major factors determining movements in interest rates. Accordingly, let's take a closer look at the determinants of interest rates. Note that it is the expectation of interest rate changes that motivates the portfolio manager into action. After interest rates have changed, it is too late to take advantage of potential capital gains or to avoid potential losses. Of course, it is not too late to try to avoid making the same mistake again and again.

RECAP The price of a bond is the discounted value of the future stream of income over the life of the bond. When the interest rate increases, the price of the bond decreases. When the interest rate decreases, the price of the bond increases.

The Determinants of Interest Rates

In previous chapters we have emphasized the role of the financial system in coordinating and channeling the flow of funds from surplus spending units (SSUs) to deficit spending units (DSUs). The interest rate is of paramount importance in this process for the following reasons: (1) since it is the reward for lending and the cost of borrowing, changes in the interest rate influence the amount of borrowing and lending; that is, the behavior of DSUs and SSUs, and (2) conversely, the borrowing and lending behavior of DSUs and SSUs influences the interest rate. In the market for loanable funds, as in other markets, supply and demand are the key to determining interest rates. This means, of course, that any change in interest rates will be the result of changes in supply and/or demand.

Demand for Loanable Funds
The demand for borrowed funds by household, business, government, or foreign DSUs.

The **demand for loanable funds** originates from the household, business, government, and foreign DSUs who borrow because they are spending more than their current income. The downward-sloping demand curve indicates that DSUs are willing to borrow more at lower interest rates, *ceteris paribus*.[9] Businesses borrow more at lower interest rates because more investment projects become profitable. Projects that would be unprofitable if the business had to pay 12 percent to borrow the funds become quite profitable if the funds can be had for only 2 per-

---

[8]In Chapter 22, we will see that the managers could also use financial futures markets to reduce the risk of losses from changes in interest rates.

[9]The federal government's demand for loanable funds is less sensitive to changes in the level of interest rates than are the other sectors. Namely, the federal government does not necessarily borrow less at higher interest rates than at lower interest rates. *Ceteris paribus*, as interest rates rise, the government may actually borrow more because of higher interest payments on the outstanding national debt.

cent. Consumers borrow more at lower interest rates, for such things as automobiles and other consumer durables.

The total **supply of loanable funds** originates from two basic sources: (1) the household, business, government, and foreign SSUs who are prepared to lend because they are spending less than their current income, and (2) the Fed, which, in its ongoing attempts to manage the economy's performance, supplies reserves to the financial system that lead to increases in the growth rate of money (and loans). We shall assume that the Fed's supply of funds is fixed at a particular amount for the time being. Adding the funds that SSUs are willing to supply to the Fed's supply of funds produces a supply curve for loanable funds that is upward sloping.[10] This indicates that SSUs are willing to supply more funds at higher interest rates, *ceteris paribus*. As Exhibit 5-3 shows, the quantity of funds supplied equals the quantity of funds demanded at point E_1. The equilibrium interest rate in the market for loanable funds is 6 percent, and the equilibrium quantity of borrowed and lent is $500 billion.

From the point of view of our portfolio manager, it is not sufficient to know the equilibrium or current interest rate. What is really of concern is the potential for

Supply of Loanable Funds
The supply of borrowed funds originating from (1) household, business, government, and foreign SSUs, or (2) the Fed through its provision of reserves.

The interest rate is measured on the vertical axis while the quantity of loanable funds is measured on the horizontal axis. At E_1, the quantity demanded is equal to the quantity supplied, and the market is in equilibrium. The supply of and demand for loanable funds determines the interest rate.

EXHIBIT 5-3
The Supply of and Demand for Funds

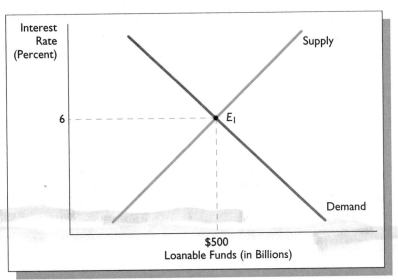

---

[10]To illustrate how the behavior of the Fed and SSUs interacts, suppose that during the current period the Fed supplies reserves to the financial system leading to $300 billion of loanable funds being supplied to the market, and that this amount of funds will not increase or decrease as the interest rate changes. As for SSUs, suppose they are willing to lend $100 billion at a 4 percent interest rate, $200 billion at a 6 percent interest rate, and $300 billion at an 8 percent rate. Adding the fixed supply of loanable funds resulting from the Fed's supply of reserves to the interest-sensitive amount that will be supplied by SSUs, we get the total supply of funds of $400 billion at a 4 percent rate, $500 billion at a 6 percent rate, and $600 billion at an 8 percent rate. This is how the supply function shown in Exhibit 5-3 is arrived at. Note that its upward slope reflects the changes in the quantity of funds supplied by SSUs at different interest rates, everything else remaining unchanged.

future changes in interest rates and the capital gains (increases in bond prices) or capital losses (decreases in bond prices) that will accompany such changes. Since any change in interest rates will be the result of a change in either the supply of funds or the demand for funds, let's take a close look at the major factors that can shift either of the curves.

Changes in the Demand for Loanable Funds

On the demand side, research has shown that movements in gross domestic product (GDP) are a major determinant of shifts in the demand for funds. In particular, when GDP rises, for example, both firms and households become more willing and able to borrow. Firms are more willing because the rise in GDP has improved the business outlook, encouraging them to expand planned inventories and engage in more investment spending such as purchases of plant and equipment. These new activities will have to be financed by borrowing. Households are more willing to borrow because the rise in GDP has increased their incomes and/or improved the employment outlook. These factors encourage them to increase their purchases of goods and services, particularly autos, other durable goods, and houses, which often require some financing. Both firms and households are more able to borrow because the improved economic outlook and the rise in incomes will make it easier to make the interest and principal payments on any new debt.[11] Another factor that affects the demand for loanable funds is an increase in the anticipated productivity of capital investments. Anticipated increases in productivity lead to a greater demand for capital investment and, hence, increase the demand for loanable funds.

The effect of an increase in the demand for funds resulting from a rise in income or an an anticipated increase in the productivity of capital investment is shown in Exhibit 5-4. The demand for funds shifts from DD to $D'D'$. Previously, the quantity of funds supplied was equal to the quantity of funds demanded at point E_1; the equilibrium interest rate prevailing in the market was 6 percent, and the quantity of funds borrowed and lent was $500 billion. When the demand curve shifts to the right, a disequilibrium develops in the market. More specifically, at the prevailing 6 percent rate, the quantity of funds demanded exceeds the quantity supplied. Given this excess demand, the interest rate rises. The higher interest rate induces SSUs to increase the quantity of loanable funds they are willing to supply (a movement along the supply curve). Such changes in plans help to close the gap between quantity demanded and quantity supplied, and a new equilibrium is eventually established at point E_2 where the interest rate is 8 percent and the quantity of funds borrowed and lent is $600 billion. To sum up, we start with an equilibrium; demand increases, creating a disequilibrium; the interest rate goes up, and a new equilibrium is established.

---

[11]Traditionally, some students are puzzled by the positive relationship between GDP (income) and the demand for funds discussed in the text. (Remember that a "positive" relationship means both move in the same direction—when one rises, the other rises; when one falls, the other falls.) They argue that these variables should be negatively related; for example, a drop in income, given expenditures, will increase a household's deficit, necessitating a rise in the demand for funds (borrowing). The problem with this reasoning is that expenditures are assumed to remain constant. In fact, the drop in income will lead to a reduction in expenditures. More generally, historical experience shows that the willingness and ability to borrow and spend will fall when income falls.

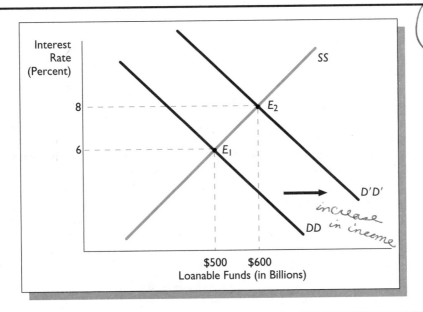

EXHIBIT 5-4
A Shift in the
Demand for Funds

Changes in the Supply of Funds

On the supply side, as you already know, one of the factors determining the supply of loanable funds is monetary policy. In particular, the Fed's ability to alter the growth rate of money in the economy means it can have a direct effect on the cost and availability of funds. To illustrate, a Fed-engineered increase in the supply of funds, as shown in Exhibit 5-5, shifts the supply curve from SS to $S'S'$. This creates a disequilibrium: The quantity supplied of funds exceeds the quantity demanded of funds at the prevailing 6 percent interest rate. The excess quantity supplied puts downward pressure on interest rates. As interest rates fall, DSUs and SSUs revise their borrowing and lending plans. For example, as the cost of borrowing falls, DSUs will be induced to borrow a larger quantity (a movement along a demand curve). Such actions, which serve to narrow the gap between quantity supplied and quantity demanded, will continue until a new equilibrium is established at point E_2. The result is a fall in the interest rate from 6 percent to 4 percent and an increase in the quantity demanded from $500 billion to $550 billion. In sum, the money supply growth rate and the interest rate are inversely related. Holding other things constant, an increase in the money supply will lower the interest rate, while a decrease in the money supply will raise the interest rate via the effect of changes in the growth rate of the money supply on the supply of loanable funds.[12]

The graphical analysis illustrates the relationship between changes in the supply of loanable funds and interest rates. However, graphs by themselves explain little and prove nothing. If the illustration is really going to aid your understanding, you need to be able to breathe some life into the picture by knowing how and why the interest rate changes; that is, what is the mechanism or process that produces this result? The answer in this case is really quite simple. Visualize financial intermediaries in the economy, particularly depository institutions, as having more funds to lend as a result of the Fed's actions of increasing the money supply.[13] In general, the

[12]Later in the text, we shall see that continuous increases in the growth rate of the money supply can lead to inflation, changes in inflationary expectations, and possible increases in interest rates.
[13]We cover the specifics of this relationship in the appendix of Chapter 14.

EXHIBIT 5-5
A Shift in the Supply
of Funds

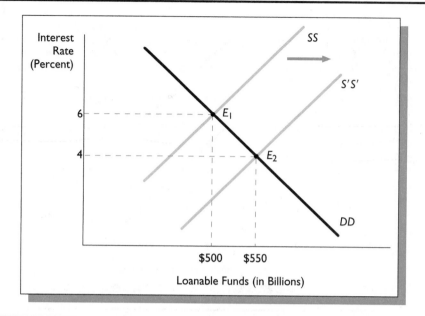

intermediaries will use these funds to acquire interest-earning assets—securities and loans, in particular. If they demand more securities (bonds), this will raise the price and lower the yield to maturity on outstanding bonds. If the intermediaries want to extend loans, they will have to induce households and firms to borrow more than they are currently borrowing or planning to borrow. How can this be accomplished? If you said, "Lower the rates charged on loans," you are correct. Thus, the movement from E_1 to E_2 in Exhibit 5-5 is not a sterile hop to be memorized and reproduced in response to some exam question. It depicts a process and a series of transactions, including the acquisition of securities, extension of loans, and accompanying changes in interest rates, that are at the heart of the operations of the financial system and its role in the economy.

The discussion of the determinants of interest rates, at least up to this point, can be summarized in a fashion that will prove quite convenient later on:[14]

$$(5\text{-}7) \qquad\qquad i = f(\overset{+}{Y}, \overset{-}{M})$$

Equation 5-7, which is really a sentence written in shorthand, says the interest rate is a positive function of income or GDP, Y, and a negative function of the money supply, M.[15] From the preceding discussion and accompanying graphical analysis, you should know that a rise in Y, holding other factors like M constant, will raise the demand for funds and, thus, the interest rate. Likewise, a rise in M, holding other factors like Y constant, will increase the supply of loanable funds and, thus, decrease the interest rate.

Of course, in the real world, other factors are not constant. Why is this important to keep in mind? Imagine that data released by the Fed indicate that both M and i are increasing. What could explain this seemingly paradoxical result? The answer is that the demand for funds must have increased by more than the increase in supply. This could result from an increase in income or, as you will learn in the next section, from

---

[14]The effects of inflationary expectations on interest rates will be added shortly.

[15]This equation is a reduced form equation resulting from simultaneously solving a demand and supply equation for loanable funds.

an increase in expected inflation. We suggest graphing this case and others like it to make sure you understand the way in which Y, M, and i interact.

RECAP The demand for loanable funds originates from DSUs. The quantity demanded is inversely related to the interest rate. The supply of loanable funds originates from SSUs and from the Fed, which supplies reserves to the banking system. The quantity supplied is directly related to the interest rate. If incomes increase, the demand for loanable funds increases and the interest rate rises. Likewise, if the anticipated productivity of capital investment increases, the demand for loanable funds increases. If the money supply increases, the supply of loanable funds increases and the interest rate falls: $i = f(\overset{+}{Y}, \overset{-}{M})$.

Inflation and Interest Rates

If you lend a friend $100 today and she agrees to pay it back in 1 year with 5 percent interest ($100 × .05 = $5), you may consider yourself $5 richer and a shrewd financier. Your $100 will earn $5 of interest income for you. However, if during the year the inflation rate is 5 percent, the real value—purchasing power—of the funds lent plus interest will be exactly the same as the real value of your funds at the beginning of the year.[16] As a result, your real reward for lending would be zero. In fact, if the inflation rate is greater than 5 percent, your friend would be paying you back an amount of money 1 year from now that would buy fewer goods and services than the amount you lent would buy today. Your real reward would be negative. The shrewd financier in this case would be your friend, not you! You might, of course, still engage in this transaction if it is your absolute best opportunity. If you hold idle cash or money in a checking account earning low interest, you would lose even more in real terms. However, we hope you would be able to find a saving opportunity that paid you a positive real return.

This example suggests that lenders are concerned about two things: (1) nominal interest, or how many dollars will be received in the future in return for lending now, and (2) inflation, or the real purchasing power the funds will be worth upon repayment. For example, a bond bearing even a relatively high interest rate may not be attractive to lenders if, due to price inflation, the money later repaid has less purchasing power than the money originally lent.

The implication of all this is that the market interest rate—called the **nominal interest rate**—is not an adequate measure of the real return on an interest-bearing financial asset unless there is assurance of price stability. Rather, the appropriate measure is the **real interest rate,** which is the return on the asset corrected for changes in the purchasing power of money. The real interest rate is the nominal interest rate minus the rate of inflation expected to prevail over the life of the asset. For example, if an investor expects inflation of 4 percent, then an asset bearing 7 percent nominal interest will be expected to yield only approximately 3 percent in real terms. If inflation of 7 percent is expected, the investor would expect the asset bearing 7 percent nominal interest to yield nothing in real terms.

Money illusion is said to occur when investors react to nominal changes (caused by price changes) even though no changes in real interest rates or other real variables have occurred. Financial investors who are not victims of money illusion will try to find an investment that pays the highest real return. Wise investors will

Nominal Interest Rate
The market interest rate, or the real return plus the rate of inflation expected to prevail over the life of the asset.

Real Interest Rate
The interest rate corrected for changes in the purchasing power of money.

Money Illusion
When spending units react to nominal changes caused by changes in prices even though real variables such as interest rates have not changed.

---

[16]The calculation is (funds received/price index) × 100. Assuming the price index was 100 in the previous year, a 5 percent inflation rate produces a price index of 105 at the end of the year (see "Cracking the Code" on page 104). Thus, the answer is ($105/105) × 100 = $100. The purchasing power or real value of $105 received 1 year from now, if the inflation rate over the year is 5 percent, is $100. This implies the real reward for lending is zero.

concern themselves with the nominal market interest rate only insofar as it enters into their calculation of the real interest rate, which is the correct measure of the reward for lending and the cost of borrowing.

The discussion to this point can be summarized with the help of some simple definitions written in the form of identities that are true by definition:

(5-8) $i = r + p^e$

Inflation Premium
The amount of nominal interest added to the real interest rate to compensate the lender for the expected loss in purchasing power that will accompany any inflation.

Equation (5-8) says that the nominal interest rate has two parts: a real interest rate, r, and an **inflation premium**. The inflation premium is the amount of nominal interest that will compensate a lender for the expected loss of purchasing power accompanying any inflation. Accordingly, the inflation premium is equal to the expected inflation rate, p^e, and therefore, nominal interest rates rise or fall as expected inflation rises or falls. Rearranging Equation (5-8) produces

(5-9) $r = i - p^e$

One of the first economists to statistically analyze the relationship between inflation and nominal interest rates was Irving Fisher, a prominent economist of the early twentieth century. The available evidence, such as that shown in Exhibit 5-6,

---

The inflation rate is measured as the percentage change in the Consumer Price Index. The nominal interest rate is represented here by the 6-month Treasury bill rate in the secondary market. When the inflation rate rises or falls, nominal interest rates also usually rise or fall. Note how the inflation rate was higher than the nominal interest rate during some years in the 1970s. What does this imply about the real rate of interest?

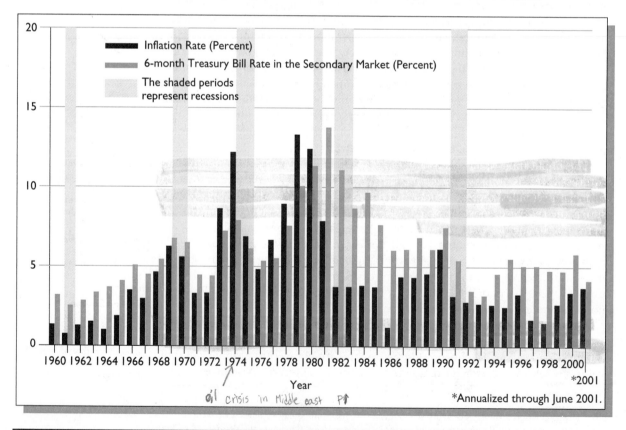

EXHIBIT 5-6

Inflation and Interest Rates: The Data (1960–2001)
SOURCE: Global Financial Data, Los Angeles, California.

does show that nominal interest rates are highly correlated with inflation and inflationary expectations.

The reason for this correlation can be seen by utilizing the equations just presented and the graphical analysis developed in the previous section. Suppose the commercial paper rate (remember this from Chapter 3?) is 6 percent and the current and expected rate of inflation is 4 percent. This means that the expected real interest rate is 2 percent. What happens if borrowers and lenders revise their expectation of future inflation upward to 8 percent? If the commercial paper rate remains at 6 percent, they will expect the real interest rate to be minus 2 percent. This is the real cost of borrowing funds. The fall in the expected real cost of borrowing will produce a rise in the nominal demand for funds. The rise in demand should, in turn, put upward pressure on the nominal commercial paper rate.

What about lenders of funds in the commercial paper market? Initially, they would have expected a real return of 2 percent (.06 – .04 = .02). If the lenders also revise their expectations of inflation upward to 8 percent, it seems reasonable to presume that an expected real return of minus 2 percent would make them less willing to lend and would thus reduce the nominal supply of funds available in the commercial paper market. The reduction in supply would also put upward pressure on the nominal commercial paper rate.

The combined effect of the increase in demand and reduction in supply, as shown in Exhibit 5-7, is a rise in the interest rate from 6 to 10 percent. With

http://www.
federalreserve.gov/
releases/h15/current/
*Provides selected interest
rates.*

We begin, as in Exhibits 5-3, 5-4, and 5-5, with an initial equilibrium at point E_1 and a prevailing interest rate of 6 percent. If the expected inflation rate, p^e, is 4 percent, this nominal rate, i, implies a real rate, r, of 2 percent ($i = r + p^e$ or 6 percent = 2 percent + 4 percent). Assume now that p^e rises to 8 percent, *ceteris paribus*. At a 6 percent nominal rate, lenders will now expect a lower real rate (–2 percent instead of +2 percent). Accordingly, they will be willing to lend less, shifting SS to $S'S'$. As for the borrowers, the rise in p^e means that the expected real cost of borrowing at a 6 percent nominal rate has fallen (from +2 percent to –2 percent). In response, they will want to borrow more, shifting DD to $D'D'$. The eventual result of the fall in supply and rise in demand is an increase in the nominal rate equal to the change in inflationary expectations.

EXHIBIT 5-7
Inflation and Interest
Rates: A Graphical
Treatment

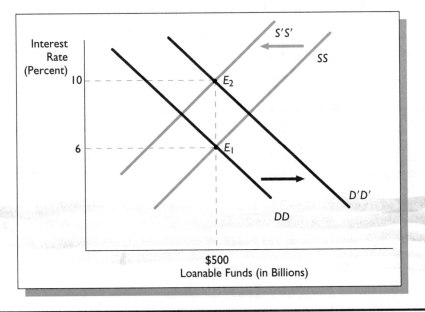

Interest
Rate
(Percent)

$500
Loanable Funds (in Billions)

CRACKING THE CODE: *Calculating the Inflation Rate*

The major price indexes in the United States—the *Consumer Price Index (CPI)* and the *Producer Price Index (PPI)*—are computed and published monthly by the government. A price index measures the changes in the costs of the items included in the index. The CPI is designed to measure changes in the cost of goods and services purchased by a typical urban consumer. The PPI measures the change in the cost of goods and services purchased by the typical producer. The *inflation rate* is generally measured by the percentage change in one of these price indexes. For example, the CPI rose from 168.9 in 1999 to 174.6 in 2000, an increase of 3.4 percent (174.6 − 168.9 = 5.7; 5.7/168.9 = .034 = 3.4 percent). Thus, the inflation rate during 2000 was 3.4 percent.

So far, so good. But where did the index number 174.6 come from, and what does it mean? The CPI is constructed by first selecting a group of goods and services—called the market basket of goods and services—representative of the purchases made by a typical urban household. Then, each month, the prices of the roughly 400 items included in this same market basket are surveyed. The hypothetical example in the following table illustrates how the resulting index and inflation rate are computed.

Year	Total Cost of Market Basket	Consumer Price Index	Annual Inflation Rate
1982–1984	$500	100	
1990	671.5	134.3	5.4%
1991	691.5	138.3	4.2
1992	712.0	142.4	3.0
1993	732.0	146.4	3.0
1994	751.0	150.2	2.6
1995	770.5	154.1	2.8
1996	796.0	159.2	3.0
1997	809.5	161.9	2.3
1998	822.5	164.5	1.6
1999	844.5	168.9	2.7
2000	873	174.6	3.4

Source: U.S. Department of Labor, Bureau of Labor Statistics.

The years 1982–1984 are the base period years for computing the index in the sense that prices of the market basket in future years are compared to the prices of the same market basket in 1982 to 1984—that is, $500. More formally, the CPI in a given year is displayed in the following equation:

CPI = (cost of the market basket in the given year)/(cost of the market basket in the base period) × 100

Accordingly, the CPI for 1982–1984 is 100, and for 2000, when the cost of the market basket rose to $873, the CPI is 174.6 [($873/$500) × 100 = 174.6]. Literally, the CPI of 174.6 for 2000 means that prices were 74.6 percent higher in 1998 than in the 1982–1984 time period.

expected inflation rising from 4 to 8 percent, the inflation premium and, therefore, the nominal interest rate, rises by 4 percent, from 6 to 10 percent. In this example, the increase in the interest rate is equal to the increase in inflationary expectations. In an imperfect world—the real world—this may not always be the case, but we can be pretty certain that the direction of the change in interest rates will match the direction of the change in inflationary expectations.

In sum, expectations of inflation affect portfolio choices that help determine the demand and supply of loanable funds. Since interest rates respond to changes in demand and supply, and expectations of inflation affect demand and supply, we can conclude that expectations of inflation affect interest rates. Given this relationship, we can rewrite Equation (5-7) as follows:

(5-10)
$$i = f(\overset{+}{Y}, \bar{M}, \overset{+}{p^e})$$

The nominal interest rate is positively related to the expected inflation rate. The accompanying Cracking the Code shows how to calculate the inflation rate from the Consumer Price Index (CPI).

RECAP The nominal interest rate is the real interest rate plus the expected inflation rate. Money illusion occurs when investors react to nominal changes when no real changes have occurred. If expected inflation increases, the nominal interest rate will rise. Borrowers are then willing to pay an inflation premium, and lenders demand to be paid an inflation premium. Thus, nominal interest rates are correlated with expected inflation:

$$i = f(\overset{+}{Y}, \bar{M}, \overset{+}{p^e})$$

The Cyclical Movement of Interest Rates

Suppose that, like Rip Van Winkle, you slept for a long time, and when you woke up, you read this chapter and Chapter 1. You would find yourself well rested and—believe it or not—quite able to explain how interest rates move over the business cycle and why they move as they do.

Recall from Chapter 1 that the stages of the business cycle are recession, trough, expansion, and peak. The recession phase is usually characterized by falling GDP, a drop in the inflation rate (especially in the later stages of the phase), and, not surprisingly, given the Fed's desire to stabilize the economy, a rising money supply growth rate. Utilizing Equation (5-10), we hope you would predict that such developments generally produce a decline in interest rates during recessions. Conversely, during the expansion phase of the cycle, income is rising, inflation usually re-accelerates (especially in the later stages of the phase), and the Fed may be trying to slow money supply growth to prevent an inflationary boom from developing. Again referring to Equation (5-10), you should not be surprised to learn that interest rates usually rise as an economic recovery proceeds. Generally speaking, although not always, interest rates tend to fluctuate pro-cyclically—that is, they move with the business cycle, rising during expansions and falling during recessions.[17]

We have covered much ground. By now you should have a clear understanding of the questions and headlines in the introduction to this chapter. This chapter contains two appendices. The first is on how the price of a special type of bond, called a *consol*, changes as interest rates change. The second reconciles the theory of interest rate determination based on the supply and demand for money discussed in Chapter 2 with the loanable funds theory presented in this chapter.

---

[17]The correlation between the business cycle and interest rates is far from perfect. For example, during the expansion of the 1990s, interest rates did not behave in the same manner described.

Summary of Major Points

- The interest rate is the return on lending today (spending in the future) and the cost of borrowing today (repaying in the future). It links the present with the future. More directly, the interest rate represents the time value of money and specifies the terms under which one can trade present purchasing power for future purchasing power.

- Compounding answers the question: What is the future value of money lent today? Specifically, it is the increase in the future value of funds that results from earning interest on interest. Discounting answers the question: What is the present value of money to be received in the future? As long as the interest rate is positive, $1,000 received today is worth more than $1,000 to be received in the future. Discounting is the procedure used to compute the present value of funds to be received in the future. Here again, the interest rate links the present with the future.

- A bond represents a stream of future payments. The price of a bond will be equal to the present value of the discounted future stream of income. When the interest rate changes, the present value of the future payments will also change. More specifically, when interest rates rise, the prices of outstanding bonds will fall. Likewise, when interest rates fall, the prices of outstanding bonds will rise.

- *Ceteris paribus*, the quantity demanded of loanable funds is inversely related to the interest rate. *Ceteris paribus*, the quantity supplied of loanable funds is directly related to the interest rate.

- Changes in interest rates are the result of changes in the supply of funds and/or changes in the demand for funds. The supply of loanable funds results from the surpluses of SSUs and the provision of reserves by the Fed to the financial system. The demand for funds originates from the deficits run by DSUs. The demand for loanable funds is positively related to income, Y, and positively related to anticipated increases in the productivity of capital investment. In general, anything that increases demand or reduces supply will tend to raise interest rates. Anything that reduces demand or increases supply will tend to lower interest rates. In summary, $i = f(\overset{+}{Y}, \overset{+}{M})$.

- The nominal interest rate, i, is composed of a real interest rate, r, and an inflation premium, reflecting the expected inflation rate, p^e: $i = r + p^e$. In general, the willingness to lend and the willingness to borrow depend on the real return

to lending and the real cost of borrowing where $r = i - p^e$. In summary, $i = f(\overset{+}{Y}, \overset{-}{M}, \overset{+}{p^e})$.

- The consumer price index (CPI) is designed to measure changes in the cost of goods and services purchased by a typical urban consumer. The producer price index (PPI) measures the change in the cost of goods and services purchased by the typical producer. The inflation rate is generally measured by the percentage change in one of these price indexes.

- Interest rates tend to fluctuate pro-cyclically. As a recession proceeds, income and GDP fall, tending to reduce the demand for funds, and the Fed's efforts to stabilize the economy generally result in a rising growth rate of the money supply. Conversely, as an expansion takes hold, GDP rises, tending to increase the demand for funds. Inflation often re-accelerates, and to prevent an inflationary boom from developing, the Fed will slow money supply growth. Reflecting such developments, interest rates will tend to rise.

- A consol is a perpetual bond with no maturity date. The price of a consol is equal to the coupon payment divided by the nominal interest rate (Appendix 5-A).

- Stocks are quantities that are measured at a point in time. Flows are quantities that are measured through time. When the Fed increases bank reserves, banks create money when they make loans. At the same time, the supply of loanable funds increases and vice versa. A theory stated in stocks can always be reformulated in terms of flows and vice versa (Appendix 5-B).

Key Terms

Compounding	Inflation Premium	Principal
Consol	Liquidity Preference	Producer Price Index (PPI)
Coupon Payments	Money Illusion	Real Interest Rate
Demand for Loanable Funds	Nominal Interest Rate	Stocks
Discount from Par	Par Value	Supply of Loanable Funds
Discounting	Premium above Par	Time Value of Money
Flows	Present Value	Yield to Maturity

Review Questions

1. Define the concepts of compounding and discounting. Use future values and present values to explain how these concepts are related.

2. Use the concept of present value to explain why a trip to Hawaii next year would mean more to most people than the same trip in the year 2010.

3. Under what conditions will a bond sell at a premium above par? At a discount from par?

4. During the Great Depression of the 1930s, nominal interest rates were close to zero. Explain how real interest rates could be very high even though nominal interest rates were very low. (Hint: Prices fell during parts of the Great Depression.)

5. Assume that after you graduate, you get a job as the chief financial officer of a small company. Explain why being able to forecast the direction of interest rate changes may be critical for your success in that position. Likewise, why are investment bankers concerned about future changes in the interest rate?

6. What factors affect the demand for loanable funds? The supply of loanable funds?

7. In general, discuss the movement of interest rates, the money supply, and prices over the business cycle.

8. A young couple is borrowing $100,000 to buy their first home. An older couple is living off the interest income from the $100,000 in financial assets they own. How does the interest rate affect each couple? If the interest rate increases, could that change the behavior of either couple? How and why?

9. What is liquidity preference? Explain how changes in flows affect stocks and vice versa. (Appendix 5-B).

Analytical Questions

10. What is the present value of each of the following income streams?
    a. $100 to be received at the end of each of the next 3 years
    b. $100 to be received at the end of each of the next 3 years plus an additional payment of $1,000 at the end of the third year

11. What is the price of a bond that pays the income stream in question 10 (b)?

12. Assume that a bond with 5 years to maturity, a par value of $1,000, and a $60 annual coupon payment costs $1,100 today. What is the coupon rate? What is the current yield?

13. The nominal interest rate is 12 percent, and anticipated inflation is 8 percent. What is the real interest rate?

14. Graph the demand and supply for loanable funds. If there is an increase in income, show what happens to the interest rate, the demand for loanable funds, and the quantity supplied of loanable funds. If the Fed orchestrates a decrease in the money supply growth rate, show what happens to the interest rate, the supply of loanable funds, and the quantity demanded of loanable funds.

15. As an enrolling freshman, would you have been willing to pay $18,000 for 4 years' tuition rather than $5,000 per year for 4 years? (Assume you would be able to do so and that you have no fear of flunking out of college before you graduate.)

16. You win a million dollar lottery to be paid out in 20 annual installments of $50,000 over the next 20 years. Assuming an interest rate of 6 percent, how large a payment would you accept today for this future stream of income?

17. Jake is given $10,000 in a CD that matures in 10 years. Assuming interest payments are reinvested during the life of the CD, how much will the CD be worth at maturity if the interest rate is 5 percent? If the interest rate is 10 percent?

18. Henry and Sheree just had a baby. How much will they have to invest today for the baby to have $100,000 for college in 18 years if the interest rate is 5 percent? If the interest rate is 10 percent?

19. Use graphical analysis to show that if Y and M both increase, the interest rate may increase, decrease, or stay the same. In each case, what happens to the equilibrium quantity demanded and supplied?

20. Using Exhibit 5-6, determine in what years real interest rates were at their highest and lowest levels.

21. If the PPI is 105 in 2002 and increases to 111 in 2003, what is the inflation rate in 2003 based on the PPI?

22. What is the price of a consol with a coupon payment of $200 per year if the interest rate is 10 percent? What is the interest rate on a consol if the coupon payment is $400 and the price of the consol is $8,000? (Appendix 5-A)

23. I purchase a consol with a coupon payment of $100 when the interest rate is 10 percent. When I sell the consol, the interest rate has risen to 20 percent. What is the amount of my capital gain or loss? (Appendix 5-A)

Internet Exercise

The realized real interest rate is the nominal interest rate minus actual inflation. Illustrate the relationship between actual inflation and nominal interest rates by accessing the following Web site for nominal interest rates: **http://www.stls.frb.org/fred/** **data/irates.html**. Use the prime rate as a measure of nominal interest rates. The actual inflation rate may be obtained from the following Web site: **http://www.stls.frb.org/fred/data/cpi.html**.

Suggested Readings

For a look at "International Linkages in Short- and Long-Term Interest Rates," see Guglielmo Maria Caporale and Geoffrey Williams' article by the same name, *Zagreb International Review of Economics and Business*, vol. 3, no. 2 (November 2000), pps. 39–61.

For an interesting book on an application of discounting, see Paul R. Portney and John P. Weyant, eds., *Discounting and Intergenerational Equity* (Washington, DC: Resources for the Future), 1999.

For a discussion of how policymakers may produce a permanent decrease in the real interest rate by accepting a permanent increase in the inflation rate, see Marco A. Espinosa-Vega, "Can Higher Inflation Reduce Real Interest Rates in the Long Run?" *Canadian Journal of Economics* 31:1 (1998): 92–103.

For a very readable article for students who would like more information about real interest rates, see Rosemary and Thomas J. Cunningham, "Recent Views of Viewing the Real Rate of Interest," *Economic Review of the Federal Reserve Bank of Atlanta*, July–August 1990, pp. 28–37. Current abstracts of the *Economic Review* are available at the following Internet site: **http://www.fbratlanta.org/publica/eco-rev/index.html**.

For a sophisticated discussion about "The Cyclical Behavior of Interest Rates," see the article by the same name in the *Journal of Finance* 52 (September 1997): 1519–1542.

A classic work dealing with interest rate determination is Irving Fisher, *The Theory of Interest* (New York: Macmillan, 1930). A more recent article, "The Fisher Hypothesis Revisited: New Evidence," finds that nominal interest rates are directly related to expected inflation rates and government borrowing. It can be found in *Applied Economics* 29 (August 1997): 1055–1059.

For an interesting article on the relationship between interest rates and inflation, see Edward Renshaw, "Inflation and the Search for a Neutral Rate of Return on T-Bills," *Challenge*, November–December 1994, pp. 58–61.

For an analysis of the relationship between interest rates and bond prices, see Dale Bremmer, "The Relationship Between Interest Rates and Bond Prices," *American Economist* 36 (Spring 1992): 85–86.

For a look at how long-term interest rates are determined in major industrialized countries, see "Determinants of the Expected Real Long-Term Interest Rates in the G7-Countries," by Klass H. W. Knot, in *Applied Economics* 30 (February 1998): 165–176.

Appendix 5-A

The Inverse Relationship between Bond Prices and Interest Rates: The Case of Consols

The discussion in the text has developed the formal analytical link between changes in interest rates and changes in bond prices. Just in case you are not yet completely comfortable with the analysis, this appendix provides a simpler, helpful example.

A type of bond called a **consol** has no maturity date. The issuer is not obligated to ever repay the principal, but makes coupon payments each year forever. Thus, if I buy a consol today, I am entitled to receive the coupon payment forever, but never to be repaid the principal. After some mathematical manipulation and simplification of Equation (5-6), which we will mercifully put in footnote a, such characteristics imply the following:[a]

$$i = C/P$$

The yield to maturity, or interest rate, i, on a consol is equal to the coupon payment, C, divided by the price of the bond, P. Suppose a new $1,000 face value consol is issued today and promises to pay $50 in interest each year. This is the coupon payment each year. Assuming the price of the new consol is $1,000, the $50 divided by the price shows that the consol yields 5 percent ($50/$1,000 = .05).

Now assume that a year later another $1,000 consol is issued by the same company. However, let's suppose the prevailing level of interest rates in the economy has risen so that the new consol will have to pay $60 a year in interest to be competitive. Clearly, the new consol is now a better investment than the 1-year-old 5 percent consol.

Suppose now that some unforeseen financial problems lead the owner of the old 5 percent consol to sell it. Who would be willing to purchase the old 5 percent consol, given that they could instead purchase a new 6 percent consol? The answer is nobody, at least not yet. The older consol will have to yield 6 percent to be sold, and it will sell if it can somehow be made to yield 6 percent.

The older consol cannot change the fact that it pays $50 a year in interest. This is a contractual arrangement. However, the old consol can sell for a lower price. If the price drops to $833.33, then $50 a year interest would represent a yield of 6 percent ($50/$833.33 =.06). In fact, this is exactly what will happen. The owner of the old consol will offer the bond for sale at $1,000—the original price. Because no buyers appear, the market maker handling the transaction will lower the price. The price cutting will continue until buyers appear; this will occur when the price falls to $833.33 because, at this point, the yield on the old consol is competitive with the yield on new consols. We suggest closing the book and working through the case in which the interest rate on new bonds falls to 4 percent. What will happen to the price of the old consol and why?[b]

> **Consol**
> A perpetual bond with no maturity date; the issuer is never obliged to repay the principal but makes coupon payments each year forever.

Appendix 5-B

Interest Rates: Which Theory Is Correct? Reconciling Stocks and Flows

In Chapter 2, we developed a theory of interest rate determination based on the supply of and demand for money. In this chapter, we developed a theory of interest rate determination based on the supply of and demand for loanable funds. Just as there is more than one way to get a job done, there is more than one way to explain interest rates. The purpose of this appendix is to convince you that the two theories presented in this text are complementary and consistent.

Liquidity preference is the name given to the theory based on the demand for and supply of money. It was developed by John Maynard Keynes in the 1930s. The

> **Liquidity Preference**
> The theory of interest rate determination based on the supply of and demand for money; first developed by Keynes.

---

[a]From Equation (5-6), the price of a consol is equal to $P = C/(1 + i)^1 + C/(1 + i)^2 + C/(1 + i)^3 + C/1 + i)^4 + \ldots = C[1/(1 + i) +1/(1 + i)^2) + 1/(1 + i)^3 + 1/(1 + i)^4 + \ldots = C(1/i) = C/i$. Therefore, $i = C/P$.

[b]The old consol represents a future stream of income of $50 per year forever. At an interest rate of 4 percent, the price rises to $1,250 ($50/.04 = $1,250), and the lucky owner makes a capital gain of $250.

supply of money is the stock of money, and the demand for money, or "preference for liquidity," is how much money that spending units wish to hold. The supply of and demand for money are both measured at a point in time and refer to actual **stocks.** The stock of money is partially determined by the central bank through its control over the stock of reserves and reserve requirements. Also, remember from Chapter 2 that the demand for money is based on the spending plans of spending units. Demand is positively related to income while quantity demanded is negatively or inversely related to the interest rate. The interest rate adjusts to equate the quantity supplied (stock) of money with the quantity demanded.

Stocks
Quantities that are measured at a point in time.

Flows
Quantities that are measured through time.

The loanable funds theory developed in this chapter is based on **flows** as opposed to stocks. Flows are measured through time whereas stocks are measured at a point in time. Thus, if I offer you a job for $10,000, you will want to know whether this is per week, per month, or per year. Not so for stocks. If I give you a $10,000 savings account, there is no relevant time dimension. The loanable funds theory develops the argument that the interest rate is determined by the supply of and demand for loanable funds. The demand for loanable funds reflects borrowing plans by DSUs while the supply of loanable funds reflects lending plans by SSUs. *Ceteris paribus*, the quantity demanded of loanable funds is inversely related to the interest rate while the quantity supplied of loanable funds is directly related to the interest rate. The interest rate adjusts to equate the quantity demanded of loanable funds with the quantity supplied.

To help you see that the theories complement each other, consider what happens when the Fed increases bank reserves. When reserves increase, banks create money by incurring deposit liabilities as they acquire loans as assets. In doing so, banks have simultaneously augmented the supply of loanable funds. According to liquidity preference, an increase in the supply of money causes the interest rate to fall, while according to the loanable funds theory, an increase in the supply of loanable funds has the same effect. Likewise, if the Fed decreases the supply of reserves, you should be able to verify that both the stock of money and the supply of loanable funds decrease, leading to a higher interest rate. Again both theories predict that the interest rate changes in the same direction.

Next consider what happens when the demand for loanable funds increases, reflecting an increased desire of people to borrow more at every interest rate. Since banks acquire loan assets when they create checkable deposits, which are also money, an increase in the demand for loanable funds corresponds to an increase in the demand for money. According to both theories, an increase in the interest rate results. Likewise, a decrease in the demand for loanable funds translates to a decrease in the demand for money and a lower interest rate.

From an intuitive standpoint, we can reconcile the two theories by recognizing that when there is a change in a stock measured at different times, a flow has occurred; that is, a flow over time results in a change in a stock. For example, if I have a gallon of milk in the morning, go to the refrigerator for a glass of milk repeatedly throughout the day, and have a half gallon left at the end of the day, then I can safely say that I consumed a half gallon of milk during the day. Consumption of milk over the course of the day represents a flow, while the amount of milk in the refrigerator at a point in time is a stock. The change in the stock of milk as measured at two different points in time depicts the flow. If I save $100 per year, at the end of the year, my stock of wealth will have increased by $100 (ignoring interest payments for the time being). Correspondingly, changes in the supply (flow) of loanable funds entail changes in the stock of money as measured at two different points in time. Likewise, changes in the demand (flow) of loanable funds entail changes in the demand for money. A theory stated in flows can always be reformulated in terms of stocks and vice versa.

chapter

The Structure of Interest Rates

6

Learning Objectives *After reading this chapter, you should know:*

- What a yield curve is
- How expectations influence interest rates
- What determines expectations
- What determines credit ratings and how these ratings affect interest rates
- Why interest rates on state and local (municipal) bonds are usually below the rates on other types of bonds

"
Time gives good advice.
—Maltese proverb

RATES & YIELDS

Bond Yields

LAST 4 h

Long bonds	5.09%	Basis points
10-year Treasuries	Down 2 b.p.	
Notes	3.85%	
2-year Treasuries	Down 7 b.p.	
Municipals	5.27%	
Bond Buyer index	Down 3 b.p.	

From One Interest Rate to Many

The "interest rate" is a familiar term we hope you have come to know and understand. Before you become too attached, however, the time has come to confess the obvious. Previous chapters have discussed in some detail what determines the interest rate as if there were just one interest rate. This simplification allowed us to abstract and focus on the essential factors influencing interest rates in general. Of course, the real world is more complicated.

Numerous types of financial claims are traded in financial markets—Treasury bills, corporate bonds, municipal bonds, commercial paper, certificates of deposit, and Treasury bonds, to name just a few. A glance at any newspaper reveals that the interest rates on the various types of financial claims differ. Lest you be overwhelmed by such differences, remember that our objective is to bring order to chaos. Specifically, we want (1) to understand the patterns and common threads that link the various interest rates together, and (2) to identify the factors that explain the differences.

Simply put, interest rates generally move up and down together. However, rates may not move the same amount, and occasionally some rates may not even move in the same direction as the rest. As a result of such disparate movements, the spreads, or patterns of relationships, between rates can change. For example, the spread between Treasury bill and Treasury bond rates may narrow while the spread between the rates on risky corporate bonds and on less risky bonds may widen.

Within this chapter, we study the factors that are primarily responsible for determining the relationships among interest rates. Financial analysts have isolated and identified four primary determinants of these relationships: (1) term to maturity, (2) credit risk, (3) liquidity, and (4) tax treatment.

Why is it important to know all this, you ask? There are many possible responses, but this hypothetical example should suffice. Suppose you have $1 million available to purchase financial claims and you have narrowed your options to 1-year Treasury notes yielding 7 percent, 2-year Treasury notes yielding 8 percent, or 2-year municipal notes yielding 5 percent. Which would you choose? More to the point, what would you need to know before you or any portfolio manager could make a rational decision? This chapter will provide answers to such questions.

The Role of Term to Maturity in Interest Rate Differentials

Treasury Notes
Securities issued by the U.S. government with an original maturity of 1 to 10 years.

Term Structure of Interest Rates
The relationship between yields and time to maturity.

The U.S. Treasury issues different types of securities—bills, notes, and bonds—as it manages the nation's debt or finances a government budget deficit. The major characteristic distinguishing one type of Treasury security from another is the term to maturity. For example, Treasury bills have short terms to maturity of 1 year or less, while **Treasury notes** and bonds have long terms to maturity of 1 year or more. We are interested in discovering what determines the relationship between interest rates on Treasury securities of different maturities. What is the relationship between the interest rate on a Treasury security with a short term to maturity and on a Treasury security with a long term to maturity? The pattern of relationships among interest rates and the time to maturity is usually referred to in financial markets as the **term structure of interest rates**.

The Yield Curve

A yield curve is a common analytical construct used as a framework for examining the role of term to maturity in explaining interest rate differentials. Formally, a **yield curve** is a graphical representation of the relationship between interest rates (yields) on particular financial instruments (securities) and their terms to maturity. A yield curve visually represents the term structure of interest rates—that is, it shows how interest rates vary with the term to maturity.

Analysts traditionally focus on Treasury securities when constructing yield curves. By focusing on one particular type of security, we can control for factors other than term to maturity, such as friskiness and tax treatment, which also could affect the structure of yields.[1] In other words, this permits us to isolate the effects of term to maturity. Although we use U.S. government securities, we could have used other types of assets to demonstrate yield curves such as corporate bonds with the same default risk (and other nonmaturity related characteristics) or municipal bonds. Just be sure you understand that each individual asset is usually represented on a single yield curve, even though several yield curves may be drawn on one graph.

To construct yield curves, we begin with Exhibit 6-1. This table shows the interest rates on U.S. Treasury securities of different maturities prevailing on January 16, 1981; January 29, 1993; and July 17, 1998. From this information, we can construct three different yield curves—one for each of the three dates. Term to maturity is always measured on the horizontal axis, while the return on an asset (yield to maturity) is measured on the vertical axis.

Utilizing the data in Exhibit 6-1, the yield curves for the three dates are plotted in Exhibit 6-2. Notice that on January 16, 1981, the yield on 3-month Treasury bills was 15.19 percent, while the yield on 10-year Treasury bonds was 12.53 percent. Thus, the slope of the yield curve at that time was negative, meaning that yields declined as the term to maturity increased. In contrast, on January 29, 1993, the yield curve had a positive slope, which means that yields rose with term to maturity. On this day, the yield on 3-month Treasury bills was 2.92 percent, while the yield on 10-year Treasury bonds was 6.46 percent. Thus, the slope of the yield curve changed over time. Notice also that all of the 1993 yields were below all of the 1981 yields. This indicates that the level of the yield curve, as well as the direction of the slope, changed.

Next look at the yield curve for July 17, 1998. On this day, the yields on 3-month Treasury bills and 10-year Treasury bonds were 5.01 and 5.49 percent, respectively,

Yield Curve
A graphical representation of the relationship between interest rates (yields) on particular securities and their terms to maturity.

TERM TO MATURITY	JANUARY 16, 1981	JANUARY 29, 1993	JULY 17, 1998
3 months	15.19%	2.92%	5.01%
1 year	13.91	3.41	5.36
2 year	13.15	4.24	5.46
5 year	12.69	6.08	5.47
10 year	12.53	6.46	5.49

SOURCE: *Federal Reserve Bulletin*, various issues, 1981–1998.

EXHIBIT 6-1
Interest Rates on Treasury Securities

---

[1]Later in the chapter, we modify the analysis to account for differences in liquidity between short- and long-term financial securities.

EXHIBIT 6-2
Yield Curves

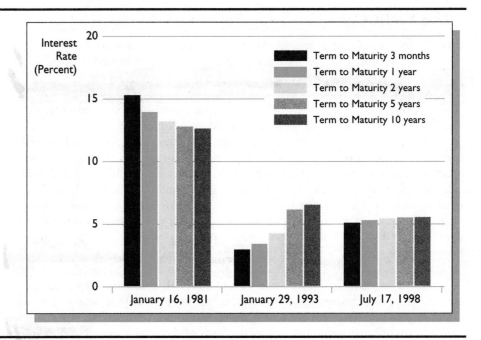

http://www.clev.frb.
org/research/nov96et/
intrat.htm
*Provides information on
yield and yield curves.*

resulting in a yield curve that was much flatter than the 1993 curve. Note also that short-term rates were higher in 1998 than in 1993, while the reverse was true of longer-term rates. As you can see, there can be much variation among yield curves!

The slope (shape) and position (level) of the yield curve are called the term structure of interest rates. We are interested in explaining what determines the term structure—that is, the shape of the yield curve and its level. Although much has been written to explain the term structure of interest rates, the conventional wisdom can be boiled down to expectations theory and some modifications of that theory. To simplify the explanation of the theory and the modifications, we shall assume that there are only two types of Treasury securities: T-bills with a short term to maturity (1 year) and Treasury notes with a long term to maturity (2 years). We shall develop our analysis in terms of the demand for and supply of these two securities.

In Chapter 5, we discussed interest rate determination in terms of the supply of and demand for loanable funds. By now you should be able to see that when we supply loanable funds, we demand financial securities, and when we demand loanable funds, we supply financial securities. Thus, developing our analysis of the expectations theory in terms of the demand for and supply of financial securities is consistent with our previous discussion.

RECAP The yield curve is a graphical representation of the relationship between the interest rate (yield) and the term to maturity. Yield curves show how interest rates vary with term to maturity.

The Expectations Theory

Expectations Theory
A theory holding that the long-term interest rate is the geometric average of the present short-term rate and the short-term rates expected to prevail over the term to maturity of the long-term security.

Simply put, the **expectations theory** postulates that the yield curve is determined by borrowers' and lenders' expectations of future interest rates and that changes in the slope (shape) of the curve result from changes in these expectations. Specifically, the expectations theory postulates that the long rate is the geometric average of the current short rate and the future short rates expected to prevail over the term to maturity of the longer-term security.

To understand the expectations theory, assume that you have funds to lend for a 2-year period and that the current yield, i_1, on a 1-year bill (a short-term security) is 5 percent per year, and the current yield, i_2, on a 2-year note (a long-term security) is 5.99 percent per year. Now suppose that you and others with funds available to lend expect that the yield on short-term (1-year) securities, i_1^e, will be 7 percent 1 year from now. Assuming you have no preference as to holding 1-year (short-term) or 2-year (long-term) securities, which would you acquire now? Drawing on the concept of maximization developed earlier in the text, we predict you will acquire the security with the higher expected rate of return. Think of yourself as having two options: Option A is to buy short-term (1-year) securities today and short-term securities again 1 year from now; Option B is to buy long-term (2-year) securities now. Which of the options gives the higher expected rate of return?

The answer is derived in two simple steps: (1) calculate the expected return from acquiring the 1-year bill now and the 1-year bill 1 year from now; and (2) compare it with the 5.99 percent return you would earn by acquiring the 2-year note now.

To calculate the expected return of the 1-year bill now and the 1-year bill 1 year from now, we find the **geometric average** of the two rates. We use the geometric average instead of the simple arithmetic average to take into account the effects of compounding, as discussed in Chapter 5. In other words, use of the geometric average assumes that the interest earned the first year will earn interest during the second year. More precisely, using the geometric average, the long rate, i_2, can be calculated as follows:

Geometric Average
An average that takes into account the effects of compounding; used to calculate the long-term rate from the short-term rate and the short-term rates expected to prevail over the term to maturity of the long-term security.

(6-1) $$(1 + i_2) = [(1 + i_1)(1 + i_1^e)]^{1/2}$$

Subtracting 1 from both sides of Equation (6-1) yields

(6-2) $$i_2 = [(1 + i_1)(1 + i_1^e)]^{1/2} - 1$$

Returning to our numerical example, if we perform these calculations we find that the expected return associated with Option A is 5.99 percent. More specifically, plugging the present 1-year rate and expected 1-year rate into Equations (6-1) and (6-2) yields

$$(1 + i_2) = [(1 + .05)(1 + .07)]^{1/2} = [(1.05)(1.07)]^{1/2} = (1.1235)^{1/2} = 1.0599$$

and

$$i_2 = 1.0599 - 1 = .0599 = 5.99 \text{ percent}$$

This is the geometric average of the short rate now, i_1, and the short rate expected to prevail 1 year from now, i_1^e. The expected return from Option B—acquiring the 2-year note—is also 5.99 percent. Since both options provide the same expected return, you and other lenders (buyers of securities) will be indifferent between the two options and perhaps will purchase both short-term and long-term securities. More formally, since the long rate is equal to the geometric average of the current short rate and the short rate expected to prevail 1 year in the future, we have an equilibrium configuration or term structure of interest rates. The associated yield curve is shown in Exhibit 6-3.

Our example does not prove the expectations theory postulated earlier; after all, we chose the numbers in the example. What happens when the numbers change? To get the answer and explain how the theory works, go back to our example and assume the 1-year rate and the 2-year rate initially remain at 5 percent and 5.99 percent,

EXHIBIT 6-3
Hypothetical Yield
Curve

If the interest rate on a 1-year security is 5 percent and the 1-year rate expected
to prevail 1 year from now is 7 percent, then the 2-year rate is 5.99 percent.
Since the future expected 1-year rate is above the present 1-year rate, the yield
curve is upward sloping.

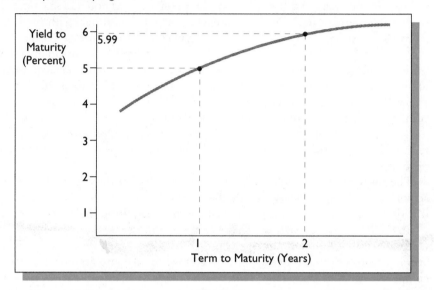

respectively, but that future rate expectations change such that the 1-year rate
expected to prevail 1 year from now rises from 7 to 9 percent. What would you and
other potential buyers of securities do, and how would those actions affect the term
structure—that is, the slope and level of the yield curve in Exhibit 6-3?

Presumably, you and other financial investors would first recalculate the expected
return from Option A (buy short-term securities now and again 1 year from now) and
compare it to the expected return from Option B (buy long-term securities now). We
use Equation (6-2) to calculate the geometric average—the expected return—of
Option A. The calculation reveals that the expected return is 6.98 percent: .0698 =
[(1.05) (1.09)]$^{1/2}$ – 1. Because this is higher than the 5.99 percent return associated
with Option B, you and others will want short-term securities. In fact, those who own
long-term securities will want to sell them and buy short-term securities. What will
happen as the demand for long-term securities falls in the market? We hope you said
the price of these long-term securities will fall and, thus, their yields will rise.

How far will this portfolio reshuffling go? Or, to put it somewhat differently,
how high will long rates rise? Given our theory, and assuming the short rate
remains at 5 percent and the expected short rate remains at 9 percent, the long rate
will have to rise to 6.98 percent.[2]

Why 6.98 percent? This is the only rate that will equate the expected returns from
Options A and B and thus leave financial investors indifferent between them. If
investors are indifferent, there is no tendency to change, and an equilibrium configuration or term structure of interest rates is realized. More formally, a 6.98 percent

---

[2]For simplicity, we are assuming the short-term rate does not change. In reality, because the demand
for short-term securities increases, their price would rise. The portfolio reshuffling would result in a fall
in the short rate in addition to the rise in the long rate.

interest rate on the 2-year note, i_2 will make it equal to the geometric average of the prevailing 5 percent 1-year rate, i_1, and the 9 percent 1-year rate expected to prevail 1 year from now, i_1^e. The relationship between long-term interest rates and short-term interest rates depends directly on interest rate expectations; as i_1^e changes, i_2 will change relative to i_1.[3]

In our example, the adjustment in the long (2-year) rate from 5.99 to 6.98 percent as a result of the change in interest rate expectations was developed from the demand side of the market for securities; that is, from the point of view of the lender. But do not forget that the securities market also has a supply side. The expectations of the borrower are also important. Suppose you need funds for 2 years and can either issue a security for 2 years with an interest rate of 5.99 percent or issue a 1-year security at 5 percent now and another 1-year security 1 year from now at an expected 9 percent rate. Which option would you choose? Again, drawing on the concept of maximization, we assume you will choose the option that minimizes the cost of borrowing and thus maximizes utility or profits. Accordingly, you would issue a 2-year security with an annual interest rate of 5.99 percent rather than sell two consecutive 1-year securities having an expected average annual interest rate of 6.98 percent.

When borrowers believe that the average of current and expected future interest rates on short-term securities exceeds the rate on long-term securities, they will increase their current supply of long-term securities, thus tending to raise the long-term interest rate. In other words, because borrowers will want to issue 2-year notes, the supply of the notes will increase (causing their price to fall), and, thus, higher interest rates will have to be paid on them. The market will be in equilibrium when the quantity of notes supplied equals the quantity of notes demanded.[4]

Taken together, the effects of interest rate expectations of investors and borrowers on the demand for and supply of securities, respectively, will determine the term structure of interest rates. More specifically, if expectations about future interest rates change such that future rates are expected to be higher, the original yield curve in Exhibit 6-3 will turn into the new yield curve in Exhibit 6-4. As the demand for longs falls and the supply of longs rises, the price of longs will fall, and the long rate will rise relative to the short rate, resulting in a steepening of the yield curve.

The previous few paragraphs have been jam-packed with information. Let's try to summarize and nail down some implications of the key points. First, the hypothetical yield curve accompanying our initial example, shown in Exhibit 6-3, is positively sloped—that is, yields rise with term to maturity. The explanation for the slope of the yield curve is directly related to the interest rate expected to prevail on short-term securities 1 year in the future—hence, the term *expectations theory*. More specifically, the positively sloped yield curve reflects expectations of a rise in the interest rate on short-term securities over the course of the year from the currently prevailing 5 percent to 7 percent.

Second, the new hypothetical yield curve accompanying our second example wherein the expected future rate rose from 7 percent to 9 percent is as shown in Exhibit 6-4, even more positively sloped than the original curve. The explanation for the change in the slope is the change in future interest rate expectations. More specifically, the steeper slope reflects expectations of an even larger rise in the interest rate

---

[3]Equation (6-2) is easily generalized for a long-term security, with, say, 10 years to maturity. In this case, the 10-year rate would be the geometric average of the current, short 1-year rate and the 1-year rates expected to prevail over the next 9 years. Thus, $i_{10} = [(1+i_1)(1+i_1^e)(1+i_2^e) \ldots (1+i_9^e)]^{1/10} - 1$, where i_n^e is the expected 1-year rate n years from now.

[4]For simplicity, we are ignoring the fact that the supply of short-term securities will also be reduced, causing their price to rise and their yield to fall.

EXHIBIT 6-4
New Hypothetical
Yield Curve

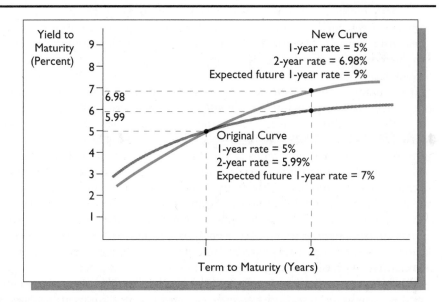

Yield to Maturity (Percent)

New Curve
1-year rate = 5%
2-year rate = 6.98%
Expected future 1-year rate = 9%

Original Curve
1-year rate = 5%
2-year rate = 5.99%
Expected future 1-year rate = 7%

Term to Maturity (Years)

on short-term securities over the course of the year—that is, from the currently prevailing 5 percent to 9 percent rather than from 5 to 7 percent as in the previous example.

Third, the change in the slope of the yield curve, which accompanies a change in interest rate expectations, does not come about magically. Rather, it reflects changes in the supply of and demand for securities, which are induced by the change in interest rate expectations.

Fourth, assuming the expectations theory is basically correct, we can solve for the interest rate expected to prevail in the future by looking at the current structure of rates and doing some simple algebra. We start by squaring both sides of Equation (6-1):

$$(1 + i_2)^2 = \{[(1 + i_1)(1 + i_1^e)]^{1/2}\}^2 = (1 + i_1)(1 + i_1^e)$$

We then divide through by $(1 + i_1)$ to get

$$(1 + i_2)^2/(1 + i_1) = (1 + i_1^e)$$

Subtracting 1 from both sides of the equation, we arrive at Equation (6-3):

(6-3) $i_1^e = [(1 + i_2)^2/(1 + i_1)] - 1$

Returning to our numerical example, if we know that the 1-year rate is 5 percent and the 2-year rate is 5.99 percent, as in our first example, we can plug the relevant numbers into Equation (6-3) and solve for i_1^e. Specifically,

$$i_1^e = [(1.0599)^2/(1.05)] - 1 = .07 = 7 \text{ percent}$$

If instead we observe in the market that the 1-year rate is 5 percent and the 2-year rate is 4.5 percent, we can use Equation (6-3) to find that the expected rate on a 1-year security bought 1 year from now is approximately 4 percent: $i_1^e = [(1 + .045)^2/(1 + .05)] - 1 = .04$. Thus, based on the expectations theory, one can look at the yield curve and infer the market's expectation for the direction and level of future short-term interest rates.

Exhibit 6-5 shows the three most common shapes of the yield curve. Exhibit 6-5a shows a rising or positively sloped yield curve. When a rising yield curve is observed in the market, the implication under the expectations theory is that market partici-

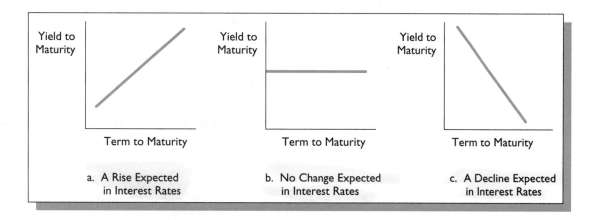

EXHIBIT 6-5
Alternative Yield Curve Shapes

pants expect future short-term interest rates, i_s^e to rise above current short rates, i_s; that is, $i_s^e > i_s$. A horizontal or flat yield curve, as shown in Exhibit 6-5b, implies that interest rates are expected to remain constant, $i_s^e = i_s$. A declining or negatively sloped yield curve, as shown in Exhibit 6-5c, implies that interest rates are expected to decrease in the future, $i_s^e < i_s$.

Believe it or not, you now know enough to say quite a lot about the actual data and yield curves shown in Exhibits 6–1 and 6–2. Referring to the yield curves shown in Exhibit 6–2, the expectations theory tells us that the shape of the January 16, 1981 curve indicates that investors expect future short-term rates to decline. According to the expectations theory, since the 2-year rate is the average of the current 1-year rate and the 1-year rate expected 1 year from now, the 1-year rate expected to prevail 1 year from now must be less than the current 1-year rate. Utilizing the data in the table in Exhibit 6–1, see if you can figure out the 1-year rate that was expected to prevail 1 year from January 16, 1981.[5]

The shape of the January 29, 1993 curve indicates that investors expected future short-term rates to rise, while the shape of the July 17, 1998 curve indicates that investors expected a much smaller increase in rates. See if you can explain how we know this.[6]

RECAP According to the expectations theory, the long-term rate is the geometric average of the short-term rate and the short-term rates expected to prevail over the term to maturity. Given the 1-year rate and the 2-year rate, we can solve for the expected 1-year rate one 1 from now.

---

[5]The answer is 12.395 percent; i_1 = 13.91 percent and i_2 = 13.15 percent. Plugging these figures into Equation (6–3) yields 12.395 percent: $.12395 = [(1 + .1315)^2/(1 + .1391)] - 1$.

[6]The January 29, 1993 yield curve is steeper than the July 17, 1998 curve. Using the expectations theory to solve for the expected future short-term rate on January 29, 1993, we get 5.08 percent: $[(1 + .0424)^2/(1 + .0341)] - 1 = .0508$. Solving for the expected future short-term rate on July 17, 1998, we get 5.556 percent: $[(1 + .0546)^2/(1 + .0536)] - 1 = .0556$. Hence, according to the expectations theory, in 1993, the short rate was expected to rise from 3.41 percent to 5.08 percent over the course of the year, while in 1998, the short-term rate was expected to rise from 5.36 percent to 5.56 percent. As you can see, the expected increase in 1993 was much larger than in 1998.

Now that you have the mechanics of yield curves and expectations nailed down, we are ready for the home stretch. For those who think they have already crossed the finish line, please note that the whole expectations theory is rather empty unless we can explain what determines future interest rate expectations and changes in those expectations. Otherwise we have a theory explaining the term structure via expectations that are left unexplained.

Determining Interest Rate Expectations

Naturally then, the question is, "What determines interest rate expectations?" The answer is much easier than you might think. In Chapter 5, we examined the determinants of the interest rate and developed a general expression—Equation (5–10)—that brought together the most important supply and demand influences on the interest rate.[7] This expression is now Equation (6–4):

(6-4) $$i = f(\overset{+}{Y}, \overset{-}{M}, \overset{+}{p^e})$$

where Y = national income or gross domestic product

M = the money supply

p^e = inflationary expectations

The signs over the variables indicate that a rise in income or inflationary expectations will tend to raise the interest rate and that an increase in the money supply will tend to reduce the interest rate.

Now, assuming we want to know what determines the expected short-term interest rate, i_s^e, how can Equation (6–4) be of help? The answer is straightforward; if the current short-term interest rate is determined by Y, M, and p^e, then the expected short-term interest rate must be determined by expectations about Y, M, and p^e. In other words,

(6-5) $$i_s^e = f(\overset{+}{Y^e}, \overset{-}{M^e}, \overset{+}{p^e})$$

The expected short-term interest rate, i_s^e is a positive function of expectations about future income and inflation and a negative function of expectations about the future money supply.[8]

Tying the Determinants of Expectations to the Changing Shape and Level of Yield Curves

We have learned that a positively sloped yield curve reflects expectations of rising interest rates. Utilizing Equation (6-5), we can be even more specific; a positively sloped yield curve reflects expectations of some combination of future increases in income and inflation and possibly some reduction in the future growth rate of the money supply—developments that would all tend to raise future short-term interest rates. Conversely, a negatively sloped yield curve usually reflects expectations of some combination of future declines in income and inflation and possibly some accompanying increase in the future growth rate of the money supply—developments that would all tend to lower short-term interest rates in the future.

---

[7]Remember that this equation is a reduced form equation derived from simultaneously solving a demand and supply equation for loanable funds.

[8]An even deeper question is what determines Y^e, M^e, and p^e. A theory of how expectations are formed is covered in the next chapter.

Everything should now be coming into focus. Ask yourself at what stage of the business cycle you would expect to observe a positively sloped yield curve. The answer is the stage when the future appears to hold some growth in income, a rise in prices, and perhaps slower growth of the money supply. This typically occurs at a business cycle trough and during the first half of a recovery. During the previous recession, real income fell, inflation decelerated, and the Fed probably responded with a more stimulative policy, resulting in a rise in the money supply growth rate. All of these developments contributed to a fall in the prevailing short-term interest rate and set in motion the forces of economic recovery. As the economy bottoms out and begins to recover, market participants expect future income and prices to rise as aggregate demand for goods and services increases, and they expect the Fed to be less stimulative so as to avoid an inflationary boom.[9] As a result, market participants expect future short-term interest rates to be higher than the prevailing level of short-term rates.

What about a negatively sloped yield curve? At what stage of the business cycle would market participants expect the future to bring a fall in income and inflation and Fed actions to increase the growth of the money supply? These developments usually occur around business cycle peaks, including the late part of a recovery or expansion and the early part of a recession. Typically, income and prices have been rising quickly, and the Fed has moved to slow monetary growth—that is, "tighten" policy—to head off further surges in the inflation rate. As Equation (6–4) would lead one to predict, such developments have pushed up the prevailing level of short-term rates and set in motion forces that in the future are expected to lead to some slowdown in income, deceleration of inflation, and, after a time, a less restrictive monetary policy. Simply put, future short-term rates are expected to be lower than the prevailing level of short-term rates; hence, we observe a negatively sloped yield curve.

Going back once again to Exhibit 6-2, we hope you are not surprised to learn that January 16, 1981 fell around a business cycle peak (the exact peak was July 1981), January 29, 1993 fell during the lengthy beginning of a weak recovery, and July 17, 1998 fell 7 years into a long expansion characterized by relatively low inflation rates.[10] The change in the shape of the yield curve among the three dates reflects changes in interest rate expectations. The changes in interest rate expectations, in turn, reflect expected changes in the performance of the economy (income and prices) and expected changes in the stance of monetary policy (specifically, the money supply growth rate). Such changes are typically observed as the economy moves from one stage of the business cycle to another.

RECAP Since $i = f(\overset{+}{Y}, \overset{+}{M}, \overset{+}{p^e})$, then $i^e_s = f(\overset{+}{Y^e}, \overset{+}{M^e}, \overset{+}{p^e})$. If Y^e, M^e, or p^e changes, then i^e_s changes. Changes in i^e_s cause the yield curve to shift.

Having identified and explained the major factors underlying the different shapes of the yield curves in Exhibit 6-2, our one task left is to explain the different levels of the yield curves—that is, why all the rates prevailing in 1993 and 1998 were below the rates in 1981 and why short-term rates were higher and long-term rates lower in 1998 than in 1993. We can address this issue in two parts:

1. In part, the difference in interest rates is due to the cyclical pattern of interest rates related to real economic activity and the supply of and demand for loanable

---

[9]In reality, the Fed may not put on the brakes until the economy is well into the recovery phase!

[10]Note that negatively sloped yield curves have also been associated with abnormally high levels of interest rates when most market makers expect future interest rates to be lower. This was particularly true in 1981.

funds. This part of the answer was discussed in Chapter 5. Expectations about the returns on financial securities and the returns to capital, the business outlook, and any other factors that influence the demand for and supply of funds will affect the level of the yield curve.

2. The second part of the answer is embedded in Equations (6-4) and (6-5). In 1993, inflationary pressures were lower than in the 1980s, and the economy was experiencing a mild recovery. In January 1981, the inflation rate was about 11 percent and in coming years was expected to fall into the 7–8 percent area. Thus, in 1993, with the prevailing and expected inflation rates below the inflation rates prevailing and expected in 1981, the inflation premiums embedded in both short- and long-term interest rates were considerably smaller than the inflation premiums embedded in short- and long-term rates in 1981. In 1993, Fed policy was keeping short-term rates abnormally low. Actual short-term rates were about equal to the inflation rate, yielding a real return of zero. The Fed adopted this strategy, which we will look at in more depth in a later chapter, to help the banking sector recover from massive losses experienced in the 1980s. But short-term interest rates could not remain so low forever, and the Fed increased them over the course of 1994. By 1998, actual inflation and inflationary expectations were even lower than in 1993. So despite higher short-term rates, long-term rates fell to their lowest level in 30 years as the inflation premium plummeted.

Some Necessary Modifications to the Expectations Theory

The expectations theory of the term structure provides a powerful and widely accepted explanation for the relationship between long- and short-term interest rates. However, many researchers, taking note of several historical and institutional features of financial markets, have argued that the expectations theory needs to be modified somewhat to make it a more complete explanation of the term structure. First, it has been observed that yield curves have almost always been positively sloped over the last 45 years. Taken literally, this would imply that financial market participants have almost always expected short-term interest rates to rise. Given the ups and downs in the economy and the accompanying fluctuations in the supply of and demand for funds, this implication is difficult to accept. Second, an assumption underlying the expectations theory is that lenders and borrowers have no preference between long- and short-term securities; they would just as soon lend or borrow for short terms to maturity than for long terms to maturity. The implication that long- and short-term securities are close substitutes for one another has been questioned in light of observations suggesting that (1) many lenders have a preference for liquidity and thus prefer to hold short-term financial claims; (2) many borrowers would prefer to issue long-term claims, avoiding the need to issue and reissue short-term claims; and (3) short- and long-term borrowers have different purposes, such as borrowing for inventory versus borrowing for capital expenditures.

Preferred Habitats
An expectations theory modification hypothesizing that many borrowers and lenders have preferred maturities, which creates a degree of market segmentation between the short-term and long-term markets.

In view of these observations the question then is how does the expectations theory need to be modified? Little doubt exists that many borrowers and lenders have preferred maturities, or what have come to be called **preferred habitats,** and that this creates a degree of segmentation between the short-term and long-term markets. Nevertheless, abundant evidence supports the proposition that the short- and long-term markets are not watertight compartments. Specifically, research suggests that investors are willing to switch preferred habitats from short-term financial claims to longer-term claims if a bonus or "sweetener" is associated with doing so. This sweetener or bonus is referred to as a **liquidity premium.** In essence, it is the extra return required to induce lenders to lend long term rather than short term or in other words, the amount of interest required to induce lenders to abandon their preferred habitats. The size of the premium presumably rises with the term to maturity; the longer the term, the larger the premium must be to induce lenders to give up their preference for liquidity.[11]

How the existence of liquidity premiums modifies the expectations theory of the term structure and yield curves can be illustrated with the help of Exhibit 6-6. Suppose the current short rate and expected short rate are both 5 percent. The expectations approach suggests that the yield curve would be flat (curve A). However, the preceding discussion suggests that the issuers of long-term bonds have to offer an interest premium to get investors to buy bonds having long-term maturities. The size of the premiums is presumed to rise with the term to maturity. Curve B in Exhibit 6-6 shows the size of the liquidity premium at each maturity. Curve C represents the yield curve actually observed. The components of the total yield (curve C) are the interest rate expectations (curve A) and the liquidity premiums (curve B).

In contrast, the expectations approach would explain the shape of the yield curve depicted by curve C as indicating that market participants expect rates to rise over time.

So far this discussion has looked at the demand side of the market for securities, but we must not lose sight of the behavior of the suppliers of debt securities (borrowers) implied by this approach. Under normal circumstances, the demand for funds (supply of securities) is usually more fickle than the supply of funds. Changes in the demand for funds, which are driven by expectations, probably account for

Liquidity Premium
The extra return required to induce lenders to lend long term rather than short term.

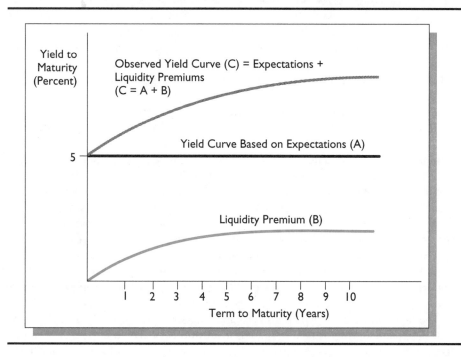

EXHIBIT 6-6
The Role of Liquidity Premiums

---

[11]Of course, the lender who goes into the short-term market also faces the risk that interest rates could fall more than expected or rise less than expected. In this case, the lender would have been better off lending long. This is called the reinvestment risk. In general, it is believed that the liquidity premium outweighs the reinvestment risk.

the largest part of the changes in interest rates. The existence of liquidity premiums means that borrowers are willing to pay them. But why would borrowers be willing to pay more to borrow for longer terms than borrowing and reborrowing for short terms? Simply put, some chance exists that short rates will be higher in the future than the 5 percent expected rate assumed in our example. If higher-than-expected rates materialize, then borrowing and refinancing in the future would prove to be more expensive than borrowing for a longer term now. Also, the firm could suffer some difficulty in the future that might reduce its credit rating and make it difficult to acquire funds later. By borrowing long term, the adverse effects of such problems can be reduced.

In sum, the fact that yield curves have almost always been positively sloped over the past 45 years suggests that liquidity premiums do exist. Theoretical considerations on both the supply and demand side of the securities markets and a variety of empirical studies seem to support such a judgment. Consider again the relatively flat yield curve in July 1998 displayed in Exhibit 6-2. Given the modifications we have just made, it seems reasonable to modify our earlier conclusions based only on the expectations theory. When a liquidity premium is taken into account, it seems reasonable that the relatively flat yield curve of July 1998 may reflect constant or even slightly declining expected future interest rates.

Our discussion of the determinants of the relationship between short- and long-term interest rates (the term structure) can be easily summarized with the aid of Equation (6-6).

(6-6)
$$i_1 = f(\overset{+}{i_s}, \overset{+}{i_s^e}, \overset{+}{l})$$

The current long-term interest rate, i_1, is a function of the current short rate, i_s; the short rates expected in the future, i_s^e; and the liquidity premium, l. The nature of the relationship between the long rate and each of the determinants is indicated by the sign over each variable. Thus, we would expect long rates to rise if current short rates rise, if expectations about future short rates are revised upward, or if liquidity premiums rise. A Closer Look discusses an alternative theory of how the shape and position of the yield curve is determined based on the segmented market hypothesis.

The Segmented Market Hypothesis: Under the expectations theory, short- and long-term interest rates adjust until the expected return from holding a series of short-term securities over a certain term to maturity is just equal to the return from holding a long-term security with that same term to maturity. To be more specific, interest rates adjust until the long-term rate is equal to the geometric average of the current short-term rate and the short-term rates expected to prevail over the term to maturity. When full adjustment has occurred, an investor is indifferent between holding a series of short-term securities or holding one long-term security. Hence, the alternatives—holding a series of short-term securities or a long-term security—are perfect substitutes for each other.

The preferred habitat and liquidity premium theories modify this analysis. Under these theories, short- and long-term securities are substitutes for each other but not perfect substitutes. In general, investors have to receive additional compensation for holding long-term securities that entail less liquidity.

The *segmented market hypothesis* takes the analysis a step further by hypothesizing that short- and long-term securities are not substitutes at all, either perfect or imperfect. Rather, under the segmented market hypothesis, markets for short- and long-term securities are completely separate markets. Accordingly, interest rates are determined by supply and demand factors in each separate market.

The segmented market hypothesis has received renewed interest in the early 2000s because of the federal government surplus and the behavior of long-term interest rates. During this period, long-term rates declined much more so than short- and mid-term rates. Analysts hypothesized this was due to the federal government using the government surplus to buy back long-term government securities. As the supply of long-term securities declined, their prices rose and long-term interest rates fell. The federal government was not buying back short- and mid-term securities so their rates were not affected by the same supply factors. As a result, the yield curve beyond a 10-year term became inverted.

RECAP The expectations theory is modified by the fact that lenders may demand a liquidity premium to lend long term and that borrowers may be willing to pay a liquidity premium to borrow long term. Also, borrowers and lenders may have preferred habitats (preferred maturities) that create a degree of segmentation between the short-term and long-term markets.

The Role of Credit Risk and Taxes in Interest Rate Differentials

The previous section dealt with interest rates on securities alike in every respect except one—term to maturity. Now we will extend our discussion and examine the relationship among interest rates on securities that have the same term to maturity but differ with regard to credit risk or taxability.

Credit Risk

The term **credit risk** refers to the probability of a debtor not paying the principal and/or the interest due on an outstanding debt. In effect, credit risk is a measure of the creditworthiness of the issuer of a security. Treasury securities are considered to have the least credit risk because they are backed by the federal government. The basic idea is that in the unlikely event the federal government collapses, we can be reasonably sure that the rest of the economy has collapsed as well. The reverse is not true since many individual firms can and do fail on a daily basis without the government collapsing. In contrast, corporate and municipal (state and local government) securities are viewed as being risky to some degree and are, therefore, analyzed and rated by firms that specialize in producing credit ratings. The two major credit-rating agencies, **Standard & Poor's** and **Moody's Investors Service,** evaluate a borrower's probability of default and assign the borrower to a particular risk class. With this information, a lender can determine to what degree a borrower will be able to meet debt obligations. Both Standard & Poor's and Moody's distinguish among several general classes of risk. Exhibit 6-7 reproduces the various credit ratings with a brief description of each.

How are borrowers classified or rated? In the case of business firms, the credit-rating agencies examine the pattern of revenues and costs experienced by a firm, its degree of leverage (dependence on borrowed funds), its past history of debt redemption, and the volatility of the industry, among other things. A firm with a history of strong earnings, low leverage, and prompt debt redemption would get an Aaa rating from Moody and an AAA rating from Standard & Poor's. A firm that has experienced net losses, has rising leverage, or has missed some loan payments would get a Baa or lower rating from Moody and a BBB or lower rating from Standard & Poor's.

The agencies also assign ratings to securities issued by state and local governments. Factors considered here include the tax base, the level of outstanding debt, the current and expected budget situation, and growth in spending.

Credit Risk
The probability of a debtor not paying the principal and/or the interest due on an outstanding debt.

Standard & Poor's
and **Moody's Investors Services**
The two major credit-rating agencies that evaluate a borrower's probability of default and assign the borrower to a particular risk class.

http://www.stockinfo. standardpoor.com and **www.moodys.com.**
Visit Standard and Poor's and Moody's sites.

EXHIBIT 6-7
Credit Ratings

MOODY'S	GENERAL DESCRIPTION	STANDARD & POOR'S
Aaa	Best quality	AAA
Aa	High quality	AA
A	Higher medium grade	A
Baa	Medium grade	BBB
Ba	Lower medium grade having speculative elements	BB
B	Lacks characteristics of desirable investment	B
Caa	Poor standing	CCC
Ca	Highly speculative	CC,C
C	Lowest grade (in default)	D

Risk Premium
The extra return or interest that a lender is compensated for accepting more risk.

To see how the credit ratings affect the spread between rates, let us make the reasonable assumption that most potential purchasers of securities would like to be compensated for risk taking. Based on real-world observations, we can say that investors are risk averse and thus, must be rewarded or compensated with extra interest for accepting more risk. The extra return or interest is called a **risk premium,** and its size increases with the riskiness of the borrower. To illustrate, the prevailing rate on securities issued by borrowers rated Aaa is less than the rate on securities issued by borrowers rated Aa, the second highest rating. The spread between the two rates $(i_{Aa} - i_{Aaa})$ is the premium necessary to induce investors to accept the extra risk associated with Aa-rated securities relative to Aaa-rated securities. Similarly, the rates on Baa-rated securities are higher than the rates on A-rated securities, and so on down the credit ratings shown in Exhibit 6-7.[12]

When we plot the spread between the interest rates on securities of the same maturity, but possessing different credit risks, we find that the spread varies over time as the perceived credit risks among the securities change. See Exhibit 6-8, which depicts the spread between Baa-rated and Aaa-rated municipal bonds. For example, if a default occurs in a major market, many investors may perceive lower-rated bonds as being relatively more risky and respond by selling lower-rated issues and purchasing higher-rated issues. This movement to higher-rated securities is usually referred to as a "flight to quality." Put another way, if investors perceive that relative risks have changed, they will demand different risk premiums and, thus, the rate spread among securities will change.

Taxability

The last major factor influencing the structure of interest rates is the taxability of securities. As you may know, interest income earned from securities issued by state and local governments is exempt from the federal income tax, while interest earned from corporate securities is taxed at the same rates as other ordinary income.[13]

---

[12]For simplicity's sake, we have used Moody's ratings in this example. We could just as easily have used Standard & Poor's ratings.

[13]In many states, interest on bonds issued by the investor's home state is also exempt from state income taxes. For example, California residents do not pay state income taxes on interest earned on bonds issued by California, but they do pay state income taxes on interest earned on bonds issued by Arizona. Although subject to federal income taxes, interest earned on federal government securities is exempt from state and local income taxes.

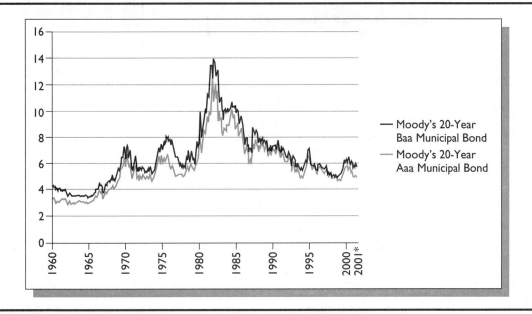

EXHIBIT 6-8

The Spread between Baa-Rated Municipal Bonds and Aaa-Rated Municipal Bonds, 1960–2001*

SOURCE: Global Financial Data, Los Angeles California.

*Through July 12, 2001.

The **marginal tax rate** is the rate paid on the last dollar of income the taxpayer earns. Because the United States has a progressive tax rate structure, higher rates apply to additional income earned beyond given tax rate brackets while income under the bracket limits is taxed at lower rates. Interest income from bonds is additional income and is therefore taxed at the highest marginal rate for each taxpayer. For bondholders who do not have much other income, interest income is taxed at a lower marginal rate than for bondholders whose other income puts them into a higher marginal tax bracket. This means that if you are in the 331/3 percent marginal federal income tax bracket, a 4 percent interest rate on a municipal bond is just as attractive as a 6 percent interest rate on a taxable corporate bond; after taxes, both yield 4 percent.[14]

As we shall see, the tax-exempt status of municipal bonds makes them quite attractive to taxpayers in high marginal tax brackets. Financial intermediaries such as commercial banks and casualty insurance companies, which are subject to the 38 percent marginal corporate income tax rate, have traditionally been heavy purchasers of municipal securities.[15]

To see how the yields on municipals are related to the yields on other types of securities, the following simple equation is helpful.

(6-6) $$\text{after-tax yield} = i - it = i\,(1 - t)$$

where t = the "marginal" tax rate on interest income

Marginal Tax Rate
The tax rate that is paid on the last dollar of income that the taxpayer earns.

---

[14]For simplicity, we are assuming equivalent safety and maturity.

[15]Commercial banks often feel subtle pressure to purchase the securities issued by municipalities in the immediate geographical area. With the bank's deposits coming from the local citizens, such purchases are viewed as an investment in the community the bank serves, an investment that demonstrates the goodwill and intentions of the bank.

This says that the after-tax yield on a bond is equal to the interest rate earned, i, minus the portion that is taxed away, it. Put another way, the after-tax yield is equal to the portion of the interest earned that is not taxed away: $i(1 - t)$.

Just as we care more about our after-tax take-home pay rather than our before-tax gross pay, financial investors making portfolio decisions care about and compare the after-tax returns on securities they might acquire. To see how this matters, suppose the rate on AAA-rated corporate bonds is 6 percent and the marginal tax rate of buyers is 33 1/3 percent, meaning that one-third of the interest income earned will be taxed away. If the only difference between the corporate bonds and AAA-rated municipal bonds is that the interest on corporate bonds is taxable while the interest on the municipal bonds is not ($t = 0$ percent), we would expect buyers to prefer the municipal securities to the corporate bonds as long as the rate on municipal bonds exceeds 4 percent. If the yield on municipal bonds equals 4 percent, investors in the 33 1/3 percent marginal tax bracket will be indifferent since the corporate bond yields 4 percent [6 percent – (.33 1/3 × 6 percent) = 4 percent] after taxes. What if the marginal tax rate of buyers of municipal securities is only 20 percent? What yield on municipal bonds would leave investors in the 20 percent tax bracket indifferent between our 6 percent corporate bond and a municipal bond? We hope you understand why the answer is 4.8 percent.[16]

In general, we would expect the buying and selling by investors—more formally, the substitution among securities—to result in the yield on municipals being approximately equal to the yield on similarly rated taxable securities, such as corporate bonds, minus the portion of the yield that is taxed away. Close the book for a moment and see if you can explain why. Suppose that the interest rate on municipals is above the after-tax yield on corporates for the typical investor; municipals are obviously the more attractive security. The resulting purchase of municipals and sale of corporates will raise the prices and lower the yields on municipals and lower the prices and raise the yields on corporates. In this example, the effect of the substitution toward municipals and away from corporates will be to equalize the interest rate on municipal securities with the after-tax return on similarly rated corporate securities.

We now know that the marginal tax rate that investors pay on interest income is the key to understanding the spread between the interest rates on tax-exempt municipal securities and the interest rates on taxable securities. We also can see that taxpayers, depending on their individual incomes, are in different marginal tax brackets—some high and some low. Thus, there is an **average marginal tax rate** somewhere between the high and low marginal tax brackets. Because of substitution, the interest rate on municipal securities will gravitate to the rate that makes the "average" taxpayer (in the average marginal tax bracket) indifferent between municipals and similarly rated corporate securities.[17]

But why are those in high tax brackets, such as banks and rich individuals, especially attracted to municipals? Simply put, they are subject to a tax rate above the average marginal rate. To see precisely how this matters, assume that the average marginal tax rate is 20 percent, the rate on municipals is 4.8 percent, and the rate on

Average Marginal Tax Rate
The average of the marginal tax rates of all taxpayers.

---

[16]4.8 percent = 6 percent – (.20 × 6 percent).

[17]Note that in actuality, the yields on municipal securities are somewhat higher than one would expect after taking account of the average tax rate of all buyers. For the most part, the quality of the secondary market in municipal issues is not as good as the secondary market for Treasuries and many corporate issues. As a result, municipal securities possess somewhat less liquidity than other types of securities and, therefore, the liquidity premium demanded by investors is larger on municipals than on other types of securities.

corporates is 6 percent. The average investor—that is, the investor in the 20 percent marginal tax bracket—is indifferent between the two securities; both have an after-tax return of 4.8 percent. Not so the investor in a higher marginal tax bracket. Someone in the 33 1/3 percent marginal tax bracket would prefer the 4.8 percent return on the municipal security to the 4 percent after-tax return on the corporate security.

RECAP Other factors that affect the interest rates on different securities with the same maturity are credit risk and taxability of interest income. Taxpayers in marginal tax brackets above the average marginal tax bracket are particularly attracted to tax-exempt securities.

A final example shows how both credit risk and taxability play a part in determining yield to maturity. Under normal circumstances, yields on 20-year general obligation AAA-rated municipal bonds are less than 80 percent of yields on comparable Treasury securities. The yield spread mainly reflects the difference in the credit risk and the tax status accorded the earnings of the two assets. In December 1994, affluent Orange County, California declared bankruptcy due to bond market losses in its investment pool. The bankruptcy created widespread uncertainty in the municipal bond market and the perception of greater risk. By year end, the municipal bond market had gone into a tailspin, and according to *Business Week*, "municipal bonds [were] trading at yields unusually close to those on Treasury bonds, so after-tax yields for many long-term muni buyers [were] roughly one-third higher."[18] Although the tax status had not changed, the relative credit risk had, causing the spread between the two categories of securities to narrow. Buyers of municipal bonds demanded a larger risk premium, and as the after-tax yields reflect, they received it.

To sum up, the yields on municipal securities are usually well below the yields on other securities with similar credit ratings and terms to maturity. The interest rate differentials observed are a reflection of the different tax treatment accorded the interest earned on each type of security and the different credit risk.

---

[18]*Business Week*, December 26, 1994, p. 140.

Summary of Major Points

- The yield curve is a graphical representation of the relationship between interest rates (yields) on a particular security and its term to maturity. It is a visual depiction of the term structure of interest rates. A unique yield curve exists for each type of financial asset such as government securities and corporate bonds, among others.

- The most widely accepted explanation for the shape (slope) and position (level) of the yield curve is the expectations theory.

- The expectations theory postulates that the long-term rate is the geometric average of the current short-term rate and the short-term rates expected to prevail over the term to maturity of the long-

term security. The geometric average is the appropriate average to use in explaining the expectations theory because it takes into account the effects of compounding. The interest earned during the first year earns interest during the second year.

- According to the expectations theory, the slope of the yield curve depends on the interest rates expected to prevail on short-term securities in the future. Specifically, a positively sloped yield curve reflects expectations of a rise in future short-term rates, relative to current short-term rates; a negatively sloped yield curve reflects expectations of a fall in future short-term rates, relative to current short-term rates.

- Expectations about future short-term rates depend on expectations about future income, the money supply, and inflation. As expectations about these variables change, expected short-term rates will change, resulting in a change in the slope and level of the yield curve.

- Because yield curves have almost always been upward sloping and some borrowers and lenders appear to have preferred habitats, many view the expectations theory as an incomplete explanation of the term structure of interest rates. Accordingly, the expectations theory has been modified to include and take into account term or liquidity premiums—the sweetener or bonus (extra return) needed to induce investors to acquire longer-term financial claims. In general, long-term rates will be determined by current short-term rates, expected short-term rates, and liquidity premiums.

- Credit risk refers to the probability of a debtor defaulting—that is, not paying the principal or interest due on an outstanding debt. Standard & Poor's and Moody's—the two major credit-rating agencies—evaluate a borrower's probability of default and assign the borrower a risk classification.

- Since investors are risk averse, they must be offered the "bonus" of extra interest to accept more risk. The extra return or interest is called a risk premium, and its size increases with the riskiness of the borrower.

- Financial investors care about the after-tax return on their investments. Since the interest earned on municipal securities is exempt from the federal income tax, the yields on municipal securities are typically well below the yields on other (taxable) securities with similar credit ratings and similar terms to maturity.

Key Terms

Average Marginal Tax Rate
Credit Risk
Expectations Theory
Geometric Average
Liquidity Premium
Marginal Tax Rate

Moody's Investors Service
Preferred Habitats
Risk Premium
Standard & Poor's Investors
  Service

Term Structure of Interest Rates
Treasury Notes
Yield Curve

Review Questions

1. Discuss the factors that determine the shape and level of a yield curve. How do term to maturity, credit risk, and tax treatment affect the interest rate on a particular asset?

2. Give an explanation of why a yield curve can be negatively sloped. Would interest rates be abnormally high or low? What would be the overall expectation of the direction of future short-term interest rates?

3. According to the expectations theory, how is the long-term interest rate determined? Why is the geometric average used instead of the simpler arithmetic average?

4. BBB-rated corporate bonds are riskier than AAA-rated bonds. Explain where the two yield curves will lie relative to each other. What could cause the spread to widen?

5. What determines expectations? Are expectations about future prices independent of

expectations about future money supply growth rates? Why or why not?

6. Could the yield curve for municipals ever lie above the yield curve for government securities? (Hint: Consider all tax rates.) What effect would an increase in marginal tax rates have on the position of the yield curve for municipals?

7. Use the liquidity premium to give an explanation for why yield curves have most often been upward sloping over the past 45 years. Could a yield curve be upward sloping even if short-term rates were expected to remain constant? If interest rates are expected to fall dramatically, under what conditions would the yield curve still be upward sloping?

8. Define preferred habitats. Explain how this modification affects the expectations theory. What could cause market segmentation based on preferred habitats to break down? How is

the market segmentation hypothesis different from the expectations theory?

9. Discuss the following statements: Over a typical cycle, the movement of the yield curve is like the wagging of a dog's tail. The entire tail wags, but short-term rates "wag" more than long-term rates.

10. If yield curves became flatter (steeper), what does this say about expectations of future interest rates?

11. What would happen to the risk premium if the economy went into a strong expansion? A deep recession?

Analytical Questions

12. If the current short-term rate is 5 percent and the expected short-term rate is 8 percent, what is the long-term interest rate? (Use the expectations theory.)

13. If the current short-term rate is 5 percent and the current long-term rate is 4 percent, what is the expected short-term interest rate? (Use the expectations theory.)

14. Rework questions 12 and 13 assuming that there is no compounding. (Hint: Use the simple arithmetic average instead of the geometric average.)

15. Assume that current interest rates on government securities are as follows: 1-year rate, 5 percent; 2-year rate, 6 percent; 3-year rate, 6.5 percent; 4-year rate, 7 percent. Graph the yield curve.

16. Given the yield curve in question 15, what is the expected direction of future 1-year rates? Under what circumstances would 1-year rates be expected to decline?

17. If a taxpayer's marginal tax rate is 33 1/3 percent, what is the after-tax yield on a corporate bond that pays 5 percent interest? If the average marginal tax rate of all taxpayers is 50 percent, will the taxpayer with the 33 1/3 percent marginal tax rate prefer a corporate or a municipal security? Assume equivalent safety and maturity.

18. Go to *The Wall Street Journal* and gather data on interest rates for government securities of various maturities for today. Graph the yield curve. (Hint: Check your answer by looking at the yield curve for Treasury securities that the *Journal* publishes daily in Part C.)

19. What would happen to interest rates, given each of the following scenarios?
    a. The government increases marginal tax rates.
    b. The tax exemption on municipals is eliminated.
    c. Corporate profits fall severely.
    d. The federal government guarantees that the interest and principal on corporate bonds will be paid.
    e. A broader secondary market for government agency securities develops.

20. Draw the yield curve assuming future short-term rates are expected to remain constant and the liquidity premium is positive. Now assume that SSUs increase their preference for short-term securities. Show what happens to the yield curve.

Internet Exercises

1. Access the glossary of terms at **http://www.ots.treas.gov/glossary/gloss-i.html.** and define the following financial terms: security, liquidity, and yield curve.

2. Use the Internet site **http://www.stls.frb.org/fred/data/irates.html** to obtain January 2001 and January 2002 data on each of the following:

a. The 3-month CD secondary market rate (a proxy for short-term interest rates)
b. The 3-year Treasury constant maturity rate (a proxy for medium-term interest rates)
c. The 30-year conventional mortgage rate (a proxy for long-term interest rates) Graph two yield curves: one for January 2001 and one for January 2002. Compare the two curves.

Suggested Readings

For an article that looks at the relationship between the slope of the yield curve and economic activity and inflation, see Arturo Estrella, Anthony P. Rodrigues, and Sebastian Schich, "How Stable is the Predictive Power of the Yield Curve: Evidence from Germany and the United States" *Staff Reports, Number 113*, Federal Reserve Bank of New York, September 2000.

For an article that looks at measuring the yield curve, see Brian Sack, "Using Treasury STRIPS to Measure the Yield Curve," *Finance and Economics Discussion Series No. 2000-42*, Board of Governors of the Federal Reserve System, 2000.

"Admiring Those Shapely Curves: The Gap between Short-Term and Long-Term Interest Rates" is an article about how the shape of the yield curve can predict future economic growth. It is found in *The Economist*, April 4, 1998, p. 83.

Many of the conclusions arrived at in this chapter are discussed in Burton Malkiel, *The Term Structure of Interest Rates* (Princeton, NJ: Princeton University Press, 1966).

For an article that reviews the economic literature on the yield curve as well as discussing a plan to shorten the maturity of the U.S. government debt to reduce interest costs, see John Y. Campbell, "Some Lessons from the Yield Curve," *Journal of Economic Perspectives* 9 (Summer 1995): 127–152.

Another article by John Y. Campbell discusses "Yield Spreads and Interest Rate Movements: A Bird's Eye View," *Review of Economic Studies* 58 (May 1991): 495–514.

For an article that discusses the tax exemption of interest on municipal bonds, see "Tax-Exempt Bonds Really Do Subsidize Municipal Capital!" *National Tax Journal*, No. 51, 1998, pps. 43–54.

The article "Does the Yield Spread Predict Real Economic Activity? A Multicountry Analysis," by Catherine Bonser-Neal and Timothy R. Morley, *Economic Review of the Federal Reserve Bank of Kansas City* 82:3 (1997): 37–54, finds that the yield spread can be used as a predictor of economic activity in several countries including the United States.

For an article that discusses the persistently downward-sloping yield curve of 1998, see "Income Uncertainty, Substitution Effect and Relative Yield Spreads," *Quarterly Review of Economics and Finance* 38:2 (1998): 217–225.

Two articles that relate growth and inflation to the shape and position of the yield curve are Stephen R. Blough, "Yield Curve Forecasts of Inflation: A Cautionary Tale," *New England Economic Review*, May–June 1994, pp. 3–16; and Campbell R. Harvey, "Term Structure Forecasts Economic Growth," *Financial Analysts Journal* 49 (May–June 1993): 6–8.

chapter

Market Efficiency

⟨ **Learning Objectives** *After reading this chapter, you should know:* ⟩

- How all prices of financial instruments are related
- How expectations are formed and what the difference is between rational and adaptive expectations
- What the efficient market hypothesis is and how it relates all financial prices
- How the sources and uses of funds can be used to integrate financial flows between sectors

❝❞
Water rises to the same level.

Stocks Rise 32 Percent while Bonds Fall by 10 Percent: Can These Price Movements Be Explained?

In earlier chapters, we covered the determination of interest rates. We learned that long-term interest rates are related to current short-term interest rates and to future short-term interest rates *expected* to prevail over the life of the long-term security. Long-term rates change whenever short-term rates or expected short-term rates change. We also saw that present short-term rates are related to income, the money supply, and inflationary expectations. A rise in income or inflationary expectations tends to raise the interest rate and an increase in the money supply tends to reduce the interest rate. However, if we do not assume that all else is equal, an increase in the money supply could increase interest rates through its effect on inflationary expectations.

We further concluded that if the current short-term interest rate is determined by national income, the money supply, and inflationary expectations, then expected short-term interest rates must be determined by expectations about these same variables. Thus, expected short-term interest rates are positively related to expectations about future income and inflation, and negatively related to expectations about the future money supply.

We have also seen that when long-term interest rates change (either because present short-term or expected short-term rates change), bond prices change inversely. That is, when interest rates rise, bond prices fall and vice versa. Recall from Chapter 6 that although we did not directly observe expected short-term rates, we were able to solve for expected short-term rates, given current short-term and long-term rates.

It is clear expectations are key determinants of long-term interest rates and bond prices. But perhaps not as clear is the difficulty in measuring expectations because they cannot be directly observed. Therefore, economists have spent a great deal of time and energy in developing various theories of how expectations are formed by market participants.

The goal of this chapter is twofold:

1. We want to identify the relationship between bond prices and the prices of other financial instruments. We shall see that prices of all financial instruments adjust so that *expected* rates of return on all financial instruments are equalized after adjustments for varying degrees of risk and liquidity have been made.[1] Again, expectations play a central role.

2. Because our discussion of how market participants form expectations has been vague, we take the analysis one step further by developing the efficient markets hypothesis, which is based on the theory of rational expectations as applied to financial markets. We conclude that prices of financial instruments adjust so that the *expected* value of financial variables is equal to the optimal forecast of those variables given all available information.

Hopefully, the analysis will go a long way toward answering the question, "Can economists explain these price movements?" We begin our discussion by relating expected rates of return to the prices of long-term financial instruments, and then

---

[1]Additional factors that can affect the prices of financial instruments are term to maturity, the taxability of earnings, and other supply and demand conditions affecting particular markets. For our purposes here, term to maturity is encompassed under risk with longer-term instruments entailing more risk. By "expected rates of return," we mean after-tax returns.

we move to the development of the efficient market hypothesis. We conclude with a look at the flow of funds among sectors and see how it is related to the efficient market hypothesis.

How Expected Rates of Return Affect the Prices of Stocks and Bonds

Stocks and bonds are two major, long-term financial instruments. Stocks represent ownership of part of the issuing firm whereas bonds represent debt of the issuer whether it is a firm, a government entity, or other deficit spending unit (DSU). To streamline the analysis, we focus on how stock and bond prices are related while recognizing that the analysis could easily be extended to other long-term financial instruments.

With regard to stocks, the size of a shareholder's ownership position depends on the number of shares owned. For example, if there are 1,000 shares outstanding, a stockholder who owns 100 shares in effect owns 10 percent of the firm. The value of each share—and, therefore, the value of the stockholder's holdings in the corporation—depends on the prevailing price of the firm's stock. For example, if the price is $50 per share, the total value of the stockholder's 100 shares is $5,000. The key question is, what determines the price per share?

Outstanding shares of stocks are traded on organized exchanges such as the New York Stock Exchange or by networks of brokers and dealers around the country (more on this in Chapter 11). Stock prices fluctuate daily—some going up, some going down—as financial investors buy and sell shares of various corporations. In part, those fluctuations occur because a share of stock represents a claim on the earnings of a firm. Tangible evidence of this sharing of earnings comes in the form of dividends, which are a distribution of profits to stockholders. If earnings prospects are improving, the share price and dividend paid per share may also be rising.[2] Financial investors will be attracted by the improved outlook (profitability) for the firm.

In general, as current and expected future earnings rise, stock prices also rise, and as current and prospective earnings decline, stock prices decline. A growing economy means that sales, production, and incomes are expanding, while a declining economy means the opposite. Since expected earnings also rise when the economy is expected to grow and tend to fall when the economy is expected to contract, a positive correlation often exists between the growth of real national income and stock prices.[3]

A portfolio usually consists of both stocks and bonds. How would you go about managing such a portfolio? Specifically, how would you decide whether to purchase stocks or bonds? We hope that you would compare the expected rates of return on the different types of financial assets, selecting those with the highest expected return consistent with the risk you are willing to take.

---

[2]If a company pays out only a small portion of its earnings as dividends, then it has retained earnings, which it invests back in the company. This usually leads to larger profits later. If the expected returns from retained earnings exceed the risk-adjusted returns that shareholders could expect to receive on alternative investments that could be made with the dividends, then a firm's stock price will rise, and the owner will earn a larger capital gain when the stock is sold. Many major companies, for example, Microsoft, pay no dividends and do not intend to do so.

[3]Real national income is national income adjusted for changes in prices or inflation. For our purposes, real national income is equivalent to real GDP.

EXHIBIT 7-1
The Expected Return to Owning Stock

As explained earlier, the expected return to owning a share of stock over, say, 1 year is the expected dividend plus the expected capital gain or loss, all divided by the share price at the time of purchase. Thus, whenever either factor changes, the expected return will change.

Assume that the stock originally costs $50 per share. The following table shows the rate of return for owning the stock, given various expected dividends and expected price changes (the capital gains or losses).

Expected Dividend	Expected Price Change (Capital Gain [+] or Loss [−])	Expected Return
$3	−$2	($3 + (−$2))/$50 = 2 percent
$3	$0	($3 + $0)/$50 = 6 percent
$3	$2	($3 + $2)/$50 = 10 percent
$3	$4	($3 + $4)/$50 = 14 percent
$4	−$2	($4 + (−$2))/$50 = 4 percent
$4	$0	($4 + $0)/$50 = 8 percent
$4	$2	($4 + $2)/$50 = 12 percent
$4	$4	($4 + $4)/$50 = 16 percent

If actual dividends or actual capital gains and losses turn out to be different from those expected, the actual return will be different from the expected. Needless to say, all investors hope that actual dividends and capital gains turn out to be higher than expected, rather than the reverse scenario of disappointing returns.

What is the expected return on stocks? Generally speaking, the expected return on a share of stock, say, over a year, is the expected dividend plus the expected change in the price of the stock, all divided by the share price at the time of purchase. For example, if you pay $50 a share, know the expected dividend is $1 per share, and expect the price to rise $3 over the year, the expected return is 8 percent [($1 + $3)/$50 = .08 = 8 percent].[4] An 8 percent expected return also would result if the expected dividend is $4 and the expected capital gain is $0 because [($4 + $0)/$50 = .08 = 8 percent]. Now would be a good time to turn to Exhibit 7-1, which looks at this relationship.

With regard to bonds the expected return is the current interest rate. Bonds represent long-term debt and pay a fixed annual coupon payment.[5] The coupon payment is the product of the face value of the bond multiplied by the coupon rate. Bondholders are entitled to be paid the coupon payment before dividends are paid to stockholders. The coupon rate is the interest rate at the time the bond is originally issued and usually appears on the bond itself. The coupon rate is not the same as the current interest rate if interest rates have changed since the bond was issued.

For instance, if the face value of a bond is $1,000 and the coupon rate is 6 percent, then the coupon payment is $60 because $60 divided by $1,000 is equal to 6 percent ($60/$1,000 = .06). This coupon payment does not change even if interest rates change after the bond has been issued. However, the bond's price will change whenever interest rates change or if the issuer's ability to make the agreed-upon interest or principal payments comes into question.

---

[4]The specifics of this relationship are flushed out in Equation 7-3 on page 141.

[5]In Chapter 5 we saw that coupon payments are usually made semi-annually. We are assuming annual coupon payments here to simplify. The assumption does not substantively change the results.

EXHIBIT 7-2
The Expected Return
on Bonds

expected percentage return on bonds

= coupon rate + expected percentage change in the bond price

= (coupon payment/bond price at the beginning of the year) + (expected bond price at the end of the year – bond price at the beginning of the year)/bond price at the beginning of the year)

As shown in Exhibit 7-2, the expected return on bonds is the coupon rate plus the expected percentage change in the bond's price over the course of the year.

Let's assume you purchase a $1,000 newly issued 30-year bond with a 6 percent coupon rate. You expect interest rates to fall to 4 percent during the next year. If interest rates fall to 4 percent, the price of the bond would approach $1,500 because $60 divided by $1,500 is equal to 4 percent ($60/$1,500 = .04). In other words, prices of previously issued bonds adjust so that they pay the new prevailing interest rate. The expected return on the bond is equal to the coupon rate (6 percent) plus the expected percentage capital gain from the change in interest rates. In our example, the new interest rate is 4 percent and the expected percentage capital gain is [($1,500 – $1,000)/$1,000 = .5 = 50 percent]. Thus, the expected return to owning the bond over the year is the coupon rate (6 percent) plus the expected percentage capital gain (50 percent), or 56 percent.

To see how bond prices fit into the picture, assume that the current interest rate on bonds is 6 percent and that the expected return on stocks is 8 percent, with the typical stock costing $50 and the expected dividend equal to $4. Also assume for simplicity that the expected capital gain is zero and that stocks and bonds have the same degree of liquidity.[6] Assume that stocks are riskier than bonds and that the portfolio managers must be compensated 2 percent for the additional risks of owning stocks. When bonds pay a 6 percent return and stocks pay an 8 percent return, the typical portfolio manager is indifferent between stocks and bonds. He or she will presumably hold some of each because the risk-adjusted returns are equalized. Equation (7-1) depicts this situation:

(7-1) risk-adjusted return on stocks = risk-adjusted return on bonds

nominal return on stocks – compensation for higher risk of owning stocks = risk-adjusted return on bonds

(8 percent – 2 percent) = 6 percent

Now suppose the Fed decides to pursue a more expansionary monetary policy. The initial result of this is a decline in the interest rate on bonds to 4 percent and a reduction in the risk-adjusted return on bonds from 6 percent to 4 percent.[7] The fall in the interest rate will tend to raise stock prices through two channels.

First, the expected return on bonds is now below the risk-adjusted expected return on stocks. Given the substitutability of stocks for bonds in investors' portfolios and the higher expected return on stocks, the demand for stocks will rise, tending to raise stock prices. Within the confines of our simple example, we

---

[6]If both stocks and bonds have highly developed secondary markets then the assumption that they have the same degree of liqudity is not that unrealistic.

[7]As noted previously, the decline in interest rates to 4 percent causes the prices of previously issued bonds to rise so that their risk-adjusted return equals 4 percent.

can even say how high stock prices will rise: Stock prices will rise until the expected return on stocks is again 2 percent higher than the expected return on bonds (4 percent). This will occur when the price of our typical share of stock rises to $66.67. because the $4 expected dividend divided by $66.67 equals 6 percent ($4/$66.67 = .06).

Second, the fall in the interest rate will be expected to raise the demand for goods and services and increase the sales and earnings of firms. With earnings expected to rise, dividends also will be expected to rise. This reinforces the first effect. For example, if the dividend is expected to rise to $5 per share, then financial investors will be willing to bid up the price per share even further to $83.33 because $5 divided by $83.33 is equal to 6 percent ($5/$83.33 =.06 = 6 percent).[8]

Again, after stock prices have adjusted to the change in interest rates, the risk-adjusted return on stocks will be equal to the risk-adjusted return on bonds.[9]

Assuming you and other portfolio managers would like to have owned the stock before all of this occurred, you now can see why actual and expected changes in the interest rate get so much attention in the stock market.

In the real world, there are many types of long-term financial instruments that offer varying degrees of risk and liquidity. Because of the substitutability of various financial instruments, prices of financial instruments will adjust so that returns to owning different instruments are equalized, after adjustments have been made for differences in risk and liquidity. Put simply, in financial markets, risk- and liquidity-adjusted rates of return are equalized.

RECAP Prices of long-term financial instruments change as current and future expected earnings change. If interest rates fall, prices of previously issued bonds rise and vice versa. If current and expected future earnings rise, stock prices also rise, and vice versa. In managing a portfolio, market participants compare expected rates of return and select those financial assets with the highest expected return consistent with varying degrees of risk and liquidity. Stock and bond prices adjust until the portfolio manager is indifferent between stocks and bonds. If interest rates change, stock prices also change. When full adjustment has occurred, differences in returns on various financial instruments reflect differences in only risk and liquidity.

To reiterate, it is the expected returns on bonds and on stocks that determine stock and bond prices. It should not surprise you that this is true of all financial instruments. Since expectations play such a central role, we turn now to a general theory of how price expectations are formed and how it is applied to financial instruments.

---

[8]A more formal approach to this relationship between stock prices and interest rates makes use of the present value (discounting) analysis developed in Chapter 5. Within this framework, the share price is viewed as the discounted present value of a firm's expected earnings (or dividends). Accordingly, a fall in the interest rate and/or a rise in the stream of expected earnings increases the expected value of the firm—that is, the share price—in the market.

[9]If the interest rate rises to 8 percent, then, in equilibrium, the risk-adjusted return on stocks will rise to 10 percent assuming the typical investor must be compensated 2 percent for the additional risk of owning stocks. The price of a typical share will initially fall to $40 because $4/$40 = .10 = 10 percent. Assuming the higher interest rate reduces demand and, hence, earnings, the dividend may be expected to fall to $3. If this is the case, the stock price falls further to $30 because $3/$30 = .10 = 10 percent.

The Formation of Price Expectations

The substantial research on the formation of price expectations suggests that the factors in Equation (7-2) are important in shaping the public's expectations of future prices.

(7-2) Price expectations = f (current and past prices, expected changes in national income, and expected changes in production costs)

This equation suggests that the formation of price expectations is both backward and forward looking. The idea that price expectations depend on the public's experience with prices, as reflected in current and past prices, is the backward-looking component. Expectations formed by looking back are typically called **adaptive expectations.** Because the recent past (the last 1 to 2 years) is likely to be more influential in forming expectations about the future, this experience is measured as a weighted average of past values with recent years weighted more heavily than earlier years. For example, if the rate of inflation was 5 percent per year for 10 years and rose 6 percent in the most recent 2 years, the public will probably expect inflation in the coming year to be closer to 6 percent than to 5 percent.

It is unreasonable to believe the public will take only the past into consideration when anticipating future prices. Expected changes in costs of production and in national income also contribute to the formation of price expectations. For example, will the price of oil rise or fall? If the public expects a large rise in the price of oil, government expenditures, or bank reserves in the coming year, expectations of inflation may be raised to, say, 7 percent. Expectations formed by looking both backward and forward, making use of all available information, are typically called **rational expectations.** Exhibit 7-3 highlights the relationship between adaptive and rational expectations.

The **theory of rational expectations** states that expectations of financial prices will on average be equal to the optimal forecast. The **optimal forecast** is the best guess arrived at by using all of the available information. Even if a forecast is rational, there is no guarantee that it will be accurate. There is an aspect of randomness in financial markets that makes the forecast either a little short or a little wide of the mark. For a forecast to be rational, all that is necessary is that *on average*, the forecast is equal to the optimal forecast. Thus, the forecast error (the difference between the actual value and the forecast) will *on average* be zero. In any given time period, it is impossible to predict what the forecast error will be.

In addition to randomness, there is another reason why the optimal forecast may deviate from the actual value of the forecasted variable: There may be additional key factors that are relevant but not available at the time the optimal forecast is made. If the information is not available, the forecast may be inaccurate. However, it is still rational because the decision maker uses all available information. This is different

Adaptive Expectations
Expectations formed by looking back at past values of a variable.

Rational Expectations
Expectations formed by looking both backward and forward.

Theory of Rational Expectations
The theory that expectations will on average be equal to the optimal forecast.

Optimal Forecast
The best guess possible arrived at by using all of the available information.

http://www.
minneapolisfed.org/
pubs/region/reg9512.
html.
Discusses the development of the rational expectations theory.

Adaptive Expectations	Rational Expectations
Expectations formed as a weighted average of past values	Expectations formed by looking at all available information
Usually more weight is given to more recent values of the variable	Looks at the past as well as all additional available information such as expected changes in national income and costs
Backward looking	Backward and forward looking

EXHIBIT 7-3
Adaptive and Rational Expectations

from the situation in which market participants fail to make use of all of the available information because they are unaware of it or because it is too costly to do so. In this latter situation, expectations formed are neither accurate nor rational.

The reasoning behind the rational expectations theory is that it is costly for market participants not to make use of all available information in forming price expectations. For example, if a producer ignores information that interest rates are going up based on a change in Fed policy, it may produce too much output, ignoring the effects the interest rate hikes have on demand, and thus, earn less profit than it otherwise would have. Or if a producer ignores the effect of higher oil prices on demand and costs, it may again produce more than the profit-maximizing output. In such cases, the errors are costly to management, employees, and stockholders, and give a strong incentive to consider readily available information in the future.

An implication of rational expectations is that as new information becomes available, market participants should adjust expectations accordingly. Current research on the formation of price expectations suggests that the public does not adjust its expectations instantaneously when new information becomes available. There are lags between when information becomes available and when it is fully incorporated into expectations. However, the evidence also suggests that as market participants (the public) have come to better understand the process of inflation, the lag in adjusting expectations has shortened considerably.

Yet another implication is that if there is a change in the way a variable moves, the way in which expectations of the variable are formed will also change. An example will help clarify this. In the early 1980s, changes in the monetary aggregate M2 were highly correlated with changes in national income. Therefore, changes in M2 played a major role in forming expectations about changes in national income. Since the late 1980s, changes in national income are no longer highly correlated with changes in M2. Therefore, changes in M2 will not be given a large weight in forming expectations about changes in national income.

RECAP Adaptive expectations are formed by looking at current and past prices. Rational expectations are formed by looking at past prices and all current available information about the economy that may affect prices. The theory of rational expectations is that expectations of financial prices will be equal to optimal forecasts, which are the best guesses arrived at by using all available information. Because of randomness in financial markets, the actual value of a financial variable is usually different from the optimal forecast. However, the forecast error (the difference between the actual value of the variable and the optimal forecast) will on average be zero.

The Efficient Market Hypothesis: Rational Expectations Applied to Financial Markets

Efficient Markets Hypothesis
The hypothesis that when financial markets are in equilibrium, the prices of financial instruments reflect all readily available information.

The **efficient markets hypothesis** builds on the theory of rational expectations. Namely, when financial markets are in equilibrium, the prices of financial instruments reflect all readily available information. Financial markets are in equilibrium when the quantity demanded of any security is equal to the quantity supplied of that security. Returns reflect only differences in risk and liquidity. As in all markets, prices—in this case, prices of financial instruments—adjust to bring financial markets to equilibrium. In an efficient market, the optimal forecast of a security's price (made by using all available information) will be equal to the equilibrium price.

Let's assume there is a financial instrument, say a share of stock, with an equilibrium return of 15 percent after adjusting for risk and liquidity. The stock clearly offers some combination of more risk and/or less liquidity than another financial asset whose equilibrium return is less than 15 percent. The dollar return in a given time period is equal to the price of the stock at the end minus the price at the beginning plus any dividend payment during that time period. To express this return as a percentage, we need to divide the total return by the price at the beginning of the period, as in Equation (7-3), to get

(7-3) $$R = (P_{t+1} - P_t + D)/P_t$$

where

R = percentage return over the time period

P_{t+1} = price of the stock at the end of the time period

P_t = price of the stock at the beginning of the time period

D = dividend payments made during the time period

If, at the beginning of the time period, we know the price and dividend payment of the stock, the only unknown variable is the price of the stock at the end of the time period (P_{t+1}). The efficient markets hypothesis assumes that expectations of future prices of financial instruments are rational. This is equivalent to assuming that the expected or forecasted price of the stock at the end of the time period will be equal to the optimal forecast of that variable arrived at by using all available information. Thus, if expectations are rational, the expected return on the stock will be equal to the optimal forecast arrived at by plugging the optimal forecast for P_{t+1} into Equation (7-3).

Returning to our example, let's assume that company A announces new profit numbers that raise the expected price of the stock at the end of the time period. The question is, how will today's price respond to the new higher expected price in the future? Assuming that the risk and liquidity of the financial asset has not changed, and that the equilibrium return (based on that risk and liquidity) of A is 15 percent, the present price will adjust so that given the new expected price, the return will still be 15 percent. Thus, the conclusion is that current price will rise to the level so that the optimal forecast of an instrument's return is equal to the instrument's equilibrium return.

http://www.investor home.com/emh.htm. *Provides a historical development of the efficient markets hypothesis.*

To clarify, let's assume that the original price and expected price of A was $100 and that the dividend was $15. Using Equation (7-3), the original return would be 15 percent, which we assumed, given the risk and liquidity of A, was also the equilibrium return. Let's assume that based on the new higher profit numbers, the expected price increases to $115.[10] What will happen to the current price? Based upon our analysis, the current price should rise to a point where the expected return on A remains at its equilibrium return of 15 percent. In this case, we solve for the new current price based on an expected future price of $115 and a dividend of $15. Plugging the numbers into Equation (7-3), we get ($115 - P_t + $15)/P_t = .15 or 15 percent. Solving for P_t, we get $113.04. Thus, the current price will immediately rise to $113.04, given the new higher expected price of $115. When the current price is $113.04, the expected return will be equal to 15 percent. At a price lower than $113.04, the expected return would be higher. For example, at the original price of $100, the expected return would be 30 percent ([$115 - $100 + $15]/$100 = 30 percent). Funds would flow in this market by investors seeking the higher than equilibrium

---

[10]For simplicity, we are assuming that despite the higher profit expectations, the dividend remains the same.

return of 15 percent based on risk and liquidity. As funds flowed in, the price of A would rise. Funds would keep flowing into the market, pushing the price up until the market returned to equilibrium. This occurs at a price of $113.04 because ($115 – $113.04 + 15)/$113.04 = 15 percent.

Two points are worth emphasizing. First, the equilibrium return is based on the risks and liquidity of this financial instrument relative to other financial instruments. Note that we are assuming the risk and liquidity of A has not changed so that the equilibrium return to A, relative to the risk and liquidity of other financial instruments, is 15 percent. Second, current prices adjust when new information that changes current expectations about future prices becomes available.

The rationale behind the efficient markets hypothesis is straightforward. Namely, if current prices do not fully reflect any changes in expectations, some market participants will earn less than what they otherwise would have. There will be unexploited opportunities to gain by purchasing those financial instruments that pay a return above equilibrium. The drive for profits ensures that all opportunities for profit will be exhausted and that prices of all financial instruments will adjust to the equilibrium return, which is the optimal forecast. Now would be a good time to read A Closer Look on the implications of the efficient market hypothesis.

Implications of the Efficient Markets Hypothesis: The efficient markets hypothesis is attractive from an intuitive sense. However, for most investors who want to believe they can consistently get above-average returns, it is unattractive. The implications are that a hot tip will not pan out unless it is based on information that is not readily available. But, buying and selling stocks based on "insider" information (information available only to someone within the corporation) is illegal.

The implications of the efficient markets hypothesis are that prices of financial instruments reflect all readily available information. Thus, if information about an issuer is already expected, when an announcement of the information is made, the announcement will have little or no effect on the instrument's price. For example, if it is believed that the bankruptcy of a firm is imminent, prices of the stocks and bonds of the failing company will already have fallen even before the actual bankruptcy is declared. Thus, prices of financial instruments change dramatically only when "*unexpected information*" becomes available.

The efficient markets hypothesis also implies that it is impossible to beat the market (earn an above-average return). This is because current prices of financial instruments reflect the optimal forecast, using all available information when markets are in equilibrium. If I read a favorable earnings report in the Sunday newspaper, by the time I buy the instrument on Monday morning, its price will already have adjusted so that I will not earn an above-average return.

Whatever the available information, markets are always moving toward an equilibrium of sorts, which can be moving toward or away from previous equilibriums, as factors affecting supply and demand for securities or funds change. A market is really not efficient unless the available information is understood by significant participants. Inasmuch as there is a learning curve in understanding, adapting to, and using information not equally shared, understood, held with equal and unvarying confidence, and subject to imminent change, volatility in the market is to be expected and may even be greater as more information becomes available and is disseminated faster.

The quality of information varies, and when traders are not sure of what they know or don't know, the market can be volatile even without any changes in the available information as confidence levels rise and fall. Add to this the rational or irrational emotions embodied in herd instinct, market momentum, market rotation, guru hypnosis, mythical mottos like "buy on the rumor, sell on the fact," and consensus forecasts, etc.

In areas of the market such as high-technology stocks in the late 1990s and early 2000s, it is unlikely that participants interpreted the available information in the same way.

With increased individual control over pension plans and the rise of managed mutual funds, many market participants make little use of information except for minimal asset allocation and the reputation of a popular guru or fund manager. Consequently, fund managers engage in highly competitive behavior to report good results. Powerful mood swings of pessimism and optimism can, by contagion, sweep the markets and become part of the changing information that affects them.

Averages being what they are, someone is always beating them and someone is always being beaten by them. Whether someone can beat the average consistently is the question. John Maynard Keynes, the well-known economist, said that the true genius is the person who can accurately forecast what the average investor will believe about the direction of the economy or the future profitability of a corporation. In reality, forecasting what the average investor will believe is more important than forecasting what will actually happen.

One final note: When interest rates change, default risk also changes. For example, if the Fed takes action to increase interest rates, the economy slows and the risk of a default increases as the economy slows. Thus, the future income stream from the financial asset becomes less certain. This, in turn, affects the risk premium that the lender will require and, hence, the price of the financial instrument.

The efficient markets hypothesis holds that the prices of all financial instruments are based on the optimal forecast arrived at by using all available information. A **stronger version of the efficient markets hypothesis** holds that the prices of all financial instruments reflect the true fundamental value of the instruments. Thus, not only do prices reflect all available information, but this information is accurate, complete, understood by all, and reflects the market fundamentals. **Market fundamentals** are factors that have a direct effect on future income streams of the instruments. These factors include the value of the assets and the expected income streams of those assets on which the financial instruments represent claims. Thus, if markets are efficient, prices are correct in that they represent underlying fundamentals. In the less stringent version of the hypothesis, the prices of all financial instruments do not necessarily represent the fundamental values of the instruments.

Extraordinary run-ups of stock or bond markets that do not seem to be related to market fundamentals have occurred, such as in Japan in the late 1980s and in the United States in the late 1990s. Some economists point out that such bubbles in financial markets can still be explained by rational expectations. It may be rational to buy a share of stock at a high price, if it is thought that there will be other investors in the future who would be willing to pay inflated prices (prices that exceed those based on market fundamentals) for the stock. This phenomenon is sometimes called the "greater fool" theory.

Other economists suspect that financial market prices may overreact before reaching equilibrium when there is a change in either supply or demand. That is, prices may rise or fall more than market fundamentals would justify before settling down to the price based on fundamentals. In these cases, it may be possible for investors to earn above-average returns or to experience above-average losses.

Stronger Version of the Efficient Markets Hypothesis The theory that the prices of all financial instruments not only reflect the optimal forecast of the financial instrument but also the true fundamental value of the instrument.

Market Fundamentals Factors that have a direct effect on future income streams of the instruments, including the value of the assets and the expected income streams of those assets on which the financial instruments represent claims.

RECAP The efficient market hypothesis states that when financial markets are in equilibrium, the prices of all financial instruments reflect all readily available information. Prices of financial instruments are based on optimal forecasts. The rationale behind the hypothesis is that if prices do not reflect all available information, there may be unexploited profit opportunities. A stronger version of the efficient markets hypothesis holds that prices of financial instruments represent underlying or fundamental values of the asset and the expected income streams of those assets on which the financial instruments represent claims. Bubbles in financial markets, wherein prices seem to exceed fundamental value, can be rational if investors believe that other investors will buy the financial instrument at higher prices. Some believe that financial prices overreact to newly available information.

So far we have seen that according to the efficient market hypothesis, financial prices adjust so that unexploited opportunities for profit are eliminated and financial markets are in equilibrium when the prices of financial instruments are based on optimal forecasts using all available information. In equilibrium, differences in rates of return on financial instruments are based on differences in risk and liquidity. In the next section, we take a broader look at the flow of funds among sectors such as the household, business, government, rest-of-the-world, and financial sectors of the economy. We shall see that there are considerable links between the responses of spending units to changes in prices of financial instruments and the flow of funds among sectors.

The Flow of Funds among Sectors

Flow of Funds
A social accounting system that divides the economy into a number of sectors including the household, business, government, foreign, and financial sectors.

Sources and Uses of Funds Statement
A statement showing the sources and uses of funds for any sector.

Sources of Funds
For any sector, income and borrowing.

Uses of Funds
For any sector, current spending and changes in financial instruments held.

Surplus Sector
A sector where the combined surpluses of the SSUs are greater than the combined deficits of the DSUs.

Deficit Sector
A sector where the combined deficits of the DSUs are greater than the combined surpluses of the SSUs.

The **flow of funds** is a social accounting system that divides the economy into a number of sectors and constructs a **sources and uses of funds statement** for each sector. This section discusses the financial flows of funds among sectors and their relationship to the economy. We then construct a hypothetical sources and uses of funds table for the U.S. economy.

The four main sectors are the household, business, government, and rest-of-the-world sectors.[11] For any sector, the **sources of funds** are current income and borrowing. The **uses of funds** are current spending and changes in financial instruments held. Any sector is composed of both surplus spending units (SSUs) and deficit spending units (DSUs). For any sector, the combined surpluses of the SSUs may be greater than the combined deficits of the DSUs. In this case, the sector would be a **surplus sector.** If the combined deficits of the DSUs are greater than the combined surpluses of the SSUs, the sector is a **deficit sector.**

For *all* sectors combined, however, borrowing (the issuance of financial claims) must be equal to lending (the acquisition of financial assets). This is because each financial claim, in turn, implies the existence of a complementary financial asset. However, in each individual sector, it is highly unlikely that the combined surpluses just equal the combined deficits. Thus, the economy is usually composed of surplus and deficit sectors where the combined surpluses of the surplus sectors is equal to the combined deficits of the deficit sectors for the economy as a whole. Exhibit 7-4 flushes out these relationships.

Although the flow-of-funds accounts divide the economy into nine sectors, Exhibit 7-5 simplifies to the household, business, government, and rest-of-the-world sectors. By adding a fifth sector, the financial sector, along with the others, we can see how intermediation facilitates the flows of funds from the surplus to the deficit sectors and vice versa. Note that for every use of funds, whether for acquiring financial assets or spending on goods and services, there must be a source, and

---

[11]Historically, the rest-of-the-world sector has been called the *foreign sector.* We use the more up-to-date terminology currently employed in the flow-of-funds accounting system maintained by the Fed.

LOOKING BACK: *The Historical Pattern of Surplus and Deficit Sectors*

Historically, the household sector was consistently a surplus sector. However, a relatively large surplus fell consistently in the early 1990s and became a deficit of $67.9 billion in 1997. After a small surplus in 1998, the household sector has continuously run a deficit with the amount equaling around $275 billion in 2000.

The nonfinancial business sector has consistently been a deficit sector with the exception of a few years in the early and mid-1990s. The business sector ran a deficit of $167.3 billion in 2000, and it appears that it will also run a significant deficit in 2001. It is expected that in future years, it will invariably remain a deficit sector.

The government sector was a deficit sector in almost all of the years from 1960 through 1997, and the deficit escalated during the 1980s. During the first quarter of 1998, the combined federal, state, and local government budgets were in surplus for the first time since 1969. During 2000, the federal government surplus was $230 billion. However, many analysts expected the government surpluses to disappear as a result of increased government spending and new tax cuts because of the September 11, 2001 attack on the World Trade Center and the Pentagon, and the resulting economic turmoil.

Since 1982, the rest-of-the-world sector has also been a surplus sector. In the 1990s, the surplus of the rest-of-the-world sector increased from $100 billion in 1992 to $263.6 billion in 1997 to $442 billion in 2000. In 2001, the rest-of-the-world has continued to be a surplus sector.

The combined surpluses of all spending units in the sector > the combined deficits of all spending units in the sector = surplus sector
The combined surpluses of all spending units in the sector < the combined deficits of all spending units in the sector = deficit sector
The combined surpluses of the surplus sectors = the combined deficits of the deficit sectors

For example, if the household and business sectors are deficit sectors and the government and the rest-of-the-world sectors are surplus sectors, the combined deficits of the household and business sectors must equal the combined surpluses of the government and rest-of-the-world sectors.

EXHIBIT 7-4
Surplus and Deficit Sectors

every source is put to some use (if not spending on goods and services, then in acquiring financial instruments). Consequently, total sources and uses of funds are not only equal in each sector, but also in the aggregate for all sectors taken together. Furthermore, the uses of funds by any one sector are the sources of funds for other sectors and vice versa.

For example, the sources for households are income and debt; for business firms, net revenues and borrowings; and for the government, taxes or borrowing. Likewise, each sector has two major uses for funds. Households use funds for spending on consumption and investment or for acquiring financial assets; firms use funds for investment or for acquiring financial assets; the government uses funds for government expenditures or for acquiring financial assets; and the rest-of-the-world sector uses funds to purchase U.S. goods or services or to invest in U.S. securities. The numbers we use in Exhibit 7-5 are hypothetical but somewhat representative of the financial flows between sectors in 2000. As can be seen, the surpluses of the government and rest-of-the-world sectors exactly offset the deficits of the business and household sectors.

http://www.federalreserve.gov
Provides current flow-of-funds data.

http://www.frcenter.org.
Analyzes flow-of-funds data.

SOURCES OF FUNDS	USES OF FUNDS
Households	
Disposable income: $8,200	Consumption spending on nondurables, durables, and services: $8,100
Net borrowing: $275	+
	Investment spending on real assets: $375
Deficit = $275	
Business Firms	
Net revenues: $1,060	Net spending on real assets (plant and equipment): $1,225
+	+
Net borrowing: $220	Net spending on real assets (inventories): $55
Deficit = $220	
Government	
Tax receipts: $3,300	Government spending on goods and services: $1,190
	+
	Government spending on transfer payments: $1,620
	+
	Interest payments on the national debt: $260
	Surplus: $230
Rest-of-the-World	
Foreign purchases of U.S. goods and services: $1,170	U.S. purchases of foreign goods and services: $1,470
+	+
Net foreign purchase of U.S. financial assets: $805	Net U.S. purchases of foreign financial assets: $240
	Surplus = $265
Financial Intermediaries	
Net acquiring of financial assets: $1,080	Net incurring of financial liabilities: $1,080

The financial sector, composed of financial intermediaries, is included to show the extent of financial intermediation in the economy. Financial intermediaries acquire funds to lend by issuing claims on themselves. They use the funds to purchase financial instruments issued by DSUs. As you may have guessed, the extent of financial intermediation in an economy has a direct relationship on the extent of economic development.

The format in Exhibit 7-5 allows us to analyze flows of funds among sectors, how those flows are intermediated, and how the Fed can monitor and influence them. During expansions, both income and interest rates normally rise along with the relative intentions to deficit spend. In recessions, the reverse happens. Nevertheless, no sector of the economy can run larger deficits unless other sectors accept larger surpluses.

LOOKING FORWARD: *The Implications of a Growing Government Surplus*

Much media attention has been devoted to the growing government surpluses in recent years. Most coverage seems to stress the benefits of a growing surplus (such as lower interest rates) and what it means for taxpayers and the public. Some of the questions that are raised are "Should taxes be cut?" "Should the surplus be used to "save" the social security system?" and so on.

Assuming the government sector does indeed continue to run surpluses, the implications are that the other combined sectors must continue to run deficits. In a way, the government sector can continue to run surpluses only if the other sectors are willing to incur deficits. If other sectors do not wish to maintain their level of spending and to continue to increase their level of debt (something highly unlikely), income will fall.

Much household spending has been fueled by the wealth effects associated with the record run-up of stock prices in the late 1990s and 2000. This led to record levels of debt for the household sector. If households rethink their burgeoning levels of debt and reduce their spending, as stock prices fall in 2001, this could indeed have serious consequences for income levels. With income levels falling, businesses would hardly keep up their level of investment spending and borrowing.

When income falls, the government surplus itself will fall as tax receipts decline. The point is that only the future will tell if the forecasted surpluses will materialize. Just as record government deficits of the 1980s and early 1990s were not viewed as healthy for the economy, record surpluses may offer their own malaise in that they may tend to have depressing effects on the level of income if other sectors do not maintain their levels of spending and borrowing. However, in all probability future government surpluses will be much smaller than projected because of the attack on the World Trade Center and the Pentagon on September 11, 2001. The projected surpluses may turn into deficits.

RECAP If the combined surpluses of the SSUs are greater than the combined deficits of the DSUs, the sector is a surplus sector. If the combined deficits of the DSUs are greater than the combined surpluses of the SSUs, the sector is a deficit sector. For all sectors combined, the surpluses must be equal to the deficits. At the present time, the household and business sectors are deficit sectors and the government and the rest-of-the-world sectors are surplus sectors. The combined deficits of the household and business sectors must equal the combined surpluses of the government and rest-of-the-world sectors.

Pulling It All Together

In this chapter, we have looked at the efficient markets hypothesis based on the theory of rational expectations. We have seen that prices of financial instruments adjust so that risk- and liquidity-adjusted returns for all financial instruments are equalized. We then looked at the flow of funds among sectors where the combined surpluses of the surplus sectors are just equal to the combined deficits of the deficit sectors.

Let's return to the example discussed earlier of expansionary monetary policy wherein the Fed takes action that leads to a fall in interest rates. When this occurs, there is a reshuffling of prices of financial instruments. Some spending units decide to spend more in response to the decline in interest rates. Some spending units that were SSUs are enticed to become DSUs. In the aggregate, the surpluses and deficits within any sector change so that a sector that was a surplus sector may become a deficit sector, or vice versa. Thus, actions by the Fed not only influence financial prices but also the flow of funds among sectors. The important point is that there are significant linkages between the response of spending units to changes in interest rates and the flow of funds among sectors.

This completes our look at interest rates and prices of stocks and bonds. We return to stocks and bonds in Chapters 10 and 11. In the next chapter, we look at the determination of foreign exchange rates and their effects on the economy.

Summary of Major Points

- Long-term interest rates are determined by current and expected short-term interest rates. Present short-term rates are determined by national income, the money supply, and inflationary expectations. Expected short-term rates are determined by expectations of those same variables.

- Prices of long-term financial instruments change as current and future expected earnings change. If interest rates fall or rise, prices of previously issued bonds fall or rise. If current and expected future earnings rise, stock prices also rise and vice versa.

- Market participants compare expected rates of return for various financial instruments and select those with the highest expected return consistent with varying degrees of risk and liquidity. In equilibrium, differences in returns on various financial instruments reflect differences in risk and liquidity only.

- Adaptive expectations are formed by looking at current and past prices. Rational expectations are formed by looking at past prices and all currently available information about the economy that may affect prices. The theory of rational expectations states that expectations will be equal to optimal forecasts or the best guesses possible based on all available information.

- The efficient market hypothesis says that when financial markets are in equilibrium, the prices of financial instruments reflect all readily available information. The rationale behind the hypothesis is that if prices do not reflect all available information, there will be unexploited profit opportunities.

- The efficient markets hypothesis does not imply that all participants in the market know the optimal forecast; it is only necessary for a few savvy investors to know the optimal forecast. The efficient market hypothesis implies that it is impossible to maintain an above-average return for a long period of time. Bubbles, investments based on insider information, or market overreaction to new information, are exceptions to the efficient markets hypothesis.

- The flow of funds is a social accounting system that divides the economy into sectors and constructs a sources and uses of funds statement for each sector. For the economy as a whole, the combined surpluses of the surplus sectors must equal the combined deficits of the deficit sectors. When interest rates change, spending changes and some SSUs become DSUs and vice versa. Thus, when deficits and surpluses for individual spending units change in response to interest rate changes, the flow of funds among sectors is affected.

Key Terms

Adaptive Expectations
Deficit Sector
Efficient Markets Hypothesis
Flow of Funds
Market Fundamentals
Optimal Forecast

Rational Expectations
Sources and Uses of Funds
  Statement
Sources of Funds
Stronger Version of the
  Efficient Markets Hypothesis

Surplus Sector
Theory of Rational
  Expectations
Uses of Funds

Review Questions

1. Explain why stock and bond prices adjust until investors are indifferent between stocks and bonds, given varying degrees of risk and liquidity.

2. When full adjustment has occurred, what do differences in returns on various financial instruments reflect?

3. If current and expected earnings rise, what happens to stock prices?

4. Interest rates are going up. What happens to the prices of previously issued bonds?

5. How do adaptive expectations differ from rational expectations?

6. Why is the actual value of a financial variable different from the optimal forecast of that variable? Assuming that expectations are rational, what on average will the difference between the actual value and the optimal forecast be?

7. What is the efficient markets hypothesis? How does it differ from the stronger version of the hypothesis?

8. What is the fundamental value of a financial instrument?

9. What is the rationale behind the efficient markets hypothesis?

10. Explain why the expected return on newly issued and previously issued bonds is the prevailing interest rate plus any expected capital gain or loss.

11. Using the flow-of-funds framework, explain why the combined deficits of the deficit sectors must equal the combined surpluses of the surplus sectors.

12. Must all market participants know the optimal forecast of a financial instrument for the price of the financial instrument to be driven to the optimal forecast?

13. What is a "bubble" in a financial market? Can financial prices ever overshoot or undershoot optimal values?

14. If the household, business, and government sectors are all deficit sectors, what does this imply about the rest-of-the-world sector?

Analytical Questions

15. Assume the equilibrium return on a financial instrument is 10 percent and the instrument pays no dividends or interest. If the current price is $100 and the expected future price 1 year from now just increased from $110 to $120, what will happen to the current price?

16. Assume the equilibrium return on a financial instrument is 10 percent. If the current price is $100 and the instrument does not pay interest or dividend, what is the price expected 1 year from now when the market is in equilibrium? If the equilibrium return on the instrument increases to 15 percent because the instrument is perceived as being more

risky, what happens to the current price, assuming the expected price 1 year from now does not change?

17. News comes out that leads investors to believe that there is more risk involved with owning financial instrument *A*. What will happen to its equilibrium return?

18. Assume that in 2002 through 2005, the government and household sectors run significant surpluses. What does this imply about the other sectors?

Internet Exercise

Go to the Internet site for the Flow of Funds of the United States at **http://www.federalreserve.gov/releases/Z1/.** Go to the *Debt Growth, Borrowing and Debt Outstanding* Tables for the current release. Compare the debt growth rates for the federal government, household, business, and foreign sectors. Verify

for each sector that if a debt growth rate is negative, the total amount of borrowing is negative and the debt outstanding is falling for that sector. Likewise, if a debt growth rate is positive, then borrowing is positive, and the debt outstanding is increasing.

Suggested Readings

For an interesting article about the efficient market hypothesis, see Justin Fox, "Efficient Markets? Hah!" *Fortune*, Vol. 139, Issue 4, March 1, 1999, p. 40.

For an extensive collection of readings on the flow of funds, see John C. Dawson, ed., *Flow-of-Funds Analysis: A Handbook for Practitioners* (New York: M.E. Sharpe, Inc, 1996).

A classic article on the flow of funds between sectors is Lawrence Ritter, "The Structure of the Flow-of-Funds Accounts," *Journal of Finance* 17:2 (May 1963, pp. 219–230).

The Federal Reserve System publishes the *Flow of Funds Account of the United States, Federal Reserve Statistical Release Z.1* on a quarterly basis. These publications make for interesting viewing because of the sometimes dramatic nature of changes in the flows of funds among sectors. They are available in hardcopy from the Fed in March, June, September, and December each year and on the World Wide Web at **http://www.federalreserve.gov.**

The Financial Market Center also puts out a quarterly publication, *Flow of Funds Review and Analysis.* It is available on the World Wide Web at **http://www.fmcenter.org.**

For an article that looks at the rise in the deficit of the U.S. private sector, see Wayne Godley, "Drowning In Debt," *Policy Notes*, Jerome Levy Economics Institute, Annandale-on-the-Hudson, New York, June 2000. This article is also available on the World Wide Web at **http://www.levy.org/docs/pn/00-6.htm.**

chapter

How Exchange Rates Are Determined

8

Learning Objectives *After reading this chapter, you should know:*

• What exchange rates are
• How exchange rates affect prices of imports and exports
• How exchange rates are determined by supply and demand in the foreign exchange market
• The factors that cause exchange rates to change
• What the balance of payments is and why it must balance

“ ”
There are three main causes that dispose men to madness: love, ambition, and the study of foreign exchange.
—Walter Leaf, 1926

The More Things Change, the More Things Stay the Same

Throughout the early and mid–1980s, typical headlines in *The Wall Street Journal* told of the strong dollar, its detrimental effects on U.S. jobs, and the eventual efforts to bring down the "overvalued" dollar. However, by the end of 1987, the value of the dollar had declined to levels experienced in the late 1970s. By the mid-1990s, the dollar had fallen to record lows against many currencies and was at less than half its mid-1980's value against the Japanese yen. In the late 1990s, the dollar again strengthened against the yen and other major currencies, but not nearly to its mid-1980's level. By mid-1998, new headlines reported "U.S. Intervenes in Currency Markets to Support the Sagging Yen." In 2000, the dollar was riding high due to the strength of the U.S. economy. Despite the slowing economy in mid-2001, the dollar remained strong.

Just what does all of this mean to the average person? How do changes in the international value of the dollar affect job opportunities for recent college graduates and other workers? How are domestic interest rates linked with interest rates in the rest of the world, and how are domestic prices affected by foreign prices? Perhaps most importantly, how are all of these questions and their answers related?

Not long ago, such questions and the interactions between the U.S. economy and the rest of the world were largely ignored by most bankers, stock market analysts, economists, accountants, corporate treasurers, policymakers—and textbook writers! The reason was simple but twofold:

1. Trading of goods, services, financial claims (securities), and monies (currencies) between the United States and other countries accounted for only a small portion of total transactions in the United States.

2. Exchange rates between currencies were fixed by the central banks of the various countries and did not change on a day-to-day basis.

Today, the value of the dollar, in terms of other currencies, changes daily. Questions about its value are often puzzling to the average person. Many diverse opinions exist about whether a strong dollar is good or bad for the economy, even though the implications of a strong dollar are not often fully understood. Chapter 8 is included in this section on financial prices because, as we shall see, exchange rates are merely prices (the price of one currency in terms of another) that are determined in a market (the foreign exchange market). As in all markets, prices (foreign exchange rates) are ultimately determined by the forces of supply and demand.

Defining Exchange Rates

Exchange Rate
The number of units of foreign currency that can be acquired with one unit of domestic money.

Foreign Currency (Money)
Supplies of foreign exchange.

Appreciated
When a currency has increased in value relative to another currency.

The **exchange rate** is the number of units of **foreign currency (money)** that can be acquired with one unit of domestic money.[1] In other words, the exchange rate specifies the purchasing power of the dollar in terms of how much it can buy of another currency. For example, if the yen/dollar exchange rate is 100 yen, this literally means that $1 will buy 100 yen.[2] If the exchange rate rises to 150 yen, meaning that $1 will now buy 150 yen, the dollar is said to have **appreciated** relative to the yen. Since it

---

[1]Remember our earlier warnings about market jargon? Well, the problem is acute in the international sphere. For example, note that the definition of foreign currency includes foreign coin, paper currency, and checkable deposits; in contrast, our definition of currency in the United States included paper currency and coin only (Chapter 2).

[2]Exchange rates can also be expressed from the other direction. For example, if $1 will buy 100 yen, then 100 yen will buy $1 and 1 yen will buy $.01 [1/(100 yen) = $.01].

CRACKING THE CODE: *How Movements in the Exchange Rate Affect the Dollar Price of Foreign Goods*

Suppose a Japanese auto costs 2 million yen in Japan. Ignoring transportation costs and the like, what will it cost in the United States? The answer is that the price depends on the exchange rate between the yen and the dollar. The middle row in the following table lists the beginning situation: If the auto costs 2 million yen and $1 buys 100 yen, then, as Equation (8-1) indicates, the dollar price will be $20,000 (2,000,000/100).

The top row in the table shows that when the dollar appreciates from 100 yen to 150 yen, the dollar price of the Japanese auto falls to $13,333 (2,000,000/150). In contrast, as illustrated in the third row, a depreciation of the dollar results in a rise in the dollar price of the Japanese auto.

YEN PRICE OF JAPANESE AUTO (1)	EXCHANGE RATE (2)	DOLLAR PRICE OF JAPANESE AUTO (1)/(2)
2,000,000 yen	$1 = 150 yen	$13,333
2,000,000 yen	$1 = 100 yen	$20,000
2,000,000 yen	$1 = 50 yen	$40,000

will now buy more yen, the dollar's purchasing power has risen or grown stronger. On the other hand, if the yen/dollar exchange rate falls from 100 yen to 50 yen, the dollar is said to have **depreciated** relative to the yen. Since it will now buy fewer yen, the dollar's purchasing power has fallen or grown weaker. Supplies of foreign currencies are called **foreign exchange.**

So what does all of this have to do with the price a U.S. importer will have to pay for Japanese autos? The following handy formula, linking prices and the exchange rate, provides the ingredients necessary to answer the question:

Depreciated
When a currency has decreased in value relative to another currency.

Foreign Exchange
Supplies of foreign currencies.

(8–1)   U.S. dollar price of foreign goods
= foreign price of foreign goods/exchange rate

The accompanying Cracking the Code box utilizes this formula and the hypothetical figures already mentioned to illustrate the key point of this discussion—the U.S. dollar price of a foreign good is inversely related to the exchange rate. More specifically, as the dollar appreciates, the price of foreign goods in the United States falls, even if the foreign price in yen is constant. Conversely, as the dollar depreciates, the price of foreign goods in the United States rises.[3]

Needless to say, the importer and its customers (whether they realize it or not) are affected by changes in the exchange rate. More generally, the exchange rate links the domestic and foreign markets for goods, services, and securities.[4] As a result, changes in the exchange rate will have repercussions in all domestic and foreign markets, including markets for both inputs and outputs. Thus, if the dollar appreciates, U.S. imports (which are now relatively cheaper than before) increase, and U.S. exports to foreign countries (which are now relatively more expensive) decrease. As the dollar becomes stronger, we lose domestic jobs in both the industries in direct competition with the imports and the industries that end up exporting less. Hopefully, we have given you some insight into how these fluctuations affect the U.S. economy. Exhibit 8-1 shows the wide fluctuations in the value of the exchange rate since 1987.

---

[3]To keep things as simple as possible, we are ignoring other factors that might influence the timing and degree to which a change in the exchange rate will actually be passed through into a change in the dollar price.

[4]Does this sound familiar? Recall how the interest rate links the present and the future.

EXHIBIT 8-1

The Exchange Rate since 1987

*Includes Canada, Japan, United Kingdom, Germany, France, Italy, Belgium, Netherlands, Switzerland, Austria, Denmark, Norway, Sweden, Australia, and Spain.

**Through September 28, 2001.

SOURCE: Global Financial Data, Los Angeles, California.

Foreign Exchange Market
The market for buying and selling the different currencies of the world.

To understand these linkages and repercussions, we first must examine what determines the exchange rate. Simply put, the exchange rate, like all prices, is determined by supply and demand. The United States and the rest of the world trade goods, services, and securities. This trading gives rise to a supply of and demand for the various currencies that are traded in the so-called **foreign exchange market.** Specifically, the supply of dollar-denominated funds comes from the demand by U.S. residents for foreign goods, services, and financial claims during a specific time period; the demand for dollar-denominated funds comes from the demand by foreign residents for U.S. goods, services, and financial claims over a period of time. For simplicity, in the remainder of this chapter, we will follow common usage and use the term *dollars* to represent dollar-denominated funds.[5]

 RECAP The exchange rate is the number of units of foreign currency that can be acquired with one unit of domestic money. The U.S. dollar price of foreign goods is equal to the foreign price of foreign goods divided by the exchange rate.

---

[5]In Chapter 2, we defined the dollar as a unit of account by which exchange values of goods and services could be measured. In this chapter, we are talking about the flow of funds—that is, the supply and demand of dollar-denominated funds—not dollars. So, when we use the term *dollars*, we really mean dollar-denominated funds.

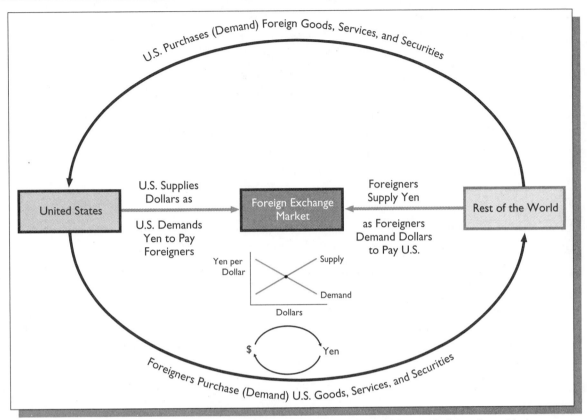

The foreign exchange market facilitates the trading of goods, services, and financial claims (securities) among countries. This global market is woven together by the market makers in foreign currencies—mostly, the foreign exchange departments of the largest commercial banks located in the world's major financial centers, such as New York, London, Frankfurt, and Tokyo. Without the ability to switch funds back and forth among the world's 100-odd currencies, Americans could neither dine in London, sell hot dogs to Japanese tourists, buy imported videocassette recorders, or export computers. Furthermore, they could not buy and sell foreign exchange to speculate on future price (exchange rates) movements.

EXHIBIT 8-2
The Foreign Exchange Market

Determining Exchange Rates

This section identifies and analyzes the most important factors affecting supply and demand in the foreign exchange market and shows how these factors determine exchange rates. Now would be a good time to look at Exhibit 8-2, which shows some of the basics of foreign exchange markets.

To understand how supply, demand, and exchange rates are related, it will be helpful to simplify and just look at how the exchange rate between two currencies is determined. The general framework we develop is directly applicable to the more complex relationships among all national currencies. For example, suppose we know the yen/dollar rate is 100 yen and the mark/dollar rate is 1.5 marks. Then, as demonstrated in the Cracking the Code feature on p. 156, it must follow that the mark/yen rate is .015 marks. This "transitivity" allows us to confine our analysis to two monies. We begin by considering how the exchange rate between the U.S. dollar and the

CRACKING THE CODE: *Finding the Yen/Mark Exchange Rate*

Since $1 = 100 yen and $1 = 1.5 marks, then 100 yen = 1.5 marks. If 100 yen = 1.5 marks, we can find how much 1 yen is worth by dividing both sides of the equation by 100:

$$100/100 \text{ yen} = 1.5/100 \text{ marks}$$
$$1 \text{ yen} = .015 \text{ marks}$$

This is the marks/yen exchange rate.

Likewise, we can find out how much 1 mark is worth by dividing both sides of the equation by 1.5:

$$1.5/1.5 \text{ marks} = 100/1.5 \text{ yen}$$
$$1 \text{ mark} = 67 \text{ yen}$$

Japanese yen is determined, recognizing that our analysis could easily be extended to relationships among more than two currencies.

The Demand for Dollars in the Foreign Exchange Market

Starting with demand, the demand for dollars in international financial markets originates from foreign purchases of U.S. goods, services, and securities. Drawing on Exhibit 8-2, we can write:

(8-2) $\overset{+}{\text{demand for dollars}} = f(\text{foreign demand for U.S. goods, services, and securities})$

The plus (+) sign over the expression simply means that the foreign demand for U.S. goods, services, and securities and the demand for dollars are positively related; when the former rises, the latter will also rise. When foreign demand for U.S. goods, services, and securities falls, the demand for dollars falls.

Now we must consider what happens to the quantity demanded of dollars/month when the exchange rate changes.[6] (Note that the quantity demanded is the amount of dollars that will be demanded at a specific exchange rate.) The answer is that, if we hold other factors constant, the quantity demanded is inversely related to the exchange rate, as depicted in Equation (8-3):

(8-3) $\text{quantity demanded of dollars/month} = f(\overset{-}{\text{exchange rate}})$

This expression says that when the exchange rate goes up, the quantity demanded of dollars/month goes down and vice versa. To see how and why the exchange rate and the quantity demanded of dollars/month are inversely related as

---

[6]In Chapters 2 and 5, we saw that the interest rate can be determined by either a stock model (the supply of and demand for money) or a flow model (the supply of and demand for loanable funds/month). Exchange rate determination is an analogous situation in that the exchange rate can be explained using a stock model, dealing with the supply of and demand for foreign exchange at a particular moment, or a flow model, dealing with flows of foreign exchange over a particular time period. In this chapter, we have opted for the flow model, noting that just as with all stock and flow models, each can generally be converted into the other without loss of substance. We hope you recall that over time, flows generate changes in stocks and that by measuring stocks at two points in time, a flow over time can be determined. For simplicity, we arbitrarily picked 1 month as our time period. The quantity demanded of dollars/month is the amount of dollars that will be demanded at a specific exchange rate.

CRACKING THE CODE: *The Cost of an IBM Computer in Japan*

If an IBM computer costs $1,500 and the yen/dollar exchange rate is 100, then in Japan, assuming transportation costs are zero, the computer will cost 150,000 yen, calculated as follows:

dollar price of U.S. goods × exchange rate = yen price of U.S. goods

$$1,500 \times 100 = 150,000 \text{ yen}$$

If the exchange rate appreciates to 150, the computer will cost 225,000 yen:

$$1,500 \times 150 \text{ yen} = 225,000 \text{ yen}$$

shown in this expression, we need to examine how the exchange rate, and changes therein, affect foreign demand for U.S. goods, services, and securities.

Focusing only on goods to simplify matters, the answer will depend on how the exchange rate affects the prices of U.S. goods in foreign markets—that is, the yen price of U.S. goods in Japan. The following formula provides the key to the entire question:

(8-4) yen (foreign) price of U.S. goods =
dollar price of U.S. goods × exchange rate

For example, as in the Cracking the Code box above, if an IBM computer costs $1,500 in the United States, and the yen/dollar exchange rate is 100 yen—meaning $1 buys 100 yen, or equivalently from a foreign perspective, it takes 100 yen to buy $1—the computer will cost 150,000 yen in Japan (1,500 × 100 yen = 150,000 yen).

To see how the exchange rate affects the foreign demand for U.S. goods and, thus, the quantity demanded of dollars, we need to examine what happens when the dollar appreciates or depreciates. Simply put, an appreciation of the dollar, from 100 yen to 150 yen would raise the yen price of the IBM computer from 150,000 yen to 225,000 yen (1,500 × 150 yen). Following standard tenets of consumer demand theory, we can reasonably assume that foreigners will respond to the price rise by reducing the quantity demanded of U.S. computers/month (and U.S. goods, more generally), thereby reducing the quantity demanded of dollars/month.[7] Conversely, a depreciation of the dollar from 100 yen to 50 yen, would lower the yen price of the IBM computer from the 150,000 yen to 75,000 yen (1,500 × 50 yen). Again, it is reasonable to assume that foreigners will respond to the fall in the yen price by raising the quantity demanded of U.S. computers/month (and U.S. goods, more generally), thereby raising the quantity demanded of dollars/month.[8]

---

[7]Actually, we are also assuming that the demand for computers, and U.S. products in general, is relatively elastic with regard to the exchange rate—that is, as the exchange rate goes up, quantity demanded/month goes down by a larger percentage than the exchange rate goes up, causing total dollar expenditures to fall. This is a reasonable assumption in the long run, although demand for U.S. products may be relatively inelastic in the short run, causing the quantity demanded of dollars to increase as the exchange rate appreciates.

[8]Again, we are assuming that demand for U.S. computers is elastic with regard to the exchange rate—that is, as the exchange rate goes down, the percentage increase in quantity demanded/month is greater than the percentage decrease in the exchange rate and, hence, total dollar expenditures on U.S. computers by foreigners increase.

To sum up to this point, the minus sign over the exchange rate in Equation (8-3) reflects the fact that an appreciation of the dollar will raise the yen price of U.S. goods in Japan and thereby reduce the quantity demanded of U.S. goods and, thus, the quantity demanded of dollars/month. The reverse is also true.

 RECAP The demand for dollars is directly related to foreign demand for U.S. goods, services, and securities. The quantity demanded of dollars/month is inversely related to the exchange rate. The foreign price of U.S. goods is equal to the dollar price of U.S. goods times the exchange rate.

The Supply of Dollars in the Foreign Exchange Market

So much for the demand side—what about supply? In international financial markets, the supply of dollars originates from domestic purchases of foreign goods, services, and financial securities, as depicted in Equation (8-5):

(8-5)   supply of dollars/month =
f (U.S. demand f$\overset{+}{\text{o}}$r foreign goods, services, and securities)

As before, the plus sign over the expression means that U.S. demand for foreign goods, services, and securities and the supply of dollars in the foreign exchange market are positively related. When the former rises, the latter rises. This occurs because when U.S. demand for foreign goods, services, and securities rises, the demand for yen to pay for those foreign goods, services, and securities also rises. But how do U.S. residents get more yen? The short simple answer is by supplying more dollars! (Remember, dollars are being supplied to purchase yen to purchase foreign goods.) You should be able to explain why a drop in the U.S. demand for foreign goods (in this case, Japanese goods) will lead to a decrease in the supply of dollars.

The next step is to consider how the quantity supplied of dollars/month is affected by changes in the exchange rate. (Note that quantity supplied is the amount of dollars that will be supplied/month at a specific exchange rate.) The answer is that, if we hold other things constant, the quantity supplied is directly related to the exchange rate, as shown in Equation (8-6):

(8-6)   quantity supplied of dollars/month = f (excha$\overset{+}{\text{n}}$ge rate)

To see why the exchange rate and the quantity supplied of dollars/month are positively related, we need to examine how changes in the exchange rate affect U.S. demand for foreign goods, services, and securities. Focusing again only on goods for simplicity, we can draw on the Cracking the Code Box on p. 153 and the discussion of Equation (8-1). As we saw, the dollar price of foreign goods in the United States is equal to the yen price divided by the exchange rate. Thus, as the exchange rate rises, the dollar price of foreign goods falls. Accordingly, we would expect U.S. residents to increase the quantity demanded of foreign goods/month, which in turn will raise the quantity of dollars supplied/month to the foreign exchange market.[9] Conversely, a fall in the exchange rate will raise

---

[9]We are also making the reasonable assumption that the quantity demanded of foreign goods/month by U.S. residents increases by a larger percentage than the percentage increase in the exchange rate. Thus, as the exchange rate appreciates, the quantity supplied of dollars/month also increases. This assumption, which is reasonable in the long run, may not hold in the short run.

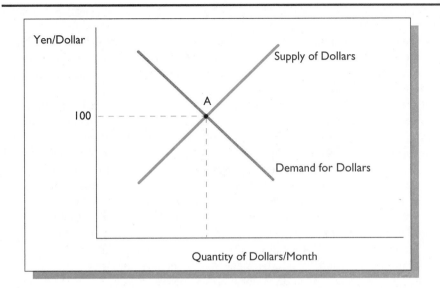

EXHIBIT 8-3
The Market
for Dollars

the dollar price of foreign goods in the United States, thereby lowering the quantity demanded of foreign goods/month and, thus, the quantity supplied of dollars/month.[10]

We have established an inverse relationship between the quantity demanded of dollars/month and the exchange rate. In addition, given our assumptions, we have confirmed a direct relationship between the quantity supplied of dollars/month and the exchange rate. These relationships are graphed in Exhibit 8-3, which depicts the determination of the equilibrium exchange rate. The foreign exchange market "clears" at the exchange rate where the demand and supply curves intersect. At this exchange rate, the quantity demanded of dollars/month is equal to the quantity supplied of dollars/month, and we have market equilibrium (at point *A*). At any other exchange rate, there is either a surplus or a shortage of dollars. Market forces generated by the surplus or shortage will cause changes in the exchange rate, which will continue until equilibrium is reached.

RECAP The supply of dollars is directly related to U.S. demand for foreign goods, services, and securities. The quantity supplied of dollars/month is directly related to the exchange rate other factors held constant.

We have made a good start, but our ultimate objective is to understand the causes and consequences of changes in the exchange rate resulting from changes in supply or demand. Accordingly, we need to examine the factors that can cause the supply and demand curves for dollars in the foreign exchange market to shift.

---

[10]Again, we are assuming that the percentage decrease in quantity demanded of foreign goods/month is greater than the percentage decrease in the exchange rate, causing the quantity supplied of dollars/month to fall.

CRACKING THE CODE: *The Foreign Exchange Market*

Suppose that you need pounds for an upcoming trip to England. You call your local bank, say, in Nashville, Tennessee, and place a buy order for 1,000 pounds. Most likely, your local bank does not have a foreign exchange department, so it will call its correspondent bank that specializes in international transactions and place an order for pounds with Citibank's foreign exchange department.[a]

Most foreign currency transactions in the United States are executed by the foreign exchange departments of the largest banks, which are linked via modern telecommunications with foreign exchange dealers around the world. Accustomed to handling transactions from around the globe daily, they stand ready to buy or sell dollars and foreign currencies at the prevailing exchange rate. Acting as auctioneers, they (and other dealers nationwide and worldwide) are prepared to adjust the exchange rate up as buy orders for dollars rise relative to sell orders, or adjust the exchange rate down as buy orders for dollars fall relative to sell orders. Of course, this is just another way of saying that the exchange rate will change as supply and/or demand changes.

So how much will your 1,000 pounds cost? If you could "crack the code" in the relevant table in *The Wall Street Journal*, you could figure out the approximate cost. We have reproduced a portion of the foreign exchange table that appeared in the *Journal* on December 13, 2001. As noted at the top of the table, it shows the exchange rates as of 4 P.M. Eastern time the preceding business day, Wednesday, December 12, 2001.

To find the exchange rate between the pound and the dollar on Wednesday, look at the fourth column ("Currency per U.S. $: Wed") in the highlighted row. The exchange rate was .6913, meaning $1 purchased .6913 pounds. Accordingly, 1,000 pounds would have cost $1,446.55 (1,000 pounds/.6913). By comparing the fourth column with the last column ("Tue"), we see that the dollar depreciated a bit on Wednesday as compared to the previous Tuesday. On Tuesday, $1 purchased .6949 pounds, slightly more than on Wednesday. Accordingly, if you had bought the 1,000 pounds on Tuesday, you would have paid slightly less than on Wednesday ($1,439.06 = 1,000 pounds/.6949).

Note that the dollar exchange rate (the number of units of foreign currency $1 can buy), shown in the fourth and fifth columns, is simply the reciprocal of the pound exchange rate (the number of dollars that can be purchased with 1 pound or, equivalently, the number of dollars needed to purchase 1 pound), shown in the second and third columns ("U.S. $ equiv."). Thus, on Tuesday, .6949 pounds to the dollar is the reciprocal of $1.4391 to the pound ($1.4391 = 1/.6949). Given this property, a depreciation of the dollar means $1 buys fewer pounds, or equivalently, it costs more ($1.4466) to buy 1 pound on Wednesday. It is crucial for you to see that these are two ways of saying the same thing.

Changes in the exchange rate have profound implications for any transactions between the two currencies. For example, suppose a hotel room in England cost 100 pounds on February 28, 2005, and is the same price 1 year later on February 28, 2006. If the pound/dollar exchange rate has changed from $1 = 2 pounds in 2005 to $1 = 1 pound in 2006, the traveler from the United States pays more for the room in 2006 (100 pounds/1 = $100 in 2006 compared to 100 pounds/2 = $50 in 2005).[b]

Exchange Rates
Wednesday, December 12, 2001

The New York foreign exchange selling rates below apply to trading among banks in amounts of $1 million and more, as quoted at 4 P.M. Eastern time by Reuters and other sources. Retail transactions provide fewer units of foreign currency per dollar.

Country	U.S. $ EQUIV.		CURRENCY PER U.S. $	
	Wed	Tue	Wed	Tue
England (Pound)	1.4466	1.4391	.6913	.6949

[a]A correspondent bank is merely a large bank, usually located in an important financial center, which provides the smaller bank with various services.

[b]The institutional details should be mentioned. First, the exchange rate quotations in the paper are for large, so-called wholesale transactions of $1 million or more among banks, as noted at the top of the table. The "retail" cost of purchasing marks for you or for us would be slightly higher than these quotes.

SOURCE: *The Wall Street Journal*, December 13, 2001, p. C14.

Changes in Supply and Demand and How They Affect the Exchange Rate

Let's first consider how and why changes in the supply of dollars in the foreign exchange market affect the exchange rate. The initial question to address is, what factors, in addition to the exchange rate, could cause U.S. residents to alter their demand for foreign goods, services, and securities and thus their supply of dollars in the foreign exchange market? In other words, what factors could cause the supply curve of dollars to shift? Previous research suggests that the following factors play a major role:

1. *Changes in U.S. real income.* Changes in U.S. real income and changes in the supply of dollars are positively related. As real income grows in the United States, households and firms have more funds to spend and save. Accordingly, they will demand more U.S. goods, services, and securities and more foreign goods, services, and securities. Thus, as U.S. real income grows, the supply of dollars will increase because U.S. residents now have more income to spend on imports. Likewise, as U.S. real income falls, the supply of dollars will decrease.

2. *Changes in the dollar price of U.S. goods relative to the dollar price of foreign goods.* Simply put, if the prices of U.S. goods rise relative to the dollar prices of foreign goods, U.S. residents will demand more foreign goods and, therefore, supply more dollars in the foreign exchange market because foreign goods are now relatively cheaper than U.S. goods. Holding the exchange rate constant, what could cause such changes in relative prices? If you said a higher inflation rate in the United States than in Japan, you are right! Likewise, using similar reasoning, if the inflation rate in the United States falls relative to that of Japan, U.S. residents will supply fewer dollars in the foreign exchange market.

3. *Changes in foreign interest rates relative to U.S. interest rates.* As foreign interest rates rise relative to U.S. rates, foreign securities become relatively more attractive. Accordingly, U.S. residents will buy more foreign securities and, thus, supply more dollars. Likewise, if foreign rates fall relative to U.S. rates, the supply of dollars decreases. To be more precise, U.S. residents will compare interest rates in the United States, i_{US}, with the expected return on foreign securities. The latter consists of the foreign interest rate, i_F, minus the expected appreciation (if any) in the value of the dollar.

For a graphical presentation of this analytical discussion of supply, see Exhibit 8-4. Study it carefully before moving on to the discussion of the demand for dollars.

Using the same logic and analytical framework, we now ask what factors, in addition to the exchange rate, could cause foreigners to alter their demand for U.S. goods, services, and securities and, thus, their demand for dollars in the foreign exchange market? Remember that changes in the demand for dollars cause the demand curve for dollars to shift. Let's begin by identifying the major factors that can alter demand:

1. *Changes in foreign real income.* Changes in foreign real income and the demand for dollars are positively related. For example, if foreign real incomes rise, foreign firms and households will have more funds to spend and save. Accordingly, they will demand more of their own goods, services, and securities and also more imported goods, services, and securities. Thus, as foreign real incomes grow, the demand for dollars, reflecting the increased supply of yen to execute transactions, will grow.[11] Following similar reasoning, if foreign incomes fall, the demand for dollars will also fall.

---

[11]We are assuming that U.S. goods are not inferior goods. Recall from your principles class that demand for inferior goods, such as bologna, falls as income increases.

EXHIBIT 8-4
Changes in the
Exchange Rate: The
Role of Changes in
Supply

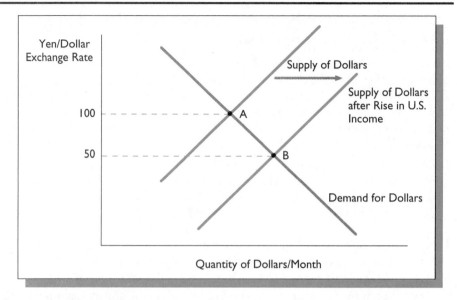

This exhibit begins with an initial equilibrium exchange rate of 100 yen. Assume that the equilibrium is now disturbed by a change in one of the factors that affect the supply of dollars, say, a rise in U.S. income, which increases the supply of dollars, as shown by the rightward shift of the supply curve. The new equilibrium at point B results in a depreciation of the dollar, as the equilibrium exchange rate falls from 100 yen to 50 yen. Note that a rise in the prices of U.S. goods relative to the dollar prices of foreign goods, or a rise in foreign interest rates relative to U.S. interest rates, would have produced a similar increase in supply and depreciation of the exchange rate.

2. *Changes in the foreign (yen) price of foreign goods relative to the foreign price of U.S. goods.* Changes in, say, the yen price of Japanese goods relative to the yen price of U.S. goods and the demand for dollars are positively related. To see why, assume inflation accelerates in Japan while there is no inflation in the United States. The Japanese inflation will raise the yen price of Japanese goods relative to the yen price of U.S. goods. As a result, foreigners will demand more U.S. goods and, thus, more dollars. If U.S. inflation rises relative to inflation in Japan, foreigners will demand fewer dollars.

3. *Changes in U.S. interest rates relative to foreign interest rates.* A positive relationship also exists between changes in U.S. interest rates relative to foreign rates and the demand for dollars. For example, suppose that initially the interest rate on both foreign government bonds and U.S. Treasury bonds is 6 percent. Portfolio managers in Japan, noticing the identical rates and recognizing the benefits of diversification, hold some of both types of bonds in their portfolios. Now interest rates in the United States rise. As a result, the demand for U.S. securities and, thus, the demand for dollars, rise. Likewise, if interest rates in Japan fall, the demand for dollars rises.

These points are illustrated graphically in Exhibit 8-5. Study this exhibit carefully before moving on. Make sure you note the similarities between the factors that cause changes in the demand for dollars and the factors that cause changes in the supply of dollars.

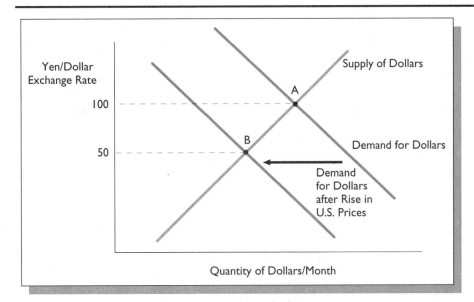

EXHIBIT 8-5
Changes in the
Exchange Rate: The
Role of Changes in
Demand

Assume that the initial equilibrium at point A is disturbed by a change in one of the
factors that affect the demand for dollars. In particular, suppose that the yen price of
U.S. goods rises relative to the yen price of foreign goods because of inflation in the
United States. As a result, foreigners' demand for U.S. goods declines, as shown by the
leftward shift of the demand curve. The new equilibrium (point B) results in a
depreciation of the dollar from 100 yen to 50 yen. Note that a fall in foreign incomes
or a rise in foreign interest rates relative to U.S. rates would have produced a similar
leftward shift in the demand curve and depreciation of the dollar.

RECAP Increases in U.S. real income, in U.S. prices relative to foreign prices,
and in foreign interest rates relative to U.S. interest rates all increase the supply of dollars and vice versa. Increases in foreign real income, in foreign prices
relative to U.S. prices, and in U.S. interest rates relative to foreign interest rates
all increase the demand for dollars and vice versa.

We have covered some important material, so now is a good time to stop and see
how we can use this analysis. Suppose that the U.S. economy is expanding at a relatively slow pace, with real GDP growing at a 1 to 2 percent annual rate, compared to
its potential growth trend of 2 1/2 to 3 percent. Against this background, the Federal
Reserve decides that a rise in the aggregate demand for goods and services is in order.
Accordingly, the Fed pursues a more stimulative monetary policy by increasing bank
reserves and the money supply. We know from previous chapters that such actions
will initially tend to lower interest rates. The question we want to focus on in the
present context is how the fall in U.S. interest rates will affect the exchange rate.

Believe it or not, the answer flows directly from the preceding discussion of
changes in supply and demand. The fall in U.S. interest rates relative to interest
rates in Japan will lead to a depreciation of the dollar—that is, a fall in the exchange
rate. The reasoning is as follows: The fall in U.S. rates reduces the attractiveness
of U.S. securities relative to foreign securities. As a result, foreigners will demand
fewer U.S. securities and, thus, will demand fewer dollars in the foreign exchange
market, while U.S. residents will demand more foreign securities and, thus, will
supply more dollars in the foreign exchange market. In sum, the dollar depreciates
as a result of the reduction in the demand for and rise in the supply of dollars

induced by the Fed's actions. Try sketching out this scenario graphically as in Exhibits 8-4 and 8-5. If the Fed's policy works, output will expand, income will grow, and demand for imports will rise, all of which will potentially further weaken the dollar, especially if the policy fuels expectations of inflation.

We have examined rather carefully the variety of domestic and foreign factors that taken together determine the exchange rate. We would be remiss if we failed to point out that changes in the factors that affect exchange rates are ongoing and, therefore, changes in exchange rates are ongoing. In reality, demands and supplies are changing all the time, so equilibrium is a constantly moving target. For example, changes in U.S. real incomes lead to changes in other countries' real incomes, which lead to changes in U.S. incomes, which lead to changes in . . . and so on. The interrelationships and interactions are increasingly significant as the world's economies become more intertwined. Now would be a good time to read A Closer Look, which discusses a theory of how exchange rates adjust in the long run.

Purchasing Power Parity: The theory of *purchasing power parity* asserts that in the long run, exchange rates adjust so that the relative purchasing power of various currencies is equalized. Thus, after full adjustment among all currencies, one currency, such as the dollar, will purchase the same market basket of goods and services in every country.

An example will help to clarify. Assume that inflation is 5 percent in the European Union and 3 percent in the United States. After the inflation and at the original exchange rate, relative prices in the European Union are roughly 2 percent higher than those in the United States. As we saw earlier in the chapter, the U.S. demand for the relatively more expensive European imports will decline and the foreign demand for relatively cheaper U.S. exports will increase. Thus, the demand for dollars will increase and the supply of dollars will decrease. As a result, the dollar will appreciate in terms of the euro. The question is "how much will the dollar appreciate?" According to purchasing power parity, the dollar should then appreciate by 2 percent, thus exactly offsetting the higher European inflation relative to the United States (5 percent – 3 percent = 2 percent) and leaving the relative purchasing power between the dollar and the euro unchanged.

The theory of purchasing power parity is based on many, often unrealistic, assumptions. These assumptions include that the goods are identical, that all goods and services are tradable, that there are no transportation costs and no barriers to trade such as tariffs, and that exchange rates are influenced only by relative inflation rates across the various countries.

In addition to the unrealistic assumptions, the theory suffers from a lack of completeness because it neglects factors that can and do cause exchange rates to vary significantly over time. These factors include changes in productivity, economic growth, market structures, and technologies across countries, and shifts in factor supplies causing commodity price shocks. Furthermore, the theory does not account for changes in tastes among countries.

Every year, the *Economist* news magazine publishes an interesting and fun Big Mac currency index based on the purchasing power parity theory. According to the theory, the dollar price of a Big Mac, the signature hamburger of the McDonald's chain, should be the same in all of the 120 countries around the world where the Big Mac is sold. Following is the most recent table from the March issue of the *Economist*.[12] To find the dollar price of a Big Mac, the price in the local currency is merely divided by the exchange rate. If the dollar price of a Big Mac is less than the $2.55 U.S. price, the currency is thought to be undervalued in terms of the U.S. dollar. Likewise, if the dollar price of a Big Mac is more, the currency is thought to be overvalued.

[12]*The Economist*, January 13, 2001.

As the table shows, the dollar price of a Big Mac around the world varies from $1.06 in the Philippines to $3.52 in Israel. Hence, according to the Big Mac index, the currency in the Philippines is thought to be undervalued by 53 percent ([$2.55 − $1.06]/$2.55 = .58). Is this the result of vestiges of the Asian currency crisis of

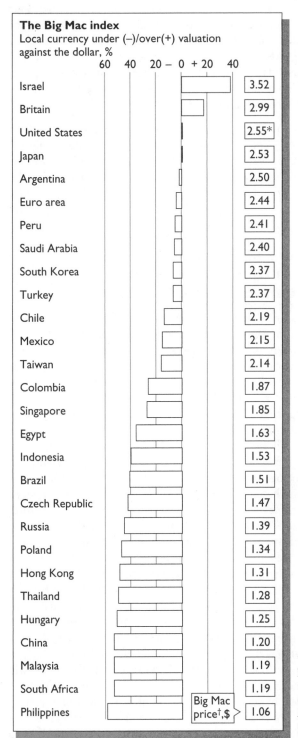

The Big Mac index
Local currency under (−)/over(+) valuation against the dollar, %

Country	Big Mac price†,$
Israel	3.52
Britain	2.99
United States	2.55*
Japan	2.53
Argentina	2.50
Euro area	2.44
Peru	2.41
Saudi Arabia	2.40
South Korea	2.37
Turkey	2.37
Chile	2.19
Mexico	2.15
Taiwan	2.14
Colombia	1.87
Singapore	1.85
Egypt	1.63
Indonesia	1.53
Brazil	1.51
Czech Republic	1.47
Russia	1.39
Poland	1.34
Hong Kong	1.31
Thailand	1.28
Hungary	1.25
China	1.20
Malaysia	1.19
South Africa	1.19
Philippines	1.06

*Average of Atlanta, Chicago, New York and San Francisco.
† At market exchange rate (Jan 8th 2001) *The Economist* using McDonald's price data.
SOURCE: *The Economist,* January 13, 2001.

1997–1998? While most currencies of emerging economies appear to be undervalued, the currency of Israel is, according to the Big Mac index, overvalued by 38 percent ([\$2.55 − \$3.52]/\$2.55 = −.38). The theory of purchasing power parity does not seem to be able to explain these disparities.

The Big Mac index is also flawed by the unrealistic assumptions and the lack of completeness of the purchasing power parity theory. For example, not all Big Macs taste the same in all countries. Local customs and tastes dictate a large part of the result. In some countries, Big Macs are quite spicy. (In others, mayonnaise is served with McDonald's french fries.) Likewise, there can be large differences in local sales taxes, trade barriers on beef, and differences in local labor and rent costs.

Thus, more factors, in addition to purchasing power parity, need to be considered in explaining exchange rate differentials and movements.

The next logical question is how developments in international trade and finance, reflected in the transactions occurring in foreign exchange markets and changes in the exchange rate, affect the U.S. financial system and the output and factor markets. The short, albeit superficial, answer is "dramatically." (Recall that a depreciation of the exchange rate causes the demand for exports to rise and the demand for imports to fall.) To develop a more informative response, it will be helpful to examine an often-mysterious concept discussed in the next section.

Defining the Balance of Payments and Its Influence on the Exchange Rate, the Financial System, and the U.S. Economy

Balance of Payments
The record of transactions between the United States and its trading partners in the rest of the world over a particular period of time.

The supply and demand forces that determine the exchange rate are reflected in the **balance of payments.** Simply put, the balance of payments for the United States is the record of transactions between the United States and its trading partners in the rest of the world over a particular period of time, such as a year. It is a record of the international flow of funds for purchases and sales of goods, services, and securities.

The accounting procedure underlying the balance of payments is based on a standard double-entry bookkeeping scheme, such as that used by business firms or households to record receipts and payments. This means that receipts (sources of funds such as income or borrowing) will, by definition, equal payments (uses of funds). In the balance of payments, all transactions that result in payments by foreigners to Americans are recorded as receipts; they are *credit* or plus items. Examples of such transactions include foreign purchases of U.S. goods, called **merchandise exports;** foreign purchases of U.S. securities (in effect, exports of securities); and expenditures by foreign tourists in the United States (in effect, exports of services). All transactions resulting in payments by Americans to foreigners are recorded as payments; they are negative or **debit** items. Examples of such payments include U.S. purchases of foreign goods called **merchandise imports;** U.S. purchases of foreign securities (in effect, imports of securities), and expenditures by U.S. residents traveling abroad.

Merchandise Exports
Foreign purchases of U.S. goods.

Debit
In the balance of payments, any transaction that results in a payment to foreigners by Americans.

Merchandise Imports
U.S. purchases of foreign goods.

Over the years, government statisticians and analysts have found it useful to divide the balance of payments into several parts by grouping various types of receipts and payments into particular accounts. These accounts are discussed in the following section and shown in Exhibit 8-6, which provides a simplified and hypothetical balance of payments for the United States. Note that for now we will ignore government transactions in foreign currencies—the so-called Official Reserve Account of the balance of payments. This complication will be taken up when we discuss international policy in Chapter 13. The balance of payments may seem imposing at first, but as we take a closer look at the various accounts, you will find that it is not so formidable.

ACCOUNT	COMPONENT	RECEIPTS	PAYMENTS	BALANCE
		Use of $ by foreigners	Sources of $ by foreigners	
Current	(2) Merchandise exports	+$400		(4) Balance of trade:
	(3) Merchandise imports		−600	(2) + (3) = −$200
	(5) Net exports of services	+ $50		(6) Balance of goods and services:
				(4) + (5) = −$150 = net exports
	(7) Net unilateral transfers		−$30	(1) Balance on current account:
				(6) + (7) = − $180
Capital	(9) Capital inflows	+$280		(8) Balance on capital account:
	(10) Capital outflows		−$100	(9) + (10) = $180
		Total uses	Total sources	
Balance of payments		+ $730	−$730	(1) + (8) = 0

EXHIBIT 8-6
A Hypothetical and Simplified Balance of Payments for the U.S. Economy in the Year 2005 (in Billions of Dollars)

The Current Account

The **current account** brings together transactions that involve currently produced goods and services. It is composed of exports and imports of goods and services, and **net transfer payments** (also called *net unilateral transfers*). The difference between merchandise exports and imports, often referred to in news reports as the **trade balance,** is taken by many observers to be an important indicator of a country's ability to compete internationally in the production and sale of goods. When merchandise imports are greater than exports, as they have been in the United States for some years, a country has a **trade deficit,** suggesting some deterioration in international competitiveness. It could just as well suggest an improvement in the country's ability to attract foreign investment. The hypothetical figure in Exhibit 8-6 shows a U.S. trade deficit—indicated by (4) in the exhibit—of $200 billion. In contrast, if exports are greater than imports, as has been the case in Japan for some time, a country has a **trade surplus,** suggesting that it is competing successfully in the world economy or that its citizens are investing heavily abroad.

When net exports of services (5), involving tourism, transportation, insurance, and financial services, are added to the trade balance (4), we get the **balance of goods and services** (6), which is often referred to as "net exports." If net exports are negative, as they were in the United States throughout the 1980s and 1990s, then we are buying more goods and services from foreigners than they are buying from the United States. Relatively speaking, the result is that GDP and, thus, production and employment in the United States, are lower than they would have been if net exports had been less negative.[13]

Current Account
Transactions that involve currently produced goods and services, including the balance of goods and services.

Net Transfer Payments
In the current account, the difference between transfer payments received from and transfer payments made to foreigners; also called net unilateral transfers.

Trade Balance
The difference between merchandise exports and imports.

Trade Deficit
When merchandise imports are greater than exports.

Trade Surplus
When merchandise exports are greater than imports.

Balance of Goods and Services
Net exports of services plus the trade balance.

---

[13]Don't let the terminology confuse you: Less negative refers to a smaller trade deficit of goods and services, meaning either more exports or fewer imports and, hence, more U.S. jobs and production in either the domestic exporting industries or those industries competing with imports. If the United States were running a trade surplus of goods and services, the greater the surplus, the greater would be the stimulus to U.S. GDP.

LOOKING OUT: *The Path to a Single European Currency*

In 1979, the *European Monetary System* was established to increase exchange rate stability among countries in Western Europe. Under the system, individual currencies had limited flexibility, and central banks intervened by buying and selling currencies if exchange rates moved outside a narrow band. If fundamental imbalances existed, exchange rates were changed to correct the imbalances. In that same year, the *European Currency Unit (ECU)* was created. The ECU was an accounting unit made up of a weighted basket of currencies. The weights were determined by the gross domestic product and other real and financial variables of the participating countries. It was hoped that the ECU would eventually lead to the creation of a single currency.

In the *Maastricht Treaty of 1991*, 15 European countries agreed to a plan to adopt a single European currency by no later than 1999.[a] During the phase-in period, the countries maintained exchange rates within a narrow range of the ECU.[b] As of January 1, 1999, 11 countries participated in the currency union. Exchange rates of the 11 participating countries were fixed and no longer fluctuated, even within a narrow range. In addition, the newly established European Central Bank, together with the national central banks, formed the Eurosystem, which took over the formulation of monetary policy. Although the new currency did not yet circulate, all newly issued stocks and government bonds, bank accounts, corporate books, credit card payments, and mortgages could be figured in *euros*.[c]

The euro did begin circulating on January 1, 2002. Europeans had until March 1, 2002, to exchange their own national currencies for euros. After that date, the national currencies will no longer be accepted as money.

To participate in the single currency, countries had to meet criteria, including having annual budget deficits not greater than 3 percent of GDP and a government debt less than 60 percent of GDP or moving toward that goal. Of the 15 countries that signed the Maastricht Treaty, Great Britain, Denmark, and Sweden decided not to participate in the currency union. Greece did not meet the criteria to join on January 1, 1999. However, Greece became the twelfth country to participate in the currency union when it was able to join on January 1, 2001.

In giving up their national currencies, countries are surrendering the right to determine their own national interest rates, exchange rates, and monetary policies. In addition, they are giving up some control over the size of their budget deficits. For example, countries may not be able to run fiscal deficits as large or lower interest rates as much as they would like in the face of unemployment, and they definitely will not be able to devalue national currencies!

Despite these potential disadvantages, the countries supported the common currency because it will lead to tremendous reductions in the transactions costs of making exchanges. Such reductions translate to higher economic growth. According to *Business Week,* "In one fell swoop, it [the euro] will create the world's second-largest economic zone. The potential benefits are limitless—and so are the risks."[d]

[a]The following countries signed the Maastricht Treaty: Austria, Belgium, Denmark, Finland, France, Germany, Great Britain, Greece, Ireland, Italy, Luxembourg, the Netherlands, Portugal, Spain, and Sweden.
[b]A currency crisis in 1992 caused the band to be widened from 2.5 percent to 15 percent.
[c]Recall the picture of the new euro that appeared in Chapter 3 and the discussion of the Eurosystem in Chapter 4.
[d]"The Euro," *Business Week,* April 27, 1998, pp. 90–94.

Net transfer payments are the difference between transfers received from foreigners and transfers made to foreigners including payments such as U.S. government aid to foreigners, aid from foreign governments to the United States, and private charitable relief. Adding net unilateral transfers (7) to the balance of goods and services, or net exports (6) yields the **balance on current account** (1), which in our example is in deficit by $180 billion.

Balance on Current Account
The balance of goods and services plus net unilateral transfers.

The Capital Account

Capital Account
The financial flow of funds and securities between the U.S. and the world.

The **capital account** summarizes the financial flow of funds and securities between the United States and the rest of the world. The globalization of the U.S. financial system—a fancy term to describe the tremendous growth of international lending and borrowing—is reflected in the surge of U.S. investment in international stocks, bonds, and mutual funds, and the increased borrowing abroad by U.S. entities to fund the U.S. current account deficit.

Purchases of U.S. financial securities by foreigners and, more generally, borrowing from foreign sources by U.S. firms and residents, result in **capital inflows** into the United States; these are receipt (credit or plus) items in the capital account, as shown in Exhibit 8-6. Purchases of foreign financial securities by U.S. residents and borrowing by foreigners from U.S. banks and other sources result in **capital outflows** from the United States; these are payment (debit or negative) items in the capital account. In our hypothetical example in Exhibit 8-6, the balance on capital account (8), which is equal to the difference between capital inflows and capital outflows, is in surplus by $180 billion—and the United States is experiencing a **net capital inflow.**

Capital Inflows
Purchases of U.S. financial securities by foreigners and borrowing from foreign sources by U.S. firms and residents.

Capital Outflows
Purchases of foreign financial securities by U.S. residents and borrowing by foreigners from U.S. banks and other domestic sources.

Net Capital Inflow
When there is a surplus in the capital account and capital inflows exceed capital outflows.

RECAP The balance of payments for the United States is the record of transactions between the United States and its trading partners in the rest of the world over a particular time period. The balance of payments consists of the current account and the capital account. The current account brings together transactions involving currently produced goods and services. It includes the balance of goods and services and unilateral transfers. The capital account measures the flow of funds and securities between the United States and the rest of the world.

So much for the components of the balance of payments. What do they have to do with the exchange rate and U.S. markets? Believe it or not, the various tools of analysis necessary to answer this question have already been developed. All we need to do is to bring them together.

The Balance of Payments and the Exchange Rate

Take a careful look at the bottom line in Exhibit 8-6. Not surprisingly, it says that the balance of payments balances; the hypothetical $180 billion deficit in the current account (1) is exactly offset by a $180 billion surplus in the capital account (8).[14] Another way of saying the same thing is that the sum of all the items in the receipts-from-foreigners column is exactly equal to the sum of all the items in the payments-to-foreigners column.

To see why this equality is not just the result of bookkeeping gimmickry and why it relates directly to the determination of the exchange rate and the role it plays in our economy, note that all of the items in the receipts column in Exhibit 8-6 represent foreign demands for U.S. goods, services, and securities—the very items that determine the demand for dollars in the foreign exchange market. Similarly, all of the items in the payments column represent U.S. demands for foreign goods, services, and securities—the very items that determine the supply of dollars in the foreign exchange market. Assuming that the exchange rate is flexible and free to move in response to any change in demand or supply, it will move to that rate where the quantity of dollars demanded/month is equal to the quantity of dollars supplied/month. Put in terms of Exhibit 8-6, the equilibrium exchange rate will change until the sum of all the items in the receipts column, which reflects the quantity of dollars demanded/month, is equal to the sum of all the items in the payments column, which

---

[14]Remember, we are ignoring any official government transactions in foreign exchange markets until Chapter 19.

LOOKING BACK: *The Gold Standard*

During the late nineteenth and early twentieth centuries, the United States, along with the other major world economies, was on a gold standard that lasted about 30 years. Under the gold standard, the amount of currency in circulation was backed by gold. Each country defined its currency in terms of gold and agreed to buy or sell unlimited quantities of gold at a pre-established price, called the *par value*.

A gold standard is a type of fixed exchange rate system. For example, if 1 ounce of gold in the United States is equal to $20 and 1 ounce of gold in England is equal to 5 British pounds, then the pound/dollar exchange rate is .25; that is, $1 equals .25 British pounds. The dollar and the pound will always trade in this fixed ratio as long as both countries redeem their currencies in gold at the par value.

A gold standard comes under strain if countries experience different growth rates. For instance, suppose that a gold standard was in existence and that the United States was growing faster than its neighbors. In that case, the United States would find that imports were increasing faster than exports. In the foreign exchange market, the quantity supplied of dollars would be greater than the quantity demanded. Foreigners would present the dollars to the U.S. Treasury to be redeemed for gold, and the United States would lose its gold supply. As the United States lost gold, its money supply would fall with resulting depressing effects on output, jobs, and so on.

If policymakers wanted to keep the U.S. economy growing faster than the economies in the rest of the world, they would be under pressure to devalue the U.S. currency. A devaluation is an increase in the number of dollars that must be presented to the Treasury to receive an ounce of gold. Fear of devaluation would cause more of the currency to be presented for redemption. Holders of dollars would convert the dollars to gold, and if devaluation did occur, they would convert the gold back to more dollars than they started with! This would exacerbate the gold loss and result in periodic financial crises as gold redemptions were suspended and the par values among currencies had to be redefined. In fact, scenarios like this actually occurred and led to the end of the gold standard.

http://www.
newyorkfed.org/
pihome/fedpoint/
fed40.html
*Provides detailed
information on the balance
of payments.*

reflects the quantity of dollars supplied/month. While the uses of funds are always equal to the sources (for every source, there is a use), the intended uses and sources may differ significantly, and these differences in plans and intentions move the exchange rate.

The Effects of Policy on Interest Rates and Exchange Rates since 1990

In the early 1990s, the need to reduce the government budget deficit led to contractionary fiscal policy. At the same time, the Fed pursued a relatively easy monetary policy due to the weak economy and reduced fears of inflation. These policies produced lower interest rates and depreciation of the dollar. In mid-1993, despite these circumstances, the trade deficit began to widen. No doubt this was due to the mild recovery of the U.S. economy and the faltering of many foreign economies. The demand for imports increased in the recovering domestic economy while the demand for exports decreased in the stumbling foreign economies. With U.S. interest rates at low levels relative to those of the rest of the world, particularly a united Germany, some economists wondered how far and for how long the dollar would fall.

By mid-1995, the dollar was again on the rise as U.S. interest rates had risen above foreign rates due to the strength of the U.S. economy and tightening actions taken by the Fed. The relatively higher U.S. interest rates led to increasing capital inflows. Continued strengthening of the U.S. economy raised expectations that the Fed would continue to take actions that led to increases in interest rates. Uncertainty abroad and the exceptionally strong performance of the U.S. economy led to further strengthening of the dollar.

During late 1997 and early 1998, the financial crisis in Asian economies caused the ongoing appreciation to escalate. A "flight to quality" in international financial markets, triggered by the crisis in Asia, often meant a flight into dollars and dollar-denominated financial instruments. During June 1998, the Fed (at the request of China) intervened to raise the value of the Japanese yen (and lower the value of the dollar in terms of the yen). Its efforts were not particularly successful, and the Bank of Japan gave up trying to support or elicit support for the yen in early August 1998. Finally, in late fall 1998, the overvalued dollar did plummet as the Fed on two occasions took action that lowered interest rates.

By mid-1999, the dollar was again on the rise as an overheating U.S. economy continued to demonstrate incredible resilience. By late 2000, the dollar was stronger than what it had been since 1986. The trade deficit was also very high, buoyed by a booming U.S. economy. As the economy began to slow in 2001, the Fed orchestrated several cuts in the interest rate and the newly elected Bush administration got a significant tax cut passed by Congress. The hope was that falling interest rates and a tax decrease would work together to offset the strong recessionary tendencies the economy was experiencing. The U.S. economy was experiencing expansionary monetary policy, which led to falling interest rates and less contractionary fiscal policy, which reduced the current budget surplus.

While examining the factors determining exchange rates, we learned that a fall in U.S. interest rates relative to foreign rates would tend to decrease the foreign demand for U.S. securities and, thus, the demand for dollars. We also learned that a fall in U.S. rates relative to foreign rates would tend to increase the U.S. demand for foreign securities and, thus, the supply of dollars. In balance of payments terminology, the relatively lower U.S. interest rates would cause increased capital outflows and decreased capital inflows. The fall in the demand for dollars and the increase in the supply of dollars, in turn, would lead to a depreciation of the dollar.

If capital outflows rise and inflows fall, the capital account surplus shown in Exhibit 8-6 will fall. If nothing happens to the current account, the balance of payments will no longer balance. Obviously, something else must change. What happens is this: As the exchange rate depreciates, a number of adjustments in foreign demands and U.S. demands ensue. Among the most important is a decrease in the current account deficit, reflecting, in large part, a decrease in the trade deficit. To be more specific, the depreciation of the dollar will tend to decrease the yen (foreign) price of U.S. goods abroad, thus increasing U.S. exports. The depreciation will also tend to raise the dollar price of foreign goods in the United States, thus decreasing U.S. imports and the trade deficit.[15] From a purely domestic perspective, the fall in U.S. interest rates pulls foreign funds from the U.S. financial system, leads to a depreciation of the dollar, and tends to increase foreign demand for U.S. output and, thus, increase U.S. employment relative to what it otherwise would have been. The tax cut leading to a smaller government surplus or a deficit, and increased consumer demand for now relatively cheaper imports reinforces this effect on the trade balance.[16]

We have now completed our three-chapter discussion of financial prices. In Part 3, we move on to a look at the major financial institutions in our economy.

http://www. newyorkfed.org/ pihome/fedpoint/ fed44.html
Discusses U.S. foreign exchange intervention.

http://www.bea.doc. gov/bea/di1.htm
Provides current information on international transactions.

---

[15]Refer back to Equations (8-4) and (8-1).

[16]However, even though interest rates fall because of the Fed's expansionary actions, the tax cut and reduction in the government surplus cause interest rates to be higher than what they otherwise would be without the less contractionary fiscal policy.

Summary of Major Points

- The exchange rate is the number of units of foreign money (currency) that can be acquired with one unit of domestic money. If the exchange rate rises, the dollar is said to have appreciated relative to other currencies. If the exchange rate falls, the dollar has depreciated.

- The dollar price of foreign goods is equal to the foreign price of foreign goods divided by the exchange rate. The foreign price of U.S. goods is equal to the dollar price of U.S. goods multiplied by the exchange rate. Accordingly, a depreciation will lower the price of U.S. goods in foreign markets and raise the price of foreign goods in the United States. An appreciation will raise the price of U.S. goods in foreign markets and lower the price of foreign goods in the United States.

- The exchange rate is a price—the price of one national currency in terms of another—and is determined by supply and demand. The demand for dollars in the foreign exchange market reflects the demand by foreign residents for U.S. goods, services, and financial claims. The supply of dollars comes from the demand by U.S. residents for foreign goods, services, and financial claims.

- The quantity demanded of dollars/month is inversely related to the exchange rate. The demand for dollars is positively related to changes in foreign income, to changes in the foreign price of foreign goods relative to the foreign price of U.S. goods, and to changes in U.S. interest rates relative to foreign interest rates. The quantity supplied of dollars/month is positively related to the exchange rate. The supply of dollars is positively related to changes in U.S. income, to changes in the dollar price of U.S. goods relative to the dollar price of foreign goods, and to changes in foreign interest rates relative to U.S. interest rates.

- A depreciation of the dollar can result from one or more of the following: a fall in U.S. interest rates relative to foreign interest rates, a rise in U.S. income, a fall in foreign income, and/or more inflation in the United States than abroad. An appreciation of the dollar can result from one or more of the following: a rise in U.S. interest rates relative to foreign interest rates, a fall in U.S. income, a rise in foreign income, and/or less inflation in the United States than abroad.

- The balance of payments is the record of transactions between the United States and its trading partners in the rest of the world over a particular period of time. Thus, it keeps track of the flow of funds for purchases of goods, services, and securities. Ignoring official government transactions, it is comprised of the current account and the capital account.

- If the exchange rate is flexible and thus free to move in response to any change in the demand for or supply of dollars, the exchange rate will move to that rate where the quantity of dollars demanded/month is equal to the quantity of dollars supplied/month. According to the purchasing power parity theory, exchange rates adjust in the long run so that the relative purchasing power of various currencies is equalized. The purchasing power parity theory is based on the assumption that goods are identical and tradable, and that there are no transportation costs or barriers to trade. Also, the theory ignores changes in tastes, productivity, economic growth, market structures, and technologies across countries. Using balance of payments terminology, the equilibrium exchange rate will equalize the sum of all receipts from foreigners with all payments to foreigners. The balance of payments always balances.

- If something, such as a policy-induced rise in U.S. interest rates relative to foreign interest rates, results in capital inflows and, say, a larger capital account surplus, it will also result in an appreciation of the dollar. In turn, the appreciation of the dollar will tend, among other adjustments, to reduce U.S. exports of goods and services and to increase U.S. imports. These adjustments will tend to produce a larger current account deficit, which will rebalance the balance of payments.

- During the early 1990s, monetary and fiscal policies in the United States produced falling real interest rates relative to the rest of the world. This fall in U.S. interest rates helped produce a depreciation of the dollar and a reduction in the nation's current account deficit. Although the dollar fell dramatically in the early 1990s, the trade deficit persisted. The dollar strengthened through late 1998, fueled by a booming U.S. economy and international financial crises that cause a "flight to quality" and increased demand for dollars. The dollar did weaken in 1999 only to further escalate in 2000.

- By early 2001, the dollar was as strong as it had been since 1986, and the trade deficit continued

to persist. However, a faltering U.S. economy, combined with expansionary monetary policy and falling interest rates, suggested that the value of the dollar and the trade deficit would fall.

Key Terms

Appreciated	Current Account	Merchandise Exports
Balance of Goods and Services	Debit	Merchandise Imports
Balance of Payments	Depreciated	Net Capital Inflow
Balance on Current Account	Exchange Rate	Net Transfer Payments
Capital Account	Foreign Currency (Money)	Trade Balance
Capital Inflows	Foreign Exchange	Trade Deficit
Capital Outflows	Foreign Exchange Market	Trade Surplus

Review Questions

1. Define exchange rate, foreign currency, and foreign exchange market.

2. Distinguish between a change in the quantity demanded of foreign exchange and a change in demand for foreign exchange. Do the same for the quantity supplied and the supply of foreign exchange.

3. Explain the relationship between the supply of dollars in the foreign exchange market and debit items in the balance of payments. Do the same for the demand for dollars in the foreign exchange market and credit items in the balance of payments.

4. Defend the following statement: The balance of payments always balances.

5. Explain how the trade balance, the balance of goods and services, and the balance of payments differ.

6. How is a surplus in the current account related to a deficit in the capital account?

How is a deficit in the current account related to a surplus in the capital account?

7. If interest rates in the United States were lower than rates in the rest of the world, would the United States be more likely to be experiencing a net capital inflow or a net capital outflow? Would the current account be in surplus or deficit?

8. If the demand for U.S. exports falls, what will happen to the exchange rate? What will happen to the trade balance and the balance of goods and services?

9. What would happen to the exchange rate if foreigners decided to sell U.S. securities?

10. What is the difference between the trade balance and the current account balance?

11. What are the assumptions of the purchasing power parity theory? What are the reasons why the theory may not offer a complete explanation of exchange rate differentials?

Analytical Questions

12. If a hotel room in downtown Tokyo costs 20,000 yen per night and the yen/dollar exchange rate is 100, what is the dollar price of the hotel room? If the yen/dollar exchange rate increases to 150, what happens to the dollar price of the hotel room?

13. If a hotel room in downtown Los Angeles costs $100 per night and the yen/dollar exchange rate is 100, what is the yen price of the hotel room? If the yen/dollar exchange rate increases to 150, what happens to the yen price of the hotel room?

14. Assume that the dollar appreciates by 10 percent in terms of the Mexican peso. Explain what happens to the dollar price of tequila from Mexico after the appreciation. What happens if the dollar depreciates by 10 percent?

15. If a bottle of rare French wine sells for 100 euros in Paris and the exchange rate is .9 euros, how much will the bottle of wine sell for in New York City? (Ignore transportation costs, etc.)

16. Use graphs to show what happens to the demand for and supply of dollars in the foreign exchange market in the event of each of the following:

a. Domestic income rises.
b. Foreign income rises.
c. Domestic inflation rises relative to foreign inflation.
d. Domestic interest rates rise relative to foreign interest rates.

17. Use graphs to demonstrate that when both domestic and foreign incomes are rising, we cannot be sure of the direction of exchange rates.

18. If merchandise exports are $600 and merchandise imports are $500, what is the trade balance?

19. If there is a surplus of $100 in the capital account, no unilateral transfers, and a $50 deficit in the net exports of services, what is the trade balance?

20. If $1 = 150 yen and 1 yen = 75 British pounds, what is the pound/dollar exchange rate? What is the dollar/pound exchange rate?

21. If the yen/dollar exchange rate is 125, how much will 25,000 yen cost? If the exchange rate appreciates to 150, how much will the 25,000 yen cost?

22. If the yen/dollar exchange rate is 125, how many yen will $15,000 be worth? If the exchange rate depreciates to 100, how many yen will $15,000 be worth?

23. Explain how, according to the purchasing power parity theory, exchange rates will adjust if inflation in the United States is 3 percent and inflation in Japan is 1 percent.

Internet Exercises

1. Go to **http://www.federalreserve.gov/ releases** for information on current exchange rates. Examine both the pound/dollar exchange rate and the mark/dollar exchange rate. Access the historical data to determine whether the dollar has appreciated or depreciated since January 1995.

2. Monthly trade statistics may be accessed at the following site: **http://www.census.gov/ foreign-trade/www/**. What is the current trade balance?

Suggested Readings

Although we ignored (for the time being) government transactions in foreign currencies, the *Federal Reserve Bulletin* includes a feature entitled "Treasury and Federal Reserve Foreign Exchange Operations" on a quarterly basis. We cite these articles here because they provide an in-depth discussion of the reasons for recent movements in exchange rates. They are also available on the World Wide Web at the Fed's site, **http://federalreserve.gov/ publications.htm**.

Are you interested in sampling Big Macs around the world? (We understand that local customs and tastes dictate the spices.) Refer to the *Economist*, which since 1986 has been tracing the dollar price of Big Macs around the world, as discussed in the body of the chapter. For the 2001 report, see "Big

MacCurrencies," the *Economist*, January 13, 2001. Information about the *Economist* can be found on the Internet by accessing **http://www.economist. com**.

We also suggest three free publications from the New York Fed. They are *Basics of Foreign Trade and Exchange* and *Balance of Payments* (*Fedpoints 40*) and *All about the Foreign Exchange Market in the United States*. For those of you who prefer comic books, request *The Story of Foreign Trade and Exchange*. All are available by writing the Federal Reserve Bank of New York, Public Information Department, 33 Liberty Street, New York, NY 10045. You may order or browse *Fedpoints* and other New York Fed publications on the World Wide Web at **http:// www.newyorkfed.org/pihome/fedpoint/**.

For a variety of articles on the international financial crisis of 1997 and 1998, see Clifford Krauss, "Argentine Leader Vows to Retain Currency Peg to Dollar," *New York Times*, September 14, 1998, p. C7; Peter Fritsch, "Brazil's Rate Boost Seems to Slow Dollar Flight," *Wall Street Journal*, September 15, 1998, p. A17; Paul Krugman, "Saving Asia: It's Time to Get Radical," *Fortune*, September 7, 1998, pp. 74–80; and Michael M. Weinstein, "Twisting Controls on Currency and Capital," *New York Times*, September 10, 1998, p. C11.

A more academic and comprehensive article on international financial crises is Robert Z. Aliber, "Capital Flows, Exchange Rates, and the New International Financial Architecture: Six Financial Crises in Search of a Generic Explanation" *Open Economies Review*, Vol. 11, No. 0, Supplement 1, August 2000, pp. 43–61.

For an interesting article on the euro and monetary policy, see David G. Mayes, "The Exchange Rate and Monetary Conditions in the Euro Area," *Review of World Economics*, vol. 136, no. 2, 2000, pp. 199–231.

For a look at the implications of the euro, see Robert A. Mundell, *The Euro as a Stabilizer in the International Economic System*, (Norwell, MA: Kluwer Academic Press, 2000).

part

FINANCIAL MARKETS AND INSTRUMENTS

3

chapter

9 The Money Market

Learning Objectives *After reading this chapter, you should know:*

- The primary participants and instruments of the money market
- How money markets are used by various participants
- Recent trends in money market instruments
- How the money markets have become international in scope
- What money market mutual funds are and why they have become important intermediaries

" "

The need for a money market arises because receipts of economic units do not coincide with their expenditures.
—Timothy Q. Cook and Robert K. LaRoche, *Instruments of the Money Market*, Federal Reserve Bank of Richmond, Chapter 1

835

FANNIE MAE
PARTNERSHIP OFFICE

Direct Lending, Instruments, and Markets

Part 3 links the process of financial price determination, discussed in Chapters 5–8, with the financial institutions we describe in Chapters 14–20. Some of these institutions provide investment banking, insurance, and pension services while others more directly facilitate lending from surplus spending units (SSUs) to deficit spending units (DSUs). As noted earlier, when intermediaries arrange the lending process, we refer to it as *indirect finance. Direct finance* refers to lending that happens without an intermediary. In direct finance, DSUs borrow from SSUs by using various types of financial instruments and markets.

In this third section of the text, we examine the instruments and markets of direct finance more closely. The subject matter is organized by the type of markets within which DSUs and SSUs connect. We begin with a discussion of the *money market*—the short-term credit market wherein debt securities having original maturities of 1 year or less are traded. This definition distinguishes it from intermediated borrower-lender relationships for short-term funds, as well as from the capital market for longer-term debt and equity transactions. Chapters 10–12 discuss various capital markets, wherein financial assets with a maturity of greater than 1 year (or no maturity at all) are traded. Capital markets include the bond, stock, and mortgage markets. Chapter 13 closes this third section of the text with an examination of various international financial institutions and markets.

This chapter on money markets is divided into two main parts. The first section explores how various participants use money market instruments to meet their borrowing and lending needs. In the second section, we turn our attention to individual money market instruments, their recent trends, and the development of money market mutual funds (MMMFs).

Money Market Characteristics

Despite their name, money markets are not used for trading currencies or the components of M1 money. Currencies are traded on foreign exchange markets, as described in the previous chapter. Similarly, none of the instruments in the M1 definition of money (currency in the hands of the public, checkable deposits, and traveler's checks) are traded in money markets. However, if one moves to broader M2, M3, and DNFD definitions of money, we do find money market instruments such as money market mutual fund shares, negotiable certificates of deposit, Eurodollars, repurchase agreements, and U.S. Treasury bills. Hence, money markets are not completely misnamed; the instruments sold there are used to raise funds and these instruments are classified as "money," but only of the broader M2, M3, and DNFD types. Money markets are also a good place to store funds when one requires that they be kept liquid in a form of near money.

Although there are as many different types of money markets as there are instruments, people often refer to these markets in the singular, as a money market. This is because money market instruments share many characteristics. First, they are *issued in large denominations*, usually of $1 million or more. This feature, along with their absence of reserve requirements and lower regulatory burdens when compared to depository institutions, make money markets an efficient means of raising and storing short-term funds. The large denominations also limit their use primarily to institutional investors in wholesale markets. With the exception of money market mutual fund shares, money market instruments are rarely used in retail markets where most individual investors purchase securities. Second, money market instruments have *short maturities*, typically less than 3 months, but ranging from

1 day to 1 year. Third, money market instruments are characterized by *low liquidity and default risk*. Short maturities and active resale markets for most instruments provide considerable insulation from liquidity risk. Exhibit 9-1 shows that only repurchase agreements and non-negotiable Eurodollar time deposits lack secondary markets. Their sale by some of the most creditworthy borrowers, namely the federal government and large financial and nonfinancial corporations, lowers an investor's exposure to default risk. Investor risk exposure is further reduced by some commercial paper and bankers' acceptance issuers contracting with banks to provide liquidity through credit lines and protection against default through payment guarantees. Fourth, and finally, unlike commodities or stocks that often trade on specific exchanges, the money market *does not occupy one particular geographic location or trading floor*. The market tends to be centered in New York City, but it consists of borrowers and lenders as well as brokers and dealers linked by computers, fax machines, and telephones throughout the nation and the world. Exhibit 9-1 summarizes the instruments used, as well as their typical maturities, principal borrowers, and the status of their secondary market, if any, for each instrument.

INSTRUMENTS	TYPICAL MATURITIES	PRINCIPAL BORROWERS	SECONDARY MARKET
Federal funds	Chiefly 1 business day	Depository institutions	Active brokers' market
Negotiable certificates of deposit (CDs)	1 to 6 months and longer	Depository institutions	Modest activity
Bankers' acceptances	90 days	Financial and business enterprises	Limited
Eurodollars			
Time deposits (non-negotiable)	Overnight, 1 week, 1 to 6 months, and longer	Banks	None
CDs (negotiable)	1 to 6 months and longer	Banks	Moderately active
Treasury bills	3 to 12 months	U.S. government	Very active
Repurchase agreements	1 day, and terms of 2 days to 3 months typical; 6 months less typical	Banks, securities dealers, other owners of securities, nonfinancial corporations, governments	None, but very active primary market for short securities
Federal agencies (Government-sponsored enterprises)		Federally sponsored agencies	
Discount notes	30 to 360 days	Federal National Mortgage Association, Federal Farm Credit Banks Funding Corporation, Student Loan Marketing Association	Active
Coupon securities	6 to 9 months		Active
Commercial paper	1 to 270 days	Financial and business enterprises	Moderately active
Municipal notes	30 days to 1 year	State and local governments	Moderately active for large issuers

SOURCE: Ann-Marie Meulendyke, *U.S. Monetary Policy & Financial Markets*, Federal Reserve Bank of New York, 1998. p. 81

EXHIBIT 9-1
The Money Market

Money Market Benefits

As the quote that opens this chapter suggests, financial and nonfinancial businesses as well as governmental entities generally experience flows of receipts and expenditures at different times. To manage this mismatch in cash flows, economic agents of all types have periods when they need to borrow and other periods where they have funds to lend. As discussed in previous chapters, banks and finance companies do provide a variety of different types of loans and lines of credit to businesses that are temporarily short on funds. Depository institutions also stand ready to serve as a place for businesses to store their excess funds and avoid the opportunity cost of lost interest earnings.

Borrowing in the money market—relative to borrowing from a bank—is a more efficient source of credit for the largest financial institutions, nonfinancial corporations, and governmental bodies. The advantages of the direct lending process over bank borrowing stem from two sources. First, banks are required to hold non-interest-bearing required reserves as vault cash or on deposit at the Fed. Thus, only 90–97 percent of their domestic transactions deposits can be lent out. Second, banks face regulatory constraints on the size of loan they can make to one particular borrower and the particular types of assets they are allowed to hold on their balance sheet. In the past, banking regulations even limited the amount of interest that banks could pay to their depositors. State-imposed usury ceilings limited the interest rates that banks could charge to customers. These regulatory strictures place banks and other lenders at a competitive disadvantage to direct finance in the less restricted and regulated money market.

Many different types of institutions reap the benefits as wholesale borrowers and/or lenders in the money market. These include commercial banks and savings associations, governments and government-sponsored enterprises (GSEs), the Federal Reserve, corporations and finance companies, pension funds and insurance companies, brokers and dealers, as well as money market mutual funds (MMMFs) and individuals. Since you have already had a brief introduction to money market instruments in Chapter 3, we will begin here with a discussion of how money market participants use these securities. This is followed with an in-depth discussion of each money market instrument.

Money Market Participants

Commercial Banks and Savings Associations

Commercial banks and savings associations play five important roles in the money market:

1. They borrow in the money market to meet their reserve needs or to make loans to their commercial or household customers. These funds are raised by borrowing in the federal (fed) funds markets, by issuing negotiable certificates of deposit (CDs), and/or through engaging in repurchase agreements (RPs). Some large bank holding companies also issue commercial paper.

2. Commercial banks and other depository institutions hold significant levels of Treasury securities on the asset side of their balance sheets. These liquid assets help them to manage their cash flow needs. T-bills also earn interest, which is an improvement over holding non-interest-bearing excess reserves.

3. Large commercial banks and savings associations assist other participants by providing credit enhancements for a fee to those issuing commercial paper and bankers' acceptances. When a corporation issues commercial paper, it often

Backup Line of Credit
A bank's promise to lend funds to a borrower on demand; often used to assist commercial paper issuers with their payment obligations.

Letters of Credit
A form of credit enhancement offered by banks that guarantees a bank will redeem a security if the issuer does not.

approaches a bank to provide a **backup line of credit.** This credit line is drawn on by the corporation in the event that it is unable to retire or roll over its payment obligations. In the case of serious credit deterioration on the part of the issuer, banks can withdraw lines of credit before they are used to pay off maturing commercial paper. **Letters of credit** are a stronger form of credit enhancement offered by banks. These guarantee that a bank will redeem a security, such as a bankers' acceptance, if the issuer does not. By reducing risk, these guarantees also lower the interest rate at which a security issuer can borrow.

4. Some large banks, such as Citibank and Bank of America, serve as agents and underwriters in the commercial paper market.

5. The largest money center banks, such as Citigroup, Bank of America, and J.P. Morgan Chase & Co., and some large savings banks, such as Chicago's Harris Trust and Savings Bank, serve as primary dealers of U.S. government securities. This enables them to trade money market securities on behalf of their corporate customers.[1]

Governments and Government-Sponsored Enterprises (GSEs)

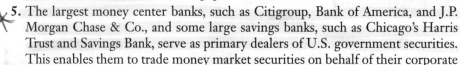

The U.S. Treasury is the world's single largest borrower in the money market. It issues U.S. Treasury bills (T-bills), which are money market instruments, as well as Treasury notes and bonds that have longer maturities and are classified as capital market instruments. Like other participants, the federal government's revenues and expenditures fail to coincide. By issuing new T-bills, the government can finance its expenditures until tax revenues are received. It can also pay off previously issued T-bills as they mature. The government budget surplus of the late 1990s and early 2000s has allowed the federal government to begin paying off national debt and to issue fewer T-bills than in the past. Privately owned, government-sponsored enterprises (GSEs) such as the Federal National Mortgage Association (Fannie Mae), Federal Farm Credit Banks Funding Corporation (FFCBFC), Student Loan Marketing Association (Sallie Mae), and others have increasingly used the money (and capital) markets as a source of funds for their various endeavors.[2] Most GSEs are engaged in assisting with the finance of housing, agriculture, or education. GSEs are widely perceived as having an implicit government guarantee on their debt. As a result, they are able to borrow at lower interest rates.

State and municipal (local governments and special districts) governments issue short-term municipal notes to finance their own expenditures as well as those of local schools, hospitals, and private firms. The interest earned by investors on these securities is generally exempt from federal taxation. This exemption allows state and local governments to borrow at a lower cost (offer lower pre-tax yields).

The Federal Reserve

The Fed plays a pivotal role in the money market and, thus, in the economy as a whole. Through the open market purchase and sale of Treasury bills or repurchase

---

[1]In addition to these roles, some commercial banks play the role of dealer in the over-the-counter interest rate derivative market. This has facilitated their use by other intermediaries in managing interest rate risk. Although short-term interest rate swaps, financial futures, and options are money market instruments, we save our discussion of these derivative instruments for Chapters 22–23.

[2]Other GSEs include Federal Home Loan Mortgage Corp. (Freddie Mac), Federal Farm Credit Banks Funding Corporation (FFCBFC), Farm Credit Financial Assistance Corp. (FACO), Student Loan Marketing Association (Sallie Mae), Financing Corporation (FICO), and Resolution Trust Corp. (RTC).

agreements, the Fed controls the level of reserves available to depository institutions. When the Fed buys securities, it pushes reserves into the system and drives down the fed funds rate. When it sells securities, the Fed pulls reserves out of the system and drives up the fed funds rate. Movements in the fed funds rate in turn affect money market and other interest rates in the same direction. Similarly, changes in interest rates influence consumer purchasing and business investment behavior, which are important components of economic output. The Fed can, of course, also influence money market rates by changing the level of required reserves and the discount rate. The Fed's monetary policy actions are conducted primarily in the money market. In addition to this important policy role, the Fed also serves as the Treasury's agent in the government securities market and helps it to make a market in Treasury securities.

http://www.
federalreserve.gov/
releases
*Provides current and
historical data on finance
companies, commercial
paper, and more.*

Corporations and Finance Companies

Finance companies and other corporations use the money markets both to raise and store funds. Finance companies, in particular, issue large amounts of commercial paper as a primary source of funds. They lend these funds to individuals to finance automobiles, boats, homes, home improvements, and other unsecured personal loans. They lend to firms so they can purchase inventories, equipment, or real estate. Other corporations tend to issue commercial paper to make up for temporary shortfalls of cash. When surplus cash is available, corporations and finance companies use it to buy the money market instruments issued by commercial banks, governmental units, and other businesses. Most of these can be easily resold if cash needs arise.

Pension Funds and Insurance Companies

Pension funds and insurance companies alike find it useful to maintain some portion of their investment portfolios in various money market instruments. These instruments can be sold easily to meet unexpected payments or to purchase additional stocks and bonds. Casualty and property insurers in particular are susceptible to less predictable claims and need a greater degree of liquidity than do life insurers or pension funds. In short, pension funds and insurance companies, like other businesses, use the money market for cash management purposes and to provide a degree of liquidity otherwise lacking in their portfolios.

Brokers and Dealers

Among the most important participants in the money market are the brokers and dealers that ensure its regular functioning. These participants market the new issues of money market securities and stand ready to purchase these securities, thereby facilitating the establishment of a secondary market for federal funds, negotiable CDs, banker's acceptances, Eurodollar CDs, T-bills, government agency securities, commercial paper, municipal notes, and various derivative products. Dealers, who take ownership positions in these securities, tend to use repurchase agreements (RPs) to finance their inventories of other money market instruments. This occurs when a dealer sells some of its securities to a lender and promises to buy them back at some point in the near future. The term is typically overnight or for a few days or weeks. When the dealer repurchases the securities, he or she repays the lender the principal amount of the loan as well as the accumulated interest. In many ways, this looks like a secured loan with the dealer's securities serving as collateral. To protect the lender, the amount loaned is generally less than the dollar value of the securities sold. Dealers also act as intermediaries in the RP market by borrowing from those who wish to lend, and lending to those who desire to borrow. Brokers do not take ownership positions. They match buyers and sellers of money market instruments and earn a commission on each sale.

Money Market Mutual Funds and Individuals

The final participants are money market mutual funds (MMMFs) and individuals. Few individuals participated directly in the money market before 1978. The denominations involved ($10,000 for a Treasury bill or $100,000 for a negotiable CD) were simply too large for all but the very wealthiest investor to purchase. However, the combination of higher interest rates and Regulation Q interest rate ceilings on deposit interest rates in the late 1970s created the incentive for financial innovation. In 1978, Merrill Lynch created short-term investment pools called money market mutual funds. These MMMFs use the proceeds they raise from selling shares to invest in commercial paper, repurchase agreements, certificates of deposit, Treasury bills, bankers' acceptances, and other U.S. and foreign short-term debt securities. This single innovation has allowed individual investors to benefit from the higher returns and safety of the money market previously restricted only to institutional investors. We will have more to say about these intermediaries at the end of the chapter.

RECAP The money market is the market for short-term credit. Instruments issued here are characterized by large denominations, short maturities, and low risk, and lack a central trading floor. Because of these characteristics and relatively little regulation, compared to depository intermediaries, the money market is a low-cost place to raise and store funds. A wide variety of institutions use the money market to manage the common mismatch in timing of revenues and expenditures they experience. Users of the market include commercial banks and savings associations, governments and government-sponsored enterprises (GSEs), the Federal Reserve, corporations and finance companies, pension funds and insurance companies, brokers and dealers, as well as money market mutual funds (MMMFs) and individuals.

Money Market Instruments

Now that you understand who the primary players are in money markets and how they use various instruments, we now turn our attention to a more detailed discussion of each of the individual money market instruments. The pie chart displayed in Exhibit 9–2 shows the relative shares of various money market instruments outstanding as of December 31, 2001. One can see that of the $4.7 trillion outstanding, the instruments in order of importance are the following: commercial paper, federal funds and repurchase agreements, CDs, Treasury bills, Eurodollars, and bankers' acceptances. We will discuss various facets of each of these instruments, as well as recent trends in the volume and interest rates associated with each of these instruments.

Commercial Paper

Corporations and foreign governments issue unsecured, short-term promissory notes called *commercial paper* as an alternative to short-term bank loans or other forms of borrowing. The primary benefit to the largest and most creditworthy commercial paper issuers is that the cost of borrowing is lower than it would be at a commercial bank. During the 1990s and early 2000s, the interest rate on commercial paper tended to be

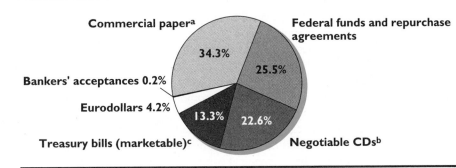

EXHIBIT 9-2
The Money Market: Relative Shares of Money Market Instruments Outstanding as of December 31, 2000 (in billions)

[a]Includes commercial paper issued by both financial and nonfinancial firms.

[b]Because of changes in data gathering, large time deposits issued by the largest commercial banks are substituted for negotiable CDs.

[c]Treasury-bill data is from June 30, 2001 and does not include nonmarketable debt used for off-budget programs such as Social Security.

SOURCE: All data (except for the T-bill data) come from Board of Governors of the Federal Reserve System, Washington, D.C. 20551 available at http://www.federalreserve.gov/releases. We used releases H and Z and their *Flow of Funds Accounts of the United States, 1995–2000*. Treasury bill data are from the Bureau of the Public Debt's "Monthly Statement of the Public Debt," available at http://www.publicdebt.treas.gov. Percentages do not sum because of rounding.

about 2 to 3 percentage points lower than the prime rate that commercial banks charge to their best corporate customers. In addition, the costs of issuance, even through a dealer, are extremely low. When one considers that there is over $1.6 trillion dollars of commercial paper outstanding, shaving even a couple of percentage points from the interest rate charged reduces the annual cost of borrowing by about $32 billion!

The characteristics of commercial paper issues are largely defined by legislation and issuers' attempts to avoid the costly disclosure requirements mandated for other types of securities. The Security Act of 1933 requires that securities sold to the public must be registered with the Securities and Exchange Commission (SEC).[3] Registration in turn requires comprehensive public disclosure, including the preparation of a prospectus describing the firm issuing the security and the details of the specific offering. However, these time-consuming and expensive requirements can be avoided if the following three requirements are met: (1) the paper issued must mature in less than 270 days; (2) it must be issued in large denomination so it is not typically purchased directly by the public; and (3) the proceeds must be used to fund current transactions. Commercial paper is designed to meet all three of these criteria and avoid disclosure requirements. Most commercial paper matures in 5 to 45 days, with the average being about 30 days. Minimum denominations are usually $100,000. However, since amounts can be customized for the buyer upon request, minimum face values sometimes fall as low as $10,000. More typically, commercial paper is sold in multiples of $1 million to meet the needs of institutional investors. Commercial paper is usually sold on a discount basis—the buyer pays something less than face value. At maturity, the buyer receives the higher face value. The difference between the two is the interest earnings. In some cases, paper can be issued on a coupon basis at the request of an investor. Finally, as required by the Security Act, the funds raised are used for current transactions or to temporarily finance construction projects until bonds can be issued.

---

[3]The Act took effect in 1934 with the creation of the SEC.

Many different types of companies and government units raise funds in the commercial paper market. Since 1995, a small but growing part of the commercial paper market comes from foreign companies and governments. In the early 2000s, foreign banks, bank holding companies, corporations, and foreign governments issued about 7 percent of the commercial paper outstanding. Japan, the United Kingdom, and France are among the countries with the largest commercial paper issuers. Exhibit 9-3 illustrates the trends in domestic and foreign commercial paper outstanding. The graph shows that the recession in Japan in the early 1990s had a dampening effect on the amount of foreign commercial paper issued in the United States. One can also see that U.S. issues dominate, generating 93 percent of all commercial paper volume.

In terms of types of companies, financial companies (specifically nonbank financial companies) are responsible for issuing the vast majority of both domestic and foreign paper. Of all commercial paper outstanding, 78 percent is issued by financial companies and 22 percent is issued by nonfinancial companies. Almost all domestic and foreign *financial* issues are made by finance companies. Finance companies use the funds raised in the commercial paper market to make loans to consumers for vehicles and real estate, and unsecured personal loans, as well as to firms for inventories, equipment, and commercial property. These nonbank finance companies include such household names as General Motors Acceptance Corporation (a finance subsidiary of General Motors), General Electric Capital (a finance subsidiary of GE), and Ford Motor Credit. These firms borrow in the commercial paper market and then lend these funds to consumers who purchase the products of the firms' parent companies.

In addition to finance companies, many other insurance and securities firms, commercial bank holding companies, public utilities, state and local governments, and industrial and service companies raise funds with commercial paper. The funds are used to finance inventory purchases, manage accounts receivables, or meet other current expenses. The liquidity raised can enable the issuer to take advantage of cash discounts on inventory deliveries and/or to maintain its bank credit lines as a reserve for unexpected cash-flow problems. Some firms and municipalities issue

EXHIBIT 9-3
U.S. and Foreign
Commercial Paper
Outstanding
1991–2000

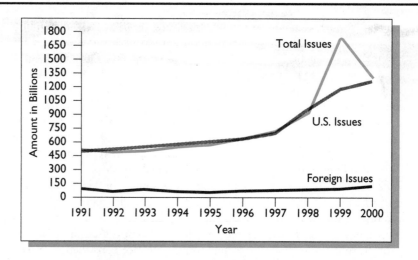

SOURCE: Federal Reserve Board of Governors. As of January of each year using total, not-seasonally-adjusted, data for U.S. and foreign financial and nonfinancial companies. http://www.federalreserve.gov. Look under *Statistics: Releases and Historical Data* and then click on commercial paper.

commercial paper monthly so that it becomes a semi-permanent form of financing. This does not violate the "current transactions" requirement of the Security Act, because the rolling over of the debt is at the discretion of the issuer. Furthermore, the buyer is under no obligation to purchase the newly rolled-over issues.

Companies can choose to issue their commercial paper through a dealer or engage in **direct placements.** As the name suggests, in a direct placement the issuer sells directly to the buyer without the assistance of an outside dealer. According to data from the Federal Reserve, approximately 25 percent of commercial paper was sold through direct placement in the early 2000s, primarily by large, well-known financial firms. These firms rely on direct placement as a semi-permanent form of financing, so it makes sense for them to create in-house dealers to manage the periodic issuance of paper. The remaining 75 percent of commercial paper is sold through dealers—up from about 55 percent in 1980. Investment banks serving as dealers, such as Merrill Lynch and Goldman Sachs, continue to dominate. However, they are being challenged by the likes of Bankers Trust, Citigroup, and Bank of America, who have established bank holding company subsidiaries to serve as dealers in the commercial paper market. Dealers earn their fees by purchasing the paper for less than they sell it. This spread is thin, equaling only about one-eighth of 1 percent (.00125 percent) of the face value of the issue. A large issuer with $400 million worth of paper outstanding for a year would generate fee revenues for the dealer of $500,000. Given the heterogeneous rates, maturities, and face values of commercial paper, it is difficult to bundle blocks of paper together to securitize and resell in a secondary market. Thus, dealers play another important role in this market, creating a modestly active secondary market by purchasing paper from investors in need of cash.

> **Direct Placements** When the issuer of a security sells straight to a buyer without the assistance of a broker or dealer.

The rates that individual issuers pay to borrow are strongly influenced by the perceived risk of the borrower. Since the first serious disruption of the commercial paper in 1970—the $82 million default of Penn Central Transportation Company—most issuers have paid to have their commercial paper issues rated. Companies such as Moody's and Standard & Poor's provide up-to-date information and ratings to investors who subscribe to their publications or information services. As noted earlier, most issuers turn to commercial banks for backup liquidity and other credit enhancements to further reduce default risk.

A variety of different kinds of investors purchase commercial paper. These include money market mutual funds, large insurance companies, nonfinancial businesses, bank trust departments, and pension funds. The attraction is that these securities are characterized by low default risk, short maturities, and relatively high yields when compared to other securities with similar risk and maturities.

Federal (Fed) Funds

Commercial banks, savings associations, and credit unions are all required by the Federal Reserve to hold reserves for the purpose of managing monetary policy. Reserves can be held as vault cash or as deposits at the Fed. Reserves do not earn interest, so depository institutions have an incentive to hold as few as possible. Other assets that will earn a return can be held. Nevertheless, depository institutions must meet their reserve requirements. When institutions anticipate that they will have insufficient reserves, they often turn to the *federal (fed) funds market*. Here they can borrow reserves from other institutions on an overnight basis. Similarly, institutions that find themselves with excess reserves can turn to the fed funds market to loan these reserves and earn interest. Typically, fed funds are lent on an overnight basis in denominations of $5 million or more. In some cases, they can be rolled over or established for a fixed term of a few days or a few weeks. The loans are usually unsecured and booked based only on an oral agreement between the lender and borrower. As an added bonus to the borrower, the funds are exempt from reserve requirements and have been free of interest rate ceilings since their creation in the summer of 1921.

A commercial bank in need of reserves has a couple of places to turn to obtain fed funds. First, if the bank has an ongoing correspondent banking relationship with another bank, it can call this bank and see if it has reserves to lend. If it does, and an oral agreement is arranged, a call is placed to the Federal Reserve district bank to wire funds from the lending bank's account to the borrowing bank's account. The arrangement is reversed the next day and the lending bank is paid 1 day's worth of interest. If the borrowing bank does not have a correspondent banking relationship or its correspondents are unable to make a loan, the bank can turn to a federal funds broker. Brokers take bids and offers from various banks and arrange federal funds transactions. The accompanying A Closer Look feature explains the broker's role in this market in more detail. In either case, fed funds transactions involve an overnight, self-reversing loan that takes place at a Federal Reserve district bank or between Federal Reserve district banks. Thus, the term "fed funds" is an appropriate name for this instrument, market, and interest rate.

The Broker's Role in the Federal Funds Market: Banks hold a portion of their reserves as deposits at the Federal Reserve. The federal funds market is where banks trade these immediately available reserve balances to meet their required reserve balances. The accompanying figure illustrates how this process typically works.[4]

Brokers do not take positions; instead, they take bids to sell and offers to buy from banks over the phone. They charge a small 50 cents per $1 million commission on trades. Although this seems small, commissions can be considerable when one considers the large volumes involved. In the early 2000s, it was common for $250 billion in fed funds to change hands—daily! When bid and offer terms correspond, the broker sends notification to both the selling and buying banks. (Bids and offers typically differ by only 1/16 or 1/8 of a percentage point.) Once the terms have been agreed upon, the bank selling its reserve balances notifies its Federal Reserve district bank to

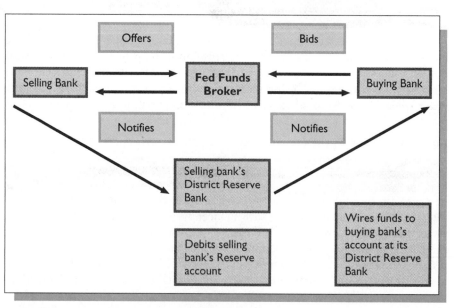

[4]Adapted from Ann-Marie Meulendyke, *U.S. Monetary Policy & Financial Markets,* Federal Reserve Bank of New York, 1998. p. 86

debit its account for the amount of the loan. The Federal Reserve district bank then wires these funds to the buying bank's Federal Reserve District Bank. On the next business day, this transaction is reversed. The buying bank transfers funds, plus a day's worth of accumulated interest, back to the selling bank.

The **federal (fed) funds rate** is determined by the interaction of supply and demand for reserves. When there is a shortage of reserves, the fed funds rate increases. When there is an excess supply of reserves, the fed funds rate decreases. As noted earlier, the Fed can manipulate the fed funds rate through open market operations—its buying and selling of government securities. When the Fed buys securities, it increases the supply of bank reserves in the banking system and puts downward pressure on the fed funds rate. Similarly, when the Fed sells securities, it is increases the demand for reserves and puts upward pressure on the federal funds rate. Although few consumers participate directly in this market, the fed funds rate does impact their lives. When the federal funds rate increases, most other interest rates follow suit. Thus, the cost of borrowing on a credit card, home mortgage, or automobile loan is also likely to increase. Higher rates, in turn, are likely to dampen consumer expenditures, business investment, and rates of economic growth.

> **Federal (Fed) Funds Rate**
> The interest rate charged on overnight loans of reserves among commercial banks.

Repurchase and Reverse Repurchase Agreements

The same shortage of reserves that leads banks to borrow funds in the federal funds market leads some banks to engage in repurchase agreements. **Repurchase agreements (RPs,** or repos) are short-term agreements in which the seller (the borrower of funds) simultaneously sells a government security to a buyer (lender of funds) and agrees to buy the government security back on a later date at a higher price. In short, from the initial seller's perspective, it looks like a collateralized loan.[5] Since collateral is usually transferred, repurchase agreements are viewed as being safer than federal funds loans. This explains why the interest rate associated with repurchase agreements is typically lower than the fed funds rate. From the lender's perspective, this is still a better deal than holding cash that earns no return or holding T-bills that usually earn an even lower rate return than repos.

The most confusing thing about repos and reverse repos is getting the name straight. When looked at from the *borrower's* perspective (from the vantage point of the one initially selling the security), the transaction just described is called a *repo*. When viewed from the *lender's* perspective (the one buying the security, agreeing to sell it back in the future, and supplying the funds), the transaction is called a **reverse repurchase agreement** or a **matched sale-purchase (MSP) agreement.** If a dealer is involved in the transaction, we usually discuss the transaction from the dealer's perspective. So, when a dealer *borrows* funds—by selling securities to an investor or the Fed, and the dealer agrees to buy them back in the future—we call it a *repo*. When a dealer *lends* funds—initially buying securities from an investor or the Fed, and the dealer agrees to sell them back in the future—we call this a *reverse repo* or MSP. One caveat: Traditionally, if the Fed is involved in a reverse repo, we avoid that term and instead call it a *matched sale-purchase transaction*.

The speculative actions of brokers and dealers have historically proven to be disruptive to the regular functioning of the money market as well as to other institutions with which they do business. The Looking Back feature explains this historical

> *DON'T WORRY*
> **Repurchase Agreement**
> Short-term contract in which the seller agrees to sell a government security to a buyer and simultaneously agrees to buy it back on a later date at a higher price.

> *DON'T WORRY*
> **Reverse Repurchase Agreement** or **Matched Sale-Purchase (MSP) Agreement**
> A repurchase agreement viewed from the perspective of the initial buyer; short-term agreements in which the buyer buys a government security from a seller and simultaneously agrees to sell it back on a later date at a higher price.

---

[5]Although repos look like a collateralized loan, legally they have been treated as sales and repurchase contracts. Regardless of this legal ambiguity, in the case of bankruptcy, lenders can liquidate the securities in their possession.

LOOKING BACK: *Disruptions in the RP Market: Drysdale and ESM*

Before its failure in 1982, Drysdale Government Securities, Inc. was a small, ambitious government securities firm and dealer in the repurchase agreement market. Drysdale made extensive use of reverse repurchase agreements. A typical set of transactions looked like this: Dealers wishing to borrow money would enter into an RP with Chase Manhattan Bank. Drysdale would then enter into a reverse RP with Chase and borrow the securities used in the initial RPs. In this respect, Chase served as a blind broker because it connected dealers who wanted to temporarily sell securities (borrow money)—and who knew nothing of Drysdale—with Drysdale, who temporarily wanted to buy securities (lend money).

Everything appeared to be working fine despite the fact that when Drysdale borrowed securities, it took advantage of the interest coupons coming due on these securities and sold the securities in the open market to capture this value. Drysdale basically bet that when it needed to pay back the coupon payments and the original securities, securities prices would have fallen because of increases in interest rates. Drysdale would then be able to purchase a cheaper security in the market to meet its payment obligations to Chase. As long as interest rates were increasing, Drysdale's strategy worked and the firm expanded rapidly. When interest rates fell, securities prices were pushed up, undermining its scheme.

On May 17, 1982, Drysdale announced that it would be unable to pay $160 million in interest payments it owed to Chase Manhattan Bank. The problem was difficult to unwind. Chase claimed it was simply playing the role of a broker and that Drysdale was responsible for paying back those dealers who had engaged in RPs with Chase. The dealers argued that they were dealing only with Chase and that Chase should be held accountable. Ultimately, Chase paid for the losses to avoid further market disorder. The Fed was forced to liberalize trading rules in the government securities market and to allow firms to borrow securities. This was done to prevent what Gerald Corrigan, then President of the Federal Reserve Bank of Minneapolis, called a "gridlock situation in the market with people failing to deliver securities." Losses wiped out Chase's second-quarter earnings in 1982, caused a sharp decrease in its stock market value, and adversely affected shareholders, regulators, and other market participants.

A similar tale can be told about ESM Government Securities, Inc. ESM, too, engaged in RPs and reverse RPs with a variety of institutions and municipalities. Its closest financial relationships were with the largest state-insured savings bank in Ohio, Home State Savings Bank of Cincinnati, and with the American Savings and Loan Associates of Miami, Florida. The essential problem was that ESM had promised the same securities to more than one lender. ESM was able to do this by offering the thrifts and municipalities with which it did business a higher rate of interest if they would avoid taking actual possession of the securities underlying their RPs. When ESM failed on March 4, 1985, total losses were estimated at $315 million. The biggest losses were Home State at $150 million and American Savings and Loan at $53.3 million. To make matters worse, when Home State's depositors learned of the problems, they started an old-fashioned bank run on the thrift. Worried depositors withdrew $90 million in just 2 or 3 days. Given that the Ohio Deposit Guaranty Fund had only $136 million to insure the remaining 70 state-insured thrifts in the state, depositors rationally started bank runs on other thrifts across the state. By March 15, 1985, Ohio's governor ordered all state-insured thrifts to remain closed—the first such declaration since the banking holiday of 1933. Before permission was granted for a thrift to reopen, it had to qualify for federal insurance. In many cases, this required that a thrift merge with another institution.

SOURCE: Closely adapted from Martin H. Wolfson's, *Financial Crisis: Understanding the Postwar U.S. Experience*, 2nd ed. M. E. Sharpe, 1994, pp. 82–84, 103–104.

phenomenon with respect to the RP market and the failure of two government securities dealers, Drysdale Securities and ESM Government Securities, Inc. The behavior of dealers in the repurchase agreement market may seem esoteric and of little practical value to consumers and financial institutions managers. However, because of the layering of financial claims in our financial system, a small disruption in one part of the financial system can adversely affect the functioning of other parts. The two examples from the 1980s described in the Looking Back feature are illustrative of this important reality.

There are two main differences between the fed funds and repo markets. First, in the repo market, nondepository institutions can participate. In addition to depository institutions, securities dealers, money market mutual funds, mutual funds, pension funds, nonfinancial corporations, and state and local governments use the RP market to borrow and lend large-denomination, short-term funds. A second difference is that no collateral is transferred with fed funds. In a typical repo, funds and securities are transferred simultaneously via Fedwire and then reversed at the end of the contract. Despite these differences, repurchase agreements and federal funds are close substitutes and their rates of return tend to move in the same direction. You can see why by thinking through an increase in the fed funds rate. Imagine a situation in which the Fed sells securities, which pulls reserves out of the banking system. This leads some depository institutions to borrow more federal funds to meet their reserve need and push up that interest rate. As the fed funds rate increases, some institutions instead turn to the RP market to raise funds. This puts upward pressure on the interest rate in this market as well. The same happens in reverse when interest rates in the fed funds market are falling.

Like other money market instruments, repos involve large-denomination, short-term loans. They can be sold through a dealer or through private placement. Transaction amounts are usually at or above $25 million for terms of 1 to 15 days. Longer-term RPs have standardized maturities of 1-, 3-, and 6- month periods and transaction amounts in blocks of $10 million. Occasionally, amounts are negotiated under $100,000, but the smallest customary amount handled by securities dealers is $1 million. Short-term repos can be renewed or arranged on a continuing basis. The borrower receives only the negotiated repo rate of return. The rate of return on the underlying security or its coupon payment has no bearing on the repo rate of return. Companies regularly using repos to raise funds create a department to find counterparties to their desired repo or reverse repo transactions. However, many repos are arranged by brokers and dealers that match the borrowing and lending needs of various participants and earn a small commission on each trade. No secondary market exists for RPs.

The exact size of the repurchase agreements market is impossible to calculate because many participants are not required to file reports. Nevertheless, estimates indicate that between 1981 and 1992, there was a 10-fold increase. Growth has continued, albeit at a somewhat less torrid pace, throughout the 1990s and early 2000s. Most government data after the 1990s combine federal funds and repurchase agreement estimates. As of the early 2000s, about $1.2 trillion in these securities are outstanding.

Most money market instruments have maturities that are so short it is impractical for the issuer to offer periodic "coupon" interest payments. Instead, most money market instruments are sold at a discount. Equation (9-1) calculates the interest earned (or payable) on an RP:[6]

(9-1)   interest earned = funds invested × RP rate × (number of days/360)

For example, an overnight, $10-million RP at a 5.0 percent repo rate would yield an interest return of $1,388.89.

$$\$10,000,000 \times .05 \times (1/360) = \$1,388.89$$

---

[6]These same equations can also be used to calculate the interest earned or rate of return for commercial paper instruments. (Just change RP rate to CP rate for commercial paper.) By changing the 360-day year used here, to a 365-day year, and the RP rate to the T-bill rate, these modified equations can also be used to calculate the accumulated interest and investment yield on Treasury bills. The difference in days per year stems from differences in customary usage by market participants.

If we instead know the purchase price, the selling price, and the term, but want to compute the repo rate, we would use the following equation (the selling price received at maturity is sometimes referred to as the *face* or *par value*):

(9-2)
$$\text{RP rate} = \frac{\text{selling price} - \text{purchase price}}{\text{purchase price}} \times \frac{360}{\text{number of days}}$$

The repo rate depends on the difference between the purchase price and the selling price, annualized over a 360-day year. For example, assume that the repo has an initial security purchase price of $9,998,611.11 and that it can be resold tomorrow for $10 million. This would yield a repo rate of 5 percent.

$$\frac{\$10,000,000 - \$9,998,611.11}{\$9,998,611.11} \times \frac{360}{1} = 5\%$$

RECAP Commercial paper, federal funds, and repurchase agreements are the three most frequently used types of money market instruments. Their outstanding balances constitute more than one-half of all outstanding money market instrument balances. Commercial paper refers to short-term, large-denomination, unsecured promissory notes issued by the most creditworthy corporations as an alternative to bank borrowing. These may be offered through brokers or as direct placements. Fed funds and repurchase agreements are used primarily by depository institutions to meet their reserve requirements. Unlike fed funds, RPs are also used by securities dealers, money market mutual funds, pension funds, nonfinancial corporations, and state and local governments. Fed funds consist primarily of overnight loans of reserves between banks. Repurchase agreements (repos) are short-term agreements in which a seller simultaneously agrees to sell government securities now and promises to buy them back in the future at a higher price. In effect, repurchase agreements look like collateralized loans secured with government securities.

Certificates of Deposit (CDs)

Certificates of Deposit (CDs)
Debt instruments issued by commercial banks having a minimum denomination of $100,000, a fixed interest rate, and return the principal at maturity; may be negotiable (tradable) or non-negotiable (not tradable).

Thrift CDs
Certificates of deposit issued by savings associations.

Certificates of deposit (CDs) are term debt instruments issued by large commercial banks. When issued by large savings associations, they are often referred to as **thrift CDs.** In either case, they pay the bearer a fixed interest rate and return the principal amount at maturity. Minimum denominations are $100,000, but $1 million is more typical. Maturities range from 1 week to 12 months. However, most are issued for 1 to 3 months. CDs cannot be redeemed prior to maturity. This term requirement distinguishes CDs from other demand deposit liabilities that can be withdrawn at any time. CDs can be either negotiable or non-negotiable. Negotiable in this context means that they may be resold after their initial purchase. A non-negotiable CD or time deposit must be redeemed by the original buyer of the instrument. As with other deposits, the first $100,000 of a CD is insured. However, since most are issued in much larger denominations, buyers are exposed to default risk if an issuer goes bankrupt. The primary purchasers of negotiable CDs are nonfinancial corporations and money market mutual funds. Most negotiable CDs are sold directly by a bank to an investor. However, brokers and dealers do assist with the sale of negotiable CDs and typically deal in round lots of $25 million.

Interest rates on negotiable CDs tend to be higher than T-bill rates for three reasons:

1. CD holders are exposed to default risk because only a portion of their deposit is insured.

2. Unlike T-bills, earnings on CDs are subject to state and local income taxes.

3. The secondary market for CDs is much thinner than that of T-bills. Thus, negotiable CDs are less liquid than Treasury bills.

The history of CDs illustrates two of the dominant themes of this text: the importance of evolutionary change in financial instruments, markets, and institutions, as well as the globalization of financial markets. Following World War II, corporations replaced many of their demand deposit holdings with purchases of other higher-earning money market instruments. To entice corporations to return these funds, banks began issuing large, negotiable CDs in 1961. National City Bank of New York (now Citibank) was the first issuer. The Discount Security Corporation, a securities dealer, agreed to make a secondary market in the instruments. The market grew rapidly until 1966, when open market interest rates rose above the Regulation Q ceilings limiting the amount of interest banks could pay on these CDs. (This problem arose again in 1969–1970.) Investors seeking higher returns turned elsewhere, leading to sharp decreases in the CD market. To manage this problem, banks turned to the commercial paper and Eurodollar markets for liquidity and, most importantly, created **Euro CDs.** Again, National City Bank took the lead, offering dollar-denominated CDs in London in 1966 to get around the Regulation Q interest rate ceilings and to avoid the reserve requirements mandated on domestic deposits. Euro CDs continue to be issued and are mostly sold primarily to institutional investors and large U.S. corporations. The term "Euro CD" has come to refer to any CD issued by the foreign branch of a commercial bank in a foreign country denominated in the currency of the corporation's home country. In contrast, we use the term **foreign CDs** to refer to instruments issued by a commercial bank in a foreign country but in the denomination of that foreign country. An example could be the U.S. branch of a French bank issuing a dollar-denominated CD in the United States. Foreign CDs issued in the United States are called **Yankee CDs.** Yankee CDs were first marketed in the United States in the early 1970s.

Following the failure of Penn Central Transportation Company in 1970 and the subsequent disruption of the commercial paper market, the Fed eliminated interest rate ceilings on large CDs with maturities of less than 3 months. This made it easier for banks to raise funds for financing commercial loans to businesses adversely affected by the disruption of the commercial paper market. In 1973, Regulation Q was eliminated for large CDs (greater than $100,000) of all maturities and has not been reimposed. Except for the recession period of the middle 1970s, the CD market expanded steadily through the late 1980s. One of the main engines of growth was the creation of money market mutual funds (MMMFs). MMMFs pooled the funds of many small investors who were dissatisfied with the Regulation Q-limited returns they were earning on their demand deposit and small (less than $100,000) CDs. The MMMFs in turn purchased large quantities of negotiable CDs.

The savings and loan (S&L) crisis of the late 1970s and early 1980s led Congress to create money market deposit accounts (MMDAs) and Super NOW accounts in 1982. Banks and S&Ls used these new instruments as a source of funds and their use of CDs fell precipitously. The secondary market in CDs was dealt a cruel blow with the failure of Continental Illinois in 1984. Active secondary-market trading depended on the perception by most participants that all CDs were pretty much the same and could be bought and sold through a broker or dealer. The failure of this large bank, as well as questions about the health of other commercial banks, led to a sharp curtailment of secondary-market participation. By June 1987, even the Federal Reserve had decided it was not worth the trouble to track negotiable and non-negotiable CDs separately. Instead, the Fed now collects data only on large time deposits issued by the largest U.S. banks.

Euro CDs
Certificates of deposit issued by the foreign branches of commercial banks but denominated in the currency of the branch's *home* country (e.g., Citibank issuing a dollar-denominated CD in Japan).

Foreign CDs
Certificates of deposit issued by the foreign branches of commercial banks and denominated in the currency of the branch's *host* country (e.g., Citibank issuing a yen-denominated CD in Japan).

Yankee CDs
A certificate of deposit issued by a foreign bank in a foreign currency, but sold in the United States (e.g., Crédit Lyonnais, France's largest bank, issuing a French franc-denominated CD in the United States).

U.S. Treasury Bills

During most of the years following World War II, the U.S. federal government ran budget deficits. This meant that in a typical year, it spent more than it took in from tax revenues. Beginning in 1998, the government began running budget surpluses. As of 2001, tax revenues are still greater than federal expenditures and experts forecast that this trend will continue for several more years. Despite this recent reversal in fiscal fortune, as of June 30, 2001, the *Monthly Statement of the Public Debt of the United States* reported that the accumulated sum of all previous deficits and surpluses—our national debt—stood at about $5.7 trillion. The federal government holds about $2.8 trillion of this, mostly in the Social Security "trust fund" and at the Fed to conduct monetary policy. This leaves a national debt of about $2.9 trillion outside of the federal government. About $1.2 trillion of this is owned by foreign investors.

The U.S. Treasury department has an entire division whose sole function is to finance the rolling over of this debt and to manage the ongoing mismatch in the timing of tax inflows and government expenditures. To manage these tasks, the Treasury sells a variety of Treasury securities with various maturities and face amounts. Of particular interest in this chapter on money markets are the Treasury's issues of short-term *U.S. Treasury bills (T-bills)*. (We will explain longer-term Treasury notes and bonds in the next chapter.) As of June 30, 2001, the total amount of U.S. Treasury bills outstanding was $620 billion. During the late 1990s and early 2000s, this amount decreased as the federal government began running budget surpluses.

Treasury bills are sold with low minimum denominations and short maturities to a variety of different types of buyers. The minimum denomination of a T-bill is $1,000. This is low compared to the usual $100,000 needed to buy commercial paper or negotiable CDs. Despite the low minimum, the bid and ask quotations in *The Wall Street Journal* are based on $1 million minimum trades. Most trades between dealers involve round lots of at least $5 million. T-bills have maturities of three different lengths: 4 weeks (28 days), 13 weeks (91 days), or 26 weeks (182 days). In February 2001, the 52-week (12-month) Treasury bill was discontinued. Among the largest buyers of Treasury bills are commercial banks, money market mutual funds, the Federal Reserve, individuals, and foreigners.

Like commercial paper, Treasury bills are sold on a discount basis. One purchases a T-bill at a price below its face or par value. An investor earns interest by receiving the difference between the purchase price paid and the face value received at maturity. For example, one might pay $9,692.10 for a $10,000 security that will mature in 26 weeks. The difference between the price paid and face value of the security, $307.90, serves as the interest earnings. We can examine yields from the example in the Cracking the Code feature on page 195. It reports and discusses the results of a T-bill auction held on August 21, 2000. We encourage you to look up more recent examples. They can be found in Section C on Tuesdays in *The Wall Street Journal's* "Credit Markets" column.

As you probably surmised, original issues of T-bills are sold at regularly scheduled auctions. It is worth understanding how the auction works and recent changes in the process. The 4-week, 13-week, and 26-week bills are sold each week and the volumes available for sale are announced every Thursday by the Treasury. Bids must be submitted to the Federal Reserve by Monday at 1:00 P.M. Eastern time. Results are typically announced at 1:30 P.M. and the securities are issued 3 days later on Thursday. Bids are of two types: competitive bids or noncompetitive bids. *Competitive bids* specify both the quantity desired and the discount rate offered. If the discount rate

CRACKING THE CODE: *Treasury Bill Auction Results, August 21, 2000*

Here are the details of yesterday's auction by the Treasury of 13-week and 26-week bills: All bids are awarded at a single price at the market-clearing yield. Rates are determined by the difference between that price and the face value.

	13-WEEK	26-WEEK
Applications	$21,781,177,000	$20,115,925,000
Accepted bids	$9,509,177,000	$8,504,675,000
Accepted noncompet'ly	$1,287,216,000	$1,229,222,000
Auction price (rate)	*98.439 (6.110%)*	96.921 (6.090%)
Coupon equivalent	6.291%	6.371%
Bids at market yield	8%	25%

Bond issues are dated Aug. 24, 2000. The 13-week bills mature Nov. 24, 2000, and the 26-week bills mature Feb. 22, 2001.

We focus on the 13-week security for purposes of illustration. One notices in the first and second rows that of the $21,781,177,000 worth of applications, only $9,509,177,000 (44 percent) were accepted. One can also see that two different interest rates are quoted for this security. The first is the T-bill discount price, labeled here as the "Auction price (rate)" at 6.110 percent. The second is the "Coupon equivalent" or annualized yield at 6.291 percent. These can be calculated in a way very similar to that used earlier with repurchase agreements. Business periodicals typically quote the T-bill discount or T-bill rate. This represents the difference of the purchase price from the par value in a simplified 360-day year:

(9-3)
$$\text{T-bill discount} = \frac{\text{par} - \text{PP}}{\text{par}} \times \frac{360}{n} = \text{"auction price (rate)"}$$

where par = face value at maturity
PP = purchase price
n = number of days of investment

We can substitute the figures from the August 21, 2000 auction for 13-week (92-day) T-bills assuming a $100 face value for calculation purposes:

$$\frac{\$100 - \$98.439}{100} \times \frac{360}{92} = .06108 \text{ or } 6.108\%$$

There is a difference of 2 one-thousandths (6.108 percent *vs.* 6.110 percent) because of rounding. To find the true investment yield, or "coupon equivalent," one must divide the difference of the purchase price from the face, by the purchase price itself, and adjust for the portion of a 365-day-year used. Equation (9-4) illustrates.[a] These bond equivalent yields are always higher because they are divided by the purchase price instead of par value.

(9-4)
$$\text{T-bill annualized yield} = \frac{\text{par} - \text{purchase price}}{\text{purchase price}} \times \frac{365}{\text{number of days}}$$

$$\frac{100 - \$98.439}{\$98.439} \times \frac{365}{92}$$

$$= .06291305099 \text{ or } 6.291\%$$

[a]Careful readers will note that Equation (9-4) is almost identical to Equation (9-2), which is used for repurchase agreements. Only the rate/yield has been renamed and "selling price" is changed to "par."

SOURCE: *The Wall Street Journal*, August 22, 2000, p. C21.

is within the range accepted, the bidder is entitled to the entire quantity sought.[6] *Noncompetitive bids* include only the number of bills desired. Noncompetitive bidders are guaranteed to receive the amount of T-bills they request. However, they must accept the market-determined price and discount yield. Since noncompetitive bids are limited to a $1 million maximum per bidder, only individuals and smaller firms participate. Collectively they purchase only a small fraction of all T-bills offered for sale. Note that in the Cracking the Code example, of the $9,509,177,000 of 13-week bills sold, only $1,287,216,000 (13.5 percent) was sold noncompetitively. Noncompetitive bids can be made at no cost by individuals directly to the Federal Reserve Bank or U.S. Treasury. Some brokerages will also make bids on a client's behalf. However, paying fees will sharply reduce effective yields if the client is purchasing a single $10,000 T-bill.

**http://www.publicdebt.
treas.gov**
*Provides more information
about the direct purchase of
Treasury securities.*

Multiple-Price Method
An auction method
whereby the seller of
securities accepts bids prior
to selling securities. Sales
are awarded beginning
with the highest bidder,
and buyers end up paying
different prices for the same
securities based upon their
respective bids. The
Treasury discontinued this
method in November,
1998.

Stop-Out Yield
The lowest accepted bid
price or yield in a
securities auction.

Uniform-Price Method
An auction method
whereby the seller of
securities accepts bids
prior to selling securities.
Sales are awarded
beginning with the
highest bidder, and buyers
pay the same price for the
securities based on the
stop-out yield. The
Treasury instituted this
method in November,
1998.

The auction-pricing method used in government securities auctions changed significantly in 1998. Before then, government securities (including T-bills) were awarded to the highest bidders using a **multiple-price method.** The number of securities requested by noncompetitive bids was set aside, and then others were awarded beginning at the highest price (lowest yield) and descending until all of the securities planned for sale were sold. This lowest accepted bid price (highest accepted yield) is called the **stop-out yield.** This method resulted in different buyers paying different prices for the securities at the same auction. Bidders had to be careful to avoid the "winner's curse," whereby a successful bidder is stuck paying a higher price (earning a lower yield) than that paid by other bidders. Noncompetitive bidders paid a price equal to the weighted average of all accepted bids. In an attempt to increase its revenue, the Treasury adopted a **uniform-price method** beginning November 2, 1998. The hope was that this method would eliminate the winner's curse and thereby evoke higher bids. Like before, the quantity of securities needed for noncompetitive bids is set aside. Bids are still ranked lowest to highest yield and orders are filled going up to the stop-out yield. However, all competitive and noncompetitive bidders now pay the same price and receive the same yield. This is noteworthy—in our preceding example, only 8 percent of bidders actually bid the final market price.

Treasury bills possess an absence of default risk and a high degree of liquidity. Because the federal government issues T-bills, they are regarded as free of default risk. Unlike individuals, when the federal government faces difficulty in meeting its debt payments, it can either raise taxes or simply create money to pay off its debts. This explains why interest yields on T-bills are lower than those from commercial paper, negotiable CDs, or other money market instruments that are characterized by at least some degree of default risk. Both the primary and secondary markets for Treasury bills are well organized, have many participants, and trades can be arranged at very low transactions costs. One measure of the degree of liquidity is the spread between the price that buyers are willing to pay (bid price) and the price at which sellers are willing to sell (ask price). Throughout the 1990s and early 2000s, bid-ask spreads have been 2 basis points (.02 percent) or less. Another distinctive quality of T-bills is that they are exempt from state and local income taxes. For investors facing these taxes, Treasury bills can offer a lower rate of interest than that of corporate securities and still provide a higher after-tax yield. Of course, investors should not expect too much from their T-bills. For the high degree of

---

[6]The one exception to this is if the bidder happens to be the one bidder offering the highest discount rate (lowest price) bid. (This is called the stop-out yield.) In this case, he or she is awarded as many T-bills as needed so that the total amount of bids accepted for purchase equals the total amount of bills offered for sale.

safety involved, investors should expect to receive rates of return only slightly above the rate of inflation. To earn a higher return, many investors turn to negotiable CDs or Eurodollar deposits.

Eurodollars

Eurodollars are dollar-denominated deposit liabilities exempt from U.S. banking regulations. Financial innovation can be induced by a variety of causes, as you have learned throughout this book. In the case of Eurodollars, the spur was the Cold War and the threat of provocation. During the 1950s, Soviet officials worried that in a crisis, the U.S. government might freeze any U.S. dollar deposits that the USSR held in the U.S. banking system. To reduce this risk, the Soviets convinced London bankers to accept dollar-denominated deposits (hence, the origin of the name). Since that time, financial institutions around the world have begun accepting dollar-denominated deposits. Regardless of whether U.S. dollar-denominated deposits are held in Canada, Hong Kong, Japan, or Panama, we still refer to them as Eurodollars. Since 1981 it has even been possible for non-U.S. residents to hold Eurodollar deposits within the borders of the United States at financial institutions called **international banking facilities (IBFs).** These facilities help meet the credit needs of foreign individuals, corporations, or governments within the United States.

International Banking Facilities (IBFs)
Financial institutions located in the United States that cater to the needs of foreign individuals, corporation, and/or governments. They allow non-U.S. residents to hold unregulated Eurodollar deposits.

Although cold war tensions have eased, the Eurodollar market has continued to grow. The reasons for its persistence are simple: The Eurodollar market avoids many of the intermediation costs faced by domestic depository institutions. As the accompanying A Closer Look feature illustrates and explains, the foreign branch of a U.S. bank receiving a Eurodollar deposit easily avoids non-interest-bearing reserve requirements and deposit insurance premiums. A Eurodollar deposit also faces lower capital standards and less onerous financial supervision. In addition, transactions negotiated in London, or other locations, can be posted in Nassau or the Cayman Islands to take advantage of lower tax rates in these locations. Some states in the United States have also changed their tax codes to provide preferential tax treatment to IBFs. These advantages allow Eurodollar-accepting institutions to pay higher rates of interest to their depositors and charge lower rates of interest to their borrowers.

Eurodollar deposits were initially held as non-negotiable, fixed-rate time deposits (TDs). Given the lack of liquidity that characterized these securities, it should not be surprising that over time, negotiable Euro certificates of deposit (Euro CDs) that could be resold in a secondary market developed. Floating rate Euro CDs have also arisen to reduce interest rate risk for bearers of the securities. All of these instruments have maturities typically ranging from 1 week to 6 months, but can range from overnight to several years. Typical denominations range from $250,000 to $10 million dollars. Some types of wholesale CDs have up to $30-million denominations that are later subdivided for individual investors. Longer-term international capital market instruments such as notes with both fixed and floating rates are also available to investors and will be discussed in Chapter 13.

Several larger London banks participate in the interbank Eurodollar market. In many ways, this market plays a role similar to that of the fed funds market among U.S. domestic banks. Although there are no reserve requirements imposed on Eurodollars, banks frequently find themselves temporarily short of reserves to meet their operating needs. In the fed funds market, we talk about only one fed funds rate. However, we acknowledge that dealers earn a spread on the difference between bid and ask rates. In the Eurodollar market, this spread is often made

London Interbank Bid Rate (LIBID)
The interest rate at which London banks are willing to *borrow* Eurodollar balances.

London Interbank Offered Rate (LIBOR)
The interest rate at which London banks are willing to *loan* Eurodollar balances.

explicit in the rates reported in the financial press. The rate at which banks are willing to borrow funds is called the **London interbank bid rate (LIBID).** The rate at which banks are willing to lend funds is the **London interbank offered rate (LIBOR).** The spread between these two rates seldom exceeds more than 1/8 of a percent. They, of course, move up and down together and are closely correlated to changes in the American federal funds rate. The correlation to the fed funds rate should not be a surprise since fed funds and Eurodollar deposits serve as close substitutes for each other.

Although the U.S. dollar is the world's dominant currency for international trade and the currency most commonly held as a Eurocurrency, it is not the only Eurocurrency. Many others exist. For example, one can hold Japanese yen-denominated, Mexican peso-denominated, or English pound-denominated deposits in the United States (or elsewhere). We refer to these as Euroyen, Europeso, and Europound deposits, respectively. As Europe's unified currency, the euro, becomes a circulating and increasingly popular currency, we can look forward to the day when euro-denominated currencies are held at U.S. banks. This could happen as early as January 1, 2002, when the euro is first issued as a circulating currency. Can you speculate as to what these euro-denominated deposits will be called?

The Anatomy of Eurodollar Borrowing: General Motors converts a $1 million demand deposit at J.P. Morgan Chase & Co. New York to a Eurodollar deposit at J.P. Morgan Chase & Co. London. The New York bank branch was holding $100,000 in required reserve assets against the $1 million demand deposit. J.P. Morgan Chase & Co. New York branch borrows the Eurodollar deposit from its London branch. The Eurodollar deposit then becomes a $1 million nondeposit liability, free of reserve requirements. General Motors earns additional interest on the deposit, and J.P. Morgan Chase & Co. New York has $100,000 in additional funds to lend.

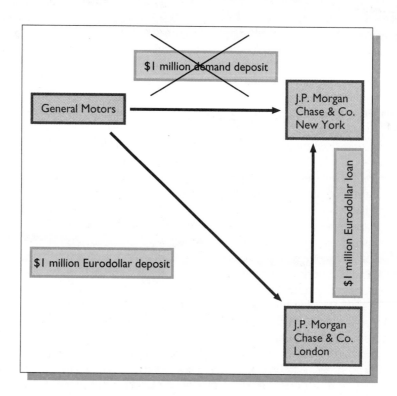

Bankers' Acceptances

Bankers' acceptances (BAs) allow a bank to "accept" responsibility or guarantee the payment of one of its customers. This is extremely important in international trade when an export company may not know or be able to easily determine the credit worthiness of a foreign company that wishes to purchase its goods. For example, suppose a small company that manufactures power washers in South Dakota may not know or trust a small import company in South Korea. However, if the import company arranges a bankers' acceptance with Citibank to pay for the imports, the exporter can confidently ship the merchandise and not worry about whether or not it will get paid. Legally, both the issuer of the BA, Citibank in this example, as well as the company using it to make the purchase, are obligated to pay at maturity. Maturities typically range from 30 to 270 days. Since there is some risk of default, BA rates are typically higher than T-bill rates. An additional benefit to the receiver of the acceptance is that there is a secondary market, albeit limited, for BAs. Thus, our power washer company does not necessarily need to wait until the BA matures, but can instead resell the instrument at a discount to meet its immediate liquidity needs. (You may want to flip back to Chapter 3, Exhibit 3-3 for a reminder of how bankers' acceptances work.)

The Federal Reserve Act of 1913 authorized U.S. banks to participate in bankers' acceptances. The Fed provided stability and liquidity to this market by regularly buying BAs from 1914 to the 1930s and again after World War II until the 1970s. By the late 1970s, the Fed was able to manage reserves by relying on Treasury securities alone and the acceptance market had matured enough to stand on its own. As a result, the Fed stopped outright purchases of BAs in 1977 and their use in repurchase agreements in 1984. From the 1960s to 1984, bankers' acceptances experienced rapid growth—from $2 billion to $75 billion outstanding. However, the rise of asset-backed and euro-commercial paper, as well as narrowing gaps between Eurodollar deposit rates and BA rates, have led to diminished use. By the end of 1998, the amount of outstanding bankers' acceptances had fallen to $14 billion.

Money Rates: Every day in *The Wall Street Journal's* Credit Markets column (Section C), a list of various short-term interest rates is published. Following is an abridged version of the information from this column with rate information on money market instruments discussed in this chapter.[7]

Money Rates for Thursday, August 15, 2001: The key U. S. and foreign annual interest rates that follow are a guide to general levels but do not always represent actual transactions.

Prime Rate: 6.75% (effective 06/28/01). The base rate on corporate loans posted by at least 75% of the nation's 30 largest banks.

Discount Rate: 3.25% (effective 06/27/01). The charge on loans to depository institutions by the Federal Reserved Banks.

Federal Funds: 3 7/8% high, 3 5/8% low, 3 11/16% near closing bid, 3 3/4% offered. Reserves traded among commercial banks for overnight use in amounts of $1 million or more. Source: Prebon Yamane (U.S.A) Inc. FOMC fed funds target rate 3.75% effective 06/27/01.

A Closer Look

Commercial Paper: Placed directly by General Electric Capital Corp.: 3.55% 30 to 34 days; 3.52% 35 to 44 days; 3.48% 45 to 59 days; 3.41% 60 to 89 days; 3.38% 90 to 270 days.

Euro Commercial Paper: Placed directly by General Electric Capital Corp.: Market closed.

Dealer Commercial Paper: High-grade unsecured notes sold through dealers by major corporations: 3.52% 30 days: 3.46% 60 days; 3.42% 90 days.

Certificates of Deposit: Typical rates in the secondary market. 3.58% one month; 3.48% three months; 3.52% six months.

Bankers Acceptances: 3.61% 30 days; 3.56% 60 days; 3.50% 90 days; 3.50% 120 days; 3.56% 150 days; 3.54% 180 days. Offered rates of negotiable, bank-backed business credit instruments typically financing an import order. Source: Reuters.

London Interbank Offered Rates (Libor): 3.6200% one month; 3.5600% three months; 3.56313% six months; 3.7100% one year. British Banker's Association average of interbank offered rates for dollar deposits in the London market based on quotations at 16 major banks. Effective rate for contracts entered into two days from date appearing at top of this column.

Foreign Prime Rates: Canada 6.00%; Germany 4.50%; Japan 1.375%; Switzerland 5.375%; Britain 5.00%. These rate indications aren't directly comparable; lending practices vary widely by location.

Treasury Bills: Results of the Monday, August 13, 2001, auction of short-term U.S. government bills, sold at a discount from face value in units of $1,000 to $1 million: 3.350% 13 weeks; 3.260% 26 weeks. Results of the Tuesday, August 14, 2001 auction; 3.470% 4 weeks.

Overnight Repurchase Rate: 3.85%. Dealer financing rate for overnight sale and repurchase of Treasury securities. Source: Reuters.

Fannie Mae: Posted yields on 30 year mortgage commitments (priced at par) for delivery within 30 days 6.87%, 60 days 6.96%, standard conventional fixed-rate mortgages; 5.30%, 6/2 rate capped one-year adjustable rate mortgages.

SOURCE: Reuters.

Money Market Mutual Funds

Many money market instruments and markets date back centuries. However, until 1978, only large institutional investors were allowed to benefit from the relative safety and higher returns of these short-term debt securities. The large denominations involved were often far beyond what most individual investors were willing and able to spend on a single security. However, as we have seen throughout this text, when the economic incentives are right, financial innovations can occur that fundamentally change the character of how financial participants and markets behave. In some cases they involve the creation of an entirely new type of intermediary. This is the case with **money market mutual funds (MMMFs)**. MMMFs are short-term investment pools that use the proceeds they raise from selling shares to invest in commercial paper, U.S. government securities (Treasury and agency securities), municipal securities, repurchase agreements, small time and savings deposits, and other domestic and foreign short-term debt securities. The interest earned on these securities, minus a small management fee, is then paid to those investing in the fund.

MMMFs emerged in the late 1970s as yet another example of financial innovation outpacing financial regulation. In this case, economic conditions changed much faster than did the structure of financial system regulation. FIs were forced

Money Market Mutual Funds (MMMFs)
Short-term investment pools that use the proceeds they raise from selling shares to invest in various money market instruments.

to evolve or go bankrupt. In the late 1970s, interest rates increased sharply and stayed above Regulation Q deposit interest rate ceilings. Initially, only the largest depositors engaged in **disintermediation**—the process of pulling deposits out of intermediaries and purchasing financial instruments directly in the open market. However, investment banks and brokerage firms began offering MMMFs as an alternative to deposits. The funds paid market rates of interest and allowed check writing. They were not insured, so investors were exposed to only slightly more default risk. MMMFs use most of their funds to purchase high-quality, short-term commercial paper and government securities that have little risk of default. This new instrument caused a great deal of problems for depository institutions. Ordinary depositors with small balances could now withdraw their funds from depository institutions and reinvest them in MMMFs.[8] Congress eventually passed legislation in the early 1980s to eliminate Regulation Q ceilings and authorized banks to offer money market deposit accounts and savings associations to offer NOW accounts.

Disintermediation
The reversal of the financial intermediation process whereby funds are pulled from financial intermediaries, like banks, and moved directly into open market instruments like commercial paper or government securities.

With most MMMFs, investors are typically required to have a minimum initial investment between $500 to several $1,000 to open an MMMF account. In some cases, if investors are willing to have regular electronic payments set up from their checking account, some companies will accept a lower initial investment. These features as well as those just noted have made MMMFs one of the fastest-growing intermediaries of the 1980s and 1990s. Although there were almost no MMMFs in 1978, they managed nearly $1 trillion in assets by the early 2000s.

RECAP Negotiable CDs are debt instruments issued by commercial banks. They typically have fixed interest rates, maturities of 1 to 3 months, and denominations of $1 million. Their most distinctive feature is that unlike non-negotiable CDs and time deposits, negotiable CDs may be resold before maturity. U.S. Treasury Bills are regularly auctioned by the federal government to finance the national debt and to manage the mismatch between government revenues and expenditures. They are characterized by typical maturities of 4, 13 or 26 weeks, denominations as low as $1,000, an absence of default risk, high liquidity, and preferential tax treatment. Eurodollars refer to dollar-denominated deposit liabilities held anywhere outside of the U.S. system of banking regulation. Bankers' acceptances facilitate international trade by allowing a bank to guarantee the payments of its customers engaged in importing goods from abroad. Money market mutual funds pool the funds of their shareholders and use them to purchase a variety of money market instruments. Their creation in the late 1970s brought the safety and high yields of the money market to individual investors.

We have covered a lot of territory in this chapter. You should now have a fuller understanding of money market instruments and markets as well as how various institutions and individuals make use of these instruments. The domestic money market has grown rapidly over the last couple of decades as financial innovations such as MMMFs emerged and corporations increased their reliance on commercial paper and reduced their use of bank loans. The money market has also become more global in scope. We have witnessed this trend with innovations such as the Eurodollar and other euro-type deposits as well as the use of euro and foreign CDs.

---

[8]Be sure you are clear that disintermediation means the removal of funds from FIs into open market instruments such as government securities, stocks, or bonds. When funds are removed from depository institutions and put into money market mutual funds, disintermediation has not occurred because money market mutual funds are intermediaries.

As technological advances are made in telecommunications and computing and as barriers to trade are eliminated, we expect these trends of continued growth, innovation, and global expansion of the money market to continue.

We continue our exploration of direct finance in the next few chapters by turning our attention to the capital market, where longer-term instruments are issued and traded. Our next stop, the market for corporate and government bonds, will be followed by chapters on the stock market and mortgage markets. We close this section of the text with a discussion of international financial markets.

Summary of Major Points

- Money market instruments share four common characteristics. They are (1) issued in large denominations, (2) have short maturities, (3) expose investors to low default and liquidity risk, and (4) do not share a common trading floor. Because of these common characteristics, the numerous instruments traded on various markets are often referred to in the singular as the "money market."

- Many different institutions make use of the money market to manage the mismatch in the timing of their revenues and expenditures. These include commercial banks and savings associations, governments and government-sponsored enterprises (GSEs), the Federal Reserve, corporations and finance companies, pension funds and insurance companies, brokers and dealers, as well as money market mutual funds (MMMFs) and individuals. These various savers and borrowers could use depository institutions to meet their needs. However, the less-regulated money market allows savers to reap higher returns and borrowers to pay lower rates of interest.

- Commercial banks and savings associations participate in the money market five main ways: (1) They borrow in the fed funds and repurchase agreement market when they need to meet their reserve requirements and issue CDs to raise funds. Large bank holding companies issue commercial paper for the same purpose. (2) Depository institutions hold large quantities of federal government-issued Treasury bills to manage their revenues and expenditures. (3) Large commercial banks assist other institutions in issuing commercial paper by providing fee-based credit enhancements. These include lines and letters of credit. (4) Some large banks serve as agents and underwriters in the commercial paper market. (5) The largest banks and savings banks serve as primary dealers in the government security market. This allows them to trade money market securities for their corporate customers.

- Many different types institutions play an active role in the money market. The federal government issues U.S. Treasury bills (T-bills) to finance its expenditures. The Fed uses these securities to manage the banking system's reserve level and interest rates. Government-sponsored enterprises (GSEs) issue commercial paper to fund expenses related to housing, agriculture, and student loans. State and local governments issue municipal notes to finance various expenditures, especially for educational purposes. Corporations and finance companies assist consumers in buying automobiles, boats, and real estate investments by issuing commercial paper and lending these funds to their customers. Pension funds, insurance companies, other businesses, and individuals use the money market and money market mutual funds for cash management purposes.

- Brokers and dealers ensure the regular functioning of the money market by marketing new issues of securities, standing ready to purchase these securities, and in some cases acting as intermediaries by borrowing from those desiring to lend, and lending to those who desire to borrow. Brokers do not take ownership positions; dealers do.

- Commercial paper, federal funds, and repurchase agreements are the three most frequently used types of money market instruments. Their outstanding balances constitute more than one-half of all outstanding money market instrument balances.

- Commercial paper refers to short-term (less than 270 days), large-denomination, unsecured promissory notes issued by the most creditworthy corporations as an alternative to bank borrowing. Commercial paper is sold on a discount basis and is used to fund current transactions. It may be offered through brokers or as direct placements.

The primary benefit to issuers is that issuing commercial paper is cheaper than borrowing from a bank. Most outstanding commercial paper has been issued by nonbank financial companies. However, other financial and nonfinancial companies make use of this market to meet short-term credit needs.

- Depository institutions use Fed funds and repurchase agreements to meet their reserve requirements. Fed funds consist primarily of overnight loans of reserves between banks. Repurchase agreements (repos) are short-term agreements in which a seller simultaneously agrees to sell government securities now and promises to buy them back in the future at a higher price. In effect, repurchase agreements look like collateralized loans secured with government securities. Reverse repurchase agreements or matched sale-purchase (MSP) agreements refer to the same transaction from the perspective of the lender of funds. Unlike fed funds, RPs are also used by securities dealers, money market and mutual funds, pension funds, nonfinancial corporations, and state and local governments.

- Commercial banks issue negotiable CDs with fixed interest rates, term maturities of 1 to 3 months, and denominations of $1 million. Their most distinctive feature is that unlike non-negotiable CDs and time deposits, negotiable CDs may be resold before maturity. Euro CDs refer to CDs denominated in a currency other than that of the country in which they are issued. In contrast, foreign CDs are issued by a foreign bank in the domestic currency of the country in which they are issued.

- The federal government regularly auctions U.S. Treasury bills (T-bills) through a uniform-price method to manage the mismatch between government revenues and expenditures. T-bills have typical maturities of 4, 13 or 26 weeks, denominations as low as $1,000, an absence of default risk, high liquidity, and are given preferential tax treatment. Because of these various features, T-bills almost always have the lowest interest rate among money market instruments. Like commercial paper, they are sold on a discount basis.

- To earn a higher rate of return than that on T-bills, investors often turn to the Eurodollar market. Eurodollars refer to any dollar-denominated deposit liabilities held anywhere outside of the U.S. banking system. This includes the use of international banking facilities (IBFs) by foreigners residing in the United States. In London, larger banks express the rate at which they are willing to borrow Eurodollars as the London interbank bid rate (LIBID). The rate at which they are willing to lend Eurodollars is called the London interbank offered rate (LIBOR). Other Eurocurrency deposits include the Euroyen, Europeso, and Europound.

- Bankers' acceptances (BAs) facilitate international trade by allowing a bank to guarantee the payments of its customers engaged in importing goods from abroad. They typically mature in 90 days and a limited resale market invests for those who wish to sell the instruments before they mature.

- The most important innovation in the money market during the post-World War II era was the creation of money market mutual fund (MMMF). MMMFs pool the funds of their shareholders and use them to purchase a variety of money market instruments. The interest earned on these securities, minus a small management fee, is then paid to those investing in the fund. Their creation in the late 1970s brought the safety, liquidity, and money market rates of interest to individual investors, while also providing access to their funds through limited check writing.

Key Terms

Backup Line of Credit
Certificates of Deposit (CDs)
Direct Placements
Disintermediation
Euro CDs
Federal (Fed) Funds Rate
Foreign CDs
International Banking Facilities (IBFs)

Letters of Credit
London Interbank Bid Rate (LIBID)
London Interbank Offered Rate (LIBOR)
Money Market Mutual Funds (MMMFs)
Multiple-Price Method
Repurchase Agreement

Reverse Repurchase Agreement or Matched Sale-Purchase (MSP) Agreement
Stop-Out Yield
Thrift CDs
Uniform-Price Method
Yankee CDs

Review Questions

1. What are the four characteristics shared by almost all money market instruments?

2. Explain how the following participate in the money market:
   a. Commercial banks and savings associations
   b. Governments and government-sponsored enterprises (GSEs)
   c. The Federal Reserve
   d. Corporations and finance companies
   e. Pension funds and insurance companies
   f. Brokers and dealers
   g. Money market mutual funds and individuals

3. What specific role do brokers play in the federal funds market? (Hint: See the related A Closer Look feature on page 188.)

4. When banks are short on reserves, why do they use the fed funds or repurchase agreement markets instead of borrowing from another bank?

5. What advantages do large institutional investors and savers receive in the money market compared to conventional bank deposits and loans?

6. What three sets of money market instruments have the largest outstanding dollar amounts? Which is the largest? Of all money market instruments, which has the smallest outstanding balance?

7. Why are commercial paper issues characterized by maturities of less than 270 days, large denomination amounts, and used exclusively for the purpose of funding current transactions?

8. What two places might a commercial bank turn to if it wants to borrow reserves in the fed funds market? How does the Fed influence the fed funds rate?

9. Explain the difference between a repurchase agreement and a reverse repurchase agreement. In what ways does the fed funds market differ from the repo market?

10. How do negotiable CDs differ from traditional demand deposits and from traditional time deposits?

11. In what ways does the history of negotiable CDs illustrate this text's dual themes of evolutionary change and globalization? (Be sure to mention the roles played by National City Bank, Penn Central Transportation Company, Regulation Q, and the rise of money market mutual funds, Euro CDs, and foreign CDs.)

12. Why are U.S. Treasury bills characterized by the lowest interest rate of any money market instrument? How do the currently used uniform-price method auctions differ from the previously used multiple-price method auctions? Why did the Treasury change auction methods?

13. When, where, why, and by whom were Eurodollars created? What advantages does a bank like J.P. Morgan Chase & Co. have in issuing a Eurodollar deposit instead of a domestic deposit?

14. How do Bankers' acceptances (BAs) facilitate international trade? Is the Fed an active participant in this market?

15. Institutions develop to solve historically specific problems and then frequently persist long after that initial problem has been resolved. In what ways does this statement apply to the creation of money market mutual funds and their continued growth? In what ways does the statement apply to the Eurodollar market and its continued growth?

16. Did money market mutual funds facilitate disintermediation in the late 1970s and early 1980s?

Analytical Questions

17. How did the failure of ESM Government Securities, Inc. lead to a thrift "bank holiday" in the state of Ohio?

18. Assume there are excess reserves in the banking system. Explain why first the fed funds rate is likely to fall and why the repurchase agreement rate is likely to follow. Can you speculate as to why other money market rates are likely to fall as well?

19. How much interest income would be generated on a $10 million, 3-day repurchase agreement, given an RP rate of 6.0 percent?

20. How much interest income would be generated on a $5 million, 5-day repurchase agreement, given an RP rate of 5.0 percent?

21. If one purchases an RP for $9,950,000 and sells it 5 days later for $10 million, what annualized rate of interest would be earned?

22. If one purchases an RP for $9,950,000 and sells it 10 days later for $10 million, what annualized rate of interest would be earned?

23. Assume that you submitted a noncompetitive bid for a $10,000 U.S. Treasury bill. The bill matures in 13 weeks and the purchase price is $9,844.50. What is the auction price rate? What is the T-bill annualized yield?

24. Assume that you submitted a noncompetitive bid for a $10,000 U.S. Treasury bill. The bill matures in 26 weeks and the purchase price is $9,600. What is the auction price rate? What is the T-bill annualized yield?

Internet Exercises

1. Go to **http://www.bankrate.com/brm/rate/mmmf_home.asp** or **http://www.bankrate.com** and do a search on money market mutual fund rates in your city (or state if you live in a non-metro area). Who offers the highest annual percentage rate in your area? What is the required minimum deposit?

2. Go to **http://www.publicdebt.treas.gov/** and find the "Summary of Treasury Securities Outstanding." Of the total marketable securities outstanding, what share is in the form of Treasury bills?

Suggested Readings

The single best source for information about money market instruments and participants is the Federal Reserve Bank of Richmond's *Instruments of the Money Market*, 7th ed, edited by Timothy Q. Cook and Robert K. Laroche. It was last updated in 1993. As chapters are revised, they become available online at **http//www.rich.frb.org/instruments/toc.html**. Marcia Stigum's, *The Money Market*, rev. ed. (Homewood, IL: Dow Jones-Irwin, 1990) and First Boston Corporation's, *Handbook of Securities of the United States Government and Federal Agencies, and Related Money Market Instruments* (July 1990) are also valuable reference materials.

The Federal Reserve Bank of New York published *U.S. Monetary Policy & Financial Markets* by Ann-Marie Meulendyke. Although primarily about monetary policy, Chapter 4 provides an overview of financial markets and includes an informative discussion of money market instruments. The *Federal Reserve Bulletin* provides monthly updates of data on money market interest rates and volumes outstanding and occasional articles of interest on this topic. The December 1999 issue has an article entitled "The Treasury Securities Market: Overview and Recent Developments" that served as an important source of information for our discussion of the T-bill market.

chapter

The Corporate and Government Bond Markets

> **Learning Objectives** *After reading this chapter, you should know:*

- The characteristics of the bond market and how the market has changed in recent years
- How corporate and government bond markets function
- The characteristics and advantages of municipals
- What government agency securities and government sponsored enterprises are
- The factors that affect bond prices
- The types of international bonds

" "
Gentlemen prefer bonds.

veri⚡on

History in the Making

In Chapter 6, we saw that small changes in interest rates can cause large changes in bond prices. The longer the term to maturity, the greater the change in price for any change in the interest rate. In an era of volatile rates, price changes can be dramatic and bond markets can be anything but dull. In recent years, there have been other noteworthy trends in the bond market, which the following scenarios illustrate. Hopefully they will convince you to give this chapter close attention.

In January 2000, Treasury Secretary Lawrence Summers announced U.S. Treasury plans to scale down the issuance of new, 30-year government bonds and to buy back as much as $30 billion of publicly held, longer-term-to-maturity government debt. As Summers stated, "Buying back old, higher interest debt allows us to manage the Federal debt in a way that saves the American taxpayer money."[1] In total, the marketable Treasury debt had been reduced by over $610 billion between the end of March 1998 and the end of June 2001. The retiring and/or purchasing back of long-term government debt caused long-term government bonds to be in short supply. Like anything else in short supply, long-term bond prices rose and long-term rates fell. Furthermore, in October 2001, the Treasury announced that it would no longer issue 30-year bonds, causing long-term rates to fall to new lows. Indeed, the 10-year note replaced the 30-year Treasury as the long-term benchmark interest rate.

In late June 2000, Deutsche Telekom, a German telecommunications firm, made history by issuing $14.5 billion in new global bonds—the largest corporate bond offering ever in the international bond market. Deutsche Telekom is part of the booming telecommunications sector and is in the forefront of bidding for government licenses for third-generation cell phone services. The bonds were issued in four different currencies (the Japanese yen, the British pound sterling, the euro, and the U.S. dollar) with maturities in the 5-, 10-, and 30-year ranges. The U.S. dollar issuance of $9.5 billion of the $14.5 billion was the largest U.S. corporate bond offering to date! There was speculation that new issues in the telecommunication sector could total $30 billion by the end of the year.

These developments point out three trends in the bond market:

1. As the federal government runs surpluses, the supply of government bonds is going down—particularly long-term Treasuries.
2. As the supply of Treasuries declines, corporations are stepping in to take advantage of relatively low long-term rates and to issue new bonds.
3. As part of the overall trend to globalization, more and more issues are in the global bond market and involve numerous currencies and maturities.

This chapter explores the government and corporate bond markets. How does a firm go about designing an initial public offering of bonds? How do the federal government, government agencies, and government-sponsored enterprises go about marketing their securities? What are the characteristics that all bonds have in common? What are the advantages and disadvantages of bonds to a firm and to investors? What is the international bond market? These are some of the questions that will be answered in this chapter.

The bond market is the market in which bonds issued by deficit spending units (DSUs) are bought by and sold to surplus spending units (SSUs). Before we can discuss the characteristics of the corporate and government bond markets, we need to know what a bond is.

---

[1]"Treasury Department Launches Debt Buyback Program," Press Release, Office of Public Affairs, Treasury Department, January 13, 2000.

The Bond Market

Bonds are debt instruments with an original maturity greater than 10 years that are issued by private and public entities. They normally pay a fixed interest rate, the **coupon rate,** which is stated on the face of the bond. The principal, also called the *par value* or face value of the bond, is repaid in full at maturity. The *coupon payments* (*C*) are equal to the coupon rate multiplied by the face value of the bond and are usually made every 6 months.

Bonds may be either bearer bonds or registered bonds. In the case of **bearer bonds,** the bond's owner clips the coupon from the bond and sends it to the issuer, who then returns the coupon payment. With **registered bonds,** the issuer keeps records of ownership and automatically sends the coupon payment to the bondholder. Today, registered bonds are far more prevalent than bearer bonds. The issuer may be the U.S. government, an agency of the government, a state or local government, a domestic or foreign corporation, or a foreign government.

Two major credit-rating agencies, *Standard & Poor's* and *Moody's Investors Service,* analyze and evaluate bonds and assign them to a particular risk class based on the probability that the issuer will fail to pay back the principal and interest in full when due. The credit-rating agencies examine the pattern of revenues and costs experienced by a firm, its degree of leverage (dependence on borrowed funds), its past history of debt redemption, and the volatility of the industry, among other things. A firm with a history of strong earnings, low leverage, and prompt debt redemption would get an Aaa rating from Moody's and an AAA rating from Standard & Poor's. A firm that has experienced net losses, has rising leverage, or has missed some loan payments would get a Baa or lower rating from Moody and a BBB or lower rating from Standard & Poor's.

Moody's and Standards & Poor's also assign ratings to municipal securities issued by state and local governments. Important factors in determining the rating include the tax base, the level of outstanding debt, the current and expected budget situation, and the growth in spending. The specific rate classes of Standard & Poor's and Moody's were summarized in Exhibit 6-7, Chapter 6.

Bond ratings are beneficial to lenders because they help the lender determine the risk involved in purchasing a specific bond. Bonds rated below investment grade are not recommended for investment and are often referred to as *high-yield* or *junk bonds,* depending on one's perspective. Of course, their high yield results from their riskiness. Exhibit 10-1 shows the spreads between yields on bonds with different credit ratings since 1960. Note that the lower the credit rating, the higher the interest rate investors require to purchase the bonds.

The Corporate Bond Market

As the name implies, corporate bonds are issued by corporations. Investment bankers like Merrill Lynch, Salomon Smith Barney, and Bear Stearns design, market, and underwrite new corporate bond issues. They design the bond indenture. The **bond indenture** is a document that spells out the terms of the offering along with many other provisions under which the bonds are issued. The indenture is made out to a trustee who represents the investors buying the bonds. The trustee usually works for a bond or trust company, or may be part of the trust division of a bank. The trustee is an expert in interpreting the provisions of the offering for the investors and sees that the issuer fulfills the terms and conditions of the indenture.

Coupon Rate
The fixed interest rate stated on the face of a bond.

[margin note: TO THE BANK]

Bearer Bonds
Bonds in which the bond's owner clips the coupon from the bond and sends it to the issuer who then returns the coupon payment.

Registered Bonds
Bonds in which the issuer keeps records of ownership and automatically sends the coupon payment to the bondholder.

[margin note: OWNER IS RECORDED FOR TAX REASONS]

Bond Indenture
A document stating the terms under which a bond is issued.

http://www.bloomberg.com/markets/ and http://www.investinginbonds.com
Provides information regarding the corporate bond market.

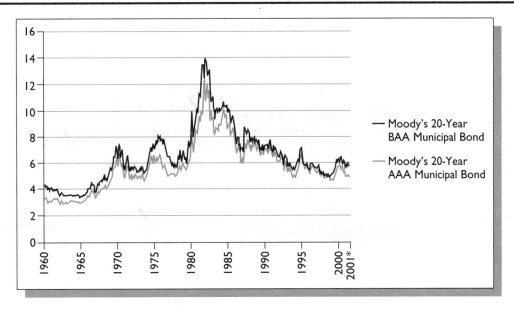

*Through July 12, 2001.

EXHIBIT 10-1

The Spread between 20-year Municipal Bonds with Different Credit Ratings 1960–2001
SOURCE: Global Financial Data, Los Angeles, California

The following are some of the provisions that an indenture may include:

1. *Sinking fund provisions:* A provision that specifies if the corporation is required to pay off (retire) a specified portion of the newly issued bonds each year is called a **sinking fund provision.** Sinking fund provisions increase the probability that all of the bonds will be paid back by maturity. For example, if a corporation issues 15-year bonds, a sinking fund provision may require that 1/15 of the issue be retired each year.

2. *Call provisions:* A provision that the corporation can pay off (retire) the bonds before maturity is called a **call provision.** Call provisions also state under what terms the bonds can be retired. A corporation may want to pay off bonds if the interest rate has fallen since the bonds were originally issued. The proceeds of a new bond issued at a lower interest rate could be used to redeem the higher-rate bonds. Another reason why a corporation may want to call bonds is to meet the sinking fund provisions just discussed. In either case, the bond indenture spells out the terms under which the bonds can be called. This includes the premium that will have to be paid above the face value of the bonds if they are retired; the premium may vary depending on the reason why the bonds are retired. Today, most corporate bonds are issued with call provisions.

3. *Convertibility provisions:* If the bondholder has a right to convert the bonds to a predetermined number of shares of common stock, the bonds are called **convertible bonds.** If the stock's price rises enough to make the conversion beneficial for the bondholder, this right will be exercised. The conversion will be beneficial if the stock's price rises such that the difference between the value of the predetermined

Sinking Fund Provisions ~PAY OFF THE DEBT~
Provisions of a bond indenture that specify whether the corporation is required to pay off a portion of the newly issued bonds each year.

Call Provisions
Provisions of a bond indenture that specify whether the corporation can pay off the bonds before they mature (and if so, under what terms).

Convertible Bonds
Bonds in which the bondholder has a right to convert the bonds to a predetermined number of shares of common stock; particularly beneficial to the bondholder if the shares of stock appreciate greatly.

number of shares of stock and the value of the bonds more than compensates for the increase in the risk of owning stocks rather than bonds. In most cases, the stock's appreciation would have to be significant for the conversion to be beneficial and thus exercised. However, convertibility provisions have value and, generally, convertible bonds will be issued at lower interest rates than bonds without this feature.

Warrant
Contracts sometimes issued with newly issued bonds; warrants give the holder the right to purchase a designated security at a price set today; warrants may be sold to a third party.

4. *Provisions for the issuance of warrants:* A **warrant** is a contract that gives the holder the right to purchase a designated security such as common stock or bonds of the issuer any time up to a future date at a price set today. If bonds are issued with a warrant, the bond indenture will include provisions about the warrants. Warrants may be held to be used at a later date, or they may be sold immediately to a third party. Bonds issued with warrants are issued at lower interest rates than bonds without this feature.

Restrictive Covenants
Stipulations within the bond indenture that limit the ability of the corporation with regards to certain activities.

5. *Restrictive covenants:* **Restrictive covenants** are stipulations within the bond indenture that limit the ability of the corporation with regard to certain activities. For example, restrictive covenants may restrict the salary and bonuses of the corporate officers, the amount of dividends the corporation can pay, or the amount of additional debt that can be incurred. Usually, the more restrictive the covenants, the lower the interest rate will be on the bonds.

6. The indenture may contain a provision that the coupon payment on the bond be increased if the credit rating of the corporation is downgraded by a certain amount during the life of the bond.

Mortgage Bonds
Bonds backed by real personal property.

Collateral Bonds
Bonds backed by financial assets.

Debenture Bonds
Bonds with no specific collateral backing but have a general claim on the other unpledged assets of the issuer.

Subordinated Debenture Bonds
Bonds with no collateral backing that have a general claim after debenture bondholders have been paid.

Some bonds are backed by specific collateral such as real or personal property. The collateral may include plant, equipment, and financial assets that the issuing corporation owns. **Mortgage bonds** are backed by real property while **collateral bonds** are backed by financial assets. **Debenture bonds** are not backed by specific collateral, but in the event of a default, they have a general claim on the otherwise unpledged assets of the issuer. Finally, **subordinated debenture bonds** are not backed by collateral and have a general claim after debenture bondholders have been paid. Thus, in the event of a default, owners of subordinated debenture bonds are the last bondholders in line to receive any funds after all other bondholders—and often after other creditors—have been paid. As expected, other factors being equal, subordinated debenture bonds pay the highest return, followed by debenture bonds, followed by mortgage and collateral bonds.

Some bonds also come with financial guarantees issued by insurance companies. The bond issuer pays a premium that guarantees the payment of interest and principal by the insurance company in the event the issuer defaults. In reality, the credit of the guarantor is substituted for the guarantee of the issuer. The issuer pays a premium for the financial guarantee. Because of the guarantee, the bonds are issued at a lower interest rate. Obviously, it is beneficial to the bond issuer to pay for the financial guarantee if the present value of the interest savings over the life of the bond is greater than the insurance premium.

Zero-Coupon Bonds
Corporate bonds sold at a discount with the difference between the amount paid for the bond and the amount received at maturity equal to the interest.

Some firms also issue **zero-coupon bonds,** which, as their name implies, do not have coupons and do not make coupon payments. Instead, the bonds are sold at a discount with the difference between the amount paid for the bond and the amount received at maturity being equal to the interest.[2] The advantage to the investor is that there is no risk that the interest will have to be reinvested at a lower rate. A disadvantage is that the interest payments are amortized over the life of the loan

---

[2]Zero-coupon bonds are similar to Treasury bills that are also sold at a discount.

LOOKING BACK: *The Junk Bond Market*

In 1909, John Moody issued the first public rating for bonds considered "too risky for investment" and called that rating "below investment grade."[a] These bonds are now called *junk bonds.* During the Great Depression of the 1930s, many bonds originally recommended for investment were downgraded to "below investment grade." After the bonds had been issued, their ratings were lowered because the issuing corporations were not doing as well as expected. At the end of the Great Depression, 42 percent of all outstanding corporate bonds were rated as junk bonds. Even so, new issues of junk were nonexistent because widespread financial failures—the brute forces of events—had caused investors to grow weary of all but the top-rated grades. As a result, by 1977, only 3.7 percent of outstanding corporate debt carried the below investment grade rating.

The market was ripe for change in the 1970s, when Michael Milken joined the small unknown brokerage house of Drexel Burnham Lambert. Under Milken's leadership, Drexel Burnham Lambert became a market maker for junk bonds. Drexel began underwriting new issues of junk bonds and created a secondary market, standing ready to buy or sell as needed. The junk bond market grew rapidly throughout the 1980s as financial intermediaries (FIs) and individuals jumped on the bandwagon. By the end of 1989, more than 22 percent of outstanding U.S. corporate bonds were junk bonds. Furthermore, three-quarters of this debt had been issued below investment grade, and Drexel Burnham Lambert had grown to rival the largest investment banking firms on Wall Street. But the junk bond market was headed for trouble, and two events would lead to its demise.

First, a large issuer of junk bonds, Campeau Corporation, defaulted, causing panic and large sell-offs among junk bondholders. And second, Congress enacted a law forcing all U.S. thrift institutions—savings and loans, credit unions, and mutual savings banks—to sell off their junk bond holdings by mid-1994.

Faced with these events, the market collapsed and Drexel Burnham Lambert declared bankruptcy. A liquidity crisis ensued and prices plummeted further. Milken, who was indicted on 98 counts of racketeering and tax and securities fraud, pleaded guilty to six charges. His sentence included a $600 million fine and 10 years in prison. He ended up serving a much shorter time in prison.

Many who rode out the declining market eventually did well. For instance, MCI, the long-distance phone company, got started by issuing junk bonds to finance its operations, and the market is extremely active today.

[a]When marketing these bonds, brokers refer to them as high-yield bonds.

and taxes are paid on the amount of the interest earned each year, even though the interest is not paid until the bond matures. The advantages for the corporation are that the interest payments are written off on an annual basis, and they do not have to be made until the bond matures.

The secondary market in corporate bonds is a loosely connected array of brokers and dealers who buy, sell, and take positions in bonds in what is called the *over-the-counter market.* In the over-the-counter market, brokers and dealers buy and sell bonds over computer links and telephone lines. Although the bulk of bond trading takes place over-the-counter, some bonds are also bought and sold on organized exchanges such as the New York Stock Exchange.[3]

Bonds trade with varying degrees of liquidity in the secondary market. Other factors being equal, the greater the expected liquidity, the lower the yield. Now would be a good time to read the Cracking the Code box on p. 212, which tells how to understand corporate bond prices and yields as reported in the financial pages of popular newspapers.

http://www.newyorkfed.org/pihome/fedpoint
Provides a New York Fed publication on zero coupon bonds (Fedpoint 42).

---

[3]Over 97 percent of the dollar value of trading activity on the New York Stock Exchange involves the trading of stocks, which is why we defer a more lengthy discussion until the next chapter on the stock market.

CRACKING THE CODE: *Corporate Bonds*

The following table shows a typical example of the way bond market information appears in the newspaper. If we look at the AT&T (American Telephone and Telegraph) bonds, we see that there are a number of different types of bonds outstanding. They were issued at different times to finance operations such as investment. Accordingly, all of these issues are "used" (or "seasoned") bonds trading in the secondary market. We will focus on the highlighted bond.

Corporation Bonds Volume, $10,851,000

Bonds	Cur Yld	Vol	Close	Net Chg
AMR 9s 16	8.3	10	108 3/8	+1 3/8
ATT 7⅛ 02	7.1	10	100 11/16	– 9/16
ATT 6½ 02	6.4	10	101 1/4	– 1/8
ATT 5⅝ 04	5.7	215	98 3/4	– 1/2
ATT 7s 05	6.8	5	103	– 1/4
ATT 6s 09	6.4	185	94 1/2	– 3/8
ATT 8⅛ 22	7.9	196	102 3/8	+3/8
ATT 8⅛ 24	8.0	80	101 3/4	– 1/2
ATT 8.35s 25	8.1	20	103 1/2	+3/8
ATT 5½ 29	7.5	70	86 3/8	– 5/8
ATT 8⅛ 31	8.3	5	104 1/8	– 5/8

SOURCE: *The Wall Street Journal*, March 26, 2001, p. C15.

First, you see the issuing company's name—AT&T. The "8 1/8" next to the name is the coupon yield. It appears on the face of the bond and indicates the amount of interest that AT&T will pay the holder annually; in this case, the 8 1/8 percent (8.125 percent) indicates that $81.25 of interest will be paid annually (usually in semi-annual installments) per $1,000 of face (or par) value of bonds held. The $81.25 is 8 1/8 percent of $1,000. Next we see "24," which means that the bond will mature in the year 2024. At that time, AT&T will give the holder of the bond the last interest payment and $1,000 of principal per $1,000 of face (or par) value. As the name suggests, the "face value" appears on the face of the bond.

The "Close" and "Net Change" columns refer to the price of the bond. As you will see, the price code in the bond market is different than the price code in the stock market; this is part of a conscious plot to confuse "outsiders." To conserve space in the newspaper, bond prices are stated as percentages of 100, with 100 representing $1,000 face value. Hence, the closing price for the day was 101 3/4, which means $1,017.50 (each point is equal to $10). The closing price was down 1/2 from the previous day's closing price, or $5 ($5 = 1/2 of $10).

The "Vol" column simply gives the volume of trading in thousands of dollars. The current yield ("Cur Yld") column is not so simple. This bond pays $81.25 annually to its holder. At the close on this day, someone could have bought the bond for $1,017.50. As a result, the current yield on the investment—that is, the bond purchased—would be 8.0 percent ($81.25/$1,017.50 = .08 = 8.0 percent). Only if a bond is selling at 100, or at par value, will the coupon yield be equal to the current yield.

RECAP Bonds are debt instruments that may be issued by domestic or foreign governments and corporations. The terms of a corporate bond issue are spelled out by the bond indenture and interpreted by the trustee. These may include sinking fund provisions, call provisions, convertibility privileges, and other restrictive covenants. Corporate bonds may be mortgage bonds, collateral bonds, debenture bonds, or subordinated debenture bonds. Mortgage and collateral bonds are backed by real or financial assets that the corporation owns. Debenture bondholders are entitled to be paid before subordinated debenture bondholders. With convertible bonds, the bondholder can convert the bonds into a predetermined number of shares of stock. Bonds sometimes come with warrants that allow the bondholder to purchase (or sell the right to purchase to another investor) a number of shares of stocks or bonds in the future.

The Treasury Bond Market

U.S. government bonds, or Treasury bonds, are issued in the primary market by the Bureau of the Public Debt in minimum amounts of $1,000. They make periodic coupon payments (usually every 6 months). The Federal Reserve system sells Treasury bonds in regularly scheduled competitive auctions during February, August, and November. Treasury notes and T-bills are sold in other regularly scheduled auctions. With the buy-back of government securities and reduction in marketable Treasury debt, there is some question whether there will continue to be as many Treasury auctions as in the past.[4] The Treasury decides the maturity structure and the amount of the various offerings.[5]

The secondary market in Treasury bonds is an over-the-counter market. A group of U.S. government securities dealers stands ready to buy or sell various issues of outstanding securities over-the-counter. Today, Treasury securities are sold in worldwide secondary markets 24 hours a day. An extensive and very active secondary market makes Treasury bonds highly liquid. The dealers' profits stem from the spread between the bid (buying) and ask (selling) prices.

How the Treasury Bond Market Works

Primary dealers are large banks and securities brokers and dealers that trade Treasury securities directly with the New York Fed and are the main participants in the Treasury auctions. They submit competitive bids, which are offers to buy the newly issued bonds that may or may not be accepted. The role of primary dealers began in 1960 when 18 were selected. By 1988, the number of primary dealers had grown to 46. Since that time, the number has fallen to 25, primarily due to mergers among the firms within the banking and security industries.

To become a primary dealer, the firm must apply to the New York Fed and must demonstrate that it meets certain criteria. Banks must be in compliance with specific mandated capital standards. Brokers and dealers must have at least $50 million in regulatory capital and must meet other criteria established by the Securities and Exchange Commission. Foreign-owned firms that meet the criteria are eligible to become primary dealers.

As noted previously, sales of government securities by the Treasury occur through a competitive bidding process in which the New York Fed asks all primary dealers to submit bids in response to an announced offering. The lowest-priced bids are accepted up to the amount of the offering.

In addition to participating in the auction of Treasury securities, primary dealers must participate in the Fed open market operations that are a part of monetary policy. The open market operations implemented under the direction of the Fed Open Market Committee involve both the selling and buying of Treasury securities. Thus, primary dealers play an important role in facilitating the implementation of monetary policy as well as the marketing of new Treasury securities.

Since 1994, bids to buy and offers to sell securities have been submitted electronically. Likewise, the Fed's responses to those bids and offers are also executed electronically. Primary dealers must participate in a meaningful way in the open market operations and the auctions, both in terms of size and competitiveness of

Primary Dealers
The large banks and government securities dealers that are approved by the Fed to be the main participants in the auctions of Treasury securities that are conducted by the Fed.

---

[4]In addition to buying back old debt, the Treasury Department has also reduced the number of scheduled auctions for 52-week Treasury bills.

[5]As we saw in Chapter 3, government securities consist of Treasury bills, notes, and bonds, depending on maturity. Bills have an original maturity of 1 year or less. Notes have an original maturity of 2 to 10 years and bonds have an original maturity of greater than 10 years.

EXHIBIT 10-2
Who Are the Primary
Dealers? Primary
Dealers as of
July 2, 2001

ABN AMRO Inc.	Fuji Securities, Inc.
BMO Nesbitt Burns Corp.	Goldman, Sachs & Co.
BNP Paribas Securities Corp.	Greenwich Capital Markets, Inc.
Bank of America Securities LLC	HSBC Securities (USA), Inc.
Bank One Capital Markets, Inc.	J.P. Morgan Securities, Inc.
Barclays Capital Inc.	Lehman Brothers, Inc.
Bear Stearns & Co., Inc.	Merrill Lynch Government Securities, Inc.
CIBC World Markets Corp.	Morgan Stanley & Co., Inc.
Credit Suisse First Boston Corp.	Nomura Securities International, Inc.
Daiwa Securities America, Inc.	SG Cowen Securities Corp.
Deutsche Bank Securities, Inc.	Salomon Smith Barney, Inc.
Dresdner Kleinwort Wesserstein	UBS Warburg LLC
Securities LLC	Zions First National Bank

SOURCE: Federal Reserve Bank of New York, http://www.newyorkfed.org/pihome/news/opnmktops/.

their positions. They must also provide the Fed with weekly reports on their trading. Failure to do so may cause the Fed to withdraw their status as primary dealers. Exhibit 10-2 is a list of 25 primary dealers as of July 2, 2001.

Individual investors seeking to participate in the auction may submit noncompetitive bids. With a noncompetitive bid, the investor agrees to accept the average rate determined at the auction and is guaranteed a security. If investors are planning to keep their securities until maturity, they may purchase the securities "treasury direct" at the Bureau of the Public Debt or at a Federal Reserve bank or branch.

In addition to the treasury direct system, the Federal Reserve also operates a commercial book-entry system. Ownership is recorded and payments are disbursed electronically. Investors who maintain their securities in this system have bought them through a financial institution or a government securities dealer, and the securities may be resold in the secondary market.

Treasury bonds are a full-faith and credit obligation of the U.S. government. Consequently, investors view Treasury securities as being free from default risk. The federal government, with its power to tax or issue currency, will definitely pay back the principal and interest as scheduled. However, Treasury bonds are not free of interest rate risk. If the interest rate goes up after the bonds are issued and before their maturity, the value of the bonds will go down. If the bonds are sold before maturity, the investor will receive less than the face value of the bonds and experience a capital loss. A desirable feature of Treasury bonds is that the interest earned is exempt from state income taxes; this feature is particularly beneficial in states with high income tax rates. Interest rates on Treasury securities serve as benchmark rates to judge the riskiness and liquidity of other securities, and their prices are widely quoted in the popular media. The Cracking the Code feature on p. 215 explains how to interpret the prices of Treasury bonds reported in major newspapers.

Treasury STRIPS are a type of government security first offered in 1984 and sold through depository institutions and government securities dealers. All newly issued Treasury notes and bonds with maturities of 10 years or longer are eligible for the STRIPS program. STRIPS allow investors to register and trade ownership of the interest (coupon) payments and the principal amount of the security. The advantage of STRIPS is that the coupon and principal payments can be sold separately at a discount.[6] Don't let these last statements fool you into thinking that

**http://www.
federalreserve.gov**
*Provides information
regarding Treasury
securities.*

**http://www.
newyorkfed.org/
pihome/fedpoint/
fed42.html**
*Describes the operation of
the Treasury STRIPS
program.*

Treasury STRIPS
A type of government
security that allows
investors to register and
trade ownership of the
interest (coupon)
payments and the
principal separately.

---

[6]Recall that Treasury bills are sold at a discount.

CRACKING THE CODE: *Treasury Bonds*

To understand how to read the accompanying table of developments that occurred in the government bond market on March 23, 2001 (taken from *The Wall Street Journal*), let us take a look at the highlighted line. Under "Rate" (first column) is listed "6." This is the coupon rate, and it indicates that the holder of this security receives $6 per year for each $100 (face or par value), usually paid in semiannual installments.

MATURITY RATE	MO/YR	BID	ASKED	ASK CHG	YLD
6	Feb 26	107:04	107:06	–28	5.47

SOURCE: *The Wall Street Journal*, March 26, 2001, p. C15.

The maturity date (second column) is Feb 26. This simply indicates that the security will mature in February 2026.

The next two columns give the "Bid" and "Asked" prices. The bid price is the price the market maker (dealer) is willing to pay to acquire this security. Prices are quoted in thirty-seconds. Thus, 107:04 bid means 107 4/32 or $107.125, per each $100. Hence, for a $1,000 bond, we need only move the decimal point to find that the bid price is $1,071.25. The asked price is the price the dealer is asking when selling the security. In this case, the asked price is 107:06, which means 107 6/32 or $107.1875, per $100. For a $1,000 bond, the asked price is $1,071.88. Prices are quoted in thirty-seconds.

The column labeled "Chg" shows that the bid for this particular government security decreased 28 on March 23, 2001, as compared with the close on the previous trading day. The change is also reported in thirty-seconds, so the decrease is really 28/32, or $.875, per $100 or $8.75 for a $1,000 bond.

The last column gives the yield to maturity on an annual basis for this bond. It is 5.47 percent—this is the interest rate, or rate of return on the bond. The yield to maturity takes into account the dollar return to the investor resulting from the coupon payment ($60 per year per $1,000 face value), the price appreciation or depreciation between the time when the security is bought and when it matures, and the price paid. In this case, there will be a depreciation at maturity. The security is selling at a premium: The market price of $1,071.88 exceeds the face value of $1,000.

Whenever the security sells at a premium, the yield to maturity is less than the coupon rate. Can you explain why the yield to maturity exceeds the coupon rate when the security sells at a discount (market price is less than the face value)?

there are actual physical securities and actual physical coupons. STRIPS are sold in book entry form, meaning that the security is issued and accounted for electronically. The investor pays less today for the future payment than he or she will receive when the security matures. The interest the investor earns is the difference between what is paid today and what is received at maturity. Because the future payments are sold at a discount, the investor avoids the uncertainty that coupon payments may have to be reinvested at a lower interest rate because rates have fallen since the security was issued. The future payments of the STRIPS securities are direct obligations of the U.S. government.[7]

Inflation-indexed bonds are a more recent hybrid, first offered for sale by the Treasury in January 1997. An inflation-indexed bond is one in which the principal amount is adjusted for inflation at the time when an interest (coupon) payment is made, usually every 6 months. Although the interest rate does not change, the

http://www.dtonline. com/bonds/basics.htm
Provides basic information about inflation-indexed bonds.

Inflation-Indexed Bonds
Bonds whose principal amount is adjusted for inflation at the time when coupon payments are made (usually every 6 months).

---

[7]Actually, starting in 1982, some brokers and dealers were discounting coupon payments and principal payments of long-term Treasuries in a way that is similar to the STRIPS program. Creation of the Treasury-sponsored STRIPS program eliminated the need for these less efficient, privately managed programs.

interest payments are based on the inflation-adjusted principal, and the inflation-adjusted principal is repaid at maturity. Inflation-indexed bonds protect the investor from the ravages of inflation.

STOP

RECAP Treasury securities are sold in competitive auctions with participation by 25 approved dealers. They may also be purchased treasury direct or from a financial institution or government securities dealer. They are considered to be free of default risk, and their interest rate serves as a benchmark to judge the risk and liquidity of other financial assets. The secondary market for government securities is a highly-developed, over-the-counter market. STRIPS are a government security that allow the investor to register and trade ownership of the coupon payments and the principal separately. Because the future payments are sold at a discount, the risk (called reinvestment risk) that coupon payments may have to be reinvested at a lower interest rate is eliminated. The principal of inflation-indexed bonds is adjusted for inflation every 6 months. The coupon payment is based on the inflation-adjusted amount and the investor receives the inflation-adjusted principal at maturity.

Municipal and Government Agency Securities

Municipal Bonds
(munis, for short)
Bonds issued by state, county, and local governments to finance public projects such as schools, utilities, roads, and transportation ventures; the interest on municipal securities is exempt from federal and state taxes for investors living in the issuing state.

Municipal bonds (munis, for short) are bonds issued by state, county, and local governments to finance public projects such as schools, utilities, roads, and transportation ventures. The interest on municipal securities is exempt from federal taxes as well as from state taxes for investors living in the issuing state. This allows the issuer to borrow at a lower rate than if taxes would have to be paid on the interest earned. Municipal bonds are particularly attractive to taxpayers in high income tax brackets. As we saw in Chapter 3, the interest rate will gravitate to the rate at which the average investor is indifferent between purchasing munis or other bonds of comparable maturity, liquidity, and risk where the interest income is not tax exempt. This rate is depicted in Equation 10-1, where t is the average marginal tax rate, i_b is the rate on comparable bonds, and i_m is the rate on munis.[8]

(10-1) $$i_b(1-t) = i_m$$

Taxpayers in a tax bracket higher than the average marginal bracket can earn a higher return by investing in munis. The cost to the state, county, or local government issuer is t percent less than it would be if the interest income were not tax exempt. Thus, if the comparable corporate rate is 8 percent, the average marginal tax bracket 25 percent, and the muni rate 6 percent, taxpayers in a tax bracket above 25 percent can earn a higher after-tax return by investing in munis. In addition, municipalities can borrow at a 2 percent lower rate than if their interest income were not tax exempt.[9]

Municipal bonds may be either *general obligation bonds* or *revenue bonds*. General obligation bonds are repaid out of general tax revenues. A default in the state-issued municipal bonds market has not occurred in the last 100 years. This is not

---

[8]As we saw in Chapter 3, the marginal tax rate is the tax rate on the last dollar of taxable income. Taxpayers, depending on their individual incomes, are in different marginal tax brackets, some high and some low. The average marginal tax rate is somewhere between the high and the low marginal tax brackets. Because of substitution, the interest rate on municipal securities will gravitate to the rate that makes the "average" taxpayer (in the average marginal tax bracket) indifferent between municipals and similarly rated corporate securities.

[9]For a more detailed explanation of the benefits of investing in munis for individuals in high tax brackets, see Chapter 3.

true for munis issued by local and county governments. Repayment of revenue bonds is tied to the success of a specific project that the bonds support. That is, the bondholder is paid back out of the cash flows of a particular project. Defaults on revenue bonds occurred when specific projects did not generate the forecasted revenues.

Most municipal bonds are marketed publicly in the primary market through an investment banker and/or the municipal bond department of a commercial bank. Some issues may also be placed privately. An official statement, a legal opinion that describes the offering, must be released with each new offering. As noted earlier, municipal bonds are rated by Moody's and Standard & Poor's. Governments often try to time their issuance of "munis" when interest rates are low. Although secondary markets are active, they do not have the breadth and depth of secondary markets for Treasury securities.

Government agency securities are issued by private enterprises that were publicly chartered by Congress to reduce the cost of borrowing to certain sectors of the economy. They may be divided into two classes: government-sponsored enterprises and federally related institutions securities markets.

Areas where **government-sponsored enterprises (GSEs)** have been established include housing, farming, the savings and loan industry, and student loans. Among others, GSEs include the Federal Home Loan Banks, the Federal National Mortgage Association, the Federal Home Loan Mortgage Corporation, the Farm Credit System, and the Student Loan Marketing Association. All are privately owned and issue long-term securities (bonds) to assist in some aspect of lending such as funding of student loans, mortgage loans, and farm credit. In most cases, the federal government has no legal obligation to guarantee the timely payment of interest and principal. However, many market participants assume that the government does "*de facto*" guarantee the payments.

The yield spread between government agency securities and U.S. government securities reflects differences in liquidity and risk. The yield spread can be significant because secondary markets do not have the breadth and depth of Treasuries.

Government-sponsored enterprises experienced tremendous growth in the 1990s. Credit market debt outstanding, most of which are long-term securities increased from about $700 billion at the end of 1994 to about $1,958 billion as of June 30, 2001. We take a closer look at the issues involved with some of the GSEs—those that relate to the mortgage market—in Chapter 12. GSEs are also covered in depth in Chapter 20.

In addition to government agency securities, the Federal Financing Bank, created in 1973, issues bonds to borrow for several federally related institutions. Among others, these institutions include the Commodity Credit Corporation, the General Services Administration, the Government National Mortgage Association, the Rural Telephone Bank, the Small Business Administration, and the Tennessee Valley Authority. The bonds issued by the Federal Financing Bank are backed by the full faith and credit of the U.S. government.

Government Agency Securities
Bonds issued by private enterprises that were publicly chartered by Congress to reduce the cost of borrowing to certain sectors of the economy such as farming, housing, and student loans.

Government-sponsored Enterprises
Private enterprises that have been chartered by Congress to reduce the cost of borrowing in such sectors as housing, farming, the savings and loan industry, and student loans.

RECAP Municipal securities are bonds issued by state, county, and local governments. The interest income on municipal securities is exempt from federal taxes and state income taxes for investors in the state where the municipals were issued. The interest on Treasury securities is exempt from state income taxes. Municipal securities may be either general obligation bonds or revenue bonds. Government agency securities are issued by government-sponsored enterprises, which are private enterprises that are publicly chartered by Congress and by the federal financing bank.

Recent Trends in the Bond Market

In the late 1990s and early 2000s, U.S. corporate debt of nonfinancial firms has increased dramatically. Corporate debt, as a share of gross domestic product, is now at an all-time high. This ratio increased from just under 30 percent in 1960 to about 47 percent in 2000, with corporate debt increasing by 10.2 percent in 2000.[10] Although not all of the debt of nonfinancial firms is long-term debt, newly issued corporate bonds were $116.3 billion, $150.5 billion, $218.7 billion, $239.9 billion, and $175 billion, respectively, in the years 1996 through 2000. In the first half of 2001, over $212 billion of new corporate bonds were issued. During this same time period, outstanding corporate bonds of the nonfinancial sector increased from approximately $1.5 trillion to approximately $2.4 trillion.[11]

Some analysts are concerned that the high level of debt could lead to problems for corporations in the event of an economic downturn, a major decline in stock prices, and/or major increases in interest rates. High debt levels make a corporation more vulnerable because a decline in revenues or a spike in interest rates could call into question the corporation's ability to service its debt.

While debt of U.S. nonfinancial firms as a share of GDP is at a historic high, debt of nonfinancial firms relative to the market valuation of firms in the market has trended steadily and significantly downward. This is due to the unprecedented run-up in stock prices during 1996 though 2000. (Stock prices represent the market valuation of firms.) This trend was reversed in 2001 due to declines in stock prices. The fact remains, however, that debt of financial firms relative to gross domestic product is very high and that this impacts the bond market. Exhibit 10-3 shows the debt of nonfinancial firms as a share of gross domestic product.

Federal budget surpluses have reversed the upward trend of the 1980s in the total amount of publicly held government debt.[12] Federal debt owed to the public fell from approximately $3,872 billion on March 31, 1998 to $3,261.4 billion on June 30, 2001. As noted in the chapter introduction, this is a decrease of $610.6 billion. The Treasury instituted a program in which the Treasury buys back previously issued securities with long terms to maturity remaining. The buyback programs enhance the liquidity of the debt and reduce the average term to maturity of the debt from what it otherwise would be.[13] Whether or not the downward trend of publicly held government debt continues depends on whether or not the government will continue to run surpluses. Given downward pressures on the economy in late 2001, caused in part by the September 11 attack on the World Trade Center and the Pentagon, future surpluses will be much less than previously thought, if they exist at all. As a result of the economic turmoil, tax receipts are expected to decline at the same time government expenditures increase.

On August 3, 2000, Fannie Mae, a government-sponsored enterprise, made the largest bond sale in U.S. history outside the global and Treasury markets. Fannie Mae, the nation's largest purchaser of mortgages, sold $11.5 billion in bonds. This

---

[10]*Flow of Funds Accounts of the United States, Z.1*, Board of Governors of the Federal Reserve System, September 18, 2001, p. 6.

[11]*Flow of Funds Accounts of the United States, Z.1*, Board of Governors of the Federal Reserve System, September 18, 2001, p. 64.

[12]Part of the public debt is held by government agencies such as the Fed and the Social Security Administration. This amount increased from $1,623 billion on September 30, 1997 to $2,474 billion on October 12, 2001. As discussed in Chapter 14, the Social Security System continues to run surpluses, which are used to purchase government securities.

[13]If the Treasury merely let the outstanding debt fall by not rolling over short-term securities as they matured, then the debt would become more heavily weighted with long-term securities and the average maturity would increase.

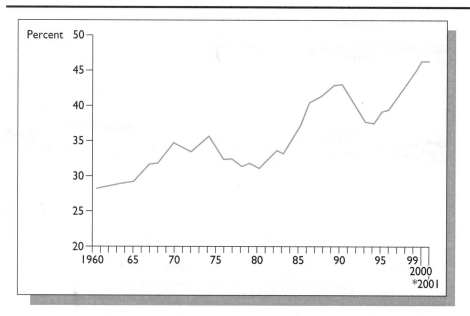

EXHIBIT 10-3
The Upward Trend
of Debt of U.S.
Nonfinancial Firms
Relative to Gross
Domestic Product
GOP 1960–2001*

*Values for 2001 are through the second quarter.
SOURCE: Board of Governors of the Federal Reserve System. *Flow of Funds Accounts, Z1,* Second Quarter, 2001, September 18, 2001

surpassed the domestic corporate offering of $9.5 billion by Deutsche Telekom made a few months earlier. Securities of government-sponsored enterprises and federally related mortgage pools increased from approximately $2.6 trillion in 1996 to over $4.5 trillion as of June 30, 2001.[14] The bulk of this debt is in long-term bonds.

The rest of the world, or foreign sector, has also dramatically increased the inflows of capital to the United States from abroad. Part of the inflow has been used to purchase government and agency securities, but inflows into corporate bonds were $83.7 billion, $84.6 billion, $122.2 billion, $160.6 billion, and $183.7 billion, respectively, in the years 1996 through 2000. In the first half of 2001, foreigners purchased over $139 billion in U.S. corporate bonds. U.S. purchases of foreign bonds were $67 billion, $61.4 billion, $34.9 billion, $16.8 billion, and $54.3 billion in the years 1996 though 2000. In the first half of 2001, U.S. holdings of foreign bonds increased by about $18 billion.[15] Thus, in net, the value of domestic bonds purchased by foreigners grew consistently and far exceeded the value of foreign bonds purchased by U.S. residents.

RECAP The bond market has grown significantly, fueled by increases in nonfinancial corporate bonds, and bonds issued by government-sponsored enterprises. The publicly held outstanding supply of Treasury bonds is going down. Foreigners have made substantial net purchases of domestic bonds, increasing the supply of funds flowing into this market. In total, the trend is for increasing capital flows across borders and the globalization of finance.

In the next section, we look at how bond prices are determined. The trends we will discuss affect the ultimate outcome in bond markets.

---

[14]*Flow of Funds Accounts of the United States, Z.1*, Board of Governors of the Federal Reserve System, September 18, 2001, p. 58.

[15]*Flow of Funds Accounts of the United States, Z.1*, Board of Governors of the Federal Reserve System, September 18, 2001, p. 22.

The Determinants of Bond Prices

The price of a previously issued bond will be equal to the present value of the future stream of income from that bond. Once the bond has been issued, the coupon rate is relevant only in determining the coupon payment. The purchaser of the bond has a claim on a future income stream that is composed of the coupon payments and the face (par) value that will be received at maturity. It is the coupon payment and the face value of the bond that are relevant. The present value of the future income stream will determine the price at which the bond will currently trade and is determined by the current interest rate, not the coupon rate. When interest rates change, the prices of previously issued bonds change.

To find its present value and, thus, the price at which the bond will trade in financial markets, we need to compute the present value of each coupon payment and the present value of the final repayment of the face value on the maturity date. The appropriate discount factor is the current interest rate on a security of equal risk, liquidity, and maturity.

The formula for the price of a previously issued bond is:

(10-2) $P = C_1/(1 + i)^1 + C_2/(1 + i)^2 + \ldots + C_n / (1 + i)^n + F/(1 + i)^n$

where

P = the price (present value) of the bond

C = the coupon payment on the bond (C_1 in year 1, C_2 in year 2, etc.)

F = the face or par value of the bond

i = the interest rate

n = the number of years to maturity (on a 5-year bond, $n = 5$)

You can see that the price of a bond is equal to its par value only when the coupon rate is equal to the current interest rate.

Simpler ways to determine the price of a bond include using either a financial calculator or present value tables. Financial calculators (along with directions) are widely available in campus bookstores and office supply stores. The appendix to this chapter discusses how to use present value tables.

As Exhibit 10-4 shows, the longer the term to maturity remaining, the larger the fluctuation in the price of the bond for any given change in interest rates.

In the case of bonds, the expected future cash flows are the coupon payment and the repayment of the face value at maturity.[16] The amount is known with certainty unless the corporation or government entity runs into financial difficulties and cannot meet its obligations. That is, unless the issuer defaults, the interest payments and the principal payments are known in advance and there is no chance that they will be more or less. This is different from the case of stocks, in which the cash flow payments in the form of dividends are uncertain.

Because of the federal government's power to print money and to tax, virtually no uncertainty exists that it will be able to meet its obligations. Therefore, Treasuries are considered to be default risk-free and the long-term government bond rate has been regarded as the risk-free rate.[17] Note that Treasuries are still subject to an interest rate risk if the interest rate increases after the bond is issued and

---

[16]In the case of callable bonds, the face value can be paid off prior to maturity. Callable bonds have not been issued by the Treasury since 1985.

[17]As noted in the chapter introduction, the 10-year rate has recently replaced the 30-year Treasury bond rate as the benchmark risk-free rate.

In this example, we are assuming that the original interest rate is 5 percent regardless of the term to maturity.[a] We consider what will happen to the bond price if the interest rate increases to 6 percent.

TERM TO MATURITY	ORIGINAL PRICE	NEW PRICE OF BOND AFTER INTEREST RATE INCREASE
10 years	$1,000	$926.41
20 years	$1,000	$885.30
30 years	$1,000	$862.35

Thus, the longer the term to maturity, the larger the change in the price of the bond for any given change in the interest rate, *ceteris paribus.*[b] Can you explain why in all cases, the bond will sell for less than its face value in the secondary market?

[a]This is not usually the case, but could be if the yield curve were flat. This simplification is used for illustrative purposes only and does not alter the results.

[b]Note that we used the present value tables found in the appendix of this chapter to calculate the new bond prices.

before it matures. In the case of Treasuries, the current Treasury bond rate is the discount factor that is used to find the bond prices of bonds with equivalent maturities. Thus, to find the price an investor would be willing to pay for a stream of income from a Treasury that has 10 years to maturity, the appropriate discount factor to use is the 10-year Treasury bond rate. If this rate is above the coupon rate of the bond (interest rates have gone up since the bond was originally issued), the price of the bond will be less than the face value, and sell at a discount from par. If the current 10-year rate is below the coupon rate at which the bond was previously issued, the bond will sell at a premium above par.

Many factors affect the risk-free rate, and one of the most important is the stance of monetary policy. If the Fed increases the supply of reserves, short-term interest rates fall and the supply of credit is expanded; long-term interest rates also fall but usually by less. Changes in inflationary expectations and the level of economic activity also affect long-term, risk-free interest rates. If inflation is expected to increase in the coming years, bond purchasers will require—and borrowers will be willing to pay—an inflation premium to compensate for the loss in purchasing power. Likewise, if income is increasing, the demand for loanable funds increases and puts upward pressure on interest rates. In the real world, these factors are interrelated. For example, expansionary monetary policy may cause market participants to expect higher inflation. Rather than leading to lower interest rates, interest rates may rise despite the expansionary monetary policy. Likewise, a recession brought on by higher oil prices may lead to higher interest rates if the impact of the higher oil prices affects inflationary expectations more than the drop in income. Other factors such as international capital flows and the amount of government borrowing also impact interest rates.

In the case of bonds that are not default-risk free, investors require that a risk premium be added to the risk-free return. The sum of the risk-free return plus the risk premium will equal the appropriate discount factor to use in determining the price of a bond, as depicted in Equation 10-3.

(10-3) $$d = R_F + R_P$$

where

d = the discount factor

R_F = the risk-free rate

R_P = the risk premium

The question that remains is how the risk premium is determined. What is the risk premium that investors require as compensation in order to purchase the bonds rather than Treasuries? A major factor affecting the ability of the bond issuer to make payments as prescribed is the level of economic activity. In a booming economy, sales, revenues, and cash flows all facilitate the timely payment of the corporation's obligations. Likewise, in a recession or depression, cash flows may fall short of what is needed to meet scheduled payments.

The capital structure of a firm is composed of debt and equity. Debt reflects borrowing whereas equity reflects ownership in the form of stocks. The capital structure of a corporation, as reflected in its leverage ratio, affects the risk premium. The **leverage ratio** is the ratio of the firm's debt relative to its equity. Other things being equal, the higher the leverage ratio, the greater the risk to bondholders and the higher the risk premium will be. The reason is that if a highly leveraged firm experiences a substantial decline in earnings, it may default on its debt obligations and be forced into bankruptcy. A firm with a low leverage ratio could weather a decline in earnings by cutting dividends to stockholders, which are residual claims, not contractual obligations. The highly leveraged firm does not have this option: It must pay its debt costs or fold. Therefore, firms that have considerable debt relative to equity will find the cost of debt financing to be relatively high.

Finally, other firm-specific or industry-specific conditions can exist that affect the ability of a corporation to meet its debt obligations. To the extent that these factors exist, the risk premium is affected. Some of these factors include labor disputes, lawsuits such as those against the tobacco industry, losses in international markets, or oil shortages.

As you may have guessed, the credit rating of the issuing corporation will affect the risk premium because it should capture the firm, industry, and economy risk factors. The factors that affect the risk-free return and the risk premium are summarized in Exhibit 10-5.

Leverage Ratio
The ratio of the firm's debt relative to its equity.

RECAP The price of a bond is the discounted value of the future stream of income over the life of the bond. When the interest rate increases, the price of the bond decreases. When the interest rate decreases, the price of the bond increases. The longer the term to maturity, the greater the fluctuation in the price of the bond for any given change in the interest rate. The discount factor used to determine the price of a bond includes a risk-free rate and a risk premium. Treasury bonds are considered to pay a risk-free rate of return. The risk premium encompasses both economy-wide and firm/industry-specific risks.

In the next chapter, we will examine stocks.

EXHIBIT 10-5
Factors That Affect
Bond Prices

Factors that affect the risk-free rate:	Factors that affect the risk premium:
• The stance of monetary policy	• The credit rating of the bond as determined by Moody's and Standard & Poor's
• Chances in inflationary expectations	• The economic outlook
• Changes in the level of economic activity	• The capital structure of the firm
• Changes in capital inflows	• Other firm-specific conditions
• Changes in government borrowing	• Losses in international markets

LOOKING OUT: *The International Bond Markets*

As financial markets become globalized, the international bond market plays an increasingly important role in the domestic bond market by augmenting the supply of funds available to the bond market and by increasing the array of bonds available to investors. The international bond market consists of primary and secondary markets for Eurobonds and foreign bonds.

Eurobonds

Eurobonds are bonds denominated in a currency other than that of the country where they are marketed. For example, dollar-denominated bonds sold outside the United States are called *Eurobonds.* Like the term Eurodollar, the term Eurobond has come to mean any bond denominated in the currency of the country from which it was issued rather than that of the country where it is sold. The Eurobond market experienced tremendous growth in the 1980s and early 1990s and now accounts for over 80 percent of new issues in the international bond market. In addition, the value of dollar-denominated Eurobonds exceeds the value of new issues in the domestic corporate bond market. No longer do domestic DSUs have to look only to domestic SSUs or domestic financial intermediaries to obtain funds. Likewise, domestic SSUs have opportunities to supply funds denominated in dollars outside the United States. The Eurobond market has greatly expanded the borrowing sources for domestic borrowers. In addition, Eurobonds are less regulated than domestic bonds and offer some tax advantages.

Up to 1984, foreign purchasers of U.S. bonds were subject to a 30 percent withholding tax on all interest payments. Because of this, many Eurobonds were issued through subsidiaries of U.S. corporations in Netherlands Antilles. This location was chosen because of a treaty between the United States and Netherlands Antilles that made non-U.S. investors exempt from the withholding tax. This effectively sidestepped the tax and allowed the bonds to be offered at a lower rate. But to issue Eurobonds, corporations had to have or establish a financial subsidiary in Netherlands Antilles. This was too costly for many firms. In July 1984, the U.S. government repealed the withholding tax and authorized U.S. corporations to sell bonds directly to non-U.S. investors without the withholding tax. This greatly increased the volume of bonds sold directly to non-U.S. investors.

Foreign Bonds

Unlike Eurobonds, foreign bonds are denominated in the currency of the country where they are underwritten and sold to investors, although the issuer of the bonds is from a foreign country. An example is a bond issued by a French corporation, denominated in dollars (as opposed to French francs), and marketed in the United States by U.S. investment bankers. Foreign bonds denominated in dollars and marketed in the United States are called *Yankee bonds;* foreign bonds denominated in Japanese yen and sold in Japan are called *Samurai bonds;* and foreign bonds denominated in British pound sterling and sold in Great Britain are called *Bulldogs.* In order to finance their overseas operations, domestic corporations often issue foreign bonds in the countries where those operations are located.

Summary of Major Points

- Bonds are debt instruments issued by the U.S. government; an agency of the government; a state, county, or local government; a domestic or foreign corporation; or a foreign government. The coupon payment is based upon the par (face) value multiplied by the coupon rate. They may be bearer bonds or registered bonds. Bonds are rated by Moody's and Standard & Poor's with regard to creditworthiness.

- The terms of a corporate bond issue are spelled out in the bond indenture and interpreted and enforced by the trustee. Bond indentures may include sinking fund provisions, call provisions, convertibility provisions, and other restrictive covenants that limit the behavior of the corporation. In addition, the newly issued bonds may come with warrants. Mortgage and collateral bonds are issued by corporations and are backed by real or financial assets. In the event of a default, debenture bondholders are entitled to be paid before subordinated debenture bondholders. Corporations also issue zero-coupon bonds that do not pay interest but are sold at a discount, with the difference between what the bond sells for and the amount that is received at maturity being equal to the interest. Secondary markets exist to trade previously issued corporate bonds.

- Treasury securities, considered to be free from default risk, may be purchased from a market maker or directly from the Federal Reserve. Interest rates on Treasury securities serve as a benchmark to judge the riskiness and liquidity of other securities. The secondary market for government securities is the largest secondary market in the world. Treasury bonds are subject to an interest rate risk.

- Hybrid Treasury securities include STRIPS and inflation-indexed bonds. STRIPS allow the coupon and principal payments of government securities to be sold separately at a discount. Investors avoid the uncertainty that coupon payments may have to be reinvested at a lower interest rate because rates have fallen since the security was issued. Inflation-indexed bonds were first offered in 1997. The principal amount of an indexed bond is adjusted for inflation at the time when an interest (coupon) payment is made. The interest rate does not change, but the interest payments are based on the inflation-adjusted principal.

- Municipal bonds are issued by state and local governments. Interest income on municipal securities is exempt from federal and state taxes for investors living in the issuing state. General obligation bonds are repaid out of general tax revenues. Revenue bonds are repaid from the revenues of a specific project that the bonds support. Government agency securities are issued by private enterprises that are publicly chartered by Congress to reduce the cost of borrowing in specific areas.

- Bond markets have grown significantly, fueled by increases in nonfinancial corporate bonds and bonds issued by government-sponsored enterprises. Foreign entities have made substantial net purchases of domestic bonds, increasing the supply of funds flowing into this market. In total, the trend is for increasing capital flows across borders and the globalization of finance.

- The price of a bond is the present value of the future cash flows associated with the bond. When the interest rate increases, the price of the bond decreases. When the interest rate decreases, the price of the bond increases. The longer the term to maturity, the greater the fluctuation in the price of the bond for any given change in the interest rate.

- The discount factor used to determine the price of a bond includes a risk-free rate and a risk premium. Treasury bonds are considered to pay a risk-free rate of return. The risk premium encompasses both economy-wide and firm/industry-specific risks. Economy-wide factors include the stance of monetary policy, expected inflation, and the level of economic activity. The major firm/industry factors include the capital structure of the firm, the economic outlook for the firm, and the credit rating of the bond issuance.

Key Terms

Bearer Bonds
Bond Indenture
Call Provisions
Collateral Bonds
Convertible Bonds
Coupon Rate
Debenture Bonds
Government Agency Securities

Government-Sponsored
  Enterprises
Inflation-Indexed Bonds
Leverage Ratio
Mortgage Bonds
Municipal Bonds (Munis)
Primary Dealers
Registered Bonds

Restrictive Covenants
Sinking Fund Provisions
Subordinated Debenture Bonds
Treasury STRIPS
Warrant
Zero-Coupon Bonds

Review Questions

1. Define par (face) value, coupon rate, coupon payment, and current yield.

2. What is the difference between bearer and registered bonds?

3. What are inflation-indexed bonds? How do they reduce the risk of holding long-term bonds? Does the interest rate on inflation-indexed bonds change after they have been issued?

4. Why are interest rates on Treasury securities used as a benchmark to judge the riskiness and liquidity of other securities?

5. What are the advantages of investing in STRIPS rather than Treasury securities that make regular interest payments?

6. What is a bond indenture? What is the role of the trustee?

7. What is the purpose of restrictive covenants? Of sinking funds? Of call provisions?

8. What are warrants?

9. Are revenue bonds as safe as general obligation bonds?

10. What are the reasons for differences in the interest rate on Treasury securities and on government agency securities? Between Treasuries and municipals?

11. What roles do Moody's and Standard & Poor's play in the bond market?

12. Discuss what will happen to the discount factors used to determine prices of previously issued bonds sold in secondary markets, given the following scenarios:
    a. A company's earnings report comes in much lower than expected.
    b. Your college is suffering from declining enrollments, particularly among students who want to live on campus. Revenue bonds have been issued to finance your college dorm.
    c. Fed policy turns expansionary.
    d. The performance of the economy is particularly strong.

13. Discuss recent trends in the bond market.

14. Why is the coupon rate irrelevant in determining the price of a previously issued bond? What factors are important in determining the price of a previously issued bond?

15. When will a bond sell in the secondary market for its face value?

Analytical Questions

16. Can you explain why the bonds in the Cracking the Code boxes on pages 212 and 215 are selling at premiums above par?

17. A Treasury bond pays a 7.25 percent coupon yield. What is the coupon payment per $1,000 face value?

18. A bond has a face value of $1,000, a coupon rate of 7 percent, and a selling price of $9,900. What is the current yield? What has happened to interest rates since the bond was issued?

19. If a bond pays $80 in interest annually and sells for $1,050, what is its current yield?

What would the bond have to sell for to have a current yield of 8 percent?

20. Compare the current yield on a 1-year T-bill that sells for $9,400 and can be redeemed for $10,000 with the yield on a bond with a face value of $10,000 that pays a coupon yield of 8 percent and sells for $9,800.

21. If the interest rate on a corporate bond is 10 percent, in equilibrium, what will the rate on a muni be with comparable risk, maturity, and liquidity if the average marginal tax rate is 20 percent?

Internet Exercises

1. **http://www.federalreserve.gov/
    releases/medterm** contains information
    about 10-year medium term corporate notes.
    In the most recent year for which there is data,
    what percent of newly-issued notes were
    investment grade? How does the amount com-
    pare to the previous year? How many firms
    issued medium term notes? Click on "Tables"
    at the bottom of the page. What are
    some of the trends in this market?

2. **http://www.dismal.com/chartroom/
    chartroom.asp** shows charts of various
    indicators for the U.S. economy. Go to U.S.
    credit markets. Compare and contrast trends
    in the 30-year T-bond, the 1-year T-bond,
    and the prime rate.

Suggested Readings

For a further discussion of some of the theoretical
issues raised in the chapter, see Franklin R. Edwards,
The New Finance (Washington, DC: AEI Press, 1996).

For a complete look at all aspects of the bond market, see Frank J. Fabozzi, *Bond Markets: Analysis and
Strategies*, 4th ed., (Upper Saddle River, NJ: Pren-
tice Hall), 1999.

For a more thorough discussion of inflation-
indexed bonds, see Pu Shen, "Features and Risks of
Treasury Inflation Protection Securities," *Economic*

Review of the Federal Reserve Bank of Kansas City 83:1
(First Quarter 1998): 23–38.

For a discussion of high-yield bonds, see Theodore M.
Barnhill, William Maxwell, and Mark R. Shenkman,
editors, *High-Yield Bonds* (New York: McGraw-Hill),
1999.

For an article that gives some perspective on the
International bond market, see Jane D'Arista,
*"Assessing International Banking and Bond Markets,"
Capital Flows Monitor*, December 19, 2000.

Appendix 10-A

The formula in Equation 10-2 for determining bond prices is based on annual
coupon payments. In reality, bonds usually make semi-annual coupon payments. In
this appendix, we consider refinements of how bond prices are determined when
semi-annual rather than annual coupon payments are made. We also look at present value tables that can be used to find bond prices.

When a bond pays semi-annual coupon payments of $\frac{C}{2}$ (assuming that C is the
annual coupon payment) and this bond has n years to maturity, then $2 \times n$ payments
(two payments per n year) will be made. The final payment at the end of n years of
will be equal to F. To find the present value (P) of the stream of income, we divide
the interest rate (i) by 2, since two payments of $\frac{i}{2}$ over the course of the year will be
equal to i. For example if the coupon rate is 8 percent, two semi-annual payments
of 4 percent would approximate an 8 percent annual return. The appropriate discount factor for the final payment (F) is again i_2 because we consider $2n$ periods.
Equation 10-2 becomes:

$$(10\text{-A1}) \qquad P = (\tfrac{C}{2})/(1 + \tfrac{i}{2})^1 + (\tfrac{C}{2})/(1 + \tfrac{i}{2})2 + \ldots + \\ (\tfrac{Cn/2}{2})/(1 + \tfrac{i}{2})2n + F/(1 + \tfrac{i}{2})2n$$

where

P = the price (present value) of the bond

$\frac{C}{2}$ = the semi-annual coupon payment on the bond

F = the face or par value of the bond

i = the interest rate

$2n$ = the number of 6-month periods to maturity (on a bond with 5 years to maturity, $n = 10$)

Note that we used word "approximate" because semi-annual coupon payments of 4 percent would be greater than an 8 percent annual return if the effects of compounding are taken into account. That is, since the coupon payment made in the first half of the year would earn interest during the second 6-month period, the annual return would actually be greater than 8 percent.

Present value tables and financial calculators can be used to simplify the process of finding bond prices. Next we discuss how to use two types of present value interest factor tables for single and multiple constant payments.

Exhibit 10A-1 presents two present value tables. Table 10A-1 shows the factor used to calculate the present value of a sum to be received in n years given various interest rates. To do so, we merely multiply the sum to be received in n years by the factor in the table for a given interest rate. Table 10A-2 shows the factor used to calculate the present value of constant payment to be made in each of n years. To calculate the present value of this stream, we merely multiply the present value of a single payment to be received in each of n years by the factor in the table for a given interest rate. Thus, with these two tables, we can calculate the prices of previously issued bonds.[a]

For example, let's assume that I own a previously issued bond that has 17 years until maturity, a face value of $1,000, and a coupon payment of $100. I want to sell the bond in the secondary market. Let's also assume that the present interest rate is 8 percent. We use Table 10A-1 to calculate the present value of $1,000 in 17 years. By reading down and across, we can see that the present value interest factor is .270. Therefore, the present value of the principal to be received in 17 years is $270.00 ($1,000 × .270). We merely multiply the payment to be received in 17 years by the present value factor. We use Table 10A-2 to calculate the present value of 17 payments of $100. In this case, the present value factor is 9.122. We used Table 10A-2 because 17 continuous equal payments were made, and thus, the value of the 17 $100 payments is $912.20 ($100 × 9.122). Therefore, the bond will sell for the sum of both present values or $1,182.20 ($270.00 + $912.20). Note this is more than the face value of the bond. However, you should be able to calculate that the original coupon rate was 10 percent. With a current interest rate of 8 percent, the price of the bond has gone up and the lucky investor makes a capital gain if the bond is sold in the secondary market.

---

[a]You should also be able to see that we could have calculated the price of a bond using just the first table. In this case, we would have had to make calculations for each of the individual coupon payments.

TABLE 10A-1 Present Value Interest Factors for a Single Constant Payment

YEARS HENCE	1%	2%	4%	6%	8%	10%	12%	14%	15%	16%	18%	20%	22%	24%	25%	26%	28%	30%	35%	40%	45%	50%
1	0.990	0.980	0.962	0.943	0.926	0.909	0.893	0.877	0.870	0.862	0.847	0.833	0.820	0.806	0.800	0.794	0.781	0.769	0.741	0.714	0.690	0.667
2	0.980	0.961	0.925	0.890	0.857	0.826	0.797	0.769	0.756	0.743	0.718	0.694	0.672	0.650	0.640	0.630	0.610	0.592	0.549	0.510	0.476	0.444
3	0.971	0.942	0.889	0.840	0.794	0.751	0.712	0.675	0.658	0.641	0.609	0.579	0.551	0.524	0.512	0.500	0.477	0.455	0.406	0.364	0.328	0.296
4	0.961	0.924	0.855	0.792	0.735	0.683	0.636	0.592	0.572	0.552	0.516	0.482	0.451	0.423	0.410	0.397	0.373	0.350	0.301	0.260	0.226	0.198
5	0.951	0.906	0.822	0.747	0.681	0.621	0.567	0.519	0.497	0.476	0.437	0.402	0.370	0.341	0.328	0.315	0.291	0.269	0.223	0.186	0.156	0.132
6	0.942	0.888	0.790	0.705	0.630	0.564	0.507	0.456	0.432	0.410	0.370	0.335	0.303	0.275	0.262	0.250	0.227	0.207	0.165	0.133	0.108	0.088
7	0.933	0.871	0.760	0.665	0.583	0.513	0.452	0.400	0.376	0.354	0.314	0.279	0.249	0.222	0.210	0.198	0.178	0.159	0.122	0.095	0.074	0.059
8	0.923	0.853	0.731	0.627	0.540	0.467	0.404	0.351	0.327	0.305	0.266	0.233	0.204	0.179	0.168	0.157	0.139	0.123	0.091	0.068	0.051	0.039
9	0.914	0.837	0.703	0.592	0.500	0.424	0.361	0.308	0.284	0.263	0.225	0.194	0.167	0.144	0.134	0.125	0.108	0.094	0.067	0.048	0.035	0.026
10	0.905	0.820	0.676	0.558	0.463	0.386	0.322	0.270	0.247	0.227	0.191	0.162	0.137	0.116	0.107	0.099	0.085	0.073	0.050	0.035	0.024	0.017
11	0.896	0.804	0.650	0.527	0.429	0.350	0.287	0.237	0.215	0.195	0.162	0.135	0.112	0.094	0.086	0.079	0.066	0.056	0.037	0.025	0.017	0.012
12	0.887	0.788	0.625	0.497	0.397	0.319	0.257	0.208	0.187	0.168	0.137	0.112	0.092	0.076	0.069	0.062	0.052	0.043	0.027	0.018	0.012	0.008
13	0.879	0.773	0.601	0.469	0.368	0.290	0.229	0.182	0.163	0.145	0.116	0.093	0.075	0.061	0.055	0.050	0.040	0.033	0.020	0.013	0.008	0.005
14	0.870	0.758	0.577	0.442	0.340	0.263	0.205	0.160	0.141	0.125	0.099	0.078	0.062	0.049	0.044	0.039	0.032	0.025	0.015	0.009	0.006	0.003
15	0.861	0.743	0.555	0.417	0.315	0.239	0.183	0.140	0.123	0.108	0.084	0.065	0.051	0.040	0.035	0.031	0.025	0.020	0.011	0.006	0.004	0.002
16	0.853	0.728	0.534	0.394	0.292	0.218	0.163	0.123	0.107	0.093	0.071	0.054	0.042	0.032	0.028	0.025	0.019	0.015	0.008	0.005	0.003	0.002
17	0.844	0.714	0.513	0.371	0.270	0.198	0.146	0.108	0.093	0.080	0.060	0.045	0.034	0.026	0.023	0.020	0.015	0.012	0.006	0.003	0.002	0.001
18	0.836	0.700	0.494	0.350	0.250	0.180	0.130	0.095	0.081	0.069	0.051	0.038	0.028	0.021	0.018	0.016	0.012	0.009	0.005	0.002	0.001	0.001
19	0.828	0.686	0.475	0.331	0.232	0.164	0.116	0.083	0.070	0.060	0.043	0.031	0.023	0.017	0.014	0.012	0.009	0.007	0.003	0.002	0.001	
20	0.820	0.673	0.456	0.312	0.215	0.149	0.104	0.073	0.061	0.051	0.037	0.026	0.019	0.014	0.012	0.010	0.007	0.005	0.002	0.001	0.001	
21	0.811	0.660	0.439	0.294	0.199	0.135	0.093	0.064	0.053	0.044	0.031	0.022	0.015	0.011	0.009	0.008	0.006	0.004	0.002	0.001		
22	0.803	0.647	0.422	0.278	0.184	0.123	0.083	0.056	0.046	0.038	0.026	0.018	0.013	0.009	0.007	0.006	0.004	0.003	0.001	0.001		
23	0.795	0.634	0.406	0.262	0.170	0.112	0.074	0.049	0.040	0.033	0.022	0.015	0.010	0.007	0.006	0.005	0.003	0.002	0.001			
24	0.788	0.622	0.390	0.247	0.158	0.102	0.066	0.043	0.035	0.028	0.019	0.013	0.008	0.006	0.005	0.004	0.003	0.002	0.001			
25	0.780	0.610	0.375	0.233	0.146	0.092	0.059	0.038	0.030	0.024	0.016	0.010	0.007	0.005	0.004	0.003	0.002	0.001	0.001			
26	0.772	0.598	0.361	0.220	0.135	0.084	0.053	0.033	0.026	0.021	0.014	0.009	0.006	0.004	0.003	0.002	0.002	0.001				
27	0.764	0.586	0.347	0.207	0.125	0.076	0.047	0.029	0.023	0.018	0.011	0.007	0.005	0.003	0.002	0.002	0.001	0.001				
28	0.757	0.574	0.333	0.196	0.116	0.069	0.042	0.026	0.020	0.016	0.010	0.006	0.004	0.002	0.002	0.001	0.001	0.001				
29	0.749	0.563	0.321	0.185	0.107	0.063	0.037	0.022	0.017	0.014	0.008	0.005	0.003	0.002	0.001	0.001	0.001					
30	0.742	0.552	0.308	0.174	0.099	0.057	0.033	0.020	0.015	0.012	0.007	0.004	0.003	0.001	0.001							
40	0.672	0.453	0.208	0.097	0.046	0.022	0.011	0.005	0.004	0.003	0.001	0.001										
50	0.608	0.372	0.141	0.054	0.021	0.009	0.003	0.001	0.001	0.001												

TABLE 10A-2 Present Value Interest Factors for an Annuity

YEARS (N)	1%	2%	4%	6%	8%	10%	12%	14%	15%	16%	18%	20%	22%	24%	25%	26%	28%	30%	35%	40%	45%	50%
1	0.990	0.980	0.962	0.943	0.926	0.909	0.893	0.877	0.870	0.862	0.847	0.833	0.820	0.806	0.800	0.794	0.781	0.769	0.741	0.714	0.690	0.667
2	1.970	1.942	1.886	1.833	1.783	1.736	1.690	1.647	1.626	1.605	1.566	1.528	1.492	1.457	1.440	1.424	1.392	1.361	1.289	1.224	1.165	1.111
3	2.941	2.884	2.775	2.673	2.577	2.487	2.402	2.322	2.283	2.246	2.174	2.106	2.042	1.981	1.952	1.953	1.868	1.816	1.696	1.589	1.493	1.497
4	3.902	3.808	3.630	3.465	3.312	3.170	3.037	2.914	2.855	2.798	2.690	2.589	2.494	2.404	2.362	2.320	2.241	2.166	1.997	1.849	1.740	1.605
5	4.853	4.713	4.452	4.212	3.993	3.791	3.605	3.433	3.352	3.274	3.127	2.991	2.864	2.745	2.689	2.635	2.532	2.436	2.220	2.035	1.876	1.737
6	5.795	5.601	5.242	4.917	4.623	4.355	4.111	3.889	3.784	3.685	3.498	3.326	3.167	3.020	2.951	2.885	2.759	2.643	2.385	2.168	1.983	1.824
7	6.728	6.472	6.002	5.582	5.206	4.868	4.564	4.288	4.160	4.039	3.812	3.605	3.416	3.242	3.161	3.083	2.937	2.802	2.508	2.263	2.057	1.883
8	7.652	7.325	6.733	6.210	5.747	5.335	4.968	4.639	4.487	4.344	4.078	3.837	3.619	3.421	3.329	3.241	3.076	2.925	2.598	2.331	2.108	1.922
9	8.566	8.162	7.435	6.802	6.247	5.759	5.328	4.946	4.772	4.607	4.303	4.031	3.786	3.566	3.463	3.366	3.184	3.019	2.665	2.379	2.144	1.948
10	9.471	8.983	8.111	7.360	6.710	6.145	5.650	5.216	5.019	4.833	4.494	4.192	3.923	3.682	3.571	3.465	3.269	3.092	2.715	2.414	2.168	1.965
11	10.368	9.787	8.760	7.887	7.139	6.495	5.937	5.453	5.234	5.029	4.656	4.327	4.035	3.776	3.656	3.544	3.335	3.147	2.752	2.438	2.185	1.977
12	11.255	10.575	9.385	8.384	7.536	6.814	6.194	5.660	5.421	5.197	4.793	4.439	4.127	3.851	3.725	3.606	3.387	3.190	2.779	2.456	2.196	1.985
13	12.134	11.343	9.986	8.853	7.904	7.103	6.424	5.842	5.583	5.342	4.910	4.533	4.203	3.912	3.780	3.656	3.427	3.223	2.799	2.468	2.204	1.990
14	13.004	12.106	10.563	9.295	8.244	7.367	6.628	6.002	5.724	5.468	5.008	4.611	4.265	3.962	3.824	3.695	3.459	3.249	2.814	2.477	2.210	1.993
15	13.865	12.849	11.118	9.712	8.559	7.606	6.811	6.142	5.847	5.575	5.092	4.675	4.315	4.001	3.859	3.726	3.483	3.268	2.825	2.484	2.214	1.995
16	14.718	13.578	11.652	10.106	8.851	7.824	6.974	6.265	5.954	5.669	5.162	4.730	4.357	4.033	3.887	3.751	3.503	3.283	2.834	2.489	2.216	1.997
17	15.562	14.292	12.166	10.477	9.122	8.022	7.120	6.373	6.047	5.749	5.222	4.775	4.391	4.059	3.910	3.771	3.518	3.295	2.840	2.492	2.218	1.998
18	16.398	14.992	12.659	10.828	9.372	8.201	7.250	6.467	6.128	5.818	5.273	4.812	4.419	4.080	3.928	3.786	3.529	3.304	2.844	2.494	2.219	1.999
19	17.226	15.678	13.134	11.158	9.604	8.365	7.366	6.550	6.198	5.877	5.316	4.844	4.442	4.097	3.942	3.799	3.539	3.311	2.848	2.496	2.220	1.999
20	18.046	16.351	13.590	11.470	9.818	8.514	7.469	6.623	6.259	5.929	5.353	4.870	4.460	4.110	3.954	3.808	3.546	3.316	2.850	2.497	2.221	1.999
21	18.857	17.011	14.029	11.764	10.017	8.649	7.562	6.687	6.312	5.973	5.384	4.891	4.476	4.121	3.963	3.816	3.551	3.320	2.852	2.498	2.221	2.000
22	19.660	17.658	14.451	12.042	10.201	8.772	7.645	6.743	6.359	6.011	5.410	4.909	4.488	4.130	3.970	3.822	3.556	3.323	2.853	2.498	2.222	2.000
23	20.456	18.292	14.857	12.303	10.371	8.883	7.718	6.792	6.399	6.044	5.432	4.925	4.499	4.137	3.976	3.827	3.559	3.325	2.854	2.499	2.222	2.000
24	21.243	18.914	15.247	12.550	10.529	8.985	7.784	6.835	6.434	6.073	5.451	4.937	4.507	4.143	3.981	3.831	3.562	3.327	2.855	2.499	2.222	2.000
25	22.023	19.523	15.622	12.783	10.675	9.077	7.843	6.873	6.464	6.097	5.467	4.948	4.514	4.147	3.985	3.834	3.564	3.329	2.856	2.499	2.222	2.000
26	22.795	20.121	15.983	13.003	10.810	9.161	7.896	6.906	6.491	6.118	5.480	4.956	4.520	4.151	3.988	3.837	3.566	3.330	2.856	2.500	2.222	2.000
27	23.560	20.707	16.330	13.211	10.935	9.237	7.943	6.935	6.514	6.136	5.492	4.964	4.524	4.154	3.990	3.839	3.567	3.331	2.856	2.500	2.222	2.000
28	24.316	21.281	16.663	13.406	11.051	9.307	7.984	6.961	6.534	6.152	5.502	4.970	4.528	4.157	3.992	3.840	3.568	3.331	2.857	2.500	2.222	2.000
29	25.066	21.844	16.984	13.591	11.158	9.370	8.022	6.983	6.551	6.166	5.510	4.975	4.531	4.159	3.994	3.841	3.569	3.332	2.857	2.500	2.222	2.000
30	25.808	22.396	17.292	13.765	11.258	9.427	8.055	7.003	6.566	6.177	5.517	4.979	4.534	4.160	3.995	3.842	3.569	3.332	2.857	2.500	2.222	2.000
40	32.835	27.355	19.793	15.046	11.925	9.779	8.244	7.105	6.642	6.234	5.548	4.997	4.544	4.166	3.999	3.846	3.571	3.333	2.857	2.500	2.222	2.000
50	39.196	31.424	21.482	15.762	12.234	9.915	8.304	7.133	6.661	6.246	5.554	4.999	4.545	4.167	4.000	3.846	3.571	3.333	2.857	2.500	2.222	2.000

chapter

11 The Stock Market

Learning Objectives *After reading this chapter, you should know:*

- The major characteristics of the stock market
- How the organized exchanges and the over-the counter markets function
- The various stock indexes and what each measures
- How the value of a share of stock is determined

" "
Buy low, sell high!!

Speculative Bubbles and Their Effects on the Economy

Most of us are familiar with the record stock market boom of the late 1990s.[1] Stock prices underwent dramatic increases despite some sharp sell-offs. Technological changes in how funds are transferred, increased globalization of financial markets, and other structural changes in the economy have facilitated the flow of funds into equity investments around the world.

At the same time, more households than ever were investing in the stock market, whether directly through a broker, an employer, or online; or indirectly through a savings or retirement plan.

When stock price movements are more pronounced, stock markets have a greater potential for speculative bubbles that cannot be sustained. A **speculative bubble** is an irrational increase in prices accompanied by euphoric expectations. When market participants realize that the speculative bubble cannot be maintained, they tend to liquidate their positions. This results in prices falling to lower levels than if the bubble had not occurred in the first place. Such volatility in stock prices can cause financial instability as gains and losses are magnified. When the bubble bursts, the resulting financial losses spill over into the economy, causing unemployment and recession.

Speculative Bubble
An irrational increase in stock prices accompanied by euphoric expectations.

Volatile stock prices also affect financial institutions and the financial system. The solvency of any institution that holds large amounts of stocks, such as an investment banker, could be threatened if prices fall unexpectedly and significantly.

In Chapter 4, we saw that the Fed attempts to minimize fluctuations in output and prices around a long-term trend. There, we were concerned about output prices of goods and services. The Fed must also be concerned about unstable stock prices. Volatile stock prices can affect employment, inflation, and the health and stability of the financial system.

In this chapter, we explore the anatomy of stock markets and how they have grown and changed.

When the Bubble Bursts

Central banks must be concerned about speculative bubbles because of the potential spillovers to other financial markets and to the economy if the bubble bursts. If severe and widespread enough, declines in stock prices can also threaten the solvency of the entire financial system. Analysts now know that the economy had turned down before the stock market crash of October 1929. Most agree, however, that the crash played a major role in the collapse of the financial system and the deepening and lengthening of the downturn that became the Great Depression.

In more recent episodes, globalized financial markets have facilitated capital flows that ultimately contributed to speculative bubbles. The Mexican crisis of 1994–1995 and the Asian crisis of the late 1990s are examples of situations wherein stock prices, supported by large capital inflows, became overvalued. When exchange rates could not be maintained, what began as currency crises quickly spread to other markets. Stock, bond, and real estate prices plummeted, causing widespread bankruptcies of financial and nonfinancial firms. The financial systems and real sectors of the affected economies collapsed. Unprecedented international

---

[1]The rally was interrupted briefly by a worldwide collapse of stock prices in October 1998. By early 1999, the market had fully recovered and was reaching new highs. But in early 2001, the market suffered a large crash and as of late 2001, it had not recovered.

intervention was needed as domestic and international investors withdrew funds from the crippled regions.

During the mid-1980s, monetary and fiscal policies in Japan were expansionary, and the central bank took actions that steadily lowered interest rates. Despite the low rates, inflation in output markets was virtually nonexistent. In response to the low interest rates, stock prices that had been trending upward since 1984 continued to rally. By the late 1980s, the market appeared to many analysts to be overvalued. During 1988, the Nikkei 225, Japan's index of the stock prices of the 225 largest firms, increased just under an unprecedented 40 percent. By the end of 1988, the stock market was in a full-fledged bubble, having gone through a period of excessive price increases accompanied by euphoric expectations. The bubble was not limited to asset prices, but also encompassed the real estate market, where prices more than doubled in 4 years. Record price increases in the stock and real estate markets continued in 1989 even though monetary policy turned contractionary in mid-1989. Interest rate increases set the stage for the bubble to burst, which it did in early 1990. Between 1990 and 1992, Japan's stock prices fell by over 60 percent, and real estate prices in some large Japanese cities plummeted as much as 50 percent. The collapse of the speculative bubbles caused a severe economic downturn that began in the spring of 1991 and lasted until the end of 1993. The health of the entire financial system was threatened by the collapse. The Japanese financial system (including the banking system and stock market) has yet to recover from the turmoil set in force by the collapse of the speculative bubbles.

In early 2001, the U.S. economy appeared to be heading into its first recession in over 10 years. If the downturn does materialize, many analysts undoubtedly will attribute it to the cataclysmic collapse of what appeared to be overvalued stock markets in early 2001. Stock prices, led by dot.com[2] and technology stocks, experienced record increases in the late 1990s. Some analysts believed that stocks were overvalued as early as 1995. Between 1995 and 2000, stock prices more than doubled. By 2001, it became clear that stock valuations were in a speculative bubble and markets collapsed, with the dot.com and technology sectors experiencing the largest price declines. The Fed responded by lowering interest rates nine times by October 2001. Further interest rate decreases were a possibility. When the markets will hit bottom and/or rebound remains to be seen. Likewise, the full effects of the bursting of the speculative bubble on the U.S. economy also remain to be seen.

The Anatomy of Stocks

Firms issue shares of stock when they need to raise long-term financial capital, usually for investment spending. If a corporation is publicly held, shares of stock are sold to the public. A share of stock represents equity in a corporation and entitles the owner to a share of the corporation's profits.[3] The stock may be **preferred stock** or **common stock.** Owners of preferred stock receive a fixed dividend to which they are entitled before owners of common stock can receive anything. The fixed dividend is similar to the interest payment that a bondholder receives. However, dividends must be paid to preferred stockholders only if the corporation earns a profit, whereas the corporation is liable for interest payments under all circumstances. In

Preferred Stock
Equity claims representing ownership of the net income and assets of a corporation that receive a fixed dividend before common stockholders are entitled to anything.

Common Stock
Equity claims representing ownership of the net income and assets of a corporation that receive a variable or no dividend after preferred stockholders have been paid and retained earnings have been put aside.

---

[2]Dot.com stocks are those of Internet companies, many of which were small start-up companies that had never earned a profit.

[3]Corporations are legal entities that own the assets of the corporation. Stocks represent ownership of the legal entity rather than ownership of the assets directly.

LOOKING BACK: *Famous Financial Quotations*

"Stock prices could double, triple, or even quadruple tomorrow and still not be too high. Stocks are now, we believe, in the midst of a one-time-only rise to much higher ground—to the neighborhood of 36,000 for the Dow Jones Industrial Average."

—James K. Glassman and Kevin A. Hasset, "Dow 36000," *The Atlantic Online*, September 1999, http://www.theatlantic.com

"In a [stock] market like this, every story is a positive one. Any news is good news. It's pretty much taken for granted now that the market is going to go up."

—*Wall Street Journal*, August 26, 1987, less than 2 months before the largest percentage drop in stock prices in history

Although there have been many stock market crashes, the most famous occurred in 1929, heralding the Great Depression. Although it was not known at the time, output had actually turned down before the market crashed. The market crash came at the end of a decade of rising stock prices and what many now realize was a speculative bubble. The following are some quotations from around that time:

"There will be no interruption of our permanent prosperity."

—Myron E. Forbes, president, Pierce Arrow Motor Car Co., January 12, 1928

"I cannot help but raise a dissenting voice to statements that we are living in a fool's paradise, and that prosperity in this country must necessarily diminish and recede in the near future."

—E. H. Simmons, president, New York Stock Exchange, January 12, 1928

"Stock prices have reached what looks like a permanently high plateau. I do not feel that there will soon, if ever, be a fifty or sixty point break below present levels, such as Mr. Babson has predicted. I expect to see the stock market a great deal higher than it is today within the next few months."

—Irving Fisher (one of the most prestigious economists of the day), October 16, 1929

"I believe that the breaks of the last few days have driven stock prices down to hard rock. I believe that we will have a ragged market for a few weeks and then the beginning of a mild bull movement that will gain momentum next year."

—Irving Fisher, October 22, 1929

addition, interest payments to bondholders are tax write-offs for the corporation; dividend payments to preferred stockholders are not.

Common stockholders receive a variable dividend after preferred stockholders have been paid and retained earnings have been set aside. Retained earnings are undistributed profits that are usually used to fund investment projects. The current trend among many corporations is to forgo paying dividends to common stockholders.[4] In this case, stockholders benefit from increases in the stock's price generated by putting the earnings back into the company or using the earnings to purchase the company's own stock. If a company buys back its own stock and does not resell it, the stock is retired. After shares of stock are retired, the remaining outstanding shares tend to appreciate in value. Common stockholders have voting rights within the firm whereas preferred stockholders do not. Stockholders who own only a minuscule share of the outstanding stock of a firm do not usually exercise voting rights.

---

[4]Some corporations such as Microsoft have never paid a dividend and have no intention of doing so.

CRACKING THE CODE: *The Stock Market*

Here is a section from a typical stock page of a major newspaper. To begin cracking the code, look at the following entry for Gap Inc., the popular clothing store.

52 Weeks High	Low	Stock	Sym	Div	Yld.	PE %	Vol	High 100s	Low	Close	Net Change
53^{12}	18^{50}	Gap Inc	GPS	.09	.4	24	34217	23^{90}	22^{25}	23^{79}	$+0^{50}$

SOURCE: *Wall Street Journal*, March 26, 2001.

The name of the company is in the third column, followed by the company ticker symbol, and then the regular annual dividend paid by the Gap, in this case, $.09. The price of the stock at the close of the preceding day's trading was 23^{79}, or $23.79 (from the column labeled "Close"). The dividend is usually divided by the closing price to get the current yield (or return). The dividend of $.09 divided by the closing price $23.79 gives a current yield of .4 percent ($.09/$23.79 = .004).

In January 2001, a plan was implemented to move away from fractions with the goal of making prices more easily understood by investors, reducing spreads, and bringing the United States into conformity with international practices. Prior to the change, the Gap's 52-week low price on the stock page would have been reported as 18 1/2 rather than 18^{50}.

The column labeled "PE" tells us that the ratio of the price per share to the earnings per share of the company—that is, the price-to-earnings (P-E) ratio—is 24. The higher the earnings per share of the company (given the price of the stock), the lower the ratio. Stocks with low PE ratios compared to other firms in the industry are sometimes thought to be undervalued while stocks with high PE ratios are thought to be overvalued.

The "Vol" column tells us the number of shares traded (in hundreds) on a given day. Thus, 34217 means that 3,421,700 shares of the Gap were traded on this particular day. Also, the high price during the course of the day was 23^{90}, the low price was 22^{25}, and the price of the stock at the close was, as we have seen, 23^{79}. In the last column, we see that the closing price per share was up 0^{50} ($.50) from the close of the previous day.

To the left of the company's name are two columns headed "High" and "Low." These are the high and low prices of the stock for the last 52 weeks. The Gap had traded at a low price of 18^{50} ($18.50) and at a high price of 53^{13} ($53.13). Those of you who bought at 18^{50} ($18.50) can smile.

Investment bankers usually market new shares of stocks, or securities. One or more securities firms design and market the new securities offering. Sometimes, employees and individuals may purchase new shares of stocks directly from the company, thus bypassing investment banks. Stocks represent liquid claims because the shares can usually be sold relatively easily in secondary markets. Previously issued shares of stock are traded either on organized exchanges or over-the-counter. As we saw in Chapter 3, the marketing of newly issued shares represents primary market activity, while the purchase or sale of previously issued securities represents secondary market activity. The Securities and Exchange Commission (SEC) has extensive authority to regulate secondary market activities. The Cracking the Code box on this page deciphers the information about stock prices reported in major newspapers.

The value of corporate equities has increased dramatically in the past decade. Exhibit 11-1 traces the outstanding value of corporate equities since 1982. At the end of 1999, the outstanding value of domestic corporate equities was $19.6 trillion. This was up from $10.26 trillion just 4 years earlier and $3.8 trillion 10 years earlier. Stocks did not fare as well in the early 2000s, as the value of outstanding corporate equities fell to about $15.8 trillion by the end of the second quarter 2001. Households, state and local governments, foreigners, and a variety of financial insti-

Year	Corporate Equities
1982	$1,562.5
1983	1,856.0
1984	1,789.2
1985	2,270.4
1986	2,682.6
1987	2,710.3
1988	3,076.3
1989	3,819.7
1990	3,542.6
1991	4,863.4
1992	5,430.9
1993	6,306.2
1994	6,333.3
1995	8,495.7
1996	10,255.8
1997	13,201.3
1998	15,427.8
1999	19,576.3
2000	17,168.8
2001*	15,863.3

*Through second quarter 2001.

SOURCE: *Flow of Funds of the United States, Z1,* Board of Governors of the Federal Reserve System, various issues.

EXHIBIT 11-1
The Value of Outstanding Shares of Domestically Issued Stock Since 1982

tutions hold domestically issued stocks. The major financial institutions that own shares of stocks are mutual funds, private and public pension funds, and insurance companies. At the end of first quarter 2001, foreigners owned about $1.6 trillion, or 11 percent of domestically issued stocks.

All companies that issue publicly traded shares of stock are regulated by the **Securities and Exchange Commission (SEC),** which was created by the Securities and Exchange Act of 1934. To protect investors, the SEC has broad disclosure requirements, requiring companies to file numerous reports that detail the financial condition of the company, information about key personnel, and any changes that would be important to stockholders.

Securities and Exchange Commission (SEC)
A government agency created by the Securities and Exchange Act of 1934 that regulates disclosure rules for companies that issue publicly traded shares of stock; the SEC also regulates disclosure rules in secondary markets.

Stock Offerings

An **initial public offering (IPO)** occurs when a corporation issues stock publicly for the first time. Many of the companies that have gone public in recent years are well known to college students. Some of them are Ben and Jerry's Ice Cream, California Pizza Kitchen, Martha Stewart Living Omnimedia, Guess?, and Krispy Kreme Doughnuts, as well as a rash of Internet start-up companies. Stock prices often move dramatically on the first day of trading. For example, on the first day of trading, California Pizza Kitchen's stock jumped 35 percent, Krispy Kreme Doughnut's stocks jumped 75 percent, and Red Hat Inc., an Internet company, saw its stock jump over 80 percent. Price jumps among many of the Internet offerings did not last through a general downturn in Internet stocks in mid-2000. For example, Red Hat

Initial Public Offering (IPO)
When a corporation issues stocks publicly for the first time.

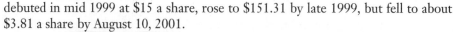

Secondary Stock Offering
An offering of newly issued shares by a firm that already has outstanding publicly held shares.

Shelf Registration
A procedure that permits a company to register a quantity of securities with the SEC and sell them over a 2-year period rather than at the time of registration.

debuted in mid 1999 at $15 a share, rose to $151.31 by late 1999, but fell to about $3.81 a share by August 10, 2001.

A **secondary stock offering** is an offering of newly issued shares by a firm that already has outstanding publicly held shares. To bring new shares to the market, a corporation must register the new issue with the SEC. Since 1982, the SEC has allowed corporations to register securities without immediately issuing them through a procedure called shelf registration. **Shelf registration** permits a company to register a quantity of securities and sell them over a 2-year period rather than at the time the shares are registered. This avoids the costs in time and money of several registration processes and also allows the firm to respond quickly to advantageous market conditions.

RECAP Stocks represent equity in a corporation. Preferred stockholders receive a fixed dividend while common stockholders receive a variable or no dividend. Firms issue stock to raise funds for long-term investment spending. An IPO is a public offering of newly issued stocks by a corporation that has not previously sold stocks to the public. A secondary stock offering is an offering of newly issued stocks by a firm that has publicly held stocks outstanding. Shelf registration permits a company to register new shares of stocks at the present time, but issue the new shares over a 2-year period.

The Stock Markets

When most people think about the stock market, they think of New York City's Wall Street, an actual street in South Manhattan that is home to New York's financial district and is also the nation's financial center. But to financial market participants, the stock market has a much broader connotation that includes many different organized stock exchanges and a nationwide network of brokers and dealers who buy and sell stock "over-the-counter."

In recent years, the volume and values of stocks traded—whether on exchanges or over-the-counter—have increased dramatically. Large institutional investors such as pension funds, insurance companies, and mutual funds have come to dominate the market. The institutional investors tend to trade large blocks of stocks (more than 10,000 shares of a given stock or trades with a market value greater than $200,000). Institutional investors now own over 40 percent of the market valuation of all stock. The expanded use of computers to execute trades has accommodated the greater volume of trading and facilitated an increase in **program trading** by institutional investors. Program trading allows institutional investors to pre-program computers to buy or sell a large number (basket) of stocks.

Program Trading
The pre-programming of computers to buy or sell a large number (basket) of stocks usually by institutional investors.

Despite the increase in institutional trading, a higher percentage of households have a stake in the stock market than ever before, usually through retirement funds, direct ownership, or ownership of mutual funds. In 1989, only 31.6 percent of households owned stocks in some form, but by 1998, that percentage had risen to 48.8. Between 1995 and 1998, the median value of a household's ownership of stock increased from $15,400 to $25,000. The proportion of stockholdings relative to all financial assets increased from 40 percent to 53.9 percent in the same time period. The increases reflect both the increased market valuations of stocks and a tendency for more households to purchase stock.[5] As stock market fluctuations occur in the early 2000s, it is unclear whether these trends will continue.

---

[5]"Recent Changes in U.S. Family Finances," *Federal Reserve Bulletin*, January, 2000, p. 14.

As Exhibit 11-2 shows, over time, investing in the stock market has paid a higher return than investing in the bond market or purchasing other financial assets. Other factors being equal, ownership of stocks entails a greater risk than ownership of bonds or other financial assets. Even though there is a higher expected return with stock ownership, there is no guarantee that any given investment will realize a higher return. Moreover, most financial assets issued by depository institutions offer the added advantage of deposit insurance. Stockholders own the excess, whether paid out in dividends or not, of what is left over after bondholders and other creditors have been paid fixed obligations. The residual may be huge, but then again it may fall short of expectations.

Investors do not have to put up funds equal to the full value of a stock purchase. Rather, they can purchase stocks on the margin by borrowing. The **margin requirement** is the percentage of a stock purchase that can be borrowed as opposed to being paid in readily available funds. The current margin requirement, which is set by the Fed, has been 50 percent since 1974 and applies only to initial purchases. Buying on the margin allows an investor to amplify gains when the stock's price goes up because the investor, in essence, has control over a larger number of shares. It is thought that margin buying fuels speculation in stocks and can be particularly dangerous in a stock market bubble.

The New York Stock Exchange and the National Association of Securities Dealers require member firms to impose a minimum 25 percent **maintenance margin requirement** on their customers. The maintenance margin requirement is the minimum amount of equity the investor needs in his or her account relative to the market value of his stock. The maintenance requirement comes into play if the stock has been purchased using borrowed funds and if the stock's value falls so that the investor has less equity than the amount required by the maintenance margin. Many individual brokerage firms set higher margin requirements and vary those requirements depending on the stocks and trading behavior of individual customers.

Margin Requirement
The percentage of invested funds that can be borrowed as opposed to being paid in readily available funds; currently margin requirements are set by the Fed at 50 percent.

Maintenance Margin Requirement
The minimum amount of equity the investor needs in his account relative to the market value of his stock.

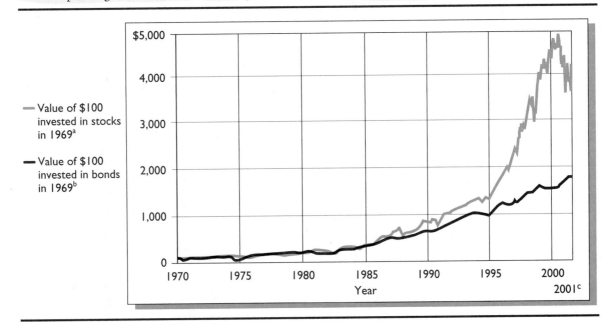

EXHIBIT 11-2
The Returns to Stocks and Bonds over Time
[a]Return to stocks is measured by the Standard and Poors 500 Composite Index and includes reinvestment of dividends.
[b]Return to bonds is measured by Moody's AAA Rated Corporate Bond Index and includes reinvestment of interest.
[c]Through September 28, 2001.
SOURCE: Global Financial Data, Los Angeles, California.

In a falling stock market, buying on the margin can present problems because losses are also amplified. If the value of a stock falls to less than what is owed, the lender may put in a margin call requiring the investor to put up more funds. If the investor fails to do so, the stock is sold at the low price for the lender to recoup part or all of its losses. Selling the stock to recoup losses puts additional downward pressure on the flagging stock price.

In late 1999 and early 2000, margin credit grew much faster than the overall appreciation of the stock market. By early 2000, margin credit relative to the total value of stocks traded in the market reached a 29-year high. Raising margin requirements has also been proposed as a monetary policy tool to reduce speculative behavior that could fuel a stock market bubble.

The mid-to-late 1990s also saw unprecedented capital inflows into U. S. markets to purchase U.S. equities. The magnitude of these inflows is dramatic and is part of the ongoing globalization of financial markets. Only life insurance companies and mutual funds purchased more U.S. equities than non-U.S. purchasers. The inflows that many contributed to booming U.S. markets also increased the demand for stocks. Without the inflow from abroad, demand for U.S. stocks would have been lower and equity prices not as high. Thus, it is difficult to say whether the inflows are the result or the cause of booming stock prices. If foreigners sell U.S. equities or slow purchases, prices of U.S. equities will be lower than what they otherwise would be. It is difficult to say what the future trend will be. Exhibit 11-3 shows the dollar value of net non-U.S. purchase of U.S. stocks since 1995.

EXHIBIT 11-3
Net Non-U.S.
Purchases of U.S.
Stocks

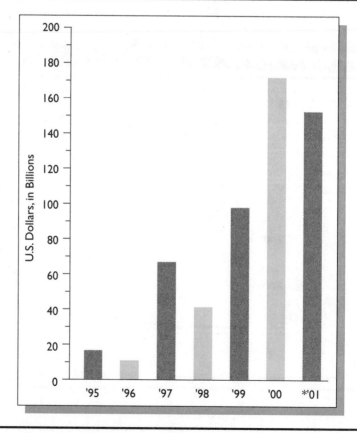

*Analyzed through second quarter 2001.

SOURCE: *Flow of Funds of the United States, Z1,* Board of Governors of the Federal Reserve System, September 18, 2001, page 22.

The Stock Market and Mutual Funds

Many individuals can tap into the higher returns of the stock market while minimizing the risk of doing so by purchasing shares of a mutual fund. Mutual funds are companies that pool the funds of many investors and then invest in several hundred or even thousands of stocks. In addition, some mutual funds invest in bonds or some combination of both stocks and bonds. The small investor who buys into the fund can own a small piece of the large basket of stocks and/or bonds. An investor would need a large sum of money to purchase the same stocks and/or bonds owned by a mutual fund. Like individual stocks, mutual funds are regulated by the SEC, which requires fairly extensive reporting.

For many investors, mutual funds may offer less risk and greater safety than individual stocks because of diversification. Since all securities do not perform equally well over the business cycle (returns are not perfectly correlated), diversification reduces risk. The risk of investing in a single company that fails is eliminated. If a mutual fund has invested in 1,000 companies, the risk that all of them will go under at once is much less than the risk that any one of them will be forced into bankruptcy. If only one or a few of the companies perform poorly, the overall returns to the mutual fund are hardly affected. Mutual fund companies offer highly trained professional management to research the best investments. This not only saves the individual investor time and effort, but is intended to improve the performance (yield) of the portfolio as well.

Mutual funds are also highly specialized to reflect the amount of risk an investor wishes to accept. One potential challenge for investors is to decide which fund to purchase. Mutual funds now number over 11,000, while only 2,825 stocks are listed on the NYSE. Thus, investors must "invest" some time in choosing the fund with the greatest probability of achieving their goals.

The Major Domestic Exchanges

The New York Stock Exchange (NYSE)

The **New York Stock Exchange (NYSE),** located on Wall Street in New York City, is the world's largest market for trading securities. The stocks of about 2,825 companies are traded, and the NYSE includes more than 425 non-U.S. companies—more than triple the number of foreign companies in mid 2001 than in 1995 and up from only 95 foreign companies in 1990. For the stock of a corporation to be listed on the NYSE, the corporation must apply to the exchange and meet several criteria dealing with the size and number of shareholders. The NYSE seeks to enhance trading by ensuring that markets for any traded stock are sufficiently broad and deep. In the first 7 months of 2001, 1,206.1 million shares worth $44.1 billion were traded on an average day. Exhibit 11-4 lists the 10 largest companies whose stocks are traded on the NYSE as of July 2001.[6]

New York Stock Exchange (NYSE)
The world's largest market for trading stocks; trades the stocks of over 3,000 companies.

The NYSE (known as the "Big Board") is a highly visible, auction-type market. Members, who act as agents for their customers, buy and sell shares of stock. Each member of the exchange has purchased a seat on the exchange. As of October 2, 2001, the price of a seat was $2.3 million, about $300,000 lower than the price of a seat in June 1999 and $600,000 higher than in July 2000. As of July 31, 2001, the NYSE had 373 member firms that owned 1,366 seats. Mergers among large financial institutions is one factor that has caused the demand and hence the price, for seats on the NYSE to fall since 1999. Another

---

[6]http://www.nyse.com

EXHIBIT 11-4
The Ten Largest
Companies
(Measured by Market
Value) Traded on the
Big Board, July 2001

Ten Largest NYSE-Listed Companies				
		JULY 2001	JULY 2001	JULY 2000
Company Name	Symbol	Market Cap ($bil.)	NYSE Average Daily Volume	Market Cap ($bil.)
General Electric Co.	Ge	432.2	20,876,540	506.9
Exxon Mobil Corp	XOM	288.1	10,958,637	278.2
Pfizer Inc	PFE	260.2	13,242,718	165.9
Citigroup Inc	C	252.7	11,257,568	237.6
Wal-Mart Stores	WMT	249.9	7,428,327	244.9
American International Group	AIG	194.1	4,849,423	203.8
AOL Time Warner Inc	AOL	193.6	13,078,036	117.4
Intl Business Machines Corp	IBM	182.8	7,748,647	202.9
Johnson & Johnson	JNJ	163.8	8,183,296	129.3
Merck & Co	MRK	155.9	6,710,387	167.0

SOURCE: http://www.nyse.com

reason is the increased ability to trade stocks electronically over the Internet, thus bypassing an exchange.

The benefits of membership include participating directly in stock trading and charging commissions for trading stocks for customers. The customers may be financial or nonfinancial institutions or individual investors. The NYSE is self-regulated—meaning that every transaction is under constant surveillance by the exchange to ensure that trades are executed fairly.

Each company whose stock is listed on the "Big Board" is assigned to a single post where a specialist in that stock manages the auction process. Members of the NYSE bring all large buy-and-sell orders to the floor either electronically or by broker on the floor of the exchange. Orders for a specific stock are funneled to the appropriate post. If the post is surrounded by more brokers looking to buy the stock than to sell at the existing price, the stock's price will rise. If the reverse is true, the price will fall. In this way, the forces of supply and demand determine prices.

When a new price is reached, a clerk records the information on a device that sends it out over the "ticker." The ticker provides a constant stream of stock symbols and prices; each symbol consists of three or fewer letters and represents the stock of a particular corporation. The ticker continuously posts stock prices electronically on displays in brokerage houses and on computer screens around the world. For small orders of fewer than 3,000 shares, the process is a little different. The brokerage firm representing the buyer or seller of the stock routes the order to the **Designated Order Turnaround (DOT)** system. DOT is a computer system that sends buy or sell orders to the specialist's post where the transaction is automatically executed. The vast majority of trades are transacted through the DOT system.

On occasion, there have been large daily fluctuations in stock prices. During the week of October 12–16, 1987, the Dow fell 250 points. On Monday, October 19, 1987, it fell 508 points, or more than 20 percent. Not only was this the largest point drop in history to that date, but it was also by far the largest percentage drop. To give you some

**Designated Order
Turnaround (DOT)**
A computer system used
for trades of fewer than
3,000 shares on the NYSE.

http://www.nyse.com
*Provides closing prices and
other information on NYSE-
listed companies.*

idea of its magnitude, the next-largest percentage decline occurred on October 28, 1929, when the market fell 12.8 percent near the start of the Great Depression.[7]

In response to the October 1987 crash, certain reforms were instituted to limit such severe declines. In particular, **"circuit breakers"** were introduced to temporarily halt market trading if prices fall by some specified amount. During the halt, market makers have a chance to take positions and evaluate new information to provide support for the market. Bargains can be snatched up, stopping the free-fall in prices.

Originally, the new rules called for trading to be halted for half an hour if the market dropped 250 points from the previous day's close. If the market dropped 400 points, trading was to be halted for 1 hour.

The circuit breakers that halt all market trading were first tripped on October 24, 1997, as stocks fell in response to the Asian crisis. Shortly thereafter, the point ranges were broadened to 350 and 550 points. At the time, many analysts called for switching to a percentage change system from the point change system because trading halts based on percentage changes would be more meaningful. The Dow had increased so dramatically throughout the 1990s that a 350- or 550-point change was not nearly as significant as when the Dow was at lower levels.

In response, the NYSE adopted a threshold percentage rule that took effect on April 15, 1998. The point threshold is adjusted quarterly based on a percentage of the average closing level of the Dow Jones Industrial Average during the previous month. The thresholds are as follows:

1. If the Dow declines 10 percent from the threshold before 2:00 P.M., the market will close for 1 hour—between 2:00 and 2:30 P.M., the market will close for 30 minutes; after 2:30 P.M., the 10 percent threshold is removed and the market will continue trading.
2. If the Dow declines 20 percent from the threshold before 1 P.M., the market will close for 2 hours—between 1 and 2 P.M., for 1 hour; after 2 P.M., for the day.
3. If the Dow declines 30 percent at any time, the market will close for the day.

Circuit breakers also limit some program trading. A 50-point movement in the Dow originally triggered these limitations, which apply to price advances and declines. On February 16, 1999, the point movement that triggers the limitations on program trading was increased to 180 points. For the first 7 months of 2001, program trading accounted for 28 percent of the average daily volume of trading on the NYSE.

Other Exchanges

In addition to being the home of the Big Board, New York City is the home of the **American Stock Exchange,** where the stocks of over 660 companies are traded.[8] The dollar value of stocks traded on the American Stock Exchange is small compared to the NYSE and the criteria for the stock of a corporation to be traded are not as stringent. Regional exchanges that primarily trade stocks listed on the NYSE are located in Boston, Cincinnati, Chicago, Los Angeles, San Francisco, Philadelphia, and Spokane. Stocks of a given company may be traded on more than one exchange, and specialists on the floor of each exchange watch prices on competing exchanges.

Many foreign countries also have stock exchanges with varying degrees of development and depth. Some European exchanges, such as the London Stock Exchange and Amsterdam Stock Exchange, pre-date those in the United States.

Circuit Breakers
Reforms introduced in 1987 on the NYSE to temporarily halt market trading if prices change by a specified amount.

American Stock Exchange
A stock exchange located in New York City that trades the stock of over 660 companies.

---

[7]Over time, movements in the Dow have been closely correlated with the overall movement of more broadly based stock market indexes.

[8]As we shall see in Chapter 22, the American Stock Exchange also trades options.

LOOKING BACK: *Would You Buy a "Seat" on the New York Stock Exchange for $400?*

The first securities were sold on New York's Wall Street just over 200 years ago. An informal network of brokers and dealers met to trade stocks, bonds, and other commodities such as furs and tobacco.

At first, the trading sessions were informal. But soon brokers started to schedule regular auctions, and Wall Street became a centralized location where securities were traded every day at noon. To sell a security, you gave it to the auctioneer who would sell it to the highest bidder for a commission. To buy a security, you could participate directly in the auction or pay a broker a fee to purchase shares for you while you were elsewhere. Some individuals would meet after the centralized auction was closed and trade securities for reduced commissions. The process was a bit disorganized and chaotic, motivating those who participated to design a better system.

On May 17, 1792, the Buttonwood Tree Agreement was signed by 24 men who agreed to trade securities only among themselves for a commission of 0.25 percent on all transactions. The agreement was named after a large buttonwood tree under which the brokers traded securities. In 1793, the exchange moved inside and eventually moved to its present home on 11 Wall Street. In March 1817, a formal constitution was adopted that created the New York Stock Exchange Board. The cost to be a member of the exchange entitled to directly trade securities was $400.

Being a member of the New York Stock Exchange was, and still is, often referred to as having a "seat" on the exchange. The terminology, although outdated, dates from the time when members who bought and sold securities were actually seated. As noted in the chapter, today's cost for a seat on the exchange is in excess of $2.3 million and, invariably, members are not sitting down as they make trades!

The Nikkei Exchange in Tokyo, the London Stock Exchange, the DAX in Germany, and the Toronto Stock Exchange in Canada are among the busiest exchanges around the world. In September 2000, the Amsterdam, Brussels, and Paris stock exchanges merged to form the Euronext Exchange. More cross-border mergers are expected, particularly in European countries that participate in the Euro. In recent years, many emerging economies have developed stock exchanges concomitant with the globalization of finance and the increase in capital flows.

RECAP Program trading by institutional investors allows for the pre-programming of computers to buy or sell baskets of stocks. Buying stocks on the margin refers to putting up only a fraction of the stock's selling price and borrowing the rest. Currently, the margin requirement is 50 percent. Stocks may be traded in organized markets such as the NYSE, the American Stock Exchange, or other regional stock exchanges. Organized exchanges operate auction-type markets where a specialist trades large blocks of shares. The NYSE is by far the largest organized exchange. Each stock is traded at a specific post, which may trade up to several dozen stocks. Smaller trades are made on the NYSE via a computer system (the DOT system) that sends buy or sell orders to the specialist's post where the transaction is automatically executed.

The Over-the-Counter Market all secondary markets are traded

Over-the-Counter Market
A network of securities dealers who trade stocks of over 30,000 companies via telephone or computer.

The **over-the-counter market** is composed of thousands of securities dealers located all over the country. Transactions in the stocks of more than 30,000 companies are executed over the telephone or via computer. The dealers or brokerage firms that make a market in a particular security or securities buy and sell the securities at publicly quoted prices. The **National Association of Securities Dealers (NASD)** regulates the market participants in the over-the-counter market under the supervision of the SEC. The NASD is privately owned. Historically, the over-the-counter market dealt mainly with stocks of small companies. Today, the over-the-counter market trades the stocks of many larger firms, including such high-tech giants as Apple Computer and Microsoft.

As of June 2001, more than 4,378 of the larger 30,000 companies whose stocks are traded over-the-counter are also members of the **National Association of Securities Dealers Automated Quotation System (NASDAQ).** NASDAQ, which was founded in 1971, is the world's first electronic stock market.[9] Stocks of NASDAQ members are traded on an advanced computer system that provides immediate information about prices and the number of shares being traded. To be listed on the NASDAQ, a company must meet several requirements, including sales volume. Over 1,000 brokers and dealers participate in the NASDAQ market, and trading information is broadcast over 350,000 computer terminals worldwide. NASDAQ has also established a pre-market and an after-hours market to trade listed stocks outside the regular trading session from 9:30 A.M. to 4 P.M. eastern time. The pre-market session is from 9:00 A.M. to 9:30 A.M. eastern time; the after-market hours are from 4 P.M. to 6:30 P.M. eastern time. The NASDAQ International market session is from 3:30 A.M. to 9 A.M. eastern time. Trading in these markets often offers less liquidity, inferior prices, and potentially greater price volatility than trading during regular hours. These discrepancies may lessen as the pre-market and after-hours market become more developed.[10]

The market capitalization value of the stocks traded on the NASDAQ is approximately $3.2 trillion in June 2001, down from approximately $5.6 trillion one year earlier. The NASDAQ's market share of trading volume of all stocks increased from under 30 percent in 1979 to 56 percent in 2000. In the same time, the market share of trading volume for the NYSE has declined from over 60 percent to 42 percent. Since 1999, the NASDAQ has also been the largest market in terms of dollar volume, increasing from under 20 percent to 54 percent between 1979 and 1999. Again, the NYSE share of the dollar volume of trading declined from around 80 percent in 1979 to 44 percent in 1999. In addition, in early 2000, the NASDAQ was the first stock market to trade 2 billion shares of stock in one day. Over 400 of the 4,378 NASDAQ companies are foreign companies, making the NASDAQ the leading U.S. market for non-U.S. corporations.

The NASDAQ's tremendous growth in the 1990s made it a rival to the NYSE and bigger than all other domestic and foreign stock exchanges. Although the market capitalization of the stocks traded on the NYSE far exceeds that of stocks traded on the NASDAQ, the NASDAQ has been growing relatively faster in terms of the number of shares and dollar volume of trading.

Stock Market Indexes

Stock market indexes measure the overall performance of the stocks included in the index. An index can be used to evaluate how well a specific stock or mutual fund is performing relative to the other stocks represented in the index. Almost 100 indexes monitor stock prices. The **Dow Jones Industrial Average** (the

National Association of Securities Dealers (NASD)
A privately owned organization that regulates the market participants in the over-the-counter market under the supervision of the SEC.

NASDAQ
An association whose members trade stocks over an advanced computer system that provides immediate information about prices and the number of shares traded.

http://www.NASDAQ. com
Updated information about the stocks traded on the NASDAQ.

Dow Jones Industrial Average (the Dow)
An index that measures movements in the stock prices of 30 of the largest companies traded on the NYSE.

---

[9]As part of the general trend in financial markets, the NASDAQ merged with the AMEX in March 1998.

[10]The NYSE is instituting pre-market and after-market hours in the second half of 2000.

EXHIBIT 11-5
The Companies That
Make Up the Dow as
of August 13, 2001

Alcoa	Intel Corp.
American Express	IBM
AT&T	International Paper Co.
Boeing	J.P. Morgan Chase & Co.
Caterpillar	Johnson & Johnson
Citigroup Inc.	McDonald's Corp.
Coca-Cola	Merck & Co.
DuPont	Microsoft Corp.
Eastman Kodak	Minn. Mining & Manufacturing
Exxon Mobil Corp.	Philip Morris Cos.
General Electric Co.	Procter & Gamble Co.
General Motors Corp.	SBC Communications
Hewlett-Packard Co.	United Technologies Corp.
Home Depot	Wal-Mart
Honeywell International Inc.	Walt Disney

Dow, for short) measures movements in the stock prices of 30 of the largest companies in the country. The Dow, first introduced in 1896, is the oldest index in use today and is the most famous. Exhibit 11-5 lists the stocks that currently make up the Dow.

The total of stocks in an index may include all the stocks traded on a particular stock exchange, selectively chosen stocks, or stocks that fall into a particular class based on the value of outstanding shares.

The following list describes the major stock indexes reported in the popular media. As a quick glance shows, indexes other than the Dow are far more broadly based. Over the long run, however, the movement of the Dow has closely paralleled other, more comprehensive indexes.

The Dow Jones Industrial Average, (the DJIA), is an unweighted average of the sum of the daily closing prices of the stocks of 30 of the largest companies in the country, the "blue chips." (See Exhibit 11-5.) The companies that make up the index are selected by Dow Jones & Company, which also publishes *the Wall Street Journal*. The companies are changed over time to reflect changes in corporate America. Note that the index is larger than the sum of the daily closing prices of the 30 stocks. The number that the sum is divided by is adjusted to take into account the effect of stock splits and stock dividends. Also, when a company is dropped and a new company added, the average is adjusted so that the new index is comparable to earlier values.

- The Dow Jones Transportation Average is calculated using the prices of 20 airline, trucking, and railroad stocks.

- The Dow Jones Utility Average is calculated using the prices of 15 gas, electric, and power company stocks.

- The Dow Jones 65 Composite Index is calculated from all stocks in the Dow Jones Industrial, Transportation, and Utility Averages.

- The Standard & Poor's 500 (the S&P 500, for short) is a weighted index of prices of 500 broad-based corporations. Stocks included in the index may be traded on the New York Stock Exchange, the American Stock Exchange, or over-the-counter. They are selected by Standard & Poor's Corporation and changed over time as needed so that the index reflects general stock market conditions. As with other weighted indexes, the stocks are weighted according to their relative values so that larger corporations contribute more to the index. Many analysts consider the S&P 500 to be a more meaningful index of overall stock market activity than the Dow.

- The New York Composite Index is a weighted average of the market value of all stocks traded on the NYSE. The index also reports four subgroup indexes representing industrial, transportation, utility, and finance stocks.

- The Wilshire Equity Index Value (the Wilshire 5000) is a weighted index of the value of all stocks listed on the NYSE, all stocks on the American Stock Exchange, and all over-the-counter stocks that are traded by NASDAQ members. As such, it includes virtually all companies headquartered in the United States and is the broadest measure of stock market activity. Today the Wilshire 5000 includes over 6,800 stocks. When the index was originally created, it included 5,000 stocks (hence the name).

- The NASDAQ Composite Index, as its name suggests, is a weighted index that measures changes in prices of all stock traded by the NASDAQ system.

Exhibit 11-6 looks at the value of the DJIA, S&P 500, NYSE Composite, and NASDAQ Composite from 1985 until August 10, 2001. Note the phenomenal increase in all of the indices. Exhibit 11-7 shows the daily averages of the stock market volume and the values traded from 1985 until July 2000. Again, note the phenomenal increase in both volume and value of stocks traded. In the next section, we look at how market analysts determine the value of stocks.

Stock Market Performance Indices (End of Period)			
DOW JONES INDUSTRIAL AVERAGE	S&P 500	NYSE COMPOSITE	NASDAQ COMPOSITE
1985	1,546.67	211.28	121.58	324.93
1986	1,895.95	242.17	138.58	348.83
1987	1,938.83	247.08	138.23	330.47
1988	2,168.57	277.72	156.26	381.38
1989	2,753.20	353.40	195.04	454.82
1990	2,633.66	330.22	180.49	373.84
1991	3,168.83	417.09	229.44	586.34
1992	3,301.11	435.71	240.21	676.95
1993	3,754.09	466.45	259.08	776.80
1994	3,834.44	459.27	250.94	751.96
1995	5,117.12	615.93	329.51	1,052.13
1996	6,448.27	740.74	392.30	1,291.03
1997	7,908.25	970.43	511.19	1,570.35
1998	9,181.43	1,229.23	595.81	2,192.69
1999	11,497.12	1,469.25	650.30	4,069.31
2000	10,786.90	1,320.28	656.87	2,470.52
2001*	10,416.30	1,190.16	608.34	1,956.47

EXHIBIT 11-6
The Value of the DJIA, S&P 500, NYSE Composite, and NASDAQ Since 1985

*As of August 10, 2001.
SOURCE: Global Financial Data, Los Angeles, California

EXHIBIT 11-7
Daily Average of Stock Market Volume and Values Traded Since 1985

	STOCK MARKET VOLUME (DAILY AVG., MILS. OF SHS.)			VALUE TRADED (DAILY AVG., $ BILS.)	
	NYSE	*AMEX*	*NASDAQ*	*NYSE*	*NASDAQ*
1985	109.2	8.3	82.1	3.9	0.9
1986	141.0	11.8	113.6	5.4	1.5
1987	188.9	13.9	149.8	7.4	2.0
1988	161.5	9.9	122.8	5.4	1.4
1989	165.5	12.4	133.1	6.1	1.7
1990	156.8	13.2	131.9	5.2	1.8
1991	178.9	13.3	163.3	6.0	2.7
1992	202.3	14.2	190.8	6.9	3.5
1993	264.5	18.1	263.0	9.0	5.3
1994	291.4	17.9	295.1	9.7	5.8
1995	346.1	20.1	401.4	12.2	9.5
1996	412.0	22.1	543.7	16.0	13.0
1997	526.9	24.4	647.8	22.8	17.7
1998	673.6	28.9	801.7	29.0	22.9
1999	808.9	32.7	1,081.8	35.5	43.7
2000*	953.8	37.1	1,542.0	40.0	79.7

*As of July 2000.

SOURCE: Securities Industry Association

RECAP In addition to purchasing stocks from an organized exchange, stocks may also be purchased over-the-counter. The over-the-counter market is an informal network of market makers who trade stocks via telephone or computer linkages. Stocks of over 30,000 companies are traded over-the-counter. NASD, a privately owned organization, regulates the over-the-counter market under the supervision of the SEC. Large companies may also be NASDAQ members. Stocks of NASDAQ members are traded on an advanced computer system that provides price quotes for the members of NASDAQ. Trading on the NASDAQ has grown faster than trading on the organized exchanges in recent years. Stock market indexes measure movements in stock prices. The Dow is an index of 30 of the largest companies in the country. The S&P 500 is a weighted average of 500 broad-based companies and is considered to be a more meaningful index than the Dow.

The Valuation of Stocks

Should you buy a particular stock or not? It depends on whether you think it is your most profitable opportunity, given your tolerance for risk. At the present price at which it is trading, is the stock undervalued or overvalued? In this section, we will attempt to shed some light on these questions.

Given some of the material covered in Chapters 5 and 7, you will not be surprised to learn that the price of a share of stock in a firm should be equal to the present value of the expected future cash flows that the share will generate.[11] If we assume that the stock will be held indefinitely into the future (forever), then the current price of the stock will be equal to the present value of the expected cash flows, as portrayed in Equation 11-1:

(11-1) $$P = C1/(1 + d) + C2/(1 + d)^2 + C3/(1 + d)^3 + . . .$$

where

(dividend cash flow)

Cn = the expected cash flow in the nth year

d = the discount factor (interest rate) applied to find the present value or price (P)

If we expect the firm to earn a constant cash flow ($C1 = C2 = C3 = . . .$), then Equation 11-1 simplifies to Equation 11-2:

(11-2) $$P = C/d$$

Assuming we can estimate the expected cash flow (C) and the discount factor (d), we can solve for the current value of a share of the stock. If the stock is trading at a lower price, the savvy investor will buy; if it is trading at a higher price, the investor will sell. If there is agreement about expected cash flows, the stock's price should converge to the value based on that expectation. In the real world, there are often very divergent opinions about future cash flows. That is why some people are buying and others are selling at any given moment.

A question that remains is how is the discount factor determined? For any stock, there is a required return that is needed by investors who purchase the stock. This is the equilibrium return that is based on a risk-free return plus a risk premium associated with owning the stock, as discussed in Chapter 7. The risk-free return is usually measured by the long-term government bond rate.

The risk premium is composed of two parts:

- A **market risk premium** based on historical data that shows how much on average the ownership of stocks pays over the risk free return.

- A **firm-specific risk premium** that is measured by a coefficient called **beta.** Beta measures the overall sensitivity or variability of the stock's return relative to changes in the entire stock market.[12] Changes in the S&P 500 can serve as a proxy for changes in the whole market. Thus, if on average, when the S&P 500 increases (or decreases) 1 percent and a particular stock's price increases (or decreases) 2 percent, then the beta for this stock is 2. This stock is more risky than the average stock in the S&P 500 index because its value fluctuates more. On the other hand, if a 1 percent change in the S&P 500 generates a .5 percent change, then beta is .5 and the stock varies less than the S&P 500.

The **capital asset pricing model** makes use of the preceding analysis to develop a model of the return needed to own a share of stock based on the market and firm-specific risks. According to the capital asset pricing model, the return needed is

Market Risk Premium
The risk based on historical data that shows how much on average the ownership of stocks pays over a risk-free return.

Firm-Specific Risk Premium
A risk measured by beta that shows the overall sensitivity of the stock's return relative to changes in the entire market.

Beta
A measure of the overall variability of a stock relative to changes in the entire stock market.

Capital Asset Pricing Model
A model that asserts that the value of a share of stock includes a risk-free return, a market risk premium, and a firm-specific risk premium that is based on beta.

---

[11]Cash flows can include dividends and retained earnings.

[12]The covariance between two variables is a measure of how the variables move together. The variance of a variable is a measure of how a variable moves relative to its mean. In reality, beta is the covariance between a specific stock's return and the market's return, all divided by the variance of the market's return.

equal to the risk-free return plus beta multiplied by the market risk premium, as depicted in Equation 11-3:

(11-3) $d = Rf + b(Rm)$

where

d = the discount factor

Rf = the risk-free return

b = beta for this particular stock

Rm = the market risk premium that the investor must be compensated for owning stocks in general

The discount factor takes into account the risk-free return, the market risk premium, and the firm-specific variance of the return as measured by beta.

In our example, if the risk-free return is 5.5 percent, the market risk factor based on historical data is 4 percent, and beta for this firm is 2, then d is equal to 13.5 percent $(5.5 + (2 \times 4)) = 5.5 + 8 = 13.5)$. 13.5 percent is the discount factor that we will plug into Equation 11-2 to find the present value of a share of the firm's stock. If the expected cash flow is $10 per year, the price of the stock will be $74.07 because $10/.135 = $74.07.

Note that the risk-free return and the market risk premium are the same for all firms, while beta is usually different and dependent on the variability of a firm's returns.

The assumption of a constant expected cash flow is rather limiting since hopefully cash flows will grow over time. If we assume that expected cash flows grow at a constant percent, g, then we can modify Equation 11-2 to account for this common growth rate. This is done in Equation 11-4:

(11-4) $P = C/(d - g)$

where

P = the stock price

C = the expected cash flow today

d = the discount factor

g = the constant growth rate of future expected cash flows

Thus, modifying the preceding example, if cash flows are expected to grow 5 percent annually $(g = .05)$, the new stock price will be $117.65 because $($10/(.135 - .05) = $117.65)$.

In Chapter 7, we looked at the efficient market's theory, which laid much of the groundwork for this section. We saw that the prices of stocks and bonds adjust until the average investor is indifferent between stocks or bonds—in other words, until the risk-adjusted returns to owning stocks or bonds are equalized. In this section, we have expanded that analysis to consider a market risk of owning stocks versus bonds plus a firm-specific risk as measured by beta. The equilibrium return to owning stocks consists of a risk-free return, a risk premium for owning stock, and a firm-specific premium. Again, if the Fed takes action that causes interest rates to change, this changes the risk-free return of government bonds, and financial prices of stocks and bonds adjust until the investor is again indifferent between stocks and bonds.

 A point needs to be emphasized: Future cash flows are, of course, unknown. Therefore, it is the discounted value of expected cash flows that is used in stock valuation. You can see why cash flow and earnings reports get so much attention in the media. If earnings reports are different than forecasted, sharp price movements can occur immediately as investors take advantage of buying and selling opportunities. A Closer Look discusses some of the current issues with regard to the performance of U.S. stock markets in recent years.

Can Recent U.S. Stock Prices Be Justified?: As shown in Exhibit 11-6, U.S. stock markets reached levels that were unimaginable before the stock market boom began in the early 1990s. Some analysts believe that the market has been in an irrational bubble that cannot be sustained and look to the downturn in mid-2001 to support their claim. Others believe that increases in information technologies have transformed the way firms do business, increased worker productivity, and promised increased cash flows that justify the high prices.

Although a definitive answer has not been found, several theories have been put forth to attempt an explanation of the high stock valuations of recent years. From the material in this chapter, we can see that the stratospheric stock prices are justified under two conditions:

1. If expected cash flows have increased sufficiently to justify the high prices and/or,
2. If the rate at which expected cash flows are discounted has decreased enough to justify the high prices.

One theory holds that the high prices are justified if the growth rate of earnings has increased from the 1.4 percent averaged over the past century to 2.4 percent in recent years and if the required rate of return has fallen from the 7.3 percent averaged over the last century to 6.6 percent.[13] It suggests that changes in stock market participation, consumer preferences, and earnings growth together could explain the higher prices. As noted earlier, a much larger percentage of the population now participates in the market. Given increased life expectancies and uncertainty surrounding future social security payments, investors now have a longer time horizon for investments. Finally, given the growth of mutual funds, cash flows are less uncertain because of the greater extent of diversification that investing in mutual funds makes possible.

Another theory suggests that the high stock prices can be accounted for because of increases in productivity.[14] Productivity increased at an 8 percent annual rate in the 1960s, 2 percent in the 1970s, 17 percent in the 1990s, and 24 percent in the last 5 years. Although many believe the explosion of information technologies has increased worker productivity, these estimates seem unrealistic at best and also raise another question. If volatile productivity growth can explain changes in stock prices, then what are the factors that cause productivity growth to be so volatile?

A third theory suggests that a major technological innovation reduces the value of existing firms and causes a reduction in the stock market that will continue until shares in new firms making use of the technology enter into the market.[15] The idea is that the information technology revolution began in the early 1970s with the invention of the microprocessor. However, older firms with existing technologies and capital were slow to adopt the changes and so their values were reduced. The higher value of the new

[13]John Heaton, and Deborah Lucas, 1999. "Stock Prices and Fundamentals," http://www.kellogg. nwu.edu/faculty/heaton/research/macroannual.pdf.

[14]Robert E. Hall, 2000. "The Stock Market and Capital Accumulation." http://www.stanford. edu/~rehall/SMCA-d%205-12-00.pdf.

[15]Bart Hobijn, and Boyan Jovanovic, 2000. "The Information Technology Revolution and the Stock Market: Preliminary Evidence." Mimeo. New York University; Boyan Jovanic, and Peter L. Rousseau. 2000. "Vintage Organization Capital." Mimeo. New York University.

innovative firms was not reflected in stock markets because these firms did not offer tradable securities. Only after the new firms issued tradable stocks via IPOs would the value of new technologies be reflected in the market. To support the hypothesis, the authors show that most of the increased values in the stock market relative to gross domestic product since 1985 are the result of increases in the value of new firms. Firms that were in existence in early 1970s lost about half of their value then and have not fully recovered.

Finally, a fourth theory holds that the run-up in stock prices is due to two factors:

1. Technological changes are being assimilated into stock valuations, and
2. Structural changes such as financial liberalization allow for more widespread participation in stock markets.[16]

In addition, there are learning curves for both the changes in technology and the increased participation that could help to explain market volatility.

In the bull market and new economy of the late 1990s, Internet stocks—referred to as dot.coms—experienced enormous gains. Some of these start-up companies had never made a profit, never produced a product, and had virtually no real or financial assets. So why were investors willing to pay such hefty prices? If you followed this chapter, you should be quick to answer, "expected future cash flows." Of course after spring 2000, when prices of many of the dot.coms collapsed, investors began to take a closer look and question whether or not the expected cash flows had been vastly over-estimated. Perhaps some Internet stocks had been caught in a speculative bubble.

Other stocks that suffered significant losses at the time included media and telecommunications stocks. Indeed, the technology-laden NASDAQ index fell over 39 percent in 2000. By March 2001, the NASDAQ index had fallen 62 percent in a bear market.

RECAP The value of a stock is the discounted present value of the expected future stream of cash flows that the stock will generate. Investors require a return that is the sum of a risk-free return plus a risk premium to account for stocks being riskier than government securities. In addition to a market risk premium, there is a firm-specific risk premium based on beta that measures the variability of a stock's return relative to the entire market. If cash flows grow by a constant percent, g, then the price of a share of stock will be equal to $C/(d - g)$ where C is the original cash flow, d is the discount factor based on the market risk and the firm-specific risk, and g is the constant growth rate of the cash flow.

We have completed our look at stocks. Hopefully you have a better understanding of these financial instruments. This chapter contains one appendix on how a firm that wishes to raise long-term financial capital chooses between issuing stocks or bonds. We will complete our discussion of capital markets with the next chapter on the mortgage market. This will lay the groundwork for our discussion in Chapter 24, where we take up the issue of how policymakers should respond to price volatility in these capital markets.

---

[16]Joseph Zeira, 1999. "Informational Overshooting, Booms and Crashes." *Journal of Monetary Economics* 43(1) pp. 237–257.

Summary of Major Points

- In recent decades, prices of stocks have become more volatile. The Fed is concerned about inflation and deflation in stock prices because of their potential to cause unemployment or inflation or to affect the solvency of financial institutions and the financial system.

- Stocks represent ownership in a corporation. Preferred stock pays a fixed dividend while common stock may pay a variable or no dividend. Under normal circumstances, publicly held stocks are liquid financial assets that may be traded in organized markets such as the NYSE, the American Stock Exchange, or regional stock exchanges. They may also be traded over-the-counter through computer networks and over the telephone lines.

- Institutional investors in the stock market are primarily insurance companies, pension plans, and mutual funds. Program trading allows institutional investors to pre-program computers to buy or sell a market basket of stocks. Buying on the margin refers to buying stocks by using one's own funds and borrowed funds. Current margin requirements for purchases are 50 percent. Exchanges set maintenance margins that apply to margins that must be maintained after the stock has been purchased. Shelf registration allows a corporation to register the stocks that will be issued over the next 2 years.

- Organized exchanges operate auction-type markets wherein a specialist trades large blocks of shares at a specific post. Smaller trades are made on the NYSE via the DOT system, which is a computer system that sends buy or sell orders to the specialist's post.

- The over-the-counter market is an informal network of market makers who trade stocks of over 30,000 companies via telephone or computer linkages. The NASD regulates the over-the-counter market under the supervision of the SEC. New issues of securities must be registered with the SEC. The NASDAQ is the world's first electronic stock market and trades the stocks of over 4,378 of the larger 30,000 corporations that are in the over-the-counter market. The stocks are traded on an advanced computer system. In recent years, the trading volume on the NASDAQ has been growing faster than on the NYSE.

- The value of a share of stock is the discounted present value of the expected future cash flows that the stock will generate. Investors require a return that is the sum of a risk-free return plus a risk premium to account for the fact that stocks are riskier than government securities. In addition to a market risk premium, there is a firm-specific risk premium based on beta that measures the variability of this stock's return relative to the entire market. If cash flows grow by a constant percent, then the price of a share of stock will be equal to $C/(d-g)$ where C is the original cash flow, d is the discount factor based on the market risk and the firm-specific risk, and g is the constant growth rate of the cash flows.

- (App.) If firms want to spend more than their receipts, they must decide between internal or external financing. If the firm uses external financing, it can issue new stocks or bonds. If a firm chooses external debt financing, it must also decide if the debt will be long term or short term. Issuing stock dilutes the ownership of the firm. Issuing debt has tax advantages because interest payments are a tax write-off whereas dividend payments are not. Issuing debt increases the leverage ratio of the firm, which makes the firm more vulnerable to a downturn in profits.

Key Terms

American Stock Exchange
Beta
Capital Asset Pricing Model
Circuit Breakers
Common Stock
Designated Order Turnaround (DOT)

Dow Jones Industrial Average (the Dow)
External Financing (app.)
Firm-Specific Risk Premium
Initial Public Offering (IPO)
Internal Financing

Maintenance Margin Requirement
Margin Requirement
Market Risk Premium
National Association of Securities Dealers (NASD)

National Association of
  Securities Dealers Automated
  Quotation System (NASDAQ)
New York Stock Exchange
  (NYSE)

Over-the-Counter Market
Preferred Stock
Program Trading
Secondary Stock Offering

Securities and Exchange
  Commission (SEC)
Shelf Registration
Speculative Bubble

Review Questions

1. How could a stock market crash affect the economy?

2. Assuming other factors remain constant, rank the following assets from highest to lowest in terms of the risk of holding them: (Hint: If needed, refer to Chapter 10 for information on bonds.)
   a. Common stock
   b. Preferred stock
   c. Collateral bond
   d. Mortgage bond
   e. Debenture bond
   f. Subordinated debenture bond

3. Assuming other factors remain constant, rank the following assets from highest to lowest in terms of the return to holding them: (Hint: If needed, refer to Chapter 10 for information on bonds.)
   a. Common stock
   b. Preferred stock
   c. Collateral bond
   d. Mortgage bond
   e. Debenture bond
   f. Subordinated debenture bond

4. Which market index would you look at to see how well the stock market is performing? Why? Why do you think the movements of the Dow and the S&P 500 are highly correlated?

5. Why are mutual funds generally perceived to be less risky than holding a market basket of individual stocks?

6. What are institutional investors, and what impact do they have on stock markets? What is program trading?

7. What is the over-the-counter market? Are only companies that are too small to be listed on an organized exchange traded over-the-counter?

8. Can a stock be listed on more than one exchange at the same time?

9. What are circuit breakers? How have the rules changed in recent years?

10. Discuss the following statement: "Organized exchanges, like dinosaurs, will disappear."

11. In a paragraph, explain how inflation in stock markets can spill over to inflation in output markets. Do the same for deflation.

12. How does a firm choose between debt and equity financing? What are the advantages and disadvantages of each?

13. What is buying on the margin? Does it increase or decrease the risk of large losses? What about gains?

14. Can Microsoft do a new IPO? Explain. What is the difference between buying stock in a secondary public offering or in the secondary market?

Analytical Questions

15. If a share of stock pays a dividend of $3 and closes today at $36, what is the current yield?

16. What is the discount factor if beta is 1.2, the market risk premium is 5 percent, and the risk-free return is 4 percent?

17. If the expected cash flow is constant and equal to $10, what is the value of a share of stock with the discount factor in problem 16? If the cash flow is expected to grow 3 percent each year, what is the value?

18. If I bought $10,000 worth of stock by putting up 60 percent of the selling price and borrowing the rest, how much have I borrowed? If the stock falls to $3,000 and a margin call is put in for the difference between the value of the stock and the amount I have borrowed, how much will I have to put up?

19. New earnings figures suggest that cash flows will experience a $100 one-time increase because of a new product being brought on line. If d is 15 percent and g is 3 percent, how much will the stock's value increase?

Internet Exercises

1. Go to the NASDAQ home page at (**http://www.nasdaq.com**) and click on major indices to determine their latest performance. How do they compare?

2. What were the 10 most actively traded stocks on the American Stock Exchange today? What were the 10 most advanced? You can find this information by clicking on the appropriate link from the homepage of the American Stock Exchange (**http://www.amex.com/**).

3. **http://www.dismal.com/chartroom/ chartroom.asp** contains a graphical glimpse of the U.S. economy over about a 10-year period. Under "U.S. equity markets", compare and contrast the performance of the S&P 500 index, the Dow Jones Index, and the NASDAQ Index over time.

4. **http://www.yardeni.com** contains information about industry performance. Under "Trackers" click on "S&P YTD." Look at the S&P sector and industry performance year-to-date. What sector has the largest percent change? How many sectors are showing year-to-date gains? Year-to-date losses?

Suggested Readings

For a sobering look at the stock market, see J. Patrick Raines and Charles G. Leathers, *Economists and the Stock Market: Speculative Theories of Stock Market Fluctuations* (Northampton, MA: Edward Elgar), 2000.

For a discussion of the linkages between asset prices and monetary policy, see "Manias and How to Prevent Them, An Interview with Charles Kindleberger" and "Market Volatility and Monetary Policy," by John Balder, Jr., both in *Challenge*, November–December 1997, pp. 21–31 and pp. 32–52, respectively.

Technology has played a part in the formation of numerous stock market bubbles. For an in-depth look at technological innovation and stock market bubbles since the early 1900s, see Robert Shiller's *Irrational Exuberance* (Princeton, NJ: Princeton University Press), 2000.

For a historical look at a time when the New York Stock Exchange nearly collapsed, see Alec Benn, *The Unseen Wall Street, 1969–1975* (Westport, CT: Greenwood Publishing Group), 2000.

For a comprehensive view of the stock market and how it affects the economy, see John Charles Pool and Robert L. Frick, *Demystifying the Stock Market* (Winchester, VA: Durell Institute of Monetary Science at Shenandoah University), 1993.

One of the best resources for a layperson to learn about the stock market is William J. O'Neill, *How to Make Money in Stocks: A Winning System in Good Times or Bad*, 3rd ed. (New York: McGraw-Hill), 2001. Another good book is *One Up on Wall Street: How to Use What you Already Know to Make Money in the Market* by Peter Lynch, John Rothchild (Contributor), (New York: Simon and Shuster), 2000.

For a look at "Mutual Funds and the U.S. Equity Market," see the article by the same name by Eric M. Engen and Andreas Lehnert, in the *Federal Reserve Bulletin*, December, 2000, pp. 797–817.

For a discussion of the linkages between asset prices and monetary policy, see "Manias and How to Prevent Them, An Interview with Charles Kindleberger" and "Market Volatility and Monetary Policy," by John Balder, Jr., both in *Challenge*,

November–December 1997, pp. 21–31 and pp. 32–52, respectively. Also see "Monetary Policy and Asset Prices," by Andrew J. Filardo, *Economic Review, Federal Reserve Bank of Kansas City*, Third Quarter 2000, vol. 85, No. 3, pp. 11–38.

For another point of view, see "The Long-Term Outlook for Stocks: Interview with Peter Diamond," *Challenge*, March–April 2000, Vol. 43, No. 2, pp. 6–16.

For an early 1998 article that predicted falling stock prices a few years before a significant downturn, see "Valuation Ratios and the Long-Run Stock Market Outlook," *Journal of Portfolio Management* 24 (Winter 1998): 11–26. Another article along the same line is Nathan S. Balke and Mark E. Wohar, "Why Are Stock Prices So High? Dividend Growth or Discount Factor?" *Working Paper No. 00-01*, Federal Reserve Bank of Dallas, January 2000.

For an article that predicts that recent high stock market returns may mean lower returns in the future, see John E. Golob and David G. Bishop, "What Long-Run Returns Can Investors Expect from the Stock Market?" *Economic Review of the Federal Reserve Bank of Kansas City* 82:3 (Third Quarter, 1997): 5–20.

A much more technical discussion of stock market prices and inflation can be found in David P. Ely and Kenneth J. Robinson, "The Stock Market and Inflation: A Synthesis of the Theory and Evidence," *Economic Review of the Federal Reserve Bank of Dallas*, March 1989, pp. 17–27.

The determinants of stock prices are discussed in Robert B. Barsky, "Why Does the Stock Market Fluctuate?" *Quarterly Journal of Economics* 108 (May 1993): 291–311.

Appendix 11-A

The Choice Between Stocks and Bonds

In the process of investing and operating on a day-to-day basis, firms experience periods when expenditures exceed receipts. As a result, a firm must make several portfolio decisions regarding the financing of excess spending. First, should the spending be financed internally or externally? **Internal financing** is simply the spending of money balances on hand or the liquidation of financial or real assets owned by the firm to finance the excess. Internal financing is the largest source of funds for business firms.

As for **external financing,** there are two types: expanding equity or expanding debt. Thus, if a firm chooses external financing—perhaps because its financing needs exceed the internal funds available—it must then decide whether to issue new debt and/or equity.

External financing via equity involves issuing shares of common stock, thereby expanding the ownership in the firm.[17] If the firm chooses external financing through borrowing, it faces the decision of whether to issue long-term or short-term debt. For example, the firm must choose between loans or market instruments, such as commercial paper and corporate bonds. In general, each decision is guided primarily by the desire for profit maximization and the existing structure of financial liabilities. A firm will choose the option that minimizes the cost of funds.

For each firm, the prevailing financial environment, the stance of monetary policy, and so forth, will determine the overall cost of funds. The relative cost of alternative sources of financial capital and, therefore, the particular financing decision reached, will be influenced by several considerations: (1) the particular type of

Internal Financing
The spending of money balances on hand or the liquidation of financial or real assets to finance spending that exceeds current receipts.

External Financing
Financing spending that exceeds current receipts by expanding either debt or equity.

---

[17]If the new shares are sold to existing shareholders, ownership is not diluted. Indeed existing shareholders are sometimes given the first option to purchase the new shares.

expenditures being financed, (2) the current financial environment and expectations about the future environment, (3) the firm's financial structure, and (4) the tax laws.

Traditionally, borrowing to finance inventories has taken the form of either short-term bank loans or the issuance of commercial paper. The usual maturity of the bank loans or commercial paper is 1 to 6 months, which is appropriate in that inventories are typically not held for long periods of time. Fluctuations in inventory investment over the business cycle explain much of the variation in short-term debt accumulated by firms. The correlation is not perfect, however. For example, if prevailing long-term rates are perceived by many firms to be temporarily high relative to short-term rates, some firms will issue short-term debt to finance the initial phases of their investment spending on new capital. These firms expect that long-term interest rates will soon drop, at which point the firms will issue long-term debt to pay off the maturing short-term debt and finance subsequent phases of their investment spending. Thus, we see how current and expected financial environments play a role in firms' financing decisions.

From the mid-1970s until 1991, a substantial portion of externally financed investment spending, which by definition is the acquisition of capital (new plant and equipment), was financed by issuing long-term debt. Why long-term debt instead of equity? The answer is that U.S. tax laws tend to bias the financing decisions of business firms toward debt and away from equity. Interest paid on debt is a tax-deductible cost and, thus, is subtracted from gross revenues before the corporate income tax is computed. Dividends paid to equity holders, however, are not tax deductible. Dividends must be paid out of after-tax earnings.[18] Thus, debt financing will initially be cheaper, on average, than equity financing, which may also entail higher flotation costs. Equity financing also dilutes the ownership of current shareholders.

Debt financing also has a downside. Increasing debt is believed to expose a firm to more risk and, therefore, to weaken the firm's financial structure. The exposure to more risk can ultimately raise the overall cost of capital, as the suppliers of funds require higher returns to compensate them for the additional risk.

The relationship among debt finance, risk, and the cost of capital is rooted in a common measure of the financial structure—the *leverage ratio*, or the ratio of debt to equity on a firm's balance sheet. Other things being equal, the higher the leverage ratio, the greater the risk to bondholders and stockholders. The reason is that if a highly leveraged firm experiences a substantial decline in earnings, it may default on its debt obligations and be forced into bankruptcy, possibly leaving its stockholders with nothing. A firm with a low leverage ratio could weather a decline in earnings by cutting dividends, which are residual claims, not contractual obligations. The leveraged firm does not have this option: It must pay its debt costs or fold. Hence, *ceteris paribus*, risk-averse investors will typically demand a higher yield on funds they lend to highly leveraged corporations. Firms that have considerable debt relative to equity will find the cost of debt financing (as well as equity financing) to be relatively high. As a result, they may decide to issue equity both to raise funds and to strengthen their balance sheets.

Another reason why firms issued new debt in the 1980s was to acquire the equities of other firms in whole or in part. Often referred to as mergers and acquisitions, this activity has sometimes been financed by the issuance of junk bonds that carry yields above prevailing yields on higher-rated conventional corporate bonds.

---

[18]Thus, dividends are subject to so-called double taxation. They are taxed as part of business income and taxed again as part of household income.

In this case, debt increases but no new investment occurs. Whatever the benefits of this activity, the resulting expansion of debt relative to equities increases the leverage ratio of the corporate sector as a whole. This, in turn, generates concerns about increased risk—that is, the increased vulnerability of individual firms and the economy as a whole to adverse developments.

Starting in 1991 and lasting until early 1994, firms altered the trend of debt financing and issued new shares of stock instead. Because of lower interest rates on CDs, savers poured funds into mutual funds that soaked up the new stock issues. With stocks trading at high values, issuing relatively fewer shares could raise large amounts of funds. By mid-1994, the trend had reversed itself. From 1994 to the present, companies bought back record amounts of stocks, with a net $2.7 trillion worth of stocks bought back in the last 5 years alone.[19] Companies were using earnings to purchase their own stock rather than to pay dividends. In the bull market, this activity was also pushing stock prices even higher. In the later years, the capital gains of those who sold the stock back to the companies were subject to lower tax rates than dividends would have been. In addition, during the same years, bank loans and the issuance of corporate bonds increased. Thus, because of the rise in debt, in the aggregate, the leverage ratios of firms increased and the creditworthiness of firms declined. In the initial high-profit environment of the late 1990s and early 2000s, companies were paying a smaller amount of interest on bank loans and bonds than their return on equity. This could bode trouble for firms in the event of a downturn in profits and/or stock prices, such as was occurring in early and mid-2001.

---

[19]"Survey of Corporate Finance," The *Economist*, January 27, 2001, pp. 5–20.

chapter

The Mortgage Market

12

┌─ **Learning Objectives** *After reading this chapter, you should know:* ─┐

- What a mortgage is and how the mortgage market functions
- How the secondary market in mortgages works and what mortgage-backed securities are
- The main risks of investing in mortgages and mortgage-backed securities
- How prices of mortgages are determined in secondary markets
- The role of the government in the mortgage market

"

We are the country's third largest corporation, in terms of assets, and the nation's largest provider of funds for home mortgages. With a book of business that currently exceeds 12 million mortgages, we are one of the largest financial services corporations in the world.

—From the homepage of Fannie Mae, www.fanniemae.com

The 100-Year Mortgage: Indebting Your Children and Grandchildren

In the late 1980s, property values escalated in Japan, so much so that the typical Japanese family was unable to purchase a home by obtaining a traditional 25- to 30-year mortgage loan. In 1990, average property values in Japan were 9 times the average household income. In the United States, the comparable ratio was 3. To make homes more affordable, many Japanese borrowers turned to 80- to 100-year mortgages. When the term of the mortgage is lengthened, the monthly payment is reduced. With these mortgages, which became the norm, borrowers were indebting their children and their grandchildren (who possibly were not yet born).

In the first half of 2000, housing prices in Great Britain soared 14.5 percent. To cope with the higher prices, first-time buyers were being offered mortgages up to 6 times their annual income. In 1980, the average mortgage was 1.67 times annual income. To keep payments lower, the terms of many of the new mortgages were increased to 40 years. Halifax, Britain's biggest mortgage lender, introduced an intergenerational mortgage for homeowners 55 years and older.[1] With the new mortgage, the original borrower pays only interest. When the borrower passes away, the loan is passed on to the children, provided their credit is satisfactory. The children then make both principal and interest payments on the loan. This can be a good deal for the children if the property has appreciated significantly because they assume their parents' loan based on the lower property value. If the children do not have acceptable credit, the property is repossessed and sold by the lender to recoup some or all of the costs.

In the United States, commercial banks, savings and loans, and mortgage brokers are active participants in the residential mortgage market today. The federal government also plays an increasingly important role both directly and indirectly. Ginnie Mae, FHA, and VA are federal agencies that facilitate mortgage lending by insuring the principal and interest payments on some mortgage loans. Fannie Mae and Freddie Mac, two government-sponsored enterprises, are the major participants in the secondary mortgage market and were involved in over 70 percent of the 6.1 million mortgage loans that were made in 1999. In addition, borrowers today have a wide variety of innovative mortgages from which to choose.

It has not always been like this in the United States. Historically, savings and loans and mutual savings banks were the primary lenders in the residential mortgage market; the government had limited involvement. Between 1930 and 1970, virtually all mortgages were 30-year, fixed-rate loans. Despite the numerous creative types of mortgages available today, the bulk of mortgage contracts are much more standardized than in the past.

In this chapter, we look at the mortgage market, which is the largest debt market in the United States.[2] Residential mortgages, our focus, make up the largest segment of the market. We shall see how the mortgage market has changed in recent years, the role of the government and government-sponsored enterprises in the mortgage

---

[1]Robert Winnett and Kathryn Cooper, "House Boom Sets Scene for 100-year Mortgage," *Sunday Times*, London, September 3, 2000.

[2]Even though outstanding mortgages are the largest debt instrument, in recent years, the value of equities (stocks) has exceeded the value of mortgages by a substantial amount. The reason is that as new mortgages are issued, old mortgages continue to mature, whereas equities have no maturity date. For example, at the end of 2000, the outstanding value of domestic equities was over $17.1 trillion while the outstanding value of mortgages was over $6.9 trillion.

market, and the risks and benefits of investing in mortgages. Although intergenerational mortgages have not emerged in the United States, some of the changes in the mortgage market in the last 20 years are no less dramatic. We also hope to explain the enigma posed at the end of the preceding paragraph—namely, that there has been a proliferation of mortgage types despite the increasing standardization of mortgages. Let's begin with a description of mortgages and how the mortgage market functions.

The Anatomy of Mortgages

A *mortgage* is a long-term debt instrument for which real estate is used as **collateral** to secure the loan in the event of a default by the borrower. Mortgages are assets to the holder (lender) and liabilities to the issuer (borrower) who signs the mortgage agreement. They are similar to bonds with the caveat that the underlying real property or land serves as collateral.

Mortgages result from loans made to individuals or businesses to purchase land, single- or multiple-family residential housing, commercial properties, or farms. Mortgages may also be made to finance new commercial or residential construction. The building (structure) or land serves as collateral. In general, borrowers put down a minimum of 5 to 20 percent to purchase a property and take out a mortgage loan for the balance of the purchase price.

As noted previously, most mortgages are made to individuals to purchase residential property. Thus, households are the major borrowers in this market. Exhibit 12-1 shows the outstanding values of the various types of mortgages. In the middle of 2001, single- and multi-family residential mortgages accounted for 82 percent of all mortgages.

With a mortgage loan, the lender puts a **lien** on the property until the mortgage is fully paid off. The lien is a public record that stays with the property title and gives the lender the right to repossess the property if the borrower defaults. In the event of a default, the property is usually sold to recoup some or all of the losses. The property cannot be sold to a third party unless it is free of liens. In this way, the lender is guaranteed that the collateral will be there if the borrower defaults.

Despite the lien on the property that comes with a mortgage, lenders are not in the business of repossessing properties. Therefore, they want to be careful in assessing the **default risk** on a loan. Keeping this in mind, what would a lender want to know to determine whether a borrower should get a mortgage loan?

The two most important factors in determining whether a borrower can obtain a mortgage loan are the borrower's **debt-to-income ratio** and **loan-to-value ratio.** The debt-to-income ratio measures the monthly payments of the borrower relative to the borrower's monthly income and reflects how easily the borrower can

Collateral
The building (structure) or land that will be foreclosed on and repossessed if the borrower fails to make the scheduled payments; the lender then sells the property to recoup some or all of the losses.

Lien
A public record that stays with the property title and gives the lender the right to repossess and sell the property if the borrower defaults.

Default Risk
The risk that the borrower will not make the principal and interest payments as scheduled.

Debt-to-Income Ratio
A ratio composed of all of the borrowers debt relative to income; generally should not exceed 36 percent for a loan to be approved.

Loan-to-Value Ratio
The loan size relative to the value of the property that is used as collateral.

EXHIBIT 12-1
The Outstanding Value of Mortgages, 2001** (in billions)

TYPE OF MORTGAGE	OUTSTANDING VALUE	PERCENT OF TOTAL*
Single-family residential	$5,449.7	76 %
Multi-family residential	414.5	6
Commercial	1,188.3	17
Farm	112.7	2
Total	$7,165.3	101 %*

*Numbers do not sum to 100 percent because of rounding.

**Through second quarter 2001.

SOURCE: *Flow of Funds, Z1*, Board of Governors of the Federal Reserve System, September 18, 2001, p. 59.

afford to make the monthly payment. For example, if a borrower with an income of $4,000 per month and no other debts is applying for a mortgage with a monthly payment of $1,000, the debt-to-income ratio is $1,000/$4,000, or 25 percent. If the same borrower has $300 in other monthly debts, say a $300 monthly car payment, the total debt, including the mortgage, would be $1,300 per month ($1,000 mortgage payment plus $300 car payment). In this case, the debt-to-income ratio would be $1,300/$4,000, or 33.3 percent. If the borrower has credit card payments of $200 per month in addition to the car payment and the proposed mortgage payment, the debt-to-income ratio would be $1,500/$4,000, or 37.5 percent. Thus, the debt-to-income ratio includes not only the new payment on the real estate but also other payments such as car payments, credit card payments, etc., for which the borrower is liable. In general, lenders want the debt-to-income ratio to be lower than 36 percent.

The loan-to-value ratio measures the loan size relative to the value of the property that the lender would receive in the event of default. For example, if the purchaser puts down $20,000 and is borrowing $80,000 on a $100,000 property, the loan-to-value ratio is $80,000/$100,000, or 80 percent. If the purchaser has only $10,000 for a down payment, the loan-to-value ratio would be $90,000/$100,000, or 90 percent. The larger the down payment, the smaller the loan-to-value ratio.

It should come as no surprise that the lower the debt-to-income and loan-to-value ratios are, the easier it is for a borrower to obtain a mortgage loan. A low debt-to-income ratio means that it is easier for the borrower to afford the loan. The larger the down payment, the smaller the amount of the loan. However, loans for 100 percent of the value of a property are sometimes available, particularly when property values are appreciating rapidly. The borrower pays a higher interest rate to procure such a loan because of the increased risk involved.

The borrower's credit rating as measured by a credit rating agency is also important in determining whether a mortgage loan will be approved. The credit history becomes less important if there is a large down payment relative to the property value.

Mortgage Amortization

Amortization
The paying off of the principal of a loan over the life of the loan.

Unlike a bond, whereby the principal is repaid at maturity, the repayment of the principal on a mortgage is generally spread out over the life of the loan. Each month, a constant payment is made that includes some part of the principal in addition to the interest payment. At the end of the loan, the mortgage has been fully repaid. This is known as **amortization**.[3] Mortgages are usually made for up to 30 years. In recent years, though, shorter-term mortgages have increased because they result in tremendous interest savings over the life of the loan. The most popular terms are 15 and 30 years.

Exhibit 12-2 shows several months in the amortization schedules for a $200,000 mortgage issued at 8 percent for 15- and 30-year terms. Note that in both cases, a small amount initially goes toward the principal of the loan. Over time, the amount applied to the principal increases. For example, with the 15-year mortgage, $577.97 goes on the principal the first month, $800.40 the 50th month, and $1,898.65 the 180th, or last, month. With the 30-year mortgage, $134.20 goes toward the principal the first month, $185.84 the 50th month, $440.84 the 180th month, and $1,457.81 the 360th, or last, month. The small, initial principal corresponds with a large interest payment. As the principal gradually falls, more of the

---

[3]The alternative to an amortized loan would be to make interest-only payments and to repay the principal in a balloon payment at the end of the loan. Although common prior to the Great Depression, this is unusual today in the mortgage market.

Principal	$200,000		
Interest Rate	8 percent		
Amortization Period	15 Years—180 Payments		
Monthly Payment	$1,911.30		

PAYMENT NUMBER	PRINCIPAL	INTEREST	BALANCE
1	$ 577.97	$ 1,333.33	$199,422.03
2	581.82	1,329.48	198,840.21
3	585.70	1,325.60	198,254.50
4	589.61	1,321.70	197,664.89
49	795.09	1,116.21	166,636.30
50	800.40	1,110.91	165,835.90
110	1,192.47	718.84	106,633.29
180	1,898.65	12.66	0
Total	$200,000.00	$144,034.75	$ 0

Principal	$200,000		
Interest Rate	8 percent		
Amortization Period	30 Years—360 Total Payments		
Monthly Payment	$1,467.53		

PAYMENT NUMBER	PRINCIPAL	INTEREST	BALANCE
1	$ 134.20	$ 1,333.33	$199,865.80
2	135.09	1,332.44	199,730.10
3	135.99	1,331.54	199,594.72
4	136.90	1,330.63	199,594.72
49	184.61	1,282.92	192,253.47
50	185.84	1,281.69	192,067.63
110	276.87	1,190.66	178,321.70
180	440.84	1,026.69	153,563.12
240	656.78	810.75	120,955.93
300	978.50	489.03	72,376.24
360	1,457.81	9.72	0
Total	$200,000.00	$328,310.49	$ 0

constant monthly payment goes toward the principal and has a much larger impact on it. Note also that $184,275.74 ($328,310.49 – $144,034.75 = $184,275.74) in interest is saved over the life of the loan if the term is 15 years instead of 30.

Although not apparent in Exhibit 12-2, which uses an 8 percent interest rate for both the 15- and 30-year loans, the interest rate on a 15-year mortgage is usually less than the interest rate on a comparable 30-year mortgage. The longer the term to maturity, the greater the risk that the lender could lose. Thus, a higher interest rate compensates the lender for the longer term. Despite the savings, many individuals opt for the 30-year mortgage because they cannot afford the higher payments associated with a 15-year mortgage. In the example in Exhibit 12-2, the difference in the monthly payments is $443.77 per month ($1,911.30 – $1,467.53).

Insured and Uninsured Mortgages

Federal Housing Administration (FHA)
A federal agency that for a .5 percent fee insures mortgage loans made by privately owned financial institutions up to a certain amount if the borrowers meet certain conditions defined by the FHA.

Veterans Administration (VA)
A federal agency that, among other things, insures mortgage loans made by privately owned financial institutions up to a certain amount if the borrowers meet certain conditions, including being military veterans.

Conventional Mortgages
Mortgages made by financial institutions and mortgage brokers without federal insurance that the principal and interest will be repaid.

Residential mortgages may also be insured by an agency of the federal government. The insurance guarantees the repayment of the principal and interest in the event that the borrower defaults. This eliminates the credit or default risk for the lender. The two federal agencies that guarantee mortgages are the **Federal Housing Administration (FHA)** and the **Veterans Administration (VA).** For a .5 percent fee, the FHA insures mortgage loans made by privately owned financial institutions up to a certain amount that varies by state, depending on average housing costs. In 1999, the typical figure was around $250,000. Borrowers must meet certain conditions defined by the FHA. Generally, the criteria deal with the income of the borrower; FHA loans are designed to help low-income families purchase homes. With the government guarantee, the lender does not have to worry about the borrower defaulting. VA loans are similar to FHA loans but are designed to insure the principal and interest payments on loans made to veterans. The purpose is to help those who have served the country in the military to purchase homes. FHA and VA loans generally have small or no down payments.

Conventional mortgages have no federal insurance and are made by financial institutions and mortgage brokers. These loans usually require a 5 to 20 percent down payment. Generally, when the down payment or equity in the property is less than 20 percent, lenders require the borrower to purchase private mortgage insurance that would make the principal and interest payments in the event the borrower defaults.

The borrower pays a higher interest rate to cover the cost of the insurance. Equity is the difference between the market value of the property and the outstanding loan balance. If the property appreciates enough or if the loan balance declines enough that the equity in the property is 20 percent or greater, the borrower may initiate the termination of the mortgage insurance. In this case, the monthly payment will fall by the amount of the insurance.

Closing Costs

Closing Costs
Costs, the bulk of which are paid by the borrower, to obtain a mortgage; include such things as loan origination fees, surveys, appraisals. credit reports, title insurance, recording fees, and processing fees.

Points
A prepayment of interest at the time a mortgage loan is made that lowers the nominal interest rate on the loan; one point is equal to 1 percent of the loan balance.

Mortgages also entail **closing costs** that are paid by the borrower. These costs include loan origination fees, appraisals, property surveys, credit reports, title insurance, recording fees, and processing fees, etc. Title insurance, purchased before the loan closes, guarantees the lender that there are no liens on the property.

Closing fees may also include **points.** One point is equal to 1 percent of the loan balance. For example, on a $150,000 mortgage, one point is $1,500, two points are $3,000, etc. Points are, in reality, a prepayment of the interest on the loan. The borrower has an option of how many points to pay. The more points paid up front, the lower the interest rate on the loan. The borrower may also choose to pay no points and pay a higher interest rate. The decision as to how many points to pay should be based on how long the borrower anticipates having the loan. Very few loans are kept the full 15- or 30-year term. If the borrower anticipates moving (or refinancing if interest rates fall) in 3 to 5 years, the loan will be paid off (prepaid) long before maturity. In this case, paying points up front may be more costly over the life span of the loan. That is, if points paid up front and are figured into the cost of the loan, the effective interest rate can be much higher even though the nominal interest rate is lower than when no points are paid.

RECAP Mortgages are long-term debt instruments used to purchase residential, commercial, and farm properties. The underlying property serves as collateral and a lien is put on the property. In the event of default, the property may be repossessed and sold to recoup all or part of the losses from the loan. The principal is generally amortized over the life of the loan. The debt-to-income ratio and the loan-to-value ratio are the two most important criteria that determine whether or not a mortgage will be funded. The borrower's credit rating is also important. The principal and interest payments may be insured by the FHA or VA, which are agencies of the federal government. Conventional loans are not federally insured and are made by financial institutions and mortgage brokers. Lenders may also require borrowers without FHA or VA loans to obtain private mortgage insurance. Closing costs include loan origination fees, appraisals, property surveys, credit reports, title insurance, and processing fees. The borrower may also pay points, which are interest prepayments. The more points a borrower pays, the lower the interest rate.

Fixed and Variable Interest Rate Mortgages

With **fixed interest rate mortgages,** the interest rate remains constant over the life of the loan; with **variable interest rate mortgages,** where the interest rate is adjusted periodically to reflect changing market conditions.

Fixed-rate mortgages have risks and benefits to both lenders and borrowers. For lenders, fixed-rate mortgages carry the **interest rate risk** that nominal interest rates will rise, causing the value of fixed-rate mortgages to decline. Remember the inverse relationship between prices of long-term financial instruments and the interest rate. In addition, if long-term mortgages are funded with short-term deposits, the lending institution can experience a negative cash flow as the costs of liabilities rise above the earnings on assets.

If rates fall, the lender is initially better off with fixed interest rate mortgages. In this case, the lender sees the value of the fixed-rate mortgages increase and profit margins generally widen. However, an additional risk to the lender, called **prepayment risk,** is that when interest rates fall, the mortgage may be prepaid early by the borrower through refinancing and the lender will have to reinvest the funds at a lower rate. If interest rates fall and stay low for a significant period of time, lenders can expect a rash of prepayments as refinancing occurs. Prepayment penalties are fees that the borrower pays if the loan is paid off early. Conventional loans do not have prepayment penalties, but VA and FHA loans do have prepayment penalties that may discourage refinancing. Prepayment risk also includes the risk that the loan is prepaid early because the property is sold.

Fixed-rate mortgages reduce the borrower's risk that loan payments will rise in the event that interest rates rise. The downside is that the borrower does not automatically benefit from falling rates. If rates fall, the borrower can refinance the loan, but there are generally substantial costs involved, such as closing costs and possibly prepayment penalties. With refinancing, the borrower gets a new loan to pay off the old loan. The new loan has a lower rate and correspondingly lower payment.

Variable interest rate mortgages, also known as **adjustable rate mortgages (ARMs),** charge an interest rate that changes with market conditions. They were first offered in the United States in 1970. The interest rate is tied to an index of short-term interest rates such as the Treasury bill rate, the cost of funds for savings institutions, or the prime-lending rate. The 1-year T-bill rate is the most popular

Fixed interest Rate Mortgages
Mortgages whose the interest rate remains the same over the life of the loan.

Variable Interest Rate Mortgages
Mortgages whose interest rate is adjusted periodically to reflect changing market conditions.

Interest Rate Risk
The risk that nominal interest rates rise and the value of long-term assets fall.

Prepayment risk
The risk that a mortgage may be prepaid early and the lender will have to reinvest the funds at a lower interest rate.

Adjustable Rate Mortgages (ARMs)
Mortgages that have a variable interest rate.

http://www.mortgage quotes.lycos.com and **http://www. mtgprofessor.com**
Discuss mortgage rates, the size of mortgage you can afford, and a payment calculator.

index. An index of short-term interest rates is used because lenders often fund mortgages with short-term deposits. In any case, the lender does not control the index. If the index rises, the interest rate and payments rise. The interest rate on the ARM is usually 2 to 3 percent above the index. The interest rate on ARMs is adjusted every month, every 6 months, or every 1, 2, or 3 years, depending on the terms specified in the loan. The maximum amount that the interest rate can rise is customarily 2 percentage points per year. There is often a cap, such as 5 to 6 percent, on the amount the rate can rise over the lifetime of the loan. If the initial rate is 6 percent and the lifetime cap is 5 percent, the maximum interest rate is 11 percent. Note that the interest rate can rise to 11 percent only if the index increases enough over time to justify an 11 percent rate.

An advantage of ARMs to the lender is that the loan payments rise if the costs of funds rise, thus preventing the possibility of a negative spread. The disadvantage is that payments fall if rates fall. Just the opposite is true for the borrower—if rates rise, payments also rise; if rates fall, payments fall. ARMs reduce the interest rate risk to the lender. However, the default risk is increased. If rates and payments rise as interest rates rise, more mortgages will go into default because borrowers cannot afford the higher payments.

Other factors being constant, the initial interest rate for an ARM is always lower than that for a fixed-rate mortgage because of the reduced interest rate risk. Closing costs charged to initiate the loan are lower also. Because the ARM has lower payments than a fixed-rate loan, it is easier for a borrower to qualify and to qualify for a higher amount. Exhibit 12-3 summarizes the risks and benefits of fixed-rate and variable rate mortgages.

In recent years, lenders have offered increasingly innovative mortgages designed to meet the needs of consumers. Technological changes in information and computer technologies have facilitated the development of innovative mortgages. Because of the diverse types of mortgages available, shopping for a mortgage can

EXHIBIT 12-3
The Risks of Investing in Mortgages

Default Risk—The risk that the borrower will not make the principal and interest payments as scheduled.

- The longer the term to maturity, the greater the default risk because the more distant future becomes more uncertain.
- The lower the down payment, the greater the default risk. The borrower has less to lose by defaulting.
- If interest rates rise, the default risk on variable-rate loans increases because monthly payments rise.

Interest Rate Risk—The risk that interest rates rise and the value of long term mortgages decline. If long-term mortgages are funded with short-term deposits, the spread between the earnings on assets and costs of liabilities narrows and may become negative.

- The longer the term to maturity, the greater the interest rate risk.
- Variable-rate loans reduce the interest rate risk.

Prepayment Risk—The risk that mortgages will be prepaid early and that the funds will have to be reinvested at a lower return.

- Increases greatly when interest rates fall, particularly if they stay low for a significant period of time.
- Much less for variable-rate loans than for fixed-rate loans.

involve much time and consideration. The Internet is a good resource for specific information about mortgages and interest rate and cost comparisons. Payment and amortization information, the size of mortgage you can qualify for given your income and debts, and a potpourri of various options regarding the terms of the mortgage loan, are all at your fingertips. You can even apply online! A Closer Look discusses some of the newer types of mortgages.

Innovative Types of Mortgages: Following are some of the major types of innovative mortgages:

Graduated payment mortgages offer initial low monthly payments with gradual escalation of the payments over the life of the loan. They are designed for borrowers who expect their incomes to rise. The downside is twofold. First, graduated payment mortgages may involve negative amortization when the initial payments do not cover the interest costs and the principal grows. The borrower ends up owing more than what was initially borrowed. Second, the borrower's income may not grow as expected, so he or she may not be able to afford the higher payments.

Reverse annuity mortgages are designed for retired individuals who want to stay in their homes but need part of the equity they have built up to supplement their income. With a reverse annuity mortgage, the lender sends the homeowner a monthly check and the mortgage balance increases by that amount. The lender puts a lien on the house for the higher amount. When the borrower passes away or sells the property, the lender is paid back through the sale of the property.

Graduated equity mortgages allow homeowners to pay off their loans in a shorter time period than what the initial payments justify. Payments start out as if the loan is amortized for 30 years. Payments grow over the life of the loan and the additional amount is applied to the principal. The result is that the loan is paid off in less than 30 years. The downside is that with graduated equity mortgages the payment goes up even if the borrower's income does not. Since most mortgage loans do not have prepayment penalties, borrowers who do not want to be locked into higher payments can achieve the same result by taking a 30-year loan and making higher payments when and if they are able to do so.

A Closer Look

With the *biweekly mortgage,* the borrower pays one-half the monthly payment every 2 weeks. Since there are 52 weeks in a year, 26 biweekly payments are made. The result is that the equivalent of 13 monthly payments are made rather than 12. Thus, the borrower pays one extra monthly payment per year. For a 30-year loan, the biweekly payment pays off the loan in roughly 22 years. The term of the 15-year loan is reduced to 12 years.

Hybrid mortgages called *fixed-period ARMs* offer combinations of fixed- and variable-rate loans. For example, an interest rate may initially be fixed for 3, 5, 7, or 10 years but then becomes variable. The advantage is that the initial interest rate for the fixed period is lower that the comparable loan with a fixed rate for 30 years. The shorter the initial fixed term, the lower the interest rate is relative to the 30-year fixed rate. Borrowers who anticipate having the loan or owning the property for less than the fixed-rate period can save with this type of mortgage. These loans sometimes have prepayment penalties, so the buyer needs to fully understand the terms.

Second mortgages allow a property owner to borrow against the equity in their property. Second mortgages are made at higher interest rates than the original mortgage because the maker of the original mortgage has a first claim on the property in the event of a default. Thus, second mortgages are more risky and the lender must be compensated. Second mortgages are often used to improve the property.

RECAP Mortgages may have fixed or variable interest rates. With fixed-rate loans, the interest rate remains the same over the life of the mortgage. With variable-rate loans, the interest rate is adjusted periodically to reflect changing market conditions. Fixed-rate mortgages carry the risk to the lender that nominal interest rates will rise and the value of the mortgage will fall. There is also a prepayment risk that when the interest rate falls, borrowers will prepay their loans and refinance at the lower rate, causing the lender to have to reinvest the funds at a lower rate. Variable-rate loans reduce the interest rate risk for the lender but increase the default risk. ARMs carry lower initial interest rates and have lower closing costs, but the borrower accepts the risk that his or her payment could rise substantially. Other types of mortgages include graduated payment mortgages, reverse annuity mortgages, graduated equity mortgages, biweekly mortgages, fixed period ARMs, and second mortgages.

The next section discusses the burgeoning secondary market in mortgages. We shall see that the federal government is involved in the secondary mortgage markets in two ways. First, an agency of the federal government insures the timely payment of principal and interest on standardized pools or packages of mortgages. Second, two government-sponsored enterprises sell securities and use the proceeds to purchase mortgages. When the mortgages are purchased, new funds are provided to the mortgage market.

Secondary Markets in Mortgages

Secondary markets trade previously issued financial claims. Mortgages have two characteristics that made the development of secondary markets difficult. First, individual mortgages are for properties with different characteristics and diverse geographic locations. They are not as standardized as shares of stock or bonds issued by a large corporation. The outstanding shares of stock and bonds of one corporation represent fairly identical claims on the corporation. Second, individual mortgages are typically for small denominations relative to other financial securities. For example, 1 million shares of identical stock with a value of $50 million can be issued by one corporation. Because of these characteristics, secondary markets for mortgages were slower to develop than secondary markets for stocks or bonds, wherein the outstanding financial claims are larger and more homogeneous.

Federal National Mortgage Association (Fannie Mae)
A privately owned, government-sponsored enterprise that sells securities and uses the proceeds to buy mortgages primarily of banks.

Prior to 1970, only mortgages insured by the FHA or VA were sold in secondary markets and directly to investors. The amount of market activity was very small. The **Federal National Mortgage Association (Fannie Mae)** was created by Congress in 1938 but did not establish a secondary market for FHA and VA loans until 1972. Fannie Mae issued bonds and bought FHA- and VA-insured mortgages. Still the market did not grow to any significant extent and was even declining by the late 1960s because of a decrease in VA loans.

Government National Mortgage Association (GNMA)
A government-owned program that guarantees the timely payment of interest and principal on bundles of at least $1 million of standardized mortgages.

Ginnie Mae

In 1968, Congress created the **Government National Mortgage Association (GNMA,** or *Ginnie Mae,* for short). Ginnie Mae was split off from Fannie Mae to provide additional support for the mortgage market. In 1970, Ginnie Mae began a program in which it guaranteed the timely payment of interest and principal on *bundles* of $1 million or more of standardized mortgages. Small-denomination mortgages (mortgages up to the FHA and VA limits) were standardized with regard to the debt-to-income ratios of borrowers and the loan-to-value ratios of properties. The standardized mortgages could be packaged together to be resold in secondary markets. Thus, Ginnie Mae guaranteed (for a fee) that the mortgages purchased with bond proceeds would be repaid and, hence, that the bonds would be repaid. The guarantee was backed up by the full faith and credit of the U.S. government. Ginnie Mae fostered the creation of large secondary markets that increased the liquidity of previously illiquid mortgages.

The secondary market in mortgages created by the Ginnie Mae guarantee operates as follows: Private financial institutions such as banks or savings and loans gather or pool several Ginnie Mae federally guaranteed mortgages into a bundle of, say, $1 million. They then sell all or parts of the $1 million security, called a **mortgage-backed security,** to third-party investors such as pension funds, mutual funds, or individual investors. If investors need their funds back before the security matures, they can sell them in a secondary market for mortgage-backed securities. The secondary market for mortgage-backed securities operates similar to the secondary market in corporate bonds. The minimum denomination for an individual to purchase a Ginnie Mae mortgage-backed security from a financial institution is $25,000. Borrowers then make their mortgage payments (on the GNMA-guaranteed mortgages) to the original lender. When the mortgage payments are received for all of the mortgages included in the $1-million bundle, the institution sends the owner(s) of the mortgage-backed security a check for the total of all payments. This constitutes the interest and principal payment on the security.

Ginnie Mae mortgage-backed securities have no default risk because of the government guarantee, provide a steady stream of income to the owner, and can be sold in secondary markets if funds are needed before the security matures. As a result, they have become highly popular with investors. Ginnie Mae is part of the Housing and Urban Development (HUD) Department of the U.S. Government. As such, it is government owned.

Despite the lack of default risk, Ginnie Mae securities are subject to an interest rate risk. Since they are long-term instruments, the value of the securities will fall if the interest rate rises after the securities have been issued.

Unlike Fannie Mae, Ginnie May does not issue bonds. Other financial institutions such as banks, savings associations, or mortgage brokers issue bonds that are guaranteed (for the fee) by Ginnie Mae.

Fannie Mae and Freddie Mac

In 1970, Congress authorized Fannie Mae to purchase conventional (non-VA- or non-FHA-insured) mortgages. Congress also created the **Federal Home Loan Mortgage Corporation (Freddie Mac)** to lend further support to the VA, FHA, and conventional mortgage markets. Congress hoped to make housing more available by increasing the funds flowing into mortgages. The goal, which remains the same today, was to expand the opportunities for low- and moderate-income families to purchase homes. Although Fannie Mae purchased and held mortgages, it did not pool the mortgages to create a mortgage-backed security until 1981. Freddie Mac issued its first mortgage-backed security, called a **participation certificate,** in 1971. It resulted from a pool of conventional mortgages. Fannie Mae primarily buys the mortgages of banks while Freddie Mac primarily buys the mortgages of thrifts.

Mortgage-Backed Securities
Securities backed by a pool of mortgages; have a low default risk and provide a steady stream of income.

http://www.ginniemae.gov
Provides information on the operations of the GNMA (Ginnie Mae).

Federal Home Loan Mortgage Corporation (Freddie Mac)
A privately-owned, government-sponsored enterprise that sells securities and uses the proceeds to buy mortgages primarily of thrifts.

Participation Certificate
A mortgage-backed security issued by Freddie Mac and backed by a pool of conventional mortgages.

http://www.fanniemae. com and **http://www. freddiemac.com**
Provides information about Fannie Mae and Freddie Mac.

Fannie Mae and Freddie Mac are government-sponsored enterprises (GSEs). They are privately owned and managed corporations chartered by Congress. Their stocks trade on the New York Stock Exchange. Fannie Mae and Freddie Mac are exempt from state and local corporate income taxes and have a $2.25 billion line of credit with the U.S. Treasury. They provide loanable funds to the housing sector by purchasing conventional loans, packaging or pooling the mortgages together, and issuing mortgage-backed securities, using the pool of mortgages as collateral.[4] The mortgages they purchase may also be held by them as investments instead of being packaged and sold as mortgage-backed securities.

Investors who purchase Fannie Mae and Freddie Mac mortgage-backed securities can then sell them in secondary markets if funds are needed before the securities mature. The secondary markets for mortgage-backed securities are created by market makers who buy and sell previously issued, mortgage-backed securities. Some mortgage-backed securities are traded on organized exchanges.

Fannie Mae and Freddie Mac purchase a specific type of conventional loan called a **conforming loan**.[5] As of 2000, conforming loans are for $252,700 or less and comply with criteria that allow them to be packaged together and resold in the secondary market to Fannie Mae and Freddie Mac.[6] The loan limit is adjusted each year in response to changes in housing prices. The securities that Fannie Mae and Freddie Mac issue are backed by the principal and interest payments on the mortgages that they have purchased. The principal and interest payment are not government guaranteed as with Ginnie Mae securities.

Conforming Loan
A specific type of conventional loan that comply with criteria that allow it to be packaged together and resold in the secondary market to Fannie Mae or Freddie Mac; as of 2000, conforming loans are for a maximum amount of $252,700.

When mortgages are sold to Fannie Mae or Freddie Mac, the lending institution receives additional funds to make new mortgages. This process is now an important source of funds to the mortgage market. In fact, this market has become so important that the bulk of mortgages are now made in accordance with the standardized lending guidelines that allow them to be sold to Fannie Mae or Freddie Mac. After being sold to Fannie Mae or Freddie Mac, the mortgages can be packaged and sold to investors as mortgage-backed securities. In the middle of 2001, the amount outstanding of federally related mortgage-backed securities was over $2.6 trillion, up from $1.2 trillion in 1991 and $.18 trillion in 1982. Thus, these markets have experienced spectacular growth in the last two decades.

Although the federal government has no legal obligation, many market participants assume that the government does "*de facto*" guarantee the timely payments of principal and interest on Fannie Mae and Freddie Mac securities. If the default risk is nil, the yield spread between these securities and U.S. government securities is due to differences in liquidity. The yield spread can be significant because secondary markets for Fannie Mae and Freddie Mac securities do not have the breadth and depth of Treasury securities. If market participants question the "*de facto*" government guarantee, as they did in mid-2000, the spread can also widen to include compensation for the perceived increased risk. A Closer Look discusses a recent controversy regarding the "implicit guarantee" for Fannie Mae and Freddie Mac securities.

---

[4]The mortgage-backed securities issued by Fannie Mae and Freddie Mac are called agency securities.

[5]Although they mainly purchase conventional loans, Fannie Mae and Freddie Mac have also purchased FHA- and VA-insured loans.

[6]Nonconforming loans are called jumbo loans and are for amounts greater than $252,700. *Ceteris paribus*, jumbo loans have higher interest rates than do conforming loans. Fannie Mae and Freddie Mac do not buy nonconforming loans.

The Implicit Fannie Mae and Freddie Mac Guarantee????: In the past decade, Fannie Mae and Freddie Mac have experienced astounding growth. In 1999, about 70 percent of the 6.1 million homes sold in the United States were purchased with loans that were bought by Fannie Mae or Freddie Mac. To do so, they issued $260 billion in long-term securities in 1999 alone. Together, in the middle of 2001, Fannie Mae and Freddie Mac had about $2.6 trillion in outstanding securities. With the federal government debt declining, it is estimated that outstanding Fannie Mae and Freddie Mac securities could exceed Treasury securities within 3 years. There has also been discussion that Fannie Mae and Freddie Mac securities should replace Treasury securities as the national and international benchmark security for low-risk debt.

As noted earlier, despite being shareholder owned, Fannie Mae and Freddie Mac were chartered by the federal government, are exempt from state and local corporate taxes, and have a $2.25 billion line of credit with the U.S. Treasury. They were established to assist low- and moderate-income families in financing the purchase of homes that they might otherwise not have been able to buy. Many investors in Fannie Mae and Freddie Mac securities believe that these characteristics imply an implicit government guarantee where no explicit guarantee exists—namely, that the government would bail out the corporations if they got in a jam, even if the government is not legally obliged to do so.

The high growth combined with the implicit guarantee have created concerns about the safety of Fannie Mae and Freddie Mac. In addition, Fannie Mae and Freddie Mac have loosened loan qualification requirements and are making less desirable, higher-risk, subprime loans. Such lending increases the possibilities that the companies could run into financial problems similar to those of the savings and loan industry in the 1980s.

Others are concerned with the stupendous growth of Fannie Mae and Freddie Mac and its effect on competition. Competitors, such as commercial banks and mortgage brokers, and many financial services industry trade groups, complain that the GSEs have an unfair advantage because of the government ties that allow them to borrow at a lower cost.

Needless to say, a bill before Congress in mid-2000 attempted to rein in Fannie Mae and Freddie Mac and to sever the ties between the corporations and the government. In addition, Fed Chairman Alan Greenspan and several Treasury officials have expressed concerns about the growth of Fannie Mae and Freddie Mac. If property values should fall and there are massive defaults, would the government have to step in and bail them out?

Private Mortgage-Backed Securities and Collateralized Mortgage Obligations (CMOs)

In 1984, some private groups started to issue their own mortgage-backed securities. The new securities did not rely on the backing of Ginnie Mae and were not issued by corporations like Fannie Mae or Freddie Mac that had ties to the federal government. Such issuers of private mortgage-backed securities include, among others, commercial banks, mortgage bankers, and investment banking firms. Like Ginnie Mae, Freddie Mac, and Fannie Mae mortgage-backed securities, privately issued mortgage-backed securities may also be sold in secondary markets. Again, the secondary markets are created by market makers who trade the previously issued securities. In the middle of 2001, the total amount of outstanding debt issued by private mortgage pools exceeded $814 billion, up from $11 billion in 1984 and $110 billion in 1991. Thus, like Fannie Mae and Freddie Mac, privately issued mortgage-backed securities have also exploded in recent years. Securities issued by private issuers are rated by the major credit-rating agencies. The credit rating may

LOOKING BACK: *The Evolution of the Mortgage Market*

Prior to the Great Depression, most mortgages were "balloon" mortgages. Only interest payments were made on a monthly basis and the entire principal was due at maturity. They required large down payments that averaged about 40 percent of the property value. At the end of the term (usually 3 to 5 years), the mortgage was usually renegotiated for a slightly amount. Because of the economic havoc created by the Great Depression, many borrowers could not renegotiate the mortgages and many lenders failed in the early 1930s. The widespread defaults caused the collapse of the mortgage market. The federal government stepped in and assisted homeowners by taking over the balloon payments and allowing borrowers to spread out the payment of both the principal and interest over a longer period of time. Thus, the first amortized mortgages were introduced. In addition, in 1934 the federal government established the FHA to insure the timely payment of principal and interest on long-term, fixed-rate mortgages that met FHA's criteria. In 1944, VA-insured loans, similar to FHA loans, were established that required no down payments for eligible veterans.

In the two decades after World War II, the mortgage market thrived and was dominated by savings and loan associations that held long-term mortgages funded with short-term deposits. By the late 1960s, an inflationary environment began to cause problems for savings and loans. The need to adjust asset maturities in the face of rising inflation and interest rates underscored the need for a secondary market. With a secondary market, the lender would not have to hold the mortgage until maturity but rather could sell it in the secondary market. Hence, the interest rate risk would be reduced. In 1968, the government established Ginnie Mae and re-chartered Fannie Mae as a privately owned, government-sponsored enterprise (rather than government owned). Advances in computer technologies and the emergence of mortgage-backed securities in 1970 fostered the growth of a secondary market.

By the 1980s, mortgage brokers and mortgage bankers were originating many mortgage loans that were then sold off in the secondary market to Fannie Mae, Freddie Mac, and other private issuers of mortgage-backed securities. Mortgage brokers and mortgage bankers originate mortgages but do not hold them as investments. Despite the collapse of the savings and loan industry in the 1980s, mortgage lending continued as other lenders, including commercial banks, stepped into fill the void.

From 1982–1984 until 2000, the dollar value of outstanding mortgages has increased from $1,666.1 billion to $6,959.1 billion, an increase of over 318 percent in nominal terms. During this same period, the consumer price index increased by 74.6 percent, nominal GDP increased about 200 percent, and real GDP increased by just under 89 percent. Thus, outstanding mortgages grew at a much faster rate than the overall level of prices and the levels of real and nominal economic activity.

Two other changes are noteworthy. First, in 1982, savings institutions held over 35 percent of all outstanding mortgages. By 2000, savings institutions held only about 10 percent. Commercial banks that held approximately 18 percent of outstanding mortgages in 1982 increased their share to about 24 percent by 2000. Both types of institutions prefer to hold ARMs because of the reduced interest rate risk.

Second, the biggest mortgage holders today are government-sponsored enterprises. In 1982, they held 23 percent of all mortgages and by 2000, this percentage had increased to 36 percent. This does not include the mortgages that are federally insured by Ginnie Mae but held by private institutions. Outside of insuring the timely payment of principal and interest on VA and FHA loans, the federal government did not play an important role in the mortgage market before 1970. With the creation of Ginnie Mae and Freddie Mac, and the growth of Fannie Mae, the federal government now has a major impact on the industry.

In the early 2000s, mortgage market activity now consists of three distinct functions: originating, investing in, and servicing mortgages. Sometimes, one institution performs all three activities. At other times, an institution may perform only one or two of the activities. For example, a mortgage broker may originate loans only, while a bank may originate, invest in, and service the mortgages. A savings and loan may originate the loan, sell it in the secondary market and, for a fee, continue to service the mortgage.

also be improved by obtaining insurance that guarantees the timely payments of principal and interest on the securities.

When mortgages are sold in the secondary market, the original lender, whether a bank or savings and loan, will sometimes continue to service the loan for a fee. Servicing a loan involves collecting the monthly payment, sending statements, and keeping records. In addition, servicing sometimes includes collecting property taxes and insurance payments, called *impounds*, and then disbursing these payments. In this way, the lender is guaranteed that the property taxes are paid and property insurance is maintained. Banks and other financial institutions are getting increasingly larger shares of their revenues from fees rather than interest. In addition to the secondary mortgage market, an active secondary market exists for trading the rights to collect the monthly payments (servicing the mortgage).

As noted previously, investors in mortgage-backed securities face the risk that the mortgages will be prepaid before they mature because the property is sold or refinanced and that the return will fall short of expectations. To reduce this risk, **collateralized mortgage obligations** have been developed by Freddie Mac. Collateralized mortgage obligations redirect the cash flows (principal and interest) of mortgage-backed securities to various classes of bondholders, thus creating financial instruments with varying prepayment risks and varying returns. Those who are most risk averse can choose an instrument wherein the principal will soon be repaid. Those who are willing to bear more risk can choose an instrument wherein the principal will not be repaid until later, and hence, is subject to a greater prepayment risk. In exchange for more prepayment risk, the investor receives a higher return. Needless to say, such provisions make attractive choices available to a wider range of investors.

Collateralized Mortgage Obligations
Securities developed by Freddie Mac that redirect the cash flows (principal and interest) of mortgage-backed securities to various classes of investors, thus creating financial instruments with varying prepayment risks and varying returns.

RECAP In recent decades, the government has become much more active in the mortgage market by guaranteeing the repayment of some mortgages and encouraging the development of a secondary market in mortgages. Most mortgages today are made in accordance with lending guidelines that allow them to be packaged and sold as mortgage-backed securities. Fannie Mae and Freddie Mac are GSEs that issue mortgage-backed securities and use the proceeds to purchase mortgages. Fannie Mae and Freddie Mac securities have no explicit government guarantee. Ginnie Mae guarantees the timely payment of principal and interest on mortgage-backed securities put together by private lenders. Ginnie Mae securities do have an explicit government guarantee. Other private groups issue mortgage-backed securities without government involvement. Secondary markets trade previously issued mortgage-backed securities and are similar to the secondary markets in bonds. Collateralized mortgage obligations redirect the cash flows (principal and interest) of mortgage-backed securities to various classes of bondholders, thus creating financial instruments with varying prepayment risks and varying returns.

The Determinants of the Price of Mortgages in Secondary Markets

A large and active secondary market exists for mortgages and mortgage-backed securities. In this section, we discuss how the price of a previously issued mortgage is determined. Since mortgage-backed securities are backed by mortgages, we will also be able to conclude how the prices of these securities are determined in secondary markets.

Like bonds, the price of a previously issued mortgage is simply the present value of the future stream of income from the ownership of the security. This consists of the monthly payment stream that includes both an interest and a principal payment, as depicted in Equation (12-1).

(12-1)
$$P_M = MP/(1 + d_M)^n$$

where

P_M = the price at which the security will trade in the secondary market

MP = the monthly payment, (including both principal and interest)

d_M = the monthly discount factor required by lenders in this market

n = the number of months remaining on the loan

Once the mortgage has been made, the original interest rate becomes irrelevant. Only the remaining monthly payments and the current discount factor are relevant in determining the mortgage's present value and, hence, the price at which the mortgage will trade.

Note that in Equation (12-1), because we are considering monthly payments instead of annual payments, d_M represents the monthly discount factor. To find the monthly discount factor, d_M, we merely divide the annualized discount factor, D_M, by 12. For example, a mortgage with 5 years remaining to maturity would have 60 more monthly payments—payments 1 through 60 spread over 5 years. If the annualized discount factor is 9 percent, the monthly discount factor is .75 percent (9/12 = .75). The payment at the end of the first remaining year is the twelfth payment and the present value of this payment is $MP/(1 + .075)^{12}$.[7]

To find the price at which the mortgage will trade in financial markets, we need to compute the present value of each monthly payment remaining. The appropriate discount factor is the current interest rate on a security of equal risk, liquidity, servicing costs, and maturity. As noted before, servicing costs are the costs associated with collecting the monthly payments.

Because mortgages require the handling of monthly payments of principal, interest, and possibly impounds, mortgages have higher servicing costs than Treasury securities that make semi-annual coupon payments. Lenders in the mortgage market must be compensated for these higher costs.

As summarized in Equation (12-2), the annualized discount factor used to determine the present value includes three components: a risk-free return, a risk premium, and a premium for the higher servicing costs that mortgages entail.

(12-2)
$$D_M = r_F + r_P + r_{SC}$$

The risk-free return is composed of the return on a Treasury security of comparable maturity.[8] When the risk-free interest rate changes, the discount factor, and the prices of previously issued mortgages, also change.

The risk premium includes the return the investor needs to be compensated for given the increased riskiness of owning mortgages. The risk premium includes compensation to the lender for the following possibilities:

- The borrower will default
- The loan will be prepaid early when reinvestment possibilities for the lender are less favorable than when the mortgage was originally made

---

[7]If annual payments were made instead of monthly payments, there would be five annual payments remaining and the present value at the end of the first remaining year would be $MP/(1 + .09)^1$.

[8]The comparable maturity for a Treasury security and a mortgage are not the same as the terms to maturity. For example, since a 30-year mortgage payment includes both a principal and interest payment each month, the comparable term of the mortgage will actually be less than a 30-year Treasury that does not repay any of the principal until the end of 30 years.

- The lower liquidity of mortgages compared to Treasury securities will cause the lender to experience losses

When the mortgage is federally insured, the risk premium will be lower than otherwise because the default risk is zero. In this case, the risk premium will include compensation for the prepayment risk and the lower liquidity of mortgages.

Treasury securities are considered to be risk-free of default, and the long-term government bond rate has been regarded as the risk-free interest rate.[9] Many factors exist that affect the risk-free rate. One of the most important factors is the stance of monetary policy. If the Fed increases the supply of reserves, short-term interest rates fall and the supply of credit is expanded. Other factors held constant, long-term interest rates will fall but usually not as much as short-term rates. Changes in inflationary expectations and the level of economic activity also affect the long-term, risk-free interest rate. If inflation is expected to increase in the coming years, lenders will require and borrowers will be willing to pay an inflation premium to compensate for the loss in purchasing power. Likewise, if income is increasing, the demand for loanable funds increases and puts upward pressure on interest rates.

In the real world, the factors that affect the risk-free interest rate are interrelated. For example, expansionary monetary policy may cause market participants to expect higher inflation. Rather than leading to lower interest rates, interest rates may rise, despite the expansionary monetary policy. Likewise, a recession brought on by higher oil prices may lead to higher interest rates if the impact of the higher oil prices affects inflationary expectations more than the drop in income. Other factors such as international capital flows and the amount of government borrowing also impact interest rates.

The risk premium investors need to be compensated with in order to purchase the mortgages is affected by the borrower's ability to make the monthly payment. The risk premium for insured mortgages is much lower than that for uninsured mortgages. A major factor affecting the risk premium for uninsured mortgages is the level of economic activity. In a booming economy, incomes and economic activity are increasing, thus reducing the number of defaults in the mortgage market. Likewise, interest rates rise and the prepayment risk also declines. The reverse is true in downturns.

Innovative changes in technology reduce servicing costs. An example of such an innovation is automatic payment deductions from a borrower's checking account. This saves the costs of sending out monthly statements and collecting and processing checks.

The factors that affect the discount factor are summarized in Exhibit 12-4.

RECAP The price of a mortgage is the discounted value of the future stream of monthly payments over the remaining life of the loan. When the interest rate increases, the price of a previously issued mortgage decreases and vice versa. In secondary markets, the price that a mortgage-backed security trades at is based on the prices of the underlying mortgages in the pool that backs the security. The discount factor includes a risk-free rate, a risk premium, and a premium for the higher servicing costs that mortgages entail. Treasury securities are considered to pay a risk-free rate of return. The risk premium encompasses economy-wide risks, the risk that the mortgage may be prepaid early when investment opportunities for the lender are less favorable, and a premium for the lower liquidity of mortgages. The premium for the higher servicing costs of mortgages is affected by changes in technology that reduce servicing costs.

---

[9]As noted earlier, the 10-year rate has recently replaced the 30-year Treasury bond rate as the benchmark risk-free rate. This is particularly relevant for mortgages because of the reasons stated in footnote 8.

EXHIBIT 12-4
Factors That Affect
the Discount Factor

Factors that affect the risk-free rate:
• The stance of monetary policy
   1. Expansionary policy—rate falls
   2. Contractionary policy—rate rises
• Chances in inflationary expectations
   1. Higher prices expected—rate rises
   2. Lower prices expected—rate falls
• Changes in the economic outlook and the level of economic activity
   1. Economy improves—rate rises
   2. Economy deteriorates—rate falls
• Changes in government borrowing
   1. Government borrowing increase—rate rises
   2. Government borrowing decrease—rate falls

Factors that affect the risk premium:
• Changes in the economic outlook and the level of economic activity (pertains to uninsured mortgages only)
   1. Economy improves—rate falls
   2. Economy deteriorates—rate rises

• The prepayment risk that the mortgage will be prepaid early and that the lenders' reinvestment options are less desirable than when the original mortgage was made (pertains to insured and uninsured mortgages)
• Changes in the relative liquidity of mortgages and mortgage-backed securities relative to Treasury securities.

Any factors that affect the servicing costs of the loan such as changes in technology that reduce servicing costs:
Note that as the economic outlook and the level of economic activity improves, the risk-free rate rises while the risk premium falls, and vice versa. Hopefully, you can explain why.

This completes our look at the mortgage market. You should be able to identify the ways in which the mortgage market is similar and different from other financial markets such as the money market, the stock market, and the bond markets. You should also be able to explain the inconsistency in the chapter introduction: The growth of the secondary market has required mortgages to be more standardized with regard to debt-to-income and loan-to-value ratios, *but* technology, innovation, and the demands of the consumer have also facilitated the development of many diverse types of mortgages. The next chapter on international financial markets completes our look at financial markets and instruments.

Summary of Major Points

• Mortgages are long-term debt instruments used to purchase residential, commercial, and farm properties. The underlying property serves as collateral that the debt will be repaid. In the event of default, the property may be repossessed and sold to recoup all or part of the losses. The principal is generally amortized over the life of the loan. The most common terms to maturity of mortgages are 15 and 30 years.

• To procure mortgage loans, borrowers generally pay closing costs that include a loan origination fee, appraisal fees, surveys, processing fees, recording fees, points, and title insurance. A point is 1 percent of the loan and is a prepayment of interest that reduces the nominal interest rate on the mortgage loan. Borrowers may choose the number of points that they pay up front. The debt-to-income ratio and the loan-to-value ratio are the two most important criteria that determine whether or not a mortgage will be funded. The borrower's credit history is also important.

- The timely payment of the principal and interest on a mortgage may also be insured for a fee by an agency of the federal government. FHA and VA insure mortgages that meet certain criteria. The purpose of FHA-insured loans is to help low-income families purchase homes. The purpose of VA loans is to help veterans purchase homes. Conventional mortgages are made by financial institutions and have no government insurance.

- Mortgages have a default risk, an interest rate risk, and a prepayment risk. Default risk is the risk that the borrower will default on the loan. The interest rate risk is the risk that the interest rate will rise and the value of the long-term mortgage will fall. The prepayment risk is the risk that the borrower will repay the loan early and that the funds will have to be reinvested at a lower rate.

- Mortgages may have a fixed or variable interest rate. With fixed-rate mortgages, the interest rate remains the same over the life of the loan. With variable interest rate mortgages, the interest rate fluctuates over the life of the loan with the general level of interest rates. The interest rate is tied to an index such as the 1-year Treasury bill rate. There is usually an annual cap and a lifetime cap with regard to how much the interest rate can increase. Variable-rate loans reduce the interest rate risk for the lender but increase the default risk because if rates and payments rise, the borrower is more likely to default.

- In recent decades, the government has become much more active in the mortgage market by guaranteeing the repayment of Ginnie Mae mortgages and sponsoring Fannie Mae and Freddie Mac. Fannie Mae and Freddie Mac are privately owned, government-sponsored enterprises that purchase a type of conventional loan called conforming loans. Most mortgages today are made in accordance with lending guidelines that allow them to be packaged and sold as mortgage-backed securities. Fannie Mae and Freddie Mac mortgage-backed securities have no explicit government guarantee. The Ginnie Mae guarantee is explicitly backed by the government. Private groups also issue mortgage-backed securities without an explicit or implicit government guarantee. Secondary markets exist that trade previously issued mortgage-backed securities.

- The price of a mortgage is the discounted value of the future stream of monthly payments over the life of the instrument. When the interest rate increases, the prices of long-term mortgages securities decrease and vice versa. Prices of mortgage-backed securities are determined by the prices of the mortgages that make up the pool that backs the security. The discount factor used to determine the price of a mortgage or mortgage-back security includes a risk-free rate, a risk premium, and a premium for the higher servicing costs that mortgages entail. Treasury bonds are considered to pay a risk-free rate of return. The risk premium encompasses economy-wide risks and includes the risk that the mortgage may be prepaid early when investment opportunities for the lender are less favorable. It also includes compensation for the lower liquidity of mortgages due to a less-developed secondary market.

Key Terms

Adjustable Rate Mortgages (ARMs)

Amortization

Closing Costs

Collateral

Collateralized Mortgage Obligations

Conforming Loan

Conventional Mortgages

Debt-to-Income Ratio

Default Risk

Federal Home Loan Mortgage Corporation (Freddie Mac)

Federal Housing Administration (FHA)

Federal National Mortgage Association (Fannie Mae)

Fixed Interest Rate Mortgages

Government National Mortgage Association (GNMA)

Interest Rate Risk

Lien

Loan-to-Value Ratio

Mortgage-Backed Security

Participation Certificate

Points

Prepayment Risk

Variable Interest Rate Mortgages

Veterans Administration (VA)

Review Questions

1. What is the difference between a fixed interest rate and a variable interest rate loan?

2. How is a mortgage similar to a bond? How is it different?

3. Is the monthly payment higher or lower if a loan is fully amortized versus if the loan calls for a balloon payment at end of the term of the loan? Explain.

4. Henry and Sheree have low debt-to-income and low loan-to-value ratios for a loan on a new home. Their credit report has some delinquent items. Should their loan request be approved?

5. Explain the process by which a mortgage-backed security is created. What roles do Ginnie Mae, Fannie Mae, and Freddie Mac play?

6. If Sandi and Juan repay their mortgage early because they are refinancing or selling their home, why is there a risk for the lender?

7. How would a fall in real estate prices affect the value of previously issued mortgages? How would a fall in interest rates affect the value of previously issued mortgages?

8. Mohammad wants to make a $100,000 down payment to purchase a $200,000 house. Discuss the factors that could jeopardize his loan approval despite the large down payment.

9. Mari and Judy have just graduated from college and are purchasing a condominium. They expect that their incomes will be increasing in the next few years. Should they consider a graduated payment or graduated equity mortgage? What are the pros and cons?

10. Alberto and Maureen have just bought their first condominium. They plan on staying in the condo for about 5 years and then buying a house. What type of mortgage loan would you advise them to get?

11. Technological advances have reduced the servicing costs on loans. What would happen to the discount factor applied to value mortgages and mortgage-backed securities? Why?

12. Discuss what would happen to the discount factor for mortgages under the following circumstances:
    a. A recession is expected in the near future
    b. The Fed has taken action to raise interest rates
    c. International financial crises have caused an inflow of funds into the United States
    d. The federal government is running a larger surplus than expected

13. How can investing in a collateralized mortgage obligation entail less risk than investing in a mortgage-backed security? Can it ever entail more risk?

14. What are the characteristics of financial assets that have highly developed secondary markets?

15. What is the difference between the secondary market in mortgages and the secondary market in mortgage-backed securities?

Analytical Questions

16. Assume that the risk-free rate is 5 percent and the risk premium for investing in mortgages is 2 percent. Also assume that it costs approximately 1 percent to service a mortgage loan. What will the discount factor for mortgages be?

17. Will the following events increase, decrease, or leave the mortgage rate unchanged?

    a. The Fed lowers the interest rate because of a slowdown in economic activity.
    b. Technological changes reduce the costs of servicing mortgage loans.
    c. The default rate on mortgages increases because of falling property values.

Internet Exercises

1. Go to the Freddie Mac Internet site at **http://www.freddiemac. com.**

   a. Click on the "economic outlook" link.
      - Summarize the economic outlook?
      - How is the housing market faring?
      - What about interest rates and Fed policy?

   b. Scroll down the left "what's new" column.
      - Summarize any information about new or previously issued freddie mac securities.

2. Go to **http://www.mtgprofessor.com.**
   - What is the monthly mortgage payment on a $200,000 mortgage amortized over 30 years? . . . over 15 years?

   - Assuming the borrower has no other debts, what is the income needed to qualify for a 30-year 8 percent mortgage on a $200,000 house with 20 percent down . . . for a 15-year 8 percent mortgage?

   - Next assume the borrower has additional car, credit card, and student loan debt payments of $700 per month. What is the income needed to qualify for 30 year loan? . . . for a 15 year loan?

Suggested Readings

Two comprehensive articles on the controversies regarding the government's ties to Fannie Mae and Freddie Mac are Patrick Barta, "Why Calls Are Escalating to Clip Fannie Mae's, Freddie Mac's Wings, *The Wall Street Journal*, July 14, 2000, and Richard W. Stevenson, "Defending Home Turf from Attack; Fannie Mae is Facing Assault by House Panel and Business Rivals" *New York Times*, April 22, 2000.

For an analysis of "The Effects of Recent Mortgage Refinancing," see the article by the same name by Peter Brady, Glenn B. Canner and Dean M. Maki, *Federal Reserve Bulletin*, July 2000, pp. 441–450.

Mortgage-backed securities are the subject of "Remarks by Chairman Alan Greenspan" before a conference on mortgage markets and economic activity sponsored by America's Community Bankers, Washington D.C., November 2, 1999. The remarks are available on the Fed's World Wide Web site at **hhtp://www.federalreserve.gov.**

Recent articles on mortgages include Paul S. Calem and Stanley D. Longhofer, "Anatomy of a Fair-Lending Exam: The Uses and limitations of Statistics," *Finance and Economics Discussion Series No. 2000–15*, Board of Governors of the Federal Reserve System, 2000; Joe Mattey, "B2B E-Commerce in Residential Mortgages," *FRBSF Economic Letter No. 2000–23*, Federal Reserve Bank of San Francisco, July 28, 2000; Stanley D. Longhofer and Paul S. Calem, "Mortgage Brokers and Fair Lending," *Economic Commentary*, Federal Reserve Bank of Cleveland, May 15, 1999; and Joe Mattey, "Mortgage Interest Rates, Valuation, and Prepayment Risk," *Economic Letter*, No. 98–30, Federal Reserve Bank of San Francisco, October 9, 1998.

Other articles of interest include Robert Winnett and Kathryn Cooper, "House Boom Sets Scene for 100–Year Mortgage," *London Sunday Times*, September 3, 2000; Kristin Downey, "Study Refutes Myth that Americans are Best-Housed People," *Minneapolis Star Tribune*, March 9, 1991.

chapter

13 The International Financial System

Learning Objectives *After reading this chapter, you should know:*

- How and why the international financial system is changing
- The role of the international financial system under the Bretton Woods Accord
- How the present managed floating exchange rate system works
- The role the dollar plays in the international financial system
- The roles of the International Monetary Fund, the World Bank, and the Bank for International Settlements

" "

This afternoon I intend to address a subject that ten years ago would have been sleep inducing. Today it is a cage rattler: the structure of the international financial system.
—Alan Greenspan, November 5, 1998

A Dramatic Metamorphosis

The **international financial system** consists of the numerous rules, customs, instruments, facilities, markets, and organizations that enable international payments to be made and funds to flow across borders. In recent years, the international financial system has experienced tremendous growth. New financial instruments have been created, and the volume of transactions has exploded. The dramatic metamorphosis of international financial markets is driven by technological changes, the growth in world trade, and the breakdown of barriers to financial (capital) flows.

From an economic standpoint, developments in the international financial system have made financial markets more efficient because funds (financial capital) can more easily flow around the world to wherever they will earn the highest return. As resources are allocated more efficiently, both developed and developing countries should experience greater economic growth over time. As a result, living standards around the world should rise.

A more globalized environment can also entail costs. A disturbance in one financial market or in one country can have immediate effects on other countries and the entire international financial system. As Alan Greenspan puts it, "These global financial markets, engendered by the rapid proliferation of cross-border financial flows and products, have developed a capability of transmitting mistakes at a far faster pace throughout the financial system in ways that were unknown a generation ago."[1] An example is the Asian financial crisis of 1997–1998 that started in currency markets in Thailand and quickly spread to other Asian countries and beyond. This "contagion effect" was exacerbated by the greater integration of financial markets that has occurred in recent years.

The international financial system includes the international money and capital markets and the foreign exchange market. The international money market trades short-term claims with an original maturity of 1 year or less; the international capital market trades capital market instruments including stocks, bonds, mutual funds, and mortgages, with an original maturity greater than 1 year. In recent years, many new international financial products have been created to facilitate the increased financial flows. These include various types of mutual funds that allow investors to invest in developed and emerging economies.

A crucial part of the international financial system is the foreign exchange market, where foreign currencies are bought and sold in the course of trading goods, services, and financial claims (securities) among countries. As we have seen in earlier chapters, this global market is woven together by the dealers in foreign currencies—mostly, the foreign exchange departments of the largest commercial banks in major financial centers such as New York, London, Frankfurt, and Tokyo. During 1995, daily trading in the foreign exchange market exceeded $1.5 trillion.

In the post-World War II period, the international financial system has operated under two distinct exchange rate regimes. The specific exchange rate regime affects the trading of all international financial instruments. During the first regime from 1944 to 1973, major industrial countries maintained a system of fixed exchange rates, and currency values rarely changed. Under the second regime, in effect since 1973, exchange rates fluctuate daily in response to changes in supply and demand (market forces). As we shall see, governments also intervene in this flexible exchange rate system.

International Financial System
The numerous rules, customs, instruments, facilities, markets, and organizations that enable international payments to be made and funds to flow across borders.

---

[1] Remarks by Alan Greenspan before the 34th Annual Conference on Bank Structure and Competition at the Federal Reserve Bank of Chicago, May 7, 1998.

So far in Part 3, we have discussed many aspects of the international financial system, including how cross-border financial flows affect domestic and foreign stock, bond, and money markets. This chapter completes our coverage of financial markets by providing the international framework in which financial instruments trade. We examine the international exchange rate systems in effect since 1944 and how these exchange rate systems form the backbone in which the international financial system operates. We also discuss the unique role the dollar plays in the international financial system. Finally, we look at the international organizations that seek to provide a framework for financial stability as the cross-border trading of all types of financial instruments continues to grow.

The International Financial System from 1944 to 1973

Fixed Exchange Rate System
An exchange rate system with currency values that do not fluctuate.

Official Reserve Currency
The currency used by other countries to define their own currency; the U.S. dollar was the official reserve currency under the Bretton Woods Accord.

Bretton Woods Accord
A 1944 agreement, negotiated by the major industrialized countries, that established fixed exchange rates with the U.S. dollar serving as the official reserve currency.

From the end of World War II until the early 1970s, the major economies of the world participated in a **fixed exchange rate system** with the U.S. dollar functioning as the **official reserve currency.** Other countries defined their currencies in terms of the U.S. dollar and agreed to buy or sell dollars to maintain the agreed-upon exchange rates.[2] The dollar, in turn, was defined in terms of gold. During the postwar period, 1 ounce of gold was set equal to $35, and the United States agreed to convert any unwanted dollars of foreign central banks into gold.[3]

This fixed exchange rate system was established by the **Bretton Woods Accord** of 1944, which was worked out by representatives from the major industrialized countries who met at Bretton Woods, New Hampshire, to design a new international financial system. Under the Bretton Woods Accord, if the trade deficit of a country other than the United States increased, that country increased the supply of its currency. Other factors remaining constant, the increased supply put downward pressure on the exchange rate. To maintain the agreed-upon exchange rate, the country's central bank had to purchase the excess supply of its currency using dollars.

An example will help clarify. Assume that the exchange rate between the dollar and the British pound was set at $1 = 2 pounds, but supply and demand were causing the market value of the two currencies to gravitate to $1 = 3 pounds. Perhaps Britain's trade deficit had increased significantly in recent months, causing Britain's balance of payments on current and capital accounts to move into a deficit position.[4] The smaller supply of dollars relative to pounds in international markets puts upward pressure on the exchange rate of the dollar while the larger relative supply of pounds puts downward pressure on the value of the pound. In such a case, the Bank of England, the central bank of Great Britain, would intervene in the market by buying pounds with dollars until the market value of the two currencies converged to the agreed-upon exchange rate. By changing the supply of dollars and pounds outstanding, the Bank of England could manipulate the market value of the dollar in terms of the pound. In this manner, the values of the dollar and the pound could be maintained at the agreed-upon exchange rate of $1 = 2 pounds.

---

[2]In this chapter, when we refer to dollar or dollars, we also mean "dollar-denominated deposits."

[3]In cases of fundamental imbalances, an orderly procedure was established to make adjustments in exchange rates and thereby avoid the disruptive changes that had occurred between World War I and World War II.

[4]Recall from Chapter 8 that the current account measures transactions that involve currently produced goods and services (exports and imports) and net transfer payments. The capital account measures the financial flows of funds and securities among countries.

Such government transactions in foreign currencies were measured in the **Official Reserve Account** of the balance of payments. We ignored this account in Chapter 8. We can now see that by supplying dollars and demanding pounds, the Bank of England would run a surplus in the Official Reserve Account that would just equal the deficit in the current and capital accounts of the balance of payments. Hence, under fixed exchange rates, it was (and always is) official government transactions in foreign exchange markets that brought the balance of payments into balance at the fixed exchange rate.

Because the Bank of England was maintaining the fixed exchange rate by buying pounds with dollars, Great Britain could continue to maintain the fixed rate only so long as it had or could acquire sufficient dollars to support the value of its currency as needed. If Great Britain (or another foreign country) ran a persistent deficit in its current and capital accounts, its central bank would eventually run out of dollars and have to **devalue,** or decrease the value of its currency in terms of the dollar, in order to reflect the diminished value of the pound. Devaluation occurs when the monetary authorities reduce the value of a country's currency under a fixed exchange rate system. In terms of our analysis, the pound is devalued if the official rate is changed from $1 per 2 pounds to $1 per 4 pounds. At the original rate, each pound was worth 50 cents while at the latter rate, after the devaluation, each pound is worth 25 cents.[5]

As we have seen, in the decades after World War II, the U.S. dollar served as the official reserve currency. Unlike Great Britain in our example, the United States was eventually in the unique position of being able to run persistent balance of payments deficits on the current and capital accounts.[6] Foreign central banks wanted to stockpile dollars to function as international reserves.

Once foreign central banks had acquired sufficient reserves, the ability of the United States to run chronic deficits in the balance of payments on current and capital accounts was also limited. In this case, the dollar would become overvalued in terms of one or more foreign currencies. Under the Bretton Woods Accord, the United States would lose gold as the unwanted dollars were presented for conversion. The United States would then pressure foreign central banks to **revalue,** or increase, the value of their currency in terms of the dollar.

Revaluation occurs when monetary authorities increase the value of a country's currency under a fixed exchange rate system. For example, the pound is revalued if the official rate is changed from $1 equals 2 pounds to $1 equals 1 pound. In the original case, each pound was worth 50 cents while in the latter case, each pound is worth $1. Other factors held constant, the revaluation would in time reduce the U.S. balance of payments deficit on current and capital accounts and slow the flow of unwanted dollars abroad. In turn, the gold outflow would diminish.

A foreign central bank might be hesitant to revalue, however, because revaluation could adversely affect its country's economy. Among other things, revaluation

Official Reserve Account
The balance of payments account that records official government transactions in the foreign exchange market to bring the balance of payments into balance.

Devalue
Under a fixed exchange rate system, to decrease the value of a country's currency.

Revalue
Under a fixed exchange rate system, to increase the value of a country's currency.

---

[5]The need to devalue could be accelerated if speculators sensed an impeding necessity to devalue and increased the supply of pounds from what it would be otherwise. The alternative to devaluing would be for Great Britain to run a severely contractionary policy designed to lower prices in pounds and make British goods more desirable. As exports increased and imports decreased, the value of the pound would be restored to the agreed-upon exchange rate.

[6]Initially after World War II, the United States was running sizable trade surpluses financed by capital outflows under the Marshall Plan. During this period, a "dollar shortage" occurred as countries scrambled for dollars not only for reserves but also to rebuild their economies.

http://www.nyse.com/
international/
international.html
Provides links to world stock exchanges.

could reduce net exports and have a negative impact on employment.[7] Consequently, foreign central banks would pressure the United States to correct the imbalance by reducing its deficit on the current and capital accounts. Note the irony of the situation and the potential for a stalemate in which each country is pressuring the other to take action.

A balance of payments deficit on current and capital accounts could also be caused by increases in the capital outflows of a country. If a country experienced a net capital outflow, this had the same effect as an increase in the trade deficit of the same magnitude.[8] Likewise, if a country experienced an increased net capital inflow, this had the same effect on the balance of payments on current and capital accounts as an increase in the trade surplus. As we have seen, such capital flows resulted from changes in domestic interest rates relative to foreign rates.

During the 1960s and 1970s, some countries, including the United States, expanded their economies and domestic money supplies faster than others, such as Japan and Germany. The United States experienced inflationary pressures in the mid- to late-1960s as a result of monetary and fiscal policies associated with the Great Society's War on Poverty and the Vietnam War buildup. Consequently, some central banks outside the United States accumulated more dollars than they wished to hold as reserve assets. Rather than revaluing their currencies, they asked the United States to convert these unwanted dollars to gold. As more central banks requested conversion, it became clear the United States would not be able to continue redeeming the dollars in gold. In late 1971, the United States suspended the international conversion of dollars into gold. At the same time, the dollar was devalued by setting the value of 1 ounce of gold equal to $42 rather than the $35 that had been in effect since the inception of the Bretton Woods Accord. Hence, the "official value" of the dollar was reduced from $1 = 1/35 ounce of gold to $1 = 1/42 ounce of gold, even though the United States was no longer redeeming dollars with gold. In 1973, most countries abandoned fixed exchange rates altogether, and the value of the dollar began to float. The Jamaica Agreement of 1974 officially adopted floating exchange rates, underscoring what had unofficially been done in 1973.

A final comment is in order. During the Bretton Woods period, the amount of cross-border trading of financial assets such as stocks, bonds, and mortgages was much less than it is today. Under normal circumstances, exchange risk was minimal during this period, but many countries had capital controls that did not allow the purchase of foreign financial instruments. Also, technology at that time did not foster cross-border financial flows.

RECAP The international financial system consists of the arrangements, rules, customs, instruments, facilities, and organizations that enable international payments to be made and funds to flow across borders. The international financial system includes the international money and capital markets and the foreign exchange market. The Bretton Woods Accord of 1944 established fixed exchange rates among major world currencies. The U.S. dollar, backed by gold, served as the official reserve currency, and other countries defined

---

[7]Note that whether the United States was running a persistent surplus or a persistent deficit in its balance of payments on current and capital accounts, the foreign central bank had to change the value of its currency in terms of the U.S. dollar. The foreign central bank had to act because under the Bretton Woods Accord, if the United States changed the value of the dollar, the change would affect the relationship between the dollar and all other currencies even though the dollar might have been out of alignment with only one of the foreign currencies.

[8]Other factors held constant, an increased net capital outflow from the United States comes from an increase in direct foreign investment by U.S. individuals or firms.

their currencies in terms of the dollar. If a country other than the United States had a deficit in its balance of payments, it used supplies of dollars to purchase its own currency to maintain fixed exchange rates. If a country other than the United States had a surplus in its balance of payments, it demanded dollars to maintain the value of its currency. The system broke down in late 1971 when the United States suspended the international conversion of dollars to gold. A flexible exchange rate system was adopted in 1973. In the Bretton Woods period, cross-border investment in financial instruments was much less than it is today.

Floating (Flexible) Exchange Rate System
An exchange rate system in which currency values are determined by supply and demand and fluctuate in response to changes in supply and demand.

The Managed Float Exchange Rate System Since 1973

The demise of the Bretton Woods Accord initiated a new era in which the exchange rates of major industrialized countries are no longer fixed. Rather, these countries participate in a **floating (flexible) exchange rate system** wherein exchange rates fluctuate by the minute and the hour as market forces change.

Like other major currencies, the exchange rate of the U.S. dollar is determined by demand and supply in international markets. The supply of dollars/month reflects the U.S. demand for foreign goods, services, and securities. If we hold other factors constant the quantity of dollars supplied is a positive function of the exchange rate. The demand for dollars reflects the foreign demand for U.S. goods, services, and securities. If we hold other factors constant, the quantity demanded is a negative function of the exchange rate. The market gravitates to the equilibrium exchange rate where quantity demanded is equal to quantity supplied.

From an initial equilibrium, if U.S. incomes, U.S. inflation, or foreign interest rates rise, U.S. demand for foreign goods, services, and securities will increase, and so will the supply of dollars. The market will gravitate to a new equilibrium at a lower exchange rate that corresponds to a depreciation of the dollar.

Likewise, if foreign incomes, foreign inflation, or U.S. interest rates rise, foreign demand for U.S. goods, services, and securities will increase, and so will the demand for dollars. The market will gravitate to a new equilibrium at a higher exchange rate that corresponds to an appreciation of the dollar.[9]

To summarize, factors such as domestic and foreign incomes, inflation rates, and interest rates affect exchange rates, and "flexible" exchange rates immediately adjust to changing market conditions and expectations. A Closer Look reviews the basics of exchange rate determination under flexible exchange rates, as first presented in Chapter 8.

The Foreign Exchange Market: In the accompanying graphs (a) and (b), the quantity of dollars is measured on the horizontal axis, and the exchange rate (euro per dollar) is measured on the vertical axis. If we hold other factors constant, the quantity supplied of dollars/month, reflecting U.S. demand for foreign goods, services, and securities, is a positive function of the exchange rate; the quantity demanded of dollars/month is a negative function of the exchange rate. In this case, quantity demanded is equal to quantity supplied at point A, producing an equilibrium exchange rate of 2 euros. Assume now that the initial equilibrium at point A in graph (a) is disturbed by one of the following developments: (1) the euro price of U.S. goods and services rises relative to the euro price of foreign goods and services because of inflation in the United States; (2) foreign interest

A Closer Look

---

[9]Because we live in a very dynamic world, the factors that determine supply and demand are always changing; hence, exchange rates change by the minute.

rates rise relative to U.S. interest rates; or (3) foreign incomes fall relative to U.S. incomes. The result is a reduction in the demand for U.S. goods, services, and financial instruments by foreigners and, thus, a reduction in the demand for dollars—shown as a leftward shift of the demand function in graph (a). The new equilibrium at point B results in a depreciation of the dollar from 2 euros to 1 euro.

Next, assume that the economy is again at the initial equilibrium exchange rate of $1 to 2 euros as in graph (b). The equilibrium is disturbed by one of the following developments: (1) a rise in U.S. income, (2) a rise in U.S. prices relative to the dollar prices of foreign goods, or (3) a rise in foreign interest rates relative to U.S. interest rates. As a result, U.S. demand for foreign goods, services, and securities increases, as does the supply of dollars—shown as a rightward shift of the supply function in graph (b). The new equilibrium at point B results in a depreciation of the dollar as the equilibrium exchange rate falls from 2 euros to 1 euro.

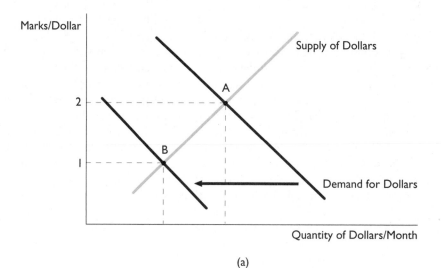

(a)

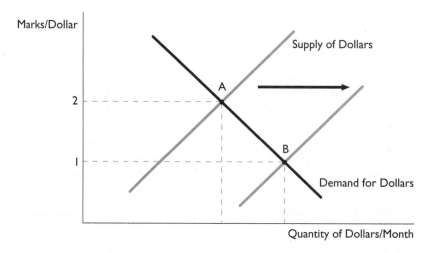

(b)

Our story does not end here, however. Market forces are not the only factor that affect exchange rates. In addition, central banks may intervene in the foreign exchange market by buying and selling currencies to influence exchange rates. Thus, the present international monetary system can be more correctly characterized as a **managed float exchange rate system.** Exchange rates are allowed to fluctuate in accordance with supply and demand, but central banks may intervene if a currency is thought to be over- or undervalued. This system is distinctly different from the fixed rate exchange system under the Bretton Woods Accord.

Interestingly, central banks have intervened more often under the managed float than under the previous fixed exchange rate system. Central banks of major countries have often agreed to pursue similar exchange rate policies and have coordinated their interventions as part of the implementation of monetary policy. Central bank intervention is discussed more fully in Chapter 25.

One final point needs to be made. Under the managed float exchange rate system, many smaller countries peg the value of their currencies to the U.S. dollar or some other major currency or basket of currencies. By doing so, a small country reduces the risk that the value of its currency will fluctuate unpredictably.[10] A financial crisis can result, however, if the country cannot maintain the fixed exchange rate. Both the Mexican peso crisis of 1994 and the Asian crisis of 1997–1998 occurred when the affected countries were unable to maintain an exchange rate that they had fixed in terms of the dollar. In both cases, the eventual depreciation of the currencies triggered widespread losses, the failure of many financial and nonfinancial firms, and financial crises.

Exhibit 13-1 gives the exchange rate arrangements for most countries in the world.

Managed Float Exchange Rate System
A system in which currency values fluctuate with changes in supply and demand but central banks may intervene if currency values are thought to be over- or undervalued.

Managing Exchange Rate Risk Under the Managed Float

Under flexible exchange rates, when market participants enter into contracts to receive or supply certain amounts of a foreign currency on a future date, there is an exchange rate risk because the future spot exchange rate is unknown.[11] Market participants may be importers or exporters who will receive or need so much foreign exchange on a future date, or they may be investors who have purchased or plan to purchase foreign financial securities that will mature in the future. If the exchange rate changes unexpectedly between now and the future date, the anticipated profits of an exporter, importer, or investor could be reduced. Worse yet, a loss could be incurred. Thus, under flexible exchange rate systems, market participants are exposed to substantial exchange rate risk.

In recent years, international financial markets have developed hybrid instruments including foreign exchange forward, futures, options, and swap agreements to hedge exchange rate risk. In Chapters 22 and 23, we shall see how these instruments, all forms of derivatives, can be used to reduce the risk of unforeseen price changes. In this case, the prices are exchange rates. Thus, these markets reduce exchange rate risk.

---

[10]If the exchange rate of a small country fluctuates unpredictably, the value of real or financial assets denominated in that currency will also fluctuate unpredictably. By tying the value of its currency to the U.S. dollar or a basket of other major currencies, a small country can reduce this risk.

[11]Hopefully you recall that the spot exchange rate is the exchange rate of foreign currency for immediate delivery.

EXCHANGE RATE REGIME (NUMBER OF COUNTRIES)	MONETARY POLICY FRAMEWORK							
	Exchange rate anchor				*Monetary aggregate target*	*Inflation targeting framework*	*Fund-supported or other monetary program*	*Other*
Exchange arrangements with no separate legal tender (39)	**Another currency as legal tender** Ecuador* Kiribati Marshall Islands, Rep. of Micronesia, Fed. States of Palau Panama* San Marino	**ECCU[2]** Antigua & Barbuda Dominica Grenada St. Kitts & Nevis St. Lucia St. Vincent & the Grenadines	**CFA Franc Zone** **WAEMU** Benin* Burkina Faso* Côte d'Ivoire* Guinea-Bissau Mali* Niger* Senegal* Togo	**CAEMC** Cameroon* C. African Rep.* Chad* Congo, Rep. of Equatorial Guinea Gabon			Benin* Burkina Faso* Cameroon* Central African Rep.* Chad* Congo, Rep. of* Côte d'Ivoire* Ecuador* Gabon* Guinea-Bissau* Mali* Niger* Senegal*	**Euro Area** [3,4] Austria Belgium Finland France Germany Greece Ireland Italy Luxembourg Netherlands Portugal Spain
Currency board arrangements (8)	Argentina* Bosnia and Herzegovina* Brunei Darussalam Bulgaria* China, P.R. Hong Kong Djibouti* Estonia* Lithuania*						Argentina* Bosnia and Herzegovina* Bulgaria* Djibouti* Estonia* Lithuania*	
Other conventional fixed peg arrangements (including de facto peg arrangements under managed floating) (44)	**Against a single currency (30)** Aruba Bahamas, The[5] Bahrain[6,7] Barbados Belize Bhutan Cape Verde China, P.R. Mainland*[6] Comoros[8] Congo, Dem. Rep of El Salvador[13] Eritrea Iran[5,6] Iraq Jordan*[6] Lebanon[6] Lesotho*	Macedonia, FYR*[6] Malaysia Maldives[6] Namibia Nepal Netherlands Antilles Oman Qatar[6,7] Saudi Arabia[6,7] Swaziland Syrian Arab Republic[5] Trinidad & Tobago* Turkmenistan[6] United Arab Emirates[6,7]	**Against a composite (13)** Bangladesh Botswana[5] Fiji Kuwait Latvia* Malta Morocco Myanmar[5] Samoa Seychelles Solomon Islands Tonga Vanuatu		China, P.R.: Mainland*[6]		Jordan*[6] Latvia* Lesotho* Macedonia, FYR*[6] Trinidad & Tobago[6]	
Pegged exchange rates within horizontal bands (6)[9]	**Within a cooperative arrangement ERM II (1)** Denmark		**Other band arrangements (5)** Cyprus Egypt[5] Libyan A.J. Suriname[5] Vietnam[6]					

Exchange Arrangements with No Separate Legal Tender: The currency of another country circulates as the sole legal tender or the member belongs to a monetary or currency union in which the same legal tender is shared by the members of the union.
Currency Board Arrangements: A monetary regime based on an explicit legislative commitment to exchange domestic currency for a specified foreign currency at a fixed exchange rate, combined with restrictions on the issuing authority to ensure the fulfilment of its legal obligation.
Other Conventional Fixed Peg Arrangements: The country pegs its currency (formally or de facto) at a fixed rate to a major currency or a basket of currencies where the exchange rate fluctuates within a narrow margin of at most ± 1 percent around a central rate.
Pegged Exchange Rates Within Horizontal Bands: The value of the currency is maintained within margins of fluctuation around a formal or de facto fixed peg that are wider than ± 1 percent around a central rate.

Crawling Pegs: The currency is adjusted periodically in small amounts at a fixed, preannounced rate or in response to changes in selective quantitative indicators.
Exchange Rates Within Crawling Bands: The currency is maintained within certain fluctuation margins around a central rate that is adjusted periodically at a fixed preannounced rate or in response to changes in selective quantitative indicators.
Managed Floating with No Preannounced Path for the Exchange Rate: The monetary authority influences the movements of the exchange rate through active intervention in the foreign exchange market without specifying, or precommitting to, a preannounced path for the exchange rate.
Independent Floating: The exchange rate is market determined, with any foreign exchange intervention aimed at moderating the rate of change and preventing undue fluctuations in the exchange rate, rather than at establishing a level for it.

**ECCU: Eastern Caribbean Currency Union; WAEMU: West African Economic and Monetary Union; CAEMC: Central African Economic and Monetary Community

Note: "Country" in this publication does not always refer to a territorial entity that is a state as understood by international law and practice; the term also covers the euro area and some nonsovereign territorial entities for which statistical data are provided internationally on a separate basis.

[1]A country with * indicates that the country adopts more than one nominal anchor in conducting monetary policy. It should be noted, however, that it would not be possible, for practical reasons, to infer from this table which nominal anchor plays the principal role in conducting monetary policy.

EXHIBIT 13-1
Exchange Rate Arrangements as of March 31, 2001

EXCHANGE RATE REGIME (NUMBER OF COUNTRIES)	MONETARY POLICY FRAMEWORK				
	Exchange rate anchor	*Monetary aggregate target*	*Inflation targeting framework*	*Fund-supported or other monetary program*	*Other*
Crawling pegs (4)[6]	Bolivia* Costa Rica Nicaragua* Zimbabwe*			Bolivia Nicaragua* Zimbabwe	
Exchange rates within crawling bands (5)[6, 10]	Israel* Uruguay* Honduras* Venezuela, Rep. Hungary Bolivariana		Israel*	Honduras* Uruguay*	
Managed floating with no preannounced path for exchange rate (33)		Jamaica[6] Slovenia Tunisia	Czech Republic Norway	Cambodia[5] Croatia Ethiopia Jamaica*[6] Kazakhstan Kenya Kyrgyz Republic Mauritania Nigeria Pakistan Romania Russian Federation Rwanda Sri Lanka Sudan Ukraine Yugoslavia, Fed. Rep of	Algeria[3] Azerbaijan Belarus[3, 5] Burundi[3] Dominican Rep.[3, 5] Guatemala[3] India[3] Lao PDR[3,5] Paraguay[3] Singapore Slovak Republic[3] Uzbekistan[3, 5]
Independently floating (47)		Gambia, The* Ghana* Guinea* Guyana* Mauritius[6] Malawi* Mexico Mongolia* Peru* Philippines* São Tomé and Principe* Sierra Leone* Turkey* Yemen*	Australia Brazil[12] Canada Chile[5] Colombia* Iceland Korea New Zealand Poland South Africa Sweden Thailand* United Kingdom	Albania Angola Armenia Colombia* Gambia, The* Georgia Ghana* Guinea* Guyana* Haiti Indonesia Madagascar Malawi* Moldova Mongolia* Mozambique Papua New Guinea Peru* Philippines* São Tomé and Principe* Sierra Leone* Tajikistan Tanzania Thailand* Turkey* Uganda Yemen* Zambia	Afghanistan[5, 11] Japan[3] Liberia[3] Somalia[5, 11] Switzerland[3] United States[3]

[2]These countries have a currency board arrangement.

[3]The country has no explicitly stated nominal anchor, but rather monitors various indicators in conducting monetary policy.

[4]Until they are withdrawn in the first half of 2002, national currencies will retain their status as legal tender within their home territories.

[5]Member maintained exchange arrangements involving more than one market. The arrangement shown is that maintained in the major market.

[6]The indicated country has a de facto arrangement under a formally announced policy of managed or independent floating. In the case of Jordan, it indicates that the country has a de jure peg to the SDR but a de facto peg to the U.S. dollar. In the case of Mauritius, the authorities have a de facto policy of independent floating, with only infrequent intervention by the central bank.

[7]Exchange rates are determined on the basis of a fixed relationship to the SDR, within margins of up to ±7.25%. However, because of the maintenance of a relatively stable relationship with the U.S. dollar, these margins are not always observed.

[8]Comoros has the same arrangement with the French Treasury as do the CFA Franc Zone countries.

[9]The band width for these countries is: Cyprus (±2.25%), Denmark (±2.25%), Egypt (±1%), Libya (±77.5%), Suriname (±1.1%), and Vietnam (0.1% daily movement, one-sided).

[10]The band for these countries is: Honduras (±7%), Hungary (±2.25%), Israel (±20%), Uruguay (±3%), and República Bolivariana de Venezuela (±7.5%).

[11]There is no relevant information available for the country.

[12]Brazil maintains a Fund-supported program.

[13]For El Salvador, the U.S. dollar is also legal tender; all financial system accounts are denominated in U.S. dollars.

SOURCE: *International Financial Statistics,* September 2001, pp. 2–3.

Forward, futures, options, and swap agreements effectively lock in an exchange rate today for a transaction that may or will occur in the future, thus reducing the risk that changes in the exchange rate will alter expected outcomes.

The development of foreign exchange forward, futures, options, and swap agreements coincides with the tremendous growth in trade and capital flows, coupled with the increased volatility of exchange rates under the managed float exchange rate system. Because these instruments reduce exchange rate risks, they facilitate trade in goods, services, and financial claims.

The Role of the Dollar under the Managed Float

Under the Bretton Woods Accord, the dollar played a dominant role in the international financial system because it served as the official reserve currency. Under the managed float system, the dollar continues to serve as the major reserve currency in the international financial system because of its relative stability.

In addition to serving as a reserve asset, the dollar is sometimes used as a medium of exchange and a unit of account in international markets. Exchanges between two currencies of smaller countries often take place through dollars. For example, rather than using its own currency for a direct purchase Peru might convert its currency to dollars and use those dollars to purchase the currency of South Africa. Prices of standardized contracts of raw materials and commodities are often quoted in dollars. For example, since the price of oil is quoted in dollars, the dollar is the medium of exchange through which oil is bought and sold around the world. The dollar is accepted for payments in many foreign countries and has been widely used in countries experiencing political and economic unrest such as Russia, Ukraine, and Mexico.

The dollar also acts as a store of value. As we have seen, 50 to 60 percent of all U.S. currency and over 70 percent of $100 bills are held abroad. The dollar is demanded as a store of value because of the United States' political stability and the dollar's acceptance over time.

Although the dollar is no longer the official reserve asset, the demand for dollars in international financial markets (either as reserves or for other uses) has continued to grow. Indeed, the demand for dollars has grown faster than domestic real incomes due to the increase in trade, capital flows, and real incomes around the world.

Today, despite these many roles, the dollar is less important in relative terms than it was under the Bretton Woods Accord. Notwithstanding this, it has gained in relative importance since 1990. Between 1990 and 1999, the percentage of official international reserve assets held in dollars or dollar-denominated assets increased from 50.6 percent to 66.2 percent. Other currencies such as the euro, the Japanese yen, and the British pound are now also used as international reserves. In coming years, the euro may also gain in relative importance if its value stabilizes after a downslide in the first years following its introduction. In 1999, the newly created euro made up 12.5 percent of international reserves. The Japanese yen and British pound sterling made up 5.1 percent and 4.0 percent, respectively.[12]

Within this changing environment, several international organizations are developing unique roles in the international financial system. These organizations include the International Monetary Fund, the World Bank, and the Bank for International Settlements. They seek to foster stability in the international financial system so that the benefits of trade and cross-border trading of financial instruments can be real-

---

[12]*Annual Report 2000*, International Monetary Fund, p. 111.

ized. Just as the financial system has evolved to deal with the growth in trade and capital flows, these organizations are redefining their roles in an increasingly globalized economy. It is to these organizations that we now turn our attention.

RECAP Since 1973, major industrialized countries have participated in a managed float exchange rate system. A currency's value is determined by supply and demand, but governments intervene by buying and selling (demanding and supplying) currencies to affect values. Smaller countries often tie the value of their currencies to the dollar or some other major currency. Foreign exchange forward, futures, options, and swap agreements have been developed to allow market participants to hedge exchange rate risks. Under the managed float, the dollar remains the major international reserve asset although other currencies also serve as international reserves. In addition, the dollar is demanded in international financial markets because of its stability. It serves as a medium of exchange, a unit of account, and a store of value in some international markets.

Major International Financial Organizations

As we have seen, the Bretton Woods Accord of 1944 established the fixed exchange rate system that remained in effect until the early 1970s. In addition, the meetings at Bretton Woods resulted in the creation of the **International Monetary Fund (IMF)** and the **World Bank.** Although the fixed rate exchange system has not survived, both the IMF and World Bank have. Indeed, in recent years, both have gained in stature. Another international organization, the Bank for International Settlements (BIS), predates the IMF and the World Bank and is the oldest major international financial institution in existence today.

The International Monetary Fund (IMF)

The IMF was designed to:

> promote international monetary cooperation; to facilitate the expansion and balanced growth of international trade; to promote exchange stability; to assist in the establishment of a multilateral system of payments; to make its general resources temporarily available to its members experiencing balance of payments difficulties under adequate safeguards; and to shorten the duration and lessen the degree of disequilibrium in the international balances of payments of members.[13]

As such, the IMF is a voluntary institution owned and directed by the countries that choose to join. The IMF is like an overseer of the monetary and exchange rate policies of its members. Member countries agree to exchange their currencies freely with other foreign currencies, to keep the IMF informed of changes in financial and monetary policies that may affect other members, and to adjust these policies based on the recommendations of the IMF for the greater common good.

When joining the IMF, each country is assessed a quota (membership fee) based on its economic importance and the amount of its international trade. A country's voting rights in the organization are proportionate to the amount of its quota. At the IMF's inception, the total quota (subscription) was $8.8 billion. The United States's share was 31 percent. Thus, the United States controlled 31 percent of the votes. Quotas are revised every 5 years to ensure that the IMF has adequate funds at its disposal. As of April 2001, 183 countries (including all major countries of the

International Monetary Fund (IMF)
An organization created in 1944 to oversee the monetary and exchange rate policies of its members who pay quotas that are used to assist countries with temporary imbalances in their balance of payments.

World Bank
An investment bank created in 1944 that issues bonds to make long-term loans at low interest rates to poor countries for economic development projects.

http://www.worldbank. org, www.imf.org and **www.bis.org**
Visit the sites of the World Bank, the International Monetary Fund, and the Bank for International Settlements.

---

[13]The homepage of the IMF is at http://www.IMF.org.

world) were members of the IMF, and the total subscription was roughly $300 billion. The size of the subscription has grown as more countries have joined the IMF and larger quotas have been assessed. Over the years, the U.S. share has fallen to 17.4 percent. Therefore, the United States today controls 17.4 percent of the votes. The IMF is headquartered in Washington, D.C., and has 2,700 employees from over 122 countries. Other offices are in Paris, Geneva, and at the United Nations in New York City.

The IMF administers the pool of funds generated by the quotas to assist member countries that do not have enough foreign exchange to pay all of the claims being presented to them because of deficits in their balance of payments. Members can borrow from the pool of funds to resolve temporary imbalances. This influx of funds gives them time to change their economic policies so that balance of payment deficits are resolved in an orderly manner with minimal damages to themselves and to other countries. Members must request assistance and abide by IMF policy recommendations while receiving the funds. In addition to the pool of funds generated from the quotas, the IMF also has standby agreements to borrow supplemental funds, if needed, from the wealthiest members.

Special Drawing Rights (SDRs)
International reserve assets created by the IMF to supplement other international reserves.

In 1969, the IMF created **special drawing rights (SDRs)**, which are international reserve assets that supplement other international reserves. SDRs were created in response to a shortage in international reserves.[14] The value of the SDR is a weighted average of the U.S. dollar, the euro, the Japanese yen, and the British pound sterling, so it fluctuates daily. Today the outstanding value of SDRs fluctuates around $30 billion, depending on the values of the four currencies. The SDRs are equal to about 2 percent of nongold international reserves of the member countries. They are bookkeeping entries not backed by other reserve assets and provide the international financial system with additional liquidity. Central banks use SDRs, rather than other national currencies, to make payments to other member countries.

In the past, SDRs have been distributed to members of the IMF according to their quotas. Although only two distributions have been made since their inception, more SDRs can be created and distributed if the IMF determines that there is a long-term global need for additional international reserves. The last distribution was in 1981. In September 1997, the IMF proposed an additional one-time allocation to spread the SDRs more equitably among members.[15] As yet, the proposal has not been ratified by the required 60 percent of IMF members with 85 percent of the total voting power.

http://www.imf.org
Provides a detailed description of the International Monetary Fund's operations.

The activities of the IMF can be divided into two distinct periods: the Bretton Woods era and the period since the managed float. During the Bretton Woods era, the IMF's activities centered on monitoring the fixed exchange rate system and assisting countries in maintaining it. The IMF would often make loans to countries to finance short-term deficits in their balance of payments so that the fixed exchange rates could be maintained. If long-term problems existed, the fixed exchange rates were adjusted to correct the imbalances. When making loans, the IMF often recommended that the recipient country change the domestic policies that had contributed to its balance of payments deficit. As already noted, loans were contingent on the borrower's acceptance of the IMF's recommendations.

When fixed exchange rates were abandoned in 1973, the IMF no longer had a fixed rate system to monitor, so its role changed. Now the IMF, in an advisory

---

[14]At the time, the Bretton Woods Accord was still in effect, and the dollar was the official reserve asset.
[15]Since the last distribution, 39 countries have joined the IMF and have never received an allocation.

capacity, oversees economic policies that affect the balance of payments and exchange rates. In addition, the IMF provides information to members about countries experiencing balance of payments difficulties that could result in financial crises. Finally, the IMF continues to provide financial assistance to members experiencing short-term balance of payments problems. As before, the financial assistance is contingent on the recipient's promise to reform its economic policies and adopt the IMF's recommendations. The IMF played a key role in resolving the international debt crisis that afflicted less-developed countries in the 1980s and the Mexican peso crisis of 1994–1995. Intervention by the IMF has also prevented many financial crises from occurring. For a discussion of the IMF's role in the Asian crisis of the late 1990s, see A Closer Look.

The Role of the IMF in the Asian Crisis: The IMF was created at the end of World War II to assist countries that were experiencing a financial crisis. The goal was to contain the crisis and prevent it from spreading to the global financial system.[16] The IMF assists countries that are experiencing a financial crisis by providing large-scale liquidity. In addition, the IMF can provide technical assistance to help policymakers find a resolution to the crisis.

The Asian crisis of 1997 arose out of a situation in which the currencies of Southeast Asia were pegged to the dollar and, thus, had appreciated along with the dollar. Given large current account deficits and relatively small supplies of international reserves, the currencies became overvalued. In addition, the countries were enjoying significant capital inflows and had large short-term loans denominated in U.S. dollars. If the currencies were devalued, more domestic currency would be required to pay back the dollar-denominated loans. The result would be many defaults and bankruptcies.

Throughout the crisis, the IMF played a significant role in helping the countries of Southeast Asia find a solution to their problems. Beginning in late 1997, the IMF recommended that the overvalued currencies be devalued. After the initial round of devaluations and the breaking of the dollar peg, the IMF called for the Asian nations to substantially increase their interest rates in an attempt to stop the continuing slide of currency values. In addition, the IMF made short-term loans to provide liquidity to the stricken economies. The goals of the rescue plans were to stabilize currency values, restore investor confidence, and reestablish the nations' access to international capital flows.

The IMF assistance did not come without strings attached. The IMF required the countries to pursue contractionary fiscal policies designed to cut consumption. The fall in consumption would lead to a decrease in imports and a reduction in the current account deficits. This policy recommendation was fairly typical for the IMF in such a situation.

In addition, the IMF required the governments to introduce structural changes into their financial systems—in particular, to improve the regulation and oversight of their banks. In the future, the countries were to avoid becoming so dependent on short-term financing (especially from abroad) to prevent their financial systems from being so vulnerable to changes in market sentiment.

By mid-1998, some economies in Southeast Asia were on the road to recovery but far from experiencing healthy growth. Without loans from the IMF, the crisis would have persisted. It is also highly likely that the countries would have defaulted on their short-term U.S. dollar loans.

Although the IMF had some success in alleviating the crisis, its policies have been criticized. Some complain that because the rescue plans did not entail a restructuring of the

---

[16]A major rationale for intervening in financial crises was that an international financial crisis could lead to a military conflict. World leaders were painfully aware of how Germany's problems with hyperinflation in the 1920s contributed to the rise of Hitler and subsequent world war.

short-term debt and left corporate sectors in very fragile financial positions, the currencies continued to depreciate, and bankruptcies persisted longer than if a restructuring plan had been part of the rescue package. At the other extreme, some critics argue that although the short-term pain would have been greater, the crisis would have had long-term, positive impact if it had been allowed to run its course without intervention from the IMF. Still others argue that the crisis could have been prevented or at least mitigated if the IMF had warned the international financial community earlier about the problems of the troubled economies.[17]

Overall, the Asian crisis has caused the IMF to reconsider its role as an international financial organization, particularly as it relates to imposing structural reforms on its members and fostering a stable international financial system.

In the 2000s, the growing economic integration of the world's goods, services, and capital markets has created new opportunities and challenges for the IMF. The IMF is taking a leading role in defining and fostering a stable international financial system.

The World Bank

Like the IMF, the World Bank was created in 1944 at Bretton Woods and is headquartered in Washington, D.C. The similarities stop there, however. The World Bank is an investment bank that issues bonds and uses the proceeds to make long-term, low-interest rate loans to poor countries for economic development projects. The bonds have the highest credit rating because the World Bank's 182 member countries guarantee repayment as of 2001.

International Bank for Reconstruction and Development
A bank that makes 12- to 15-year loans to poor, but not the poorest, countries, charging an interest rate just above the rate at which the bank borrows.

International Development Association
An association that makes interest-free loans with a maturity of 35–40 years to the world's poorest countries.

The World Bank is really two organizations: the **International Bank for Reconstruction and Development** and the **International Development Association.** The latter makes interest-free loans with a maturity of 35–40 years to the world's poorest countries (those having an annual per capita gross domestic product of less than $865). The former makes 12- to 15-year low-interest-rate loans to poor countries with annual per capita gross domestic product between less than $5,225 but greater than $865. Countries with per capita gross domestic products between $865 and $1,445 may receive some combination of 35–40 year interest-free loans and 12–15-year low-interest loans. Thus, the World Bank makes loans to developing countries that would not have other sources of funds or other venues from which to borrow. The interest rate charged is slightly above the rate the bank pays to borrow when it issues the bonds.

Many of the loans financed by the World Bank are used to build infrastructure such as electric power plants and roads. The bank also finances projects to improve drinking water, waste disposal, health care, nutrition, family planning, education, and housing. In addition to loans, the bank also provides technical assistance. Many countries that borrowed from the World Bank in the past have developed sufficiently that they no longer need to borrow funds, so the bank can direct its aid to other poorer countries.

International Finance Corporation
An organization that mobilizes funding for private enterprise projects in poor countries.

The World Bank focuses on public projects, rather than providing direct assistance to private enterprises in developing countries. Another organization, the **International Finance Corporation,** seeks to mobilize funding for private enter-

---

[17]Others believe that early warning systems may cause some crises to occur that otherwise would not.

prises. Although legally separate from the World Bank, the corporation is associated with it and is the organization through which the World Bank encourages small business development. The International Finance Corporation has also helped to establish stock markets in many developing countries, thus increasing their ability to attract international capital flows.

The Bank for International Settlements (BIS)

The **Bank for International Settlements (BIS)**, headquartered in Basel, Switzerland, is an independent international financial organization created in 1930, 14 years before the Bretton Woods Accord. As such, it is the world's oldest international financial organization. The purpose of the BIS was "to promote the cooperation of central banks and to provide additional facilities for international financial operations."[18] The BIS was originally established to monitor and administer the reparations that countries defeated in World War I were required to pay to victorious nations. In addition, the BIS was to provide specialized services to central banks and, through them, to the international financial system.

Since 1960, the BIS has become an important international monetary organization with expanding functions. The BIS acts as a trustee for many international financial agreements and monitors compliance with the agreements. It is very active in identifying, negotiating, and monitoring international standards for banking regulation and supervision. The BIS seeks to establish international reporting standards for financial institutions and to assist countries in developing safe and sound financial practices. It encourages cooperation among member and nonmember central banks.

At the present time, 49 countries are members of the BIS, and the bank's directors come from the central banks of 11 countries (Belgium, Canada, France, Germany, Italy, Japan, the Netherlands, Sweden, Switzerland, the United Kingdom, and the United States). Central bankers from Belgium, France, Germany, Italy, the United Kingdom, and the United States are permanent members of the board of directors. A country does not have to be a member of the BIS to have an account with the bank. Central banks of 120 countries have deposit accounts with the BIS totaling just over $128 billion in March 2001.[19] The bank has 500 employees from 35 countries.

In addition to acting as a bank for central banks, the BIS is also a meeting place where central bankers consult on a monthly basis. Since the early 1960s, a group of 11 nations (Belgium, Canada, France, Germany, Italy, Japan, the Netherlands, Sweden, Switzerland, the United Kingdom, and the United States), widely known as the G-10, has held regular monthly meetings at the bank to discuss international financial matters. As financial markets have become more globalized, these informal meetings have taken on more importance and led to greater international cooperation. In Chapter 17, we will look at the details of the Basel Accord of 1988, which established international standards for banking regulation among the 12 nations that signed the agreement. The agreement was negotiated at the BIS.

At the present time, the BIS is expanding its relationships with central banks in emerging economies, thus increasing its stature in the international financial system.

Bank for International Settlements (BIS)
An international financial organization that promotes international cooperation among central banks and provides facilities for international financial operations.

http://www.bis.org
Provides the mission statement of the Bank for International Settlements, its latest annual reports, and more.

---

[18]The homepage of the BIS at http://www.bis.org.
[19]Article 3 of the original statute creating the Bank for International Settlements.

A Framework for International Financial Stability

Leaders from Canada, Germany, France, Italy, Japan, the United Kingdom, and the United States (known as the G-7 countries), have met annually since 1975 to discuss such common concerns as macroeconomic management, human rights, trade, energy, the environment, crime and drug trafficking, arms control, and the international financial system. Discussions before and after meetings are sometimes broadened to include leaders from other countries, including but not limited to the leaders of the G-10 countries mentioned earlier who also meet annually. The financial crisis in Asia in the 1990s revealed several deficiencies in the international financial system. As a result, the purpose of the G-7 meetings in Birmingham, England, in May 1998 was to discuss ways to strengthen the international financial system. The goal was to devise a system that would produce fewer crises in the future and to improve the response by the international financial community in the event of a crisis. Out of these meetings and others came an "emerging consensus" with regard to changes that need to be made in the international financial system to maximize the benefits of globalization while minimizing the costs.

The leaders agreed that as a prerequisite for participating in a stable international financial system, a country must have sound economic policies that foster noninflationary growth. Emerging countries that want to take advantage of increased international capital flows need support and encouragement to develop stable financial systems and markets that are appropriately supervised both internally and externally. Developing countries must establish banking systems that encourage the appropriate amount of risk taking. The system may include deposit insurance and a lender of last resort, but it should still allow private lenders to bear the costs of their decisions as well as to reap the rewards. If lenders know that national or international regulators will bail them out in the case of failure, they are likely to engage in too much risk taking.[20] At the same time, the financial system should be strong enough that private failures rarely spill over to the entire financial system.

In addition to establishing healthy national financial systems, countries must also standardize the reporting of qualitative and quantitative information about their financial markets, institutions, laws, and regulations. Reporting of fiscal conditions should include information about international reserves, external debt (both short and long term), and the health of the banking sector. At the same time, financial and nonfinancial institutions should adopt international accounting standards that allow for effective international comparisons. International standards should be developed for auditing, disclosure, bankruptcy, corporate governance, and the valuation of stocks, bonds, and other assets.

Finally, the surveillance of international organizations that oversee the international financial system must be improved. Organizations such as the IMF and BIS should work to see that the international financial system is more transparent and that surveillance is more open.

More meetings and discussion will undoubtedly occur in the future if the full potentials of globalization are to be realized.

---

[20]The case in which lenders are encouraged to take too many risks because they know they will be bailed out is an example of the moral hazard problem confronting institutions.

RECAP The IMF, the World Bank, and the BIS all have unique roles in the international financial system. The IMF promotes exchange rate stability, oversees the international financial system, and lends to member countries experiencing temporary balance of payments deficits. The World Bank promotes the economic development of the world's poorest countries by raising funds to make development loans. The BIS acts as a bank for central banks and seeks to establish and monitor international reporting and capital standards for financial institutions and to assist countries in developing safe and sound financial practices.

This chapter contains one appendix on how to compare returns in a globalized financial system. In Part 4, we turn our attention to how financial market participants and institutions manage risk.

Summary of Major Points

- The international financial system consists of the arrangements, rules, customs, instruments, facilities, and organizations that enable international payments to be made and funds to flow across borders. The international financial system has experienced tremendous growth in recent years because of the increase in trade in goods, services, and financial instruments; technological advances; and the removal of barriers to capital flows. The international financial system is composed of the international money and capital markets and the foreign exchange market.

- The Bretton Woods Accord of 1944 established fixed exchange rates between the U.S. dollar and other major currencies. Under the accord, foreign countries defined their currencies in terms of the U.S. dollar and agreed to buy or sell dollars, the official reserve asset, to maintain the agreed-upon exchange rates. The dollar, in turn, was defined in terms of gold, and the United States agreed to convert any unwanted dollars of foreign central banks into gold.

- Under fixed exchange rates, if a country other than the United States had a deficit in its balance of payments on current and capital accounts, it used supplies of dollars to purchase its own currency to maintain the exchange value. Likewise, if such a country had a surplus in its balance of payments on current and capital accounts, it demanded dollars to maintain or support the value of its currency. Persistent deficits and surpluses resulted in foreign countries having to devalue or revalue their currencies, respectively.

- The United States was in the unique position of being able to run persistent deficits in its balance of payments on current and capital accounts while foreign central banks were accumulating dollars to serve as international reserves. Once foreign central banks had acquired sufficient reserves, the ability of the United States to run deficits in its balance of payments on current and capital accounts was also limited. Eventually, the United States was unable to continue to convert dollars into gold, and the Bretton Woods system of fixed exchange rates collapsed in 1973. It was replaced by a system of flexible exchange rates. During the Bretton Woods period, trade in goods, services, and financial instruments was much less than it is today.

- Under flexible exchange rates, the value of the dollar is determined by the demand for and supply of dollars, and the exchange rate will gravitate to the value at which quantity demanded is equal to quantity supplied. The demand for dollars is determined by foreign demand for U.S. goods, services, and financial instruments. The supply of dollars is determined by U.S. demand for foreign goods, services, and financial instruments. Ultimately, the demand for and supply of dollars are determined by domestic and foreign incomes, inflation rates, and interest rates.

- Since 1973, the major industrialized countries have participated in a managed float exchange rate system. Under a managed float, exchange rates are determined by market forces, but governments may intervene by demanding or supplying currencies to affect exchange rates. Smaller countries often tie the value of their currencies to the dollar or some other major currency.

- The dollar is very important in the international financial system because it serves as the major international reserve asset. Other currencies such as the euro, the Japanese yen, and the British pound also serve as international reserves. In addition, dollars are demanded in international financial markets to serve as a medium of exchange, a unit of account, and a store of value. Even though the dollar is no longer the official reserve currency, the international demand for dollars has increased because of the growth of trade in goods, services, and capital flows.

- Foreign exchange forward, futures, options, and swap markets are used by market participants to hedge exchange rate risk. They effectively allow those who will need or will receive foreign exchange in the future to lock in an exchange rate today.

- The IMF is an international organization owned and operated by its 183 member countries. The IMF promotes exchange rate stability, oversees the international financial system, and lends to member countries experiencing temporary balance of payments deficits. In addition to quotas from its members, the IMF also has lines of credit from the major industrial countries to lend, if needed, to member countries with balance of payments difficulties. SDRs are an international reserve asset created by the IMF to supplement the supply of international reserves.

- The World Bank promotes the economic development of the world's poorest countries by raising funds to make development loans. A total of 182 countries belong to the World Bank. Whereas the World Bank funds public projects, the International Finance Corporation seeks to encourage private enterprise and development. The corporation is separate from the World Bank but works closely with it.

- The BIS acts as a bank for central banks and seeks to establish and monitor international reporting and capital standards for financial institutions and to assist countries in developing safe and sound financial practices. Leaders from the G-7 countries meet on an annual basis to discuss common problems, such as establishing a stable international financial system.

- (App.) Financial market participants compare expected rates of return on instruments denominated in different currencies. In equilibrium, interest rates adjust so that after adjustments have been made for expected inflation and exchange rate risk, returns are equalized across countries. Foreign exchange forward and futures contracts can be used to hedge exchange rate risk. Interest rate parity has been achieved when interest rates have adjusted so that rates between countries differ only by the expected appreciation or depreciation of the currency.

Key Terms

Bank for International
    Settlements (BIS)
Bretton Woods Accord
Devalue
Fixed Exchange Rate System
Floating (Flexible) Exchange
    Rate System
Interest Rate Parity (App.)
International Bank for
    Reconstruction and
    Development

International Development
    Association
International Finance
    Corporation
International Financial System
International Monetary Fund
    (IMF)
Managed Float Exchange Rate
    System
Official Reserve Account
Official Reserve Currency

Revalue
Special Drawing Rights (SDRs)
World Bank

Review Questions

1. What is the international financial system, and how has it changed in recent years? What opportunities does the new system offer? What are the challenges?

2. Identify and explain three differences between the international monetary system under the Bretton Woods Accord and the managed float exchange rate system that replaced it.

3. Why did the Bretton Woods Accord break down?

4. What was the role of the dollar under the Bretton Woods Accord?

5. Why has the demand for dollars in international financial markets continued to grow, even though the dollar is no longer the official reserve currency?

6. When a country ran a deficit in its balance of payments under the Bretton Woods Accord, how was that deficit resolved?

7. Leticia is a small country that is experiencing a deficit in its current account in its balance of payments. The value of Leticia's currency is tied to the U.S. dollar, which has been appreciating. What options could the IMF recommend to correct the imbalance in Leticia's balance of payments?

8. Under flexible exchange rates, what happens if a country experiences a deficit in its balance of payments? How long can a deficit in the balance of payments persist?

9. Why and how do central banks intervene in foreign exchange markets under the managed float exchange rate system?

10. How do the roles of the IMF and the BIS differ? How are they similar? What is the primary function of the World Bank?

11. What is the difference between the types of projects financed by the World Bank and those funded by the International Finance Corporation?

12. What factors have contributed to the increase in capital flows among countries?

13. What is the contagion effect? Why is it more pronounced today than it was 20 years ago?

14. What were the causes of the Asian crisis? What did the IMF do to mitigate the Asian crisis?

15. Which international financial organization do you think is most important: the IMF, the World Bank, or the Bank for International Settlements? Give reasons to support your choice within the context of the international financial system. When and why was each organization created?

16. (App.) What is interest rate parity? Describe the process by which currencies will move toward interest rate parity.

Analytical Questions

17. Go to today's *Wall Street Journal* and find the yen/dollar exchange rate. Has the dollar appreciated or depreciated since April 2, 2001, when $1 equaled 126.68 yen?

18. Graphically demonstrate what would happen to the exchange rate in each of the following situations:
    a. The U.S. trade deficit increases.
    b. The U.S. trade deficit decreases.
    c. Capital outflows increase.
    d. Capital inflows increase.

19. Assume the nominal U.S. rate is 8 percent, the nominal foreign rate is 9 percent, expected U.S. inflation is 3 percent, expected foreign inflation is 5 percent, and the exchange rate risk is –1 percent. What is the real U.S. interest rate? What is the real foreign interest rate? Is there interest rate parity? Explain.

20. Foreigners are buying $100 billion in U.S. securities. U.S. residents are buying $300 billion in foreign securities. Is the United States experiencing a capital inflow or outflow? How much?

Internet Exercises

1. From the homepage for the International Monetary Fund (**http://www.imf.org**), provide some information on the organizational structure of the IMF. Where does the IMF get its resources and who can borrow money from the IMF? What are some criticisms being leveled at the IMF in the wake of the Asian crisis?

2. What are some of the differences and the similarities between the operations of the IMF and the World Bank? You may obtain answers to this question from the Web site of the IMF (**http://www.imf.org**).

Suggested Readings

An article that looks at the role of the U.S. dollar in the global financial system is Stephan Schulmeister, "Globalization Without Global Money: The Double Role of the Dollar as National Currency and World Currency," *Journal of Post Keynesian Economics*, Vol. 22, No. 3, Spring 2000, pp. 365–396.

For a discussion of "The IMF and Global Financial Crises," see Joseph Joyce's article by the same name in *Challenge*, Vol. 43, No. 4, July–August 2000, pp. 88–107. For another interesting article, also in *Challenge*, see Jane D'Arista's "Reforming International Financial Architecture, Vol. 43, No. 3, May–June 2000, pp. 44–82.

For a blending of theory and application to the changing international financial system, see Hans Visser, *A Guide to International Monetary Economics*, 2nd ed., (Northampton, MA: Edward Elgar, 2000).

For a look at "Liberalizing Capital Movements: Some Analytical Issues," see the article by the same name by Barry Eichengreen, Michael Mussa, Gjovanni Dell'Ariccia, Enrica Detragiache, Gian Maria Milesi-Ferretti, and Andrew Tweedie, *Economic Issues*, 17, International Monetary Fund, 1999.

For an in-depth look at the Asian crisis, see Uri Dadush, Dipak Dasgupta, and Marc Uzan, eds., *Private Capital Flows in the Age of Globalization: The Aftermath of the Asian Crisis* (Northampton, MA: Edward Elgar, 2000).

For a discussion of *European Monetary Integration*, see the book by the same name, Eric J. Pentecost and Andre Van Poeck, eds. (Northampton, MA: Edward Elgar, 2001). For a look at the euro as a global currency, see Pier Carlo Padoan, ed., *Monetary Union, Employment and Growth: The Impact of the Euro as a Global Currency* (Northampton, MA: Edward Elgar, 2001).

For a pessimistic view about the global financial system, see James L. Clayton, *The Global Debt Bomb* (Armonk, NY: M.E. Sharpe, 1999).

An article that touches on many of the issues of this chapter is Jane D'Arista, "Reforming International Financial Architecture," *Challenge*, Vol. 43, No. 3, May–June, 2000, pp. 44–82.

A book titled *Maintaining Financial Stability in a Global Economy* contains a collection of articles resulting from a symposium sponsored by the Federal Reserve Bank of Kansas City at Jackson Hole, Wyoming, August 28–30, 1997. The 367-page book is available from the Federal Reserve Bank of Kansas City, and articles from the book are online at the Web site **http://www.kc.frb.org**.

For a comprehensive article on the IMF, see Jane Sneddon Little and Giovanni P. Olivei, "Rethinking the International Monetary System: An Overview," *New England Economic Review*, Federal Reserve Bank of Boston, November 1999, pp. 3–24.

A recent article that touches on many of the subjects in this chapter is Charles Morris, "Maintaining Financial Stability in a Global Economy," *Economic Review of the Federal Reserve Bank of Kansas City* 82:4 (1997): 23–38.

Toward a Framework for Financial Stability, prepared by the staff of the International Monetary Fund, January 1998, 81 pages, is a very useful publication. It can be ordered directly from the IMF in Washington, D.C., or over the Internet by e-mailing publications@IMF.org.

Another new book that pertains to the material in this chapter is *Global Financial Crises: Lessons from Recent Events*, Joseph R. Bisignano, William C. Hunter, and George G. Kaufman, eds., (Norwell, MA: Kluwer Academic Publishers, 2000).

A article that looks at how a currency crisis in one country can cause a banking crisis in another and vice versa is Victoria Miller, "The Double Drain with a Cross-Border Twist," *The American Economic Review* 88: 2 (May 1998): 439–43.

A short article that looks at the origins of the Asian crisis, the international response, and the role of the IMF is "The International Community's Response to the Asian Financial Crisis" by Thomas M. Hoenig. It can be found in the *Economic Review of the Federal Reserve Bank of Kansas City* 83:2 (1998): 5–7.

Two other articles on the Asian Crisis are Stephen Poloz, "Fallout from Asia's Currency Turmoil,"

World Economic Affairs 2:1 (Autumn 1997):64; and Ramon Moreno, "What Caused East Asia's Financial Crisis?" *Federal Reserve Bank of San Francisco Economic Letter 98–24*, August 7, 1998.

A discussion of the new euro can be found in Malcolm Surry, "Great Expectations: Can the Euro Break the Dominance of the Dollar?" *Asian Business* 34:6 (June 1998): 6–7.

The annual report of the Bank for International Settlements can be found at **http://www.bis.org**.

Appendix 13-A

Comparing Returns in a Globalized Financial System

When comparing financial instruments denominated in the same currency, investors consider the return, the maturity, and the default risk. If instruments are denominated in different currencies, investors and borrowers must also consider the exchange rate risk, or the risk that the exchange rate between two currencies will change and alter the real return of the investment. For example, suppose that a U.S. investor converts dollars to Mexican pesos to make an investment denominated in pesos that earns a 10 percent nominal return. The investor expects the exchange rate to remain constant, but if the peso unexpectedly depreciates by 10 percent, the entire 10 percent return is wiped out when the pesos are converted back to dollars. Thus, exchange rate risk must be factored into any international investment.

In globalized financial markets, financial market players compare expected rates of return on instruments denominated in various currencies, including their own. To do so, they must convert all returns to an equivalent return in the domestic currency. The nominal rate of return in a domestic currency on an investment that is denominated in a foreign currency is the nominal foreign interest rate, plus the expected change in the exchange rate, less an adjustment for risk that results from the uncertainty of the future exchange rate. Equation (13A-1) depicts such a situation:

(13A-1) $$I_{US} = I_{FOR} + E$$

where

I_{US} = the nominal U.S. return on an investment in a foreign instrument that earns the nominal foreign interest rate, I_{FOR}

E = the expected percentage change in the exchange rate plus an exchange rate risk factor

Lenders compare this nominal U.S. return, I_{US}, with the U.S. interest rate and choose the instrument that offers the highest return. Borrowers choose to borrow in the market that offers the lowest rate as expressed in their domestic currencies. Because of market adjustments, if the nominal U.S. return is greater than the nominal foreign return plus the exchange rate adjustment, lenders will supply more

Interest Rate Parity
The condition when interest rates have adjusted so that rates between countries differ only by the expected appreciation or depreciation of the currency.

funds in the U.S. market and borrowers will borrow more funds in foreign markets. The adjustments will continue until the U.S. and foreign nominal interest rates are equal except for the expected exchange rate adjustment and risk. When interest rates have adjusted so that rates between countries differ only by the expected appreciation or depreciation of the currency, **interest rate parity** has been reached.

In reality, borrowers and lenders are making decisions based on the expected real return, rather than nominal returns. The real interest rate (return) is the nominal return less expected inflation. At times, we may wish to express returns between nations in terms of real interest rates as opposed to nominal rates. To do so for the United States, we must subtract expected U.S. inflation from each nominal rate in Equation (13A-1) as in Equation (13A-2). In equilibrium, the real U.S. interest rate, R_{US}, will be:

(13A-2) $$R_{US} = I_{US} - P_{US} = I_{FOR} + E - P_{US}$$

where

P_{US} = the expected U.S. inflation rate

Likewise, we can express the nominal foreign rate, I_{FOR}, in terms of the real foreign rate, R_{FOR}, plus the expected foreign inflation, P_{FOR}, to arrive at the equilibrium real U.S. interest rate in terms of the foreign real rate and domestic and foreign expected inflation. The results are summarized in Equation (13A-3):

(13A-3) $$R_{US} = R_{FOR} + P_{FOR} + E - P_{US}$$

Just as in foreign trade, foreign exchange forward and futures contracts can be used to hedge the exchange rate risk when investing in foreign financial instruments. By doing so, the exchange rate risk—E in Equation (13A-3)—can be greatly reduced or eliminated. We can conclude that with greater capital mobility, the real U.S. and foreign interest rates will tend to be equalized after differences in expected inflation have been taken into account.[21]

RECAP Financial market participants compare expected rates of return on instruments denominated in different currencies. The expected nominal rate of return on a foreign investment is the foreign interest rate, plus the exchange change in the exchange rate, less an adjustment for risk from the uncertainty of the future exchange rate. The expected real return includes an adjustment factor for expected inflation in both countries. In equilibrium, interest rates adjust so that after adjustments have been made for expected inflation and exchange rate risk, returns are equalized across countries. Foreign exchange forward and futures contracts can be used to hedge exchange rate risk.

---

[21]Another fact, which we ignore here for simplicity, is that P_{FOR} and E are not independent.

part

FINANCIAL INSTITUTIONS

chapter

An Introduction to Financial Intermediaries and Risk

> **Learning Objectives** *After reading this chapter, you should know:*

- The characteristics common to all types of financial intermediaries (FIs)
- The services provided by FIs and the types of risks they must manage
- The major types of depository institutions and other FIs
- The principal assets and liabilities of the various FIs
- The characteristics that distinguish one type of FI from another

" "
Presume Not That I Am the Thing I Was.
—William Shakespeare

Are All Financial Intermediaries More or Less Alike?

It is the last day of the month. Sandi and Dave have both been paid by their employers, and it's now time to pay the family's bills and save something for their upcoming vacation. Sitting at the kitchen table, they write checks on their account at HLT National Bank to Prudential Insurance Company for the premium due on Sandi's life insurance policy, APEI Credit Union for the car loan payment, and the local savings and loan (S&L) association for the mortgage payment. When these and other bills are paid, a check for the surplus funds to be saved is sent to their money market mutual fund account at Merrill Lynch.

In this hypothetical series of transactions, Sandi and Dave dealt with five different financial intermediaries (FIs)—a commercial bank, an insurance company, a credit union, an S&L, and a money market mutual fund. Why five instead of one? Can't one provide all of the relevant services? Put another way, how are these intermediaries similar to one another, and how do they differ? These are the questions we will address in this chapter. In essence, we will examine the functioning and role of those institutions that provide the public with a wide range of financial services and play a central role in coordinating and channeling the flow of funds in the economy.

As we begin, it should be emphasized that **financial innovation,** which is the creating of new financial instruments, markets, and institutions, has often been the key to growth and survival in the financial services industry, particularly during the past 35 years and at the present time.[1] As in many other firms and industries, institutional details in the financial services industry are evolving at a rapid pace due to changes in technology and the globalization of finance. Thus, we can provide you only with a snapshot of the current state of affairs and point out how and why this snapshot differs from the picture of the financial landscape prevailing in the recent past. This will lay the groundwork for subsequent chapters in which we analyze the forces that previously produced major changes in the financial system and that are likely to remain influential in the future.

Financial Innovation
The creation of new financial instruments, markets, and institutions in the financial services industry.

Common Characteristics

To the untrained eye, an insurance company and a commercial bank appear to be quite different institutions. However, the trained eye sees more. Both are FIs that link up deficit spending units (DSUs) and surplus spending units (SSUs) and, in the process, provide the public with a wide range of financial services. Recall from Chapter 1 that a SSU is a spending unit such as a firm or household wherein spending on consumption and investment is less than income. SSUs are the net lenders in society. Likewise, a DSU is a spending unit wherein spending is greater than income. DSUs are net borrowers. The linking or channeling function involves the acquisition of financial claims on DSUs by the FIs and the acquisition of claims on the FIs by the SSUs. (You might want to take a quick look at Exhibit 1-1 in Chapter 1.) The DSUs (borrowers) sell financial claims against themselves, which the intermediaries purchase. The financial claims may be signed loan papers, equities, or securities. In this context, when we say FIs make loans to DSUs, the FIs are purchasing financial claims—signed loan papers—from the DSUs. The intermediaries get the funds to lend by selling their own financial claims that the SSUs (lenders) purchase. The financial claims against the FIs include checking, time, and saving

---

[1]We look in depth at financial innovation in Part 5.

deposits, among others. Even though funds flow ultimately from SSUs to DSUs, the intermediaries do more than act as a go-between. The SSUs acquire claims against the FIs, which sell their own liabilities; thus, the FIs are in debt to the SSUs.[2]

The characteristics common to intermediaries can be identified with the aid of A Closer Look, which conceptualizes the notion that FIs are firms that produce services just as nonfinancial firms in the economy produce goods. We call these firms, collectively, the financial services industry. More specifically, in the process of acquiring and providing funds, FIs provide the public with a wide range of financial services. Two questions are pertinent: (1) Why do FIs do this? and (2) What types of services are we talking about?

FIs as Firms: FIs are firms. We generally think of manufacturing firms, for example, as acquiring inputs—including labor, capital, and natural resources—and using these inputs to produce outputs. In the case of FIs, their inputs—their sources of funds—are found on the liability side of their balance sheets. These funds are used to extend loans and acquire securities. Such financial claims appear on the asset side of the balance sheets and represent the outputs of the FIs. Banks, for example, incur deposit liabilities as a source of funds and use the funds to increase their asset holdings of loans and securities. Insurance companies receive premium payments from policyholders and provide benefits (protection) in return. The funds received are used to acquire assets—mainly loans and securities.

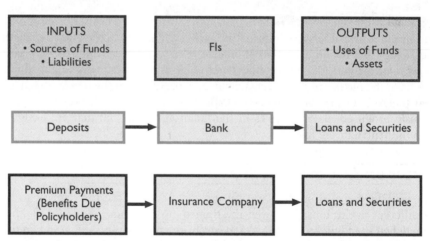

The answer to the first question is straightforward and represents a feature common to FIs and nonfinancial corporations. Intermediaries are, by-and-large, profit seeking.[3] In this context, it means FIs provide financial services because doing so is profitable. By extension, it means the quantity, quality, and type of financial services offered will expand or contract as the perceived profitability of this activity grows or shrinks.

To illustrate, banks "hire" funds from depositors. The interest a bank pays on its deposits is a cost of doing business, akin to the wages a manufacturing firm pays its workers. The bank then lends out the acquired funds to farmers, consumers, businesses, and governments. The interest earned on the loans represents revenue to

---

[2]For the time being, we are ignoring the money creation process by depository institutions, which may also generate funds that are lent to DSUs. This process will be covered in depth in the appendix of this chapter.

[3]The exceptions, such as credit unions, will be discussed later in the chapter.

the bank, akin to the revenue generated by a manufacturing firm's sales. The difference between the interest earned and the interest paid is a primary determinant of the bank's profitability. If funds can be hired more cheaply by providing a new type of deposit service, FIs have an incentive to act accordingly. Similarly, if a particular type of lending turns out to be less profitable than expected, FIs have an incentive to lend less in this area or to attempt to increase the expected revenue associated with such lending.[4] As we shall see, the link between expected profitability and the specific services provided by FIs is a crucial part of the explanation of why FIs change over time.

With this point, we come to our second question concerning the types of services FIs provide. In general, FIs provide services to the public for the following purposes:

1. To reduce the risks and costs associated with borrowing, lending, and other financial transactions.
2. To fulfill the demand for various financial assets and services, including protection against the financial losses associated with various exigencies.

More specifically, FIs use their expertise to appraise the risk of default associated with lending to particular borrowers. They usually do a better job of assessing these risks than individuals could do on their own. FIs pool the surpluses of many SSUs and lend to thousands of DSUs. Diffusing this risk, in effect, spreads out the individual surpluses of SSUs among numerous borrowers and further reduces risk. The SSUs are no longer putting all of their eggs in one basket.

On the flip side, by buying the financial liabilities of DSUs, the FIs provide borrowing opportunities for DSUs. The liabilities may be long- or short-term loans, equity, or debt. Without the FIs, the DSUs would have to rely on direct finance and would have far fewer or no borrowing sources. If there were no FIs, think how difficult it would be for individuals to find someone to lend them funds to purchase a new car—or for firms to borrow funds to purchase new machinery and equipment. When they did borrow, undoubtedly DSUs would be charged higher interest rates to compensate for the greater risks. Thus, the significant overall economic function of financial intermediation is to facilitate borrowing and lending that result in the allocation of resources to capital (plant, equipment, and the like) formation and other spending—the investment and spending processes.

In addition, FIs provide a menu of financial claims and depository services tailored to meet the needs of SSUs and, more generally, society at large. The menu includes (1) relatively safe and liquid claims, such as checking, time, and savings deposits at banks and other depository institutions, and (2) **contingent claims,** such as casualty and life insurance benefits that offer the public some protection from the often catastrophic financial effects of theft, accidents, natural disasters, and death. Thus, the wide array of menu choices fulfills the demand for various financial assets by the SSUs.

With FIs playing such a vital role in the economy, it should not be surprising that they share another common feature. They are regulated by various levels and agencies of government. Government regulators establish and enforce operating regulations aimed at promoting a smooth-running, efficient financial system and protecting the public from fraud and other abusive practices. The regulators seek to promote competition in the market for financial services, while preserving the public's confidence in the safety and soundness of the system.

Contingent Claims
Claims such as casualty and life insurance benefits that offer the public protection from the often catastrophic financial effects of theft, accidents, natural disasters, and death.

---

[4]As you may know, the default rate on student loans has been on the rise. If you are following the discussion, you should now understand why banks have been increasingly reluctant to make such loans.

By their nature, regulations represent an attempt to constrain or restrict an activity that might otherwise occur. In the financial system, regulations take many forms. Entry into the industry is tightly controlled. For example, someone cannot just open a bank. A charter from the federal government or relevant state government is needed to engage in the business of banking. There are also restrictions on particular types of assets and liabilities specific FIs can acquire. S&Ls, for example, cannot acquire common stock. In the past, regulations limited the interest rates FIs could pay to hire certain types of deposits and charge on certain types of loans. Lastly, regulations have restricted the geographical areas in which some FIs can operate. Until recently, for example, banks could not establish branches across state lines.

Such regulations, examined in detail in Chapter 17, have had at least three major effects:

1. For quite a while, they tended to reinforce and encourage specialization by FIs (in particular financial services). For example, life insurance companies usually stuck to providing life insurance, and S&Ls stuck to purchasing mortgages. More directly, the regulations tended to limit competition among different types of FIs.
2. Such specialization helps to explain the different types and mix of assets and liabilities found on FIs' balance sheets.
3. Over time, FIs became aware of the benefits of diversifying. In particular, they realized that providing the public with a wider range of financial services could be profitable. Attempts to move in such a direction often involved innovations to get around some existing regulations, particularly restrictions limiting the range of services FIs could provide and the competition among FIs in general. As we shall see in Chapters 15 and 17, legislation in late 1999 has also allowed commercial banks, securities firms, and insurance companies to affiliate under common ownership. Thus, one firm can offer its customers a complete range of financial services.

These more recent developments, which include the emergence of "financial supermarkets," are discussed in this and the next chapters. As we shall see, Sandi and Dave, whom we met at the beginning of the chapter, may be dealing with far fewer than five FIs if they do business with one of these one-stop financial supermarkets.

In addition to these regulatory effects, the 1990s brought increasing competition for FIs from nonfinancial institutions and from direct finance through the commercial paper market.[5] For example, many nonfinancial corporations such as General Motors, AT&T, Sears, and General Electric, now offer financial services and products such as consumer loans and credit cards. Whereas most firms used to rely on bank loans for funds to finance inventories and day-to-day expenses, firms of all sizes now have much greater access to borrow through the commercial paper market.[6]

RECAP FIs possess many common traits. In general, they are regulated, profit-seeking firms that provide the public with a wide range of financial services. These services help to reduce the risks associated with channeling funds from SSUs to DSUs. The services provided include the appraisal and diversification of risk, the pooling of funds, and the provision of a menu of claims, including contingent claims, tailored to the needs of customers.

---

[5]In Chapter 3, we saw that commercial paper is a short-term IOU issued by creditworthy corporations to finance short-term borrowing needs.

[6]The commercial paper may be issued through a broker who places it with a large corporation or other lender.

Types of Risks Faced by All FIs

To understand how the services that FIs provide reduce the risks associated with borrowing and lending, visualize the various FIs as being exposed to and having to deal with several types of risks and uncertainties. FIs face each type of risk in varying degrees depending on the composition of their assets and liabilities. Before turning to the balance sheets of the specific intermediaries, we first review the types of risks common to all FIs and SSUs and DSUs in general.

Credit or Default Risk

If a stranger knocked on your door and asked to borrow $1,000, you would probably react quite negatively, regardless of the interest rate the stranger was willing to pay. Your reluctance is, of course, tied to the risk or likelihood that the borrower will default and not repay the loan. You don't know the person's financial history and current situation, and you are suspicious about why anyone would show up at your home to make such a request.

Every time an intermediary makes a loan or purchases a security issued by a DSU, it faces the same risk. Credit, or *default risk* is the risk that the DSU will be unwilling or unable to live up to the terms of the liability it has sold. Perhaps the DSU is a firm that uses the funds for expansion, but the business it thought would boom turns out to be a bust because of some unanticipated complication or a general slowdown in the economy. Perhaps the borrower is morally unscrupulous and takes the money and runs. Thus, when making a loan or buying a financial asset issued by a DSU, the intermediary—whether it be a bank, mutual fund, or insurance company—is exposed to the risk that the DSU will default.

We have already seen that a primary function of an intermediary's management is to evaluate or assess the credit risk associated with purchasing the financial claims of DSUs. To do this, FIs employ experts in risk assessment who generally do a better job of assessing default risks than individuals could do on their own. Cynics say it is quite easy to get a loan as long as you can prove you don't really need the funds. In reality, managing credit risk does not mean denying loans to all borrowers who may default, or failing to make any investments that could go sour. Maintaining and enhancing profitability in the financial services industry, as in other industries, entails taking some risks. Unforeseen events can turn an otherwise profitable endeavor into a losing and perhaps bankrupt situation. Thus, a "good" credit risk can become a "bad" investment. It is a fact of economic life that despite good intentions, decent planning, and a successful track record, some borrowers will default. Conversely, some who have experienced financial difficulties in the past will "turn the corner" and become quite profitable.

Given this background, the task of financial managers is to lend and invest prudently. In general, this means gathering all relevant information on potential borrowers and using this information to avoid exposing the FI to excessive risk. The information should include balance sheets, income statements, credit checks, how funds are to be used, and so on. Recognize that the terms *prudent* and *excessive* are somewhat nebulous. One cannot find a precise, quantitative definition in the dictionary, so an FI's management team must establish guidelines that quantify the terms. This is what management is all about. Losses will occur, but the trick is to cover losses with profits on other loans and investments.

Interest Rate Risk

Another type of risk that must be managed is the *interest rate risk*—the risk that the interest rate will unexpectedly change so that the costs of an FI's liabilities exceed the earnings on its assets. This risk emanates from the relationship between the interest rate (return) earned on assets and the cost of, or interest rate paid on, liabilities. An FI's profitability is directly related to the spread between these rates. FIs obviously strive for a large, positive spread in which the return on assets significantly exceeds the cost of liabilities.

The potential problem is that a positive spread today can turn into a negative spread when the cost of liabilities exceeds the return on assets. For example, whenever intermediaries borrow short term through passbook savings deposits or commercial paper and make long-term loans or purchase long-term, fixed-rate financial assets such as bonds or mortgages, they are exposed to an interest rate risk. This risk has been a chronic problem for some intermediaries, particularly the S&L industry during the 1970s and 1980s as the financial system was deregulated and interest rates fluctuated over a fairly wide range. FIs have responded to this changing environment in a variety of ways, including utilizing adjustable rate loans (discussed in Chapter 16) and financial futures, options, and swaps. The latter three instruments, which will be analyzed in detail in Chapter 22, are now used extensively by FIs to hedge interest rate risk.[7]

In addition, as first discussed in Chapter 5, any intermediary holding long-term bonds is subject to the risk that the value of these bonds will fall if interest rates rise. The value of other long-term fixed rate assets will also fall when rates rise.

Liquidity Risk

Liquidity Risk
The risk that an FI will be required to make a payment when the intermediary has only long-term assets that cannot be converted to liquid funds quickly without a capital loss.

Liquidity risk is the risk that an FI will be required to make a payment when the intermediary has only long-term assets that cannot be converted to liquid funds quickly without a capital loss. Such a situation could occur when depositors unexpectedly withdraw funds or when an insurance company incurs unexpectedly high claim losses as a result of an earthquake, fire, flood, or hurricane. All intermediaries may experience a sudden need for funds, but depository institutions are particularly vulnerable to a deposit run that can cause a financial crisis. Their reserves are only a fraction of their liabilities and those liabilities are often payable on demand. In Chapter 4, we saw that the Fed stands ready to provide liquidity for depository institutions by acting as a lender of last resort. Intermediaries can reduce their liquidity risk by holding highly liquid assets that can be converted quickly into the funds needed to meet unexpected withdrawals or contingencies. They can also make other arrangements to mitigate this risk, such as backup lines of credit to meet unexpected needs.

Exchange Rate Risk

Financial markets have become increasingly international in scope. Consequently, many large intermediaries and corporations maintain stocks of foreign exchange to use in international transactions. In addition, some FIs may hold financial assets (investments) that are denominated in foreign currencies. In either case, the FI is

---

[7]An FI can be exposed to losses if it has fixed-rate liabilities, such as fixed-rate CDs, and variable-rate assets, such as variable-rate loans. In this case, if interest rates fall, the return on assets falls while the cost of liabilities does not.

exposed to a risk that the dollar exchange rate between the two currencies will appreciate, causing the dollar value of the foreign currency or foreign financial assets to fall. Thus, an FI, like any holder of foreign exchange or foreign financial assets, is subject to an **exchange rate risk**—the risk that changes in the exchange rate will cause the dollar value of foreign currency or foreign financial assets to fall. For example, assume an intermediary holds 10,000,000 yen or a financial asset valued at 10,000,000 yen. If the exchange rate is $1 = 100 yen, then 10,000,000 yen are worth $100,000. If the dollar exchange rate appreciates to $1 = 200 yen, then the 10,000,000 yen are worth only $50,000. In this case, the FI incurs a loss proportional to the amount of foreign currency or foreign financial assets it holds and to the change in the exchange rate. As we shall see in Chapters 22 and 23, foreign exchange forward contracts, futures, options, and swaps can be used to mitigate this risk.

Exchange Rate Risk
The risk that changes in the exchange rate will adversely affect the value of foreign exchange or foreign financial assets.

RECAP All FIs face several risks in varying degrees. Default risk is the risk the borrower will not pay the financial claim. Interest rate risk is the risk interest rate changes will turn a profitable spread into a loss. Liquidity risk is the risk that funds will not be available when needed. Exchange rate risk is the risk that changes in exchange rates will change, causing the FI to experience losses in the dollar value of foreign currency or foreign financial assets.

By now you should have a clearer picture of the similarities among FIs. We turn now to the differences among FIs, which are manifested in the composition of their balance sheets. An examination of FI balance sheets will not only highlight the differences among FIs, but will also make clear why FIs are exposed to many risks in varying degrees.

A Guide to FIs and Their Balance Sheets

In this section, we examine the balance sheets of the major FIs. A **balance sheet** is an accounting statement presenting the monetary value of an economic unit's assets, liabilities, and net worth at a specific point in time such as the last day of a year. In this case, the economic unit is an FI; the assets are financial assets such as loans and securities, and the liabilities are financial liabilities such as deposits and borrowed funds. The fundamental balance sheet identity is that assets equal liabilities plus net worth. If each dollar of assets is matched by a dollar of liabilities, net worth is zero. If the value of liabilities exceeds the value of assets, call the bankruptcy lawyer!

As we examine the balance sheets of the major FIs, it will be helpful to group FIs according to the nature of their liabilities or the major financial service they provide. Classifying "like with like" facilitates the development of a lucid "snapshot" and brings the relationship between past and current snapshots into focus. We shall see that the nature of the liabilities sold by a particular type of FI bears a close relationship to the nature of the assets acquired. More specifically, the maturity, stability, riskiness, and liquidity of an FI's liabilities affect the maturity, liquidity, and safety of the assets it acquires. In other words, the structure of an FI's assets and liabilities affects the degree to which it manages each of the specific risks discussed in the preceding section.

Balance Sheet
An accounting statement that presents the monetary value of an economic unit's assets, liabilities, and net worth on a specific date.

Deposit-Type FIs

Depository institutions include commercial banks, S&Ls, savings banks, and credit unions. The S&Ls, savings banks, and credit unions are called **thrifts**. As the term

Thrifts
Depository institutions known as S&Ls, savings banks, and credit unions.

"depository institution" implies, a large portion of the liabilities of these FIs are deposits. The deposits have been issued by the depository institutions in order to obtain funds (inputs) that can be used to make loans and other investments (outputs). Deposit-type FIs are also important in the nation's money supply process because many of their deposit liabilities are checkable deposits.[8] Let's take a closer look at the institutions within this category.

Commercial Banks

Commercial Banks
Depository institutions that issue checkable, time, and savings deposit liabilities and, among other things, make loans to commercial businesses.

The word "bank" is derived from the Italian word *banca*, which referred to the table, counter, or place of business of a money changer. Although modern banks bear little physical resemblance to ancient money changers, their functions remain quite similar. In modern parlance, **commercial banks** are typically defined as institutions that issue checkable deposit liabilities and extend loans to commercial businesses. These two characteristics help to differentiate banks from other FIs but, of course, banks do many other things. For example, banks issue time and savings deposits and offer other types of loans including mortgages and consumer loans. They also provide electronic funds transfers, debit cards, international trade-related payments, credit cards, leasing, trust services, financial guarantees, and advisory and accounting services. Chapter 15 explains more about bank services. For now, Exhibit 14-1 presents aggregate balance sheet data for all banks in the United States.

CHECKING ACCOUNT

Transactions Deposits
Deposits that can be exchanged for currency and are used to make payments through writing a check or making an electronic transfer.

Savings Deposits
Highly liquid deposits that can usually be withdrawn on demand but not by writing a check.

Time Deposits
Deposits that have a scheduled maturity and a penalty for early withdrawal.

A bank's success depends on many factors, but especially important is its ability to attract funds by offering deposit liabilities. Deposits fall into three categories: transactions deposits, savings deposits, and time deposits. **Transactions deposits** can be exchanged for currency and are used in transactions to make payments. The deposit claim is transferred by writing a check or making an electronic transfer. **Savings deposits** cannot be withdrawn by writing a check but are highly liquid. By custom, banks usually allow withdrawals on demand although a waiting period can be required. **Time deposits** have a scheduled maturity, and if funds are withdrawn before that date, a penalty is paid—usually the forfeiture of some interest that has already been earned. As we first saw in Chapter 2, a money market deposit account has the characteristics of both transactions and savings deposits.[9] Since deposits are by far the main source of bank funds, banks continually strive to increase deposits. In addition, banks have recently developed other nondeposit sources of funds such as fed funds, repurchase agreements, and Eurodollar borrowings. A bank's success depends on local and regional factors, such as the population and economic vitality of the service area, and its ability to attract deposits away from competing FIs or from banks in other geographical regions.[10]

Turning to the asset side of the balance sheet, a bank must decide how best to use its funds to meet its objectives. Obviously one objective is to maximize profits. Stockholders will see that the bank's management does not lose sight of this goal. Banking can be a risky business, however, and the management and stockholders will also want to minimize the risks faced in the pursuit of profits. In particular, the

---

[8]To clarify, banks attract deposits (inputs) in order to make loans and other investments (outputs). Because banks hold only a fraction of their deposits in reserve, when they make loans, they create checkable deposits and are part of the money supply process. More on this in the appendix of this chapter.

[9]To refresh your memory, money market deposit accounts are individual accounts authorized by Congress in 1982 that offer limited check writing (say, up to three checks per month) and generally pay higher interest than other checkable deposits.

[10]National factors, such as monetary policy, are also an important determinant of a bank's success.

	TOTAL[a]	PERCENT OF TOTAL ASSETS[a]
Financial assets	**$6,592.2**	**100.0%**
Reserves	56.2	.09
Vault cash	37.2	.07
Deposits at the Fed	17.6	.03
Loans	3,899.2	59.00
Business loans	1,462.9	22.20
Mortgages	1,723.1	26.10
Consumer credit	540.2	8.20
Security credit	173.0	2.60
U.S. Government securities	875.5	13.30
Treasury securities	178.1	2.70
Government agency securities	699.5	10.60
Municipal securities	116.2	1.80
Corporate and foreign bonds	326.1	4.90
Miscellaneous	1,319.4	20.00
Liabilities	**6,503.1**	**98.8%**
Checkable deposits	503.4	7.60
Small time and savings deposits		
(including money market deposit accounts)	2,342.1	35.50
Large time deposits	904.8	13.70
Fed funds and repurchase agreements (net)	823.6	12.50
Commercial paper	69.4	1.00
Corporate bonds	295.4	4.50
Loans and advances	179.0	2.70
Miscellaneous	1,277.8	19.40
Net Interbank liabilities	107.6	1.60
To the Fed	−0.2	<−.03
To domestic banks	5.3	<−.10
To foreign banks (Eurodollar Borrowings)	102.5	1.50
Net worth (capital)	**$89.1**[b]	**1.4%**[b]

EXHIBIT 14-1
Financial Assets and Liabilities of Commercial Banks, June 30, 2001 (in billions of dollars)

[a]Details may not sum to totals because of rounding.

[b]This item is not proposed as a measure of capital for use in capital adequacy analysis.

SOURCE: *Flow of Funds Accounts, Z1,* Second Quarter 2001, Board of Governors of the Federal Reserve System, September 18, 2001, p. 69.

bank will try to diversify its portfolio in a way that ensures a considerable margin of liquidity and safety for the bank. Banks seek safety because they are highly leveraged institutions. That is, their assets are overwhelmingly supported by borrowed funds, which are either deposit or nondeposit liabilities. As Exhibit 14-1 shows, liabilities accounted for 98.8 percent of bank assets on June 30, 2001. The exhibit also shows that banks held a mix of loans (including business loans, consumer credit, and mortgages), government securities, municipal securities, corporate and foreign bonds, and other assets. Note that in mid 2001, banks' holdings of mortgages exceeded their holdings of business loans. This represents a dramatic change over the past 30 years. Business loans were traditionally the lending venue for banks while mortgages were held by S&Ls. With the passage of new legislation in 1999, banks may also underwrite and deal in municipal revenue bonds.[11]

http://www.fdic.gov/ bank/statistical/index. html
Provides banking statistics for the latest quarter.

---

[11]The new legislation is the Gramm-Leach-Bliley Act, which was passed in November 1999. This landmark legislation is further discussed in Chapters 15 and 17.

In addition to these interest-earning assets, banks also hold reserve assets to help meet their liquidity and safety objectives and because the Fed forces them to do so. As we first saw in Chapter 4, the Fed sets reserve ratios that require banks to possess reserve assets equal to a certain percentage of checkable deposit liabilities.

Banks' concerns about liquidity are partly generated by the nature of their sources of funds. For example, checkable deposits, which are obviously payable on demand, can and often do fluctuate widely. Nondeposit liabilities have the potential to fluctuate even more. For instance, if a bank's solvency is questioned or if another depository institution offers better rates, a bank can quickly lose some nondeposit funds such as fed funds, repurchase agreements, and Eurodollar borrowings, which are usually placed for a relatively short time period.[12] When deposits and nondeposit liabilities fall, even the most solvent bank must have a cushion of liquidity enabling it to meet these withdrawals. Such liquidity needs can be satisfied by holding some highly liquid assets, such as Treasury bills and non-interest-bearing cash reserves.[13] If profits were all that mattered, a bank would never hold a Treasury bill yielding 5 percent if another, equally safe asset, such as a guaranteed student loan yielding 6 percent, was available.[14] However, the liquidity of Treasury bills in effect provides an implicit return to banks in addition to the explicit yield.

Guided by its liquidity, safety, and earnings objectives, a bank must make portfolio decisions regarding the optimal mix of loans, securities, and reserves it will hold. Simply put, this means the bank must decide on the best way to use its funds.

The *capital base* is the value of the bank's assets less the value of its liabilities. In general, the smaller the capital base, the more vulnerable the bank is to adverse developments. Assume that some of a bank's larger loans go sour when the borrowers default and fail to pay the principal and interest due. These defaults will reduce the cushion provided by the bank's capital base and push the bank toward insolvency and bankruptcy. For example, suppose the bank's capital base amounts to 8.4 percent of assets. Thus, for every $1 million in assets, the bank holds only $84,000 in capital. If loans are 65 percent of assets, the bank's capital will be gone if 12.9 percent of its loans go sour.[15] We hope you can see why regulators are concerned that banks maintain adequate capital.

Savings Associations

Savings associations include S&Ls and savings banks. **Savings and loan associations (S&Ls),** originally known as building and loan associations, were founded in the United States in the early 1830s. Their express purpose was to pool the savings of local residents to finance the construction and purchase of homes. **Savings banks** predate the S&Ls by about 20 years and are located mostly on the East Coast of the United States. Sixty percent are in New York and Massachusetts. Like

Savings Associations
S&Ls and savings banks.

Savings and Loan Associations (S&Ls)
Depository institutions established for the purpose of pooling the savings of local residents to finance the construction and purchase of homes; S&Ls have offered checkable deposits since 1980.

Savings Banks
Depository institutions set up to help finance the construction and purchase of homes; located mainly on the East Coast.

---

[12]Small depositors do not have to worry about the solvency of their bank as long as it is a member of the Federal Deposit Insurance Corporation (FDIC). Currently, the deposits of all FDIC member banks are insured up to $100,000.

[13]Banks may also hold liquid assets so that they will be able to accommodate unexpected loan demands from valued customers.

[14]Don't forget that by holding long-term, fixed-rate financial assets, banks are exposed to an interest rate risk. If the interest rate rises, the value of the asset falls. This risk is minimal for Treasury bills, which will be maturing in the near future.

[15]If loans are 65 percent of all assets and 12.9 percent go bad, then 8.4 percent (= .65 × .129) of the assets will be worthless. This is an equivalent way of saying that the bank has lost all of its capital.

S&Ls, savings banks were founded to encourage thrift and to help finance the construction and purchase of homes.[16]

In the mid-1990s, the assets of S&Ls were more than three times those of savings banks. Nevertheless, because their assets and liabilities have a similar composition and the institutions share other commonalities, we have lumped S&Ls and savings banks together as savings associations. Their combined balance sheet appears in Exhibit 14-2.

The major sources of funds for savings associations are time, savings, and checkable deposits. In the aggregate, these deposits accounted for about 60 percent of total liabilities on June 30, 2001. As in commercial banks, most deposits are insured up to $100,000. Savings associations were first allowed to issue negotiable order of withdrawal (NOW) accounts (interest-earning checkable deposits) nationwide in 1980. Checkable deposits make up a growing source of funds for savings associations. Savings associations use the funds mainly to acquire mortgage loans, which

	TOTAL[a]	PERCENT OF TOTAL ASSETS[a]
Financial assets	**$1,273.9**	**100%**
Reserves at the Fed	1.0	<.1
Checkable deposits and currency	21.7	1.7
Time and savings deposits	2.4	.2
Fed funds and repurchase agreements	22.0	1.7
U.S. government securities	158.2	12.4
Municipal securities	4.0	.3
Corporate and foreign bonds	93.1	7.3
Mortgages	751.7	59.0
Consumer credit	65.3	5.1
Corporate equities	25.6	2.0
Loans and advances	43.8	3.4
Miscellaneous	85.1	6.7
Liabilities	**$1,241.3**	**97.4%**
Deposits	755.5	59.3
Checkable	291.9	22.9
Small time and savings	307.2	24.1
Large time	156.4	12.3
Repurchase agreements	69.6	5.5
Corporate bonds	6.4	.5
Loans and advances	288.1	22.6
Miscellaneous	121.7	9.5
Net worth (capital)	**$32.6[b]**	**2.6%[b]**

EXHIBIT 14-2
Financial Assets and Liabilities of Savings Associations, June 30, 2001 (in billions of dollars)

[a]Details may not sum to totals because of rounding.

[b]This item is not proposed as a measure of capital for use in capital adequacy analysis.

SOURCE: *Flow of Funds Accounts, Z1,* Second Quarter 2001, Board of Governors of the Federal Reserve System, September 18, 2001, p. 73.

---

[16]The original savings banks were "mutuals," which meant that the depositors were really the owners of the institutions. They were actually benevolent philanthropic institutions set up to encourage the poor and the working class to save to relieve poverty and pauperism. The poor deposited whatever pennies they could, and the funds were managed by wealthy entrepreneurs. Today, roughly two-thirds of the savings banks retain this form of ownership, while one-third have sold stock and converted their ownership to stock savings banks.

comprised about 59 percent of total assets held in mid 2001. U.S. government securities made up another 12.4 percent of assets.

Although still specializing in mortgage lending, savings associations diversified somewhat during the 1980s into other forms of lending previously prohibited by regulations. Other regulatory changes allowed the institutions to offer time deposits with rates that went up and down in tandem with rates on money market instruments like Treasury bills.

Prior to the 1980s, savings associations were not only prohibited from offering checkable deposits, but they could not exceed a ceiling rate or cap set by regulators on the rates paid on time and savings deposits. In this earlier environment, small savings deposits were the major source of funds for savings associations. Small savers found passbook savings accounts attractive relative to the alternatives available to them. The accounts were liquid, safe, insured stores of value with fixed interest rates. In the new environment, savings associations have more flexibility and now offer the public diverse types of liabilities. As a result, there is more competition among banks, S&Ls, and savings banks to attract checkable and flexible rate time deposits.

During the 1980s, the S&L industry experienced multiple strains that came to be known as the savings and loan crisis or debacle. More than 500 institutions became insolvent and were seized by regulators during the late 1980s at the taxpayers' expense.[17] The **Financial Institutions Reform, Recovery, and Enforcement Act (FIRREA) of 1989** attempted to resolve the crisis by creating a new federal regulatory structure, limiting the assets S&Ls can acquire, and requiring S&Ls to maintain adequate capital. As of December 31, 1999, the final cost to the taxpayers for the bailout was approximately $124 billion, which was much less than initial estimates.

Although heavily committed to the mortgage market, savings banks were somewhat more diversified than were the S&Ls during the 1980s. They held a substantial quantity of federal, municipal, and corporate securities. This diversification, plus higher reserve ratios, allowed the savings banks to avoid some of the strains experienced by the S&Ls.

The changes in the structure of the assets and liabilities of savings associations over time suggest that FIs' areas of specialization increasingly overlap. Furthermore, recent legislation now allows banks and savings associations to merge. Reflecting this trend, the term "bank" is often used by the press and the public in reference to commercial banks, S&Ls, and savings banks.

Credit Unions

Credit unions cater almost exclusively to small (in terms of dollars) savers and borrowers. They are cooperative, nonprofit, tax-exempt associations operated solely for the benefit of members. By law, members must share "a common bond" such as an employer, a church, or a labor union. Not just anybody can "join"—deposit in or borrow from—a particular credit union. Although there are about 20,000 credit unions, most are small in size; 75 percent have total assets of $5 million or less. As in other depository institutions, deposits may be insured up to $100,000. Exhibit 14-3 lists the major assets and liabilities of credit unions.

Credit unions get most of their funds from members' savings accounts. Additionally, as with S&Ls, regulatory changes first permitted credit unions to offer checkable deposits in 1980. Interest-earning checking accounts at credit unions are

Financial Institutions Reform, Recovery, and Enforcement Act (FIRREA) of 1989
An act that attempted to resolve the S&L crisis by creating a new regulatory structure, limiting the assets S&Ls can acquire, and requiring S&Ls to maintain adequate capital.

Credit Unions
Depository institutions that are cooperative, nonprofit, tax-exempt associations operated for the benefit of members who share a common bond.

---

[17]We should also note that the bailout benefited the taxpayers by maintaining the solvency of the financial system.

	TOTAL[a]	PERCENT OF TOTAL ASSETS[a]
Financial assets	**$476.2**	**100%**
Checkable deposits and currency	18.1	3.8
Time and savings deposits	18.7	3.9
Fed funds and repurchase agreements	8.3	1.7
U.S. government securities (Treasury and agency securities)	72.2	15.2
Mortgages	130.3	27.4
Consumer credit	187.0	39.3
Miscellaneous	41.5	8.7
Liabilities	**$431.3**	**90.6%**
Shares/deposits	426.3	89.5
Checkable	54.2	11.4
Small time and savings	342.8	72.0
Large time	29.3	6.2
Miscellaneous	5.0	1.0
Net worth (capital)	**44.9[b]**	**9.4%[b]**

[a]Details may not sum to totals because of rounding.

[b]This item is not proposed as a measure of capital for use in capital adequacy analysis.

SOURCE: *Flow of Funds Accounts, Z1,* Second Quarter 2001, Board of Governors of the Federal Reserve System, September 18, 2001, p. 74.

EXHIBIT 14-3
Financial Assets and Liabilities of Credit Unions, June 30, 2001 (in billions of dollars)

called *share drafts*, and as Exhibit 14-3 shows, they are now a significant liability for credit unions. As of June 30, 2001, about 39 percent of the assets held by credit unions were in the form of consumer loans to members while over 27 percent were mortgages. Just over 15 percent of the assets held were U.S. Treasury and government agency securities. The remaining assets were deposits at other FIs, fed funds, repurchase agreements, and miscellaneous items. Credit unions, which are exempt from most taxes, generally do not hold municipal securities. Municipals pay a lower interest rate because their interest is exempt from federal taxation.

Although these proportions have been remarkably stable over time, the total funds acquired and loaned by credit unions have grown rapidly. In 1970, for instance, their assets totaled only $18 billion while in 2000, this figure was over $441 billion. Thus, credit union assets increased roughly 20-fold while prices a little more than quadrupled! Being nonprofit institutions, credit unions have often offered depositors slightly higher rates and loan applicants slightly lower rates than offered by competing FIs. This advantage, along with the convenient locations of many credit unions (close proximity to businesses or the company cafeteria, for example), helps to explain their growth.

RECAP The major sources of funds for commercial banks are checkable, savings, and time deposits plus nondeposit liabilities. Banks' major uses of funds are loans, government securities, and reserves. Because of legislation in 1999, banks have also been authorized to underwrite and deal in municipal revenue bonds. The major sources of funds for S&Ls are time, savings, and checkable deposits. The major use of funds is to make mortgage loans. Credit unions are tax-exempt and small in size but numerous. Their main sources of funds are share drafts and small savings accounts. They primarily make small personal and mortgage loans to their members and invest in government securities.

Contractual-Type FIs

As the name suggests, contractual-type FIs have liabilities defined by contract. These contracts generally call for regular payments to be made to the FIs in exchange for future payments under specified conditions. As mentioned earlier, these claims are often referred to as *contingent claims*. Specifically, life and property and casualty insurance companies require premium payments in exchange for insurance coverage. Public and private pension funds require regular contributions, usually with each paycheck, in exchange for retirement benefits.

Life Insurance Companies
Intermediaries that offer protection against the financial costs associated with events such as death and disability in exchange for premiums.

Life insurance companies offer the public protection against the financial costs, losses, and reductions in income associated with death, disability, old age, and other health problems. Based on the principle of risk sharing, the public makes payments, generally called *premiums*, in exchange for this protection. The companies lend out the funds collected to other households, businesses, and governments. The interest and dividend income received from the loans and the stocks and bonds, along with the premiums, is used to pay benefits to policyholders as they come due. The influx of premium payments is relatively steady and predictable, and statisticians (actuaries) can predict fairly well the proportion of policyholders likely to become disabled, die, or become ill in a given year. Thus, life insurance companies have a reasonably predictable stream of benefit payments to policyholders distributed over time. This allows these institutions to use a fairly large portion of their funds to acquire longer-term assets or financial investments. Longer-term instruments generally provide higher yields than shorter-term assets but are not as liquid. Given the nature of the companies' liabilities, holding a large portion of liquid assets is not as essential for them as it is for banks, for example.

Exhibit 14-4 shows that on June 30, 2001, about 39 percent of life insurance companies' assets were corporate and foreign bonds, about 30 percent were equities, about 8 percent were mortgages, about 9 percent were U.S. government securities, and the remainder were miscellaneous items. The liabilities are the policy benefits (reserves) that are due and will be paid to policyholders in the future.

Pension Funds
Tax-exempt intermediaries set up to provide participants with income at retirement in exchange for premiums.

Pension funds are tax-exempt institutions set up to provide participants with retirement income that will supplement other sources of income, such as Social Security benefits. Some pension plans are run by private corporations while others are associated with government units. Like life insurance companies, pension funds have little need for a large amount of liquid assets. The number of people likely to retire each year is quite predictable. As a result, private pension funds and those associated with government units place about 81 percent of their funds—acquired through contributions by employees and employers—in corporate equities, U.S. government securities, corporate and foreign bonds, and mutual funds. Exhibit 14-5 shows that on June 30, 2001, of the approximate $6.7 trillion of assets held by these funds, $3,137.8 billion were in corporate equities, $834.6 billion were in U.S. government securities, $690.8 billion were in corporate and foreign bonds, and $800.0 billion were in mutual funds. In fact, pension funds are the largest single class of investors in equities![18] The liabilities are the policy benefits that will be paid out to policyholders in the future.

---

[18]This being the case, it is worth noting that the often-heard calls to "tax corporations more" might, if implemented, have the effect of reducing corporate profits and, thus, dividends paid to shareholders, such as pension funds. The result would be smaller pensions for retirees. This is an example of the interdependencies we have been emphasizing.

	TOTAL[a]	PERCENT OF TOTAL ASSETS[a]
Financial assets	**$3,223.6**	**100%**
Checkable deposits, currency, and money market fund shares	216.9	6.7
Corporate and foreign bonds	1,280.3	39.7
Corporate equities	955.1	29.6
U.S. government securities	297.7	9.2
Mortgages	236.1	7.3
Policy loans	103.1	3.2
Mutual fund shares	46.1	1.4
Open market paper	53.5	1.7
Miscellaneous	29.6	.9
Liabilities	**$3,006.2**	**93.3%**
Life insurance reserves	807.5	25.0
Pension fund reserves	1,405.1	43.6
Miscellaneous	791.7	24.6
Net worth (capital)	**$217.4[a]**	**6.7[a]**

EXHIBIT 14-4
Financial Assets and Liabilities of Life Insurance Companies, June 30, 2001 (in billions of dollars)

[a]Details may not sum to totals because of rounding.

[b]This item is not proposed as a measure of capital for use in capital adequacy analysis.
SOURCE: *Flow of Funds Accounts, Z1,* Second Quarter 2001, Board of Governors of the Federal Reserve System, September 18, 2001, p. 75.

	TOTAL[a]	PERCENT OF TOTAL ASSETS[a]
Financial assets	**6,651.8**	**100%**
Checkable deposits and currency	17.0	.26
Time and savings deposits	118.8	1.80
Repurchase agreements	70.8	1.10
Money market mutual funds	85.9	1.30
Mutual funds	800.0	12.00
Corporate equities	$3,137.8	47.20
U.S. government securities (Treasury and agency securities)	834.6	12.50
Municipals	1.5	.02
Corporate and foreign bonds	690.8	10.40
Mortgages	38.6	.58
Commercial paper	72.1	1.10
Miscellaneous	783.8	11.80
Liabilities	**6,755.5**	**100%**
Pension fund reserves	$6,755.5	100%

EXHIBIT 14-5
Financial Assets and Liabilities of Public and Private Pension Funds, June 30, 2001 (in billions of dollars)

[a]Details may not sum to totals because of rounding.
SOURCE: *Flow of Funds Accounts, Z1,* Second Quarter 2001, Board of Governors of the Federal Reserve System, September 18, 2001, p. 76.

In contrast to life insurance companies, which provide financial protection against adverse developments affecting individuals, **property and casualty companies**—in exchange for premiums—provide protection against the untoward effects of unexpected occurrences on property, particularly automobiles and homes. Two factors are relevant in trying to understand the composition of assets held by these FIs: (1) Unlike pension funds, which are nontaxable, and life insurance companies, which are taxed at

Property and Casualty Companies
Intermediaries that provide protection against the effects of unexpected occurrences on property.

	TOTAL[a]	PERCENT OF TOTAL ASSETS[a]
Financial assets	**$866.1**	**100%**
Checkable deposits, currency, and repurchase agreements	38.6	4.5
Corporate equities	184.7	21.3
Municipal securities	186.1	21.5
U.S. government securities	131.8	15.2
Corporate and foreign bonds	191.2	22.0
Trade receivables	68.6	7.9
Miscellaneous	63.7	7.4
Liabilities	**572.3**	**66.1%**
Net worth	293.8	33.9[b]

[a]Details may not sum to totals because of rounding.

[b]This item is not proposed as a measure of capital for use in capital adequacy analysis.

SOURCE: *Flow of Funds Accounts, Z1,* Second Quarter 2001, Board of Governors of the Federal Reserve System, September 18, 2001, p. 75.

a very low rate, property and casualty companies are taxed at the full 35 percent corporate rate; and (2) compared to life insurance companies and pension funds, the stream of benefit payments made by these companies is less predictable. Accidents and natural disasters do not follow regular patterns. Hurricane Andrew in 1992 was followed by the great Mississippi flood of 1993, the Northridge earthquake in 1994, and Hurricane Opal in 1995. Indeed, the attack on the World Trade Center and the Pentagon on September 11, 2001 is expected to be the largest loss for property and casualty companies in history, dwarfing all other single accidents or natural disasters. Tax considerations lead property and casualty companies to hold about 23 percent of their assets, which totaled $866.1 billion on June 30, 2001, in the form of tax-exempt municipal securities. (See Exhibit 14-6.) The need for liquidity helps to explain the 19.7 percent of assets held in the form of Treasury securities, checkable deposits, currency, and repurchase agreements.

Investment-Type FIs

The major types of intermediaries in the investment category are mutual funds, also known as investment companies, and money market mutual funds. Generally, **mutual funds** acquire and pool funds from the public, invest the funds in capital market instruments, and return the income received, minus a management fee, to the investors. Some funds invest in particular types of securities, such as corporate stocks and bonds, while others have broader asset portfolios that include stocks, bonds, mortgages, gold, and so on. In the 1990s, mutual funds experienced tremendous growth. Small depositors, seeking higher returns than the low rates offered by depository institutions at the time, poured funds into mutual funds. Mutual funds began expanding to offer other financial services previously provided by banks. Some have expressed concern regarding the adequacy of the regulation of mutual funds, given their growth in the 1990s (more on this in Chapter 20).

Money market mutual funds, mentioned briefly in Chapters 2 and 9, are a good example of funds that limit the type of financial claims they purchase.[19] They

Mutual Funds
Investment-type
intermediaries that pool
the funds of SSUs,
purchase the long-term
financial claims of DSUs,
and return the income
received minus a fee to
the SSUs.

---

[19]In reality, money market mutual funds are a subcategory of the general category of mutual funds. However, when we refer merely to mutual funds, we mean those that invest primarily in capital market instruments as opposed to money market instruments.

Mutual Funds		
	TOTAL[a]	PERCENT OF TOTAL ASSETS[a]
Financial assets	**$4,269.9**	**100%**
Repurchase agreements	91.2	2.10
Corporate equities	3,225.9	70.10
U.S. government securities (Treasury and agency)	426.7	9.90
Municipal bonds	239.7	5.60
Corporate and foreign bonds	397.4	9.30
Commercial paper	87.7	2.10
Miscellaneous	1.6	.04
Liabilities	**$4,269.9**	**100%**
Mutual fund shares	**$4,269.9**	**100%**

Money Market Mutual Funds		
	TOTAL[a]	PERCENT OF TOTAL ASSETS[a]
Financial assets	**$2,014.8**	**100%**
Checkable deposits and currency	−2.8	<−.14
Small time and savings deposits	171.5	8.50
Repurchase agreements	208.2	10.30
Foreign deposits	110.4	5.50
U.S. government securities (Treasury and agency)	361.3	17.90
Municipals	255.2	12.70
Commercial paper	638.2	31.70
Corporate and foreign bonds	159.9	7.90
Miscellaneous	112.8	5.60
Liabilities	**$2,014.8**	**100%**
Money market fund shares	**$2,014.8**	**100%**

[a]Details may not sum to totals because of rounding.

SOURCE: *Flow of Funds Accounts, Z1,* Second Quarter 2001, Board of Governors of the Federal Reserve System, September 18, 2001, p. 77.

EXHIBIT 14-7
Financial Assets and Liabilities of Mutual Funds and Money Market Mutual Funds, June 30, 2001 (in billions of dollars)

. acquire funds from individual investors and pool them to purchase money market instruments such as Treasury bills, bank CDs, and commercial paper. The interest earned, minus a management fee, is then paid to investors. Exhibit 14-7 shows the major assets and liabilities of mutual funds and money market mutual funds.

Finance Company-Type FIs

Finance companies, such as Household Finance Corporation, Beneficial Finance, Commercial Credit Corporation, and the General Motors Acceptance Corporation lend funds to households to finance the purchase of consumer durables such as automobiles, appliances, and furniture and to businesses to finance inventories and the purchase or leasing of equipment. In the past, finance companies often loaned to borrowers considered risky by other types of FIs, particularly depository institutions. Today finance companies lend to all types of borrowers. As Exhibit 14-8 shows, finance companies held assets totaling $1,123.8 billion on June 30, 2001. Their major sources of funds come from selling commercial paper and issuing long-term bonds.

Finance Companies
Intermediaries that lend funds to households to finance consumer purchases and to firms to finance inventories.

EXHIBIT 14-8
Financial Assets and
Liabilities of Finance
Companies, June 30,
2001 (in billions of
dollars)

	TOTAL[a]	PERCENT OF TOTAL ASSETS[a]
Financial assets	**$1,123.8**	**100%**
Checkable deposits and currency	29.3	2.6
Mortgages	157.1	14.0
Consumer credit	191.0	17.0
Other Loans	481.5	42.8
Miscellaneous	264.9	23.6
Liabilities	**$1,160.2**	**103.2%**
Corporate bonds	504.6	44.9
Bank loans	45.2	4.0
Commercial paper	177.3	15.8
Miscellaneous	423.6	37.7
Net worth (capital)	**−36.4[b]**	**−3.2%[b]**

[a]Details may not sum to totals because of rounding.

[b]This item is not proposed as a measure of capital for use in capital adequacy analysis.

SOURCE: *Flow of Funds Accounts, Z1,* Second Quarter 2001, Board of Governors of the Federal Reserve System, September 18, 2001, p. 79.

RECAP **Contractual-type intermediaries offer contingency claims in return for regular payments. They include life insurance companies, property and casualty companies, and pension funds. Investment-type intermediaries (mutual funds and money market mutual funds) pool funds from the public, invest the funds, and return the income received—less a management fee—to the investors. Finance company-type intermediaries lend to households to purchase consumer durables and to businesses to finance inventories.**

Pulling Things Together

FIs can be classified into four groups:

1. Deposit types (banks, S&Ls, savings banks, and credit unions)
2. Contractual types (insurance companies and pension plans)
3. Investment types (mutual funds and money market mutual funds)
4. Finance company types

As Exhibit 14-9 shows, contractual-type FIs are now the largest group of FIs in terms of total assets, while pension plans are the single largest type of FI. Just a few years ago, banks were the largest FIs. Each group can be distinguished from other groups by the financial services it specializes in and the composition of the group's balance sheets. Such factors also help to distinguish one member of a group from other members of the same group. Specifically, the composition of each FI's balance sheet depends mainly on (1) the range of financial services offered to the public; (2) any specialization in particular services offered to the public, perhaps as a result of custom; (3) the tax status of the institution; (4) the nature of the institution's liabilities; and (5) legal constraints or regulations governing the types of assets and liabilities that can be acquired.

Examples of these factors at work include the following:

1. S&Ls, reflecting custom and regulations, specialize in mortgage lending because they have a perceived competitive advantage and some tax advantages in that area.

	1970	1984	1991	1998	2001*
Deposit type:					
Commercial banks	$505	$1,951	$3,414.4	$5,635.5	$6,592.2
Savings associations	252	1,180	1,144.9	1,088.1	$1,273.9
Credit unions	18	116	240	394.5	476.2
Contractual type:					
Life insurance companies	201	697	1,499.5	2,819.5	$3,223.6
Property and casualty companies	50	251	575.8	884	866.1
Pension funds	170	1,211	1,892.1	6,675.3	6,651.8
Investment type:					
Mutual funds	47	368	840.7	3,626.1	4,269.9
Money market mutual fund	—	—	535	1,334.2	2,014.8
Finance company type	64	306	559.7	826.6	1,123.8

EXHIBIT 14-9
Total Financial Assets
of Principal FIs
(in billions of dollars)

*Figures for 2001 are as of June 30, 2001.
SOURCE: Figures for 1970 are from the *Annual Statistical Digest,* Federal Reserve Board, 1991, various pages.
Figures for 1984 and 1990 are from the *Flow of Funds Accounts, Z1,* Fourth Quarters, 1984, 1990, 1998.
Figures for 2001 are from the *Flow of Funds Accounts, Z1,* Second Quarter, 2001, various pages.

2. Tax-exempt FIs, such as credit unions and pension funds, generally do not hold tax-exempt municipal securities. Institutions subject to the full corporate income tax, such as banks and property and casualty insurance companies, do hold such assets.

3. FIs, such as life insurance companies, that have a relatively steady and predictable inflow of funds and a fairly predictable stream of liabilities (payment outflows) hold more long-term and less-liquid assets than do FIs, such as banks, that have a greater need for liquidity because a considerable portion of their liabilities (deposits) are payable on demand.

4. Banks do not hold corporate equities because regulations prohibit it.

In addition, the nature of an FI's assets and liabilities determines the degree to which it must manage specific risks. For instance, an FI with a high percentage of long-term, fixed-rate assets must manage interest rate risks to a greater degree than an FI whose assets and liabilities do not have such a maturity configuration. Likewise, an FI with uncertain payment contingencies must manage the liquidity risk to a greater degree than an FI whose payments are more certain and stable.

Together, regulations and customs can account for many of the differences among FIs. Nevertheless, while such distinguishing characteristics should not be ignored, it is equally important to keep sight of the "common threads" that bind all types of FIs together. Moreover, as this chapter has suggested, FIs are undergoing fundamental changes.

At the risk of oversimplification, we can say banks are increasingly trying to enter markets for financial services traditionally provided by other FIs, while other FIs are increasingly trying to enter markets traditionally served by banks. This process of homogenization and the trend toward financial supermarkets mean that Sandi and Dave, whom we met at the beginning of the chapter (and the rest of us), no longer have to deal with five different types of FIs. One FI may provide the services previously supplied by many.

Although not all attempts at creating financial supermarkets have been successful, Merrill Lynch is a prime example of a supermarket that has prospered. It is the nation's largest brokerage firm, the second-largest mutual fund company, the largest investment underwriter, and a major insurance broker. In addition, it manages retirement accounts, makes mortgages and other business loans, and manages a successful

Gramm-Leach-Bliley Act (GLBA)
Legislation that removed decades-old barriers between banking and other financial services by creating financial holding companies that linked commercial banks with securities firms, insurance firms, and merchant banks; passed by Congress in November 1999 and became effective March 2000.

money market mutual fund. The trend toward supermarkets eroded the effectiveness of various regulations and thereby produced fundamental changes in regulations and traditional competitive positions. The tendency toward consolidation of financial services was given new impetus by the passage of the **Gramm-Leach-Bliley Act (GLBA)** in November 1999. This act, effective in March 2000, removed decades-old barriers between banking and other financial services by creating financial holding companies that linked commercial banks with securities firms, insurance firms, and merchant banks. (More on the GLBA in Chapters 15 and 17.)

Even though banks and other intermediaries have experienced tremendous growth, they are losing ground to other nonfinancial institutions and direct financing venues, which have grown even faster. As mentioned previously, many large and small corporate borrowers now borrow by issuing commercial paper rather than obtaining bank loans, and many nonfinancial corporations such as Sears, AT&T, and General Motors now issue credit cards. Additionally, more and more consumers bypass S&Ls to obtain mortgage loans directly from mortgage brokers.

Despite these ongoing developments, banks (and other depository institutions) probably remain the most important type of FIs because they have been central to the Fed's conduct of monetary policy and the determination of the money supply. They have also been at the forefront of innovation and deregulation. The appendix of this chapter looks at the money-creation process that results when a depository institution creates a checkable deposit in the loan-making process. The next chapter focuses on banks and the banking industry.

Summary of Major Points

- In general, FIs are profit-seeking firms that link up DSUs and SSUs and, in the process, provide the public with a wide range of financial services. The linking or channeling function involves the acquisition of financial claims on DSUs by the FIs and the acquisition of claims on the FIs by SSUs.

- The quantity, quality, and type of financial services offered by FIs varies with the perceived profitability of engaging in various activities.

- FIs provide services to the public to reduce the risks and costs associated with borrowing and lending and other financial transactions. They also afford the public protection against the financial costs associated with various contingencies and fulfill the demand for various financial claims.

- Most FIs are heavily regulated. Historically, regulations tended to encourage specialization by certain types of FIs, in particular, financial services and, thus, limited competition among different types of FIs. More recently, FIs have come to appreciate the benefits of diversifying and providing the public with a wider range of financial services. This trend has led to various, often successful attempts to innovate around existing

regulations, and competition has increased as a result. Recent changes in regulations have allowed banks, insurance companies, and securities firms to affiliate under common ownership.

- All FIs are exposed to various risks in varying degrees. Credit or default risk is the risk that a DSU will not live up to the terms of the liability it has sold. Interest rate risk is the risk that unexpected changes in the interest rate will cause the value of fixed-rate financial assets to fall or that the FI will experience a negative spread between assets and liabilities. Liquidity risk is the risk that the FI will not have funds available to make required payments and will be unable to convert long-term assets to liquid funds quickly without a capital loss. Exchange rate risk is the risk that changes in exchange rates will cause the FI to experience looses in the dollar value of foreign currency or foreign financial assets that the FI holds.

- The differences among FIs manifest themselves in the financial services the institutions specialize in and the composition of their balance sheets. The composition of a balance sheet depends mainly on the range of financial services offered;

any specialization in particular services, perhaps as a result of custom; the tax status of the institution; the nature of the FI's liabilities; and legal constraints or regulations.

- FIs can be grouped or classified according to the nature of their liabilities or the major activity (financial service) they engage in. The major groups are deposit type, including banks, S&Ls, savings banks, and credit unions; contractual type, including insurance companies and pension plans; investment type, including mutual funds and money market mutual funds; and finance company type. The contractual-type group is the largest group, and pension plans are the single largest FI.

- The major sources of funds for commercial banks are checkable, savings, and time deposits plus nondeposit liabilities such as corporate bonds, fed funds, repurchase agreements, and Eurodollar borrowings. The major uses of funds for banks are loans, government securities, and reserves. The major sources of funds for S&Ls are time, savings, and checkable deposits. The major use of funds is to make mortgage loans. Credit unions are tax-exempt, small in size, and numerous. Their main sources of funds are share drafts and small savings accounts. They primarily make small personal and mortgage loans to their members and invest in government securities. Savings banks, located mostly on the East Coast, lend heavily in the mortgage market.

- Contractual-type intermediaries offer contingency claims in return for regular payments. They include life insurance companies, property and casualty companies, and pension funds. Investment-type intermediaries (mutual funds and money market mutual funds) pool funds from the public, invest the funds, and return the income received, less a management fee, to the investors. Finance company-type intermediaries lend to households to purchase consumer durables and to businesses to finance inventories.

- (App.) Open market purchases increase the supply of reserves while open market sales decrease the supply of reserves. Any one institution can safely lend only its excess reserves. When the proceeds of a loan are spent, however, deposits and reserves flow into another depository institution, which responds by expanding loans and creating additional deposition. Deposits and the money supply expand by a multiple of the injection of reserves.

- (App.) $ER = TR - RR$. If depository institutions are loaned up, then $TR = RR = r_D \times D$. The simple money multiplier is $1/r_D$, since $\Delta D = 1/r_D \times \Delta TR$.

- (App.) The monetary base is reserves, TR, plus currency in the hands of the public, C. The money supply will be equal to the monetary base, MB, times the money multiplier. The actual money multiplier is more complicated than the simple money multiplier because depository institutions may hold excess reserves, ER, equal to some fraction of deposits and the public may withdraw cash as deposits expand to maintain a desired currency-to-deposits C/D ratio. Taking both effects into account, the money multiplier is $[(1 + c)/(r_D + e + c)]$ since $[(1 + c)/(r_D + e + c)] \times \Delta MB = \Delta M$.

Key Terms

Balance Sheet
Commercial Banks
Contingent Claims
Credit Unions
Excess Reserves (ERs) (App.)
Exchange Rate Risk
Finance Companies
Financial Innovation
Financial Institutions Reform, Recovery, and Enforcement Act (FIRREA) of 1989
Fractional Reserve Banking System (App.)

Gramm-Leach-Bliley Act (GLBA)
Life Insurance Companies
Liquidity Risk
Loaned Up (app.)
Monetary Base (MB) (App.)
Money Multiplier (App.)
Mutual Funds
Pension Funds
Property and Casualty Companies
Required Reserves (RRs) (App.)

Savings and Loan Associations (S&Ls)
Savings Associations
Savings Banks
Savings Deposits
Simple Money Multiplier (App.)
Thrifts
Time Deposits
Total Reserves (TRs) (App.)
Transactions Deposits

Review Questions

1. List two services that FIs provide to the public. Why do intermediaries provide these services? What is a contingent financial claim? Give two examples.

2. "With financial intermediation, SSUs can earn a higher return on their surplus funds, and DSUs can acquire funds at a lower cost." Explain how this seemingly contradictory statement can be true. (Hint: Consider a risk-free return.)

3. How are FIs like other firms? How are all FIs similar? How are they different?

4. If an FI has mainly long-term liabilities with few payment uncertainties, in what type of assets is it most likely to invest? Why?

5. What is a depository institution? What are the main types of depository institutions? What distinguishes them from other intermediaries?

6. Why do banks hold reserve assets?

7. Identify the major contractual-type FIs. What are their main sources of funds (liabilities) and their main uses of funds (assets)?

8. What are the main sources of funds (liabilities) and uses of funds (assets) for finance company-type FIs?

9. Why does A-1 Student Auto Insurance Company need to hold more liquid assets than Senior Life Insurance Company? How do depository institutions manage liquidity risk?

10. John, a recent college graduate, is buying his first house. From which FIs could he obtain a mortgage loan?

11. How do money market mutual funds differ from mutual funds? How are money market mutual funds similar to depository institutions? As an investor, Sam holds both mutual funds and money market mutual funds. Holding which asset entails greater interest rate risk for him? Why?

12. Would a property and casualty company hold municipal securities in its portfolio of assets? What about a credit union and a life insurance company? Why or why not?

13. How can diversification reduce credit or default risk? In the event of widespread economic collapse, will diversification always reduce this risk?

14. What are the major determinants of an FI's liability structure? Give examples of each.

15. What was the purpose of the Financial Institutions Reform, Recovery, and Enforcement Act (FIRREA) of 1989? Why was the act needed?

16. Which FIs have deposit insurance?

17. What is a mutual savings bank? (Hint: See footnote 16.)

18. (App.) If a depository institution has excess reserves, how much can it safely lend? If e increases given c and r_D, how can the Fed offset this change in e?

Analytical Questions

19. If a bank has assets of $100 million and liabilities of $95 million, what is its net worth? If 60 percent of its assets are loans, what percentage of the loans could go sour before the bank would lose all of its capital?

20. Make a chart listing the main sources of funds (liabilities) and main uses of funds (assets) in order of importance for the following depository institutions: commercial banks, S&Ls, mutual savings banks, and credit unions. Describe how the sources and uses of funds have changed through the years for the various depository institutions.

21. What type of risk does each of the following situations portray?
    a. After the Northridge earthquake, several major insurance companies did not have sufficient cash assets available to meet casualty claims.
    b. ABC Bank, located along the U.S.-Mexican border, was holding a large quantity of Mexican pesos when the value of the peso collapsed.
    c. Friendly S&L specializes in fixed-rate mortgages. There is a sharp increase in short-term interest rates.
    d. A family needs funds immediately to meet a medical emergency. All of its assets are tied up in real estate.
    e. I am planning a trip to Europe next summer and have exactly $5,000. At the present exchange rates, I will have a great time. Is there any doubt?
    f. Chad takes a loan for an expensive racing truck and then loses his job.

22. (App.) If $r_D = .25$, what is the simple money multiplier? If reserves increase by $100, how much do loans and deposits increase?

23. (App.) Assume the Fed sets the required reserve ratio equal to 10 percent. If the banking system has $20 million in required reserve assets, what is the amount of checkable deposits outstanding?

24. (App.) If $c = .35$, $r_D = .10$, and $e = .10$, what is the money multiplier? If a depository institution's excess reserves increase by $400, how much can it safely lend? *Ceteris paribus*, how much money will the banking system create?

25. (App.) In each of the following fictitious examples, tell whether the money multiplier will increase, decrease, or stay the same:
    a. Depositors become concerned about the safety of depository institutions, and there is no deposit insurance.
    b. Depository institutions do not see any creditworthy borrowers.
    c. The Fed lowers the required reserve ratio.
    d. Depository institutions believe that overall default risk has decreased.

Internet Exercises

1. The FDIC maintains a web page at **http://www.fdic.gov**. A useful link at this site provides quarterly banking statistics. Click on the "Statistical" link under bank data. Access the latest balance sheet of all FDIC-insured depository institutions and answer the following:
   a. What is the total number of commercial banks in the United States?
   b. What is the amount of total assets that are owned by all FDIC-insured depository institutions in the United States?
   c. What are the various components on the liability side of commercial banks' balance sheets?

2. Some interesting facts about the FDIC can be found at the following Web site: **http://www.fdic.gov/about/learn/learning/index.html**. Access this site and answer the following:
   a. Whose deposits does the FDIC insure, and what does the federal deposit insurance cover?
   b. What is the amount of FDIC insurance coverage? If you have deposits in several different FDIC-insured banks, will your deposits be added together for insurance purposes?

Suggested Readings

The *Journal of Financial Intermediation* has numerous articles that deal with material in this chapter. It is available on the Internet at **http://www.academicpress.com/jfi**.

For a look at how technology is impacting on financial intermediation, see "Earthquake on the Street", *Economist*, May 20, 2000.

For a look at "The Future of Financial Intermediation and Regulation: An Overview," see the article by Stephen Cecchetti, *Current Issues in Economics and Finance*, Federal Reserve Bank of New York, Vol. 5, No. 8, May 1999.

For a review of the role of financial intermediation in the current financial environment, see Allen Franklin, "The Theory of Financial Intermediation," *Journal of Banking and Finance* 21:11–12 (December 1997): 1461–1485.

An interesting article that touches on the history of financial institutions is Eugene N. White, "Were Banks Special Intermediaries in Late Nineteenth Century America?" *Federal Reserve Bank of St. Louis Review* 80:3 (May/June 1998): 13–32.

Two rather fun books to read about FIs (and lots of other related subjects) are Tom Wolfe, *The Bonfire of the Vanities* (New York: Farrar, Strauss, & Giroux, 1987); and Martin Mayer, *The Money Bazaars* (New York: Mentor, 1984).

Appendix 14-A

Depository Institutions, and the Money Supply Process

http://www.newyorkfed.org/pihome/fedpoint/fed32.html

Provides an excellent description of the Federal Reserve's open market operations and a discussion of how they enable the Fed to influence short-term interest rates.

http://www.newyorkfed.org/pihome/fedpoint/fed08.html

Provides information on the Federal Reserve float and its consequences for the banking system.

As we have seen, depository institutions include banks, savings and loan associations, credit unions, and mutual savings banks. They issue checkable deposits and hold reserve assets equal to a fraction of deposit liabilities. Taken together, depository institutions make up the banking system.

This appendix focuses on the ways in which the operations of the Fed affect the banking system and the ways that depository institutions, in turn, influence the supply of money and credit in the economy.

Open market operations are the buying and selling of government securities by the Fed. They affect the supply of reserves available to depository institutions. The volume of reserves has a direct effect on the banking system's ability to extend loans and thereby expand checkable deposits and the supply of money. When the Fed buys securities, reserves of depository institutions rise. When the Fed sells securities, reserves of depository institutions fall.[20] In practice, most of the Fed's transactions are conducted electronically and occur quickly. Regardless of timing, however, the essential point is that through its open market operations, the Fed can inject or remove reserves from the banking system.

---

[20]Other factors besides open market operations can affect reserves. One of the major factors is changes in discount loans. As discussed in Chapter 4, the Fed operates a lending facility called the discount window through which depository institutions caught short of reserves can borrow. Another factor that influences reserves is Federal Reserve float, which results from the check-clearing process. Federal reserve float is the excess in reserves that results from a check being credited to one depository institution before it is debited from another. If one of these other factors causes an unexpected increase in reserves, the Fed can use an open market sale to decrease reserves. Likewise, if an unexpected decrease in reserves occurs, the Fed can use an open market purchase to increase reserves. In general, these offsetting open market sales and purchases are designed to counter movements in the reserves of depository institutions caused by other factors so as to maintain existing reserve conditions in the banking system.

Changes in reserves affect the volume of deposits and loans in the banking system. To simplify, we will employ a balance sheet for a bank in our hypothetical banking system.

PROTOTYPE BALANCE SHEET FOR A BANK

Assets	*Liabilities*
Reserves	Checkable deposits
Loans	

On the assets side are reserves and loans. For simplicity, other assets are ignored. On the liabilities side, we shall assume that there are only checkable deposits, the major component of the nation's money supply. Thus, we are ignoring other deposit and nondeposit liabilities and net worth. In addition, we focus only on changes in assets and liabilities resulting from various transactions.

Look at Exhibit 14A-1. Let's assume that HLT National Bank begins with $1,000 of new **total reserves (TRs)** and $1,000 of new deposit liabilities, which resulted from an open market purchase. Here we are assuming that the Fed purchased the security from the public and paid for the security with a check drawn on the Fed. The public deposited the check in HLT. HLT owes the public $1,000 of new checkable deposit liabilities. HLT submits the check to the Fed for collection and, hence, receives $1,000 of new reserves.

Where do we go from here? HLT is not in business to hold idle funds as reserves; it uses funds deposited with it to acquire assets that earn interest income. If the Fed insists that HLT hold **required reserves (RRs)** equal to 10 percent of its checkable deposit liabilities, the remaining 90 percent of reserves are **excess reserves (ERs).** In this example, required reserves are $100 (10% × $1,000) and excess reserves (total reserves minus required reserves) are $900 ($1,000 – $100).

Given their desire for profits, we assume that HLT and other depository institutions in our system will not wish to hold any excess reserves and will, therefore, use such funds to acquire assets. In our simple model, loans are the only assets that are acquired. Assuming new loan customers are readily available, we are ready to consider the first stage of what will be a multistage process of loan and deposit expansion.

It just so happens that J. P. Young needs $900 to purchase a new stereo. Given the excess reserves it has on hand, HLT agrees to lend J.P. $900. He signs a loan contract, which HLT puts in its vault, and HLT credits $900 to J.P.'s deposit balance. The loan contract is an asset while the deposit balance is a liability. Exhibit 14A-1 also shows the

Total Reserves (TRs)
Required reserves plus excess reserves.

Required Reserves (RRs)
The amount of reserve assets that the Fed requires a depository institution to hold.

Excess Reserves (ERs)
Reserves over and above those required by the Fed.

EXHIBIT 14A-1
Loan and Deposit Expansion at HLT National Bank

HLT NATIONAL BANK

Assets		Liabilities	
Total reserves	$1,000	Checkable deposits	$1,000

HLT has just seen both its total reserve assets and its checkable deposits increase by $1,000. Assuming the bank was loaned up to begin with, this represents an increase of $100 in required reserves and $900 in excess reserves. The bank can safely lend out its excess reserves. When a loan is made, the proceeds are disbursed by creating a checkable deposit. The bank's assets increase by the amount of the loan.

Assets		Liabilities	
Total reserves	$1,000	Checkable deposits	$1,000
Loan	900	New checkable deposits	900
Total	**$1,900**	**Total**	**$1,900**

EXHIBIT 14A-2

Transactions between HLT National Bank and Second National Bank

HLT NATIONAL BANK

Assets		Liabilities	
Total reserves	$ 100	Checkable deposits	$1,000
Loan	900		
Total	$1,000		$1,000

SECOND NATIONAL BANK

Assets		Liabilities	
Total reserves	$900	Checkable deposits	$900
Total	$900		$900

balance sheet entries for HLT and J.P. after this transaction. Combining this stage with the initial situation, HLT's balance sheet shows a $900 rise in assets—the $900 loan is added to the original $1,000 in reserves. There is also a $900 increase on the liability side—the new $900 deposit in J.P.'s account is added to the original $1,000 deposit. Since deposits increase when the $900 loan is made, $900 of money has been "created."

Remember, however, that J.P. did not borrow the money to keep in his account. J.P. writes a check for $900 to pay I.M. Loud, Inc. for the stereo equipment. We will assume I.M. Loud, Inc. does its banking at Second National Bank. Accordingly, I.M. Loud deposits the check received from J.P. in its deposit account at Second National. Second National credits I.M.'s account, and when the check is cleared, the Fed will debit (decrease) HLT's deposit account at the Fed by $900 and credit (add to) Second National's deposit account at the Fed by the same amount. HLT will, in turn, debit J.P.'s account for $900 for the check written to I.M. This series of transactions is shown in Exhibit 14A-2.

So what is the net effect of those transactions on the supply of money and credit in the economy? When J.P. writes a check for $900 against his account at HLT, this reduces HLT's deposit liabilities and reserve assets by $900. (The $900 in reserve assets is credited to I.M. Loud's bank, Second National.) If we sum up the charges on HLT's balance sheet (bottom row), we see that the initial $1,000 deposit inflow is balanced by a $100 rise in reserves and a $900 rise in loans. HLT is now fully **loaned up,** which means that it has no excess reserves left to serve as a basis for lending. The $100 of reserves it holds are all required reserves. HLT responded to the initial deposit inflow by expanding its loans and deposits by 90 percent of the inflow. Thus, HLT, and indeed any individual depository institution, can make additional loans and thereby "create" deposits equal to its excess reserves.

The process has not ended, however. Take a close look at Second National's balance sheet. With $810 of excess reserves, it is clearly not loaned up. Just as HLT did, Second National will react to the deposit inflow ($900) by setting aside enough to meet the Fed's reserve requirement and lending out the rest. In this case, given our assumption of a 10 percent reserve requirement, it will keep $90 as required reserves and will have $810 of excess reserves. The excess reserves will serve as the basis of lending to, say, Jane Collins, who happens to need exactly $810 to pay her fees at State University. Jane gives a check to the university, which then deposits it in Third National Bank, as depicted in Exhibit 14A-3. As was the case before, the clearing of the check results in the Fed crediting Third National's account at the Fed by the same amount. Second National will, in turn, debit Jane's account by the same $810, leaving it fully loaned up with the original gain of $900 in deposits on the liability side of its balance sheet and a rise of $90 in required reserves and $810 in loans on the asset side of its balance sheet. (Again, $810 in total reserve assets have been credited to Third National, State University's bank, because Jane's

Loaned Up
When a bank has no excess reserves left to serve as a basis for lending.

SECOND NATIONAL BANK

Assets		Liabilities	
Total reserves	$ 900	Checkable deposits	$ 900
Loans	810	Checkable deposits	810
Total	$1,710		$1,710

The proceeds of the loan from Second National are spent and deposited in the university's account at Third National. Second National loses $810 in reserve assets, and the $810 deposit of the loan proceeds is extinguished. The resulting balance sheets of Second National and Third National are as follows:

SECOND NATIONAL BANK

Assets		Liabilities	
Total reserves	$ 90	Checkable deposits	$900
Loans	810		
Total	$900		$900

THIRD NATIONAL BANK

Assets		Liabilities	
Total reserves	$810	Checkable deposits	$810
Total	$810	Total	$810

check is written to State.) If you are with us, you should now be able to describe what will happen in the next stage.

We have shown that each individual bank was able to increase its earnings assets by the amount of the excess reserves that resulted from a deposit inflow. But why can't an individual bank (or other depository institution for that matter) expand deposits by more than its excess reserves (90 percent of the inflow)? In general, a bank cannot assume that new deposits created in conjunction with loans will be spent and redeposited in its coffers. Rather, it should expect to lose reserves equal to the loans extended and deposits created. If it loaned out, say, $1,000 (100 percent of the inflow) and subsequently lost $1,000 of reserves, it would find itself with the original $1,000 inflow of deposits on the liability side. If you think this is okay, you've forgotten one important factor—the Fed's reserve requirements. All depository institutions must have $100 of required reserves for each $1,000 of checkable deposits. To ensure that it meets the requirement, an individual institution will normally limit lending and deposit creation to its excess reserves.

As the loans of one depository institution increase, however, the use of the loan proceeds by the borrower lead to a deposit inflow at another institution. A deposit inflow increases total deposit liabilities and reserve assets. The depository institution will adjust to the inflow of reserves and deposits by expanding its loans and "creating" additional deposits. Subsequently, the individual institution will lose reserve assets and the additional deposit liabilities as the borrower uses the loan proceeds to pay for a purchase. However, one institution's loss is another's gain. Note that as this process occurs, the total volume of reserves in the banking system does not change. Instead, at each stage, deposits rise and the composition of total reserves in the banking system changes—required reserves rise and excess reserves fall.

The size of these changes can be stated precisely. As deposits flow through the banking system, the change in deposits at each depository institution can be represented as the change in required reserves plus the change in excess reserves. The change in required reserves is equal to 10 percent of the deposit inflow while the change in excess reserve assets is equal to 90 percent of the deposit inflow. Hence, the change in loans and deposits "created" by each depository institution is equal to 90 percent of the inflow to that institution. In our example, the $1,000 increase in deposits at HLT is followed by a $900 increase in deposits at Second National, which is followed by an $810 increase in deposits at Third National. Taken together—that is, adding up the changes in all the individual balance sheets, the increase in total deposits in the banking system at each stage as loans are extended is 90 percent of the new deposits "created" at the previous stage. This means that, ultimately, the new deposits created at subsequent stages approach zero and the process ends. To illustrate, $.9 \times \$1,000 = \$900$; $.9 \times \$900 = \$810$; $.9 \times \$729 = \$656.10$; $.9 \times \$656.10 = \$590.49$ and so on.

Perhaps the most important aspect of the process to fix in your mind is that the total expansion of loans and deposits ($1,000 + $900 + $810 +. . .) is much greater than the initial injection of reserves into the banking system. In fact, the expansion of loans and deposits turns out to be a multiple of the initial injection of reserves. Some simple algebra presented in the next section will help confirm this point.

RECAP Open market purchases increase the supply of reserves while open market sales decrease the supply of reserves. Any one institution can safely lend only its excess reserves. When the proceeds of a loan are spent, however, deposits and reserves flow into another depository institution, which responds by expanding loans and creating additional deposition. Deposits and the money supply expand by a multiple of the injection of reserves.

The Simple Multiplier Model of the Money Supply Process

In our simple example, the process of creating money and credit from increases in reserves will end when all reserves in the banking system become required reserves—that is, when the banking system is fully loaned up. This situation is reached gradually as individual depository institutions "create" deposit liabilities and at the same time increase assets (loans in this case) in response to deposit inflows. When no excess reserves are left in the banking system, new loans cannot be made and new deposit creation ceases. The net result of the actions taken by individual depository institutions for the banking system and the economy as a whole can be illustrated with the aid of a simple model.

Required reserve assets, RR, are by definition equal to the **required reserve ratio,** r_D, multiplied by the amount of deposit liabilities, D:

(14A-1) $$RR = r_D \times D$$

Excess reserves, ER, are by definition equal to total reserves, TR, minus required reserves.

(14A-2) $$ER = TR - RR$$

If total reserves equal required reserves, there are no excess reserves to serve as the basis of lending. As already discussed, this is the case when the banking system is fully loaned up. Therefore, when ER equals zero,

(14A-3) $$TR = RR = r_D \times D$$

Rearranging terms yields:

(14A-4) $$D = TR/r_D$$

or

$$D = 1/r_D \times TR$$

Total deposits are equal to the quantity of reserves multiplied by the reciprocal of the required reserve ratio. We shall refer to $1/r_D$ as the **simple money multiplier.**

For any change in reserves, TR, the change in deposits, D, is equal to the simple money multiplier ($1/r_D$) multiplied by the change in reserves, TR. Assuming excess reserves equal zero, we can rewrite Equation (14-4) as:

(14A-5) $$\Delta D = 1/r_D \times \Delta TR$$

Simple Money Multiplier
The reciprocal of the required reserve ratio, $1/r_D$.

Since we assumed that r_D was fixed at 10 percent (.1) in our example, the simple money multiplier is 1/.1, which is equal to 10. Therefore, the increase in deposits resulting from the $1,000 increase in reserves will be $10,000, assuming depository institutions hold no excess reserves. Although in our example reserves increased by $1,000, make sure you understand that the simple money multiplier works in both directions. If reserves decrease by $1,000, assuming depository institutions hold no excess reserves, there would be a corresponding decrease in deposits of $10,000.

Sometimes students come away from the preceding analysis feeling that they do not really understand how an injection of reserves into the banking system by the Fed leads to multiple increases in the money supply and credit. For those of you who fall into this category, we can illustrate this phenomenon without resorting to equations. Here is another way to understand this process.

The simple multiplier process is a reflection of what is called the **fractional reserve banking system.** A depository institution must hold reserve assets equal to some fraction of deposit liabilities. The fraction it must hold is determined by the reserve requirements set by the Fed. If the reserve requirement is 100 percent, any increase in deposits would result in an identical dollar-for-dollar increase in required reserves. In this case, the simple money multiplier would equal 1. If the reserve requirement is less than 1, however, a given dollar increase in deposits will result in the need to hold required reserves equal to only some fraction of the increase in deposits. The remaining fraction of reserve assets is excess reserves and can serve as the basis of lending, which becomes new deposits as described earlier. In this latter case, the total change in deposits is greater than the amount of required reserves, and therefore, the multiplier is greater than 1. In general, the change in deposits and credit, which accompanies a given change in reserves, will be inversely related to reserve requirements. That is, for a given change in reserves, the smaller the required reserve ratio is, the larger the change in deposits and credit will be. Exhibit 14A-4 shows various combinations of required reserve ratios and the resulting simple money multiplier.

Fractional Reserve Banking System
A banking system in which individual banks hold reserve assets equal to a fraction of deposit liabilities.

The original injection by the Fed leads to increased reserve assets and deposit liabilities and provides individual depository institutions with excess reserves. They adjust to this abundance of reserves by expanding loans and deposits. The deposits, when spent by loan recipients, flow to other depository institutions, which, in turn, expand loans and deposits. The process continues because profit-maximizing institutions are, in general, not interested in holding non-interest-earning excess reserves. As a result, the original injection of reserves can support a multiple expansion in loans and deposit. The whole process is not unlike a family tree. A husband and wife have children, who, in turn have children, and so forth.

http://www.ny.frb.org/ pihome/fedpoint/ fed45.html
Provides details on reserve requirements and their role in monetary policy.

Even though we have ignored many real-world details, several policy implications flow from the preceding analysis. First, a given dollar change in reserves will lead to a larger (multiple) change in the money supply and credit extension. Since the Fed can ultimately control the supply of reserves in the banking system with its open market operations, the Fed has considerable influence on the lending activity of depository institutions and, therefore, the availability of funds in the financial system. Second, if the multiplier was really as simple as $1/r_D$, the Fed could actu-

EXHIBIT 14A-4
The Required Reserve
Ratio and the Simple
Money Multiplier

r_D	Simple Money Multiplier
.05	1/.05 = 20
.10	1/.10 = 10
.20	1/.20 = 5
.25	1/.25 = 4
.50	1/.50 = 2

As the required reserve ratio increases, the simple multiplier decreases. Intuitively, if the Fed increases the required reserve ratio, depository institutions have to hold more reserve assets and have fewer excess reserves to lend.

ally control the money supply precisely. Simple arithmetic is all that would be required. If the Fed could control total reserves, TR, because it sets reserve requirements, r_D, it could make deposits, D, in Equation (14A-4) or, more generally, the money supply, do anything it wanted, assuming depository institutions wish to maintain zero excess reserves.

As the next section explains, however, the multiplier is actually more complicated than $1/r_D$ and is not under the Fed's complete control. Nevertheless, such complications should not obscure two features of monetary control: (1) the Fed's enormous influence on the value of borrowing and lending in the economy, and (2) the cumulative process linking the Fed's actions to deposit creation and, hence, to the money supply. Simply put, whenever the Fed reports a large monthly decrease in the money supply, such as the one described at the beginning of the chapter, you can be reasonably sure that the decrease, to a large extent, is due to prior Fed actions, particularly open market sales.

RECAP $ER = TR - RR$. **If depository institutions are loaned up, then** $TR = ER = r_D \times D$. **The simple money multiplier is** $1/r_D$ **because** $\Delta D = 1/r_D \times \Delta TR$.

Some Complicating Realities in the Multiplier Model

Let us take a look at the simplifying assumptions we made in developing our model of how money and credit are created and their implications. First, we assumed that depository institutions never hold any excess reserves. When deposits flow in and reserve assets increase, depository institutions continue to lend by creating new deposit liabilities until excess reserves equal zero. In fact, depository institutions do hold excess reserves, and the amount fluctuates over time. The excess reserves are a leakage from the flow of increases in deposits and credit extension. The effect of this leakage is similar to the effect of an increase in reserve requirements. The amount of loans and deposits created at each stage will be reduced by the volume of excess reserves held. The net effect will be to lower the simple money multiplier.

Second, we have ignored currency. If the stereo dealer (I.M. Loud) in our example exchanges J.P.'s $900 check for a $675 deposit at Second National and $225 of currency from the vault at Second National, the net change in the reserves of Second National is less than J.P.'s check. Second National has an increase in its reserve account at the Fed of $900, a reduction in vault cash of $225, and a net change in reserves of $675. In other words, the stereo dealer exchanges the $900 check for a deposit equal to three-fourths of the amount of the check and currency equal to one-fourth of the amount. This will reduce the flow of reserves and deposits from Second National to subsequent depository institutions by 25 percent and, hence, reduce the overall expansion of the money supply.

As a result of these implications, the actual multiplier is clearly not as simple as the one presented in Equation (14A-4). We can develop a somewhat more realistic multiplier model by taking into account the factors already mentioned. Let us see what happens when we recognize that depository institutions hold excess reserves. Now total reserves, TR, are equal to required reserves, RR, against checkable deposits, $r_D \times D$, plus excess reserves, ER.

(14A-6) $$TR = RR + ER$$

or

$$TR = (r_D \times D) + ER = r_D D + ER$$

Next, assume that depository institutions hold excess reserve assets equal to a constant proportion of checkable deposit liabilities, D. For example, say they hold a few cents of excess reserve assets per dollar of deposits. Given this assumption, we can define ER as being equal to eD, where e is the ratio of excess reserves held to checkable deposits, ER/D. More directly, e is the ratio of excess reserves depository institutions choose to maintain relative to the size of their deposit liabilities. Substituting this expression into Equation (10-6) yields:

(14A-7) $$TR = r_D D + eD = (r_D + e)D$$

Solving this equation for D yields:

(14A-8) $$D = 1/(r_D + e)TR$$

And in terms of changes in reserves and deposits, we have:

(14A-9) $$\Delta D = 1/(r_D + e) \, \Delta TR$$

Equation (14A-9) defines the new relationship between deposits and reserves. Two things are important to note about this relationship. First, the multiplier in Equation (14A-9), $1/(r_D + e)$, is smaller than the simple multiplier, $1/r_D$, in Equation (14A-5). For example, if r_D is .10 and e is .02, the multiplier is 8.33 [$1/(.10 + .02) = 8.33$], rather than 10 ($1/.10 = 10$). Second, the multiplier is not under the complete control of the Fed. Depository institutions can control the excess reserve ratio, e, which suggests that control by the Fed is not a matter of simple arithmetic.

In recent years, the excess reserves held by depository institutions have generally fluctuated between $.75 billion and $1.8 billion. (During this time, total reserves fluctuated between $45 billion and $65 billion.) The changes in excess reserves contribute to fluctuations in the multiplier and make it difficult to predict precisely. This difficulty is especially relevant in the short run (week to week and month to month). Over a longer period, say, 3 to 6 months, the fluctuations largely average out. That is, a large increase during one week is offset by a large decrease during another week. Hence, controlling the money supply is less difficult for the Fed over longer periods than over shorter periods.

Having shown that depository institutions can affect the multiplier through e, let us examine how the public can affect the money supply through its currency-holding behavior. Recall that the total money supply, M, is equal to checkable deposits, D, plus currency in the hands of the public, C. Let us assume that the public also desires to maintain its currency holdings as a constant proportion of its checkable deposits. Currency held by the public, C, is equal to cD, where c is the desired ratio of currency to checkable deposits, C/D. Thus, we can write:

(14A-10) $$M = D + C = D + cD = (1 + c)D$$

Monetary Base (MB)
Reserves plus currency in the hands of the public; denoted as *MB*.

Taking account of the public's desire to maintain its currency holdings equal to cD, we can see that open market purchases of securities by the Fed may result in an increase in both reserves and currency in the hands of the public. As members of the public sell securities, their checkable deposits increase, and they exchange some of those deposits for currency to maintain the desired currency-to-deposits ratio, c.

We define the **monetary base (MB)** as the sum of reserves and currency in the hands of the public, $TR + C$. Although open market purchases initially show up as increases in reserves, which lead to new lending and deposit creation, the reserves become severely depleted as the newly created deposits are exchanged for currency to maintain the desired currency-to-deposits ratio. Thus, when the Fed engages in open market operations, both reserves and currency in the hands of the public can change. In reality, open market operations change the monetary base. The multiplier is affected because some of the newly created deposits are exchanged for currency. Making the appropriate substitution for reserves from Equation (14A-7) and substituting cD for C, as noted previously, we arrive at Equation (14A-11):

(14A-11)
$$MB = TR + C$$
$$= (r_D + e)D + cD$$
$$= (r_D + e + c)D$$

Rearranging terms, we get:

(14A-12)
$$D = [1/(r_D + e + c)]MB$$

Equation (14A-12) shows the relationship between the monetary base and deposits. By combining Equations (14A-10) and (14A-12), we can derive the relationship between the monetary base and the money supply, M:

(14A-13)
$$M = D + C$$
$$= [1/(r_D + e + c)]MB + C$$
$$= [1/(r_D + e + c)]MB + cD$$
$$= [1/(r_D + e + c)]MB + c[1/(r_D + e + c)]MB$$
$$= [1/(r_D + e + c)]MB \times (1 + c)$$
$$= [(1 + c)/(r_D + e + c)]MB$$

In terms of changes in the monetary base and the money supply and assuming r_D, e, and c remain constant, we have:

(14A-14)
$$[(1 + c)/(r_D + e + c)]\Delta MB = \Delta M$$

Money Multiplier
The multiple of the change in the monetary base by which the money supply will change.

Equation (14A-14) defines the change in the money supply in terms of the monetary base and the expanded multiplier, which we will now refer to simply as the **money multiplier.** Taking account of another complication (the currency drain) has reduced the multiplier; if c is equal to .3, the multiplier is $(1 + .3)/(.1 + .02 + .3) = 3.1$, rather than the 8.33 in Equation (14A-9). Because we are using M1 as our measure of the money supply, our money multiplier is actually the M1 multiplier.

To summarize, in this more complete model, the money multiplier is the multiple of the change in the monetary base by which the money supply will change. Thus, in our example, when the Fed uses open market purchases to increase the monetary base by $1,000, the money supply will increase by $3,100. The new money multiplier takes into account excess reserves and the currency drain. In the simple money multiplier case, the simple multiplier is the multiple by which a change in reserves leads to a change in deposits and loans without considering other factors.

RECAP The monetary base is reserves, *TR*, plus currency in the hands of the public, *C*. The money supply will be equal to the monetary base, *MB*, times the money multiplier. The actual money multiplier is more complicated than the simple money multiplier because depository institutions may hold excess reserves, *ER*, equal to some fraction of deposits, and the public may withdraw cash as deposits expand to maintain a desired currency-to-deposits, *C/D*, ratio. Taking both effects into account, the money multiplier is $[(1 + c)/(r_D + e + c)]$ since $[(1 + c)/(r_D + e + c)] \, \Delta MB = \Delta M$.

The Fed's Control over the Money Supply

We could go on adding complications, but we hope you get the point. When the Fed engages in open market operations, reserves and the monetary base change. Compare Equations (14A-5) and (14A-14). In Equation (14A-14), the multiplier is smaller, and the Fed's control of the money supply is not so straightforward. The public, rather than the Fed, controls *c* and depository institutions determine *e*.

Since *c* and *e* vary over time, the multiplier linking the monetary base and the money supply is not perfectly stable or predictable, especially in the short run. And what does that mean? It means that even if the Fed can control the monetary base, it may find controlling the money supply somewhat more difficult, especially in the short run. Over a longer period, fluctuations in the *c* and *e* ratios and, thus, the multiplier, tend to offset one another. That is, a large increase is offset by a large decrease in some other period. Consequently, the Fed's ability to predict the money multiplier and, thus, control the money supply, improves considerably over a longer time period.

The multiplier model presented in this chapter yields many insights into the money supply process, the interaction among depository institutions, and the effect of Fed actions. You should recognize, however, that it is really a "sausage grinder" model—the Fed increases the monetary base, you crank the handle, and loans, deposits, and currency held by the public come out at the other end. This model leaves out some of the points developed in earlier chapters. Nevertheless, when the Fed engages in open market operations, the effects ripple through the entire financial system, including loans, deposits, credit availability, currency held by the public, and the monetary aggregates.

Remember that depository institutions are firms, and like other firms they are interested in maximizing profits. Given this objective, firms will consider the costs and revenues associated with alternative courses of action, such as lending versus not lending or borrowing reserves versus not borrowing reserves. The multiplier model simplifies away such notions. In particular, the cost of deposits and the return on loans—in other words, interest rates—were ignored. We simply assume that depository institutions always have customers ready, willing, and able to borrow.

The model also neglects to consider the creative ways that banks and other depository institutions develop to get around reserve requirements when the banking system is demanding more reserves than the Fed is willing to supply. The Eurodollar market is a prime example of a way that a bank can change a deposit liability with its corresponding reserve requirement into a nondeposit liability free of a reserve requirement. Credit extension can continue, even without the Fed feeding additional reserves into the system.

Also remember that the discount window can affect the supply of reserves and the monetary base as well. Acting as the lender of last resort through its discount facility, the Fed could supply depository institutions with all the reserves they demand. In reality, the Fed can discourage discount window borrowing by raising the discount rate and making it uncomfortable for depository institutions to borrow from the discount window. Borrowing, after all, is a privilege, not a right, and should be exercised only to cover temporary shortfalls of reserves, never to extend new loans.

Given the preceding clarifications, some economists suggest that teaching this multiplier model should only be done from a historical perspective. They believe that in the complex financial system today, the model is merely a historical artifact with little relevance to the way depository institutions behave. If viewed with caution, we believe that the model gives some insight into the workings of the banking system. Perhaps that is why we have relegated the material to an appendix.

chapter

Commercial Banking Structure, Regulation, and Performance

15

> **Learning Objectives** *After reading this chapter, you should know:*

- Who regulates whom in the banking system and why
- What a bank holding company is and why virtually all large banks are now organized as holding companies
- What a financial holding company is
- The nature of and reasons for the recent wave of bank mergers
- The profitability of the banking system in recent years

" "
A holding company is the people you give your money to while you're being searched.
—Will Rogers

The Biggest Intermediary in Town

The chief executive officer (CEO) convenes the regular Monday morning meeting of the managers of the bank's key divisions. As the division heads report, the managers learn that several large corporate customers are requesting short-term loans and that deposit growth has slowed in recent weeks. In response to this and other information, the CEO instructs the manager of the bank's liabilities to borrow more funds in the certificate of deposit (CD) market and directs the senior loan officer to pursue the corporate loan business aggressively by offering attractive terms on the requested loans. Since the slowdown in deposit growth appears to be related to increased competition from other financial intermediaries (FIs) in the area, particularly one large savings and loan (S&L), the managers endorse a major marketing plan designed to inform the public about several new services now available to depositors. The CEO also brings the committee members up-to-date on bank mergers among some key competitors. She also discusses several possible mergers upper management is considering. Although mergers are supposed to exploit economies of scale and make the bank more profitable, committee members silently worry that they may translate to a loss of jobs. Lastly, "the chief" directs the members of the committee to be "on their toes." Bank regulators have arrived to conduct their periodic examination of the bank's books and operations.

This story depicts the start of a fairly normal week at a bank. We hope it conveys the flavor of the dynamic world of banking and helps to introduce the issues to be examined in this chapter. What risks must banks manage? What competition do banks face in the markets for loans and deposits? What new services are banks offering? Why have there been so many bank mergers in recent years? What is a financial holding company? Who are the regulators, and what are the auditors looking for?

As discussed in Chapter 14, banks are one of the largest types of FIs and play an important role in transferring funds from surplus spending units (SSUs) in our economy to deficit spending units (DSUs). Banks borrow or hire funds from SSUs (lenders) and pay interest on the borrowed funds. They lend funds to DSUs (borrowers) and earn interest on the loaned funds. Ignoring some of the details for the moment, the excess of the interest earned on the loaned funds over the interest paid on the borrowed funds is the profit earned from financial intermediation.

As they "intermediate," commercial banks make a number of decisions. These decisions include (1) the interest rates they will pay to borrow or "hire" funds, (2) the types of deposits they will offer the public, (3) the interest rates they will charge to lend funds, (4) the types of loans they will make, and (5) the type of securities they will acquire. Each of these decisions affects the DSUs' demand for funds (borrowing) from banks and/or the SSUs' supply of funds (lending) to banks. Ultimately, we need to know much more about the macroeconomic and microeconomic aspects of banking. On the macro side, how does bank behavior affect interest rates, the money stock, the volume of credit extended by banks, and economic activity? On the micro side, how do banks make the pricing and quantity decisions just mentioned, how do regulations affect such behavior, and how has bank behavior changed over time? We begin by examining the banking regulations that have led to our current commercial banking system. We then look at how the system's structure has been changing in recent years. Finally, we discuss bank efforts to increase profits and look at how banks have performed in this area in recent years.

Again, we emphasize that banks, like many other firms and industries in our society, are continually changing and innovating. As a result, many institutional details will change as time passes. Nevertheless, we can look at how the banking system evolved to its current state, provide a picture of the current system, and offer a glimpse at where the industry may be going.

The Banking Regulatory Structure

As we saw in Chapters 1 and 4, the banking system is regulated primarily to preserve its safety and soundness and ensure the fair and efficient delivery of banking services to the public. From the regulator's perspective, continual oversight is needed to ensure that banks are operated prudently and in accordance with standing statutes and regulations. Broadly speaking, regulation involves the formulation and issuance of specific rules to govern the structure and conduct of banks.

For the most part, the regulatory structure prevailing at the beginning of the 1970s was inherited from and the product of the 1930s. This structure was put in place as a result of events that occurred at the start of and during the Great Depression. In October 1929, prices on the New York Stock Exchange collapsed. The Dow Jones Industrial Index, a measure of stock market values, stood at 200 in January 1928, rose to 381 in September 1929, and then collapsed, eventually reaching a low of 41 in July 1932. From 1929 through 1933, more than 8,000 banks failed, industrial production fell more than 50 percent, and the nation's unemployment rate rose from 3 percent to 25 percent. At the time, people believed that these events were intimately connected and that the Great Depression was caused and/or severely aggravated by serious defects in the structure and regulation of the financial system. The failure of many financial institutions was alleged to be the result of (1) "excessive and destructive competition" among banks, which had led to the payment of unduly high interest rates on deposits, and (2) the granting of overly risky loans, particularly those extended to stock market speculators. Further, it was believed that banks sought out such loans, and the high yields they carried, because of the high rates being paid on deposits. When the stock market crashed, the value of the speculators' portfolios collapsed, leading them to default on their bank loans. The banks, in turn, became insolvent (bankrupt) or were left so weakened that depositors rushed to withdraw their funds.

Given this diagnosis, the legislative and regulatory remedies established at the time are understandable.[1] Among the most widespread and ultimately pernicious "cures" was the establishment of maximum ceilings on the interest rates banks could pay on deposits. The ceilings, imposed under the **Glass-Steagall Act of 1933,** or the Banking Act of 1933, were popularly known as **Regulation Q.** Interest payments on demand deposits, the only type of checkable deposit in existence at the time, were prohibited, and interest payments on time and savings deposits were not to exceed the rate ceilings set by the relevant regulatory authority. The rationale for the ceilings was seductive and attractive: By holding down the rates on deposits (sources of bank funds), the rates on loans (uses of funds) could be held down. Banks would no longer need to seek out and grant high-risk, high-yield loans.

To further limit bank failures, the Glass-Steagall Act created the **Federal Deposit Insurance Corporation (FDIC).** As noted in Chapter 14, the individual deposits of most banks and other depository institutions are now fully insured up to $100,000. The presence of deposit insurance eliminated bank runs or bank panics in which depositors, fearing their bank would fail, "ran" to get their funds out.

Glass-Steagall Act of 1933
Banking legislation, enacted in response to the Great Depression, that established Regulation Q interest rate ceilings, separated commercial and investment banking, and created the FDIC.

Regulation Q
Interest rate ceilings on deposits at commercial banks that were established during the Great Depression and phased out after 1980.

Federal Deposit Insurance Corporation (FDIC)
The federal agency that insures the deposits of banks and savings associations.

---

[1]Subsequent research has seriously questioned this analysis. For example, it appears that the banks that were paying the very highest rates on deposits prior to the Great Depression were not the most likely to fail.

In addition, the Glass-Steagall Act separated commercial banking from investment banking, which is the underwriting and marketing of primary corporate securities. Banks were no longer allowed to own or underwrite corporate securities. Thus, the assets held by commercial banks were effectively limited to cash assets, government securities, and loans. The commercial banks' role was to accept deposits, paying up to the Regulation Q interest rate ceilings, and to make predominantly commercial loans.

Comptroller of the Currency
The federal agency that charters national banks.

We have already seen the Fed is the most important regulator of commercial banks that are its members. The Fed also sets reserve requirements and provides discount facilities for all depository institutions. Under the regulatory structure that prevailed from the 1930s until the early 1980s, the Fed shared regulatory responsibilities with two federal bodies—the **Comptroller of the Currency** and the FDIC—and with state banking departments. Prior to the 1980s, the scope of regulation included restrictions on entry, branching, types of assets and liabilities permitted, financial services that could be offered, and interest that could be paid on certain types of deposits and charged on certain types of loans. Today, banks have found ways around many of these regulations, and many regulations have been relaxed if not totally eliminated. Recently, other regulations dealing mainly with bank capital requirements and risk management have gained in importance. In Chapter 17, we look at major legislation in recent years that will drastically alter the structure of the banking system.

Chartered
Given permission to engage in the business of commercial banking: banks must obtain a charter before opening.

National Bank
A bank that has received a charter from the Comptroller of the Currency.

To aid in understanding this complex regulatory structure, it is useful to begin with the birth of a bank. Unfortunately (or should we say fortunately), none of us can just decide to open a bank tomorrow. Commercial banks in the United States are **chartered**—that is, they are given permission to engage in the business of commercial banking by either the federal government or one of the 50 state governments. When applying for a charter, the applicant must demonstrate a knowledge of the business of banking and have a substantial supply of capital funds.[2] If a bank's charter is granted by the federal government, the bank is called a **national bank.** The office of the Comptroller of the Currency is the federal government agency charged with chartering national banks. For example, Wells Fargo Bank of San Francisco is a federally chartered bank. A bank can also be chartered by a state banking authority. This system, in which commercial banks are chartered and regulated by the federal government or a state government, is usually referred to as the **dual banking system.** Think of it as a dual chartering system.

Dual Banking System
The system whereby a bank may have either a national or a state charter.

http://www.fdic.gov/ lawsregs
Provides general information about the FDIC, as well as related links.

Federally chartered banks must belong to the Federal Reserve System and subscribe to federal deposit insurance with the FDIC. As mentioned, the latter provides insurance for individual deposit accounts up to $100,000 per account and charges banks an insurance premium that varies with the reserves the insurance fund has available. The premium is slightly more for high-risk banks. Thus, national banks are subject to the regulatory and supervisory authority of the Comptroller, the Fed, and the FDIC.

A state-chartered bank will be regulated by its state banking authority. If it chooses to join the Federal Reserve System, the state bank will also have to subscribe to federal deposit insurance since all Fed members must have FDIC insurance. Thus, in this case, the state-chartered bank will be subject to regulation by the Fed and the FDIC. Finally, state banks may also subscribe to FDIC insurance without joining the Fed.[3]

---

[2]In addition, the applicant must be free of a criminal record.

[3]In 1989, the FDIC was also given the responsibility of insuring the deposits of savings associations (S&Ls and savings banks) that wished to join. At that time, the FDIC was divided into two parts. The Bank Insurance Fund insured commercial bank deposits of member banks while the Savings Association Insurance Fund insured deposits of member savings associations.

LOOKING BACK: *The Origins of the Dual Banking System*

How did we end up with a dual banking system? Actually, it was not the intent of Congress. The National Currency Act of 1863 and the National Banking Act of 1864 established the Comptroller of the Currency, which chartered national banks for the first time. Prior to that time, all banks were chartered by the states. The state banks issued their own bank notes, which, under normal circumstances, were redeemable at face value in the bank's geographic trade area. Outside the bank's geographic area, the notes were often redeemable at less than face value. The bank notes issued by the national banks circulated at full value and were backed by government bonds.

The national acts imposed a 10 percent tax on bank notes issued by state banks. The purpose of the restrictive tax was to make state bank notes so undesirable that state banks would be driven out of business. If they were unable to issue notes, they could not make loans. A financial innovation—the acceptance of demand deposits—saved the state banks from extinction. State banks could stay in business without issuing their own bank notes. The innovation foiled the plans of Congress to put an end to state banks.

Incidentally, if you have any old state or national bank notes lying around your house, you may want to check out how much they're worth. At a recent show in St. Louis, a $10 bank note from Platteville National Bank sold for $9,500.[a]

[a]"The Currency Dealer," *Greensheet Newsletter* (Torrance, CA: December 1995).

One of the interesting and unique features of the system is that those being regulated can choose the regulator. In effect, they can "vote with their feet." By this we mean that banks can apply for either a state or a federal charter or attempt to shift from one to the other.

The decisions made by banks on chartering, branching, and membership in the Fed are captured in Exhibit 15-1. Presumably, these decisions are based on expected profitability. The data in Exhibit 15-1 indicate that as of March 31, 2001, about 73 percent of all banks had state charters while about 27 percent had national charters. Although there are fewer national banks, they have many more branches on average than do state banks. Thus, national banks have more total banking offices (home offices plus branches) than state banks have. Most state-chartered banks do not belong to the Federal Reserve System, although larger state banks do tend to be Fed members.

Historically, most banks, especially smaller ones, found it more profitable to be state-chartered, non-Fed members. State banking authorities were often viewed as being more friendly in regulating and supervising institutions and more lenient in allowing nonbanking activities than their federal counterparts. In addition, the reserve requirements, which specify that a bank must hold reserve assets equal to a portion of its deposit liabilities, were often lower for state-chartered/regulated banks than for national banks regulated by the Fed. Lower reserve requirements

EXHIBIT 15-1
FDIC-Insured Banks, March 31, 2001

	NUMBER OF BANKS	DEPOSITS (IN BILLIONS OF DOLLARS)	ASSETS (IN BILLIONS OF DOLLARS)
Total domestic banks	8,237	$5,764.57	$6,310.81
National charter	2,201	3,134.04	3,440.22
State charter	6,036	2,630.53	2,870.50
Fed member	980	1,540.25	1,666.83
Non-Fed member	5,056	1,090.28	1,203.76

SOURCE: Federal Deposit Insurance Corporation.

meant more potential profits. Because a smaller portion of deposits were held as reserve assets, a larger portion could be used for loans and other interest-earning investments. (Reserve requirements are now the same for all depository institutions.) Larger banks, usually Fed members, often provided nonmembers with many of the services the Fed would normally have provided. Fed members also have to buy stock in the Fed equal to 3 percent of their assets. The stock pays dividends that are lower than what banks could earn by making loans.

More than 97.5 percent of all banks have elected to be part of the FDIC. Apparently, banks feel it is important to offer depositors the safety and peace of mind that federal deposit insurance engenders. For those who think this point is trivial, recall that in the midst of the Great Depression, between 1929 and 1933, more than 8,000 banks failed in the United States. As those banks failed, depositors in other banks rushed to withdraw their funds out of fear that the problems would spread. Such a "run" on even a healthy, solvent bank can cause severe difficulties because the bank's asset portfolio may not have enough cash or liquid assets on hand to pay off the many depositors making withdrawals. Limiting cash withdrawals (to, say, $25 a week) or closing the bank temporarily, reinforced the public's perception that this bank, and perhaps all banks, were in serious difficulty. As the epidemic spread, such illiquid banks were often forced out of business, and the entire financial system was threatened. In what must be judged one of the most successful pieces of legislation in history, Congress created the FDIC in 1933. By and large, this halted the runs on solvent but illiquid banks and thus restored some stability to the banking and financial systems.[4] Deposit insurance was first made a "full faith and credit obligation" of the federal government in 1989. Prior to that year, the FDIC was on somewhat the same footing as private insurance companies in that the federal government was not required by law to pay off depositors if the FDIC ran out of funds in the face of widespread bank failures.

Having a dual banking system with a variety of regulatory authorities leads to a considerable overlap of responsibilities, with some institutions subject to regulation and supervision by as many as three regulatory authorities. In an attempt to minimize the overlap, primary regulatory responsibility for each category of banks has been assigned to one regulator, who then shares the resulting information. Regulatory responsibility has been distributed in the following manner: (1) the FDIC for state-chartered, insured banks that have not joined the Fed; (2) the Comptroller of the Currency for national banks, which also must be FDIC insured and Fed members; (3) the Fed for state-chartered, insured members of the Fed and all bank holding companies (more on them later); and (4) the states for state-chartered banks that do not subscribe to FDIC insurance or belong to the Fed. Exhibit 15-2 gives additional details for each category.

Some people believe that the current set of regulations, supervisory authorities, and statutes of the dual chartering system provides an incentive for state-chartered local banks to structure their services so as to fulfill the needs of their communities. In contrast guidelines for federally chartered banks may relate more to national and international concerns. They also argue that the dual system fosters competition and innovation among banks. Opponents of the dual system argue that the overlapping of regulatory agencies breeds considerable confusion and leads to

---

[4]During 1985 some state-insured (as opposed to federally insured) S&Ls in Maryland and Ohio experienced "runs." This, once again, illustrated the attractiveness of federal insurance to depositors.

EXHIBIT 15-2
Regulatory
Responsibilities

- **FDIC:** Regulates state-chartered, insured non-Fed members and insured branches of foreign banks.
- **Comptroller of the Currency:** Regulates national banks that are not bank holding companies and federally chartered branches of foreign banks.
- **Fed:** Regulates state-chartered, insured members of the Fed, all bank holding companies, all financial holding companies and branches of foreign banking organizations operating in the United States and their parent bank.
- **States:** Regulate state-chartered, non-FDIC-insured banks that are not Fed members.

SOURCE: Federal Deposit Insurance Corporation.

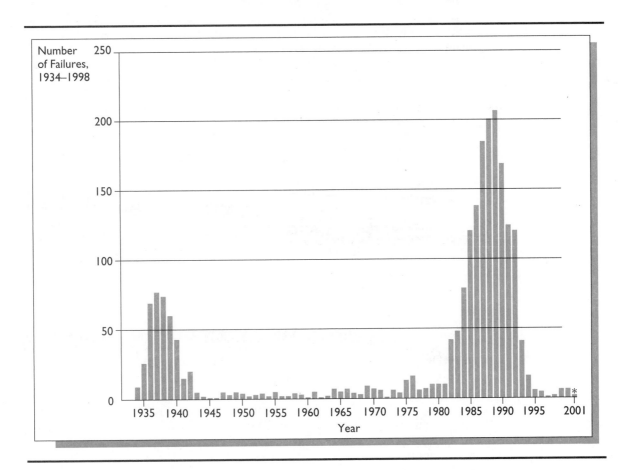

EXHIBIT 15-3
Bank Failures since the Inception of the FDIC, 1934–2001
*Through June 30, 2001.
SOURCE: *FDIC Annual Report,* 1993, Table A, and various FDIC press releases.

lax enforcement. They maintain that this system gives banks considerable freedom to escape proper supervision and regulation.

As Exhibit 15-3 shows, bank failures in the mid- and late 1980s were at the highest level since the inception of the FDIC in 1933. Between 1955 and 1981, bank failures averaged 5.3 per year. Between 1987 and 1990, they averaged a whopping 189 per year! By the late 1990s, bank failures had fallen dramatically, averaging around five per year between 1995 and mid-2001.

Even though bank failures fell to an insignificant level by the early 2000s and bank profits increased dramatically, the experience of the 1980s has left many industry observers nervous. In the aftermath, Congress has questioned the various agencies responsible for regulating banks, asking how so many banks could have failed if regulation and supervision were adequate.[5] In Chapter 17, we look at how regulators have implemented existing regulations to ensure adequate banking supervision. We also look at suggestions for overhauling the federal regulatory structure of banking and other financial services.

RECAP Federally chartered banks are called national banks. They must belong to the Fed and subscribe to FDIC deposit insurance. State-chartered banks can, if they choose, belong to the Fed and/or subscribe to FDIC insurance. Nearly all banks subscribe to FDIC insurance. This dual banking system has allowed banks to choose their regulators. Seventy-two percent of banks have state charters while 28 percent have national charters. National banks tend to be much larger and have many more branches than state banks.

The Structure of the Commercial Banking System

In establishing the statutes and regulations that have contributed to the evolution of the commercial banking system's structure, Congress and the regulatory agencies were guided by several considerations. It was assumed that a large number of small banks would encourage competition and efficiency, which would result in conduct or behavior by firms that was beneficial to the public and society at large. At the same time, the more competitive the market, the greater is the risk of failure of an individual firm from the pressure of intense competition. Although the public would be provided with the largest quantity of financial services at the lowest prices, more banks could fail in a highly competitive environment.

In contrast, a structure characterized by a few large firms would result in limited competition, inefficiencies, and fewer benefits for the public in the form of lower prices and improved quality and quantity of financial services.[6] At the same time, fewer banks would fail in a noncompetitive market. Because of a lack of competition, banks could charge higher prices for their services and earn higher profits. Nevertheless, with only a few large banks, the failure of just one bank could have major ramifications throughout the economy. With many small banks, the failure of one would not be catastrophic. Presumably, regulators attempt to balance all of these considerations by encouraging bank behavior that is beneficial to society while at the same time ensuring the safety and soundness of the financial system.

Against this background, it should not be surprising that regulators were interested in monitoring and influencing, if not controlling, the structure of the market for banking services. In particular, regulators used their powers to control entry into the market, mergers among existing firms, and branching in an effort to main-

---

[5]In addition to what appeared to be lax regulation, many banks had problems during years of prosperity because leveraging was high and bad loans had been made to developing countries.

[6]Note that this argument is in sharp contrast to one of the reasons given for the recent wave of bank mergers in the late 1990s. Presumably, because of technological changes in the 1990s, large banks now can be more efficient than small ones. A recent study suggests, however, that most economies of scale are exhausted by the time banks reach the size of $10 billion to $25 billion in assets, which is certainly small by today's standards.

tain many small firms and a so-called competitive environment, while at the same time protecting small banks from excessive competition. But, as we shall see, the regulators' attempts to maintain a competitive environment often resulted in a noncompetitive environment. Even though there were many banks, each bank was shielded from competition.

A local environment can become more competitive in several ways. One way occurs when a new institution secures a charter and sets up in competition with local banks. Competition also can increase if existing banks located elsewhere in the state are allowed to open new branch offices in the area. In the past decade, barriers to branching within states have been significantly reduced. All states now allow some branching, and the vast majority of states allow statewide branching.

Until recently, however, branching generally had to stop at the state line. The **McFadden Act,** passed by Congress in 1927, prohibited federally chartered national banks from branching across state lines. It also required national banks to abide by the branching laws of the state in which they were located. State banks that are Fed members can operate only in the state that grants them a charter. Generally, other state-chartered banks cannot open branches across state lines, although some states permitted entry by state-chartered banks that were not Fed members. Although it is now history, the McFadden Act is substantially responsible for the structure of the commercial banking system we have today.

Initially, state and federal restrictions on intrastate and interstate branching were motivated by a desire to prevent undue concentration and reduced competition in banking. For example, it was believed that with unrestricted statewide branching, a few large city banks would open branches across a state and drive the small community banks out of business. The result would be a worrisome concentration of economic and perhaps political power in a few large institutions and a reduction in the quality and quantity of financial services available in smaller communities.

This concern about "bigness" or "concentration"—along with the fear that more competition in local banking markets might lead to more bank failures—resulted in restrictions on entry and branching. This, in turn, led to a large number of small banks being located in relatively small communities. Despite the alleged competitiveness, many of these institutions have faced little or no competition because larger, and perhaps more efficient, banks were prohibited from entering the local market. Thus, entry and branching restrictions ultimately served to limit competition, not increase it. In part, this is why in 1994, Congress decided to allow interstate branching. The McFadden Act was effectively abrogated in September 1994 when President Clinton signed the **Interstate Banking and Branching Efficiency Act (IBBEA).** The IBBEA allowed unimpeded nationwide branching beginning on June 1, 1997.

Another reason for the enactment of the IBBEA was that Congress and the president were merely following the lead of the states. In 1985, the Supreme Court gave states the freedom to form regional banking pacts. Two years later, 45 of the 50 states allowed some form of interstate banking. More importantly, as we shall see in the next section, banks had found ways to engage in interstate branching even before the law allowing branching was passed.

As Exhibit 15-4 shows, on June 30, 2001, there were 8,178 FDIC-insured banks in the United States. Of these, 57.3 percent had assets of less than $100 million each. Although $100 million might sound like a lot, it is small for a bank. At the same time, over 95 percent of FDIC-insured banks had assets less than $1 billion while almost 5 percent had assets greater than $1 billion.

A look at total banking assets for the industry reveals even more. The smallest 57.3 percent of all banks own less than 4 percent of total banking assets. The

McFadden Act
The 1927 act by Congress that outlawed interstate branching and made national banks conform to the intrastate branching laws of the states in which they were located.

Interstate Banking and Branching Efficiency Act (IBBEA)
Signed into law in September 1994, an act by Congress that effectively allows unimpeded, nationwide branching.

EXHIBIT 15-4

Size Distribution of FDIC-Insured Banks as of December 31, 2000

ASSET SIZE	NUMBER OF INSTITUTIONS	PERCENT OF TOTAL	CUMULATIVE PERCENT	TOTAL ASSETS	PERCENT OF TOTAL*	CUMULATIVE PERCENT*
< $100 million	4,685	57.3	57.3	$228.0	3.5%	3.5%
$100 million–$1 billion	3,101	37.9	95.2	789.8	12.4	16.3
$1–$10 billion	313	3.8	99.0	899.6	14.1	30.4
> $10 billion	79	.9	99.9*	4,442.8	69.8	100.2*
Total	8,178	100%	100%	$6,360.2	100%	100%

*Percents may not sum to 100% because of rounding.
SOURCE: Federal Deposit Insurance Corporation.

smallest 99 percent of banks had about 30 percent of total assets. Less than 1 percent of all banks had assets of more than $10 billion, but they owned almost 70 percent of total banking assets! By any measure, it is clear that the industry is composed of a large number of banks that have a small percentage of total banking assets.

At the same time, there are a small number of very large banks; 25 banks had total assets of more than $40 billion while 8 banks had assets of $100 billion or more. Although the largest 10 banks account for less than .1 percent of the total number of banks, collectively they have over 37 percent of all bank assets. As you might guess, most of the industry giants have extensive branching networks and are located in states that had liberal branching laws long before the IBBEA.

But the numbers alone conceal additional relevant attributes of the banking structure—namely, that the numbers are changing dramatically as mergers occur. Virtually all of the large banks are organized as bank holding companies or as financial holding companies. We now turn to these subjects.

RECAP The McFadden Act outlawed interstate branching by national banks. The Act required national banks to abide by the branching laws of the state in which they were located. As of June 1, 1997, the IBBEA effectively allowed unimpeded, nationwide branching. Today, there are a large number of small banks and a small number of large banks. The largest 10 banks, out of 8,315, control about 37 percent of banking assets.

Bank Holding Companies and Financial Holding Companies

When we hear the name Johnson & Johnson, many of us probably think of baby powder, shampoo, and Band-Aids. These are major products associated with the J&J brand name. In fact, J&J is a conglomerate, producing numerous other products through its many subsidiaries, including Tylenol, surgical instruments, sausage casings, toys, tranquilizers, and contraceptives. In other words, J&J is a company that owns and operates many firms that produce a wide variety of products.

Bank Holding Company
A corporation that owns several firms, at least one of which is a bank.

A **bank holding company** is a corporation that owns several firms, at least one of which is a bank. The remaining firms are engaged in activities that are closely

- Making, acquiring, brokering, or servicing loans, issuing and accepting letters of credit
- Real estate and personal property appraising
- Commercial real estate equity financing
- Check-guaranty services
- Collection agency services
- Credit bureau services
- Asset management, servicing, and collection activities
- Acquiring debt in default
- Real estate settlement services
- Leasing personal or real property
- Operating nonbank depository institutions
- Performing trust company functions
- Financial and investment advisory activities
- Providing feasibility studies
- Agency transactional services
- Investment transactions as principal including underwriting and dealing in government obligations, money market instruments, foreign exchange, forward contracts, options, futures, options on futures, swaps, and similar contracts
- Management consulting and counseling activities
- Courier services
- Printing and selling checks, deposit slips, etc.
- Insurance agency and underwriting
- Community development activities
- Issuing money orders, savings bonds, and traveler's checks
- Data processing

EXHIBIT 15-5
Allowable Activities for Bank Holding Companies (Federal Reserve Regulation Y, Revised January 1, 2001)

SOURCE: Federal Reserve System, *http://www.federalreserve.gov/regulations/default.htm*

related to banking. If the holding company owns one bank, it is called a *one-bank holding company*. If it owns more than one, it is called a *multi-bank* holding company.

Many banks organize themselves into holding companies because they expect this organizational form to be more profitable than a simple bank would be. Specifically, this corporate form allows banks (1) to circumvent restrictions on branching and thus seek out sources and uses of funds in other geographical markets, and (2) to diversify into other product areas, thus providing the public with a wider array of financial services, while reducing the risk associated with limiting operations to traditional banking services.

Thus, organizing as a bank holding company allowes banks to effectively circumvent prohibitions on intrastate and interstate branching, which now have been virtually eliminated, and to participate in activities that otherwise would be barred. Such activities include data processing, leasing, investment counseling, and servicing out-of-state loans. For a summary list of non-banking activities that bank holding companies can engage in, see Exhibit 15-5.

Almost all large banks are owned by holding companies. By the middle of 2001, bank holding companies numbered over 7,100. The largest holding company is Citigroup, which resulted from the September 1998 merger of Citicorp and Travelers Group. Citigroup currently has over $953 billion in assets, over 100 million customers, and a presence in more than 100 countries. Although the list is rapidly changing, the 25 largest bank holding companies appear next to a list of the 25 largest banks in Exhibit 15-6. You can observe how the two lists overlap and see the additional assets that the bank holding companies add to the largest banks.

EXHIBIT 15-6

The Giants: Banks and Bank Holding Companies

	Banks by Total Assets as of March 31, 2001			
RANK	NAME	CITY	STATE	TOTAL ASSETS (IN THOUSANDS OF DOLLARS)
1	Bank of America, National Association	Charlotte	NC	584,284,000
2	Citibank, N.A.	New York	NY	382,106,000
3	Chase Manhattan Bank, The	New York	NY	377,116,000
4	First Union National Bank	Charlotte	NC	231,837,000
5	Morgan Guaranty Trust Company of New York	New York	NY	185,762,000
6	Fleet National Bank	Providence	RI	166,281,000
7	Wells Fargo Bank, National Association	San Francisco	CA	115,539,000
8	Bank One, National Association	Chicago	IL	101,228,538
9	Suntrust Bank	Atlanta	GA	99,528,008
10	U.S. Bank National Association	Minneapolis	MN	82,023,123
11	HSBC Bank USA	Buffalo	NY	80,121,433
12	Keybank National Association	Cleveland	OH	77,760,463
13	Bank of New York, The	New York	NY	74,266,429
14	Firstar Bank, National Association	Cincinnati	OH	72,593,553
15	Wachovia Bank, National Association	Winston-Salem	NC	69,187,160
16	State Street Bank and Trust Company	Boston	MA	64,643,911
17	PNC Bank, National Association	Pittsburgh	PA	63,185,903
18	Wells Fargo Bank Minnesota, National Association	Minneapolis	MN	53,117,860
19	Lasalle Bank, National Association	Chicago	IL	48,852,837
20	Branch Banking and Trust Company	Winston-Salem	NC	46,991,799
21	Southtrust Bank	Birmingham	AL	45,170,172
22	Bankers Trust Company	New York	NY	44,324,000
23	Regions Bank	Birmingham	AL	43,528,061
24	Merrill Lynch Bank USA	Salt Lake City	UT	43,171,125
25	Mellon Bank, N.A.	Pittsburgh	PA	41,974,315

Financial Holding Companies

Holding companies that can engage in a broader array of financial-related activities than bank holding companies, including securities dealing, insurance underwriting, merchant banking and more.

Even more dramatic than the conversion of large banks to bank holding companies is the ongoing trend for bank holding companies to convert to **financial holding companies.** Under the Gramm-Leach-Bliley Act (GLBA) of 1999, bank holding companies, securities firms, insurance companies, and other financial institutions can affiliate under common ownership to form financial holding companies. A financial holding company can offer its customers a complete range of financial services. The activities of a financial holding company include:

- Securities underwriting and dealing
- Insurance agency and underwriting activities
- Merchant banking activities.
- Any other activity that the Fed determines to be financial in nature or incidental to financial activities.
- Any nonfinancial activity that the Fed determines is complementary to the financial activity and does not pose a substantial risk to the safety or soundness of depository institutions or to the financial system

EXHIBIT 15-6
Continued

	Bank Holding Companies by Total Assets as of June 30, 2001			
RANK	NAME	CITY	STATE	TOTAL ASSETS (IN THOUSANDS OF DOLLARS)
1	Citigroup Inc.	New York	NY	953,427,000
2	J. P. Morgan Chase & Co.	New York	NY	712,702,000
3	Bank of America Corporation	Charlotte	NC	625,524,000
4	Wells Fargo & Company	San Francisco	CA	289,758,000
5	Bank One Corporation	Chicago	IL	272,412,000
6	First Union Corporation	Charlotte	NC	245,941,000
7	Taunus Corporation	New York	NY	216,513,000
8	Fleetboston Financial Corporation	Boston	MA	202,113,000
9	U.S. Bancorp	Minneapolis	MN	165,156,000
10	ABN AMRO North America Holding Company	Chicago	IL	164,699,748
11	HSBC North America Inc.	Buffalo	NY	107,445,340
12	Suntrust Banks, Inc.	Atlanta	GA	100,822,534
13	National City Corporation	Cleveland	OH	95,247,453
14	Keycorp	Cleveland	OH	85,522,573
15	Bank of New York Company, Inc., The	New York	NY	76,831,453
16	Wachovia Corporation	Winston-Salem	NC	74,828,414
17	State Street Corporation	Boston	MA	70,317,346
18	PNC Financial Services Group, Inc., The	Pittsburgh	PA	70,034,428
19	Fifth Third Bancorp	Cincinnati	OH	69,833,640
20	BB&T Corporation	Winston-Salem	NC	64,733,769
21	Comerica Incorporated	Detroit	MI	49,494,169
22	Southtrust Corporation	Birmingham	AL	46,534,992
23	Regions Financial Corporation	Birmingham	AL	45,392,788
24	Mellon Financial Corporation	Pittsburgh	PA	43,705,445
25	MBNA Corporation	Wilmington	DE	40,418,814

SOURCE: Federal Financial Institutions Examination Council, http://www.ffiec.gov/.

Merchant banking is the making of direct equity investments (purchasing stock) in start-up or growing nonfinancial businesses. Under GLBA, financial holding companies will be able to own up to 100 percent of commercial, nonfinancial businesses as long as (1) ownership is for investment purposes only, (2) the financial holding company is not involved in the day-to-day management of the company, and (3) the investment is for 10 years or less. Prior to the recent law, bank holding companies could own only 5 percent of a commercial company directly and up to 49 percent through certain subsidiaries.

To become a financial holding company, bank holding companies that meet certain criteria must file a declaration with the Federal Reserve.[7] The declaration must certify that, among other things, all of the bank holding company's depository institution subsidiaries are well capitalized and managed.

Merchant Banking
Direct equity investment (the purchasing of stock) by a bank in a start-up or growing company.

---

[7]Banks that are not bank holding companies may apply simultaneously to become bank holding companies and financial holding companies.

As of March 11, 2000, the effective date of the GLBA, 117 institutions were certified as financial holding companies. As of October 12, 2001, 582 financial holding companies had been formed.

To summarize, banks, under the holding company corporate umbrella, have been expanding the geographical areas they serve and the array of financial services they offer the public. Bank holding companies may also apply to become financial holding companies if they meet certain criteria. Under the financial holding company status, bank holding companies, insurance companies, and securities firms can affiliate under common ownership. In addition, financial holding companies can engage in an even broader array of financial and nonfinancial services than those offered by bank holding companies. The expansion by banks into areas traditionally served by other, more specialized FIs has been matched, as discussed in the last chapter, by other FIs and other nonfinancial institutions. These nonbank institutions are expanding into areas traditionally served mainly by banks, such as the checkable deposits offered by S&Ls and the credit cards offered by General Motors.

Ongoing Changes in the Structure of the Banking Industry

The breakdown of barriers to intra- and interstate branching has resulted in increased competition in the financial services industry and considerable erosion in the domain and effectiveness of many long-standing financial regulations. The changes in the structure of U.S. banking and banking laws have been revolutionary and resulted in a drastic decline in the number of banks in the past few years. Between 1980 and 1997, over 1,450 banks failed, about 7,000 mergers occurred, and 3,600 new banks were started. The result was a net decline in the number of banks from over 14,400 in 1980 to under 8,200 in mid-2001. The passage of the GLBA is expected to maintain or even accelerate the pace of change within the financial services industry as banks and other financial institutions become more integrated through the formation of financial holding companies.

A related trend is a significant increase in the share of total bank assets controlled by the largest banks. For example, in 1980, the 100 largest banking organizations (banks and bank holding companies) accounted for about one-half of total banking assets. By mid 2001, the largest 79 banks accounted for about 70 percent of banking assets. The increased concentration of banking assets in the largest bank holding companies has resulted from the removal of branching restrictions, particularly across state lines, and bank mergers. Despite the decline in the number of banks, the number of branches has actually increased since 1980.

In the 1990s, the pace and dollar volume of mergers increased significantly. Some of the largest mergers in history that took place during the early and mid-1990s include Chase–Chemical Bank, Wells Fargo–First Interstate, NationsBank–Barnett, and First Union–Core States. However, these mergers are much smaller than the more recent mergers of Citicorp and Travelers, Wells Fargo and Norwest, Banc One and First Chicago, and NationsBank and BankAmerica. These mergers have set a new standard for sheer size in U.S. banking organizations. Recent mergers are occurring not only between banks, but also, like the Citicorp-Travelers merger, between banks and other companies in the financial services industry.[8] Exhibit 15-7

---

[8]This merger actually occurred prior to the passage of the Gramm-Leach-Bliley Act. Because it involved the merger of a bank and an insurance company, it would not have been legal without the ultimate passage of the GLBA.

EXHIBIT 15-7
The Declining
Number of Banks

In the 1980s and early 1990s, some of the decline was due to bank failures. In the mid- and late 1990s, the decline was due to the record number of mergers among healthy institutions. The data do not reveal that many of the mergers were between the largest banks.
PDIC-Insured Commercial Banks 1980–2001*

Year	Institutions	Year	Institutions
2001*	8,178	1990	12,347
2000	8,315	1989	12,715
1999	8,581	1988	13,137
1998	8,774	1987	13,723
1997	9,143	1986	14,210
1996	9,530	1985	14,417
1995	9,942	1984	14,496
1994	10,452	1983	14,469
1993	10,960	1982	14,451
1992	11,466	1981	14,414
1991	11,927	1980	14,434

*As of June 30, 2001.

*Reflects the number of banks as of December 31, 2000.

SOURCE: Federal Deposit Insurance Corporation.

shows how the number of banks has declined during the 1990s, largely due to bank mergers. A Closer Look examines some of the recent mega-mergers.

Megamergers of the Late 1990s: The provisions of the Interstate Banking and Branching Efficiency Act of 1994 were fully phased in by mid-1997. After this time, mergers entered a new era, as the size, geographical area, and number of mergers increased sharply. Moreover, bank holding companies merged with other financial services firms, producing mega-financial supermarkets. Here we review four mergers that occurred during the fall of 1998:

A Closer Look

1. The largest bank holding company arose from another mega-merger—the merger of Citicorp and Travelers Group. The new firm, Citigroup, is the largest financial services firm in the world with over $950 billion in assets, outstanding stock valued at $82 billion, and 100 million customers in 100 countries. It can offer customers one-stop shopping for all of their financial service needs including retail and investment (securities) banking, credit cards, brokerage services, and property, casualty, and life insurance.

2. BankAmerica Corporation of San Francisco merged with NationsBank Corporation of Charlotte, North Carolina. The merger entailed a stock-for-stock swap between the two banks valued at $60 billion. The new mega-bank has assets in excess of $570 billion and a network of 3,800 branches in 27 states. Both NationsBank and BankAmerica purchased securities firms in 1997. In 1991, BankAmerica purchased Security Pacific in what at that time was the largest-ever bank merger. In 1997, NationsBank purchased Florida-based Barnett Bank and Missouri-based Boatman's Bancshares. The combined bank—called BankAmerica—is the second-largest bank holding company in the country.

3. Ohio-based Banc One Corporation and First Chicago NBD Corporation swapped $30 billion of stock in order to merge. The result was the largest retail and commercial

bank network in the Midwest. The new bank—called Bank One Corporation—has over 2,000 branches and assets in excess of $275 billion.

4. Minneapolis-based Norwest Corporation merged with San Francisco-based Wells Fargo to become the nation's sixth-largest bank with assets over $191 billion and operations in 21 states throughout the West and Midwest. The new bank, known as Wells Fargo, is the nation's leader in offering banking services over the Internet.

These mergers resulted from the desire to slash costs (and often employees), boost stock prices, and offer customers more diversified services. The trend is from traditional, local banks with limited services to multiregional and national banks that offer customers in a wider geographical area a larger menu of services including bank accounts, loans, and investment and insurance services.

Two things are certain: (1) The structure of the banking system is changing rapidly and looks far different than it looked 15 years ago; and (2) profit-seeking banks will continue adapting to change in regulations and the financial environment in which they operate in ways that will produce further structural changes.

As we have seen, new legislation passed that allows bank holding companies, under the financial holding company status, to enter the securities, insurance, and merchant banking industries, and to engage in other financial and nonfinancial activities as determined by the Fed. Since the trough of the Great Depression in 1933, banks were barred from these activities for more than 60 years although they have *de facto* found ways into some of these areas through nonbank subsidiaries. As the new legislation, which allows extensive financial integration, gets phased in, additional changes will continue to occur in the financial services industry.

The Evolution of International Banking

The banking environment has also changed dramatically in the international arena. A striking increase in international borrowing and lending by domestic banks began in the 1970s with the expansion of world trade that occurred shortly after the first OPEC oil crisis.[9] Not only did the amount of international lending increase but also the number of participating banks. Petrodollars, as they came to be known, flowed into the OPEC nations in payment for oil. In turn, the OPEC nations deposited a large part of these funds in U.S. and European banks in exchange for deposit claims. Many U.S. banks began to loan funds denominated in dollars to less-developed countries. In the early 1980s, a crisis arose when the less-developed countries were unable to service their loans. As a result, many large banks had to write off or restructure these loans and incurred losses that took many years to absorb. Consequently, the 1990s have seen less emphasis on growth, more caution, and more emphasis on asset quality and rate of return.

In addition, many foreign banks made significant inroads into U.S. markets by the 1980s. Many of these foreign banks got caught up in the same types of problem loans that plagued domestic banks in the 1980s, and their growth slowed considerably. Nevertheless, foreign banks still have a major presence in the United States. On December 31, 2000, 279 foreign banks from more than 50 countries operated branches in the United States. Branches of foreign banks controlled more than 15 percent ($943 billion) of banking assets in the United States. Additionally, foreign banks owned more than 25 percent of 85 U.S. commercial banks, with about $315 billion in assets. Another 70 foreign banks operated agencies in the

---

[9]OPEC stands for the Organization of Petroleum Exporting Countries, a cartel dominated by the Middle Eastern oil-producing nations.

United States. An **agency of a foreign bank** is a more restrictive form of operation than a foreign branch in that the agency can raise funds only in the wholesale and money markets, whereas the branch of a foreign bank can accept retail deposits as well as borrow in the wholesale and money markets.

In the 1990s, the banking system became truly international in scope. Advances in electronics and telecommunications allowed domestic and foreign banks to participate in worldwide transactions without leaving home. Funds can now be transmitted easily anywhere in the world. Deregulation has also made it possible for U.S. banks to open offices and enter foreign markets more easily than before and vice versa.

In this new environment, bankers have discovered the tremendous competition for international transactions involving the electronic transfer of funds—and, consequently, profit margins are declining. Scores of banks from around the world can bid on loans with the result that the interest rate and, hence, the return, are driven to rock-bottom levels. What appeared to be new lending opportunities have been somewhat disappointing because of the reduced profit margins. As a result, banks again are looking to more traditional markets for expansion.

The time has come to round out our examination of commercial banking by focusing on the management of individual banks, with particular emphasis on the risks that banks face. In this way, we will gain a greater appreciation for what banks do and why.

Agency of a Foreign Bank
A U.S. banking office of a foreign bank that can borrow funds only in the wholesale and money markets and is not allowed to accept retail deposits.

RECAP Under the holding company corporate umbrella, banks have succeeded in expanding the geographical areas they serve and the array of financial services they offer the public. Barriers to interstate branching were removed in 1997 by the IBBEA. GLBA allowed banks, securities firms, and insurance companies to affiliate under common ownership and to provide their customers with an extensive array of financial services. Since the 1980s, the number of banks has declined because of bank failures and mergers. In the 1990s, many mega-mergers have occurred, and banking is becoming increasingly concentrated. Banking also has become truly international in scope. Foreign banks own over $943 billion of U.S. banking assets.

Bank Management: Managing Risk and Profits

After the ribbon is cut and the new bank or branch opens, the bank's managers swing into action. In essence, it is the bank's balance sheet—assets, liabilities, and capital—that is "managed." The decisions involve what kinds of loans are to be made, what the prime rate should be, what interest rate to offer on 1-year time deposits, and so forth. These decisions reflect an interaction between the bank's liquidity, safety, and earnings objectives and the economic and financial environment within which the bank operates.

To clearly picture this interaction, visualize bank management as having to face and deal with several types of risks and uncertainties, including credit or default risk, interest rate risk, liquidity risk, and exchange rate risk. A primary function of a bank loan officer is to evaluate or assess the default risk associated with lending to particular borrowers, such as firms, individuals, and domestic and foreign governments. To do this, the loan officer gathers all of the relevant information about potential borrowers, including balance sheets, income statements, credit checks, and how the funds are to be used.

In addition to developing reports that quantify risks, loan officers must also be aware that they are making decisions about whether to fund a loan under conditions of asymmetric information. **Asymmetric information** means that a potential borrower

Asymmetric Information
When a potential borrower knows more about the risks and returns of an investment project than the bank loan officer does.

knows more about the risks and returns of an investment project than does the bank loan officer. Thus, the borrower and the lender do not have equal, or symmetric, information. After all, don't many of those who apply for a loan obviously try to put their best foot forward and conceal any blemishes? Further, those with the most to hide and those willing to take the biggest risks are often the most likely to be less forthright and/or to pursue a loan most diligently. If the bank funds these less-desirable loans, the result is an **adverse selection problem,** which increases the risk of default.

Moreover, after the loan is made, it may be difficult to guarantee that the loan is used only for the stated purpose and not for a more risky venture. This so-called **moral hazard problem** results from the fact that once borrowers get the funds, they may have an incentive to engage in a more risky venture that pays a higher return.[10] After all, the borrowers are now risking the bank's funds. If the borrowers win, they keep the bigger profits. But if they lose, the bank bears the loss if the borrowers default. Under these conditions, members of a bank's management team must be experts at assessing and evaluating risk. They must recognize that asymmetric information, adverse selection, and the incentive to engage in more risky ventures are facts of life.

Bank managers must manage interest rate risk as well. As noted in Chapter 14, a positive spread today can turn into a negative spread later when the cost of liabilities exceeds the return on assets. For example, suppose LHT National Bank is about to make a 2-year loan to a local restaurant. The loan officer is satisfied that the credit risk is not excessive, and an interest rate of 7 percent is agreed upon. In effect, the bank, in view of the economic and financial outlook and its existing balance sheet, plans to finance the loan by issuing ("hiring") 1-year time deposits paying 4 percent. The 3 percent spread will yield a handsome gross profit over the first year. What about the second year? As a great economic philosopher once said, "It all depends."

At the end of the first year, the time deposit matures, and LHT has to "rehire" the funds needed to continue financing the outstanding loan to the restaurant. If the funds can be rehired at 4 percent, the spread will not change. However, suppose that the overall level of interest rates has risen dramatically, perhaps due to restrictive policy actions being pursued by the Fed, and the bank must now pay 10 percent on 1-year time deposits. The 3 percent positive spread (7 percent minus 4 percent) in the first year of the loan is exactly offset by a 3 percent negative spread (7 percent minus 10 percent) in the second year. When various administrative and processing costs are considered, the loan turns out to be quite unprofitable.

We have already seen that banks can use financial futures, options, and swaps to manage interest rate risk. We have not yet discussed in detail how **adjustable- (variable-) rate loans** can also be used to hedge interest rate risk. The basic idea is quite simple. The loan contract specifies that the rate charged on a loan—be it a consumer loan, business loan, or mortgage loan—will be adjusted up or down, say once a year, as the cost of funds rises or falls. The aim is to preserve a profitable spread and to shift the interest rate risk onto the borrower.

Going back to our example, suppose the loan contract with the restaurant calls for an adjustable rate of 3 percentage points above the bank's cost of funds, instead of the fixed rate originally assumed. Such an arrangement produces the same 7 percent rate in the first year (4 percent plus 3 percent), but a 13 percent rate (10 percent plus 3 percent) in the second year. In effect, the bank has succeeded in shifting the interest rate risk to the borrower.[11] It is worth emphasizing here that

Adverse Selection Problem
When the least desirable borrowers pursue a loan most diligently.

Moral Hazard Problem
When the borrower has an incentive to use the proceeds of a loan for a more risky venture after the loan is funded.

Adjustable-(Variable-) Rate Loan
When the interest rate on a loan is adjusted up or down as the cost of funds rises or falls.

---

[10]Deposit insurance causes a moral hazard problem in a macro sense. The presence of deposit insurance causes financial intermediaries to take more risks than they otherwise would because they know that if they lose, their depositors still get their funds back.

[11]Note that even though the interest rate risk for the bank has been reduced, default risk increases because the borrower is less certain of future payment obligations.

adjustable-rate loans have become an important risk-management tool. In the early 1990s, interest rates on liabilities fell faster than rates on assets, resulting in record bank profits. Imagine a positive spread becoming bigger over time.[12]

Like other intermediaries, banks need to manage liquidity risk. As noted in Chapter 14, a large proportion of bank liabilities are payable on demand, checkable deposits and savings deposits being two prominent examples. Banks must be prepared to meet unexpected withdrawals by depositors and to accommodate unexpected loan demands by valued customers. The resulting need for liquidity can be satisfied by holding some highly liquid assets, such as Treasury bills or excess reserves, or by expanding particular types of liabilities as needs develop. One way to expand liabilities is to attract large negotiable CDs, possibly by offering higher rates than those offered by the competition. Other ways include borrowing more reserves from the Fed's discount facility or in the federal funds markets, or increasing borrowing in the repurchase agreements or overnight Eurodollar markets.

Last, as banking has become more international in scope, some banks maintain stocks of foreign exchange that are used in international transactions and to service customers who need to buy or sell foreign currencies. If the exchange rate between two currencies changes, the value of the stocks of foreign exchange will also change. Thus, a bank, like any holder of foreign exchange, is subject to an exchange rate risk. As we shall see in Chapters 22 and 23, banks and other holders of foreign exchange now use exchange rate futures and options, forward agreements, and swaps to hedge this risk.

Perhaps the business of banking is beginning to sound somewhat more complex and challenging than you originally envisioned. But then again, most senior bank executives don't make six- and even seven-figure incomes just for showing up in gray pinstripe suits.

Bank Performance

As seen, banks are facing increasing competition from other FIs and nonfinancial corporations in a global environment. They have confronted a volatile economic and regulatory environment. In the face of such challenges, bank profitability, which was low in the 1980s, improved significantly in the 1990s. For example, banks reported a record $15.9 billion in profits in April 1998—the fifth consecutive quarter in which a new record profit level was established. The profits were attributed to the strong economy that reflected favorably on bank assets, low interest rates, and growing sources of noninterest income.[13] Most analysts ascribed the better performance by banks to their more diversified portfolios and environment. The problem loans to less-developed countries such as Mexico, Brazil, and Argentina, which caused major loan losses for many large banks in the 1980s, were resolved. Banks shored up capital due to new regulations. All of these factors led to record profit levels and high bank stock valuations.

Bank stocks performed below average in the late 1980s but did very well in the early 1990s and extremely well in the late 1990s, outperforming the S&P 500 index. Proceeding on the premise that the market value or price of a firm's stock—be it a bank or a manufacturing firm—is a function of current and expected earnings and the riskiness associated with the firm's operations, the better performance in the 1990s

---

[12]In a falling interest rate environment, a bank heavily into adjustable loans would be worse off than one that contracted at fixed rates on its assets.

[13]In the early 1990s, profits rose mostly as a result of falling interest rates on liabilities, which lowered the cost of borrowing. The return on bank assets was also falling during the 1990s, but the cost of liabilities was falling faster, which resulted in increased profits.

suggests that financial investors had gradually come to view bank stocks as much more attractive investments than they were in the 1980s due to their record profit levels.[14]

As we enter the new millennium, the major challenge facing banks is competition from other intermediaries and other nonfinancial companies that have taken an increasing share of intermediation. These **nonbanks,** as they have come to be called, face less regulation and often lower costs. Costs may be lower because nonbanks are less regulated than banks are with regard to what they can do and where they can locate. In addition, nonbanks do not face reserve requirements, nor do they have to maintain full-service branches. As Exhibit 15-8 shows, despite the

Nonbanks
Other intermediaries and nonfinancial companies that have taken an increasing share of intermediation.

EXHIBIT 15-8
Commercial Banks' Declining Share of Intermediation

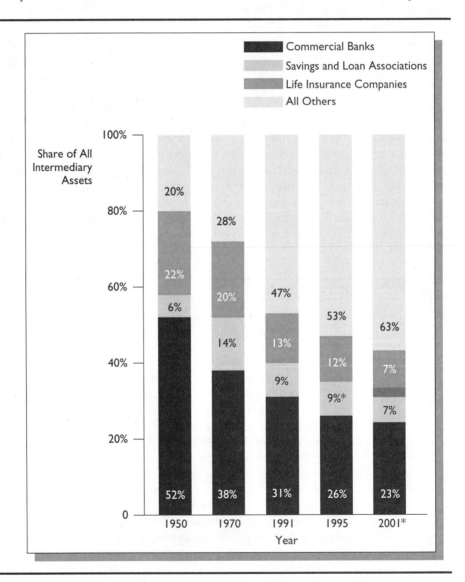

*As of June 30, 2001.
SOURCE: *Budget of the U.S. Government—Fiscal Year 1993:* "Modernizing the Financial Services Sector," U.S. Government Printing Office, 1992, p. 259. Figures for 1995 are from *Flow of Funds Account, Z1,* Fourth Quarter 1995, March 8, 1996, p. 72 and *Flow of Funds Accounts, Z1,* Second Quarter, 2001, September 18, 2001, p 58.

[14]The poor performance in the 1980s reflected troubled loans, which included loans to less-developed countries, and energy and commercial real estate loans. Concerns about the safety of the financial services industry, given the general climate surrounding the savings and loan crisis, were also quite prevalent.

record profits, banks' share of total intermediation is declining. Banks must increasingly adapt to a changing industry to maintain profits as well as to maintain market share. It is no wonder that banks are merging with other financial services firms and expanding into areas previously prohibited to banks.

The next chapter looks at savings associations and credit unions. In Chapter 21, we take a closer look at how banks manage risk on a day-to-day basis.

RECAP Bank management must deal with the problems of asymmetric information, adverse selection, and moral hazard, as well as default risk, interest rate risk, liquidity risk, and exchange rate risk. Banks made record profits in the 1990s after performing very poorly in the 1980s. Despite record profits, banks' share of intermediation continues to decline.

Summary of Major Points

- Banking is a heavily regulated industry. Regulatory policy aims at promoting competition and efficiency, while preserving the safety and soundness of institutions. The Glass-Steagall Act of 1933 was enacted in response to the financial collapse in the Great Depression. The law established interest rate ceilings that could be paid to depositors, separated investment and commercial banking, and created the FDIC.

- Banks in the United States are chartered by either the federal government or one of the 50 state governments. Federally chartered banks are called national banks and must belong to the Fed and subscribe to FDIC deposit insurance. State-chartered banks can, if they choose, belong to the Fed and/or subscribe to FDIC insurance. In fact, nearly all banks subscribe to FDIC insurance. Although only about 30 percent have federal charters and belong to the Fed, these banks tend to be the largest and have the most deposits and banking offices.

- The McFadden Act outlawed interstate branching by national banks. With regard to intrastate branching, the Act required national banks to abide by the branching laws of the state in which they were located.

- Restrictions were imposed on entry and branching as a result of fears that more competition in local banking markets might lead to more failures and that letting big-city banks enter markets served by small community banks might result in concentration. These restrictions have resulted in a banking structure in which a large number of small banks control a small portion of total banking assets and a small number of large banks control the bulk of total banking assets. Many bank mergers occurred in the 1990s—some of them between banks and other financial services firms.

- Banking is becoming more heavily concentrated. As of June 1, 1997, the Interstate Banking and Branching Efficiency Act (IBBEA) of 1994 effectively allowed unimpeded, nationwide branching. With the passage of the Gramm-Leach-Bliley Act of 1999, banks, securities firms, and insurance companies have been able to affiliate under common ownership and to offer the public a vast array of financial services under one umbrella.

- Under the holding company corporate umbrella, banks have been expanding the geographical areas they serve and the array of financial services they offer the public. The expansion by banks into areas traditionally served by other more specialized FIs has been matched by other FIs and nonfinancial institutions expanding into areas traditionally served mainly by banks. The result has been more competition in the financial services industry and considerable erosion in the domain and effectiveness of many long-standing regulations. Under GLBA, bank holding companies can be certified as financial holding companies. In addition to banking, financial holding companies can engage in securities underwriting and dealings, insurance activities, merchant banking activities, and other financial and nonfinancial activities determined by the Fed.

- Banking has become internationalized as U.S. banks have increased their participation in international lending and domestic banks have faced competition from foreign banks. Foreign banks now own over $943 billion, or over 15 percent, of U.S. banking assets. Electronic and telecommunication advances have helped to increase the competitiveness of international lending, thereby reducing the profit margin.

- Bank managers supervise a bank's balance sheet. In the process, they have to face and deal with default risk, interest rate risk, liquidity risk, and exchange rate risk. They must make decisions despite asymmetric information, adverse selection, and moral hazard.

- Regulators periodically audit (examine) banks. Conducting more of a management appraisal than a financial audit, the examiners pay particu-

lar attention to the quality of a bank's assets and, thus, how the bank is managing risk.

- In the early 1990s, the cost of liabilities fell faster than the earnings on bank assets, resulting in record profits. The record profits continued into the late 1990s due to the strong economy, low interest rates, and increases in noninterest income. Despite their success, banks' share of total intermediation is declining.

Key Terms

Adjustable (Variable) Rate Loan
Adverse Selection Problem
Agency of a Foreign Bank
Asymmetric Information
Bank Holding Company
Chartered
Comptroller of the Currency
Dual Banking System

Federal Deposit Insurance
   Corporation (FDIC)
Financial Holding Company
   (FHCs)
Glass-Steagall Act of 1933
Interstate Banking and
   Branching Efficiency Act
   (IBBEA)
McFadden Act

Merchant Banking
Moral Hazard Problem
National Bank
Nonbanks
Regulation Q

Review Questions

1. We have stressed that the goals of efficiency and competition may conflict with the goals of safety and soundness. Give an example of when this could occur.

2. What is meant by a dual banking system?

3. What is a bank holding company? Why have most large banks become bank holding companies? What is a financial holding company? What must a bank holding company do to become a financial holding company?

4. What are the two major provisions of the McFadden Act? What was the motivation behind its passage?

5. What is the IBBEA? What was the motivation behind its passage?

6. How did multibank holding companies "get around" the McFadden Act before the passage of the IBBEA? Defend the following statement: The IBBEA did nothing more than endorse what was happening in the marketplace.

7. Critique the following statement: Since there are over 8,100 commercial banks in the United States, banking is obviously a highly competitive industry.

8. What is interest rate risk? Explain several ways that banks can reduce interest rate risk.

9. What is liquidity risk? Discuss how banks deal with this risk. Does the development of non-deposit liabilities increase or decrease liquidity risk?

10. Identify two factors that have contributed to the growth of international banking. What factors contribute to reduced profit margins in this area?

11. What is adverse selection? What is moral hazard? How can a bank manager deal with these risks?

12. Discuss the factors that have contributed to the revolutionary changes in the structure of U.S. banking in recent years. Which factors

are most important? Could regulators have prevented many of the changes?

13. Will the revolutionary changes in banking increase or decrease the competitiveness of the industry? Why?

14. Discuss the following statement: The breakdown of barriers to interstate and intrastate banking means that competition in banking is decreasing.

15. What is the difference between a bank holding company and a financial holding company?

16. What is merchant banking?

Analytical Questions

17. On June 30, 2001, what percentage of bank assets did the smallest 99.9 percent of banks control? What percentage of bank assets did the largest .1 percent of banks control?

18. Explain whether each of the following situations involves asymmetric information, adverse selection, or moral hazard:
    a. I am financing a new car. In applying for a loan, I withhold information about my student loan, and the loan does not show up on my credit report.
    b. Just before quitting my job, I take out all the credit cards I can. I plan to run them up to the limit and declare bankruptcy.
    c. I take out a loan to manufacture a product. My costs end up being higher than expected, and there seems to be little market for my product. I am unable to repay the loan.

19. Use Exhibit 15-1 to calculate the following:
    a. What percentage of state banking offices with FDIC insurance are members of the Fed?
    b. What percentage of FDIC-insured banking offices are members of the Fed? What percentage of total deposits do they hold?
    c. What percentage of total deposits is in national banks?

Internet Exercises

1. The U.S. commercial banking system is unique in the sense that it is a dual banking system with side-by-side federal and state-chartered commercial banks. Access the Internet site for the FDIC at **http://www.fdic.gov** and obtain data on the current status of commercial banks in the United States.
    a. What percentage of commercial banks operates with a national charter? What percentage has a state charter?
    b. Classify the number of FDIC-insured commercial banks by asset size. What do you observe?

2. Browse the Quarterly Banking Profile for the most recent quarter found on the Internet site **http://www.fdic.gov/.** Locate information on the total deposits and income of banks with deposit insurance and the number of bank failures.

Suggested Readings

For an in-depth look at "Changing Technology and the Payment System" with emphasis on the role of banks, see the article by the same name by Jamie B. Stewart, Jr. in *Current Issues in Economics and Finance*, Federal Reserve Bank of New York, Vol. 6, No. 11, October 2000, 6 pgs.

Another interesting article is Robert R. Bliss and Mark J. Flannery, "Market Discipline in the Governance of U.S. Bank Holding Companies: Monitoring Vs. Influencing," *Working Papers*, No. WP-00-3, Federal Reserve Bank of Chicago, March 2000.

For a fascinating article about the sometimes harrowing experiences of a bank examiner, see "Follow the Money," by David Fettig, ed., in *The Region* 12:2 (June 1998): 16–21, published by the Federal Reserve Bank of Minneapolis.

A fairly comprehensive article on the ramifications of large bank mergers is David Greising, "Are Megabanks—Once Unimaginable, Now Inevitable—Better . . . ," *Business Week*, April 27, 1998, pp. 32–39. For a more academic view, see Fred Furlong, "New View of Bank Consolidation," *Federal Reserve Bank of San Francisco Economic Letter*, no. 98-23, July 24, 1998; or Kevin Stiroh and Jennifer Poole, "Explaining the Rising Concentration of Banking Assets in the 1990s," *Current Issues in Economics and Finance*, Federal Reserve Bank of New York, Vol. 6, No. 9, August 2000.

For a discussion of the trends likely to influence banking, see Dev Strischek, "Commercial Lending and Lenders in the 21st Century," *Journal of Lending and Credit Risk Management* 80:12 (August 1998): 16–22.

An article that concludes that regulation accounts for a small, but not insignificant, share of bank costs is Gregory Elliehausen, "The Cost of Bank Regulation: A Review of the Data," *Federal Reserve Bulletin* 84:4 (April 1998): 252–253.

For a glimpse into the future, see Robert T. Parry, "Financial Services in the New Century," *Federal Reserve Bank of San Francisco Economic Letter*, no. 98-15, May 8, 1998.

For an interesting discussion of bank mergers, see Y. Amihud and G. Miller, eds., *Bank Mergers and Acquisitions* (Amsterdam: Kluwer Academic Press, 1998).

A collection of 124 articles in four volumes, see *The Regulation and Supervision of Banks*, Maximilian J.B. Hall, ed., (Northampton, MA: Edward Elgar, 2001). The series covers articles that span from 1973 to 1998.

For a look at "The Emerging Role of Banks in E-Commerce" see John Wenninger's article by the same name in *Current Issues in Economics and Finance*, Federal Reserve Bank of New York, Vol. 6, No. 3, March 2000.

Two relatively new books that look at banking systems abroad may be of interest. They are *Islamic Banking* by Mervyn K. Lewis and Latifa M. Algaoud, (Northampton, MA: Edward Elgar, 2001) and *Banking and Financial Stability in Central Europe* by Karl Petrick and David M.A. Green, (Northampton, MA: Edward Elgar, 2001).

chapter

Saving Associations and Credit Unions

16

Learning Objectives *After reading this chapter, you should know:*

- The origins, purposes, and recent trends in thrifts—mutual savings banks, savings and loans, and credit unions

- The risks faced by thrifts and how they manage these risks

- The similarities and differences among the sources and uses of funds for savings associations and credit unions

- The primary causes of the S&L crisis and the regulatory attempts to address it

" "

One question had to do with whether my financial support in any way influenced several political figures to take up my cause. I want to say, in the most forceful way I can, I certainly hope so.
—Charles Keating

STJ St. Jean's
CREDIT UNION
MON - WED
9:00AM-4:00PM

THUR - FRI
9:00AM-6:00PM

Savings, Mortgages, and the American Dream

Homeownership has long been a part of the American dream. Although you may not yet own your own home, you likely know someone who does. Perhaps you have even watched as your parents, siblings, or friends have gone through the home purchase process. One needs first to organize his or her financial affairs, accumulate savings to make a down payment, and then go to a bank to be pre-qualified or pre-approved for a loan.[1] The next step is to search for a home in one's price range with a realtor or, increasingly, through the many real estate Web pages on the Internet. The process can be intimidating and especially frustrating for those with spendthrift habits, a credit history blemished by too much credit card debt, or a record of late payments. Nevertheless, most Americans today own their own homes. During the economic expansion of the 1990s, homeownership rates rose steadily. As the Department of Housing and Urban Development recently noted, the percentage of households owning their own homes increased from 64 percent in 1993 to 66.2 percent by the end of 2000. However, it has not always been this way.

Many of us take for granted the savings institutions we use to set aside funds, to apply for mortgage loans, or to meet our other consumer lending needs. It is hard to imagine that less that 200 years ago, working-class Americans had few alternatives to deposit the savings they had amassed or to borrow the funds they needed for home purchases or other consumer credit needs. Commercial banks of the era were, for the most part, just that—commercial banks. They took commercial business deposits and made commercial business loans. The homebuyers of the early 1800s not only had to save and borrow like we do, but many of them also helped create and manage the financial institutions used to hold their savings, grant their mortgages, and meet their other borrowing needs. A strong democratic, cooperative, and—in some cases—philanthropic impulse aided these pioneers in creating local savings banks, savings associations, and credit unions.

Since their inception, savings associations and credit unions have continued to evolve. Savings associations lost their nonprofit status during the 1950s as their operations expanded. Commercial banks have gone to court to challenge the nonprofit status of credit unions for similar reasons. The high and persistent interest rates of the late 1970s and early 1980s challenged the existence of savings associations (a challenge hundreds failed to meet), changed the risks these lenders faced, exposed problems in the regulatory structure, and forced lenders, legislators, and regulators to adapt to changing circumstances. One notable change in this evolutionary process has been the manner in which lenders manage home mortgages. In the past, lenders (primarily savings associations) made mortgage loans and held them until maturity. The interest revenue generated was the primary source of revenue for the lenders. As you learned in Chapter 12, lenders today are more likely to make mortgage loans and resell them in the secondary mortgage market. Instead of relying on interest income, lenders increasingly rely on fee income generated from loan processing.

---

[1] To be pre-qualified for a loan means that you have met with a banker to discuss your current assets and debts and have estimated how much house you can afford. In contrast, to be pre-approved for a loan means that you have actually completed a loan application for a particular loan amount and had the lender examine your credit report.

Chapter 14 introduced you to financial institutions and financial conglomerates. In this chapter, we will take a closer look at *thrifts*.[2] savings banks, savings and loans, and credit unions. We begin by describing savings associations (savings banks and savings and loan associations), why they were created, how they compare to each other, and how they are distributed by asset size. We also describe trends in their number and size, the ways they raise and use funds, and the ways they manage risk. We look at the savings and loan crisis of the 1980s and regulatory changes that played a part in encouraging and resolving the crisis. Finally, we discuss credit unions—their history and regulation, size distribution, trends, sources and uses of funds, and management of risk.

Savings Associations

History and Regulation

The early 1800s were a tough time for working-class people to find a place to store funds or obtain a home *mortgage*. Providing depository and lending services to the nonrich was perceived by bankers and entrepreneurs as an expensive and unprofitable proposition. Nevertheless, the financial needs of this class did not disappear. In response to growing needs, an absence of commercial interest, and a sense of philanthropy, businesspeople and, sometimes, clergy took it upon themselves to create local savings associations. These *savings associations* were created to encourage personal thrift by generating returns for depositors. They took two forms in the United States: *savings banks* and *savings and loan associations (S&Ls)*. Congressional legislation allowed for the state-level chartering of mutual savings banks in 1816 followed by chartering for savings and loans in 1831. Federal chartering of savings and loans came first in 1933. Savings banks had to wait until 1978 for federal chartering approval. Congress hoped that state and federal chartering of these institutions would provide a reliable source of local funding for families who wanted to buy a home. A review of savings association history shows that this hope has been largely realized.

Since the early 1880s, state-chartered savings banks and S&Ls weathered the ups and downs in the business cycle with varying degrees of success and were left relatively unregulated. The despair and disruption accompanying the Great Depression led financial regulators to write regulations that compartmentalized the financial services industry to reduce competition and enhance safety and soundness. Hence, insurance companies were to specialize in insurance, banks in commercial loans, and savings associations in mortgage lending, In addition, depository institutions were restricted from branching within and across state lines and limited in the interest rates they could charge to borrowers or offer to savers.

Between 1932 and 1934, a series of legislative acts was passed to address the specific needs of savings associations. These acts allowed for the federal chartering of S&Ls, created a federal savings association oversight board, and provided deposit insurance. The regulatory structure coming out of these acts established the **Federal Home Loan Bank Board (FHLBB)** and its network of 12 regional home loan

Federal Home Loan Bank Board (FHLBB)
The primary federal regulatory agency for savings associations from 1932 until 1989; replaced by the Office of Thrift Supervision (OTS).

---

[2]According to the Office of Thrift Supervision (OTS), the thrift industry is defined as the following: "All of the operating financial institutions that primarily accept deposits from individual savers and loan funds primarily for home mortgages. These include savings and loan associations and savings banks." Throughout this text we also include credit unions in our definition of thrifts. We justify this by pointing out that savings associations and credit unions are primarily concerned with the provision of saving and lending to individuals and households. In contrast, commercial banks tend to be more concerned with the saving and borrowing needs of business enterprises.

banks. This network created a flexible source of credit to meet the liquidity needs of member institutions engaged in home mortgage lending. The FHLBB also served as the primary regulator of federally chartered savings associations. In 1934, Congress created the **Federal Savings and Loan Insurance Corporation (FSLIC)** to insure savings association deposits in the same way the FDIC serves commercial banks. These institutions and accompanying regulations served the industry and the needs of homebuyers well until the late 1970s. After this time, the industry faced a severe crisis that will be discussed shortly.

Today, savings associations have become second only to commercial banks in terms of savings deposits and asset holdings. Mortgage brokers and commercial banks have significantly increased their share of mortgage loans originated and eliminated the supremacy that savings associations once had. However, savings associations continue to play an important role in the home mortgage origination process.

Savings Banks

The famous English author, Daniel DeFoe, is credited with originating the concept of the savings bank. In 1697, he suggested the organization of "Friendly Societies for Provident Habits in General." The First Friendly Society, however, was not created for almost 70 years and the term "savings bank" was not applied until 1810. The first savings bank was established in 1810 by the Scottish clergyman, the Reverend Henry Duncan, for his parishoners in Ruthwell Village, Dumfrieshire, Scotland.[3] Its purpose was to encourage the poor and the working class to save and thereby reduce poverty.

The concept of a savings bank and its charitable objectives was transferred to the United States 6 years later. In 1816, Congress allowed savings bank charters, and The Philadelphia Savings Fund Society began operations as the first **mutual savings bank** in the United States. Others followed thereafter. These original savings banks were "mutuals." A mutual savings association or savings bank does not issue capital stock, but instead is owned and controlled by its savings depositors and, in some cases, by its borrowers. Owners called "members" do not usually receive a share of the profits, but do exercise other ownership rights such as electing the board of governors. Today, roughly two-thirds of the savings banks retain this form of ownership, while one-third have sold stock and converted their ownership to **stock savings banks.** Mutual savings banks are chartered in only 17 states, mostly on the East Coast of the United States. Sixty percent of all of these are located in New York and Massachusetts. Mutual savings bank continue to promote savings deposits by individuals and use these funds primarily to make residential mortgage loans, to purchase government and corporate securities, and to offer other banking services.

Savings and Loan Associations (S&Ls)

Like their savings bank companions, savings and loan associations (S&Ls) were created to assist their members in saving and attaining that essential element of the

---

[3]In his *History of Money: From Ancient Times to the Present Day* (University of Wales Press, Cardiff, 1994) Glyn Davies (pp. 332–333) points out that earlier examples of savings banks existed before 1810 in Britain and abroad. However, he argues that these earlier forms of savings banks, "had little influence beyond their own localities, whereas Duncan's experiment quickly became imitated worldwide."

Federal Savings and Loan Insurance Corporation (FSLIC)
The federal agency that insured the deposits of member savings associations from 1934 until 1989; replaced by the FDIC's Savings Association Insurance Fund (SAIF).

Mutual Savings Bank
Savings banks that lack stockholders and whose assets are managed to benefit its collective owners—present and future depositors.

Stock Savings Bank
A type of savings bank charter in which ownership is held by the stockholders.

American dream—homeownership. Their express purpose was to pool the savings of local residents to finance the construction and purchase of homes. The first S&L established in the United States was the Oxford Provident Building Association in Frankfort, Pennsylvania in 1831. Oxford Provident was originally organized as a self-terminating mutual institution. To ensure loan quality, membership and loans were geographically limited to a 5-mile radius of Frankfort, Pennsylvania. In these early associations, shareholders were encouraged to leave their funds in the institution until all members had an opportunity to purchase a home. To withdraw funds earlier, 1 month's notice was required and a 5 percent penalty was applied. After everyone in the building or savings association had an opportunity to purchase a home, the association was dissolved.

These early savings and loans functioned more like modern-day mutual funds than like the S&Ls of today. Mutual funds consist of a pool of funds taken from a variety of investors and used to buy a diverse selection of stocks and bonds. In a similar manner, these early building associations or S&Ls pooled the funds of a variety of "investors" to buy local mortgages. The repayment of mortgages with interest generated the incentive for investors to participate.

As savings and loans expanded in number and geographic location, institutions began to operate on a perpetual basis. Over time, the concepts of "saving" and "loaning" became viewed as separate services. Those who came to save were not necessarily those who came to borrow. Similarly, those who came to borrow did not necessarily come to the institution to save. Institutions also began to accept new members, first on a periodic (quarterly, semiannual, or annual) basis and then on a daily basis. Over time, regulations and insurance were provided to protect consumers. Following World War II, S&Ls spread rapidly with the growth of new housing construction, but many failed during the 1980s.

Savings and Loans versus Savings Banks

There are a few differences between savings and loan associations and savings banks:

1. S&Ls are located throughout the country whereas savings banks are located predominately on the East Coast.
2. Deposits in most S&Ls are insured by the Savings Association Insurance Fund, which is administered by the Federal Deposit Insurance Corporation. In contrast, some savings banks are insured by state insurance fund programs.
3. On average savings banks hold a slightly smaller share of their assets in home mortgages as compared to S&Ls.
4. Savings banks are typically larger than S&Ls in terms of assets and deposits.

Nevertheless, the similarities between S&Ls and savings banks are much greater than their differences. The central mission of both types of institutions is to encourage thrift and to fund home purchases. This creates similar asset and liability structures—both raise funds from the same types of deposit accounts and use these funds for mortgages or mortgage-backed securities. Both types of institutions can be either state or federally chartered. At the federal level, they share the same primary federal financial regulator, the **Office of Thrift Supervision (OTS),** and the same insurer, the *Federal Deposit Insurance Corporation (FDIC)*. Given these similarities between savings banks and S&Ls, it seems useful to group them together for purposes of analysis and discussion.

Office of Thrift Supervision (OTS)
An agency created by the FIRREA to replace the Federal Home Loan Bank Board as the overseer of the S&L industry.

http://www.ots.treas. gov
Provides information about the Office of Thrift Supervision.

EXHIBIT 16-1
Distribution of
Insured Savings
Institutions by Asset
Size, 1999

ASSET SIZE	NUMBER	% NUMBER	ASSETS (IN BILLIONS OF DOLLARS)	% ASSETS
$0–$24.9 million	139	8.5	2.2	0.2
$25–$49.9 million	198	12.1	7.4	0.6
$50–$99.9 million	327	19.9	24.1	2.1
$100–$499.9 million	705	43.0	159.5	13.9
$500–$999.9 million	124	7.6	85.2	7.4
$1–$2.9 billion	96	5.9	161.5	14.1
$3 billion or more	51	3.1	708.9	61.7
Total	**1,640**	**100.0**	**$1,148.7**	**100.0**

SOURCE: U.S. Census Bureau, *Statistical Abstract of the United States, 2000,* Table No. 799, "Selected Financial Institutions—Number and Assets by Asset Size: 1999." Available online at http://www.census.gov; click on Statistical Abstract. Totals fail to sum because of rounding.

Distribution of Insured Saving Institutions

Exhibit 16-1 shows the distribution of federally insured savings institutions by asset size. At year-end 1999, there were 1,640 insured savings institutions holding assets of over $1.1 trillion. The vast majority—1,369, or 83.5 percent—of these institutions have assets of less than $500 million. In contrast, the largest 271 institutions making up 16.6 percent of the industry had an asset size of $500 million or more. They controlled $955.6 billion of the $1.148.7 billion (or 83.2 percent) of the total saving institution assets. Further, the largest 51 institutions—3.1 percent—had an asset size of $3 billion or more and controlled 61.7 percent of total savings institution assets. Thus, most savings associations are small (less than $500 million in assets). However, most savings institution assets (61.7 percent) are controlled by the 51 largest savings institutions that have over $3 billion in assets.

Recent Trends

Between 1984 and 2000, the number of insured savings associations fell by more than 50 percent. Exhibit 16-2 shows that in 1984, there were 3,418 insured savings institutions operating in the United States. By year-end 2000, this number had fallen to 1,590—a decline of about 53 percent. Although new savings institutions continue to open, existing institutions merged with other savings institutions or converted to commercial bank or credit union charters.

During the period of consolidation from 1984 to 2000, the average size of savings associations continued to increase. In 1984, total assets for the industry stood at a little over $1.1 trillion and there were 3,418 institutions. This meant that the average savings institution had an asset size of nearly $335 million. By 2000, the industry had slightly fewer assets—$1.2 trillion. However, these assets were spread out over only 1,590 firms. Thus, the average savings institution in 2000 had an asset size of about $769 million. In short, saving institution nominal assets have increased slightly between 1984 and 2000 while the number of institutions has fallen by more than half. The result is that savings associations on average have more than doubled in nominal size since the mid-1980s.

In the mid-1990s, the assets of S&Ls were more than three times larger than those of savings banks. Nevertheless, as mentioned earlier, their assets and liabilities have a similar composition and, since the institutions share other commonalities, we have lumped S&Ls and savings banks together as savings associations for purposes of discussion.

As first discussed in Chapter 14 (Exhibit 14-2), the major sources of funds for savings associations are time, savings, and checkable deposits. In the aggregate, these

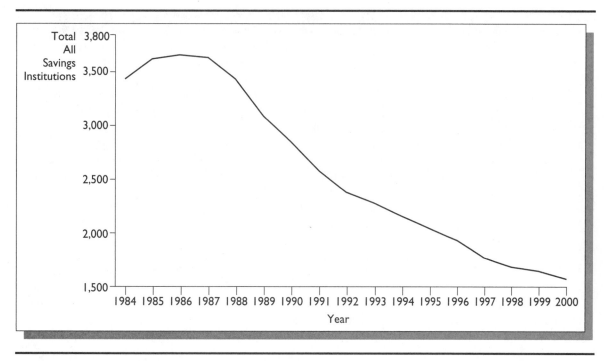

EXHIBIT 16-2

Number of Insured Savings Institutions December 31, 1984– December 31, 2000, United States and Other Areas
SOURCE: FDIC, Historical Statisitcs on Banking, http://www.fdic.gov

deposits accounted for almost 60 percent of total liabilities on December 31, 2001. As is the case with commercial banks, most deposits are insured for up to $100,000. Savings associations were first allowed to issue *negotiable order of withdrawal (NOW)* accounts (interest-earning checkable deposits) nationwide in 1980. Checkable deposits make up a growing source of funds for savings associations. They use the funds mainly to acquire mortgage loans, which comprised 59 percent of total assets held in 2001. U.S. government securities made up another 12 percent of assets.

Although they still specialized in mortgage lending, savings associations diversified somewhat during the 1980s into other forms of lending that were previously prohibited by regulations. Other regulatory changes allowed the institutions to offer time deposits with rates that went up and down with rates on money market instruments, such as Treasury bills.

Prior to the 1980s, savings associations were not only prohibited from offering checkable deposits, but the rates they could pay on time and savings deposits were not allowed to exceed an interest rate cap. This cap was set by *Regulation Q*, which put a ceiling on the maximum interest rate that could be paid on deposits. Commercial banks also faced this cap, but to assist savings associations and encourage homeownership, this cap was set one-half percentage point higher to make their deposit products more attractive to savers. In this earlier environment, small savings deposits were the major source of funds for savings associations. Small savers found passbook savings accounts attractive relative to the alternatives available to them. The accounts were liquid, safe, insured stores of value with fixed interest rates. In the new environment, savings associations have more flexibility and offer the public more diverse types of liabilities. As a result, there is more competition among banks, S&Ls, and savings banks to attract checkable and flexible rate time deposits, and the earlier caps on deposits have been eliminated for all institutions.

LOOKING OUT: *Savings Institutions in Other Countries*

In the United States, thrifts serve as important institutions for encouraging and managing consumer saving. In other countries with other needs, risks, and regulatory structures, different institutions are used to meet citizens' savings needs.

The state-owned postal savings system in Japan was founded in 1875 to offer a risk-free place for small savings. Savers deposit their funds at the local post office. The funds are then used to finance government infrastructure projects and other government spending, rather than consumer loans or mortgages as in the United States. By offering branches in even the smallest villages, the postal system has, according to *The Economist*, become the "world's biggest repository of private savings." Since it is controlled by the state, the postal system can offer higher interest rates than those offered by commercial banks. It also guarantees higher interest rates for 10 years and charges no penalty for early withdrawal. The accounts are understandably popular with consumers because of their convenience, return, and safety. Since Japan's 1996 "big bang" of financial deregulation, the Japanese postal system has faced pressure from private banks to pursue privatization and its alleged efficiencies.

The United Kingdom has mutually owned building societies similar to U.S. savings and loan associations. Until very recently, the building societies were the main lender of mortgages. They have come under pressure to be more competitive and many are converting from mutual building societies to stockholder-owner banks. Many of the building societies are becoming banks to prevent customers from leaving them in search of higher returns. People have been using traditional savings accounts less and turning to riskier forms of investment. The result has been a diminished share of the mortgage market for Britain's building societies.

SOURCE: *The Economist,* "Japanese Finance—Sleeping with the Enemy," April 22, 2000, Vol. 355, 8167, p. 73; "Public Affairs: Building Societies," (Britain) Feb. 3, 1996, Vol. 338, No. 7951, p. 67(1); "Japan's Dangerous Post Office," (editorial) Oct. 29, 1994, Vol. 333, No. 7887, p. 20(2).

RECAP Thrift institutions consist of savings associations (savings banks and S&Ls) and credit unions. All were created to encourage thrift and provide a place for the nonwealthy to accumulate savings and provide home purchase financing. The similarities between S&Ls and savings banks are much greater than their differences. The central mission of both types of institutions is to encourage thrift and to fund home purchases. Almost 85 percent of all savings associations have assets of less than $500 million. However, the largest 15 percent of savings institutions control more than 80 percent of all savings association assets. Since the mid-1980s, the number of savings associations has fallen in half while the average size of savings associations has doubled. The major sources of funds for savings associations are time, savings, and checkable deposits. The major uses of funds are for mortgage loans and U.S. government securities.

Savings Association Management of Risk

All financial intermediaries face varying degrees of default, interest rate, liquidity risk, and exchange rate risk. Since savings associations, in general, do not engage in transactions that involve foreign exchange, exchange rate risk is usually minimal. Therefore, we focus on how savings associations manage these three other types of risk.

Default, or credit, risk is the probability of a debtor not paying the principal and/or interest due on an outstanding debt. Savings associations are most exposed to default risk when making mortgage loans. One underlying facet of mortgage loans is that they require the loan be secured by land and real property. This collateral serves as a potent force to discourage default.

Early savings associations dealt with default risk by requiring that loans be made in a local area where the owners and managers of the firm could have knowledge about the value of the property and about the character of the borrower. Today's managers rely on expert credit analysis and insurance to reduce default. Mortgage insurance is provided through the Federal Housing Authority (FHA) and Veterans Administration (VA) government programs to qualified savings association borrowers. For conventional mortgages, lenders often require that the borrowers take out private mortgage insurance (PMI) for highly leveraged properties—transactions whereby the purchaser borrows more than 80 percent of the property's value. For those less highly leveraged loans (less than 80 percent loan-to-value ratio), the lender usually bears the remaining risk directly. However, as long as the underlying property value does not collapse, the lender should be in a position to resell the property at a profit in case of default.

Interest rate risk is the threat that the interest rate will unexpectedly change so that the costs of a savings association's liabilities exceed the earnings on its assets. Savings associations were established to make long-term mortgages and fund them by taking in short-term deposits. As long as the interest rate on the savings association's assets (loans) exceeds the interest rate on its liabilities (deposits), this spread, or gap, will yield positive earnings. If an intermediary pays his or her depositors 3 percent and then loans these funds out as 6 percent, the spread is a positive 3 percent. Problems occur when interest rates increase and the interest rates on short-term deposits increase more rapidly than those on long-term loans. The spread can quickly turn negative, thus creating losses, reducing capital, and as we saw in the early 1980s, creating widespread insolvency in the industry. Imagine a situation in which an intermediary has to pay depositors 9 percent to attract deposits, but most of its assets are held as long-term mortgage loans paying only 6 percent. In this case, the intermediary faces a negative interest rate spread of 3 percent.

One way that savings associations manage interest rate risk is through the use of **adjustable- (variable-) rate mortgages (ARMs)**. As the cost of funds rise or fall, the interest rates on these mortgage loans adjust upward or downward with the cost of funds. This adjustable rate helps savings associations maintain a positive interest rate spread between their loans and deposits even in the face of rising interest rates. It is worth noting that the risk has not been eliminated by ARMs. Variable-rate mortgages simply shift the interest rate risk from the lender to the borrower. If interest rates rise so that some borrowers are unable to make their payments, the savings association is exposed to a higher degree of default risk than it otherwise would have been with fixed-rate mortgages.

Adjustable- (Variable-) Rate Mortgages
Mortgages made with an interest rate that is adjusted up or down as the cost of funds rises or falls.

Savings associations have also reduced interest rate risk over time by holding fewer longer-term assets. As mentioned earlier, savings associations today often resell mortgages soon after they grant them. In addition, they also make prudent use of interest rate futures contracts and interest rate swaps to reduce interest rate risk.

Savings associations also face liquidity risk—the threat that a savings association will be required to make a payment when it holds only long-term assets that cannot be quickly converted to cash without a capital loss. Savings associations rely on short-term liabilities (small savings and time deposits) to finance long-term assets (home mortgages). This makes them especially susceptible to liquidity problems when deposit withdrawals are greater than incoming deposits. To meet these withdrawal requests, savings associations can either sell some of their assets or take on more liabilities.

In terms of the asset side of the balance sheet, savings associations can sell mortgages, Treasury bills, or other assets to raise funds. On the liability side, the institution can borrow in the fed funds market, engage in repurchase agreements, or issue higher-interest rate CDs to attract depositors. In case of severe liquidity problems, they may borrow at the discount window of their Federal Reserve District bank.

RECAP Like all financial intermediaries, savings associations must deal with credit, interest rate, and liquidity risk. Default or credit risk is the probability of a debtor not paying the principal and/or interest due on an outstanding debt. It is managed by securing loans with collateral, using expert credit analysis, and requiring mortgage insurance. Interest rate risk is the threat that the interest rate will unexpectedly change so that the costs of a savings association's liabilities exceed the earnings on its assets. This can be managed through the prudent use of adjustable rate mortgages and by selling mortgages into the secondary mortgage market. Liquidity risk is the threat that a savings association will be required to make a payment when it has only long-term assets than cannot be converted to liquid funds quickly without capital loss. Savings associations manage this risk by borrowing in the fed funds market, through the use of repurchase agreements, or through the discount window at the Fed. They can also sell mortgages, Treasury bills, or other assets.

The S&L Crisis

The high interest rates of the late 1970s created problems for the savings associations because they primarily funded long-term mortgage loans with short-term deposits. When interest rates rose, a positive spread could turn negative because the savings associations had to pay more for the use of deposits than they were earning on their assets. In addition, as we first saw in Chapter 5, as interest rates rose, the value of their long-term, fixed-rate mortgage assets fell. Thus, savings associations were exposed to a great deal of interest rate risk and had not yet developed the tools, such as adjustable rate loans and secondary markets, to manage that risk.

The problems for savings associations that began in the 1970s increased in the 1980s. Changes in regulations compounded the problems and a severe financial crisis developed. More than 1,500 institutions failed or went out of existence. Many others downsized and the industry as a whole shrunk considerably. Taxpayers spent billions of dollars to bail out the industry because the financial crisis threatened the health and stability of the entire economy. The result is an industry far different from what it was at the start of the 1980s. To understand today's S&L industry, we need to first understand the crisis it underwent in the 1970s and 1980s as well as the legislative attempts to ameliorate this crisis.

As in most crises, the seeds of the S&L debacle were planted long before the first sprouts of trouble appeared and can be found in the way S&Ls do business. Unless interest rates remain fairly stable for long periods of time, as they did from the early 1950s until the 1970s, it is risky to fund long-term loans or purchase long-term assets with short-term deposits. If interest rates rise, the cost of the funds borrowed over the short term can increase above what long-term assets are earning. As we saw earlier, S&Ls were literally established for the express purpose of borrowing short-term from passbook savers and lending long-term to finance mortgage loans. That is, they were designed to engage in behavior that would be dangerous in an environment of volatile or rising interest rates.

From the early 1950s on, the U. S. economy experienced a slow, upward drift in interest rates. Regulation Q, which put a ceiling on the interest rate that could be paid on deposits, applied to S&Ls as well as commercial banks. With Regulation Q in place, the cost of the funds borrowed, mostly from passbook savers, was maintained at or below the ceiling limits. Small savers, at least for a time, had few alternatives to passbook savings accounts in depository institutions. Consequently, disintermediation (the removal of funds from financial intermediaries) was relatively minor when interest rates on other financial assets such as Treasury bills or commercial paper went above the Regulation Q limits. The other financial assets were generally unavailable to small savers who did not have the minimum amounts required to purchase them (at the time $10,000 was the minimum amount needed to purchase a Treasury bill). By the 1970s, however, small savers did have money market mutual funds as an alternative to passbook accounts in depository institutions.[4] Still, the situation fermented for some time before the crisis occurred. By the late 1970s and early 1980s, events had begun to unfold that would result in total collapse of the industry and a large taxpayer bailout.

To understand the burgeoning crisis, recall that nominal interest rates are approximately equal to real interest rates plus the expected inflation rate. In the late 1970s, high nominal rates reflected expectations about inflation—that is, the high nominal rates were the result of large inflation premiums, not from high real interest rates. In fact, in the 1970s real rates were often abnormally low and sometimes even negative despite the high nominal rates. Negative real interest rates exist whenever the rate of inflation is higher than the nominal interest rate. This happened in the early 1970s when the rate of inflation was over 10 percent and the interest rate was below 10 percent.

In late 1979, the Fed orchestrated a huge spike in already high nominal rates as part of a policy aimed at reducing inflation. Interest rates climbed far above the Regulation Q ceilings, which capped nominal rates while ignoring real rates. The spike in nominal rates caused severe disintermediation and/or the transfer of funds from S&Ls to money market mutual funds. In 1980, Congress passed the **Depository Institutions Deregulation and Monetary Control Act (DIDMCA),** which pertained to all depository institutions including savings associations. This Act allowed S&Ls to issue checkable deposits in the form of negotiable orders of withdrawal (NOW) accounts and increased the asset and liability powers for thrifts. Additional legislation, the **Garn-St. Germain Act of 1982,** authorized S&Ls to offer **money market deposit accounts (MMDAs)** that competed with money market mutual funds. Money market deposit accounts actually had an advantage over money market mutual funds because they were insured by the Federal Savings and Loan Insurance Corporation (FSLIC), whereas money market mutual funds were not. Garn-St. Germain slowed the disintermediation and the transfer of funds from the S&Ls to money market mutual funds, but it was probably too little too late. It also left the S&Ls with another problem: S&Ls had mostly long-term, fixed-rate assets, primarily low-rate mortgages, that were now funded by high-interest, variable-rate accounts. Thus, the S&Ls faced two related problems. First, their profits fell as their costs of funds increased faster than their earnings on assets. Second, the value of their assets fell. Recall that when interest rates rise, the value of long-term bonds falls. Long-term, fixed-rate mortgages are similar to long-term bonds in that when interest rates rise, the present value of long-term, fixed-rate mortgages goes down.

In 1981, economists estimated that the S&L industry had a substantial negative net worth that was far greater than the assets of the Federal Savings and Loan Insurance Corporation (FSLIC), which insured the deposits of the sickly S&Ls.[5]

Depository Institutions Deregulation and Monetary Control Act of 1980 (DIDMCA)
The statute that removed many of the regulations enacted during the Great Depression, phased out Regulation Q, established uniform and universal reserve requirements, increased the assets and liabilities depository that institutions could hold, authorized NOW accounts, and suspended usury ceilings.

Garn-St. Germain Act of 1982
A statute that, along with DIDMCA, deregulated the financial structure; authorized money market deposit accounts and Super NOW accounts.

Money Market Deposit Accounts (MMDAs)
Financial claims with limited check-writing privileges, offered by banks since 1982; they earn higher interest than fully checkable deposits and require a higher minimum balance.

---

[4]Actually, as we saw earlier, a person transferring funds from a depository intermediary to a money market mutual fund is not "disintermediating," but is transferring funds from one type of intermediary to another.

[5]The now defunct FSLIC was the federally sponsored agency that insured the deposits of S&Ls for up to $100,000. It was dissolved in 1989. Since this time, S&Ls can obtain deposit insurance from the Savings Association Insurance Fund (SAIF), which is part of the Federal Deposit Insurance Corporation (FDIC).

Rather than confronting the problem head on in the early 1980s, which would have required injecting taxpayer funds into the system, Congress responded with actions that would eventually make the situation much worse. As noted previously, the legislation of 1982 expanded the lending powers of the S&Ls. S&Ls were allowed to enter new product lines that paid a high return but were unfamiliar to S&L managers and entailed considerable risk. Capital requirements—the cushion against losses—were also lowered so that the S&Ls could aggressively enter the new lending arenas. Rather than having to hold capital equivalent to 5 percent of assets, S&Ls were required to hold capital equal to only 3 percent of assets.

With expanded lending powers and lower capital requirements, the industry made new high-earning investments in such ventures as junk bonds and commercial real estate. What happened next? The S&Ls ended up losing even more and literally went broke. In late 1986, Congress granted the FSLIC $10.8 billion funded by borrowing against future deposit insurance premiums to be paid by the thrifts themselves. In 1988, the Federal Home Loan Bank, the equivalent of the Fed for S&Ls at the time, liquidated more than 200 insolvent thrifts by selling the institutions to individuals and firms. In the liquidation process, the buyers were compensated for the negative net worth of the institutions with an array of future guarantees and obligations, including tax breaks. None of these compensations required congressional authorization or appropriation and have subsequently been viewed with suspicion.

In 1989, Congress responded with the *Financial Institutions Reform, Recovery, and Enforcement Act (FIRREA)*, which attempted to resolve the problems of widespread failures within the industry and insufficient insurance funds to settle the crisis. Besides providing funds to resolve the S&L crisis, the most important changes of this Act were the elimination of the FHLBB system and the FSLIC as the savings association insurer. In their place, the Office of Thrift Supervision (OTS) now serves as the primary federal regulatory agency for the industry. FSLIC's responsibilities were folded into the FDIC and its newly created **Savings Association Insurance Fund (SAIF).** The Act also created the **Resolution Trust Corporation (RTC)** as a temporary agency to dispose of thrift properties that failed between 1989 and 1995. The FDIC was put in charge of overseeing the RTC. The provisions of the DIDMCA, Garn-St. Germain Act, and FIRREA are covered in more detail in the next chapter.

The financial bailout shifted the costs from the owners of S&Ls and their depositors to the public (taxpayers) at large.[6] According to Timothy Curry and Lynn Shibut in the *FDIC Banking Review,*[7] by the end of 1999 the total cost of the cleanup was approximately $153 billion. About $124 billion was paid by taxpayers and the other $29 million was paid for by savings associations. This estimate is significantly higher than initial estimates in the late 1980s and substantially less than estimates of a half a trillion dollars put forward in the mid-1990s.

What can we conclude about the causes of the crisis? Undoubtedly, the inherent problem of lending long and borrowing short when interest rates were rising was a major factor. Another factor was the extension of lending powers to the thrifts in the early 1980s. These new powers, which allowed for more risk-taking, also seem to have attracted some dishonest folk to the industry. Finally, regulators were slow to move in and shut down troubled thrifts, which caused eventual losses to be greater

Savings Association Insurance Fund (SAIF)
An organization created by FIRREA in 1989 and managed by the FDIC to provide insurance for savings association deposits. It replaced the defunct FSLIC.

Resolution Trust Corporation (RTC)
An agency created by the FIRREA in 1989 to dispose of the properties of failed S&Ls.

---

[6]We should point out that the bailout was to the benefit of taxpayers by maintaining the solvency of the financial system as well as at the expense of taxpayers.

[7]Fall 2000-Vol. 13, No. 2 or http://www.fdic.gov/bank/analytical/banking/2000dec/.

LOOKING BACK: *The Lincoln Savings Scandal*

Lincoln Savings was a pristine S&L in the idyllic planned community of Irvine, California. It was purchased for $51 million in 1984 by American Continental of Phoenix, a large real estate development company controlled by Charles Keating. With hindsight, it is surprising that Keating was allowed to buy Lincoln, since he had been accused of fraud by the Securities and Exchange Commission only 4 years earlier. As a state-chartered institution, Lincoln was permitted unlimited direct investment in real estate, a potential gold mine for a real estate developer. Within days of taking the helm, Keating fired moderate loan officers and rushed into high-risk investments including junk bonds, desert land in Arizona, hotels, common stock, currency futures, and real estate developments, including those of his own American Continental.

The Federal Home Loan Bank Board (FHLBB) was responsible for regulating and insuring Lincoln Savings. Although under the state charter Lincoln was free to make unlimited direct investments in real estate, the FHLBB balked and announced a regulation that limited direct investment in real estate to 10 percent of total assets for S&Ls insured with the FSLIC. In 1986, regulators from the Federal Home Loan Bank in San Francisco realized that Lincoln exceeded this limit for federally insured thrifts by some $600 million. By 1987, the regulators realized that Lincoln Savings was in serious trouble, and they wanted to move in and seize the institution.

Keating responded by seeking the help of influential politicians. He made large political contributions, in particular giving $1.3 million to five U.S. senators who became known as the "Keating Five."[a] They intervened with the FHLBB on behalf of Lincoln and met with Edwin Gray, chair of the FHLBB, and top regulators from the San Francisco office. The senators alleged that the regulators were being too hard on Lincoln and asked for regulatory leniency.

In September 1987, M. Danny Wall replaced Edwin Gray as chair of the FHLBB. He later continued on at the Office of Thrift Supervision (OTS). Wall transferred the regulation of Lincoln from the San Francisco office to the Washington office, a most unconventional move. No regulator walked into Lincoln for the next 10 months. In early 1987, Lincoln had assets of $3.9 billion. By early 1989 when Lincoln failed, its assets had grown to $5.5 billion. Obviously, a lot of lending had been done. The Lincoln failure ended up costing taxpayers about $2.5 billion. M. Danny Wall was forced to resign because of his involvement in the scandal, and both Charles Keating and his son were sentenced to prison for numerous convictions for negligence and fraudulent acts.[b]

Of the many fraudulent practices that Lincoln engaged in, perhaps the most pernicious was misrepresentation in the sale of subordinated debt. Subordinated debt is unsecured debt that in the event of default will not be repaid until other creditors are repaid. Buyers of this debt, who later swore to investigators they had been guaranteed that the debt was insured just like other deposits in an S&L, lost about $200 million. Many of these unsuspecting investors were senior citizens who lost their life savings.

[a]The senators were Dennis DeConcini and John McCain of Arizona, Alan Cranston of California, John Glenn of Ohio, and Donald Riegle of Michigan. Check the reelection results after the scandal, and you may be surprised at what you find.
[b]After serving almost 5 years in prison, Keating was released in December 1996, when his convictions were thrown out on technicalities.

than they otherwise might have been, and Congress was also slow to act. Fraud also played a supporting role in the crisis, as described in the accompanying Looking Back feature on the Lincoln Savings scandal. Many hard lessons were learned as taxpayer funds were diverted to bail out the S&L industry rather than being used to build schools, improve our nation's infrastructure, or for any other worthwhile projects.

http://www.fdic.gov/ bank/historical/s&l/ index.html
Provides a chronologically organized list of bibliographic resources on the S&L crisis.

RECAP The S&L crisis resulted primarily because the structure of lending long and borrowing short was seriously disrupted by volatile and high interest rates of the late 1970s and early 1980s. The Financial Institutions Reform, Recovery, and Enforcement Act (FIRREA) of 1989 served as the S&L bailout bill. It created the Office of Thrift Supervision (OTS) to oversee the savings association industry, moved FSLIC's responsibilities to the FDIC's Savings Association Insurance Fund (SAIF), and created the Resolution Trust Corporation (RTC) to manage the liquidation of assets from failed S&Ls.

Credit Unions

History and Regulation

Credit unions, the third type of thrift organization, are cooperative, nonprofit, member-owned, tax-exempt depository institutions operated for the benefit of the member savers and borrowers who share a common bond. Credit unions are frequently managed by boards of directors and supervisory committees composed entirely of volunteers who wield substantial decision-making power over the institution. Unlike savings associations, which specialize in the provision of long-term housing credit, credit unions specialize in small, short-term consumer loans. Also unlike a savings association, the general public cannot "join"—deposit into or borrow from—a particular credit union. By law, members must share a *common bond* such as an employer, a church, a labor union, or a geographic region. Almost 80 million Americans, many of them federal government, state government, and public utilities employees, were members of the 10,684 credit unions in operation at year-end 2000. Among the 20 largest federally insured credit unions in the United States are the Navy, the North Carolina State Employees, the Pentagon, the Orange County Teachers, and the Boeing employees credit unions.

The history of credit unions is similar to that of savings institutions—they arose out of frustration with the lack of attention commercial banks gave to the saving and credit needs of ordinary working people. Although savings institutions were created to help address these needs with respect to mortgage credit, the need for small loans to buy automobiles, furniture, home improvements, and other personal expenses remained unmet. The credit union filled this niche. The first credit unions began in Germany in the 1840s. They spread to Quebec in 1900 and finally to the United States in 1909, with the establishment of St. Mary's Cooperative Credit Association in Manchester, New Hampshire.

In 1914, the Massachusetts Credit Union (MCU) was organized both to serve as a regular credit union and to assist others with the creation of new credit unions. Over time it evolved into a kind of central credit union and trade association for the industry. In 1921, the MCU became the **Credit Union National Extension Board (CUNEB)**, whose primary purpose was to expand the credit union movement across the country. In 1935, it was reorganized again to become the **Credit Union National Association (CUNA).**

Today, CUNA serves as the "premier national trade association" in the country for credit unions. CUNA works in partnership with state credit union leagues to assist credit unions with legislative and regulatory advocacy, professional education, and market research. CUNA also works with other organizations to provide quality products and services to credit unions more cheaply than individual institutions could acquire on their own.

The federal government also had a hand in facilitating credit union growth. On June 26, 1934 the Federal Credit Union Act was signed into law by President Roosevelt "to establish the Federal Credit Union System, to establish a further market for securities of the United States, and to make more available to people of small means credit for provident purposes through a national system of cooperative credit, thereby helping to stabilize the credit structure of the United States." In the debate over the Act, neither the Federal Reserve Board nor the Comptroller of the Currency (OCC) wanted regulatory responsibility over federal credit unions. The Farm Credit Administration took initial responsibility, and over the years responsibility shifted to bureaus within the FDIC, the Federal Security Agency, and the Department of Health, Education and Welfare.

Credit Union National Extension Board (CUNEB)
A privately created organization formed in 1921 to expand the credit union movement across the country; a forerunner to the CUNA.

Credit Union National Association (CUNA)
The largest credit union trade association in the United States provides bulk purchases of supplies, automated payment services, credit card programs, and various investment options to member credit unions.

http://www.cuna.org
Provides more information about CUNA.

Credit union membership and assets continued to grow steadily in the post-World War II period as has the need for stronger federal regulatory oversight. To meet this need, the National Credit Union Act of 1970 established the **National Credit Union Association (NCUA)** as an independent federal agency to charter and regulate federally chartered credit unions and state member institutions.[8] The Act also created the **National Credit Union Share Insurance Fund (NCUSIF)**—which is managed by the NCUA board—to "insure" credit union deposits. All federally chartered credit unions are required to join the NCUSIF system. State-chartered credit unions that qualify for and choose to become members of NCUSIF may also join. As is the case with commercial banks and savings associations, each account at an insured credit union has coverage of up to $100,000 per account. Some state-chartered credit unions continue to be insured by their state depository agency.[9] Unlike a bank or savings association that pays an explicit premium for deposit insurance, credit union insurance is more like a mutually owned investment pool—credit unions set aside 1 percent of their deposits in the NCUSIF.[10] If credit unions fail, they dip into the fund to pay off their depositors. When necessary, the NCUA board can charge an additional premium. Fortunately, this has not been necessary since the early 1990s. Congress has also mandated that when the insurance fund holds more than 1.3 percent of total credit union insured deposits, these additional funds must be returned to credit unions as dividends on their investments. It is worth noting that as of 2000, more than two-thirds of the NCUA's annual expenses are paid for out of earnings on the NCUSIF. In the last few years of the 1990s, credit unions received dividends on their "insurance" investment.

The common bond requirement and limited geographic diversification of credit unions leave them especially vulnerable to short-term liquidity problems. If a credit union has short-term liquidity needs, it can borrow from other credit unions or from a network of (corporate) state central credit unions. Since 1974, these corporate state central credit unions (34 in 2000) have worked in conjunction with the **U.S. Central Credit Union** (the credit union equivalent of a central bank) to provide their member credit unions with electronic settlement services and access to national and international money and capital markets.

In addition to this network of state credit unions the **Central Liquidity Facility (CLF)** was created in 1978 to serve as a lender-of-last-resort for credit unions. To use this facility, credit unions must become members and prove that they need the liquidity. This is similar to how the Fed's discount window serves commercial banks. Temporary *emergency* loans are commonly used to boost the liquidity of troubled credit unions or to meet their short-term seasonal funding needs. For most day-to-day liquidity needs, state central credit unions are sufficient. However, in case of a nationwide crisis, the CLF can borrow directly from the Federal Reserve and thus provide liquidity to credit unions across the country. Membership in the CLF is voluntary.

National Credit Union Association (NCUA)
A federal regulatory agency created in 1970 to charter and regulate federally chartered credit unions and state member institutions.

National Credit Union Share Insurance Fund (NCUSIF)
A federal agency created in 1970 to insure the deposits of federally chartered credit unions and state member institutions.

U.S. Central Credit Union
The central bank for credit unions.

http://www.uscentral.org
Provides more information about the U.S. Central Credit Union and its member owners.

Central Liquidity Facility (CLF)
A lender-of-last-resort created in 1978 for credit unions experiencing temporary liquidity problems.

http://www.ncua.gov
Discusses more about NCUA, the NCUSIF, and the Central Liquidity Facility.

---

[8]The NCUA is managed by a three-member board, one of which serves as chair. Board members are appointed by the president and confirmed by the Senate. They serve staggered 6-year terms.

[9]As of September, 1999 nonfederally insured state chartered credit unions are located in Alabama, California, Idaho, Illinois, Indiana, Maryland, Montana, Nevada, Ohio, and Puerto Rico. As of July 2001, the states of Delaware, South Dakota, and Wyoming, and the District of Columbia, allow only federal chartering of credit unions.

[10]Some bankers have begun suggesting that the FDIC should adopt a similar mutual ownership structure.

ASSET SIZE	NUMBER	% NUMBER	ASSETS (IN MILLIONS OF DOLLARS)	% ASSETS
$0–.2 million	304	2.85	37	0.01
.2–.5 million	541	5.06	188	0.04
.5–1 million	745	6.97	551	0.12
1–2 million	1,001	9.37	1,472	0.33
2–5 million	1,823	17.06	6,095	1.36
5–10 million	1,648	15.42	11,761	2.61
10–20 million	1,456	13.63	20,761	4.62
20–50 million	1,544	14.45	49,064	10.91
50–100 million	732	6.85	51,503	11.45
100–200 million	448	4.19	63,301	14.07
200–500 million	310	2.90	96,691	21.50
500+ million	132	1.24	148,375	32.99
Total	**10,684**	**100.00%**	**$449,799**	**100.00%**

SOURCE: Credit Union National Association (CUNA), Credit Union report. Available online at http://www.cuna.org/data/cu/research/cu_stats.html#annualdata.

Distribution of Credit Unions

Although there are about as many credit unions (10,684) as there are commercial banks and savings associations combined, most credit unions are small in size. Some 6,332 (59 percent) are chartered under federal law, while the other 4,352 (41 percent) are chartered under the laws of various states and Puerto Rico.

At year end 2000, the total assets of credit unions stood at about $450 billion compared to the roughly $1.2 trillion controlled by savings associations and $6.5 trillion for commercial banks. Exhibit 16-3 shows that most credit unions (56.74 percent) have total assets of less than $10 million. Almost one-quarter (24.25 percent) have less than $2 million in assets. The largest credit unions—those with $100 million or more in assets—constitute 8.33 percent of credit unions and control 68.56 percent of credit union assets. The 11 largest federally insured credit unions with assets of over $2 billion—.1 percent of the industry—possess over $44 billion in assets, or almost 10 percent of total credit union assets. Thus, like the savings associations and commercial banks, a few larger credit unions control the majority of the industry's assets. In comparison to savings associations, the typical credit union is likely to possess less than $10 million in assets. The typical (median) savings association has an asset size between $100 million and $500 million, making the typical savings association at least 10 times larger than the typical credit union.

Recent Trends

Exhibit 16-4 shows that the number of credit unions in the U.S. more than doubled between 1950 and 1975. Since then the total number of credit unions has declined steadily because of changes in charter and because of mergers, and to a lesser degree, failures. Since 1975, one-half of U.S. credit unions have closed, changed their charter, or merged with other institutions. By the end of 2000 there were 10,684 credit unions in operation in the U.S.

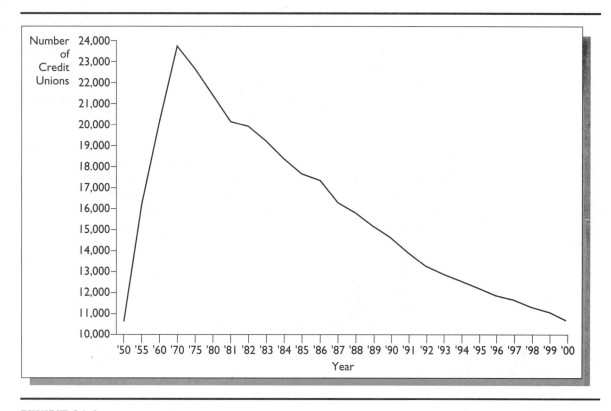

EXHIBIT 16-4

Number of Total (federal and state) U.S. Credit Unions December 31, 1950– December 31, 2000

SOURCE: Credit Union National Association. Available online at http://www.cuna.org.

Credit Unions, Corporate Taxes, and the Community Reinvestment Act: Should credit unions be exempt from corporate taxes and the Community Reinvestment Act (CRA)?[11] These questions are at the center of a debate between commercial banks and credit unions. Commercial banks, even small community banks, are subject to corporate taxes as well as CRA requirements. Many bankers believe that credit unions behave similarly to banks—they lend money and take deposits. However, due to the nonprofit status of credit unions, they are tax-exempt. Some bankers believe that this leads to an unfair advantage. Because of their tax exemption, credit unions are allowed to pay higher interest rates and charge lower fees to their members.

Bankers also believe that credit unions have another advantage in the area of community reinvestment. Since banks must comply with CRA in order to merge with other banks, many pay millions each year to provide services to low-income areas. Bankers charge that credit unions should be required to comply because many are failing when it comes to investment in low-income areas.

A Closer Look

---

[11]The Community Reinvestment Act (CRA) of 1977 requires banks and savings associations to meet the convenience and needs of the entire community (including low and moderate income areas) in which they are located. It was passed in response to allegations that banks were refusing to make loans to particular neighborhoods based on their racial and income composition of the area. The Act requires lenders to document their lending patterns and community participation. Credit unions are exempt.

Credit unions, of course, have a response to the claims made by banks. Credit union officials believe that banks want increased control over the financial services industry. By forcing credit unions to pay taxes and comply with CRA, many credit union officials believe that banks will succeed in reducing price competition from credit unions. Because some credit unions are small, community-based entities, forcing them to pay corporate taxes could threaten their solvency. Credit unions would also have to increase their fees and lower the interest rates paid to their members in order to have the extra revenue needed to pay taxes.

Credit union officials also disagree with bankers about CRA. Community-based credit unions serve the people within their designated community, thus making loans to low-income members without the coercion of federal regulation. Contrary to the assertions of many bankers, credit unions argue that they do serve low-income individuals who would not otherwise be able to receive loans or other financial services. Resolution of this debate will likely be left to the courts, with the loser appealing to Congress.[12]

Share Accounts
Highly liquid credit union deposits that can be withdrawn on demand, but not by writing a check.

Share Draft Accounts
Interest-bearing checking accounts of credit unions.

Share Certificates
The credit union equivalent of a CD.

Credit unions are mutual institutions because they are owned by their depositors. This affects how we talk about credit union deposits and returns. Member deposits are called *shares*. Like the earnings from stock ownership, the interest paid on these deposits is called *dividends*. As of June 30, 2001, credit unions received the vast majority (72 percent) of their funds from members' small time/savings accounts—called regular **share accounts.** (You may want to refer to Exhibit 14-3 from chapter 14.) **Share draft accounts** are interest-bearing checking accounts that were developed in the early 1970s and made available nationally in the 1980s by changes in federal regulation. At mid-year 2001, share draft accounts constituted 11.4 percent of credit union liabilities. They compete favorably with the money market deposit accounts (MMDAs) offered by commercial banks and NOW accounts offered by savings associations. Credit unions also offer **share certificates,** which are similar to the CDs offered by other depository institutions. The depositor agrees to leave the funds for a specified length of time and is rewarded with a higher interest rate return. These larger time deposits constitute 6.2 percent of credit union liabilities.

Not every credit union offers every financial product. According to the Credit Union National Association (CUNA), at the end of 1999, 61 percent offered share draft (personal checking) accounts; 46 percent offered credit cards; 49 percent offered ATM cards; and 41 percent offered first mortgages. Most (79 percent) credit union members hold accounts at credit unions that offer seven of the following eight services: share drafts, certificates, ATM cards, guaranteed student loans, first mortgages, direct deposit of federal recurring payments, credit cards, and travelers checks.

We turn now to credit union uses of funds. As of mid 2001, 39.3 percent of the assets held by credit unions were in the form of consumer loans (for automobiles, furniture, appliances, boats, and other personal needs) to members, while 27.4 percent were for mortgages. About 15.2 percent of the assets held were U.S. Treasury and government agency securities. The remaining assets were deposits at other financial intermediaries, fed funds, repurchase agreements, and miscellaneous items.

Although these statistics have been remarkably stable over time, the total funds acquired and loaned by credit unions have grown rapidly over the years. In 1970,

---

[12]For more on this topic see Kelly Culp, "Banks v. Credit Unions: The Turf Struggle for Consumers," *Business Lawyer.* November 1997, Vol. 53, No. 1, pp. 193–216.

for example, their assets totaled only $18 billion. The comparable 2001 figure was over $475 billion. Nevertheless, credit union assets remain only about one-third of savings association assets and one-fourteenth of commercial bank assets.

RECAP Credit unions are cooperative, nonprofit, member-owned, tax-exempt depository institutions operated for the benefit of the member savers and borrowers who share a common bond. They are regulated at the federal level by the National Credit Union Association (NCUA) and insured by the National Credit Union Share Insurance Fund (NCUSIF). The majority of credit unions (75 percent) have assets of less than $25 million. Almost half (45 percent) have assets less than $5 million. The largest 7 percent of credit unions control 65 percent of credit union assets. The number of credit unions peaked in the 1970s. Since then, mergers have reduced their numbers. Despite the recent consolidation in numbers of credit unions, membership and total assets have continued to increase. The main sources of funds for credit unions are savings/small time deposits and share draft accounts. These funds are used primarily to make small personal and mortgage loans and to purchase government securities.

Credit Union Management of Risk

Because of their common bond requirement and balance sheet structure, credit unions face different degrees of default, interest rate, and liquidity risk, as do other financial intermediaries. Like savings associations, they generally do not experience significant exchange rate risk. Credit unions are exposed to default risk primarily through the loans they make to their members. Most of these loans are secured by real property in the case of mortgages, or by titles to automobiles or boats for other types of loans. This holding of collateral reduces risk. Like their savings association peers, credit unions also require various forms of mortgage insurance and engage in expert analysis to lessen default risk.

One concern is that credit unions often rely on volunteers to assist potential borrowers. These volunteers may lack the necessary training and/or emotional distance from the borrower to engage in effective analysis. A second concern is that the common bond requirement of credit unions makes them vulnerable to a downturn in the local economy. Credit unions are designed to meet local needs and, in some cases, the needs of employees of a single company. If that company experiences a decrease in sales and responds by laying off workers or, in the worst case, shuts down its local facility, the credit unions catering to these workers will face sharply higher rates of default. These risks, of course, will be worsened by weak local economic conditions.

Like savings associations, credit unions fund long-term assets with short-term liabilities. However, they tend to hold a smaller proportion of their assets in mortgages and the personal loans they grant tend to be for shorter periods of time. As of 2001, savings associations and credit unions hold roughly 59 percent and 27 percent, respectively, of their assets as mortgages. Thus, savings associations have a larger degree of interest rate risk than do credit unions. For the mortgages that credit unions do offer, the use of variable-rate mortgages and the sale of mortgages to the secondary market help limit exposure to interest rate risk.

In the case of unanticipated deposit withdrawals, credit unions face the need to raise cash quickly. To meet these withdrawal requests, credit unions can turn to the

Central Liquidity Facility (CLF). Unlike their banking and savings association counterparts, they are less able to bring in funds through higher CD rates because their common bond requirement severely limits the number of new customers available. The desire to reduce exposure to liquidity risk through credit union mergers has been one of the driving forces for consolidation among credit unions today.

RECAP Like all financial intermediaries, credit unions must deal with credit, interest rate, and liquidity risk. Default risk is handled in a way similar to that of savings associations: Collateral is held, mortgage insurance is required, and expert credit analysis is utilized. Interest rate risk is less of an issue for credit unions than for savings associations because of the shorter-term assets held by credit unions. Nevertheless, adjustable rate mortgages and use of the secondary mortgage market can assist credit unions in maintaining a positive interest rate spread. Liquidity risk or an illiquid financial position can be dealt with by accessing funds through the Central Liquidity Facility (CLF). Recent mergers among credit unions have, in part, been motivated by a desire to broaden the liability base of credit unions and thereby reduce liquidity risk.

The Evolution of Thrifts

Savings banks, savings and loans associations, and credit unions share a common theme in their birth and subsequent evolution. All were created out of a need for ordinary people to have access to convenient and affordable savings and lending services. However, these institutions today bear little resemblance to their institutional ancestors. As economic conditions (especially high and volatile interest rates) and telecommunications technology have changed, so have the risks facing these intermediaries. Thrifts have responded by creating new savings and lending instruments, expanding the range of services provided, widening the geographic areas over which they do business, and competing more directly with other types of financial intermediaries. Since the creation of thrifts, Congress and federal regulatory agencies have assisted their development with the creation of deposit insurance, various forms of federal regulatory oversight, as well as various attempts at deregulation and reregulation. The interplay among these changes in economic conditions, technology, regulation, and risks continues to cause the financial innovation that we have described in this chapter. In the next chapter, we take a closer look at how commercial banks, savings associations, credit unions, and other financial services firms are regulated.

Summary of Major Points

- Thrift institutions consist of savings associations (savings banks and S&Ls) and credit unions. All were created, in part, because of the failure of commercial banks to fulfill the savings, housing finance, and consumer credit needs of working-class individuals.

- State chartering of savings banks began in 1816 and federal chartering in 1978. Chartering of savings and loan associations (S&Ls) began at the state level in 1831 and at the federal level in 1934. At the federal level, the Federal Home Loan Bank Board (FHLBB) served as the primary regulatory agency for both types of savings associations until 1989. It was replaced by the Office of Thrift Supervision (OTS). The Federal Savings and Loan Insurance Corporation (FSLIC) insured savings associations until 1989, when its functions were assumed by the Federal Deposit Insurance Corporation's (FDIC's) Savings Association Insurance Fund (SAIF).

- Savings banks may be either mutual savings banks or stock savings banks. Mutuals do not issue capital stock, but instead are owned and controlled by their depositors and, in some cases, their borrowers. Member owners do not usually share in the profits of the firm, but often elect the governing board of the institution. Stock savings banks do issue stock and are controlled by their shareholders.

- Early savings and loan associations functioned more like temporary mutual funds with limited membership than like the S&Ls of today. Over time, they began to operate on a perpetual basis and to regularly accept new members.

- The similarities between S&Ls and savings banks are much greater than their differences. The central mission of both types of institutions is to encourage thrift and to fund home purchases. The major sources of funds for savings associations are time, savings, and checkable deposits. Their major uses of funds are for mortgage loans and U.S. government securities.

- Most (almost 83.5 percent) savings associations have assets of less than $500 million. However, the remaining 16.5 percent of savings institutions control more than 83 percent of all savings association assets. From 1984 to 2000, the number of savings associations has fallen in half— from 3,418 to 1,590—while the average size of savings associations has more than doubled— from about $335 million to about $769 million.

- Like all financial intermediaries, savings associations must deal with credit, interest rate, and liquidity risk. (Exchange rate risk typically plays a minor role for savings associations and credit unions.) Default or credit risk is managed by securing loans with collateral, using expert credit analysis, and requiring mortgage insurance. Interest rate risk is managed through the prudent use of adjustable rate mortgages and by selling mortgages into the secondary mortgage market. Savings associations manage liquidity risk by borrowing in the fed funds market, through the use of repurchase agreements, or through the discount window at the Fed. They also sell mortgages, treasury bills, or other assets.

- The S&L crisis resulted primarily because S&Ls were created to make long-term loans that were funded by borrowing in the short term. This balance sheet structure was seriously disrupted by volatile, high interest rates of the late 1970s and early 1980s. The Financial Institutions Reform, Recovery, and Enforcement Act (FIRREA) of 1989 served as the S&L bailout bill. It created the Office of Thrift Supervision (OTS) to oversee the savings association industry, moved FSLIC's responsibilities to the Federal Deposit Insurance Fund's (FDIC's) Savings Association Insurance Fund (SAIF), and created the Resolution Trust Corporation (RTC) to manage the liquidation of assets from failed S&Ls.

- Credit unions are cooperative, nonprofit, member-owned, tax-exempt depository institutions operated for the benefit of the member savers and borrowers who share a common bond. They are regulated at the federal level by the National Credit Union Association (NCUA) and insured by the National Credit Union Share Insurance Fund (NCUSIF). Many are members of the Credit Union National Association (CUNA), which serves as a trade association for the industry. The Central Liquidity Facility (CLF) serves as a lender-of-last-resort for credit unions with temporary liquidity problems.

- The majority of credit unions (75 percent) have assets of less than $25 million. Almost half (45 percent) have less than $5 million. The largest 7 percent of credit unions control 65 percent of credit unions assets. The number of credit unions peaked in the 1970s. Since then mergers have reduced their numbers. Despite the recent consolidation in numbers of credit unions, membership and total assets have continued to increase. Their main sources of funds for credit unions are savings/small time deposits and share draft accounts. These funds are primarily used to make small personal loans, mortgage loans, and to purchase government securities.

- Credit unions manage default risk by holding collateral, requiring mortgage insurance, and utilizing expert credit analysis. Adjustable rate mortgages and use of the secondary mortgage market assist credit unions in managing interest rate risk. An illiquid financial position can be dealt with by accessing funds through the Central Liquidity Facility (CLF), selling assets, or increasing one's liabilities.

Key Terms

Adjustable (Variable) Rate Mortgages

Central Liquidity Facility (CLF)

Credit Union National Association (CUNA)

Credit Union National Extension Board (CUNEB)

Depository Institutions Deregulation and Monetary Control Act of 1980 (DIDMCA)

Federal Home Loan Bank Board

Federal Savings and Loan Insurance Corporation (FSLIC)

Garn-St. Germain Act of 1982

Mortgage

Mutual Savings Bank

National Credit Union Association (NCUA)

National Credit Union Share Insurance Fund (NCUSIF)

Office of Thrift Supervision (OTS)

Resolution Trust Corporation (RTC)

Savings Association Insurance Fund (SAIF)

Share Accounts

Share Certificates

Share Draft Accounts

Stock Savings Bank

U.S. Central Credit Union

Review Questions

1. Briefly discuss the primary motivations for the creation of savings banks and savings and loan associations in the early nineteenth century.

2. What are the two possible forms of ownership for savings banks and how do they differ?

3. Savings and loan associations have significantly changed the way in which they finance mortgages. Compare the process in 1831 to the process used in the early twenty-first century.

4. List and explain the similarities and differences between savings and loans and savings banks.

5. Describe the size distribution of savings associations. What size category is the most numerous? What size category controls the greatest share of assets?

6. How has the number of savings associations changed since 1984?

7. Before being phased out in 1980, why were Regulation Q ceilings set one-half percent higher for savings associations than for banks?

8. List and describe the major sources and uses of funds for savings associations. How have these changed since the early 1980s?

9. List and explain the major ways in which savings associations manage default risk, interest rate risk, and liquidity risk.

10. Have adjustable rate mortgages eliminated interest rate risk? Explain.

11. Who is Charles Keating and why did he go to jail?

12. Describe the functions of the following credit union agencies:
    a. CUNEB
    b. CUNA
    c. NCUA
    d. NCUSIF
    e. U.S. Central Credit Union
    f. CLF

13. Describe the size distribution of credit unions. What size category is the most numerous? What size category controls the greatest share of assets? How does the size of a typical credit union compare to the size of a typical savings association?

14. How has the number of credit unions changed since 1950?

15. Give the name of the credit union equivalent of the following savings association deposit liabilities:
    a. Passbook savings account
    b. NOW or MMDA account
    c. CDs

16. List and describe the major sources and uses of funds for credit unions.

17. List and explain the major ways in which credit unions manage default risk, interest rate risk, and liquidity risk.

Analytical Questions

18. Explain why credit unions and pension funds rarely purchase municipal securities while casualty companies do. (Hint: It has something to do with the tax status of credit unions.)

19. How has savings association management of credit risk changed over time?

20. Imagine that you are the manager of an S&L. Deposit withdrawals have been $3 million more than anticipated during the morning hours. There is little vault cash remaining and it is 4 hours until closing time. What options do you have to address this liquidity problem?

21. Write one paragraph that accurately identifies and describes the primary causes of the S&L crisis of the 1980s. In a second paragraph, list and explain the actions and effects of the regulatory acts passed in 1980, 1982, and 1989 that attempted to address the S&L crisis.

Internet Exercises

1. One of our favorite resources on the Web is the U.S. Census Bureau's *Statistical Abstract of the United States*, which is updated annually. Go to **http://www.census.gov** and then click on the Statistical Abstract link. (This is sometimes found under the Special Topics link. Click on the "Adobe Acrobat PDF files" link.) The section on Banking, Finance and Insurance provides a wealth of information. Pull up this file and find a table or tables entitled something like "Selected Financial Institutions—Number and Assets by Asset Size." Use this data to do two things: (1) Briefly compare the current size distribution of insured savings institutions with those of credit unions; and (2) describe how the size distribution of insured savings institutions has changed since this book went to print. You will need to refer back to Exhibit 16-1.

2. Let's update the recent trends for credit unions that have occurred since this book went to press. Go to **http://www.ncua. gov.** Click on the Reference Information link and then on Statistics for FICUs. A menu will emerge for the most recent "mid-year" or "year-end" statistics for federally insured credit unions. Click on the most recent data. This PDF (Adobe Acrobat) file usually contains a section on federally insured credit unions. Find that page and print out the most recent 5-year trends for credit unions. Report what has happened to (1) the number of federally insured credit unions, (2) the number of credit union members, and (3) credit union assets under management.

Suggested Readings

The early history of the credit union movement both in Germany and the United States is summarized by J. Carroll Moody in *The Credit Union Movement: Origins and Developments, 1850–1970*, 1971, published by the University of Nebraska Press in Lincoln, Nebraska. Despite the unique historical role played by credit unions, they have continued to evolve over time. As a result, some credit unions have come to look more like their more heavily regulated and corporate-taxed commercial bank competitors. The result has been a heated debate about whether credit unions should be forced to comply with the Community Reinvestment Act (CRA) and/or allowed to maintain their tax-exempt status. George Cleland argues that "Bank-like Credit Unions Should Face Bank-like Taxes" in his *ABA Banking Journal* article of January 1989 (Vol. 81, No. 1, p. 14). In contrast, the March 13, 1998 (Vol. 163, No. 49, p. 4) *American Banker* article entitled "Compromise by Banks is Bait-and-Switch Tactic" discusses the recent banking lobby proposal that separates credit unions into various categories and then imposes category-specific restrictions on these credit unions. Finally, Kelly Culp outlines the many legal battles between banks and credit unions in her "Banks v. Credit Unions: The Turf Struggle for

Consumers" in *Business Lawyer* (November 1997, Vol. 53, No. 1, pp. 193–216).

The S&L crisis has served as a magnet for a large number of scholars assessing its causes and consequences. Right-leaning authors tend to see deposit insurance and the moral hazard problems it created as a primary cause of the problem. For an eloquent and thoughtful discussion on this topic, see Edward J. Kane's *The S&L Insurance Mess: How Did it Happen?* (Washington DC: Urban Institute Press, 1989). Kane argues that the undercapitalization of S&Ls, combined with the flat-rate deposit insurance premiums charged, caused the large number of failures and high resolution costs. Regulatory reluctance and legislative lethargy further exacerbated the crisis. He suggests that the crisis could have been lessened with better accounting practices and more reliable reporting procedures. In James R. Barth's 1991 book, *The Great Savings and Loan Debacle*, Barth concurs with Kane that deposit insurance plays a central role. However, Barth also provides an historical approach to understanding S&Ls while proffering the need for higher capital standards and the more free-market-oriented remedies of geographic deregulation and an expanding macroeconomy. In contrast to Kane and Barth, left-leaning Lawrence J. White argues in his book, *The*

S&L Debacle: Public Policy Lessons for Bank and Thrift Regulation (New York: Oxford University Press, 1991) that deposit insurance is not the root cause. Instead he posits that inadequate regulation and insufficient capital requirements bear the primary burden for the crisis. He strongly opposes remedies that would weaken the deposit insurance system. For a lighter approach to understanding the debacle, try Martin Mayer's *The Greatest-Ever Bank Robbery: The Collapse of the Savings and Loan Industry* (New York: C. Scribner's Sons, 1990). Mayer describes a rich cast of mostly Wall Street investment bankers, accountants, regulators, and lawyers who helped cause and directly profited from the crisis. He also cautions against the current move away from the specialized housing finance institutions that are founded on using local funds to meet local housing needs. The quote from Charles Keating that opens this chapter is recounted by William G. Kastin, Esq. during a hearing on campaign spending and the first amendment. It can be found at **http://www.fordham.edu/law/pubs/iplj/html/article.html.** Finally, for a romantic portrayal of savings and loan associations during the 1930s and the bank runs they faced, it is hard to beat the Christmas classic "It's a Wonderful Life" staring Jimmy Stewart. Reading from this list should help you to earn your wings.

chapter

17

Regulation of the Banking and Financial Services Industry

Learning Objectives *After reading this chapter, you should know:*

- Why regulation is needed in the financial services industry
- Who regulates whom in the banking system
- Some of the major pieces of legislation important to the banking industry today
- Regulatory challenges facing Congress and the regulators

" "

The dogmas of the quiet past are inadequate to the stormy present. As our case is new, so we must think anew and act anew. We must disenthrall ourselves, and then we shall save our country.
—Abraham Lincoln

The people's right to change what does not work is one of the greatest principles of our system of government.
—Richard Nixon

The Role of Regulation

The ability of certain industries within a market economy to regulate themselves has long been the subject of controversy. Some analysts believe that virtually no regulation is needed and that the market can handle almost every situation far better than can a government regulatory agency. For example, they believe that airlines can regulate themselves better than can a government regulatory agency.[1] They argue that if an airline is unsafe, it will experience more accidents than other airlines. As passengers become aware of this accident record, they will avoid flying on the unsafe airline, and it will be driven out of business. Likewise, the market can better regulate the financial services industry than any regulatory agency such as the Fed or the Office of Thrift Supervision. According to this argument, a bank that takes too many risks will be driven out of business when cautious depositors become aware of the risks and withdraw their deposits or when the bank sustains losses and is unable to pay back depositors.

At the other extreme are those who believe that the economy needs much regulation because the quest for profits is so strong that without regulation, consumer welfare will be jeopardized. For example, an airline may skimp on costly maintenance to keep its planes in the sky because planes on the ground do not generate profit. Or a financial intermediary (FI) might take a large risk because the potential payoff is great, and the bulk of the funds the intermediary is risking belong to depositors.[2] Although the unsafe airline may eventually be driven out of business in a market economy, that won't bring back the loved ones who were killed in a plane crash. Likewise, depositors may feel some satisfaction when the depository institution that lost their life savings is driven out of business, but the institution's demise does not reduce their losses.

In Chapter 15, we looked at the Glass-Steagall Act, which was implemented in response to the financial collapse of the Great Depression. Glass-Steagall made the banking sector a highly regulated industry. Although the crisis in the Great Depression might suggest the need for some regulation, by the late 1970s sentiment in the United States had shifted to the belief that the economy had become a victim of over-regulation. This change led to a *deregulation* movement that continues in varying degrees today. Industries such as airlines, trucking, and financial services have been deregulated.

After deregulation, some industries experienced severe stresses and bankruptcies, particularly in the 1980s. The financial services sector went through the collapse of the savings and loan (S&L) industry and the largest wave of bank failures since the Great Depression. Some blamed deregulation, at least to some extent, for these problems. Others, however, argued that the failures were the result of previous regulations that had protected inefficient operations and that the problems would be resolved in time. Indeed, as we have seen, the banking system has recovered and made record profits in recent years.

The banking system, composed of depository institutions, is a major part of the financial services industry. In this chapter, we focus primarily on the regulatory structure of the banking system today and look at the major pieces of legislation that have created it. We begin with deregulation acts in 1980 and 1982 that removed many of the regulations imposed in the Great Depression. We look at the regulatory structure that was implemented in response to the financial crises of the 1980s and to new regulations that were designed in response to technological changes and the globalization of financial markets. We look at recent sweeping legislation that promises to overhaul the banking system and the financial services industry. Finally,

---

[1]The regulatory agency for the airline industry is the Federal Aviation Administration (FAA).

[2]In a world with deposit insurance, the problem is even greater because the depositors will be paid off even if the venture fails.

because of the growing integration of banking and financial services firms, we summarize the major regulators of the financial services industry in general.

The How and Why of Financial Services Regulation

"Free to compete" means "free to fail." Because the failure of a significant number of FIs will undermine the public's confidence in the system, there is a potential conflict between the two objectives of regulation: competition and efficiency, on the one hand, and safety and soundness, on the other hand. The regulatory authorities attempt to balance these objectives by issuing regulations that govern banks and other financial intermediaries.

As we have seen, most bank activities were regulated by various government regulators from the Great Depression in the 1930s until the 1980s. Given the despair and disruption accompanying the Great Depression, the financial regulators wrote regulations that limited "price" competition, restricted entry, controlled the various types of products and services banks and other FIs could offer the public, and specified prudent capital positions for intermediaries. Specific regulations included Regulation Q interest rate ceilings, chartering and branching restrictions, assets and liabilities restrictions, and net worth requirements.

During the 1980s, banks and most other intermediaries were substantially deregulated. A series of financial crises followed that culminated in widespread insolvencies within the S&L industry and many bank failures.[3] The crises triggered attempts at re-regulation and the thought that regulations needed to be overhauled.

Throughout this text, we have repeatedly emphasized the role of regulation in ensuring the safety and soundness of the financial system. Regulations were deemed necessary because of the nature of the financial system and the trade-off between high returns for surplus spending units versus safety and soundness. As we have seen, FIs can earn higher returns by assuming more risks. Indeed, some intermediaries offer higher returns for the acceptance of more risks. However, depository institutions, within limits, offer a guaranteed but lower return.

When deciding how much risk to take on, an FI should evaluate the risks of an activity. Generally speaking, when the expected benefits outweigh the expected costs, the activity will usually be profitable to undertake. But in the process of assessing the expected costs associated with various levels of risk, the intermediary considers only the costs to the stockholders, creditors, and depositors that would result from an investment or portfolio of investments going sour.[4] Because they are so highly leveraged, some FIs may fail to adequately consider how much risk they should take and may ignore the costs to the community at large that could result from the failure of the institution. The collapse of an FI not only affects those directly involved, but could also impede the smooth functioning of a local community or the entire economy. The failure could lead to a bank run and a simultaneous financial collapse. Thus, we arrive at the crux of the problem: If left to decide the level of risk on their own, banks or other intermediaries will generally accept too much risk because they fail to consider the additional costs of failure that the community at large must bear. If banks and other intermediaries were left unregulated, the drive for profits might jeopardize the goals of safety and soundness for the system as a whole.

http://www.dot.gov/
affairs/faaind.htm
Provides information on the Federal Aviation Administration, an example of a regulatory body.

http://www.state.ma.
us/dob/feds.htm
Describes general information on federal bank regulatory agencies.

---

[3]Correlation does not imply causality, which means that deregulation did not necessarily cause the subsequent insolvencies.

[4]Actually, as we have seen, in a world with deposit insurance, the intermediary may consider only the costs to the stockholders and creditors, because large portions of the deposits are insured. In reality, bank managers may consider only the risk of losing their own jobs if investments go sour.

Prior to the 1980s, regulations encouraged specialization that resulted in the segmentation of the financial services industry. For decades, the industry remained highly segmented. The limitations on portfolios were predicated on the alleged benefits of compartmentalizing FIs into various specialties. Insurance companies were to specialize in insurance and banks in banking and "never the twain shall meet." Thus, in the belief that competition needed to be limited among the compartments, the regulators effectively segmented the financial markets.

Slowly over time though, barriers between intermediaries began to break down as financial institutions made inroads into each other's areas of specialty. The segmentation gave way as banks increasingly engaged in traditional nonbanking activities, and nonbanks increasingly engaged in traditional banking activities. Finally in 1999, landmark legislation underwrote the changes in the marketplace by allowing the full financial integration of banking, securities, and insurance firms.

Historically, the regulatory structure was as segmented as the financial services industry. As the industry segmentation broke down, however, the regulatory segmentation failed to break down concurrently.[5] Who said government bureaucrats were flexible anyway? Today, although the historical segmentation of regulatory responsibilities persists, it has begun to gradually change.

Regulation can focus on either financial markets (products) or financial institutions. For example, stocks, bonds, and futures are financial products that are regulated, while banks, S&Ls, and insurance companies are financial institutions that are regulated. In addition, sometimes a particular financial product or institution may be regulated by more than one agency, and a single agency may regulate more than one financial product or institution. Given this background, read A Closer Look, which surveys the many agencies currently regulating the financial services industry. Many of these nonbanking system regulators are covered in more depth in subsequent chapters.

A Closer Look

Regulators in the Financial Services Industry

- *Banks:* We have already discussed the dual banking system in which federal and state-chartered banks exist side by side. Federal banks are regulated by the Office of the Comptroller of the Currency, the FDIC, and the Fed. State banks are regulated by the state banking commissioner and possibly the Fed and/or the FDIC, depending on whether they choose to be members of the Fed and/or subscribe to deposit insurance. With regard to reserve requirements, all banks are regulated by the Fed.
- *Bank holding companies and financial holding companies:* These are regulated by the Federal Reserve. However, unless the Fed suspects a problem, the Fed relies on the reports of a subsidiary's functional regulator, such as the Securities and Exchange Commission or the state insurance commission.
- *Savings and loan associations:* S&Ls are regulated by the Office of Thrift Supervision (OTS) of the Treasury and, with regard to reserve requirements, the Fed. Those that subscribe to deposit insurance are also regulated by the FDIC.
- *Credit unions:* Federally chartered credit unions (CUs) are regulated by the *National Credit Union Administration* while those with state charters are regulated by state banking commissioners. The *National Credit Union Share Insurance Fund* insures deposits in CUs up to $100,000. Because they are nonprofit, tax-exempt institutions, CUs have generally engaged in less risk taking than their for-profit competitors. They have larger reserves and fewer losses, and consequently experienced

---

[5]Perhaps the only exception to this is the creation of the SAIF under the auspices of the Federal Deposit Insurance Corporation (FDIC) in 1989.

much milder strains. Unlike other depository institutions, credit unions do not pay an insurance premium, but rather put up capital equal to 1 percent of their insured deposits with the insurance fund. If this reserve is ever depleted because of losses, credit unions are required to replenish it out of capital.

- *Finance companies:* Finance companies must obtain permission to open an office for business from the state in which they want to operate. Once that permission is obtained, there are virtually no restrictions on branching. The *Federal Trade Commission (FTC)* regulates finance companies with regard to consumer protection. However, there are no restrictions on the assets they hold or how they raise their funds, other than those generally applying to the issuance of securities.

- *Financial futures:* Financial futures are regulated by the *Commodity Futures Trading Commission* and the *National Futures Association.* The latter was set up by the industry for self-regulation.

- *Financial options:* Financial options are regulated by the *Securities and Exchange Commission (SEC),* which was established in 1933. Options on futures are regulated by the Commodity Futures Trading Commission. The *Options Clearing Corporation* has been set up by the industry for self-regulation.

- *Mutual funds:* The SEC was given regulatory control over mutual funds (MFs) by the *Investment Company Act of 1940.* Mutual funds have experienced tremendous growth in the 1980s and early 1990s. Partially as a result, some people believe that additional regulation may be needed for two reasons: (1) Sales offices for mutual funds are now allowed to be located inside commercial banks, even though the funds are not sold directly by the bank. Apparently, a significant portion of customers erroneously believe that mutual funds purchased in a bank are insured by the bank. (2) Mutual funds have grown to be a significant portion of total intermediation while the regulatory structure has not grown at the same pace.

- *Insurance companies:* Insurance companies are regulated by the insurance commissioner of the state in which they do business.

- *Pension funds:* Pension funds are regulated by the Department of Labor. The *Pension Benefit Guaranty Corporation* provides insurance in the event that a pension plan is unable to pay the benefits defined in the pension agreement. The pension rights of more than 40 million Americans are protected by this insurance.

- *Stocks and bonds:* Securities markets are overseen by the SEC, which requires that companies fully disclose their financial condition before issuing bonds and while the bonds are outstanding. Likewise, issuers of new securities must register with the SEC and disclose all important financial information. If the equities are to be publicly traded, ongoing disclosure is required, and *insider trading* is forbidden. The Fed sets margin requirements for the purchase of stocks and bonds.

- *Securities firms:* Securities firms are regulated by the SEC, the New York Stock Exchange (NYSE), and other exchanges. In addition, securities firms are self-regulated by the *National Association of Securities Dealers.* The *Securities Investor Protection Corporation* insures retail customers of securities brokerage firms for up to $500,000 of their portfolios in the event the brokerage firm becomes insolvent.

- *U.S. government securities:* U.S. government and U.S. government agency securities are regulated by the Fed and the SEC.

Noticeably absent from this list is a regulator of the money markets including the market for commercial paper, bankers' acceptances, and negotiable CDs, the mortgage-backed securities market, and the Eurodollar and Eurobond markets. Since the regulatory structure will continue to change as the financial services industry evolves, innovative regulations for new and existing markets and products may be just around the corner.

A final point needs to be reiterated. The regulatory structure of the financial services is undergoing constant change because of the ongoing evolution of the industry resulting in new products and markets, technological changes in the delivery of financial services, and the globalization of financial markets. All of these changes leave many concerns about the adequacy of regulation.

 RECAP Regulation must balance the goals of competition and efficiency versus safety and soundness. FIs should balance the expected benefits and costs of assuming various levels of risk. Initially, regulation encouraged market segmentation and so regulation was segmented. Although segmented markets are breaking down, regulations have been slower to change. Either financial products or financial institutions can be regulated. The regulatory structure is continually undergoing change because of the evolution of the financial services industry.

We now turn our attention to the most recent pieces of regulatory legislation, which will govern the banking system in the early years of the new millennium.

Depository Institutions Deregulation and Monetary Control Act of 1980 and Garn-St. Germain Act of 1982: Deregulation in the Early 1980s

The burdens associated with complying with the regulations and the benefits associated with innovating around them produced numerous forms of adaptive behavior by banks and other FIs. For example, banks developed new types of liabilities to sidestep Regulation Q (interest rate ceilings that could be paid to depositors) and reserve requirements. These need-types of liabilities included borrowings in the fed funds, the negotiable CDs market, repurchase agreements, and the Eurodollar markets. Because these new types of liabilities were borrowings but not deposits, they were not subject to interest rate caps or to reserve requirements. Banks also used the holding company corporate form to evade certain entry and branching restrictions and to engage in nonbanking activities. The financial regulations and structure that had been designed and erected during the Great Depression were increasingly ill-suited to the changing economic and technological environment of the 1970s. As innovations weakened the effectiveness of various regulations, regulators recognized the difficulty, if not the impossibility, of controlling financial flows and the market for financial services. Accordingly, Congress decided to deregulate by dismantling the regulations. Landmark legislation enacted in 1980 and 1982 was the result.[6]

The first legislation was the **Depository Institutions Deregulation and Monetary Control Act of 1980 (DIDMCA).** Its numerous provisions reflect the compromises necessary to enact such an all-encompassing piece of legislation. As its title suggests, however, the major provisions of interest to us can be divided into two groups:

1. Deregulation:
   a. The remaining Regulation Q ceilings were phased out over a 6-year period that ended in 1986.

Depository Institutions Deregulation and Monetary Control Act of 1980 (DIDMCA)
The statute that removed many of the regulations enacted during the Great Depression, phased out Regulation Q, established uniform and universal reserve requirements, increased the assets and liabilities held by depository institutions, authorized NOW accounts, and suspended usury ceilings.

---

[6]In addition to the analytical factors, as noted earlier, the general "political wind" had shifted in the late 1970s toward less regulation.

b. Asset and liability powers of banks and thrifts were expanded:

- Assets: S&Ls and savings banks were allowed to extend loans to businesses and offer more services to customers.

- Liabilities: All depository intermediaries were permitted to offer households NOW accounts (interest-bearing checkable deposits).

c. State **usury ceilings** (maximum interest rates FIs are allowed to charge borrowers on certain types of loans) were suspended.

2. Monetary control:

a. All depository institutions were subject to reserve requirements (so-called **universal reserve requirements**).

b. Reserve requirements were to be the same on particular types of deposits across institutions (so-called **uniform reserve requirements**); this provision was phased in over an 8-year period that ended in 1987.

Usury Ceilings
Maximum interest rates that FIs may charge on certain loans.

Universal Reserve Requirements
Reserve requirements to which all depository institutions are subject.

Uniform Reserve Requirements
Reserve requirements that apply to particular types of deposits and are the same in all depository institutions.

Generally, the deregulation provisions put some explicit price competition back into banking and permitted more competition among depository institutions. In the future, banks and thrifts would be more alike in terms of the products and services offered to the public. Congress hoped the net result of more competition would be greater efficiency, an accompanying reduction in costs, and an improvement in the quantity and quality of financial services.

By mandating universal and uniform reserve requirements, the act strengthened the effectiveness of the regulatory process and expanded the powers of the Fed. Henceforth, when the Fed changed the amount of funds available for reserves, its control over the money supply and supply of loanable funds would be more direct. All in all, the DIDMCA was a landmark piece of legislation that brought many long-overdue changes to the financial structure—changes that had been recommended by numerous federal studies over the previous 20 years.

Two years later, the *Garn-St. Germain Depository Institutions Act of 1982* was enacted. Like its 1980 predecessor, the 1982 act had many provisions. Chief among them was one that sped up the pace of deregulation by allowing depository institutions to offer two types of deposit accounts designed to compete directly with money market mutual funds: (1) money market deposit accounts, which have no rate ceiling and permit six third-party payment transactions per month, and (2) super NOW accounts, which also have no rate ceiling but are fully checkable.

Since this legislation was enacted, competition among FIs and between FIs and the open market has increased dramatically. For instance, depository institutions now offer rates on all deposit liabilities that are closely correlated with market rates. Such dramatic changes in the competitive environment within which banks and other FIs operate have noticeable effects on the portfolio behavior and operations of depository institutions.

http://www.fdic.gov/
The Federal Deposit Insurance Corporation (FDIC) is an exception to regulatory segmentation.

RECAP Because market participants had found ways around many regulations, Congress passed two major statutes that deregulated financial markets. The DIDMCA in 1980 phased out Regulation Q ceilings and expanded the asset and liability powers of banks and thrifts. It also established uniform and universal reserve requirements for all depository institutions. The Garn-St. Germain Act of 1982, among other things, authorized money market deposit accounts and Super NOW accounts.

Basel Accord—The Introduction of International Capital Standards

Until 1980, banks were generally free to establish their own capital requirements as the Fed and other regulators pursued different avenues of control such as reserve requirements, asset restrictions, chartering, and Regulation Q. Since the deregulation of these traditional avenues of regulation in the early 1980s, regulators have attempted not only to impose stricter capital requirements, but also to use them as a primary vehicle of regulation.

The trend toward stricter standards received further impetus in November 1988, when the United States and 11 other countries entered into the **Basel Accord,** which established uniform international capital standards for banks. The accord specified the amount of capital that banks must hold relative to assets. This standard was stricter than that imposed on U.S. banks at the time. Despite the regulators' efforts, many banks were holding less capital relative to assets than the new regulations required. As a result of the Accord, many U.S. banks had to alter their behavior—to shore up bank capital relative to assets—in the early 1990s to meet the stricter standards. A Closer Look explains the standards and gives an example of how they are implemented.

Basel Accord
A 1988 agreement among 12 countries that established international capital standards for banks.

A Closer Look

Bank Capital Standards under the Basel Accord: The Basel Accord established requirements for core capital and for total capital. *Core capital* is the historical value of outstanding stock plus retained earnings. *Total capital* is core capital plus supplemental capital (loan-loss reserves plus subordinated debt). *Subordinated debt* is long-term debt that is paid off after depositors and other creditors have been paid in the event that the institution goes under. The amount of capital that must be held is based on the larger of two measures: One measure is based on risk-adjusted assets and the other on total assets.

The method based on risk-adjusted assets assigns different weights to different types of assets according to their risks. For instance, ordinary loans are counted at 100 percent of their value while mortgages are counted at 50 percent. Only half of the value of mortgages is counted because the property is held as collateral and repossessed in the event of default. Deposits between banks (interbank deposits) count at 20 percent while T-bills and cash count at 0 percent. In addition, off-balance-sheet activities that result in an obligation or potential obligation for the bank are also counted in risk-adjusted capital at their full value. For example, if a bank gives a standby letter of credit for $1,000, that letter of credit is counted at its full value ($1,000) in calculating risk-adjusted assets, even though it is not an asset. The reason for this is that if the standby letter of credit is exercised, the bank stands to lose $1,000 just as if it had made a bad loan. For safety, a bank with off-balance-sheet activities that expose the bank to greater risk must maintain greater capital. The risks of some activities such as futures, options, and swaps may be difficult to evaluate, however.

Once risk-adjusted assets have been determined, they are subject to two capital constraints: (1) Core capital must be equal to at least 4 percent of risk-adjusted assets; and (2) total capital must be equal to at least 8 percent of risk-adjusted assets. Presently, risk-adjusted assets account for only credit risk. They do not consider interest rate, liquidity, or exchange rate risks. Additional requirements that consider these risks may be implemented in the future.

In addition to the constraints based on risk-adjusted assets, banks are also subject to a leverage requirement stated in terms of total assets. In this case, all assets are weighted at 100 percent, and there is no accounting for off-balance-sheet activities. (The weight assigned to off-balance-sheet activities is 0.) According to the Basel Accord requirements, a bank must have core capital equal to at least 3 percent of total assets.

The use of international capital requirements has many desirable effects. All banks from the countries that abide by the standards are put on a more-or-less equal footing. The accompanying table provides an example of how the standards are implemented.

CORE CAPITAL	$775,000		
Stock issued	$500,000		
Retained earnings	$275,000		
TOTAL CAPITAL	**$1,535,000**		
Core capital	$775,000		
Loan-loss reserves	$260,000		
Subordinated debt	$500,000		
RISK-ADJUSTED ASSETS			
Loans	$14,000,000 @ 100%	$14,000,000	
Mortgages	$3,500,000 @ 50%	1,750,000	
Interbank deposits	$2,000,000 @ 20%	400,000	
Government securities	$3,000,000 @ 0%	0	
Reserves	$1,800,000 @ 0%	0	
Standby letters and other lines of credit	$3,000,000 @ 100%	3,000,000	
TOTAL RISK-ADJUSTED ASSETS	**$19,150,000**		
TOTAL ASSETS			
Loans	$14,000,000 @ 100%	$14,000,000	
Mortgages	$3,500,000 @ 100%	3,500,000	
Interbank deposits	$2,000,000 @ 100%	2,000,000	
Government securities	$3,000,000 @ 100%	3,000,000	
Reserves	$1,800,000 @ 100%	1,800,000	
Standby letters and other lines of credit	$3,000,000 @ 0%	0	
TOTAL ASSETS	**$24,300,000**		

Core capital must equal at least 4 percent of risk-adjusted assets:
  4% × $19,150,000 = $766,000.
Total capital must equal at least 8 percent of risk-adjusted assets:
  8% × $19,150,000 = $1,532,000.
Core capital must equal at least 3 percent of total assets:
  3% × $24,300,000 = $729,000.

Financial Institutions Reform, Recovery, and Enforcement Act of 1989—Re-regulation in Response to Financial Crisis (Bailing Out the Thrifts)

The *Financial Institutions Reform, Recovery, and Enforcement Act (FIRREA)* was signed into law in August 1989. The FIRREA was passed in response to the S&L crisis of the 1980s and was an attempt at re-regulation following the deregulation and subsequent crises of the 1980s (see Chapter 16). The provisions of the FIRREA include the following:

http://www.fdic.gov/laws
Explains the Financial Institutions Reform, Recovery, and Enforcement Act.

1. An initial $50 billion was injected into the newly created Savings Association Insurance Fund (SAIF). The SAIF was established to provide insurance for the deposits of S&Ls, thereby replacing the Federal Savings and Loan Insurance Corporation (FSLIC). Additionally, the SAIF provided funding for government takeover of failed S&Ls. The original $50 billion was raised by selling bonds known as bailout bonds, and the money was used to compensate institutions that took over a failed S&L by making up the difference between the value of the

LOOKING OUT: *Basel Committee Announces 25 Core Principles for Effective Bank Supervision*

The Asian meltdown of 1997–1998 demonstrated how crisis-prone the international financial system can be as financial markets become more globalized. Long before this crisis, the Basel Committee on Banking Supervision had related concerns and was meeting on a regular basis at the Bank for International Settlements in Basel, Switzerland. The committee consists of central bank governors from the G-10 countries. Its goal is to improve banking supervision at the international level and enhance international financial stability.

In September 1997, the Basel Committee announced 25 core principles that the committee believes must be in place for a supervisory system to be effective. In addition to the G-10 nations, 15 other emerging economies participated in the discussions. Supervisory authorities throughout the world were asked to endorse the principles by October 1998. Endorsement includes a review of current supervisory arrangements and the changes that would have to be implemented for a country to be in compliance with the principles.

The core principles address "the preconditions for effective banking supervision, licensing and structure, prudential regulations and requirements, methods of ongoing banking supervision, information requirements, formal powers of supervisors and cross-border banking."[a] They are intended to serve as a reference for regulators to apply when supervising banks in their countries. In addition, the principles are designed to be verifiable by domestic and international regulators and the market. It is hoped that if countries strengthen areas where they fall short of the core principles, domestic and international financial stability will be improved.

[a]Press Release, Bank for International Settlements, September 23, 1997.

http://www.ots.treas.
gov
Provides information about the Office of Thrift Supervision.

Federal Home Loan Bank Board
The regulatory body of the S&L industry until 1989.

http://www.nils.com/
rupps/5300.htm
Provides information about the Resolution Trust Corporation.

assets and liabilities of the defunct institution. Administration of the SAIF was made the responsibility of the Federal Deposit Insurance Corporation (FDIC). The FSLIC was dissolved. It had virtually gone bankrupt because of the S&L crisis of the 1980s and was unable to cover the losses of insured deposits.

2. Two new government agencies were created. The *Office of Thrift Supervision (OTS)* was established to oversee the S&L industry, replacing the **Federal Home Loan Bank Board.** The *Resolution Trust Corporation (RTC)* was set up as a temporary agency to dispose of the properties of the thrifts that failed between January 1, 1989, and July 1, 1995. The FDIC was put in charge of the RTC, and the board of the FDIC was expanded from three to five members with the addition of the director of the OTS and an additional appointment by the president of the United States.

3. For the first time, deposit insurance was made a full faith and credit obligation of the federal government, rather than the FDIC. Until 1989, neither Congress nor the taxpayers were legally required to bail out an insolvent deposit insurance company. In reality, the government was *de facto* required to bail out a failed deposit insurer, as it did with the FSLIC, but only because failing to do so might cause a systemwide collapse. Contrary to what most Americans thought, there was no legal responsibility for the bailout.

The new deposit insurance funds, the SAIF and the Bank Insurance Fund (BIF), both under the FDIC, were required to maintain reserves of at least 1.25 percent of insured deposits. Premiums paid are a percentage of total domestic deposits, including deposits over $100,000. As of December 31, 2000, the BIF had assets of $30.9 billion, which amounted to 1.38 percent of insured banking deposits. The SAIF had assets of $10.8 billion, or 1.43 percent of insured S&L deposits.

In the early and mid-1990s, the SAIF was seriously underfunded, with reserves of only 0.38 percent of insured deposits. A special $2.1 billion assessment on insured institutions in 1996 and a substantial decline in thrift failures returned the SAIF to a healthy position by the late 1990s.

4. New regulations restricted the investments of S&Ls by limiting commercial mortgage lending and by phasing out junk bond investments by 1994. Investments in junk bonds had first been authorized in 1982 by the Garn-St. Germain Act. In addition, S&Ls were required to hold at least 70 percent of their assets as mortgages or mortgage-backed securities. Commercial real estate loans were restricted to 400 percent of total capital.

5. Capital requirements were imposed on the S&Ls. The requirements were similar to those placed on banks under the Basel Accord. Risk-based capital standards were phased in, just as they had been for banks in participating countries (see A Closer Look on pp. 392-393). Core capital for S&Ls was to be 3 percent by 1995, and total capital was to be at least 8 percent of risk-adjusted assets by 1992. These new requirements more than doubled the amount of capital that had to be held under the previous standards. As of December 31, 1997, the total capital-to-asset ratio of S&Ls was 8.33 percent, which is higher than it was in the 1940–1970 period, when the ratio fluctuated around 7 percent.

Federal Deposit Insurance Corporation Improvement Act of 1991— Tightening Up Deposit Insurance

Although it might seem that deposit insurance would solve the problem of excessive risk taking by protecting small depositors in the event of a depository institution's insolvency, it actually increases the problem of excessive risk taking. Deposit insurance reduces market discipline because depositors no longer have to be concerned about the level of risk their bank engages in. This risk, known as the *moral hazard problem*, results from financial intermediaries taking more risks than they otherwise would because they know that if they lose, their depositors still get their funds back through deposit insurance.[7] This encourages a financial institution to take on more risk because the greater the risk, the greater the possibility of higher returns. It's like going to Las Vegas to gamble with your neighbor's funds—if you win, you get to keep the winnings and if you lose, your neighbor still gets paid back, but not by you.

In response to growing concern about this problem, Congress passed the **Federal Deposit Insurance Corporation Improvement Act (FDICIA)** in 1991. The FDICIA attempted to secure the safety and soundness of the banking and thrift industries (S&Ls, savings banks, and credit unions) through regulatory changes and enacted several reforms including the following:

1. Insurance premiums were scaled to the risk exposure of the banks or thrifts. Now banks or thrifts that engage in high levels of risk or have low capital ratios are charged higher deposit insurance premiums. Thus, higher-risk institutions contribute more to deposit insurance funds than do lower-risk institutions. As noted previously, since both funds are currently above the statutory reserves limit of 1.25 percent of insured deposits, healthy banks are not being charged premiums for deposit insurance. Higher-risk institutions are charged up to 27 cents per $100 in deposits depending on their risk profile. Those with the most risk pay premiums at the higher end of the range. Approximately 95 percent of all insured institutions are in the lowest risk category and currently pay nothing for deposit insurance.

Federal Deposit Insurance Corporation Improvement Act (FDICIA)
Legislation passed by Congress in 1991 to enact regulatory changes to ensure the safety and soundness of the banking and thrift industries.

http://www.occ.treas. gov/launder/sotf.htm
Provides information on the Federal Deposit Insurance Corporation Improvement Act of 1991.

---

[7]In Chapter 15, we discussed moral hazard from a micro standpoint. In that case, borrowers have an incentive to use borrowed funds for a more risky venture once loan funds had been received.

Payoff Method
The method of resolving a bank insolvency by paying off the depositors and closing the institution.

Purchase and Assumption Method
The method of resolving a bank insolvency by finding a buyer for the institution.

"Too Big to Fail"
The position adopted by FDIC regulators in 1984 whereby the failure of a large bank would be resolved using the purchase and assumption method rather than the payoff method.

2. As of December 31, 1999, the FDICIA limited insurance coverage of regular accounts to a maximum of $100,000. On retirement accounts, the limit is $100,000 per depository institution.[8]

3. The FDIC was also required to use the least costly method to resolve any insolvency. Prior to this time, an insolvency could be resolved by either the payoff method or the purchase and assumption method. Under the **payoff method,** depositors of a failed institution are paid off, the assets liquidated, and the institution closed. Depositors with balances greater than $100,000 lose their balances over $100,000. Under the **purchase and assumption method,** an insolvency is resolved by finding a buyer for the failed institution. In this case, all deposit liabilities (even those above the $100,000 limit) are assumed by the purchasing institution and depositors do not lose anything. The payoff method is usually cheaper for the FDIC. Being required to use the least costly method to resolve insolvencies could prevent the FDIC from *de facto* insuring deposits over $100,000 by using the purchase and assumption method to dispose of insolvent banks that are "too big to fail." Under the **"too big to fail"** practice, adopted by FDIC regulators in 1984, the failure of a large bank would be resolved using the purchase and assumption method rather than the payoff method. This clause of FDICIA formally ended this practice. Despite this provision, if the failure would result in a systemic risk (a risk to the entire financial system), the least costly method does not have to be used. An exception requires the approval of the Treasury in consultation with the president and the approval of two-thirds of the members of the Board of Governors of the Fed and the FDIC. Needless to say, an exception is unlikely to be granted unless the failure would cause serious adverse effects to the economy and the financial system.

4. The FDIC established a system that divided weak banks into different categories such as "undercapitalized," "significantly undercapitalized," and "critically undercapitalized." Banks in each category are subject to appropriate treatment. The greater the degree of undercapitalization, the more severe the restrictions on the bank's operations.

5. The ability of foreign banks to use certain categories of deposits in the United States was limited. Foreign banks desiring to keep insured deposit accounts can do so only through insured U.S. subsidiary banks.

Thus, as a result of the Basel Accord, the FIRREA, and the FDICIA, banks and other depository institutions are now subject to both risk-based capital standards and risk-based insurance premiums. We turn now to the Community Reinvestment Act, which was actually passed in 1977 and was not really well known outside the banking industry until recent years.

 RECAP The Basel Accord of 1988 established international capital standards for financial institutions. Twelve countries signed the original accord. The FIRREA of 1989 bailed out the S&L industry, imposed new risk-based capital standards on S&Ls, and restricted the assets that S&Ls could hold. The FDICIA of 1991 imposed risk-based insurance premiums and eliminated the "too big to fail" practice by requiring the FDIC to resolve insolvencies in the least costly way.

---

[8]This limit is rather easy for many families to circumvent. For example, a family of four can open 14 different accounts, each with $100,000 deposit insurance coverage, thus effectively giving them $1.4 million in deposit insurance at every institution. In case you are wondering how four people can have 14 accounts, it is by grouping them together in different ways. Thus, each can have an individual account; then there can be six accounts with two people on each account (such as father and mother, and mother and oldest child), three accounts with three people each, and one account with all four.

Community Reinvestment Act—Outlawing Discriminatory Lending Practices

The original purpose of the **Community Reinvestment Act** was to increase the availability of credit to economically disadvantaged areas and to correct alleged discriminatory lending practices. Minority borrowers and neighborhoods had long been the victims of redlining. **Redlining** refers to the practice of drawing a red line (or any colored line) around a certain area on a map and restricting the number or dollar amount of loans made in that area regardless of the creditworthiness of the borrower with respect to income or collateral.

The Community Reinvestment Act did not get much attention because it provided no means of enforcement for regulators. However, activist groups believed that many banks were not making significant efforts to comply with the law, and in recent years, many mainstream community groups have joined their calls for more stringent enforcement of the act.

During the late 1980s and the 1990s, a means of enforcing the act became available due to the wave of bank mergers and acquisitions that began in the late 1980s and accelerated in the late 1990s. In deciding whether to approve a bank merger or acquisition, the Fed now assesses how well the bank is meeting the lending criteria of the Act, and compliance statements are judged critically.[9] As a result, the law is getting more "teeth." Banks are finding it in their best interest to take notice. Bank performance in this area is often difficult to judge, however, because banks are required to practice nondiscriminatory lending while at the same time focusing on safety and soundness.

To clarify some of the confusion over what compliance entails, on March 21, 1989, four regulatory agencies—the Fed, the Comptroller of the Currency, the FDIC, and the now defunct Federal Home Loan Bank Board—issued a policy statement. Among other things, the guidelines call for banks to do the following:

1. Continue efforts to discover community needs through outreach to local government, business, and community organizations.
2. Develop, market, and advertise products and services that the community needs, such as low-cost checking accounts.
3. Participate in government-insured lending programs.
4. Train employees to be responsive to the guidelines of the Community Reinvestment Act.
5. Market credit services directly to target groups such as small business owners and real estate agents in low- and moderate-income neighborhoods.

The policy statement also lists specific activities banks should engage in to ensure compliance. Although banks used to regard the law as a burden, their views are changing as the environment in which they operate changes. The nation is experiencing growing diversity and will continue to do so. To the extent that the Community Reinvestment Act forces financial institutions to recognize and respond to the changing demographics before they would otherwise have done so, the law provides an important service to the industry and community. Many bankers are now of the opinion that they will need to develop new markets, products, and services and that these new activities will turn out to be quite profitable.

Community Reinvestment Act
Legislation passed by Congress in 1977 to increase the availability of credit to economically disadvantaged areas and to correct alleged discriminatory lending practices.

Redlining
The practice of restricting the number or dollar amounts of loans in an area regardless of the creditworthiness of the borrower.

http://www.occ.treas.gov/cra/info.htm
Provides information on the Community Reinvestment Act.

---

[9]In the next section, we shall see that the Interstate Branching and Banking Efficiency Act of 1994 also emphasized compliance with the Community Reinvestment Act.

Interstate Banking and Branching Efficiency Act of 1994—The Dawn of Nationwide Branching?

The *Interstate Banking and Branching Efficiency Act (IBBEA)* of 1994 eliminated most restrictions on interstate bank mergers and made interstate branching possible for the first time since the passage of the McFadden Act in 1927.[10] The law permits all bank holding companies to acquire banks anywhere in the nation as long as certain conditions are met. In addition, under the same conditions, banks in one state may merge with banks in another state, thus effectively branching. The conditions include meeting requirements for the safety and soundness of the institutions involved (they must be well capitalized and well managed) and making commitments to community reinvestment under the Community Reinvestment Act. Under no circumstances will banks be permitted to use a branch to generate deposits without considering community reinvestment needs. Prior to the law, some states had limited or put additional conditions on the acquisition of banks by out-of-state bank holding companies.

Further, as of June 1, 1997, bank holding companies were permitted to convert their multiple banks in various states into branches of a single interstate bank. This reduced duplicative overhead expenses, such as maintaining a separate board of directors for each bank. Whether significant savings will be realized remains to be seen.

We turn now to the final major piece of banking legislation in the twentieth century. With the passage of the Gramm-Leach-Bliley Act in 1999, the financial services industry of the twenty-first century will be far different from that of the twentieth century.

The Gramm-Leach-Bliley Act (GLBA) of 1999—The Final Demise of Glass-Steagall

Until 1999, the most significant piece of banking legislation in the twentieth century had been the Glass-Steagall Act of 1933, which separated investment and commercial banking, created the FDIC, and limited the range of assets and liabilities that a commercial bank could hold and issue. After 67 years, this Act was effectively repealed with the passage of the *Gramm-Leach-Bliley Act (GLBA)* in November 1999. This landmark legislation became effective March 11, 2000 and significantly impacts the financial services industry. Rather than segmentation among financial service providers, the Act allows for considerable financial integration in the financial services industry.

Major Provisions of GLBA

The Act allows bank holding companies meeting certain criteria to be certified as *financial holding companies (FHCs)*. FHCs may engage in a broad array of financial and nonfinancial activities. To become a FHC, a bank holding company must file a declaration with the Fed certifying that all of its depository institutions are well capitalized and well managed and have a "satisfactory" or better rating under the Community Reinvestment Act.

---

[10]In Chapter 15, we saw that the McFadden Act outlawed interstate branching and made national banks conform to the intrastate branching laws of the states in which they were located.

FHCs may engage in the following:

1. Financially related activities including securities underwriting and dealing, insurance agency and underwriting activities, and merchant banking activities.

2. Other financial activities that the Fed determines are financial in nature or incidental to financial activities.

3. Nonfinancial activities that the Fed determines are complementary to a financial activity and do not pose a substantial risk to the safety or soundness of depository institutions or the financial system.

The Act also authorizes expanded powers for banks and their subsidiaries. Under the new law, banks are:

4. Authorized to underwrite and market municipal revenue bonds.

5. Authorized to own or control a "financial subsidiary" that engages in activities that national banks are not permitted to directly engage in if prior approval of the Office of the Controller of the Currency is received. The activities of the financial subsidiary do not include insurance underwriting, real estate development or investment, or complementary activities.

Under the GLBA, the Fed is given the ultimate responsibility for supervising FHCs. This is similar to its ultimate regulatory responsibility for bank holding companies. However, under the law, the Fed is to rely on reports of examination prepared by the subsidiary's primary functional regulator as much as possible. For example, the primary banking regulator may be the FDIC, the Fed, or the Office of the Controller of the Currency; for securities activities, the primary regulator is the Securities Exchange Commission; and for insurance activities, the state insurance commissioner is the primary regulator. The exceptions to this are in cases in which the Fed believes the activities of a subsidiary may pose a threat to an affiliated depository institution or if the subsidiary is in violation of any federal law that the Fed has jurisdiction to enforce.

As of March 2000, when the law became partially effective, 117 bank holding companies had been certified as FHCs. By fall 2001, the number had increased to about 580. Full phase-in of the law will be effective November 12, 2004, when financial subsidiaries of FHCs may engage in merchant banking activities.

There are two important additional provisions of the Act that protect consumers. The first requires that ATM operators post a notice of any fees that may be imposed and inform the consumer through an on-screen or paper message of the amount of the fee before the consumer is irrevocably committed to completing the transaction. The second includes a number of new requirements relating to the disclosure of financial information about consumers. Namely, financial institutions cannot sell information for marketing purpose, and are required to disclose prior to the opening of an account and at least annually thereafter, the institution's policies regarding the disclosure of nonpublic personal information to third parties.

RECAP The Community Reinvestment Act of 1977 was designed to eliminate discriminatory lending practices. The IBBEA of 1994 allowed unimpeded nationwide branching as of June 1, 1997. The GLBA of 1999 allowed for the certification of financial holding companies that could engage in banking, securities, and insurance activities. The GLBA effectively repealed the provisions of the Glass-Steagall Act, which separated commercial and investment banking.

To summarize, by the turn of the century, many regulatory changes had already occurred, including the following: (1) scaling insurance premiums to the risk exposure of banks, (2) limiting foreign deposit coverage, (3) intervening early when a bank begins experiencing problems so that measures will be taken before bank capital is fully depleted, (4) ending the practice of "too big to fail," (5) increasing capital requirements, (6) expanding interstate banking, (7) allowing banks, securities firms, and insurance companies to affiliate under common ownership, and (8) authorizing FHCs to engage in many previously prohibited financial and nonfinancial services. We now focus on other existing concerns and possible areas of future reform that could alleviate these concerns.

Other Possible Areas of Reform

Both the FIRREA and the FDICIA tightened regulations by requiring higher capital standards and risk-based deposit insurance premiums. This legislation has generally been praised as a much needed remedy to the moral hazard dangers of deposit insurance.

Nevertheless, some critics contend that the reforms do not adequately address the problem of moral hazard. Others argue that the reforms do not go far enough in establishing market-based incentives for financial institutions to avoid engaging in excessively risky activities.

One suggested reform is to privatize deposit insurance. Proponents argue that government-sponsored deposit insurance reduces the ability of banks to compete with other financial intermediaries by subjecting them to excessive regulations and imposing restrictions on the products they can offer. Opponents of this proposal suggest that a private system of deposit insurance might not be able to withstand a catastrophic wave of bank failures. For reasons we have already suggested, bank failures often occur in waves. In the event of a crisis, Congress may again have to step in, but only after the system and the economy have suffered significant damage. Others argue that even with private deposit insurance, the government would still regulate banks in order to ensure the safety and soundness of the system. Moreover, the moral hazard problem would still exist with private deposit insurance. Any private insurance scheme would also need to set capital and management standards to reduce moral hazard.

Another recommended reform involves capping or limiting deposit insurance. Proponents contend that lowering the amount of an insured deposit to less than $100,000 would increase market discipline by causing depositors to monitor the activities of their banks more closely. After all, if deposits are insured, why worry about the health of the institution in which they are placed? Another suggestion is to limit systemwide coverage of deposits by an individual to $100,000, regardless of how many accounts the individual has. This could be implemented by using Social Security numbers to track accounts.

An additional suggested reform would not only reduce the insurance limit but also make deposit insurance optional for bank customers. A bank forgoing all insurance would not be subject to any regulation with the exception of required disclosures to consumers. With this reform, depositors and banks would get to choose their level of regulation or lack thereof.

In response to the existing regulatory potpourri and confusion, as well as the new risks and challenges that the financial services industry will face in the future, some people have suggested consolidating and streamlining the regulatory agencies. Most analysts believe that a complete regulatory overhaul is inevitable. Look at A Closer Look on pp. 388–89. Current regulatory responsibility for the banking

LOOKING BACK: *A Time Line of Banking Legislation*

The twentieth century has seen a number of pieces of major banking legislation that have shaped the industry and its evolution.

- 1913: The Federal Reserve Act created the Federal Reserve System.
- 1927: The McFadden Act prohibited interstate banking.
- 1933: The Glass-Steagall Act established the FDIC as a temporary agency, separated commercial and investment banking, established Regulation Q interest rate ceilings, and set the interest rate ceiling on demand deposits at 0 percent.
- 1935: The Banking Act established the FDIC as a permanent agency.
- 1980: The depository Institutions Deregulation and Monetary Control Act (DIDMCA) authorized NOW accounts nationwide, thereby ending the monopoly of commercial banks on checkable deposits; phased out Regulation Q; established uniform and universal reserve requirements; granted new powers to thrifts; eliminated usury laws; and increased deposit insurance from $40,000 to $100,000 per account.
- 1982: The Garn-St. Germain Act expanded the asset and liability powers of banks and thrifts, expanded the power of the FDIC to help troubled banks, and created money market deposit accounts and Super NOW accounts.
- 1989: The Financial Institutions Recovery, Reform, and Enforcement Act (FIRREA) authorized a taxpayer bailout of the S&L industry, brought deposit insurance for thrifts under the FDIC, created the OTS to replace the Federal Home Loan Bank Board, created the RTC as a temporary agency to dispose of the assets of failed institutions, and imposed new restrictions on S&Ls.
- 1991: The Federal Deposit Insurance Corporation Improvement Act (FDICIA) abolished the "too big to fail" policy, limited brokered deposits, established new capital requirements for banks, established risk-based insurance premiums, gave the FDIC new powers to borrow from the U.S. Treasury, and restricted activities of foreign banks and insured state banks.
- 1994: The Interstate Banking and Branching Efficiency Act (IBBEA) allowed virtually unimpeded interstate branching by adequately capitalized and managed banks that meet CRA requirements starting June 1, 1997.
- 1999: The Gramm-Leach-Bliley Act (GLBA) allowed banks, insurance companies, securities firms, and other financial institutions to affiliate under common ownership and to offer a complete range of financial services that were previously prohibited; created financial holding companies (FHCs), which could engage in financially related activities, other financial activities, and complementary nonfinancial activities; expanded allowable activities for banks and their subsidiaries; repealed key provisions of the 1933 Glass-Steagall Act, which separated commercial and investment banking.

system (including banks and S&Ls) is distributed among four supervisory agencies: the FDIC, the Office of the Comptroller of the Currency, the OTS, and the Fed. Many analysts think that the present system causes duplication of regulatory functions and bureaucratic delays. They believe that multiple, decentralized supervisory agencies result in costly systems that potentially decrease the effectiveness and efficiency of bank supervision. In response to these concerns, the Fed, the FDIC, and state banking departments are working together to make bank regulations more consistent and to make bank examinations more efficient and less burdensome.

Currently, the impetus for major reform beyond the GLBA has declined due to the record profits that the banking system earned in recent years. Congress rarely makes substantial changes without a crisis occurring first.

We would be remiss, however, if we did not discuss one final aspect of banking regulation. As we have seen, the Glass-Steagall Act separated commercial banking from investment banking. After 20 years of debate, Congress finally passed the Gramm-Leach-Bliley Act (GLBA) in late 1999, which repealed key provisions of Glass-Steagall and allowed full integration of banks and other firms that provided financial services as of March 2000. Nevertheless, even before the comprehensive GLBA was passed, banks had made substantial inroads into investment banking by the late 1990s because over time the regulatory barriers have been relaxed. For instance, in 1986, a Fed ruling allowed bank holding companies (in certain cases) to obtain 10 percent of their revenues from securities that were previously barred, including corporate debt and equities, commercial paper, municipal revenue bonds, mortgage-backed securities, and asset-backed securities. In February 1996, the Fed raised the limit to 25 percent, and as a result, most large bank holding companies not already in the securities industry are scrambling to get in. After all is said and done, the repeal of Glass-Steagall with the passage of the GLBA is similar to the passage of the IBBEA; that is, it underwrote what the regulators and markets have already accomplished. One thing we can be sure of is that the financial services industry and its regulation will continue to change in the twenty-first century.

Summary of Major Points

- Because the failure of a depository institution has systemwide repercussions, Congress has enacted legislation to regulate the financial services industry with the goal of averting such a failure. A segmented financial services industry resulted in a segmented regulatory structure.

- Regulation is by institution group or financial market (product). All depository institutions are regulated by the Fed with regard to reserve requirements. The FDIC also regulates banks and thrifts that opt for federal deposit insurance. Many other regulatory agencies regulate specific institutions. In addition, agencies such as the SEC regulate stocks and bonds. Other agencies regulate other financial products such as futures and options. Some product groups establish self-regulatory bodies. At the present time, no agency is in charge of regulating the money market. The regulatory structure is in an ongoing evolutionary process.

- Beginning in 1980, the banking system was deregulated. The Depository Institutions Deregulation and Monetary Control Act (DIDMCA) of 1980 phased out Regulation Q interest rate ceilings and expanded the asset and liability options for banks and thrifts. All depository institutions were allowed to offer interest-bearing checkable deposits, and S&Ls and savings banks were allowed to make business loans. DIDMCA also expanded the powers of the Fed by authorizing uniform and universal reserve requirements.

- The Garn-St. Germain Depository Institutions Act of 1982 allowed all depository institutions to offer money market deposit accounts, which had

no interest rate ceilings, permitted limited check writing, and were fully insured up to $100,000. Also authorized were Super NOW accounts, which are checking accounts that pay a market interest rate.

- The Basel Accord, an agreement among 12 countries, sets uniform international capital requirements for financial institutions as a primary vehicle of regulation. Requirements for core capital and total capital are based upon risk-adjusted assets and total assets. Core capital is the historical value of outstanding stock plus retained earnings. Risk-adjusted assets are calculated by assigning different weights to different types of assets depending upon risk.

- The Financial Institutions Reform, Recovery, and Enforcement Act (FIRREA) of 1989 attempted to resolve the S&L deposit insurance crisis. It created the OTS and assimilated the defunct FSLIC into the FDIC. New regulations restricted the investments that S&Ls could make, and capital standards similar to those imposed on banks by the Basel Accord were adopted. Deposit insurance was made a full faith and credit obligation of the U.S. government, and bonds, which would eventually be paid off by taxpayers, were sold to obtain the funds necessary to bail out the defunct S&Ls.

- The Federal Deposit Insurance Corporation Improvement Act (FDICIA) of 1991 required higher deposit insurance premiums for banks or thrifts that undertake high levels of risk. The "too big to fail" practice that had been in effect since 1984 was ended. Under the "too big to fail" practice, the failure of large banks was resolved using the purchase and assumption method rather than the payoff method. Weak banks were categorized as either "undercapitalized," "significantly undercapitalized," or "critically undercapitalized" and subject to appropriate treatment.

- The Community Reinvestment Act of 1977 gained prominence in the late 1980s as the Fed used compliance with this Act as a criterion for approving or disapproving bank mergers. The Act requires banks to lend in economically disadvantaged areas and to end the practice of redlining.

- The Interstate Banking and Branching Efficiency Act (IBBEA) of 1994 allowed interstate branching by mergers of well-capitalized and well-managed institutions as of June 1, 1997. Under this law, bank holding companies can also convert separate banks into branches.

- With the passage of the Gramm-Leach-Bliley Act (GLBA) in 1999, the final vestiges of the Glass-Steagall Act separating investment and commercial banking were removed. The stage is set for full financial integration of the banking, securities, and insurance industries. The GLBA allowed for bank holding companies to be certified as financial holding companies (FHCs), which could engage in financially related activities, including securities underwriting and dealing, and insurance and merchant banking activities. The GLBA also allowed FHCs to engage in other financial activities and complementary nonfinancial activities. Banks had previously found ways into the securities industry through bank holding company subsidiaries. They have been able to do this because the Fed has relaxed or weakened many of the provisions of Glass-Steagall.

- Despite the enactment of higher capital standards and risk-based insurance premiums, many believe that the reforms do not go far enough in dealing with the moral hazard problem. One recommendation is to privatize deposit insurance. Critics of this proposal contend that private deposit insurance might fail in the event of catastrophic bank failures and that regulators would still want to regulate banks to ensure the safety and soundness of the financial system. Others have suggested limiting deposit insurance or making it optional. Still others have suggested streamlining financial services regulation to make it more efficient and less burdensome.

Key Terms

Basel Accord

Commodity Futures Trading Commission

Community Reinvestment Act

Depository Institutions Deregulation and Monetary Act (DIDMCA)

Federal Deposit Insurance Corporation Improvement Act (FDICIA)

Federal Home Loan Bank Board

Federal Trade Commission (FTC)

Financial Holding Companies (FHCs)

Payoff Method

Purchase and Assumption Method

Redlining

"Too Big to Fail"

Uniform Reserve Requirements

Universal Reserve Requirements

Usury Ceilings

Review Questions

1. How is the failure of an FI different from the failure of a video rental store? What do these differences imply about the need for regulation?

2. Discuss the major provisions of the FIRREA and the FDICIA.

3. What is redlining? How is the Community Reinvestment Act supposed to affect redlining? Discuss some of the difficulties with assessing compliance with the law. Could my bank be violating the law if it fails to lend to businesses located in the deteriorating downtown area?

4. What is the Basel Accord? Why is it desirable to have uniform international capital standards for banks?

5. What is the intent of the 25 core principles for effective bank supervision?

6. Some contend that the passage of the IBBEA will have little effect on the banking industry. What is the basis of their argument? On what date were banks allowed to branch across state lines by merging with a bank in a different state?

7. Explain at least three suggestions for deposit insurance reform to deal with the moral hazard problem.

8. Would a wealthy individual with bank accounts greater than $100,000 prefer the FDIC to use the purchase and assumption method or the payoff method to liquidate failed banks? Why?

9. What is core capital? How do risk-adjusted assets differ from total assets?

10. Who regulates money markets? Who regulates capital markets?

11. What are the major provisions of the Depository Institutions Deregulation and Monetary Control Act of 1980? The Garn-St. Germain Depository Institutions Act of 1982? Which act expanded the powers of the Fed? How?

12. Explain the difference between risk-based capital standards and risk-based deposit insurance premiums.

13. What are the regulatory responsibilities of the Securities and Exchange Commission? What is insider trading? Who sets margin requirements?

14. Identify three self-regulating agencies and explain which industries they regulate. Speculate as to why an industry would self-regulate.

15. Explain the function of each of the following:
    a. National Credit Union Share Insurance Fund
    b. Pension Benefit Guaranty Corporation
    c. Securities Investor Protection Corporation
    d. FDIC

16. Explain the difference between the purchase and assumption method and the payoff method of resolving a bank insolvency. What does "too big to fail" mean?

17. What are the major provisions of the GLBA? What is a FHC? How does a bank holding company become a FHC? What conditions must be met to become a FHC?

18. Was investment banking effectively separated from commercial banking prior to the passage of GLBA? Explain.

Analytical Questions

19. Assume that a bank has core capital of $1 million and total capital of $2 million. Its total risk-adjusted assets are $25 million and total assets are $30 million. According to the Basel Accord, does the bank have adequate capital?

20. Assume that a bank has the following:

Stock issued	$15 million
Retained earnings	$2.75 million
Loan-loss reserves	$2.6 million
Subordinated debt	$5 million

What is its core capital? What is its total capital?

Internet Exercises

1. From the latest Quarterly Banking Profile, **http://www.2fdic.gov/qbp,** access the most current balance sheet for FDIC-insured commercial banks and report the numbers for the total assets for all FDIC-insured commercial banks in the latest quarter. Compare this number to the assets figure for the same quarter of the previous year. Report the latest data on the equity capital (net worth) of all commercial banks.

2. Access information about the following regulatory agencies:
    a. OTS: **http://www.ots. treas.gov/**
    b. Office of the Comptroller of the Currency: **http://www.occ.treas.gov/**
    c. FDIC: **http://www.fdic.gov/**
    Do you believe that the present system involves multiplicity and duplication of regulatory functions?

Suggested Readings

For an excellent book on the material in this chapter, see Ken Spong, *Banking Regulation: Its Purposes, Implementation, and Effects*, 5th ed., Federal Reserve Bank of Kansas City, 2000. The book is available online at **http://www.kc.frb.org/BS&S/publicat/bks &pamp.htm.**

For a look at "The Future of Financial Intermediation and Regulation Overview," see the article by Stephen Cecchetti, "The Future of Financial Intermediation and Regulation," *Current Issues in Economics and Finance*, Federal Reserve Bank of New York, Vol. 5, Issue 8, May 1999.

For an analysis of the effects of IBBEA, see Ann B. Matasar and Joseph N. Heiney, "Lemonade or Lemon?: Riegel-Neal and the Consolidation of American Banking" *International Advances in Economic Research*, Vol. 6, No. 2, May 2000, pp. 249–258.

For an analysis of the success of the Community Reinvestment Act, see Robert B. Avery, Raphael W. Bostic, and Glenn B. Canner, "CRA Special Lending Programs," *Federal Reserve Bulletin*, November, 2000, pp. 711–731; also see "Does the Community Reinvestment Act Influence Lending? An Analysis of Changes in Bank Low-Income Mortgage Activity," *Working Paper* No. WP-00-6, Federal Reserve Bank of Chicago, May 2000.

A recent study of "Bank Merger Policy and the New [Community Reinvestment Act] CRA Data" by Anthony W. Cyrnak appeared in the *Federal Reserve Bulletin*, September 1998, pp. 703–714. A related article, "New Information on Lending to Small Businesses and Small Farms: The 1996 [Community Reinvestment Act] CRA Data," appeared in the *Federal Reserve Bulletin*, January 1998, pp. 1–21.

An article that concludes that bank regulation is needed to protect the payments system is Thomas M. Hoenig, "Bank Regulation: Asking the Right Questions," *Economic Review of the Federal Reserve Bank of Kansas City* 82:1 (First Quarter 1997): 5–10.

Two articles that deal with comprehensive regulatory reform are Gary H. Stern, "Market Discipline as Bank Regulator," and Roger W. Ferguson, Jr., "The Changing Banking Environment and Emerging Questions for Public Policy," in *The Region* 12:2 (June 1998): 2–3 and 34–39, respectively, published by the Federal Reserve Bank of Minneapolis.

An article that looks at a novel approach to bank regulation is Charles Calomiris, "Could Banks Police Each Other?" *The Economist*, October 17, 1998, p. 94.

Matthew T. Billett looks at the topic of market discipline in "The Cost of Market versus Regulatory Discipline in Banking," *Journal of Financial Economics* 48:3 (June 1998): 333–358.

Gregory Elliehausen looks the labor costs of regulatory compliance in "The Cost of Bank Regulation: A Review of the Evidence," *Federal Reserve Bulletin* 84:4 (April 1998): 252–253.

For an empirical study of banking regulations, see "The Efficiency of Financial Institutions: How Does Regulation Matter?" *Journal of Economics and Business* 50:2 (March–April 1998): 79–234.

An interesting article on the future is Charles S. Sanford, Jr., "Financial Markets in 2020," *Economic Review of the Federal Reserve Bank of Kansas City*, First Quarter 1994, pp. 19–28.

Helen A. Garten offers *Why Bank Regulation Failed: Designing a Bank Regulatory Strategy for the 1990s* (Westport, CT: Quorum Books, 1991).

For a look at how difficult true banking reform legislation is, see Sarkis Joseph Khoury, *U.S. Banking and Its Regulation in the Political Context* (Lanham, MD: University Press of America, 1998).

For an international perspective, see David Gowland, *The Regulation of Financial Markets in the 1990s: Issues and Problems in an Age of Innovation* (Brookfield, VT: Edward Elgar, 1990).

For a collection of essays on the state of the financial system and rationales for reform, see *Reforming Financial Institutions and Markets in the United States*, George Kaufman, ed. (Hingham, MA: Kluwer Academic Publishers, 1994).

For a discussion of the realities of expanded activities for U.S. banks, see Anthony Saunders and Ingo Walter, *Universal Banking in the United States* (New York: Oxford University Press, 1994).

For an engaging analysis of the present state of the financial system, along with a blueprint for change, see *Transforming the U.S. Financial System*, Gary Dymski, Gerald Epstein, and Robert Pollin, eds. (Armonk, NY: M. E. Sharpe, 1993).

A book that looks at banking and securities regulation in both the United States and the European Community is *International Financial Market Regulation*, Benn Steil, ed. (New York: Wiley, 1994.)

chapter

Insurance Companies

Learning Objectives *After reading this chapter, you should know:*

- What life insurance, health insurance, and property and casualty companies do
- How adverse selection and moral hazard create risks for insurance companies and how these are managed
- The various types of life insurance policies available
- Recent trends for these financial intermediaries and how they are regulated

" "
Life is uncertain, eat dessert first.
—Unknown

Life Is Uncertain

Two fundamental assumptions underlie how financial theorists think about financial risk and its management. First, most people are **risk averse.** We desire to reduce the likelihood that we will be subject to an unfortunate mishap and its accompanying financial loss. Second, the future is uncertain. As much as we would like to, we simply cannot foresee the future. The best we can do is to behave rationally—to make probabilistic calculations about those risks and base our behavior on playing those odds. Although this rational behavior does not insulate us from unfortunate mishaps, it does provide a starting point from which we can make logical financial decisions.

Many economic and financial theorists find it useful to distinguish between the notions of risk and uncertainty. Risk implies that an *a priori* calculation of an event can be probabilistically computed.[1] For instance, the odds or risk of pulling the ace of diamonds from a deck of ordinary playing cards (with jokers) is 1 in 54, or a little less than 2 percent. In contrast, uncertainty often refers to those situations with no basis for a probabilistic calculation. For instance, there is no corresponding basis on which we can make a mathematical probability calculation to infer the price of oil 20 years from now. We simply do not know how many different outcomes are possible. Instead, we resort to various types of conventions. We might presume that the world (and its prices) 20 years from now will be pretty similar to what they are today. This convention can be made slightly more complicated by building in an assumed price level increase over the period. Alternatively, we might turn to the most distant futures prices and use them to guess about future oil prices. Note, however, the use of these conventions to make statistical inferences is a different kind of mental process than engaging in a probabilistic computation wherein the possible outcomes are known beforehand. This type of calculation lies at the heart of much of the risk management discussed in this chapter.

Risk-averse behavior can be observed in the way most people make insurance-buying decisions. When given a choice between living uninsured in a $100,000 house or paying $400 per year to insure against its loss, most of us choose to buy the insurance. It is likely that one could live in a house for an entire lifetime and never experience a major catastrophe. However, most of us also know that the loss of house—regardless of its unlikely destruction—would leave us with an unbearable financial loss. Rather than taking the wager that our house will not burn down, we instead do the opposite of gambling—we purchase coverage from an insurance company. This coverage ensures that in the unlikely occurrence of our house being burned to the ground, we will be reimbursed financially for the loss.

Chapter 14, introduced financial institutions and financial conglomerates. This chapter examines insurance companies more closely. The first section explains risk-pooling and two special kinds of risk created by insurance, adverse selection and moral hazard, and examines professional employment in the insurance industry. Later sections discuss various aspects of the life, health, and property and casualty insurance businesses, how insurance companies manage adverse selection and moral hazard, and insurance industry regulation.

Risk Averse
A state of being wherein one is reluctant to fully bear the financial or physical loss of an event.

---

[1]An *a priori* calculation refers to one in which deductive reasoning—moving from cause to effect—is used to make a decision. This differs from *a posteriori*, or inductive reasoning, which is based upon experience or inference. One deductively *knows*, based on probability theory, that the odds of pulling the ace of diamonds from a deck of cards is 1 in 54. One does need to infer from hundreds of observed experiments that this statement is true. Predicting future commodity prices requires an entirely different approach.

Insurance Companies

Overview

Insurance Company
A contractual-type financial intermediary that offers the public protection against the financial costs associated with the loss of life, health, or property in exchange for a premium.

Insurance companies are a form of contractual-type financial intermediary that offer the public protection against the financial costs associated with the loss of life, health, or property. For a fee, called a *premium*, insurance companies agree to make a payment contingent upon the occurrence of a certain event. Premiums are used to purchase financial assets until policyholders present their claims. As long as a company's combined premium revenue and investment earnings are greater than the insurance claims made against it, the company will earn a profit.

The essential principle underlying insurance is that through the pooling of risks, a loss that would be unbearable if borne by one person becomes bearable if shared with enough other people. Imagine a situation in which we can compute actuarially that, on average, 3 ships out of 100 leaving a particular port will sink or be captured by pirates each year. We do not know which three ships will be lost. Without insurance, the owners of the sunken and captured ships will face potential financial ruin. They may not be able to afford to stay in business. However, if the 100 ship owners band together and each pays a small premium whose sum equals the cost of replacing three ships each year, the actual loss becomes bearable. Those losing insured ships are not financially submerged but are instead able to continue their nautical pursuits. It is this basic concept that medieval merchants understood when they created the property and casualty insurance agreements to insure each other's ships. This practice continued for centuries. In the 1690s, a London coffeehouse owned by Edward Lloyd became a regular meeting place for shipowners and merchants. Before a ship set sail, its cargo was listed on a statement and read to those in the coffeehouse. Those willing to guarantee or underwrite the risk of insuring the cargo wrote their name and the share of risk they were willing to bear on the statement. Over time, Lloyd's of London grew into one of the most famous names in insurance, introducing insurance coverage for a wide variety of misfortunate occurrences.

Adverse Selection and Moral Hazard

Insurance coverage creates two additional forms of risk that must be actively managed. As explained in Chapter 15 with regard to commercial bank deposit insurance, these two additional types of risk are *adverse selection* and *moral hazard*. Adverse selection occurs when the least desirable individuals are those most likely to pursue and be selected for a transaction. Banks worry that the least creditworthy applicants are likely to pursue a loan with the most vigor. When applied to insurance, adverse selection means that those people most likely to file an insurance claim are those who will most likely apply for and be granted insurance. Continuing with our ship example, those owning the least seaworthy ships and hiring the most daring sea captains are likely to be those most interested in insuring their vessels. To prevent losses, insurance and banking firms need to actively manage this adverse selection problem.

Moral hazard is the risk that a policyholder will behave in a more risky manner than he or she would have in the absence of insurance coverage. In banking, this occurs when a borrower has an incentive to use a loan's proceeds for a venture with a higher expected return, but a riskier outcome, than stated on the loan application. In insurance, moral hazard means that the policyholder will be less careful with the insured item than he or she would be if uninsured. When faced with an impending storm, our uninsured ship owners might move their ships into a safe harbor. However, insured ship owners may be less careful in protecting their ships because they know they will receive a new ship in the case of severe damage. In the worst case, they may actually move the ship into harm's way or pay an arsonist to destroy it, hoping to profit from the damage. As with adverse selection, insurance companies must actively manage this moral hazard problem to avoid unforeseen losses. Some economists argue than even mundane items like seatbelts cause moral hazard problems. People might buckle up more often but may drive faster and more aggressively than they would without a seatbelt, reducing the benefit of the seatbelt.

Employment

The insurance industry is a significant employer in the U.S. economy. According to the U.S. Department of Labor's Bureau of Labor Statistics, 2.3 million people worked in the insurance field in 1999. To develop, sell, and manage insurance policies, insurance companies hire four primary types of insurance professionals: actuaries, agents, underwriters, and claims adjusters. **Actuaries** are employed to forecast the likelihood of insurance claims being filed by insured clients. Although life, health, and property and casualty companies find it difficult to predict when any one particular person will die, or if the person will become sick or wreck his or her car, forecasts for the population as a whole are extremely accurate. By collecting and analyzing statistical data, actuaries can predict—within some margin of error—the likelihood of claimable events occurring. This information is used in the development and pricing of investment products. To sell their products, insurance companies use large numbers of licensed agents whose income is generated primarily from sales commissions. Agents can be *exclusive agents*, selling only the products of one particular company, or *independent agents* who sell policies issued by a wide number of companies. To ensure that agents do not sell policies to people who are too risky to insure, insurance companies employ *underwriters* who review, approve, or reject policy applications written by the insurance agents. Underwriters have the authority to reject applicants who fail to meet application criteria or otherwise appear unacceptably risky. *Claims adjusters* assist policyholders with filing claims by verifying losses and determining the insurance company's liability.

> **Actuaries**
> An insurance professional trained in the mathematical aspects of insurance who is responsible for calculating policy premiums.

All types of insurance and insurance companies—life insurance companies, health insurance companies, and property and casualty companies—employ these types of employees. We now turn to a more detailed discussion of each of these three types of insurance companies.

RECAP Risk-averse behavior in an uncertain world creates profitable opportunities for insurance companies to assist businesses and consumers with the management of risk. Insurance companies offer the public protection against the financial costs associated with the loss of life, health, or property. Unfortunately, insurance also creates adverse selection and moral hazard problems. Adverse selection exists when the least-insurable applicants pursue an insurance policy more aggressively than other applicants and, as a result, are more likely to be insured. Moral hazard is the threat that once insured, policyholders engage in riskier behavior than they would if uninsured. Actuaries, agents, underwriters, and claims adjusters play important roles in the design, sale, management, and loss determination of insurance products.

LOOKING BACK: *The Intellectual Roots and Philosophical Applications of Risk Assessment*

This use of insurance to hedge against risk has a long intellectual history and broader application. The Code of Hammurabi, a collection of laws from a famous eighteenth-century B.C. Babylonian king and lawyer, refers to a kind of credit insurance that predates our medieval ship insurance example by over 2,500 years. A borrower's loan was forgiven if personal circumstances made it such that he was unable to pay. He, of course, had to pay an extra amount in addition to interest payments to receive this coverage. Ancient Greek and Roman societies also used burial insurance and rudimentary forms of old-age pensions. Medieval guilds provided similar protection to their members centuries later.

Insurance salesmanship has also been applied to philosophical and religious realms. Blaise Pascal, the famous seventeenth-century French philosopher and mathematician, used risk management logic in his attempt to persuade atheists to believe in God. He argued that nonbelievers might be right—God might not exist. These nonbelievers could save time and money by avoiding a lifetime of religious services, obligations, and time in prayer. However, if these nonbelievers were wrong, they faced an eternity in hell. Pascal asserted that professing a faith in God was a small "premium" to pay to avoid the unbearable loss of eternal damnation. In this light, "Pascal's wager" brings new meaning to the concept of *life* insurance.

Life Insurance Companies

Overview

Life insurance companies are intermediaries that offer protection against the financial costs associated with events such as death and disability in exchange for premiums. When a policyholder dies or becomes disabled, a life insurance company agrees to make either a lump sum payment or an annuity (a series of payments) to the **beneficiary** of the policy. According to the American Council of Life Insurers' *Fact Book 2000*, most life insurance policies and annuities in the United States are sold through one of the 1,470 (as of 1999) U.S. life insurance companies.

Beneficiary
The person who receives an insurance payment or annuity stream after a policyholder dies.

http://www.acli.org
Find more on life insurance issues.

Most insurers (1,356 of the 1,470, or 92 percent) are organized as stock companies. Stock companies issue shares of stock and are owned by their stockholders. In contrast, only 7 percent (106 companies) of life insurers are organized as mutual companies, which are owned by their policyholders. Mutual insurance companies include some familiar names—Prudential of America, New York Life, John Hancock, and Citigroup, a financial conglomerate that was created from the merger of Citicorp and Travelers. Exhibit 18-1 shows the top 20 life/health insurance companies ranked by their asset size. In addition to stock and mutual insurance companies, life insurance products are also sold through a variety of fraternal societies; savings banks in Connecticut, Massachusetts, and New York; and the U.S. Department of Veterans Affairs.

As of year-end 1999, approximately 366 million life insurance policies with a total face value of more than $15.5 trillion were in force in the United States. Some people are covered by multiple policies. The Fed's 1998 *Survey of Consumer Finances* shows that ownership of any type of life insurance has actually declined from 75.2 percent of families in 1989 to 69.2 percent in 1998.

1. Prudential of America Group	$211,529,476,000
2. Metropolitan Life and Affiliated	198,574,177,000
3. Hartford Life, Inc.	134,406,906,000
4. Aegon USA, Inc.	123,441,677,000
5. TIAA Group	110,570,305,000
6. American General Group	97,373,516,000
7. American International Group	96,064,931,000
8. New York Life Group	96,053,789,000
9. Equitable Group	95,305,316,000
10. Nationwide Group	90,051,093,000
11. Aetna, Inc. Group	88,743,160,000
12. Northwestern Mutual Group	85,982,484,000
13. Lincoln National Corp.	83,383,911,000
14. Principal Life Insurance Co.	76,017,652,000
15. Cigna Group	75,568,895,000
16. John Hancock Financial Services Group	71,433,890,000
17. MassMutual Financial Group	70,642,867,000
18. American Express Financial	61,998,150,000
19. Citigroup	58,990,482,000
20. GE Financial Assurance Group	52,805,628,000

EXHIBIT 18-1

Top 20 Life/Health Insurance Groups and Unaffiliated Companies (Total Assets, 1999 Year-End Data)

SOURCE: *Best's Review,* October 2000, Vol. 101, No. 6, pp. 72–73.

Types of Coverage

Life insurance products can be divided into five main types of coverage:

1. Term life insurance (pure insurance) covers a policyholder for a specific time period or "term."

2. Permanent insurance provides coverage for one's "whole life" and embodies both an insurance component and an investment vehicle; examples include whole life, universal life, and variable life policies.

3. Annuities provide a stream of future income payments to their holder to serve as a form of protection against the risk of outliving one's income.

4. Disability insurance provides insurance coverage when workers are unable to work because of accident or illness.

5. Long-term care insurance covers the costs of services for policyholders unable to perform certain activities of daily living without assistance.

Term Life Insurance

Term life insurance is the least expensive type of life insurance. *Straight term insurance* provides a death benefit to an insured policyholder's beneficiary only if the insured dies within the specified period of time, or "term," of the policy. It ends automatically after a stated number of years. Term insurance policies are often set with a fixed premium for 1-, 5-, 10-, or more year periods. Premiums are based on statistical data called **mortality tables.** Actuaries develop and use these tables to estimate the number of people of a given age who are expected to die during a year. This information is used in conjunction with estimates of administrative costs and expected earnings on investments to establish appropriate premiums.

Term Life Insurance
Life insurance that provides a death benefit to an insured policyholder's beneficiary only if the insured dies within the specified period of time or "term" of the policy.

Mortality Tables
Schedules used to estimate the number of people of a given age who are expected to die during a year.

Term insurance policyholders know the premium and the death benefit for the term in which the policy is in force. *Renewable term life insurance* allows a policyholder to continue the policy for an additional term after the original policy expires. In some cases, renewal requires the policyholder to undergo a physical examination to continue insurability. Some term policies revert to 1-year renewable term policies wherein premiums increase annually. In almost all cases, term policy premiums increase steeply with the age of the policyholder. Most companies do not permit renewal after a person reaches 65 or 70 years of age.

Term insurance plans are also provided by many businesses, labor unions, and professional groups to their employees or members as *group life insurance*. Since group coverage is cheaper to administer, often because of subsidies from the sponsoring organization, these plans are often less expensive than individual plans. Regardless of whether the term insurance is straight, renewable, or group-sponsored, it has no investment component or cash build-up. Once the term has expired, the policyholder—if living—has nothing to show for the premiums paid.

Two types of financial innovations overcome this shortcoming. First, insurance companies have developed whole, universal, and variable life policies that accumulate cash values. Second, some term insurance policies are **convertible** into these other kinds of insurance. Under specified conditions, the policyholder has the right to change his or her term life insurance policy into a whole, universal, or variable life product. This may often be done without providing evidence of insurability if it is changed within some given period stated by the policy.

Permanent Life Insurance

Like term life insurance, **whole life insurance** (sometimes called a *straight life policy* or *continuous premium policy*) charges a fixed premium and pays a fixed death benefit as long as the policyholder makes timely premium payments. However, whole life policies differ from term insurance in two fundamental respects. First, whole life policies are not limited to a particular term. Instead, they are a form of permanent life insurance that provides protection for as long as the insured lives and makes premium payments. Second, the premiums for whole life insurance are substantially higher than those for term life insurance, especially at the beginning of the contract. These additional premium amounts accumulate in a separate account as a cash reserve that is invested by the insurance company for the policyholder's benefit.

There are two main tax advantages of accumulating a cash reserve in this way. First, under current tax law, cash reserves accumulated within an insurance policy grow tax deferred—no tax is paid unless the funds are withdrawn. However, tax law does require that the cash value of a policy cannot exceed its death benefit. Second, death benefits usually pass to beneficiaries free of taxation. In addition to these benefits, cash reserves can be borrowed by the policyholder at low interest rates, used to make premium payments, or taken as a cash *surrender* (turn-in) value. If the policy is canceled, the policyholder is entitled to this cash surrender value minus any outstanding loans against the policy. In the case of death, the beneficiary receives only the policy's face value, regardless of the cash value of the separate account.

In the high-interest rate environment of the late 1970s and early 1980s, whole life insurance policy holders found that the growth in the cash reserve portion of their policies failed to keep up with the rate of inflation or even the rates of return on conservative money market instruments. In response, many policyholders

Convertible
Insurance policies containing a clause allowing the policyholder to change a term insurance policy into a permanent (whole, universal, variable) life insurance product.

Whole Life Insurance
A permanent type of life insurance that charges a fixed premium and pays a fixed death benefit, and whose separate account is invested by the insurance company for the policyholder's benefit.

allowed their policies to lapse. They began instead to follow the financial planning advice of the day, which said "buy term and invest the difference" to reap higher rates of return than could be earned with traditional whole life policies.

To attract customers in this more volatile interest rate climate, insurance companies created **universal life insurance** in 1979. This product maintains a similar pure life insurance product, but allows the interest rate on cash reserves to adjust with market interest rates. Policyholders effectively pay a premium that covers the cost of term insurance and funds a separate account as well. The separate account grows at a fluctuating interest rate similar to that received on money market accounts or short-term CDs. Policyholders are also allowed to vary the amount of their premium as long as they meet the minimum amount needed to fund the pure insurance part of their policy.

A more recent variation on this theme is the creation of **variable life insurance,** or equity-linked policies. (These policies are sometimes referred to as *universal variable life insurance.*) Like regular universal life policies, variable life policies have an insurance component and a separate account. The fundamental innovation is that variable life insurance policies allow policyholders to more actively manage their separate account and use it to purchase mutual fund shares from an array of insurance company-approved funds. This policy innovation allows for the possibility of even greater returns than those possible with universal life and allows policyholders to take advantage of tax-deferred growth. Like universal life, the combination of premium payments and/or policy cash values must be sufficient to pay the pure cost of the insurance to maintain the policy. As long as sufficient premiums are paid or adequate cash reserves in the policy pay the cost of insurance, a minimum death benefit is guaranteed. Exhibit 18-2 summarizes the differences in life insurance products.

Universal and variable life insurance products help insurance companies compete against other kinds of financial products. They also help insurance companies manage risk. By allowing the funds in separate accounts to adjust with market interest rates—like those in universal life insurance policies—or to be managed by policyholders in various kinds of mutual funds within variable life insurance policies, insurance companies no longer need to guarantee a particular rate of return. In short, universal and variable life insurance products shift the risk of inadequate account appreciation from insurance companies to policyholders. If interest rates or mutual fund valuations change such that policyholders receive low returns, it is not the insurance company that loses. Rather, policyholders suffer the loss and end up with a lower death benefit or higher premium costs than they had expected.

Term life and permanent life insurance products insure against the risk of death. Products that insure against the risk of living longer than expected are also available, and include annuities, disability insurance, and long-term care insurance.

Universal Life Insurance
A form of permanent life insurance that provides a pure insurance product as well as a separate account. This separate account grows at a fluctuating rate of interest similar to that received on a money market account or short-term CD. Premium payment amounts may be flexible as long as the minimum premium for the pure insurance benefit is met.

Variable Life Insurance
A form of permanent life insurance that provides a pure insurance product as well as a separate account. The separate account may be used by the policyholder to purchase mutual funds from a list of insurance company approved funds. These equity-linked funds pay a minimum death benefit as long as sufficient premium payments are received.

	TERM	WHOLE	UNIVERSAL	VARIABLE
Pure insurance coverage	Yes	Yes	Yes	Yes
Permanent protection (not limited to a particular term)	No	Yes	Yes	Yes
Cash reserves accumulate	No	Yes	Yes	Yes
Cash reserves accumulate at money market rates of interest	*NA*	No	Yes	No
Cash reserves accumulate at rates tied to mutual fund performance	*NA*	No	No	Yes

EXHIBIT 18-2
A Comparison of Term, Whole, Universal, and Variable Life Insurance Products

Annuities

Imagine a retiree who lives longer than she expects and spends down all of her retirement funds. She spends herself into poverty and is forced to rely on her family, Social Security, Medicare, and/or Medicaid to manage her remaining years of retirement. (Medicaid is a joint federal-state program that funds long-term care for low-income people once they have spent down most of their assets. Medicare is the federal program that pays for medically related recovery and rehabilitation services for those above a qualifying age.) Our retiree could have avoided this outcome if she had foreseen this difficulty early enough and had the funds available to purchase an annuity. An **annuity** is a contract that promises either (1) periodic payments over the lifetime of the **annuitant** (owner of the annuity) or (2) periodic payments for a specified period of time. Some policies guarantee the refund of all money contributed by the annuitant minus a fee for administrative costs. In this case, if the annuitant dies before receiving all of the proceeds of the annuity, the cash value is passed to the beneficiary. Annuities can be characterized as either immediate or deferred. Immediate annuities begin to pay income at once; deferred annuities increase in value before payments begin at some time in the future.

Annuity
An insurance contract that provides a periodic income at regular intervals for a specified amount of time, such as a number of years of for the life of the beneficiary.

Annuitant
The owner of an annuity.

Disability Insurance

According to the American Council of Life Insurance (ACLI), "nearly one-third of all Americans will suffer a serious disability between ages 35 and 65." Many of these illnesses or accidents result in prolonged periods of unemployment and its concomitant loss of income. To address this problem, life insurance companies offer **disability insurance.** These policies provide a portion (commonly 50–70 percent) of an insured worker's previous income while the worker is unemployed. During the latter half of the 1990s and early 2000s, disability income products became more customized with a variety of different benefit levels and definitions of what qualifies as a claimable disability. Most disability policies are sold through group plans.

Disability Insurance
Policies, exchanged for premiums, that are designed to cover a portion of an insured worker's previous income if the worker becomes unable to work because of illness or injury.

Long-Term Care Insurance

As the American population ages, there is a growing need for services to help those unable to carry out the daily tasks of bathing, eating, dressing, and moving about without assistance. **Long-term care insurance** was developed to help fund the provision of these services. The U.S. government currently pays for more than half of long-term care expenditures through Medicaid and Medicare. Increasingly, insurance companies are making policies available for skilled nursing home care and for services that allow the insured to stay at home and benefit from assisted living and home care medical services.

Long-Term Care Insurance
Policies, exchanged for premiums, that are designed to compensate insured policyholders needing assistance with the daily tasks of bathing, eating, dressing, and moving about. Medicare and Medicaid currently pay more than one-half of these expenditures.

Recent Trends and Balance Sheet Composition

The Financial Services Modernization Act of 1999 (Gramm-Leach-Bliley Act) allows for a fundamental change in the way in which insurance companies compete. The Act removed the last vestiges of the Glass-Steagall Act provisions that prohibited commercial banks, security firms, and insurance companies from joining forces. The first firm to test the waters—actually 1 year before the Act passed—was Citibank in its merger with Traveler's Insurance Group, creating Citigroup. Insurance companies that are not owned by banks or that have not purchased banking affiliates will likely find themselves at a competitive disadvantage as combined

LOOKING OUT: *International Life Insurance Markets*

According to the American Council of Life Insurers (ACLI's) *Life Insurance Fact Book 1999,* Asia is the largest life insurance market in the world. When measured in terms of premium dollars, Asia (primarily Japan) comprises slightly less than 40 percent of the world life insurance market. Europe is second, accounting for about 30 percent, and North America is third, with about a 25 percent share. That leaves the combined populations of Oceania, Africa, and Latin America to share the remaining 5 percent of the world life insurance market share.[a]

During 1997, Asia experienced the slowest real growth rate for any of the world's regions at a 5.4 percent rate. (Oceania had the highest rate at 19.8 percent followed by Latin America at 15.6 percent, Africa at 10.8 percent, Europe at 10.5 percent, and North America at 6.9 percent.) Asia's slow rate of growth was due primarily to Japan's sluggish economy and its slow recovery from the Asian financial crisis. Nevertheless, this was a vast improvement over 1996 when the Asian market as a whole shrank by one-fifth!

Despite relatively large market shares in Europe and North America, the greatest growth potential for life insurance is in developing economies where economic growth is increasing most rapidly. A strong correlation exists between growth in income and life insurance premium volume. Furthermore, in many of these countries, the industry is controlled by "inefficient domestic monopolies." As markets around the world are opened, global insurance companies will have increased access to these markets and will likely provide more affordable insurance products. In any case, global life insurance companies expect to sharply increase their market penetration in developing economies over the next few decades. Recent changes, such as the privatization of Chile's pension system, will enhance premium growth there and in other countries pursuing similar reforms.

[a]Oceania includes Australia, New Zealand, and Pacific Island chains. North America excludes and Latin America includes Mexico.
SOURCE: ACLI *Life Insurance Fact Book 1999,* pp. 155–156.

organizations market their products to customers throughout the combined firm. Reflecting the blurring lines between insurance and banking, this combination of banking and insurance is known as *bancassurance.*

Insurance companies and their agents have been moving away from an almost exclusive focus on insurance products to a broader focus on overall financial planning services. This new approach relies on providing clients with financial planning advice and access to mutual funds, stocks, bonds, and money market instruments.

As we saw in Chapter 14, life insurance company balance sheets hold a large share of corporate stocks and bonds. As of mid-year 2001, life insurance company assets consisted of 40 percent corporate and foreign bonds, 30 percent stocks, 9 percent government securities, and 7 percent mortgages. This high degree of long-term asset holdings can be explained by the relatively predictable payments that insurance companies can be expected to make. The reserves set aside to fund policy benefits in the future make up the vast majority of insurance company liabilities.

RECAP Life insurance companies offer protection against the financial costs associated with death and disability in return for premiums. The five main types of coverage include term life insurance, permanent life insurance (whole, universal, and variable), annuities, disability insurance, and long-term care insurance. Since the payments made by life insurance companies are relatively predictable, they are able to hold a large share of bonds and stocks on their balance sheets. The Financial Services Modernization Act of 1999 allows insurance companies to merge with banks and securities firms. This deregulation of the financial services industry allows financial conglomerates to market and sell insurance products alongside other banking and investment services.

Health Insurance Companies

Health Insurance Companies
Intermediaries that offer protection, in exchange for premiums, against the financial costs associated with events such as doctor visits, hospital stays, and prescription drugs.

Health insurance companies are a second kind of contractual-type intermediary. In return for premiums, health insurance companies pay part or all of the costs of hospitalization, surgery, doctor's visits, laboratory tests, prescription drugs, and other medical expenses. The provision of health insurance has been a contentious political issue since President Clinton proposed fundamental reform of the health insurance industry in 1992. At that time, 34 million Americans were uninsured, the costs of health care and health insurance were escalating, and the share of U.S. GDP spent on health care expenditures was growing.

Between 1992 and 2000, the number of uninsured Americans grew by about 10 million, costs continued to increase—albeit at a slower rate—and the share of GDP spent on health care continued to swell. Higher medical costs were putting a strain on the government programs (Medicaid and Medicare) used to provide health insurance coverage for the indigent and the elderly. Although fundamental reforms have not been passed, the media's attention to rising costs and to the millions of uninsured Americans has forced many to take notice.

The rising cost of health care has also put a strain on the many company-sponsored health insurance plans. As costs rose, companies have dealt with rising premium costs by curtailing coverage, asking employees to bear a bigger share of the burden, and attempting to control costs. To control costs directly, firms have negotiated with physicians' groups to provide particular medical services at a set fee. They have also created managed care plans that require patients to have medical services approved before any nonemergency medical procedure is completed.

Health Maintenance Organizations (HMOs)
Specialized health care insurers that provide almost complete medical care in exchange for fixed per person premiums.

Many insurance companies have created **health maintenance organizations (HMOs)** to assist with the controlling of medical costs. HMOs provide almost complete health care services in return for a fixed, per-person premium. In return, most medical expenses are paid subject to a deductible and copayment by the insured. Three primary problems have arisen from HMO arrangements. First, health care costs have continued to increase and HMOs have frequently underestimated these costs. This has caused HMOs to experience financial losses and has led many insurance companies to sell their HMO affiliates. Second, HMO providers have an incentive to limit medical services to cut costs. This has led to criticisms that bureaucrats—not doctors—are making decisions about which medical procedures are most appropriate. Third, medical services must usually be provided by a medical staff designated by the HMO. Consumers have chafed at this mandate and at laws prohibiting them from suing their HMOs for providing substandard medical services. These complaints have led to calls for a Patients Bill of Rights that would enhance consumer choice and hold HMOs financially liable for their actions. Despite these problems and the clamor for reform, American membership in HMOs has increased from about 3.5 million in 1970 to over 50 million in 2000.

Property and Casualty Companies
Intermediaries that provide protection against the effects of unexpected occurrences on property.

Property Insurance
Contingent claims, exchange for premiums, that protect insured policyholders from the financial costs of property loss, damage, or destruction.

Property and Casualty Companies

Property and casualty companies are the third form of contractual insurance intermediary. **Property insurance** protects insured property owners (or renters) against the effects of property loss, damage, or destruction caused by various natu-

ral perils such as fire, theft, storm, or acts of God[2] or human perils such as automobile accidents, vandalism, arson, or burglary. Property insurance is most frequently used to protect automobile owners and home owners. Businesses use property insurance to protect commercial property and the accompanying loss of
income caused by its damage or loss.

Casualty (liability) insurance protects a policyholder from financial responsibilities to those harmed by an accident, product failure, or professional malpractice. It
also provides coverage to commercial and individual property owners when a person
is injured on the property. Manufacturing companies purchase casualty insurance to
protect themselves against product defects that cause injury or death to consumers.
Doctors, lawyers, and other professionals purchase liability insurance to protect
themselves from claims of negligence or malpractice. While property insurance lends
itself to the actuarial calculations of risk, liability risk exposure is more uncertain and
is virtually impossible to predit accurately. The liability suits and high putative damage awards successfully brought against tobacco companies in the late 1990s and in
the early 2000s were unimaginable to most only 10 years earlier.

Most automobile policies are a combination of both property insurance and casualty insurance. The property insurance portion protects against loss or damage to
the vehicle in case of an accident, vandalism, damaging weather, or theft. The casualty insurance portion of the policy provides the owner with liability coverage if he
or she harms another or another's property with the vehicle. Assume a two-car accident. Your car hits another car and causes injuries both to yourself and to the other
driver. You, the insured driver, are at fault, so the property insurance part of your
policy will pay for the repair of your car. The casualty part of your insurance policy
will pay for any medical injuries to yourself and for the repair of the automobile you
hit. It will also cover the medical bills (up to some prescribed limit) of the other
driver. If the case had to first go through court, the liability insurance would also, in
some cases, cover the defendant's court costs. In some states, **no-fault insurance**
coverage enables insured auto accident victims to collect damages from their own
insurance company regardless of whether or not they caused the accident.

Exhibit 18-3 lists the 20 largest property and casualty insurance companies in
rank order. There are 3,800 property and casualty companies in the United
States—more than twice the number of life insurance companies (1,563). However,
the total assets of the life insurance industry were more than three times those of
the property and casualty industry, at about $2.8 trillion versus $884 billion. A cur-
sory comparison between Exhibits 18-1 and 18-3 suggests why. Even among the
largest 20 firms in each segment of the industry, life insurance companies tend to
be much larger than property and casualty insurers.

The composite balance sheets of life insurance companies and property and
casualty companies differ not only in asset size but also in asset composition. Life
insurance companies hold about 70 percent of their assets in the form of corporate
and foreign bonds and corporate equities. In contrast, property and casualty companies hold only about 43 percent of their assets in this form. This is because life
insurance companies sell longer-term policies with more predictable payments and

Casualty (Liability) Insurance Insurance exchanged for premiums, that protects insured policyholders from the financial responsibilities to those harmed by an accident, product failure, or professional malpractice.

No-Fault Insurance Insurance coverage that pays an accident victim regardless of who caused an accident or damage.

http://www.housingcenter.com/insur/coverage/property.html. *Examine factors to consider when planning commercial property insurance needs.*

---

[2]"Act of God" is a catch-phrase that refers to any other unforeseeable occurrence caused by nature
not explicitly exempted by the insurance contract. Most homeowners policies state specific exemptions
from coverage. For example, flood damage is not covered in a typical homeowner's policy. Nearly all
policies have exemptions for war or nuclear contamination.

EXHIBIT 18-3
Top 20 Property/
Casualty Groups and
Unaffiliated
Companies (Total
Assets, 1999 Year-End
Data)

1.	State Farm Group	$95,158,000
2.	Berkshire Hathaway Insurance Group	69,141,000
3.	American International Group	45,650,000
4.	Allstate Insurance Group	39,060,000
5.	Travelers PC Group	35,197,000
6.	CAN Insurance Companies	34,798,000
7.	Liberty Mutual Insurance Companies	30,895,000
8.	Nationwide Group	23,230,000
9.	Hartford Insurance Group	23,178,000
10.	St. Paul Companies	22,153,000
11.	Chubb Group of Insurance Companies	15,930,000
12.	Farmers Insurance Group	15,821,000
13.	Employers Re US Group	15,486,000
14.	Allanz of America, Inc.	14,786,000
15.	USAA Group	11,763,000
16.	CGU Group	11,448,000
17.	Zurich US	11,336,000
18.	Fairfax Financial (US) Group	10,191,000,
19.	Kemper Insurance Companies	9,785,000
20.	Safeco Insurance Companies	9,754,000

SOURCE: *Best's Review.* October 2000, Vol. 101, No. 6, pp. 76–79.

with more clearly defined loss exposure. In contrast, the total losses on property and casualty claims, especially liability claims, are more difficult to predict. Similarly, many property and casualty policies are for short periods of time and are more prone to the problems of adverse selection and moral hazard than are typical life insurance products.

A Closer Look

Alleged Racial Bias in Property and Casualty Insurance and Life Insurance: During the late 1990s, property and casualty insurance companies faced allegations of racial bias in their treatment of minority applicants and others living in minority neighborhoods. This allegation was forcefully made by various authors in Gregory D. Squires's compiled volume, *Insurance Redlining: Disinvestment, Reinvestment, and the Evolving Role of Financial Institutions* (Washington, DC: The Urban Institute Press, 1997). The book documents that residents of minority neighborhoods travel farther to find an insurance agent's office, are less likely to have agents return their phone calls, are denied coverage more often, are offered less comprehensive insurance coverage, are charged higher premiums, and have their insurance claims processed more slowly. Because of these actions and policies, blacks and other people of color, as well as those living in minority neighborhoods, experience unequal access to housing, mortgage finance, home improvement loans, and business loans. The authors collectively and persuasively demonstrate that the insurance industry has created institutional barriers that unfairly hinder people of color and others living in minority neighborhoods in accumulating financial wealth. These barriers to wealth accumulation perpetuate inequality and produce poverty within the inner city. The authors claim that the government's response to these grievances has been haphazard and incomplete because the industry lacks a federal regulatory agency.

Life insurance companies also face allegations of racial bias. As recently as 2000, there have been allegations of life insurers using race as a basis for charging higher premium costs. *U.S. News & World Report* shares the story of Bessie Smith, who paid more than $1,600 for a burial policy worth $1,000. The price was obviously unfair and caused even more hurt to Ms. Smith when she learned that white policyholders were charged less for the same policy. She was not alone. In June of 2000, Smith and millions of other minority policyholders settled charges of racial discrimination with American General Life and Accident Insurance Co. for $215 million. The words of American General's chairman and CEO, Richard Devlin, are hard to improve upon as a statement of prudent insurance company management: "It was imperative that we move swiftly and responsibly to correct an unfortunate historical practice."

Other life insurance companies also face allegations of racial discrimination. According to Scot J. Paltrow of *The Wall Street Journal,* lawyers representing millions of African-American policyholders sued Prudential Insurance Co. of America and MetLife Inc. in July 2000. The plaintiffs sought damages on past life insurance sales for an alleged "nationwide scheme of racial discrimination." Prudential even admitted that "like many other insurance companies, Prudential, at certain points in its history, used race-based underwriting." However, the company went on to argue that it had stopped this practice "many years ago." The suits facing these two companies contend that in the past, policies carrying lower benefits and higher premiums had been specifically marketed to blacks. The key issue is the allegation that although the companies stopped selling these policies, they did not do enough to make up for past discrimination. The companies failed to increase the benefits owed to African-American policyholders or to refund their excess premium payments.[3]

RECAP Health insurance companies offer contingency claims in return for health insurance premiums. Recent increases in health care costs have led to new ways to manage care and control costs. Property and casualty companies offer policies that are complementary for both individuals and businesses. Property insurance offers financial protection against the effects of property loss, damage, or destruction caused by fire, theft, storm, or acts of God. Casualty insurance protects the insured from financial claims of others who are harmed by an accident, product failure, or professional malpractice.

Managing Adverse Selection and Moral Hazard in the Insurance Industry

All insurance companies must actively manage their clients to prevent adverse selection and moral hazard problems. Remember, adverse selection suggests that those entering the insurance pool are more likely than the population as a whole to file a claim. Those needing insurance have an incentive to pursue its acquisition most aggressively. Moral hazard suggests that once people get into the pool, their behavior will be altered and they will behave in a more reckless manner than they would be if they were uninsured. Insurance coverage tends to attract higher-risk clients and tends to make insured policyholders behave in a more reckless manner than they would otherwise. Insurance companies have created a variety of management practices to address these problems as summarized in Exhibit 18-4.

The first line of defense is for insurance underwriters to screen out those applicants who would be poor insurance risks. Life insurance companies routinely refuse coverage to those in poor health or past a certain age. Property and casualty companies check driving records before agreeing to provide automobile coverage. A

---

[3]Angie Cannon, "Paying for a Bad Policy," *U.S. News & World Report,* July 3, 2000, Vol. 129, i1, p. 24; Scott J. Paltrow, "Prudential Insurance, MetLife Face Suits Over Alleged Racist Practices," *The Wall Street Journal,* July 13, 2000; Reynold F. Nesiba, Review for *Insurance Redlining: Disinvestment, Reinvestment, and the Evolving Role of Financial Institutions,* edited by Gregory D. Squires, The Urban Institute Press, Washington, DC, 1997; *Journal of Economic Issues,* 32:3 (September 1998): 901–904.

EXHIBIT 18-4
Top 10 Ways to Manage Adverse Selection, Moral Hazard, and Other Risks in the Insurance Industry

1. Effective screening
2. Risked-based premiums
3. Deductibles
4. Coinsurance
5. Threaten or cancel coverage
6. Restrictive provisions
7. Fraud prevention
8. Limit the amount of insurance
9. Reinsurance
10. Effective credit, interest rate, liquidity, and exchange rate risk management

Risk-Based Premiums
Insurance charges that increase with the perceived risk of the policyholder.

Deductibles
A fixed amount that the insured policyholder is required to pay before insurance coverage becomes effective.

Coinsurance
The percentage share or fixed amount of a claim that must be paid by the policyholder. Many health insurance companies require 80/20 cost sharing, with the insurer bearing 80 percent of the cost and the policyholder paying 20 percent. The policyholder's share is sometimes capped at some maximum out-of-pocket expense.

driver with a history of frequent accidents is likely to be denied coverage. Until prevented by federal regulation, health insurance coverage routinely denied coverage to patients with "pre-existing conditions" that would increase the likelihood of costly medical care.

A second line of defense is to charge substantially higher **risk-based premiums** instead of denying coverage. The elderly can obtain life insurance, poor drivers can get automobile coverage, and the chronically ill can buy health care coverage. However, they will be charged higher premiums to compensate for the higher expected pay-outs they will generate from the insurer.

A third defense, used primarily to prevent moral hazard in almost all health and property insurance policies, is to require insured policyholders who file claims to pay deductibles. **Deductibles** are the fixed amount an insured must pay when a claim is paid off. Automobile coverage, for instance, may require the insured to pay the first $250 of a $2,000 hail damage claim. This has two effects: First, since insured policyholders stand to lose in the wake of a damage claim, they have an incentive to get the car into the garage if a menacing storm is approaching. Secondly, since policyholders are forced to bear the costs of low-dollar-amount claims, insurance companies avoid handling the paperwork associated with frequent small claims.

Coinsurance (requiring a copayment) serves as a fourth line of defense against moral hazard. By requiring the insured to pay 20 percent of a medical bill while the insurance company pays the other 80 percent, a financial incentive effect similar to a deductible is imposed. The policyholder has an incentive to avoid needless medical care. Many prescription drug policies use a similar arrangement by requiring a $5 to $20 copayment when a policyholder purchases prescription medication.

A fifth tool companies can use to reduce unnecessarily risky action by their policyholders is to threaten to cancel their insurance coverage. An automobile insurer can warn a policyholder with frequent accident claims that further claims will result in the cancellation of coverage. Of course, management by idle threat is likely to be ineffective. If policyholders continue to cost more than they are worth, companies do cancel policies.

Restrictive provisions stand as a sixth management tool to reduce insurance company exposure to risk. Some life insurance companies refuse to pay claims if the insured commits suicide. Similarly, some health insurance companies restrict coverage of medical liability claims for injuries sustained from parachuting or skydiving. Some property and casualty companies deny liability coverage for injuries sustained while jumping on a trampoline.

For restrictive provisions to be effective, insurance companies use a seventh tool—fraud prevention. Insured policyholders have an incentive to file fake claims or to make claims on injuries sustained while engaging in restrictive activities. A home owner whose house has been completely destroyed may be tempted to claim the loss of assets that she never owned. To prevent this, insurance companies require documentation that the home owner actually possessed the item. Many home owners periodically videotape the contents of their house with a camcorder to create this documentation.

An eighth management tool is to limit insurance coverage to the value of the insured property. If a home owner could insure his $100,000 house for $200,000, he could be tempted to torch the house in hopes of reaping a $100,000 gain. Limiting insurance to the value of a property or less helps eliminate this moral hazard.

A ninth way to manage insurance company risk is to engage in **reinsurance**, which involves sharing the risk of a policy with other insurance companies. A small insurance company may write a large property and casualty policy to a large corporation. Rather than face the possibility of paying a large claim alone, the small insurance company may allocate a portion of the risk to other companies for a share of a portion of the premiums. In this way, total exposure is reduced as well as any adverse selection or moral hazard problems that accompany it.

Reinsurance
The practice by smaller insurance companies of sharing the risk of a large policy with other insurance companies to reduce risk exposure.

A tenth and final way for insurance companies to manage risk really has nothing to do with adverse selection and moral hazard. Instead, it is a reminder to be vigilant in the management of the credit, interest rate, liquidity, and exchange rate risks faced by all FIs. The bonds, stocks, and real estate held on insurance company balance sheets are subject to credit or default risk and market fluctuations. Care must be taken in diversifying portfolios. Insurance companies have become insolvent because of losses on junk bonds and real estate holdings. Similarly, insurance companies—particularly life insurance companies—are subject to interest rate risk because of their holdings of long-term securities. As interest rates increase, the value of these long-term securities falls. This can be managed with increased use of floating rate securities and prudent use of futures contracts and interest rate swaps. Liquidity risk is particularly problematic for property and casualty companies that are subject to a large number of simultaneous claims due to a natural disaster. This can be reduced by geographically diversifying where policies are sold and by maintaining an adequate level of liquid assets. Exchange rate risk plays a small but growing role as insurers become more international in scope. Diversification of asset holdings and avoiding large foreign currency denominated assets and policies are effective ways of reducing this risk.

Regulation

Despite the active management of risk by insurance companies, government agencies have also been created to provide outside supervision of the industry. Unlike the depository institutions examined in earlier chapters, life, health, and property casualty insurance companies are regulated almost exclusively by state-level insurance commissioners. It did not always appear that it would work out this way. In 1944, the Supreme Court ruled that insurance was subject to federal regulation because it involved interstate commerce. However, Congress lost little time in writing the **McCarran-Ferguson Act of 1945,** which exempts the insurance industry from federal regulation. The agencies that serve as federal regulators are the Internal Revenue Service (IRS), which administers special taxation rules, and the Securities and Exchange Commission (SEC), which requires insurance companies with publicly traded stock to comply with its requirements.

McCarran-Ferguson Act
Federal statute passed in 1945 that exempts life insurance companies from federal regulation and defers its oversight to state insurance commissioners in each state.

In addition, each state establishes its own set of safety and soundness regulations with regard to the types of securities insurance companies may hold, the levels of capital required, and the accounting standards adopted. Insurance companies are

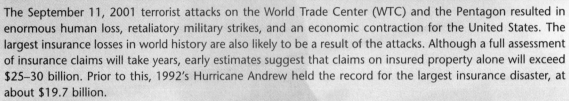

LOOKING BACK: *Terrorist Attacks Cause Record Insurance Losses*

The September 11, 2001 terrorist attacks on the World Trade Center (WTC) and the Pentagon resulted in enormous human loss, retaliatory military strikes, and an economic contraction for the United States. The largest insurance losses in world history are also likely to be a result of the attacks. Although a full assessment of insurance claims will take years, early estimates suggest that claims on insured property alone will exceed $25–30 billion. Prior to this, 1992's Hurricane Andrew held the record for the largest insurance disaster, at about $19.7 billion.

Unfortunately, property losses are not the only type of claim the industry must meet. Herb Perone of the American Council of Life Insurers posits that the attacks caused the largest number of life insurance claims ever for a single day. These claim amounts cannot be determined until thousands of people are accounted for. Leslie Jacobs, president of Hiberia Rosenthal Insurance, says the death benefit on workers' compensation policies of employees in the WTC alone will likely exceed $5 billion. Accidental death benefits could add another $2–5 billion to the ultimate tab. Financial ripples further away from the attack include insurance claims for lost revenues caused by postponed or cancelled National Football League games.

Companies with the largest financial exposure are expected to be re-insurers, such as Munich Re, Swiss Re, Berkshire Hathaway, and Lloyd's of London. While losses may wipe out some individual firms, experts confidently assert that the global insurance industry has more than sufficient capital to manage these losses. Thus, despite the tremendous loss of life and property and issues related to specific policy exclusions, the insurance industry is expected to sufficiently absorb the financial losses of September 11, 2001 without serious disruption.

http://www.naic.org/ splash.htm
Read more about insurance regulations.

compelled to follow the standards set by the state in which they are chartered as well as the regulations in any state in which they do business. To help manage the crazy quilt of 50 possible regulatory approaches, the National Association of Insurance Commissioners (NAIC) develops model laws and regulations. These models are often used by state legislatures when revising or writing new legislation. Since the state of New York comprises a large life insurance market and is the headquarters for many insurance companies, its laws and regulations have a widespread impact on the industry. To ensure that agents are familiar with the products they sell to consumers, all states require that agents be licensed in each state that they sell insurance.

RECAP Since insurance creates the dual problems of adverse selection and moral hazard, it must be actively managed. This can be done through careful screening, risk-based premiums, deductibles, coinsurance, threatening policy cancellation, restrictive provisions, fraud protection, limiting insurance coverage, engaging in reinsurance, and managing other risks. Because of the McCarran-Ferguson Act of 1945, insurance companies are primarily regulated at the state level.

Evolution and Globalization

The insurance industry caters to the risk-averse desires of individuals and businesses by pooling risks and allowing policyholders to purchase appropriate protection for life, health, and property and casualty needs. Although the fundamental benefit of risk pooling has remained unchanged for centuries, the insurance industry continues to evolve and to expand globally. As we have seen with other financial service providers, financial modernization and the desire to remain competitive have encouraged insurers to combine with banks and securities firms to provide a wide range of savings, investing, payment, and financial planning services. Recent lawsuits and the pursuit of profit have forced insurance companies to change the way they do business with minority individuals and in minority neighborhoods. The volatile interest rates of a few decades ago served as an impetus for the development of new universal and variable life insurance products. These products better meet the needs of consumers and allow insurers to better manage their own risk exposure. The life insurance industry has become more global in nature, with the fastest growth occurring in developing countries where income growth is the most rapid.

Summary of Major Points

- Many economists and financial experts find it useful to distinguish between risk and uncertainty. Risk refers to those situations wherein one can calculate the odds of a particular outcome. It requires *a priori* knowledge of all possible outcomes and some data on which rational decision making can be based. In contrast, uncertainty refers to situations in which there is no basis for a probabilistic computation. These arise when a decision maker lacks knowledge regarding possible outcomes on which to compute a mathematical probability.

- Risk aversion refers to the desire of financial decision makers to reduce the likelihood of an unfortunate mishap and its accompanying financial loss. In an uncertain world, risk-averse behavior creates profitable opportunities for insurance companies and pension plans to help others manage risk.

- Insurance companies are a form of contractual-type financial intermediary. The financial costs associated with the loss of life, health, or property can be reduced by buying insurance from life, health, and property and casualty companies, respectively. For a premium, insurance companies agree to make a payment contingent upon a certain event occurring. The design, sale, management, and loss determination of insurance policies are respectively carried out by actuaries, agents, underwriters, and claims adjusters.

- The use of insurance by policyholders creates the dual challenges of adverse selection and moral hazard that must be actively managed by insurance companies. Adverse selection occurs when the riskiest or least-profitable policy applicants pursue an insurance policy more vigorously than other applicants and are therefore more likely to become insured. Moral hazard refers to the possibility that an insured policyholder's behavior will be riskier than it was in the absence of insurance.

- The financial costs of unexpected events such as death and disability can be managed by purchasing life or disability insurance. Types of life insurance overage include term life insurance, permanent life insurance (whole, universal, and variable life), annuities, disability insurance, and long-term care insurance.

- Health insurance companies offer contingency claims in return for health insurance premiums. Recent increases in health care costs have led to new ways to manage care and control costs, including managed care and health maintenance organizations (HMOs). Rising costs to pay for Medicare, Medicaid, and private insurance coverage, as well as a growing number and share of Americans without health insurance coverage, continue to be pressing public policy problems.

- Property insurance offers financial protection to individuals and businesses from the effects of property loss, damage, or destruction caused by fire, theft, storms, or acts of God. Casualty insurance protects an insured policyholder from the financial claims of others who are harmed by accidents, product failures, or professional malpractice.

- Ten ways to manage risk in the insurance industry are through effective screening, risked-based premiums, deductibles, coinsurance, threatening and/or canceling a policy, restrictive provisions, effective fraud prevention, limits on the amount of insurance, reinsurance, and active management of credit, interest rate, liquidity, and exchange rate risk.

- The McCarran-Ferguson Act of 1945 prohibits federal regulation of insurance companies. As a result, they are primarily regulated at the state level. The National Association of Insurance Commissioners (NAIC) develops model laws and regulations that are often used by state legislatures when revising or writing new legislation. This is done in an attempt to create some consistency among the 50 different states. All states require that agents be licensed before they are allowed to sell insurance.

Key Terms

Actuaries

Annuitant

Annuity

Beneficiary

Casualty (Liability) Insurance

Coinsurance

Convertible

Deductibles

Disability Insurance

Health Insurance Companies

Health Maintenance
 Organizations (HMOs)

Insurance Company

Long-Term Care Insurance

McCarran-Ferguson Act

Mortality Tables

No-Fault Insurance

Property and Casualty
 Companies

Property Insurance

Reinsurance

Risk Averse

Risk-Based Premiums

Term Life Insurance

Universal Life Insurance

Variable Life Insurance

Whole Life Insurance

Review Questions

1. Explain the difference between risk and uncertainty. Give an example of a decision influenced by each of these concepts.

2. List and explain the two primary sources of revenue and the main use of funds for insurance companies in general.

3. Briefly explain the primary responsibilities of actuaries, agents, underwriters, and claims adjusters.

4. Explain how adverse selection differs from moral hazard.

5. Explain the salient characteristics of term, whole, universal, and variable life insurance policies.

6. Give a specific example of how a bowling alley would benefit from having both property and casualty insurance.

7. List and explain the 10 ways insurance companies actively manage risk.

8. List and explain four types of professional positions in the insurance industry and their job responsibilities.

9. List and describe the coverage provided by the three main types of insurance companies described in this chapter.

Analytical Questions

10. Briefly explain risk pooling, the essential principle underlying insurance coverage, by using an automobile insurance example.

11. Why might health insurance companies hold fewer long-term assets than life insurance companies?

12. Why is most disability insurance sold through group plans?

13. How do the large number of malpractice suits against doctors and the large jury awards to victims affect the price of casualty insurance and health insurance? Explain the possible effect of caps on awards to victims on health insurance costs.

14. Discuss the evidence that racial bias exists in the insurance industry.

15. Can you explain why male college students usually pay more than female college students for exactly the same automobile insurance coverage? Make the case that this is unfair to male students. Make the rebuttal that an insurance company would give to defend its policies.

16. Your instructor has decided that the best way to explain adverse selection and moral hazard is to sell "grade insurance" policies to students in your class. Policyholders who are unhappy with their final course grade can file a claim for any grade they desire. Policies are sold for $20. However, only three policies will be sold

in your class. Describe how adverse selection and moral hazard would likely play themselves out in your course. Give specific examples of how your instructor could amend these policies in an attempt to reduce adverse selection and moral hazard.

Internet Exercises

1. Go to **http://www.insurance.com/** or another Internet site that allows you to generate price quotes online. (A Google.com search in August 2001 generated 1.7 million hits on "term insurance.") What would it cost you to purchase $100,000 of term life insurance at a fixed rate over 10 years? Go back and do the process again. However, this time apply as a male born January 1, 1950 who smokes, has high blood pressure, and is overweight. What would it cost this fictional person? Drawing on the material in the chapter, explain why this second person would likely pay more. If your quote was more expensive than this person's, explain why.

2. Go to **http://insurance.yahoo.com/** and take the "savings quiz." Are you a savvy auto insurance shopper? What suggestions did this site give for you to reduce your premiums? Now go back and click on "quick" quotes for auto insurance. What would it cost you to insure your current automobile? Apply for a second quote and take all of the suggestions from the savings quiz. In addition, pretend that you live in South Dakota. How much did your quoted premium decrease? Why?

Suggested Readings

The American Council of Life Insurers' *Life Insurance Fact Book* (**http://www.acli.com**) provides an annual statistical profile of trends and important statistics about the life insurance industry. Tables and figures provide a wealth of information, including numbers of Americans covered, number of insurance companies, consolidated balance sheet information, mortality and life expectancy tables, and more.

For information on discrimination in the property and casualty industry, see Gregory D. Squires, ed., *Insurance Redlining: Disinvestment, Reinvestment, and the Evolving Role of Financial Institutions* (The Urban Institute Press, Washington, DC, 1997). This is reviewed by Reynold F. Nesiba in *Journal of Economic Issues*, 32:3 (September 1998): 901–904. Recent articles on discrimination in the life insurance industry include Angie. Cannon, "Paying for a Bad Policy," *U.S. News & World Report*, July 3, 2000, Vol.129, i1, p. 24; and Scott J. Paltrow, "Prudential Insurance, MetLife Face Suits Over Alleged Racist Practices," *The Wall Street Journal*, July 13, 2000.

chapter

10 Pension Plans and Finance Companies

> **Learning Objectives** *After reading this chapter, you should know:*
>
> - The various kinds of pension plans and finance companies
> - The benefits provided by pension plans and finance companies
> - The principal sources and uses of funds for both of these financial intermediaries
> - The primary regulations and regulatory agencies with which both of these FIs must comply
> - Recent changes in the way these FIs do business

" "

In 1949 the nation's pension assets totaled only $14.3 billion . . . At the end of 1998 the nation's pension assets totaled more than $8.7 trillion, more than 600 times what they were in 1949.
—Michael J. Clowes

New or expanding small business may be denied traditional bank loans because of limited track records or high debt. . . . In these situations, a commercial finance company may be an alternative source of financing for your business.
—http://www.scoredelaware.com/financing.com.company.htm

Retirement Planning and Liquidity Management

Chapter 18 explained that the existence of uncertainty, combined with the desire to avoid excessive risk, led to risk pooling and the eventual creation of insurance companies. This chapter examines two different types of institutions: pension plans and finance companies. Pension plans (like insurance companies) exist in part to help risk-averse people deal with the uncertainties of retirement planning. However, the goals of finance companies are somewhat different. They help consumers and firms manage liquidity risk by providing a variety of leasing and lending services.

Individuals who are planning for retirement want to amass a sufficient level of wealth to maintain their standard of living after they quit working. If these investors hold funds solely in low-interest-earning savings accounts, they face the possibility that inflation will erode the purchasing power of their assets. Insufficient funds will be available to finance their years of retirement. If investors attempt to avoid this inflation risk by purchasing higher-yielding individual stocks and bonds, they expose themselves to significant default and interest rate risk. Thankfully, pension plans have been developed to assist us in managing these risks and achieving our desired financial goals.

Where pension plans assist individuals and groups with their retirement needs, finance companies provide various types of leasing and lending services to consumers and firms. They aid leasees in avoiding additional debt and standardizing their payment streams. Specialized commercial finance companies also purchase the accounts receivables of other business firms. This provides liquidity to the selling firm and transfers the default risk associated with extending credit from the selling firm to the finance company.

The first section of this chapter describes the various types of pension plans (including the difference between defined-contribution and defined-benefit plans), discusses recent trends in the industry, and explores regulatory issues. We conclude this first section of the chapter with a discussion of the largest public pension system, Social Security. Here we discuss recent stresses on this system and plans for its reform. The second section examines finance companies. We compare them to banks and thrifts and describe consumer finance, business finance, and real estate loan companies. We also explain recent trends in the industry and discuss how finance companies manage risks, and conclude with a discussion of finance company regulation.

Pension Plans

Overview

Pension plans have been around almost since the birth of our nation. The first pension plans in the United States were created to provide income for the disabled American veterans of the Revolutionary War. In the early 1800s, benefits were also extended to retired veterans. The federal government continues to be one of the primary providers of pensions through its plans for veterans and retired government employees and through the Social Security program. The first private pension plan in the United States was offered in 1875 by the American Express company, then an important transportation firm. Railroads followed by adding pensions in the 1880s. Labor unions created funds for their members in the early 1900s. Before the creation of Social Security in 1935, however, most Americans worked until they died. If they outlived their ability to care for themselves, they relied on family members to provide long-term care. Contemporary notions of retirement and the prospect of years of retirement (and, increasingly, decades) are a relatively new social, economic, and financial phenomenon.

To assist workers and future retirees with this new reality, tax-exempt intermediaries called *pension plans* or *pension funds* have been set up to provide income to workers and/or their spouses after a worker retires, becomes disabled, or dies. They are currently the fastest-growing type of financial intermediary. This rapid growth is often attributed to the steady increase in wealth and income generated in the United States since World War II, the growing need to plan financially for the retirement years, and the significant tax advantages Congress has created for these funds.

Types of Pension Plans

Pension plans are often categorized by: (1) who makes the contributions, (2) the type of sponsorship, and/or (3) the manner in which either contributions or benefits are defined. First, in terms of contributions, most pension plans are **contributory plans** in which both the employee and the employer make contributions. In **noncontributory plans,** only the employer makes contributions.

Contributory Plans
Pension plans in which both the employee and employer contribute.

Noncontributory Plans
Pension plans in which only the employer contributes.

Public Pension Plans

Pension plans can be sponsored publicly (governmental units) or privately (corporations, unions, small businesses, or individuals). *The Life Insurers Fact Book 2000* notes that total U.S. retirement plan assets reached $12.7 trillion in 1999. A little more than one-third of these assets are managed by public pension plans sponsored by state and local government employees, federal civilian employees, railroad retirement, and Social Security's Old-Age, Survivors, and Disability Insurance program. Almost all government employees are covered by pension plans. Exhibit 19-1 shows that the four largest employer-sponsored pension funds in the country, California Public Employees, the New York State Common, California State Teachers, and the Florida State Board, are at the state government level. Each of these funds has over $100 billion in assets under management. The City of New York has a plan for its workers with almost $69 million in assets. Plans such as the Old-Age, Survivors, and Disability Insurance program, the Federal Civilian Employees, and the Railroad Retirement Plan all manage substantial sums not listed here.

Private Pension Plans

A private pension plan is sponsored by a single corporation, union, small business, or individual. As of September 20, 2000, two-thirds of all pension assets—$8.2 trillion—were sponsored and managed by private pension funds, mutual funds, banks, brokerage firms, and life insurers. The two largest private (corporate) pension funds listed in Exhibit 19-1 are General Motors (number 5) with $105.8 billion in assets and General Electric (number 8) with $88.49 billion in assets. Privately sponsored pension plans currently cover about half of private sector employees. The Teamsters, Sheet Metal Workers, and various other unions have their own pension plans.

Pension plans have historically been sponsored by large employers to cover their employees. However, as of 2000, only 46 percent of employees in firms with fewer than 100 employees were participating in employment-based retirement plans. Most small-business employees have missed out on these tax-preferred savings vehicles. The Small Business Protection Act of 1996 attempts to meet this need. This Act created a retirement savings vehicle for employees of firms with 100 or fewer workers: the **SIMPLE plans (Savings Incentive Match Plan for Employees of Small Employers).** SIMPLE plans provide an affordable way for small firms to

SIMPLE Plans (Savings Incentive Match Plan for Employees of Small Employers
Simplified defined-contribution plans created by Congress in 1996 to assist small businesses in offering salary deductions and matching contributions to fund retirement savings for their workers.

1. California Public Employees	$171,542
2. New York State Common	124,973
3. California State Teachers	111,552
4. Florida State Board	106,328
5. General Motors	105,800
6. Federal Retirement Thrift	100,191
7. New York State Teachers	90,093
8. General Electric	88,490
9. Texas Teachers	87,150
10. New Jersey Division	82,052
11. New York City Retirement	68,701
12. IBM	68,274
13. Lucent Technologies	67,505
14. Wisconsin Investment Board	66,225
15. Boeing	65,162
16. SBC Communications	63,674
17. Ford Motor	60,000
18. North Carolina	59,328
19. Ohio Public Employees	58,707
20. Ohio State Teachers	56,786

EXHIBIT 19-1

Top 20 Pension Fund Sponsors, Ranked by Asset Size (in millions of dollars, as of September 30, 2000)

SOURCE: http://www.pionline.com/pension/2001charts\top200.html Pensions & Investments online

offer retirement benefits through employee salary deductions and matching contributions. Employers are generally required to match the contributions of participating workers up to 3 percent of pay or put in a flat 2 percent for all workers regardless of participation. Contributions are set aside pre-tax and grow tax-deferred until they are withdrawn in retirement. Like many other types of tax-deferred retirement plans, employee withdrawals before age 59 1/2 are subject to a 10 percent penalty.

Individually Sponsored and Self-Employed Private Pension Plans

Although most pension plans are group plans, they can also be set up for individuals. There are three types of privately sponsored individual pension plans: individual retirement accounts (IRAs), Keogh plans, and simplified employee pensions (SEPs).

Individual retirement accounts (IRAs) are unique savings accounts administered by insurance and pension companies and various types of depository institutions. In a traditional tax-deferred IRA, individuals are allowed to deposit a certain sum of money ($2,000 maximum for an individual, $4,000 for a couple as of 2000) into the account without having to pay tax on it or on the interest it earns until the funds are withdrawn at retirement. To qualify for a traditional IRA, a person must not have any other private pension. If the person has another private pension, he or she must earn less than some maximum amount. If funds are withdrawn before the age of 59 1/2, a penalty usually applies. Exceptions are made for the purchase of a home or to finance college expenses. At the age of 70 1/2, the IRA holder must begin withdrawing funds. Congress has recently created the **Roth IRA** (named after Delaware Senator William Roth, who sponsored the legislation). Roth IRAs offer better tax advantages for many investors. Contributions to traditional IRAs are tax-exempt; taxes on the gains are postponed until the funds are withdrawn. Although funds deposited into a Roth IRA are not tax-exempt, the accumulated earnings are never taxed. Hence, they are sometimes called *tax-free Roth IRAs*. Tax law changes in 2001 (The Economic Growth and Tax Relief Reconciliation Act) increased maximum annual contributions for Roth IRAs from $2,000 in 2001 to

Individual Retirement Accounts (IRAs)
Tax-advantaged savings accounts administered by insurance companies, pension funds, and other intermediaries for the purposes of accumulating wealth for retirement.

Roth IRA
A special type of individual retirement account in which one's contributions are taxed, but the earnings accumulated within the account are tax-exempt.

$5,000 by 2008 for those earning $95,000 or less. Individuals with incomes above $110,000 (single) or $160,000 (married) are excluded from Roth IRA participation.

Self-employed individuals sometimes find it more difficult to set aside funds for retirement. **Keogh plans** (named after New York Congressman Eugene Keogh, who initiated the legislation) were established specifically to create a tax-preferred savings vehicle for self-employed people. Like traditional IRAs, Keogh accounts are handled by banks and other financial institutions. Interest accrues on a tax-deferred basis. Keoghs come in two main types. For most self-employed people, a "profit-sharing" Keogh is the best choice. It allows a self-employed person to contribute up to as much as 13 percent of net income (up to some maximum dollar limit) of income each year. The percentage and amount can change each year and payments can be skipped if one is having a bad year. "Money-purchase" Keoghs allow for higher contribution limits, but one has to set aside the same percentage of funds each year. Failure to do so results in a tax penalty.

The 1978 Revenue Act created **simplified employee pensions (SEPs),** sometimes called *SEP-IRAs,* to allow small-business owners to make tax-deductible IRA contributions on behalf of their employees and themselves. These plans are similar to Keoghs but have lower administrative costs, greater flexibility in contributions, and fewer reporting requirements. There is one hitch for one-man or one-woman firms. If you have a Keogh or SEP-IRA for yourself and you subsequently hire employees, you must also make the plan available to them and make employee contributions.

Defined-Benefit and Defined-Contribution Plans

Pension plans can be divided into two main types—defined-benefit or defined-contribution plans—regardless of who makes the contributions or the kind of sponsor. A **defined-benefit pension plan** promises employees a specific benefit based on factors such as age, earnings, and years of service. Plans can be modified to pay in the event of death, disability, or retirement. Retirement benefits usually take the form of periodic payments for the lifetime of participants and/or their spouses and are sometimes received as a lump-sum payment.

A long-time employee with a firm may receive a pension of, say, two-thirds of her salary if she has been at the same firm for 30 years. However, if an individual jumps from firm to firm, the pension may be far smaller. This is because most defined-benefit plans require an employee to be *vested*—that is, after some period of time, the employee is entitled to benefits. If the employee moves to another employer, he will be able to move the balance of the fund to his next employer. However, if an employee leaves a firm before becoming fully vested, he sacrifices part or all of his retirement benefits. Vesting periods vary by employer. Some require as little as 1 or 2 years of service to be fully vested; other employers require up to the legal maximum of 7 years.

Benefit calculations can be specified in a variety of ways for eligible employees. The following three examples show the different ways to calculate benefits. Assume that John has been working for the same company for 30 years. His final salary is $40,000 and his average salary over the last 5 years is also $40,000. A plan may state his benefit as a percentage of salary and years of service with the company; for example, 2 percent of final pay, times years of service, or:

$$2\% \times \$40,000 \times 30 = \$24,000 \text{ annually}$$

In some cases, a specific percentage (here, 68%) of the employee's highest 5-year average earnings is used to calculate retirement benefits; for example:

$$68\% \times \$40,000 = \$27,200 \text{ annually}$$

Keogh Plans
Tax-advantaged savings accounts, administered by banks and other financial intermediaries for the retirement needs of self-employed people.

Simplified Employee Pensions (SEPs)
Small-business pension plans allowed by Congress in 1978 with fewer reporting requirements and less administrative complexity and costs than traditional pension plans.

Defined-Benefit Pension Plan
Contract promising a specific level of income upon retirement based on the worker's years of service and level of earnings.

In other cases, the calculation may be based on a specific dollar amount and years of service (say $70 per month at retirement times the number of years worked). In annual terms for John, this would be:

$$\$70 \times 12 \times 30 = \$25,200$$

Some firms also offer the retiree the option to take a lump-sum payment at retirement based on similar sorts of calculations.

In all of the preceding cases, the employer bears the burden and investment risk of funding the pension plan to meet these defined-benefit payment obligations. To fund these promises, employers employ professional money managers who decide the level of contributions necessary to meet the plan's future obligations. These contributions are supplemented by the investment earnings generated by the plan's assets. In all three of the examples, the amount of annual benefit is a function of either pay (final or average) or years of service, or both. Thus, in many cases workers can significantly increase their annual pension benefit by working a few extra years, especially if they receive regular salary increases.

When actuaries determine that sufficient funds have been set aside to meet future pension disbursements, the plan is *fully funded*. In the unlikely situation that more than enough funds are available, a plan is *overfunded*. *Underfunding*, which means that the funds available are estimated to be insufficient to meet the plan's future payment commitments, occurs more frequently. Exhibit 19-2 lists the 10 largest defined-benefit plans as of September 30, 2000. Most of these plans are sponsored by state-level government organizations such as California, New York, and Florida employees. The largest defined-benefit plan, the California Public Employees, has over $171 billion in assets under management.

A **defined-contribution pension plan** is a contract in which specific and periodic contributions to an investment fund are made by employers, employees, or both. For instance, an employer may require an employee to pay 4 percent of pretax earnings into the pension plan with the understanding that the employer will contribute an additional 8 percent. These contribution percentages may remain fixed or may change depending on the employee's length of service, age, or the firm's profitability. Only the contribution is defined. No promise is made regarding the benefit the employee will receive upon retirement. The account is managed by the employee like an individual mutual fund with investment gains, losses, and contributions credited to the employee's account. From the firm's perspective, the primary advantage of defined-contribution plans over defined-benefit plans is that the interest rate and default risk associated with ensuring an adequate retirement is

Defined-Contribution Pension Plan
Contract specifying that a particular and periodic share of an employee's wages will be contributed by employers, employees, or both.

EXHIBIT 19-2
Top 10 Employer-sponsored Defined-benefit Plans (in millions of dollars)

1. California Public Employees	$171,372
2. New York State Common	124,973
3. California State Teachers	111,500
4. Florida State Board	106,328
5. New York State Teachers	90,093
6. Texas Teachers	87,150
7. General Motors	82,200
8. New Jersey Division	80,717
9. New York City Retirement	68,701
10. Wisconsin Investment Board	64,980
Total	$988,014

Note: Small differences between Exhibit 19-1 and 19-2 are caused by some of the largest pension fund sponsors in Exhibit 19-1 managing both defined-benefit and defined-contribution assets.
SOURCE: *Pensions & Investments, http://www.pionline.com,* data as of September 30, 2000.

EXHIBIT 19-3

Top 10 Employer-
sponsored, Defined-
contribution Plans
and Top 10
Managers of Multi-
firm, Defined-
contribution Assets
(in millions of dollars)

EMPLOYER-SPONSORED, DEFINED-CONTRIBUTION PLANS	
1. Federal Retirement Thrift	$100,191
2. General Electric	36,828
3. Boeing	24,281
4. General Motors	23,600
5. IBM	21,907
6. Lucent Technologies	20,561
7. Ford Motor	20,000
8. SBC Communications	18,399
9. Exxon Mobil	17,744
10. Bell Atlantic	14,413
Total	$297,924

TOP 10 MANAGERS OF MULTI-FIRM, DEFINED-CONTRIBUTION ASSETS[a]	
1. Fidelity	$360,400
2. TIAA-CREF	285,447
3. State Street Global	195,930
4. Barclays Global	101,200
5. Vanguard	89,831
6. Deutsche Asset	87,000
7. Capital Research	77,037
8. Prudential	62,393
9. Putnam	57,400
10. T. Rowe Price	53,981
Total	$1,370,619

[a]U.S. institutional, tax-exempt assets managed internally. These pension assets are managed for a variety of different companies. For instance, TIAA-CREF manages retirement pensions for teachers and professors across the country.

Note: Small differences among Exhibit 19-1, 19-2, and 19-3 are caused by some of the largest pension fund sponsors in Exhibit 19-1 having both defined-benefit and defined-contribution assets.

SOURCE: *Pensions & Investments*, http://www.pionline.com, all data as of September 30, 2000.

moved from employer to employee. As one might expect, this advantage has been partially responsible for the trend away from defined-benefit plans and toward defined-contribution plans over the last 20 years.

As shown in Exhibit 19-3, the two largest employer-sponsored, defined-contribution plans are managed by Federal Retirement Thrift and General Electric. This exhibit also illustrates that some of largest defined-contribution plans are managed by financial services organizations like Fidelity and TIAA-CREF. These companies manage the pension plans of many different individual firms. Fidelity alone has as many pension-defined contribution assets under management as the 10 largest employer-based, defined-benefit contribution plans combined.

RECAP Pension plans provide participants with income at retirement in exchange for premiums now. They are currently the largest and fastest-growing type of financial intermediary. Pension plans can be categorized three main ways: by who contributes to the plan, by sponsorship, and by the manner in which contributions or benefits are defined. In contributory plans, both the employee and the employer make contributions. In noncontributory plans, only the employer makes contributions. Privately sponsored plans can be for groups (individual firms, industry groups, or unions) or individuals (IRAs, Keoghs, SEPs). Publicly sponsored plans cater to local, state, or federal government bodies. A defined-benefit pension plan promises employees a specific retirement pay-out based on factors such as age, earnings, and years of service. A defined-contribution pension plan is a contract in which specific and periodic contributions to an investment fund are made by employers, employees, or both.

Recent Trends in Private Pensions

According to Richard Ippolito of the Pension Benefit Guaranty Corporation (1997), of all worker pension plans in 1979, defined-benefit plans made up the vast majority (82 percent). Approximately 18 percent of workers were covered by defined-contribution plans. Over time, coverage with defined-benefit plans has decreased while defined-contribution plans have increased. By the mid-1990s, the numbers were nearly equal—about half of workers were covered by each type of plan. This trend away from defined-benefit plans is explained by three main factors. First, there was a decrease in the share of employment at large, unionized manufacturing companies, traditionally the largest users of defined-benefit plans. Second, legislation was passed in the 1980s to ensure that adequate reserves were being set aside in defined-benefit plans. As a result, the administrative costs and regulatory burden of managing defined-benefit plans increased. This further discouraged their use. A third and, perhaps, primary reason for the recent trends was the introduction of **401(k) plans** in 1981.

401(k) Plans
A special type of defined-contribution plan introduced in 1981 allowing for greater flexibility in employer and employee contributions.

This special type of defined-contribution plan increased the flexibility that employers and employees have in saving for retirement. They are also more portable than traditional plans, which is important as employees change jobs more frequently. Employers are still allowed to give a flat percentage contribution to all employees like a traditional pension. However, 401(k)s also allow workers to make voluntary, pretax contributions to the plan. These plans grow on a tax-deferred basis—contributions to the plans are exempt from taxes and the earnings accumulate tax free until they are withdrawn during retirement. In many cases, voluntary worker contributions are fully or partially matched by the employer up to some predetermined share of the worker's salary. For instance, a firm might make a 4 percent contribution for each employee. Employees are allowed to make additional voluntary contributions that are matched by the employer up to a total of 7 percent of the employee's salary. In many corporations, employer matches are made with company stock. The newest innovation in 401(k) plans began in 1999 with Fidelity's marketing of *e-401(k)s*. These low-cost plans are easy to set up and manage and are targeted at small businesses that are less likely to offer retirement benefits to their employees.

Pension funds have grown rapidly over the post-war period, continuing over the last two decades. According to *Pensions & Investments* (September 20, 1979), the top 100 pension plans held assets of $270 billion. By September 1999, the top 100 pension funds held $3.1 trillion in assets! In addition to the increase in size, the asset structure of pension funds has evolved toward greater diversification. Between 1979 and 1999, the largest corporate pension funds increased the share of assets held in stock from about 56 percent to 63 percent. Among public funds, equity allocation increased from about 22 percent to 61 percent. These changes were driven by recognition that asset allocation greatly influenced returns. Portfolio management benefited from increases in computing power and enhanced modeling techniques. In addition, legal changes allowed investments to be considered on a portfolio-wide basis rather than requiring every investment to be viewed as prudent. Finally, the use of index funds has increased since their inception in the late 1970s. These funds now comprise more than 25 percent of the assets at the largest funds.

Since contributions are received regularly and payments to retirees are fairly predictable, pension funds as a whole hold mostly nonliquid assets. The vast majority of these assets are held in corporate equities (57.3 percent), U.S. Government securities (13.5 percent), mutual funds (8.5 percent), and corporate and foreign bonds (8.2 percent) comprise the remainder. Pension fund liabilities are simply the benefits paid out to pension policyholders.

Despite having a fairly steady revenue stream and predictable future payment obligations, pension funds have had problems. In the early 1960s, the fiscal integrity of pension fund companies was brought into question by allegations of mismanagement, overly restrictive age and service requirements, and the termination of employees nearing retirement. The 1964 failure of the Studebaker automobile plant in South Bend, Indiana inflicted heavy pension losses on workers and brought the issue national attention. This led to congressional hearings and eventually the passage of federal pension fund regulation and government insurance.

Pension Plan Regulation and Insurance

On Labor Day, 1974, Congress passed the Employee Retirement Income Security Act (ERISA). The Act established the first federal standards for the financing and operation of private, defined-benefit pension plans. It in no way mandates firms to provide pension plans. It merely sets the rules if a firm, union, or other group chooses to operate a pension plan. The Act has six main features:

1. A plan's sponsor must make minimum contributions such that projected benefit payments are actuarially sound. Firms are prohibited from waiting until an employee's retirement to set aside funds.

2. All contributions must be invested in a prudent manner. Portfolio managers who fail this "prudent expert" fiduciary rule can face prosecution and conviction. This ensures that the pension manager is looking out for the employees' best interest.

3. Plans must have minimum vesting requirements. Vesting refers to the length of time an employee must work for a company before he or she is eligible for pension benefits. These rules were amended again in 1989, shortening the maximum vesting period to 7 years.

4. Plans must increase disclosure of information to employees regarding the contents and financial health of their plans.

5. The Department of Labor was named as the primary regulator to enforce ERISA's provisions.

6. The Act created the *Pension Benefit Guarantee Corporation (PBGC)*.

http://www.pbgc.gov/
Provides more information about the Pension Benefit Guarantee Corporation.

http://www.pionline.com/
Provides more information on pension funds.

PBGC, or Penny Benny, as it is often called, guarantees that the approximately 43 million American workers and retirees with defined-benefit pension funds will receive their promised benefits upon retirement and for life. If a company with an underfunded pension goes bankrupt or if a pension fund is unable to fully provide promised benefits, Penny Benny will step in and make up the difference. In short, PBGC insures defined-benefit pension plans in the same way the FDIC insures the deposits of commercial banks and savings associations. It does not receive any federal funding, but instead charges premiums to participating pension plans. In case of emergency, it can borrow up to $100 million from the U.S. Treasury.

RECAP Decreases in manufacturing sector employment and the advent of 401k plans have led to a trend away from defined-benefit plans and toward defined-contribution plans. Because of unacceptable management practices and pension losses on the part of workers, the federal government intervened to regulate the industry and provide insurance for defined-benefit pension plans. The Employee Retirement Income Security Act (ERISA) of 1974 established standards that must be met by all pension plans and created a pension guarantor. The Pension Benefit Guarantee Corporation (Penny Benny) insures defined-benefit pension plans against the risk that a plan's sponsor goes bankrupt or otherwise fails to meet its payment obligations.

Social Security

In addition to playing a significant role in regulating and insuring defined-benefit pension funds, the federal government also manages the best-known public pension plan, **Social Security.** A Closer Look asks whether we should think about the Social Security program as a social insurance program or as a pension plan. We will let you make up your own mind about this. However, since many people use and view this program as a their primary source of retirement funds, we will discuss it as a public pension plan.

Social Security
Federal government program that provides retirement and survivors pensions, and disability and health insurance benefits to qualifying individuals.

Social Security: Insurance Policy or Pension Plan? Should we think of Social Security as a life, disability, and health insurance policy or as a pension plan? The metaphor we use to think about Social Security influences the way we evaluate the value of the program and plans for its reform. Some argue that Social Security is a social insurance program. The name of its core benefit program, Old Age Survivors and Disability *Insurance* (OASDI), suggests as much and distinguishes it from the health *insurance* (Medicare and Medicaid) aspects of the program. Like automobile, homeowner, or term life insurance premiums, our Social Security tax payments are paid with the understanding that, under certain conditions such as disability or retirement, we (or our surviving dependents) will be eligible to file a claim for benefits. However, if these particular events never happen, we lack the grounds to file a claim and no accumulated asset value is awarded to us or passed to our heirs.

If we view Social Security in this manner, we assess its value by evaluating how much insurance protection we receive for the premiums paid, not by the rate of return on assets. The amount paid in FICA taxes and received in insurance benefits varies based a person's earnings record, general health, and age. The reason we buy pure insurance products is to provide financial protection in case something unexpected happens. In the case of Social Security, we pay premiums into an insurance system that will provide retirement, disability, and medical benefits to us and/or our dependents when particular conditions are satisfied. From this perspective, criticisms leveled at the low rates of return earned by some Social Security recipients are unfair and moot. We do not inquire about the "rate of return" on premiums paid on automobile, health, or term life insurance. If a person never makes a claim, there is no return whatsoever. If Social Security is just another example of an insurance plan, it is inappropriate to inquire about its rate of return.

A Closer Look

Of course, not everyone views Social Security in this way. Valid reasons exist for viewing Social Security as a pension plan. The fixed contributions—15.3 percent of earnings—paid into the system, the monthly "pension" checks received by retirees, and the statements sent out by the Social Security Administration all resemble features of a pension plan. Many of us are familiar with pension plan statements and how to read them. We read our statements regularly to see how rapidly our investments are growing and how much retirement income we can expect to receive in the future. Computing rates of return and comparing these to other investment vehicles is an essential element in assessing the quality of our pension plans. If Social Security is viewed in this way, it fares less well. Recent studies show that workers who retired 20 years ago received back everything they had paid in, plus interest, several times over. Those retiring in the early 2000s are expected to receive only about a 2 percent real return on their investment. Those younger than 30 are expected to experience negative rates of return—their typical contributions are expected to be greater than their benefits. Expected returns also differ by income level. Low-income workers are likely to pay lower premiums but receive more generous insurance benefits because of the income redistribution aspects of the program. Minimum wage earners, for instance, are likely to receive about one-half of their current pay level in benefits. In contrast, higher-income workers will pay higher premiums but will not receive the correspondingly high retirement benefits. Instead, many workers who earn more than $70,000 per year will receive less than one-quarter of their previous salary from Social Security benefits. From a higher-income individual's "pension plan perspective"—and ignoring the insurance aspects of the plan—we can see that Social Security appears to be a less-than-optimal retirement vehicle. Nevertheless, it remains an important part of almost everyone's retirement planning. Future beneficiaries of the program should pay attention to proposals for its reform.

http://www.ssa.gov/
Provides more information on Social Security.

The Social Security Act was enacted in 1935 to provide old-age retirement benefits. Since that time, it has been amended repeatedly to broaden eligibility and increase benefits. In 1939, the Act was amended to include benefits for dependents and survivors. Disability benefits were added in 1956. Medicare and Medicaid insurance programs were added in 1966. In addition to these new benefit programs, minimum retirement ages were lowered (and more recently, raised), more types of employees were covered, and benefit levels were increased. To keep the system solvent, both the tax rate and the amount of income subject to tax have been increased.

Social Security is funded through payroll taxes. (You can see the amount of this payroll tax on your paycheck stub in a box marked *FICA*. FICA stands for the Federal Insurance Contribution Act, another name for the Social Security Act of 1935.) FICA taxes include withholdings for both the **Old Age Survivors and Disability Insurance (OASDI)** program and health insurance (Medicare and Medicaid) benefit programs. Since 1990 (and as of 2001), the OASDI portion of the payroll tax rate stands at 12.40 percent. Half of this (6.2 percent) is paid by the employee; the other half is matched by the employer. The health insurance portion (Medicare and Medicaid) of the payroll tax is 2.9 percent, again split (1.45 percent each) between the employee and employer. Thus, the combined payroll tax for these programs is a flat tax of 15.30 percent. Self-employed workers pay the full combined amount on their federal income tax return. For the vast majority of people, these taxes apply to their entire earned income. However, higher-income earners receive a substantial break. In 2001, the OASDI tax applied only to the first $80,400 of income. After this maximum is reached, no further tax is withheld. In effect, the tax rate falls to zero. This maximum income level or cap normally increases each year based on increases in average wages. In contrast, the health insurance portion of the tax applies to an individual's entire earnings.

Old Age Survivors and Disability Insurance (OASDI)
Core program of Social Security that is funded by payroll taxes to pay retirement and disability payments to eligible individuals and their dependents.

A worker becomes eligible for Social Security benefits by earning 40 "credits." In 2001, each $830 of self-employment income or wages earned 1 credit. A maximum of 4 credits may be earned in any 1 year. Thus, for most workers, 10 years of part-time employment is sufficient to qualify for retirement benefits. Young people can qualify for survivors and disability benefits with even fewer credits. Monthly benefits are determined by a worker's average earnings and age when he or she begins receiving benefits. The higher the worker's lifetime earnings, the higher the benefits. Similarly, the longer a worker waits to accept benefits, the higher the monthly benefit. If a worker begins receiving benefits at age 62 rather than his full retirement age (age 67 for those of us born after 1960), his monthly benefit will be about 30 percent lower. The Social Security Administration provides various benefit calculators at its Web site at http://www.ssa.gov. Benefit estimates can also be obtained by phone by calling 1-800-772-1213 or, for those with hearing-related problems, 1-800-325-0778 for "TTY" services.

If you are over the age of 25, the Social Security Administration should send a personalized benefits statement about 3 months before your birthday. If you have enough credits—10 years of paid work is usually sufficient—your statement will include an estimate of retirement, disability, and survivor benefits. If you do not receive a statement, or if it contains errors or omissions, call 800-772-1213.

Given the sources and uses of funds, Social Security is set up on a "pay-as-you-go" basis—today's workers are paying the retirement benefits of today's Social Security recipients. Future Social Security recipients will rely on the taxes of the next generation of workers to fund their retirement. Social Security tax receipts are currently greater than payments. A portion of these excess funds are being "deposited" into a trust fund that, in turn, uses the surplus to purchase government securities.

The "Social Security crisis" so prominent in the news media refers to the predicted problem of sustaining Social Security through the 2030s. The crux of the problem is that the 76 million members of the "baby boom" generation born between 1946 and 1964 will begin retiring in 2011. These increased numbers of retirees are expected to live longer and, therefore, receive more benefits. In 1940, the average life expectancy for a 65-year-old was 12 1/2 more years. Today's typical 65-year-old is expected to live an additional 17 1/2 years. Further exacerbating these problems, the number of workers supporting each retired person is declining. In 1940, there were approximately 30 workers for each retiree. In 1999, there were 3.3 and by 2030 there will only be 2. The Medicare portion of Social Security is also stressed from these issues and additional pressure from increases in current and expected per capita medical costs. What all of this means is that the surplus in the Social Security trust fund will begin to be depleted in about 2013 when its payments will begin to exceed its revenues. By 2034, the trust fund will have been spent. Without additional funding, Social Security will be able to pay only 75 percent of its expected benefits. This is far from being a threat of bankruptcy, but it is nevertheless a cause for concern and will likely entail changes in public policy. To address this expected funding shortfall, several proposals, including increasing revenues, decreasing benefits, or altering the structure of the system, have been put forward to reform the system.

Social Security: Plans for Reform

One way to ensure that Social Security meets 100 percent of its future payment commitments is to increase revenues coming into the system. This can be done by either raising the tax rate or increasing the tax base on which it is applied. The current OASDI portion of the Social Security tax stands at 12.4 percent, shared equally by the employer and the employee with each paying 6.2 percent. Without any other reforms, this tax would need to be raised to 18 percent to fully meet the system's needs. Both employers and employees would need to increase their contributions to 9 percent of the wage earner's taxable income. Although this increase of 2.8 percentage points (5.6 percentage points combined) represents a substantial tax increase, the "crisis" rhetoric that has so far characterized the debate appears overstated. This is made even more evident by the realization that revenues could also be raised by expanding the tax base. As noted previously, in 2001, OASDI taxes were collected on only the first $80,400 of earned income. By raising this cap, or eliminating it entirely—as is done with the health insurance tax portion of Social Security—considerable revenue could be raised. Some estimates suggest that eliminating the cap would erase half of the predicted deficit. Others, including the system's creator, President Franklin Delano Roosevelt, have suggested using tax revenues raised from corporate and personal income taxes to enhance the revenues flowing into the system.

A second way to address the system's fiscal problems is to reduce benefits. This could be done in a variety ways. Proposals have suggested increasing the retirement age, making it more difficult to qualify for disability; reducing annual cost of living increases; or initiating "means-testing" of benefits. Means-testing refers to the process by which applicants to the program show evidence of financial need to determine what level of benefits, if any, they should receive. Clearly, this would lower and, in some cases, eliminate the benefits paid to many wealthy retirees. The disadvantage is that this would reduce the universal nature of the plan and further reduce political support for the plan among the wealthy.

A more controversial way of reforming Social Security and meeting the needs of future retirees is to turn the system into a true pension system. This partial or total "privatization" would be done by using the system's funds to purchase corporate securities. Plans under this rubric include three main approaches. The first would allow a portion of workers' payroll taxes to be invested in individual retirement accounts. As the Looking Out feature on Chile's Second Revolution explains, this South American country has pursued privatization aggressively. Chile requires all workers to deposit 10 percent of their earnings into an individual retirement account. The hope there, as well as in the United States, is that higher rates of return can be earned on stocks and bonds, thereby providing retirees with more retirement income. The drawbacks are that this plan would substantially increase workers' exposure to market risk and would likely lead to some retirees receiving much more at retirement than others. Democrats and their organized labor constituents have opposed this type of reform. In contrast, the securities industry sees the prospect of tens of millions of new accounts and ardently supports it.

A second approach to privatization would be to have the federal government use the current Social Security surplus to purchase stocks and bonds. This, too, would hold the prospect of earning higher rates of return for retirees and would eliminate the costs and bureaucracy of setting up tens of millions of individual retirement accounts. The main drawback of this plan is that the U.S. government would become the country's largest shareholder for many companies. Some fear that politicians would use this power to control individual corporations.

A third approach to privatization is to encourage workers to contribute to personal accounts in addition to their FICA contributions. This would likely lead to most retirees having more funds at retirement. The drawback is that it requires current workers to set aside more of their current earnings. Others point out that these kinds of IRAs already exist.

The biggest problem with all of these privatization schemes, except the last, is that in the short-run, they make the problem worse. Diverting funds from current programs to purchase securities means that there is less revenue available to pay current retiree benefits. The costs of moving to privatization would be enormous.

The easiest solution to all of Social Security's financial problems is to have faster wage growth than expected. Forecasts of the plans' demise are highly dependent on conservative estimates of future revenues and expenses. If the economy continues to expand faster than expected, and if this leads to faster wage growth, it is possible that the feared day of reckoning may never come. During 1999, the economy's faster rate of growth led the Social Security Administration to change its prediction from 2032 to 2034 as the year it will be unable to meet all of its payment com-

LOOKING OUT: *Chile's Second Revolution:*
A Privatized Social Security System

In 1973, General Augusto Pinochet led an armed revolution in Chile and quickly rose to power. In 1981, Pinochet led a second—this time, financial—revolution. His country was among the first to privatize its public pension system. At the time, the existing public pension system was nearing bankruptcy, caused primarily by an aging population. Chile's leaders believed that only through radically restructuring the system could the benefits of future retirees be assured. Further, they hoped that this restructuring would lead to an increase in savings, boosting domestic investment, and stimulating more rapid economic growth. To address these needs, they imposed a system of individual retirement accounts. Workers were required to invest at least 10 percent of their taxable income into a privately managed, defined-contribution pension fund. The plan appears to have worked.

Between 1981 and 1995, national savings rose from 8.2 percent of GDP to 27.6 percent of GDP. Employment has sharply increased, stock market capitalization has quadrupled, and Chile has created one of the few active, long-term corporate bond markets in South America. Of course, not all of the kudos can go to privatization. Trade liberalization, the privatization of other government-owned entities, and economic growth among its trading partners have helped to transform the Chilean economy into the most dynamic economy in South America. Robert Holzmann, an economist at the University of Saarland in Germany, asserts that pension privatization plan has had two indirect effects that are often overlooked. First, the savings plan forced the government to trim its budget. This increased government savings may be the most important reason for Chile's economic recovery. Second, capital markets simply work better now than they did before. The new funds pouring into the system made the markets more liquid and increased the efficiency with which savings were used.

Privatization has not come without problems. The administrative costs of operating individual accounts for each worker are high. These were unnecessarily inflated at the beginning by the need for competing pension funds to spend enormous sums on marketing to attract clients. The costs of maintaining the old system while funding the new pension plan were also significant. The government remains responsible for losses in the old system and serves as a guarantor of a minimum benefit level to workers and retirees in the new system. Thus, even with privatization, it remains exposed to considerable market risk.

Despite these shortcomings, Argentina, Colombia, Peru, Mexico, and Bolivia are all attempting plans similar to Chile's. One lesson from all of these experiments is that in a democracy, privatizing pensions is a more difficult matter than under a dictatorship like Pinochet's. A second lesson is that pension reforms appear to work better in the context of other simultaneous economic reforms. A full assessment must wait until today's pension contributors become pensioners themselves. In the meantime, we can nevertheless hope that these plans will assist these countries in avoiding the economic instability that in the past has led to social unrest and political revolution.

SOURCES: *The Economist,* "Retirement Revolution," November 23, 1996, Vol. 341, No. 7993, p. 95; and "Paying for Greying: Latin American Pensions," November 26, 1994, Vol. 333, No. 7891, p. 88.

mitments. If robust economic growth is restored in 2002 and beyond, calls for Social Security reform are likely to recede.

RECAP The largest and best-known pension plan is Social Security. It was created to provide old-age retirement benefits under the Old Age Survivors and Disability Insurance (OASDI) program. Since that time, it has been amended repeatedly to broaden eligibility and increase benefits, including Medicare and Medicaid in 1966. The program is funded on a pay-as-you-go basis—current payroll taxes are used to pay current retirees. With growing numbers of retirees, longer expected life spans, fewer workers for each retiree, and growing per capita health care costs, Social Security is expected to face mounting financing pressures. Plans to address this need include increasing taxes, increasing the tax base, reducing benefits, or various forms of privatization. Faster economic growth would also assist this endeavor by raising incomes and payroll tax revenues more rapidly than expected.

Finance Companies

Overview

Finance companies are a second type of specialized, nondepository financial intermediary. They are best described as intermediaries that lend funds (1) to households to finance consumer purchases; (2) to firms to finance inventories and accounts receivable, and to purchase machinery or equipment; and (3) to both consumers and businesses for real estate loans. Finance companies are not commercial banks, savings associations, or credit unions, although some bank holding companies have finance company subsidiaries. Finance companies differ from banks and thrifts in their sources and uses of funds. Banks and thrifts gather many small deposits and other kinds of purchased funds. These funds are used primarily to make large commercial loans. In contrast, finance companies do not issue deposits.[1] Instead, they issue relatively large-denomination bonds or commercial paper, or take out large loans from commercial banks. These funds are then used to make relatively small consumer, business, and real estate loans. A second characteristic distinguishing finance companies from their deposit-dependent cousins is that finance companies tend to target higher-risk borrowers. To compensate for this greater default risk exposure, finance companies often charge higher rates of interest. They are able to do this because their nondepository status leaves them less regulated than banks and thrifts. Finally, the finance company industry is more heterogeneous in size and services than the bank and thrift industry. Finance companies range in size from multibillion-dollar multinational corporations, to small, single-unit loan companies. Services offered range from diversified providers of financial services to firms that specialize in one particular type of lending. According to the Federal Reserve's 1996 *Survey of Finance Companies*, there are approximately 1,250 finance companies operating in the United States. However, the top 20 firms account for 75 percent of finance company receivables, implying a high degree of industry concentration. As of April 2000, finance companies had just over $1 trillion in receivables outstanding. These receivables were divided into three broad categories: 37 percent consumer, 47 percent business, and 16 percent real estate. Some finance companies are active participants in all three lending categories.

Types of Finance Companies

Finance companies are most easily classified into consumer finance, business finance, and real estate loan companies. Real estate loans can be for either household or commercial property. However, in most cases, these loans are made to consumers for a second mortgage on their home.

Consumer Finance Companies

Consumer finance companies offer personal loans to consumers to purchase (or often lease) motor vehicles, mobile homes, furniture, and appliances. They also provide credit card services and assist in the refinancing of debt. These loans are

---

[1]A few states do allow finance companies to offer deposits under certain conditions; however, these are the exceptions. Deposits remain a very small source of funds for the industry.

often made to borrowers who are unable to obtain credit elsewhere because of their checkered credit history, low income, or discontinuous work history. To reduce their default risk, finance companies often require some sort of collateral as security. Some finance companies are willing to make personal loans based on a car or mobile home title as collateral. By stopping in and signing over the title to the property, the borrower can obtain a short-term, high-interest rate loan. In most cases, the consumer can continue to drive his car or live in the mobile home. If the consumer fails to make timely payments, the finance company has the title to his property and can sell it. This is essentially the same idea that pawnbrokers, another type of finance company, employ. If someone brings in a piece of personal property, the pawnbroker will make a loan for some amount less than the value of the property. If the loan is not repaid, the pawnbroker has the right to sell the collateral left behind, pocketing the difference.

This same basic idea applies when consumers buy furniture or appliances. In some cases, consumers can apply for "in-store credit" with apparently attractive "90 days same as cash" or "no payments for 6 months" financing. In most cases, the in-store credit application is really being provided by a finance company, which may be the finance company subsidiary of a bank like Wells Fargo or a separately owned corporation such as Beneficial Finance. The finance company allows the store to fax, telephone, or electronically transmit the loan application for on-the-spot approval or rejection. Once a loan has been approved, the furniture or appliance store originates the loan. It then immediately sells the paper or loan at a discount to the finance company. This benefits the store three ways: (1) It generates a sale that was otherwise unlikely to be made; (2) it eliminates the store's exposure to default risk; and (3) it allows the store to avoid becoming involved in bill processing and collections.

The finance company also benefits. It identifies new customers, some of whom may apply for credit cards. Also, once the initial teaser rate expires, the effective interest rate rises dramatically—to the high teens and low 20s, as of the early 2000s—and sometimes retroactively. If the loan is not paid in the first 90 days, interest begins to accrue as of the date of purchase. Besides being profitable, these loans are also secure. In case of default, the finance company retains the right to repossess the property. **Repossession** occurs when a borrower fails to make payments on time and the finance company goes to the borrower's residence and takes the asset back. Repossession is even easier if the asset in question is being leased rather than purchased. With a lease, the property is technically owned by the finance company. This negates the usual need to transfer the title of ownership back to the lender. Many rent-to-own contracts are set up in this way. The finance company or "leasing company" retains the title on the property until all payments have been received.

Consumer finance companies are of two types: ordinary finance companies and sales finance companies. The companies described previously are ordinary finance companies—they make secured loans for a variety of different products or firms. In contrast, **sales finance companies,** or **captive finance companies,** make secured loans to consumers to purchase a product from a particular manufacturer or retailer. The "big three" U.S. automakers all have substantial sales finance companies. The General Motors Acceptable Corporation (GMAC) provides attractive financing terms to those interested in purchasing a new GM vehicle. Ford Motor Company and DaimlerChrysler have similar affiliates. Sears, Roebuck Acceptance Corporation does the same for purchases made at Sears. Finance companies also offer their services to businesses.

Repossession
The process whereby a lender takes back the assets used to secure a loan.

Sales Finance Companies (Captive Finance Companies)
Companies that make loans to consumers so they can purchase a product from a particular manufacturer or retailer.

Business Finance Companies

Business loans, the most common type of loan made by finance companies, are made for three main purposes. The largest category is for equipment leasing and loans. Finance companies also make loans for retail and wholesale motor vehicle loans and leases, as well as for loans on accounts receivables or factored commercial accounts.

Businesses with a high debt level may find it difficult or undesirable to take on the greater level of debt needed to purchase the equipment or machinery needed in the production process. The down payment may even be too costly. The purchase of railroad cars, jet airplanes, and computer systems all involve substantial expenditures. Instead of purchasing these assets outright, businesses may instead have a finance company purchase the assets for them. The finance company then agrees to lease the equipment back to the firm. The business avoids the appearance of debt on its balance sheet and avoids using a large chunk of working capital as a down payment. The finance company receives a steady stream of rental income and, in the case of missed lease payments, simply sells the equipment to recoup its investment. Given the substantial depreciation on big-ticket capital expenditures, the finance company may also reap tax advantages that the business itself may not have been able to utilize because of its lower income level. Some firms set up finance company subsidiaries specifically to take advantage of these benefits. Finance companies also provide outright financing for business equipment purchases and for the purchase of business inventories. This gives firms access to supplies needed in production. The firm repays the loans with the sales of the final product. In some cases, finance companies even make loans so a company can buy the assets of another company. These leveraged buyouts or (LBOs) are riskier ventures because of the difficulty in judging the market value of another firm's assets. However, they promise higher returns than other forms of business lending.

The second largest category of loans made to businesses by finance companies involves retail and wholesale motor vehicle loans and leases. Some dealers of automobiles, boats, and construction equipment are required to purchase fleets of vehicles for their yearly inventory. These often do not sell immediately. To manage this mismatch between expenditures and revenues, finance companies pay for the dealer's new inventory through **floor-plan loans.** As the dealer sells each new vehicle, the revenues from the sale are used to pay off these wholesale loans. In many cases, the same finance company makes the wholesale loan to the dealer and the retail loan to the customer. Few other lenders have an opportunity to make both a wholesale and a retail loan on a car when it is sold to a customer for the first time. Increasingly, loans secured by a automobile, boat, or other title are pooled together and securitized. The finance company generates fee income from the granting of wholesale and retail loans, but avoids exposure to default risk by issuing a security backed by these loan bundles. Automobile leases have become extremely popular. Businesses and individuals both engage in vehicle leases to glean the benefits of lower down payments and the avoidance of taking on debt. Automobile finance companies like GMAC are able to take full advantage of the tax benefits of depreciation and the relatively easy repossession process if a customer fails to make his or her payments.

A third type of business loan offered by finance companies involves loans based on the purchase of accounts receivables. Imagine a business that sells its product on credit, but for a variety of reasons, is not particularly skilled at bill collections, processing, or otherwise managing its accounts receivables. Some of this firm's best customers may make irregular payments. The firm does not wish

Floor-Plan Loans
Finance company loan product that allows dealers of automobiles, boats, and construction equipment to use their inventory as collateral for loans that are repaid when vehicles are sold.

to offend customers by making aggressive telephone calls or mailing harassing letters demanding payment. To overcome these problems, specialized finance companies, called **factoring companies,** have been created to purchase the accounts receivables of other firms. In a traditional factoring arrangement, a business firm sells its accounts receivables to a factoring company at a discount. The factor takes over the bill processing and collections of these debts. The firm benefits because it is free of the default risk stemming from these receivables and is provided with immediate liquidity to use for other endeavors. The factoring company benefits by buying debts at a discount. Assuming that the factor has carefully checked the quality of the firm's receivables, the factor will have earned itself a profit when the debts are collected. In some cases, finance companies do not actually take over the management of the accounts receivable, but instead make a loan secured by these accounts receivable. If the business fails to make timely payment, the finance company then has the right to collect and retain the funds owed to the business itself.

Factoring Companies
Specialized finance companies that purchase the accounts receivables of other firms at a discount.

Real Estate Loan Companies

Finance companies also offer real estate loans to businesses and individuals. Finance companies tend to specialize in second mortgages, wherein a homeowner takes out an additional mortgage loan against the accrued equity in his or her property. They also make home purchase and commercial real estate loans.

During the last half of the 1990s, the real estate segment of finance company receivables grew at an annual percent rate higher than its overall receivables.[2] Several factors have contributed to this trend over the last two decades. Continued residential real estate appreciation has led to increases in home owner equity—the difference between the market value of the property minus the debt owned against it. To use this equity, home owners must either sell their property or borrow against it. Because of their less-regulated structure and lower costs, finance companies have become more adept than other real estate lenders at creating **home equity loans** with longer maturities and higher loan-to-value ratios. Some finance companies offer 125s—second mortgage loans allowing home owners to borrow up to a total of 125 percent of the value of their home. Finance companies also issue **home equity lines of credit** that function like a credit card but are secured by the home owner's equity.

Home Equity Loans
Mortgage loans of a specific amount in which one's private residence serves as collateral for the loan.

Home Equity Lines of Credit
Credit cards that are secured by a second mortgage on one's home.

Finance company real estate loans, particularly home equity loans and home equity lines of credit, have become more popular because of changes in the tax code. In 1986, Congress eliminated the tax deductibility of consumer credit interest payments but retained it for mortgage interest expenses. This change encourages homeowners to borrow against their property rather than using other unsecured kinds of consumer credit.

Finance company real estate lending has also increased by the adoption of credit scoring techniques. Credit scoring involves taking a wide variety of information from a borrower's loan application and applying a mathematical rating technique to assess the borrower's creditworthiness. Recent advances in telecommunications and computer technology allow finance companies to compute credit scores rapidly and to customize the rates charged to an applicant's credit score.

---

[2]In 1996, the annual growth rate for real estate receivables increased 54.5 percent as finance companies aggressively entered the subprime and manufactured housing mortgage markets.

Recent Trends

Four important trends currently characterize the finance company industry:

1. The industry grew steadily during the 1980s, then experienced a brief downturn with the recession of the early 1990s. Since then, the industry has rebounded. During the last half of the 1990s, the industry experienced rapid growth in total receivables.[3] Between year-end 1996 and April 2001, total receivables (consumer, real estate, and business) grew from $762.4 billion to $1,171.4 billion, an increase of 54 percent in less than 5 years.

2. Although real estate remains the smallest category of finance company receivables, real estate receivables grew by 63 percent from 1996 to 2001. Much of this lending has been in the form of subprime and manufactured housing lending targeted primarily at low-income and minority borrowers. **Subprime lending**[4] refers to loans in which a borrower has a blemished (or nonexistent) credit record. A lender makes a higher-fee, higher-interest-rate loan to compensate for the greater risk of delinquency and higher costs of loan servicing and collection. Thus, the term "subprime" technically refers to the perceived riskiness of the loan (less than "prime" quality), not to the interest rate charged, which is typically much higher than that charged for prime loans. **Manufactured housing lending** refers to mortgages made on homes that are built in factories rather than those built on site. This recent insurgence of finance companies into the mortgage market has raised questions about the nature of this type of lending. Are finance companies "predatory lenders" preying on uninformed borrowers, or are they serving a valuable function not provided by other traditional types of lenders? The jury is still out, and Congress appears poised to debate legislation regarding the need for greater regulation in these markets.

3. To finance the industry's growth, finance companies have increasingly relied on securitization to provide the liquidity necessary to fund their entry into the real estate market. Securitization of automobile loans and leases for both consumers and businesses have also steadily increased, facilitating finance company growth overall.

4. The composition of finance company sources and uses of funds continue to evolve. As noted earlier, finance companies do not take deposits. They instead issue bonds and commercial paper or rely on loans from banks and other lenders. The fastest-growing part of this mix is the use of commercial paper. Its issuance by finance companies has grown from around $400 billion in 1990 to almost $1 trillion in 2000. In terms of the uses of funds, real estate receivables have grown as a share of total receivables while consumer and business receivables have decreased.

Managing Risk

Like banks and thrifts, most finance companies have little exposure to exchange rate risk. However, they do face credit, interest rate, and liquidity risk. Default risk is a major concern for all lenders and particularly so for finance companies, which typically offer credit to higher-risk borrowers. As a result, finance companies can

---

Subprime Lending
High-fee, high-interest-rate loans typically made to a borrower with blemished (or nonexistent) credit records.

Manufactured Housing Lending
High-fee, high-interest-rate loans made to homebuyers whose homes were built in factories instead of being built on site.

---

[3]According to the Federal Reserve (Release *G.20, finance companies,* July 12, 2001) the total receivables rubric "includes finance company subsidiaries of bank holding companies, but not of retailers and banks."

[4]The term "subprime lending" can also refer to credit cards and automobile loans as well as mortgage loans. Finance companies have been playing a growing role in these markets.

be expected to have higher rates of default. By requiring adequate collateral on their loans, charging higher risk-adjusted interest rates, securitizing when appropriate, and prudently applying credit scoring and other credit assessment techniques, finance companies can obtain the higher returns that come with higher-risk lending. Regardless of these techniques, finance companies remain vulnerable to cyclical downturns in the economy. A general downturn in the economy can adversely affect the collateral values securing these loans and the employment prospects of these higher-risk borrowers.

The interest rate risk faced by finance companies is less than that of its depository institution counterparts. Finance companies tend to make short-term loans and rely on short-term financing. Thus, fluctuations in interest rates are quickly repriced on the liability side and almost as rapidly on the asset side of the balance. Nevertheless, this risk can be reduced by greater reliance on shorter-term and/or adjustable-rate loans and increased use of securitization.

The liquidity risk faced by many lenders comes from unexpected deposit withdrawals. Finance companies do not use deposits, so they have less exposure to liquidity risk than do their depository peers. If liquidity is needed, some finance company assets, such as real estate and automobile loans, lend themselves to securitization or to resale. On the liability size, larger finance companies can issue commercial paper or draw on a line of credit at a bank or thrift. Smaller firms will likely need to rely on bank loans. We discuss risk management for all financial institutions in greater detail in Chapter 21.

Regulation

Although finance companies compete directly with banks and thrifts, they face much less regulation. Finance companies do not accept deposits, so federal regulators have less reason to restrict their activities. Finance companies that operate within a bank holding company structure are an exception. All bank holding companies fall under the regulatory purview of the Fed. Similarly, all lenders are subject to federal fair-lending laws prohibiting discrimination in lending and truth-in-lending laws that require disclosure regarding the annual percentage rate charged and the total interest paid over the life of the loan. Like insurance companies, finance company regulation occurs primarily at the state level and varies significantly. State-level regulations limit the maximum size and maturity of loans and the interest rates charged. Some states offer a greater degree of protection to consumers from aggressive collections personnel. Restrictions include the time of day and other actions by collections people in pursuing repayment.

http://www.ftc.gov
Provides a wealth of consumer protection and business guidance information.

RECAP Finance companies are non-depository intermediaries that lend funds to households to finance consumer purchases; to firms to finance inventories, accounts receivable, and to purchase machinery or equipment; as well as to both consumers and businesses for real estate loans. Some consumer loans are made by captive finance companies that make loans only for a particular manufacturer's or retailer's products. Business finance companies make loans to help businesses pay for inventory, manage accounts receivables, or provide leasing services. Real estate lending has been the most rapidly growing portion of finance company receivables. However, this lending has been targeted primarily at the subprime and manufactured housing segments of the market. Finance companies face less interest rate and liquidity risk than do banks and thrifts, but remain vulnerable to default risk, especially in a recession. Since finance companies do not accept deposits, they remain less strictly regulated than other types of lenders.

Financial Modernization Changes Everything

The Financial Modernization Act of 1999 changed the way depository institutions do business. The most significant impact of this Act is the combining of the pension fund and finance companies with the banking and insurance services and the securities companies. It has finally become possible for all of these various types of companies to be brought together onto one corporate organizational chart.

These new financial conglomerates expect to meet your home-buying needs with a mortgage and to efficiently assist you with financing a car to park in your driveway and a refrigerator for your kitchen. They will also be able to provide your basic banking services, manage your pension and mutual funds, provide property and casualty insurance services—as well as a life insurance policy to pay off the loans (in case the stress of all this financing leads to your premature demise).

We have yet to see if consolidation will allow financial conglomerates to offer this menu of services cheaper than can specialized companies and if consumers really want one-stop financial services shopping. The cost benefits of information sharing among various financial subsidies and the synergies of cross-selling multiple products are still relatively unproven. But regardless of these concerns, the next decade or two will be an exciting time to work in or be an observer of the financial services industry. The fundamental structure of the systems used to deliver financial services will be forever altered.

Summary of Major Points

- Pension plans, or funds, provide income to workers and/or their spouses after a worker retires, becomes disabled, or dies. They are currently the largest and most rapidly growing type of financial intermediary.

- Pension plans are categorized by contribution-type, sponsorship, and/or whether contributions or benefits are defined. Defined-benefit plans have declined in importance over the past 20 years as defined-contribution plans have increased in popularity.

- Pension plan standards were set with the passage of the 1974 Employee Retirement Income Security Act (ERISA). Defined-benefit pension plans are insured against a firm's failure to meet payment obligations by the Pension Benefit Guarantee Corporation (Penny Benny).

- Social Security provides retirement, disability, survivor, and health benefits to qualifying citizens. Unlike ordinary pensions, Social Security is funded on a pay-as-you-go basis. The system pays current benefits from current payroll taxes.

- Over the next 3 decades, the Social Security system will face funding challenges from a growing numbers of retirees, longer expected life spans, fewer workers for each retiree, and growing per capita health care costs. These will likely be met by increasing tax revenues or decreasing benefits, or by creating some form of privatization to boost future earnings. Faster rates of economic growth and increases in wage rates may raise tax revenues sufficiently to indefinitely postpone the day of crisis.

- Finance companies are non-depository intermediaries that lend funds to households to finance consumer purchases; to firms to finance inventories, accounts receivables, and to purchase machinery or equipment; and to both consumers and businesses for real estate loans. The real estate segment of receivables, including sub-prime and manufactured housing lending, has experienced the most rapid growth.

- Like all intermediaries, finance companies face credit, interest rate, and liquidity risk. Compared to banks and thrifts, finance companies are more vulnerable to default risk because of the riskier types of loans they offer. Finance companies are less vulnerable to interest rate and liquidity risk because of the similar maturities between their assets and liabilities and their absence of reliance on deposits.

- Finance companies face less regulation at the federal level than other intermediaries because they do not accept deposits. Nevertheless, regulation regarding fair lending and truth-in-lending still apply, as do state level regulations about the size and maturity of loans and the maximum interest rate that may be charged on loans.

- Financial modernization will likely lead to a melding of financial intermediaries.

Key Terms

401(k) plans
Contributory Plans
Defined-Benefit Pension Plan
Defined-Contribution Pension Plan
Factoring Companies
Floor-Plan Loans
Home Equity Lines of Credit
Home Equity Loans

Individual Retirement Accounts (IRAs)
Keogh Plans
Manufactured Housing Lending
Noncontributory Plans
Old Age Survivors and Disability Insurance (OASDI)
Repossession
Roth IRA

Sales Finance Companies (Captive Finance Companies)
SIMPLE Plans (Savings Incentive Match Plan for Employees of Small Employers
Simplified Employee Pensions (SEPs)
Social Security
Subprime Lending

Review Questions

1. Explain the fundamental difference between the following category pairings: contributory versus noncontributory pension plans; public versus private pension plans; and defined-benefit versus defined-contribution pension plans.

2. What advantage do Roth IRAs have over traditional IRAs?

3. What kind of organization would be most likely to offer SIMPLE plans?

4. Why has there been a trend away from defined-benefit and toward defined-contribution pension plans?

5. Would you rather have a defined-benefit or a defined-contribution pension plan? Why? (Hint: What are the advantages and disadvantages of each of these types of plans?)

6. What are the six main features of ERISA? Who or what is Penny Benny?

7. Summarize the primary causes of the Social Security crisis and possible plans for the system's reform.

8. What are the three main types of finance company receivables? Which is growing the most rapidly? Why?

9. Explain the differences among captive finance companies, factoring companies, and floor-plan loans.

10. Why are finance companies subject to less regulation than banks and thrifts?

11. What is the difference between subprime mortgage and manufactured housing lending? Why have finance companies pursued it more vigorously than have banks and thrifts?

Analytical Questions

12. Given the current funding structure of Social Security, why should a college-aged student be interested in the education received by today's elementary students?

13. Make the case that Social Security should be viewed as a pension plan. Make the opposite case that it should be thought of as an insurance plan.

14. Why is it easier to set up a privatized pension plan under a dictatorship than in a democratic society?

15. Assume that Jaciel has been working for the same firm for 25 years. Over the last 5 years, her salary has increased by $1,000 each year from $41,000 to $45,000. The average salary of her final 5 years with the company is $42,000.

Which of the following defined-benefit plans will Jaciel prefer? Why?

a. Plan A: 2.5 percent of final salary times years of service

b. Plan B: 68 percent of her highest 5-year average earnings

c. Plan C: $90 per month times the number of years worked

16. What strategies do finance companies employ to reduce default risk?

17. Why have home equity loans and lines of credit become so popular over the last decade?

Internet Exercises

1. Go to **http://www.pionline.com/** and click on the "pension funds" link. Scroll down to "US Pension Funds" and click on the "Rankings" link. Under "Rankings," scroll down or do a search to find the "Fund Rankings" link. Compare the current rankings with Exhibit 19-1. Have any of the top-10 funds changed places? If so, explain. Hit the "back" button and then find the link for "Rank by Category." List the names and asset levels of the largest corporate, public, union, and miscellaneous pension funds.

2. Go to **http://www.ssa. gov/** and click on "Benefits Planners." Scroll down and find the calculators to estimate Social Security Benefits in today's dollars. Use the "1. Quick Calculator" to compute an estimate of monthly retirement benefits at age 66 and the family maximum monthly disability/survivor benefits for two different workers. The first worker is 50 years old and earns $20,000 per year. The second worker is 50 years old and earns $200,000 per year.

Suggested Readings

Thinking about retirement planning? A comprehensive overview entitled "Everything You Need to Know about Managing Your Finances—for Every Stage of Life" is provided by *The Wall Street Journal's Lifetime Guide to Money*, C. Frederic Wiegold, ed. (New York: Hyperion, 1997). To learn more about pensions, try Richard A. Ippolito, *Pension Plans and Employee Performance: Evidence, Analysis, and Policy* (The University of Chicago Press, 1997). It provides an overview of the effects of pensions on worker behavior, productivity, and recent trends.

Michael J. Clowes, *The Money Flood: How Pension Funds Revolutionized Investing* (John Wiley & Sons, 2000) explains how the rise of managed pension funds have come to dominate financial markets. He also provides a haunting scenario of what is likely to happen to stock and bond markets when baby boomers stop pouring money into pension funds and instead begin taking it out.

For information on Latin American and Chilean pension systems, see *The Economist*, "Paying for Greying: Latin American Pensions," (November 26, 1994, Vol. 333, No. 7891, p. 88), and "Retirement Revolution." November 23, 1996, Vol. 341, No. 7993, p. 95).

For an engaging history and overview of fringe finance companies (such as pawn shops and check-cashing outlets), as well as who uses them and why, see John P. Caskey's *Fringe Banking: Check-Cashing Outlets, Pawnshops, and the Poor* (Russell Sage Foundation: New York, 1994).

chapter

Securities Firms, Mutual Funds, and Financial Conglomerates

Learning Objectives *After reading this chapter, you should know:*

- What securities firms are and what financial services they provide
- The various types of mutual funds
- What hedge funds and real estate investment trusts (REITs) are
- The role of government-sponsored enterprises (GSEs)
- What financial conglomerates are and why they have grown so much in recent years

" "
People tell their friends about their winners and the IRS about their losers.

The Boiler Room

In earlier chapters, we covered depository institutions, insurance companies, pension plans, and finance companies. All these financial intermediaries play major roles in the financial system. In this chapter, we bring together the remaining important financial institutions and we introduce the subject matter with a story about a likeable character named Seth Davis.

Seth is a young, intelligent, upper-middle-class, frustrated college dropout who wants to make a "quick, easy buck." In the fast-track economy of the 1990s, he sees that many people have struck it rich in the stock market. Out of his apartment, Seth has been running a successful but illegal gambling operation catering to college students who play cards between classes. His chance to make it big comes when a customer offers him a job at J.T. Marlin, a securities firm on Long Island. He is told that like many other young stockbrokers in New York, he will be able to make $1 million within 3 years if he works hard. Seth goes for the bait.

He soon discovers the securities he will be selling are bogus. The corporations issuing them have no assets or products and the securities exist only on paper. Friends of Michael Brantley, the owner of J.T. Marlin, own the fake corporations. The funds raised go to these friends, who then share them with Brantley. In this way, the brokers working for J.T. Marlin can be paid commissions that exceed the maximum allowed by securities regulations. Prices are pushed artificially high because of aggressive brokers who work in a "boiler room" and create a false demand for the stock. Unscrupulous brokers employ high-pressure sales techniques and tell lies to potential investors about the prospects of the fake corporations. Apparently, not all the brokers know the depths of the scam and choose to look the other way as they make millions.

After all shares of the spurious corporations have been sold, the brokers no longer push the stock and the stock's price falls through the floor. Investors are left with worthless securities. Many unsuspecting investors who hoped to make a killing in the market lose everything they have. Brantley, his friends, and the brokers who work for J.T. Marlin make a bundle.

Needless to say, the firm is violating many government regulations and committing many crimes. Regulators are hot on its trail. Eventually, J.T. Marlin is closed down, and the owner is hopefully brought to justice. For immunity and to save his father's career (his father is a judge), Seth Davis turns state evidence.[1]

If you saw the hit movie "The Boiler Room," then you recognize our story as the movie's plot. It is far from realistic; the overwhelming majority of securities firms operate above board and regulators keep a close watch over the industry. It does, however, capture some aspects of how securities firms operate, particularly in a booming economy. Brokers can be aggressive while investors can be naïve, conducting minimal research into the quality of the securities they purchase. Finally, financial prices can change dramatically based on rumors or whims.

In this chapter, we look at securities firms—investment banks, securities brokers, and dealers. Not many securities firms are like J.T. Marlin—they do not deal with phony securities or pay illegal commissions. Instead, securities firms are important in the marketing of newly issued and previously issued financial claims. They "grease the wheels" in the raising of funds for deficit spending units (DSUs) and the transferring of debt and equity securities among investors.

---

[1] What the firm was doing would not have been illegal as long as there was no connection between the corporation issuing the stock and the securities firm. However, in reality, J.T. Marlin was undoubtedly committing many other acts of securities fraud.

We also look at mutual funds and government-sponsored enterprises (GSEs). Investment banks, brokers and dealers, mutual funds, and GSEs are the major financial institutions that make up the securities industry. These institutions play central roles in the financial system and help it function smoothly.

To conclude this section on financial institutions, we look at the emergence of financial conglomerates that meld together financial services once provided separately by several intermediaries and differing financial institutions. These new financial conglomerates offer a variety of financial services under one roof and operate on a nationwide and global basis. We hope this chapter gives you a more representative picture of the dynamic trends among major financial institutions and the key roles they play in the financial system. Keeping Seth in mind, we begin with a look at securities firms.

Securities Firms

Securities firms aid in the smooth functioning of the financial system. The two main functions of securities firms are investment banking and the buying and selling of previously issued securities. Investment banking deals with the marketing of newly issued securities in the primary market. Brokers and dealers assist in the marketing of previously issued securities in the secondary market. Some securities firms provide both functions, while others provide only one or the other.

During the 1990s, securities firms experienced tremendous growth as the average daily trading volume of U.S. securities increased 512 percent. Households shifted their financial assets away from bank deposits and into financial securities. In 1975, 55 percent of household financial assets were in bank deposits, 43 percent in stocks and bonds, and 2 percent in mutual funds. By the end of first quarter, 2001, 24 percent of household financial assets were in bank deposits, 51 percent were in stocks and bonds, and 25 percent were in mutual funds and money market mutual funds.[2]

Investment Banks: The Primary Market

Investment banks are financial institutions that design, market, and underwrite new issuances of securities—stocks or bonds—in the primary market.[3] Merrill Lynch, Salomon Smith Barney (part of Citigroup), Morgan Stanley, Dean Witter, and Goldman Sachs are some of the better-known investment banks. Their main offices usually are located in New York City, but they are electronically linked to branch offices in other major cities in the United States and around the world.

Investment Banks
Financial institutions that design, market, and underwrite new issuances of securities in the primary market.

The design function of the investment bank is important. A corporation may need assistance in pricing the new financial instruments that it will issue in the open market. The corporation looks to the investment bank to provide advice about the design of the new offering. In return for their services, the investment bank is paid a fee. Many investment banks, in addition to their primary market activity, are also brokers and dealers in the secondary markets.

---

[2]In this case, household financial assets include only deposits, stocks and bonds, and mutual funds and money market mutual funds. Flow of Funds Accounts of the United States, Z1, Board of Governors of the Federal Reserve System, June 9, 2000.

[3]The Glass-Steagall Act of 1933 separated investment banking from commercial banking. As we have seen, this Act was effectively repealed in 1999 with the passage of the Gramm-Leach-Bliley Act (GLBA) of 1999. The passage of the GLBA is partially responsible for the emergence of financial conglomerates discussed later in this chapter.

Responsibilities for New Offerings

There are two types of new offerings. When a company has not previously sold financial stocks or bonds to the public, the offering is an *initial public offering (IPO)*. The investment bank will try to establish an appropriate price by looking at stock prices of other firms in the industry with comparable characteristics. Because there are no previously issued securities being publicly traded, it is usually much more difficult to determine the price at which securities in an IPO should be offered. In the case of bonds, investment banks look to the market prices of existing bonds with comparable maturity, risk, and liquidity. The existing degree of leverage (reliance or borrowed funds) of the issuer is also a determinant of how much can be raised and at what price in the bond market.

Seasoned Issuance
The offering of new securities by a corporation that has outstanding previously issued securities.

When stocks or bonds have been previously issued, the offering is called a **seasoned issuance.** The price of the new issue should be the same as the market price of the outstanding shares. However, the investment bank must still anticipate how the new issue will affect the market price of the outstanding shares. Likewise, with a seasoned issuance of bonds, the investment bank must anticipate how the greater degree of leverage will affect the price at which the new bonds can be sold.

Timing. Timing is one of the most important factors affecting the selling price of new securities. For example, it may be a good time to sell equities if a corporation's outstanding stock is trading at relatively high prices, if favorable earnings reports have recently been issued, and if the economy is particularly strong. A relatively larger amount of funds can be raised by issuing fewer shares at a higher price, than if the stock was trading at a lower price. Likewise, if long-term interest rates are relatively low and profit expectations are high, it may be a good time to issue bonds.

The Role of the Securities and Exchange Commission. Once the amount, type, and pricing of securities have been established, the investment bank assists the corporation in filling out and filing the necessary documents with the *Securities and Exchange Commission (SEC)*. The SEC is a government regulatory agency created in 1934 to regulate the securities industry. Primary areas of regulation include "disclosure" requirements for new securities issues and the monitoring of illegal and fraudulent behavior in securities markets.

Registration Statement
A statement that must be filed with the SEC before a new securities offering can be issued.

The SEC maintains active supervision of investment banks, particularly with regard to information that must be disclosed to potential investors. A **registration statement** must be filed with the SEC before the offering can be issued. This statement contains information about the offering, the company, and other disclosure information,[4] including relevant information about management, what the funds will be used for, and the financial health of the corporation. Once the registration statement has been filed, the SEC has 20 days to respond. If the SEC does not object during the 20-day period, the securities can be sold to the public. The lack of an objection by the SEC in no way means that the new securities are of high quality or that the price is appropriate. It simply means that it *appears* the proper information has been disclosed to potential investors. The **prospectus,** which is a subpart of the registration statement, *must* be given to investors before they purchase the securities. It contains all of the disclosures and pertinent information required by the SEC about the new offering.

Prospectus
A subpart of the registration statement that must be given to investors before they purchase the securities.

---

[4]A corporation must go through the formal procedure of filing with the SEC if the securities issuance is greater than $1.5 million and if the term to maturity of the securities is greater than 270 days.

Credit Rating.   Investment banks assist in obtaining credit ratings for new bond issuances from Standard & Poor's or Moody's Investors Services. A trustee is selected that will monitor whether or not a corporation fulfills the terms of the offering as outlined in the **bond indenture.** The terms of the offering, along with many other provisions, are spelled out in the bond indenture before the bonds are issued. Investment banks may also help arrange the listing (trading) of an issuance of new stock on an exchange and or in the over-the-counter market.

Underwriting and Marketing.   Once the necessary steps to issue the new securities have been taken, the investment bank underwrites and markets the securities. In underwriting the security, the investment bank purchases the entire issuance at an agreed-upon price and then assumes responsibility for marketing the newly issued securities. If the price at which the bank sells the securities is greater than the price it paid, it will earn a profit on the spread. If the securities sell for less than the agreed-upon price, the bank accepts the loss.

Sometimes one investment bank may be reluctant to take full responsibility for a new issuance. In this case, the bank may form a **syndicate** by asking other investment banks to underwrite part of the new offering. The syndicate is merely a group of investment banks, each of which underwrites a portion of a new securities offering. In a syndicate, each participating investment bank earns the profit—or assumes the loss—on the portion of the new offering it underwrites.

Syndicate
A group of investment banks, each of which underwrites a proportion of new securities offering; reduces the risk to one investment bank of underwriting the entire new offering.

Investment Banks and the Functioning of the Primary Market

As a key player in financial markets, investment banks facilitate the smooth and orderly functioning of primary markets. They stand ready to buy, sell, and adjust prices—literally making a market. If there are 100,000 shares of a stock for sale at a particular price and if buyers take only 80,000 shares at that price, the investment bank that bought the securities may hold them for a time to keep the price from falling erratically. Or the investment bank may alter prices until all, or most, of the shares are sold. Thus, the investment bank enables the ongoing shuffling and rearranging of portfolios by being prepared to hold the securities if there is no immediate buyer. These actions, although they can involve risk for the investment bank, enhance market efficiency and contribute to a smooth functioning financial system. The investment bank is rewarded with profits from fees for designing the offering and underwriting the new securities, and as we saw earlier, from (hopefully) selling the securities at a higher price than what it paid for them.

Exhibit 20-1 show U.S. corporate underwriting activity since 1985. Note that new debt issuances exceeded new equity issues in every year between 1985 and 2000. Outstanding debt does not grow as fast as the new issuances would suggest because some debt issues mature each year while equity issues do not mature. However, in some cases, stocks are bought back and retired by the corporations that issued them. Note also the relatively large issuances of equity in the late 1990s, when stock valuations were particularly high.

Private Placement

Investment banks also handle **private placement.** This is an alternative for a corporation issuing new securities that bypasses the process described previously and places the new securities offering privately. In a private placement, new securities are sold to a limited number of investors. Because the number of investors is small,

Private Placement
A method of issuing new securities by selling to a limited number of large investors.

EXHIBIT 20-1
U.S. Corporate
Underwriting Activity
(in billions of dollars,
rounded)

YEAR	NEW DEBT ISSUES	NEW EQUITY ISSUES	TOTAL UNDERWRITINGS
1985	$ 203.9	$ 35.5	$ 239.4
1986	355.3	68.4	423.7
1987	325.7	66.6	392.3
1988	352.9	57.8	410.7
1989	318.3	57.8	376.1
1990	299.3	40.2	339.5
1991	389.8	75.4	465.2
1992	471.5	88.3	559.8
1993	641.5	124.1	765.6
1994	498.0	85.1	583.1
1995	573.2	100.6	673.8
1996	651.1	122.0	773.1
1997	811.4	117.9	929.3
1998	1,001.7	182.0	1,183.7
1999	941.3	223.9	1,165.2
2000	807.3	283.7	1,091.0
2001*	689.5*	124.9*	814.4*

*Through July 2001 only.

SOURCE: Board of Governors of the Federal Reserve System, *Federal Reserve Bulletin*, various issues.

they are, of necessity, very large investors such as commercial banks, insurance companies, pension plans, or mutual funds. Private placements occur more frequently with bonds than with stocks.

RECAP Investment banks design, market, and underwrite the issuance of new securities (stocks and bonds) in the primary market. The securities may be an IPO or a seasoned offering. In addition to advising the issuer about market conditions and prospective prices, the investment bank also assists in filing the necessary forms with the SEC so that the new securities can be publicly sold. A registration statement must be filed with the SEC. Part of the registration statement is the prospectus, which contains information and disclosures about the issuance. The prospectus is distributed to investors. The SEC is concerned that appropriate information is disclosed to the public. Approval by the SEC to sell the securities is in no way an endorsement of their quality or that the price is proper. Private placement of securities to a limited number of investors is an alternative to going through the underwriting process.

http://www.tfsd.com
*has information about
capital markets around the
world.*

Brokers and Dealers: The Secondary Market

Brokers and dealers make up brokerage firms, which are securities firms that also facilitate the smooth and orderly functions of secondary financial markets. *Brokers* arrange trades between buyers and sellers—that is, they arrange for a buyer to purchase securities from a seller. The broker charges a brokerage fee, or commission, for arranging the trade. *Dealers* are market makers who, in addition to arranging trades between buyers and sellers, stand ready to be a principal in a transaction and may maintain an inventory of securities. Dealers are prepared to purchase and hold previously issued securities sold by investors. The dealer carries an inventory of securities and then sells them to other investors. Since the dealer holds a stock of securities, the risk exists that the securities' price will fall and the brokerage firm will experience a capital loss.

Types of Orders

Three types of orders may be placed with brokerage firms: market orders, limit orders, and short sells. **Market orders** direct the broker or dealer to purchase or sell the securities at the present market price. **Limit orders** instruct the broker or dealer either to purchase the securities at the market price up to a certain maximum if possible or to sell the securities at the market price if it is above a certain minimum. Securities are bought at one price (the *bid price*) and sold at a higher price (the *asked price*).

A **short sell** instructs the broker or dealer to borrow shares of stocks and sell them today with the guarantee that the borrowed stocks will be replaced by a particular date in the future. The investor engages in a short sell if he or she believes that the stock's price is going to fall in the future and that the borrowed shares will be paid back with shares purchased in the future at the lower price. If the volume of short sells is very high, it is an indication that investors believe the stock's price is going to fall. If the price does not fall, the buyer of the short sell must purchase the shares at a higher price and thus loses money. If many buyers of short sells are in this position, the market price is pushed even higher.

Market Orders
Orders by an investor that direct the broker or dealer to purchase or sell the securities at the present market price.

Limit Orders
Orders that instruct the broker or dealer to purchase securities at the market price up to a certain maximum or sell them at the market price if above a certain minimum.

Short Sell
Instructions to brokers or dealers to borrow shares of stocks and sell them today with the guarantee that the investor will replace them by a date in the future.

Margin Loans

Full-service brokerage firms not only arrange for the trading of securities, but they give investment advice to potential investors as well. They may also make loans, called **margin loans,** to help investors purchase securities. In this case, investors do not have to put up funds equal to the full value of the purchase. Rather, they can purchase stocks on the margin by borrowing. The *margin requirement* is the percentage of a stock purchase that can be borrowed as opposed to being paid in readily available funds. The current margin requirement, which is set by the Fed, has been 50 percent since 1974 and applies only to initial purchases. Many individual brokerage firms set higher margin requirements and vary those requirements depending on the stocks being traded and the trading behavior of individual customers.

Margin Loans
Loans to investors wherein the proceeds are used to purchase securities.

Brokerage Fees

Until 1975, all brokerage firms charged investors virtually the same brokerage fees for executing trades of financial securities. Brokerage firms distinguished themselves among investors by engaging in nonprice competition. Some attempted to offer better and more attentive advice established through market research. Others had geographical advantages, name recognition, or other attributes that led to better customer relationships. All this began to change when Congress passed the Securities Acts Amendment of 1975, which eliminated fixed commissions. Instead of engaging only in nonprice competition, brokerage firms could compete by offering lower fees.

Discount brokerage firms provide only limited or no investment advice, but their fees are much lower than those of full-service brokerage firms. In recent years, due to increased competition among brokerage firms and the emergence of discount brokers and online trading, brokerage fee revenues have fallen. In place of trading fees, brokerage firms are earning more from advising fees and from interest income on margin loans. The development of the Internet further evolved securities marketing by allowing online trading. A Closer Look explores the emergence of online trading.

Online Trading: What is "online trading"? In general, it means trading stocks, mutual funds, and money market shares on the computer. Brokers and dealers, of course, use computers for most of their trading. However, "online trading" usually refers to the individual's use of computers for trading.

Online trading offers the public more control over trading and over their financial accounts. However, even more significantly, it offers lower fees for executing trades and hosting financial accounts. Online trading brokerage firms can do this because they use technology to automate these processes. This makes trading less costly and increases the volume that can be handled.

Before the Internet, there were only a few firms that offered computerized trading, mainly through direct dial-up connections. The customer base was very small. However, with the explosive growth of the Internet, the number of online trading brokerage firms and customers has shot upward. The following table shows the growth.

YEAR	NUMBER OF ONLINE BROKERAGES	NUMBER OF ACCOUNTS (IN MILLIONS)	TOTAL VALUE OF ONLINE ACCOUNTS (IN BILLIONS)
1994	0	0	$ 0
1996	18	1.5	111
1999	150	5.5	400
2000	200	10	
2003*		20*	3,000*

*Projected

SOURCE: Securities Industry Association

A Closer Look

The rising popularity of online trading brought about a new set of brokerage firms, coming from three major sources. One source is discount brokerage firms seeking new ways to offer low-cost trading services. The second is new companies created as online trading brokerage firms. The third source is existing full-service brokerage firms coming late into the online trading market; these firms have added online trading to their list of services in order to prevent the loss of customers to other online trading firms.

Even though many traditional full-service brokerage firms have added online trading to their list of services, they still have experienced a rapid decline in commission revenues. Consequently, they have concentrated on improving information services such as advising and consulting, and offering other advanced trading services such as making margin loans to their customers.

Other types of online traders include people who do not work for brokerage firms but still trade for a living—commonly called daytraders—and people who earn a living in other jobs and trade only as frequently as they wish. The latter group includes people with savings who want to earn extra money in addition to their primary income, often to build funds for retirement.

Both types of online traders use the services of online trading brokerage firms. Daytraders, however, typically utilize specialized online trading firms because they need more sophisticated services. The brokerage firms used by daytraders provide more sophisticated software and more real-time, direct, and detailed access to information and stock exchanges. This is often referred to as direct access trading. An example of this is NASDAQ Level II quotes. Typically, the general public and other online traders see only one price at a time listed for a particular security (for example, IBM stock). NASDAQ Level II, however, shows several prices and volumes for recent trades of a particular stock. This level of information is of little use to most non-daytraders, although it is sometimes offered to those with large accounts who engage in heavy trading.

Online brokerage firms engaged in price wars in the mid- to late 1990s. However, pricing stabilized, and firms now compete more on features such as ease of use and quality of information. This competition has brought about two new services to the online trading market: (1) trading in foreign stock markets, and (2) using remote, hand-held devices such as cellular phones and two-way pagers to get online information and to execute online trades.

In addition to regulation by the SEC, the securities industry is self-regulated by the *National Association of Securities Dealers (NASD)* and various securities exchanges such as the New York and American stock exchanges. Brokerage firms that are registered with the SEC must also purchase insurance for their customers from the **Securities Industry Protection Corporation (SIPC).** SIPC is a nonprofit, membership corporation that U.S. registered brokers and dealers are required by law to join. Congress established SIPC in 1970. The purpose of SIPC is to protect investors' securities from liquidation by the brokerage firm. Each investor is insured for $500,000. Note that this does not protect investors from losses because of falls in securities prices. Rather, it protects the investor from losses resulting in the bankruptcy or insolvency of the brokerage firm.

Securities Industry Protection Corporation (SIPC)
A nonprofit membership corporation established by Congress in 1970 that provides insurance up to $500,000 per investor to protect investors' securities from liquidation by the brokerage firm.

The income of securities firms is dependent upon the fees and commissions they generate in their day-to-day activities. In a booming economy, markets tend to be much more active and, hence, the income of securities firms increases. The reverse is true in downturns. At the end of 1999, the financial assets of security brokers and dealers was just under $1 trillion, an increase from $83.3 billion in 1982.

RECAP Brokerage firms are important financial institutions because they facilitate the smooth functioning of securities markets. Brokers arrange the trading of financial securities among corporations and investors in exchange for a brokerage fee. Dealers not only arrange trades but also buy and sell financial securities for their own portfolios in order to make a market. Market orders direct the broker or dealer to purchase or sell the securities at the present market price. Limit orders instruct the broker or dealer either to purchase the securities at the market price up to a certain maximum if possible or to sell the securities at the market price if it is above a certain minimum. A short sell instructs the broker or dealer to borrow shares of stocks and sell them today with the guarantee that the borrowed stocks will be replaced by a date in the future. The investor engages in a short sell if he or she believes that the stock's price is going to fall in the future and that the borrowed shares will be paid back with shares bought at a lower price.

Investment Companies

Unlike the securities firms just described, **investment companies** are financial intermediaries that raise funds from many small investors by selling shares in the company. The funds are then pooled together and used to purchase financial securities. Investment companies reduce risk for individual investors by purchasing hundreds or even thousands of different securities. This allows individual investors to diversify to a much greater extent than possible by purchasing individual securities on their own. In addition, because large blocks of securities are bought and sold, the investment company can take advantage of volume discounts, and the transactions costs per share are less than if smaller amounts of securities were purchased or sold. Investors share in the gains and losses proportionate to the size of their investment.

Investment Companies
Companies that own and manage a large group of different mutual funds.

Open-End and Closed-End Companies

Open-End Fund
A mutual fund that continually sells new shares to the public or buys outstanding shares from the public at a price equal to the net asset value.

Closed-End Fund
Mutual funds that sell a limited number of shares like other corporations but usually do not buy back outstanding shares.

Net Asset Value
The difference between the market value of the shares of stock that the mutual fund owns and the liabilities of the mutual fund.

Investment companies may be **open-end** or **closed-end**. An open-end fund continually sells new shares to the public or buys outstanding shares from the public at a price equal to the net asset value. The **net asset value** per share is found by subtracting the liabilities of the mutual fund from the market value of the securities that the fund owns and then dividing the difference by the outstanding number of shares.

The vast majority of investment companies are open-end companies called *mutual funds*. Mutual funds that deal in money market instruments with an original maturity of 1 year or less are called *money market mutual funds*. They issue more shares as investors demand them. Because they buy and sell their own shares, mutual fund shares are not traded on organized exchanges. Mutual funds sell their own new shares to investors and stand ready to buy back outstanding shares.

Closed-end investment companies sell shares like other corporations but usually do not buy back outstanding shares. Once the sale of a limited number of shares is completed, the fund is "closed" to new purchases, but the shares may be traded like shares of stock on organized exchanges. Because the price of a share of a closed-end fund is determined by supply and demand, it can differ from the net asset value.

Load and No-Load Companies

Load
A sales commission paid to a broker to purchase mutual funds; by law the load cannot exceed 8.5 percent.

No-Load
Mutual funds that are purchased directly from the mutual fund company and are not subject to a load.

Some investment companies require that a **"load,"** or sales commission, be paid to a broker to buy into a fund. By law, the load cannot exceed 8.5 percent of the investment. **"No-load"** funds are purchased directly from the mutual fund company without a broker or a sales commission.

Both load and no-load companies deduct a percentage from the net asset value each year to administer the funds. The fees are usually in the range of 0.2 to 1.5 percent. A fund may also deduct a fee called "12b-1" (named for the SEC regulation that authorizes the fee) for marketing and advertising expenses. Finally, there can be a redemption fee, called a "back-end" load, to sell the investment company shares. An investor should know all the fees before investing in a fund.[5]

Growth of Investment Funds

Investment funds, particularly mutual funds, have experienced incredible growth since the late 1980s. One reason for this trend is that recent legislation gives individuals control over where their pension funds are invested, and many have chosen mutual funds. In 1999, nearly half of all U.S. households (48.4 million households) owned mutual funds. Exhibit 20-2 shows the growth of mutual funds, money market mutual funds, and closed-end investment funds from 1982 to 2001. Note that increases in mutual funds in each year in the late 1990s often exceeded the total amount outstanding prior to 1990. This was due not only to additional funds flowing into mutual funds, but also to increases in market valuations due to the booming stock market. Note, too, that the dollar amounts invested in open-end mutual funds are much greater than those invested in closed-end investment companies.

---

[5]In most cases, the SEC requires that total fees including all loads and 12b-1 fees not exceed 8.5 percent.

YEAR	MONEY MARKET MUTUAL FUNDS	OPEN-END MUTUAL FUNDS	CLOSED-END INVESTMENT COMPANIES
1982	$ 219.9	$ 76.9	$ 7.5
1983	179.5	112.1	7.4
1984	232.2	135.6	6.4
1985	242.4	245.9	8.3
1986	290.6	426.5	14.5
1987	313.8	480.2	21.3
1988	335.0	500.5	43.2
1989	424.7	589.6	52.5
1990	498.3	608.4	52.9
1991	535.0	769.5	71.2
1992	539.5	992.5	93.5
1993	589.6	1,375.4	116.1
1994	602.9	1,477.3	117.8
1995	745.3	1,852.8	134.4
1996	891.1	2,342.4	144.7
1997	1,048.7	2,989.4	149.4
1998	1,334.2	3,610.5	151.0
1999	1,584.8	4,552.4	156.3
2000	1,812.1	4,457.2	142.8
2001*	2,014.8*	4,269.9*	136.3*

EXHIBIT 20-2
The Value of Outstanding Shares of Investment Companies 1982–2001 (in billions of dollars)

*Through second quarter 2001 only

SOURCE: *Flow of Funds Account of the United States*, Z.1, Board of Governors of the Federal Reserve System, various issues.

Exhibit 20-3 outlines various types of funds investors can select depending on their particular goals and risk tolerance.

Many types of mutual funds are often offered by a single investment company. Investors can own several different funds within the one investment company. Depending on their investment needs, they can choose the funds they prefer. Investors can also move funds in and out of various funds within one company at a relatively low cost. Some of the better-known and larger investment companies are Fidelity, Vanguard, American Fund, Putnam, Janus, Franklin, and T. Rowe Price. Fidelity Fund had $653 billion in assets as of April 2000.[6] Note that the assets of Fidelity at that time exceeded the amounts in all open-end mutual funds prior to 1991.

Investment companies also create new funds that invest in several mutual funds. In reality, the investor purchases a **"fund of funds."** For example, Vanguard's STAR fund invests in nine different Vanguard funds. In general, 60 to 70 percent of investments are held in stock funds, 20 to 30 percent in bond funds, and 10 to 20 percent in money market mutual funds. The advantages to investors are that they achieve much greater diversification than if they invested in only one mutual fund, and they save the time and effort of investing in several different mutual funds on their own. A disadvantage is that costs can be high because both the individual funds and the "fund of funds" charge fees. If investors pick different funds on their own, they can avoid the "fund of funds" fees.[7] At the present time, there are about 600 mutual fund families that offer more than 11,000 mutual funds. To put these numbers in perspective, remember that stocks of only 3,025 individual companies trade on the New York Stock Exchange.

Fund of Funds
A mutual fund that invests in a portfolio of other mutual funds rather than individual stocks and/or bonds.

---

[6]Jeanne Sahadi, Fund Family Lowdown, http://cnnfn.cnn.com/2000/06/08/mutualfunds/q_funds_family/.

[7]With the Vanguard STAR Fund, Vanguard waives the "fund of funds" fee so that investors pay only the fees of the individual mutual funds.

Stock Funds
- *Aggressive growth funds* seek capital appreciation by investing in small companies with potential for growth; such funds are risky but often pay high returns.
- *Global equity funds* invest in stocks from around the world, thereby achieving greater diversification than that achieved by investing in comparable stocks provided by; one country the downside is exposure to losses if exchange rates change adversely.
- *Growth and income funds* invest in companies that are expected to grow and that pay dividends.
- *Income-equity funds* invest in companies expected to pay high dividends.
- *Index funds* invest in a market basket of stocks that replicates the basket included in a stock market index such as the S&P 500; index funds attempt to match the performance of the index.
- *Sector funds* invest in stocks of particular industries such as biotechnology or health care; because diversification is less than that achieved in more broadly based funds, returns can be more volatile.
- *Socially conscious funds* invest in companies believed to be ethically responsible; depending on the specific values and goals, these funds may avoid stocks of companies involved with cigarettes, alcohol, gambling, weapons, or nuclear power; they may also avoid stocks of a country whose leadership they believe is repressive.

Bond Funds
- *Corporate bond funds* invest only in corporate bonds.
- *Global bond funds* invest in bonds from around the world; the exchange rate risk can be high.
- *Ginnie Mae funds* invest in Ginnie Mae mortgage-backed securities.
- *High-yield bond funds* invest most of their portfolio in junk bonds; these funds offer the potential for high returns but also entail high risk.
- *Long-term municipal bond funds* invest in a broad base of municipal bonds; earnings are exempt from federal taxes.
- *State municipal bond funds* invest in municipal bonds from one state; earnings are exempt from federal and state taxes for investors living in the issuing state.
- *U.S. government income funds* invest in U.S. government bonds and government agency securities.

Stock and Bond Funds
- *Balanced funds* invest in some combination of stocks and bonds to preserve principal, generate income, and achieve long-term growth.
- *Flexible portfolio funds* can vary relative investments among stocks, bonds, and money market instruments depending on management strategy.
- *Income-mixed funds* invest in stocks and bonds to earn high dividend and interest income.
- *Convertible securities funds* invest in securities (such as preferred stock or bonds) that can be converted to common stock; such securities offer the potential to share in earnings if the company does very well by converting to common stock.

EXHIBIT 20-3
A Sample of the Types of Mutual Funds

RECAP Investment companies are financial intermediaries that pool the funds of many investors to invest in several hundred or even thousands of stocks. For any given investment, investment companies offer greater safety and more diversification than offered by investing in one or a few stocks. Money market funds invest in financial instruments with an original maturity of 1 year or less. Some mutual funds invest in bonds or some combination of both stocks and bonds. An open-end fund continually sells new shares or buys shares from the public at the net asset value and is called a mutual fund. Closed-end investment companies sell a limited number of shares that may be traded on the open market and on organized exchanges. The value of open-end funds (mutual funds) greatly exceeds that of closed-end investment companies. The price of closed-end investment companies is determined by supply and demand and can differ from the net asset value. Mutual funds and closed-end investment companies can be either load or no-load funds. Both have experienced tremendous growth in recent years.

CRACKING THE CODE: *Mutual Funds*

Toward the back of the "Money and Investing" section of *The Wall Street Journal,* you can find quotations for open-end and closed-end mutual funds. This Cracking the Code feature will familiarize you with how to decipher those quotes.

NAME	NAV	NET CHG	YTD % RET
Eclipse Funds			
AssetMgr	13.18	+0.02	– 0.8
Balanced	21.44	+0.01	+ 3.7
Bond	9.76	+0.01	+ 2.5
GrEq	25.58	–0.01	– 11.8
IdxBd	10.62	+0.01	+2.1
IdxEq	31.34	+0.09	– 1.7
IdxEqSv	31.18	+0.08	– 1.9
MidCpVal	17.58	–0.01	+ 3.8
SmCpVal	12.27	+0.03	+ 15.2
ValEq	14.41	+0.10	+4.7

Open-End Funds

The following quotes from *The Wall Street Journal* of May 21, 2001 show a group of 10 different mutual funds offered by Eclipse Funds.[a] The funds differ by the amount of risk. Their names often describe the type of financial instruments in which the fund invests. Look at the highlighted row.

In the first column, "Bond" is the name of the fund within the group of Eclipse Funds. As the name implies, this fund invests in bonds. The second column gives the net asset value (9.76). The third column gives the net change in the net asset value from the previous day (+0.01), while the fourth and final column gives the year-to-date percent return to the fund (2.5). In this example, the net asset value is $9.76, up $.01 from the previous day, and the year-to-date percent return is 2.5 percent.

Note that if you invest in the bond fund of the Eclipse Funds, you are investing in one of 10 funds offered by Eclipse Funds and not a "fund of funds." An investor can invest in one or more of the funds to tailor the amount of overall risk to his or her specific needs. Some larger mutual fund companies offer far more than 10 different funds. For example, Fidelity Investments offers over 80 different mutual funds.

Closed-End Funds

Following is a portion of the "Closed-End Funds" section of *The Wall Street Journal* of May 21, 2000.[b] This portion looks at U.S. government bond funds. Look at the highlighted row.

FUND NAME (SYMBOL)	STOCK EXCH	NAV	MARKET PRICE	PREM /DISC	12 MONTH YIELD 5/18/01
U.S. GOVT. BOND FUNDS					
ACM Govt Incm (ACG)	N	8.30	8.29	– 0.1	10.5
ACM Govt Oppty (AOF)	N	8.01	8.11	1.2	9.6
EIS Fund Ltd (EIS)-c	♣N	18.67	17.10	– 8.4	6.2
MFS Govt Mkts (MGF)	N	7.07	6.39	– 9.6	7.5
MSDW Govt Inc. (GVT)	N	9.41	8.71	– 7.4	6.3
KEMPER Int. Govt (KGT)	♣N	7.27	6.85	– 5.8	7.8

In the first column is the fund's name (MFS Govt Mkts) followed by the fund's ticker symbol (MGF). The second column gives a one-letter abbreviation of the exchange (N) on which the fund is traded. The "N" stands for the New York Stock Exchange. The third column gives the net asset value. The fourth column gives the market price of the fund, which, since this is a closed-end fund, can be greater than or less than the net asset value. In this case, the net asset value ($7.07) is greater than the market price of the fund ($6.39) and the fund is trading at a discount. The fifth column gives the percentage premium or discount (above or below the net asset value) at which the fund is trading ([$6.39 – $7.07] / $7.07 = –.096 = –9.6 percent). The final column gives the percentage 52-week market return (7.5 percent). For bond funds, the 52-week market return is based on the past 12-month income distributions as a percent of the current market price.

[a]*The Wall Street Journal,* May 21, 2001, p . C16.

[b]*The Wall Street Journal,* May 21, 2001, p . C14.

Hedge Funds

Hedge Fund

A nontraditional type of mutual fund that attempts to earn maximum returns regardless of whether financial prices are rising or falling.

Historically, a **hedge fund** was a nontraditional investment fund formed as a partnership of up to 99 "accredited" investors who invested in a variety of often risky securities. An accredited investor was one who had at least $1 million in investable assets. In April 1997, the SEC expanded the rules by allowing some hedge funds to raise money from 499 "qualified" investors. In this case, a qualified investor is an individual who has a minimum net worth of $5 million, or an institution such as a pension fund or mutual fund with at least $25 million in capital. Today, both types of hedge funds exist.[8]

For all hedge funds, a general partner usually organizes the fund and is responsible for making day-to-day trading decisions. Limited partners put up most of the funds but have limited or no say in the day-to-day decision making. Partners who buy into the hedge funds are wealthy individuals and institutions—minimum investments start around $250,000, and many hedge funds have much higher minimum requirements. Hedge funds may also limit withdrawals or require that funds be invested for a minimum time period such as 10 years.

Because there are a limited number of wealthy investors, hedge funds are not regulated in the same way as traditional investment pools or mutual funds. They are not required to file a registration statement and may engage in many trading strategies from which traditional mutual funds are barred. These strategies include borrowing funds to invest, purchasing many types of option and derivative instruments, short selling, and dealing in real estate and commodities.

Hedge funds attempt to earn high or maximum returns regardless of whether prices in broader financial markets are rising or falling. The funds trade securities and other creative financial instruments and try to outperform traditional investment funds by employing novel trading strategies.

In general, hedge funds use riskier investment strategies than those used in traditional mutual funds. As we have seen, the funds often rely on borrowed funds (leveraging) as well as the funds of the partners. This leverage increases the potential for profits but also magnifies the potential for losses. Short selling to take advantage of falling prices, and the use of some risky financial instruments, can also result in large losses if prices do not move in the anticipated direction. In general, hedge funds outperform other mutual funds when markets are falling.

Hedge funds traditionally charge high fees and take a large percent of the profits. For example, some charge a 2 percent annual management fee and take 25 percent of the profits. The remainder of the profits is distributed to the partners based on their percentage of ownership in the fund.

Although the first hedge fund was established more than 50 years ago, the number and assets of hedge funds have grown tremendously since the mid-1990s. Domestic hedge funds now number over 3,000. Offshore hedge funds are located outside the United States, and are difficult for most U.S. investors to invest in because of certain tax consequences.[9] The number of partners in offshore hedge funds is unrestricted.

---

[8]As used here, "hedge fund' means any kind of private investment partnership. The most common meaning of "hedge" is to reduce risk. This can be misleading, since hedge funds often engage in very risky activities.

[9]The tax consequences are net losses cannot be used to offset gains and deferred interest payments are taxable in current years. Investors are often not provided the information by the hedge fund that would allow them to make current tax payments and to avoid tax penalties. Offshore hedge funds·are easily available to a small number of tax-exempt, wealthy U.S. investors.

At the present time, hedge funds are becoming more accessible for investors because of the development of funds of hedge funds. A fund of hedge funds invests in multiple hedge funds, each usually employing a different investment strategy. Because of pooling, they have lower required minimums for participation and offer less risk due to diversification.

To summarize, some of the strategies employed by hedge funds include the following:

1. Selling borrowed securities (short selling) in the hopes of profiting by buying the securities at a lower price on a future date

2. Exploiting unusual price differences between related securities in anticipation of making a profit when the prices come into more traditional alignment

3. Trading options and other derivatives

4. Borrowing to invest (leveraging) so that returns are increased

Real Estate Investment Trusts (REITs)

Real estate investment trusts (REITs) are a special type of mutual fund that pools the funds of many small investors and uses them to make investments. Whereas other mutual funds invest only in financial instruments, REITs may invest in real property as well. Their funds are used to buy or build income property or to make or purchase mortgage loans, unlike those of traditional mutual funds. Another difference is that, to some extent, they also raise funds by taking out bank loans or issuing debt. REITs are "pass-through" enterprises; rents from income property and/or interest income from the mortgages are "passed through" to shareholders. Shareholders are also entitled to any capital gains from the properties that the REITs own.

At least 75 percent of the assets of REITs must be either real property (generally commercial or industrial real estate) or mortgages. The majority of REITs invest in real property such as shopping malls, apartment complexes, hotels, golf courses, and other commercial buildings for income. REITs may either buy or provide the funding to build income property. The income from property provides a steady, dependable stream of income for investors. Some REITs either make or purchase mortgage loans on commercial property, and some do both.

REITs resulted from legislation passed by Congress in 1960. The intent of the legislation was to give small investors an opportunity to invest in commercial real estate. At that time, REITs could own income property but not manage it. REITs did not take off until 1986 when the restrictions on managing income property were removed. Now individual REITs have different characteristics and may be highly specialized, depending on the investment strategy and management style of the fund's manager. They are virtually diversified holdings of real estate investments that are professionally managed.

By law, REITs must return 95 percent of their earnings to shareholders each year. Therefore, if they want to expand, they must issue new equity or debt or take out bank loans. REITs are also attractive because most of their earnings (95 percent are passed through) are exempt from corporate federal and state income taxes, thereby avoiding double taxation and allowing for fairly predictable income streams.

Shares of REITs are traded on organized exchanges like shares of stock. Thus, they are liquid investments even though their equity is in real property and long-term mortgages. In recent years, the spreads between the bid and asked prices have narrowed significantly, signaling that the secondary markets are becoming more highly developed. Prices of REITs are determined by supply and demand. In this

Real Estate Investment Trusts (REITs)
A special type of mutual fund that pools the funds of many small investors and uses them to buy or build income property or to make or purchase mortgage loans.

sense, they are like closed-end investment companies because the price can deviate from the underlying value of the assets owned.

Prices of REITs fell over 20 percent in the 1998–1999 period as investors flocked to high-tech stocks that promised higher returns. Global financial crises in 1998 also contributed to the fall in prices. In the first half of 2000, funds flowed into REITs as prices increased over 10 percent at the same time that prices of other securities were falling or earning far less. In the first half of 2000, REITs controlled about $300 billion of the $4 trillion real estate market.[10]

RECAP Hedge funds are a type of mutual fund that has fewer then 99 very wealthy investors. The SEC does not regulate them. Hedge funds attempt to earn high returns for their investors regardless of whether financial prices are going up or down. Hedge funds engage in sometimes-risky investment strategies. REITs are a type of mutual fund that pools the funds of many small investors and uses them to buy or build income property or to make or purchase mortgage loans. They are pass-through institutions in that the rents from the income property and/or the interest income from the mortgages are passed through to shareholders. Whereas other mutual funds invest only in financial instruments, REITs may invest in real property as well as financial instruments. Shares of REITs are traded on organized exchanges. By law, REITs must return 95 percent of their income to shareholders each year. REITs allow for the integration of commercial real estate markets and capital markets.

Government-Sponsored Enterprises

Government-Sponsored Enterprises (GSEs)
Publicly held corporations that are chartered by Congress.

http://www.HUD.gov
Provides other information on government-sponsored enterprises.

Government-sponsored enterprises (GSEs), as the name suggests, are corporations sponsored or chartered by Congress. Despite the federal charter, most GSEs are privately owned and privately managed. Some GSEs have issued shares of stock that are publicly held like shares in other corporations. The stocks of these GSEs are traded on organized exchanges.

GSEs issue short-term securities that sell at a discount and long-term bonds that pay semi-annual coupon payments. The majority of the issuances are long term. The proceeds are used to assist in some aspect of lending that the federal government has deemed desirable. GSEs operate mainly in the areas of housing, farm credit, and student loans. The securities that GSEs issue, called *government agency securities,* are considered government securities for SEC purposes.

In most instances, the federal government has no legal obligation to guarantee the timely payment of interest and principal of GSE securities. However, many market participants assume that the government does "*de facto*" guarantee the payments. The yield spread between government agency securities and U.S. government securities is due to differences in liquidity and risk. The yield spread can be significant because secondary markets do not have the breadth and depth of Treasuries. If market participants question the "*de facto*" government guarantee, the spread can also widen.

Exhibit 20-4 shows the financial assets and liabilities of GSEs from 1982 to 2001. In recent years, GSEs have increased significantly in terms of their size and market share. This is particularly true with respect to lending in the housing sector.

---

[10]*Economic Letter,* Federal Reserve Bank of San Francisco, Number 2000–02, January 28, 2000.

YEAR	TOTAL FINANCIAL ASSETS	GSE SECURITIES OUTSTANDING	TOTAL LIABILITIES
1982	$ 254.8	$ 205.4	$ 249.1
1983	256.5	206.8	250.3
1984	297.7	237.2	291
1985	324.0	257.8	319.6
1986	346.4	273.0	342.8
1987	374.4	303.2	370.1
1988	421.7	348.1	416.1
1989	454.2	373.3	447.6
1990	477.6	393.7	469.1
1991	496.8	402.9	486.0
1992	552.3	443.1	538.7
1993	631.1	523.7	614.4
1994	781.8	700.6	761.7
1995	896.9	806.5	873.4
1996	988.6	896.9	964.1
1997	1,099.4	995.3	1,070.3
1998	1,403.8	1,273.6	1,368.1
1999	1,720.6	1,591.7	1,681.1
2000	1,969.4	1,825.9	1,922.6
2001[b]	2,125.3[b]	1,957.6[b]	2,076.3[b]

EXHIBIT 20-4

Financial Assets and Liabilities of Government-Sponsored Enterprises (in billions of dollars)

[a]Note that GSEs have other miscellaneous liabilities in addition to outstanding securities. The difference between total assets and total liabilities represents stockholder equity.

[b]Through second quarter 2001.

SOURCE: *Flow of Funds Accounts of the United States, Z1*, Board of Governors of the Federal Reserve System, Washington DC, various issues.

The GSE Housing Market

The GSEs that pertain to the housing market are the *Federal National Mortgage Association (Fannie Mae)*, the *Federal Home Loan Mortgage Corporation (Freddie Mac)*, and the *Government National Mortgage Association (Ginnie Mae)*.[11] Fannie Mae and Freddie Mac provide loanable funds to the housing sector by selling their own securities and using the proceeds to purchase mortgages or mortgage-backed securities in the secondary mortgage market. The securities that Fannie Mae and Freddie Mac issue are backed by the principal and interest payments on the mortgages or mortgage-backed securities that they have purchased. However, there is no explicit government guarantee—Fannie Mae and Freddie Mac are privately owned and their stocks trade on the New York Stock Exchange. The difference between Fannie Mae and Freddie Mac is that Fannie Mae primarily buys the mortgages of banks while Freddie Mac primarily buys the mortgages of thrifts.

Ginnie Mae is part of the Housing and Urban Development (HUD) Department of the U.S. government. As such, it is government owned. For a fee, Ginnie Mae guarantees that the mortgages purchased with bond proceeds will be repaid and, hence, the bonds will be repaid. Unlike Fannie Mae and Freddie Mac, Ginnie Mae does not issue bonds. Other financial institutions such as banks, savings associations, or mortgage brokers issue the bonds that are guaranteed by Ginnie Mae,

---

[11]Fannie Mae and Freddie Mac are exempt from state and local corporate income taxes and have a $2.25 billion line of credit with the U.S. Treasury.

http://www.
freddiemac. com,
http://www.fanniemae.
com and http://www.
ginniemae.gov
*Provide more information
about GSEs.*

referred to as Ginnie Mae bonds. The minimum denomination for Ginnie Mae Bonds is $25,000. Unlike Fannie Mae and Freddie Mac, Ginnie Mae securities are fully backed by the U.S. government and, thus, have no default risk.

These GSEs were created by Congress to make housing more available by increasing the funds flowing into mortgages. The goal is to expand opportunities for low- and moderate-income families to purchase houses. HUD regulates these GSEs with regard to meeting this goal and ensuring the financial safety and soundness of the corporations.

The GSE Farm Loan Market

**Federal Farm Credit
Banks Funding
Corporation (FFCBFC)**
Issues bonds and discount
notes to make loans to
farmers.

**Farm Credit Financial
Assistance Corporation
(FACO)**
Issues bonds with explicit
government guarantee
and uses the proceeds to
assist the FFCBFC.

The **Federal Farm Credit Banks Funding Corporation (FFCBFC)** issues bonds and discount notes and uses the proceeds to make loans to farmers to facilitate the funds flowing into agriculture. The bonds carry no explicit government guarantee that the principal and interest will be repaid. The FFCBFC ran into financial problems in the 1980s because many farmers defaulted on high-interest loans made in the late 1970s and early 1980s. Congress created the **Farm Credit Financial Assistance Corporation (FACO)** in 1987. FACO issues bonds and uses the bonds to assist the FFCBFC. Unlike the bonds of the FFCBFC, FACO bonds do have an explicit government guarantee.

The GSE Student Loan Market

**Student Loan
Marketing Association
(Sallie Mae)**
Issues securities to
purchase student loans,
increasing the amount and
liquidity of funds flowing
into student loans

http://www.salliemae.
com
*Provides more information
on Sallie Mae.*

The **Student Loan Marketing Association (Sallie Mae),** a publicly traded company, issues securities and uses the proceeds to purchase student loans. The securities are not backed by an explicit federal government guarantee. However, the federal government guarantees repayment of many of the student loans. The purpose of Sallie Mae is to increase the funds flowing into student loans and to make student loans more liquid. The company, which is the nation's largest supplier of student loans, owns or manages student loans for more than 5 million borrowers.

Other GSEs

**Financing Corporation
(FICO)**
Issues bonds and uses the
proceeds to help resolve
the savings and loan crisis.

In 1987, Congress created a new GSE, the **Financing Corporation (FICO)** in response to the savings and loan crisis.[12] FICO was to issue up to $10.825 billion in 30-year bonds to help shore up the insurance company (the FSLIC) that at the time insured deposits in the failed thrifts.[13] FICO was capitalized by nonvoting stock purchased by the 12 regional Federal Home Loan Banks. It is to be dissolved by 2026 or earlier.

In 1989, Congress created another GSE, the Resolution Trust Corporation (RTC), in response to the savings and loan crisis. The RTC was to dissolve or find buyers for the failed thrifts and liquidate the $450 billion of real estate properties owned by the thrifts being dissolved. Thirty-year bonds were issued to help finance the RTC, but the federal government did not explicitly guarantee the bonds. The RTC went out of business on December 31, 1995, after it had completed its work. By that time, it had resolved the insolvencies or closed over 750 savings associations.

---

[12]The savings & loan crisis is covered in detail in Chapter 11.

[13]FICO was not successful in bailing out the failed thrifts, so additional legislation and the creation of the RTC were needed.

With the paying down of the federal debt, government agency securities, as they are known, have taken a more prominent position in financial markets.

RECAP GSEs are privately owned, government-sponsored enterprises that issue financial securities. The funds raised are used to provide funds to areas that the government deems desirable, including housing, farm credit, and student loans. The major GSEs that pertain to the housing market are Fannie Mae, Freddie Mac, and Ginnie Mae. The FFCBFC issues securities and uses the proceeds to make loans to farmers. Congress created FACO in 1987 because of financial troubles of the FFCBFC. Sallie Mae is a publicly traded company that issues securities and uses the proceeds to purchase student loans.

The Growth of Financial Conglomerates

Financial conglomerates are firms that own and operate several different types of financial intermediaries and financial institutions. As a rule, they operate on a global basis. Financial conglomerates usually result from the mergers of several firms. For example, one financial conglomerate may own a commercial bank, a savings institution, a mutual fund, a pension fund, a securities firm, and an insurance company. The alleged advantages of forming financial conglomerates include taking advantage of economies of scale, economies of scope, and diversification.

Economies of scale, which are gains from large size, may result when separate firms owned by a conglomerate and offering the same product streamline management and eliminate duplication of effort. Thus, the conglomerate may have fewer boards of directors and may also share a common technology infrastructure.

Economies of scope refer to the advantages of a conglomerate has in offering several financial services under one roof. This one-stop shopping is supposedly an advantage to financial services customers and, hence, gives financial conglomerates advantages over several separate firms providing the same set of services. In addition, the subsidiaries can share information about customers and seek new customers from other subsidiaries.

Diversification refers to the financial conglomerate branching out into several product lines. Diversification reduces the dependence of the financial conglomerate on one service, which in turn reduces the risk of failure for the financial conglomerate. If one division is performing poorly, the conglomerate can still be earning a profit if other divisions pick up the slack. For instance, if the credit card division is losing money, it can be subsidized by the insurance division for a while. If credit cards were the dominant product line of a financial services institution, losses in this area could affect the solvency of the institution. This is not so in the case of a financial conglomerate.

Financial conglomerates have been emerging in the financial world since the early 1970s. Some of the first attempts were started by nonfinancial giants, such as Sears, that bought financial subsidiaries. Not all the early attempts at forming financial conglomerates met with success, particularly when they originated with a nonfinancial firm purchasing financial institutions. For example, in 1981, Sears purchased Dean Witter Stock Brokerage and Coldwell Banker Real Estate, only to sell them in 1989 because of losses in these subsidiaries.

Regulations dating back to the Glass-Steagall Act during the Great Depression attempted to prevent different types of financial firms from merging and providing a vast array of financial services. However, by the mid-1990s, many institutions were already finding loopholes in existing regulations, and impetus was building to form financial conglomerates. In November 1999, Congress passed

Financial Conglomerates
Firms that own and operate several different types of financial intermediaries and financial institutions on a global basis.

Economies of Scale
Gains from large size that may result from several firms being able to streamline management and eliminate the duplication of effort of several separate firms.

Economies of Scope
Advantages to firms being able to offer customers several financial services under one roof.

Diversification
The branching out of financial conglomerates into several product lines.

the Gramm-Leach-Bliley Act (GLBA), also known as the Financial Modernization Act, which gave new impetus to the formation of financial conglomerates. The law effectively repealed Glass Steagall and allowed for the formation of financial holding companies (FHCs). FHCs may own securities firms, banks, and insurance companies. They may also engage in ancillary financial and complementary nonfinancial enterprises. By March 2000, the effective date of GLBA, there were already 111 FHCs, and by October 2001, the number of FHCs had increased to about 600.

Rather than maintaining the status quo of segmentation among financial service providers, the GLBA encourages considerable financial integration in the financial services industry and the formation of financial conglomerates. Read A Closer Look, which discusses Citigroup, a financial conglomerate actually formed in 1998 before the passage of GLBA.

Citigroup: In April 1998, Citicorp, the nation's second-largest bank holding company, announced that it would merge with Travelers Group, the parent company of Travelers Insurance and Salomon Smith Barney. Salomon Smith Barney was the nation's third-largest securities firm. Citigroup was on its way to becoming the quintessential financial conglomerate, operating globally and providing a vast array of financial services.

The rationale behind the merger was to take advantage of economies of scale and scope and diversification. Experts had forecasted that the merger would save at least $1 billion per year in expenses. Citigroup's first-year performance was disappointing due to losses related to the severe financial crises in Russia and Brazil. However, in the first half of 2000, Citigroup's revenues increased 16 percent and net income rose 35 percent. In mid 2000, Citigroup's 4.49 billion shares of stock outstanding were trading between $55 and $60 per share, and on an average day, 7.66 million shares changed hands. The value of Citigroup's assets as of June 30, 2001 was $953.4 billion.

The 1998 merger occurred before the passage of GLBA and, in its present configuration, Citigroup would not be a legal entity if GLBA did not pass. Indeed, the Fed approved the merger in September 1998 with the understanding that Citigroup would divest itself of several banned services—such as insurance underwriting—within 5 years if Glass-Steagall was not repealed. But GLBA passed and the merger was consummated in October 1998. At that time, Citigroup had over $700 billion in assets, over 100 million customers, and a presence in more than 100 countries.

Citibank, which is owned by Citicorp, is the nation's second-largest bank. In addition to Citibank, Citigroup has nonbank subsidiaries that provide such services as investment banking, credit cards, global asset management, trust services, buying and selling stocks, mutual funds, bonds, consumer finance, commercial lending, mortgage banking, data processing, leasing, securities advising and management, and insurance services.

On September 6, 2000, Citigroup announced the purchase of Associates First Capital Corporation, the largest U.S. consumer finance company, for about $31 billion in stock. The deal boosts Citigroup's consumer-oriented business lines. After the purchase, Citigroup will have about 2,000 retail locations in the United States and will be the top U.S. provider of credit cards, home equity loans, and commercial leasing services. In addition, the acquisition strengthens Citigroup's international position. Associates First has 700,000 customers in Europe and is the fifth-largest consumer finance company in Japan.

Hopefully, the description of Citigroup gives you a better understanding of financial conglomerates. As in this case, they often result from mergers and acquisition, operate on a global basis, and provide a vast array of consumer and business financial services.

LOOKING OUT: *The Growth of Global Financial Markets*

U.S. investors have increasingly purchased foreign securities, and foreign investors have purchased U.S. securities in increasing amounts. The following table shows the extent of the increases in cross-border flows in selected years since 1982.

YEAR	U.S. HOLDINGS OF FOREIGN STOCKS (IN BILLIONS OF DOLLARS)	U.S. HOLDINGS OF FOREIGN BONDS (IN BILLIONS OF DOLLARS)
1982	$ 17.4	$ 61.1
1991	279	130.4
1998	1,407.1	462.6
1999	1,939.5	479.4
2000	1,786.2	533.7
2001*	1,610.7*	551.0*

YEAR	FOREIGN HOLDINGS OF U.S. STOCKS (IN BILLIONS OF DOLLARS)	FOREIGN HOLDINGS OF U.S. TREASURIES (IN BILLIONS OF DOLLARS)	FOREIGN HOLDINGS OF U. S. CORPORATE BONDS (IN BILLIONS OF DOLLARS)
1982	$ 88.3	$ 160.4	$ 68.3
1991	299	535.1	233.4
1998	1,175.1	1,622.2	660.0
1999	1,537.8	1,633.6	820.8
2000	1,748.3	1,772.4	1,003.9
2001*	1,732.2*	1,820.8*	1,143.8*

Note that domestic investors have a preference for foreign stocks over bonds, while foreign investors prefer U.S. Treasuries, although the largest percent increase over the 1982–2001 period has been in foreign ownership of U.S. stocks.

*Through second quarter 2001.

SOURCE: *Flow of Funds of the United States, Z1*, Board of Governors of the Federal Reserve System, various issues.

Since the 1990s, there have been three trends in financial markets: growth, consolidation and globalization. These trends have been emphasized repeatedly throughout this text. We expect these trends to continue in the future and that financial markets and institutions will be most influenced by these factors as they evolve.

RECAP Financial conglomerates operate several different financial intermediaries and financial institutions that provide an array of financial services on a domestic and global basis. They result from consolidation in the financial services industry due to economies of scale, economies of scope, and diversification. Passage of the GLBA encouraged the formation of financial conglomerates.

This completes our look at financial institutions. You now should have a better understanding of the evolution and current state of financial institutions. In the next chapters, we will focus on financial markets and instruments and begin with a look at the money market.

Summary of Major Points

- Investment banks design, market, and underwrite the issuance of new securities in the primary market. The newly issued securities may be an IPO or a seasoned offering. In addition to advising the issuer about market conditions and prospective prices for the new securities, the investment bank also assists in filing the necessary reports with the SEC so that the new securities can be sold publicly. The securities may be stocks or bonds. A registration statement must be filed with the SEC. Part of the registration statement is the prospectus that will be distributed to investors. The SEC is concerned that appropriate information about the issuance is disclosed to the public.

- Mutual funds pool the funds of many investors to invest in several hundred or even thousands of stocks or bonds. Mutual funds may offer greater safety and more diversification than investing in one or a few stocks. Mutual funds have experienced tremendous growth in recent years. Money market mutual funds invest in securities with an original maturity of 1 year or less.

- An open-end fund continually sells new shares or buys outstanding shares from the public at the net asset value. Closed-end investment companies sell a limited number of shares that may be traded openly. The price is determined by supply and demand and can differ from the net asset value. The net asset value per share is the difference between the market value of the shares of stock that the fund owns and the fund's liabilities, all divided by the outstanding number of shares. Mutual funds can be either load or no-load funds.

- Government-sponsored enterprises (GSEs) are corporations that are sponsored or chartered by Congress. Most GSEs are privately owned and privately managed. Some GSEs have issued shares of stock that are publicly held like other corporations. The stocks of these GSEs are traded on organized exchanges. GSEs issue short-term securities that sell at a discount and long-term bonds. The majority of the issuances are long term. The proceeds are used to assist in some aspect of lending that the federal government has deemed desirable. The major areas that GSEs operate in are housing and farm credit and student loans. The securities that GSEs issue are called government agency securities.

- In most cases, the federal government has no legal obligation to guarantee the timely payment of interest and principal of GSE securities. However, many market participants assume that the government does "*de facto*" guarantee the payments. The yield spread between government agency securities and U.S. government securities reflects differences in liquidity and risk. The yield spread can be significant because secondary markets do not have the breadth and depth of Treasuries.

- Hedge funds are a type of mutual fund that has fewer then 99 very wealthy investors. They are not regulated by the SEC. Hedge funds attempt to earn high returns for their investors regardless of whether financial prices are going up or down. Sometimes, hedge funds engage in risky investment strategies. GSEs are privately owned, government-sponsored enterprises that issue financial securities. The funds that are raised are used to provide funds to areas that the government deems desirable including housing, farm credit, and student loans.

- Real estate investment trusts (REITs) pool the funds of many small investors and use them to buy or build income property or to make or purchase mortgage loans. They are pass-through institutions in that the rents from the income property and/or the interest income from the mortgages are passed through to shareholders. At least 75 percent of the assets of REITs must be either real property (generally commercial or industrial real estate) or mortgages. By law, REITs must return 95 percent of their earnings to shareholders each year. Shares of REITs are traded on organized exchanges like shares of stock.

- Financial conglomerates are financial firms that provide an array of financial services previously provided by several financial intermediaries and financial institutions. In theory, financial conglomerates offer economies of scale, economies of scope, and diversification. Changes in technology and regulations have given new impetus to the formation of financial conglomerates in recent years.

Key Terms

Closed-End Fund
Diversification
Economies of Scale
Economies of Scope
Farm Credit Financial
  Assistance Corporation
  (FACO)
Federal Farm Credit Banks
  Funding Corporation
  (FFCBFC)
Financial Conglomerates
Financing Corporation (FICO)
Fund of Funds

Government-Sponsored
  Enterprise (GSE)
Hedge Fund
Investment Banks
Investment Companies
Limit Orders
Load
Margin Loans
Market Orders
Net Asset Value
No-Load
Open-End Fund
Private Placement

Prospectus
Real Estate Investment Trusts
  (REITs)
Registration Statement
Seasoned Issuance
Securities Industry Protection
  Corporation (SIPC)
Short Sell
Student Loan Marketing
  Association (Sallie Mae)
Syndicate

Review Questions

1. What are the functions of investment banks? Do they engage in primary or secondary market activity? What is a syndicate?

2. What is a prospectus? What are the differences among a prospectus, a registration statement, and a bond indenture?

3. What is the difference between a securities broker and a securities dealer? What roles do brokers and dealers play in the financial system?

4. How does a hedge fund differ from a traditional mutual fund? What are the two types of hedge funds and how are their requirements for participation different? What is the difference between a mutual fund and a money market mutual fund?

5. Are investment banks financial intermediaries? Explain why or why not.

6. The spread between the bid and asked price widens. What does this mean about the securities?

7. What is the difference between a load and a no-load mutual fund? Could a load fund ever result in higher total sales commissions and costs?

8. Miguel expects a stock's price to rise. Should he short-sell the stock? Explain.

9. What is the different between a market order and a limit order? What are the two types of limit orders?

10. What type of securities do GSEs sell? What is the purpose of GSEs? Does the federal government guarantee the securities of GSEs? Who owns the GSEs?

11. What are some of the factors for the growth of mutual funds in recent years?

12. List some reasons why Henry should consider purchasing a fund of funds. Are there any reasons he should not?

13. How do REITs differ from other mutual funds? Are all REITs pretty much the same? What are their differences?

14. What is a financial conglomerate? Discuss the factors that contribute to the formation of financial conglomerates.

15. How does diversification reduce the risk that a financial conglomerate will fail? What is the difference between economies of scale and economies of scope?

Analytical Questions

16. A mutual fund owns stocks with a market value of $1 billion and has liabilities of $1 million. What is the net asset value? If there are 2 million shares of stock outstanding, what is the net asset value per share?

17. What are some of the factors that determine the spread between the bid and asked price? If the bid-asked spread narrows, what does this mean?

18. What are the factors that determine the spread between agency securities and Treasuries?

19. Make a chart listing the similarities and differences among the following institutions: money market mutual funds, mutual funds, hedge funds, government-sponsored enterprises, and REITs.

20. Jessie has bought a share of stock for $100. She has borrowed $50 from her broker. There is a 25 percent maintenance margin requirement. The price of the stock falls to $80. Will her broker put in a margin call to her asking her to put up more funds? If so, how much? What if the price falls to $50? In each case, if so, how much more funds will she need?

21. Comment on the following: Frank calls his broker to complain that the stock the broker sold him has fallen in value and Frank has lost a lot of money. The broker says: "Look, I made money and the brokerage firm made money on the deal. Two out of three is not bad!"

Internet Exercises

1. Go to the internet site for Ginnie Mae at **http://www.ginniemae.gov**. Click on "About Us." Summarize the material about Ginnie Mae.

2. Summarize the testimony on the supervision and regulation of GSEs by Treasury Under-Secretary Gary Gensler before a Congressional subcommittee on March 22, 2000. The testimony is available on the U.S. Treasury World Wide Web site at **http://www.ustreas.gov/press/releases/ps479.htm**.

3. Go to **http://www.hedgeworld.com**. Click on "News." Pick two recent articles about hedge funds and summarize their content.

Suggested Readings

For an engaging article on "Why We Do What We Do: The Views of Bankers, Insurers, and Securities Firms on Specialization and Diversification," see the article by the same name by Tony Candito, Michael J. Castellano, Richard Heckinger, presenters, Darryll Hendricks, moderator, summary by Kevin J. Stiroh, *Economic Policy Review*, Federal Reserve Bank of New York, Vol. 6, No. 4, October 2000, pp. 81–87.

For a discussion of many of the topics in this chapter, see Dimitri B. Papadimitriou, ed., *Modernizing Financial Systems*, (London and Basingstroke: Macmillan/St. Martin's Press, 2000).

For a historical look at the securities industry at a time of dramatic change, see Alec Benn, *The Unseen Wall Street, 1969–1975*, (Westport, CT: Greenwood Publishing Group, 2000).

For an analysis of mutual funds, see Peter Fortune, "Mutual Funds, Part I: Reshaping the American Financial System," *New England Economic Review*, Federal Reserve Bank of Boston, July, 1997, pp. 45–72; and Peter Fortune, "Mutual Funds, Part II: Funds Flows and Security Returns," *New England Economic Review*, January, 1998, pp. 3–22.

For a discussion of the size, number, behavior, regulation, and policy implications of hedge funds, see Barry Eichengreen and Donald Mathieson, "Hedge Funds: What Do We Really Know?" *Economic Issues*, 19, International Monetary Fund, September 1999.

part

MANAGING FINANCIAL RISK

chapter

21 Risk Assessment and Management

Learning Objectives *After reading this chapter, you should know:*

- how financial managers use the "Five Cs" of credit to assess default risk
- a few strategies for managing default risk
- how GAP analysis is used to measure the threat of interest-rate risk to bank earnings
- balance sheet strategies for managing interest-rate risk
- how to assess and manage liquidity risk
- how the threat of interest-rate risk to bank capital can be assessed using duration analysis (Appendix)

Risk exists, and banks must accept risk if they are to thrive and meet an economy's needs. But they must manage the risks and recognize them as real. Risk matters. Whether or not it is temporarily ignored, it will eventually come out.
—Federal Reserve Governor,
Laurence H. Meyer

• customize

stment Services   Planning & Tools   Products & Services   Help Desk

Welcome to Citibank® Online

The one-stop solution for all your financial needs

Free Online Bill Payment
Pay virtually anyone, anytime

Smart Deals
Enjoy savings & special values

Safe, Secure Banking

Managing Balance Sheet Risk and Return

The goal of financial management is to enhance an institution's earnings and market value. The central problem is that strategies designed to achieve the highest rates of return are also characterized by the highest risk. Thus, management must pursue profitability in a manner that maintains the institution's solvency by avoiding excessive exposure to credit, interest rate, liquidity, and foreign exchange-rate risk. To pursue this dual mandate of high returns and acceptable levels of risk, most banks utilize an asset-liability committee. The committee is usually composed of senior management including the president, the chairperson, and those in charge of major functions, such as asset management (domestic/international lending and securities purchases), liability management (attracting and retaining various types of deposits), and economic analysis. The asset-liability committee is responsible for shaping a bank's basic borrowing and lending strategy. The committee meets several times each month to shape, coordinate, and direct a strategy that will sustain and enhance profitability without exposing the bank to excessive risk.

The basic issue for the asset-liability committee is the rate spread between the return on assets (interest rates received on loans and other assets) and the cost of liabilities (rates paid on deposits and other liabilities). After reviewing the bank's current balance sheet, regulatory requirements, the degree of competition from other lenders, the economic outlook, pending loan applications, and recent deposit growth, the committee will make decisions on loan pricing. Decisions such as where to set the prime rate and whether to offer loan applicants fixed- or variable-rate loans are made. In addition, the committee will decide how to raise the funds needed to support the planned expansion of assets. This is accomplished by altering the interest rates paid on various kinds of deposits and deciding how deposit products will be marketed to consumers. The resulting integrated strategy operates on both sides of the bank's balance sheet. Underlying all of the committee's decisions is a desire to limit the institution's exposure to levels of risk that compromise its long-term survival.

This focus on managing risk is the subject of the four chapters (Chapters 21–24) that make up this fifth section of the text. This chapter emphasizes how bankers assess their exposure to credit, interest-rate, and liquidity risk. We emphasize how the "Five Cs" of credit management can be used to assess default risk and describe how income gap analysis can be used to assess the effects of interest-rate changes on bank income. The discussion of duration analysis in the chapter appendix examines the effects of interest-rate changes on a bank's net worth. Our discussion of assessing and managing liquidity risk is less extensive. We save our approach to managing foreign exchange-rate risk for Chapter 22, where we explain how forwards, futures, and options can be used to hedge against foreign exchange as well as interest-rate risk. Similarly, in Chapter 23 we examine the reasons for the increased use of asset-backed securities, interest-rate swaps, and other derivative instruments, as well as how each can be used to reduce risk exposure. Although our discussion of risk assessment and management in this chapter focuses on commercial banks, the techniques and management strategies presented here can be used in many types of financial institutions.

When we talk about risk management, it is the bank's balance sheet—assets, liabilities, and capital—that is "managed." Consider the balance sheet of a typical depository institution. The asset side of the balance sheet records the business, consumer, and mortgage loans; government and municipal securities; corporate and foreign bonds; reserves; and other real assets owned by the bank. On the liability side of its balance sheet, our bank tracks the funds it owes to others in various kinds of deposits (small and large time deposits, savings deposits, and checkable deposits) commercial paper, corporate bonds, and borrowed funds such as Fed funds, repurchase agreements, and Eurodollar borrowing. These liabilities, and the interest rates paid to borrow them, determine a lender's cost of funds. The goal is to maintain a **positive spread**—wherein the rate of return on assets rises above the cost of funds on liabilities—to ensure profitability. If the cost of funds rises above the rate of return on assets, the bank faces a **negative spread,** causing the bank's net income and equity to fall. If this persists, the value of the bank's liabilities will become greater than the value of its assets. The bank is then deemed **insolvent** and either sold or closed by financial regulators. Regardless of how the insolvency is resolved, the bank managers will lose their positions.

The asset side of a bank's balance sheet generates its revenue stream. Earnings received on loans and leases, interest earned on securities holdings, and realized appreciation in the value of assets sold by the bank all contribute to a lender's earnings. However, these returns are not risk-free. Generally, higher rates of return are associated with greater risk. In the absence of regulation and prudence, a bank manager could lend all of the bank's funds to a single borrower and earn high returns—assuming the borrower repaid the note. This high return strategy would also be accompanied by a high risk of default. Since the single loan dominates the bank's portfolio, this single default could also cause the bank's insolvency. Similarly, lower rates of return are associated with less risk. A bank manager could simply fill the asset side of its balance sheet with risk-free U.S. Treasury bills. However, he or she would also have to be content to accept low returns. The key is to balance the tradeoff between the pursuit of high earnings with the need to avoid an inappropriate level of credit, interest-rate, and liquidity risk. The first step toward managing this tradeoff is to effectively assess each of these risks.

The Five Cs of Credit

Credit or default risk is the risk that a DSU (our borrowers) will be unwilling or unable to repay a loan or satisfy the terms of a security it has issued. In short, there is some chance that DSUs who have borrowed funds from a bank or who have issued debt securities will not pay them back. Banks are exposed to credit or default risk whenever they make commercial or personal loans or buy the debt security of a corporation or governmental unit. In either case, the bank is serving as an intermediary channeling funds from SSUs to DSUs.

Inherent in the loan process are the ever-present problems of *asymmetric information, adverse selection,* and *moral hazard.* Typically, potential borrowers know more about the risk and return of an investment project, and the likelihood of a loan being repaid, than does a bank loan officer. The balance of information between borrower and lender is not equal or symmetric. Instead, borrowers have the best knowledge about the project they are funding and will likely put the best possible spin on any credit report or project shortcoming. We refer to this problem as asymmetric information. Adverse selection also creates a need for active risk management. If those most likely to default pursue loans more determinedly than others, a bank will select borrowers whose actions will have the most adverse affect on its balance sheet. The bank will grant a disproportionate share of its loans to those least likely to repay. Higher loan rates exacerbate the adverse selection problem in two ways. First, the higher rates drive "responsible" borrowers out of the market, leaving only those willing to pursue high-return/high-risk investment projects. Second, the higher interest rates make the debt payments of those who do borrow more onerous and, therefore, default risk is increased. Once a loan is

Positive Spread
When the rate of return on assets is *greater than* cost of funds on liabilities. This occurs when loan rates are *above* deposit rates.

Negative Spread
When the rate of return on assets is *less than* cost of funds on liabilities. This occurs when loan rates are *below* deposit rates.

Insolvent
When the value of a bank's liabilities are greater than the value of its assets.

granted, a moral hazard problem emerges. Borrowers may be tempted to use loan proceeds in a manner that enhances the borrower's possibility of gain while endangering the lender with increased default risk.

To reduce default risk and its attendant problems, lenders have developed the **Five Cs of credit**—the most important factors credit managers must actively and prudently assess, monitor, and manage to avoid defaults among their loan and security holdings. These factors include the following borrower or investment project characteristics:

1. *Capacity:* The borrower's ability to repay a loan
2. *Character:* The competency and willingness of a business firm's management or an individual borrower to repay his or her debts
3. *Capital:* The amount of equity or wealth a borrower has at stake in the proposed project
4. *Collateral:* The amount and liquidity of assets a borrower uses to secure a loan
5. *Conditions:* Forecasts of economic conditions, revenues, market share, degree of competition, and other variables—largely beyond a borrower's control—that may affect his or her ability to repay the loan

Capacity

To effectively assess an individual loan applicant's capacity—his or her ability or potential for repaying a loan—requires careful evaluation of an applicant's income and wealth relative to other payment obligations. After gathering accurate financial information from an individual or business entity, the lender examines the applicant's expected future income stream that could be drawn upon to make debt payments. When evaluating a mortgage application, many lenders use various financial ratios to determine whether a loan applicant (or security issuer) can handle the additional debt load. A common rule of thumb is that an applicant's **debt-to-income ratio**—total mortgage, automobile, credit card, and student loan payments, etc. as a share of gross income—should not exceed 36 percent. Similarly, his or her **housing-to-income ratio**—mortgage payment, insurance, property taxes, and private mortgage insurance relative to one's gross monthly income—should not exceed 28 percent. Both of these ratios are commonly computed on a monthly basis. Effective risk management begins with an accurate assessment of a borrower's capacity to repay a loan. This also applies to commercial loan applicants or security issuers. In either case, the borrower needs to show that his or her projected income will be sufficient to service all outstanding and proposed payment commitments.

Character

The techniques used to assess a potential borrower's character have changed significantly over the last two or three decades. In the past, local bankers gave important consideration to the personal reputation of the loan applicant. The difference between a loan being accepted or rejected might have been how well the banker knew the applicant through various civic organizations, family interactions, social activities or, most importantly, through one's previous dealings at the bank. The role played by character in the credit process created a strong incentive on both the part of the customer and the banker to maintain long-term relationships. If a borrower was having short-term cash flow problems and needed a small loan, he could apply for a "character loan" based simply on his reputation—as long as he had managed to repay loans regularly in the past. Similarly, bankers would often cover a

Five Cs of Credit
The primary factors lenders must assess and manage to avoid excessive default risk exposure; these include a loan applicant's capacity, character, capital, collateral, and conditions.

Debt-to-Income Ratio
A financial ratio used to assess a loan applicant's capacity for repaying a loan, based on the share of one's total monthly debt payments relative to his or her gross monthly income.

Housing-to-Income Ratio
A financial ratio used to assess a mortgage loan applicant's capacity to repay a loan, based on the share of total housing expenses relative to one's gross monthly income.

bounced "insufficient fund" check to avoid offending a good banking customer and losing future deposits or loan business. This system worked as long as banking was a local business predicated primarily on business relationships. However, as banking became national and international in scope, most of the requisite relationships necessary for this type of character assessment have broken down. As a result, the techniques used to assess character have also needed to evolve.

Today most bankers are less familiar with their clients. Character assessment is done empirically by examining various facets of one's past. An applicant's credit and work history suggests how strongly a potential borrower is attached to the work force and how diligently past debts have been repaid. These are the primary proxies used today to assess one's ethical make-up. If a borrower has a checkered work history and/or has defaulted on past loans, he is presumed to be less likely to repay a debt than one who does not have these shortcomings. A similar assessment is extended to a business firm with a poor record of paying previous debts.

These measures are not perfect. Some borrowers may have had child-rearing or other responsibilities that prevented them from having a continual employment record. Similarly, the effects of a divorce and/or an uninsured and unanticipated medical expense may create a flawed credit history that may or may not accurately reflect a applicant's true willingness and ability to discharge future debts. Businesses also face competitive issues beyond their control that may adversely affect their ability to meet debt payments. If an applicant has an opportunity to meet with a banker face-to-face, these "flaws" can sometimes be explained and an adjustment can be made prior to the loan decision. In other circumstances, this interaction is impossible and the loan application is simply rejected.

Capital

Perhaps the best predictor of a default risk is the amount of equity or capital that a borrower has at stake in the project. On a balance sheet, capital equals assets minus liabilities. The same holds here. Capital is the difference between the market value of the property being purchased (the asset) and the amount borrowed (the liability). The greater the amount of capital a borrower has in a property, the lower the default risk to the lender. The reverse is also true. The less equity a borrower has in a project, the more likely he is to default.

One frequently used measure of capital, the **loan-to-value ratio,** is used to assess the degree of risk involved in mortgage, automobile, commercial equipment, and other types of lending. The loan-to-value ratio is computed by dividing the total loan amount by the total market value of the property. For example, if you wish to purchase a $100,000 house, a mortgage banker may be willing to finance only 90 percent of the home's market value. To qualify for financing, you would first need to put forward a 10 percent down payment. This $10,000 stands as your equity (your capital) or share of ownership in the project. (The value of the house itself—including your equity in it—will serve as collateral for the loan.) Lenders often require some minimum down payment for loans on homes, automobiles, and other real property. If the borrower is unable to come up with a down payment, the lender will either (1) deny the loan, (2) charge a higher interest rate to compensate for the higher risk, and/or (3) require the borrower to purchase insurance that guarantees payments if the borrower defaults.

The amount of equity a borrower has in a project is good measure of default risk and a strong predictor of default. Recent studies cited by Avery, Bostic, Calem, and Canner found that "conventional mortgages with loan-to-value ratios of 91 percent to 95 percent at origination default more than *twice as frequently* as loans with loan-to-value ratios in the range of 81 percent to 90 percent and more than *five times as often* as loans with loan-to-value ratios in the rage of 71 percent to 80 percent" (emphasis added).[1] Making loans to those who have more equity in an investment gives the bank a larger cushion if real estate values fall. When the borrower in the previous example purchases a $100,000 home with a 10 percent down payment, the buyer has $10,000 worth of equity in the property. If the price of the home falls to $95,000, the borrower still has a strong incentive to make payments to retain the remaining $5,000 in equity. However, if the home value falls to $85,000 and the borrower still owes $90,000, he would have negative equity of $5,000. The incentive to repay is much weaker. It may make sense for the borrower to default to avoid owing more than the property is worth. Even in circumstances in which borrowers experience negative equity, most continue to make their payments to protect their credit ratings and/or in the hope that the property will again appreciate in the future, creating positive equity.

This fact that most loans are repaid even when there is negative equity helps explain why **"125s"** have become so popular. With these special home equity loans, the bank loans the borrower up to 125 percent of a home's value. Lenders charge higher interest rates to compensate for the increased default risk caused by the negative equity. A combination of factors, such as negative equity combined with a "triggering event" that causes instability in one's income (divorce, loss of a job, or uninsured medical expenditures), cause borrowers to default. In the absence of these triggering events, most 125s are repaid. Bankers who successfully screen potential borrowers and price appropriately for the default risk are likely to receive financial reward.

> **125s**
> A specialized and increasingly popular type of home equity loan in which the borrower is allowed to borrow up to 125 percent of a home's value.

Collateral

It is easy to confuse the notions of capital and collateral. The previous section explained that capital is to the difference between the value of a borrower's property and the amount owed against it. Collateral is the value of the borrower's property given as security to the lender as a promise of loan repayment. Thus, collateral includes capital, but both are important elements of default risk assessment and management.

For auto or mortgage loans, banks require that the property being purchased serve as security (collateral) for the loan. In the case of a loan default, the bank has a right to repossess the auto or the real property. Let's say that a borrower has defaulted on a automobile loan that has an outstanding balance of $15,000. The bank can repossess the car, which it now owns, and resell it to generate funds for repaying the note. If the car sells for $10,000, the bank can still pursue the $5,000 unsecured debt obligation owed by the borrower. Although the bank repossesses the property, the borrower is not off the proverbial hook. The lender has a right to the property used as collateral. If its value is insufficient to pay off the loan—which was caused by the existence of negative equity—the lender continues to have a claim against the borrower. The same concept applies for commercial loans when a business firm is purchasing a new piece of equipment. Collateral works because it ensures—even in the presence of adverse selection and default—the lender will

---

[1]For details, see the article entitled "Credit Risk, Credit Scoring, and the Performance of Home Mortgages" by Robert B. Avery, Raphael W. Bostic, Paul S. Calem, and Glenn B. Canner in the *Federal Reserve Bulletin*, July 1996, p. 624.

not lose the entire loan amount. This is why mortgage bankers require that a title search be completed on a property before granting a loan. The banker wants to ensure that the property pledged as collateral is, in fact, owned by the person pledging it.

Banks use collateral when lending in the fed funds market or participating in various derivative markets. The value of collateral can change given changes in the economic conditions. To avoid this problem, especially with business loans, some lenders require **compensating balances,** a special form of collateral that requires a portion of loan proceeds to be maintained on deposit at the bank. If a business firm is borrowing $100,000, the lender may require that $10,000 be held in a checking account at the bank as a form of security. In case of default, the lender can utilize these funds to partially compensate for its losses.

Compensating Balances
A form of collateral that specifies a portion of loan proceeds to be maintained on deposit at the bank making the loan.

Conditions

Prudent financial managers consider how a borrower's capacity, capital, and collateral may change when economic growth slows or credit conditions tighten. Thus, financial institutions employ economic forecasters to predict what will likely happen over the short- and long-term time horizons. They also employ credit analysts who use various scenarios to predict how a particular loan will perform given changes in the economy. If the bank's economists predict a recession, we can presume greater unemployment, decreased sales revenues for many firms, and perhaps even a fall in the value of assets used for collateral. Before making a highly leveraged commercial real estate loan—in which the buyer has little equity in the property—the bank should consider the possibility that the value of the real estate may fall. In this case, the value of the borrower's capital and the value of his collateral are reduced. If his job or other investment income is threatened by the slowdown in economic activity, his capacity for repaying the loan will also be reduced. The opposite occurs when forecasters predict continued economic growth, increased employment, increased sales revenues, and rising asset values.

Forecasts of economic conditions can also influence the aggressiveness with which a bank pursues various types of loans. An institution's forecast of continued strong economic growth, low unemployment, and stable prices may suggest that default risk is relatively low. Based on this insight, the bank may choose to hold a smaller portfolio of Treasury securities and instead hold a higher proportion of its assets as loans or even as higher-risk loans. In contrast, if the future is characterized by a business cycle downturn and higher unemployment, it may make sense to tighten up lending standards (avoid higher risk loans) and hold a larger proportion of total assets as lower-risk securities and cash rather than loans. Forecasted changes in interest rates also influence bank behavior.

RECAP The ultimate goal of bank management is to enhance an institution's earnings and market value. This requires that the bank create a positive spread between its rate of return on assets and the cost of its liabilities. If a negative spread persists, the institution will face insolvency. To avoid this misfortune, financial managers must carefully assess and manage default risk. The first step in this process is to identify the key elements involved in the credit decision—the Five Cs of credit: capacity, character, capital, collateral, and conditions. Before any loan is granted or security purchased, these five elements of default risk should be assessed carefully.

Default Risk Assessment and Management Techniques

The Five Cs of credit require active assessment and management. To successfully counter the problems of asymmetric information, adverse selection, and moral hazard, managers must (1) engage in accurate discernment and pricing, (2) carry out careful observation, (3) encourage long-term banking relationships, and (4) manage asset portfolios actively.

Engage in Accurate Discernment and Pricing

Managers must *discern* which applications are characterized by a sufficient combination of capacity, character, capital, collateral, and favorable economic conditions such that a loan is approved and *priced* accordingly. Various laws prohibit banks from discriminating on the basis of sex, race, religion, and marital status. The techniques used to discern acceptable credit risks from unacceptable credit risks focus on economic factors. To assess these factors, the bank (our SSU) requires the potential borrower to submit a considerable amount of information. This includes the commercial or individual applicant's balance sheet (assets and liabilities), income statement (revenues and expenditures), credit history (including a credit check with a credit reporting agency), work history, and, if applicable, an inspection of any property involved in the transaction. This information is then used to discern whether the Five Cs are sufficiently met. Weaknesses in one of the Five Cs may be compensated by strengths in another.

Over the last decade or two, default risk assessment has been profoundly altered by the growing importance of the three major **credit reporting agencies** (Experian, Equifax, and Trans Union) and technological innovation. Credit reporting agencies play an increasingly important role in overcoming the asymmetric information problem and in the decision to grant and price credit. They gather a wealth of public and private information and sell it to prospective creditors, insurers, and employers. Civic documents such as court records regarding lawsuits, judgments, bankruptcies, and tax liens are gathered by the agencies from publicly available databases. The agencies gather private information on the types and amounts of credit outstanding, bill-paying habits, and credit history from various lenders with whom the agencies maintain relationships, including credit card companies, department stores, banks, mortgage companies, and finance companies. The agencies compile this public and private information on individual borrowers into a **credit report** (sometimes referred to as a *credit file*). This report summarizes a person's debt profile and bill-paying habits and highlights any lingering legal issues. The advance of telecommunications technology, statistical analysis, and computers has allowed the data in credit reports to be quickly and efficiently merged with loan application data and other information to generate credit scores. A Closer Look explains how to go about obtaining your credit report.

Credit Reporting Agencies
Companies such as Experian, Equifax, and Trans Union that gather credit and legal information on individuals, compile it into a credit report, and then provide it to prospective creditors, insurers, and employers for a fee.

Credit Report
An account or file of an individual's legal and credit history. It includes information about previous legal judgments as well as information about the types and amounts of one's outstanding debts as well as a record of one's payment history.

Obtaining and Correcting a Credit Report: Credit reports play a critical role in influencing one's credit score, access to credit, and in some cases, access to employment and insurance. Given this significance, it seems prudent to ensure that the information in one's credit file is accurate. It is fairly easy to request a copy, analyze the report, close unused accounts (or those you thought were already closed), and report errors. If you find an error, you should file a dispute with your local credit bureau. It must investigate your claim and either verify the item in dispute or clear it from your record. Adverse and accurate entries stay on one's credit report for 7 years and a bankruptcy case stays on

A Closer Look

for 10 years. Thus, failure to pay your bills can have lasting consequences. The credit reporting agencies may charge a reasonable fee (about $8.50) for a copy of your credit report. However, if you have been denied credit, employment, or insurance as a result or your credit report and you request a copy within 30 days of receiving notice, the credit bureau reporting the information must provide you with a free copy of your credit report. Residents of Vermont and Massachusetts are entitled to one free credit report from each of the three credit bureaus annually. To complicate matters slightly, there are three main credit reporting agencies: Equifax, Experian, and Trans Union. To request a copy of your credit report, contact the agencies at their phone number or Internet address:

Equifax	1-800-685-1111	http://www.equifax.com
Experian	1-888-397-3742	http://www.experian.com
Trans Union	1-800-916-8800	http://www.tuc.com

You may purchase a copy of your credit score for $12.95 from Fair, Isaac, and Company, Inc., at http://www.myfico.com.

A new credit reporting and scoring system for businesses has been developed by LiveCapital.com. Business owners can learn more about this automated credit approval system at http://livecapital.com.

Credit Score
The three-digit number that predicts a loan applicant's likelihood of default based upon his or her credit history.

A **credit score** refers to the three-digit number between 300 to 850 that predicts a loan applicant's likelihood of default based upon his or her credit history. (A score over 700 means you are viewed as a low credit risk; a score of 300–500 means you are a high credit risk.) Credit scores go by a variety of names. The most popular type, FICO® scores, are prepared using software from the firm that created credit scoring in 1956—Fair, Isaac and Co. Other brand names include Beacon or Empirica scores. Many lenders use their own in-house versions tailored to their own particular needs. Regardless of the name, credit scores are based on an individual's bill-paying history, current debt levels, types of debt outstanding, requests for new credit, and the length of time credit has been in use. Loan decisions that used to take days or weeks to approve can now be discerned and priced in a matter of hours. More importantly, these scores allow for far more subtle distinctions between various risk classifications and can be priced accordingly.

Risk-Based Pricing
Charging different interest rates to borrowers based on an assessment of a loan applicant's default risk; highly rated applicants are charged the lowest rates.

Instead of dividing applications into just "good" versus "bad" credit risks, bankers now engage in **risk-based pricing.** This involves grouping applicants into various risk tiers ranked by quality. The best "prime" borrowers are rated as A. The ranking continues down through various "subprime" categories of A–, B, C, and D tiers. Highly rated borrowers are charged the lowest rates. The interest rates charged increase as credit score declines. As of early 2001, the difference between A and D rated credit could be the difference between paying 10.1 percent and 15.75 percent for a home equity loan. The use of this more sophisticated discernment mechanism has allowed lenders to reclassify some borrowers from prime to subprime and to charge rates according to the best estimate of default risk exposure. Improved discernment and pricing have resulted in higher earnings.

Credit Rationing
Charging a lower interest rate than some borrowers are willing to pay and apportioning loans and loan amounts only to those with sufficient credit.

Lenders need to be careful about making higher interest loans. We know from our experience with adverse selection that the riskiest borrowers are likely to pursue a loan with the most persistence. Lenders that specialize in the subprime market—lenders making loans to those with A– or lower credit scores—often have the highest loan rejection rates. These lenders may engage in **credit rationing**—purposely charging a lower interest rate than some borrowers are willing to pay and then apportioning loans only to those with sufficient credit. This lower rate reduces adverse selection and default risk in two ways. First, the riskiest borrowers are simply denied

LOOKING FORWARD: *Credit Scoring and Fair Lending*

Are minorities and women unfairly denied credit because of credit scoring techniques? Will legal action be taken against lenders as a result? Authors of articles published in the banking and business press suggest that the answer to both questions is "Yes." Critics of credit scoring say that blacks and other minority members are at a disadvantage with credit scoring techniques because the scores give little or no weight to the loan products used in minority neighborhoods. The loans extended in minority neighborhoods are often from community groups, subprime lenders, or finance companies. These lenders are less likely to report information to credit bureaus. In some cases, predatory lenders may withhold positive credit information to ensure that a borrower cannot refinance at a lower rate elsewhere. This lack of information in the file leaves minority borrowers at a disadvantage. Women, too, are likely to be at a disadvantage. Married women find that when they apply for credit, the joint accounts they hold with their spouse are often listed in only their husband's name. The result: Female borrowers have less positive credit information on record and their lower credit scores reflect it.

Given the broader conceptions of discrimination used by the federal regulators, this apparent bias against minorities and women may be grounds for legal action. In 1994, federal financial regulators issued a statement on fair lending that identified three types of illegal discrimination: *overt discrimination* (intentional denial or adverse loan terms because of bigotry), *disparate treatment* (treating equally qualified applicants differently), and *disparate impact* (using a policy or practice that disproportionately and adversely affects a protected group). It is this last category that may cause problems for bankers who use credit scoring techniques to assess loan applicants. One appeal of credit scoring is that it would eliminate overt discrimination as a criterion for denying a loan or determining loan terms. However, it may simultaneously increase disparate impact discrimination. *Forbes* quotes John P. Relman of the Washington Lawyers' Committee for Civil Rights & Urban Affairs, who makes just such a claim. "I'm positive credit scoring is going to have an adverse effect on African-Americans and Latinos. If it continues to be used, it will be challenged by either private-sector plaintiffs or the Justice Department." At this writing, the case law is beginning to be assembled. According to compliance expert Jo Ann Barefoot, the current environment calls for "proactive risk management." Bank managers must use statistically valid scoring systems, regularly revalidate them, and employ fair-lending "best practices" to avoid a lawsuit or at least to avoid losing one.

SOURCES: Jo Ann S. Barefoot, "The Next Fair-Lending Risk: Disparate Impact," *ABA Banking Journal,* May 1997 pp. 28, 30, 32.; *Business Week,* May 22, 2000, p. F50, "No Credit Where Credit Is Due"; and Janet Novack, "The Coming Fight Over FICO," *Forbes,* December 18, 1995, Vol. 156, No. 14 p. 96(1).

credit. Second, the lower rate makes it easier for those who are granted loans by lowering their debt payments. Credit rationing can also be used to reduce moral hazard. In some cases, a lender may ration credit by approving a loan but then lending less than the full amount desired by the borrower. This leaves the borrower with fewer funds to spend in an inappropriate manner.

Carry Out Careful Observation

The second step to effective risk management occurs after a loan has been originated. The borrower's financial actions must be *observed* to ensure moral hazard is avoided and that the borrower continues to meet the conditions of the Five Cs under which the loan was approved. In some cases, a borrower is encouraged or required to move his checking account, credit card, and/or savings account to the lender's bank. This arrangement allows the bank to monitor the borrower's spending and savings behavior. Unusual levels of spending or lower-than-usual bank balances may suggest moral hazard or changes in a borrower's capacity to discharge the loan. At a minimum, the lender must closely track the borrower's repayment history and respond with requests for payments or begin foreclosure through the bank's collections department.

Encourage Long-Term Banking Relationships

The third step, despite changes in how in character is assessed, requires bank managers to develop professional *relationships* with clients. Long-term banking relationships make the discernment and observation processes easier for both the borrower and lender. It also serves as a basis for repeat and referral business for the bank and greater flexibility for DSUs. Borrowers can benefit by establishing credit lines or **loan commitments**—promises by a bank to lend a given amount of funds at a particular rate for a specified period of time that can be drawn on when the borrower experiences cash-flow problems.

Loan Commitments
Promises made by banks to a firm to lend a given amount of funds at a particular rate for a specified period of time.

Manage Asset Portfolios Actively

Even after all Five Cs are satisfied and the previous three steps are followed, credit or default risk problems can emerge if our fourth and final step is not followed. Loan portfolios must be managed prudently. Lenders need to strike a balance between specialization and diversification. For example, during the "go-go" years of the oil patch in the 1980s, some banks in Oklahoma and Texas found it profitable to become experts in analyzing loan applications from firms working in the oil fields. The banker's ability to understand the needs of the industry, develop ongoing relationships with borrowers, and develop techniques to appropriately discern borrower's Five Cs and price loans according to risk proved profitable. Because of this expertise, many of these lenders ended up with large proportions of oil loans on their balance sheets. When oil prices collapsed and companies went bankrupt, these lenders struggled and many failed. Had these lenders made loans in other parts of the country or to businesses in other industries, or simply held larger shares of Treasury securities, smaller shares of their portfolios would have defaulted and many of these lenders would still be in business. The recent trend to nationwide mergers is motivated at least in part by the desire of banking firms to diversify their loan portfolios both nationally and internationally.

In some cases, it is in a banker's interest to reduce credit or default risk by sharing it with others or eliminating it entirely by selling the loan. Sometimes a bank makes a loan that is simply too big—legally or from a risk management perspective—for its own balance sheet. In these cases, banks create **loan participations**—an agreement that allows an originating bank to give partial interest in the loan to one or more banks. This practice is common among large money center banks to reduce default risk and to avoid the legal maximums allowed for loans made to a single borrower. As we discussed with respect to mortgages in Chapter 12, many banks reduce their default risk exposure entirely by selling loans to another bank or to a firm specializing in **securitization**—the pooling and repackaging of similar loans into marketable securities. Because of the decreased default risk, as well as reduced liquidity and interest-rate risk, securitization has spread from mortgage loans to automobile, small business, and student loans.

Loan Participations
A loan agreement that allows an originating bank to give partial interest in a loan to one or more additional banks.

Securitization
The pooling and repackaging of similar loans into marketable securities.

A final word of caution. We have framed our discussion of default risk management as the prudent management of an institution's balance sheet. Over the last few decades, off-balance sheet activities—such as unused lines of credit, overdraft protection, unused credit card balances, and various commitments for which a bank is liable but do not appear on the balance sheet—have been growing in importance. The use of these instruments by the bank's clients, followed by a subsequent default, could harm the earnings and perhaps the solvency of a banking institution as certainly as a loan or security default. Effective default risk management also requires consideration of off-balance sheet activities.

RECAP There are four main steps to effective credit or default risk assessment and management. First, managers must engage in accurate discernment and pricing. This includes using various credit scoring techniques, employing risk-based pricing, and engaging in credit rationing. Second, once a loan has been made, the borrower's actions should be observed to prevent moral hazard and to determine whether the borrower has experienced a reduction in his or her capacity and/or collateral that will adversely affect the likelihood of repayment. Third, long-term banking relationships reduce the costs of discernment and observation, encourage repeat business, and allow borrowers greater flexibility in meeting their credit needs. Fourth, financial managers need to manage their portfolios. This includes balancing the costs and benefits of specialization and diversification, sharing the risk with other lenders, and prudently using securitization. Off-balance sheet activities should not be ignored.

Assessing Interest-Rate Risk

As noted earlier, the operating goal of a bank manager is to maintain a positive rate spread between the return on assets and the cost of liabilities in an attempt to maximize the institution's market value. Our discussion of default risk emphasized how bankers try to avoid making loans or buying securities that result in default. The problem we now need to confront is that bank balance sheets tend to be asymmetric with respect to the time it takes to *reprice* or to adjust for changes in short-term interest rates.

Chapter 16 discussed the savings and loan industry's problems with interest-rate risk. S&Ls held almost 80 percent of their assets in 30-year, fixed-rate mortgages and funded these with short-term, flexible-rate savings, checking, and time deposits. When interest rates rose in the late 1970s and early 1980s, the costs of funds rose much faster than the interest rates charged on loans. You know the end of the story—many institutions failed and the federal government used taxpayer funds to bail out the industry.[2] The problem illustrated by the structural mismatch between the interest-rate sensitivity of S&L assets and liabilities remains relevant for our discussion of interest-rate risk. Changes in interest rates—particularly increases in interest rates—create the possibility of a positive spread narrowing or turning into a negative spread. Higher interest rates also decrease the market value of loans previously originated and securities previously purchased. These changes can cost a lender earnings and equity, and like the S&L debacle, may lead to an institution's demise. Given the increased volatility of interest rates over the last 30 years, managing interest-rate risk has become a fundamental managerial task. The chapter appendix discusses ways to readjust balance sheets to manage risk. Chapters 22 and 23 will discuss how various types of financial derivatives can also be used to manage interest rate- and other types of risk without restructuring bank balance sheets.

Income GAP Analysis

Despite its potentially serious consequences, interest-rate risk is both measurable and manageable. The first step in any risk management strategy is to identify which

---

[2]Of course, just the opposite occurred in the early 1990s. When interest rates fell, bank profitability rose, averting a bail-out of the commercial banking system from its deposit insurance crisis.

EXHIBIT 21-1
Balance Sheet for
First South-Western
Bank

ASSETS		LIABILITIES	
Reserves and cash	$100 million	Checkable deposits (fixed rate)	$50 million
Securities		Money Market deposit accounts	50 million
Less than 1 year	80 million	Savings deposits (fixed rate)	50 million
Greater than 1 year	20 million	CDs	
Commercial loans		Variable rate	50 million
Less than 1 year	20 million	Less than 1 year	70 million
Greater than 1 year	80 million	Greater than 1 year	30 million
Residential mortgages		Fed funds	20 million
Variable rate	50 million	Other borrowing	
Fixed rate	50 million	Less than 1 year	60 million
		Greater than 1 year	70 million
All other assets	100 million	Bank capital	50 million
Total assets	$500 million	*Total liabilities and capital*	$500 million

assets and liabilities are interest-rate sensitive over a particular time period. Take a moment to do that with the simplified balance sheet from First South-Western Bank in Exhibit 21-1. Which assets and liabilities will experience a change in their returns or costs over the next 12 months if interest rates increase?

On the asset side, interest-rate-sensitive assets (ISAs) will include those with maturities of less than 1 year and those with variable interest rates. In this example, we would include those securities ($80 million) and commercial loans ($20 million) with maturities of less than 1 year, as well as all variable-rate mortgages ($50 million). Summing these asset values together yields a sum of ISAs equal to $150 million. These represent the bank's assets, whose earnings will increase (decrease) if interest rates rise (fall). On the liability side, we again identify those instruments that will mature in less than 1 year or are otherwise characterized by variable interest rates. We will refer to these interest-rate-sensitive liabilities as ISLs. These include money market deposit accounts ($50 million), variable-rate CDs ($50 million), short-term (less than 1 year) CDs ($70 million), fed funds ($20 million), and other short-term (less than 1 year) borrowings ($60 million), for a total of $250 million. These represent the bank's ISLs, whose costs will increase (decrease) if interest rates rise (fall). To compute the **income GAP**—to distinguish it from the duration gap discussed in the appendix to this chapter—we use Equation 21-1. It directs us to subtract our interest-sensitive assets (ISAs) from our interest-rate-sensitive liabilities (ISLs) to compute the GAP.

Income GAP
The difference between a bank's interest-rate-sensitive assets and its interest-rate-sensitive liabilities.

(21-1)   GAP = ISAs – ISLs

where

    ISAs = interest-rate-sensitive assets

    ISLs = interest-rate-sensitive liabilities

First South-Western has *ISAs* of $150 million and *ISLs* of $250 million. So,

GAP = $150 million – $250 million
GAP = **–$100 million**

South-Western's interest-rate-sensitive liabilities (ISLs) are greater than its interest-rate-sensitive assets (ISAs), creating a negative income GAP. Most banks find themselves in a similar situation. This means that the cost of attracting the bank's liabilities (the interest rate on various kinds of deposits) will go up more rapidly than the interest-rate earnings received on its assets (loans and securities). It follows logically that if interest rates increase, bank income will fall. However, if interest rates fall, just the opposite would occur. With a negative income GAP and falling interest rates, our cost of funds will fall more quickly than the rates we receive on our assets. Bank income will rise because of the widening positive spread.

We should also consider the case of a bank characterized by a positive income GAP. This would happen whenever ISAs are greater than our ISLs. In this second case, an increase in interest rates would cause the rates on assets to rise faster than the rates on liabilities. This, too, would cause a bank's income to rise. However, if we have a positive GAP and falling interest rates, bank income would fall because of a narrowing spread. This is caused by the rates of return on loans and securities falling more quickly than the rates we pay to our depositors.

In the third possible case, when ISAs equal ISLs, the income GAP is zero. An increase or a decrease in interest rates causes the interest rates on liabilities and assets to move in tandem. Bank income remains unchanged by interest-rate movements. These relationships are summarized in Exhibit 21-2.

Income GAP analysis is widely used because it is simple, powerful, practical, and flexible. Our example covering a 1-year time period could easily be applied and adapted to other time periods. This type of assessment is called *maturity-bucket gap analysis*. Bank managers may be interested in examining the bank's GAP over the next week, month, quarter, year, or even over multiple periods. The key to tailoring this analysis is to identify which assets and liabilities are sensitive to interest-rate movements in the time periods—the relevant maturity buckets—one wishes to analyze. To perform a GAP analysis of First South-Western's balance sheet for next 3 months, we start by identifying ISLs and ISAs whose earnings or costs could change in the next 3 months (that level of detail is not shown in Exhibit 21-1). Similarly, if our asset-liability committee wants a GAP report for the next year broken down by quarters, it identifies which ISLs and ISAs are sensitive to interest-rate changes in each of the four quarters and then applies the analysis. As long as the bank maintains careful records regarding the maturity of its assets and liabilities, the bank's analysts will have little trouble applying Equation 21-1 to whatever time period or periods the asset-liability committee wishes to examine.

To further guide our asset-liability committee's strategic management, GAP analysis can be used to predict not only the effect of interest-rate movements on the *direction* of bank income over various time periods—increase, decrease, or no

Income GAP Analysis
An evaluation of the bank's exposure to interest-rate risk that involves subtracting the institution's interest-rate sensitive liabilities (ISLs) from its interest-rate sensitive assets (ISAs). The resulting "gap" describes the degree to which bank income will be affected by changes in interest rates.

	POSITIVE GAP INTEREST-RATE-SENSITIVE ASSETS ARE *GREATER THAN* INTEREST-RATE-SENSITIVE LIABILITIES (ISAs>ISLs)	NEGATIVE GAP INTEREST-RATE-SENSITIVE ASSETS ARE *LESS THAN* INTEREST-RATE-SENSITIVE LIABILITIES (ISAs<ISLs)	ZERO GAP INTEREST-RATE-SENSITIVE ASSETS ARE *EQUAL TO* INTEREST-RATE-SENSITIVE LIABILITIES (ISAs = ISLs)
Interest rates increase	Bank income rises	Bank income falls	Bank income is unchanged
Interest rates decrease	Bank income falls	Bank income rises	Bank income is unchanged

EXHIBIT 21-2
The Effects of Gap and Interest Rate Changes on Bank Income

change—it can also be used to estimate the *magnitude* of the change. What effect will a 3 percent increase in the interest rate have on First South-Western Bank's income? By using Equation 21-2, the solution is calculated easily. We take the GAP and multiply it by the change in the interest rate to solve for the change in bank income. *Caution:* Make sure you use the correct signs (positive or negative) for both the GAP and the change in the interest rate.

(21-2) $$\Delta BI = GAP \times \Delta i$$

where

$\quad \Delta BI$ = change in bank income

$\quad$ GAP = ISAs – ISLs from Equation 21-1

$\quad \Delta i$ = change in interest rates

First South-Western had a GAP of –$100 million. Assuming a 3 percent increase (+.03) in the interest rate we find:

$$\Delta BI = -\$100 \text{ million} \times .03$$
$$\Delta BI = -\$3 \text{ million}$$

In this case, the bank can expect its income to fall by $3 million because of its negative gap combined with the 3 percent rise in interest rates. If interest rates fell by 3 percent instead, the symbol in front of .03 would be a minus sign and our $3 million loss would become a $3 million gain.[3]

Managing Interest-Rate Risk in Response to Income GAP Analysis

Understanding the connections among GAP, interest-rate changes, and changes in bank income is essential for the effective management of interest-rate risk. In short, the larger the absolute value of the GAP, the greater the bank's exposure to interest-rate risk. Forecasts of future interest rates and the degree of risk the bank's asset-liability committee is willing to embrace determine how much risk it is willing to assume. If the bank expects interest rates to rise over the upcoming year, it should move the bank's balance sheet toward a positive GAP. The asset-liability committee should direct those in charge of liability management to seek

---

[3]In more sophisticated forms of income GAP analysis, analysts estimate the portion of long-term commercial loans and fixed-rate mortgages that are likely to be refinanced in the event of falling interest rates. Look back at the balance sheet in Exhibit 21-1. By examining historical data, an analyst might estimate that 10 percent of long-term (greater than 1 year) commercial loans ($8 million) and 20 percent of fixed-rate mortgages ($10 million) are repaid during the year. Thus, these assets should also be considered interest-rate sensitive. Combining this $18 million of interest-rate sensitive assets to the $150 million brings our adjusted total of interest-rate sensitive assets to $168 million. This same reasoning applies on the liability side. Assume that our analyst determines that 20 percent of First South-Western's checkable deposits ($10 million) and 50 percent of its savings deposits ($25 million) should be considered interest-rate sensitive. Summing these adjusted totals to our analysis brings our total to $285 million of interest-rate sensitive liabilities. Applying Equation 21-1 yields a recomputed GAP of $168 million—$285 million = –$117 million. If we use Equation 21-2 and assume a similar 3 percent increase in the interest rate, we find an expected decrease in income of $3.51 million (–$117 million × .03 = –$3.51 million). GAP analysis has become increasingly sophisticated over the last several decades. However, the basic equations here have not been fundamentally changed. Instead, improved estimation techniques and refinements in determining and matching the maturity of instruments to various time periods has improved the data used in the equations.

less interest-rate-sensitive liabilities. This could be done by locking in depositors with more fixed-rate, longer-term CDs. Engaging in fixed-rate, longer-term borrowing through the issuance of bonds might also be recommended. Similarly, managers would be discouraged from increasing the bank's holdings of short-term, variable-rate sources of funds like variable-rate CDs, fed funds borrowing, Eurodollar borrowing, and money market deposit accounts. The committee should also direct asset managers to pursue assets that are *more* interest-rate sensitive. This would lead to the origination of more variable-rate mortgages, more short-term commercial loans, as well as an increase in short-term security holdings.[4] Longer-term mortgages and securities could be sold to facilitate this move toward a positive gap.

If the committee expects interest rates to fall, the bank's balance sheet should be moved toward a negative GAP by doing the opposite of the previous process. Here, our committee would advocate holding *more* interest-rate-sensitive liabilities and *fewer* interest-rate-sensitive assets. The liability side would move toward the use of shorter-term and variable deposits, fed funds, and other borrowings. The asset side of the balance sheet would be biased toward fixed-rate, longer-term mortgages, loans, and securities. The absolute size of the GAP in either case will depend on the committee's degree of risk aversion. This process makes the management of interest-rate risk fairly straightforward. A bit of the real-world complexity can be appreciated by remembering that a bank's depositors and borrowers also rely on interest-rate forecasts. If interest rates rise, borrowers want fixed-rate mortgages and loans when banks are trying to move their balance sheets toward variable-rate and shorter-term loans. Thus, this adjustment process is easier to describe theoretically than it is to implement in practice. Fortunately, a number of new financial instruments have been created to hedge interest-rate risk that do not require the restructuring of the balance sheet. You will learn more about these in the next two chapters.

RECAP Interest-rate risk is the danger that changes in interest rates will adversely impact a lender's income or capital. GAP (or income GAP) analysis is a frequently used, powerful, and flexible technique for evaluating the impact of interest-rate changes on bank income. It is calculated by taking an institution's interest-rate sensitive assets (ISAs) minus its interest-rate sensitive liabilities (ISLs). The resulting "GAP" describes the degree to which the bank income will be affected by changes in interest rates. The higher the absolute value of the GAP, the greater the degree of interest-rate risk. Typically banks have negative GAPS. Thus, increased interest rates cause bank income to fall. One can predict the magnitude of change in bank income due to interest rate changes by multiplying the GAP by the percentage point change in the interest rate. If a bank's asset-liability committee believes interest rates will rise in the future, it should move the bank's balance sheet toward a positive GAP. Similarly, if the committee expects interest rates to fall, it should move the bank's balance sheet toward a negative GAP.

---

[4]Increased use of variable-rate mortgages is a great way to take advantage of expected increases in interest rates and manage interest-rate risk. The downside is that this also increases the bank's exposure to default risk. Higher future interest rates will increase the likelihood that some variable-rate mortgage borrowers will be unable to meet their higher debt payment obligations.

Assessing Liquidity Risk

Liquidity risk is the third and final risk discussed in this chapter. Liquidity risk is the danger that a financial institution will be required to make a payment when the intermediary has only long-term assets that cannot be converted to liquid funds quickly without a capital loss. As with credit and interest-rate risk, assessment and management of liquidity risk is primarily about the balance sheet.

Liquidity Ratio
A commonly used measure of liquidity and interest-rate risk. It is computed by taking the difference between a bank's short-term investments and liabilities and dividing them by the bank's assets.

The **liquidity ratio** is a tool frequently used by depository institutions to assess liquidity risk. It measures the difference between a bank's short-term investments and its short-term liabilities all divided by the bank's assets. This is similar to the income GAP measure shown in Equation 21-1 (GAP = ISAs − ISLs) divided by a bank's total assets.[5] We will allow our interest-rate-sensitive assets and liabilities to serve as proxies here for short-term assets and liabilities. This measure is summarized in Equation 21-3.

$$(21\text{-}3) \qquad \text{Liquidity Ratio} = \frac{\text{ISAs} - \text{ISLs}}{\text{total assets}}$$

where

ISAs = interest-rate-sensitive assets

ISLs = interest-rate-sensitive liabilities

We can compute a liquidity ratio using the data from the First South-Western Bank balance sheet shown in Exhibit 21-1. We can take our GAP measure (the numerator) of −$100 million and divide it by the total assets of $500 million.

$$(21\text{-}4) \qquad \text{liquidity ratio} = \frac{-\$100 \text{ million}}{\$500 \text{ million}}$$

$$\text{liquidity ratio} = -.20 \text{ or } -20\%$$

Liquidity ratios are typically less than plus or minus 10 percent. Had we computed this liquidity ratio earlier in the chapter, we could have suspected that First South-Western Bank was facing serious liquidity problems and substantial interest-rate risk.

Managing Liquidity Risk

The causes of illiquidity come from both sides of the balance sheet. On the asset side, we may run short of funds because we make more commercial or mortgage loans than expected, receive fewer loan and interest payments than expected, and/or because we hold securities that are less marketable than anticipated at their purchase. On the liability side, liquidity problems can emerge when bank customers withdraw more checkable, savings, and/or money market deposits than expected. Fortunately, federal deposit insurance and the Fed's lender of last resort actions have curbed the bank runs of earlier times, averting the substantial liquidity problems that accompanied them. Regardless of which side of the balance sheet causes the problem, the result is the same—a shortage of cash and/or reserves.

---

[5]There are a multitude of various refinements to this technique. Many analysts include checking and savings deposits (or some fraction thereof) in the computation of short-term liabilities and, thus, the liquidity ratio. We have excluded them here for ease of exposition and clarity. This measure can also be referred to as a GAP ratio and used as a measure of interest-rate risk.

One additional cause of illiquidity involves off-balance sheet use of unused credit lines and letters of credit. Banks offer credit cards and home equity lines of credit to consumers and letters and lines of credit to commercial customers. These individuals and businesses use these lines and letters to manage their own liquidity needs. Despite their absence from bank balance sheets, these untapped credit sources can be a real source of liquidity risk. Imagine a business cycle downturn that causes increased unemployment and decreased sales revenue. To meet other debt payment obligations, individual and business customers may draw on their unused lines of credit. This sudden and, possibly, large demand for cash may leave banks scrambling for liquidity. Traditional measures of liquidity risk, such as the liquidity ratio, do not account for this very real danger. Prudent managers monitor the balance sheet and off-balance sheet activities for risk exposure.

Like most causes of illiquidity, the solutions can come from either side of the balance sheet. If the problem is expected to be a temporary, bankers generally turn to the liability side of the balance sheet for a solution. This might involve raising the advertised rates on CDs, savings accounts, or money market accounts to attract depositor funds. If this is insufficient, the bank may turn to other forms of borrowing, such as repurchase agreements, the fed funds market, the Eurodollar market, and/or the Fed's discount window. If the liquidity problem is perceived to be a longer-term problem, the bank's managers reluctantly turn to the asset side of the balance sheet. On the asset side, funds are raised by selling securities, commercial loans, mortgage loans, and other assets. Sales of near-reserves like Treasury bills are often tapped for liquidity needs. The increased ability to securitize mortgage, automobile, educational, and even credit card loans has greatly increased the liquidity of these types of loans. Not only do these sales reduce liquidity risk, they also reduce default risk. Nevertheless, managers are reluctant to asset sales because they decrease the institution's size and are likely to reduce future earnings.

The assessment and management of credit, interest-rate, and liquidity risk are essential to enhancing a bank's earnings and its market value. The increased volatility of interest rates and financial asset prices over the past 30 years, the increasingly competitive markets for lending, the growing international connections among markets, and the relentless development of computing, communications, and statistical analysis have made effective risk management more technically sophisticated, rapid, and important to an FI's bottom line. The core of the management strategies posited in this chapter involve the restructuring of the bank balance sheet to manage risk. The next two chapters explain a number of new instruments that allow the management of risks without restructuring the balance sheet.

RECAP Liquidity risk is the danger that a financial institution will be required to make a payment when the intermediary has only long-term assets that cannot be converted to liquid funds quickly without a capital loss. The liquidity ratio is frequently used to measure liquidity risk exposure. It involves taking the difference between a bank's short-term assets and liabilities and dividing this by its total assets. Illiquidity can be managed on both sides of the balance sheet. On the liability side, the bank can take on additional liabilities by attracting various kinds of deposits or by tapping other sources of borrowing. On the asset side, banks can sell loans or securities to raise cash. Generally, banks prefer to avoid asset sales because it makes the institution smaller and may lower future earnings. Recent changes in the financial system have increased the sophistication, speed, and importance of effective risk management.

LOOKING OUT: *Managing Risk in a Global Economy: Are Other Countries Up to the Task?*

The credit, interest rate, and liquidity risk assessment tools are powerful and practical. Given the greater degree of global interdependence and greater volatility in interest rates, risk management has become an increasingly sophisticated, holistic, and important part of a financial institution's management. The quote from Federal Reserve Governor Laurence H. Meyer that opens this chapter comes from a story in the September 1, 2000 *American Banker* by Rob Garver. The author notes that Mr. Meyer was speaking in Bangkok, Thailand and was raising concerns about the lack of adequate management of risk in many banking systems around the world.

Mr. Garver notes, "Without naming any countries, Mr. Meyer cited lax regulators, government-directed lending, and the lack of managerial accountability as current impediments to effective risk management. Coupled with 'credit cultures' in which lending decisions are based on relationships rather than an assessment of the borrower's ability to repay, such conditions create danger not only for the lending institutions themselves but also for regional economies." To address these problems requires not only the admonishment from respected financial experts, but also institutional change. That is exactly what the Bank for International Settlements (BIS) and the International Monetary Fund (IMF) have been doing.

These institutions have been encouraging improvements in global risk management by requiring participating members to use reporting methods and capital standards that allow for increased transparency and international comparisons. In the wake of the 1997 Asian crisis, the agencies have also pushed for improved domestic government regulation and supervision of banking systems throughout the world. By illuminating and regulating risk exposure in these ways, the BIS and IMF ensure that financial risk can be more readily assessed, managed, and regulated. These institutional changes, as well as widespread adoption of tested risk management techniques, will lessen, but not eliminate, the risks of global financial intermediation. As Mr. Meyer says at the opening of this chapter, "Risk matters. Whether or not it is temporarily ignored, it will eventually come out." We couldn't have said it better ourselves.

SOURCES: Rob Garver, "In Brief: Many Nations' Banks Seen Unequal to Risk," *American Banker*, September 1, 2000, vol. 168, No. 166, p. 20.

Summary of Major Points

- To generate earnings and to increase market value, banks must maintain a positive spread between the rate of return on their assets and the interest-rate cost of their liabilities. This endeavor requires careful assessment and management of credit, interest-rate, and liquidity risk.

- Before any loan is granted or security purchased, credit analysts must assess a borrower's Five Cs of credit: capacity, character, capital, collateral, and conditions. Capacity refers to a borrower's ability to repay a loan. Character refers to a borrower's competency and willingness to repay. Capital is the amount of equity a borrower owns over and above the amount financed. Collateral describes the assets used to secure a loan. Conditions involve changes in economic conditions that may make it more difficult for a borrower to pay back a loan.

- Effective credit or default risk management requires four steps. Managers must (1) engage in accurate discernment and pricing, (2) observe borrower behavior, (3) establish long-term banking relationships, and (4) actively manage their portfolios. In addition, off-balance sheet exposure to credit risk should not be ignored.

- Interest-rate risk is the danger that changes in interest rates will adversely impact a lender's income or capital. Threats to a bank's income can be assessed using GAP analysis. GAP (or income GAP) analysis involves subtracting an institution's interest-rate sensitive liabilities (ISLs) from its interest-rate sensitive assets (ISAs). The higher the absolute value of the GAP, the greater the degree of interest-rate risk. Generally, increases in interest rates cause decreases in bank income because of negative income gaps. The magnitude of these changes in bank income can be computed by multiplying the GAP by the percentage-point change in the interest rate.

- If bank managers believe interest rates will rise, they should steer the bank's balance sheet toward a positive GAP to increase future bank income. Similarly, if bank managers believe interest rates will fall, they should steer the bank's balance sheet toward a negative GAP.

- Liquidity risk is the danger that a financial institution will be required to make a payment when the intermediary has only long-term assets that cannot be converted to liquid funds quickly without a capital loss. This risk can be measured using the liquidity ratio.

- Liquidity risk can be managed on the liability side of the balance sheet by attracting various kinds of deposits or by tapping other sources of borrowing. On the asset side, liquidity problems can be addressed by selling loans or securities to raise cash.

- (Appendix) The effect of interest-rate movements on capital can be measured using duration, and/or duration gap analysis. These include price risk—the hazard that *increases* in interest rates will lower the present value of asset holdings—and reinvestment risk—the chance that *decreasing* interest rates will lower the returns on current and future investment holdings.

- (Appendix) Duration analysis measures the responsiveness of a bank's assets, liabilities, and net worth (in chronological terms) to changes in interest rates. Securities with longer maturities and less frequent payment streams are characterized by higher duration and greater interest-rate risk.

- (Appendix) Duration gap analysis allows the assessment of both the direction and magnitude of interest-rate changes on bank capital given a particular duration gap. An increase in interest rates and positive duration gap will cause bank capital to fall; an increase in interest rates with a negative duration gap causes bank capital to rise. The reverse is also true. A decrease in interest rates and positive duration gap will cause bank capital to rise; an increase in interest rates with a negative duration gap will cause bank capital to fall. By matching asset and liability durations—reducing the duration gap to zero—banks insulate themselves from interest rate movements that affect their capital.

Key Terms

125s	Five Cs of Credit	Negative Spread
Compensating Balances	Housing-to-Income Ratio	Positive Spread
Credit Rationing	Income GAP	Price Risk (Appendix)
Credit Report	Income GAP Analysis	Reinvestment Risk (Appendix)
Credit Reporting Agencies	Insolvent	Risk-Based Pricing
Credit Score	Liquidity Ratio	Securitization
Debt-to-Income Ratio	Loan Commitments	
Duration Analysis (Appendix)	Loan Participations	
Duration GAP Analysis (Appendix)	Loan-to-Value Ratio	

Review Questions

1. What are the main objectives of the asset-liability committee and how does it pursue these goals?

2. Define default risk. What are the Five Cs of credit? List and explain each. What three ratios can be used to assess two of these five elements of default risk?

3. Why are 125s so popular if they create negative equity and increase the risk of default?

4. What is the difference between collateral and capital?

5. List and explain the four steps of effective credit-risk management.

6. Explain the differences among a credit report, a credit score, and credit rationing.

7. How can loan participations and securitization be used to reduce default risk?

8. What are the two problems that cause bank managers to be concerned about higher interest rates?

9. What are the two ways higher interest rates increase adverse selection?

10. If a bank is characterized by a positive *income* gap and interest rates rise, what will happen? What will happen if the bank is characterized by a negative *income* gap and interest rates rise? How would your answer to these questions change if we assumed that interest rates were falling? How can banks insulate themselves from the threat posed by volatile interest rates on bank income?

11. What is liquidity risk? How can it be managed on the liability side of the balance sheet?

What can be done on the asset side of the balance sheet to ease illiquidity pressures?

12. (Appendix) What is the difference between price risk and reinvestment risk? How are these two concepts related to duration analysis?

13. (Appendix) If a bank is characterized by a positive *duration* gap and interest rates rise, what will happen? What will happen if the bank is characterized by a negative *duration* gap and interest rates rise? How would your answer to these questions change if we assumed that interest rates were falling? How can banks insulate themselves from the threat posed by volatile interest rates on capital?

Analytical Questions

14. Discuss the costs and benefits of credit scoring. Is anyone hurt by credit scoring?

Use the following balance sheet for First ITP Bank to answer questions 15–17.

ASSETS		LIABILITIES	
Reserves and cash	$50 million	Checkable deposits (fixed rate)	$25 million
Securities		Money Market deposit accounts	25 million
Less than 1 year	40 million	Savings deposits (fixed rate)	25 million
Greater than 1 year	10 million	CDs	
Commercial loans		Variable rate	25 million
Less than 1 year	10 million	Less than 1 year	35 million
Greater than 1 year	40 million	Greater than 1 year	15 million
Residential mortgages		Fed funds	10 million
Variable rate	25 million	Other borrowing	
Fixed rate	25 million	Less than 1 year	30 million
		Greater than 1 year	35 million
All other assets	50 million	Bank capital	25 million
Total assets	$250 million	*Total liabilities and capital*	$250 million

15. Using data from the ITP balance sheet, what is its current income GAP? Given this answer, what will happen to bank income if interest rates fall?

16. Given your answer to the first part of question 15 and assuming a 5 percentage-point increase in interest rates, by what magnitude will bank income change?

17. What is the liquidity ratio for First ITP Bank? Is this unusually high? How do you know?

18. Assume that First ITP bank customers have unexpectedly increased their use of previ-

ously unused credit card balances and home equity lines of credit. What can the bank do to meet this unexpected and unplanned rush for liquidity?

19. (Appendix) Suppose that First ITP Bank's research staff has determined that the average duration of the bank's assets equals 1.9 years and the average duration of its liabilities equals 3.4 years. What would be its duration gap?

20. (Appendix) Given your answer to question 19 and assuming that interest rates increase from 8 percent to 10 percent, what would happen to First ITP Bank's net worth?

Internet Exercise

Go to **http://minneapolisfed.org/** and find the link or do a search to find the *Fed Gazette*. Once there, do a search on "interest-rate risk" and locate the article entitled "Interest Rate Risk: What Is It, Why Banks Would Want It, and How to Evaluate It" from the July 2000 edition of the magazine. The article may still be available at **http://minneapolisfed. org/pubs/fedgaz/00-07/banking. html**.

Answer the following questions based on your reading of this article. Why is the Fed interested in interest rate risk (IRR)? What do the authors mean when they say "Think of IRR as blood pressure for banks"? Why do banks refuse to eliminate IRR? What happened to IRR in the commercial banking industry from 1998 to 1999? (Hint: Be careful in analyzing both the diagrams and their discussion.)

Suggested Readings

Are credit scores useful for measuring relative levels of risk by mortgage loan applicants and existing mortgage holders? Robert B. Avery, Raphael W. Bostic, Paul S. Calem, and Glenn B. Canner think so. In their "Credit Risk, Credit Scoring, and the Performance of Home Mortgages" (*Federal Reserve Bulletin*, July 1996 pp. 621–64), they provide a comprehensive overview of the connections among credit risk, credit scoring, and loan performance. Despite an overemphasis on mortgage loan denials rather than differences in mortgage pricing, their work provides valuable insights into how credit scores can be used to predict the likelihood of a borrower's delinquency and/or default. In contrast, the January 2001 issue of *Consumer Reports*, "New Assault on your Credit Rating" (**http://www.consumerreports.org**) suggests that the increased use of credit scoring and lenders' refusal to share credit scores leaves borrowers at an unfair disadvantage. (Credit scores have recently become available to consumers.) The article explains how the "tiering" of credit quality scores affects the interest rates charged and pro-

vides tips for consumers to protect themselves from subprime lenders.

Methods to manage interest-rate risk have continued to evolve over the last 20 years. In this chapter and its appendix, we highlight two of the most common techniques—GAP and duration analysis. Steven Davidson, in a January 1996 *America's Community Banker* article entitled, "Measuring Interest Rate Risk" explains a new method for measuring interest-rate risk in investment securities portfolios. The method, risk point analysis, assesses how changes in the shape of the yield curve affect the value of particular portfolios as well as instruments within them.

In the May 2000 (No. 00-01) issue of the *FDIC's Bank Trends*, Allen Puwalski explains the reasons for and implication of "Increasing Interest Rate Risk at Community Banks and Thrifts." He argues that during the 1990s, the average maturity of bank and thrift assets has been rising. At the same time, these lenders have increasingly relied on volatile liabilities. Together these trends threaten both bank income and market values.

Appendix 21–A

Risk Assessment with Duration and Duration GAP Analysis

Income GAP analysis is a powerful technique for examining the effects of interest-rate changes on a bank's income. But what if we want to know the effect of interest-rate changes on the value of a bank's assets, liabilities, and net worth? There are two possible threats to a bank's portfolio when interest rates change: price risk and reinvestment risk. **Price risk** is the threat that an increase in interest rates will reduce the market value of our bond and loan portfolio. **Reinvestment risk** is the threat that falling interest rates will reduce future rates of return on our reinvested cash flows. These risks move in opposite directions. Higher interest rates will decrease the present value (the price) of security holdings. However, the higher rates will allow us to earn a higher return on those funds we reinvest. Similarly, lower inter-

Price Risk
The threat that an increase in interest rates will reduce the market value of security holdings.

Reinvestment Risk
The threat that falling interest rates will reduce future rates of return on current and future cash flows.

est rates will increase present values (our asset prices) but cause returns on current and future investments to be lower.

Bond prices and interest rates move in opposite directions. The price of long bonds will fall by more than the price of short-term bonds given the same increase in interest rates. Banks also face this price risk problem. If interest rates rise, the present value (and market value) of the loans and securities in their portfolios will fall. However, not all of the assets will fall by the same degree. If interest rates increase, the present value of their loans with long outstanding maturities is going to decrease more rapidly than their short-term securities or loans. Equation 21-5 illustrates this relationship. This equation was first introduced as Equation 5-6 with slightly different notation.[6] We use this slightly more complicated notation format here to explain the concept of duration.

$$(21\text{-}5) \qquad\qquad \text{present value} = \sum_{t=1}^{n} \frac{CP_t}{(1 + i)^t}$$

where,

CP_t = the future stream of cash payments
(principal and/or interest) made at time t

i = interest rate

n = number of years until the loan or security matures

The interest rate is on the bottom of this equation, so when interest rates rise, present value must fall. Similarly, when interest rates fall, present value must rise.

Two examples of present value calculations are illustrated in the top and bottom parts of columns 3 and 4 in Exhibit 21A-1.[7] Here we compare two securities with face values of $10,000 and a coupon rate of 10 percent. They differ only by their maturities. The security in the top half of the table matures in 5 years while the security in the bottom part of the table matures in 10 years. Column 3 shows that both have a present value of $10,000 when prevailing interest rates remain at 10 percent. However, column 4 shows that if interest rates rise to 20 percent, the 5-year note falls in value to $4,605.67 and the 10-year note falls even further to $4,234.60, a difference of $371.07. When we remember that securities trade at their present value (adjusting for risk and preferred habitats), we can see that the market or resale values of these instruments are going to fall as well. If the changes in interest rates cause the asset side of the balance sheet to fall by more than the bank's net worth—its level of capital—the bank will become insolvent. Thus, interest-rate risk is a threat not only to bank income, as we explained with GAP analysis, it also threatens the net worth and solvency of an institution.

Given these implications, we can see why bankers needed to develop a measure of how responsive the value of a bank's assets and liabilities is to changes in interest rates. The basic measure is called **duration analysis** and is illustrated in column 6 of

Duration Analysis
A measure of interest-rate risk that seeks to measure how responsive the value of a bank's assets, liabilities, and net worth are to changes in interest rates. Duration is reported in chronological terms.

---

[6]Equation 5-6 was introduced in this form $P = C_1/(1 + i)^1 + C_2/(1 + i)^2 + \ldots + C_n/(1 + i)^n + F/(1 + i)^n$ where: P = the price (present value) of the bond, C = the coupon payment on the bond (C_1 in year 1, C_2 in year 2, etc.), F = the face or par value of the bond, i = the interest rate, and n = the number of years to maturity (on a 5-year bond, n = 5). Here we have generalized the separate coupon payment (C) and face value of the bond (F) into one variable called future cash payments (CP). We also use t instead of n to denote the passage of time.

[7]We engage is a minor distortion of reality here to make two points. Under the normal circumstances of an upward sloping yield curve, the interest rate for the 10-year note would be higher than the rate for the 5-year note. Here, we have imposed a flat yield curve to illustrate the following: (1) how increases in interest rates adversely affect the value of securities that differ only by their maturities, and (2) how duration differs for these same two securities. Our distortion plays no material role in these illustrations, but it does make the comparison easier to examine.

One can see by comparing the top and bottom totals of column 3 that notes that differ only by their maturity have the same present value (they both equal $10,000). An examination of the top and bottom totals of column 4 shows how an increase in interest rates (from 10% to 20%) have a larger adverse effect on the 10-year security than on the 5-year security. (The 5-year note falls in value to $4,605.67 while the 10-year note falls to $4,234.60.) Similarly, by comparing the top and bottom totals of column 6, we can see that the longer-term security has a significantly higher duration (6.75902) than does the shorter-term security (4.16987).

DETAIL FOR A $10,000 NOTE WITH A COUPON RATE OF 10 PERCENT AND A 5-YEAR MATURITY

1	2	3	4	5	6
Year	Annual Cash Payments of Interest and Principal in $	Present Value (PV) of Cash Payments (i=10%) in $	Present Value (PV) of Cash Payments (i=20%) in $	Weights (share of total present value =PV/10,000) in Percentage Terms	Duration: Weighted Maturity (cln1*cln 3) /10,000) in years
1	$1000	$909.09	$833.33	9.091%	0.09091
2	1000	826.45	694.44	8.264	0.16529
3	1000	751.31	578.70	7.513	0.22539
4	1000	683.01	482.25	6.830	0.27321
5	1000	620.92	401.88	6.209	0.31046
5	10,000	6,209.21	1,615.06	62.092	3.10461
Totals	$15,000	$10,000.00	$4,605.67	100.000	4.16987

DETAIL FOR A $10,000 NOTE WITH A COUPON RATE OF 10 PERCENT AND A 10-YEAR MATURITY

1	$1,000	$909.09	$833.33	9.091%	0.09091
2	1,000	826.45	694.44	8.264	0.16529
3	1,000	751.31	578.70	7.513	0.22539
4	1,000	683.01	482.25	6.830	0.27321
5	1,000	620.92	401.88	6.209	0.31046
6	1,000	564.47	334.90	5.645	0.33868
7	1,000	513.16	279.08	5.132	0.35921
8	1,000	466.51	232.57	4.665	0.37321
9	1,000	424.10	193.81	4.241	0.38169
10	1,000	385.54	161.51	3.855	0.38554
10	10,000	3,855.43	42.13	38.554	3.85543
Totals	$20,000	$10,000.00	$4,234.60	100.000%	6.75902
Diff			–$371.07		+2.58916

EXHIBIT 21A-1
Present Value, Interest Rates, and Duration

Exhibit 21A-1. Its calculation requires a bit of algebra, but bankers and financial analysts get paid for more than their golf game. Duration can be computed for an individual asset or liability. To compute the duration for an entire portfolio requires using a weighted average of all loans and securities in a portfolio. A common form for computing duration—called *Macaulay duration* after its inventor—is shown in Equation 21-6. It states:

$$(21\text{-}6) \qquad duration = \sum_{t=1}^{n} \frac{CP_t(t)}{(1 + i)^t} \Bigg/ \sum_{t=1}^{n} \frac{CP_t}{(1 + i)^t}$$

where

CP_t = the future stream of cash payments (principal and/or interest) made at time t

(t) multiplies the present value in each period by the number of each year

i = interest rate

n = number of years until the loan or security matures

At first glance, the equation appears complex, but it can be programmed easily into a spreadsheet and explained with an example like that shown in columns 5 and 6 of Exhibit 21A-1. The numerator (the top part) of this equation is the present value formula from Equation 21-5 multiplied by each year. The denominator (the bottom half of Equation 21-6) is Equation 21-5. This adjustment by (t) and the denominator adjusts our numerator for two things. First, the (t) adjusts for the share each payment contributes to the total present value. We illustrate this in column 5 of Exhibit 21A-1. Second, the denominator converts the dollar figures into a measure of years. This is the weighted average maturity of the *present value* of the cash flows: duration. We illustrate this in column 6 of Exhibit 21A-1. The note with the 10-year maturity has a higher duration—6.75002 years compared to the 4.16987 years of the 5-year security. Securities or loans that make less frequent periodic payments (compared to those with more frequent payments) are also characterized by higher durations.

Understanding what duration for an individual security means requires us to reconsider price and reinvestment risk. The duration of the 5-year note shown in Exhibit 21A-1, is 4.16987. This means that after 4.16987 years, this note will have yielded a 10 percent return, *regardless of changes in the interest rate*. After this point in time, any increase in the interest rate, which normally would decrease the security's present value, will be offset by the increased investment returns on the security's past and future cash payments. The reduction in value caused by an increase in the interest rate—the price risk—is offset by an increase in value from previous and future reinvested cash payments—the reinvestment risk—made by the security. While the 5-year note reaches this point after only 4.16987 years, the 10-year security fails to reach this point until 6.75902 years have expired. The longer-term security, thus, presents its holder with more interest-rate risk than does the shorter term security. The same phenomenon would apply if our object of analysis were a loan instead of a note.

Applying Duration to Portfolios and Capital Management

The preceding examples involve computations for individual assets. By computing the duration for each instrument on our balance sheet and multiplying it by its share of the balance sheet's total asset value, we can arrive at a weighted-average duration measure for our assets and our liabilities.[8] By subtracting the weighted average of our liability duration from the weighted average of our asset duration, we arrive at a new measure called **duration GAP analysis,** described in Equation 21-7[9].

Duration GAP Analysis
A type of duration analysis that involves subtracting the duration of a bank's interest-rate-sensitive assets from its interest-rate-sensitive liabilities.

(21-7)   duration GAP = DURAs – DURLs

where

DURAs = the average duration of our assets

DURLs = the average duration of our liabilities

Our financial analysis department has undertaken this process for the balance sheet of First South-Western Bank introduced in Exhibit 21-1. The analysis yielded:

---

[8]Note: We are talking about making a weighted average of duration, which is itself a weighted average maturity of our cash flow's present value.

[9]This equation could be restated as duration gap = duration of assets – (market value of liabilities/ market value of assets) × duration of liabilities. To make your life easier, we allow you to subtract the average durations. This avoids the extra step of (1) dividing the market value of the assets by the market value of the liabilities and then (2) multiplying this fraction by the liability duration.

DURAs = 3.2

DURLs = 1.4

Applying Equation 21-7 yields:

$$\text{duration GAP} = 3.2 - 1.4$$
$$\text{duration GAP} = 1.8$$

When duration GAP is positive, as in this example—the typical case for banks—it means that the market value of the bank's assets is more sensitive to changes in interest rates then are its liabilities. You can see this because of the higher average duration on assets than on liabilities. If duration GAP is positive and if interest rates rise, asset values will fall more rapidly than liability values. This is a problem! Since net worth, or capital, equals assets minus liabilities, a positive duration GAP and rising interest rates mean that bank capital will fall. This was the problem with S&Ls during the early 1980s. In contrast, a positive GAP coupled with falling interest rates will cause bank capital to increase. The larger the duration GAP, the stronger these tendencies.

In the opposite case, when a financial institution is characterized by a negative duration GAP, rising interest rates will decrease bank capital as the value of assets falls more quickly than that of liabilities. Similarly, a negative duration GAP combined with falling rates causes bank capital to swell. If a bank insulates itself from interest-rate risk by matching the duration of its assets and liabilities, changes in interest rates will have no effect on bank capital. The relationships among duration GAP, interest-rate movements, and bank capital are summarized in Exhibit 21A-2.

Like we did with income GAP analysis, duration GAP analysis can also be used to discern not only the *direction* bank capital moves when interest rates change, it too can be used to estimate the *magnitude* of the change. Equation 21-8 explains how we can take the duration GAP computed in Equation 21-7 and multiply it by the percentage change in the interest rate to determine how much the bank's net worth—its capital—will change due to a given change in the interest rate.

(21-8) $$\%\Delta\text{NW} \approx -\text{duration GAP} \times \frac{\Delta i}{1 + i}$$

where

$\%\Delta \text{NW}$ = the percent change in the bank's net worth

i = interest rate

	POSITIVE DURATION GAP INTEREST-RATE SENSITIVE ASSETS ARE *GREATER THAN* INTEREST-RATE SENSITIVE LIABILITIES (DURAs >DURLs)	NEGATIVE DURATION GAP INTEREST-RATE SENSITIVE ASSETS ARE *LESS THAN* INTEREST-RATE SENSITIVE LIABILITIES (DURAs <DURLs)	ZERO DURATION GAP INTEREST-RATE SENSITIVE ASSETS ARE *EQUAL TO* INTEREST-RATE SENSITIVE LIABILITIES (DURAs =DURLs)
Interest rates increase	Bank capital falls	Bank capital rises	Bank capital is unchanged
Interest rate decrease	Bank capital rises	Bank capital falls	Bank capital is unchanged

EXHIBIT 21A-2

The Effects of Duration GAP and Interest-Rate Changes on Bank Capital

In Equation 21-7 we computed a positive duration GAP of 1.8. Let us also assume that interest rates are expected to increase from 10 percent to 20 percent.

(21-9) $\%\Delta NW = -1.8 \times 10/1.1$
                                 $\%\Delta NW = -16.364\%$

This means that the bank's net worth, its capital, will fall by 16.364 percent. To convert this into dollar terms, we take the –16.364 percent and multiply it by First South-Western's Bank's level of assets ($500 million) (Exhibit 21-1).

$$-.16364 \times \$500 \text{ million} = -\$81,818,181.82$$

This yields a loss of about $81.8 million. Given that First South-Western only had $50 million worth of capital to start with, this hypothetical doubling of interest rates would lead to the bank's insolvency, just like increases in the interest rates in the late 1970s and early 1980s led to the demise of many savings and loans. Thus, if management expects a sharp rise in future interest rates, it is time for First South-Western to take aggressive action.

Managing Interest-Rate Risk in Response to Duration GAP Analysis

If First South-Western's asset-liability committee thought that interest rates were going to rise, it could have attempted to reduce its positive duration GAP and thereby reduce its interest-rate risk. This could be done by *increasing* the average duration of its liabilities (DURLs) or *decreasing* the average duration of its assets (DURAs). How might that be done? A lengthening of the liability portfolio could be done by using more long-term CDs and borrowings rather than relying on short-term fed funds or money market deposit accounts as sources of funds. Asset duration could be shortened by holding a larger share of short-term and/or variable rate assets. In short, by matching the bank's asset duration to its liability duration, banks are able to insulate themselves from movements in interest rates that positively or negatively affect their capital positions. As we will see in the next two chapters, there are other instruments and techniques that can be used to avert this type of calamity without restructuring a bank's balance sheet.

RECAP Changes in interest rates threaten not only bank income as described with income GAP analysis, they also threaten the value of a bank's assets, liabilities, and capital. Increases in interest rates pose a price risk by lowering the present value of asset holdings. Similarly, falling interest rates pose a reinvestment risk by lowering the returns received on current and future investments. These types of interest-rate risk can be assessed using duration analysis and duration GAP analysis. Duration analysis measures the responsiveness of a bank's assets, liabilities, and net worth (in chronological terms) to changes in interest rates. We find that securities with longer maturities and less frequent payment streams are characterized by higher duration and interest-rate risk. Duration GAP analysis allows us to assess both the direction and magnitude of interest rate changes on bank capital given a particular duration GAP. In the usual case, a positive duration GAP combined with an increase (decrease) in interest rates causes bank capital to fall (rise). A negative duration GAP combined with an increase (decrease) in interest rates causes bank capital to rise (fall). By matching asset and liability durations—reducing the duration GAP to zero—banks can insulate themselves from interest rate movements that affect their capital.

chapter

Forward, Futures, and Options Agreements

Learning Objectives *After reading this chapter, you should know:*

- The difference between a forward contract and a futures contract
- The scope and nature of organized financial futures and options markets
- The relationship between spot and futures prices
- The difference between put and call options
- The reasons for the astounding growth of financial forward, futures, and options agreements in recent years

❝ ❞
Never let the future disturb you. You will meet it, if you have to, with the same weapons of reason which today arm you against the present.
—Marcus Aurelius

A Single Solution

It is 5:10 P.M. on Friday, the last day of a month in late 2001. The CEO's meeting with his staff has run later than usual, and a sense of uneasiness pervades the room. Doz-All, a newly emerging conglomerate, is involved in diversified financial and manufacturing areas. The mortgage banking division has committed to make $10 million in loans at 8 percent to be funded in 60 days; $25 million in bonds issued 10 years ago for start-up money is maturing in 3 months, and the company plans to pay off the existing bondholders by issuing new bonds. The newly formed international division is converting $20 million to Japanese yen to invest in Japanese securities over the next few months. The stock adviser points out that although the corporation has a diversified portfolio, there is a general fear that the market may be heading down.

All of these situations expose the corporation to risks—the risks that interest rates (and, hence, bond prices), stock prices, or foreign exchange rates will move in an unexpected direction, causing the corporation to experience a loss. The senior vice president appears tired. She cannot help but perceive that the risks associated with everyday business seem to have escalated in recent years.

In the past two decades, financial prices, such as interest rates, stock prices, and exchange rates, have become more volatile. This greater volatility has created greater risks.[1] The chief financial officer (CFO) is a young business school graduate whom senior management has come to rely on. He assures them that there are ways to deal with the increased risk although doing so will cost money. In this case, however, his recommendations are the source of the tension felt in the room. To reduce Doz-All's risk exposure, the CFO is recommending that the corporation use the financial forward, futures, or options markets. In days long past, futures and options on agricultural products and commodities were considered to be highly risky. Forward agreements, which could be costly, had other drawbacks. Could the new financial forward, futures, and options markets that have emerged in the past 25 years actually be used to reduce or manage the risks inherent in everyday business?

In this chapter, we explore financial forward, futures, and options contracts. We shall see that risk-averse financial intermediaries and corporations increasingly use these markets in their everyday business for just this purpose—to reduce the risks associated with price fluctuations. The adage "necessity is the mother of invention" aptly applies because financial forward, futures, and options markets have experienced incredible growth in the past two decades in response to increased price volatility.

Forward Transactions

Financial Forward Agreements
Transactions in which the terms, including price, are completed today for a transaction that will occur in the future.

Financial forward agreements can be used to hedge the risks associated with price changes of any financial instrument. Although virtually all financial prices have become more volatile in recent decades, forward agreements are primarily used to deal with the risks created by price fluctuations in foreign exchange markets. Thus, foreign exchange forward markets are the focus of this section.

The exchange rate is the price of one currency in terms of another. As we have seen in earlier chapters, *exchange rate risk* is the risk that changes in the exchange rate will cause someone to experience unexpected losses. Exchange rate risk is

---

[1]For example, small changes in interest rates can lead to large changes in the prices or value of long-term, fixed-rate assets such as bonds or mortgages.

greater when exchange rates are unpredictable and unstable. Exchange rates have become much more volatile since the major industrialized countries adopted the flexible exchange rate system in 1973.[2] Also, as international trade has increased and as financial markets have become more globalized, the demand for foreign financial instruments has soared. This has led to the increased trading of foreign currencies with more volatile prices and a dramatic increase in exchange rate risk for market participants. These participants have found ways to **hedge** this greater exchange rate risk through the development of forward markets.

Hedge
Reduced risk.

In Chapter 8, we discussed how exchange rates are determined by supply and demand in the foreign exchange market. In that chapter, we were referring to spot rates—that is, the exchange rates of foreign currency for immediate delivery. In financial forward agreements, the terms (including prices and amounts) are completed today for a transaction that will occur on a specified date in the future. Financial intermediaries, acting as brokers or agents, can link up two parties in a forward transaction. As noted earlier, the most common type of *financial* forward agreements is in foreign currencies (foreign exchange). These agreements have been highly developed by large commercial banks to provide services to their customers who will need or receive foreign currencies on a future date. In this case, the bank is one of the two parties in the forward transaction. Commercial banks also sometimes hold large quantities of foreign currencies and, hence, can use forward markets to hedge their own exchange rate risk.

Large banks have many customers that operate on a global basis. These customers may know that they will receive and/or need foreign currencies on a future date. The foreign currencies are used by the bank's customers to purchase or to pay for goods, services, and financial instruments. For instance, perhaps one U.S. company will be liquidating its holding of French stocks in 6 months to pay off a maturing domestic bond issue while another U.S. company plans to increase its investment in Europe. The first company will be receiving euros; the latter company will need euros. Another customer may be an importer, an exporter, or a securities firm that sells domestic and foreign financial instruments globally. Large banks not only buy and sell foreign exchange at spot rates for present delivery, but they also buy and sell foreign exchange for future delivery at a **forward rate.** The forward rate for a foreign currency will gravitate toward the *expected* future spot exchange rate for that currency. The forward rate is affected by the same factors that affect spot rates, as discussed in Chapter 8. These factors, which affect the supply and demand for foreign exchange, include expected inflation and interest rate differentials between the two counties, the economic outlook in both countries, and domestic and foreign monetary and fiscal policies. The forward rate can be used as a market-based forecast of the future spot rate.

Forward Rate
The price today for a delivery on a future date.

A bank buys foreign exchange forward agreements from some customers and sells foreign exchange forward agreements to others. The bank engages in these forward agreements to earn profits and to provide a service to its customers who wish to hedge the exchange rate risk. The bank's profit comes from buying the currency at one price—the bid price—and selling the currency at a slightly higher price—the asked price. Predating flexible exchange rates, large banks had a long history of providing exchange facilities for foreign currencies as a service to their

---

[2]With the fixed exchange rate system of the Bretton Woods Accord, under normal circumstances, there was no exchange rate risk. When situations were not normal—when there was a currency crisis—there could be substantial exchange rate risk if a country was seriously considering changing the value of its currency.

customers. Forward agreements arranged by large banks were a natural outgrowth of this service under the post-1973 flexible exchange rate system.

A typical foreign exchange forward agreement works as follows: The forward agreement is a contract with a bank to purchase or sell on a future date a specific amount of foreign exchange at a forward rate (exchange rate) determined today.

For example, assume a customer of Citibank is to receive 1 million euros in 6 months and another customer will need 1 million euros in 6 months. Both customers know the present spot rate but are worried that future exchange rate changes could reduce their profits. Citibank can enter into a forward agreement with each that will hedge this risk, and the agreements will also earn a small profit for Citibank. Just as in spot markets, Citibank buys forward contracts at one rate and sells forward contracts at a slightly higher rate. The difference between the bid and asked prices represents the profit margin on the transaction. If the forward rate for Citibank to buy euros from a customer with a delivery date in 6 months is 1 euro = $1.109, then 1 million euros can be sold to the bank by a customer for $1,109,000 (1,000,000 × 1 euro = 1,000,000 × $1.109).[3] Thus, 1 euro = $1.109 is the bid price. A customer that will be receiving 1 million euros in 6 months may enter into this transaction to reduce the risk that the euro will depreciate and that she will receive fewer than $1,109,000 in exchange for the 1 million euros. For example, if the euro depreciated to 1 euro = $1.108, then without the forward agreement, the customer would be able to sell the euro for only $1,108,000 instead of $1,109,000.

Assume that the forward rate (exchange rate) for Citibank to sell euros with a delivery date in 6 months is 1 euro = $1.11. This is the forward asked price. A customer that will be needing 1 million euros in 6 months may enter into a forward agreement in order to reduce exchange rate risk. The 1 million euros will cost the customer $1,110,000 (1,000,000 × 1 euro = 1,000,000 × $1.11) in 6 months. A customer needing 1,000,000 euros in 6 months may enter into this transaction to reduce the risk that the euro will appreciate and that he will have to pay more than $1,110,000 for 1 million euros. For example, without the forward agreement, if the euro appreciated to 1 euro = $1.112, then 1 million euros would cost the customer $1,112,000 instead of $1,110,000.

The profit to Citibank in the forward markets is, as noted previously, just as it is in spot markets: Citibank buys at one forward rate (the bid price) and sells at a slightly higher forward rate (the asked price). The bank makes a profit on the difference between the bid and asked prices multiplied by the number of euros bought and sold. In this case, the profit on the forward transactions in 1 million euros is $1,000 ($1,110,000 − $1,109,000). Exhibit 22-1 highlights these relationships.

EXHIBIT 22-1
Citibank Engages in
Forward Agreements

6-Month Forward Rates Today	
BID (BUY) PRICE	ASKED (SELL) PRICE
1 euro = $1.109	1 euro = $1.11
1,000,000 euro = $1,109,000	1,000,000 euro = $1,110,000
Profit to Citibank = $1,000 ($1,110,000 − $1,109,000)	

[3]The exchange rate can also be expressed as $1 = .90 euro.

CRACKING THE CODE: *Foreign Exchange Spot and Forward Rate Quotations*

You can find foreign exchange quotations in *The Wall Street Journal*. Spot rates are reported for about 55 countries while forward rates are reported for only the major foreign currencies including the British pound, the Canadian dollar, the the Japanese yen, and the Swiss franc. For both spot and forward exchange rates, the rate that is reported is the mid-range rate between the bid and the asked prices. The name of the currency and the country it is from appear in the first column. The second and third columns give the mid-range rates for the current and previous days in terms of U.S. dollar per unit of foreign currency. The fourth and fifth columns give the mid-range rates in terms of foreign currency per U.S. dollar.

For example, the column for the 6-month forward rate for the British pound is highlighted. On May 31, 2001, the mid-range of the 6-month forward bid and asked rates was 1 British pound = $1.4093. The pound had depreciated slightly from the rate of 1 British pound = $1.4188 the previous day, May 30, 2001. Columns four and five are merely the reciprocals of columns two and three. Thus, on May 31, the forward rate was $1 = .7096 British pounds (1 British pound/1.4093 = $1.4093/1.4093 = $1). Likewise, on May 30, the forward rate was $1 = .7048 (1 British pound/1.4188 = $1.4188/1.4188 = $1). Note that $1 is worth more on May 31 than on May 30 and, hence, has appreciated slightly.

Country	U.S. $. EQUIV.		CURRENCY PER U.S. $	
	Thu	Wed	Thu	Wed
Britain (Pound)	1.4177	1.4271	.7054	.7007
1-month forward	1.4164	1.4257	.7060	.7014
3-months forward	1.4134	1.4228	.7075	.7028
6-months, forward	1.4093	1.4188	.7096	.7048

Source: From Currency Trading, WSJ, June 1, 2001, p. C9.

The 1-month, 3-month, and 6-month forward rates for major foreign currencies such as the British pound, the Canadian dollar, the Japanese yen, and the Swiss franc are reported daily in *The Wall Street Journal* along with the spot exchange rates. The accompanying Cracking the Code feature discusses how to read the spot and forward exchange rates reported by the *Journal* on June 1, 2001. Note that for both spot and forward rates, only one exchange rate is reported. This is the mid-range rate between the bid and the asked prices. The spot and forward rates for the euro are also reported.[4]

If the bid and asked spot exchange rates 6 months from now are equal to the current forward rates, the customers both buying and selling forward agreements would be no better or no worse off financially. In addition, they may have slept more soundly at night because of the reduced exchange rate risk. However, if in 6 months the actual bid and asked spot exchange rates are more or less than the forward rates today, one of the customers will be worse off and one will be better off than without the forward agreement, depending on how rates diverged from what was expected.

---

[4]The euro is the single currency that 12 countries of the European Union adopted on January 1, 2002.

Neither customer knows who will lose and who will gain without the forward agreement, but both customers can reduce the uncertainty of the future exchange rate by engaging in a forward agreement with Citibank today. Thus, for reducing the possibility of a loss, they are both giving up the opportunity to gain. However, as noted earlier, the forward rate will converge to the market's general expectation of the future spot rate. Thus, market participants will give up the opportunity to gain only if there were unexpected changes in the future spot rate.

An example may help to clarify. As depicted in Exhibit 22-2, assume the current bid and asked spot rates in 6 months are 1 euro = $1.099 and 1 euro = $1.1. This is different from the respective forward rates of 1 euro = $1.109 and 1 euro = $1.11 of 6 months previous. Without the forward agreement, Customer A, receiving the 1 million euros, would be able to exchange them for only $1,099,000, or $10,000 less than the $1,109,000 the euro could be exchanged for with the forward agreement. This customer would be better off with the forward agreement and worse off without it. Without the forward agreement, Customer B, needing or buying the 1,000,000 euros, would pay only $1,100,000, or $10,000 less than the $1,110,000 the euro would cost if she entered into the forward agreement. This customer would be worse off with the forward agreement and better off without it. However, since the future rate is uncertain, with the forward agreement both have hedged the risk of being worse off.

Any market participant that holds supplies of foreign currencies is exposed to exchange rate risk. This includes financial and nonfinancial firms that operate in many countries with many different currencies. Since the forward agreements arranged between banks and their customers are often not perfect offsetting matches, the bank can be exposed to an exchange rate risk. For example, if one customer is to receive 1 million euros in 6 months and another needs 900,000 euros in 6 months, the bank can still arrange the forward agreements with both, but is then

EXHIBIT 22-2
The Mechanics of Spot and Forward Markets

	CURRENT SPOT RATES	FORWARD RATES 6 MONTHS PREVIOUS
Bid	1 euro = $1,099	1 euro = $1.109
Asked	1 euro = $1.100	1 euro = $1.110

No forward agreement (exchanges at current spot rates):

Customer A receives 1,000,000 euros and exchanges them for $1,099,000
Customer B needs 1,000,000 euros and pays $1,100,000 for them

With forward agreement entered into 6 months earlier:

Customer A receives 1,000,000 euros and exchanges them for $1,109,000
Customer B needs 1,000,000 euros and exchanges $1,110,000 for them

Reconciling:

With no forward agreement, Customer A receives $10,000 less ($1,099,000 versus $1,109,000) and Customer B pays $10,000 less ($1,100,000 versus $1,110,000). Customer A is worse off and Customer B is better off.

With the forward agreement, Customer A receives $10,000 more ($1,109,000 versus $1,099,000) and Customer B pays $10,000 more ($1,110,000 versus $1,100,000). Customer A is better off and Customer B is worse off.

subject to an exchange rate risk on the difference between what the receiving customer will receive and what the customer who needs euros will need. In this case, the amount of exposure to the bank is for 100,000 euros (1 million euros received less 900,000 euros needed). If the euro depreciates from 1 euro = $1.11 to 1 euro = $1.10, then 100,000 euros would fall in value $1,000 from $111,000 to $110,000. Likewise, if the euro had appreciated from 1 euro = $1.11 to 1 euro = $1.12, then 100,000 euros would increase in value $1,000 from $111,000 to $112,000.

Forward agreements can also be used to speculate about future exchange rates. The speculator may be a customer of the bank or the bank itself. If the speculator thought the future spot price in 6 months would be lower than the current 6-month forward rate, he would enter into a forward agreement to sell foreign exchange at the higher forward rate. If the speculator was correct, he could enter the spot market in 6 months and purchase the foreign exchange at a lower price than what he sold it for in the forward market. Likewise, if the speculator thought the future spot price of the currency would be greater than the current forward rate, he would enter into a forward agreement to buy the currency in 6 months. If correct, the speculator buys the currency in the forward market at a lower price than what it can be resold for in the spot market. Indeed, it is the buying and selling by speculators that causes the forward rate to converge to the market's expectation of future spot prices.

Limitations of Forward Agreements

As we have seen, forward transactions can reduce the risks of future price changes, which reduce profit. As with most things in life, though, appearances may not reveal the whole picture. The forward market in foreign currencies described previously works well because large banks have developed the market. For other financial instruments such as stocks and bonds, forward markets are not as highly developed. In this case, there are two general problems with arranging forward agreements:

1. Finding partners may be difficult; the transactions costs may be high and outweigh the possible gain. Finding partners who want the exact amount of the financial instrument on the exact date can be difficult at best.[5]
2. One party to the agreement may default—that is, not keep its part of the agreement. The party who is likely to default is the one that is worse off down the road by entering into the forward agreement earlier. Getting compliance may require legal action and may be costly, if not impossible.[6]

Although volatile prices of financial instruments other than foreign exchange may lead to large losses that could be reduced with forward agreements, the forward markets are not highly developed. Consequently, the costs of finding a partner and then enforcing the forward contract may be prohibitively high. But all hope is not lost! To minimize the costs and risks involved with arranging forward transactions, standardized agreements called **futures contracts** have been developed for many types of financial instruments including stocks, T-bills, notes, bonds, and foreign currencies.

Futures Contracts
Standardized agreements in agricultural and commodity markets to trade a fixed amount of the instrument on specific dates in the future at a price determined today.

---

[5]Note that in the case of foreign exchange forward markets, large banks are actually the partners to forward transactions—namely, the bank buys currency from one customer and resells all or part of it to another in two separate forward contracts between each customer and the bank. The point is that the transactions are not between the two customers.

[6]The risk of default is greatly reduced when one of the partners to the forward transaction is a large bank, as in the case of the foreign exchange forward markets.

RECAP Forward contracts are agreements to buy or sell something at a price determined today for delivery on a later date. Forward agreements between individual market participants are arranged by intermediaries. In financial markets, forward contracts in the most widely traded currencies have been established by large commercial banks. In addition to buying and selling foreign currencies at spot prices, the banks also buy and sell the major currencies at forward rates. In this case, the bank is an actual partner in the transaction. When there are not exact offsetting transactions, the bank has some exposure to exchange rate risk. Foreign currency forward agreements can be used to hedge exchange rate risk or to speculate about future currency values. Forward markets are not highly developed for financial instruments other than foreign currencies.

Financial Futures

Because agricultural and commodity markets historically have experienced large price fluctuations, futures markets evolved more than a century ago. In the case of agricultural products, demand is relatively stable and price fluctuations are related to weather: bad weather greatly reduces supply and leads to higher prices, and vice versa. Prices of commodities such as oil, copper, and gold fluctuate because of large changes in supply or demand.

As noted earlier, prices of financial securities, stocks, and foreign currencies have become unstable during the past 25 years. Consequently, *financial futures markets*, which trade financial futures, appeared and are now used by most major financial institutions and other large corporations to manage risk. **Financial futures** are contracts in which two parties agree to trade standardized quantities of financial instruments on standardized future dates, according to the terms (including the price) that are determined today. Financial futures can be used to reduce the risk associated with future price changes of financial instruments.

Futures contracts differ from forward agreements in that the amounts and delivery dates are standardized, whereas for forward agreements they are not. Forward agreements for specific amounts and dates are negotiated with commercial banks and other financial intermediaries. Futures contracts with standardized amounts and dates are traded on the floors of organized exchanges for a small fee.

Financial futures markets trade a wide variety of contracts in underlying financial instruments such as government securities (Treasury bills, notes, and bonds), stock market indexes, Eurodollars, and numerous foreign currencies.[7] The contracts are traded on major exchanges around the world. For example, financial futures are traded on the Chicago Board of Trade, the Financial Instrument Exchange Division of the New York Cotton Exchange, the International Monetary Market of the Chicago Mercantile Exchange, the London International Financial Futures Exchange, the Sydney Futures Exchange, and the Singapore International Monetary Exchange. Futures markets for various currencies and U.S. government securities are available virtually 24 hours a day, somewhere in the world. A Closer Look lists the most actively traded financial futures, the exchanges that trade them, and the size of the contracts that are traded.

Financial Futures
Standardized futures contracts that trade financial instruments at a future date according to terms (including the price) determined today.

http://www.cme.com/
Provides information on the trading of futures and options at the Chicago Mercantile Exchange.

---

[7]As we saw in Chapter 3, Eurodollars are dollar-dominated deposits held abroad.

Futures, Exchanges that Trade Financial Futures, Minimum Amounts, and Open Interest: Consider for a moment the many types of futures markets that exist: grains and oil seeds (including corn, oats, soybeans, wheat, barley, flaxseed, and canola); livestock and meat (including cattle, hogs, and pork bellies); food and fibers (including cocoa, coffee, sugar, cotton, and orange juice); metals and petroleum (including copper, gold, platinum, palladium, silver, crude oil, heating oil, gasoline, natural gas, brent crude, and gas oil); interest rates (including 10-year, 5-year, and 2-year U.S. Treasury notes, 30-day federal funds, Eurodollars, 1-month LIBOR, Treasury bills, and Treasury bonds); currencies (including Australian dollars, British pounds, Canadian dollars, German marks, Japanese yen, Mexican pesos, and Swiss francs); and indexes (including Dow Jones Industrial, Mini Value Line, Municipal Bonds, Nasdaq 100, Nikkei 225, Russell 2000, S&P Composite, S&P Midcap 400, S&P Mini, and Value Line).[8]

Grain and commodities futures have been around for some 100 years. Financial futures including interest rate, currencies, and stock index futures are a relatively recent innovation (during the last 25 years) that has experienced tremendous growth.

The accompanying table shows some of the major financial futures, the contract size, the futures exchange, and the total open interest (number of outstanding contracts) as of May 18, 2001.[9]

TYPE OF FUTURE	CONTRACT SIZE	EXCHANGE[10] AT WHICH TRADING OCCURS	OPEN INTEREST MAY 18, 2001
Interest Rates			
10-year agency notes	$100,000	CBOT	52,272
10-year U.S. Treasury notes	$100,000	CBOT	666,360
5-year U.S. Treasury notes	$100,000	CBOT	445,395
2-year U.S. Treasury notes	$200,000	CBOT	62,754
30-day federal funds	$5 million	CBOT	100,095
Eurodollar	$1 million	CME	4,333,138
LIBOR—1 month	$3 million	CME	22,364
U.S. Treasury bills	$1 million	CME	2,472
U.S. Treasury bonds	$100,000	CBOT	512,641
Currencies			
Australian dollar	$100,000 Australian	CME	26,591
British pound	£62,500 British	CME	39,856
Canadian dollar	$100,000 Canadian	CME	63,752
Euro	125,000 euro	CME	89,103
Japanese yen	12.5 million yen	CME	95,455
Mexican peso	500,000 pesos	CME	29,862
Swiss franc	125,000 Swiss francs	CME	51,812
Index Futures			
Dow Jones Industrial	10 × Index	CBOT	35,004
Municipal Bonds	1,000 × Index	CBOT	12,340
Nasdaq 100	100 × Index	CME	51,450
Nikkei 225	500 × Index	CME	22,573
Russell 2000	500 × Index	CME	20,776
S&P Composite	250 × Index	CME	491,544
S&P Midcap 400	500 × Index	CME	15,518
S&P Mini	50 × Index	CME	123,474

[8]Our list includes both financial and other futures because we believe you may find them interesting. Since these are information items only, we are not defining all of the terms.

[9]SOURCE: *Barron's*, May 21, 2001, pp. MW64 and MW65.

[10]Exchanges: CBOT (Chicago Board of Trade); CME (Chicago Mercantile Exchange)

A futures contract trades a fixed amount of the instrument for delivery on specific dates in the future. For example, Treasury bond futures trade in contracts of $100,000 face value for delivery in March, June, September, and December, over the course of the following 2 years. There are eight prices today for delivery of $100,000 of Treasury bonds on the eight future dates. Likewise, Treasury bill futures, which trade in contract amounts of $1 million, are also available for delivery on the same eight dates at prices set today. Note that the futures contract can be bought or sold on any given day between now and the future delivery date. The predicament for the buyers and sellers is that the spot price on the delivery date may be different from the futures price agreed upon today.

The seller of a September $1 million T-bill future has the right and obligation to deliver $1 million in T-bills in September for a price set today. The purchaser of the $1 million September T-bill future has the right and obligation to buy $1 million in T-bills in September at a price set today. Hence, both parties know the terms of a transaction that will occur in September, a point in time in the future, and the risk to either party of a price change between now and then is eliminated.[11]

If the price of T-bills rises between now and September, the seller has given up an opportunity to make a profit because she agreed to sell at the lower futures price established today. If the spot price falls in September, the buyer has given up the right to purchase the securities at the lower price in the spot market because he agreed to the higher futures price today. Without the futures contract, however, either party could lose if the price changes in an adverse direction. Without the agreement, the seller would be worse off if the price falls, and the buyer would be worse off if the price goes up.

Let's consider a simple numerical example. Assume the futures price is $96,000 for the delivery of $100,000 of Treasury bonds next December. The seller agrees to deliver and the buyer agrees to pay this much. (Make sure you are clear that December is the delivery date of the securities and not the maturity date of the securities, which may be several years hence.) When December actually arrives, if the spot price is $97,000, the seller still must make good on the contract for $96,000, even though he could sell them for $97,000 in the spot market. The buyer still pays $96,000 for the Treasury bond contract, even though she would have had to pay $97,000 for the same contract in the spot market. In this example, the seller is worse off by $1,000, and the buyer is better off by $1,000. (Remember that the securities are not usually physically delivered but, rather, a financial settlement is made between the buyer and the seller.)

However, if the spot price is $95,000, when December arrives, the seller gets to sell at $96,000, even though he would get only $95,000 in the spot market. The buyer has to pay $96,000 even though she could have paid $95,000 to buy in the spot market. The seller is better off by $1,000 and the buyer is worse off by $1,000. Again, a financial settlement is usually made between the buyer and the seller.

The point is that at the time of the agreement, neither party knows what the spot price will be on the future date. Both were willing to accept the known outcome as opposed to an uncertain future spot price even though after the fact one

---

[11]Note that the buyer rarely takes physical possession of the securities—or any futures contract instrument for that matter—on the delivery date. Likewise, the seller rarely delivers. If the price changes, the buyer or seller merely settles up financially for any changes in value, usually by executing an opposing transaction. For example, if Suzanne purchases a futures contract, rather than taking delivery on the delivery date, she can sell a futures contract involving the same asset for the same delivery date. The sale effectively cancels out the purchase. Or, if she had sold a futures contract, she can purchase a futures contract with the same delivery date, effectively canceling out the sale. Most futures contracts are settled in this manner: Purchases in the futures market are reversed by sales in the futures market; sales in the futures market are reversed by purchases in the futures market. This fact does not alter the analysis, however.

CRACKING THE CODE: *Futures Prices*

Midway through the "Money and Investing" section of *The Wall Street Journal,* you will find a table entitled "Futures Prices." Part of the "Interest Rate Futures" section of this table for May 21, 2001, is reproduced here. We can crack the code to futures prices by looking at the highlighted row starting on the left with June under "Treasury Bills (CME)."

TREASURY BILLS (CME)–$1 mil.; pts. of 100%

	Open	High	Low	Settle	Chg	Yield	Chg	Open Interest
June	96.62	96.62	96.59	96.59	–.03	3.41	+.03	2,472

Est vol 55; vol Thu 8; open int 2,472 +1.

SOURCE: *Wall Street Journal,* May 21, 2001, p. C12.

The 96.62 in the second column means that on May 13, the agreed-upon opening price for June delivery of Treasury bills was 96.62 percent of the face value of the contract. The low price for that day (fourth column) was 96.59. The high for the day (third column) was 96.62 percent, and the settle for the day (fifth column) was 96.59. The "–.03" in the sixth column indicates that there was a negative .03 change from the previous day. To verify this, we would have to check the preceding day's newspaper to see if the settle price was 96.62. Remember that T-bills sell at a discount, which is reflected in the price being less than 100 percent of the contract amount. For the T-bill contract, the contract amount (face value) is $1 million. The seventh column ("Yield") indicates the percentage discount on the settle price. In this case, the settle price of 96.59 means that the contract sells at a 3.41 discount (100 – 96.59 = 3.41). Therefore, a T-bill futures contract sells at a 3.41 percent discount. The open interest is the number of contracts outstanding for the month of June—in this case, 2,472.

To give some meaning to these numbers, let's assume we purchased a T-bill futures for June delivery. We pay a small brokerage fee (on May 18, 2001) for the right and obligation to purchase $1 million face value in T-bills (of 90-day maturity) in June 2001 for a price that is based on a discount of 3.41 percent. To find this price (*P*), we solve for *P* using the following formula: $3.41 = [(\$1,000,000 - P)/\$1,000,000] \times (360/90)$.[a] In this case, the price is $991,475 because $3.41 = [(\$1,000,000 - \$991,475)/\$1,000,000] \times (360/90)$. In June, if the spot price of $1 million in T-bills is greater than $991,475 plus the small brokerage fee, we win. If it's less, we lose!

[a]The 360 approximates the number of days in a year while the 90 represents the number of days until the T-bill matures.

could have been better off without the agreement. Because the contracts are standardized with respect to type (90-day T-bills, 10-year Treasury notes, and the like) and quantity ($1 million and $100,000 contract sizes), and because volume is large, brokerage fees for buying and selling futures are relatively small.

So far, we have been discussing futures in which the parties are hedging, or reducing, the risk of a price change in the future. Futures markets can also be used for speculation. Consider the case in which the ABC Government Securities Firm believes that the spot price of T-bills is going to be much higher in September than today's futures price. If ABC holds this belief firmly, it can put its money behind the belief and buy a futures contract. If ABC is correct, it can resell the futures contract at the higher spot price on the delivery date. Contrarily, if the firm believes the price will be lower, it can sell a futures contract to make its profit.[12] Futures prices are reported daily in most major newspapers. Now would be a good time to read the accompanying Cracking the Code feature on futures prices.

Because financial futures are written only in standardized contract amounts for delivery on a few specific dates, a perfect offsetting transaction between the buyer

---

[12]In case you want to check, the answer is that if ABC's guess is right, it can go into the spot market in September and purchase the T-bills at the lower price for immediate delivery to the buyer of the future. The difference between the futures price and what ABC pays in the spot market is its profit—ABC is good at counting this.

and seller, as in forward markets, is rarely made. For instance, suppose a bank has loans that will be repaid next August and suspects that interest rates are heading down. The bank may have to reinvest the funds at a lower rate. The bank can buy a September T-bill futures contract today to hedge this risk. If interest rates do move down, the funds will be reinvested in August at a lower rate, but the reduction in earnings from the level the bank is currently receiving will be at least (partially) offset by the profit made on the September futures contract. (Recall that T-bills are sold at a discount, and, as with other securities, if interest rates go down, the price of the newly issued T-bills goes up.) Even though the standardized contracts do not provide an exact match (either by amount or by date), they do provide an offsetting transaction that reduces risk. Because a perfect match need not be found, the high transactions costs of finding a unique trading partner, as in forward agreements, are greatly reduced.

The futures price is set by bidding and offering in an auction-like setting on the floor of the exchange. Each financial instrument that is traded usually has its own **pit** (trading area on the floor) where authorized brokers gather to buy and sell for their customers. Bid and asked prices (to buy or sell) are called out until the brokers become aware of the prices in the market. The most favorable transactions (from the point of view of both the buyers and sellers) are consummated. Once an agreement is struck in the pit, the transaction becomes depersonalized, and the agents of the buyer and seller never meet again for that transaction. Instead, a **clearinghouse**, operated by the exchange, takes on the responsibility of enforcing the contract.

The futures contract is a standardized agreement to make a trade at a later date, and both the buyer and seller rely on the clearinghouse to execute the transaction. Specifically, the seller looks to the clearinghouse to deliver, and the buyer looks to the clearinghouse to pay the amount due on the delivery date. In exchange for the small brokerage fee, the clearinghouse of the organized exchange guarantees that the terms of the agreement will be met, and thus, the default risk associated with a forward transaction is greatly reduced. To facilitate this guarantee, the exchange requires buyers and sellers of futures to put up a **performance bond,** called a *margin requirement,* set by the exchange. Brokers are required to collect margin requirements from their customers before they make any futures purchases or sales. Note that the performance bond or margin is required of both the seller and the buyer and that the brokerage fee plus the margin requirements are relatively small compared to the dollar value of the futures agreement. An example of how financial futures can be used to hedge interest rate risk is given in A Closer Look.

Pit
The trading area on the floor of an organized exchange where authorized brokers gather to buy and sell for their customers.

Clearinghouse
The part of an organized exchange that takes on the responsibility of enforcing the contract after an agreement is made.

Performance Bond
A bond required by an organized exchange from both the buyer and the seller of a futures agreement to ensure that both parties abide by the agreement.

LHT Inc. Enters the Futures Market: Let's consider an example in which financial futures are used to hedge. Assume that LHT Inc. issued bonds 10 years ago and those bonds will mature in a year. When the bonds come due, LHT Inc. will not be in a position to pay off the debt. Instead, LHT will issue new bonds (borrow) to raise the funds to pay off the owners of the original bonds.[13] Let's further assume that LHT fears interest rates could rise over the next year, causing the new bonds to be issued at a higher interest rate. If this scenario materializes, the firm will have to make higher interest payments on the new bonds, which will cut sharply into profits. But something as important as profits need not be left to the vicissitudes of unknown interest rates 1 year from now! LHT can protect itself against an undesirable increase in rates by selling a T-bill future today. The T-bill futures agreement will oblige LHT to deliver so many T-bills on a later date, say, in 1 year, at a price set today. If the interest rate does rise over the course of the year, as LHT expects, the spot price of the T-bills will fall. Remember the

---

[13]Borrowing to repay maturing debt is called rolling over and is actually quite common.

inverse relationship between the price of securities and the interest rate that we discussed in Chapter 5. LHT can buy the T-bills in the spot market at the lower price for delivery to the purchaser of the futures contract, who pays the higher price agreed upon earlier. If the interest rate does rise, the loss due to issuing new bonds at a higher interest rate is offset by the profit LHT makes on the T-bill futures contract.

But what happens if LHT Inc. is wrong about the direction of the interest rate over the next year and the interest rate falls or, equivalently, the price of T-bills rises? LHT takes a loss on the T-bill future because it buys the T-bills in the spot market at the higher price to deliver to the buyer of the futures contract for the lower price previously agreed upon. However, LHT Inc. is not really worse off. The loss in the futures market is offset by the savings on the new bonds the corporation issues at a lower rate because interest rates have fallen.

As we have seen, the securities usually are not actually delivered physically. Instead, the buyer or seller of the futures agreement merely pays any price difference between the spot price and the futures price. In this case, if the interest rate does go up, LHT receives a payment from the seller of the T-bill futures agreement that offsets the loss incurred by having to issue bonds at the higher interest rate. If the interest rate goes down, LHT makes a payment to the seller of the T-bill futures agreement, but issues the new bonds at the lower interest rate.

LHT Inc. has successfully used the futures market to reduce the risk of losses if interest rates go up while sacrificing the possibility of gains if interest rates go down—a trade that the firm may be happy to make. Can you explain what happens if interest rates stay the same over the course of the next year?[14] Think about it before checking the answer in the footnote.

In summary, financial futures markets have experienced spectacular growth in the past 25 years because the financial world has become a much more volatile place and financial futures can be used to reduce risks associated with this volatility. Because interest rate swings are larger, the prices of government securities (or the value of any fixed-rate instrument) oscillate more rapidly and over a broader range. Stock prices now fluctuate over a wider range, and, as we saw in Chapter 8, flexible exchange rates have increased the movement of currency prices while foreign trade in goods, services, and securities has escalated sharply. Futures markets may be used to hedge all of these risks. We now turn to how the futures price is determined.

RECAP Financial futures are standardized contracts in which two parties agree to trade financial instruments at a future date according to terms, including the price, that are determined today. Financial futures are different from forward agreements because the quantities and delivery dates are standardized and, thus, the brokerage fees are relatively small. Financial futures markets exist for government securities, stock market indexes, Eurodollars, and foreign currencies. Both the buyer and the seller have obligations and rights. Financial futures can be used to hedge the risk of future changes in prices or to speculate. Organized exchanges trade the standardized contracts.

Determining the Futures Price

Financial futures are traded each day on exchanges around the world. The exchange delivers, or accepts for delivery, the futures contract at the specified future time and place at a price agreed upon today. The buyer or seller accepts the risk of a price

---

[14]LHT Inc. buys T-bills in the spot market to deliver to the purchaser of the futures contract at the same price for which it sold the contract. Aside from a small brokerage fee to purchase the futures contract (that can be thought of as an insurance premium), LHT Inc. is no worse off.

change of the contract and agrees to pay off any financial losses or to receive any financial gains. There are several different futures prices depending on the expiration date of the futures contract. In this section, we pose the question, "How are those prices determined?" We hope that buzzers and alarms are going off in your head and that your immediate response is "supply and demand." Of course, you are right! But, in this case, it may prove beneficial to look more closely at what determines the supply and demand for financial futures and, hence, their prices.

First, the most important thing to point out is that the futures price and the spot price are highly correlated—that is, they move up and down together. This is not accidental, but rather due to actions of individuals called **arbitrageurs** who seek a riskless profit.

Consider what happens if a futures contract for Treasury bonds to be delivered in 3 months is much higher than the present spot price. An arbitrageur could purchase the Treasury bonds in the spot market while selling a futures contract. She could hold the bonds purchased in the spot market for delivery at the later date to fulfill the futures contract. Granted, she would incur some **carrying costs** in holding the Treasury bonds (or the gold or whatever), but as long as the futures price was greater than the current spot price plus the carrying costs, she would make a riskless profit. (Carrying costs generally consist of the interest costs for the use of the funds to purchase the securities, less the interest earned on the securities while the arbitrageur is holding them, plus other transactions costs of the exchange.) On the other hand, if the futures price was below the spot price plus carrying costs, arbitrageurs (who owned some of the securities) would buy futures, driving the futures price up, and sell in the spot market, driving the spot price down. Can you explain how a riskless profit would be made?[15]

If such an opportunity for riskless profit opens up, arbitrageurs move in and purchase in the spot market (driving up the price) and sell in the futures market (driving down the price) and vice versa. As the delivery date of the futures contract comes closer, the length of time in which funds are borrowed to establish the position is reduced. Therefore, as the delivery date nears, the carrying costs are reduced and the futures price approaches the spot price. Arbitrage continues until the futures price is bid up (down) to the spot price plus carrying costs—a phenomenon called **convergence**. Thus, on the last day before the expiration date, the futures price is practically equal to the spot price because the carrying costs are negligible since only 1 day is left. Because futures prices are highly correlated with spot prices and because convergence occurs, futures prices are ultimately determined by the spot prices of the underlying contract instruments. Now would be a good time to look at A Closer Look, which discusses stock index futures and the October 1987 crash of the stock market.

Arbitrageurs
Traders who make riskless profits by buying in one market and reselling in another market.

Carrying Costs
Interest costs for funds used to purchase the security underlying a futures contract plus any transactions costs.

Convergence
The phenomenon in which the futures price is bid up or down to the spot price plus carrying costs.

A Closer Look

Stock Index Futures and the '87 Crash: A stock market index such as the Dow Jones Industrial Average is an index that measures price changes of a market basket of stocks included in the index. *Stock index futures* are contracts that give the purchaser (seller) the right and obligation to purchase (sell) a multiple of the value of the index at some specified date in the future at a price determined today. Stock index futures are available for several indexes of stock market activity, and the futures contract calls for the delivery of the cash value of a multiple of a particular stock index.

Perhaps the two most prominent stock index futures are the futures contracts for the S&P 500 and the NYSE Composite Indexes. In both cases, the contract size is $500 times the index on the delivery date. The financial futures contracts are available for the quarterly dates (during March, June, September, and December) over the next 2 years. For example,

---

[15]Likewise, forward prices cannot diverge from spot prices by more than the carrying costs.

if Jamal purchases a December contract for the S&P 500, this gives him the right and obligation to receive on the delivery date $500 times the value of the S&P 500 stock index on that date. The price for the future delivery is negotiated today. Let's say Jamal negotiates a price today of $275,000, which he will pay on the delivery date. Consider the two cases for the delivery date on which the S&P Index is (1) 525 or (2) 575. If it is 525, the seller pays $262,500 (500 × $525) but receives $275,000 from Jamal. If it is 575, Jamal pays $275,000 but receives $287,500 (500 × $575). In the first case, the seller makes a profit. In the second case, Jamal makes a profit. If $500 times the value of the index is greater than the futures price, the buyer of the futures makes a profit. If it is less, the seller makes a profit.

Just as in all futures, the spot and futures prices move up and down together. In the case of stock index futures, arbitrage prevents the futures price from deviating a tremendous amount from the spot price. For instance, if the futures price is far above the spot price, an arbitrageur could make a riskless profit by buying a market basket of stocks that made up the index while simultaneously selling a futures contract. As long as the futures price exceeded the spot price plus the cost of carrying the inventory of stocks, the arbitrageur could make a riskless profit. But by doing so, she would be increasing the demand for stocks in the spot market (pushing up the index) and increasing the supply of futures contracts (pushing down their price). As in other futures markets, arbitrage would keep the spot and futures prices in close alignment with one another.

But wouldn't it be difficult to recognize every opportunity for arbitrage and go into the spot market to purchase the stocks that make up the stock index? After all, in the case of the S&P 500, one would have to purchase (or sell) 500 different stocks. Not even the largest of most small investors can do this. As we saw in Chapter 11, however, the advent of sophisticated computer technology has allowed brokerage houses and institutional investors (such as mutual funds and pension plans) to program automatic purchases and sales of stock index "market baskets" into a computer. Sales or purchases can be triggered automatically when the stock index futures price gets out of alignment with the spot price. This program trading allows every opportunity for arbitrage to be exploited immediately. As advantageous as this may seem to the brokerage house that uses it, program trading can be controversial.

As we saw in Chapter 11, during the week of October 12–16, 1987, the Dow Jones Industrial Average fell 250 points, and on Monday, October 19, 1987, it plummeted 508 points, or more than 20 percent—the largest percentage drop in history and the largest point drop to that time. Could program trading have been the culprit in this major downturn?

Consider what would happen if a stock index futures suddenly fell steeply. Program trading would trigger spot market sales of the stocks that made up the index and purchases of index futures. A major fall in the futures price could bring about large sales (and plummeting prices) in the spot market for stock. *Stop orders* (or orders to automatically sell if the stock price falls to a certain level) would be triggered, which would cause further plummeting of spot prices and could reverse the trend of purchases in the futures market. Indeed, the October 1987 crash was triggered by program trading and stop orders.

To prevent a reoccurrence of the 1987 crash, many exchanges have put in "circuit breaker" restrictions that, among other things, limit computerized program trading if the index falls more than a certain amount on any day. They have been activated many times.

Other analysts are less concerned about program trading than about the cause of the fall in futures prices to begin with. If futures prices fall because of the expectation that spot prices will be falling, the arbitrage causing the present spot price to fall may simply be rational price adjustment in a declining market. By restricting computerized trading, we may only be treating the symptoms of a problem without treating the cause. Maybe the market, like a virus, should be allowed to run its course, or maybe a little preventive medication will stop a mild virus from turning into a severe infection. Opinions about the extent of intervention needed continue to differ.

RECAP The futures price is determined by supply and demand. If the futures price is above the spot price plus the carrying costs, an arbitrageur will sell a futures agreement while at the same time purchasing securities in the spot market. The increased supply of futures will push the price down until the difference between the spot price and the futures price is equal to the carrying costs. If the futures price is below the spot price plus carrying costs, arbitrageurs (who own some of the underlying instruments) will buy futures and sell in the spot market. The futures price will go up, and the spot price will come down until the difference equals the carrying costs. As the delivery date nears, the spot and the futures prices converge.

Options

As shown in previous sections, business firms (financial and nonfinancial) or individuals can use the futures market to reduce the risk of price changes inherent in everyday business. Thus, if they need to buy or sell a financial instrument in the future, they can use the futures market to offset any possible loss due to an unanticipated price change between now and the day when they will be making the purchase or sale. An unattractive feature of the futures market, however, is that it also eliminates a possible gain from a price change.

For example, consider the case in which Michael needs to borrow $1 million in a month. He knows what the interest rate is today, but is concerned that it will be higher in a month. He can sell a T-bill future for $1 million that gives him the right and obligation to sell the T-bills in 30 days at a price determined today. If the interest rate goes up, he borrows at a higher rate, but the price of the T-bill futures contract falls and he makes a profit. This profit offsets the higher borrowing costs (and accomplishes his goal of reducing the risk of losses if the interest rate goes up). If the interest rate goes down, Michael gains by borrowing at a lower rate. However, he loses money on the T-bill futures (because lower interest rates cause the T-bill futures price to rise and he is locked into selling at the lower price). Therefore, to reduce the risk of losses from the interest rate rising, he forgoes the chance of a gain if the interest rate falls.

Could there be another way of getting risk protection from a loss without giving up the possibility of a gain? If you said, "Surely there must be because markets are so quick to respond to changing needs and conditions," you are correct (or, as we shall see, almost correct). Let's turn our attention to options to demonstrate how our friend Michael can use them to reduce the risk of an interest rate increase over the next month without forgoing a gain if rates fall.

Options
Standardized contracts that give the buyer the right—but not the obligation—to buy or sell an instrument in the future at a price determined today.

Strike Price
The agreed-upon price in an options contract.

Options on Futures
Options that give the buyer the right—but not the obligation—to buy or sell a futures contract up to the expiration date on the option.

Options are similar to futures in that they are used to reduce the risk of future price changes or to speculate. Options give the buyer the right—but not the obligation—to buy or sell an instrument in the future for a price determined today. The agreed-upon price is called the **strike price.** This right continues until an expiration date specified in the contract. Options exist for many agricultural products, commodities, individual stocks (such as AT&T, IBM, and EDS), and other financial instruments. In addition, options are also available on the major types of futures contracts, including stock index futures, currency futures, and interest rate futures. These options, called **options on futures,** give the buyer of the option the right (but not the obligation) to buy or sell a futures contract up to the expiration date of the option. Financial options are available for specific dates in the future, often for the two nearest months and then for March, June, September, and December for the next 9 months. As in the case of futures, the clearinghouse of the exchange enforces the contract and, for a fee, takes on the default risk. Many of the similarities between futures and options stop here, however.

There are two kinds of options, and we will outline each of them briefly, focusing mainly on financial options. A Closer Look lists the major U.S. options and the exchanges on which they are traded.

http://www.cbot.com
Provides information about options trading.

Major Options, Exchanges, and Open Interest: Options are available for hundreds of individual stocks, for many stock indexes, and for foreign currencies. Most options must be exercised in less than 1 year. However, there are long-term options (both equity and index) in which the specified time to exercise the option is over 1 year. *Barron's* reports weekly on the 1,350 most actively traded stock, index, and long-term options. In addition, the Chicago Board Options Exchange also makes an option market in 10-year Treasury notes. This option can be used to hedge interest rate risk.

The following list includes the open interest (number of contracts outstanding) of total options, long-term options, index options, and foreign currency options.[16]

TYPES OF OPTIONS	EXCHANGE[17] AT WHICH TRADING OCCURS	OPEN INTEREST MAY 18, 2001
All options		
Stock, equity, currency, interest rate (short and long term)	CBOE	52,249,007 calls 31,551,488 puts
	AMEX	21,614,894 calls 8,935,607 puts
	PHLX	32,104,243 calls 16,157,973 puts
	PS	48,105,749 calls 27,431,883 puts
Long-Term Options		
Equity and index options	CBOE	10,778,541 calls 5,387,981 puts
	AMEX	0 calls 0 puts
	PHLX	0 calls 0 puts
	PS	10,375,774 calls 4,813,888 puts
Index Options		
Various stock market indexes	CBOE	2,000,650 calls 2,710,146 puts
	AMEX	51,142 calls 48,306 puts
	PHLX	127,931 calls 126,845 puts
	PS	53,593 calls 4,071 puts
Currency Options (Australian dollar, British pound, Canadian dollar, euro, Japanese yen, and Swiss franc)	PHLX	13,200 calls 18,065 puts
Interest Rate 10-year U.S. Treasury notes	CBOE	1,830 calls 4,551 puts

A Closer Look

---

[16]SOURCE: *Barron's*, May 21, 2001 p. MW63.

[17]Exchanges: AMEX (American Stock Exchange); CBOE (Chicago Board Options Exchange); PHLX (Philadelphia Stock Exchange); PS (Pacific Exchange).

Put Options

Put Options
Options that give the buyer of the option the right—but not the obligation—to sell a standardized contract of a financial instrument at a strike price determined today.

Put options give the buyer of the option the right—but not the obligation—to sell a standardized contract of a financial instrument or a futures agreement at a strike price determined today. The seller has the obligation—but not the right—to buy the contract if the buyer exercises it before the expiration date.[18] Therefore, Michael, who has to borrow $1 million in the next month, can hedge the risk of a future interest rate increase by buying a put option on, say, a T-bill or Treasury bond contract. If the interest rate does go up, he exercises the option at a profit to offset the loss incurred by having to borrow at the higher rate. Like futures, financial options are written only in standardized contract amounts for delivery on a few specific dates, and a perfect offsetting transaction is rarely found. Nevertheless, risk is still reduced. Unlike futures, put options allow the risk of an interest rate increase to be hedged without losing the possibility of a gain if the interest rate goes down. If rates do fall, Michael simply does not exercise the option. He has used put options to reduce the risk of an interest rate increase when he has to borrow in the future. Put options could also be used to reduce the risk of a price decrease by anyone who has to sell a financial instrument in the future.

Call Options

Call Options
Options that give the buyer of the option the right—but not the obligation—to buy a standardized contract of a financial instrument at a strike price determined today.

Call options give the buyer the right—but not the obligation—to buy a financial instrument, at a strike price determined today, anytime before the expiration date. Note that the buyer has the right—but not the obligation—to buy. The buyer exercises the option (buys the instrument or futures contract at the strike price) only if it is in his or her interest to do so—that is, only if the price of the financial instrument is greater than the strike price. If the price of the financial instrument or futures contract falls, the buyer is not obliged to exercise the option and will let it expire. The option allows the buyer to limit the losses from a price increase without limiting his or her ability to take advantage of a price decrease.

RECAP Options give the buyer of the option the right—but not the obligation—to buy or sell an instrument in the future for a price determined today. Put options give the buyer the right—but not the obligation—to sell a standardized contract, at a price determined today, anytime before the expiration date on the option. A call option gives the buyer the right—but not the obligation—to buy a financial instrument, at a price determined today, anytime before the expiration date on the option.

The Option Premium

Why would individuals or firms hedge risk with futures that limit both losses and gains when they could use options that limit only losses? If you answered, "Because futures must be cheaper," you may have a future as an economist! Futures cost very little—basically only a small brokerage fee, which is low because the contracts are standardized and the volume in the market is very large. Both parties to the agreement have rights and obligations. With options, however, one party has rights with no obligations, and the other party has obligations with no rights. From the buyer's

---

[18]In this chapter, we are limiting our discussion to American options, which can be exercised anytime before their expiration date. European options can be exercised only on the expiration date of the option.

position, put or call options give the right—but not the obligation—to sell or buy the contract at the agreed-upon price if the buyer exercises the option. In addition to paying the exchange a brokerage fee, the party with the rights but no obligations (the buyer) pays an **option premium** to the party with the obligations but no rights (the seller).[19] The premium is the reward to the seller of either a put or a call option for accepting the risk of a loss with no possibility of a gain.[20]

So far, we have been discussing situations in which options are used to hedge. As you might have guessed, put and call options also can be used to speculate. However, speculation in this manner can be extremely costly because option premiums are often quite substantial (several thousands of dollars). If the option is not exercised, the buyer of the call or put option loses the option premium. Hedgers can think of the option premium as an insurance premium, limiting the amount of losses they will incur if a financial instrument must be purchased or sold at a later date. For speculators, the option premium is the amount that they are willing to bet when they believe that the price will change significantly from the strike price, thereby creating potential profit.[21]

On the one hand, someone who needs to buy a financial security or instrument in the future can hedge the risk of an inopportune price increase by paying a premium to purchase a call option, which gives the buyer the right to purchase the instrument at a price agreed upon today up to the expiration date of the option. On the other hand, someone who needs to sell a financial security or instrument in the future can hedge the risk of a price decrease by paying a premium to purchase a put option, which gives the buyer the right to sell the contract at a price agreed upon today up to the expiration date. The sellers of the call or put options are not hedging, but are accepting risk for a price—in this case, the option premium. The buyer of a call or put option is hedging risk without giving up any potential for gains, as in the case of futures. Like futures, options can also be used to speculate about future price changes. The downside to options is the option premium, which can be quite substantial as compared to the usually small brokerage fee for buying or selling a futures contract.[22] Economists are famous for saying "There is no such thing as a free lunch!" If options are used to exploit gains while limiting losses, this is certainly true.

Like futures, option prices are quoted in many daily newspapers. The accompanying Cracking the Code feature explains how to read option prices.

In this section, we looked at financial options and saw that they can also be used by business firms for managing risk due to price changes. Like futures, options can be used to reduce the risks of price changes in future time periods.

RECAP The option premium is paid by the party who has rights but no obligations. The seller of the option receives the premium to compensate for accepting the risk of a loss with no possibility of gain.

---

[19]Make sure you are clear that the buyer of a put option has the right but not the obligation to sell while the buyer of a call option has the right but not the obligation to buy.

[20]In the case of interest rate options, for the hedger to be better off, the loss from the interest rate increase must be larger than the put option premium.

[21]As with hedgers, for the speculator to benefit from the option, the price must increase (in the case of call options) or decrease (in the case of put options) enough to more than cover the option premium.

[22]The option still entails a small brokerage fee for arranging the option in addition to the option premium.

Option Premium
The premium paid by the buyer of an option to compensate the seller for accepting the risk of a loss with no possibility of a gain.

CRACKING THE CODE: *Cracking the Code on Options*

The following table shows a typical example of how option market information appears in the newspaper. We use the example of an option on a interest rate futures agreement because this is the preferred way of hedging. Using an options on a futures agreement is preferable to an option on the underlying asset because of the liquidity and homogeneity of the futures market. In this example, we are considering options on $100,000 of Treasury bond futures with a coupon rate of 8 percent and a 15-year maturity. In the T-bonds (CBT) section, we will consider the highlighted row that starts with the strike price of 100. The second, third, and fourth columns give the settle (final of the day) option premium for call options for July, August, and September, respectively. The last three columns give the settle option premium for put options on May 31, 2001 for July, August, and September.

T-BONDS (CBT)
$100,000; points and 64ths of 100%

STRIKE PRICE	CALLS-SETTLE			PUTS-SETTLE		
	Jly	Aug	Sep	Jly	Aug	Sep
99	1–15	. . .	2–06	0–43	. . .	1–34
100	0–46	1–18	1–38	1–10	. . .	2–02
101	0–25	0–57	1–12	1–53	2–21	2–39

SOURCE: *Wall Street Journal,* June 1, 2001, p. C13.

Thus, on May 31, for a strike price of 100, or 100 percent of the face value of the contract (in this example, $100,000), the option premium for a July call option was $718.75 or (46/64% × $100,000). For a September put option, the premium (column 7) is $2,031.25 or (2 02/64% × $100,000). If no price is given, as for an August put option with a strike price of 100, then the contract did not trade on this day.

To give some meaning to these numbers, let's assume we purchased an August Treasury bond call option with a strike price of 100 for $718.75 on May 31, 2001. We pay a small brokerage fee (on May 31) for the right (but not the obligation) to purchase $100,000 face value in Treasury bonds (of 15-year maturity and 8 percent coupon rate) for $100,000 in August ($100,000 × 100% = $100,000). If the spot price of $100,000 in Treasury bonds in July is greater than $100,000, we exercise the option. If the spot price is greater than $100,000 plus the option premium of $718.75, we make money. If it's less, we do not exercise the option. In this case, we lose the option premium of $718.75! However, we can consider the $718.75 as an insurance premium, insuring us against having to pay much more for the Treasury bond futures in July.

Derivatives
Financial contracts whose values are derived from the values of other underlying instruments, such as bonds or an index.

One final note: All of the markets that we have been discussing—financial forward, futures, and options—are examples of derivatives. **Derivatives** are financial contracts whose values are derived from the values of other underlying instruments, such as foreign exchange, bonds, equities, or an index. For example, the value of a financial futures contract in Treasury bonds derives its value from the underlying bonds. There are many kinds of derivatives, and those described in this chapter are relatively simple. As you may suspect, we discuss other types of derivatives in the next chapter. This chapter contains two appendixes. The first examines foreign exchange futures markets; the second discusses how the mysterious option premium is determined.

Summary of Major Points

- In forward markets, the terms of a transaction (including the price) that will occur on a future date are arranged today. Forward transactions are used to reduce the risk that future price changes will eliminate profit. Forward agreements between individual parties are arranged by intermediaries. Forward agreements can have high transactions costs because they usually require the exact matching of two parties and because each party has a default risk in that the other party may not fulfill the agreement.

- In financial markets, forward contracts in the most widely traded currencies have been established by large commercial banks. The bank is an actual participant in the agreement. In addition to buying and selling foreign currencies at spot prices, the banks also buy and sell the major currencies at forward rates. There does not have to be an exact matching of two parties. When there is not an exact offsetting match, the bank has some exposure to exchange rate risk. Foreign currency forward agreements can be used to hedge exchange rate risk or to speculate about future currency values.

- Financial futures are standardized contracts between two parties to buy or sell financial securities, such as government securities, stock indexes, Eurodollars, and numerous foreign currencies, on a future date at a price determined today. They are traded on major exchanges and are used to hedge interest rate risks, exchange rate risks, and the risk that stock prices will change. They can also be used to speculate about future price changes.

- Because futures contracts are standardized, they have low transactions costs and high volume. They often do not provide an exact offsetting match with regard to the quality, the quantity, or the due date of the contract. The clearinghouse of the exchange enforces the contract and, for a fee, takes on the default risk. Both the buyer and the seller put up performance bonds. Arbitrageurs ensure that the futures price is equal to the spot price plus carrying costs. The futures price converges to the spot price on the delivery date.

- Options are financial contracts that can also be used to hedge or speculate. They are available for many of the same financial instruments as futures. In addition, two kinds of options are offered for buying or selling futures contracts. A call option gives the buyer of the option the right—but not the obligation—to purchase the contract by the expiration date at a price determined today. A put option gives the buyer of the option the right—but not the obligation—to sell the contract by the expiration date at a price determined today. The buyer of a call or put option pays an option premium because she or he has rights but no obligations. The seller of the call or put option takes on the risk that the option will be exercised for a price, the option premium. Futures limit both gains and losses, while options limit losses without limiting gains.

- On October 19, 1987, the Dow Jones Industrial Average fell 508 points. Program trading has been implicated in the fall. The collapse was triggered by declines in the prices of stock index futures. Since that time, reforms have been put in place to limit a collapse from program trading.

- A foreign exchange futures market trades standardized contracts to buy or sell some amount of foreign exchange on a future date at a price determined today. These futures are widely used to hedge risks involving the delivery of one currency that must be converted to another currency at a later date. (Appendix 22-A).

- The option premium is dependent on the volatility of the financial instrument in the contract (such as T-bills), the difference between the strike price and the spot price, and the length of time until the expiration date on the option (see Appendix 22-B).

Key Terms

Arbitrageurs
Call Options
Carrying Costs
Clearinghouse
Convergence
Derivatives
Financial Forward Agreements

Financial Futures
Foreign Exchange Futures
  Contract
Forward Rate
Futures Contracts
Hedged
Option Premium

Options
Options on Futures
Performance Bond
Pit
Put Options
Strike Price

Review Questions

1. Define financial futures, forward agreements, and options. What are the advantages and disadvantages of each?

2. How do spot markets differ from forward markets? How do spot markets differ from futures markets?

3. A government report forecasts both higher inflation and higher interest rates in the future. Yvette needs to borrow money in 6 months. What can she, as a future borrower, do now to protect herself from the risk of an increase in the interest rate? What if she is the lender?

4. Why do both the buyer and the seller of futures contracts have to put up performance bonds? When does the seller profit? When does the buyer profit? How is the clearinghouse protected from losses?

5. Explain why the futures price is very close to the spot price on the day before the delivery date of a futures contract.

6. How do arbitrageurs and speculators differ?

7. Explain how arbitrage causes the futures and spot prices to converge.

8. Explain the difference between call and put options. Does the buyer or the seller of an option pay the option premium? Why does the seller of an option take on the risk?

9. What are options on futures?

10. Explain how an investor could use a stock index future to hedge the risk of a fall in stock prices.

11. Assume that an intermediary uses futures only to hedge risk and never to speculate. Is it as vulnerable to losses as an intermediary that uses futures to speculate? Explain.

12. What factors determine the size of the option premium (see Appendix 22-B)?

Analytical Questions

13. Angela buys a Treasury bond futures agreement for $94,000. On the delivery date, the spot price is $95,000. Does she win or lose? How much? If Angela bought the futures contract to hedge, can she lose? Explain. (Hint: What if she is willing to give up the opportunity for gain to reduce the risk of loss?)

14. IBM sells a Treasury bond futures agreement for $94,000. On the delivery date, the spot price is $95,000. IBM sold the futures agreement to speculate. Does IBM win or lose? Explain.

15. A firm buys a December $100,000 Treasury bond call option with a strike price of 110. If the spot price in December is $108,000, is the option exercised?

16. An investment firm buys a December $100,000 Treasury bond put option with a strike price of 110. If the spot price in December is $108,000, is the option exercised?

17. If the settle price for a T-bill futures contract is 96.75, what is the percent discount?

18. A brokerage house purchases an S&P 500 futures agreement for $300,000. On the delivery date, the S&P 500 Index is 575. Does the brokerage house make a profit? What if the S&P 500 is 625?

19. If I buy a T-bill future for $950,000 and interest rates go up between now and the delivery date, what will happen to the price of the T-bill future? Will I make money or lose money? Explain.

20. Assume that you will inherit a $1 million trust fund from your family when you turn 21 next year. Interest rates are high right now, and you fear they may be lower in a year. Explain in detail how you can use futures or options to alleviate your fears.

21. Ruben is importing Colombian coffee to the United States. He will be paid $100,000 in 6 months, but he is concerned about how much of his domestic currency (Columbian pesos) he will receive for the $100,000. Explain in detail how he can reduce the risk that, in 6 months, the peso will depreciate in value against the dollar and he will receive fewer pesos than he anticipates (see Appendix 22-A).

Internet Exercises

1. The Chicago Mercantile Exchange (CME) is the world's largest financial exchange where firms buy and sell financial instruments. A glossary of financial instruments such as futures and options is available from the CME at **http://www.cme. com/**. Access this site, locate the glossary and find the meaning of futures and options. From the information at this site, explain the difference between a call option and a put option.

2. Go to the Chicago Board of Trade Internet site at **http://www.cbot.com/**. Summarize the latest news about the exchange as reported on the *CBOT Today* link.

Suggested Readings

For a comprehensive analysis of futures markets, see A. B. Malliaris, *Foundations of Futures Markets: Selected Essays of A. G. Malliaris* (Northampton, MA: Edward Elgar, 2000).

For a collection of 70 articles written over the last 25 years on options, see George M. Constantinides and A. G. Malliaris, eds., *Options Markets* (Northampton, MA: Edward Elgar, 2001).

An article that looks at how futures can be used to hedge risk or to speculate is Lorayne Fiorillo, "Back to the Futures: Ups and Downs Aside, Futures Investing Could Help You Diversify Your Portfolio," *Entrepreneur*, August 1998, p. 661.

A study that looks at recent developments in futures markets is Ahmet E. Kocagil, "Return-Volume Dynamics in Futures Markets," *Journal of Futures Markets*, 18:4: 399–426.

For an article that looks at the recent performance of Asian futures exchanges after the Asian financial crisis, see Rachael Horsewood, "After the Crash, It's Back to the Futures," *Asiamoney*, March 1998, pp. 15–17.

An article that discusses options and option pricing is John Krainer, "The Nobel Prize in Economics," *Federal Reserve Bank of San Francisco Economic Letter*, 98-05, February 13, 1998.

For a discussion of the risks that derivatives pose for banks, see Chapter 7 of Franklin R. Edwards, *The New Finance: Regulation and Financial Stability* (Washington, DC: The AEI Press, 1996), pp. 120–147.

For a look into the future, see Asani Sarkar and Michelle Tozzi, "Electronic Trading on Futures Exchanges," *Current Issues in Economics and Finance*, No. 1, January 1998.

Two comprehensive and somewhat technical articles are "Money Market Futures" and "Options on Money Market Futures," both found in *Instruments of the Money Market*, 7th ed., Timothy Q. Cook and Robert K. LaRoche, eds. (Federal Reserve Bank of Richmond, 1993). Additional information on futures and other financial instruments may be found at **http://www.e-analytics.com**.

Appendix 22-A

The Foreign Exchange Futures Market

In the body of this chapter, we discussed foreign exchange forward agreements that are offered by large banks to allow their customers to hedge exchange rate risk. In addition to these forward markets, large futures markets that trade foreign exchange futures contracts have also developed to hedge exchange rate risk. Both forward and futures agreements in foreign currencies facilitate cross-border trading in goods, services, and financial claims. Both achieve similar results. This appendix looks at foreign exchange futures contracts.

Foreign Exchange Futures Contract
A standardized contract to deliver a certain amount of a foreign currency on a date in the future at a price determined today.

A **foreign exchange futures contract** is a standardized contract to deliver a certain amount of a foreign currency on a date in the future at a price determined today. The agreed-upon price is the futures price. Like spot markets, foreign exchange futures markets have experienced remarkable growth due to the tremendous increase in trade and foreign investment, and in the volatility of exchange rates. Foreign exchange futures markets have been organized since the mid-1970s and allow importers, exporters, and investors in foreign securities to hedge. Like other futures markets, they also provide the opportunity for speculation.

The foreign exchange markets, including both spot and futures markets, actually form the largest market in the world in terms of the volume of transactions. Spot markets do not have a single location, such as the New York Stock Exchange, but rather are located at large banks in the world's financial centers in London, New York, Tokyo, and Frankfurt. Large banks in financial centers in other countries are usually linked to the major banks in one of the financial centers, which, in turn, are linked by telephone and telex. Standardized futures contracts are traded on the Chicago Mercantile Exchange and require a relatively large minimum purchase. In reality, one worldwide foreign exchange market (either spot or futures) is open somewhere in the world 24 hours each day. Since supplies and demands change from day to day, exchange rates (both spot and futures prices) fluctuate day-to-day, hour-to-hour, and even minute-by-minute![23]

Foreign exchange futures markets, like all futures markets, offer the opportunity to hedge risk or to speculate. Importers and exporters often enter into agreements to deliver goods in the future for a price determined today. Because the price is agreed upon today without knowing the future spot exchange rate, there is a risk that the exchange rate between the two currencies will change between now and the delivery date. Thus, there is a possibility that the anticipated profit could be eliminated or, worse yet, that a loss could occur. This risk is referred to as *exchange rate risk*.

To hedge, an importer can enter the foreign exchange futures market. An example will help to clarify. Assume Jean is exporting computers to a firm (Choca Firm) in Switzerland that plans to resell them at a profit.[24] She agrees to deliver 500 computers in September, 3 months from now, at a price of $1,000 per computer, or $500,000. Choca Firm will have to come up with $500,000 in September to pay for the computers.[25] Checking the exchange rate today, Choca finds that the Swiss

---

[23]The relationship between the spot and futures exchange rate is the same as the relationship between any spot and futures price.

[24]Choca Firm has previously specialized in Swiss chocolates but now is trying to diversify by importing computers.

[25]In this example, we are assuming that the importer must exchange domestic currency for the foreign currency—that is, Choca Firm must pay for its imports with the currency of the exporting country. The situation could work in reverse. In that case, the exporter would be paid in the currency of the importing country and have to exchange it for the exporting country's currency. Either way, the risk is the same; the only difference is in who bears the risk.

chapter

23

Asset-Backed Securities, Interest-Rate Agreements, and Currency Swaps

> **Learning Objectives** *After reading this chapter, you should know:*

- How asset-backed securities work and why they were created
- The most common types of asset-backed securities
- The benefits and risks associated with the use of asset-backed securities
- How interest-rate swaps, caps, floors, and collars can be used to reduce interest-rate risk
- How and why currency swaps are used to manage exchange-rate risk

" "

Corporations that shelter their cash flows from volatility can afford to take greater internal risks in the form of higher levels of investment or expenditures on research and development. Financial institutions themselves are vulnerable to volatility in interest rates and exchange rates; to the extent that they can hedge that volatility, they can extend more credit to a wider universe of deserving borrowers.
—Peter L. Bernstein, *Against the Gods: The Remarkable Story of Risk,* 1996, p. 327

South Dakota, Scholarships, and Securitization

Risk assessment and management techniques that reduce cash flow volatility not only increase earnings, but also allow credit to be allocated more broadly. If a non-financial corporation can hedge against adverse interest-rate, price, and/or currency movements, less capital needs to be set aside for reserves. These financial resources can then be redirected to internal research and development and higher levels of capital investment rather than used as a reserve against volatility. This will likely increase the firm's productivity and profitability. At the same time, since fewer funds are needed for reserves, credit can be allowed to flow to a wider array of deserving borrowers. In this chapter we will investigate how securitization, interest-rate agreements (interest-rate swaps, caps, floors, and collars) and currency swaps can be used to achieve these objectives and beneficial outcomes. We begin with a case involving the state of South Dakota's proposed use of securitization.

It is January 2001 and the South Dakota legislature is in session. The governor has proposed a new Regents Scholarship that will pay South Dakota high school students up to $9,500 over 4 years of college at a public school if they meet certain GPA and course selection criteria and promise to abstain from tobacco use. The scholarship is to be funded by future receipts from South Dakota's portion of the recent federal tobacco industry settlement. The governor and the state legislators are nervous. What if the nationwide restrictions on tobacco advertising and decreased tobacco use cause tobacco firm earnings to decline? What if these companies go bankrupt? This exposure to default risk could undermine the stream of future earnings upon which the governor's proposed scholarship is funded. Is there a way that the state of South Dakota could decrease its exposure to default risk, move up receipt of its tobacco payments, and reduce the uncertainty of future funding for the proposed scholarship plan?

The answer to all of these questions is an enthusiastic "Yes—for a price!" During the 2001 legislative session, South Dakota's governor signed legislation into law that allowed the state to make more certain its receipts from the federal tobacco settlement. *Securitization* refers to this process whereby relatively illiquid financial assets—here, future tobacco industry receipts—are packaged together and sold off to individual investors as securities. In short, rather than take the $25 million or so in annual tobacco payments over the next 30 years, the state of South Dakota would sell the rights to these future payments for an estimated $240 million today. This amount could be reinvested with the annual interest earnings used to partially fund the governor's scholarship plan. The $240 million would be paid by those purchasing the securities, and the securities themselves would be backed by the promise of future tobacco payments. As annual payments from the tobacco industry are received by the state, they would be passed through to the holders of the securities. In essence, securitization turns relatively illiquid instruments (like a promise of future tobacco payments) into liquid investments called **asset-backed securities (ABSs)**. The tobacco companies' promise to pay (a financial asset) serves as collateral or "backing" for the state's issuance of securities.

Asset-Backed Securities
Securities that result from the process of securitization.

Many benefits could result from the state's participation in this sort of arrangement. The state would receive its money up front and generate interest earnings. Securitization would also eliminate any exposure to default risk from the earnings shortfall or failure of a tobacco company. However, there is a downside. The process is very expensive. Securitization would cost several million dollars to arrange. In addition, if the tobacco companies do not fail, the state would be forgoing tens and perhaps hundreds of millions of dollars in potential revenue over the next two decades. Thus, there are both advantages and disadvantages of the governor deciding to use his new authority to securitize. If at some point in the future this issue is referred to the voters of South Dakota or some other state, how should they vote? Should voters favor or oppose the securitization of future tobacco payments?[1]

To answer this question, we first need to understand how the securitization process works. The first section of this chapter describes the securization process, discusses the origins of securitization, explores its benefits and costs, and describes trends among the most common types of asset-backed securities. The second section of the chapter describes instruments for managing interest-rate risk and examines how various interest-rate agreements (swaps, caps, floors, and collars) can be used to hedge against or speculate on interest-rate changes. We then examine how currency swaps can be used to manage foreign exchange-rate risk.

The management of financial risk has grown increasingly sophisticated. To be a successful financial manager—and in the case of South Dakota, a responsible citizen—requires a basic familiarity with these new types of financial instruments.

The Anatomy of a Securitization

Exhibit 23-1 provides a diagram of a typical securitization structure. There are seven main sets of players: borrowers, loan originator, special-purpose trust, rating agency, credit enhancer, underwriter, and investors. To understand each of these players and their roles, let's talk through the anatomy of a hypothetical securitization. As is the case with human anatomy, we need to understand not only the individual parts, but also how the parts work together to create an organized system.

Step 1: Our borrowers need to take out loans. Let's assume that our borrowers use credit cards issued by First South-Western, a credit card bank and the loan originator of our example. When its customers use their credit cards to buy goods and services (or to take a cash advances), they are creating credit card receivables for First South-Western. Our bank has been careful to screen credit card applicants according to predetermined criteria to ensure that these credit card balances will conform to the requirements of the resale market.

Step 2: First South-Western can pool or group these credit card receivables together into $1 million bundles to be sold to a **special-purpose trust.** We call ours *ITP Credit Card Receivables Trust.* A trust is often the subsidiary of the loan originator or an investment underwriter. In either case, the special-purpose trust buys the rights to the future credit card payments and, with the help of the underwriter, issues the asset-backed securities. The special-purpose trust is also often responsible for monitoring the value of the collateral and managing the cash flows of the receivables pool. In some cases, a separate loan servicer is employed to manage the collections process.

Special-Purpose Trust
A corporate agent that buys financial obligations from a loan originator and works with a security underwriter, credit enhancer, and rating agency to issue asset-backed securities; sometimes responsible for loan-servicing responsibilities.

---

[1]This example is a bit more complicated than appears here for at least three reasons. First, on March 20, 2001, South Dakota's governor successfully vetoed his own scholarship bill because private colleges had been added by amendment. This disconnected the securitization process (which passed and was signed into law) from its stated use for college scholarships. Second, in early April 2001, a bipartisan group of dissenting legislators organized a petition drive to refer the securitization law to a vote of the people. They failed to gather enough signatures by the mid-June deadline to put the issue on the statewide ballot. Third, the South Dakota constitution requires that all appropriation bills pass the legislature by a two-thirds majority. The securitization bill passed by only a simply majority. Thus, with the failure of the petition drive, legal action may be taken against the bill on constitutional grounds since securitization appears to require an appropriation to hire professionals to package the offering.

EXHIBIT 23-1
The Anatomy of
an Asset-Backed
Security Offering

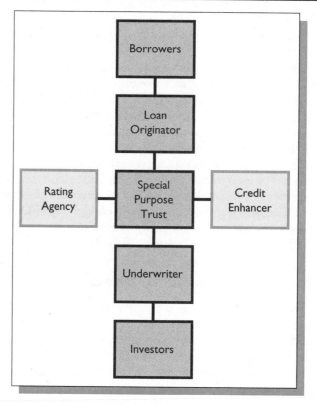

SOURCE: Adapted from Leon T. Kendall and Michael Fishman (1996), *A Primer on Securitization,* The MIT Press, Cambridge, Massachusetts, p. 3.

The trust structure is employed for two main reasons. First, it allows the trust and the loan originator to be exempt from taxes. The trust simply acts as a conduit through which future payments are passed from credit card borrowers to the owners of the asset-backed securities. Thus, no taxable gain is created. The loan originator is allowed to account for the transaction as the discounted sale of receivables. This ensures that the loan originator shows no taxable profit on the transaction. Second, by buying the receivables outright, the transaction becomes bankruptcy remote. If First South-Western Bank (the loan originator) went bankrupt, the asset-backed security offering would be unaffected. Once ITP Credit Card Receivables Trust (the special-purpose trust) owns the receivables, the credit worthiness of the loan originator is immaterial.[2]

Step 3: As Exhibit 23-1 illustrates, ITP Credit Card Receivables Trust works with one of the largest credit-rating agencies, such as Moody's Investors Service or Standard and Poor's Corporation. Financial regulators and, perhaps more importantly, financial markets and investors, accept the assessment of national credit-rating agencies as equal to **due diligence**—research performed to assure offerings financial statements are accurate—required in other loan and security offerings. Thus, ratings agencies create a basis by which investors can compare perceptions of default risk.

Due Diligence
The investigative process used by a lender, investor, or investment banker to ensure that a borrower's or security issuer's financial statements are accurate.

[2]There is at least one exception to this. Sometimes a form of credit enhancement called "recourse to issuer" is used. If there were losses to the security buyers, the issuer could be held liable. In this case, the loan originator forfeits its bankruptcy remoteness in order to achieve a higher credit rating for the issue.

Step 4: To obtain the highest possible rating and lowest possible interest rate, ITP Credit Card Receivables Trust and the underwriter will work with a **credit enhancer** or find alternative means to enhance the perceived quality of the issue. A credit enhancer might be an insurance company or a bank that, for a fee, guarantees an issuance or offers a letter of credit in support of the offering. The creditworthiness of the asset bundle can also be enhanced by overcollateralizing the offering or establishing an outside reserve account to meet any future underpayments on the part of the borrowers. For example, if the principal amount of the issue is for $50 million, the pool of assets "backing" it may be $52 million. In this example, if $2 million worth of loans go into default, the investors are protected by the extra collateral. Similarly, the issuer may simply set aside an additional cash reserve that can be drawn on if the obligations backing the security issue fail to perform as expected.

Another way to enhance the pool's credit is to use a **superior/subordinated debt structure.** In this type of structured issue, the securities are sold in at least two different classes, or tranches. A **tranche** is one part of a total asset-backed security offering. It might be backed by a portion of the principal or by the interest payments, or some combination of both. Each tranche is often given a different credit rating, coupon rate, and repayment period. The first class (the superior tranche) consists of highly rated and lower-yielding securities. These investors are paid before the subordinated (lower-rated and higher-yielding) security holders are paid. This allows the superior parts of the offering to be rated as investment grade while the subordinated class of securities is not. This is the key to the success of securitization. By selling the pool of payments in parts (with various credit enhancements and ratings), investors are willing to pay more for the security offering than they would if it was sold as a whole without credit enhancements and with lower ratings because the highest quality (lowest risk) portions of a security offering are sold at a premium. In many cases, this premium for quality more than makes up for the modest discount on the subordinated (highest risk) portions of the offering.

Step 5: The underwriter works out the details with ITP Credit Card Receivables Trust, the credit enhancer, and the rating agency. Most importantly, the underwriter makes the market for the securities by arranging the sale of the securities and standing ready to buy those securities that fail to be sold in the market. The investors (either individual investors or institutional investors such as pension funds or insurance companies) themselves receive payments made by credit card customers that are passed through the loan originator and special trust. These payments ultimately end up as the interest and/or principal payments to the security holder. It is hard to believe that the use of a simple credit card can be the impetus for creating such sophisticated and layered financial relationships. We turn now to a discussion of why borrowers, issuers, and investors engage in securitization. As with most financial and economic reasoning, the benefits of securitization appear to outweigh the costs.

> **Credit Enhancer**
> An insurance company or a bank that guarantees a security issue or offers a letter of credit in its support for a fee.

> **Superior/Subordinated Debt Structure**
> A framework that allows securities to be sold in at least two different classes or tranches.
>
> **Tranche**
> A particular class or part of a securitization issue; some parts may be backed only by principal payments, others only by interest payments.

Securitization Benefits to Borrowers, Issuers, and Investors

Borrowers, issuers, and financial investors all appear to benefit from the asset-backed securitization process. As we saw earlier in the text with mortgages, the primary benefits to borrowers are twofold. First, securitization *increases the funds available* for home equity, auto finance, credit card, commercial lending, student loans, and manufactured housing. Second, *the costs of borrowing are lower* than they would be through traditional intermediated (indirect) finance.

However, there are at least two possible disadvantages to borrowers. If a potential borrower fails to meet the established criteria for a loan intended for securitization, it is possible that the lender will reject the application or charge the applicant a substantially higher loan fee or interest rate. A second possible disadvantage is that the profitability of asset-backed securities (ABSs) has made some lenders more aggressive in pursuing loan business. This may have the effect of encouraging credit card companies to extend credit to borrowers that may be of questionable credit quality or at rates higher than some borrowers could get elsewhere. Given that these disadvantages are harder to calculate than the benefits, most see securitization as a boon to borrowers.

The primary benefit accruing to issuers of asset-backed securities has already been noted. By carefully employing various credit enhancements and tranche structures, a lender can lower its cost of funds and thereby enhance its profitability. By issuing securities, banks can broaden their base of funding sources. Investors willing to buy ABS issues are unlikely to have made deposits at the bank, but through ABSs they become a source of funds for the issuer. The kinds of earnings generated are also altered, as earnings are shifted from interest earnings generated over time to more immediate loan origination and servicing fees.

In addition to enhancing earnings, securitization also enhances a lender's ability to reduce exposure to liquidity, credit, and interest-rate risk. For instance, imagine a lender having a short-term cash-flow, credit, or interest-rate risk problem. Because of the increased use of securitization, our lender's holdings of home equity loans, credit card receivables, auto loans, and other types of credit are now increasingly marketable to investment banking firms wishing to underwrite ABS issues. The ability to sell portions of its loan portfolio (or issue its own ABSs) allows it to avoid the liquidity, credit, and interest-rate risk associated with lending long and financing with short-term deposits. Furthermore, from a bank's perspective, by enabling it to sell assets, capital requirements are easier to meet and/or avoid. Securitization allows earnings to be generated without increasing the assets or liabilities held on the balance sheet.

Investors also have benefited from the securitization of financial assets—they are given the possibility of purchasing relatively high-yielding, highly-rated securities or to purchase even higher-yielding, higher-risk securities to meet their various investment needs. Tranches can be customized to meet almost any investor's need with respect to rating, yield, average term-to-maturity, and other aspects. Most issues are backed by a highly diversified pool of loans. Many issues also benefit from various forms of credit enhancement.

An ABS involves risk; investment losses are possible. One of the least understood facets of ABSs is their ratings, which focus on assessing the default risk of the underlying assets given various economic scenarios. These scenarios are based on assumptions about future economic activity, likely default rates, and possible prepayment rates. Problems result if the assumptions depart significantly from reality. Investment grade securities are expected to weather a downturn similar to that of the Great Depression without significant risk of default. However, ratings generally do not attempt to assess the likelihood of borrower prepayment. If interest rates fall, it is possible that borrowers will refinance their loans and prepayments will significantly reduce expected yields. Similarly, higher interest rates may increase default rates on variable-rate loans and also leave investors with unexpected reductions in yields or outright losses.

Given the widespread benefits of securitization to borrowers, loan originators, and investors, securitization will continue to increase in the financial markets where it is already available and in new types of financial markets over the foreseeable future. Nevertheless, investors need to realize that losses are possible and sometimes substantial.

RECAP A typical securitization involves seven types of agents: borrowers, a loan originator, a special purpose trust, a rating agency, a credit enhancer, an underwriter, and financial investors. Through the pooling of financial obligations, prudent credit enhancement, favorable credit ratings, and appropriate structuring, a securitization can significantly reduce the transactions costs associated with moving funds from lenders to borrowers. The result is that borrowers can pay lower borrowing costs, issuers can earn higher profits, and investors can receive higher yields and more customized investment vehicles. Given these widespread benefits, securitization will likely continue to expand.

The Origins of Securitization

Now that you understand how securitization works and its benefits, you can better appreciate how pressures in the mortgage market of the 1970s and 1980s encouraged the rise of securitization. Home prices were increasing steadily and expectations of future increases bolstered demand for residential housing and mortgages. At the same time, savings and loan associations—the primary originators of home mortgages—watched as interest rates rose over and stayed above Regulation Q interest rate ceilings. Depositors withdrew their funds and moved them into money market securities or money market mutual funds that paid higher rates of interest. This, in turn, caused the supply of credit available for mortgages to shrink dramatically. The increased demand and decreased supply of loanable funds created a shortfall of funds for mortgage finance. Wall Street, specifically Solomon Brothers, tried to come up with an alternative funding source.

However, before mortgages or any other financial assets could be securitized, three essential legal, institutional, and technological changes had to be made. First, tax laws had to be changed so that payments could be allowed to pass tax-free from those making loan payments to those owning the asset-backed securities. Second, government guarantees and new government-sponsored enterprises (GSEs) facilitated the development of a secondary market. The Government National Mortgage Association (Ginnie Mae) began guaranteeing the timely principal and interest payments on mortgage-backed securities. The Federal National Mortgage Association (Fannie Mae) and Federal Home Loan Mortgage Corporation (Freddie Mac) created standardized underwriting criteria and an active secondary market for mortgage-backed securities beginning in the early 1970s. In fact, Freddie Mac and Solomon Brothers worked together to carry out the first mortgage-backed securitization issue. Third, computer technology improved enough to track the cash flows of mortgage bundles with differing interest rates, terms to maturity, and face values. Without these legal, institutional, and technological changes, the new securities would have been impossible to create. By 1984, private groups, without the assistance of the GSEs, were issuing their own mortgage-backed securities that were traded in secondary markets. Since then, securitization has continued to expand in the mortgage market not only in volume, but also in kind. Securitizations are created for a variety of fixed- and variable-rate mortgages and commercial real estate loans. In addition, securitization has rapidly spread to other types of assets.

Trends in Common Types of Asset-Backed Securities

Home Equity Loans
A type of mortgage that allows a borrower to use the equity in one's home as backing for a loan or revolving line of credit.

Securitizations have been and are completed for a wide variety of different kinds of financial assets besides first mortgages. The term "specialty finance asset-backed securities" is used to differentiate these types of issues from those of mortgage lending securitization. The most important of these includes **home equity loans,**

EXHIBIT 23-2

Shares of Specialty
Lending Asset-Backed
Security Issues in
2000 Ranked by
Sector as of
December 31, 2000
(in millions of dollars)

	NUMBER OF ISSUES	DOLLAR AMOUNT OF ISSUES	PERCENT OF ALL SPECIALTY LENDING
Home equity loans	159	$65,686.50	29.36
Auto finance	62	61,680.30	27.57
Credit cards	71	50,855.80	22.73
Commercial loans	35	22,176.30	9.91
Student loans	10	13,818.00	6.18
Manufactured housing	23	9,158.30	4.09
Other	00	359.90	0.16
Total		**$223,735.10**	**100.00%**

SOURCE: Bjorn Turnquist, "Investors Secure on Securitization," *Specialty Lending,* February 2001, Vol. 7, No. 2, pp. 1, 8–10.

http://www.ftc.gov/
bcp/conline/pubs/
homes/homequt.htm

Provides information to
consumers on home
equity loans.

automobile and truck loans and leases (including RVs and motorcycles), credit card balances, commercial loans,[3] student loans, and manufactured housing loans. Despite the "asset-backed" label, physical (hard assets) do not serve as collateral for all ABS issues. Credit card issues, for instance, are backed only by credit card receivables, a form of consumer loan.

Exhibit 23-2 summarizes the number, dollar amounts, and share of total specialty lending ABSs constituting each sector. Almost one-quarter of a trillion dollars ($224 billion) in specialty finance asset-backed securities was issued in 2000. The largest category, home equity loans, was responsible for almost 30 percent of this total, followed closely by auto finance (27.57 percent) and credit card—sometimes called plastic—issues (22.73 percent). Thus, these three types of issues made up almost 80 percent of all 2000 issues. In addition, commercial loan, student loan, and manufactured housing loan securitizations made up the other 20 percent of specialty finance asset-backed security issues.

As securitization has grown in popularity and spread from mortgages to the many other types of activities, the outstanding value of asset-backed security has increased tremendously. Exhibit 23-2 examines the issues made in one particular year. Exhibit 23-3 illustrates the growth in the total amounts of asset-backed securities outstanding.[4] Prior to 1982, the Federal Reserve reported no securitizations. By 1987, asset-backed securities outstanding passed the $100 billion mark. By 1998, the amount outstanding increased 10-fold and surpassed the $1 trillion mark. During the early 2000s, the $2 trillion milestone will be passed. Given its phenomenal growth in the 1990s and early 2000s, it now appears that securitization, which is a form of direct finance, will replace much of the lending that historically has gone through traditional intermediaries (indirect finance).

---

[3]These include operating leases, equipment sales finance, floorplan, small business loans, and trade receivables.

[4]We have included mortgage securitization in the totals for Exhibit 23-3. Some reserve the term "asset-backed securities" to refer solely to securitizations that are not backed by traditional mortgages. We use the term "specialty lending asset-backed securities" to refer to ABS lending that excludes mortgage-backed lending.

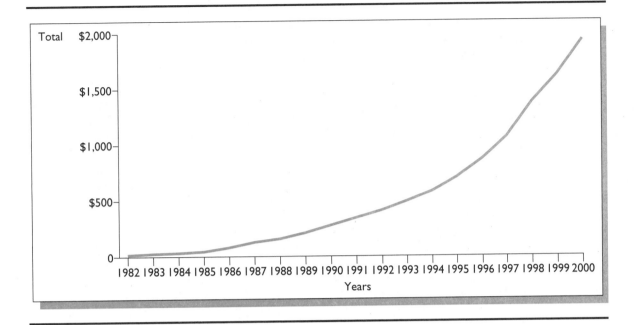

EXHIBIT 23-3

Zero to $2 Trillion in 20 Years: Trends in Total Asset-Backed Securities Outstanding (includes mortgages)

SOURCE: http://www.federalreserve.gov/releases/z1/current/data.htm Table L.126 various years.

The ability to dream up possibilities for securitization seems to be limited only by one's imagination. As the list of securitized assets in Exhibit 23-2 suggests, any dependable stream of revenue has the potential to be securitized. The tobacco bonds proposal that opens this chapter is just one example. A Closer Look describes the first securitization of small business loans.

Securitization of Small Business Loans: Although one might think that after 30 years of financial innovations few unexploited opportunities to significantly reduce costs or increase benefits are left, we should not jump to conclusions. In another innovation in late 1993, small business loans were packaged into securities (securitization), creating a secondary market. Indeed, a secondary market makes the securitization process much more successful because it increases the liquidity of the new securities.

In the early 1990s, small businesses were particularly hard hit by a credit crunch due to new capital adequacy requirements imposed on depository institutions by the Financial Institutions Reform and Recovery Act (FIRREA) of 1989. The situation was particularly critical because small businesses did not have the same access to the commercial paper market as did medium-sized and large firms. For a long time, securitization of the small business loan market had not seemed feasible because small business loans are particularly diverse and are often funded on a subjective basis. In other words, small business loans are by nature heterogeneous—a characteristic that did not make them good candidates for securitization. Generally speaking, securitization develops most easily in markets in which financial assets are fairly homogeneous. For example, to be securitized and sold in a secondary market, mortgages are made to specific criteria regarding the income

of the borrower and the loan-to-property value ratio. Under these circumstances, pools of mortgages are a fairly homogeneous lot. Auto loans, likewise, are made to certain income criteria with the vehicles serving as collateral. In the case of small business loans that are packaged and sold as securities, the backing includes accounts receivables, inventories, and equipment.

In early 1993, Fremont Financial Corporation of Santa Monica, California sold $200 million of variable rate certificates backed by a pool of loans to small and medium-sized businesses. Merrill Lynch underwrote the offering, which quickly sold out, with the securities being bought by insurance companies, pension funds, and other large investors. The novelty of this offering was that unlike Small Business Association loans, which are guaranteed by the federal government, the Fremont offering had no government guarantee.

In general, as more small business loans become securitized, the risks involved in lending to small businesses will be spread among many investors, fast-growing companies will be funded, and income will be generated for the innovators. As Fed Chair Alan Greenspan put it, a secondary market for business loans "would be a major contribution to the financial vitality of this country."[5]

However, these two examples are not the most eccentric. In 1997, a Wall Street underwriter issued $55 million worth of 10-year securities based on expected royalties from the future sales of 25 previously released albums by rock star David Bowie. Prudential Insurance Company of America bought the entire issue. Some see the securitization of revenues from other types of intellectual property rights such as best-selling novels, screen plays, and patents as being the new frontier for asset-backed security offerings. Perhaps J.K. Rowling, Steven Spielberg, or Oprah Winfrey security issues are not far behind.

 RECAP The high and volatile interest rates of the 1970s and 1980s encouraged large banks to pursue securitization as a means of increasing funding for traditional home mortgages. Changes in tax laws, the creation of Government Sponsored enterprises (GSEs), and technological innovation facilitated this process. Since then, securitization has spread to many other types of asset-backed issues including home equity loans, auto finance, credit cards, commercial loans, student loans, and manufactured housing. The securitization of revenues from intellectual property rights may be the next frontier in asset-backed security issues.

Interest-Rate Swaps

Interest-Rate Swaps
Financial instruments that allow financial institutions to trade their interest payment streams to better match payment inflows and outflows.

Some interest-rate agreements are used to hedge interest-rate risk: interest-rate swaps, interest-rate caps, floors, and collars. **Interest-rate swaps** involve two parties that trade interest payment streams to guarantee that their respective payment inflows will more closely match their outflows. They can be used by some businesses (primarily intermediaries) to manage interest-rate risk over long periods of time. Originating around 1982, they are a totally new instrument used mainly by commercial banks, saving and loans, other intermediaries, government agencies, and securities dealers to reduce interest-rate risk. The use of swaps is growing fast, particularly at large banks. Swaps make markets more efficient and reduce risks, but they are often complex. Because of their complexity, we limit our discussion to a simple case involving two commercial banks: Bank A and Bank B, as illustrated in Exhibit 23-4.

[5]Kenneth H. Bacon and Eugene Carlson, "Market Is Seen in Small-Business Loans," *The Wall Street Journal,* October 18, 1993.

EXHIBIT 23-4

A Simple Interest Rate Swap

THIS YEAR	
Bank A	*Bank B*
Two-year loans earn 9% fixed	Two-year loans earn 8% variable
Deposits cost 5% variable	Deposits cost 6% fixed
Spread: 9%–5% = 4%	Spread: 8%–6% = 2%

NEXT YEAR RATES GO UP—NO SWAP	
Bank A	*Bank B*
Loans earn 9% fixed	Loans earn 12% variable
Deposits cost 9% variable	Deposits cost 6% fixed
Spread: 9%–9% = 0% ☹	Spread: 12%–6% = 6% ☺

NEXT YEAR RATES GO DOWN—NO SWAP	
Bank A	*Bank B*
Loans earn 9% fixed	Loans earn 5% variable
Deposits cost 2% variable	Deposits cost 6% fixed
Spread: 9%–2% = 7% ☺	Spread: 5%–6% = –1% ☹

NEXT YEAR RATES GO UP—THEY SWAP	
Bank A	*Bank B*
Loans earn 9% fixed	Loans earn 12% variable
Deposits cost 6% fixed	Deposits cost 9% variable
Spread: 9%–6% = 3% ☺	Spread: 12%–9% = 3% ☺

NEXT YEAR RATES GO DOWN—THEY SWAP	
Bank A	*Bank B*
Loans earn 9% fixed	Loans earn 5% variable
Deposits cost 6% fixed	Deposits cost 2% variable
Spread: 9%–6% = 3% ☺	Spread: 5%–2% = 3% ☺

The swap allows both banks to be happy all the time!

Bank A has long-term, fixed-rate loans, such as mortgages, that it funds with floating or variable-rate money market accounts. The interest payments on money market accounts fluctuate with market interest rates, but the interest payments earned on the loans do not. The other bank—Bank B—has made floating or variable-rate loans. The interest payments on these loans go up and down with an index of market interest rates, such as rates on government bonds. The bank funds these loans with long-term, fixed-rate deposits. The interest payments on these deposits do not change.

Both banks make a profit on the spread, or the difference between what the banks earn on their loans and what they pay depositors for the use of their deposits. But there is a problem: As the loans and deposits are now configured, both banks have some interest-rate risk. In other words, both banks are in a position in which a change in interest rates can cause them to experience either no gain or a loss. If interest rates go up, Bank A (with fixed-rate loans and variable-rate deposits) ends up earning as much on its loans as it pays for its deposits. If interest rates go down,

Bank B (with variable-rate loans and fixed-rate deposits) ends up paying more for the use of its deposits than it earns on its loans.

All is not lost, however. These two intermediaries can get together through an interest-rate swap arranged by another bank. Bank A and Bank B can trade the interest payments on their deposits (liabilities), but not the principal payments. After the swap, Bank A will be funding fixed-rate assets with fixed-rate liability interest payments, and Bank B will be funding variable-rate assets with variable-rate instruments. Both can hedge risk by engaging in the swap. The interest payments received by Bank A are fixed because it has fixed-rate loans. After the swap, the interest payments it makes to fund the loans will also be fixed. A rise in interest rates will no longer put Bank A in a losing position. Bank B's earnings on its loans will continue to move up and down with market interest rates, but the interest payments it makes to fund the loans will also be flexible. A fall in interest rates will no longer put Bank A in a break-even position.

We have described a simple swap, but as noted previously, these instruments can be—and usually are—complex. A swap is often arranged for up to 15 years and has the advantage over forwards, futures, and option agreements of allowing the participants to hedge for longer periods of time.

Risk-averse, profit-seeking financial market participants are resourceful and ingenious in dealing with risk. When risks increase (as they do when markets become more volatile), market participants develop new ways to "handle" or manage the risk. Thus, we have witnessed the phenomenal growth of swaps. Financial and nonfinancial corporations must now be aware of and take every opportunity to reduce risks. If they fail to do so, they may find that they are not playing on a level field. Even the most skeptical of players may become convinced that it should be using the flashy, new **derivative instruments,** rather than be vulnerable to risk. If prices settle down (become less volatile), the growth of these markets may slow, but it is doubtful they will ever disappear. Once such markets are so highly developed, they will continue to be a means to capitalize on even small opportunities to reduce risk.

Derivative Instruments
Financial contracts (e.g., forwards, futures, options, and swaps) whose values are "derived" from the values of other underlying instruments, such as foreign exchange, bonds, equities, or an index.

RECAP Swaps entail two parties trading interest payment streams to guarantee that the inflows of payments will more closely match the outflows. Thus, an intermediary with fixed-rate assets and variable-rate liabilities will trade with another intermediary that has variable-rate assets and fixed-rate liabilities. By trading interest payment streams, both reduce interest rate risk.

Interest-Rate Caps, Floors, and Collars

In addition to the securitization process and the creation of interest-rate swaps, a variety of other interest-rate agreements have emerged to assist with the management of interest-rate risk. These include interest-rate caps, floors, and collars. Like interest-rate swaps, these instruments help firms reduce income fluctuations caused by movements in interest rates. They also allow financial institutions to hedge against interest-rate risk without requiring a firm to restructure its balance sheet. If you read about option contracts in Chapter 22, you have an conceptual framework of how these instruments work. Options allow a buyer to hedge against adverse price movements by giving the buyer the right, but not the obligation, to buy or sell an asset in the future at a strike price determined today. Interest-rate caps, floors, and collars do the same thing, but become effective based on changes in interest rates rather than on changes in asset prices.

Interest Rate Caps

Imagine that you are managing First South-Western Bank. Remember from Chapter 21 that most banks have a negative income gap—the amount of their interest-rate-sensitive assets (i.e., commercial loans, mortgages, and security holdings) is less than the amount of their interest-rate-sensitive liabilities (i.e., checkable, savings, money market, and time deposits and other forms of borrowing). This means that higher interest rates will reduce bank income because deposit rates will reprice (increase) faster than loan rates for the bank's portfolio as a whole. If interest rates fall, your bank's income will rise because the deposit rates (the cost of funds) will reprice more quickly than loan rates. Your asset-liability committee wishes to hedge against the possibility of higher interest rates, but does not want to sacrifice the possibility of benefiting from lower interest rates. Strategies discussed in Chapter 21 such as seeking *less* interest-rate-sensitive liabilities and *more* interest-rate-sensitive assets would reduce the problems caused by higher interest rates. Securitizing some of your assets or engaging in an interest-rate swap would also be reasonable alternatives. However, all of these strategies would also reduce the benefit that would be gained from lower interest rates. Is the asset-liability committee asking you to do the impossible?

Fortunately, the answer is no. These apparently contradictory goals of reducing risks associated with higher interest rates without losing the benefits of lower interest rates can be achieved. One way to achieve these goals is to purchase as **interest-rate cap**—an agreement whereby the seller of the cap agrees, for a fee, to compensate the cap buyer when an interest-rate index (the reference rate) *exceeds* a specified **strike rate**. Agreements often specify LIBOR as the reference rate. The strike rate is simply the interest rate specified in the agreement.

The amount of compensation due the buyer, if any, is determined by the principal amount specified in the agreement and the degree to which the interest-rate index exceeds the strike rate. By purchasing this interest-rate cap, the committee can achieve its desire to reduce the risks associated with higher interest rates without eliminating the benefits of lower interest rates. Of course, a premium or fee has to be paid to achieve this risk reduction. A buyer of an interest-rate cap is often a bank that would be adversely affected by higher interest rates. In that event, the payments received from the interest-rate cap partially offset the loss of income caused by the higher costs of attracting deposits.

The example illustrated in Exhibit 23-5 will make this clearer. Let's assume that First South-Western agrees to buy a 2-year, $10 million interest-rate cap from ITP Capital. The parties agree to settle once per year, employ a strike rate of 6 percent, and use a particular 1-year interest rate as the reference rate. The premium for this contract is 3 percent of the principal amount ($10 million × .03 = $300,000), or

Interest-Rate Cap
An agreement whereby the seller of the cap agrees, for a fee, to compensate the cap buyer when an interest-rate index *exceeds* a specified strike rate.

Strike Rate
The agreed-upon rate in an interest agreement.

Principal amount = $10 million		
Premium = 3% of $10 million principal = $300,000		
Payments received from an interest rate cap = (LIBOR–strike rate) × principal amount		
	YEAR 1	YEAR 2
LIBOR (reference rate)	8%	9%
Strike rate	6%	6%
Payments received	$200,000	$300,000

EXHIBIT 23-5
A Simple Interest Rate Cap

$300,000. First South-Western pays this fee with the understanding that if the interest rate exceeds the 6 percent strike rate, First South-Western will be compensated by ITP Capital. In effect, by buying a cap, a ceiling rate is placed on the cost of funds. Higher interest rates will increase the cost of funds, but they will also increase the compensation from the interest-rate cap.

Total compensation is determined by the difference between the actual interest rate and the strike rate, times the principal amount of the transaction. Let's assume that the interest rate 1 year from now is 7 percent and the rate 2 years from now is 8 percent. In year 1, ITP Capital will pay the difference between the actual and strike rates (8 percent–6 percent) × $10 million = $200,000. In year 2 it will pay (9 percent–6 percent) × $10 million = $300,000. Thus, over the 2-year period, ITP Capital pays First South-Western $500,000. This is $200,000 more than the $300,000 fee First South-Western paid for the cap. If the interest rate had remained below the strike rate, ITP Capital would have made no payments to First South-Western despite the fee paid. If interest rates would have been higher, ITP Capital would have been paid even more. Regardless of what happens with actual interest rates, First South-Western is able to reduce the possibility of lower income resulting from higher interest rates and retain the possibility of benefiting from lower interest rates by purchasing an interest-rate cap.

Interest-Rate Floors

One can easily imagine the opposite case with a bank facing risks caused by lower interest rates.—for example, a credit card bank has a positive income gap caused by more interest-rate-sensitive assets (floating rate credit card receivables) than interest-rate-sensitive liabilities (fixed-rate bonds outstanding). An increase in interest rates would lead to higher credit card rates, enhancing the firm's revenue stream. However, higher short-term rates would have little or no effect on the bank's cost of funds. Lower interest rates would be a problem. Credit card rates could float downward while its costs of funds remain unchanged, thus narrowing or reversing the interest-rate spread. This bank could hedge against falling interest rates by engaging in a securitization, restructuring its balance sheet, or employing an interest-rate swap. However, all of these solutions would also limit the bank's ability to profit from higher future interest rates. To avoid the downside risk of lower rates without eliminating the upside potential of higher rates, our bank can buy an interest-rate floor.

Interest-Rate Floor
An agreement whereby the seller of the cap agrees, for a fee, to compensate the cap buyer when an interest-rate index *falls below* a specified strike rate.

An **interest-rate floor** is an agreement whereby the seller of the floor agrees, for a fee, to pay the buyer of the floor when the actual interest rate *falls below* the strike rate. Like a cap, the amount of compensation is determined by the difference between the actual interest rate and the strike rate, times the principal amount of the transaction. Our seller will pay only if interest rates fall below the strike rate. Let's again assume that First South-Western (here, our credit card bank) is the buyer and the ITP Capital is the seller. The terms are the same except that this is now an interest-rate floor instead of an interest-rate cap. In effect, by buying a floor, a guaranteed minimum rate of return is ensured on earnings. This example is illustrated in Exhibit 23-6.

Let's assume that First South-Western agrees to buy a 2-year, $10 million interest-rate *floor* from ITP Capital. The parties agree to settle once per year, employ a strike rate of 6 percent, and use a particular 1-year interest rate as the reference rate. The premium for this contract is 3 percent of the principal amount ($10 million × .03 = $300,000), or $300,000. First South-Western pays this fee with the understanding that if the interest rate *falls below* the 6 percent strike rate, First South-Western will be compensated.

EXHIBIT 23-6
A Simple Interest Rate
Floor

Principal amount = $10 million
Premium = 3% of $10 million principal = $300,000
Payments received from an interest rate floor = (strike rate–LIBOR) × principal amount

	YEAR 1	YEAR 2
LIBOR (reference rate)	4%	4.5%
Strike rate	6%	6%
Payments received	$200,000	$150,000

Let's assume that the interest rate 1 year from now is 4 percent and the rate 2 years from now is 4.5 percent. In year 1, ITP Capital will pay the difference between the actual and strike rates (6 percent–4 percent) × $10 million = $200,000. In year 2 it will pay (6 percent–4.5 percent) × $10 million = $300,000. Thus, over the 2-year period in nominal terms, ITP Capital pays First South-Western $350,000. The fee paid was $300,000, so First South-Western gained $50,000 in this transaction. If interest rates had been lower, ITP Capital would have paid even more. If the interest rate had remained *above* the strike rate, the premium would still have been paid and ITP Capital would have made no payments to First South-Western.

Why would a financial institution be willing to *sell* an interest-rate cap or floor? A seller of an interest-rate cap would typically be a financial institution whose financial analysis department has predicted stable or lower future interest rates. If the prediction is correct, it receives the cap fee and makes no payments. Alternatively, it may be a firm that, because of its balance sheet structure, would be hurt by lower rates. Thus, it is hedging against this scenario by selling the interest-rate cap. If rates do fall, the income from the rest of its portfolio may fall, but the fee income from the interest-rate cap would partially offset this affect and no payments would need to be made to compensate the buyer. In contrast, the seller of an interest-rate floor expects stable or higher interest rates. If the seller is correct, it receives the fee for the floor and makes no payments to the buyer. Similarly, the seller of an interest-rate floor may be a firm hurt by higher rates. By selling a floor, income is generated to help offset the losses occurring elsewhere on the firm's balance sheet. Appreciating the motivations of both buyer and sellers helps us to understand why firms buy an interest-rate cap and sell an interest-rate floor simultaneously.

Interest-Rate Collars

An *interest-rate collar* is created when one simultaneously *buys* an interest-rate cap and *sells* an interest-rate floor. Think back to the two examples given in our discussion of interest- rate ceilings and floors. If a financial manager believes that interest rates are going to rise, it makes sense to pay the fee to buy an interest-rate cap. If one is especially confident, he or she can simultaneously sell an interest-rate floor. The fee income generated from the sale of the floor may partially or fully offset the fee paid to purchase the interest-rate cap in the first place. As long as the prediction of higher interest rates holds, the holder of the collar will generate earnings. If interest rates do fall, the seller of the floor will need to pay the buyer the compensation contractually due. However, in most circumstances, this will not be an undue burden. Typically, as discussed in our interest-rate cap example, lower interest rates increase a bank's ordinary earnings by lowering the cost of funds faster than the earnings on loans. Thus, a collar may be an effective way for a bank to hedge against interest-rate risk.

Currency Swaps

Just as interest-rate swaps, caps, floors, and collars have proliferated for managing interest-rate risk, currency swaps, forwards, futures and options have originated to help financial institutions manage the adverse effects of currency movements.

Currency Swaps
Agreements whereby one party agrees to trade periodic payments, over a specified period of time, in a given currency, with another party who agrees to do the same in a different currency.

Currency swaps are an agreement whereby one party agrees to trade periodic payments, over a specified period of time, in a given currency, with another party who agrees to do the same in a different currency. Currency swaps function like a series of currency future contracts. The difference is that rather than contracting for a single time period, a swap can be used to hedge against foreign exchange-rate risk over a multi-year period.

Like many financial innovations, currency swaps originally developed as a means to circumvent regulation. In the past, many countries employed capital controls to encourage greater foreign investment by domestically based foreign subsidiaries. By delaying the conversion of foreign-denominated earnings into a parent company's domestic currency, countries hoped that foreign subsidiaries would engage in increased investment within the country. Imagine a U.S. soft drink company with bottling and sales operations in China. If China delays the conversion of yuans into dollars, the bottling company will forgo interest earnings it could earn if it could convert yuans to dollars now. China hopes that delay will encourage the bottling company to invest its yuans within the country to foster economic development. However, American corporations have found ways to get around this regulation.

http://www.risk.net
Visit the Risk Waters Group for a variety of information on risk management, including currency swaps.

To avoid both lost interest earnings and investing in China, it makes sense for the soft drink company to engage in a currency swap. This is arranged in three steps: (1) Our bottling company borrows using a yuan-denominated bond issue or loan; (2) it asks another company to borrow using a dollar-denominated bond issue or loan; and (3) the two companies "swap" the proceeds from their respective loans. They do not, however, swap the repayment of their loans. Our bottling company pays off its loan with funds from its Chinese operations. Similarly, the other company pays off its loans in dollars from its ongoing operations. Both companies get immediate access to the currency that they want and innovate around the capital control regulations.

In addition to avoiding capital controls and allowing for the multi-year hedging of foreign-generated earnings, currency swaps can, under certain circumstances, create profitable opportunities for intermediation and reduced borrowing costs.

Imagine a U.S. company that wants to build an office complex in London, England. At the same time, a U.K. company wants to build a new strip mall in Los Angeles, California. Each of these projects will cost $30 million dollars, or 15 million pounds at the current exchange rate of $1 = £.5 (or £1 = $2). For the sake of simplicity, we assume the loans (or bond issues) are interest-only for 5 years and the principal is repaid at maturity. To pay for its project in pounds, the U.S. firm could either (1) issue a fixed-rate, £60 million-denominated bond in the United Kingdom or (2) a fixed-rate, $30 million dollar-denominated bond in the United States and then convert the proceeds into pounds to pay for the new office complex. The U.K. firm engaging in the U.S. mall project faces similar choices in obtaining dollars. It could either (1) issue a fixed-rate, $30 million dollar-denominated bond in the United States or (2) a fixed-rate, £15 million denominated bond in the United Kingdom and then convert the proceeds into

Suppose that a U.S. and a U.K. firm can borrow in their respective countries for 5 years at the following fixed rates of interest:

	$	£
U.S. firm	5.0%	**9.5%**
U.K. firm	**8.0%**	10.0%

Structure and potential benefits of a currency swap

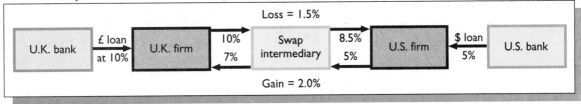

EXHIBIT 23-7
Structure and Potential Benefits of a Currency Swap

dollars to pay for construction of the new mall.[6] Which of these options is the best for each firm?

As with many things in finance, it depends. Exhibit 23-7 summarizes the hypothetical loan rates facing each of our firms in each country and the structure of a currency swap. The U.S. firm has a higher credit rating and can borrow more cheaply in both the U.S. and U.K. markets. However, the U.S. firm has a bigger comparative advantage in the United States (3 percentage points—8.0 percent–5.0 percent) than it does in the United Kingdom (.5 percentage point—10.0 percent–9.5 percent). This might be because the U.S. firm is better known in the States than it is in the British Isles. Note that in this particular example, interest rates for both firms are higher in the United Kingdom than in the United States.

If the U.S. firm borrows in pounds (at 9.5 percent) and the U.K. firm borrows in dollars (at 8 percent), they will be paying a combined interest rate of 17.5 percent (9.5 percent + 8.0 percent = 17.5 percent). If, instead, each firm borrows in its home country and engages in a currency swap, both can reduce their borrowing costs. The U.S. firm can borrow dollars at 5.0 percent and the U.K. firm can borrow pounds at 10.0 percent. In this case, the total interest paid is 15.0 percent (5.0 percent + 10.0 percent = 15.0 percent). Thus, the firms can reduce the annual interest payments by 2.5 percentage points by borrowing in their own currencies and then swapping the proceeds.

Examine the bottom half of Exhibit 23-7 beginning at the far left. The U.K. bank lends £15 million to a U.K. firm at a 10 percent interest rate. The U.K. firm, in turn, lends the loan proceeds to an intermediary coordinating the swap at the same 10 percent interest rate. The intermediary takes these pounds and loans them to the U.S. firm at 8.5 percent. This 8.5 percent rate is 1.0 percentage point lower than the 9.5 percent rate the U.S. firm could get in the U.K. market on its

---

[6]Either or both of our firms could engage in variable-rate borrowing. If one used fixed-rate and the other variable-rate financing, they could combine an interest-rate swap with a currency swap. This combination of instruments is called a cross-currency swap. We ignore these instruments for ease of exposition and because our students find currency swaps complicated enough. We have also simplified this example by making the principal amounts of the loans for both firms the same. However, this does not materially change our results.

own. It also means that the intermediary takes a loss of 1.5 percent on this loan. Before you dismiss the intermediary's sanity, we need to also examine the bottom half of Exhibit 23-7 from right to left. A U.S. bank lends $30 million to a U.S. firm at a 5 percent interest rate. Like its English counterpart, the U.S. firm lends its dollars to the swap intermediary at the same 5 percent interest rate. The intermediary in turn lends these dollars at a 7 percent interest rate to the U.K. firm. This 7.0 percent rate is 1.0 percentage point lower than the U.K. firm would have had to pay borrowing on its own. Here, the intermediary also makes a gain of 2 percent by borrowing dollars at 5 percent from the U.S. firm and then lending them to the U.K. firm again at 7 percent. Thus, this 2 percentage point gain minus the earlier 1.5 percentage point loss leaves the intermediary .5 percent ahead of where it started. In summary, the U.S. firm borrows pounds at an interest rate 1 percent below what it otherwise could have obtained, the U.K. firm borrows dollars at an interest rate 1 percentage point lower than it could otherwise, and the shrewd intermediary who arranged the entire transaction receives a net .5 percent spread.

The currency swap has allowed our firms to borrow at lower rates. However, both firms remain exposed to considerable exchange-rate risk. The U.K. firm has to make five annual loan payments on a dollar-denominated loan and repay the $30 million in principal in 5 years. If the dollar appreciates during this period, it will take even more in pound terms to repay the loan. Similarly, our U.S. firm has to make five annual payments on a pound-denominated loan and pay back £15 million in principal. If the pound appreciates, it will take even more dollars than expected to repay the loan. The good news is that this exchange-rate risk exposure can be completely discharged. If the U.S. firm agrees to make the U.K. firm's interest and principal payments and the U.K. firm agrees to make the U.S. firm's interest and principal payments, the exchange-rate risk is eliminated. Thus, under certain circumstances, firms borrowing in their home markets, "swapping" their initial loan proceeds, and then again "swapping" their payment obligations, can lead to lower borrowing costs and provide multi-year protection from exchange-rate risk.

Recent Trends in Interest-Rate Agreements and Currency Swaps

The best data from tracking the derivative instruments come from surveys done by the International Swaps & Derivatives Association (ISDA). These data are illustrated in Exhibit 23-8, which is based on the outstanding notional principal of interest-rate swaps, caps, floors, and currency swaps.[7] *Notional principal* is the base amount used for calculating the exchange of payments (we refer to it as simply the *principal amount* in our examples of caps and floors). This greatly overstates the amount of market risk, but serves as a useful yardstick for measuring changes over time.

By any measure, these derivative instruments have grown rapidly in popularity. In 1995, $17 trillion of these were outstanding. By year end 2000, this amount increased to over $63 trillion worth of notional principal outstanding. As global trade and investment expand and users become increasingly sophisticated in their risk management strategies, we expect the popularity of these instruments to continue their rapid growth.

---

[7] Also included are data on the volume of swaptions, a type of interest-rate option not discussed in this text.

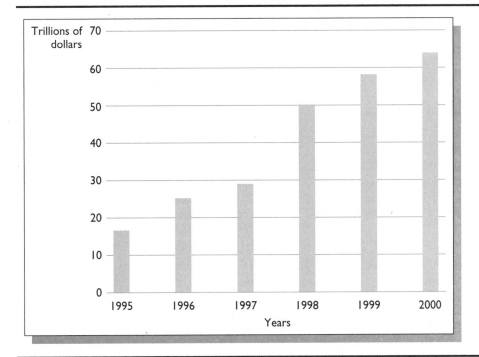

SOURCE: http://www.isda.org, International Swaps and Derivatives Association.

EXHIBIT 23-8
Recent Trends in Interest-Rate Agreements and Currency Swaps (In trillions of dollars of outstanding notional principal)

RECAP Interest-rate caps, floors, and collars can be used to manage interest-rate risk when securitization, interest-rate swaps, or balance sheet restructuring is inappropriate An interest-rate cap is an agreement whereby the seller of the cap agrees, for a fee, to compensate the cap buyer when an interest-rate index exceeds a specified strike rate. In contrast, an interest-rate floor is an agreement whereby the seller of the floor agrees, for a fee, to pay the buyer of the floor when the actual interest rate falls below the strike rate. In either case, the amount of compensation is determined by the difference between the actual interest rate and the strike rate, times the principal amount of the transaction. An interest-rate collar is created when one simultaneously buys an interest-rate cap and sells an interest-rate floor. Currency swaps are used to reduce a firm's exposure to foreign exchange risk. The main benefit of currency swaps over currency future contracts is that swaps can be done for multiple-year periods whereas future contracts are used to hedge foreign exchange risk for shorter periods of time. Over the last half of the 1990s, the volume of interest-rate agreements and currency swaps has increased dramatically.

Conclusion

This concludes our three chapter practical introduction to financial risk assessment and management. We have discussed essential risk assessment techniques, (applying the five Cs of credit and income gap analysis), financial instruments (forwards, futures, options, swaps), and risk management strategies (balance sheet restructuring and securitization) that can be used to manage credit, interest-rate, liquidity, and exchange-rate risks. This subject matter is essential for the effective financial manager and the overall efficiency of our financial system.

The final two chapters of the text (Chapters 24 and 25) will explore how the Federal Reserve System uses monetary policy to manage the money and credit supply and interest rates. The Fed's aim is to encourage economic growth and maintain stable prices. By doing so, the Fed's policies—like the risk assessment and management techniques explored here—have the potential to reduce economic uncertainty and enhance both the efficiency and equity of the financial system.

Summary of Major Points

- Securitization, interest-rate agreements (swaps, floors, ceilings, and collars), and currency swaps can be used to manage various kinds of risk. However, issuers and purchasers of these various instruments need to understand and employ these instruments correctly to manage risk and avoid losses.

- The process of securitization involves a variety of important players, including borrowers, a loan originator, a special purpose trust, a rating agency, a credit enhancer, an underwriter, and financial investors. Securitization reduces the transactions costs associated with financial intermediation through the pooling of financial obligations, prudent credit enhancement, favorable credit rating, and appropriate structuring of tranches.

- The benefits of securitization include lower borrowing costs for borrowers, enhanced earnings and customized investment vehicles for investors, and risk reduction and earnings for issuers.

- Securitization began in response to a shortage of funds for mortgages during the 1970s and 1980s. Tax law changes, the creation of government-sponsored enterprises, and technological advances in computing further facilitated this process. Over time, securitization has spread to many other types of asset-backed issues, including home equity loans, automobile loans, credit cards, commercial loans, student loans, and manufactured housing loans.

- Interest-rate swaps allow two parties to trade interest payment streams such that their interest inflows more closely match their outflows. An intermediary with fixed-rate assets and variable-rate liabilities will trade with another intermediary that has variable-rate assets and fixed-rate liabilities. The result is that both parties to the agreement reduce their risk exposure.

- The seller of interest-rate cap agrees, for a fee, to compensate the buyer of an interest-rate cap whenever an interest-rate index *exceeds* a specified strike rate. The seller of an interest-rate floor, agrees, for a fee, to pay the buyer of the interest-rate floor when the actual interest rate *falls below* the strike rate. The amount of compensation due to the buyer in either situation is determined by the difference between the actual interest rate and the strike rate, as well as the principal amount of the transaction. An interest-rate collar is created when one simultaneously *buys* an interest rate cap and *sells* an interest rate floor.

- Currency swaps are used to reduce a firm's exposure to foreign exchange risk. The main benefit of swaps over currency future contracts is that swaps can be done for multiple-year periods whereas future contracts are involve shorter time periods.

- Over the last half of the 1990s, the volume of interest-rate agreements and currency swaps has increased substantially.

Key Terms

Asset-Backed Securities	Home Equity Loans	Strike Rate
Credit Enhancer	Interest-Rate Cap	Superior/Subordinated Debt Structure
Currency Swaps	Interest-Rate Floor	
Derivative Instruments	Interest-Rate Swaps	Tranche
Due Diligence	Special Purpose Trust	

Review Questions

1. What are the costs and benefits of securitizing South Dakota's tobacco revenue?

2. What different kinds of assets "back" asset-backed securities? Which three constitute the largest shares of ABS issues?

3. Describe the historical trend in total asset-backed securities outstanding between 1982 and 2000.

4. What financial, legal, institutional, and technological changes encourage and facilitate the use of securitization?

5. Why is the trust structure important to the securitization process?

6. How can credit enhancement and a superior/subordinated debt structure be used to allow an A-rated company to issue AAA-rated securities?

7. How do borrowers, issuers, and investors benefit from the securitization process? Are there any losers from this process? Why?

8. What is a tranche?

9. Why would a bank with variable-rate money market deposits and fixed-rate, long-term mortgages enter into an interest-rate swap with another bank that has long-term, fixed-rate deposits and short-term, variable-rate mortgages? How would each benefit?

10. What advantage do interest-rate caps or floors have over interest-rate swaps?

11. What is an interest-rate collar? Under what circumstances would a financial manager employ one?

12. What is a currency swap? How does it differ from a currency futures contract?

Analytical Questions

13. Explain the role played by each of the seven types of players in the securitization process.

14. Imagine two banks: Bank A has short-term, variable-rate deposits and long-term, fixed-rate mortgages; Bank B has fixed-rate, long-term deposits and short-term, variable-rate mortgages. Which would be harmed by an increase in interest rates? Which would be harmed by a decrease in interest rates?

15. Which of the two banks described in question 14 would most likely buy an interest-rate cap? Why? Which would be most interested in buying an interest-rate floor? Why?

16. First South-Western agrees to buy a 2-year, $20 million interest-rate cap, settled once a year from ITP Capital. The strike rate is 5 percent. The premium is 2.5 percent of the principal amount. The interest rate 1 year from now is 7 percent and 2 years from now is 4 percent. How much will First South-Western pay for this contract? How much will First South-Western receive from ITP Capital in years 1 and 2?

17. First South-Western agrees to buy a 2-year, $25 million interest-rate floor, settled once a year from ITP Capital. The strike rate is 4 percent. The premium is 2.5 percent of the principal amount. The interest rate 1 year from now is 5 percent and 2 years from now is 3 percent. How much will First South-Western pay for this contract? How much will First South-Western receive from ITP Capital in years 1 and 2?

18. Assume that First South-Western enters into an interest-rate collar. It buys an interest-rate cap like that described in question 16 and simultaneously sells an interest-rate floor to West Capital that has the following characteristics: 2-year, $20 million interest-rate floor, settled once a year. The strike rate is 3 percent. The premium is 2.0 percent of the principal amount. The interest rate 1 year from now is 7 percent and 2 years from now is 4 percent. How much will First South-Western pay for these contracts? How much will First South-Western receive in years 1 and 2?

Internet Exercises

1. Go to Google (**http://www.google.com**) and do a search on "Asset-Backed Alert " (currently at **http://www.abalert.com**). When you find the site, click on "The Marketplace" button. Using the data on this page, do the following:

   a. Explain the distribution of ABS issues by sector (auto, cards, subprime, etc) year-to-date.

   b. Describe how this year's *total* year-to-date volume compares to last year's.

   c. Describe how this year's *non-US* year-to-date volume compares to last year's.

2. Go to **http://www.isda.org** and find the link for statistics. Use this to update the data shown in Exhibit 23-8. Describe what has happened to the overall trend in outstanding interest-rate swap, currency swap, and interest-rate option transactions since 2000. Were the authors right in predicting a continued upward trajectory?

Suggested Readings

Peter L. Berstein asserts that "The revolutionary idea that defines the boundary between modern times and the past is the mastery risk . . ." His *Against the Gods: The Remarkable Story of Risk* (John Wiley & Sons, Inc., 1996) is an engaging and entertaining history of our ability to measure and manage risk. He begins with the writings of the ancient Greeks and continues through a variety of writings of great minds such as Pascal, Fermat, Leibniz, Bernoulli, Knight, Keynes, von Neumann, Black, and Scholes. His history also gives us a longer-term perspective on the more recent failings of institutions such as Bankers Trust caused by investment in financial derivatives.

Felxi Kloman assembles, "A List of Treasured Risk Management Tomes" in his recent *Bank Insurance* article (May 21, 2001, Vol. 35, p. 10). All readers interested in this topic will find intriguing books worthy of further study among his brief reviews.

An excellent introduction to all aspects of securitization is assembled by Leon T. Kendall and Michael J. Fishman (1996) in *A Primer on Securitization* from MIT Press, Cambridge, Massachusetts. He provides an engaging overview of how securitization works and applies it to housing, commercial property automobile, and the financing of developing nations. In addition, various authors explain the roles played by ratings agencies, mortgage bankers, pension funds, and other investors. SNL Securities' monthly *Specialty Lending* and Merrill Lynch's annual *ABS Market Outlook* provide excellent analyses regarding trends in the industry and issuer market shares, and a wealth of information on asset-backed securities by sector.

For a comprehensive article on the history and types of interest-rate swaps, see "The Use of Interest Rate Swaps," *Asiamoney*, June 1998, pp. 2–5. For a clear discussion of interest-rate swaps, see Anatoli Kuprianov, "The Role of Interest Rate Swaps in Corporate Finance," *Economic Quarterly of the Federal Reserve Bank of Richmond*, Summer 1994; or J. Gregg Whittaker, "Interest Rate Swaps: Risk and Regulation," *Economic Review of the Federal Reserve Bank of Kansas City*, March 1987. Mary S. Ludwig's *Understanding Interest Rate Swaps* (New York: McGraw-Hill, 1993), reviews the mechanics and pricing of the swap market, swap jargon, and several potential applications of swaps. It also has a standardized interest-rate swap agreement.

Interest-rate caps, floors, and collars are the subject of Anatoli Kuprianov's "Over-the Counter Interest Rate Derivatives' in Chapter 16 of the Federal Reserve Bank of Richmond's *Instruments of the Money Market*, 7th ed, edited by Timothy Q. Cook and Robert K. Laroche. It was last updated in 1993. As chapters are revised, they become available on-line at **http://www.rich.frb.org/instruments/toc.html**.

Fuad A. Abdullah and Virginia L. Bean's "At Last, a Swaps Primer" published in the July–August 1988 *Financial Executive* remains a useful introduction to both currency and interest-rate swaps and their uses. For more up-to-the minute information on currency swaps and other derivatives, see **http://www.derivativesweek.com** and **http://www.euroweek.com**. These two sites require a fee for full access. However, both offer trial memberships that allow students to learn a great deal about these increasingly important financial instruments.

part

MONETARY POLICY

chapter

24 Monetary Policy and the Financial System

Learning Objectives *After reading this chapter, you should know:*

- How the monetary policy goals of sustainable economic growth and price stability affect the financial system
- How numerical goals are formulated for unemployment, inflation, and growth
- The time lags inherent in the policy process
- How intermediate targets are used in executing policy
- The role of the policy directive
- How monetary policy is implemented on a day-to-day basis in the market for reserves

" "

Now, it is not only necessary to do the right thing, but to do it in the right way and the only problem you have is what is the right thing to do and what is the right way to do it. That is the problem. But this economy of ours is not so simple that it obeys to the opinion of bias or the pronouncements of any particular individual.

—Dwight D. Eisenhower

The Fed and the Financial System

Monetary policy involves the Fed's use of its policy tools to affect the cost and availability of funds in the economy and to achieve its policy goals. Changes in monetary policy lead to changes in economic activity that affect prices, real output, employment, and the health and stability of the financial system.

In conducting monetary policy, the Fed works through the financial system. Recall that the Fed's primary tools for influencing the financial system include the use of open market operations, changes in the required reserve ratio, and changes in the discount rate. Open market operations are the most important monetary policy tool. These operations involve the buying or selling of U.S. government securities by the Fed. They are implemented by the Federal Reserve Bank of New York under the guidance and direction of the Fed Open Market Committee (FOMC). When the Fed buys securities, reserves rise; when the Fed sells securities, reserves fall. Open market operations have a direct effect on the reserves that are available to depository institutions and on interest rates.

Monetary policy influences the borrowing, lending, spending, and saving behavior of the household, business, government, and rest-of-the-world sectors. Monetary policy also affects the flow of funds throughout the economy and, thus, the prices of financial instruments. Prices of financial instruments are influenced both directly and indirectly. For example, when the Fed engages in open market operations, interest rates are nudged in one direction or the other. As discussed earlier, when interest rates change, prices of previously issued, long-term financial instruments change and holders of those instruments experience capital gains or losses. Additionally, changes in interest rates affect changes in economic activity as spending accelerates or slows down. Changes in economic activity lead to further changes in the prices of financial instruments.

A major responsibility of the Fed is to ensure the safety and soundness of the financial system. In conducting monetary policy, the Fed must be cognizant of its effect on the financial system because monetary policy has a direct and major effect on financial markets and institutions. Changes in reserves and interest rates affect the ability of depository institutions to make loans and to extend credit, which in turn affects their ability to earn profits. If financial institutions do not earn sufficient profit, the safety and soundness of the entire financial system can be threatened.

Likewise, when the Fed takes action that speeds up or slows down the economy, stock prices, bond prices, and the prices of foreign exchange are affected. Changes in these prices then affect the economy by causing changes in wealth and in spending.

In this chapter, we look first at the broad goals of monetary policy and the economic projections based on those goals over the next 12- to 18-month period. We then discuss the role of time lags and the use of intermediate targets in the policy process. Finally, we examine the policy directive issued by the FOMC and the day-to-day implementation of monetary policy in the market for reserves.

The Goals of Monetary Policy

As depicted in Exhibit 24-1, the long-run goals of monetary policy are to design and implement policies that will achieve sustainable economic growth and price stability over time. **Sustainable economic growth** is output growth along the economy's potential growth path. **Price stability** means inflation is so low and stable over time that it is ignored by households and firms in making decisions.

Sustainable Economic Growth
Output growth along the economy's potential growth path as determined by the growth of labor, capital, and productivity.

Price Stability
Inflation so low and stable over time that it is ignored by households and firms in decision making.

EXHIBIT 24-1
The Goals of
Monetary Policy

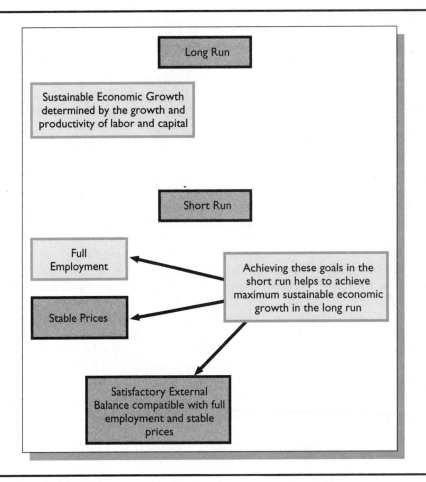

Sustainable Economic Growth

The size of the "economic pie" divided up among a nation's citizens is determined by the quantity of goods and services produced—that is, the size is determined by real output or real gross domestic product (GDP). *Real GDP* is the real or inflation-adjusted quantity of final goods and services produced in an economy in a given time period, usually 1 year. Simply put, if the size of a nation's economic pie and, thus, its potential standard of living are to rise over time, the productive capacity of the economy must expand.

Most economists agree that the growth of potential output over time is determined primarily by the growth of capital, labor, and productivity. Thus, growth of the key inputs in the production process and technological improvements are critical to long-run growth of output. So far so good—but what determines the growth of these factors?

The growth and productivity of the capital stock depends directly on the amount of investment spending undertaken by firms. By definition, the change in the capital stock is equal to the net amount of investment spending. The productivity of capital is thought to depend on the amount of resources devoted to research and development and on the resulting technological advances that lead to new and more productive plants and machines.

http://www.frbsf.org/
publications/
federalreserve/
monetary/reading.html
*Provides resources that
describe the general
purpose and goals of
monetary policy.*

In general, a thriving nation's productive capacity grows over time. Labor force growth flows from population growth and from increases in the portion of the population that participates in the labor force. The productivity of labor is thought to depend on the educational attainment and health of workers, the quantity and quality of the capital stock with which they work, and, perhaps, the competitive environment faced by firms and their employees.

Policymakers must also be concerned about unemployment, as measured by the unemployment rate, if the economy is to reach its full economic potential. Unemployment means slower economic growth because some resources are being wasted. The economy is operating below its economic potential and firms will be hesitant to invest when there is under-utilization of existing resources. From an economic standpoint, output that could have been produced last year by the unemployed is lost forever and can never be made up. Our nation's leaders operate with a clear mandate to pursue policies that encourage full employment to achieve sustainable economic growth.

Beyond these fairly obvious influences, the overall economic environment within which firms and households are making decisions is also important. A stable environment where workers are fully employed is likely to be more conducive to farsighted planning and decision making that enhance an economy's long-run growth potential. On the other hand, an unstable environment characterized by a series of inflationary booms and busts is likely to inhibit long-run growth. In such a situation, economic activity almost always grows faster or slower than the economy's capacity, thereby generating either heightened inflationary pressures or economic weakness. In any case, a stable and healthy financial system is necessary for the economy to achieve its goal of sustainable economic growth.

Price Stability

Inflation is the rate of increase in the general price level. The *Consumer Price Index (CPI)* is the most frequently cited measure of the price level in the United States. It measures the average level of prices of a market basket of goods and services purchased by a typical urban consumer. The month-to-month percentage change in this index gives us a somewhat reliable measure of inflation.[1]

Measurement aside, why do policymakers worry about inflation? After all, if the prices of all goods and services rise, then, under normal circumstances, incomes also rise. In this case, aren't all individuals and, thus, the nation as a whole, unaffected? The short answer is no. To see why, it is useful to distinguish between expected inflation and unexpected inflation.

Suppose households expect inflation to be about 3 percent in 2005. How will this expectation affect household behavior?

First and foremost, the workers in the households will try to secure wage increases of at least 3 percent so that the purchasing power of their incomes will not decline. Ideally, they would hope for wage increases greater than 3 percent so that their real incomes would rise. Regardless, wage increases will be based on the expectation of 3 percent inflation. If inflation is 3 percent as expected, all is well. But if inflation turns out to be 6 percent, workers will be worse off because wage

http://www. whitehouse.gov/fsbr/ esbr.html
Provides information on unemployment and inflation.

http://www.stls.frb. org/fred/index.html
Provides data and tables on inflation.

---

[1]Although widely used and, as we have said, "somewhat reliable," the CPI in recent years has been criticized for overstating inflation. Economists believe that the upward bias was between 0.2 and 1.5 percent per year. Currently, the method of calculating the CPI is being changed to correct the upward bias. The changes are expected to be completed in the next few years.

increases were based on the expectation of a 3 percent increase, and producers will be better off because output prices have gone up 6 percent.

Second, if households are net lenders, they will be looking for financial assets with nominal interest rates or nominal returns high enough to produce an adequate expected real (inflation-adjusted) return. As discussed in Chapter 5, a nominal return of 6 percent, given expected inflation of 3 percent, is expected to produce a real return or real interest rate of about 3 percent. If inflation turns out to be close to 3 percent as expected, all is well. But if prices actually rise by 6 percent, the real return on financial assets acquired will be less than anticipated. If lenders accepted a 6 percent interest rate, then with actual inflation of 6 percent, the lenders' real return would fall to 0 percent. In this case, the beneficiaries will be borrowers who find that the actual real cost of borrowing is well below what they expected. Beyond these types of redistribution, citizens living on fixed incomes, including many retirees, will find their purchasing power shrinking.

These simple examples illustrate a central reason why inflation, particularly unexpected inflation, is worrisome. Inflation redistributes income in arbitrary and unpredictable ways from workers to firms and from lenders to borrowers.

Additionally, due to several features of the U.S. tax system, many firms and households will pay proportionately more taxes to the government in an inflationary environment. Let us compare two scenarios. First, suppose that a household earns 4 percent interest on its surplus funds, the actual and expected inflation rate is 0 percent, and the household is in the 25 percent tax rate bracket. The household's real after-tax return is then 3 percent, as Equation (24-1) shows:

(24-1)   nominal interest rate – inflation rate –   taxes   = real after-tax return
$$.04 \quad\quad - \quad\quad 0 \quad\quad - (.25 \times .04) = \quad\quad .03 \text{ or } 3\%$$

Next, suppose that expected and actual inflation rises to 2 percent and the nominal interest rate rises from 4 to 6 percent to compensate lenders for the loss in purchasing power. The real after-tax return will again be the nominal rate minus the expected inflation rate and taxes. In this case, the real after-tax return equals 2.5 percent, as shown in Equation (24-2):

(24-2)   nominal interest rate – inflation rate –   taxes   = real after-tax return
$$.06 \quad\quad - \quad\quad .02 \quad\quad - (.25 \times .06) = \quad\quad .025 \text{ or } 2.5\%$$

Since nominal returns are taxed rather than real returns, inflation results in government taxes taking a larger portion of interest income than taken in a noninflationary environment.[2]

As the inflation rate rises, the variability of inflation tends to increase and the relationship among relative prices tends to become volatile and difficult to predict. Consequently, pricing, production, saving, and investment decisions have to be made in a more uncertain environment. Firms and households are likely to be much more cautious about making long-term commitments to spend, save, produce, or invest. They focus instead on near-term opportunities. This perspective does not enhance long-run stability and growth and can aggravate short-run instabilities and cyclical fluctuations.

Monetary policymakers do not make policy decisions in a vacuum. They are not oblivious to the domestic and international environment and the health and safety of the financial system. Nor do they aim at abstract, long-run theoretical goals of sustainable economic growth and price stability. Rather, they have specific numerical

---

[2]Inflation also reduces the real value of nominal money balances held. In this way, it acts as a tax on such holdings.

LOOKING OUT: *International Effects of Inflation*

Inflation can have an adverse effect on the nation's international competitiveness and, thus, its role in the world economy. For instance, if the prices of U.S. goods rise relative to prices of competing goods in the rest of the world, the demand for U.S. products will fall, with attendant effects on domestic production and employment. Although the resulting depreciation of the dollar will help to offset and reverse the negative effects on the trade balance over time, there is no assurance this will occur quickly. In the meantime, U.S. firms will lose a portion of their share of world markets.

As the U.S. economy becomes more globalized, monetary policymakers must be aware of the international effects of policy. For example, if the Fed raises domestic interest rates relative to foreign rates, a substantial appreciation of the dollar and augmented capital inflows can result. The dollar's appreciation may have a dramatic effect on the economy through its effect on net exports. Net exports fall as the foreign prices of U.S. goods increase and the domestic prices of foreign goods decrease. As a result, employment and output in the United States would decrease.

If monetary policymakers establish policy goals for inflation and growth that are widely divergent from those of other countries, substantial fluctuations in exchange rates can result. In addition to the price effects on net exports and the interest rate effects on capital flows, fluctuations in exchange rates greatly increase the exchange rate risks of international trade and finance. Central bank intervention may then be needed to stabilize exchange rates, but such intervention can dampen or conflict with the pursuit of other policy goals.

To summarize, monetary policy can cause dramatic changes in exchange rates and the balances on the current and capital accounts—that is, the external balance— which then feed back to the domestic economy. Exchange rate volatility can necessitate central bank intervention. The bottom line is that in designing and implementing monetary policy, policymakers must seek to achieve an acceptable external balance that is compatible with the domestic goals of full employment and stable prices. In Chapter 25, we take a more in-depth look at the international effects of monetary policy. We shall see that this increasingly globalized environment will necessitate more coordination among countries as they establish policy goals.

projections in mind for the growth of nominal and real GDP, unemployment, and inflation when they make policy adjustments that are consistent with the economic environment. It is to these projections we now turn.

RECAP The goals of monetary policy are sustainable economic growth and price stability. Sustainable economic growth is determined by the growth of the labor force, the capital stock, and productivity. Policies that achieve full employment and a noninflationary environment in the short run help to achieve sustainable growth and price stability in the long run. A stable and healthy financial system is necessary for the economy to achieve its goals. A stable price level is desirable because unexpected inflation redistributes income in arbitrary and unpredictable ways and causes distortions in the U.S. tax system. Policymakers must be aware that monetary policy can cause changes in exchange rates and the external balance that feed back to the domestic economy.

The Source of Numerical Projections for Unemployment and Inflation

General guidelines for policymakers are contained in the **Employment Act of 1946** and the **Humphrey-Hawkins Full Employment and Balanced Growth Act of 1978.** Both statutes direct policymakers to pursue policies consistent with achieving sustainable economic growth and price stability in the long run. This legislation, in effect, leaves it to policymakers, their staffs, and economists to determine what unemployment and inflation rates are consistent and feasible with the long-run goals.

Employment Act of 1946
The first statute that directed policymakers to pursue policies to achieve full employment and noninflationary growth.

Humphrey-Hawkins Full Employment and Balanced Growth Act of 1978
A statute that required policymakers to pursue policies to achieve full employment and noninflationary growth.

Natural Rate of Unemployment
The rate of unemployment that is consistent with stable prices; estimated to be 4.0 to 4.5 percent in the early 2000s.

In the early twenty-first century, most estimates of sustainable employment imply an unemployment rate of about 4.0 to 4.5 percent. This rate, also called the **natural rate of unemployment,** is believed to be the unemployment rate that is consistent with stable prices in the early 2000s.[3] Economists believe that a measured unemployment rate much below this level will trigger inflation as labor shortages appear in some markets and drive up wages and prices. The natural rate can change over time for various reasons, including the changing gender and age composition of the labor force and the changing safety net of benefits available to the unemployed.

On the inflation front, policymakers desire price stability and often stress that this should be the primary objective of monetary policy over time. To some analysts, price stability means zero inflation; others associate it with low and stable inflation rates in the 1 to 2 percent range that are ignored by households and firms. At the same time, short-term goals, such as for inflation, are not selected in a vacuum. In setting the inflation goal over the near term, such as the next year or two, policymakers consider recent experience and attempt to balance their desire to reduce inflation further with their desire to minimize the accompanying and possibly adverse near-term effects on unemployment and output growth. Thus, recent historical experience, judgments about what is feasible, and the political environment all play a role. Times change and so do economic goals.

http://www. federalreserve.gov/ boarddocs/hh
Provides the latest monetary policy testimony and report to Congress by the chair of the Board of Governors of the Fed.

Finally, based on our historical experience, economists estimate that the potential long-run growth rate for real GDP is around 2.5 to 3.0 percent per year over time. Growth beyond 3.0 percent per year does not seem to be sustainable over a long period. Sustainable growth in the 2.5 to 3.0 percent range is compatible with the other numerical goals for full employment and stable prices. If the economy grows at this sustainable rate, real GDP would increase by 2.5 to 3.0 percent per year.

In the long run, after all adjustments are completed, the goals of sustainable economic growth and price stability are believed to be perfectly compatible. Thus, there is no need for trade-offs between goals. However, we all live in the short run. History, as well as theory, tells us that policymakers' attempts to lower inflation can reduce output growth and increase unemployment for a time while attempts to raise output growth and employment can aggravate inflation. In this context, concerns do arise about the short-run versus the long-run effects of policy actions and the price versus the output effects of policy actions in the short run.

In summary, the prevailing economic and political environment and the nation's historical experience all play a role in setting the priorities that guide policy actions in the short run with the long-run goals of sustainable economic growth and price stability. Since the policymakers and the environment can change over time, so can the weight given to each priority.

Economic Projections
Goals for nominal and real GDP, unemployment, and inflation for the next 12- to 18-month period established by the FOMC at its meetings in February and July.

Against this backdrop, the FOMC establishes **economic projections** (goals) for nominal and real GDP, unemployment, and inflation at its meetings in February and July of each year. The projections are usually for 12 to 18 months. In compliance with the 1978 Humphrey-Hawkins Act, the chair of the Fed reports these long-term forecasts to Congress shortly after the meetings. Exhibit 24-2 shows the forecasts presented to Congress in July 2001.

---

[3]In the late 1980s and early 1990s, the natural rate of unemployment was believed to be in the 5.5 to 6.0 percent range. Low unemployment in the mid-1990s with moderate inflation convinced many economists that the natural rate had fallen to the 5.2 to 5.5 percent range. By the late 1990s, actual unemployment had fallen to the 4.3 to 4.7 range, with no increase in actual inflation. Many economists believed that wage pressure would soon lead to price increases. Nevertheless, by the early 2000s, the natural rate of unemployment was probably in the 4.0 to 4.5 range.

LOOKING BACK: *The Fed's Response to the Terrorist Attack of September 11, 2001*

The attack on the World Trade Center and the Pentagon on September 11, 2001 was the worst terrorist attack ever on U.S. soil. Civilian casualties exceeded 4,500 and property damage was enormous, surpassing all other single natural disasters. The attack struck at the core of the U.S. financial system, virtually closing down U.S. financial markets for one week. Key industries such as travel, airlines, and entertainment were devastated, leading to thousands of lay-offs in an economy that was already slowing. Consumer confidence plummeted.

The Fed's response to the attack was immediate and direct. First, the Fed used open market operations to supply unprecedented liquidity to the financial system in the form of increases in reserves. Reserves that had been trending downward jumped from roughly $40 billion in August 2001 to $58 billion in September 2001—a 45 percent increase in one month. In any prior month in recent years, reserves had changed by less than $1 billion.

The injection of reserves was reflected in dramatic increases in excess reserves and in all of the monetary aggregates. Excess reserves, which had been fluctuating narrowly between $1 and $1.4 billion, increased to over $19 billion in September 2001. M1 increased over $50 billion in September 2001, greatly surpassing any recent monthly increase.

In addition, the Fed made an intermeeting decrease in the fed funds rate on the morning of September 17, shortly before the re-opening of U.S. stock markets. The Fed also announced a corresponding decrease in the discount rate. The Fed coordinated the decrease in interest rates with other central banks including the European Central Bank, and central banks in Canada, England, and Sweden. The Fed also arranged a $50 billion currency swap agreement with the European Central Bank to aid European banks whose U.S. operations were disrupted by the terrorist attack.

Finally, in a related action, the U.S. Treasury announced that it would no longer issue 30-year bonds. Many believed that this move was made to help the Fed bring down long-term interest rates.

Looking back, few will say that the Fed was slow to respond to the crisis!

EXHIBIT 24-2
Economic Projections for 2001 and 2002 (in percents)
SOURCE: *Monetary Report to the Congress,* July 2001.

Indicator	BOARD OF GOVERNORS AND RESERVE BANK PRESIDENTS	
	Range	*Central tendency*
	2001	
Change, fourth quarter to fourth quarter[a]		
Nominal GDP	3–1/4 to 5	3–1/2 to 4–1/4
Real GDP[b]	1 to 2	1–1/4 to 2
PCE prices	2 to 2–3/4	2 to 2–1/2
Average level, fourth quarter		
Civilian unemployment rate	4–3/4 to 5	4–3/4 to 5
	2002	
Change, fourth quarter to fourth quarter[a]		
Nominal GDP	4–3/4 to 6	5 to 5–1/2
Real GDP[b]	3 to 3–1/2	3 to 3–1/4
PCE prices	1–1/2 to 3	1–3/4 to 2-1/2
Average level, fourth quarter		
Civilian unemployment rate	4–3/4 to 5-1/2	4–3/4 to 5–1/4

[a]Change from average for fourth quarter of previous year to average for fourth quarter of year indicated.

[b]Chain-weighted.

SOURCE: *Monetary Report to Congress,* July 2001.

RECAP General guidelines for numerical projections are found in the Employment Act of 1946 and the Humphrey-Hawkins Full Employment and Balanced Growth Act of 1978. Full employment is believed to be about 4.0 to 4.5 percent. Price stability means inflation that is low enough to be ignored by households and firms. The projections for unemployment and inflation depend upon recent experience and the political and historical environment. Sustainable growth is thought to be in the 2.5 to 3.0 percent range.

The Policy Process

Economic projections—combined with the expected economic performance—guide policy actions that, in turn, alter spending, saving, borrowing, and lending decisions, as depicted in Exhibit 24-3.

At first glance, the challenges facing policymakers do not seem all that imposing: If the economy's performance is expected to be close to the projections, leave the policy unchanged; if the economy's performance is expected to fall well short of the projections and there are signs of either economic weakness or heightened inflationary expectations, alter the policy accordingly. The reasoning is so simple and seemingly sensible that it leads one to wonder how policy and policymakers can ever go astray. However, any policymaker will tell you that making policy is both difficult and frustrating, laden with a never-ending series of problems and pitfalls. Obviously, we need to reflect more deeply about the process depicted in Exhibit 24-3.

EXHIBIT 24-3
A Conceptual
Overview of the
Macroeconomic
Policy Process

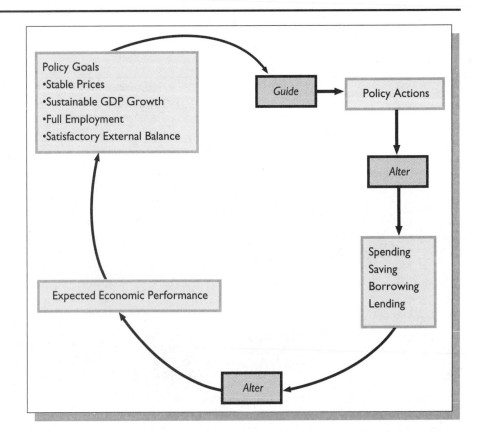

To begin, let's assume policymakers have already established numerical projections, as discussed previously. The next step is to determine the likely performance of the economy if policy remains unchanged. How do policymakers do this?

The basic approach is to use various statistical methods and models, judgment based on historical experience, and incoming data on the full range of factors affecting the economy to develop a forecast for the variables of major concern such as nominal and real GDP, inflation, and unemployment. The data include information about retail sales, industrial production, consumer confidence, business capital spending plans, business inventories, wages, personal income, profits, exchange rates, and the external balance of payments. Assuming it is January, forecasts for key variables typically cover the first quarter of the year (January to March) and extend over a 12- to 18-month horizon.

As data reports are published, policymakers ask themselves two questions: Are the data consistent with our economic outlook and desires, so no change in policy is needed? Or is the data signaling that the economy's performance has deviated so markedly from the projections that a change in policy should be considered? In reality, the process of filtering and assessing incoming data—much of which is estimated—is somewhat more difficult than one might imagine. The problem is that many monthly data releases are quite volatile, possessing a large element of randomness. The random fluctuations make the data unreliable as policy indicators. As a result of potentially large month-to-month fluctuations, it is often necessary to have data for 2 to 3 months on hand before the underlying cyclical or trend movements in an individual data series become evident.

When analysts try to extrapolate from individual data series (or sectors of the economy) to the strength of the economy as a whole, they often encounter another problem. The randomness in the individual series may cause a collection of different series to transmit conflicting signals. For example, the data reported for February might show that retail sales are stronger than expected, suggesting that the rate of consumption spending is increasing. At the same time, new orders for capital goods and housing starts are weak, suggesting that the rates of business fixed investment and residential investment spending are slowing. If the economy is in fact deviating from its expected track, it will usually take several months of data releases covering the full spectrum of the economy's performance before the ambiguities in the monthly data are resolved.

Policymakers need time to recognize that a change in the economy's performance has occurred. This time between a significant and unexpected change in the economy's performance and policymakers' recognition of that change is called the **recognition lag** in the policy-making process.

As evidence begins to accumulate that the economy is deviating significantly from the desired path, a consensus develops among policymakers that policy needs to be altered. For instance, if the economy is strengthening considerably and inflationary pressures are building, there is a need to reduce the growth of demand somewhat. At this point, the focus shifts from assessing the economy and considering whether anything needs to be done to deciding exactly what should be done. What policy tools should be used, how large or small should the policy adjustment be, and when should the policy change take place?[4]

http://www. federalreserve. gov/pf/pf.htm
Describes the goals and the process of implementing monetary policy.

Recognition Lag
The time between when a significant and unexpected change in the economy's performance occurs and when policymakers recognize that change.

---

[4]This aspect of the policy-making process, especially in the case of fiscal policy, can be agonizingly slow. It's one thing to decide to cut demand by reducing government spending and/or raising taxes. It's quite another to decide whose taxes to raise and exactly where spending should be cut. The latter inevitably involves political considerations.

Policy Lag
The time between when the need for action is recognized and when an adjustment policy is decided upon and set in motion.

Impact Lag
The time between when an action is taken and when that action has a significant impact on economic activity and prices.

Resolving these questions also takes time. The policy-making process includes a **policy lag**—the time between the point when the need for action is recognized and the point when an adjustment policy is decided upon and set in motion. The net result is that policy actions can be paralyzed for a while and policymakers may do too little too late.

When policymakers act, does the economy respond immediately? In general, the answer is no. The policy action will set in motion a series of adjustments in the economy that will gradually alter the performance of the economy relative to what it would have been in the absence of any new policy actions. To illustrate, suppose the economy has been growing quickly with inflation accelerating, so the Fed decides to pursue a more restrictive monetary policy. The Fed takes actions that reduce the supply of funds, and interest rates rise. Will firms cut their investment spending right away? Not necessarily. If a firm's new plant is half-completed, with high capacity utilization in its existing plants and with an expectation of a continuing demand for its products, the firm will continue spending on investment projects. Gradually, however, as the rise in interest rates and reduction in the availability of funds slow the growth of demand, sales and capacity utilization will fall, and expectations about the future will be modified. At this point, investment spending plans will be reevaluated and possibly postponed or canceled, leading to a further deceleration in the growth rate of economic activity.

This result is an **impact lag** in monetary policy—the time between when an action is taken and when that action has a significant impact on prices, employment, and output. How much time, you ask? Available research suggests that significant effects from policy change generally begin to show up after 6 months to 1 year or more and continue accumulating for several years. Exhibit 24-4 brings together the various lags comprising the policy process.

Despite policymakers' good intentions, monetary policy does not always produce an economic performance that coincides with the nation's economic projections. No simple explanations exist for the periodic lack of correspondence between policymakers' plans and economic performance. As in all endeavors, hon-

EXHIBIT 24-4
Lags in the Policy Process

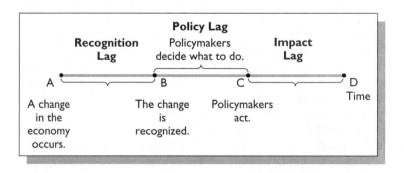

The *economy* begins to need corrective action at point A, but the need is not recognized until point B 3 months later. The time that elapses between point A and point B is called the recognition lag. Between point B and point C, policymakers think about what actions to take and reach a decision. The time that elapses between point B and point C is called the policy lag. Once action has been taken at point C, it takes time before the economy's performance is materially affected. The distance from point C to point D represents this impact lag.

est mistakes can be made, analysis can be faulty, and unexpected events beyond the policymakers' control can occur. Against this background, let's briefly examine some of the most prominent problems affecting the successful conduct of policy.

Economic Uncertainty

Economic developments today are largely the result of policies pursued over the past several years. There is little that policymakers can do today to materially affect the current performance of the economy, but they can affect the future performance of the economy. Because economic forecasts, in particular, can be quite wide of the mark, policymakers cannot know for certain what should be done today to improve the economy's future performance. To complicate matters further, large month-to-month fluctuations in economic data prevent policymakers from knowing how the economy is currently performing.

The net result is that policymakers are generally quite cautious in adjusting policy. Unless there is a crisis, they prefer to move gradually rather than precipitously in the general direction suggested by the current data on the economy and the policy projections. As understandable and reasonable as this approach sounds, some potentially serious pitfalls are lurking here.[5]

To illustrate, imagine that you are in the shower adjusting the hot water faucet to attain the desired temperature. The problem, especially in an older building, is that there is often a lag between when you turn the hot water faucet and when the water becomes warmer. Moreover, the lag can vary depending on how many other showers have been taken in the recent past, how many are currently being taken, and how much hot water is left in the tank. In other words, you lack the knowledge you need to "fine-tune" the hot water. When nothing happens after several gradual adjustments, you grow increasingly impatient and keep turning the knob. At some point, a rush of scalding water bursts out and you burn yourself. You never intended to burn yourself, but it happened anyway.

Policymakers have the same problem. They don't really intend, for example, to raise the inflation rate (and get burned), but it happens. The economy is performing sluggishly and policymakers want to increase economic growth. They increase demand (turn up the heat), but nothing seems to happen. They—and the nation— become increasingly impatient and demand increasing policy actions. Eventually, economic growth spurts ahead at an excessive pace, causing an unintended acceleration of inflation.

In sum, the existence of lags in an uncertain world complicates policymakers' efforts to act appropriately in a timely fashion regardless of whether economic weakness or heightened inflationary pressures are building. Acting or failing to act today may aggravate inflation and cyclical fluctuations later. The economy may be destabilized rather than stabilized. In the case of recession, the push *to do* something now to improve the situation as soon as possible interacts with the difficulties associated with lags and uncertainty and may lead to higher inflation later. In the case of inflationary pressures, the pressure *not to do* something now may cause higher inflation later. When there is pressure "to do something now" or "not to do something now," consistent formulation and implementation of policies conducive to economic growth and stability become even more problematic.

---

[5]For instance, in early 1994 the Fed was accused of destabilizing financial markets by making several small increases in interest rates rather than a few larger increases.

RECAP Policy projections, combined with expected economic performance, guide policy actions. The recognition lag is the time that it takes for policy-makers to recognize that economic conditions have changed and that a policy change is necessary. The policy lag is the time between the recognition of the need for action and the implementation of the policy adjustment. The impact lag is the time that it takes for the policy action to have a significant impact on the economy. The existence of lags in an uncertain world complicates policymakers' efforts to act appropriately in a timely fashion. In a recession, the push to do something now to improve the situation as soon as possible interacts with the difficulties associated with lags and uncertainty and may lead to higher inflation later. In the face of inflation, the pressure not to do something now may cause further instability later.

Intermediate Targets

Given the complexities, uncertainties, and time lags involved in the monetary policy process, the Fed has long utilized an intermediate target approach to the formulation of policy rather than solely focusing on the ultimate goals of sustainable economic growth and price stability. The basic idea, illustrated in Exhibit 24-5, is that the Fed selects a variable, such as a monetary aggregate or an interest rate, that is, in some sense, midway between its policy instruments and the ultimate or final goals or targets of policy.[6] The **intermediate target** is then used to guide day-to-day open market operations. The rationale is that if the Fed hits the intermediate target, it will come reasonably close to its economic projections.

Intermediate Target
The use of a target midway between the policy instruments and the ultimate policy goals.

Why an intermediate target? Suppose you have a bow and arrow and want to hit the center of a distant target you can barely see. The bow is your instrument, and the distant target you want to hit is your final target. The distance and poor visibility, however, make it difficult to hit the final target, so you select an intermediate target—a clearly visible target between you and the less-visible final target. You then align the intermediate target between you and the final target so that if you hit the center of the intermediate target, your arrow will continue on and strike the final target. In this way, you can hit the final target even though you can barely see it.

How does the Fed select a particular intermediate target and a particular range of values for it? The Fed could pick a monetary aggregate or domestic nonfinancial debt (DNFD), the broadest measure of credit, as an intermediate target and choose a growth rate range of, say, 5 to 9 percent. Or the Fed could use an interest rate as an intermediate target and select a target range such as 5.5 to 6 percent for nominal short-term rates. In either case, the basic criteria for selecting an intermediate target variable are related to the characteristics of economic data and policy actions discussed earlier.

First, the variable should be reliably and predictably related to the goal variables. If the variable was not related, hitting the intermediate target range would not necessarily help achieve the goals. To illustrate, a sailor traveling between point A and point B often finds it useful to guide the ship by initially aiming for a buoy firmly anchored midway between the two points. If the buoy was floating aimlessly instead of being anchored, it would not be a useful guide.

Second, policymakers should be able to observe the intermediate target regularly. That is, the data about the target should be readily available.

---

[6]Recall that the basic policy instruments that the Fed uses to manipulate the economy are open market operations, reserve requirements, and the discount rate, and that the major policy goals are full employment, stable prices, economic growth, and the external balance.

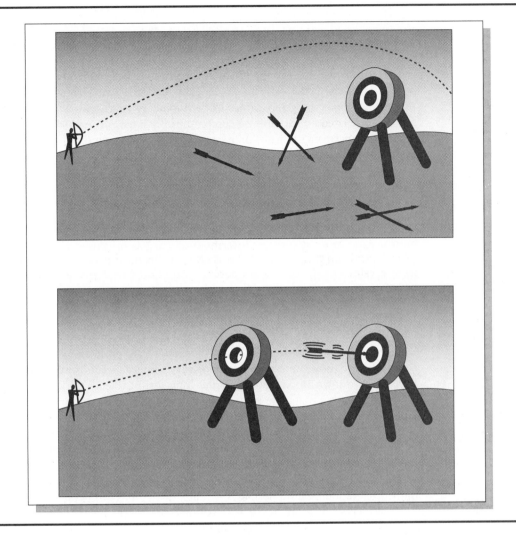

EXHIBIT 24-5

The Use of an Intermediate Target in Hitting the Final Target

Third, the Fed should be able to hit the target range of the intermediate variable—that is, they should be able to control the intermediate variable with policy instruments with a reasonable degree of precision. Obviously, a variable that cannot be readily observed and controlled would be of little practical use to policymakers. Our intrepid sailor, for example, would find a navigation buoy of little use without a working compass and good visibility.

Since mid-1993, the Fed has emphasized interest rate targeting. Under such a regime, the Fed increases the interest rate target if it perceives a need to slow down the level of economic activity and decreases the target if it perceives a need to speed things up. The Fed carries out this procedure by announcing a target for the fed funds rate and using open market operations to hit the target. In this case, the fed funds rate is an **operating target** that is highly responsive to open market operations, the Fed's main policy tool. The Fed adjusts the fed funds rate with an eye toward raising or lowering other short- and long-term interest rates. When interest rates change, the level of economic activity is affected. The Fed has more control over the operating target than over the intermediate target.

Operating Target
A target amenable to control by the policy tools and highly correlated with the intermediate target.

From the late 1970s until the early 1990s, the monetary aggregates and DNFD were monitored and used to guide monetary policy because there was a stable relationship between changes in one or more of the aggregates and the level of economic activity. The breakdown in the traditional relationships between these variables caused an abandonment of the use of monetary aggregates as either targets or information variables in the early 1990s. In July 2000, the Fed even stopped providing projections about the growth rates of the monetary aggregates and DNFD. Other models have fared no better in explaining the inflationary and growth processes. The result is an increasing reliance on a broad set of economic indicators to gauge monetary policy that is then implemented through changes in the fed funds rate.

http://www.
federalreserve.gov/
FOMC/transcripts
*Provides transcripts of
FOMC meetings.*

 RECAP The Fed uses intermediate targets to gauge policy. Monetary aggregates and nominal or short-term interest rates have been used as intermediate targets. The intermediate target must be highly correlated with the ultimate target and must be amenable to control by the Fed. In recent years, the Fed has emphasized interest rates as intermediate targets and used the fed funds rate as an operating target. The Fed has chosen this path because of the instability in the relationship of the monetary aggregates and the level of economic activity.

The Policy Directive

We already know that the Fed establishes long-term projections for nominal and real GDP, inflation, and unemployment at the February and July meetings of the FOMC. As shown in Exhibit 24-2, the long-term projections are thought to be compatible with sustainable economic growth and price stability and are likely to emerge over the coming year, given the current stance of monetary policy. At the six other FOMC meetings over the course of the year (in addition to the February and July meetings), the long-term projections are reviewed and sometimes revised, but the short-term strategies are emphasized.

Once the long-term policy stance is set, the focus of the FOMC shifts to the immediate period. In most periods, the policy discussions center on the fed funds rate itself, as well as other interest rates. As noted previously, interest rates have gained center stage as intermediate targets in the mid- and late 1990s and early 2000s.

At the same time, policy has been somewhat eclectic, and "the process of probing a variety of data to ascertain underlying economic and financial conditions has become even more essential to formulating sound monetary policy."[7] As a result, the Fed now looks at many indicators.

Given its assessment of current economic conditions and the economic outlook, the FOMC comes up with short-term strategies consistent with its longer-range projections. The FOMC issues a *policy directive* to the Trading Desk of the New York Fed. This directive guides the conduct of open market operations until the next FOMC meeting approximately 6 weeks later. The policy directive takes the following format, puts in a specific fed funds rate target, and chooses one of the bracketed phrases to communicate the exact targeted rate:

The Federal Open Market Committee seeks monetary and financial conditions that will foster price stability and promote sustainable growth in output. To further its long-run objectives, the Committee in the immediate future seeks condition in reserve markets consistent with [reducing] [increasing] [leaving unchanged] the federal funds rate to an average of around [xx] percent.

[7]*Federal Reserve Bulletin*, September 1995, p. 853.

LOOKING FORWARD: *E-Money and Monetary Policy*

Some concern exists that the evolution of the payments system to an e-money system will reduce the ability of the Fed to execute monetary policy through traditional channels. Namely, the growth of e-money may supplant traditional payment mechanisms. E-money is privately created "money" that uses the Internet to execute payments. E-money bypasses both the use of currency and reserves. Depository institutions, other intermediaries, and nonfinancial firms may create e-money. E-money consists of credits similar to IOUs that are used to make payments and are accepted as payment for goods and services. The firms that create e-money settle with each other rather than with the central bank. The concern is that if more payments are made in this way, the demand for currency and reserves will fall (and could theoretically fall to zero), thus reducing the ability of the Fed to control interest rates by affecting the supply of the monetary base.

We are very far from the scenario in which the demand for reserves and currency becomes so insignificant that it interferes with the conduct of monetary policy. The demand for currency continues to increase, driven by both the growth of cash transactions in the United States and the international demand for dollars. This trend may slow in the future with the widespread adoption of smart cards to make payments.

The demand for reserve balances has rapidly decreased in recent years due to lower reserve requirements and the growth of retail sweep accounts. These developments do not seem to have reduced the ability of the Fed to control interest rates.

However, given that a high proportion of e-money could displace traditional payment mechanisms in the future, the job of the Fed in forecasting the demand for reserves and currency and, thus, implementing monetary policy may become more difficult. Consequently, e-money could have far-reaching implications for central banks.

The policy directive, along with the following statement, is released to the public to communicate the FOMC's assessment of the risks to satisfactory economic performance in the foreseeable future. Again, the FOMC chooses one of the bracketed phrases to describe the committee's view.

> Against the background of its long-run goals of price stability and sustainable economic growth and of the information currently available, the Committee believe that the risks are [balanced with respect to prospects for both goals] [weighted mainly toward conditions that may generate heightened inflation pressures] [weighted mainly toward conditions that may generate economic weakness] in the foreseeable future.

The Fed can also make an intermeeting adjustment. Intermeeting changes occurred in 1998 in response to a crisis in Russia, twice in early 2001, in response to a weak economy and once in late 2001 in response to the terrorist attack on September 11, 2001. Historically, an intermeeting change has been rare.

In the next section, we look at the specifics of how the directive is implemented.

RECAP At each FOMC meeting, a policy directive that directs the stance of monetary policy is sent to the New York Fed. In recent years, the Fed has looked to interest rates to guide policy and downplayed the use of the aggregates.

The Reserves Market and the Day-to-Day Execution of Monetary Policy

To implement the policy directive, the Trading Desk of the New York Fed tries to manage reserve levels of depository institutions so that the fed funds rate will be equal to the targeted rate. To do this, the Trading Desk develops estimates of the likely demand and supply of total reserves. The demand for reserves consists of (1) the demand for required reserves, plus (2) the demand for excess reserves. Depository institutions may demand excess reserves to avoid unintended shortages of required reserves. Recall that the supply of reserves has two major components: (1) borrowed reserves, which are reserves borrowed by depository institutions from the Fed's discount facility, and (2) nonborrowed reserves, which are reserves available in the open market. In equilibrium, the quantity demanded of reserves will equal the quantity supplied, making the market for reserves like any other market. Exhibit 24-6 reviews the basic reserve components and determinants.

But how does this equilibrium come about? Suppose that under current market conditions, including the current fed funds rate, the quantity demanded of reserves is greater than the quantity supplied. What will happen? Simply put, the excess quantity demanded would be reflected in the fed funds market where reserves are bought and sold among depository institutions. Given the excess of quantity demanded over quantity supplied, market forces will cause the fed funds rate to rise. Likewise, if the quantity of reserves supplied of reserves at the current fed funds rate is greater than the quantity demanded, the fed funds rate will fall.

In recent years, the Fed has implemented policy by guiding its open market operations with an eye toward achieving the targeted fed funds rate. Suppose the directive calls for "maintaining the federal funds rate at an average of around 5 1/2 percent." Immediately after the FOMC meeting, the Trading Desk derives the **reserve need,** which is the difference, if any, between actual reserves and those projected to keep the fed funds rate at the desired level. The reserve need must be met with open market operations in order to fulfill the policy directive. If the Trading Desk supplies more than the reserve need, the fed funds rate will fall. If the Trading Desk supplies less than the reserve need, the fed funds rate will rise. Note that the reserve need may be negative; reserves may need to be withdrawn by open market sales to meet the directive.

Reserve Need
The difference, if any, between actual reserves and those projected to be needed to keep the fed funds rate at the target level.

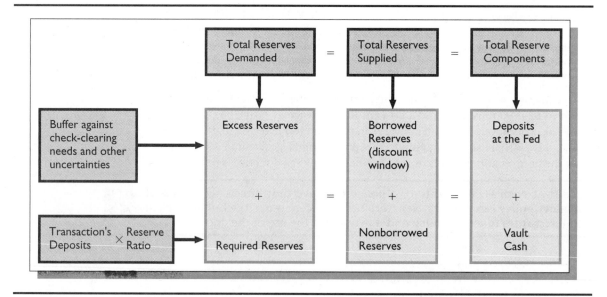

EXHIBIT 24-6
Total Reserves
SOURCE: Adapted from Ann-Marie Meulendyke, *U.S. Monetary Policy and Financial Markets* (New York: Federal Reserve Bank of New York, 1998).

As the weeks between FOMC meetings pass, various pieces of information accumulate. Each day, the Fed updates its estimates of the supply of reserves, given yesterday's change, if any, in the Fed's portfolio and new information on the other factors affecting reserves. Using updated information, the manager revises his estimate of the reserves that need to be supplied or absorbed to maintain the desired reserve conditions that coincide with the targeted fed funds rate. Thus, in response to the incoming data, the reserve need may be revised.

In recent years, required reserves have declined substantially and are continuing to decline. This is due to the widespread growth of retail sweep accounts. A financial innovation that first appeared in 1994, **retail sweep accounts** "sweep" balances out of transactions accounts that are subject to reserve requirements and into other deposits (usually money market deposit accounts) that are not.[8] Required reserves fall by the amount of funds in sweep accounts multiplied by the required reserve ratio. Balances in sweep accounts grew from $5.3 billion in January 1994 to $434.5 billion in August 2001. In the aggregate, required reserves dropped about $22 billion between December 1993 and August 2001.[9] Depositors are not affected because the funds are swept back into the transactions account when they are needed. Banks benefit because of the resulting reduction in required reserves that do not earn interest. They also have the ability to make more loans and other investments with the funds that otherwise would be held as required reserves.[10] Declines in required reserves are expected to taper off in future years, as all the opportunities to reduce reserves will have been exploited.

The significant decline in required reserves in recent years due to sweep accounts has raised concern that the fed funds rate may become more volatile and may affect the implementation of monetary policy. This increased volatility would result from depository institutions attempting to manage reserve accounts with very low balances at the Fed. Although there is some evidence that the fed funds rate has become more volatile with the growth of retail sweep accounts, the increased volatility does not seem to be significant enough to cause major disruptions in the fed funds market or general instability in financial markets.[11] So far, the implementation of monetary policy has not been affected.

To summarize, if the fed funds rate rises above the targeted rate, the Trading Desk increases the amount of reserves available to depository institutions to bring the fed funds rate back to the targeted level. Likewise, if the fed funds rate falls below the targeted rate, the Trading Desk decreases the amount of reserves.

Retail Sweep Accounts
An innovation that sweeps balances out of deposits subject to reserve requirements and into other deposits that are not.

---

[8]Wholesale sweep programs have been in existence since the 1970s. With wholesale sweep programs, the depository institution sweeps funds in a business's demand deposit into a money market instrument such as a repurchase agreement, Eurodollar deposit, or money market mutual fund. For wholesale sweep accounts, the deposits are swept into an account that may or may not be a liability of the depository institution. For retail sweep accounts, the swept funds stay on the books of the depository institution.

[9]"Open Market Operations in the 1990s," *Federal Reserve Bulletin*, November 1997, p. 870.

[10]In recent years, Congress has considered authorizing the Fed to pay interest on reserves. This could affect the amount of funds that are "swept" out of checkable deposits and into money market deposit accounts.

[11]See Paul Bennett and Spence Hilton, "Falling Reserve Balances and the Federal Funds Rate," *Current Issues in Economics and Finance*, Volume 3, Number 5, Federal Reserve Bank of New York, April 1997.

RECAP The Trading Desk derives the reserve need to fulfill the policy directive. The reserve need is based on the discrepancy between actual reserves and projections of the amount that will be needed to fulfill the policy directive. The reserve need must be met with open market purchases or sales. As new data come in about interest rates, the Trading Desk may adjust the reserve need. New data about the economy may also lead to changes in the stance of monetary policy, which will also change the reserve need. The growth of retail sweep accounts since 1994 has reduced the amount of required reserves and led to concerns about (1) increased volatility of the fed funds rate and (2) the Fed's ability to implement monetary policy using changes in the fed funds rate. So far, monetary policy does not seem to be affected.

We have considered the formulation and implementation of monetary policy given the goals of sustainable economic growth and price stability. Whatever the case may be, the policy responses discussed in this chapter suggest ways to achieve full employment and stable prices, albeit in an uncertain world where the effects of policy actions occur with lags. Keep in mind that healthy and stable financial markets are a prerequisite for the Fed to achieve its goals. The next chapter further explores the specifics of how monetary policy affects the global financial system.

Summary of Major Points

- The goals of monetary policy are sustainable economic growth and price stability. Long-run growth is influenced by increases in the labor force, the capital stock, and productivity. Government policies affect growth through the mix of monetary and fiscal policies and the resulting tax and interest rate structures. To the extent that government policies encourage a stable environment, growth is also affected. A stable and healthy financial system is a prerequisite for sustainable growth.

- Full employment is a goal if a nation is to reach its full economic potential. Price stability is a goal because inflation tends to redistribute income in arbitrary and unpredictable ways, especially if the change is unexpected. Monetary policy can cause dramatic changes in exchange rates and the balances in the current and capital accounts. Monetary policy must seek to achieve an acceptable external balance compatible with full employment and stable prices.

- General guidelines for the macroeconomic goals are contained in the Employment Act of 1946 and the Humphrey-Hawkins Act of 1978. Specific guidelines and the setting of priorities and projections are the result of historical experience, judgments about what is feasible, and the political environment.

- In general, a comparison between the expected performance of the economy and the economic goals guides policy actions. More specifically, given the long-run goals, policymakers establish projections for nominal and real GDP, unemployment, and inflation. The projections are based on what is feasible for the economy to achieve over the next 12 to 18 months. If the economy's performance is expected to be close to the projections, policy is likely to remain unchanged. Conversely, if the economy's performance is expected to deviate markedly from the projections, policy will be altered.

- The policy process involves three lags: the recognition lag, the policy lag, and the impact lag. The recognition lag is the length of time it takes for policymakers to recognize that an unexpected and significant change in the economy's performance has occurred. The policy lag is the time between the point when the need for action is recognized and when an adjustment policy is decided upon and set in motion. The impact lag is the time between when an action is taken and when that action has a significant effect on prices, output, and employment.

- The existence of lags in an uncertain world makes it difficult for policymakers to act appropriately in a timely fashion. Their actions today may increase price and cyclical fluctuations later, so they tend to be quite cautious in adjusting policy. The inflationary process was more uncertain in the late 1990s and the early 2000s than in previous decades.

- Because of the complexities and lags involved with monetary policy, the Fed uses intermediate targets such as monetary aggregates, DNFD, and interest rates to guide policy. The basic idea is that the Fed selects a variable, such as a monetary aggregate or an interest rate, midway between its policy instruments and the ultimate or final goals or targets of policy. The intermediate target is then used to guide day-to-day open market operations. If the Fed hits the intermediate target, it will come reasonably close to achieving its economic projections.

- At the present time, the Fed targets the fed funds rate in the day-to-day execution of policy with an eye toward affecting the overall level of interest rates. In the 1970s and 1980s, the Fed tracked, monitored, and set projections for the monetary aggregates and DNFD to guide policy. The Fed no longer sets projections for the monetary aggregates and DNFD because their relationship with the level of economic activity is uncertain. The Fed can control either an interest rate target or an aggregate target but not both simultaneously.

- The Fed estimates the reserve need and uses open market operations to inject or withdraw reserves from the banking system as the need arises.

Key Terms

Economic Projections	Impact Lag	Price Stability
Employment Act of 1946	Intermediate Targets	Recognition Lag
Humphrey-Hawkins Full Employment and Balanced Growth Act of 1978	Natural Rate of Unemployment	Reserve Need
	Operating Target	Retail Sweep Accounts
	Policy Lag	Sustainable Economic Growth

Review Questions

1. What are the goals of monetary policy? How are these related to a stable and healthy financial system? How does monetary policy affect the level of economic activity and the level of prices?

2. How is the goal of full employment related to the long-run goal of sustainable economic growth? How can policymakers affect long-run growth?

3. Why do policymakers have to be aware of the external balance?

4. Explain why the goal for inflation is not always 0 percent. What is the natural rate of unemployment? Why can short-term goals sometimes differ from long-term goals?

5. Why are policymakers concerned about inflation?

6. Explain why the numerical projections of policy change.

7. What are the ultimate targets of monetary policy?

8. What is an intermediate target? Why does the Fed use intermediate targets instead of focusing on the ultimate targets? What is an operating target?

9. Give two criteria for intermediate targets.

10. How would the recognition, policy, and impact lags differ with regard to monetary and fiscal policy? What role does uncertainty

play in determining monetary policy? Has uncertainty increased in recent years?

11. When is it most difficult to interpret incoming data? (Hint: Consider the case in which retail sales are weak, but new orders for capital goods are strong, etc.)

12. What are retail sweep accounts and how do they affect required reserves? How does the Fed develop the reserve need?

Analytical Questions

13. The nominal interest rate is 6 percent, expected inflation is 3 percent, and the tax rate is 20 percent. What is the real after-tax return? If the nominal interest rate and the expected inflation rate both decrease by 2 percent, what is the real after-tax return?

14. The nominal interest rate is 3 percent but prices are expected to fall by 4 percent. What is the real interest rate? If the tax rate is 20 percent, what is the real after-tax return?

Internet Exercises

1. "Formulating a Consistent Approach to Monetary Policy" is an extremely interesting article that is obtainable at **http://woodrow. mpls.frb.fed.us/pubs/ar/ar1995.html**. Read the introduction and answer the following:

   a. What is the principal long-run goal of monetary policy?

   b. How can monetary policy improve economic performance over the short run?

2. The chapter describes the natural rate of unemployment as the unemployment rate that is consistent with stable prices. Consider the behavior of unemployment, inflation, and the rate of growth of M1 from 1961 to 1971. Provide a "natural rate of unemployment" explanation for inflation in the late 1960s and the high unemployment rate of the early 1970s. Data on the unemployment rate may be accessed at **http://www. stls.frb.org/fred/data/employ/unrate**. Data on the money supply growth rate may be found at **http://www.stls.frb.org/fred/ data/monetary/m1s1**. Data on inflation rates may be found at **http://www.stls. frb.org/fred/data/cpi/cpiaucsl**.

Suggested Readings

For a look at the nature and consequences of uncertainty in monetary policy formation, see Jan Marc Berk's, "The Preparation of Monetary Policy," (Norwell, MA: Kluwer Academic Press, 2000).

For a discussion that relates higher inflation to a relatively larger financial sector, see Michael Frenkel, "Inflation and the Misallocation of Resources," *Economic Inquiry*, Vol. 38, No. 4, October 2000, pp. 616–28.

For a discussion of Nobel laureate economist William Vickery's view that under normal conditions, inflation and unemployment are separable issues, see David Colander, "Macroeconomics: Was

Vickery Ten Years Ahead?" *Challenge*, September–October 1998, pp. 72–86.

Stephen G. Cecchitti, "Policy Rules and Targets: Framing the Central Banker's Problem," discusses many of the topics in this chapter. It can be found in the *Federal Reserve Bank of New York, Economic Policy Review*, 4:2 (June 1998): 1–14.

For an article that discusses current and future challenges of monetary policy given ongoing changes in financial markets, see "Monetary Policy in a Changing World," by Thomas M. Hoenig, *Economic Review of the Federal Reserve Bank of Kansas City*, Third Quarter 2000, Vol. 85, No. 3, pp. 5–10.

It can be viewed and/or ordered on the World Wide Web at **http://www.kc.frb.org/**.

Each year, the March and September issues of the *Federal Reserve Bulletin* contain the Fed's "Monetary Policy Report to the Congress," as mandated by the Humphrey-Hawkins Act of 1978. These reports make for interesting reading regarding monetary policy and the economic outlook. The Monetary Policy Testimony and the Report to Congress are available on the World Wide Web at **http://www.federalreserve.gov/**.

For a discussion of the challenges of monetary policy given recent structural changes in the economy, see Robert T. Parry, "Monetary Policy in a New Environment: The U.S. Experience, *Economic Letter,* Federal Reserve Bank of San Francisco, No. 200–31, October 13, 2000.

For a reliable reference, see *Guide to Economic Indicators* by Norman Frumkin (Armonk, NY: M.E. Sharpe, 2000).

For a discussion of "Current Challenges for U.S. Monetary Policy," see J. Alfred Broaddus, Jr.'s article by the same name, *Economic Quarterly*, Federal Reserve Bank of Richmond, Winter 2000, pp. 1–6.

chapter

25 Monetary Policy in a Globalized Financial System

Learning Objectives *After reading this chapter, you should know:*

- How international trade and capital flows affect monetary policy in a globalized financial system
- The limitations of domestic monetary policy under fixed and flexible exchange rate systems
- Why monetary policy will most likely require increased global coordination in the future, regardless of the exchange rate system

If countries don't discipline themselves, the world market will do it.
—Morris Offit, Offitbank

Monetary Policy and the Globalization of Finance

We have seen that one of the Fed's most important roles is to formulate and implement the nation's monetary policy. The Fed attempts to ensure that sufficient money and credit are available to allow for a stable and healthy financial system. In this way, the economy can expand in accord with its long-run growth potential with little or no inflation and with minimum fluctuations in output and employment.

We have also seen that financial markets have experienced ongoing and dramatic changes. The financial system is experiencing a dramatic metamorphosis, driven by technological improvements in computers and telecommunications, the breakdown of barriers to capital flows, and an increasingly globalized environment. As a result, the international financial system has experienced inordinate growth, and economies have become much more interdependent in just a few short years. After international financial crises in Mexico, Asia, and Russia, most of us are keenly aware of just how interdependent the world's economies are and how events in one country can spill over to other countries, including the United States.

In this final chapter, we look at the policy implications of the continuing growth of international trade and the globalization of the financial system. We consider the effects of monetary policy under both fixed and flexible exchange rate systems. We shall see that the globalization of finance may, of necessity, change the modus operandi of the Fed even though the goals of monetary policy remain the same.

Monetary Policy under Fixed Exchange Rates from 1944 to 1973

From 1944 until 1973, the major economies of the world participated in the *Bretton Woods Accord*, which was a *fixed exchange rate system* with the U.S. dollar serving as the *official reserve asset*. Other countries defined their currencies in terms of the dollar and bought or sold dollars to maintain the fixed exchange rates. Supporters of the Bretton Woods Accord believed that the fixed exchange rate system offered several advantages.

One advantage was that under some conditions, inflation and unemployment could be self-correcting. If inflation or unemployment accelerated in one country relative to the rest of the world, market forces in international markets would come into play and cause the inflation and unemployment to be reduced.

Under a fixed exchange rate system, when a country experienced inflation higher than that of its trading partners, its balance of payments would go into a deficit position as net exports fell and capital outflows increased. Net exports would fall because the country's domestic prices were relatively higher than prices in the rest of the world. If the inflation was due to increases in the money supply, lower interest rates initially could also lead to a capital outflow. Under Bretton Woods, the inflation-ridden country would be forced to buy back its currency to maintain fixed exchange rates. The act of buying back its currency tended to reduce the country's domestic money supply and the inflationary pressures, and to improve the trade imbalance. Thus, inflation would be self-correcting.

Likewise, if unemployment in a country increased, income would fall, causing imports to decrease and net exports to increase. The balance of payments would move into a surplus position and the country would experience an increase in international reserves. If policymakers allowed the increase in international reserves to also increase the domestic money supply, the level of economic activity would speed up, and employment would increase.[1]

Another advantage of a fixed exchange rate system was that it minimized *exchange rate risk*—the risk that changes in the exchange rate will cause the value of foreign currencies or foreign financial instruments to fall. Under a fixed rate system, such as the Bretton Woods Accord, currency values did not change under normal circumstances. Exchange rate risk was therefore very small and related only to the probability that the monetary authorities would redefine the currency in terms of the official reserve asset. Lower exchange rate risk is an advantage because it leads to increases in trade, capital flows, and economic efficiency.[2]

Despite these advantages, the Bretton Woods system also entailed some disadvantages. The ability of foreign countries to pursue their own monetary policies was limited because each country had to support its currency if market forces caused the currency's value to deviate from the agreed-upon exchange rate. For example, when a country wanted to pursue a more expansionary policy, its monetary authorities would increase the supply of reserves available to the banking system. Interest rates would fall and the monetary and credit aggregates would increase. This policy might result in a deficit in the balance of payments on current and capital accounts for two reasons. First, net exports (exports minus imports) would decrease due to the rise in domestic income.[3] Second, because of the falling interest rates, the country would also experience a capital outflow that would further contribute to the deficit in the balance of payments on current and capital accounts.

The central bank of the deficit country would then have to use its supplies of dollars to purchase its own currency to maintain the agreed-upon exchange rate. The act of buying back its currency would at least partially undo the stimulatory effects of the injection of reserves and would limit the monetary authorities' ability to pursue an expansionary policy. If the country ran out of dollars, it might have to devalue its currency. *Devaluation* entails discreet changes in the official exchange rate by the central bank but can destabilize financial markets and the domestic economy.

Likewise, if a country wished to pursue contractionary policies relative to those of the rest of the world, its balance of payments on current and capital accounts would move toward a surplus position. Net exports would increase as imports fell relative to exports.[4] The higher interest rate would also lead to a capital inflow. Both factors would put upward pressure on the exchange rate. The ability of the monetary authorities to limit the growth of the money supply would be reduced by the necessity to supply the country's currency to maintain fixed exchange rates. The supplying of the currency would at least partially undo the contractionary effects. After a time, if the trade surplus and capital inflow persisted, the country would be under pressure to revalue its currency.[5] In a *revaluation*, the monetary authorities

---

[1]Note that if the increase in international reserves did not lead to an expansion of the domestic money supply, employment would not rise.

[2]As we saw in Chapters 22 and 23, derivatives can be used to hedge exchange rate risk. Under a fixed exchange rate system, there is less need for derivatives because exchange rate risk is less than under flexible exchange rates. Since derivatives involve some fees, the transactions costs of exchanging currencies are also reduced.

[3]An increase in domestic income causes imports to increase. If the expansionary policy also causes domestic prices to increase, exports decrease at the same time.

[4]If prices also fell due to the contractionary policies, exports would increase.

[5]Although a country that is running a balance of payments deficit and losing international reserves must at some point devalue, the situation is different for a balance of payments surplus. If a country is running chronic surpluses, it does not have to revalue. Since a country can always print more money, the country could keep supplying its own currency, although this is a highly unlikely scenario.

increase the value of a currency relative to the official reserve asset. Again, financial markets and the economy would be destabilized.

Under normal circumstances, exchange rate risk is less with fixed exchange rates. When the situation is not normal, however, this advantage can turn into a major disadvantage. If a country is running a deficit in the balance of payments and devaluation seems likely, market participants will attempt to supply more of the currency to the central bank in exchange for dollars, the official reserve asset. But by supplying more of the currency, they will further deplete the country's international reserves. Devaluation, which may have been only a possibility, would become a necessity. Thus, the expectation of devaluation may become a self-fulfilling prophecy.

For example, suppose that market participants expect the value of the peso to fall from $1 = 3.5 pesos to $1 = 7 pesos. Before the devaluation, an investor could exchange 350 pesos for $100 at the exchange rate of $1 = 3.5 pesos. If the investor is correct and the peso is devalued, the $100 will net 700 pesos after the devaluation. Note that the investor starts with 350 pesos and ends up with 700 pesos! As savvy investors exchange pesos for dollars, the country loses more of its international reserves and the need to devalue becomes more imminent. In an attempt to stop the outflow of international reserves, policymakers may deny that devaluation is a possibility. In this manner, the situation goes from bad to worse as devaluation is postponed until the problem becomes critical.

Another disadvantage of the Bretton Woods system was that it could be maintained only if all countries were willing and able to support their currencies and, if necessary, to periodically and orderly revalue or devalue them. As we have seen, foreign central banks had to adjust their currencies in terms of the dollar because the dollar was the official reserve asset. As long as foreign central banks were accumulating dollars to serve as international reserves, the United States could pursue expansionary domestic policies that resulted in balance of payment deficits on current and capital accounts. There was no need to worry about exchange rate pressures on its own or foreign currencies. Once foreign countries had acquired sufficient reserves, persistent U.S. deficits on current and capital accounts would result in the need for foreign countries to revalue their currencies. By the same token, persistent U.S. current and capital accounts surpluses would result in the need for foreign countries to devalue.

The need to periodically revalue or devalue was also related to the divergent domestic monetary and fiscal policies pursued by the Bretton Woods countries. Over time, if different countries pursued different policies, some countries would expand relatively faster than others, leading to exchange rate imbalances. For instance, expansionary fiscal or monetary policy could cause one country to grow faster than another while contractionary fiscal and monetary policy could cause a slower rate of growth.

To the extent that countries experienced different growth rates, inflation rates, and interest rate structures, imbalances in the current and capital accounts would persist. If a country had more expansionary policies than the United States, it would experience chronic deficits in the current and capital accounts and the need to devalue. If a country had more contractionary policies, it would experience persistent surpluses and the need to revalue. If countries refused to make the necessary changes in their exchange rates, the system of fixed exchange rates established at Bretton Woods would break down.

As we saw in Chapter 13, the system did eventually break down when it became clear that the United States would not be able to continue to redeem dollars in gold. The breakdown occurred because U.S. policymakers were pursuing more expansionary policies than were some foreign economies, notably Germany and

http://www.yardeni.com/finmkts.html#C3
Provides foreign exchange rate data.

Japan. The result was an outflow of gold from the United States. With the suspension of the international conversion of dollars to gold in late 1971 and the official establishment of flexible exchange rates in 1974, the Bretton Woods fixed exchange rate system came to an end.

RECAP The Bretton Woods Accord of 1944 established fixed exchange rates among major world currencies with the U.S. dollar serving as the official reserve asset. Supporters of the system believed that inflation and unemployment would, under some circumstances, be self-correcting and that exchange rate risk would be reduced. The need to maintain fixed exchange rates limited the ability of a country to pursue its own monetary policy. If a country wished to pursue more expansionary policies, lower domestic interest rates and higher income could lead to a deficit in the balance of payments. The need to buy back one's own currency would thwart the expansionary policies.

Monetary Policy under Flexible Exchange Rates since 1974

Flexible Exchange Rate System
An exchange rate system in which the value of a currency is determined by supply and demand.

Under a **flexible exchange rate system,** market forces determine the value of a nation's currency. For the U.S. dollar, this means that the exchange rate is determined by the demand for and supply of dollars in international markets. The supply of dollars/month reflects U.S. demand for foreign goods, services, and securities. If we hold other factors constant, quantity supplied is a positive function of the exchange rate. The demand for dollars reflects foreign demand for U.S. goods, services, and securities. If we hold other factors constant, quantity demanded is a negative function of the exchange rate. The market, if left alone, will gravitate to the exchange rate where quantity demanded is equal to quantity supplied. As we saw in Chapters 8 and 13, factors such as domestic and foreign income, inflation rates, and interest rates affect exchange rates, and "flexible" exchange rates immediately adjust to changing market conditions and expectations.

With the enactment of a flexible exchange rate system in late 1974, countries in some ways gained more control over their own monetary policies. A monetary objective or policy would not be compromised by a country's need to maintain the agreed-upon exchange rate as it was under the Bretton Woods Accord. No longer would a country have to support its domestic currency if market forces were causing the currency to depreciate or appreciate. As discussed in Chapter 8, *depreciation* occurs when the value of a currency falls in terms of another currency under a flexible exchange rate system. *Appreciation* occurs when the value of a currency rises in terms of another currency.

If monetary policymakers in a country are pursuing more expansionary policies than those of their neighbors, the balance of trade can move into a deficit position, with resulting deterioration in the balance of payments. Likewise, if a more contractionary policy is pursued, the balance of payments can move into a surplus position. Even though the country no longer has to defend its currency to maintain fixed exchange rates, it must consider other international ramifications of its monetary policy. Perhaps the most important effects are capital flows and the potential depreciation or appreciation of its currency. Depreciation and appreciation, in turn, can feed back to the domestic economy and cause changes in the growth rate of income through net exports.

If international trade and capital flows are small relative to the aggregate level of economic activity, monetary authorities may have greater latitude in the execution of policy. However, international trade and capital flows have increased significantly since 1970, so policymakers must consider how their policies will affect foreign countries and what the feedback to the domestic economy will be.[6] For example, in 2000, U.S. exports slightly exceeded $1,097 billion while imports slightly exceeded $1,468 billion in an economy with gross domestic product (GDP) just over $10,114 billion. In 1960, exports were roughly $25.3 billion and imports $22.8 billion, while gross national product (GNP) was $526.6 billion. Thus, in 1960, exports and imports were 4.8 and 4.3 percent of GNP, respectively ($25.3/$526.6 and $22.8/$526.6). By 2000, exports had grown to 10.8 percent of GDP ($1,097/$10,114), and imports had increased even more to 14.5 percent of GDP ($1,468/$10,114).

Coinciding with the growth in trade in the 1970s, governments began removing barriers to international capital flows. The dismantling was virtually complete by the 1980s. In addition, major breakthroughs in telecommunications technologies and the electronic transfer of funds allowed funds to be transferred almost instantaneously anywhere in the world. These two factors have created a worldwide foreign exchange market where the buying and selling of different currencies take place and the "wheels are greased" for international trade and capital flows among nations. In 1998, the foreign exchange market traded more than $1.5 trillion every day—the equivalent of over $250 per day per person in the world—making it the largest market in the world. Since enormous sums of funds flow with lightning speed, the ability for funds to find their highest return is greatly increased. From an economic standpoint, economic efficiency is enhanced when funds flow to the location with the highest risk-adjusted return.

Capital flows jeopardize or weaken the intended effects of monetary policy. To illustrate, we will consider the case of contractionary monetary policy wherein the Fed raises interest rates to slow the level of economic activity. If U.S. interest rates move up relative to interest rates abroad, foreigners will demand more U.S. financial instruments, which now pay a relatively higher return. The demand for dollars increases and puts upward pressure on the exchange rate. Capital flows in from abroad as the dollar appreciates. The augmented supply of funds from abroad causes U.S. interest rates, although higher than before the Fed acted, to be lower than they otherwise would be. Thus, slowing the level of economic activity is more difficult because of the offsetting effect of capital flows on the supply of loanable funds.

Additionally, because of the reduced demand for foreign financial instruments, there is also a tendency for prices of foreign financial instruments to fall and foreign interest rates to rise. Changes in the supply of and demand for financial instruments cause capital flows that will bring real interest rates between countries into closer alignment. Given a change in U.S. interest rates, freer capital movements will bring about immediate changes in the exchange rate and eventual interest rate adjustments in foreign economies.

Continuing with our example of contractionary U.S. policy, if the increase in the domestic interest rate causes the dollar to appreciate, the dollar price of foreign goods falls while the foreign price of U.S. goods rises. The result is a decrease in exports and an increase in imports. Thus, net exports will also fall in response to an appreciation of the exchange rate. This latter effect reinforces the contractionary effects of a rise in domestic interest rates.

---

[6]In some ways, U.S. monetary authorities have always recognized that their monetary policies can affect interest rates, inflation, and growth in other countries. In recent decades, U.S. policymakers have also become increasingly aware that foreign events can at times influence the U.S. economy and, hence, the formulation and effects of policy.

LOOKING FORWARD: *Dollarization and Currency Boards*

Full dollarization occurs when a country abandons its own currency to adopt another country's currency as its official currency. The adopted currency becomes the medium of exchange and unit of account. The U.S. dollar is the currency that has been most widely adopted and used by other countries. Although the U.S. dollar is the most dollarized currency, the term "dollarization" is generic and, in many cases, has little to do with the United States or the U.S. dollar. For example, Greenland has adopted the Danish krone; the Vatican City, the Italian lira; Tuvalu, the Australian dollar; etc.

Panama dollarized in the early twentieth century. Since 1999, El Salvador, Ecuador, and Guatemala have dollarized by adopting the U.S. dollar and abolishing their domestic currencies. Argentina has seriously considered full dollarization. Full dollarization with the U.S. dollar is discussed as a way to help developing countries, particularly those in South and Latin America, to overcome monetary and exchange rate volatility and to stabilize prices.

There are both benefits and costs to full dollarization. On the benefits side, there can be no balance of payment crises or speculative attacks on the domestic currency if the currency does not exist. The increased stability should lead to increased capital inflows, lower interest rates, and greater investment and growth. Lower interest rates also reduce the government's cost of financing the public debt. Another possibility is greater trade and financial integration with the United States and reduced inflationary expectations.

The costs of full dollarization include the loss of identity associated with one's national currency. Many of the European countries that participated in the euro had a difficult time giving up their domestic currencies. A more direct cost is seigniorage. *Seigniorage* is the difference between the cost of producing and distributing currency and any revenues earned through the distribution. For example, the Fed issues currency by purchasing government securities that earn interest. The interest goes to the Fed and eventually to the government. On the other hand, the currency issued by the Fed does not pay interest. The amount of interest earned on the government securities less the cost of producing the Federal Reserve notes is seigniorage. If a country fully dollarizes with U.S. dollars, that country forgoes earning seigniorage and the United States earns additional seigniorage related to the amount of U.S. dollars circulating in the foreign country. If electronic payments reduce the use of currency in the future, the amount of seigniorage will be reduced.

Another cost of full dollarization is that the country that dollarizes loses the ability to pursue an autonomous monetary policy. Small countries that wish to become more integrated with larger economies to increase trade and attract capital inflows have limited ability to pursue an independent monetary policy anyway.

A close alternative to full dollarization is the creation of a currency board. A *currency board* is an organized body within a country with the sole responsibility and power to defend the value of a country's currency. The currency board pegs, or fixes, the currency value to the value of the currency of the dominant trading partner. The country commits to a fixed exchange rate and the currency is fully convertible with the pegged currency. The government cannot print money unless it is backed by reserves of the currency to which it is pegged. Finally, the currency board has the power to force the government to eliminate a budget deficit that may be inflationary. Argentina, Bulgaria, Bosnia, and Hong Kong have had successful currency boards.

A currency board can achieve many of the benefits of full dollarization, and additionally, the value of the seigniorage from issuing one's own currency is not lost. However, the currency board may not be perceived to be as permanent as full dollarization. Given the perception that the currency board could be abolished or modified quite easily, the full benefits of greater trade and investment, and lower interest rates, would not be realized. The currency could still be subject to speculative attacks if speculators sold the currency at the preset price, putting tremendous pressure on the currency board to devalue.

Finally, it should be noted that dollars already circulate and are widely used in many of the countries that could benefit from full dollarization. To the extent that the dollar displaces the national currency, seigniorage is already reduced.

At the same time that these forces are working to decrease net exports, two other effects are working in the opposite direction—to increase net exports. First, the increase in domestic interest rates could cause a reduction in domestic demand as the demand for interest-sensitive expenditures falls. The reduction in aggregate demand decreases the demand for imports. Second, if the slowing of the economy causes domestic prices to fall relative to foreign prices, both foreign and domestic customers have an incentive to switch to domestically produced goods and services. These two effects work to increase net exports and to mitigate the decline in net exports that results from the appreciation of the dollar.

Nevertheless, in most cases, the decrease in net exports caused by the appreciation of the dollar will be larger than the increase in net exports resulting from these two additional factors. Hence, the total effect of contractionary monetary policy is to decrease net exports. Although that may not always be the case, we usually assume that higher U.S. interest rates lead to an appreciation of the domestic currency, capital inflows, a decrease in net exports, and a larger trade deficit (or smaller trade surplus). Exhibit 25-1 provides a schematic diagram of the results of U.S. contractionary monetary policy under flexible exchange rates.

The impact of U.S. monetary policy also depends upon the monetary and fiscal policies of other countries. If other central banks attempt to slow their economies when U.S. monetary authorities are doing so, the resulting effects on exchange rates depend upon the relative magnitudes of the interest rate changes among the various countries.[7] Thus, we can conclude that interest rates and exchange rates are determined jointly by the monetary and fiscal policies of the various interdependent countries and the resulting market forces.

In summary, the growth of trade and capital flows has occurred in a world that switched from fixed to flexible exchange rates. Because central banks are no longer necessarily committed to maintaining the value of their respective currencies, policymakers have more independence in formulating and executing monetary policy. A country's ability to run a monetary policy far different from that of its neighbors

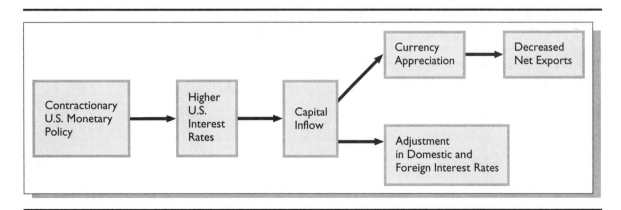

EXHIBIT 25-1
A Schematic View of the Results of U.S Contractionary Policy under Flexible Exchange Rates

[7]On the other hand, note the continual prodding of Japan by U.S. officials in mid-1998 to resolve its banking crisis to prevent spillovers to the U.S. economy and other parts of the world. When the Japanese finally adopted comprehensive banking reform in October 1998, international financial markets were stabilized.

LOOKING OUT: *Capital Flows and the Mexican Peso Crisis*

The Mexican peso devaluation of late 1994 is a striking example of the implications of international capital flows and how quickly they can occur. In the early 1990s, large amounts of international financial capital poured into Mexico. Given its proximity and ties to the United States, and the proposed North American Free Trade Agreement, Mexico appeared to be a safe haven. The market value of stocks traded on the Mexican stock exchange increased from $4 billion in 1985 to over $200 billion in 1993. In 1993, it was estimated that foreigners owned around 75 percent of the stocks traded on the exchange.[a] But the bubble could not last forever.

In the second half of 1994, Mexico began to experience capital outflows that resulted in a dramatic loss of international reserves, particularly the dollar. By December 20, 1994, Mexico found it necessary to devalue the peso by 15 percent from 3.50 to 4.00 pesos per dollar. Despite this move, the loss of international reserves continued, and 3 days later, when this exchange rate could not be maintained, the peso was allowed to float freely. The result was a 50 percent depreciation of the peso, massive capital outflows from Mexico, falling stock prices, skyrocketing interest rates, and an international financial crisis.

The capital outflow caused Mexico to lose most of its international reserves. Reserves fell from $17.1 billion on November 1, 1994, to $3.8 billion by January 30, 1995. There were fears that the government would default on the Tesobonos, which were dollar-indexed government bonds issued in pesos with maturities up to 1 year. Foreign investors, many in the United States, held half of the Tesobonos. President Clinton authorized a $20 billion rescue package that would enable Mexico to redeem all maturing Tesobonos with U.S. dollars. (An additional rescue package later arranged by Clinton amounted to $30 billion.) As a result of the crisis, Mexico experienced a severe recession.

In addition to political instability in Mexico, many analysts believe that the crisis was caused by two international events. The first was the reversal of Japanese capital flows into Mexico in response to the domestic crisis in Japan. The second was the rise in U.S. interest rates orchestrated by the Fed starting in early 1994. Both caused capital flows out of Mexico and contributed to the subsequent crisis. Writing in the *Columbia Journal of World Business,* Michael Adler made three observations about the crisis:

- Markets are extremely sensitive to uninsured risks and react quickly and massively when risks are perceived to rise.

- Any rush to sell in one sector of the market produces liquidity shortages that cause selling pressures to cascade into other market sectors. [As a result of the Mexican peso crisis, other emerging markets and even other developed economies also experienced international capital outflows.]

- Markets need some kind of insurance when governments, by suddenly changing the interest rate environment as the Federal Reserve did . . . can confront investors with the risk of ruin.[b]

As noted in this chapter and in Chapter 13, the potential for crisis is augmented because capital flows are larger and more volatile than in the past.

[a]Tom Petruno, "Global Money-Free Flows, Free Falls," *Los Angeles Times,* March 19, 1995, p. A11.
[b]Michael Adler, "Mexico's Devaluation: The Beginning, Not the End, of Its Problems," *Columbia Journal of World Business,* Spring 1995, pp. 112–120.

is limited by the increased interdependence of economies and the ease with which capital flows across borders. Capital flows and changes in the exchange rate offset the effects. The effects are larger the more important trade is to the domestic economy and the greater the ease with which capital flows between nations. Thus, for the United States, external factors are likely to dampen the effects of any Fed actions that result in relative interest rate or income changes. In the near term, an increase in U.S. rates relative to foreign rates usually increases the exchange rate of the dollar and capital inflows. Similarly, a decrease in U.S. rates relative to foreign rates usually leads to decreases in the exchange rate of the dollar and capital outflows. Note that as a result of capital flows, these financial adjustments to U.S. monetary policy action will occur in advance of the slower response of output and prices.

Thus, the crux of the dilemma is that under fixed exchange rates, countries are limited in running their own monetary policies because of the need to maintain the value of their currency. Under flexible exchange rates, they can also be limited. If they try to run a policy different from the rest of the world, capital and real flows will occur that will complicate the results and jeopardize that policy. What does all of this mean for the future? In a nutshell, it means that nations will have to be more concerned about coordinating their monetary policies. The next section looks at the specifics.

RECAP **Under flexible exchange rates, the value of a currency is determined by supply and demand. Flexible exchange rates free a country from the need to supply or demand dollars to maintain fixed exchange rates. In this way, flexible exchange rates allow policymakers more freedom in pursuing policies that diverge from those of other countries. At the same time, however, policymakers must also be concerned about the effects of their domestic policies on exchange rates and capital flows. Under flexible exchange rates, a country can pursue its own policy, but if it differs from policies in the rest of the world, changes in net exports and capital flows can mitigate the intended effects of the policy.**

The Globalization of Monetary Policy

A new reality is having a profound influence on the conduct and effectiveness of domestic policies. Simply stated, the economies of the world are becoming more interdependent. What goes on in Tokyo, London, Hong Kong, Paris, and Buenos Aires has an increasingly important effect on the financial system and the economy in the United States. Consequently, U.S. policymakers have somewhat less control over the performance of the U.S. economy than in previous eras when the U.S. economy was more isolated from international trade and finance. As Alan Greenspan said about the effects of the ongoing crises in Russia and Asia on the U.S. economy: "It is just not credible that the United States can remain an oasis of prosperity unaffected by a world that is experiencing greatly increased stress."[8]

Such observations have given rise to calls for cooperation and coordination among world policymakers. Although the difficulties some countries have in coordinating their own domestic monetary and fiscal policies suggest that coordinating policies across countries will never be easy, the existence of globalization does highlight the new challenges and complexities facing policymakers.

As we first saw in Chapter 13, policymakers are attempting to meet the challenges of globalization through informal discussions among the major industrialized countries and through international organizations such as the International Monetary Fund and the Bank for International Settlements. The dialogues suggest that to achieve a stable international financial system, countries around the world must have healthy financial systems with noninflationary policies. In addition, countries must standardize the reporting of information about financial markets, institutions, laws, regulations, international reserves, external debt (both short and long term), and the health of the banking sector. Finally, the surveillance of international organizations that oversee the international financial system must be more

---

[8]Speech by Alan Greenspan at the University of California, Berkeley, September 4, 1998.

LOOKING OUT: *The Eurosystem*

One of the best examples of increased cooperation and coordination in the formulation of monetary policy is the Eurosystem. As we saw in Chapter 4, the Eurosystem consists of the European Central Bank and the central banks of the 12 countries that participate in the euro, Europe's single currency. As such, the Eurosystem implements and carries out monetary policies for the eurozone, with the primary goal of achieving price stability. To do this, the Eurosystem decides on a quantitative definition of price stability, such as 2 percent inflation or less.

In addition, "two pillars" are used to achieve the goal. The first pillar is a quantitative reference value for the growth rate of a broad-based monetary aggregate, such as M2 in the United States. The second pillar consists of a broad collection of indicators that policymakers use to make an assessment of the outlook for price developments in the area as a whole. The former is similar to targeting a monetary aggregate to guide policy formulation. The latter is similar to using a more eclectic approach in policy formulation.

To achieve its goals, the Eurosystem uses tools similar to the Fed's, including open market operations, a lending facility like the discount window called a "standing facility," and reserve requirements. The 12 national central banks hold the required reserves, carry out open market operations, and operate the standing facility. The Eurosystem must approve of the financial instruments to be used in open market operations. The system also sets reserve requirements and interest rates on standing facility loans. It also take actions that nudge interest rates and the monetary aggregates in one direction or the other as part of monetary policy.

transparent and open. In such an environment, the full benefits of globalization could be reached while minimizing the costs.

When considering the future, one must consider a wide range of possibilities. In the broadest sense, major world economies will either remain on a version of the present system of flexible exchange rates or return to a version of fixed exchange rates. In either case, the ramifications for monetary policy will be considerable.

A fixed exchange rate system can be sustained only if the growth and inflation rates of the participating countries are similar and only if devaluations and revaluations occur in an orderly manner. To maintain the system for any period of time, both the monetary policies and the fiscal policies of the participating countries must be coordinated. As we have seen, divergent monetary and fiscal policies will lead to different growth rates of income, different inflation rates, and different interest rate structures. If economies grow at different rates, changes in net exports and interest rates will cause exchange rate pressures.

If the participants' monetary and fiscal policies are similar, however, it is possible for them to reap large benefits from the increased trade and integration that fixed exchange rates could encourage. Not only would increased trade allow the countries to enjoy a higher standard of living, but capital flows would allow surplus funds to flow to their highest return. The downside is twofold: Countries that value their independence or have divergent goals with respect to unemployment and inflation would not do well under a fixed exchange rate system. In addition, countries may not have the political discipline to stick with fixed exchange rates if domestic problems become paramount.

Under flexible exchange rates, capital flows limit a country's ability to execute policies that deviate significantly from those of the rest of the world. Thus, incentive exists for nations to cooperate to find a workable policy acceptable to all. There is already a great deal of monetary policy coordination among developed countries. Some coordination is spearheaded by international organizations such as the International Monetary Fund, which was created at the Bretton Woods Conference, and the Bank for International Settlements in Basel, Switzerland. Informal groups of major trading partners meet regularly to discuss policy regimes and options and often communicate and work together to coordinate policies. One group, called the G-7 nations, includes the United States, the United Kingdom, France, Germany, Japan, Canada, and Italy.[9] A Closer Look discusses some examples of coordinated intervention.

Foreign Exchange Market Intervention: On occasion, the U.S. Treasury and the Fed intervene in the foreign exchange market to restore orderly conditions or to influence exchange rates. Since the mid-1980s, intervention has often been coordinated with the governments and central banks of the other G-7 countries. Given the large volume of foreign currency transactions—averaging more than $1.5 trillion per day—intervention by the central bank to directly affect exchange rates would have to be on a very large scale, even for a central bank. Therefore, intervention affects the market primarily by influencing market sentiment, although on occasion several central banks will try to directly affect exchange rates through coordinated intervention.

An example of coordinated intervention occurred in 1985 when leaders of France, Germany, Japan, Great Britain, and the United States met and decided to intervene in foreign exchange markets to reduce the value of the dollar.[10] The plan was named the Plaza Accord after the hotel where the meeting took place. Since then, these nations and others have met on a more or less regular basis in an attempt to coordinate economic policy and to open international markets.

A Closer Look

Two more recent examples of coordinated intervention occurred in mid-1998 and mid-2000. The first involved intervention by the United States and Japan to boost the value of the Japanese yen. On June 17, 1998, the Fed bought about $2 billion worth of yen—the first intervention on behalf of the yen in 6 years. The value of the yen had been declining for 3 years and the exchange rate was near an 8-year low. On June 16, 1998, the yen/dollar exchange rate was $1 = 142 yen. After the intervention on June 17, 1998, the yen appreciated to $1 = 137 yen. There were two major reasons for the intervention. First, the sagging yen put additional pressures on the struggling economies of Southeast Asia, which needed to sell their goods to Japan. The weak yen made goods from Southeast Asia more expensive in Japan. Second, there was fear that the weak yen would pressure China to devalue its currency. A Chinese devaluation could set off another round of devaluations and defaults throughout Southeast Asia, intensifying the Asian crisis just as the stricken economies were beginning to recover. A unique aspect of this episode is that China had asked the United States and Japan to intervene. The intervention was basically a failure, however, because by late August, the yen was trading at $1 = 145 yen.[11]

The second example involved intervention by the G-7 major industrialized nations, including the United States, to boost the value of the euro.[12] The euro was launched on

[9]Actually, the G-7 nations resulted from the 1986 expansion of a group of five (G-5) nations that had consulted since the flexible exchange rate system was put into place in the early 1970s. The G-5 nations were the United States, the United Kingdom, France, Japan, and West Germany. In a "managed" flexible exchange rate system, exchange rates are determined by the forces of supply and demand, with occasional central bank intervention. The central banks of the G-5 or G-7 nations have frequently intervened by buying and selling in currency markets to affect exchange rates since 1971.

[10]U.S. interest rates were high relative to the rest of the world, causing large capital inflows and a strong dollar. The strong dollar fueled trade deficits that were having a negative impact on U.S. employment.

[11]In the fall of 1998, the value of the yen in terms of the dollar did fall dramatically. However, the fall was not directly related to the intervention in June 1998.

[12]The G-7 nations are Canada, Germany, France, Italy, Japan, the United Kingdom, and the United States.

January 1, 1999 at a debut price of $1.17 against the dollar. By September 2000, the euro had fallen over 28 percent to $.8439 against the dollar. Many analysts felt the euro was significantly undervalued but feared that a speculative attack on the euro would drive its value down even further. On September 22, 2000, the G-7 nations initiated a concerted intervention by buying euros in currency markets. The initial result was an increase in the value of the euro to over 88 cents against the dollar. However, the increase was short lived. Within 2 weeks, the euro began a downward slide. By late October, it was trading at its all-time low and below its value when the intervention was initiated. Several reasons were posited for why the intervention failed. First, the European Central Bank followed it up with only a small increase in interest rates. Some felt that larger interest rate increases were necessary to support the currency. Second, with presidential elections in the United States in early November 2000, U.S. Treasury officials reiterated on several occasions that there was no change in the U.S. position on the strong dollar. Finally, others felt there were imbalances in the eurozone economies that would require structural changes in labor markets and tax laws before the euro would appreciate.

When central banks and governments decide to intervene in foreign exchange markets, they do so for three reasons:

1. To resolve a severe but temporary liquidity crisis and to stabilize international financial markets
2. To signal that regulators believe exchange rates are deviating significantly from fundamental underlying values (that is, the dollar is overvalued or undervalued because of speculation in the market)
3. To signal a change in exchange rate policy or to clarify an existing policy

When the Fed participates in an intervention, it does so by purchasing or selling dollars for other foreign currencies. Since the dollars go through the banking system, reserves are either augmented or decreased. Reserves are augmented when the Fed buys foreign currencies with dollars. Reserves are decreased when the Fed buys dollars with foreign currencies that it has accumulated previously.

To limit the effects on reserves, the Fed can engage in sterilization. In this process, the full amount of the foreign exchange operation is offset by an open market operation so that the monetary base is unaffected by the foreign exchange operation. For example, suppose that the Fed, in conjunction with Japan, decides that the dollar is overvalued and the yen is undervalued. To prop up the value of the yen, the Fed sells dollars to purchase yen. If the transaction is unsterilized, the monetary base increases and the domestic money supply and interest rates are affected. If the transaction is sterilized, the Fed uses open market sales to offset the increase in the monetary base. In general, foreign exchange transactions are sterilized in the United States.

As we move into the twenty-first century, it is difficult to predict how the Fed will execute monetary policy. The Fed's current intermediate targets may no longer be relevant or effectively related to the level of economic activity in a globalized financial system. In a globalized financial system, the Fed must increasingly consider domestic exchange rates, capital flows, and foreign policies. Although the Fed's function will remain the same, it may have to work with new procedures and regulations, including some international regulations. International considerations will necessarily play a bigger role. The Fed will have to design policies for a world with increasing trade and minimal barriers to international capital flows that can occur with great speed.

In conclusion, we can say that whether the world returns to fixed exchange rates or maintains the current flexible exchange rate regime, some policy coordination will be needed. Although flexible exchange rates increase the potential independence of monetary policy, the increasing openness of world trade and finance has heightened the interdependencies among nations. Flexible exchange rates allow a central bank to set its interest rates somewhat independently of other countries, but capital mobility means that a change in the interest rates relative to other countries is compensated for by changes in exchange rates and capital flows. Thus, a central bank's freedom to set interest rates is only as great as its acceptance of the foreign exchange rate movements and the capital flows connected with a change in interest rates. Amid all the uncertainties, one factor seems highly probable: Monetary policy in the future will most likely involve more global coordination and cooperation whether it be under fixed or flexible exchange rates.

RECAP The future will require countries to coordinate their monetary policies regardless of whether exchange rates are fixed or flexible as countries become more interdependent due to the growth of trade and capital flows.

Summary of Major Points

- The Bretton Woods Accord of 1944 established fixed exchange rates between the U.S. dollar and other major currencies. Supporters of the fixed exchange rate system believed that under some circumstances, inflation and unemployment would be self-correcting.

- The need to maintain the value of the currency under fixed exchange rates limited the ability of a country to pursue its own monetary policy independently of other participants in the agreement.

- Because countries had divergent monetary and fiscal policies, exchange rate imbalances persisted. Eventually, the United States was unable to maintain the conversion of dollars into gold, and the Bretton Woods system of fixed exchange rates collapsed in 1971. It was replaced by a system of flexible exchange rates.

- Under flexible exchange rates, the value of the dollar is determined by the demand and supply of dollars. Flexible exchange rates freed countries from the need to support their currencies to maintain fixed exchange rates. Each country, in some ways, gained greater latitude in adjusting its domestic monetary policy.

- Even though countries do not have to support their currencies under flexible exchange rates,

they must be aware of the effects that their monetary and fiscal policies have on the exchange rate, capital flows, and net exports. Monetary policy must be executed with an understanding of the international ramifications and the feedbacks to the domestic economy. This is particularly true if net exports are a relatively large component of aggregate demand and if capital flows are unrestricted.

- Trade has increased because of the concerted efforts of developed nations since World War II. These efforts result from the recognition of the gains from trade to all trading partners. Capital flows have also increased because of the removal of capital barriers and because of technological advances that have increased the speed of such flows.

- Under flexible exchange rates, there is an incentive for countries to work together to coordinate monetary policy. Indeed, there is already considerable monetary policy coordination, particularly among such groups as the G-7 countries. Regardless of whether exchange rates are fixed or flexible, monetary policy in the future will most likely entail greater global coordination as economies grow more interdependent because of the growth in trade and capital flows.

Key Term

Flexible Exchange Rate System

Review Questions

1. Briefly explain the Bretton Woods exchange rate system. When was it created? When and why did the system collapse?

2. Under the Bretton Woods system, the U.S. dollar was the official reserve asset. How did this affect the U.S. balance of payments on current and capital accounts? Could the United States experience large balance of payments deficits on current and capital accounts indefinitely?

3. Assume you work at the central bank of a small country that is considering an expansionary monetary policy to speed up the level of economic activity. Given fixed exchange rates, advise the president of your country what will happen to net exports if the country pursues a policy of monetary expansion. What action will the central bank have to take to support the agreed-upon exchange rate? How will that action affect the expansionary policy?

4. Argue that fixed exchange rates are preferable to flexible exchange rates. Then present the opposite argument.

5. For each of the following situations, assuming fixed exchange rates, tell what will happen to the balance of payments on current and capital accounts in the United States:
    a. Domestic income increases.
    b. Domestic interest rates fall.
    c. Foreign income increases.
    d. Foreign interest rates fall.
    e. Domestic inflation increases.
    f. Foreign inflation increases.

6. For each of the situations in question 5, tell what will happen to the exchange rate assuming flexible exchange rates.

7. Explain whether you agree or disagree with the following statement: Flexible exchange rates allow nations to pursue their own monetary policies.

8. What are the advantages of fixed exchange rates? What are the disadvantages? Does it matter if the country is large or small?

9. Briefly explain how interest rates on instruments of comparable risk and maturity will tend to be equalized in a world without capital barriers.

10. Under a flexible exchange rate system, what effect does contractionary monetary policy have on the exchange rate?

11. Why is a country limited in executing its own monetary policy under a fixed exchange rate system? How is it limited under a flexible exchange rate system?

12. How can monetary policy coordination among countries increase the degree to which monetary policy can be used to pursue macroeconomic goals under fixed exchange rates? Under flexible exchange rates?

13. Could high U.S. interest rates affect investment spending in foreign countries? Explain.

14. What is the Eurosystem? Briefly discuss how the Eurosystem conducts monetary policy.

15. What is full dollarization? How does it differ from a currency board? What is seigniorage?

Analytical Questions

16. Use graphs to demonstrate what will happen to the value of the dollar in terms of the Japanese yen in each of the following situations:

    a. U.S. income increases.
    b. Japanese income increases.
    c. U.S. interest rates fall.
    d. Japanese interest rates fall.
    e. U.S. inflation increases.
    f. Japanese inflation increases.

17. If the nominal U.S. interest rate is 10 percent and U.S. inflation is 6 percent, what is the real U.S. interest rate? What is the real U.S. rate in terms of foreign interest rates?

18. The Fed exchanges $1 million for 139 million yen. If the Fed sells $1 million worth of T-bills in the open market, what will happen to domestic interest rates and the money supply? If the Fed does not do the open market sale, what will happen to domestic interest rates and the money supply? In which case is the foreign exchange transaction sterilized?

Internet Exercises

1. The minutes of FOMC meetings contain the committee's authorization for foreign currency operations. Access the most recent minutes at **http://woodrow.mpls.frb.fed.us/info/policy/fomcmin/index.html** and arrow down to the committee's "Authorization for Foreign Currency Operations." According to this directive, which foreign currencies are to be bought and sold by the Fed?

2. "Strong Dollar, Weak Dollar," an article that examines how the U.S. dollar's value relates to other currencies and how changes in its value affect international trade and the open economy, is available at: **http://www.chicagofed.org/publications/**. Access the article and answer the following:

    a. What is meant by a "strong" dollar? Who gains from a strong dollar?
    b. Where are foreign exchange trades completed?
    c. During the 1980s, the value of the U.S. dollar was high relative to other currencies. What effect did this have on the U.S. economy?

Suggested Readings

An informative article, "Why Is Financial Stability a Goal of Public Policy?" by Andrew Crockett, can be found in the *Economic Review of the Federal Reserve Bank of Kansas City* 82:4, Fourth Quarter, 1997, pp. 5–22. Another insightful article in that same publication is Charles Morris and Klara Parrish, "Maintaining Financial Stability in a Global Economy: A Summary of the Bank's 1997 Symposium," 23–38.

Three articles that discuss material covered in this chapter are Jeffrey D. Sachs, "Global Capitalism: Making It Work," *The Economist*, September 12, 1998, pp. 23–25; Jack Guynn, "The Role of Economic Policy in Current Economic Performance," *Business Economics* 33 (January 1998): 18–22; and Tibor Scitovsky, "On More 'Trouble' with Globalization," *Challenge* (July–August) 1998, pp. 134–135.

For a discussion of how interest rates are determined in the United States, Japan, Germany, France, and Switzerland, see Gulielmo Maria Caporale, "Domestic and External Factors in Interest Rate Determination," *Applied Financial Economics* 7 (October 1997): 465–471. The discussion concludes that monetary policy in Germany significantly affects both U.S. and Japanese interest rates while German rates are fairly responsive to developments in Europe. With regard to domestic factors, inflationary expectations are very important.

For a discussion of "Short-Run Independence of Monetary Policy under Pegged Exchange Rates and Effects of Money on Exchange Rates and Interests," see the article by Lee E. Ohanian and Alan C. Stockman, *Journal of Money, Credit and Banking* 29:2 (November 1997): 783–806. Enrique G. Mendoze, "Comment on Short-Run Independence of Monetary Policy under Pegged Exchange Rates," can be found in the same issue, pp. 807–810.

For a broad view of critical international financial events since World War II and their effects on U.S. monetary policy, see Paul Volcker and Toyoo Gyohten, *Changing Fortunes* (New York: Times Books, 1992).

In this chapter, we have argued that interest rates are interdependent because of the elimination of barriers to capital flows. For an opposing view, see Adrian W. Troop, "International Financial Market Integration and Linkages of National Interest Rates," *Economic Review of the Federal Reserve Bank of San Francisco*, 3 (1994). Back issues of the *Economic Review* may be ordered online from the Web site for the San Francisco Fed: **http://www.frbsf.org/**.

For students interested in a "famous" fixed exchange rate system, the gold standard, see *The Key to the Gold Vault*, published by the New York Fed in 1991. It is free for the asking from the Public Information Department, Federal Reserve Bank of New York, 33 Liberty Street, New York, NY 10045.

For a look at how European central banks coordinated monetary policy and the effects on the Eurosystem, see Aerdt C.F.J. Houben, *The Evolution of Monetary Policy Strategies in Europe* (Norwell, MA: Kluwer Academic Publishers, 2000).

A

Actuaries An insurance professional trained in the mathematical aspects of insurance who is responsible for calculating policy premiums.

Adaptive Expectations Expectations formed by looking back at past values of a variable.

Adjustable Rate Mortgages (ARMs) Mortgages that have a variable interest rate.

Adjustable-(Variable-) Rate Loan When the interest rate on a loan is adjusted up or down as the cost of funds rises or falls.

Adjustable-(Variable-) Rate Mortgages Mortgages made with an interest rate that is adjusted up or down as the cost of funds rises or falls.

Adverse Selection Problem When the least desirable borrowers pursue a loan most diligently.

Agency of a Foreign Bank A U.S. banking office of a foreign bank that can borrow funds only in the wholesale and money markets and is not allowed to accept retail deposits.

American Stock Exchange A stock exchange located in New York City that trades the stock of over 660 companies.

Amortization The paying off of the principal of a loan over the life of the loan.

Annuitant The owner of an annuity.

Annuity An insurance contract that provides a periodic income at regular intervals for a specified amount of time, such as a number of years of for the life of the beneficiary.

Appreciated When a currency has increased in value relative to another currency.

Arbitrageurs Traders who make riskless profits by buying in one market and reselling in another market.

Asked Price The price at which a market maker is willing to sell securities.

Asset-Backed Securities Securities that result from the process of securitization.

Asymmetric Information When a potential borrower knows more about the risks and returns of an investment project than the bank loan officer does.

Average Marginal Tax Rate The average of the marginal tax rates of all taxpayers.

B

Backup Line of Credit A bank's promise to lend funds to a borrower on demand; often used to assist commercial paper issuers with their payment obligations.

Balance of Goods and Services Net exports of services plus the trade balance.

Balance of Payments The record of transactions between the United States and its trading partners in the rest of the world over a particular period of time.

Balance on Current Account The balance of goods and services plus net unilateral transfers.

Balance Sheet An accounting statement that presents the monetary value of an economic unit's assets, liabilities, and net worth on a specific date.

Bank for International Settlements (BIS) An international financial organization that promotes international cooperation among central banks and provides facilities for international financial operations.

Bank Holding Company A corporation that owns several firms, at least one of which is a bank.

Bankers' Acceptances Money market instruments created in the course of international trade to guarantee bank drafts due on a future date.

Banking Reform Acts of 1933 and 1935 Statutes passed by Congress in response to the collapse of the banking system between 1930 and 1933.

Barter Trade of goods for goods.

Basel Accord A 1988 agreement among 12 countries that established international capital standards for banks.

Bearer Bonds Bonds in which the bond's owner clips the coupon from the bond and sends it to the issuer who then returns the coupon payment.

Beneficiary The person who receives an insurance payment or annuity stream after a policyholder dies.

Beta A measure of the overall variability of a stock relative to changes in the entire stock market.

Bid Price The price at which a market maker is willing to buy securities.

Board of Governors The seven governors of the Fed appointed by the president with Senate approval for 14-year terms.

Bond Indenture A document stating the terms under which a bond is issued.

Bretton Woods Accord A 1944 agreement, negotiated by the major industrialized countries, that established fixed exchange rates with the U.S. dollar serving as the official reserve currency.

Broker A person who arranges trades between buyers and sellers.

Business Cycle   Short-run fluctu-ations in economic activity as measured by the output of goods and services.

C

Call Options   Options that give the buyer of the option the right-but not the obligation-to buy a standardized contract of a financial instrument at a strike price determined today.

Call Provisions   Provisions of a bond indenture that specify whether the corporation can pay off the bonds before they mature (and if so, under what terms).

Capital Account   The financial flow of funds and securities between the U.S. and the world.

Capital Asset Pricing Model   A model that asserts that the value of a share of stock includes a risk-free return, a market risk premium, and a firm-specific risk premium that is based on beta.

Capital Inflows   Purchases of U.S. financial securities by for-eigners and borrowing from for-eign sources by U.S. firms and residents.

Capital Market   The market for financial assets with an original maturity of greater than 1 year.

Capital Outflows   Purchases of foreign financial securities by U.S. residents and borrowing by foreigners from U.S. banks and other domestic sources.

Carrying Costs   Interest costs for funds used to purchase the secu-rity underlying a futures con-tract plus any transactions costs.

Casualty (Liability) Insurance   Insurance exchanged for premi-ums, that protects insured poli-cyholders from the financial responsibilities to those harmed by an accident, product failure, or professional malpractice.

Central Liquidity Facility (CLF)   A lender-of-last-resort created in 1978 for credit unions experi-encing temporary liquidity problems.

Certificates of Deposit (CDs)   Debt instruments issued by commercial banks having a minimum denomination of $100,000, a fixed interest rate, and return the principal at maturity; may be negotiable (tradable) or non-negotiable (not tradable).

Chartered   Given permission to engage in the business of com-mercial banking: banks must obtain a charter before opening.

Checkable Deposits   Deposits that are subject to withdrawal by writing a check.

Circuit Breakers   Reforms intro-duced in 1987 on the NYSE to temporarily halt market trading if prices change by a specified amount.

Clearinghouse   The part of an organized exchange that takes on the responsibility of enforc-ing the contract after an agree-ment is made.

Closed-End Fund   Mutual funds that sell a limited number of shares like other corporations but usually do not buy back out-standing shares.

Closing Costs   Costs, the bulk of which are paid by the borrower, to obtain a mortgage; include such things as loan origination fees, surveys, appraisals. credit reports, title insurance, record-ing fees, and processing fees.

Coinsurance   The percentage share or fixed amount of a claim that must be paid by the policy-holder. Many health insurance companies require 80/20 cost sharing, with the insurer bearing 80 percent of the cost and the policyholder paying 20 percent. The policyholder's share is sometimes capped at some maxi-mum out-of-pocket expense.

Collateral Bonds   Bonds backed by financial assets.

Collateralized Mortgage Obliga-tions   Securities developed by Freddie Mac that redirect the cash flows (principal and inter-est) of mortgage-backed securi-ties to various classes of investors, thus creating financial instruments with varying pre-payment risks and varying returns.

Collateral   The building (struc-ture) or land that will be fore-closed on and repossessed if the borrower fails to make the scheduled payments; the lender then sells the property to recoup some or all of the losses.

Commercial Banks   Depository institutions that issue checkable, time, and savings deposit liabili-ties and, among other things, make loans to commercial businesses.

Commercial Paper   Short-term debt instruments issued by cor-porations.

Common Stock   Equity claims representing ownership of the net income and assets of a cor-poration that receive a variable or no dividend after preferred stockholders have been paid and retained earnings have been put aside.

Community Reinvestment Act   Legislation passed by Congress in 1977 to increase the availabil-ity of credit to economically dis-advantaged areas and to correct alleged discriminatory lending practices.

Compensating Balances   A form of collateral that specifies a por-tion of loan proceeds to be maintained on deposit at the bank making the loan.

Compounding   A method used to determine the future value of a sum lent today.

Comptroller of the Currency   The federal agency that charters national banks.

Conforming Loan   A specific type of conventional loan that comply with criteria that allow it to be packaged together and resold in the secondary market to Fannie Mae or Freddie Mac; as of 2000, conforming loans are for a maximum amount of $252,700.

Consol   A perpetual bond with no maturity date; the issuer is never obliged to repay the principal but makes coupon payments each year forever.

Contingent Claims Claims such as casualty and life insurance benefits that offer the public protection from the often catastrophic financial effects of theft, accidents, natural disasters, and death.

Contributory Plans Pension plans in which both the employee and employer contribute.

Conventional Mortgages Mortgages made by financial institutions and mortgage brokers without federal insurance that the principal and interest will be repaid.

Convergence The phenomenon in which the futures price is bid up or down to the spot price plus carrying costs.

Convertible Insurance policies containing a clause allowing the policyholder to change a term insurance policy into a permanent (whole, universal, variable) life insurance product.

Convertible Bonds Bonds in which the bondholder has a right to convert the bonds to a predetermined number of shares of common stock; particularly beneficial to the bondholder if the shares of stock appreciate greatly.

Corporate Bonds Long-term debt instruments issued by corporations.

Coupon Payments The periodic payments made to bondholders, which are equal to the principal times the coupon rate.

Coupon Rate The fixed interest rate stated on the face of a bond.

Credit The flow of money from SSUs or financial intermediaries to DSUs in a given time period, and vice versa.

Credit Enhancer An insurance company or a bank that guarantees a security issue or offers a letter of credit in its support for a fee.

Credit Rationing Charging a lower interest rate than some borrowers are willing to pay and apportioning loans and loan amounts only to those with sufficient credit.

Credit Report An account or file of an individual's legal and credit history. It includes information about previous legal judgments as well as information about the types and amounts of one's outstanding debts as well as a record of one's payment history.

Credit Reporting Agencies Companies such as Experian, Equifax, and Trans Union that gather credit and legal information on individuals, compile it into a credit report, and then provide it to prospective creditors, insurers, and employers for a fee.

Credit Risk The probability of a debtor not paying the principal and/or the interest due on an outstanding debt.

Credit Score The three-digit number that predicts a loan applicant's likelihood of default based upon his or her credit history.

Credit Union National Association (CUNA) The largest credit union trade association in the United States provides bulk purchases of supplies, automated payment services, credit card programs, and various investment options to member credit unions.

Credit Union National Extension Board (CUNEB) A privately created organization formed in 1921 to expand the credit union movement across the country; a forerunner to the CUNA.

Credit Unions Depository institutions that are cooperative, nonprofit, tax-exempt associations operated for the benefit of members who share a common bond.

Currency Swaps Agreements whereby one party agrees to trade periodic payments, over a specified period of time, in a given currency, with another party who agrees to do the same in a different currency.

Current Account Transactions that involve currently produced goods and services, including the balance of goods and services.

D

Dealer A person who arranges trades between buyers and sellers and who stands ready to be a principal in a transaction; a market maker.

Debenture Bonds Bonds with no specific collateral backing but have a general claim on the other unpledged assets of the issuer.

Debit In the balance of payments, any transaction that results in a payment to foreigners by Americans.

Debt-to-Income Ratio A financial ratio used to assess a loan applicant's capacity for repaying a loan; generally, the ratio should not exceed 36 percent of the borrower's debt to total income for a loan to be approved.

Deductibles A fixed amount that the insured policyholder is required to pay before insurance coverage becomes effective.

Default When a borrower fails to repay a financial claim.

Default Risk The risk that the borrower will not make the principal and interest payments as scheduled.

Deficit Sector A sector where the combined deficits of the DSUs are greater than the combined surpluses of the SSUs.

Deficit Spending Units (DSUs) Spending units such as households and firms whose spending exceeds their income.

Defined-Benefit Pension Plan Contract promising a specific level of income upon retirement based on the worker's years of service and level of earnings.

Defined-Contribution Pension Plan   Contract specifying that a particular and periodic share of an employee's wages will be contributed by employers, employees, or both.

Demand Deposits   Non-interest-earning checking accounts issued by banks.

Demand for Loanable Funds   The demand for borrowed funds by household, business, government, or foreign DSUs.

Demand for Money   The entire set of interest rate-quantity demanded combinations as represented by a downward-sloping demand curve for money.

Depository Institutions   Financial intermediaries that issue checkable deposits.

Depository Institutions Deregulation and Monetary Control Act of 1980 (DIDMCA)   The statute that removed many of the regulations enacted during the Great Depression, phased out Regulation Q, established uniform and universal reserve requirements, increased the assets and liabilities depository that institutions could hold, authorized NOW accounts, and suspended usury ceilings.

Depreciated   When a currency has decreased in value relative to another currency.

Deregulation   The removing or phasing out of existing regulations.

Derivative Instruments (Derivatives)   Financial contracts (e.g., forwards, futures, options, and swaps) whose values are "derived" from the values of other underlying instruments, such as foreign exchange, bonds, equities, or an index.

Designated Order Turnaround (DOT)   A computer system used for trades of fewer than 3,000 shares on the NYSE.

Devalue   Under a fixed exchange rate system, to decrease the value of a country's currency.

Direct Finance   When SSUs lend their funds directly to DSUs.

Direct Placements   When the issuer of a security sells straight to a buyer without the assistance of a broker or dealer.

Disability Insurance   Policies, exchanged for premiums, that are designed to cover a portion of an insured worker's previous income if the worker becomes unable to work because of illness or injury.

Discount from Par   When a bond sells below its face value because interest rates have increased since the bond was originally issued.

Discount Rate   The rate depository institutions are charged to borrow reserves from the Fed.

Discounting   A method used to determine the present value of a sum to be received in the future.

Disintermediation   The reversal of the financial intermediation process whereby funds are pulled from financial intermediaries, like banks, and moved directly into open market instruments like commercial paper or government securities.

Diversification   The branching out of financial conglomerates into several product lines.

Domestic Nonfinancial Debt (DNFD)   An aggregate that is a measure of total credit market debt owed by the domestic nonfinancial government and private sectors.

Double Coincidence of Wants   In barter, the situation when each person involved in a potential exchange has what the other person wants.

Dow Jones Industrial Average (the Dow)   An index that measures movements in the stock prices of 30 of the largest companies traded on the NYSE.

Dual Banking System   The system whereby a bank may have either a national or a state charter.

Due Diligence   The investigative process used by a lender,

investor, or investment banker to ensure that a borrower's or security issuer's financial statements are accurate.

Duration Analysis   A measure of interest-rate risk that seeks to measure how responsive the value of a bank's assets, liabilities, and net worth are to changes in interest rates. Duration is reported in chronological terms.

Duration GAP Analysis   A specific type of duration analysis that involves subtracting the duration of a bank's interest-rate-sensitive assets from its interest-rate-sensitive liabilities. For most banks, duration GAP is positive, indicating that increased interest rates will adversely affect their net worth.

E

Economic Projections   Goals for nominal and real GDP, unemployment, and inflation for the next 12- to 18-month period established by the FOMC at its meetings in February and July.

Economics   The study of how society decides what gets produced and how, and who gets what.

Economies of Scale   Gains from large size that may result from several firms being able to streamline management and eliminate the duplication of effort of several separate firms.

Economies of Scope   Advantages to firms being able to offer customers several financial services under one roof.

Efficient Markets Hypothesis   The hypothesis that when financial markets are in equilibrium, the prices of financial instruments reflect all readily available information.

Employment Act of 1946   The first statute that directed policymakers to pursue policies to achieve full employment and noninflationary growth.

Euro CDs Certificates of deposit issued by the foreign branches of commercial banks but denominated in the currency of the branch's home country (e.g., Citibank issuing a dollar-denominated CD in Japan).

Eurodollars Dollar-denominated deposits held abroad.

Excess Reserves (ERs) Reserves over and above those required by the Fed.

Exchange Rate The number of units of foreign currency that can be acquired with one unit of domestic money.

Exchange Rate Risk The risk that changes in the exchange rate will adversely affect the value of foreign exchange or foreign financial assets.

Expansion The phase of the business cycle in which economic activity increases and unemployment falls.

Expectations Theory A theory holding that the long-term interest rate is the geometric average of the present short-term rate and the short-term rates expected to prevail over the term to maturity of the long-term security.

External Financing Financing spending that exceeds current receipts by expanding either debt or equity.

F

401(k) plans A special type of defined-contribution plan introduced in 1981 allowing for greater flexibility in employer and employee contributions.

Factoring Companies Specialized finance companies that purchase the accounts receivables of other firms at a discount.

Farm Credit Financial Assistance Corporation (FACO) Issues bonds with explicit government guarantee and uses the proceeds to assist the FFCBFC.

Federal Deposit Insurance Corporation (FDIC) The federal agency that insures the deposits of banks and savings associations.

Federal Deposit Insurance Corporation Improvement Act (FDICIA) Legislation passed by Congress in 1991 to enact regulatory changes to ensure the safety and soundness of the banking and thrift industries.

Federal Farm Credit Banks Funding Corporation (FFCBFC) Issues bonds and discount notes to make loans to farmers.

Federal (Fed) Funds Loans of reserves (deposits at the Fed) between depository institutions, typically overnight.

Federal (Fed) Funds Rate The interest rate charged on overnight loans of reserves among commercial banks.

Federal Home Loan Bank Board (FHLBB) The primary federal regulatory agency for savings associations from 1932 until 1989; replaced by the Office of Thrift Supervision (OTS).

Federal Home Loan Mortgage Corporation (Freddie Mac) A privately-owned, government-sponsored enterprise that sells securities and uses the proceeds to buy mortgages primarily of thrifts.

Federal Housing Administration (FHA) A federal agency that for a .5 percent fee insures mortgage loans made by privately owned financial institutions up to a certain amount if the borrowers meet certain conditions defined by the FHA.

Federal National Mortgage Association (Fannie Mae) A privately owned, government-sponsored enterprise that sells securities and uses the proceeds to buy mortgages primarily of banks.

Federal Open Market Committee (FOMC) The principal policy-making body within the Federal Reserve System.

Federal Reserve Act The 1913 congressional statute that created the Federal Reserve System.

Federal Reserve (Fed) The central bank of the United States that regulates the banking system and determines monetary policy.

Federal Reserve System The central bank of the United States that regulates the banking system and determines monetary policy.

Federal Savings and Loan Insurance Corporation (FSLIC) The federal agency that insured the deposits of member savings associations from 1934 until 1989; replaced by the FDIC's Savings Association Insurance Fund (SAIF).

Finance The study of how the financial system coordinates and channels the flow of funds from lenders to borrowers-and vice versa-and how new funds are created by financial intermediaries during the borrowing process.

Finance Companies Intermediaries that lend funds to households to finance consumer purchases and to firms to finance inventories.

Financial Conglomerates Firms that own and operate several different types of financial intermediaries and financial institutions on a global basis.

Financial Forward Agreements Transactions in which the terms, including price, are completed today for a transaction that will occur in the future.

Financial Forward Markets Markets that trade financial forward agreements usually arranged by banks or other brokers and dealers.

Financial Futures Standardized futures contracts that trade financial instruments at a future date according to terms (including the price) determined today.

Financial Futures Markets Organized markets that trade financial futures agreements.

Financial Holding Companies Holding companies that can engage in a broader array of financial-related activities than bank holding companies, including securities dealing, insurance underwriting, merchant banking and more.

Financial Innovation The creation of new financial instruments, markets, and institutions in the financial services industry.

Financial Institutions Firms that provide financial services to SSUs and DSUs; the most important financial institutions are financial intermediaries.

Financial Institutions Reform, Recovery, and Enforcement Act (FIRREA) of 1989 An act that attempted to resolve the S&L crisis by creating a new regulatory structure, limiting the assets S&Ls can acquire, and requiring S&Ls to maintain adequate capital.

Financial Intermediaries Financial institutions that borrow from SSUs for the purpose of lending to DSUs.

Financial Markets Markets in which spending units trade financial claims.

Financing Corporation (FICO) Issues bonds and uses the proceeds to help resolve the savings and loan crisis.

Firm-Specific Risk Premium A risk measured by beta that shows the overall sensitivity of the stock's return relative to changes in the entire market.

Fiscal Policy Government spending and taxing decisions to speed up or slow down the level of economic activity.

Five Cs of Credit The primary factors lenders must assess and manage to avoid excessive default risk exposure; these include a loan applicant's capacity, character, capital, collateral, and conditions.

Fixed Exchange Rate System An exchange rate system with currency values that do not fluctuate.

Fixed Interest Rate Mortgages Mortgages whose the interest rate remains the same over the life of the loan.

Flexible Exchange Rate System An exchange rate system in which the value of a currency is determined by supply and demand.

Floating (Flexible) Exchange Rate System An exchange rate system in which currency values are determined by supply and demand and fluctuate in response to changes in supply and demand.

Floor-Plan Loans Finance company loan product that allows dealers of automobiles, boats, and construction equipment to use their inventory as collateral for loans that are repaid when vehicles are sold.

Flow of Funds A social accounting system that divides the economy into a number of sectors including the household, business, government, foreign, and financial sectors.

Flows Quantities that are measured through time.

Foreign CDs Certificates of deposit issued by the foreign branches of commercial banks and denominated in the currency of the branch's host country (e.g., Citibank issuing a yen-denominated CD in Japan).

Foreign Currency (Money) Supplies of foreign exchange.

Foreign Exchange Supplies of foreign currencies.

Foreign Exchange Futures Contract A standardized contract to deliver a certain amount of a foreign currency on a date in the future at a price determined today.

Foreign Exchange Market The market for buying and selling the different currencies of the world.

Forward Rate The price today for a delivery on a future date.

Fractional Reserve Banking System A banking system in which individual banks hold reserve assets equal to a fraction of deposit liabilities.

Freedom of Information Act A 1966 law that requires more openness in government and more public access to government documents.

Fund of Funds A mutual fund that invests in a portfolio of other mutual funds rather than individual stocks and/or bonds.

Futures Contracts Standardized agreements in agricultural and commodity markets to trade a fixed amount of the instrument on specific dates in the future at a price determined today.

G

Garn-St. Germain Act of 1982 A statute that, along with DIDMCA, deregulated the financial structure; authorized money market deposit accounts and Super NOW accounts.

General Obligation Bonds Bonds that are paid out of the general revenues and backed by the full faith and credit of the issuer.

Geometric Average An average that takes into account the effects of compounding; used to calculate the long-term rate from the short-term rate and the short-term rates expected to prevail over the term to maturity of the long-term security.

Glass-Steagall Act of 1933 Banking legislation, enacted in response to the Great Depression, that established Regulation Q interest rate ceilings, separated commercial and investment banking, and created the FDIC.

Government Agency Securities Bonds issued by private enterprises that were publicly chartered by Congress to reduce the cost of borrowing to certain sectors of the economy such as farming, housing, and student loans.

Government National Mortgage Association (GNMA) A government-owned program that guarantees the timely payment of interest and principal on bundles of at least $1 million of standardized mortgages.

Government-Sponsored Enterprises (GSEs) Publicly held corporations chartered by Congress to reduce the cost of borrowing in such sectors as housing, farming, the savings and loan industry, and student loans.

Gramm-Leach-Bliley Act (GLBA) Legislation that removed decades-old barriers between banking and other financial services by creating financial holding companies that linked commercial banks with securities firms, insurance firms, and merchant banks; passed by Congress in November 1999 and became effective March 2000.

H

Health Insurance Companies Intermediaries that offer protection, in exchange for premiums, against the financial costs associated with events such as doctor visits, hospital stays, and prescription drugs.

Health Maintenance Organizations (HMOs) Specialized health care insurers that provide almost complete medical care in exchange for fixed per person premiums.

Hedge Reduced risk.

Hedge Fund A nontraditional type of mutual fund that attempts to earn maximum returns regardless of whether financial prices are rising or falling.

Home Equity Lines of Credit Credit cards that are secured by a second mortgage on one's home.

Home Equity Loans Mortgage loans of a specific amount in which one's private residence serves as collateral for the loan.

Housing-to-Income Ratio The share of total housing expenses (including mortgage payment, insurance, property taxes, private mortgage insurance, etc.) relative to one's gross monthly income. This financial ratio is used to assess a mortgage loan applicant's capacity to repay a loan.

Humphrey-Hawkins Full Employment and Balanced Growth Act of 1978 A statute that required policymakers to pursue policies to achieve full employment and noninflationary growth.

I

Impact Lag The time between when an action is taken and when that action has a significant impact on economic activity and prices.

Income GAP The difference between a bank's interest-rate-sensitive assets and its interest-rate-sensitive liabilities.

Indirect Finance When DSUs borrow from financial intermediaries that have acquired the funds to lend from SSUs.

Individual Retirement Accounts (IRAs) Tax-advantaged savings accounts administered by insurance companies, pension funds, and other intermediaries for the purposes of accumulating wealth for retirement.

Inflation-Indexed Bonds Bonds whose principal amount is adjusted for inflation at the time when coupon payments are made (usually every 6 months).

Inflation Premium The amount of nominal interest added to the real interest rate to compensate the lender for the expected loss in purchasing power that will accompany any inflation.

Initial Public Offering (IPO) When a corporation issues stocks publicly for the first time.

Insolvent When the value of a bank's liabilities are greater than the value of its assets.

Insurance Company A contractual-type financial intermediary that offers the public protection against the financial costs associated with the loss of life, health, or property in exchange for a premium.

Interest Rate The cost to borrowers of obtaining money and the return (yield) on money to lenders.

Interest-Rate Cap An agreement whereby the seller of the cap agrees, for a fee, to compensate the cap buyer when an interest-rate index exceeds a specified strike rate.

Interest-Rate Floor An agreement whereby the seller of the cap agrees, for a fee, to compensate the cap buyer when an interest-rate index falls below a specified strike rate.

Interest Rate Parity The condition when interest rates have adjusted so that rates between countries differ only by the expected appreciation or depreciation of the currency.

Interest Rate Risk The risk that nominal interest rates rise and the value of long-term assets fall.

Interest-Rate Swaps Financial instruments that allow financial institutions to trade their interest payment streams to better match payment inflows and outflows.

Intermediate Target The use of a target midway between the policy instruments and the ultimate policy goals.

Internal Financing The spending of money balances on hand or the liquidation of financial or real assets to finance spending that exceeds current receipts.

International Bank for Reconstruction and Development A bank that makes 12- to 15-year loans to poor, but not the poorest, countries, charging an interest rate just above the rate at which the bank borrows.

International Banking Facilities (IBFs) Financial institutions located in the United States that cater to the needs of foreign individuals, corporation, and/or governments. They allow non-U.S. residents to hold unregulated Eurodollar deposits.

International Development Association An association that makes interest-free loans with a maturity of 35-40 years to the world's poorest countries.

International Finance Corporation An organization that mobilizes funding for private enterprise projects in poor countries.

International Financial System The numerous rules, customs, instruments, facilities, markets, and organizations that enable international payments to be made and funds to flow across borders.

International Monetary Fund (IMF) An organization created in 1944 to oversee the monetary and exchange rate policies of its members who pay quotas that are used to assist countries with temporary imbalances in their balance of payments.

Interstate Banking and Branching Efficiency Act (IBBEA) Signed into law in September 1994, an act by Congress that effectively allows unimpeded, nationwide branching.

Investment Banks Financial institutions that design, market, and underwrite new issuances of securities in the primary market.

Investment Companies Companies that own and manage a large group of different mutual funds.

K

Keogh Plans Tax-advantaged savings accounts, administered by banks and other financial intermediaries for the retirement needs of self-employed people.

L

Laissez-Faire The view that government should pursue a hands-off policy with regard to the economy.

Lender of Last Resort The responsibility of the Fed to provide an elastic currency by lending to commercial banks during emergencies.

Letters of Credit A form of credit enhancement offered by banks that guarantees a bank will redeem a security if the issuer does not.

Leverage Ratio The ratio of the firm's debt relative to its equity.

Lien A public record that stays with the property title and gives the lender the right to repossess and sell the property if the borrower defaults.

Life Insurance Companies Intermediaries that offer protection against the financial costs associated with events such as death and disability in exchange for premiums.

Limit Orders Orders that instruct the broker or dealer to purchase securities at the market price up to a certain maximum or sell them at the market price if above a certain minimum.

Liquidity The ease with which a financial claim can be converted to cash without loss of value.

Liquidity Preference The theory of interest rate determination based on the supply of and demand for money; first developed by Keynes.

Liquidity Premium The extra return required to induce lenders to lend long term rather than short term.

Liquidity Ratio A commonly used measure of liquidity and interest-rate risk. It is computed by taking the difference between a bank's short-term investments and liabilities and dividing them by the bank's assets.

Liquidity Risk The risk that an FI will be required to make a payment when the intermediary has only long-term assets that

cannot be converted to liquid funds quickly without a capital loss.

Load A sales commission paid to a broker to purchase mutual funds; by law the load cannot exceed 8.5 percent.

Loan Commitments Promises made by banks to a firm to lend a given amount of funds at a particular rate for a specified period of time.

Loan Participations A loan agreement that allows an originating bank to give partial interest in a loan to one or more additional banks.

Loaned Up When a bank has no excess reserves left to serve as a basis for lending.

Loan-to-Value Ratio A financial ratio used to assess the degree of equity or capital a loan applicant has at stake in an investment project. It is computed by dividing the total loan amount financed by the total market value of the property.

London Interbank Bid Rate (LIBID) The interest rate at which London banks are willing to borrow Eurodollar balances.

London Interbank Offered Rate (LIBOR) The interest rate at which London banks are willing to loan Eurodollar balances.

Long-Term Care Insurance Policies, exchanged for premiums, that are designed to compensate insured policyholders needing assistance with the daily tasks of bathing, eating, dressing, and moving about. Medicare and Medicaid currently pay more than one-half of these expenditures.

M

M1 Currency in the hands of the public plus checkable deposits.

M2 Everything in M1 plus other highly liquid assets.

M3 Everything in M2 plus some less-liquid assets.

Macroeconomics The branch of economics that studies the

aggregate, or total, behavior of all households and firms.

Maintenance Margin Requirement The minimum amount of equity the investor needs in his account relative to the market value of his stock.

Managed Float Exchange Rate System A system in which currency values fluctuate with changes in supply and demand but central banks may intervene if currency values are thought to be over- or undervalued.

Manufactured Housing Lending High-fee, high-interest-rate loans made to homebuyers whose homes were built in factories instead of being built on site.

Margin Loans Loans to investors wherein the proceeds are used to purchase securities.

Margin Requirement The percentage of invested funds that can be borrowed as opposed to being paid in readily available funds; currently margin requirements are set by the Fed at 50 percent.

Marginal Tax Rate The tax rate that is paid on the last dollar of income that the taxpayer earns.

Market Fundamentals Factors that have a direct effect on future income streams of the instruments, including the value of the assets and the expected income streams of those assets on which the financial instruments represent claims.

Market Maker A dealer who links up buyers and sellers of financial securities and sometimes takes positions in the securities.

Market Orders Orders by an investor that direct the broker or dealer to purchase or sell the securities at the present market price.

Market Risk Premium The risk based on historical data that shows how much on average the ownership of stocks pays over a risk-free return.

McCarran-Ferguson Act Federal statute passed in 1945

that exempts life insurance companies from federal regulation and defers its oversight to state insurance commissioners in each state.

McFadden Act The 1927 act by Congress that outlawed interstate branching and made national banks conform to the intrastate branching laws of the states in which they were located.

Means of Payment (Medium of Exchange) Something generally acceptable for making payments.

Merchandise Exports Foreign purchases of U.S. goods.

Merchandise Imports U.S. purchases of foreign goods.

Merchant Banking Direct equity investment (the purchasing of stock) by a bank in a start-up or growing company.

Microeconomics The branch of economics that studies the behavior of individual decision-making units such as households and business firms.

Monetary Aggregates The measures of money-including M1, M2, and M3-monitored and tracked by the Fed.

Monetary Base (MB) Reserves plus currency in the hands of the public; denoted as MB.

Monetary Policy The Fed's efforts to promote the overall health and stability of the economy.

Money Something acceptable and generally used as payment for goods and services.

Money Illusion When spending units react to nominal changes caused by changes in prices even though real variables such as interest rates have not changed.

Money Market The market for financial assets with an original maturity of less than 1 year.

Money Market Deposit Accounts (MMDAs) Financial claims with limited check-writing privileges, offered by banks since 1982; they earn higher interest than fully checkable deposits and require a higher minimum balance.

Money Market Mutual Funds (MMMFs) Short-term investment pools that use the proceeds they raise from selling shares to invest in various money market instruments.

Money Multiplier The multiple of the change in the monetary base by which the money supply will change.

Moral Hazard Problem When the borrower has an incentive to use the proceeds of a loan for a more risky venture after the loan is funded.

Mortality Tables Schedules used to estimate the number of people of a given age who are expected to die during a year.

Mortgage-Backed Securities Securities backed by a pool of mortgages; have a low default risk and provide a steady stream of income.

Mortgage Bonds Bonds backed by real personal property.

Mortgages Loans made to purchase single- or multiple-family residential housing, land, or other real structures, with the structure or land serving as collateral for the loan.

Multiple-Price Method An auction method whereby the seller of securities accepts bids prior to selling securities. Sales are awarded beginning with the highest bidder, buyers end up paying different prices for the same securities based upon their respective bids. The Treasury discontinued this method in November, 1998.

Municipal Bonds (munis, for short) Bonds issued by state, county, and local governments to finance public projects such as schools, utilities, roads, and transportation ventures; the interest on municipal securities is exempt from federal and state taxes for investors living in the issuing state.

Mutual Funds Investment-type intermediaries that pool the funds of SSUs, purchase the long-term financial claims of

DSUs, and return the income received minus a fee to the SSUs.

Mutual Savings Bank   Savings banks that lack stockholders and whose assets are managed to benefit its collective owners-present and future depositors.

N

NASDAQ   An association whose members trade stocks over an advanced computer system that provides immediate information about prices and the number of shares traded.

National Association of Securities Dealers (NASD)   A privately owned organization that regulates the market participants in the over-the-counter market under the supervision of the SEC.

National Bank   A bank that has received a charter from the Comptroller of the Currency.

National Credit Union Association (NCUA)   A federal regulatory agency created in 1970 to charter and regulate federally chartered credit unions and state member institutions.

National Credit Union Share Insurance Fund (NCUSIF)   A federal agency created in 1970 to insure the deposits of federally chartered credit unions and state member institutions.

Natural Rate of Unemployment   The rate of unemployment that is consistent with stable prices; estimated to be 4.0 to 4.5 percent in the early 2000s.

Near Monies   Highly liquid financial assets that can be converted easily to transactions money (M1) without loss of value.

Negative Spread   When the rate of return on assets is less than cost of funds on liabilities. This occurs when loan rates are below deposit rates.

Negotiable Certificates of Deposit (CDs)   Certificates of deposit with a minimum denomination of $100,000 that can be traded in a secondary market,

most with an original maturity of 1 to 12 months.

Negotiable Order of Withdrawal (NOW) Accounts   Interest-earning checking accounts.

Net Asset Value   The difference between the market value of the shares of stock that the mutual fund owns and the liabilities of the mutual fund.

Net Capital Inflow   When there is a surplus in the capital account and capital inflows exceed capital outflows.

Net Transfer Payments   In the current account, the difference between transfer payments received from and transfer payments made to foreigners; also called net unilateral transfers.

New York Stock Exchange (NYSE)   The world's largest market for trading stocks; trades the stocks of over 3,000 companies.

No-Fault Insurance   Insurance coverage that pays an accident victim regardless of who caused an accident or damage.

No-Load   Mutual funds that are purchased directly from the mutual fund company and are not subject to a load.

Nominal Interest Rate   The market interest rate, or the real return plus the rate of inflation expected to prevail over the life of the asset.

Nonbanks   Other intermediaries and nonfinancial companies that have taken an increasing share of intermediation.

Noncontributory Plans   Pension plans in which only the employer contributes.

O

125s   A specialized and increasingly popular type of home equity loan in which the borrower is allowed to borrow up to 125 percent of a home's value.

Office of Thrift Supervision (OTS)   An agency created by the FIRREA to replace the Fed-

eral Home Loan Bank Board as the overseer of the S&L industry.

Official Reserve Account   The balance of payments account that records official government transactions in the foreign exchange market to bring the balance of payments into balance.

Official Reserve Currency   The currency used by other countries to define their own currency; the U.S. dollar was the official reserve currency under the Bretton Woods Accord.

Old Age Survivors and Disability Insurance (OASDI)   Core program of Social Security that is funded by payroll taxes to pay retirement and disability payments to eligible individuals and their dependents.

Open Market Operations   The buying and selling of government securities by the Fed to change the reserves of depository institutions.

Open-End Fund   A mutual fund that continually sells new shares to the public or buys outstanding shares from the public at a price equal to the net asset value.

Operating Target   A target amenable to control by the policy tools and highly correlated with the intermediate target.

Optimal Forecast   The best guess possible arrived at by using all of the available information.

Option Premium   The premium paid by the buyer of an option to compensate the seller for accepting the risk of a loss with no possibility of a gain.

Options   Standardized contracts that give the buyer the right-but not the obligation-to buy or sell an instrument in the future at a price determined today.

Options on Futures   Options that give the buyer the right-but not the obligation-to buy or sell a futures contract up to the expiration date on the option.

Over-the-Counter Market   A network of securities dealers who trade stocks of over 30,000 companies via telephone or computer.

P

Participation Certificate   A mortgage-backed security issued by Freddie Mac and backed by a pool of conventional mortgages.

Par Value   The face value printed on a bond; the amount the bond originally sold for.

Payments Mechanism   The ways in which funds are transferred to make payments.

Payoff Method   The method of resolving a bank insolvency by paying off the depositors and closing the institution.

Pension Funds   Tax-exempt intermediaries set up to provide participants with income at retirement in exchange for premiums.

Performance Bond   A bond required by an organized exchange from both the buyer and the seller of a futures agreement to ensure that both parties abide by the agreement.

Pit   The trading area on the floor of an organized exchange where authorized brokers gather to buy and sell for their customers.

Points   A prepayment of interest at the time a mortgage loan is made that lowers the nominal interest rate on the loan; one point is equal to 1 percent of the loan balance.

Policy Directive   A statement of the FOMC that indicates its policy consensus and sets forth operating instructions regarding monetary policy.

Policy Lag   The time between when the need for action is recognized and when an adjustment policy is decided upon and set in motion.

Positive Spread   When the rate of return on assets is greater than cost of funds on liabilities. This occurs when loan rates are above deposit rates.

Preferred Habitats   An expectations theory modification hypothesizing that many borrowers and lenders have preferred maturities, which creates a degree of market segmentation between the short-term and long-term markets.

Preferred Stock   Equity claims representing ownership of the net income and assets of a corporation that receive a fixed dividend before common stockholders are entitled to anything.

Premium Above Par   When a bond sells above its face value because interest rates have decreased since the bond was originally issued.

Prepayment Risk   The risk that a mortgage may be prepaid early and the lender will have to reinvest the funds at a lower interest rate.

Present Value   The value today of funds to be received or paid on a future date.

Price Risk   The threat that an increase in interest rates will reduce the market value of security holdings.

Price Stability   Inflation so low and stable over time that it is ignored by households and firms in decision making.

Primary Dealers   The large banks and government securities dealers that are approved by the Fed to be the main participants in the auctions of Treasury securities that are conducted by the Fed.

Primary Market   The market in which a security is sold for the first time.

Principal   The original amount of funds lent.

Private Placement   A method of issuing new securities by selling to a limited number of large investors.

Program Trading   The preprogramming of computers to buy or sell a large number (basket) of stocks usually by institutional investors.

Property and Casualty Companies   Intermediaries that provide protection against the effects of unexpected occurrences on property.

Property Insurance   Contingent claims, exchange for premiums, that protect insured policyholders from the financial costs of property loss, damage, or destruction.

Prospectus   A subpart of the registration statement that must be given to investors before they purchase the securities.

Purchase and Assumption Method   The method of resolving a bank insolvency by finding a buyer for the institution.

Put Options   Options that give the buyer of the option the right-but not the obligation-to sell a standardized contract of a financial instrument at a strike price determined today.

Q

Quantity Demanded of Money   The specific amount of money that spending units wish to hold at a specific interest rate (price).

Quantity Supplied of Money   The specific amount of money that will be supplied at a specific interest rate.

R

Rational Expectations   Expectations formed by looking both backward and forward.

Real Estate Investment Trusts (REITs)   A special type of mutual fund that pools the funds of many small investors and uses them to buy or build income property or to make or purchase mortgage loans.

Real Interest Rate   The interest rate corrected for changes in the purchasing power of money.

Recession   The phase of the business cycle in which economic activity falls and unemployment rises.

Recognition Lag   The time between when a significant and unexpected change in the economy's performance occurs and when policymakers recognize that change.

Redlining   The practice of restricting the number or dollar amounts of loans in an area regardless of the creditworthiness of the borrower.

Registered Bonds   Bonds in which the issuer keeps records of ownership and automatically sends the coupon payment to the bondholder.

Registration Statement   A statement that must be filed with the SEC before a new securities offering can be issued.

Regulation Q   Interest rate ceilings on deposits at commercial banks that were established during the Great Depression and phased out after 1980.

Reinsurance   The practice by smaller insurance companies of sharing the risk of a large policy with other insurance companies to reduce risk exposure.

Reinvestment Risk   The threat that falling interest rates will reduce future rates of return on current and future cash flows.

Repossession   The process whereby a lender takes back the assets used to secure a loan.

Repurchase Agreement   Short-term contract in which the seller agrees to sell a government security to a buyer and simultaneously agrees to buy it back on a later date at a higher price.

Required Reserve Ratio   The fraction of deposit liabilities that depository institutions must hold as reserve assets.

Required Reserves (RRs)   The amount of reserve assets that the Fed requires depository institutions to hold against outstanding checkable deposit liabilities.

Reserve Bank   One of the 12 Federal Reserve Banks; each is located in a large city in its district.

Reserve Need   The difference, if any, between actual reserves and those projected to be needed to keep the fed funds rate at the target level.

Reserves   Assets that are held as either vault cash or reserve deposit accounts with the Fed.

Resolution Trust Corporation (RTC)   An agency created by the FIRREA in 1989 to dispose of the properties of failed S&Ls.

Restrictive Covenants   Stipulations within the bond indenture that limit the ability of the corporation with regards to certain activities.

Retail Sweep Accounts   An innovation that sweeps balances out of deposits subject to reserve requirements and into other deposits that are not.

Revalue   Under a fixed exchange rate system, to increase the value of a country's currency.

Revenue Bonds   Bonds used to finance specific projects with the proceeds of those projects being used to pay off the bondholders.

Reverse Repurchase Agreement or Matched Sale-Purchase (MSP) Agreement   A repurchase agreement viewed from the perspective of the initial buyer; short-term agreements in which the buyer buys a government security from a seller and simultaneously agrees to sell it back on a later date at a higher price.

Risk Averse   A state of being wherein one is reluctant to fully bear the financial or physical loss of an event.

Risk-Based Premiums   Insurance charges that increase with the perceived risk of the policyholder.

Risk-Based Pricing   Charging different interest rates to borrowers based on an assessment of a loan applicant's default risk; highly rated applicants are charged the lowest rates.

Risk Premium   The extra return or interest that a lender is

compensated for accepting more risk.

Roth IRA   A special type of individual retirement account in which one's contributions are taxed, but the earnings accumulated within the account are tax-exempt.

S

Sales Finance Companies (Captive Finance Companies)   Companies that make loans to consumers so they can purchase a product from a particular manufacturer or retailer.

Saving   Income not spent on consumption.

Savings and Loan Associations (S&Ls)   Depository institutions established for the purpose of pooling the savings of local residents to finance the construction and purchase of homes; S&Ls have offered checkable deposits since 1980.

Savings Association Insurance Fund (SAIF)   An organization created by FIRREA in 1989 and managed by the FDIC to provide insurance for savings association deposits. It replaced the defunct FSLIC.

Savings Associations   S&Ls and savings banks.

Savings Banks   Depository institutions set up to help finance the construction and purchase of homes; located mainly on the East Coast.

Savings Deposits   Highly liquid deposits that can usually be withdrawn on demand but not by writing a check.

Seasoned Issuance   The offering of new securities by a corporation that has outstanding previously issued securities.

Secondary Market   The market in which previously issued financial securities are sold.

Secondary Stock Offering   An offering of newly issued shares by a firm that already has outstanding publicly held shares.

Securities and Exchange Commission (SEC) A government agency created by the Securities and Exchange Act of 1934 that regulates disclosure rules for companies that issue publicly traded shares of stock; the SEC also regulates disclosure rules in secondary markets.

Securities Industry Protection Corporation (SIPC) A nonprofit membership corporation established by Congress in 1970 that provides insurance up to $500,000 per investor to protect investors' securities from liquidation by the brokerage firm.

Securitization The pooling and repackaging of similar loans into marketable securities.

Share Accounts Highly liquid credit union deposits that can be withdrawn on demand, but not by writing a check.

Share Certificates The credit union equivalent of a CD.

Share Draft Accounts Interest-bearing checking accounts of credit unions.

Shelf Registration A procedure that permits a company to register a quantity of securities with the SEC and sell them over a 2-year period rather than at the time of registration.

Short Sell Instructions to brokers or dealers to borrow shares of stocks and sell them today with the guarantee that the investor will replace them by a date in the future.

Simple Money Multiplier The reciprocal of the required reserve ratio, $1/rD$.

SIMPLE Plans (Savings Incentive Match Plan for Employees of Small Employers Simplified defined-contribution plans created by Congress in 1996 to assist small businesses in offering salary deductions and matching contributions to fund retirement savings for their workers.

Simplified Employee Pensions (SEPs) Small-business pension plans allowed by Congress in 1978 with fewer reporting requirements and less administrative complexity and costs than traditional pension plans.

Sinking Fund Provisions Provisions of a bond indenture that specify whether the corporation is required to pay off a portion of the newly issued bonds each year.

Social Security Federal government program that provides retirement and survivors pensions, and disability and health insurance benefits to qualifying individuals.

Sources and Uses of Funds Statement A statement showing the sources and uses of funds for any sector.

Sources of Funds For any sector, income and borrowing.

Special Drawing Rights (SDRs) International reserve assets created by the IMF to supplement other international reserves.

Special-Purpose Trust A corporate agent that buys financial obligations from a loan originator and works with a security underwriter, credit enhancer, and rating agency to issue asset-backed securities; sometimes responsible for loan-servicing responsibilities.

Speculation The buying or selling of financial securities in the hopes of profiting from future price changes.

Speculative Bubble An irrational increase in stock prices accompanied by euphoric expectations.

Spot Market A market in which the trading of financial securities takes place instantaneously.

Standard & Poor's and Moody's Investors Services The two major credit-rating agencies that evaluate a borrower's probability of default and assign the borrower to a particular risk class.

State and Local Government Bonds (Municipals) Long-term instruments issued by state and local governments to finance expenditures on schools, roads, and the like.

Stock Savings Bank A type of savings bank charter in which ownership is held by the stockholders.

Stocks Equity claims that represent ownership of the net assets and income of a corporation; quantities that are measured at a point in time.

Stop-Out Yield The lowest accepted bid price or yield in a securities auction.

Store of Value Something that retains its value over time.

Strike Price The agreed-upon price in an options contract.

Strike Rate The agreed-upon rate in an interest agreement.

Stronger Version of the Efficient Markets Hypothesis The theory that the prices of all financial instruments not only reflect the optimal forecast of the financial instrument but also the true fundamental value of the instrument.

Student Loan Marketing Association (Sallie Mae) Issues securities to purchase student loans, increasing the amount and liquidity of funds flowing into student loans

Subordinated Debenture Bonds Bonds with no collateral backing that have a general claim after debenture bondholders have been paid.

Subprime Lending High-fee, high-interest-rate loans typically made to a borrower with blemished (or nonexistent) credit records.

Superior/Subordinated Debt Structure A framework that allows securities to be sold in at least two different classes or tranches.

Supply of Loanable Funds The supply of borrowed funds originating from (1) household, business, government, and foreign SSUs, or (2) the Fed through its provision of reserves.

Supply of Money The stock of money (M1), which includes

currency in the hands of the public plus checkable deposits.

Surplus Sector   A sector where the combined surpluses of the SSUs are greater than the combined deficits of the DSUs.

Surplus Spending Units (SSUs)   Spending units such as households and firms whose income exceeds their spending.

Sustainable Economic Growth   Output growth along the economy's potential growth path as determined by the growth of labor, capital, and productivity.

Sweep Accounts   A financial innovation that allows depository institutions to shift customers' funds out of checkable accounts that are subject to reserve requirements and into highly liquid money market deposit accounts (MMDAs) that are not.

Syndicate   A group of investment banks, each of which underwrites a proportion of new securities offering; reduces the risk to one investment bank of underwriting the entire new offering.

T

Term Life Insurance   Life insurance that provides a death benefit to an insured policyholder's beneficiary only if the insured dies within the specified period of time or "term" of the policy.

Term Structure of Interest Rates   The relationship between yields and time to maturity.

Term to Maturity   The length of time from when a financial security is initially issued until it matures.

Theory of Rational Expectations   The theory that expectations will on average be equal to the optimal forecast.

Thrift CDs   Certificates of deposit issued by savings associations.

Thrifts   Depository institutions known as S&Ls, savings banks, and credit unions.

Time Deposits   Deposits that have a scheduled maturity and a penalty for early withdrawal.

Time Value of Money   The terms on which one can trade off present purchasing power for future purchasing power; the interest rate.

"Too Big to Fail"   The position adopted by FDIC regulators in 1984 whereby the failure of a large bank would be resolved using the purchase and assumption method rather than the payoff method. 1-12 months.

Total Reserves (TRs)   Required reserves plus excess reserves.

Trade Balance   The difference between merchandise exports and imports.

Trade Deficit   When merchandise imports are greater than exports.

Trade Surplus   When merchandise exports are greater than imports.

Tranche   A particular class or part of a securitization issue; some parts may be backed only by principal payments, others only by interest payments.

Transactions Costs   The costs associated with borrowing and lending or making other exchanges.

Transactions Deposits   Deposits that can be exchanged for currency and are used to make payments through writing a check or making an electronic transfer.

Treasury Notes   Securities issued by the U.S. government with an original maturity of 1 to 10 years.

Treasury STRIPS   A type of government security that allows investors to register and trade ownership of the interest (coupon) payments and the principal separately.

U

U.S. Central Credit Union   The central bank for credit unions.

U.S. Government Agency Securities   Long-term bonds issued by various government agencies including those that support real estate lending and student loans.

U.S. Government Securities   Long-term debt instruments of the U.S. government with original maturities of 2-30 years.

U.S. Treasury Bills (T-bills)   Short-term debt instruments of the U.S. government with typical maturities of 3-12 months.

Uniform-Price Method   An auction method whereby the seller of securities accepts bids prior to selling securities. Sales are awarded beginning with the highest bidder, and buyers pay the same price for the securities based on the stop-out yield. The Treasury instituted this method in November, 1998.

Uniform Reserve Requirements   Reserve requirements that apply to particular types of deposits and are the same in all depository institutions.

Unit of Account   A standardized accounting unit such as the dollar that provides a consistent measure of value.

Universal Life Insurance   A form of permanent life insurance that provides a pure insurance product as well as a separate account. This separate account grows at a fluctuating rate of interest similar to that received on a money market account or short-term CD. Premium payment amounts may be flexible as long as the minimum premium for the pure insurance benefit is met.

Universal Reserve Requirements   Reserve requirements to which all depository institutions are subject.

Uses of Funds   For any sector, current spending and changes in financial instruments held.

Usury Ceilings   Maximum interest rates that FIs may charge on certain loans.

V

Variable Interest Rate Mortgages   Mortgages whose interest rate is adjusted periodically to reflect changing market conditions.

Variable Life Insurance   A form of permanent life insurance that provides a pure insurance product as well as a separate account. The separate account may be used by the policyholder to purchase mutual funds from a list of insurance company approved funds. These equity-linked funds pay a minimum death benefit as long as sufficient premium payments are received.

Veterans Administration (VA)   A federal agency that, among other things, insures mortgage loans made by privately owned financial institutions up to a certain amount if the borrowers meet certain conditions, including being military veterans.

W

Warrant   Contracts sometimes issued with newly issued bonds; warrants give the holder the right to purchase a designated security at a price set today; warrants may be sold to a third party.

Whole Life Insurance   A permanent type of life insurance that charges a fixed premium and pays a fixed death benefit, and whose separate account is invested by the insurance company for the policyholder's benefit.

World Bank   An investment bank created in 1944 that issues bonds to make long-term loans at low interest rates to poor countries for economic development projects.

Y

Yankee CDs   A certificate of deposit issued by a foreign bank in a foreign currency, but sold in the United States (e.g., Crédit Lyonnais, France's largest bank, issuing a French franc-denominated CD in the United States).

Yield Curve   A graphical representation of the relationship between interest rates (yields) on particular securities and their terms to maturity.

Yield to Maturity   The return on a bond held to maturity, which includes both the interest return and any capital gain or loss.

Z

Zero-Coupon Bonds   Corporate bonds sold at a discount with the difference between the amount paid for the bond and the amount received at maturity equal to the interest.

Index

Photo Credits

Part 1 Opener	© PhotoDisc
Part 2 Opener	© PhotoDisc
Part 3 Opener	© PhotoDisc
Part 4 Opener	© PhotoDisc
Part 5 Opener	© PhotoDisc
Part 6 Opener	© PhotoDisc

CH1	© PhotoDisc
CH2	© PhotoDisc
CH3	© PhotoDisc
Page 61	© PhotoDisc
CH4	Courtesy of Chicago Federal Board of Trade
CH5	© Susan Van Etten
CH6	© Deanna Ettinger/2001 Thomson Learning
CH7	© Susan Van Etten
CH8	© PhotoDisc
CH9	© Susan Van Etten
CH10	© Susan Van Etten
CH11	© PhotoDisc
CH12	© AFP/CORBIS
CH13	© PhotoDisc
CH14	© Susan Van Etten
CH15	© Susan Van Etten
CH16	© Susan Van Etten
CH17	© AFP/CORBIS
CH18	© PhotoDisc
CH19	© Jonathan Blair/CORBIS
CH20	© Reuters NewMedia Inc./CORBIS
CH21	Courtesy of Citibank
CH22	© PhotoDisc
CH23	© Kevin Su/CORBIS
CH24	© AFP/CORBIS
CH25	© PhotoDisc